QUEEN ANNE

QUEEN ANNE

PATRONESS OF ARTS

JAMES ANDERSON WINN

OXFORD
UNIVERSITY PRESS

OXFORD
UNIVERSITY PRESS

Oxford University Press is a department of the
University of Oxford. It furthers the University's objective
of excellence in research, scholarship, and education
by publishing worldwide.

Oxford   New York

Auckland   Cape Town   Dar es Salaam   Hong Kong   Karachi
Kuala Lumpur   Madrid   Melbourne   Mexico City   Nairobi
New Delhi   Shanghai   Taipei   Toronto

With offices in

Argentina   Austria   Brazil   Chile   Czech Republic   France   Greece
Guatemala   Hungary   Italy   Japan   Poland   Portugal   Singapore
South Korea   Switzerland   Thailand   Turkey   Ukraine   Vietnam

Oxford is a registered trade mark of Oxford University Press
in the UK and certain other countries.

Published in the United States of America by
Oxford University Press
198 Madison Avenue, New York, NY 10016

Library of Congress Cataloging-in-Publication Data
Winn, James Anderson, 1947–
Queen Anne : patroness of arts / James Anderson Winn.
pages   cm
Includes bibliographical references and index.
ISBN 978–0–19–937219–5 (acid-free paper)   1. Anne, Queen of Great Britain, 1665–1714.
2. Great Britain—History—Anne, 1702–1714.   3. Queens—Great Britain—Biography.
4. Anne, Queen of Great Britain, 1665–1714—Art patronage.   I. Title.
DA495.W56   2014
941.069092—dc23
[B]   2013044384

Tin-glazed earthenware plate commemorating the Union of England and Scotland (c. 1707)

For Lucy

Pay your homage chearful hearts,
Greet the Patroness of Arts.
With song your tribute to her bring,
Who best inspires you how to sing;
None better claims your lays than she
Whose very soul is Harmony.
O happy those whose art can feast
So just, and so refined a taste.

—*Anonymous birthday ode for Princess Anne (1701)*

CONTENTS

About the Companion Website / x
List of Illustrations / xi
List of Musical Examples / xiv
Preface / xvii
Notes on Style / xxi

1 A LITTLE STAR / 1

2 HAIL, WELCOME PRINCE / 43

3 PRAY FOR THE PEACE OF JERUSALEM / 91

4 SHE REIGNS WITHOUT A CROWN / 139

5 SWEET REMEMBRANCE SHALL REMAIN / 201

6 ENTIRELY ENGLISH / 249

7 DOMINION OVER THE MIGHTY / 305

8 WHAT FRUITS FROM OUR DIVISIONS SPRING / 369

9 THE BREATH OF OUR NOSTRILS / 437

10 TO FIX A LASTING PEACE ON EARTH / 513

11 ALL A NATION COULD REQUIRE / 597

Acknowledgments / 637
Abbreviations Used in the Notes / 641
Notes / 643
Bibliography / 747
Index / 771

ABOUT THE COMPANION WEBSITE

WWW.OUP.COM/US/QUEENANNE

Because of Queen Anne's keen interest in music, this book includes twenty-eight musical examples, which appear in score at various points in the text. Commercial recordings of a few of these pieces exist, but most have never been recorded. With the help of a group of Boston-based specialists in early music, I have produced recordings of all twenty-eight examples, which you may hear by going to the companion website. Next to each example in score, you will see a symbol 🔊 that directs you to the website, to which you may gain access with username Music2 and password Book4416.

LIST OF ILLUSTRATIONS

ii   Tin-glazed earthenware plate commemorating the Union of England and
     Scotland (c. 1707). © The Trustees of the British Museum. 1924, 1023.1.CR.
     Frontispiece.

 6   John Dunstall, *Clarendon House* (1687–1692). © The Trustees of the British
     Museum. 1978, U.3552.

19   Frontispiece to *Ariane, ou le Mariage de Bacchus* (1674).

23   John Roettier, *Medal with Frances Stuart as Britannia* (1667). © The Trustees
     of the British Museum. G3, EM.4.

45   After John Closterman, *Henry Purcell* (1695?). © National Portrait Gallery,
     London. NPG 2150.

46   *Prince George*. Frontispiece to *The Present State of Denmark* (1683).

55   Peter Vanderbank (Vandrebanc), *Princess Anne* (1684). Possibly after
     Sir Peter Lely. © National Portrait Gallery, London. NPG D19644.

56   Peter Vanderbank, *Princess Anne*, detail.

59   Richard Tompson, *Her Highness the Lady Ann.* Mezzotint after Sir Peter Lely
     (c. 1675–1690). © The Trustees of the British Museum. 1902,1011.5230.

77   Richard Tompson, *Georg Ludwig, Prince of Hanover.* Mezzotint after
     Godfrey Kneller (c. 1675–1690). © The Trustees of the British Museum.
     1874,0808.1299.

92   Illustration from Francis Sandford, *The History of the Coronation of James II*
     (1687).

98   *The Proceeding to the Coronation of their Majesties King William and Queen
     Mary… 11 Apr. 1689* (1689), detail. Courtesy of the Boston Athenæum.

118 Regnier Arondeaux, *Silver Medal Commemorating the Executions of
     Monmouth and Argyle.* © The Trustees of the British Museum. Coins and
     Metals, MB1p615.27.

120 *An Account of his Excellence Roger Earl of Castlemaine's Embassy, From his
     Sacred Majesty James the IId.… To His Holiness Innocent XI* (1688). © The
     Trustees of the British Museum. 1895,1031.112.

150   John Smith, *William, Duke of Gloucester.* mezzotint after Sir Godfrey Kneller (1691). © The Trustees of the British Museum. 1902,1011.4580.

152   Sir Godfrey Kneller, *Barbara, Viscountess Fitzharding and Sarah, Duchess of Marlborough Playing Cards* (1691). Blenheim Palace, Oxfordshire, UK / The Bridgeman Art Library.

157   *The Northern Ditty* (1692).

159   "Forgive me" from *The Banquet of Musick* (1688).

182   *A Copy of Verses...By Thomas Bamber, Bellman* (1692). detail.

195   John Smith, *William Duke of Gloucester; Benjamin Bathurst,* mezzotint after Thomas Murray (1697). © The Trustees of the British Museum. P,8.62.

218   Illustration from Dryden's *Virgil* (1697). Boston University, Howard Gotlieb Collection.

∽

COLOR PLATES (*after page* 394)

Plate 1.   Sir Peter Lely, *Queen Anne, when a Child* (c. 1667–68). Royal Collection RCIN 404918. Supplied by Royal Collection Trust/© Her Majesty Queen Elizabeth II 2013.

Plate 2.   Sir Peter Lely, *Queen Anne, when a Child,* detail.

Plate 3.   Sir Peter Lely, *Mary II when Princess* (c. 1672). Royal Collection. RCIN 405810. Supplied by Royal Collection Trust/© Her Majesty Queen Elizabeth II 2013.

Plate 4.   Pierre Mignard, *Louise Kéroualle, Duchess of Portsmouth* (1682). © National Portrait Gallery, London. NPG 497.

Plate 5.   Pierre Mignard, *The Marquise de Seignelay and Two of her Sons* (1691). Bequeathed by Sir John Murray Scott, 1914. © National Gallery, London / Art Resource, New York. NG2967.

Plate 6.   Peter Paul Rubens, oil sketch for *Peace Embracing Plenty* (1633–34). Yale Center for British Art, Paul Mellon Collection. B1977.14.70.

Plate 7.   Studio of Sir Peter Lely, *Mary "Moll" Davis* (c. 1668). Private Collection / Photo © Philip Mould Ltd., London / The Bridgeman Art Library.

Plate 8.   Benedetto Gennari, *Annunciation* (1686). Ringling Museum, Sarasota, FL. SN131.

Plate 9.   Anne Killigrew (1660–1685), *Venus Attired by the Three Graces* (c. 1683), oil on canvas, 112 x 95 cm. Falmouth Art Gallery Collection, Cornwall. Purchased with funding from the V & A Purchase Grant Fund, Heritage Lottery Fund, The Art Fund, The Beecroft Bequest, Falmouth Decorative and Fine Arts Society, The Estate of Barry Hughes in memory of Grace and Thomas Hughes and generous donations from local supporters. FAMAG 2012.22.

Plate 10. Anne Killigrew, *Venus Attired by the Three Graces,* detail.

Plate 11. Studio of Sir Godfrey Kneller, *Princess Anne with William Duke of Gloucester* (c. 1694). © National Portrait Gallery, London. NPG 5227.

Plate 12.   Studio of Sir Godfrey Kneller, *William, Duke of Gloucester* (c. 1699). © National Portrait Gallery, London. NPG 5228.

Plate 13.   Anonymous English artist, *"Coronation Portrait" of Queen Elizabeth I* (c. 1600). © National Portrait Gallery, London. NPG 5175.

Plate 14.   Sir Godfrey Kneller, *Queen Anne* (c. 1705). Private Collection / Photo © Philip Mould Ltd., London / The Bridgeman Art Library.

Plate 15.   John Riley (or John Closterman), *Anne Morrice* (c. 1692). Antony House and Gardens, Cornwall. By kind permission of Sir Richard Carew Pole.

Plate 16.   Sir Godfrey Kneller, *John Duke of Marlborough* (1706). © National Portrait Gallery, London. NPG 902.

Plate 17.   Sir Godfrey Kneller, *Queen Anne presenting the plans of Blenheim to military Merit* (1708). Blenheim Palace, Oxfordshire, UK / The Bridgeman Art Library.

Plate 18.   Sir Godfrey Kneller, *Portrait of John Churchill, the First Duke of Marlborough, in full length* (1712). From the Collection at Althorp.

288   *The Proceeding of the Queen to her Coronation* (1702). © The Trustees of the British Museum. Y,1.139.

290   John Croker, *Coronation Medal for Queen Anne* (1702). Courtesy of A. H. Baldwin & Sons Ltd.

326   Studio of John Closterman, study for *Queen Anne* (c. 1702). © National Portrait Gallery, London. NPG 215.

327   John Faber, Jr., *Queen Anne*, mezzotint after John Closterman (c. 1725–1756). © The Trustees of the British Museum. 1887,0406.77.

362   John Croker, *Medal commemorating Queen Anne's Bounty* (1704). Courtesy of A. H. Baldwin & Sons Ltd.

393   James Thornhill, *Queen Anne's Patronage of the Arts* (1704). © Courtesy of the Huntington Art Collections.

424   Frontispiece to *England's Glory* (1706).

428   H. Vale, *The Relief of Barcelona* (c. 1706). © National Maritime Museum. BHC0345.

435   *The Union* (1707), couplet 10.

519   Judocus de Vos, *The Battle of Malplaquet* (1711). Reproduced by kind permission of His Grace, the Duke of Marlborough, Blenheim Palace.

520   *An Historical Emblematical Fan* (1711). © The Trustees of the British Museum. 1868,0808.3449.

524   Anonymous print after Jan Verelst, *The true Effiges of the four Indian kings* (1710). © The Trustees of the British Museum. 1851,0308.376.

538   John Croker, *Medal Commemorating the Battle of Almenara* (1710). © The Trustees of the British Museum. M.8117.

556   Joseph Skelton, *St. John's Smith Square* (1814). © The Trustees of the British Museum. 1880,1113.2513.

LIST OF MUSICAL EXAMPLES

Mus. Ex. 1.1.   Nicholas Staggins, "Augusta is inclin'd to fears." From *Calisto* (1675). Score: transcribed from GB-Lbl Add. MS 19759, fol. 33. Performers: Teresa Wakim, soprano; Peter Sykes, harpsichord; Laura Jeppesen, viola da gamba. Bass line reconstructed by Peter Sykes.

Mus. Ex. 2.1.   Henry Purcell, excerpt from *From Hardy Climes* (1683). Score: *Royal Welcome Songs,* pt. 1, ed. Bruce Wood (Kent: Novello, 2000), in *The Works of Henry Purcell,* XV. Performers: Paul Guttry, bass; Peter Sykes, harpsichord; Reinmar Seidler, cello.

Mus. Ex. 2.2.   John Blow, excerpt from *Hear my voice, O God* (1683). Score: *John Blow, Anthems IV: Anthems with Instruments,* ed. Bruce Wood (Stainer and Bell, 2002), in *Musica Britannica,* vol. 79. Performers: Paul Guttry, bass; Peter Sykes, organ; Reinmar Seidler, cello.

Mus. Ex. 3.1.   Henry Purcell, excerpt from *I was glad* (1685). Score: *I was glad: anthem for the coronation of James II,* ed. Bruce Wood (Kent: Novello, 1977). Performers: Teresa Wakim and Shari Wilson, sopranos; Douglas Dodson, countertenor; Patrick Waters, tenor; Paul Tipton, baritone; Peter Sykes, organ.

Mus. Ex. 3.2.   Henry Purcell, excerpt from *I was glad* (1683). Score: *Sacred Music, Part II: Nine Anthems with Strings,* ed. Lionel Pike (Kent: Novello, 2003), in *The Works of Henry Purcell,* XV. Performers: Owen McIntosh and Marcio de Oliveira, tenors; Bradford Gleim, baritone; Peter Sykes, organ.

Mus. Ex. 3.3–3.5.   Luis Grabu, excerpts from *Albion and Albanius* (1685), act 1, no. 5; act 1, no. 9; act 2, no. 39. Score: *Albion and Albanius,* ed. Bryan White (Stainer and Bell, 2007). Performers: Teresa Wakim, soprano; Jason McStoots, countertenor; Sumner Thompson, baritone; Scott Metcalfe and Karina Fox, violins; Scott Metcalfe, Karina Fox, Laura Jeppesen, and Sarah Darling, violas; Peter Sykes, harpsichord; Reinmar Seidler, cello.

Mus. Ex. 4.1–4.4.   Henry Purcell, excerpts from *Who can from Joy Refrain?* (1695). Score: *A Song for the Duke of Gloucester's Birthday, 1695*, ed. Ian Spink (Kent: Novello, 1990), in *The Works of Henry Purcell*, IV. Performers: Bradford Gleim, baritone; Teresa Wakim and Brenna Wells, sopranos; Jesse Irons and Megumi Stohs Lewis, violins; Peter Sykes, harpsichord; Sarah Freiberg, cello.

Mus. Ex. 4.5.   Henry Purcell, "Lovely Albina" (1695). Score: *Secular Songs for Solo Voice*, ed. Margaret Laurie (Kent: Novello, 1985), in *The Works of Henry Purcell*, XXV, omitting the editorial realization of the continuo. Performers: Teresa Wakim, soprano; Peter Sykes, harpsichord; Sarah Freiberg, cello.

Mus. Ex. 6.1.   Jeremiah Clarke, excerpt from *Let Nature Smile*, birthday ode for Princess Anne (1701?). Score: GB-Lbl Add. MS 31812, fol. 39r–v. Performers: Owen McIntosh, tenor; Jesse Irons and Megumi Stohs Lewis, violins; Sarah Darling, viola; Peter Sykes, harpsichord; Sarah Freiberg, cello.

Mus. Ex. 7.1.   Henry Purcell, "Serene and calm," aria from *King Arthur* (1691), act 5. Score: *The Music in King Arthur*, ed. Margaret Laurie (Kent: Novello, 1972), in *The Works of Henry Purcell*, XXVI. Performers: Bradford Gleim, baritone; Roy Sansom and Héloïse Degrugillier, recorders; Peter Sykes, harpsichord; Sarah Freiberg, cello.

Mus. Ex. 7.2.   John Blow, excerpt from *Awake, awake, utter a song* (1704). Score: John Blow, *Selected Verse Anthems*, ed. Fredrick Tarrant (Middleton, Wis.: A-R Editions, 2009). Performers: Owen McIntosh and Marcio de Oliveira, tenors; Peter Sykes, organ; Sarah Freiberg, cello.

Mus. Ex. 8.1.   Giovanni Bononcini, aria from act 1 of *Camilla* (1696, 1706). Score: *Camilla: Royal College of Music ms 79*, ed. Lowell Lindgren (Stainer and Bell, 1990), 5–6. Performers: Teresa Wakim, soprano; Scott Metcalfe, violin; Peter Sykes, harpsichord; Sarah Freiberg, cello.

Mus. Ex. 8.2.   Thomas Clayton, recitative from act 1 of *Arsinoe* (1705). Score: GB-Lbl Egerton MS 3664, fol. 5r. Performers: Patrick Waters, tenor; Michael Barrett, tenor; Shari Wilson, soprano; Paul Tipton, baritone; Peter Sykes, harpsichord; Sarah Freiberg, cello.

Mus. Ex. 8.3.   Jeremiah Clarke, excerpt from *I Will Love Thee, O Lord* (1705). Score: *The Gostling Manuscript*, ed. Franklin B. Zimmerman (Austin: University of Texas Press, 1977). Performers: Patrick Waters, tenor; Peter Sykes, organ; Sarah Freiberg, cello.

Mus. Ex. 8.4.   Jeremiah Clarke, excerpt from *O Harmony where's now thy Pow'r?* (1706). Score: GB-Ob MS Mus. C. 6, fols. 17v–19r. Performers: Patrick Waters, tenor; Paul Tipton, baritone; Peter Sykes, harpsichord; Sarah Freiberg, cello.

Mus. Ex. 9.1.   Thomas Clayton, aria from act 1 of *Rosamond* (1707). Score: *Songs in the new Opera call'd Rosamond* (1707), 15. Performers: Teresa Wakim, soprano; Peter Sykes, harpsichord; Sarah Freiberg, cello.

Mus. Ex. 9.2.   William Croft, excerpt from *Sing unto the Lord* (1709). Score: William Croft, *Musica Sacra*, 2 vols. (1724), II, 25–28. Performers: Shari Wilson, soprano; Douglas Dodson, countertenor; Patrick Waters, tenor; Paul Tipton, baritone; Peter Sykes, organ; Sarah Freiberg, cello.

Mus. Ex. 10.1.   George Frideric Handel, aria from *Eternal Source of Light Divine* (1713). Score: *Ode for the Birthday of Queen Anne*, ed. Walther Siegmund-Schultze (Kassel: Bärenreiter, 1962), in *Hallische Handel-Ausgabe*, ser. 1, vol. 6. Performance: Jason McStoots, tenor; Robinson Pyle, trumpet; Dorian Bandy and Emily Dahl, violins; Anna Griffis, viola; Peter Sykes, harpsichord; Denise Fan, cello.

Mus. Ex. 10.2.   Giovanni Baptista Draghi, excerpt from *Song for St. Cecilia's Day, 1687*. Score: *"From Harmony, from Heav'nly Harmony,"* ed. Bryan White (Novello, 2010), 11–12. Performers: Teresa Wakim, soprano; Peter Sykes, organ; Sarah Freiberg, cello.

Mus. Ex. 10.3.   George Frideric Handel, "Sarabande—Tanz von Asiatern," from *Almira* (1705), act 3, no. 52. Score: *Almira*, ed. Dorothea Schröder (Kassel: Bärenreiter, 1994), in *Hallische Handel-Ausgabe*, ser. 2, vol. 1. Performers: Scott Metcalfe, Emily Dahl, Asako Takeuchi, Dorian Bandy, violins; Peter Sykes, harpsichord; Sarah Freiberg, cello.

Mus. Ex. 10.4.   George Frideric Handel, aria from *Rinaldo* (1711), act 2, no. 22. Score: *Rinaldo*, ed. David R. B. Kimball (Kassel: Bärenreiter, 1993), in *Hallische Handel-Ausgabe*, ser. 2, vol. 4. Performers: Teresa Wakim, soprano; Scott Metcalfe, Emily Dahl, Asako Takeuchi, Dorian Bandy, violins; Anne Black, viola; Peter Sykes, harpsichord; Sarah Freiberg, cello.

Mus. Ex. 10.5.   Francesco Gasparini, aria from *Ambleto* (1712). Score: *Songs in the Opera of Hamlet* (1712), 16–17. Performers: Teresa Wakim, soprano; Robinson Pyle, trumpet; Scott Metcalfe, Emily Dahl, Asako Takeuchi, Dorian Bandy, violins; Peter Sykes, harpsichord; Sarah Freiberg, cello.

Mus. Ex. 11.1.   William Croft, aria from *Prepare, ye Sons of Art* (1714). Score: GB-Lbl Add. MS 31455; bass figures added from GB-Lbl R.M.24.d.5. Performers: Paul Tipton, baritone; Peter Sykes, harpsichord; Sarah Freiberg, cello.

PREFACE

In his influential edition of the works of Alexander Pope, the Victorian clergyman Whitwell Elwin described Queen Anne as "ugly, corpulent, gouty, sluggish, a glutton and a tippler."[1] Modern historians may be more polite, but they still underestimate Anne's intelligence and ability.[2] By approaching the life and reign of this popular and successful monarch through her knowledge and patronage of the arts, I hope to provide a more balanced picture. She was a competent performer on the guitar and the harpsichord, an excellent dancer and actress in her youth, a fluent speaker of French, a promoter of opera, a shrewd connoisseur of painting and architecture, an experienced judge of political and religious oratory, and a reader able to quote contemporary poets from memory. In crafting works designed to flatter and please her, poets, composers, painters, architects, preachers, journalists, and performers of all kinds engaged in nuanced negotiations between the political and the aesthetic, evidently believing that Anne would appreciate the subtleties of the works they crafted for her.

During her years as a princess (1665–1702), Anne devoted considerable attention to the arts. By the time she was three, her parents had provided her with a music master and a dancing master; when she was ten, they encouraged her to display her skills in John Crowne's *Calisto,* a court masque written to feature her older sister Mary, with a subservient but substantial role for Anne. In her teens, she acted in two productions of *Mithridates,* a seamy tragedy by Nathaniel Lee, playing the male lead in one and the female lead in the other. She took music lessons from Francesco Corbetta, the leading guitarist in Europe, and from Giovanni Baptista Draghi, the harpsichord player who composed the first setting of Dryden's "Song for St. Cecilia's Day, 1687." Henry Purcell wrote the music for her wedding and for several later occasions at her small court. During the brief rule of her father, James II, she witnessed the flowering of a baroque court culture emulating French and Italian models; while recognizing the sophistication of the artworks promoted by James's court, his enemies feared them as foreign and Catholic. The Revolution of 1688, which deposed him, brought in William and Mary, who established a court with a much more ascetic and hostile stance toward the arts. Disagreements about liturgical and secular music were a symptom of Anne's strained relations with her sister, which eventually led to a complete estrangement. After Mary's death, songs and poems in praise of Princess Anne were a medium for expressing dissatisfaction with King William. Anne's letters of this period reveal her as a reader of poems and plays and a fan of popular songs; the players marked her visits to the theatre with special prologues and sometimes with special music. Prominent artists also celebrated William, Duke of Gloucester, her only child to survive infancy: Sir Godfrey Kneller painted him on several occasions; Purcell wrote the music for his sixth birthday party. When he died at eleven in 1700, poets from schools and universities devoted three large volumes to poems in Latin mourning the nation's loss.

During Anne's reign as queen (1702–14), her devotion to her duties and her limited mobility kept her from attending theatrical and musical performances in the commercial theatres. On important occasions, however, she enjoyed plays and operas at court, New Year's and birthday odes performed by her own musicians, and special church music sung at services of thanksgiving for military victories in the War of the Spanish Succession. The arts flourished under her scepter: Sir John Vanbrugh designed Blenheim Palace, her gift to the Duke of Marlborough, and Sir Christopher Wren finished St. Paul's Cathedral; Alexander Pope published his astonishing early poems, Jonathan Swift and Daniel Defoe emerged as political journalists, Joseph Addison and Richard Steele established their influential journals, and Delarivier Manley wrote scandalous popular fictions; Kneller, Michael Dahl, and John Closterman painted portraits of the monarch and other prominent people; George Frideric Handel brought first-class Italian opera to London and wrote a beautiful birthday ode for the queen, who awarded him a generous pension. The causes of this cultural abundance were many: the lapse of the Licensing Act in 1695 made daily newspapers possible; the relative prosperity of the nation increased the audience for theatrical and musical entertainments; and partisan politics began to replace aristocratic patronage as a source of employment for artists. If the court was no longer the sole center of patronage, the queen played a crucial part in creating an environment in which artistic production could flourish.

Recent scholarship on this period is rich but highly specialized, often addressed to experts in only one discipline. The work of Winton Dean on Handel, to take but one example, has greatly increased our understanding of his compositional genius but has not had much influence in fields other than musicology.[3] Parliamentary historians have clarified our understanding of the frequent general elections and cabinet shifts during this period but have not given much attention to the way both parties employed writers and artists, a process exemplified when Sidney Godolphin, Anne's lord treasurer, commissioned Addison to write *The Campaign*, a poem on Marlborough's victory at Blenheim, rewarding him with a salaried position in the government. Focusing on foreign affairs, parliamentary and ministerial politics, and Anne's personal relations with her female confidantes, her biographers have neglected the insights we may gain by considering the arts of her period, which are often rich in explicit or implicit political content.[4] In bringing these materials to bear upon the life and reign of Queen Anne, I have cast my nets widely, considering not only the masterworks made for her by gifted artists but many revealing lesser works, including the obscene lampoons, topical ballads, cheap woodcut images, and novels of scandal that undermined the official court myth of the queen as the "nursing mother" of her people. Anne was the first queen to rule on her own since Elizabeth, and she sought to appropriate some aspects of her great predecessor, including Elizabeth's motto, "semper eadem" (always the same). Her presence on the throne encouraged women playwrights and poets, some of whom promoted the reformation of manners, but sexual gossip about prominent people, including the queen herself, circulated widely, and women authors participated in that process as well. If we wish to understand the aesthetic and ideological struggle over the royal image, we need to consider these materials as well as more polite artistic productions.

By declining to analyze the styles in architecture, painting, oratory, poetry, drama, music, opera, and dance that flourished during Anne's period, scholars have missed opportunities to gain a fuller knowledge of the culture that surrounded the last of the Stuarts. In order to provide a more comprehensive view of her life and reign, I have emphasized the dynamic and often competitive relations among the arts, as well as the interplay between all the arts and the religious, scientific, intellectual, and political developments of the period.

Because these complex issues sometimes come together in a single event, I have chosen to begin each chapter with a detailed account of a particular occasion: a court masque, a wedding, a coronation, a child's birthday celebration, a funeral, an allegorical pageant, a service of thanksgiving, an opera, a state trial, a musical ode, and another funeral. After the detailed account, I provide a historical narrative of events and ideas leading up to that pivotal moment. I hope this book will have an impact on scholars working in the fields of history, literature, art history, and musicology, but I have also sought to make it readily available to interested readers of all kinds. Anne's life had moments of glory and pathos, and I hope my focus on the arts will help readers understand how it felt to live in her times, and even how it felt to be the queen she became.

Boston—London—Brattleboro
June 17, 2013

NOTES ON STYLE

Dating

During the years covered by this book, England used the Julian calendar, as opposed to the Gregorian calendar in use on the Continent. The two calendars were eleven days apart, so that 9 April in England was already 20 April in France or Holland. Further confusion arises because the new year in England, though sometimes reckoned as beginning on 1 January, was traditionally marked by Lady Day (25 March). A letter dated 13 February 1701, was thus *probably*, though not necessarily, written on 13 February 1702. All dates in the text and notes are Old Style, meaning that they follow the English calendar then in use, but the year is treated as beginning on 1 January. When describing events on the Continent, I have normally given both dates, e.g. 3/14 July 1703.

Texts

When quoting material from the period of Anne's life and reign, I have sought to present the texts in versions close to what she and her contemporaries read. In quoting her letters and other manuscripts, I have preserved most of the original spellings, occasionally and silently correcting spellings that might be misleading. I have expanded "wch" to "which," "yt" to "that," and "ye" to "the," lowered all superscripted letters, and silently added punctuation marks for clarity. When I have used modern scholarly editions, such as the California Dryden and the Twickenham Pope, I have chosen old-spelling texts rather than modernized versions.

CHAPTER I

A LITTLE STAR

22 February 1675

Covered with jewels and clothed in silk, the twelve young ladies stood waiting for the music to begin. For six months, they had been memorizing their lines, practicing their dances, and trying on their special shoes. During the last two months, they had often rehearsed *Calisto: or, The Chaste Nimph* in costume before large audiences, and tonight—after months of rehearsals, revisions, and delays—they were at last presenting the official premiere of the whole masque. Six operatic scenes performed by professional musicians now framed and adorned the five acts of rhyming dialogue that the ladies had learned to declaim. As the musical prologue began, the audience saw a group of singers in allegorical costume, including "a Nymph leaning on an Urne, representing the River *Thames*," "two Nymphs, representing *Peace* and *Plenty*," and four male singers dressed as Europe, Asia, Africa, and America. After receiving symbolic gifts from the singing continents, the singing river cued the courtly amateurs for "an Entry of Shepherds and Nymphs, Dancing round the *Thames*, &c. as they stood in their Figure." Performing the sarabande, a slow dance with castanets, "the Princesses and the other Ladies" formed their circle around the professionals playing Peace, Plenty, the Thames, the continents, and the "Genius of England." In this fanciful tableau, the ring of youthful dancers enclosed the world.[1]

The "Princesses" named in the stage directions were two future queens of England: Princess Mary, aged twelve, and Princess Anne, who had just turned ten.

Their father—James Stuart, Duke of York—was next in line to the throne, and in the absence of a male child, his daughters would succeed him. King Charles II, brother to James and uncle to Mary and Anne, had no legitimate heirs of either sex, though his paramours had already borne him at least eight illegitimate children. Barred from the succession, these royal offspring participated openly in the life of the court: two of them took part in *Calisto*. Anne Palmer, Countess of Sussex, recently married though not quite fourteen, danced the sarabande with her legitimate cousins and the other ladies, while James Scott, Duke of Monmouth, a dashing young man of twenty-five, concluded this entry by performing a solo minuet. His father and his uncle, the king and the Duke of York, had the best seats in the audience: the king next to his long-suffering wife, Queen Catharine of Braganza; the duke next to his second Duchess, Maria Beatrice of Modena, an Italian beauty of sixteen—just four years older than his daughter Mary. Despite her youth, Maria had given birth to a daughter of her own six weeks before the performance, which was delayed until she recovered.[2]

By giving prominent parts in *Calisto* to Mary and Anne, the court was offering them a special opportunity to display their skills in acting and dancing, accomplishments that polite young ladies were supposed to acquire along with drawing, singing, speaking French, and playing musical instruments. The princesses had begun their training in these courtly arts as soon as they could walk and talk. In 1669, when Mary was "a little child in hanging sleeves," the diarist Samuel Pepys saw her "dance most finely, so as almost to ravish me," and gave due credit to Jeremiah Gohory, the French dancing master who taught both sisters.[3] Even earlier, when Mary was five and Anne was two, their father appointed "Anthony Robart," a French singer and viol player, as "musick-maister to the Lady Mary and Lady Anne" at £100 a year, a salary equal to that of the poet laureate. Still active in his seventies, Robart was among the professional musicians who performed in *Calisto*.[4]

Court ladies grew up quickly, and frequent plays and balls prepared the princesses for a life in which they would constantly be on stage. *Calisto* was Anne's first public performance, but her sister Mary had made her theatrical début in a leading role some five years earlier. On 6 April 1670, three weeks before her eighth birthday, the older princess presented "a comedy" before the king and queen with the other "little young ladies of the Court, who appeared extraordinarily glorious and covered with jewels."[5] The play chosen for this occasion was *The Faithful Shepherdess* by John Fletcher, with Mary playing the title character, Clorin, who enters mourning her dead swain and retains her chastity through five acts of high-minded rhyming dialogue. First acted in 1609, Fletcher's play reflects the values of an earlier era, yet John Crowne's *Calisto*, specially commissioned for performance at court in 1675, shares some of its basic features: both are poetic pastorals involving magical transformations and celebrating sexual innocence. Because the little princesses studied French, not Latin, they had no firsthand knowledge of Crowne's source, a story from Ovid in which Jupiter impregnates Diana's attendant Calisto, but they were certainly familiar with the myth of the virginal huntress. Sir Peter Lely, chief painter to the king, had already painted Mary as Diana with all the usual props: a bow and arrow, a crescent headpiece, and an eager hound (color plate 3).[6]

The education provided for Mary and Anne, with its heavy emphasis on the arts, attracted criticism from puritanical enemies of the court—and even from some in the aristocracy. In a letter published a year before Anne's birth, Margaret Cavendish, Duchess of Newcastle, complained that the skills taught to upper-class girls might lead to sexual immorality:

> Women are not Educated as they should be, I mean those of Quality, for their Education is onely to Dance, Sing, and Fiddle, to write Comple-mental Letters, to read Romances, to speak some Language that is not their Native, which Education, is an Education of the Body, and not of the Mind, and shews that their Parents take more care of their Feet than their Head, more of their Words than their Reason, more of their Musick than their Virtue, more of their Beauty than their Honesty, which…makes the Body a Courtier, and the Mind a Clown, and oftentimes it makes their Body a Baud, and their Mind a Courtesan, for though the Body procures Lovers, yet it is the Mind that is the Adulteress, for if the Mind were Honest and Pure, they would never be guilty of that Crime.[7]

The outspoken duchess, who had been a Maid of Honor during the 1640s, was not alone in these views. Elizabeth Livingston, a Maid of Honor in the 1660s, com-plained that her time was "waisted in dressing, in dancing, in seing and in acting of play's, in hunting, in musick, in all sorts of devertions, which moderately us'd had been harmelesse, but makeing them the busyness of my life, they soon became sinfull vaine pleasures."[8] Even Princess Mary, an enthusiastic dancer in her youth, had embraced a similarly ascetic position by the time she came to the throne, re-ferring to dancing as "that which used to be one of my prettiest pleasures in the world, and that I feard might be a sin in me for loving it too well."[9] Her sister Anne, by contrast, remained an avid dancer until her lameness and obesity made it im-possible for her to continue;[10] she never described the pleasure she took in any of the arts as sinful.

By emphasizing the innocence and beauty of the young performers, which was evidently part of his assignment, Crowne was countering those who disapproved of courtly graces, as well as reminding the princesses that their chastity was a pre-cious commodity, a national asset that could prove valuable in diplomatic negotia-tions of real importance. Yet only by knowing something about foreign, domestic, and courtly politics could Mary and Anne appreciate the emphasis placed on their maintaining their sexual innocence. A special epilogue written for the court performance of *The Faithful Shepherdess* in 1670, most likely the work of John Dryden, points toward some of these ironies by invoking diplomacy and warfare, ideas entirely absent from the pastoral drama itself.[11] The speaker of this epilogue, Lady Mary Mordaunt, would later play the jealous nymph Psecas in *Calisto*. She was only eleven years old at the time of the court production of *The Faithful Shepherdess*, yet the epilogue depends upon the idea that she and the other "little young ladies" of the court will soon be the objects of erotic ogling:

> When Princes in distress, would peace implore,
> They first take care to choose th' Ambassadour,
> And think him fittest for a charge so great,
> Who best can please the King with whom they treat:
> Our Play they threaten'd with a tragique Fate,
> I, Sir, am chose for this affair of State,
> And, hope, what ever errors we confess,
> You'l pardon to the young Ambassadress.
> If not though now these little Ladies are,
> In no condition, to maintain a Warr:
> Their beauties will in time grow up so strong,
> That on your Court, they may revenge the wrong.[12]

When a defeated king seeks to make peace, he is careful to choose an attractive ambassador, so the speaker poses as an "Ambassadress" to the king on behalf of the young actresses, hoping that her beauty will induce him to forgive any "errors" in their performance. Charming and witty, this simile also had specific political resonance. Three years earlier, as everyone knew, Charles II had been a prince in distress, imploring peace from the Dutch, who had sailed up the Medway, burned thirteen ships at anchor, and towed away the *Royal Charles*, effectively ending the Second Dutch Naval War (1665–1667). As his ambassadors, the king chose Denzil Holles, a punctilious old parliamentarian, and Henry Coventry, a younger man who had served as a captain in the Dutch army in the 1650s and was therefore likely to be pleasing to the Dutch negotiators. One month after attending this performance, Charles signed a secret treaty with Louis XIV of France, his first cousin, committing both nations to a new joint war against the Dutch, an ill-conceived attempt to "revenge the wrong" of the earlier defeat. In the magical, perfumed world of the Stuart court, this epilogue turns the tables, with Charles now cast in the role of the victorious monarch and little Mary Mordaunt, pretty and precocious, appealing to him on behalf of his niece and her friends. The political sophistication of the poem, which sails very close to recent embarrassments, mirrors the social and sexual sophistication of the court.

One year before *Calisto*, the Third Dutch Naval War (1672–1674) had come to a similarly unsatisfactory conclusion, as a series of defeats and a lack of domestic support forced Charles to seek peace with the Dutch once more. Crowne did his best to paper over this failure. In the musical passage announcing the entrance of the dancing nymphs, the Thames implies that the play is an "innocent delight," a way to keep the princesses and their ladies from fretting about war and politics:

> These beautious Nymphs unfrightned too,
> Not minding what on other Shores they do,
>   Their innocent delights pursue.[13]

Yet the very prologue in which she sings these lines, an operatic allegory depicting world trade in the context of the recent war, completely invalidates her description of *Calisto* as a harmless diversion designed to maintain the innocence of the young ladies. Crowne's insistence on the political innocence of the "beautious Nymphs" resembles his treatment of the play's central theme, the sexual purity and innocence of the "Chaste Nimph" Calisto, acted by Princess Mary. In both cases, the author's sly rhetoric encourages his audience to enjoy the way his knowing, worldly play engages adult concerns while pretending to be a harmless pastoral acted by ladies too young and innocent to grasp its content.[14] For the princesses and their ladies, it was a lesson in worldliness.

§

Though fancifully described as "unfrightened nymphs," the princesses featured in *Calisto* had already lived through some frightening history. Both girls were born in St. James's Palace in London, but their nursery was at York House, a handsome brick building in the riverside village of Twickenham.[15] The country setting chosen by their mother—Anne Hyde, Duchess of York—protected her children from the noise and filth of London, but not from all knowledge of the wider world. Perhaps from their parents, perhaps from the "rockers" and "dressers" who tended them, the little princesses would have learned that their paternal grandfather, Charles I, was a controversial king, executed at the end of a bloody civil war. They would also have been aware that their maternal grandfather—Edward Hyde, Earl of Clarendon, the owner of the building that housed their nursery—was an important politician now serving their uncle Charles II as his trusted Lord Chancellor. At some point, they would have heard the romantic tale of their parents' clandestine marriage in 1660, a match initially deplored by both families because

Anne Hyde, as the daughter of a self-made lawyer, was not considered noble enough to marry the brother of a reigning monarch. Princess Anne's fascination with courtly rituals, which carried over into her reign as queen, may have originated in her need to efface this supposed deficiency in her ancestry.

Sir Peter Lely's delightful portrait of the little princess at two or three shows her holding a bird on a string, but she did not have the control over events that the picture shows her exerting over her pet (color plates 1, 2). In 1665, a few months after Anne was born, the family decamped to the North to avoid the plague, and in 1666, London was ravaged by the Great Fire. In 1667, when she was only two, her four-year-old brother James, Duke of Cambridge, died in the royal nursery. Later in the same year, her grandfather's enemies made him their scapegoat for the mismanagement of the Second Dutch Naval War. Removed from office and impeached by Parliament, Clarendon fled to France, where he devoted his remaining years to writing his *History of the Rebellion*, an influential Royalist account of the English Civil War. The splendid town house he had built in London may have contributed to his fall from power; not only was it ostentatious, but the materials included stones purchased (some said stolen) from the rebuilding project at St. Paul's Cathedral.[16] Although Princess Anne was far too young to have appreciated this intersection of politics and architecture, it is intriguing that she erected no new buildings for her own use when queen, but warmly embraced a project to build fifty new churches in London.

John Dunstall, *Clarendon House* (1687–1692).

In 1668, at the age of three, the little girl went to France to be treated for an eye ailment.[17] At first she stayed with her grandmother—Henrietta Maria, the widow of Charles I—but the dowager Queen, who had long been unwell, died during her visit. The princess then moved to a nursery kept by her aunt, Charles II's beloved sister Minette, who also died, quite suddenly, in June 1670. The widowed "Monsieur," younger brother to Louis XIV, put his own daughters and their cousin Anne into "long trailing mantles of violet velvet" so that they could receive "formal visits of condolence" in the nursery.[18] Princess Anne was five years old, her cousin Marie-Louise was eight, and the baby, Anne-Marie, was not yet one. Anne's lifelong insistence on the proper observance of mourning may have owed something to this formative experience. When she returned to England, death pursued her; she lost three members of her family in 1671. Her mother died of cancer in March, and in June her three-year-old brother Edgar, the next Duke of Cambridge, followed his mother to the grave; the remaining infant, Catherine, born a few weeks before her mother's death, died in December.[19] Needing another male heir, the Duke of York was soon in search of a wife; in September 1673 he informed his daughters of his second marriage by telling Mary that he had "provided a playfellow for her."[20]

Even as children, then, both princesses had experienced death, loss, political conflict, and the courtly spectacles associated with royal weddings and funerals. They already knew quite a lot about wars on "other Shores," politics in England, and the not-so-innocent delights of the court in which they lived. Courtly protocol gave them constant reminders of where they stood in the succession to the throne, though they could not yet know how urgent the succession would become in both their lives. Gossip and controversy taught them that their father's second marriage, like the marriages they would both be constrained to make, was a political event. Although Princess Mary was not yet thirteen when she came onstage as Calisto, courtiers and diplomats had already begun to discuss the match that would join her to her first cousin William of Orange, who was twenty-four and fully engaged in the political and military affairs of Europe.

The sexually charged atmosphere of the court provided other lessons. In order to act her roles as Clorin and Calisto, fending off rude advances by shepherds and satyrs in the first play and an attempted seduction by Jupiter himself in the second, little Mary had to understand the concepts of virginity and temptation; her sister Anne, less than three years younger, would not have been far behind. If they lived in a world devoted to dressing, dancing, acting, and other diversions, the Stuart princesses were nonetheless required to be worldly. They were constantly reminded of the many kinds of desire on display in their philandering uncle's court and never allowed to forget the major traumas that had shaken their nation and their family over the past thirty-five years: the Civil Wars, the Commonwealth, the Restoration, and the naval wars against the Dutch.

Like many of his contemporaries, the playwright had lived a life shaped by those events. Born in London, John Crowne emigrated to America during the Interregnum and attended the dourly Puritan Harvard College. When he returned to England after the Restoration, he denounced his Harvard teachers as enemies to the king and began a literary career designed to gain royal patronage.[21] In his preface to the printed version of *Calisto*, Crowne described himself as "*invaded*, on the sudden, by a Powerful Command, to prepare an Entertainment for the Court." It was a welcome opportunity but a challenging one, especially for a playwright who had no experience in writing words for music. The choice of plot also presented problems. In the source, a tale from Ovid's *Metamorphoses*, the impatient Jupiter rapes the virgin Calisto, which put the playwright in a difficult position: "I employed myself," Crowne confessed, "to write a clean, decent, and inoffensive Play, on the Story of a Rape, so that I was engaged in this Dilemma, either wholly to deviate from my Story, and so my Story would be no Story, or by keeping to it, write what would be unfit for Princesses and Ladies to speak, and a Court to hear."[22]

Crowne's dilemma took on more urgency because Princess Mary was to play the title role. Aware of the court's interest in using this drama to feature the duke's young daughters, the playwright made no effort to maintain the already thin distinction between the mythical nymphs and the real princesses. As soon as Calisto appears, Diana praises her in terms clearly applicable to Mary:

> Princess Calisto, most admir'd belov'd,
>   The Fairest, Chastest, most approv'd
> Of all that ever grac'd my Virgin Throng,
> You, who of great and Royal Race are sprung,
>   Born under Golden Roofs, and bred to ease,
>   To every kind of soft delight,
>   To Glory, Power, and all that might
>   A Royal Virgin please.

As Nyphe, a character invented by Crowne, Anne had to make a speech extending this flattery and deferring to her sister:

> How am I pleas'd my Sisters praise to hear,
> Though like a little Star I near appear,
> Nature and Friendship do enough prefer
> My Name to Honour, whilst I shine in her.[23]

Even at ten, however, the "little Star," like younger siblings in many families, probably hoped to shine on her own, and she can hardly have escaped the knowledge that the play's high-minded talk of chastity and purity masked other realities. For the ladies of the court, including the maids of honor serving the queen and the duchess, sexual intrigue was constant and dangerous, and with no reliable contraception, pregnancies among their ranks were frequent. A few months after *Calisto*, Mary Kirk, Maid of Honor to the Duchess of York, gave birth to a short-lived child and fled to France in disgrace. According to those aware of Kirk's recent affairs, her baby's father might have been the Duke of York (Anne's father), the Duke of Monmouth (Anne's first cousin), or the Earl of Mulgrave (later an aspirant for Anne's own hand).[24] For an audience accustomed to such scandals, there was obviously some comedy inherent in Crowne's asking the court ladies to impersonate the "Virgin Throng" of Diana's nymphs.

One of Princess Mary's earliest surviving letters, written before she was fourteen, shows how well she understood the prevailing conventions: "men are always wery of their wifes," she writes, "and look for mistresses as sone as thay can get them."[25] Nor was such restlessness confined to men. Anne Palmer, daughter of the king by his longtime mistress Barbara Palmer, Countess of Castlemaine, was married in 1674 at the age of thirteen, gaining the title of Countess of Sussex. A few years after acting in *Calisto*, she began an affair with Ralph Montagu, ambassador to France and one of her mother's many lovers. As if the story of the teenaged countess stealing a lover from her mother were not sufficiently salacious, court gossips also hinted at an amorous connection between Anne Palmer and Hortense Mancini, Duchess of Mazarin, one of her father's many mistresses.[26]

Living as they did in a court where such intrigues were constant topics of speculation, the little princesses could not long remain naive. Another early letter in Mary's hand describes the pain and damage caused by the discovery of an affair between the Duke of Monmouth and Eleanor Needham, another Maid of Honor: "Mrs. Needam is gone away & says nobody shal never hear of her more," writes Mary. "But the Duches of Munmoth thay say dos take it mightily to harte and since it has been known has never bin abrode nor never has seen the duke of Munmoth since."[27] Anne Scott, Duchess of Monmouth, had married the king's handsome bastard on 20 April 1663, when she was twelve; their union was officially consummated on 9 February 1665, three days after the birth of Princess Anne, for whom the young duchess stood godmother. Princess Mary's understanding of the sexual culture of the court, soon shared by her sister, was not the result of disinterested observation; the scandals touched people with whom both princesses were personally familiar.

In the same letter, Mary mentions Sarah Jenyns, a participant in *Calisto* and a Maid of Honor to her stepmother. Sarah, now fourteen, was destined to be Princess

Anne's most intimate confidante for much of her adult life. She had recently caught the eye of a young courtier and soldier named John Churchill, whose military exploits as the Duke of Marlborough would be among the great events of Queen Anne's reign. At the time of *Calisto*, however, Colonel Churchill was best known at court for audaciously supplanting the king in the arms of the countess of Castlemaine, and for being the brother of Arabella Churchill, mistress to the Duke of York. For Sarah, who was fully aware of the sexual histories of John Churchill and his sister, dealing with his advances required confidence and courage—attributes her society coded as male. Crowne's preface does not tell us who was responsible for assigning roles to the young ladies who acted in *Calisto*, but the bold, opinionated Sarah was quite well suited for her part: the male god Mercury. "I am confydent," she wrote in 1714, "I should have been the greatest Hero that was known in the *Parliament Hous*, if I had been so happy as to have been a Man."[28]

Whoever cast Sarah as Mercury also thought it might be droll to cast Anne Palmer, daughter of a prominent royal mistress, as Juno, the neglected wife of the roving Jupiter. This callous joke reflects the social attitudes of the court, in which the maids of honor, explicitly chosen for their beauty, were generally regarded as fair game. With the possible exception of Princess Anne, who was only ten, all the young ladies in *Calisto* could expect ogling glances from the men of the court. Even pious Margaret Blagge, the oldest of the group at twenty-two, had two admirers watching her every move as the virgin goddess Diana: the much older scientist and scholar John Evelyn, her instructor in religion and manners, and the able courtier Sidney Godolphin, later Queen Anne's faithful Treasurer, whom Margaret secretly married a few months after the premiere.

§

Admiring the court beauties was by no means the only attraction provided by *Calisto*. In addition to the noble amateurs, the production featured no fewer than ninety professional performers: dancers, singers, and two large groups of instrumentalists.[29] The composer was Nicholas Staggins, a violinist and flutist who had already written songs for two plays by Dryden. Although most of the music he wrote for *Calisto* is lost, the surviving songs and instrumental pieces are tuneful,[30] and Staggins could count on having his work well played: thanks to his recent appointment as Master of the King's Music, he had access to the best available performers. Among the four "guitar masters" who appeared in "Indian gowns" was Francesco Corbetta, whose book of compositions, *La Guitarre Royalle*, had established him as the leading exponent of his instrument in the world. Earlier in his career, Corbetta had given guitar lessons to both Louis XIV and Charles II; he was now giving lessons to Princess Anne.[31] The female vocal soloists included Mary (or Moll) Davis and Mary Knight—both of them performers from the commercial theatres and former mistresses of the king—while the men included the bass James Hart and the countertenor William Turner, the best soloists from the all-male choir of the Chapel Royal.

The production was also lavish. Although Christopher Wren, Surveyor General of the King's Works, was busy designing the new St. Paul's Cathedral, the court asked him to supervise the extensive repairs and alterations required to prepare the Hall Theatre for *Calisto*. Robert Streeter, who had painted the ceiling of Wren's Sheldonian Theatre in Oxford a few years earlier, provided the scenery, which included a Temple of Fame and a device called a "glory," a translucent frame that bathed the actors in front of it with heavenly light.[32] Crowne called attention to all of this work by concluding his prologue with "An Entry of Carpenters"—a dance by professionals costumed as laborers.[33]

Few of those in attendance were old enough to remember the famous court masques staged for James I and Charles I, in which the fanciful costumes and sets designed by Inigo Jones had often overshadowed the poetic texts devised by Ben Jonson and his followers. Yet even without specific memories of those entertainments, many would have recognized this defiantly expensive production as a revival of the styles and attitudes of past Stuart courts. Like other attempts to recover past splendor, *Calisto* inevitably reminded its audience of the fate of the earlier Stuarts. Three weeks before the premiere of *Calisto*, the little princesses, dressed in black and fasting all day, joined the court and the nation in the annual day of mourning for their grandfather Charles I, beheaded on 30 January 1649 on a scaffold erected in front of the Banqueting House where his beloved masques had been performed. This shocking execution, the last act in a bitter and bloody struggle between king and Parliament, led to a decade of nominally republican government that was, in practice, a military dictatorship. Only the collapse of order after Oliver Cromwell's death made it possible for the Stuart line to be restored in 1660, and if Charles II, a shrewd survivor, had now clung to power for fifteen years, he was always aware of continuing opposition.

In the sermon heard by the king and his family on this most recent day of mourning, the preacher, George Stradling, compares Charles I to Jesus Christ:

> And now, *Behold the man*. Such a Person this day dying not like *one of the Princes*, but the vilest of Malefactors; murdered with all the Formalities of Justice and Devotion, by such as had no power at all over the life of the meanest of their fellow subjects.... The Common Shepherd *led like a Sheep to the slaughter*, after so many Declarations published and Professions made for his Safety and Honour, in cold blood, most barbarously Butchered on a Scaffold, by the hand of the Hangman, before that part of His Palace where He had so often appeared in State: What name shall we

find for such a wickedness? A crime black as that Hell it came from, and which nothing can equal but the defence of it.[34]

Sermons on the martyred king typically used such language, but when Stradling equates the crime of *defending* the execution with the crime of committing it, he is acknowledging the continuing existence of political forces determined to limit the authority of King Charles II and his brother James. The illegal chapels of the Non-conformists or Dissenters—Baptists, Quakers, Presbyterians, and many smaller groups—were centers of resistance to the Crown, and many conforming members of the established Church of England also harbored doubts about autocratic power. The City of London, home to mercantile interests, recent immigrants, stubborn Dissenters, and underground printers, was especially troublesome to the king, as it had been to his father.

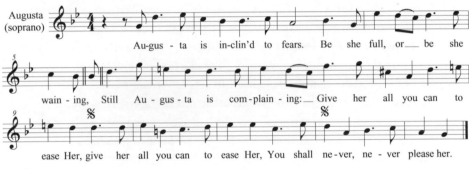

Mus. Ex. 1.1: Nicholas Staggins, *"Augusta is inclin'd to fears."* From *Calisto* (1675).

Like Stradling's sermon, Crowne's masque acknowledges the existence of this political opposition, but while Stradling vilifies the Dissenters as perpetrators of black crimes, Crowne personifies the City as a difficult woman. In a song from *Calisto* that gained some popularity, he gives London her traditional name, "Augusta," and describes her as fearful, complaining, and impossible to please.[35] Augusta is as changeable as the moon, that most conventional image of female mutability, but whether full or waning, she never stops complaining. Although the City was supposedly the last refuge of Puritan values, Augusta is also sexually insatiable: "Give her all you can to ease Her, / You shall never, never please Her."[36] Princess Anne was probably too young to understand all the political and sexual implications of this song, or of *Calisto* as a whole, but her training had already prepared her to understand that the glittering court masque, like the solemn sermon, was a defiant assertion of royal power and privilege, made in the face of troubling opposition.

The extravagance of the production was part of the defiance. Existing bills for the carpentry, costumes, and music required for *Calisto* total £3,526.19s.11³/⁴d., and some records are evidently missing; a conservative estimate of the total cost is "well over £5,000."[37] Converting seventeenth-century money into modern equivalents is notoriously difficult, but 200 is a fairly conservative "multiplier," which would give us a cost of £1,000,000, and the actual equivalent may well be more. A seventeenth-century comparison may also help to put this amount in perspective: the maximum gross for a full house at one of the commercial theatres at this date was £105, so this one production cost more than the King's Theatre might have taken in for forty-seven sellout performances.[38]

In the ideology of the Stuart court, excess was a sign of royalty. A few years earlier, in 1669, the compiler of *Angliæ Notitia*, a systematic guide to the royal establishment, lovingly chronicled the court's "prodigious" consumption of food, describing it as a way of impressing foreigners and solidifying domestic support:

> All Noblemen or Gentlemen, Subjects or Strangers that came accidently to Court were freely entertained at the plentiful Tables of His Majesties Officers.... The Magnificence and abundant plenty of the Kings Tables hath caused amazement in all Forreigners, when they have been informed that yearly was spent of gross Meat 1500 Oxen, 7000 Sheep, 1200 Veals, 300 Porkers, 400 Sturks or young Biefes, 6800 Lambs, 300 Flitches of Bacon, and 26 Boares.... This prodigious plenty caused Forreigners to put a higher value upon the King, and caused the Natives who were there freely welcome to encrease their affection to the King, it being found as necessary for the King of *England* this way to endear the English, who ever delighted in Feasting; as for the Italian Princes by Sights and Shews to endear their Subjects, who as much delight therein.[39]

Edward Chamberlayne, the nostalgic author of this account, was actually remembering how the royal tables had been furnished at the court of Charles I, a notable exponent of "Regall Magnificence."[40] Charles II, though attentive to all the rituals of monarchy, could not afford to provide meals for casual visitors, or even for all of his servants, but he often dined in public with members of his family, receiving his food from kneeling servants proffering golden dishes.[41] Her contemporaries believed that Princess Anne, who became an obese adult, inherited a propensity for gluttony from her mother, who was notorious for her love of eating,[42] but this parental example was hardly unique: Anne's courtly surroundings, before and after the early death of the duchess, gave her many opportunities to absorb the idea of magnificent consumption.

Chamberlayne was not alone in dismissing "Sights and Shews" as foreign pleasures, while praising excessive eating as authentically English, but this old-fashioned view was not applicable to Charles II, whose remarkable appetites for women and wine did not extend to gluttony and who actually showed keen interest in court theatricals. In 1663, not long after his restoration, the king complained to his sister that not one of his courtiers could execute an acceptable solo dance as part of a masquerade.[43] His agile son James, Duke of Monmouth, had learned to perform this function by the time of *Calisto*; the minuet he danced just after the ladies' sarabande was a last-minute addition to the program—and evidently one intended to please his father.[44] Charles loved French music and Italian opera, and in the early years of his reign, he explored various schemes for competing with Continental courts in staging costly musical entertainments, all of which failed because of his chronic lack of funds. In light of Chamberlayne's linking of "Sights and Shews" with "Italian Princes," it is intriguing that the second Duchess of York, an Italian princess, appears to have been keenly interested in *Calisto*. The form of the play, in which five acts in verse performed by the court ladies alternated with six musical scenes performed by professionals, closely resembles the form of the five-act spoken plays with musical *intermedii* performed at weddings of Italian nobles in the late sixteenth century, and Maria, a knowledgeable music-lover, may have suggested this structure to Crowne.[45] *Calisto* engaged all parts of the court in substantial work and expense for six months, and evidently enjoyed the support of the king and the duke, who often attended rehearsals. Henry Bennett, Earl of Arlington, a sophisticated courtier who had recently become Lord Chamberlain, clearly took overall responsibility, but Maria would have wanted her stepdaughters and their ladies-in-waiting to appear to advantage. Attentive to the personalities and positions of her attendants, who were close to her in age, she may even have been the one who assigned the speaking parts. Although she was pregnant, she continued to attend rehearsals until her time came. The decision to delay the premiere one last time so that she could be present after recovering from childbirth suggests that she had a real stake in the success of the performance.[46]

§

Observing the money and attention lavished on *Calisto*, a visitor might have concluded that Charles II was passing through a period of prosperity and leisure, and the masque may have been intended to produce that impression. In reality, the monarch's failures in warfare and vacillating policies about religion made his situation precarious. In May 1670, five years before *Calisto*, Charles had signed a treaty with Louis XIV, later known as the Secret Treaty of Dover, in which he promised better conditions for his Roman Catholic subjects and held out the hope that he would eventually declare himself a Catholic. In return for this dangerous undertaking, the wealthy Louis promised substantial financial support, and these private funds, not scrutinized by Parliament, probably paid for *Calisto*.

Only a few trusted courtiers knew about the Secret Treaty; others saw a bogus version signed in December 1670, which omitted the clauses on religion. In both versions, the monarchs agreed to attack the Dutch, whose large merchant fleet continued to dominate the lucrative trade between Africa and the West Indies: the British promised to take the lead on the seas while the French invaded Holland by land.[47]

Needless to say, the Duke of York was among those who were in on the secret. Together with his first Duchess, Anne Hyde, James had privately embraced Catholicism before the signing of the treaty; his wife's refusal of Anglican rites on her deathbed in 1671 increased the duke's devotion to his new faith. The king, whose skill at playing on both sides was remarkable, ultimately accepted his brother's conversion, but insisted that his two nieces be reared in the Church of England. He had already appointed Frances Villiers, impeccably descended and safely Protestant, as their governess and sent them to live with Lady Villiers and her six daughters in the royal palace at Richmond. Now he selected Henry Compton, a cavalry officer turned clergyman and a determined opponent of Catholicism, as their spiritual preceptor. For Princess Anne, this early training was decisive. Affection for the Church of England and disdain for the Church of Rome were constants in her adult life and principles of her reign as queen. Compton himself was also a constant: he performed her wedding ceremony in 1683, christened and buried most of her children, protected her during the revolutionary turmoil of 1688, and consoled her on the death of her husband in 1708. Although her own faith was unwavering, Anne's childhood gave her personal experience with the religious conflict that unsettled English politics for centuries. Her mother's death, a traumatic event for any six-year-old, gained added poignancy because of the conflict between her parents' Catholic beliefs and the Protestant training imposed on her by her crypto-Catholic uncle the king.

The Duke of York later represented himself as a keen supporter of the religious part of the Secret Treaty and a skeptic about the attack on the Dutch.[48] As an investor in African trade, however, he had a strong economic motive for backing a war designed to gain control of the trade routes. Catharine of Braganza had brought Charles outposts in Tangiers and Bombay as her dowry, and if Britain was not yet an imperial power, English merchants were already realizing large profits from trading in spices, gold, dyes, rare woods, and African slaves; they resented sharing that business with the Dutch. In 1660, the year of his restoration, Charles issued a charter to the Company of Royal Adventurers into Africa, whose shareholders included himself, his brother, and nine other members of the Stuart family.[49] The hope of monopolizing the lucrative slave trade was among the king's reasons for starting the Second Dutch Naval War, a debacle from which the English economy was still struggling to recover at the time of the Secret Treaty, and the loss of the war did not extinguish that hope. When the Company of Royal Adventurers folded in 1672, Charles chartered a successor, the Royal African Company; his brother James, one of the largest investors, became Governor of the Company and took an active role in its management.[50] The new war agreed to in the Secret Treaty was another attempt to secure a trading monopoly. The Duke of York, who had been a hero in the Second Dutch Naval War, expected to regain glory by commanding the fleet; the Duke of Monmouth, an aspirant for glory on the battlefield as well as the dance floor, was to share command of a small detachment of English ground troops serving under French generals.

If the alliance with France had brought control of the trade routes to England, the resulting economic prosperity might have helped the Crown repay its mounting debts; Charles may also have hoped that military and economic success would make his subjects more willing to swallow a new religious policy. But as events soon showed, this alliance was a desperate, doomed gamble. Charles needed public money for the war, and in order to gain funding from a suspicious Parliament, he took extreme measures, stirring up fears of a French invasion, ignoring his private promises to Louis, and issuing a proclamation requiring "Jesuits and Romish priests" to leave England by 1 May 1671. He also ordered the enforcement of existing laws against "popish recusants," the derogatory term used to refer to the beleaguered minority (certainly less than 10 percent, probably less than 5) who clung to the Roman Catholic faith of their ancestors.[51]

Few were convinced that the king was acting sincerely. His Portuguese queen, after all, maintained a Catholic chapel, and his brother was widely (and correctly) suspected of papist leanings. True to form, Charles reversed himself as soon as he had secured some funding for the war. First, he prorogued his Parliament, exercising his right to suspend their meetings. Then, on 2 January 1672, he took the bold step of closing the Exchequer. By suspending all payments to those expecting government funds, including creditors and salaried employees, the Treasury hoped to keep sufficient funds on hand to carry on the war, though of course those payments would eventually need to be made. The moralist John Evelyn later complained that this action had "ruined many *Widdows & Orphans* whose stocks were lent" to the government,[52] but the court lost no time in demonstrating that the stringent economy it had imposed on its creditors did not apply to its own entertainments: two days after the Stop of the Exchequer, on 4 January, "Lady Mary, daughter to his Royall Highness, gave the young ladys about the Court a ball, wherein herself bore a part, ... to the great satisfaction of their Majestys and Royall Highness there present."[53] With Parliament safely prorogued and a short-term supply of money secured by the Stop, Charles turned his religious policy around. On 15 March, claiming that he wished to unite the nation, he issued a Declaration of Indulgence, suspending all the laws against Protestant Nonconformists and Catholic recusants that he had recently ordered enforced, and on 17 March, England declared war on Holland.

Only a quick and convincing victory could have made this plan work. But in the first major battle of the war, fought off Sole Bay on 28 May, the Duke of York had to move his command post twice from disabled ships; his personal valor was not sufficient to attain a decisive victory, in part because the French ships with whom the English were allied failed to obey orders and became separated from the main fleet. Although both sides claimed victory, Sole Bay was at best a costly draw. In June, the army of Louis XIV invaded Holland, occupying large portions of its territory. Prince William of Orange, appointed Stadholder in recognition of his leadership in resisting these armed incursions, would spend the rest of his life, including his years as King William III of England, struggling to limit the power of the French. The spectacle of Protestant Holland invaded by a Catholic army was not likely to gain popular or parliamentary support in England—especially in light of the Stop of the Exchequer, the failure of the navy to secure a decisive victory, and a growing suspicion, fueled by pamphlets and rumors, about the actual provisions of the Secret Treaty of Dover.[54]

When Parliament returned from its long prorogation on 4 February 1673, antagonism toward the court was intense. Faced with a clear majority unwilling to renew financial supplies for the war unless the Declaration of Indulgence was withdrawn, Charles surrendered, canceling the Declaration on 8 March. Pressing their advantage, the parliamentary majority now passed the Test Act, which required all those holding public offices to declare that transubstantiation did not occur during the Eucharist. Among the victims was the Catalan violinist and composer Luis Grabu, who had been installed as Master of the King's Music in 1666 in order to teach the musicians to play in a French style. As a Catholic, he now had to resign; the safely Protestant Staggins, composer of *Calisto*, was his replacement.[55]

Far more important figures were also affected: on Easter Sunday, the day after Parliament recessed, the Duke of York failed to take Anglican Communion, an act that amounted to admitting his Catholicism. In June, after refusing to take the oath required by the Test, York resigned his post as Lord Admiral of the Fleet, and the English navy suffered defeat in the two battles of Schooneveld. In August, York's cousin Prince Rupert, who replaced him as Admiral, fought another costly and inconclusive naval battle at Texel Bay. Despite urgent signals, the French fleet did not join the fight, and news of that failure did further damage to the policy of the court, so Charles adroitly shifted his ground and began to seek a separate peace with the Dutch. Although most of his hopes had gone unfulfilled, there was one welcome consequence: as long as France and Holland were preoccupied with their own war, the Royal African Company was able to seize a large and lucrative share of the slave trade.[56]

Barred by the Test Act from engaging in the war, the king's brother defiantly displayed his Catholicism by taking a new bride. Not only was Maria Beatrice an Italian and a Catholic; she was the goddaughter of Louis XIV and the grandniece of Cardinal Mazarin, chief minister to the French king. Henry Mordaunt, second Earl of Peterborough, whose daughter Mary would play a part in *Calisto*, went to Italy to arrange the marriage; he stood in for James at a proxy wedding in Modena on 30 September 1673, a few days before the bride's fifteenth birthday. When Parliament met in October, the members immediately voted an address expressing their desire "that the intended Marriage of his Royal Highness with the Dutchess of Modena be not consummated; and that he may not be married to any Person, but of the Protestant Religion."[57] Prorogued for a week, they returned in an even uglier mood, refused to vote funds for the war, and expressed their grievances against the French alliance and the ministry. Charles prorogued them again on 4 November.

Maria's arrival in England later that month sparked the public burning of effigies of the pope, but at court her presence inspired an immediate increase in musical activities. The sequence of political and musical events following the wedding suggests that the court was using masques and operas as displays of monarchial power in the face of increasingly shrill parliamentary criticism. On 8 December 1673, one of Maria's Italian maids wrote a letter mentioning plans for a play with music, and on 5 January 1674, John Evelyn saw "an Italian opera in music," probably involving a new group of Italian musicians brought to London to serve the Roman Catholic chapel of the duchess. This may have been Francesco Cavalli's opera *L'Erismena*, for which a complete singing version in English survives in a contemporaneous manuscript.[58] On 7 January, the Members of Parliament, some of whom would have been as scandalized by the opera as by the chapel, convened again, and in late January or early February, a group of French musicians led by Robert Cambert performed a sung pastoral drama "for the diversion of the King," with a text designed to celebrate York's controversial marriage.[59] On 11 February, the king announced that he had concluded a peace treaty with the Dutch, and on 24 February, in order to kill bills under debate that would have further limited his power or begun the process of excluding his brother from the succession, he again prorogued his Parliament, which did not meet again for more than a year. On 30 March, Pierre Perrin's opera *Ariane*, with music by Cambert and the unfortunate Grabu, opened as a commercial production at the King's Company's new theatre at Drury Lane. Presented exactly six months after the proxy marriage between York and Maria, the opera depicted the marriage of Bacchus to Ariadne.

Like the later *Calisto*, *Ariane* alternates scenes featuring classical gods and goddesses with pastoral interludes in which shepherds and shepherdesses sing

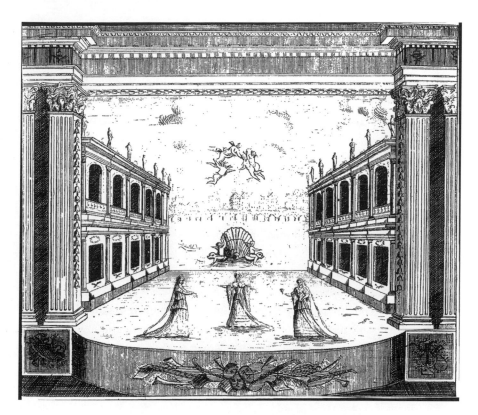

Frontispiece to Ariane, *ou le Mariage de Bacchus* (1674).

about the pleasures and pains of love. In a special prologue prepared for the London performances, the scenery depicted "a Prospect of *Thamise* opposite to *London*, on the waves of which is seen floating, a Great Shel as it were of Mother of Pearl, bearing 3. *Nimphs*, representing 3. Rivers, *Thamis, Tyber* and *Seine*, which *Nimphs* sing the *Prologue*."[60] As a compliment to Maria, a fourth nymph representing the Italian river Po joins her sister rivers in singing the praises of the Stuarts and celebrating England as the island of love. In welcoming the Po, the Thames expresses the fond hope that Maria's charms will win her popular support:

> Sweet Nimph, thy friendly care and pain,
>   Of this Great King, their just reward obtain:
>   And thou maist see his People now,
> To thy Princess, both love and honor shew:
> This Bliss, thou ow'st to her alone, whose Charm
> In 'spight of Fate, all resistance disarm:

And makes Envy itself t'adore
Her now, whom it oppos'd before.[61]

Parliamentary resistance, needless to say, was not disarmed. The Duchess of York, allegorically celebrated in this opera as a princess and a goddess, was now known to be pregnant. She would miscarry in May, but from this moment forward, James's enemies had reason to fear that she might produce a son whose claim to the throne would take precedence over those of Mary and Anne, raising the specter of a continuing Catholic succession.

§

Crowne had evidently studied the libretto for *Ariane* before writing the prologue to *Calisto*, which also featured a female singer as the river Thames. But while the French performers of *Ariane* sang in their own language, the amateurs and professionals performing *Calisto* spoke and sang in English, which provided fewer opportunities for evasion. In composing his prologue, Crowne had to gloss over several recent embarrassments. He followed the song about the ungrateful Augusta with a passage meant to compliment the king, the Duke of York, and the Duke of Monmouth by presenting the Third Dutch War as a chivalric allegory in which the king and his kinsmen save the "distressed Nymphs" of Europe from giants and monsters:

> *Europe.* From the mild power of this happy place
>   Who is inclin'd,
> To make the World as peaceful as his mind,
>   They have already gain'd the grace:
> Two Heroes of his own Celestial Race
> Are sent; the one to Triumph o're the Seas,
> And all the watery Divinities.
> The other, Monsters of the Land to quell,
>   And make the Nymphs in safety dwell.

Dancing figures representing the two dukes appear with appropriate attendants: "Sea-gods and Tritons" for York, "Warriors" for Monmouth, who played himself as the "Hero of the Land."[62] But as everyone knew, York had long since resigned his position as Admiral. Despite this inconvenient fact, the singer cast as Peace had to celebrate his imaginary victories and England's dubious command of the seas:

> Rejoice you watry Deities:
> The mighty Monsters of the Seas,
>   This valiant Prince has slain.

> The God of this fair Isle shall now
> Command (as all his Right allow)
>   The Empire of the Main.[63]

The Dutch had successfully held off the Royal Navy at sea and opened their dikes to limit the French invasion by land; they would hardly have included themselves among those who supposedly conceded "The Empire of the Main" to Charles. But in their eagerness to make peace with one of their two powerful enemies, they had agreed that Dutch ships would strike their topsails when they encountered a British vessel north of Cape Finisterre, and Crowne made the most of this symbolic concession in his text.

He also emphasized the thriving slave trade, apparently following instructions from the court. "I was obliged to invent proper Occasions, to introduce all the Entries," wrote the poet in his preface, "and particularly, for the closing of all with an Entry of *Africans*."[64] Whoever told Crowne to write that scene wanted to highlight the one area in which trade was improving despite the failure of the recent war, and Crowne took the hint. Not only did he provide the requested entry, with dancers and singers in blackface, but he also referred to the slave trade in his opening scene, in which the four continents join Peace and Plenty in offering gifts to the Thames: "Thou for thy Slaves shalt have these Scorched Sons of mine," sings the actor costumed as Africa. In staging this allegorical tableau of world trade, Crowne drew on a poetic tradition stretching back to the fourth-century Roman poet Claudian, who had pictured Rome as the "mother of arms and law," exerting her power over all.[65] Later poets reworked this personification of Empire as a mother, portraying cities and rivers as nubile women receiving the grateful tribute of exotic peoples, usually in the form of jewels and spices. In an example well known to Crowne, Dryden had pictured London, reborn from the ashes of the Great Fire of 1666, as a royal virgin:

> Now, like a Maiden Queen, she will behold,
>   From her high Turrets, hourly Sutors come;
> The East with Incense, and the West with Gold,
>   Will stand, like Suppliants, to receive her doom.
>
> The silver *Thames*, her own domestick Floud,
>   Shall bear her Vessels, like a sweeping Train;
> And often wind (as of his Mistress proud)
>   With longing eyes to meet her face again.[66]

Here politics and economics appear through a scrim of delicately erotic imagery: the distant lands come into view as suitors courting the "Maiden Queen," while the "domestick" Thames, personified as a faithful servant, gazes upon his mistress with pride and "longing eyes."

The prologue to *Calisto* gives dramatic life to a similar scene, with the crucial addition of slaves to the list of gifts brought to England by the world:

> *Plenty.* Thy Stores with all my Plenty shall be fill'd.
> *Peace.* My Halcion on thy Banks her Nest shall build.
> *Europe.* Thou shalt in all my noblest Arts be skill'd.
> *Asia.* My Jewels shall adorn no Brow but Thine.
> *America.* Thy Lovers in my Gold shall shine,
> *Africa.* Thou for thy Slaves, shalt have these Scorched Sons of mine.
> *Peace, Plenty.* Thy beautious streams we never will forsake.
> *Europe, Asia, Africa, America.* And we our Presents still will make.[67]

Trained as they were by French dancing masters and Italian instrumentalists, Princess Mary and Princess Anne could readily understand why Europe might be personified as the source of "Noble Arts." The costumes they were wearing featured precious jewels, including some from Asia, and their father's wealth had recently increased as the Royal African Company received payments of American gold for slaves brought from West Africa. But Crowne did not depict the continents presenting their gifts to Calisto and Nyphe. By changing the traditional gender of the Thames, he allowed Empire to be represented not by a virginal princess or a "Maiden Queen" but by an attractive royal mistress, the singing actress Moll Davis.[68]

There was some precedent for this transformation: Frances Stuart, Duchess of Richmond, whom Charles II pursued for years and who may briefly have been his mistress, posed in 1667 for the image of Britannia on a medal later used to commemorate the Peace of Breda, and her likeness appeared on British coins until 1971. For Charles, using "la belle Stuart" as the emblem of Empire was a way of making naval and economic power mythical and erotic, while casting himself as the lover of his country. Pepys, who took a voyeuristic interest in court ladies, understood the insouciance of the king's choice of model: "At my goldsmith's did observe the King's new Medall, where in little there is Mrs. Stewards face as well done as ever I saw anything in my whole life I think—and a pretty thing it is that he should choose her face to represent Britannia by."[69] In *Calisto*, the giving and receiving of treasure gains similar overtones when America promises the Thames that her lovers will shine in his gold. For the courtly audience, most of whom knew that Charles had been a lover of the actress playing the Thames, this tableau connected the king's generosity to his mistresses with a more general prediction of economic prosperity fueled by the slave trade.

John Roettier. *Medal with Frances Stuart as Britannia* (1667).

Glancing at those who opposed the policies of the court, the Thames complains that Augusta (London) remains unsatisfied by the gifts of Empire:

> Do you not see *Augusta*, Rich and Fair,
> (Though to her Lap, I all my Treasure bear)
> Will for no comfort stay her Tears?[70]

The merchants and Nonconformists whom Crowne personifies as the ungrateful Augusta had ample reason to believe that Charles II was not bringing all his treasure to the City, as he was pouring much of it into the lap of Louise Kéroualle, the baby-faced Catholic Frenchwoman who was his most prominent mistress at the time of *Calisto*. In 1673, the king made Louise Duchess of Portsmouth and installed her in a grandly decorated suite of twenty-four rooms in Whitehall Palace, where she hosted lavish meals and musical soirées. Robert Cambert, one of the composers of *Ariane*, was in charge of her private music, which featured French singers and wind players. Although Grabu, the other composer of *Ariane*, had lost his post as Master of the King's Music because of the Test Act, no one now sought to prevent French dancers and musicians from taking part in *Calisto*; the roster of performers includes several who regularly entertained the duchess. There was even a Frenchwoman among the courtly amateurs: six months before the premiere, the king had arranged for Louise's sister Henriette to marry Philip Herbert, the violent Earl of Pembroke, and the new Countess of Pembroke was one of the ladies who danced with the princesses. For those suspicious of Portsmouth and her entourage, *Calisto* looked like further evidence of an ominous trend toward styles associated with France and Catholicism, a combination that aroused fears of an arbitrary style of government. In the political struggles of the next eight years, the enemies of the Crown would fully exploit those fears.

§

Pierre Mignard, an artist associated with the French court, painted the Duchess of Portsmouth during a visit she made to France in 1682. In keeping with Stuart mythology, he depicted the controversial duchess receiving the gifts of a far-flung empire, a scene quite similar to the prologue to *Calisto*. In his picture, an African slave offers the royal mistress pearls and coral, precious gifts symbolic of the white skin and red lips of traditional European beauty (color plate 4). Unlike the ungrateful Augusta of Crowne's song, the painted duchess accepts the treasures poured into her lap. Although Crowne and Mignard were both working within the tradition established by Claudian, the painting goes further than the prologue in suggesting an affectionate relation between mistress and servant. The "Scorched Sons" promised in *Calisto* are possessions, but the African child in Mignard's painting receives the embrace of the duchess, who places her hand on the girl's shoulder. The same gestures appear in Mignard's later painting of the Marquise de Seignelay (color plate 5), depicting the noblewoman as the sea-goddess Thetis and her sons as Achilles and Cupid: the younger child presents coral and pearls to his mother, whose hand rests on the older son's shoulder.

The affectionate embrace in the later painting is clearly maternal, and if the racial difference in the earlier portrait makes it harder to see the African child as a daughter to the duchess, Mignard certainly suggests the more general notion of affection between master and slave. An erotic version of this idea was inherent in the traditional language describing courtly lovers as the slaves of their mistresses; Dryden's description of the Thames gazing at his mistress London with pride and longing is a subtle instance. In the portrait of Portsmouth, it appears in its most seductive guise, ostensibly made more "innocent" because both figures are female. In light of ancient traditions associating African women with homoerotic desires and practices, however, some viewers may have found this pose a titillating suggestion of same-sex love linking partners of different races.[71] The placement of the pearls is especially suggestive—one in Louise's ear, one on the shoulder of her low-cut gown, a string around the slave girl's neck (perhaps a polite version of a collar), and a cornucopia held just over the royal mistress's genitals.

The full-scale "Entry of *Africans*" with which Crowne ended his masque develops similar racial and sexual myths. In search of material for this scene, Crowne evidently consulted Ben Jonson's *Masque of Blackness* (1605), in which Queen Anne of Denmark, consort of James I, had appeared in blackface with her attendants.[72] As the "daughters of Niger," the Jacobean court ladies appeared "in a great concave shell, like mother of pearle." Their attire was "*azure*, and *silver*; but returned on the top with a scroll and antique dressing of feathers, and jewells interlaced with ropes of pearle. And, for the front, eare, neck, and wrists, the ornament was of the most choise and orient pearle; best setting off from the black."[73] The costumes in *Calisto* were similar; the women dressed as "Africans" wore "Black satin Cutt upon gold tinsell," "silver tinsell with all pretty furniture," and "24 strings of pearl."[74]

In addition to hints about costume, Crowne's entry borrows language and imagery unscrupulously from Jonson's masque. Three "African women" come seeking their beauty, supposedly lost when Phaeton, another Ovidian character, stole the chariot of the Sun and "powr'd whole streams / Of melting beams, / Red, and glowing hot upon us."[75] When they discover the "lovely White and Red" of their original beauty in the youthful faces of Calisto and Nyphe, one of the women sings a lyric that claims erotic power for blackness:

> No Losers we shall prove,
>   By parting with our Red and White;
> If black will serve the turn of Love;
>   For Beauty's made for Loves delight.

"Serve the turn," a deliberately vulgar idiom, threatens to reduce beauty and delight to a commercial transaction, as Crowne's language blurs the distinction between economic and sexual exploitation. Just after this song, "*Calisto* and *Nyphe* enter under a Canopy supported by *Africans*."[76] The canopy, a traditional sign of royalty, presumably shades their delicate complexions, but in economic terms, the Stuarts themselves were "supported by *Africans*." As major stockholders in the Royal African Company, they profited significantly from the slave trade. One piece of doubling in the casting of *Calisto* may be a recognition of this fact: Charlotte Butler, who sang the role of Plenty in the prologue, appeared again as one of the African women.[77]

The allegorical figures representing Peace and Plenty also had a long history in the masque tradition. Although genuine peace and plenty were in short supply under the Stuarts, artists and poets frequently invoked those figures, using aesthetic and erotic elements to soften a history of unfulfilled hopes.[78] When Peter Paul Rubens painted his canvases for the ceiling of Inigo Jones's splendid Banqueting House in 1636, he depicted Peace and Plenty as female figures embracing each other (color plate 6); five years later, the Civil Wars began, initiating a decade of violence and privation. In 1675, Crowne brought Mary Knight and Charlotte Butler, beautiful singers from the theatre, onstage as Peace and Plenty, but quietly admitted that the plan to secure peace and plenty through imperial expansion had not yet succeeded. In the operatic prologue, the Thames expresses her fear that the "gentle Nymphs of Plenty and of Peace / Shall now go seek some other Shore" and that the continents, visibly waiting to give her presents, will "bring [their] gifts no more." In response, Peace, Plenty, and the continents promise never to forsake her, singing "We our Presents *still* will make."[79] Buried in that adverb is the hope that a profitable trade with the rest of the world might somehow continue, even though efforts to improve it by military means had fallen short. As Dryden pointed out in *The Secular Masque* (1700), his last completed work, none of the wars pursued by English monarchs in the seventeenth century produced real gains for the nation. Adopting the form of previous masques but satirically altering the content, Dryden used singing mythological figures to expose the failures of the concluding century. Momus, god of laughter and criticism, pokes fun at Diana, Venus, and especially Mars, whom he taunts with the truth: "Thy wars brought nothing about."[80]

As she watched the beautifully costumed singers in *Calisto* enact their pageant of empire, with servile suppliants offering arts, jewels, gold, and slaves to enrich an England blessed with peace and plenty, Princess Anne, at ten, could hardly have been able to grasp the hard truths that Dryden would later express in his parody masque. By the time she came to the throne, however, just two years after *The Secular Masque*, she had gained a firm understanding of the economic and military realities that Jonson, Crowne, Rubens, and Mignard had thinly veiled in courtly art. In the real world, as her reign would demonstrate, gaining lasting control of the mercantile routes to distant continents was not a matter of erotic mythology or good luck; it required sustained and effective military force. When Anne as queen signed the Peace of Utrecht, ending the War of the Spanish Succession (1702–1713), Britain gained new possessions including Hudson Bay, Nova Scotia, Newfoundland, St. Christopher, Gibraltar, and Minorca—significant steps toward her eventual empire. Surveying Anne's accomplishments in *Windsor-*

Forest (1713), his poem on the Peace, Alexander Pope praised the queen by invoking once more the traditional figures of Peace and Plenty, linking these blessings, as Crowne had done, to the Stuart line:

> Rich Industry sits smiling on the Plains,
> And Peace and Plenty tell, a STUART reigns.[81]

In light of Queen Anne's childhood participation in the "Entry of *Africans*," it is a striking fact—and from our perspective a sad one—that the Peace of Utrecht, signed in the last year of her life, finally gave England one of the glittering prizes repeatedly sought in the failed wars of the seventeenth century: a monopoly on the delivery of African slaves to the Spanish New World.

§

Reality and myth clash awkwardly in the parts of *Calisto* dealing with war, empire, slavery, peace, and plenty. Erotic imagery, whether delicate or overt, was one means of directing attention away from political failures, but in Charles II's court, eroticism itself was also problematic. At the end of the prologue, for example, the Thames leads her attendants to the palace of "our Divinity," clearly the king, explaining that

> Pleasure, Arts, Religion, Glory,
> Warm'd by his propitious Smile,
> Flourish there, and bless this Isle.

Suddenly recognizing the king and queen, she grows warm in their praise:

> The God and Goddess too of this blessed Isle!
> Chaste Beauty in Her Aspect shines,
> And Love in His does smile.[82]

Although very much in the tradition of the earlier Stuart masque, in which panegyrics addressed to the monarch watching from his throne were often worked into the drama, these lines were sure to provoke some smiles in the court audience, and some blushes from the queen, because Moll Davis, who sang this passage in her role as the Thames, had intimate experience with the "Love" in Charles's "Aspect": she had become his mistress in 1668, and had borne him a child, Lady Mary Tudor, as recently as 1673. With Anne Palmer, another of the king's many illegitimate children, in their group of dancing nymphs, Mary and Anne can hardly have been unaware that their uncle had mistresses. But Crowne, despite his sanctimonious claim that he sought to write words "fit for Princesses and Ladies to speak, and a Court to hear," actually called attention to the court's libertine practices by asking a royal mistress to sing the praises of the amorous king and his neglected queen. His giving Moll Davis these lines in praise of the flourishing of religion under Charles II was the poetic equivalent of Lely's portraying her as Mary Magdalen with a jar of precious ointment (color plate 7).

In the opening scene of the spoken play, Crowne presented two Olympian gods discussing their need for mortal mistresses in language transparently applicable to the court. The fact that two young women spoke these lines in male costume added to the comedy, though the audience could not know that Henrietta Wentworth, who played Jupiter, would soon become the mistress of Monmouth, or that Sarah Jenyns, who played Mercury, would become the favorite of Princess Anne. Mercury, who has come to earth in search of a woman, admits his susceptibility to human flesh, and Jupiter replies in kind:

> *Mercury.*—I own these Joys, sometimes I try,
> To pass away Eternity:
> But are they not for *Jove* too low?
> *Jupiter.*—The World must not the Secret know.
> We boast great things to be ador'd and sought;
> (There is some Pleasure to be happy thought)
> But for all Joys of our abode,
>   From Earth I would not move;
> Nor be content to be a God,
>   To be depriv'd of Love.[83]

This comic exchange embodies the attitudes of the Stuart court. Like the Olympian gods, Charles and James were not beyond the need for sexual intimacy, and they evidently believed they had a right to satisfy that need. There was "some pleasure," to be sure, in being "ador'd and sought" as persons of nobility and power, and in being thought happy in their royal ease and grandeur. But those pleasures did not make it possible for the king or the duke to live "depriv'd of Love." Everyone knew about the king's mistresses, several of whom were present on this special occasion, and the duke's amour with Arabella Churchill, Maid of Honor to his first Duchess, had been public knowledge since 1665, the year of Anne's birth. James acknowledged several children by Arabella and continued to "visit" her, as the court wits comically put it, after his second marriage.[84]

Crowne also dramatized the jealousy of abandoned wives, writing a speech for Juno in which she complains, as Queen Catharine often did, of her husband's neglect:

> Must every trifling Nymph, that looks but fair,
> Entice from my Embrace my *Jupiter*?
> Must all my Charms be every Strumpets scorn,
> Only because they by a Wife are born?
> Oh! Servile State of Conjugal Embrace!
> Where seeming Honour covers true disgrace.
> We with reproaches Mistresses defame;
> But we poor Wives endure the greatest shame.
> We to their Slaves are humble Slaves, whilst they
> Command our Lords, and rule what we obey.
> Their Loves each day new kindnesses uphold,
> We get but little, and that little cold![85]

Glancing once more at the idea of slavery, Crowne has Juno complain that neglected wives are slaves to their husbands, who in turn are slaves to their mistresses. It is hard to imagine anyone in the audience, even the little princesses, missing the evident parallel between Jupiter and Juno and Charles and Catharine (or James and Maria). In another ironic twist, the decision to give the part of Juno to Anne Palmer—a choice Maria herself may have made—meant that this diatribe against mistresses was actually spoken by a child of one of the royal mistresses.

§

Within the largely female world in which the princesses were reared, there were also passionate attachments and jealousies. "Ther is no true love without jelossee," writes Mary in one of her early letters to Frances Apsley, an older girl who received frequent letters from both princesses, in which they expressed ardent devotion in language drawn from French romances and stage plays, and in which, like some of the young actresses in *Calisto*, the correspondents assumed male roles.[86] Perhaps as a result of working with the young ladies in the rehearsals, Crowne appears to have been aware of the special qualities of these relationships; his drama gives voice to emotions close to those expressed by the princesses in their early letters.[87] In the very first scene, the scornful nymph Psecas, played in the premiere by Mary Mordaunt, expresses her fury at Diana's fondness for Calisto and complains that her own merits are "unregarded":

> Oh! with what pride! and feign'd neglect of Art
> This Royal Favourite storms our Goddess Heart,
> Conquers it too, and rules her Power Divine,
> Whilst all our Merits unregarded shine.[88]

Princess Mary felt similar outrage and envy when she believed her sister Anne had replaced her in the affections of Frances Apsley:

> I consider with what eger hast you cald my hapy rival…& with what coldness she fain'd to come but at last how you wispred and then lauft, as if you had said, now we are rid of her, let us be hapey, whilst pore unhappy I sate reading of a play my heart redy to breake.

In both cases, the displaced favorite accuses her successful rival of "feigning" negligence. Living as they did in a social milieu where courtiers and ladies habitually lied to each other, presided over by a king who lied constantly to his mistresses, his Parliament, his ministers, and the other crowned heads of Europe, Mary and Anne had considerable direct experience with feigning. Yet despite their unavoidable awareness of the cynical and rapacious customs of the court, the princesses drew on literature in order to imagine an alternative to that ugly reality—a romantic, pure, and passionate world in which they would be free to express their fervent feelings toward other young women, free to take on male names and identities, free to cast themselves as characters in the refined and artificial atmosphere of the French romance or the rhymed heroic play.

In this very letter, Mary reports reading a play while experiencing her paroxysms of jealousy. She continues by comparing herself to one of the characters:

> for I was reading where Massanisa coms first to sophonisba & thought that saene so like my misary it made me ready to cry but before my hapy rival I wode not show my wekness but now with Sophonisba I may cry out she thinks me fals though I have bin most true & thinking so what may her furie do.[89]

The references here are quite specific. Mary was reading Nathaniel Lee's *Sophonisba*, first acted in April 1675, shortly after *Calisto*, and first published in 1676. Her easy reference to the characters in Lee's tragedy and her partial quotation of one couplet, in which she alters only the pronouns, make it clear that she assumed Frances Apsley had also seen or read the play. In the scene evoked here, Sophonisba awaits the arrival of the victorious general Massanissa, who has slain her husband Syphax. Expecting to be made a slave, she contemplates suicide, and when her serving maids urge her to remind Massanissa of his earlier love for her, she rightly fears his wrath:

> When breach of faith joyn'd hearts does disingage,
> The Calmest temper turnes to wildest Rage.
> He thinks me false, though I have been most true:
> And thinking so what may his fury doe?[90]

In the ensuing dialogue, Massanissa admits his continuing infatuation with Sophonisba and rails at her for marrying Syphax. Sophonisba persuades him that she has not consummated her marriage:

> Think me not false though I did Syphax wed,
> Who ever was a stranger to my bed.
> Forc'd by my Father's positive command;
> I must confess I suffer'd him my hand.
> Heaven curse me if I ever granted more,
> Cou'd I be his having bin yours before?[91]

In light of the fact that the issue between Massanissa and Sophonisba is sexual faithfulness, it may seem remarkable that Princess Mary, at perhaps thirteen, thought this scene so like her own situation with Frances Apsley that it made her ready to cry. Yet Crowne's *Calisto*, performed for a large audience by an all-female cast, also insists on an erotic element in relations between women. In the Ovidian fable, Jupiter disguises himself as the goddess Diana in order to get closer to Calisto, whom he then assaults and impregnates. In Crowne's version, the chaste Calisto rejects the god's advances, but when Jupiter is pretending to be Diana, the declaration of same-sex passion is overt:

> Oh! Princess! it is I that pity need,
> (shall I the secret tell?) your merits breed
> In my last Heart, a strange uncommon flame:
> A kindness I both fear and blush to name;
> Nay, one for which no name I ever knew,
> The Passion is to me so strange, so new![92]

The emphasis here on the lack of a name for same-sex love between females reflects a linguistic absence. Although the earliest recorded use of the word *homosexual* in English comes in the 1890s, seventeenth-century writers had some available vocabulary for relationships between males. If sympathetic to such relationships, they might speak of "masculine friendship," adducing such well-known classical examples as Nisus and Euryalus, soldier-lovers in Virgil's *Aeneid;* if attacking an enemy, they might accuse him of sodomy, which had been a capital crime since 1553.[93] In the case of women, however, there was neither a criminal code nor a widely available vocabulary.[94] Seventeenth-century women writers seeking to describe ardent feelings for other women, notably the poet Katherine Philips, usually spoke of "friendship" when they needed a noun, and male writers, of whom Crowne is typical, tended to express confusion or embarrassment when speaking of same-sex relations between women. Jupiter's claim to have "no name" for the passion he is attempting to feign in his disguise as Diana reflects this larger cultural denial. Yet despite the period's reluctance to give such feelings a name, some women in the seventeenth and eighteenth centuries evidently had strong and passionate same-sex relationships, which did not—in their minds or in the minds of their contemporaries—preclude their having close heterosexual relationships, including marriages. Again, the visual evidence is telling: when Rubens portrayed Peace and Plenty, both female, he gave them dreamy eyes, smiles of pleasure, and a frank and fleshly embrace (see color plate 6). If the culture lacked words for these feelings, it still knew how to depict them.[95]

In seeking to express their affection for other women, Mary and Anne drew not only on literary language depicting the love of men and women, which they felt free to apply to themselves by shifting the pronouns, but also on literary expressions of same-sex love. In another early letter to Frances Apsley, Mary gives further evidence of her reading of both kinds:

> I have more love for you than I can posibly have for al the world besids you do not expect from me a letter like your own this morning for I am sure Mr. Draden and al the poets in the world could not make such another. I pretend to nothing in this world but if it be posibel to tell my love I have for my Aurelia to my dearest dearest husband & ever beg of her to exept me as her most obedaint wife
>
> "MARY
"CLORINE
>
> "From al things in the world my hart
> has escaped but from cupits blody dart
> I no resistance could find
> love is the noblest frialty of the mind."[96]

"Mr. Draden" is of course Dryden, who counted the Duke of York and both his Duchesses among his patrons and was known to the princesses in person, not merely in print. Mary displays her knowledge of the Laureate's work by quoting it: the final line of her four-line poem comes from a high-minded scene about love and honor in *The Indian Emperour*. When Cydaria, the Indian woman with whom the hero Cortez has fallen in love, asks him to refrain from battle against her people, Cortez replies that his duty to his monarch gives him no choice:

> *Cortez.* Now I am sent, and am not to dispute
> My Princes orders, but to execute.

But when she tells him that she will be in the forefront of the Indian army, "with empty Quiver, and unbended Bow," he chooses love over duty:

> No more, your kindness wounds me to the death,
> Honour be gone, what art thou but a breath?
> I'le live, proud of my infamy and shame,
> Grac'd with no Triumph but a Lovers name;
> Men can but say Love did his reason blind,
> And Love's the noblest frailty of the mind.[97]

By quoting the final line of this speech, Mary chose to identify herself not with the seductive and manipulative Cydaria, but with the tortured Cortez, caught between ardor and honor. Already aware of the severe limits placed on her emotional life by her royal status, she may well have shared Cortez's bitter view of honor as "A painful burden which great minds must bear."[98] She may even have envied those among her attendants who could choose to "live, proud of . . . infamy and shame, / Grac'd with no Triumph but a Lovers name." When Eleanor Needham left the court after the discovery of her affair with Monmouth, one newsletter reported that there were "romantick stories told of her, which exceed all the adventures of Errant Ladies that were ever yet heard."[99] For the impressionable Mary, sadly aware that such romantic errantry was not to be hers, and already fearful of being married to the short, asthmatic, and unromantic William, the appeal of love as the "noblest frailty of the mind" was powerful.

Mary's drawing on the language of Cortez to express her own feelings for Frances Apsley is a further indication of the remarkable fluidity of gender at this time. By promising "to tell my love I have for my Aurelia to my dearest dearest husband," she casts Frances as both male and female, simultaneously the loved one and the confidante to whom that love must be told; and in constructing her poetic postscript, she borrows from writers of both genders, describing love of several kinds. The first three lines, shaky and uncertain in their meter, look like Mary's own work, but some of the language is drawn from her reading. The odd phrase about "cupits blody dart," for example, comes from the scene of same-sex seduction in *Calisto*. When "Diana," actually Jupiter in disguise, declares her passion for Calisto, the chaste nymph, played by Mary herself, wonders whether the goddess has contracted this "strange disease" by drinking from "some infectious spring." Picking up and expanding that imagery, the seducer speaks of "Some Spring where *Cupid* wash'd his bloody Darts, / When the young Tyrant had been murdring Hearts."[100]

The poet Katherine Philips, who memorably expressed both her passionate affection for other women and her continuing devotion to her husband, had used strikingly similar imagery in a poem to one of her female friends:

> Subduing fair! what will you win
>   To use a needless Dart:
> Why then so many to take in
>   One undefended heart?
> I came expos'd to all your Charms,
>   'Gainst which the first half hour
> I had no will to take up Armes,
>   And in the next no Power.
> How can you chuse but win the Day,
>   Who can resist your Siege,
> Who in one action know the way
>   To Vanquish and Oblige?[101]

The imagery of Cupid's "Dart," the rhyme with "heart," and the idea of a woman unable to resist the erotic power of another woman appear again in both Crowne's drama and Mary's poetic lines; the poet and the princess were evidently familiar with Philips's work, though Philips herself had died in 1664. The posthumous publication of her poems, organized by Sir Charles Cotterell, Master of Ceremonies to the King, was a crucial step in the process by which Philips, grandly described as "the matchless Orinda," became a model of the virtuous woman writer, who supposedly continued and exemplified the *précieuse* cult of Platonic love encouraged by Queen Henrietta Maria in the court of Charles I.[102] Among her poems is one addressed "To Her Royal Highness the Dutchess of York," the mother of Mary and Anne, "on her commanding me to send her some things that I had written," and in 1668, just two years before Mary's performance in *The Faithful Shepherdess*, a cast of noble amateurs including the Duchess of Monmouth and the Countess of Castlemaine presented Philips's translation of Corneille's play *Horace* at court. Staged with "a masq and antiq daunce…Twixt each act," this performance was a forerunner to the more elaborate *Calisto*.[103]

In some of her poems, Philips celebrates her passionate friendships with women in Platonic terms, as "Love refin'd and purg'd from all its dross." Such love, she argues, is preferable to the connections imposed by kinship or by arranged marriages because it is freely chosen and unconstrained:

> Nobler then Kindred or then Marriage-band,
>   Because more free; Wedlock-felicity
> It self doth only by this Union stand,
>   And turns to Friendship or to Misery.

Conscious of the long classical tradition honoring friendships among males, Philips goes on to assert the right of women to have and enjoy similar friendships:

> If Souls no Sexes have, for Men t' exclude
>   Women from Friendship's vast capacity,
> Is a Design injurious or rude,
>   Onely maintain'd by partial tyranny.
> Love is allow'd to us and Innocence,
> And noblest Friendships do proceed from thence.[104]

This high-minded talk of sexless souls, innocence, and noble friendships claims for women a classical and Cartesian tradition from which they had long been excluded,[105] but when Philips addresses a specific woman, calling her "Soul of my Soul, my joy, my crown, my Friend," the language quickly becomes more physical:

> I have no thought but what's to thee reveal'd,
> Nor thou desire that is from me conceal'd.
> Thy Heart locks up my Secrets richly set,
> And my Breast is thy private Cabinet.
> Thou shed'st no tear but what my moisture lent,
> And if I sigh, it is thy breath is spent.[106]

Poetic models of this kind may provide a context for some of the strongly physical language Princess Mary used in her letters to Frances Apsley, such as this plea for forgiveness when Frances imagined that she preferred another young woman:

> I hope you have so much goodness as to forgive and belive that hence forward there is nothing in this heart or brest guts or bowels but you shal know it.

Or this, from the letter expressing jealousy of Princess Anne:

> but since you have forsaken me quite I have still the marks that you loved me once.[107]

Male writers of the period, however, had such difficulty imagining how two women could give each other physical pleasure that they often hinted that women who were fond of other women had some form of genital abnormality, an idea implied in *Calisto* when "Diana" (actually Jupiter) wonders how Calisto can ease her pain:

> I always sigh, when I your Beauties view,
> And wish (but wonder why!) I wish for you.
> Something I fain would crave, but do not know
> What I should ask, or what you can bestow.
> Some Charms about you for my ease you bear,
> But know not how they cure, nor what they are;
> But I am certain they could give me ease.[108]

In this period, rumors concerning close attachments between two women often cast one of the women as a hermaphrodite or a man in disguise.[109] In his scandalous account of erotic adventures in the Restoration court, published toward the end of Queen Anne's reign, Anthony Hamilton told a tale about "Mrs. Hobart," one of the Maids of Honor to the first Duchess of York, "whose *Sensibility*, some pretended, was in Favour of the *Fair Sex*." According to Hamilton, rumors of Mrs. Hobart's sexual preference quickly developed into allegations of a different sort:

> 'Twas not long before the Report, whether true or false, of this *Singularity*, spread through the whole Court, where *People* being yet so unciviliz'd as never to have heard of that kind of *Refinement* in *Tenderness* of *ancient Greece*, some imagin'd, that the *illustrious H____t*, who was so fond of the *fair Sex*, was something more than she appeared to be.
>
> The *Lampoons* began to *Compliment* her upon those new Attributes; and her Companions began to be afraid of her, upon the Credit of those *Lampoons*.[110]

Hamilton, originally writing in French, claims to be more worldly about sexual variety and better informed about ancient Greece than the "unciviliz'd" people in the English court, but his mockery touches Mrs. Hobart as well as those gullible enough to believe lampoons claiming that she had impregnated her own maid.[111] The anonymous authors of manuscript satires were often willing to disparage those feelings for which they supposedly had no name, but others were more tolerant. According to Hamilton, Anne's mother dealt kindly with Mrs. Hobart: "The *Dutchese*, who was too generous not to treat as *Chimeras* what was charged upon Mrs. H____t, and too just to condemn her upon Songs, made her from a *Maid of Honour*, a *bed-chamber-woman*."[112] Far from being a dismissal, this change of status would have been financially advantageous, as a bedchamber woman at this time drew an annual salary of £150, while a maid of honor received only £20.[113]

Hamilton's account of Mrs. Hobart is suspiciously literary,[114] but the attitudes he dramatizes were real enough. From her earliest childhood, spent as it was with her sister Mary, her Governess Lady Villiers, the six Villiers sisters, and her female "rockers" and "dressers," Princess Anne formed close emotional ties to women. In a world where all her male relatives kept mistresses and fathered bastards, and in a court where female virtue, the supposed theme of *Calisto*, typically attracted irony or ridicule, it was far safer to seek intimacy with other women than with men. Yet early experiences also made Anne aware that her feelings for other women might be misunderstood, criticized, or lampooned. The scabrous lampoons on the court ladies that circulated in manuscript at this time, not content with accusing them of having rotten teeth, smelly feet, and heterosexual lovers, also mentioned physical encounters between women, for which the most common vulgar term was "playing at flats"[115]—a phrase made slightly euphemistic by the fact that "flats" was also a term for playing cards, an obsessive activity among the court ladies throughout Anne's life. In another early letter from Princess Mary to Frances Apsley, certainly no later than 1675, there is a mysterious passage that may reflect that usage: "It is very trew that I play at cards," writes Mary, "but it is not trew what Mrs. Dolly sais of my sister and I."[116] Dorothy Howard, known as "Doll," had been a Maid of Honor to the first Duchess of York and served as a Maid of Honor to Queen Catharine until her marriage in 1675. Could she have made a bad joke about Mary and Anne "playing at flats," prompting this pained denial?

§

Although she enjoyed widespread popularity, Queen Anne's obese body was subject to ridicule, and her female favorites, always suspected of holding vast political power, were mercilessly lampooned in the partisan pamphlet warfare of her reign. A ballad circulating in 1708, for example, treated the queen's fondness for her attendant Abigail Masham as completely incongruous for a monarch with responsibilities to the state and the Church:

> When as Q[ueen] A[nne] of great Renown
>   *Great Britain*'s Scepter sway'd,
> Besides the Church, she dearly lov'd
>   A Dirty Chamber-Maid.[117]

Like most lampoons, this is nasty, though certainly less shocking than the lampoon on Charles II by the rakehell poet John Wilmot, Earl of Rochester, who also spoke of swaying a scepter:

> In the Isle of Brittain long since famous growne
> For breeding the best C———s in Christendome,
> Not long since Reign'd (oh may he long survive)
> The easiest King and best-bred Man alive.
> . . . .
> Peace was his Aime, his gentleness was such,
> And Love, he lov'd, For he lov'd Fucking much.
> Nor was his high desire above his Strength:
> His Scepter and his Prick were of a length,
> And she may sway the one who plays with t'other,
> Which makes him litle wiser then his Brother.[118]

Rochester, who took a keen interest in court theatricals, was probably in attendance at *Calisto*.[119] His poem is a deliberately vulgar version of the themes politely emphasized in the courtly language of the masque, which celebrated the king's love of peace and gave him credit for the flourishing of "Pleasure, Arts, Religion, Glory." As the placing of "Pleasure" first in that line suggests, Crowne meant to connect these benefits to the "propitious Smile" of an amorous monarch. If he avoided the overtly sexual imagery in which Rochester delighted, he pointed clearly enough to the same ideas by using Moll Davis to address the king in the sung prologue and by emphasizing the parallels between Jupiter and Charles in the spoken play. He concluded *Calisto* by asking Henrietta Wentworth, who had played Jupiter, to "dissolve into a Nymph again,"

> Which will no less this fair Assembly please;
> For Nymphs, in Courts, have sway like Deities.

Though far more decorous, the claim that "Nymphs, in Courts, have sway" repeats a key idea and a crucial word from Rochester's rude lines on the royal prick, written just one year earlier. Turning directly to the king, Henrietta concluded the evening by celebrating his right to pleasure:

> You, Sir, such blessings to the World dispence,
> We scarce perceive the use of Providence.
> And since Your Rule such joy to all procures,

All should contribute what they can to Yours.
Wit by Your Smiles a Lustre do's maintain,
And Beauty keeps a long and happy Reign.
Your Right in them is therefore so entire,
They, above all, Your Pleasure should conspire.

Like much else in *Calisto*, these courtly lines express a myth that the king hoped his subjects might embrace. Despite recent disasters at home and abroad, Charles wanted his people to believe that his rule had brought blessings to the world and joy to all, and that the wit and beauty presented in the masque had flourished under his patronage. The closing verb is telling. Because Charles has smiled upon the wit of his poets and the beauty of his court ladies, Crowne argues, Wit and Beauty should *conspire* to bring him pleasure—as they had evidently done in *Calisto*—and the nation should allow him to enjoy carousing with his witty courtiers and toying with his beautiful mistresses. In the magical world of the masque, these worldly pleasures were no more troubling than the "innocent delights" of Diana's nymphs. In a court constantly subject to rumors of political and religious intrigue, about to be shaken to its core by wild tales of papist conspiracy, the notion of Wit and Beauty conspiring to give the king pleasure was a pleasant conceit, but one perhaps betraying the author's hope that the only conspiracies in Charles's future would be those designed to bring him pleasure.

By any measure, Anne as queen delivered more substantial blessings and joy to her subjects than did her uncle Charles. In Crowne's line crediting Charles with "Pleasure, Arts, Religion, Glory," the ordering of the nouns may result from metrical considerations, but it also reflects Charles's priorities. A similar accounting for Anne's reign would run in reverse: she brought England unprecedented glory in world affairs and did her best to support the Church, while paying less public attention to the arts than Charles and far less attention to pleasure. There was no public rhetoric encouraging her to indulge in pleasure, as there had been for Charles, and her experiences as a child had already taught her not to expect her court or her subjects to value her needs or desires.

At the end of Crowne's masque, when Calisto and Nyphe are about to be translated to heaven as stars, a singing shepherdess tactlessly points out that this supposed honor has unnaturally deprived them of sexual pleasure:

Must these be Stars? And to Heaven remove,
Before they have tasted the pleasures of Love.
That the Gods so ill, such Beauty should use!
What mighty Cost must Nature lose?

But before the promised apotheosis can take place, Jupiter intervenes—not in order to give the nymphs an opportunity for pleasure, but in order to oblige two kings, binding them to loyalty through arranged marriages:

> With each of you I can oblige a Throne,
> I'll keep you then to grace some Fav'rite Crown,
> On that design you here shall still remain.[120]

In the real world as in the fantasy world of the masque, royal virgins and little stars would be ill-used, and would have to play the roles that others designed for them. Unlike kings and dukes, they had no assumed right to pleasure. Two years after *Calisto*, when her chaplain informed Princess Mary that she was to be married to William of Orange, she wept all that afternoon and most of the next day.[121]

Anne learned a number of lessons from her experience as a child actress. In real life, she often played a role as dutiful as the one she enacted as Nyphe. Without shedding a tear, she married the man her uncle and father chose for her, and she strove for decades to produce an heir, at "mighty Cost" to her body and soul. She deferred to her sister and her sister's husband, often unhappily, until her own time came. But once on the throne, she showed how well she understood the limits of myth and how firmly she grasped the importance of economic and military action. She dressed carefully and symbolically for her official appearances and smiled upon the birthday odes, allegorical pageants, and anthems of thanksgiving created to praise her reign, but she never sought to parade her affairs of the heart in public. Although she adopted Queen Elizabeth's motto, "semper eadem" (always the same), virginity was not among the forms of immutability she could claim, nor were her feelings of love confined to one sex. As she had also learned from *Calisto*, a culture that lacked a name for love between women often expressed its unease as mockery. The ridicule directed at same-sex love in *Calisto* is far more delicate than the contempt in the later ballad excoriating Abigail Masham as "A Dirty Chamber-Maid," but if little Princess Anne understood any of the weak jokes Crowne made at the expense of girlish affections, she gained an early warning against being too explicit about her feelings for other women. Although Princess Mary had called Frances Apsley her "dear husband" and referred to herself as an "obedient wife," Anne reversed this practice in her own letters to Frances. Drawing on her experience in an amateur performance of Lee's *Mithridates*, she called herself "Ziphares," the male hero she had played, and addressed Frances as "Semandra," his beloved. By taking on the male role in this correspondence, Anne was claiming the strength and authority that her culture typically regarded as male, as she would do in some future relationships—and in her reign.

Believing in their own myths was the fatal flaw of the Stuarts, though less pronounced in the shrewd and evasive Charles II than in his unworldly father or his stubborn brother. Even at ten, however, Anne had every opportunity to recognize that *Calisto* was a disingenuous celebration of heroism and purity, performed for a court that was neither heroic nor pure. Despite Crowne's ironies, through which he conveyed his awareness of the impossibility of the task he was assigned, and despite the best efforts of an army of musicians, carpenters, and dressmakers, this dazzling production could not conceal the huge gap between the myths the court of Charles II wished to believe about itself and the military, economic, religious, and sexual realities of his reign. As the last Stuart monarch, Queen Anne occupied the throne during a period of military victory and economic expansion; the vigorous partisan and religious politics of her reign did not boil over into revolutionary violence, as such struggles had under the previous Stuarts. Though "Born under Golden Roofs, and bred to ease," she paid close attention to events "on other Shores," and was therefore a more successful ruler than her father, uncle, or grandfather—not least because she understood the distinction between myth and reality.

CHAPTER 2

HAIL, WELCOME PRINCE

29 July 1683

With a confidence earned by years of official appearances and a grace developed in public and private theatricals, Princess Anne moved deliberately through the crowded room to the pair of grand chairs. At ten o'clock the previous evening, she had married Prince George of Denmark in the brightly lit Tudor chapel in St. James's Palace. Her girlhood chaplain, Henry Compton, now Bishop of London, read the Anglican service, and her uncle Charles, claiming his royal prerogative, gave away the bride, as he had at Princess Mary's tearful wedding, conducted in her bedchamber six years earlier. Though modest in size, Anne's wedding was a happier occasion than Mary's. "The chiefest of the Nobility" were in attendance; the king and queen ate a celebratory supper with the newlyweds; bells and bonfires signaled public joy; and the bride was splendidly arrayed. Two weeks before the wedding, a correspondent from Paris reported rumors that Richard Graham, a loyal supporter of the Duke of York, had "brought over with him an hundred and fourscore thousand pound towards buying of wedding garters for the Princess."[1] Though the sum named here is surely exaggerated, the bridegroom's gifts, precisely described and appraised by the veteran politician Thomas Clarges, were expensive enough: "a necklace of pearle, valewd at six thousand pound, a rich jewell of diamonds to weare before, and a paire of pendants and bodkin guess'd to be worth fifteen thousand pound, besides a box of massie gold set with diamonds (wherein they were inclosed)."[2] Now, on the morning after their wedding, the bride and groom were ready to receive formal congratulations from "the Foreign Ministers residing in Court"[3] and to hear the musicians of the royal band and the Chapel Royal perform some special music composed for the occasion.[4]

Although many of the performers were the same, the music for this event—a substantial cantata in seven movements for soloists, chorus, and orchestra—was much more advanced than anything in *Calisto*. Most of the musicians who had performed in the masque were still active; the countertenor William Turner, cast as the "Genius of England" in *Calisto*, probably sang the lyrical aria praising Prince George for his "immortal worth" and Princess Anne for her beauty. But the composer of the new piece, now seated at the harpsichord and directing the performance, had not taken part in the festivities in 1675. Henry Purcell's voice broke late in 1673, when he was about fourteen, ending his career as a boy chorister. At the time of *Calisto*, he was acting as a "mender, maker, repairer, and tuner" of instruments—essentially a way for the court to keep him employed until a more important position came open—and in 1677, when the gifted composer Matthew Locke died, Purcell replaced him as "composer in ordinary...to his Majesty." Two years later, he became one of the regular organists at Westminster Abbey.[5] Purcell was about twenty-four when asked to compose the music for the royal wedding, and if a surviving portrait that may date from this period is accurate, he still had the face of a cherubic choirboy.[6] Those who had heard his music, however, recognized that this young man had a rare and precious gift. The musical bride, who was continuing her lessons on the guitar and the harpsichord, had the training and the ear to appreciate his talents.

From 1680 forward, Purcell's official duties included composing "welcome songs" for those occasions when the king or the Duke of York returned to London after being absent. Working in haste and with uninspired poetry, he nonetheless provided fresh and vibrant music for each of those events. The anonymous poets whose words he set were attempting to give formal expression to the nation's joy in welcoming royalty to London, and in this case the prince being welcomed was a bridegroom, so the poet could draw on the traditions of wedding poetry as well as those of "welcome songs." He compared the new couple to Adam and Eve, used birds and flowers to invoke the goddess Venus, and prophesied a race of "future kings and queens of Christendom...from your great loins to come." But in his opening stanza, he wrote as if Prince George had come straight from the battle-field to the court, deliberately linking the art of war and the art of love:

> From hardy climes and dangerous toils of war,
> Where you for valour unexampled are,
> Where you on honour look'd when you were young,

After John Closterman, *Henry Purcell* (1695?).

As bold as eagles gaze upon the sun,
Hail, Welcome Prince, to our benigner Isle,
Where stars denouncing gentler battles smile
On your arrival which portend you'll prove
As happy as victorious in your love.[7]

In literary terms, there was nothing new or striking about describing courtship as warfare. The epilogue to the court performance of *The Faithful Shepherdess* in 1670 had included a typical instance, describing the little court ladies as "In no condition, to maintain a Warr." Katherine Philips's question to another woman—"How can

Prince George. Frontispiece to *The Present State of Denmark* (1683).

you chuse but win the Day, / Who can resist your Siege?"—is scarcely less conventional.[8] In this case, however, the lover actually had a legitimate claim to military "valour": at the disastrous battles of Lund (4 December 1676) and Landskrona (14 July 1677), Prince George had fought the Swedes by the side of his brother, King Christian V. According to a pamphlet published to promote the match, he had given "extraordinary Testimonies of his Gallantry and Courage, in the Battle of *Lunden,* when that the King his Brother being taken Prisoner by the *Sweeds,*…he rush'd in amongst them, cut his way through all Opposition, and Slew those Persons with his own Hand, who had dared to lay hold on his Royal Brother."[9] The poet could therefore praise the prince's martial courage as suitable for the "hardy climes" of Scandinavia while implying that it would be unnecessary in the "benigner Isle" of England, where George could win his victories in the "gentler battles" of love.

For the composer, however, this was not a promising text. The poet gave him lines clogged with consonants, provided very little material encouraging lyrical smoothness, and chose to write in iambic pentameter—a form not well-suited to musical setting. Yet Purcell found a brilliant solution to the problems inherent in these lines. He decided to set the first two couplets in one musical style and meter, the next two in another, expressing the ideas of difficulty and danger in a slow recitative, then celebrating joy and victory in a rapid aria. He also made a shrewd choice of performer, giving this opening material to a remarkable bass soloist named John Gostling, whose rumbling low notes provided a musical equivalent of the virility the poet was celebrating and encouraging in the prince. In Purcell's setting, the first four lines, evoking George's military prowess, become an ominous, unsettled recitative, dramatizing the danger of warfare with a leap of a seventh and a drop of a tritone on the word *dangerous,* suggesting pain and effort with a surprising chromatic shift on *toils,* and sending Gostling near the top of his range on *valour* and *bold.* At *Hail, welcome Prince* (bar 11), the meter changes to triple time, and the harmonies become brighter and simpler. Although most of the syllables stressed in the poet's pentameter retain their stress, the lines now take on a completely different rhythm. Purcell adds to the cheerful character of this section by choosing the words *happy* and *victorious* for melismatic treatment, creating a sprightly dotted figure for *happy* and expressing *victorious* with a rapid downward scale and two wide leaps, giving Gostling a chance to display both ends of his wide range.[10]

Purcell's later career would give him better opportunities to display his gift for dramatic expression, but even here, he produces a satisfying musical narrative by dividing the poetic text into contrasting sections, creating a musical structure clearer and stronger than the rhetoric of the poem. His effective juxtaposition of contrasting styles is not merely a way of paying a polite compliment to Prince George on the occasion of his marriage; it also reveals the composer's awareness

to - rious in your love, As hap - py, hap -

- - - py as vic - to - rious in your love.

🔊 Mus. Ex. 2.1: Henry Purcell, excerpt from From *Hardy Climes* (1683).

of the wedding's place in a larger political narrative. The motion from "dangerous toils" to happy victory mirrors the political sentiments felt at this moment by many in the court. A long, strained period of political danger had at last subsided, and the sense of relief was palpable.

§

Just eleven days earlier, on Sunday, 18 July, Charles II attended a Chapel Royal service giving thanks for his escape from a recent plot against his life, where he heard the same group of musicians perform a substantial new anthem composed for the occasion by Purcell's friend and colleague John Blow. According to witnesses who came forward in June, this most recent conspiracy had come close to success. A one-eyed Cromwellian soldier named Richard Rumbold owned a property called Rye House, which the king often passed when traveling to the horse races at Newmarket, as he did in the spring of 1683 with a group including the Duke and Duchess of York and Princess Anne. As they amused themselves with riding, dancing, and cockfights,[11] the court party was not aware that a large group of political radicals, perhaps as many as forty men, had made plans to attack the royal coaches on their return journey by blocking the road with a cart full of hay at a narrow place near Rumbold's house, then firing at the coaches with blunderbusses, killing the king and the Duke of York as a prelude to a revolution in London. The royal party escaped because a fire in Newmarket on 22 March prompted them to return to London a week sooner than planned, catching the plotters unprepared.[12] For those inclined to see the hand of God in daily events, the fire looked like divine intervention; for Charles, the revelation of the Rye House Plot was a splendid opportunity to complete the defeat of the political enemies who had plagued him during the previous five years.[13]

The text for Blow's anthem was Psalm 64, in which King David asks God to save him from his enemies. Thanks to many poems and sermons linking Charles II and David, most recently Dryden's *Absalom and Achitophel* (1681), those hearing this anthem would readily identify the king with his Old Testament counterpart, and would read this particular psalm, rich in images of dark conspiracy, as a prophecy of the most recent plot:

> Hear my voice, O God, in my prayer: preserve my life from fear of the enemy.
> Hide me from the gath'ring together of the froward: and from the insurrection of wicked doers;
> Who have whet their tongue like a sword: and shoot out their arrows, even bitter words.
> That they may privily shoot at him that is perfect: suddenly do they hit him, and fear not.
> They encourage themselves in mischief, and commune among themselves how they may lay snares; and say, that no man shall see them.
> They imagine wickedness: that they keep secret among themselves, ev'ry man in the deep of his heart.
> But God shall suddenly shoot at them with a swift arrow: that they shall be wounded.
> Yea, their own tongues shall make them fall: insomuch that whoso seeth them shall laugh them to scorn.
> And all men that see it shall say, This hath God done: for they shall perceive that it is his work.[14]

In a world where people across a wide spectrum of political and religious belief all turned to the Bible to support their views and justify their actions, this text was a godsend for the king. Although his flaws were obvious, he could temporarily pose as "him that is perfect" by claiming the part of a beleaguered victim. His enemies had indeed communed among themselves about laying snares, and because so many people were involved, there was no chance of their keeping the failed plan secret. "Their own tongues," in this case the testimony of a poor Baptist oilman named Josiah Keeling, had made them fall. Perhaps the most urgent message the court hoped to convey by choosing this psalm was the idea that both the Newmarket fire and the betrayal of his fellows by Keeling were examples of God's care for his divinely anointed monarch.

Hastily composed after the plotters were found guilty on 12 July, Blow's solemn anthem dramatized the danger to the throne with dark, foreboding

🔊 Mus. Ex. 2.2: John Blow, excerpt from *Hear my voice, O God* (1683).

harmonies in the key of e minor. Purcell was about to use Gostling's deep bass notes to express the masculine vigor and energy of Anne's new consort, but Blow deployed the same register to signal the depths of depravity to which the conspirators in the Rye House Plot had sunk. By featuring the same range, and the same singer, in his wedding music, Purcell was reminding the many courtiers who heard both pieces that danger and toils were not confined to distant battlefields in Scandinavia. The court itself had just escaped a serious threat, and the marriage of the princess, which offered the prospect of a Protestant succession, represented a hope for happiness and victory.

The royal musicians, who had to learn two substantial new works very quickly in order to respond to the political trial and the royal marriage, would have had a lively sense of the way these two events collided. Prince George's arrival at Whitehall on 19 July, the day after the performance of Blow's anthem, came just one day before the execution of three of the Dissenting radicals involved in the assassination plot, and two days before the beheading of William, Lord Russell, a political opponent of the Crown whose association with the plotters sealed his doom. Thomas Clarges, in a letter detailing the news of the day, felt no unease about juxtaposing the two events:

> This day, about four in the afternoon, the Prince of Denmark arrived at Whitehall.... He is a very comely person, faire hair, few pock holes in his visage, but of very decent and graceful behaviour.... The style used to him is Royal Highness. To-morrow Walcot, Rous and How, three of the

traytors that conspired the King's death, are to be hung, drawn, and quartered, and the next day my Lord Russell is to be beheaded in Lincoln's Inn Fields.[15]

There was, of course, no actual connection between the plot and the wedding. The English and Danish courts had begun discussing a possible marriage early in 1683, and news of the match was public in May, well before Keeling came forward with his astonishing story. Narcissus Luttrell, the compiler of a voluminous digest of newsletters and rumors, was aware of the engagement by 11 May,[16] and by 4 June, Princess Anne was writing to Frances Apsley, who was now married to Sir Benjamin Bathurst, as if her own marriage were a settled fact, though she continued to use her masculine persona: "do not have so ill opinions of your Ziphares for tho he changes his condition yet nothing shall ever alter him from being the same to his deare Semandra that he ever was."[17] During the short period between George's arrival and the wedding ceremony, the young couple attended the theatre and played cards, but gave no overt signal of interest in the public drama of the executions.[18] Nonetheless, many of the poets who contributed to the volume of congratulatory verses in Latin, Greek, and English published by Cambridge University in September were quick to connect the marriage with the plot, treating both events as evidence of God's care for the Stuarts and the nation. Richard Duke of Trinity College, a protégé of Dryden, addresses the newlyweds with a prediction of political harmony:

> The shaken Throne more surely fixt shall stand,
> And curs'd Rebellion fly the happy Land!
> At Your blest Union Civil Discords cease,
> Confusion turns to Order, Rage to Peace.[19]

Thomas Lawrence of King's College, who also rhymes "cease" with "Peace," pictures George exorcising the "ghastly Ghosts" conjured up by the various plots:

> Well! Then we're safe; and all our careful fears
> (Like ghastly Ghosts when the bright Morn appears)
> Hast to be gone, for now all Plots may cease,
> And gently yield to a perpetual Peace:
> For *George* the Great rises so Ray'd with light,
> The Fiends run trembling to eternal night.[20]

And Charles Montagu of Trinity, later an important politician in the reigns of William and Anne, explicitly mentions the assassins, if only for the sake of a fanciful contrast between their blunderbusses and "*Cupids* Darts," a phrase he might have borrowed from *Calisto:*

> Great *CHARLES*, and His Illustrious Brother here,
>   No bold Assassinate need fear,
>   Here is no harmfull Weapon found,
> Nothing but *Cupids* Darts, and Beauty here can wound.[21]

Anne had always known that her marriage would be a public event with dynastic consequences, but as the music, the poems, and the grisly executions reminded her, the timing made the wedding even more significant politically than she might have expected. Although the king had escaped this latest assassination attempt, it was another reminder of his mortality and his lack of legitimate issue. His brother's Duchess, Maria Beatrice, had no living children in 1683; his nephew William and his niece Mary were also childless—and likely to remain so. The hope for a Protestant succession therefore rested with the Danish Lutheran George and the firmly Anglican Anne. This was the victory to be sought in the "gentler battles" to which Purcell's anonymous librettist urged the prince.

§

Wedding customs in seventeenth-century England were more openly sexual than those in some later periods. A French visitor to England during this period, Henri Misson, gives a full account of throwing the stockings and drinking the posset, both evidently survivals from folk rituals encouraging fertility:

> And when Bed-time is come, the Bride-men pull off the Bride's Garters, which she had before unty'd, that they might hang down, and so prevent a curious Hand coming too near her Knee. This done, and the Garters being fasten'd to the Hats of the Gallants, the Bride-maids carry the Bride into the Bed-chamber, where they undress her, and lay her in Bed. The Bridegroom, who by the Help of his Friends, is undress'd in some other Room, comes in his Night-gown, as soon as possible, to his Spouse, who is surrounded by Mother, Aunt, Sister, and Friends, and without any farther Ceremony gets into Bed.... The Bride-men take the Bride's Stockings, and the Bride-maids the Bridegroom's: Both sit down at the Bed's Feet, and fling the Stockings over their Heads, endeavouring to direct them so as that they may fall upon the marry'd Couple.... While some amuse themselves agreeably with these little Follies, others are preparing a good *Posset,* which is a Kind of Cawdle, a Potion made up of Milk, Wine, Yolks of Eggs, Sugar, Cinnamon, Nutmeg, &c. This they present to

the young Couple, who swallow it down as fast as they can to get rid of so troublesome Company; the Bridegroom prays, scolds, entreats them to be gone, and the Bride says ne'er a Word, but thinks the more. If they obstinately continue to retard the Accomplishment of their Wishes, the Bridegroom jumps up in his Shirt, which frightens the Women, and puts them to Flight; the Men follow them, and the Bridegroom returns to the Bride.[22]

Royal couples were not exempt from such foolery: on the day of Anne's wedding, her father wrote to his niece, the Countess of Litchfield, telling her that the king and queen "will be both there and I beleve will stay at St Jamess till they are bedded."[23] In light of the need for Protestant heirs, the traditional insistence on seeing the new couple "bedded" took on special urgency.

From the outset, the private details of Anne's marriage had public meaning. A painting of the new Princess of Denmark made shortly after the wedding, possibly by Lely but now known only from an engraving, deliberately presents Anne as a dewy, desirable bride. The visible shape of her right leg, the suggestive pouching of the dressing gown in her genital area, and the gesture of her left hand, which deliberately lowers her bodice, are all invitations to view the subject as a sexual being, and the figures in the tapestry in the background are carrying baskets laden with a fruitful harvest.

The poems celebrating the wedding are scarcely less overt. In his Pindaric ode, William Ayloffe of Trinity College describes the sexual union of the royal couple as a "Noble *Publick* Good":

> Blest be Ye all, Ye Powers above,
> Ye bright Seraphick flames of Love;
> Blest be the hour, (and sure it must be blest)
> When from Your skies, Ye sweetly did dispence
> The happy powerfull influence,
> That gently touch'd each Princely Lovers breast;
> And with an equal fire
> Did mutual warmth to both inspire:
> It was a Noble Publick Good, and all
> Confess the blessing Epidemical;
> The vigorous heat through every part does move,
> And tunes our Discords to harmonious Love;
> The numerous fears, and jealousies of State,
> And all our lowd Divisions silent lie
> United in the Happy Marriage tie:

Her Royal Highnefs Princefs. Ann of Denmark

Peter Vanderbank (Vandrebanc), *Princess Anne* (1684).

Peter Vanderbank, *Princess Anne*, background figures (magnified).

> Thus, when wild Chaos in confusion strove,
> Love spoke, and warring nature's faction ceas't,
> And the dissenting Elements were wedded into peace.[24]

"Mutual warmth" and "vigorous heat" are conventional poetic metaphors for sexual desire, recently deployed with comic effect in Dryden's *Absalom and Achitophel,* where the polygamous David functions as a type for Charles II:

> When Nature prompted, and no law deny'd
> Promiscuous use of Concubine and Bride;
> Then, *Israel's* Monarch, after Heaven's own heart,
> His vigorous warmth did, variously, impart
> To Wives and Slaves: And, wide as his Command,
> Scatter'd his Maker's Image through the Land.[25]

For Dryden, Charles's "vigorous warmth" is a sign of his kingship, his sexual potency signaling his monarchial power. For the more cautious Ayloffe, the "mutual warmth" of Anne and George, dispensed like a powerful prescription, is an "Epidemical" cure for the diseased body politic.

At the end of the stanza, the procreation prayed for in many of the poems celebrating the wedding becomes an act of primal Creation, described in musical terms: the happy marriage "tunes our Discords" and silences "our lowd Divisions." This imagery is also political. Ayloffe imagines Love calming "warring nature's faction"—a phrase sure to remind his readers of the political parties or "factions" of the last few Parliaments. Before being "wedded into peace," the "Elements" are "dissenting"—a term also used for the religion of the Rye House plotters. With its varying line lengths and improvisatory rhyme scheme, the Pindaric form Ayloffe chose for his poem is an ideal vehicle for depicting the taming of chaos, as Dryden would demonstrate four years later in his virtuoso "Song for St. Cecilia's Day, 1687." But Ayloffe is not quite able to enact in his poetry the control and peace he seeks to celebrate. In this stanza, the line describing "numerous fears, and jealousies of State" lacks a rhyming partner; like an unresolved dissonance in music, it leaves the reader waiting for a cadence that never comes. Neither in verse nor in real life could the "fears, and jealousies of State" be easily contained.

As Anne accepted their congratulations, the court and its followers earnestly hoped they were witnessing the end of the intense political fears and jealousies that had darkened the years between 1678 and 1683. The rituals of monarchy, including "welcome songs," had continued in those years, but now when Charles returned from a summer at Windsor or a racing week at Newmarket, his poets pictured him curing "the plague of rebellion" or "Scatt'ring the mists of faction."[26] Purcell did what he could to enliven their lines, but no one could ignore the presence of a passionate and organized opposition party in Parliament, strengthened by widespread fears of papist conspiracy. The main target of revolutionary fervor during this period was James, Duke of York, and the enmity felt toward her father significantly affected Princess Anne's life. In Purcell's song welcoming James "at his return from Scotland in the year 1682," the anonymous poet described the Duke as a man

> Whose conduct abroad
> Has his enemies aw'd
> And ev'ry proud rebel affrighted.[27]

But neither the overblown verbs nor the rollicking meter could quite efface York's recent history. In fact, his enemies were so numerous and powerful that his brother found it necessary to send him into exile—first in Brussels, then in Scotland—until the storm blew over. Princess Anne, who visited her father in Brussels in 1679 and stayed with him in Edinburgh from the summer of 1681 until the late spring of 1682, shared the poet's hope that "all factious troubles" would now cease. In his report on the wedding, Thomas Clarges called her "a princess of a very ingenious and debonaire demeaner, full of goodness in all her aire."[28] If he was correct in inferring that she was happy, her reasons were both personal and political.

§

Understanding the feelings of the princess on this happy day, as well as the sense of relief expressed in Purcell's music and the Cambridge poems, requires exploring the troubled years between her sister's marriage and her own. When Princess Mary married William of Orange in 1677, she was only fifteen; her stepmother, Maria Beatrice, had also married at that age, and Anne probably expected to do so as well, gaining an independent establishment and the status of an adult woman. A recently rediscovered portrait by Lely, dating from about 1678, reflects her liminal situation. Unlike the voluptuous later portrait, it shows a girlish Anne making a garland of flowers, a traditional emblem of innocence. Hidden in the background, however, is another message: the figures on the wine ewer behind the seated princess are Maenads, dancing in celebration of Bacchus, figures of fertility reminding the viewer that the subject will soon reach the age her culture thought appropriate for marriage. Read in this way, the portrait is a visual analogue to *Calisto:* it presents the princess as an innocent child but slyly reminds us that she will soon be available as an object of desire.[29] Curiously enough,

Richard Tompson, *Her Highness the Lady Ann*. Mezzotint after
Sir Peter Lely (c. 1675–1690).

Richard Tompson, the artist who made the popular mezzotint copy shown
here, altered this aspect of Lely's image, replacing the Maenads with two male
figures.

Alert to the fact that he might "grace some Fav'rite Crown" with the hand of
his niece,[30] Charles was probably expecting to find a princely suitor for her in the

next few years, but a series of unexpected public events now threatened and pre-occupied the court, placing Anne herself in an unsettled and unsettling series of surroundings. Her personal troubles began with her sister's marriage. According to Anne Hobart, mother of the elusive Frances, the news of Mary's wedding brought "gret joy to all the sety [City] & everybody." But in the days before the wedding, she adds, the "Duck, the Duchis, and Lady Ann set and cry 2 or 3 houres together, thay ar loth to part."[31] Even if exaggerated, this touching letter suggests the inevitable tension between the pressures of statecraft and the feelings of families, increased in this case by Maria's continuing efforts to expand her family. Little Catherine Laura, whose birth delayed the premiere of *Calisto,* had lived for only nine months, but Isabella (born 28 August 1676) was now past her first year, and Maria was in the last stages of another pregnancy. She gave birth to a son, christened Charles, on 7 November 1677, three days after Mary's wedding. Just at this moment, however, Anne fell ill with the smallpox; by the time she was well again, William and Mary had sailed for Holland. Although the princess made a complete recovery, she infected her governess, Lady Frances Villiers, and her half-brother Charles, the infant heir. Both died.

After this series of domestic calamities, Anne had urgent emotional reasons for wanting to see her sister, and in September 1678, King Charles gave permission for the princess to make a brief trip to the Hague to visit Mary, who was lonely and in poor health, having miscarried the previous spring. Together with the Duchesses of York and Monmouth (her stepmother and her godmother), the princess embarked on 27 September. Before her departure, however, an ominous sequence of political troubles had already begun to unfold. On 13 August 1678, a chemist named Christopher Kirkby, whom the king knew well through his interest in science, approached him and warned him that his life was in danger. Charles, who was generally skeptical of conspiracy theories, showed no undue alarm. When Kirkby and his associate, a crack-brained apocalyptic preacher named Israel Tonge, handed him a long written document describing a "Popish Plot" to assassinate him in order to place his Catholic brother on the throne, the king calmly asked Thomas Osborne, Earl of Danby, his Lord Treasurer and chief minister, to conduct an investigation, but made no alteration in his usual activities.[32] On 28 September 1678, the day after the ladies sailed for Holland, the author of the document Kirkby and Tonge had given the king appeared before the Privy Council.[33] Titus Oates, a defrocked Jesuit with a markedly strange manner and appearance, testified for three consecutive days and succeeded in convincing some of the Council that the plot was real, in part because he had the good luck or prescience to implicate a man who had indeed written letters expressing the hope that England would return to the Catholic fold: Edward Colman, Secretary to the

Duchess of York. So intense was the hysteria that the Catholic Duchess immediately fell under suspicion of having arranged her trip to Holland in order to spirit out of the country some priests who were supposedly "concerned" in the plot.[34] A sensational murder increased the sense of panic: on 17 October, Sir Edmund Berry Godfrey, a magistrate to whom Oates and Tongue had delivered a sworn statement about the plot, was found strangled and stabbed on Primrose Hill. His mysterious death, which has yet to be explained, convinced many that the plot was authentic. When the ladies returned on 24 October, after just three weeks abroad, the political landscape had changed dramatically. Lurid accounts of the murder of Godfrey poured forth from the press, and on 25 October, five aged Catholic peers were arrested, accused of high treason, and sent to the Tower; two of them had close relatives among Maria's Ladies of the Bedchamber.[35] On 27 November came Colman's trial. Incriminating correspondence found in his lodgings appeared to confirm Oates's testimony, and the Duchess's Secretary was condemned and promptly executed on 3 December 1678. Over the next two years, numerous Catholic priests and laymen followed Colman to the scaffold, most on much flimsier evidence.

Although Anne herself was never under suspicion, the anti-Catholic panic that now gripped the nation affected many close to her. Colman had been in her father's court in one capacity or another since before her birth, and in constant attendance on her stepmother from the time Maria arrived in England in 1673.[36] At this moment of crisis, Anne would have heard many express the fear that Colman might implicate others in the duke's court. Her friend Sarah Jenyns, now Sarah Churchill, dined with "several of the Duke's old servants at St. James's" on the day Colman was hanged and reported that her companions "were transported with Joy when they brought word he was dead without confessing any Thing."[37] There is no way to know whether Anne shared this cynical joy at the death of Colman, but she could not ignore the plot, as it touched several people in her own intimate circle. Among the bedchamber-women serving the second Duchess of York was Katherine Cornwallis, a widow who lived at court with her four daughters, two of whom—Cicely and Mary—were close to Anne.[38] Born into the prominent Arundell family, Katherine retained the Catholic faith of her ancestors and reared her daughters as Catholics. Sometime in the fall of 1678, Cicely left London, and on 13 December, she was arrested in York with another woman and a man who was correctly suspected of being a Roman Catholic priest. After admitting to being Catholics but disclaiming any knowledge of the plot, the women were eventually released. Cicely entered a convent in Hammersmith and lived a long, quiet life as a nun, but the priest, Father Jeremiah Pracid, remained in jail, where he died in 1686.[39] It was just at this time that Mary Cornwallis, the only one of the four Cornwallis sisters who did not enter a convent, emerged as Princess Anne's closest confidante, so Anne certainly knew about Cicely's arrest and imprisonment. Despite her own devotion to the Church of England, she can hardly have been unconcerned about the jailing of a childhood companion who posed no threat whatsoever to the state.

Over the next four years, Anne sent Mary Cornwallis "above a thousand letters full of the most violent professions of everlasting kindness." Although this relationship was clearly significant, the only surviving account of it was written years later by Sarah Churchill, at a time when she felt great bitterness toward Anne. Despite her scornful and dismissive tone, Sarah acknowledges that the relationship lasted "three or four years" and remembers King Charles saying "No man ever loved his Mistress, as his niece Anne did Mrs. Cornwallis."[40] She does not mention some powerful factors that worked to bring the two young ladies together. Anne's other girlhood friends were now less accessible than they had formerly been. In 1676, Frances Apsley's family moved from their lodgings at court to a new house in St. James's Square, next door to the house where the Duke of York had installed his mistress Arabella Churchill.[41] In 1677, Sarah Jenyns secretly married Arabella's brother John; she made her marriage public and resigned her post as a Maid of Honor in the spring of 1678, just before the beginning of the plot scare.[42] Both the princess and her new favorite had recently been separated from their sisters—Anne when Princess Mary married William and moved to Holland, Mary when Cicely left the court, probably fearing reprisals against all Catholics. They also had in common the experience of becoming more vulnerable as their male relatives were caught up in the Popish Plot hysteria. Among the five Catholic peers sent to the Tower in October was Henry Arundell, Third Baron Arundell, who was the uncle of Mary and Cicely. As a prominent courtier who had worked openly to promote toleration of his fellow Catholics, Arundell had every reason to fear the worst, and the Middlesex jury, acting on evidence given by professional informers, found him and the others guilty of high treason on 3 December 1678, the very day Colman was executed. Fortunately for the five Catholic lords, titled aristocrats had the right to a trial by their peers, and the king dissolved Parliament in order to interrupt impeachment proceedings against them. Despite Charles's efforts, however, all five were imprisoned in the Tower. One of them, Viscount Stafford, was tried and executed in 1680, and another, Baron Petre, died in the Tower in 1684, shortly before the other three were at last released.

Although the king had hoped for a more sympathetic legislature, the election of the first new Parliament in eighteen years resulted in a House of Commons more strongly opposed to the court than the one he had dismissed. In the fall of 1678, Charles had managed to have the Duke of York exempted from a bill banning all Catholics from sitting in Parliament, but the margin of victory was only two votes in the Commons, so he prudently ordered his unpopular brother to sail for Brussels on 3 March 1679, a few days before the new Parliament met.[43] Princess Anne expected to travel abroad with her family, but at the last minute, the king insisted that she remain behind in England with her half-sister Isabella. After sending his brother and heir away, Charles may have thought it wise to have at least one legitimate Protestant successor visible in England. Fourteen, frightened, and more alone than ever, Anne "cried as much as the rest to part company," according to one contemporary source.[44] At this trying moment, the presence of Mary Cornwallis, similarly alone, similarly terrified about the fate of her kin, would have offered some special comfort. With her father long dead and her uncle in jail, Mary had no immediate prospect of finding a husband; with her father and stepmother in exile, Anne was in a similar position. The "violent professions of everlasting kindness" that she regularly sent to Mary were expressions of a passion intensified by fear and loneliness.

§

Yet Anne was never one to wallow in tears, and she soon found another outlet for her feelings. Sometime during this period, most likely in the spring of 1679, the princess and her ladies staged Nathaniel Lee's seamy tragedy Mithridates, which had its professional premiere early in 1678.[45] Unlike the staging of Calisto at court, this performance was evidently a private affair: the date, venue, and cast remain uncertain, and we do not know who chose the play. Surviving letters, however, make it clear that the princess played the leading male role of Ziphares, with Frances Apsley playing his beloved Semandra. Perhaps Mary Cornwallis or Frances Apsley thought the work of preparing a major role would take Anne's mind off her troubles; perhaps her royal uncle, aware of her unhappiness at being separated from her family, took steps to encourage this activity. According to a much-repeated anecdote, Charles "was so pleased with the natural sweetness" of his niece's voice "that he ordered Mrs. Barry, a famous actress, should teach her to speak, which she did with such success that it was a real pleasure to hear her."[46] This story is difficult to date, but Elizabeth Barry, a gifted actress and the mistress of the Earl of Rochester, had first come to prominence two seasons earlier as Mrs. Loveit in George Etherege's play The Man of Mode, and these lessons in elocution were apparently for Anne alone—a detail suggesting that they took place after Mary's marriage, perhaps in preparation for this performance. With her sister abroad, the younger princess was no longer confined to the small role of an attendant nymph. Now she could take a leading role and even play a man, which might not have been possible had her stepmother been in England.[47] Sarah Churchill, who had starred as Mercury in Calisto, was married, pregnant, and probably not available for this production; by playing Ziphares, Anne had an opportunity to show what she could do in the kind of part for which Sarah had gained acclaim. Like many of her actions when queen, her taking the role of Ziphares was an exercise in strength, a refusal to appear weak or vulnerable.

Lee's plays, exploring extravagant passions in highly expressive language, had an appeal to female readers, and his original prologue to *Mithridates* nodded in that direction: "In the first draught," he confessed, "'twas meant the Ladies Play."[48] As a drama, however, *Mithridates* was a very strange choice for an all-female cast. The world Lee presents is dark and confusing; violence and cruelty are constants; purity and honor find no reward. In his first scene on stage, Mithridates orders a horrible torture to punish a Roman prisoner for his supposed "Desire of Wealth":

> Guards, strait convey him to the Market-place,
> Take off his wealthy Chains, and melt 'em down;
> Then, for a terrible Example to
> All sordid Wretches, Souls made up of Avarice,
> Pour down his Throat the rich dissolved Mass,
> And gorge his Entrails with the burning Gold.[49]

The central event of the play is a rape, and unlike the rape smoothly censored from the more lighthearted *Calisto,* this one actually takes place: Mithridates brutally violates Semandra. His previous favorite Monima, the only other female character in the play, exits in act 2 after just nine speeches, and the male characters include scheming courtiers, a grizzled old general, and the monstrous emperor; it is hard to imagine any of the court ladies wanting these parts or acting them effectively. The most plausible explanation for their choosing this play is that the princess wanted to play the part of Ziphares. For the fourteen-year-old princess, the beleaguered court of Charles II, hounded by enemies and swirling with rumors, might sometimes have seemed almost as frightening as the spectacularly corrupt court of Mithridates. Under these circumstances, playing a high-minded hero was an effective way of dealing with her emotions.

As the play begins, Ziphares, the heroic and upright son of Mithridates, has fallen in love with Semandra, the daughter of the veteran general Archelaus. But as Semandra tearfully reminds Ziphares, she is not of sufficient rank to marry a prince:

> First then, I must complain of my hard Stars,
> That did not dart kind Lustre on my Birth;
> For tho at present, while your young Blood boyls,
> Your Reason cannot get the Rein of Passion,
> Yet it will come, when long possession cloyes you,

Then you will think what Queens you might have had,
With Kingdoms for their Dower; perhaps you may
Prove so unkind, to tell me of it too;
Or, if you shou'd not, yet your Eyes wou'd speak—[Weeping.
Enough to break the heart of poor Semandra.[50]

For Princess Anne, this situation had personal resonance in two generations. When her parents married, just after the Restoration, there was consternation about James's having contracted himself to Anne Hyde, who was not of royal blood, when he might have had queens "with Kingdoms for their Dower." The supposed taint of her mother's ancestry lasted long enough to touch Anne herself. In 1678, a Prussian diplomat suggested a match between Anne and Georg Ludwig of Hanover (later George I of England), only to have Georg's mother, Sophia, Electress of Hanover, haughtily reply that she was not interested in a princess whose mother had been "born into a very mediocre family."[51] Faced with that kind of snobbery, Anne could identify with Semandra. But when she considered the likelihood that her own marriage would be determined by some international alliance, not by her personal preferences, she could also identify with Ziphares, prevented from wedding his true love by considerations of state. Anne would often long for kinds of intimacy that her royal status made unattainable. In 1684, she begged Sarah Churchill "not to call me Your Highness at every word, but to be as free with me as one friend ought to be with another"[52]—a request that led the two friends to correspond as "Mrs. Freeman" and "Mrs. Morley," assumed names designed to make them imaginary equals. In this earlier episode, the conventions of the drama allowed Anne to address tender words of love to Frances Apsley while safely disguised as Ziphares, enacting her lifelong fantasy of love unconstrained by rank, custom, or gender.

When Mithridates refuses to grant Ziphares permission to marry Semandra, his public motive is pride in his ancestry, but his private motive is lust for the beautiful young woman. Despite her low birth, he claims Semandra for his court, ordering her to "attend our Queen," just as Charles II regularly installed his mistresses as Ladies-in-Waiting to the neglected Catharine. The stage direction for the emperor's first appearance—"Mithridates holding Monima by the Hand; his Queens, Concubines, Sons and Daughters attending"—comes uncomfortably close to the way the king sometimes appeared in public, and in political terms, the title character embodies the worst nightmares of those opposed to the Stuart court.[53] He is arbitrary, vengeful, and a prisoner of his own lust. Not long after his refusal to approve the match, Mithridates realizes that he needs Ziphares to lead his troops against the Romans, so he relents, gives his blessing to a future marriage, asks Semandra to veil herself, and promises to avoid looking at her; but with

Ziphares off fighting the Romans, the evil courtiers, led by Ziphares's scheming younger brother Pharnaces, arrange for him to see her at her most attractive, and his lust returns. When Ziphares comes back from the wars in triumph, Mithridates tells Semandra that she must not greet him warmly, lest he die on the spot:

> If when Ziphares, at your first appearance,
> Runs to your Arms, fir'd with expected joys,
> You thrust him not away, and slight him strangely,
> With all the marks of the most proud disdain,
> That a most faithless and ambitious Woman
> Cou'd show to gain the Empire of the World;
> He shall be stab'd, be murder'd by my Guards,
> Before your eyes.

Hoping to save Ziphares, Semandra complies, and Ziphares, baffled by his cold reception, kisses her hand, only to receive a shocking rebuff:

> *Semandra.* The kiss you ravish, Prince, is dangerous;
> And let me now Conjure you, by your Love,
> If you can love after what I injoyn you,
> Upon your life, offer the like no more.
> *Ziphares.* O Man me, Reason, with thy utmost force;
> Or Passion, with the dreadful starts it makes,
> Will soon Divorce my Soul from this weak Body.

As spoken by Princess Anne in the court production, this last speech took on additional meaning. By asking reason to *man* her, Anne was enacting not only her right to play a male role in this play, but her right to claim male prerogatives in her life. She may have wept when her family departed in March, but her royal future depended on her ability to subdue her passions and keep her soul contained in her "weak Body." The role of Ziphares was an exercise in that kind of restraint.

From Semandra's coldness, Ziphares concludes that she is now his father's mistress; he curses her inconstancy and bids her farewell:

> Corrupted are her Noble Faculties,
> The temper of her Soul is quite infected:
> Inconstancy, the Plague that first or last
> Taints the whole Sex, the catching Court-disease,
> Has spotted all her white, her Virgin Beauties.
>
> . . . .

Farewel, *Semandra*. O, thou'lt never find,
In all thy search of Love, a heart like mine.
Once more, Farewel for ever, false *Semandra*.[54]

Again, this speech took on special meaning when spoken by Anne. She was all too familiar with the "Court-disease" of inconstancy, which had infected many male and female courtiers well known to her, and she was keenly aware of the need to maintain her own "Virgin Beauties." In light of the virulence of the "Court-disease," not to mention the risks of pregnancy or syphilis, her tendency to form strong relationships with women shows her prudence as well as her emotional nature. Ziphares's claim that Semandra will never again find a heart as faithful as his comes very close to Anne's habitual expressions of devotion in her letters to Frances, such as this one, written in 1679:

> I am not one of those who can express a great deale & therefore it may be thought I do not love so well, but whoever thinks so is much mistaken, for tho I have not may be so good a way of expressing my self as some people have yet I assure you I love you as well as those that do & perhaps more than some.[55]

With Ziphares out of the way, Mithridates immediately tells Semandra that she must be his queen:

> This moment I will take you in my Chariot,
> Streight to the Temple, and in publick Wed you;
> Tho you refuse to joyn in Ceremony,
> Instead of sacred words venting loud Curses,
> 'T will not avail; for when the Mystery's done,
> I'll bear you back, and as my Queen enjoy you.

He is as good as his word, and Semandra, though she refuses the marriage and resists the rape, considers herself forever ruined and dishonored. In a scene of great pathos, she seeks out Ziphares and explains the cold reception she was earlier forced to give him. In acting this scene, Anne could draw on her own recent experience of parting with her family, and more generally on her sense of having to face a hostile world on her own:

> *Ziphares.* What shall we do, Semandra?
> *Semandra.* Part, and die.
> *Ziph.* Die, 'tis resolv'd; but how? that, that must be

My future care: and with that thought I leave thee.
Go then, thou Setting-star; take from these eyes,
(These eyes, that if they see thee, will be wishing)
O take those languishing pale fires away,
And leave me to the wide, dark Den of Death!
Sem. Something within me sobs to my boding heart,
Semandra ne're shall see Ziphares more.
Ziph. Away then; part, for ever part, Semandra:
Let me alone sustain those rav'nous Fates,
Which, like two famish'd Tygers, are gone out,
And have us in the Wind. Death come upon me;
Night, and the bloodi'st deed of darkness, end me.
But, oh, for thee, for thee, if thou must die,
I beg of Heav'n this last, this only favour,
To give thy life a painless dissolution:
Oh, may those ravish'd Beauties fall to Earth
Gently, as wither'd Roses leave their Stalks:
May Death be mild to thee, as Love was cruel;
Calm, as the Spirits in a Trance decay:
And soft, as those who sleep their Souls away.[56]

Here as elsewhere, Lee creates extravagant metaphors to express the supercharged emotions of his characters: the "wide, dark Den of Death," the "famish'd Tygers," the "wither'd Roses." For Anne, who was "not one of those who can express a great deale," speaking these phrases was an opportunity to borrow a poetic eloquence not naturally hers. In addition to giving her an opportunity to act heroically in the face of doom, clinging in death to a faithful lover, the role of Ziphares allowed her to be grandly expressive, to borrow apt words for her feelings.

The final act of the play is all death: Ziphares mistakenly stabs Semandra in the dark, thinking she is an enemy, then takes poison; Mithridates, wounded in battle, beholds the dead lovers before bleeding to death. From beginning to end, the play features horror and pain, yet the court ladies acted it not only in this private performance but in a later, more public production in Edinburgh in 1681, which has left a more substantial record.[57] Anne's fascination with the corrupt and frightening world of Lee's plays is intriguing, especially in light of the long tradition of pastoral dramas at court, including *The Faithful Shepherdess* and *Calisto*. One motive the princess may have had for acting in Lee's play was to insist on her status as an adult. Princess Mary, at thirteen, had used her reading of *Sophonisba* as a way of expressing and understanding the adult emotions of passion and jealousy;[58] Anne took that process one step further by performing in *Mithridates*. If maids of honor and even princesses could be married off at fourteen or fifteen, as they often were, the belief that innocent pastorals were the only plays they should act was absurd. By acting an emphatically adult play, Anne and her ladies were insisting on their knowledge of a world in which marriages were often unhappy, promises were frequently broken, political alliances shifted, and loyalty was rare. Years later, when her physician told her that some of her subjects were expecting her to alter the succession to the throne, the queen retorted angrily: "O fye says she, there is no such thing. What, do they think I'm a Child, and to be imposed upon?"[59] Somewhere behind that outburst lay her memory of needing to insist, as a teenaged princess, that she was no longer a child.

§

Meanwhile, Anne's uncle Charles was scrambling to survive. In March, he consented to the resignation of Danby, his chief minister, but he could not prevent Danby's being impeached and sent to the Tower, where he languished for years. In April, the king appointed a new Privy Council, including Anthony Ashley Cooper, Earl of Shaftesbury, the most vocal leader of the parliamentary forces arrayed against him. Despite this conciliatory gesture, Shaftesbury's allies soon proposed a bill excluding James from the succession. Charles felt compelled to resist this and all subsequent Exclusion Bills as attacks on the fundamental principles of monarchy and responded by first proroguing, then dissolving his Parliament. He was elated in July when Titus Oates, whose testimony had now sent a number of men to their deaths, suffered his first setback: Sir George Wakeman, the queen's Catholic physician, accused of plotting to poison the king, was acquitted when Oates had to admit that he could identify neither Wakeman's face nor his handwriting.[60] Rejoicing at this verdict and hopeful that it would prove a turning point, the king at last gave Anne and Isabella permission to visit their family in Brussels, though only for a month or two. Anne's reunion with her father and stepmother was a happy one, made more so by the presence of Sarah Churchill, whose husband had joined James in exile in May; Sarah herself arrived in Brussels in August, a few days before Anne.[61] But no sooner had the princess settled into her comfortable chamber than news came that the king was seriously ill, and the Duke of York hurried home in disguise, taking John Churchill with him. He spent the night in St. James's Square, nominally at the home of the Apsleys, who conveniently lived next door to his mistress Arabella Churchill, John's sister. Wherever he slept, the duke rose early the next day and rode on to Windsor to see his brother.

Anne's trip to Brussels, always planned as a short, personal visit, now became uncertain as to length and outcome. The king had nearly recovered by the time James reached his bedside, but once in England, the duke lobbied hard for a permanent homecoming, and his daughter shared his hopes. A remarkable letter to

Lady Apsley, the mother of Frances, written just at this moment, catches Anne's shifting moods:

> I find you weare mightily surprised to see the Duke, indeed we weare all mightily surprised at it heare at first & did not know what to think, but now I hope in god it will be for the best & that I shall be so happy to bring the Dutchess over with me, but I know not whethere I have any ground for these hopes, I hope I have for I have a good heart thank God or els it would have bin down long ago. I was to see a ball at the court incognito which I liked very well; it was in very good order & some dancd well enough; indeed there was Prince Vodemont that danced extreamly well, as well if not better then ethere the Duke of Monmouth or Sr E. villiers which I think very exstrodinary.[62]

Although the Duchess of York was her stepmother, Anne does not speak of returning with the duchess but hopes instead "to bring the Dutchess over *with me.*" Even at fourteen, she is claiming a leading role in political affairs. Congratulating herself on her courage and perhaps remembering how she had systematically overcome her distress at parting with her family the previous March, she tells a great truth about her morale: "I have a good heart thank God or els it would have bin down long ago." And then the door into her emotional life slams shut, as she moves on to assess the quality of dancing at the ball, and from there to the fireworks, the condition of the streets in Brussels, and the details of her accommodations.

By the end of September, the Duke of York was back in Brussels. With careful attention to balance, the king also sent the dangerously popular Duke of Monmouth into exile. Monmouth left England on 24 September; York sailed the next day. Within a week, Charles ordered his brother to proceed to Scotland, where he had appointed him Lord Commissioner. At this moment of renewed uncertainty, Anne again turned her attentions to a play, evidently performed by the ladies-in-waiting Maria had brought with her in March, as well as those attendants who traveled with the princess herself. "The play," she wrote to Frances, "is practisde to night[.] Miss Watts is to be Lady townly which part I believe wont much become her." A young lady addressed as "Miss Watts" rather than "Mrs. Watts" would have been very young indeed, perhaps as young as Anne herself had been when she played Nyphe.[63] Yet someone, clearly not Anne, thought it would be funny to cast a child as Lady Townley, one of the older characters in *The Man of Mode,* the popular comedy that had launched Elizabeth Barry's career. Etherege's play features sexually explicit dialogue and action, so the young ladies of the court were again asserting their status as adults by choosing to perform it, though Anne's comment about the casting suggests some unease. She writes as if she has already told Frances about this play; an earlier letter, now lost, might tell us whether she herself took a part, and whether Sarah Churchill was among the actors. The quoted letter, however, is the only trace left, and the play may never have gotten past rehearsal, as the Duke of York's whole party left Brussels a day or two later, making a short visit to Mary at The Hague before arriving back in England on 12 October.[64] Two weeks later, the Yorks departed for Scotland.

Once again, the king wanted Anne and Isabella to stay in London. The princess kept the duke and duchess company on the first day of their journey by land, a trip that was to take them nearly a month, but returned to Whitehall the next day. She missed more theatricals in Scotland: in a letter to Susan Belasyse, a Lady of the Bedchamber who remained in London, Maria reported that her maids were rehearsing Dryden's *Aureng-Zebe,* another tale of a father and son in love with the same woman.[65] In London, however, Anne was able to see the leading professional actors at both theatres while witnessing the playing out of the highly theatrical struggle over the succession, which was increasingly focused on fathers and sons. Members of Shaftesbury's party, who were now called "Whigs," were pressuring the king to declare his bastard son Monmouth legitimate, bypassing York and establishing a Protestant succession. In addition to his unwillingness to tamper with the succession, Charles suspected that a king who had gained the throne in such an irregular way would be a weak puppet, controlled by those who had put him there; he believed that the ultimate aim of Shaftesbury and his party was to abolish the monarchy altogether. On 14 October 1679, irritated by Shaftesbury's questioning his appointment of James as Commissioner for Scotland, the king removed his leading opponent from the Privy Council; on the next day, he again prorogued his troublesome Parliament. Despite a well-organized wave of petitions urging that Parliament be allowed to meet, Charles continued to postpone the inevitable confrontation.

The king was still strong enough to insist on his royal prerogatives, but he could not prevent his adversaries from stirring up trouble. The anniversary of the accession of Queen Elizabeth on 10 November had long been an occasion for anti-Catholic demonstrations, and in 1679, a crowd estimated at two hundred thousand witnessed the most elaborate and expensive pope-burning procession yet mounted, featuring torches, costumed actors, and musical dialogues; some put the cost at £2,500.[66] Ten days later, Monmouth returned from exile without permission, an act of rebellion he would scarcely have undertaken without powerful supporters, doubtless including some of the wealthy Whigs who had paid for the antipope pageant. The king responded by stripping his son of his offices and banning him from court, but the young duke's presence in England was very useful to those who hoped to alter the succession. Charles prorogued his Parliament once more on 26 January 1680, summoning his brother home from Scotland as an additional gesture of defiance, but the Whigs continued to promote the idea of

Monmouth as an alternative successor through a series of carefully stage-managed appearances outside the capital. In February 1680, the "Protestant Duke" made a journey to Chichester on the model of a royal "progress," and in the summer he toured the West, where his stops included Shaftesbury's country house.[67] The court had traditionally promoted its own image through progresses and masques, so the Whigs now provided a rival myth, with their own allegorical touches. An account of Monmouth's visit to Exeter, published by an alleged "Eyewitness," gives an example of the deliberately theatrical flourishes surrounding this quasi-royal appearance:

> The Citizens, together with the people of all the adjacent parts, (verily believed to exceed 20000 persons) came all forth to meet the Duke with their Souls and Mouths filled with love and joy, trumpeting forth his welcome, and shouting out thus, God bless our Gracious Sovereign King *Charles*, God bless the Protestant Duke, God bless the Protestant Prince, *&c.* But that which most deserves remark, was the appearance of a company of brave stout young men, all clothed in linen Wast-coats and Drawers, white and harmless, having not so much as a stick in their hand, but joining hands, their number was reputed to be 10 or 1200 (the least conjecture of them was 800) these met the Duke within 3 miles of the City, being put into order on a small round hill, and divided into two parts, and so attended the coming of the Duke, who when arrived rode up between them, and after rode round each company, who then united, and went hand in hand in their order, before the Duke into the City.

Monmouth, whose skill in dancing was essential to his reputation at court, had also now demonstrated his military abilities, most recently by putting down a rebellion at Bothwell Bridge in Scotland. The "stout young men" of Exeter, with their "white and harmless" costumes, "joining hands" like dancers, combined choreography with military drill. Although they carried "not so much as a stick in their hand," their display of discipline and order was a thinly veiled threat. The "Eyewitness" concluded his account by declaring that the event "suited (at this time) the reception that a Protestant people was willing to give to an illustrious Protestant Prince."[68] The implication was that a Catholic prince who attempted to claim the throne that was his by the laws of succession would not get such a reception, that the "stout young men" would resist, this time with more than sticks in their hands. Monmouth claimed princely status on these journeys by "touching for the King's Evil," an ancient ritual in which the sovereign touched those afflicted with scrofula, many of whom believed that the slightest physical contact with a sacred monarch could cure them.[69] Queen Anne's insistence on reviving this practice during her reign, even though the process taxed and exhausted her, was an act of filial piety toward her father and uncle, but it may also have owed something to her memory of Monmouth's audacious attempt to claim it.

Further prorogations, issued at regular intervals, kept Parliament from convening until 21 October 1680, so that James and Maria were able to remain in England for seven months, a period made tentative and uneasy by the certainty that the next session of Parliament would again require them to leave. Anne, whose natural place as the duke's unmarried daughter was within his court, had now experienced two long periods of living in Whitehall without the protection and company of the Yorks and their servants, and would soon begin another. Although she retained her own entourage, which included a dancing master, a guitar teacher, and a French tutor, she was subject to the control of her aunt Henrietta Hyde, wife of her uncle Laurence, who had become her governess after the death of Frances Villiers. Born in 1646, Lady Hyde was a less congenial companion than the duchess, who was much closer to Anne in age. As she dealt with these unnerving changes, the princess, who turned fifteen a few weeks before her father returned from Scotland, had good reasons to hope for a settled establishment of her own, a goal she could only achieve by being married. But with the nation in turmoil, that happy change was still far away.

§

In the absence of a Parliament, the debate about the succession found other venues. The Licensing Act of 1662, which had given the government tight control over newspapers, expired on 27 May 1679, and the government's tame official *Gazette* lost its monopoly, as shrill partisan newspapers sprang up on both sides. Ballads, sermons, and poems now frequently carried overt political messages. In the theatre, old plays acquired new prologues and epilogues suggesting political implications their authors could not possibly have intended, and new plays made direct references to current controversies. Nor was political activity limited to the actors. In February 1680, there was "a great dispute in the Duke's Play-House, some Gentlemen in their Cupps entering into the Pitt, flinging Links [torches] at the Actors, and using several reproachfull speeches against the Dutchess of P[ortsmouth] and other persons of Honour." According to another source, the drunken gentlemen also abused the Duke of York and ended by shouting, "God bless his Highness, the Duke of Monmouth."[70] These intoxicated young blades were by no means the only Whigs attacking the king's Catholic mistress and his Catholic brother: on 26 June 1680, Shaftesbury went before a Middlesex grand jury and audaciously denounced the Duke of York as a recusant and the Duchess of Portsmouth as a prostitute. This was a propaganda stunt, undertaken in the full expectation that the king would stop the proceedings, but it forced Charles to interrupt his summer idyll at Windsor in order to come to the City and disband the jury—an irritating and embarrassing task.

The most overtly political of the new plays came on stage at the end of May, when the King's Company presented *The Female Prelate, Being the History of the Life and Death of Pope Joan,* a virulently anti-Catholic drama by Elkanah Settle. The apocryphal female pope depicted in this play, a stock figure of anti-Catholic broadsides, allegedly gained the papacy in the ninth century by hiding her gender beneath priestly robes. According to the usual account, she was found out when she delivered a child during an ecclesiastical procession. Settle portrays her as a lustful murderess at the heart of a thoroughly corrupt papal court; his version of the story includes forged correspondence, accusations of treasonous conspiracies, and plenty of sexual corruption. Among the passages most clearly designed to please the Whigs is an exchange between the fraudulent pope and the Duke of Saxony, who claims that the pope has poisoned his father. When the pope orders him chained in a dungeon, the duke asks "By what authority the power of *Rome* / Commands the Fortunes, Crowns and Lives of Princes." The pope's answer celebrates his Church's power over secular rulers:

> The Lives and Crowns of Princes, what are they
> But the Creation of our Breath! shall we
> Who from immediate Heaven derived have right
> To make or unmake Saints, want power t'enthrone
> Or depose Kings, dispose of Crowns above,
> And yet not place 'em here! command Eternity,
> And have mortality controul us?[71]

It was deep, irrational fear of the attitudes caricatured in this speech that fueled the fierce opposition to James, who had repeatedly tried to assure his countrymen that he would not, as king, be subject to papal authority. Settle dedicated the printed play to Shaftesbury, who promptly hired him to script the next year's pope-burning.[72] The supporters of the Duke of York, however, found a way to express their disapproval. Playwrights received the proceeds of the third performance when there was one, so on 2 June 1680, the afternoon of the third showing of *Pope Joan,* "the Duchesse of Portsmouth to disoblige Mr Settle the Poet carried all the Court with her to the Duke's house to see Macbeth,"[73] a play about the tragic consequences of altering a royal succession. The spectacle of a large, elaborately dressed party of courtiers, possibly including Princess Anne, trooping off to Dorset Garden in the hope that the rival theatre in Drury Lane would be left empty was itself a piece of political theatre.

Although Anne had every reason to support the legitimate succession, she had written a scornful letter from Brussels poking fun at the Catholic devotional objects for sale in the shops there.[74] Her political sympathies necessarily rested with her uncle and father, but she also shared the disdain for Catholic superstition that found expression in pope-burnings and in Settle's play. If she found an opportunity to see or read *Pope Joan,* there was much in that play to interest her. Settle's "tragedy," though crude and farcical, nonetheless presented a female figure claiming a normally male role, a process the princess knew might be part of her political future—and a process she had already enacted as Ziphares. In the third act, with a clumsiness all too typical of Settle's dramaturgy, Pope Joan tells Cardinal Lorenzo, long her secret lover, the story of her early life, as if he would not already have known it. Describing the years before she disguised herself as a man and a priest, Joan speaks of the tension between desire and power:

> Thus far I kept my Virgin Whiteness fair.
> Not but I had all
> That high Spring Tide within my youthful Veins
> That bursts the Adamantine Wall of Honour,
> And makes that Breach where Love and Ruine enter.
> But 'twas my pride preserved my guarded Innocence.
> Who yields to Love, makes but vain man her Lord:
> And I who had studied all the greater Globe
> Scorn'd to be Vassal to the lesser world.[75]

At fifteen, Anne was now experiencing the "high Spring Tide" of youth. The surviving letters to Frances Apsley, with their epistolary cross-dressing, open a small window into her emotions; the lost letters to Mary Cornwallis, with their "violent professions of everlasting kindness," may have been even more intense. Anne's exposure to the power of eros, in the theatre and in real life, gave her some appreciation of the way her passions might breach the walls of honor, but she continued to be wary of men. As she "studied all the greater Globe," especially an England now in turmoil, she could see many instances of the dangerous consequences of passion. The king himself, at this very moment, was having to discount rumors of a "black box" containing evidence that he had been married to Lucy Walter, Monmouth's mother. But as Pope Joan's speech makes clear, a woman— even a princess—risked everything in yielding to love, especially if the "vain man" who became her lord was the wrong kind of master.

§

Anne was not alone in being concerned about these issues. When Parliament finally met on 21 October, an event that sent James and Maria hurrying back to

Scotland by sea, the most important topic at issue was the second Exclusion Bill, passed by the House of Commons on 11 November, but decisively rejected by the House of Lords on 15 November, to the great relief of the king and his court. Yet Anne's possible role in a future succession did not go unnoticed: on 18 December, Sir Robert Markham asked "that a motion be made to his Majesty for the disposing the Lady Anne in marriage to a Protestant Prince."[76] A visit from an eligible suitor probably gave Markham the idea for his motion: Georg Ludwig of Hanover had arrived in London on 8 December, and after kissing the hem of the queen's petticoat, had sought permission to kiss Lady Anne on her lips.[77] In light of her emotional development and her desire for an independent establishment, it is reasonable to suppose that Anne was at least interested, possibly thrilled, to receive a formal visit from a possible husband who was only five years older than she was. As Georg did not speak English, they probably spoke French, a language Anne had mastered as a small child during her long stay in France, and a language thought ideal for romantic dalliance. By 28 December, according to one newsletter, it was "all the discourse at Court that the Prince of Hanover is to marry the Lady Anne,"[78] yet for reasons that remain maddeningly uncertain, there was no proposal. Despite her negative opinion of Anne's ancestry, the Electress Sophia, Georg's mother, did not prevent him from making this visit to England, which lasted until March. Giacomo Ronchi, an envoy from Maria's native Modena, wrote a letter describing Anne as attracted to the idea of the match, but he was hardly an eyewitness.[79] Like Anne's father and step-mother, Ronchi was far away in Edinburgh and therefore dependent on correspondents in London. With the court still preoccupied by the continuing clamor for Exclusion, and with the exiled duke unable to assess his daughter's suitor in person, this apparently promising opportunity for Anne to be "disposed . . . in marriage" slipped away.[80]

As Anne's eventual marriage to George of Denmark would come hard on the heels of the trial and execution of the Rye House plotters, her flirtation with Georg Ludwig happened at a time when Parliament, frustrated in its attempts at Exclusion, was taking revenge by trying Viscount Stafford, the weakest and most vulnerable of the five Catholic peers imprisoned in the Tower since the fall of 1678. Found guilty after a highly theatrical trial, the old man was beheaded on 29 December. Georg Ludwig, who appears to have witnessed the execution, describes the event to his mother in the same letter in which he reports kissing Anne: "They cut off the head of Milord Stafford yesterday, yet made no more fuss than if they had beheaded a chicken."[81]

In the absence of anything like hard evidence, those in charge of prosecuting Stafford spoke of the alleged threat of Catholicism in sweeping terms. The charges read out in court and promptly published included the claim that Stafford, with

Richard Tompson, *Georg Ludwig, Prince of Hanover*.
Mezzotint after Godfrey Kneller (c. 1675–1690).

Divers other Jesuites, Priests, Fryers, and other Persons, as false Traytors
to his Majesty, and this Kingdom, . . . have Traiterously Consulted, Contrived, and Acted to, and for the accomplishing of . . . wicked, pernitious
and Traiterous designs, and for that end did most wickedly, and Traiterously agree, Conspire, and Resolve to Imprison, Depose, and Murder his
Sacred Majesty; . . .

And also to subject this Kingdom and Nation to the Pope, and to his Tyrannical Government,

And to seize and share amongst themselves the Estates and Inheritances of his Majesties Protestant Subjects.

And to Erect and restore Abbeys, Monasteries, and other Convents and Societies, which have been long since by the Laws of this Kingdom suppressed for their Superstition and Idolatry, and to deliver up and restore to them the Lands and Possessions now vested in his Majesty and his Subjects by the Laws and States of this Realm.[82]

It had been over 140 years since Henry VIII's dissolution of the monasteries, which allowed him to grant large tracts of land to his supporters, yet the patently absurd fear that monks and friars might suddenly evict the families who had owned these estates for generations remained a surefire way to alarm the public. Charles Blount's *Appeal from the Country to the City,* a notorious Whig pamphlet published a year earlier, had used similarly inflammatory rhetoric: "If any men (who have Estates in Abby-Lands) desire to beg their Bread, and relinquish their Habitations and Fortunes to some old greasie bald-pated Abbot, Monk, or Friar, then let him Vote for a Popish Successor."[83] In *The Spanish Fryar,* a popular play first acted during this session of Parliament, Dryden borrowed some of Blount's language to describe the title character,

> ...a reverend, fat, old gouty Fryar;
> With a Paunch swoln so high, his double Chin
> Might rest upon't: A true Son of the Church;
> Fresh colour'd, and well thriven on his Trade,
> Come puffing with his greasy bald-pate Quire,
> And fumbling o'er his Beads.[84]

Although Dryden was willing to lift words from a Whig pamphlet to enliven his comic subplot, he was careful to deliver a loyal or "Tory" message in his serious plot. As in most of his plays, romance is inseparable from politics. Queen Leonora of Castile, played by Anne's sometime speech coach Elizabeth Barry, is the daughter of a usurper, clinging to a shaky throne as the Moors besiege her city. Although betrothed to a political ally of her late father, she falls in love with the victorious soldier Torrismond, who will eventually be revealed as the son of the deposed king. In the last act, three different armies, significantly called "Parties" in the stage directions, march into the palace courtyard; each claims to represent true loyalty and denigrates the others as "Rebels." Only a miracle, restoring a true succession, can avert disaster, and at the last instant, a miracle duly occurs: old King Sancho, earlier said to be dead, turns out to be alive. Torrismond, now the lawful successor, delivers the moral in a rhyming couplet:

> But let the bold Conspirator beware
> For Heaven makes Princes its peculiar Care.[85]

It may have been possible for some Whigs to believe that the pathetic old Lord Stafford had been a "bold Conspirator," but for Dryden and the court he served, such terms were more immediately applicable to Shaftesbury and Monmouth, who were boldly and overtly conspiring to alter the succession. In his resistance to their efforts, King Charles took comfort in the belief that he and his brother enjoyed the "peculiar Care" of Heaven.

Anecdotal history reports that Charles was especially fond of *The Spanish Fryar*; his theatrical niece is unlikely to have missed it.[86] Designed to admit a variety of political interpretations, Dryden's play was a cagey response to a dilemma he shared with Princess Anne. Neither the poet nor the princess was a Roman Catholic, and both were willing to poke fun at Catholic excesses. Both of them, however, had Catholics in their families: Anne's father and stepmother were of that faith, as was Dryden's wife, who was a cousin of the unfortunate Stafford. Both had Catholic friends, in Anne's case her favorite, Mary Cornwallis. In the face of the current unrest, both were committed to the succession as a bedrock principle of political stability. But in 1683, neither could predict the changes that lay ahead: Dryden, despite having written brilliantly in defense of the Anglican "middle way," would convert to Catholicism in 1686, and in 1688, Anne would support a conspiracy to remove her Catholic father from the throne, altering the succession forever.

A master of literary ambiguity, Dryden could use his art to explore the complexities of the Exclusion Crisis, but neither his poetic skill nor his position as Poet Laureate could protect him from reprisals. A year before *The Spanish Fryar*, in December 1679, hired thugs beat him senseless in Rose Alley; the motive for this unsolved crime was probably political.[87] In Dryden's plays, and in those of Lee and even Settle, Anne, who was not creative, found language and imagery that helped her understand her political and emotional plight, but in these troubled times her natural reticence also served her well. If she was aware that some discussions of the succession included the idea that she herself be named Charles's heir, she maintained a dignified silence.[88] Mindful of the fate of her grandfather, she knew that royal blood was no sure protection against violence: if the Rye House plot had succeeded, she might herself have been among the victims.

In the absence of effective medical care, royal blood was also no protection against disease. On 2 March 1681, Princess Isabella, not yet five, died a lonely death in London, far away from her mother and father in Edinburgh. For Anne, who had already lost three siblings and two half-siblings, this death was particularly poignant: with the rest of her family away, she was the only close relative left in London to mourn the little girl. Although the king kindly sent a special messenger to convey the sad news to James and Maria in Edinburgh, the nation was so fixated on the continuing political struggle that the death of the younger princess went almost unnoticed. Fearing the potential for popular violence from the City if Parliament met in London, Charles summoned them to meet on 21 March in Oxford, long a Royalist stronghold. Both parties staged their arrivals with elaborate theatrical symbolism. The king came up in his coach on 14 March (Monday), accompanied by the queen, the Duchess of Portsmouth, and the comic actress Nell Gwyn; his right to keep mistresses was evidently one of the prerogatives on which he was insisting. Provided with free wine, the crowd drank the monarch's health on their knees, while Charles assured them of his determination to keep both staff and sword in his own hands, received a Bible from the Vice-Chancellor, settled his various women, and went off to the horse races at Brunton. Shaftesbury arrived on 19 March (Saturday), accompanied by two hundred armed men on horseback; in their hats, his followers wore blue ribbons with a combative slogan: "No Popery, No Slavery."[89]

On Monday, in a "subtle crafty" opening speech, the king insisted on his prerogatives and refused to alter the succession; his answer to demands for "the Peoples right" was a vague promise "to remove all reasonable fears that may arise from the possibility of a Popish successor." On Tuesday, Monmouth, who had delayed his arrival for added drama, rode into town with thirty armed comrades, and on Thursday, Shaftesbury contrived to pass Charles a paper "in an unknown hand" proposing that Monmouth be declared the successor. The king, delighted to have finally maneuvered his foes into openly supporting a bastard, delivered a stinging reply:

> The *K.* surpriz'd, told the Earl, that he wonder'd that after so many Declarations to the contrary, he should press him upon that Subject, that if either with Conscience, or Justice, or Nature, he could do such a thing, he would have done it before; it being reasonable that if he had had ever a Child of his own Legitimate, he would much rather have him reign, than his Brother, or any of his Brothers Children: That his Majesty was none of those that grew more timorous with age, but that rather he grew the more resolute the nearer he was to his grave.

The specific reference to "any of his Brothers Children" shows that Charles's consideration of the succession included Mary and Anne, and if the rhetoric of this reported exchange treats both princesses as less desirable successors than a legitimate son, the king was nonetheless vigorously defending a succession that included his nieces. When "the Loyal Earl... cry'd out that it chill'd his blood to hear of such an expression," the king sarcastically expressed his doubts about Shaftesbury's loyalty, assuring him that he "would much sooner lose this Life, of which you pretend to be so watchful Preservers, than ever part with any of my Prerogative, or betray this Place, the Laws, or the Religion, or alter the true Succession of the Crown."[90]

This exchange was immediately printed; the rapid reporting of all the events during this Parliament indicates the urgency of the crisis, which many expected to erupt into civil war. But the drama was short-lived. On Monday (28 March), having created the expectation of a longer sitting by agreeing to have the Sheldonian Theatre refurbished as a meeting place for the House of Commons, Charles came into the House of Lords, apparently ready to hear the day's proceedings. Then, like an actor making a lightning change of costume, he donned his formal robes and crown, which had been hidden in his sedan chair, sent for the Commons, and dissolved Parliament. It was not the military coup some had feared, but it was a decisive coup de théâtre. According to a passage that the Whig Bishop Gilbert Burnet decided to omit from his history, Charles employed a splendidly rude gesture to dramatize his contempt for his foes:

> He came to the parliament house in a very indecent manner, being carried in a chair to the house of lords, with the crown between his legs; and having sent for the house of commons, he pulled it out from thence—
> i. e., from his codpiece, as the factious party made the story pass—and put it on his head, and so dissolved the parliament.[91]

Whether true or not, Burnet's story embodies the naked claim to potency that Charles employed in dismissing the Oxford Parliament. This time the gamble worked, as the tide of public support turned toward the king, who never summoned another Parliament, and who felt strong enough by the next fall to have Shaftesbury arrested and tried for high treason.

§

As previous events had shown, Anne's chances to be united with her family depended on the king's perception of his own strength. In the summer of 1679, buoyed up by the acquittal of Dr. Wakeman, he had let Anne travel to Brussels, and in the summer of 1681, with his confidence growing once more, he allowed her to travel to Edinburgh. Accompanied by "severall ladyes of quality,"[92] the princess arrived in Scotland on 17 July and stayed until the following May. In addition to the satisfaction of being reunited with her father and stepmother, Anne found plenty to amuse her in Edinburgh. As her father wrote to his niece, "we here do not passe our tyme so ill as you in England think we do, for we have plays, ride abroad, when tis good weather, play at Bassett and have a great deele of good company."[93] Much of the company was female; "Scots letters" dated 11 August, less than a month after Anne's arrival, reported that "their Royal Highnesses, the Lady Ann and 8 coaches full of ladies attended by about 80 of the nobility and gentry went to Poletowne about 4 miles from Edinburgh to see the gardens."[94] Although Sarah Churchill was not among the ladies who enjoyed this outing, she joined the court in exile in September and stayed for the next eight months, renewing her close friendship with Anne.[95] The princess and her stepmother went horseback riding "almost every day" until December, when Maria had a dangerous fall that forced her to stop dancing for a few months. Anne, however, continued to participate in "country dances" and card-playing for high stakes.[96]

There was also theatre. The Smock Alley troupe from Dublin, a company of some thirty actors, arrived in July to begin regular performances that James considered "prety tolerable."[97] The presence of professionals, however, did not preclude amateur performances by the court ladies. Sir John Lauder, in a contemporary diary, gives an account of another production of Lee's *Mithridates:*

> 15 Novembris 1681, being the Queane of Brittaine's birth-day, it was keeped by our Court at Halirudhouse with great solemnitie, such as bonfyres, shooting of canons, and the acting a comedy, called Mithridates King of Pontus, before ther Royal Hynesses &c., wherein Lady Anne, the Duke's daughter, and the Ladies of Honour were the onlie actors.[98]

As with *Calisto,* there was more than one performance; James's letter of 26 November mentions three:

> My Daughter acted on thursday last, for the third and last tyme her play, there were five of them that did their parts very well, and they were very well drest, so that they made a very fine show, and such a one as had not been seen in this country before.[99]

Neither Lauder nor James gives the cast, but other sources tell us that Joseph Ashbury, the leader of the Smock Alley players, coached Anne in the role of

Semandra.[100] No surviving document explains why she played this part instead of repeating her performance as Ziphares. The fact that she was now sixteen was probably a factor: having already been courted in some fashion by Georg Ludwig, the princess may have wanted to play a female role, and her stepmother probably thought Semandra a better part for an eminently marriageable young lady. Perhaps Sarah Churchill was eager to undertake Ziphares; given her theatrical experience, it seems likely that she was one of the five principal performers James mentions. Even though the details remain elusive, the larger pattern is clear enough: at times of stress, Anne took comfort in the work of preparing and performing theatricals, and there was still plenty of tension in the air. If the king had been sufficiently confident to allow Anne to leave London, he was not yet ready to recall his brother. Despite the amusements and the company, Anne had reasons to feel that she was in exile. Her continuing concern about the political crisis shows in one of her letters from Edinburgh to Frances Apsley, in which she asks her friend to send her "ye Gazett & other printed papours that are good,"[101] a phrase suggesting that she preferred to read the news in either the official government *Gazette* or one of the Tory journals. Despite her care in choosing her sources, there was no way for her to be unaware of the outcome of Shaftesbury's trial, in which a jury carefully chosen by the Whig sheriffs of London returned a verdict of *ignoramus,* allowing the court's chief antagonist to go free.

Although Shaftesbury escaped with his life, his power was broken, and supporters of the king became increasingly confident in expressing their disdain for the Whigs. In Scotland, Anne had an opportunity to participate in the Tory revenge: when Thomas Cartwright, a rabid Tory, preached a pointedly political sermon before her on the anniversary of Charles I's execution, the princess insisted on its publication "for the benefit of them that could not croud in to hear it," and the sermon promptly appeared, first in Edinburgh and then in London, with a dedication emphasizing Anne's royal virtues:

> I hope, we shall never live to see the *Defender of the Faith* any more destroyed for *Conscience-sake,* as we did that *Glorious Martyr,* of whom the World was not worthy. His *Blood* does still run in your *Royal Veines*; and you have prov'd your self to have such an eminent share of his *Piety* hitherto, that we have no reason to question, but you will continue a *Glorious Pattern* of the same to your Lives end and remain constant in that *truly Catholick Religion* for which he dyed.[102]

By March 1682 the Duke of York was joining his brother for the races at Newmarket, where he was "waited on by most of the nobility to pay their respects to him."[103] The time was ripe for York's entire court to make a triumphant return, but on his voyage to Scotland, where he planned to collect his wife and daughter, his yacht, the *Gloucester*, ran aground and sank, with considerable loss of life. Among those drowned was the violinist and flageolet player Thomas Greeting, who had served Princess Anne. Four silver trumpets and a set of kettledrums were also lost, along with at least two of the men who played them.[104] James escaped in the longboat, accompanied by John Churchill and a few others. Despite this terrifying event, Maria and Anne bravely embarked with the duke on the return voyage, arriving in London on 27 May. Maria was six months pregnant; a daughter, Charlotte Maria, would be born on 15 August. Unlike previous returns from exile, this one felt permanent, and the duchess now reestablished her court, which many regarded as more sophisticated and magnificent than the queen's.[105]

Among the new maids of honor named to serve Maria Beatrice at this time was Anne Kingsmill, who would later gain fame as a poet under her married name, Anne Finch; she was already writing lyric poetry, dramatic scripts, and libretti.[106] Also present at the court of the Yorks was the poet and painter Anne Killigrew, whose death in 1685 would be the occasion for one of Dryden's greatest poems.[107] The duchess and her ladies often attended plays, though the merger of the two theatre companies into a single United Company in May 1682 meant that fewer productions were now on offer. Anne may have joined them on occasion, but there is no surviving evidence, and as neither of the poetical ladies in her stepmother's court addressed a poem to the princess, it is difficult to speculate about her relations with them. According to Gregorio Leti, who wrote a lengthy account of the British court at this time, Princess Anne now had a court of her own, with at least thirty salaried employees. Although he politely singled out Viscountess Hyde, Anne's governess, for her constant and particular attention to the princess, he also emphasized the presence of "masters of every sort of noble profession"—certainly including musicians, artists, and choreographers.[108]

§

Despite Lady Hyde's vigilance, Anne was now secretly receiving poems of courtship from John Sheffield, Earl of Mulgrave, a competent amateur poet nearly twenty years her senior. In 1682, the year in which the Yorks returned to London, Mulgrave published his *Essay on Poetry*, an imitation of Horace that had probably received some polishing touches from his friend Dryden; two years earlier, the laureate and the earl had collaborated on a translation of one of Ovid's *Heroides*. As a veteran of the last two naval wars, a loyal supporter of the Duke of York during the Exclusion Crisis, and a Gentleman of the Bedchamber to the king, Mulgrave enjoyed easy access to both courts, but he was nonetheless overplaying his hand if he imagined that he might seriously woo the princess. When the liaison came to light, early in October 1682, Charles banished Mulgrave from court and stripped him of his offices; although the courtier-poet protested that he had been "only ogling," the court gossips were quick to claim that he had "ruined" the princess.[109] The death of her infant half-sister Charlotte Maria on 6 October may have added to the stress Anne felt in this crisis.[110]

There are, of course, no poems explicitly addressed to Princess Anne in Mulgrave's published works, which did not appear until 1723, though some poems he wrote to her may survive in that collection. In 1682, it would have been daring of him to send her a poem like "The Dream," in which the speaker imagines his loved one naked in his arms:

> There my *Celia*'s snowy Arms,
>   Breasts, and other Parts more dear,
> Exposing new and unknown Charms,
>   To my transported Soul appear.
>
> Then you so much Kindness show,
>   My Despair deluded flies;
> And indulgent Dreams bestow
>   What your Cruelty denies.
>
> Blush not that your Image, Love
>   Naked to my Fancy brought;
> 'Tis hard, methinks, to disapprove
>   The Joys I feel without your Fault.

According to the speaker, the woman should neither blush nor disapprove of his masturbatory fantasy. In the crucial rhetorical turn of the poem, he asks her to believe that the honor on which she has been insisting is as much an illusion as his erotic dream:

> Wonder not a fancy'd Bliss
>   Can such Griefs as mine remove;
> That Honour as fantastick is,
>   Which makes you slight such constant Love.
>
> The Virtue which you value so,
>   Is but a Fancy frail and vain;
> Nothing is solid here below,
>   Except my Love, and your Disdain.[111]

Even though the "Celia" of this poem has not yet yielded, it would have been embarrassing for Anne to be found reading a poem of this sort. It is nonetheless possible that Mulgrave sent her works of this kind, trusting in the male myth his rival Rochester invoked by praising Sir Charles Sedley for his skill at the "mannerly Obscene," a "prevailing gentle Art / That can with a resistless Charme impart / The loosest wishes to the chastest heart."[112] In light of his rakish reputation, however, Mulgrave might more wisely have chosen to write poems for Anne stressing his capacity for reform. A surviving lyric called "The Convert" looks suspiciously like such a poem:

> Dejected as true Converts die,
>   But yet with fervent Thoughts inflam'd,
> So, fairest! at your Feet I lie,
>   Of all my Sex's Faults asham'd.
>
> Too long, alas, have I abus'd
>   Love's innocent and sacred Flame,
> And that divinest Pow'r have us'd
>   To laugh at as an idle Name.
>
> But since so freely I confess
>   A Crime which may your Scorn produce,
> Allow me now to make it less
>   By any just and fair Excuse.
>
> I then did vulgar Joys pursue,
>   Variety was all my Bliss;
> But ignorant of Love and you,
>   How could I chuse but do amiss?

The speaker breezily excuses his previous promiscuity on the grounds that he was actually ignorant of true love before meeting the woman he addresses. In her luminous presence, he is ashamed not only of his own faults but of the faults of all men. He wittily appropriates religious language—"convert," "fervent," "sacred," "divinest"—for erotic purposes, and emphasizes his supposed reform by invoking curses on himself if he reverts to his habitual unfaithfulness:

> If ever now my wandring Eyes
>   Seek out Amusements as before,
> If e'er I look, but to despise
>   Such Charms, and value yours the more;

> May sad Remorse, and guilty Shame,
>   Revenge your Wrongs on faithless me;
> And, what I tremble ev'n to name,
>   May I lose all in losing thee.[113]

For Anne, who had written often of her own constancy to her female favorites, such high-minded expressions of reform and faithfulness might have been appealing, but as in the case of Georg Ludwig, there is no reliable evidence about her response to Mulgrave's approaches. She certainly had reason to regard him as dangerous: he had shared Mary Kirk with her father and her first cousin, and his poems proudly claim other adulterous liaisons.[114] Princess Mary, writing from Holland to Frances Apsley (now Lady Bathurst), fretted about her sister's possible loss of reputation, calling Mulgrave an "insolent man":

> If I could love you better then I did before your last letter would make me
> do so, to see the concern you are in for my pore sister. I am sure all who
> are truelly her friands must be so, for my part I never knew what it was to
> be so vext & trobled as I am at it, not but that I believe my sister very in-
> nocent however I am so nice upon the point of reputation that it makes
> me mad she should be exposed to such reports, & now what will not this
> insolent man say being provokt.[115]

Mary's fears proved groundless, as Anne was evidently not "ruined." Mulgrave said nothing further to damage her, and was restored to favor shortly after Anne's wedding.[116]

A significant consequence of Mulgrave's brief disgrace was the dismissal of Anne's longtime favorite Mary Cornwallis, who had apparently carried messages between the princess and the poet.[117] When she learned about this part of the episode, Princess Mary wrote again to Lady Bathurst, expressing her strong disapproval:

> I think all you said very well & am very much of your mind conserning
> that persone you there mention [evidently Mary Cornwallis] & had
> I known of the friendship at first I should have done all I coud in the
> world to have brock it off but I never knew any thing in the world till
> such time as she [again Mary Cornwallis] was forbid when I heard it
> from my sister herself & was very much surprised & trobled to find her
> concern as great.
>   You will oblidge me very much to lett me know if there be any new
> ones [i.e. new female favorites] in hand that I may endeavor to stop it if it

be not to her advantage or at least do my best for I think nothing more prejudiciell to a young woman than ill company.[118]

In light of her own girlhood crush on the recipient of this letter, Mary's haughty attitude toward her sister's friendship with Mary Cornwallis is intriguing. Her sneering reference to "ill company" probably reflects her disapproval of Mrs. Cornwallis's Catholicism, which others describing this episode also mention as a danger, yet the final and bitter estrangement between the two sisters, nine years later, would also turn on Anne's loyalty to a female favorite—and that favorite, Sarah Churchill, was a Protestant. Another explanation for Mary's stance is that she now disapproved of Anne's tendency to form passionate relationships with other women, a disapproval intensified by her own guilty memory of having done the same thing herself in her earlier years. By expressing her views to Frances, the very object of her own prepubescent passion, she may have been attempting to enlist an ally in support of the view that such relationships, perhaps inevitable for girls of thirteen, were inappropriate for young women of seventeen.

Curiously enough, the dismissal of Mary Cornwallis in 1682 completed the ascendancy of Sarah Churchill, who was to be Anne's closest companion for the next twenty-five years.[119] By her own admission, Sarah now "began to employ all her Wit, & all her Vivacity, & almost all her Time, to divert, & entertain, & serve the *Princess:* & to fix that Favour, which now one might easily observe to be increasing towards Her every day." Her motives for wanting to secure Anne's preference are not hard to seek, but she may not have been prepared for the form that preference took. "The favour," she continues, "quickly became a Passion: & a Passion which possess'd the Heart of the *Princess* too much to be hid."[120] Deprived of Mary Cornwallis, to whom she had made "violent professions of everlasting kindness,"[121] Anne evidently transferred her passionate feelings to Sarah. In one of the earliest letters preserved from their massive correspondence, she candidly expresses her urgent longing for Sarah's company:

I have bin in aspectation of you a long time but can stay no longer without desireing to know what you intend to do with me for it is most sertin I cant go to bed without seeing you. If you knew in what a condition you have made me I am sure you would pity her that is Sincerly yours.[122]

Sarah's replies are lost, so it is difficult to know how fully she reciprocated Anne's passion, but she was alert to the opportunities Anne's friendship opened up for her and her husband.

Alarmed by the Mulgrave episode, the court was now seeking a husband for Anne with renewed urgency, and in searching for a Protestant prince, they set their sights on Denmark. The princess's great-grandmother, the wife of James I, had been Anne of Denmark, diplomatic relations between the two countries were cordial, and the Churchills had a connection to the Danish court. Charles Churchill, John's youngest brother, had gone to Denmark as a page to King Christian in 1669 and had served Prince George, the king's younger brother, since 1672. When the diplomats of both nations had settled the terms of the marriage, John Churchill went to Gluckstadt in the royal yacht to fetch the prince;[123] when the time came to organize her new court, one of Anne's most pressing requests to her father was that she have Sarah among her Ladies of the Bedchamber.[124] Her uncongenial governess, Henrietta Hyde, retired when Anne married, but she was forced to trade one eccentric aunt by marriage for another. Laurence Hyde, who became Earl of Rochester in 1682, and his brother Henry, Earl of Clarendon since 1674, used their considerable influence to have Henry's wife Flower appointed as Anne's Groom of the Stole, and Anne immediately began complaining about her to Sarah. A few years later, Clarendon was appointed Lord Lieutenant and went to Ireland, taking his wife with him; Anne promptly seized the opportunity to appoint Sarah as Groom of the Stole, officially confirming her position as the chief royal favorite.

§

As she looked back over the previous seven years, the newly married Anne had many reasons to rejoice. Those most vigorously opposed to her father's right to succeed were now defeated: Shaftesbury had died in Holland early in 1683, and the Duke of Monmouth, wanted in the wake of the Rye House revelations, was lying low at the country house of his mistress Henrietta Wentworth. For her new household, her uncle Charles had given her an attractive section of Whitehall Palace called the Cockpit, and there were valuable appointments to be made. Benjamin Bathurst, husband of her dear friend Frances Apsley, immediately became the Treasurer of her household, and soon John Berkeley, husband of her girlhood companion Barbara Villiers, became her Master of the Horse.[125] At this point, the money granted her by her uncle and her father, together with her husband's expected income from his estates in Denmark, seemed adequate to support a comfortable life, though events would prove otherwise. Prince George, already regarded as dull by King Charles, was nonetheless a compatible and obedient consort, and for the kinds of emotional support Anne most needed, her beloved Sarah was readily at hand. Herself in reasonably good health, enjoying riding, hunting, and dancing, the eighteen-year-old princess could now hope for children—not only for the joys and satisfactions they might bring to her, but also because, as the Cambridge poets reminded her, her offspring would give a grateful nation the assurance of a Protestant succession. Her private pleasures, as Ayloffe had suggested, might now prove "a Noble Publick Good." Perhaps it was her lifelong disappointment at being unable to provide an heir—a disappointment she had no reason to expect as a bride—that gave Queen Anne her remarkable determination to provide other public benefits to her subjects.

CHAPTER 3

PRAY FOR THE PEACE OF JERUSALEM

23 April 1685

From the private box she shared with her husband, Princess Anne had a privileged view of her father's coronation in Westminster Abbey on St. George's Day, the auspicious date Charles II had chosen for his coronation in 1661—and the date she would choose for her own in 1702. She was comfortably seated when the grand procession began at noon with the entry of "The Kings Herb-woman, & her 6. Maids, with Baskets of Sweet Herbs & Flowers, strewing the way."[1] Behind the herb-women, who scattered their petals on the cloth-covered walkway from Westminster Hall to the Abbey, came a fife-player, a full complement of trumpets and drums, and two large choirs, as well as aldermen, judges, bishops, and virtually all the peers of the realm. The queen and the king, each covered by a canopy and grandly attended, came near the end, followed by the Yeomen of the Guard, resplendent in their new uniforms.[2] All the participants wore formal costumes designed to reflect their ranks, and there were specific instructions for making those costumes. According to orders sent out by the Earl Marshall, "The *Robe* or *Mantle* of a BARONESS," was to be "of *Crimson Velvet*, the *Cape* to be…Powdered with Two *Bars* or *Rows* of *Ermine*"; her train was to measure "Three Foot on the Ground." A viscountess was allowed "Two Rows and a Half of *Ermine*" and a train of "a Yard and a Quarter." A countess had "*Three Rows* of *Ermine*" and a train of "a Yard and a Half."[3] Even the unfortunate lad who carried the kettledrums wore high-heeled shoes and his finest livery.

Illustration from Francis Sandford, *The History of the Coronation of James II* (1687).

For Princess Anne, now twenty, courtly rituals had long been a way of life, beginning with the bizarre ceremonies in which she was compelled to participate as a five-year-old in France.[4] If the English court was not quite so formal as the French, it nonetheless made much of funerals, weddings, christenings, and royal birthdays, as Anne knew from frequent experience. A few months after her own wedding, for example, she had attended the christening of Charles Fitzroy, son of her cousin Henry, Duke of Grafton, who was another of Charles II's many children by the Countess of Castlemaine. Despite the father's illegitimacy, the cast of characters was impressive: Henry Compton, Bishop of London, who had officiated at Anne's wedding, performed the ceremony; the King and the Prince of Orange (represented by the Duke of Ormond) were the godfathers; and Anne herself was the sole godmother.[5] Yet familiar as she was with courtly pomp, Anne had never seen anything quite so elaborate as this coronation, which was clearly designed to underscore James's place in the historical succession of monarchs and to mollify or silence those who had opposed him.

The succession, to everyone's amazement, had been smooth. Charles II awoke with convulsions on 2 February 1685; he died four days later, on Anne's twentieth birthday. Proclaimed immediately, James II made reassuring statements that won him widespread support, though he also gave immediate signals of his intention to make a grand public display of his Roman Catholic faith. In the month after his accession, he confirmed the appointment of Antonio Verrio, an Italian Catholic, as "chief and 1st painter" to the Crown.[6] Verrio's specialty was baroque decorative painting on a large scale; Charles had employed him to paint the ceilings at Windsor Castle and to devise grand decorative schemes for the new royal palace at Winchester, but James set him to work painting a new chapel at Whitehall in a style befitting the Roman Catholic services he was planning to hold there.[7]

Mindful of the power of ritual in establishing legitimacy, the new king also took a personal interest in planning his coronation ceremony, which required frequent committee meetings, royal letters summoning those who were to attend, and rulings settling rival claims of precedence. According to Francis Sandford, who wrote the official account,

> His *Majesty* (Our now most Gracious *Sovereign*,) had no sooner taken Care for the Funerals of His Dear and Royal Brother Deceased, ... but He forthwith took Order for his Own and His Royal Consorts *Coronation*. To which end having appointed a *Committee* of all the Lords of his *Privy Council*, to consider of the manner thereof; and having Gratiously condescended, not only to be Present, and Assist thereat, in His Own Royal Person, but also, for the greater Ease and Dispatch, to Debate and Adjust most of the *Previous Matters* in a Select Committee of those Lords; and particularly to Model the *Proceeding* thereunto; in that Glorious Manner in which it appeared. And having thought fit, that the Memory thereof should remain to Posterity, and that the several Advances which were made towards the Performing this Great *Solemnity*, should be carefully Digested and Recorded, was Pleas'd to Order; That the whole *Ceremony*, with all its Circumstances, should be *Printed* and *Illustrated* with *Sculpture*.[8]

Preparing the elaborate illustrations for this large and expensive volume, however, took longer than expected, and it did not appear until 1687, by which time James had lost the support of many of the aristocrats for whom the book was designed.[9]

Most of the records related to the coronation of Charles I, the committee noted, had been "lost in the late *War*,"[10] but they read over the records of the coronations of Charles II in 1661 and James I in 1605 with close attention to the particulars and costs of those ceremonies. Everyone was keenly interested in making this coronation as traditional as possible, but the religion of the new monarch necessitated adjustments in the liturgy. "His Grace the Lord Archbishop of Canterbury was desired to view the Forms of Divine Service used at former Coronations, and ... to abridge, as much as might be, the extream length thereof."[11] But length was not the real issue. In asking for a shorter service, the committee was asking the archbishop to omit the Eucharist, conveniently sparing everyone the embarrassment that might have ensued when the Catholic king refused the chalice. With some reluctance, William Sancroft obeyed their instructions.[12]

If the stated desire to reduce the length of the service had been genuine, Sancroft might also have proposed omitting the sermon, but that would have meant missing a chance to have a skilled orator emphasize the new king's legitimacy. The man chosen to preach, Francis Turner, Bishop of Ely, was well known to Princess Anne. He had been chaplain to her mother, Anne Hyde, in the 1660s and chaplain to the Anglicans in James's household, of whom Anne was the most important, during the duke's recent exile in Scotland. Taking a strong Tory line, Turner delivered a stern warning to those who had questioned the succession:

> Be the *Title* of a King as good as a Warrant from heaven can make it; ... Yet if His Subjects will be the *Sons of Belial, Sons of the Devil,* ... Men that will bear no Yoke: 'tis still in their power to be as miserable as they please.... Thô the Maintenance of *Religion* is commonly made the most plausible Pretence for *Rebellion* (as it was for the last among us, and has been made use of since towards the encouraging of another,) yet *Rebellion* almost constantly proves (as that last prov'd) the Means to destroy *Religion.* My meaning is not only this, That as soon as ever Men begin to be *Rebels,* They cease to be inwardly Religious and truly good Men; but I drive it farther, That to *Rebel* is the ready way to ruine the Constitution of the outward, Profest, and *Establisht Religion* in a Nation.[13]

James did his part toward supporting Turner's position by promising publicly to uphold the established church. When the Bishop of Gloucester formally petitioned him on behalf of the bishops, the king gave the prescribed reply:

> With a Willing and Devout Heart, I Promise...that I will Preserve and Maintain to You, and the Churches committed to your Charge, all Canonical Privileges, and due Law and Justice: And that I will be Your Protector and Defender to my Power, by the Assistance of God; as every good King in His Kingdom ought in Right to Protect and Defend the Bishops and Churches under Their Government.[14]

Protocol for the coronation dictated that Anne, now second in line to the throne behind her sister Mary, be an onlooker, not a participant. Neither she nor Prince George marched in the procession, nor were they expected to make a symbolic gesture of assent. Yet with William of Orange refusing to attend the ceremony, Anne was the most prominent Protestant member of the royal family in attendance, and to the delight of many, she was visibly with child. This was her second pregnancy. The first, which came immediately after her marriage, had ended in disappointment when she delivered a stillborn daughter in May 1684. Less than a year later, she was again drawing close to her time, and the Catholic queen, mindful of her condition, honored her stepdaughter by coming over to sit with Anne and George in their box before the recessional.[15] On 22 May, Anne returned the favor by joining Maria in attending the opening of Parliament, despite the advanced state of her pregnancy. Just ten days later she delivered a daughter, christened Mary in honor of her sister, who was a godmother in absentia. Bishop Compton performed the ceremony of baptism; Anne's uncle Rochester, now Lord Treasurer, stood godfather; and the Duchess of Grafton, whose child Anne had sponsored two years earlier, was the second godmother.[16]

Anne's passive role at the coronation gave her an opportunity to contemplate the significance of the day's events. Turner's sermon, with its stern dismissal of the Exclusionists as *"sons of the Devil,"* was in keeping with her own views. Years later, the Duchess of Marlborough, herself a Whig, complained that Anne "had been always bred with an utter aversion to all that went under the name of *Whigs.* She had been told strange frightfull things of Them: ... She believed them sworn Enemies to the Rights of Princes: & had been taught to look upon them all as *Rank Republicans,* & as always in readiness to rebel."[17] With her equally strong prejudice against Roman Catholicism, Anne needed to believe that her father was serious in his promise to preserve the Church of England, though she already had reasons to doubt his sincerity. As a lifelong lover of ceremony, she could take pleasure in the grandeur and symbolism of the costumes, thrones, crowns, swords, and orbs whose details Sandford lovingly describes and illustrates in his printed account. Always fond of food, she could look forward to the splendid dinner that was to follow, which included 145 separate dishes in the first course and 30 more in the second. And if she was concerned about where her father's policies might lead him, Henry Purcell's anthem, a setting of Psalm 122, offered her and others a moment for reflection. The traditional Psalm text, beginning "I was glad when they said unto me, Let us go into the House of the Lord," was fitting for a grand ceremony, and Purcell's effective setting was designed to be sung as an introit. As the choir marched in, their cheerful and harmonically simple music expressed the Psalmist's gladness at entering the Temple. Once inside, however, they gave a more complex and fervent expression to the Psalmist's hope for peace. In setting the verse asking the congregation to "pray for the peace of Jerusalem," Purcell used passing dissonances to dramatize a need for prayer that was inwardly felt by many in attendance.[18]

Significantly, the most dissonant moments in this phrase occur on the words *peace* and *love,* where one might have expected more comforting harmonies. Though resolved on *Jerusalem,* these dissonances reflect Purcell's awareness of how difficult it had been to achieve domestic peace in recent years. For Anne as for many others, Purcell's subtle treatment of this passage would have been a reminder of the political dissonances that remained unresolved as James took the throne, not least the question of whether a convinced Roman Catholic could effectively rule a country whose culture was partly defined by demonizing Catholicism.

Mus. Ex. 3.1: Henry Purcell, excerpt from *I was glad* (1685).

11 April 1689

Less than four years later, Anne witnessed another coronation, designed to give official sanction to a coup that had effectively deposed her father and placed her sister Mary and her brother-in-law William on the throne. She probably occupied the same box she had used in 1685, and once again, she was pregnant. Many aspects of the ritual were identical: once more the herb-women, drummers, trumpeters, bishops, and peers processed from hall to abbey, in much the same order; once more the choir, with different boys but most of the same men, sang Purcell's splendid introit; once more the symbolic swords and orbs were on display. As Anne understood, the similarities between the two coronations were a way of claiming cultural continuity, despite the fact that this second coronation was the direct result of a revolution, but the differences were also significant. Archbishop Sancroft was not presiding. Having crowned James II, he could not in conscience crown William, and would soon be deprived of his position, joining a number of other clergy as "non-jurors," men unwilling to take the oaths to the new monarchs. In his place stood Anne's girlhood chaplain, Henry Compton, Bishop of London. Suspended from his office in 1686 for opposing James II's religious policies, the triumphant Compton, an active supporter of the Revolution, was delighted to crown the Protestant king and queen. Yet in light of the claim that William had invaded in order to save the Church of England, it was an ominous irony that there were fewer bishops in attendance at this coronation than at the last. According to the diarist John Evelyn, who was present, "There were but five bishops and four judges; no more had taken the oaths."[19] Other sources list nine bishops in attendance, but even that number compares poorly with the total of fourteen bishops who marched in 1685.[20]

Evelyn also noticed that "several noblemen and great ladies were absent," and in this assertion he was correct. On the back of a manuscript listing the peers in the procession, the scribe set down a kind of score-sheet comparing the attendance of aristocrats at the two events:

K. J. 2		W. & M.	
7	–	9	Dukes
1	–	2	Marq[esses]
45	–	38	Earls
<u>39</u>		<u>28</u>	Barons
97		81	

His arithmetic is faulty, but his conclusion is accurate: there were clearly more nobles at James's ceremony.[21] Although a substantial majority of peers demonstrated their acceptance of the Revolution by appearing in their robes, a significant number stayed away, uneasy about the legality of the new regime. Some who had helped bring about the coup marched under new titles: Thomas Osborne, Earl of Danby, who had organized support for the Revolution in Yorkshire, was rewarded for his efforts by becoming Marquess of Carmarthen; John Churchill, who had been a baron under James, became Earl of Marlborough just in time to enjoy his new status at William's coronation.

Decades later, in her "hints toward a character" of Queen Anne, the Duchess of Marlborough emphasized the queen's knowledge of protocol: "She has the greatest memory that ever was, especially for such things as are all forms, & ceremonys, giving people their due Ranks at Processions & their proper

The Proceeding to the Coronation of their Majesties King William and
Queen Mary...11 Apr. 1689 (1689), detail.

Places at Balls, & having the right order at Installments & funerals."[22] On this
occasion, Anne would have noticed the many symbolic differences between
this coronation and the last one. Instead of sitting by her side, Prince George
marched in the procession, with a train long enough to require an attendant
to hold it; his presence in a place of honor was a recognition of the significance
of the actions he and Anne had taken in support of the Revolution. Instead of
appearing under separate canopies, as James and his queen consort had done,
William and Mary marched together under one canopy, a visual representation
of the plan to have them rule together, with Mary's status as a queen regnant
preserving the polite fiction of a succession. Immediately before that canopy
marched three bishops holding the chalice, the paten, and the Bible; the sacrament was an integral part of this ceremony because William was eager to demonstrate his Protestant credentials and his willingness to conform to Anglican
practice.[23]

In her diary, however, the new queen fretted over the emphasis placed on the
sacrament, which she believed arose from "worldly considerations," including reminding all present that her father had omitted the sacrament from his coronation.[24] During her years in Holland, Mary had absorbed some of the Calvinist
rigor of her surroundings;[25] by the standards of the Stuart court, she had become
prudish. In January 1689, a few weeks before she sailed for England, she played
hostess to the Elector and Electress of Brandenburg at the Hague. Reflecting on

their visit, she deplored her departures from her usual pious routine but congratulated herself on declining to dance:

> The stay they made there, though but short, shewd me my weackness, let me see my own frailty. I found the world had still too much power over me; for I toock so much care to be civil to the elector and divert the electress, that I gave my self no time for any thing else. The circumstances of time were such that we could have no publick entertainments but onely treating them at my several houses, which I did and played cards out of complaisance so late at night, that it was ever neer two before I got to bed; yet I bless my God I did not neglect prayers in the morning, but went both to French and English ones in my own house, but I considered too much the public and my private interest, and toock so much care of my guests, that I neglected going to church in the afternoon when they were there.... One thing pleased me very much, which was, that tho' I had seen the electress dance, I was not tempted, so that I believed I had overcome that which used to be one of my prettiest pleasures in the world, and that I feard might be a sin in me for loving it too well.[26]

Mary's personal doubts about the "pomp and vanity" of the coronation ceremony were in keeping with this self-denying and ascetic strain. Her sister Anne, though equally devout, was fond of liturgical splendor, interested in issues of precedence and protocol, and enthusiastic about dancing. Within a short time, these differences would spawn a bitter quarrel.

The contrast between the sermon preached in 1689 and the one preached four years earlier may suggest the political dimensions of the looming conflict between the sisters. In 1685, emphasizing the obedience owed to legitimate monarchs, Francis Turner, chaplain to Anne when she was in Edinburgh, preached on a verse from 1 Chronicles: *"Then Solomon sate on the Throne of the Lord, as King, instead of David his Father, and prospered, and all Israel obeyed him."* In 1689, Gilbert Burnet, chaplain to William during the invasion, cunningly invoked the same Old Testament succession but chose a verse from 2 Samuel in which King David gives advice to his son Solomon, emphasizing the moral qualities of kings, not their genealogy: *"The God of Israel said, The Rock of Israel spake to me: He that ruleth over men must be just, ruling in the fear of the Lord."* In explicating his text, Burnet interpreted this verse as an early statement of Whig political theory:

> Here are the true measures of Government; it is a *Rule,* and not an Absolute Dominion; it is a *Rule over men,* and not a Power, like that which we have over Beasts. In a word, it is the Conduct of free and reasonable

Beings, who need indeed to be governed, but ought not to be broken by the force and weight of Power.[27]

Turner had spoken scornfully of those favoring Exclusion as "Men that will bear no Yoke," but for Burnet, even those who opposed the Crown were "free and reasonable Beings, who…ought not to be broken by the force and weight of Power." Although she had helped to bring about the Revolution, Anne's fundamental views on monarchy were much closer to Turner's than to Burnet's. That a princess with her reverence for heredity and tradition should have supported a revolution based in part on Whiggish principles that she deeply deplored is an indication of how aberrant her father's rule had become—not only to the Whigs but to many Tories as well.

§

The coronation of James II and Maria Beatrice in 1685 was the first in twenty-four years. Few in attendance could have imagined that there would be another coronation in less than four years, especially one caused by a coup. Although the king was already fifty-two, he was in robust health and expected to reign for decades. While his queen had no living children, she was only twenty-seven and had been pregnant within the last year; there was a distinct possibility that she might yet produce a male heir who could be reared as a Roman Catholic. The vigorous voices of opposition heard in poems and pamphlets during the Exclusion Crisis had become all but silent in the closing years of Charles II's reign and remained inaudible in the early months of James's. Charles's sudden death and the unopposed succession of his brother initially called forth effusions of loyalty, even from the ballad-mongers. An anonymous song, "To the Tune of, *The Cannons Roar*," for example, cautioned the Whigs against disobedience while expressing hope for an heir:

> Now the Bells of *London* Ring,
> Whiggs be wise, obey your King,
> While the Loyal-hearted Sing,
>   and banish all vexation:
> That our joys may more abound,
> Let the glass go freely round,
> Since our King and Queen is Crown'd
>   the glory of the Nation.
> . . . .
> Let it be the Subjects Prayer,
> That our Gracious Queen may bear
> To Great *James* a Princely Heir,
>   to Reign in after Ages.[28]

Yet despite enjoying widespread goodwill, James proceeded to alienate the clergy, the aristocracy, the Members of Parliament, and the English people with alarming speed. Even his dutiful daughter Anne was eventually persuaded to take drastic action by the king's increasingly bald attempts to promote his own religion and its adherents. In May 1687, writing to her sister about their father's insistence on appointing Roman Catholics to key posts in the universities, she complained that "the priests have so much power with the King as to make him do things so directly against the Laws of the Land, & indeed contrary to his own promises."[29] She was correct on both counts. In attempting to advance those who shared his faith, James ignored many existing laws, though he claimed that his "dispensing power" allowed him to do so; he also violated his coronation oath to "Protect and Defend" the established church.

When she decided to support William's invasion in 1688, Anne placed a greater value on protecting the Church of England than on obeying a legitimate king who was also her father. Her choice had already been made by the time William's forces landed at Torbay. On 18 November 1688, as James marched west to confront the invaders, the princess wrote to William to promise him that her husband, who was a part of the royal entourage, would soon defect, as he did on the evening of 24 November, following three of Anne's most loyal male supporters who defected together in the early morning hours of the same day: John Churchill, husband of her favorite Sarah; John Berkeley, husband of her childhood friend Barbara; and Henry, Duke of Grafton, her illegitimate first cousin, for whose child she had stood godmother. As soon as she received word of that decisive action, Anne escaped down the back stairs of her Whitehall lodgings with Sarah Churchill and Barbara Berkeley, stepped into a coach where the Bishop of London and the Earl of Dorset were waiting, and began a progress toward the North that provided another focal point for those hoping for political change.[30] Moderates who were appalled by James's policies but not yet willing to join an invading army could easily rally to the cause of protecting the princess, and thousands did.

Although Anne felt compelled to oppose her father's policies, her decision set in conflict two kinds of belief that she held dear. Because of her respect for tradition, she was probably uneasy about the changes made in the coronation service for 1689. In 1685, James II had given his assent to an ancient oath:

SIR, Will you Grant and Keep, and by Your Oath Confirm to the People of England, the Laws and Customes to them Granted by the Kings of *England*, your Lawful and Religious Predecessors; and namely, the Laws, Customs, and Franchises Granted to the Clergy by the Glorious King *St. Edward* Your Predecessor, according to the Laws of God, the True Profession of the Gospel Established in this Kingdom, and agreeing to the Prerogative of the Kings thereof, and the Antient Customs of this Realm?[31]

But before the coronation of William and Mary, Parliament passed an act establishing a new oath. Characterizing the traditional oath as "framed in doubtful words and expressions, with relation to ancient laws and constitutions at this time unknown," Parliament required William and Mary to accept a new version recognizing the importance of the legislature:

> *A[rch] Bish[op].* Will you solemnly Promise and Swear to Govern the People of this Kingdom of *England*, and the Dominions thereto belonging according to the statutes in Parliament agreed on, and the Laws and Customs of the same?
> King. *I solemnly Promise so to doe.*
> *A. Bish.* Will you to your Power cause Law and Justice in Mercy to be executed in all your Judgments?
> King. *I Will.*
> *A. Bish.* Will You to the utmost of Your Power Maintain the Laws of God the true Profession of the Gospel and the Protestant Reformed Religion Established by Law? And will You preserve unto the Bishops and Clergy of this Realm, and to the Churches committed to their Charge, all such Rights and Priviledges as by Law doe, or shall appertain unto them, or any of them?
> King. *All this I Promise to doe.*[32]

Gone forever was the reference to laws granted to the people by their kings, replaced by a recognition of Parliament as the source of law. Gone as well were the references to the royal prerogative and the unbroken relationship between King and Church stretching back to Edward the Confessor. Disregarding "Antient Customs" for which Anne had great affection, the new oath emphasized the power of the forces behind the Revolution: Parliament and "the Protestant reformed religion."

In her diary, Mary referred to these changes as "very good alterations in the Office," but Anne is unlikely to have shared that view. When she herself succeeded to the throne, she was constrained by the Act of Settlement of 1701 to take the oaths established in 1689, but the speech she made to Parliament on 11 March 1702, delivered just days after William's death, reordered many of the terms used in the oaths, producing a different emphasis:

> The true Concern I have for our Religion, for the Laws and Liberties of *England*, for maintaining the Succession of the Crown in the Protestant

Line, and the Government in Church and State, as by Law established, encourages me in this great Undertaking, which, I promise my self, will be successful, by the Blessing of GOD, and the Continuance of that Fidelity and Affection of which you have given me so full Assurances.[33]

First comes religion, then laws and liberties, then the Protestant succession. The description of "the Government in Church and State, as by Law established" quietly omits any explicit recognition of parliamentary claims. If Anne was a realist, understanding that the Revolution was necessary to preserve England as a Protestant nation, she was also a traditionalist, firmly believing that the members of her Parliament should feel "Fidelity and Affection" for their queen.

§

Historians disagree about the causes of the Revolution of 1688. Some regard James II as vain and incompetent; others see a struggle between a court determined to move the government toward the autocratic and Catholic model of France and a Whig opposition that looked to Holland for a more democratic model.[34] Not often considered in these discussions is the evidence provided by the artistic productions of James II's reign, which reveal some of the reasons for his failure. Like his unfortunate father, James habitually ignored the hard realities of public opinion, taking refuge in the Stuart myth of monarchial privilege. For Charles I, the court masque had been a perfect medium for expressing and celebrating that myth, and for Charles II, a high baroque style in painting and music served the same purpose, though his chronic lack of funds limited his capacity to support the arts he loved. Only after triumphing over his enemies in 1683 did the king give full expression to his baroque taste, commissioning spectacular allegorical ceiling paintings in Windsor Castle (most now lost), planning a splendid new castle at Winchester (never finished), and commissioning a full-scale opera (not performed until after his death). James II inherited these baroque projects, and the works he himself commissioned, self-consciously imitating French and Italian models, were often overtly Roman Catholic in concept and detail. He seems never to have understood that his subjects, while recognizing the splendor of the artistic productions his court promoted, would find many aspects of those works disturbing and foreign.

The king's artistic choices contributed to his losing the support of his Parliament, his army, and his daughters. His stubborn belief that he could return his kingdom to the Catholic fold, a fantasy encouraged by his Italian wife and the papal emissaries who now gained access to his court, was especially apparent in the paintings made for the new Catholic chapel by Antonio Verrio and his colleague Benedetto Gennari, nephew and heir of the famous painter Guercino. Gennari's

altarpiece, an Annunciation in which the Virgin Mary looks suspiciously like Maria
Beatrice, is not only an unabashed example of Counter-Reformation splendor, but
an expression of the king's fervent hope for a son (color plate 8). For Anglicans at
court, who could hardly have avoided seeing it, the painting stirred up the fears that
Anne expressed in a candid letter to her sister Mary, written in 1686:

> I must tell you that I abhor the principles of the Church of Rome as much
> as 'tis possible for any one to do, & I as much value the Doctrine of the
> Church of England, & certainly there is the greatest reason in the world
> to do so. For the Doctrine of the Church of Rome is wicked & dangerous,
> & directly contrary to the Scriptures, & their ceremonies most of them
> plain down right Idolatry. But God be thanked we were not bred up in
> that communion, but are of a church that is pious & sincere, & conform-
> able in all it's principles to the Scriptures.[35]

Although Anne's fears were widely shared, artists of all kinds embraced a deliberately ornate style during the early months of James's reign. Professional poets
saw the events of early 1685 as an occasion for Pindarics, loosely constructed odes
whose metrical flexibility was supposedly a signal of emotional intensity and a
license for employing extravagant metaphors. Dryden's *Threnodia Augustalis*, lamenting the death of Charles but devoting considerable space to praising James,
pointed in that direction, and others followed suit. In her *Pindarick Poem on the
Coronation*, a work of nearly eight hundred lines, the dramatist and poet Aphra
Behn looked forward to a long reign, extolling "the *Prospect* that appears / In the
vast Glories of *succeeding years!*" For Behn, a Tory loyalist who may have been a
crypto-Catholic, James was a "*Royal HERO, . . . Rough* as a *useful Storm*" and comparable to the archangel Michael,

> To whom the great Command was giv'n
> The first Born *Rebells* to chastise;
> Who, while the flaming Sword he bore,
> 'Twas only to declare his Pow'r,
> And *unusurpt* maintain his *Paradice.*

According to this little allegory, the Whigs who sought to exclude James from
the succession were reenacting the primal disobedience of Adam and Eve. His
task as king is to keep them from attempting a re-entry into the garden from which
they have been banished, and the recommended weapon is not persuasion but a
"flaming Sword." If he read this poem, James might well have interpreted it as encouraging his natural tendency toward asserting arbitrary power. At the time of
the coronation, however, neither the king nor the poet could have guessed that

there would be two armed invasions during his reign, or that the second would succeed. Despite Behn's praise, James proved unable to keep his kingdom *"un-usurpt."*

Like earlier court panegyrics, Behn's expansive poem treats feminine beauty as a sign of royal power. If James is a rough, military hero, balking usurpers with a flaming sword, Maria is a *"Conqueress"* in her own right, armed for victory and decorated with trophies. As she describes Maria dressing for the coronation, Behn evokes the adorning of Venus by the Graces and Cupids, a mythological scene much loved by baroque painters:

> And now the *Nymphs* ply all their Female arts
>> To dress Her for Her *victory* of hearts;
>>> A Thousand little *LOVES* descend!
>> Young waiting *Cupids* with officious care
>>> In smiling order all attend:
> This, decks Her *Snowy Neck*, and that Her *Ebon Hair*.
>> The Trophies which the *Conqueress* must adorn,
>>> Are by the *busie wantons* born;
>>> Who at Her Feet the shining burdens lay,
> The *Goddess* pleas'd to see their Toyls,
> Scatters Ten Thousand *Graces* from Her *Smiles*;
>> While the wing'd Boys catch ev'ry *flying Ray*.
> This bears the valu'd *Treasure* of the *East*,
>> And lugs the Golden casket on His Breast;
>>> Anothers little hand sustains
>>> The weight of *Oriental* Chains;
>>> And in the flowing jetty *curles*
>>> They weave and braid the luced *Pearls*.[36]

The scene Behn describes had special resonance in Maria's court. In the libretto for the court masque *Venus and Adonis* (c. 1683), the poet Anne Kingsmill, Maid of Honor to Maria, included directions for a live tableau accompanied by John Blow's music: "While the Graces dance, the Cupids dress Venus, one combing her head, another ties a bracelet of pearls round her wrist."[37] At about the same time, her friend Anne Killigrew, the "Accomplisht Young LADY" of Dryden's great ode, painted a *Venus attired by the Graces* in a style derived from Continental masters (color plate 9).[38] The Graces in Killigrew's painting "weave and braid the luced *Pearls*" into the goddess's curls exactly as the Cupids do in Behn's poem (color plate 10). In the painting, as in the poem and the masque, the pearls are "valu'd *Treasure* of the *East*," imperial imports like the pearls in Mignard's portrait of the Duchess of Portsmouth (color plate 4).

Almost thirty years later, with Anne on the throne, Alexander Pope drew heavily on these lines in his sparkling mock-epic, *The Rape of the Lock*. His coquette heroine, Belinda, also has a "Casket" on her dressing-table filled with treasures from exotic locations, and the locks of her hair, like Maria's, have "well conspir'd to deck / With shining Ringlets her smooth Iv'ry Neck."[39] So much had changed in the culture, however, that the fanciful imagery Behn had deployed in her courtly panegyric could serve Pope only as an opportunity for playful mockery. In Behn's poem, the king and queen are mythic figures, larger than life, imbued with superhuman courage and beauty, monarchs to be adored and obeyed, not questioned or challenged. For Pope and Queen Anne, living as they did in a world forever altered by the Revolution of 1688, those ancient assumptions of divine monarchy, shrouded in myth and incense, might be remembered with fond nostalgia, but could not be treated as truth. Anne revived the practice of touching for the King's Evil, which William had brusquely dismissed as a superstition, but in the real political world, she knew she had to operate within the limits imposed on her by the Revolution Settlement. In a comic poem occasioned by a social quarrel among the Catholic gentry, Pope could appropriate baroque imagery from Behn without anyone taking it seriously, but while he was writing *Windsor-Forest*, his public celebration of the Peace of Utrecht, the Whig journalist Joseph Addison cautioned poets against using "Fawns and Satyrs, Wood-Nymphs, and Water-Nymphs"[40] to applaud the Peace. Although Pope did not purge his poem of myth, he deployed his mythic elements with an awareness that baroque panegyric had become a nostalgic, endangered style.

Behn's poem is a poetic parallel to the old coronation oath, with its talk of royal prerogatives and ancient customs. As they rejected the traditional oath for being "framed in doubtful words and expressions," the architects of the Revolution also questioned the ornate artistic styles in which the painters, poets, and composers favored by James had expressed royal myth. This shift was partly the result of the more secular and modern political assumptions behind the Revolution; the Whig aesthetic that developed in the 1690s and carried over into Anne's reign was suspicious of mythology, though of course unable to dispense with it altogether.[41] But the Stuarts themselves also played a part in this process. Though deeply committed to a traditional view of monarchy, Charles II and James II compromised the power of royal myth by their own actions, including their private amours. Deploying ancient mythology as poets had always done on such occasions, Behn argues that the "Artillery" of Maria's beauty is

> Fatal to *All* but Her Lov'd *Monarchs* heart,
> Who of the *same* Divine Materials wrought;
>   Cou'd equally exchange the dart,
> Receive the wound with Life, with Life the wound impart;
>   And mixt the Soul as gently as the thought:

So the Great *Thund'rer Semele* d'stroy'd,
  Whil'st only *Juno* cou'd embrace the *God!*[42]

In celebrating Maria as the only woman able to embrace the new king without being destroyed, the Juno to his Jupiter, Behn presumably means to emphasize the allegedly "Divine Materials" in the royal blood of the king and queen, but the comparison to Olympian deities inevitably suggests other more embarrassing parallels. Like the notoriously adulterous Jupiter, with his string of earthly women, James was habitually unfaithful to Maria. He had fathered children by both Arabella Churchill and Catharine Sedley, and his resolution to break with his mistress on becoming king lasted only three months.[43] Like the coronation ceremony, in which two men costumed as the Dukes of Aquitaine and Normandy kept up the pretense that Charles or James or Anne was the ruler of "England and France,"[44] Behn's poem was an expression of comforting myths that could not bear close scrutiny. Although James encouraged and supported artistic expressions of those traditional myths, the events of his reign exposed them as hollow and false.

§

In the early months of the reign, however, Royalist myths were on display not only in the pageantry of the coronation and the expansiveness of Pindaric poetry, but in an expensive and unfamiliar musical medium. Six weeks after the coronation, with the town full for the opening of Parliament, the Dorset Garden Theatre presented the long-awaited premiere of *Albion and Albanius,* the only full-length, through-sung opera in English publicly presented in London before the eighteenth century. The plans for this performance began shortly after Anne's wedding in 1683, when Charles II dispatched the actor-manager Thomas Betterton to France to arrange for an opera to be performed in London. Rather than importing a French production, Betterton persuaded the composer Grabu, who had fled to France at the height of the Popish Plot, "to go over with him to endeavour to represent something at least like an Opera in England for his Majestyes diversion." Significantly, this description comes in a letter to the Duke of York from Richard Graham, the English envoy to the French court, in which Graham asks James "to speake a good word…to the King" on behalf of Grabu.[45] His appeal to York for patronage and support probably reflects Graham's hope that the women of York's court would look favorably on this project: Maria had enjoyed operatic performances in her native Modena and promoted them in England; Princess Anne, after years of instruction in singing, dancing, harpsichord, and guitar, remained keenly interested in music.

As Graham conceded by hoping for "something at least *like* an Opera," opera was not a familiar form in England. The major European capitals had supported opera companies since the early seventeenth century, but London was an exception, and English audiences associated through-sung opera with the absolutist court of Louis XIV, where Jean-Baptiste Lully was the resident composer. The plays previously called "operas" in England had combined spoken dialogue with elaborate musical interludes featuring singers who were not the major actors in the drama, typically appearing as shepherds, nymphs, sprites, or mythological figures. When Dryden and Sir William Davenant made their adaptation of *The Tempest* (1667), they added more singing and dancing to a Shakespearean original that was already musical. An even more elaborate "operatic" *Tempest* staged in 1674, with music by Matthew Locke and others, did much to establish the conventions of English "semiopera." *Calisto* (1675), which Crowne called a "masque," alternated spoken drama acted by the court ladies and pastoral interludes sung by professional musicians; its all-sung prologue, effectively a short opera, was a model for *Albion and Albanius*. Later musical dramas in the public theatres, such as Thomas Shadwell's *Psyche* (1675) and Charles Davenant's *Circe* (1677), also featured spoken dialogue, doubtless in deference to English tastes.[46]

In the years after *Calisto,* Charles's court was preoccupied by the political struggle over Exclusion, and James's court was often in exile. Only after Charles's victory over his political opponents was there another court theatrical: *Venus and Adonis,* probably performed in 1683.[47] On this occasion, aware of the court's renewed interest in opera, John Blow set Anne Kingsmill's libretto to music from beginning to end, with recitatives rather than spoken dialogue. The resulting small-scale opera, identified in one surviving manuscript as "a masque for the entertainment of the King," looks like a private trial run for the longer, more elaborate opera that Charles's servants, including his Poet Laureate, were preparing for public performance.

When he first became involved in creating the new opera, Dryden's plan was to write a semiopera based on the story of King Arthur, but in deference to the king's interest in French-style opera, he also wrote a fully sung prologue designed as an allegory of the Restoration. Perhaps because both Grabu and Charles were more interested in this part than in the Arthurian semiopera, the prologue grew into a three-act allegory bringing the political history up to the present, in which Charles appeared as "Albion" and his brother, the Duke of York and Albany, as "Albanius." The descent of this drama from the prologue to *Calisto* is apparent, but while *Calisto* had featured both courtly amateurs and paid professionals, *Albion and Albanius* was planned from the start as an all-professional production with scenery and machines of unprecedented splendor, supported by the court but performed in the Dorset Garden Theatre, not at Whitehall or Windsor. Charles II's sudden death in February 1685 was the last of many factors delaying the performance, but Dryden deftly salvaged the text by adding a brief apotheosis in which Albion is summoned to heaven, and on 3 June 1685, the opera finally had its premiere. Before the action began, the audience saw a painted "frontispiece" with figures representing peace, plenty, poetry, painting, and music. In the middle, in a "very large Pannel," was "a Woman representing the City of *London*, leaning her Head on her Hand in a dejected Posture" and "a Figure of the *Thames* with his Legs shakl'd, and leaning on an empty Urn."[48] Many details of this iconography, including the urn, come straight from *Calisto,* and Dryden's cast of characters included a number of mythical figures who had appeared in *Calisto,* such as Augusta, Thames, Mercury, and Juno.[49]

In the most memorable song from *Calisto,* Crowne had described "Augusta" as a fickle woman, and in *Albion and Albanius,* Dryden constructed his first act as an allegory of the unfaithful London of the Interregnum. Mercury descends from heaven to find a dejected Augusta lamenting the absence of her "Plighted Lord" (Charles II). As he forces her to confess, Augusta has caused her husband's departure by her unfaithfulness. Like Behn's poetic allegories, this account of the Interregnum as an episode of marital infidelity bears scant resemblance to the truth. Some eighteen years earlier, in dedicating *Annus Mirabilis* to "The Most Renowned and Late Flourishing City of London," Dryden had described the City, a center of active opposition to the Crown, as the passive victim of a series of violent rapists:

Mus. Ex. 3.3: Luis Grabu, excerpt from *Albion and Albanius* (1685), Act 1, no. 5.

Never had Prince or People more mutual reason to love each other, if suffering for each other can indear affection. You have come together a pair
of matchless Lovers, through many difficulties; He, through a long Exile,
various traverses of Fortune, and the interposition of many Rivals, who
violently ravish'd and with-held You from Him: And certainly you have
had your share in sufferings.⁵⁰

In 1667, as he praised the City in terms his readers knew were false, Dryden
was urging the citizens of London to embrace the loyal role in which he offered to
cast them. In 1685, having lived through the Popish Plot and the Exclusion Crisis,
he returned to the same allegory, but presented it more darkly and dramatically. No
sooner has Augusta expressed her hope to free herself "From force of Usurpation"⁵¹
than Dryden gives that force bodily form, bringing on a trio of adversaries who
threaten a gang rape more terrifying than anything dreamt of in *Calisto*, indeed far
closer to the violent world of Lee's *Mithridates*. Democracy, here portrayed as male,
and Zelota, a female representative of religious zeal, seize Augusta, urging a character named Archon to help them ravish her. Much to the surprise of his would-be
partners, however, Archon rescues Augusta and declares his intention to bring back
Albion, just as the real George Monck, who had been a general and an admiral in
the service of the Protectorate, used his power to effect the restoration of Charles II
during the chaotic spring of 1660.

Throughout the Exclusion Crisis, Tory writers had accused the Whigs of
wanting to bring back the chaos caused by the Civil Wars and the unpopular governmental structures established during the Commonwealth, so reminding the
nation of the blessings secured by the Restoration was an effective plan for an
opera celebrating the Stuart line. Grabu's music, however, vitiates the force of
Dryden's rhetoric. The major-key recitative in which Democracy and Zelota announce their violent intentions has neither rhythmic nor harmonic tension. If
Purcell had set this text, he would surely have provided some minor sonorities
and grinding dissonances to make these figures more frightening. The cheerful air
in which Archon announces his arrival to save the day, soon repeated as a chorus,
is a little more appropriate for its text, but would have been much more effective if
presented as a contrast to some darker music for the villains.

At the end of this act, silent figures representing Albion and Albanius come
on stage for an entry reenacting the Restoration and Charles's coronation, complete with triumphal arches. Despite having been planned as a celebration of both
the royal brothers, this scene turned out to be highly appropriate when it was
finally produced, reminding the audience of the continuities linking Charles's coronation in 1661 with James's in 1685. But in order to present more recent events,
Dryden and Grabu had to use singing actors to represent the royal brothers. For

Democracy (countertenor): Pull down her gates! ex-pose her bare! I must en-joy the

Figured bass

Zelota (soprano): I'll hold her proud dis-dain - ful fair; Haste, Ar - chon haste To lay her waste!

4 # 6

fast to be em - brac'd.

And she shall see A thou - sand ty - rants are in

4 # 6 ♮5

Violins 1 and 2

thee, A thou-sand, thou-sand more in me.

Archon (bass): From the Ca - le-do-nian

Shore Hith-er am I come, to save thee, Not to force or to en - slave thee, But thy Al - bion

🔊 Mus. Ex. 3.4: Luis Grabu, excerpt from *Albion and Albanius* (1685), Act 1, no. 9.

audiences used to the conventions of semiopera, in which the kings and heroes played by the leading actors never sang, there would have been something unnerving about seeing James II, present in the royal box at the premiere, portrayed by a warbling countertenor, while Charles II, just four months dead, appeared as a baritone. The scene in which a singing Albion tells a singing Albanius that he must go into exile borders on bathos.

Recognizing this dialogue as a sad scene, Grabu provides lugubrious minor harmonies in the four viola parts. But he misses the rhetoric of Dryden's dialogue, providing no musical support for Albanius's pious declaration that he will make a merit of his sufferings, or for Albion's agonized alternation between brusque orders and expressions of regret. Again, the music is palpably weaker than the verse.[52]

In act 3, the banished Albanius returns from exile in a maritime scene that resembles the opening of *Ariane*.

> A Machine rises out of the Sea: It opens and discovers *Venus* and *Albanius* sitting in a great Scallop-shell, richly adorn'd: *Venus* is attended by the Loves and Graces, *Albanius* by *Hero's*: The Shell is drawn by Dolphins: It moves forward, while a simphony of Fluts-Doux, &c. is playing.[53]

As in *Calisto*, a figure representing James appears with a retinue of martial heroes; as in Behn's coronation ode, a goddess surrounded by mythological attendants represents Maria; as in *Venus and Adonis*, there is a dance tune "for the Loves and Graces." But the repetition of these familiar allegories could not entirely efface

Viola 1 and 2

Viola 3 and 4

Albanius
(countertenor)

Oh Al - bion, hear the gods and___ me! Well am I

Figured bass

♮6   5

lost in sav - ing thee! Not ex - ile or dan - ger can fright a brave

spi - rit, With in - no-cence guard -ed, With vir - tue re - ward - ed I make of my

6
♮4

suf - f'rings a me-rit.

Albion (baritone)

Since then the gods and thou wilt have it

6   6 4 ♮

♮6

🔊 Mus. Ex. 3.5: Luis Grabu, excerpt from *Albion and Albanius* (1685), Act 2, no. 39.

some inconvenient facts: James's actual voyage to Scotland to bring back Maria and Princess Anne in 1682 had resulted in a fatal shipwreck. There were no dolphins to save the hapless hundreds who drowned, and as the musicians in the orchestra played Grabu's "simphony," with its prominent recorder parts, they could hardly help missing their colleague Thomas Greeting, a virtuoso wind-player who had been among those lost in the wreck of the *Gloucester*.

Princess Anne was unable to join the king and queen for the premiere of this opera because she had given birth to a daughter just two days earlier, but it is possible that she had heard some of the music. Like *Calisto*, which was practiced at court for months before its official performances, *Albion and Albanius* was often rehearsed for Charles. There is a clear record of such rehearsals in the apartments of the Duchess of Portsmouth during the winter of 1684–1685, and a newsletter reports that the king, at Windsor, was "Entertained with mr drydens new play the subject of which is the last new Plott" on 29 May 1684, his birthday.[54] In 1684, "the last new Plott" could only mean the Rye House Plot, which is fancifully enacted in act 3 of the opera: a "one-Ey'd Archer," obviously a stage version of the one-eyed conspirator Richard Rumbold, advances to shoot at Albion but is thwarted when "A fire arises betwixt them." If Anne heard the court rehearsals of *Albion and Albanius,* as seems quite likely, she was in a position to understand the allegory in detail and to recognize the musical innovations of the form. Decades later, when operas began to be presented in London on a regular basis, Queen Anne invited the singers to perform at court on her birthdays, and when a permanent company began to present operas sung in Italian, she smiled on their efforts. The celebration of her birthday in 1711 included a performance by the castrato Nicolini and "the other celebrated Voices of the Italian Opera: with which her Majesty was extreamly well pleas'd."[55]

§

Mocking the "brave stout young men"[56] in white linen who had greeted Monmouth on his symbolic journey to the West in 1680, Dryden included a "Confus'd Dance" for the "Fighting White Boys and Sectaries" in the third act of *Albion and Albanius*. When he invented this allegorical episode, he could hardly have imagined that the opera would ultimately fail when some real Whigs and Dissenters took up arms in support of Monmouth's claims. Ten days and six performances after the premiere, news reached London that the Protestant duke had landed at Lyme Regis with an army. Monmouth had only eighty-two followers and four cannon when he came ashore, and he had hired the three ships in which they came by pawning the jewels of his mistress Henrietta Wentworth, whom he probably first met during the rehearsals for *Calisto*. Although the scale of the invasion was small, discontented men rallied to Monmouth's standard in significant numbers, and the fevered correspondence that followed his landing shows that many considered it a genuine threat.[57] The panic caused by the revolt ruined the run of the opera, and one specific character whom Dryden had treated as a mythic figure now reappeared in the flesh: Richard Rumbold, the model for Dryden's one-eyed archer, had been in hiding on the Continent since 1683; now he returned as a colonel in the rebel army led by Archibald Campbell, ninth Earl of Argyll, who invaded Scotland as Monmouth invaded England.

Monmouth issued a declaration claiming to be the rightful king, accusing his uncle of having poisoned his father, and deploring James's absolutism. But the most telling language in this document takes aim at the king's Catholicism:

> He not only began his Usurpation and pretended Reign, with a barefaced avowing himselfe of the *Romish Religion*, but hath call'd in multitudes of *Preists* & *Iesuits* (for whom the Law makes it *treason* to come into the Kingdom) and hath impower'd them to exercise their *Idolatries*, and besides his being dayly present at the worship of the *Mass*, hath publickly assisted at the *grossest Fopperies* of their superstition.[58]

It is remarkable that Monmouth—or his associate Robert Ferguson, who drafted the declaration—should have expressed disdain for Catholic practices with the term *Fopperies,* more normally used to criticize the affected dress and manner of dandified characters in plays. Even in the midst of a daring attempt to alter the political landscape, the rebels specified the liturgical style of James's chapel as a central instance of the attitudes and practices they hoped to overthrow.

The men from the western counties who rallied to Monmouth's cause, perhaps seven thousand at the moment of greatest enthusiasm, outnumbered the forces dispatched by the king to meet them, but they were completely undisciplined and barely armed. James, who had been attentive to the state of the army in the months since his accession, received an immediate grant of £400,000 from his Parliament for the purpose of putting down the rebellion. He augmented the local militia, some of whom had deserted to Monmouth, by sending two regiments from his well-armed regular forces to head off the rebels. John Churchill, promoted to brigadier, rode west immediately with a cavalry contingent, but the king appointed the Frenchman Louis Duras, Earl of Feversham, whom he had known and trusted for years, as commander. Churchill rightly concluded that he would do most of the work and get none of the credit.[59] After several weeks of skirmishes and maneuvers, Monmouth led his army across Sedgemoor in the fog on the night of 5 July, hoping to surprise the encampment of regular troops at Weston Zoyland. It was a brave move, and his best chance for success, as even Feversham was asleep in his tent. By design or accident, however, one of the sentries fired his weapon and woke the sleeping troops, who quickly formed up to defend the camp. Confusion, poor cavalry leadership, and the superior discipline of the outnumbered regulars ultimately led to a disastrous rout, followed by a disorganized flight. Early on 8 July, a search party found the bearded, dirty, and exhausted Monmouth asleep in a ditch; a week later, having begged everyone for mercy, he was beheaded on Tower Hill. The Scottish rebellion also failed. Argyll and Rumbold, defiant to the end, were executed in Edinburgh, and James saw to it that one of Rumbold's quarters was put on display at Rye House.

There are only tantalizing scraps of evidence from which to speculate about Anne's response to these events. She certainly shared the fears of Catholicism that motivated Monmouth's supporters; her letter to Mary deploring Catholic ceremonies uses the term *Idolatry,* which also appears in Monmouth's declaration. But a ragtag army made up of rabid Whigs and Dissenters, with no aristocratic support at all, was unlikely to attract her sympathy, and politically, she had every reason to side with her father, as the crowning of Monmouth would have effectively removed her from the succession. On a personal level, she had concerns and connections on both sides. Monmouth was her first cousin and the husband of her godmother, with whom she remained close. In early June, the Duchess of Monmouth was in residence at Whitehall with her children, specifically in the part of the palace called the Cockpit, where her goddaughter Anne was recovering from childbirth.[60] As a music-lover and a longtime patroness of Dryden, the duchess probably attended *Albion and Albanius* during the first week of June, but when news of the invasion reached London, the king placed her family under house arrest at the Cockpit; after Sedgemoor, he sent the children to the Tower, where the duchess voluntarily joined them, and where her daughter died in August. Although she had long been estranged from her husband, who declared on the scaffold that he regarded himself as married to Henrietta Wentworth, the duchess could not be unconcerned about the fate of her children's father; she swooned at their final interview.[61] Princess Anne may have had some sympathy for her godmother, but she showed greater concern for her closest friend. When news of the victory at Sedgemoor reached Whitehall, Anne wrote to Sarah Churchill, congratulating her on John Churchill's safety and jealously claiming that her rejoicing at his survival was greater than that felt by any of Sarah's other correspondents.[62]

At this point, James II was in a very strong position: with solid support from the aristocracy, he had disposed of the most obvious pretender to the throne; his large and proven army, with a number of Roman Catholic officers added to its ranks in response to the invasion, was encamped at Hounslow Heath; a cooperative Parliament had voted him a generous financial supply. As the diarist Sir John Reresby shrewdly pointed out, the king was made "the faster in the throne by this endeavour to cast him out."[63] But he fatally overplayed his hand. Not content with having defeated Monmouth, he took sweeping revenge against those caught up in the rebellion: in the "Bloody Assizes" held in the West during the late summer and early autumn, Chief Justice Jeffreys sent hundreds of Monmouth's followers to the gallows and the plantations. Very few of those who appealed to the Crown for mercy were pardoned. This uncompromising vengeance was a striking contrast to Charles II's judicious treatment of his former enemies at the time of the Restoration—and an indication of more trouble to come.

There were artistic signals of the same intractable attitudes. Shortly after putting down the rebellion, James had a medal struck showing the decapitated corpses of Monmouth and Argyle. The imagery was in abysmal taste, and the artist, Regnier Arondeaux, was a Frenchman normally employed by Louis XIV. As he celebrated a victory in which he had enjoyed widespread support, James again displayed his disregard for the feelings of his countrymen, both in his political actions and in his choice of artisans and images. Intent on keeping the Catholic officers in the army, he now asked Parliament to abolish the Test Act of 1673, a high-handed action that sparked immediate protests. On 19 November, "there were very great debates in the house of lords concerning that part of his majesties speech which referrs to the popish officers in the army,"[64] and on the very next day, the haughty and impatient king prorogued his Parliament, which never met again in his reign.

Regnier Arondeaux, *Silver medal commemorating the executions
of Monmouth and Argyle.*

Before the end of the year, James's insistence on having his way in all things
directly touched his daughter: the king dismissed Henry Compton, Bishop of
London, who had officiated at Anne's marriage and at the christening of her
daughter, from his seat on the Privy Council and his position as Dean of the
Chapel Royal, where Anne worshiped. Compton had spoken out against James's
plan to repeal the Test Act, but the real reason for his dismissal, according to
Reresby, was "his being industrious to preserve the Princess Ann of Denmarke in
the Protestant religion, whom there were some endeavours to gain to the Church
of Rome."[65] For Anne, who was concerned about her sickly daughter Mary and
expecting another child in the spring, such pressure to convert was unwelcome,
and the loss of the trusted Compton as a regular celebrant in her chapel was a
serious blow.

In the case of Compton, as in the later case of the Seven Bishops, James failed to grasp that his punishment of those who opposed him might make them heroes in the eyes of the public. By 5 January 1686, witnesses were reporting that "the Bishop of London's fame runs high in the vogue of the people" and that "London pulpits ring strong peals against Popery,"[66] appropriating for a different purpose an image Dryden had used in his opera, where "the People" ring peals for the Restoration:

> Hark! the Peals the People ring,
> Peace, and Freedom, and a King.[67]

But instead of seeking compromise and conciliation, James continued to persecute outspoken Anglicans. John Sharp, who would later become a trusted advisor to Queen Anne, preached a sermon "reflecting on the new converts to the Roman Catholic faith" on 2 May 1686, and on 17 June James ordered Compton, Sharp's bishop, to suspend him from preaching. Looking for a compromise, Compton encouraged Sharp to write a petition to the king, who refused to hear it and used his new Ecclesiastical Commission to suspend Compton from his bishopric.[68]

§

Events on the Continent made James's high-handed punitive actions toward Compton and others look even more ominous. The Edict of Nantes, issued in 1598, had allowed the Protestant minority in France to practice their religion in peace for generations, but in October 1685 Louis XIV suddenly revoked it. Faced with violent coercion to convert to Catholicism, Huguenot refugees came flooding into Holland and England, bringing horror stories that found sympathetic ears. At such a moment, James would have been well advised to minimize opportunities for his subjects to compare him to the Catholic monarchs of Europe. Instead, he dispatched Roger Palmer, Earl of Castlemaine, on an official embassy to the pope and began preparations for the arrival of Count Ferdinando d'Adda, sent by Innocent XI as his envoy to England. This exchange of ambassadors was an act of treason in the eyes of many Englishmen, but James insisted on publicizing it. He appointed the Catholic portrait painter John Michael Wright, who had studied painting in Rome, as Castlemaine's steward, and Wright produced a lavishly illustrated folio volume describing Castlemaine's mission, published in Italian and later in English at the urging of the court. The volume opens with an unguarded and explicit account of James's purposes:

> It having still been the Custom of all the Great Princes, in Communion with the Church of *Rome* (on their first accession to the Throne) to send an Embassador to that court, His Majesty thought it became Him also to do the like.[69]

An Account of his Excellence Roger Earl of Castlemaine's Embassy, From his Sacred Majesty
James the IId....To His Holiness Innocent XI (1688).

By encouraging this publication, which includes illustrations and descriptions of
the symbolic decorations on the coaches made for the embassy, James was foolishly keeping his attempts to emulate Continental monarchs in the public eye, even
though some elements of the account were embarrassing. James chose Castlemaine for this mission because of his religion, and Wright's frontispiece shows him

making an elaborate obeisance to the pope. Neither seems to have thought that the ambassador, as the cuckolded husband of Charles II's longtime mistress, might be a target for ridicule. Nor do they appear to have worried about contradictions within the book. In one egregious passage, Wright describes at length a "florid Italian Oration" praising King James for "His *Clemency*, in being ever readier to pardon, than offenders to ask it," an encomium distinctly at odds with the king's refusal to pardon those involved in Monmouth's rebellion.

Castlemaine arrived in Rome at Easter and met privately with the pope, but his official entry, delayed by the making of new coaches and liveries, did not occur until January 1687. A month after this formal audience, Queen Christina of Sweden, who was resident in Rome, entertained Castlemaine with a cantata in praise of James II, performed by 250 musicians under the direction of Arcangelo Corelli:

> The composition, was sung in Dialogue, by five persons, representing *London, Thames, Fame, The Ruling Genius, and The Genius of Rebellion;* with a Chorus of an hundred Voices, and an hundred and fifty musical Instruments.
>
> The subject was, The Encomiums of the English Nation, and their Great Monarch, *James* the Second; with the Augury also, and Assurance, of happy successes, under the Dominion of so mighty a Prince.[70]

Not to be outdone, the court of Modena, birthplace of the Queen of England, presented an allegorical oratorio called *L'Ambitione Debellata overo La Caduta di Monmuth (Ambition Defeated, or the Fall of Monmouth).* James appeared as Innocence, Maria as Faith, and Monmouth as Ambition.[71] Both these works bear a strong family resemblance to *Albion and Albanius,* but Italian audiences were more accustomed to this kind of musical allegory than English theatergoers, for whom reports of these performances would have reinforced the notion of musical drama as foreign, extravagant, and absolutist.

In London, there was no prospect of another English opera celebrating the increasingly unpopular monarch. With the theatre company deeply in debt from expenditures on scenes and machines for *Albion and Albanius,* which they were unable to recoup when the run was spoiled by the rebellion, James had to make do with an imported French opera, Lully's *Cadmus et Hermione,* sung in French by French performers on 11 February 1686.[72] Like *Ariane,* this opera celebrates a mythological marriage; like *Calisto,* it draws its plot from Ovid and includes an entry of Africans. In the climactic scene, which the king probably saw as an analogue to Monmouth's rebellion, Cadmus sows the teeth of a dragon in the field of Mars, where they spring up as armed men who threaten him. He defeats this army by tossing a grenade provided by Amour into their midst, which magically induces them to fight with each other. The survivors lay their arms at his feet, determined to save their remaining blood to serve a hero beloved by the gods.[73]

In the opera, this episode is a ballet danced to a lively dotted tune; as one English witness admitted, Lully's music was "very fine."[74] Like other myths deployed in praise of the Stuarts, however, the story of Cadmus was open to various interpretations, and it was already apparent to some that James, through his vindictive treatment of the rebels and the clergy, was sowing the dragon's teeth that would spring up against him in the next invasion. Moreover, by appropriating an opera first performed for Louis XIV in 1674, he was again imitating the hated Sun King, now notorious for his persecution of Protestants. In his prologue to *The Devil of a Wife*, a comedy staged a few weeks later, Thomas Jevon poked fun at the opera, singing the French lyrics to one of its songs in an affected falsetto. In *his* play, he proudly declared, even the dances were "*English* all, all *English* quite." The sentiments to which Jevon was appealing were not merely nationalistic. Satirizing Lully's song as "a pretty *Whyne*"[75] was an indirect way of expressing concern about the king's taking his autocratic French cousin as a model.

The performance of *Cadmus et Hermione* has left just three small traces: Jevon's prologue, a brief description in a letter, and a bill for tickets for the king and queen to "the French opera," with a box for the maids of honor. If Anne, now six months pregnant, attended the performance, no one recorded her presence, but there is contemporaneous evidence of her interest in French dance music. In a letter to Mary written in 1687, she reports enjoying a dance "called the Rigadoon which the D[uke] of St. Albans brought out of France," which was "mightily liked, & indeed it was a very pretty one I thought," though she patriotically remarks that "we have some that are much finer." She then blames the Rigadoon for a personal disaster: "I have no reason to like it now, for I believe it was the dance that made me miscarry, for there is a great deal of jumping in it."[76] Many of Anne's pregnancies ended in miscarriages, and it is impossible at this distance to assess her suspicion that vigorous dancing caused the one she suffered on 22 January 1687. Her willingness to lay the blame on a French dance, however, is suggestive.

§

Anne's pregnancy in 1686 had a happier outcome, and appears to have intensified the king's efforts to convert her. On 6 April 1686, the government official John Ellis, in Dublin, heard that "poor Princess Ann is sadly tezed about a new declaration in matter of faith, so that at last it is agreed to after lying in; but I hope it may not be thus, say nothing of it."[77] At this point, Anne's "lying in" was imminent; she gave birth to a second daughter on 12 May. Although James reportedly came to visit her with a Roman Catholic priest, a tactless act that made his daughter cry, she did not, as the writer had feared, make any new declaration of faith after the birth.[78] The list of participants in the christening of little Anne Sophia may suggest the pressures under which the princess was now suffering. With Compton dismissed as Dean of the Chapel Royal, the ceremony was performed by Nathaniel Crew, Bishop of Durham, long a close friend of James II. The king appointed Crew to replace Compton in December and would soon add him to the notorious Ecclesiastical Commission. The Earl of Feversham, victor at Sedgemoor, stood godfather; Anne may have admired his skills as a dancer, which were apparently remarkable, but he was also a choice sure to please the king. The recently widowed Countess of Roscommon, a Lady of the Bedchamber to the queen, was one godmother, and Sarah Churchill was another.[79] In assembling this group, Anne was evidently trying to placate her father and stepmother, while at the same time enlisting the formidable Sarah to support and protect her.

The birth of Anne Sophia marks the beginning of the only period in Anne's life when she had two living children. Barbara Berkeley, Anne's childhood companion and the daughter of her first governess, was in charge of the nursery, but Anne, whose friendship with Barbara was marked by episodes of jealousy and distrust, frequently consulted with Sarah Churchill about the care of her daughters, drawing on her favorite's experience as a mother.[80] A letter of August 1686 affords a rare glimpse into this world. Edward Greeting, son of the drowned musician Thomas Greeting, had the job of playing music for the little girls, but he had done something to offend Anne, who wrote about the situation to Sarah:

As for young Greeting, Since the Queen has commanded Mrs Berkly to take him I shall not contradict it, but the next little fault he comites he shall never play at my nursery again, for he is so very bold & impertinent that he is not fitt to be theire & to tell you true I was very glad of this to putt him away & since he is one of the Kings musick & has nothing from me but what I give him at newyeares tide, tis no charety to heare him play. however if you do desire it he shall never be forbid again, for I will ever obey my deare Lady Churchills commands since I am sure you will never desire anything but what is reasonable. It may be Mrs Berkly may think that since She went people has spoke to me against him, but I asure you since I heard what he did to Mr Wentworth no body has ever opened their lips about him.[81]

Without more context, much in this letter will remain obscure, but it is still valuable for what it reveals about the dynamics of the court and the psychological state of the princess. In commanding that Greeting be appointed, the queen may have been claiming expertise in musical matters or hoping to help her husband provide for the families of those lost in the wreck of the *Gloucester*, but she was also pulling rank. Although Anne does not "contradict" the queen's appointment, she reserves the right to dismiss Greeting if he gives renewed offense. Maria had no living child at this time, while Anne had two, as she indicates by the pointed reference to "*my* nursery." In speaking of "charity," Anne demonstrates that detailed knowledge of family and rank for which Sarah would later give her grudging praise: she remembers that Greeting's dead father was among her own servants and shows some concern for his family, but she also points out that the younger Greeting has a salaried post in the king's band, so that she may dismiss him from the nursery without consigning him to poverty. Yet after constructing a strong case for dismissing him, she leaves the decision to Sarah, whose commands she promises to obey. Still only twenty-one, Anne was feeling the stress of motherhood and watching her once-cordial relations with her stepmother deteriorate. Her willingness to defer to her "deare Lady Churchill" was a way to have someone else make decisions and defend them.

It was also an act of love. In her later account of this period, carefully constructed to show her actions in the best possible light, Sarah describes Anne's need for her as if all the feeling were on one side:

> This favour quickly became a Passion: & a Passion which possess'd the Heart of the *Princess* too much to be hid. They were shut up together, for many hours, daily. Every moment of Absence was counted a sort of a tedious, lifeless, state. *To see* the Dutchess *was a Constant Joy;* & *to part with* Her, for never so short a time, *a constant Uneasiness: as the Princess's* own frequent expressions were. This work'd, even to the jealousy of a Lover. She used to say, *She desired to possess Her wholy.*

But as this passage continues, and as Sarah tells once more the story of how the two women chose the assumed names under which they would correspond, the mask begins to slip:

> But the *Dutchess* had too great a Sense of Her Favour, not to Submitt to all such Inconveniences to oblige *One*, who, she saw, loved Her to Excess.... [The Princess] chose the feign'd name of *Morly*; & the *Dutchess*, with some regard to Her own frank & open Temper, chose that of Freeman. And, from this time, Mrs *Morly*, & Mrs *Freeman* are to converse as *Equals*, made so by *Love.*[82]

If Anne and Sarah were now "*Equals*, made so by *Love*," there was necessarily love on both sides, though it is impossible to know to what extent that love was expressed in physical intimacy. Both women were married, frequently pregnant, and concerned for their children; both had numerous responsibilities. Yet they managed to be "shut up together, for many hours, daily," and both of them evidently drew comfort and strength from their time together.

Anne's lifelong desire for a converse of equals often found expression as unease about rank and power: "I am more yours than can be exprest & had rather live in a Cottage with you than Reinge Empresse of the world without you,"[83] she wrote in another letter to Sarah. This fantasy of a simple life, removed from the strain of courtly power, had an especially strong appeal at a time when her father was behaving like an emperor and stubbornly insisting on his prerogatives. In April 1686, a packed panel of judges ruled that the king had the power to dispense with laws made by Parliament, and James, who had been unable to force Parliament to repeal the Test Act, promptly used his "dispensing power" to appoint Catholics to posts in many sectors of society. In July, he named Powis, Arundell, and Belasyse—the three Catholic peers who had languished in the Tower from 1678 until 1684—to his Privy Council. He cannot have believed that he would gain much in the way of shrewd advice from these elderly and inexperienced men, but he evidently relished showing his enemies that he could now honor and reward the very men the Whigs had indicted for high treason just eight years earlier.

Later in the same month, the king staged a show of armed might as a compliment to his queen and laid plans for a progress to the western counties from which Monmouth had drawn his support:

> His Majesty, as a piece of gallantry, made all his 4000 horse march at two in the morning into Staines Meadow, and attend the Queen from thence to the Heath, where she honoured Lord Arran with dining with him. But his Sacred Majesty designs a farther graciousness in a few days, viz. to go and let all his good friends of Bristoll, Taunton, and the towns about see him, and judge how decent an attendance 4000 men at arms are.... then we shall see how that corner which was so zealous to receive a mock-king, will behave themselves when their true one appears.[84]

The newswriter is surely sarcastic in calling the king's progress to the West "a farther graciousness." James's journey to the Bristol area with a large contingent of heavily armed troops, many of them commanded by Catholic officers, was designed to intimidate his subjects. When the court returned to London, the king gave a similarly deliberate display of his religious arrogance. In December, he began to hear Mass in his new Roman Catholic chapel in Whitehall, with its splendid paintings by Verrio and Gennari. The ever-curious diarist John Evelyn admired "the carving & Pillars of exquisite art & greate cost" and described the paintings in detail. He found the whole effect both riveting and troubling; it was "a world of mysterious Ceremony, the Musique playing and singing: & so I came away: not believing I should ever have lived to see such things in the K. of Englands palace, after it had pleas'd God to inlighten this nation." Despite his disapproval, Evelyn returned a few weeks later to hear "the famous *Cifeccio* (Eunuch) sing, in the new popish chapel, ... which was indeede very rare, & with greate skill. He came over from Rome, esteemed one of the best voices in *Italy*, much crowding, little devotion."[85]

For James, the display of Italian art and music in his chapel, like the appointment of Catholic peers to the Privy Council or the show of military power in the West, was a way of demonstrating his belief that he could cow his enemies into silence by insisting on his monarchial privileges. As even those inclined to support him recognized, this was a shortsighted, doomed approach. In a letter to the playwright George Etherege, who was receiving a pension from the king, the poet Dryden, a recent convert to Catholicism, described himself as "great in idleness," staying in the country and avoiding the court. Developing that theme, he expressed his wish that James would also embrace idleness, as Charles II had done: "Oh that our Monarch wou'd encourage noble idleness by his own example, as he of blessed memory did before him for my minde misgives me, that he will not much advance his affaires by Stirring."[86] Like Anne's dream of living in a cottage with Sarah, Dryden's preference for a quiet life in the country was an expression of deep unease as James's insistence on "Stirring" increasingly alienated his people.

Dryden wrote his letter to Etherege in February 1687, a month in which personal disaster struck the Denmarks: Prince George contracted the smallpox, as did both their daughters. Princess Anne, who had already had the disease, tried to nurse them all, but Anne Sophia died on 2 February, Mary died on 8 February, and while George survived, his recovery was slow and difficult. For Anne, who had miscarried on 22 January, the sudden loss of both children was a bitter blow. A sad letter from Lady Russell, widow of the alleged Whig plotter, describes Anne and George in their grief: "Sometimes they wept, sometimes they mourned; in a word, then sat silent, hand in hand; he sick in bed, and she the carefullest nurse to him that can be imagined."[87] In addition to the personal trauma, the loss of her daughters altered Anne's status vis-à-vis the queen; later in the same spring, she wrote bitterly to Mary of her dislike for Maria, whom she now described as having "a very proud, haughty humour" and as "the most hated in the world by all sorts of people. For every body believes that she presses the King to be more violent then he would be of Himself, which is not unlikely, for she is a very great Bigott in her way." Of course, Anne was not in a position to express these sentiments openly; indeed, she complained in the same letter that it was "a sad & a very uneasy thing to be forc'd to live civilly, & as it were freely with a woman that one knows hates one, & does all she can to undo every body which she certainly does."[88]

Once he began to mend, George made plans to visit his native Denmark, and Anne proposed to visit her sister in Holland at the same time. But after initially agreeing to this plan, James peremptorily refused to allow Anne to go, presumably fearful of collusion between his daughters.[89] While this personal struggle was playing out at court, the king made two ill-considered political gambles. When Henry Clerke, President of Magdalen College, Oxford, died on 24 March, James insisted on naming a candidate for the vacant post, and when the Fellows refused to vote as instructed, he saw to it that most of them were deprived of their positions. This was a direct assault on the independence of the universities, whose primary function was to train the Anglican clergy, and Anne was involved in the drama. Dr. John Younger, her personal chaplain, was also a Fellow of Magdalen, and had been thought likely to succeed Clerke. The dead man's daughter gave Younger early notice of her father's death, advising him to "procure by the interest of Princess Anne...the King's recommendatory letters to the College."[90] It was not unreasonable to think that Younger might be acceptable to the king, as he was married to a daughter of James's close associate Richard Graham, the man who had bought wedding garters for Anne and promoted the operatic project that led to *Albion and Albanius*. But Younger, who was in a position to observe the court closely, knew that James wanted to appoint Catholics to such positions, so he chose not to be a candidate. He contrived to retain his fellowship by absenting himself from the ensuing meetings, pleading the necessity to attend the princess. There is no surviving record of Anne's response to this episode, but when she wrote to Mary in May, describing a parallel case at Cambridge, she complained that "the priests have so much power with the King as to make him do things so directly against the Laws of the Land, & indeed contrary to his own promises."[91] Was she perhaps alluding to a broken promise from her father—or at least a fond hope of her own—that her chaplain would have the presidency of Magdalen?

On 4 April 1687, one day before "willing and requiring the College to elect and admit into the place of President his trusted and well-beloved Anthony Farmer, M.A.," who was ineligible, undistinguished, and widely believed to be a Roman Catholic, the king issued a sweeping Declaration of Indulgence, abolishing all penalties for those who did not conform to the Church of England. "It has of long time been our constant sense and opinion," he wrote, "that conscience ought not to be constrained nor people forced in matters of mere religion." An earlier sentence in the same paragraph, however, reveals the real impulse behind the high-minded talk of religious freedom: "We cannot but heartily wish," wrote the king, "that all the people of our dominions were members of the Catholic Church."[92] James's intention was to forge an alliance between the Roman Catholics and the Protestant Dissenters, but the language in which he made the Declaration was bound to give offense to many, and while both groups were doubtless glad for relief from the fines and penalties they had often suffered, they were hardly natural allies.

In taking these actions, James fatally underestimated the resilience and determination of the Anglican establishment. He also underestimated his daughter Anne, who lent her considerable prestige and support to Anglicans speaking out against the Crown. On 20 March 1687, by which time James's intentions about his Declaration were widely known, she heard Bishop Thomas Ken preach in Holborn, and on 25 March, Dr. Sharp, whose sermon against opportunistic conversions had led to Compton's suspension, preached "at the Chapel at Whitehall before the Princess of Denmark," who probably had something to do with his being invited to speak there.[93] Neither sermon survives, though there is every reason to think both had political resonance. John Evelyn, who habitually set down details of sermons in his diary, was present on both occasions. His notes on Sharp's sermon are instructive:

> Dr. *Sharp*, at White-hall,…shewing the stupendious efficacy of the Gospel, that the Scandal of the Crosse & the preaching thereof so plainely, & inartificialy; should prevaile so infinitely beyond all the Rhetoric & Eloquence of other Sects, Philosophers & Orators.[94]

Sharp's emphasis on preaching "plainely, & inartificialy" pointed to the marked contrast between Protestant practice and the ornate and mysterious services in the king's new chapel. Small wonder that Paul Barillon, the French ambassador, complained to Louis XIV on 3 April that Anne was going incognito to churches to hear popular preachers. He reported her plan to spend the late spring in Richmond, absenting herself from court, and her distress that her planned voyage to Holland had been forbidden. He also noted that James still hoped to convert her, a further instance of the king's limitless capacity for wishful thinking.[95] In fact, Anne was not only attending sermons; she was reading works of theological controversy. In a letter to her sister, written from Richmond on 9 May, she reported that "a great many books come out every day about religion, & a great many of our side, that are very well writt: if you care to see any of them let me know it, & I will send you those that are best worth reading."

In the same letter, Anne predicted that she would be especially vulnerable when her husband set sail for Denmark, which he did on 17 June, leaving his pregnant wife behind: "when he is away," she fretted, "I fancy the King will speak to me about my religion, for then he will find me more alone, then yet he has done."[96] Chosen as Anne's consort for his Protestant faith, her Lutheran husband was thought impervious to proselytizing by the priests of James's court;[97] his determination helped protect Anne from her father's efforts to convert her. During his absence there was another spectacular display of courtly Catholicism. Count d'Adda, who had now taken orders and assumed the position of a nuncio, an official papal ambassador, made his formal visit to the king at Windsor on 3 July. His entourage included thirty-six coaches with six horses each, a display designed to match the parade in Rome organized by Castlemaine. Charles Seymour, Duke of Somerset, who would support Anne at several critical moments in later decades, refused to introduce the nuncio to the king, maintaining that it would be treason to do so, and promptly lost all his offices.[98] However much she may have admired Somerset's courage, Anne was not in a position to make a similar gesture of defiance. According to Thomas Cartwright, the Tory clergyman who had preached before the princess in Edinburgh, she attended two sermons on 10 July in St. George's Chapel at Windsor, where the services were Anglican, and later that evening allowed the nuncio to "pay his compliments to her."[99] Prince George followed a similar policy when he returned from Denmark, joining the king and the nuncio at the Lord Mayor's feast in October but remaining faithful in attendance at Anglican services. By inviting the nuncio to their feast, the City fathers, who included many Protestant Dissenters, were attempting to show their support for the alliance between Catholics and Nonconformists envisioned in the king's Declaration of Indulgence, but the attempt quickly backfired. According to a shrewd Italian observer, there was "a grave contest between the Lord Mayor and the Aldermen" in which the invitation to the nuncio had become "a crime which every one wishes to lay on his neighbour."[100]

§

From Anne's point of view, the focus of politics now became personal. Distressed by her father's policies, she urgently wanted to produce an heir, and the hopes for a Protestant succession now rested with her, as her sister was evidently incapable of bearing children; Mary's last failed pregnancy had occurred in 1678. In striving to bear a living son, Anne necessarily thought of herself as competing with the queen, and she probably believed her chances were better than the queen's. Maria had no living children and had last been pregnant in 1684, though she was still under thirty. Anne, just twenty-two, had proved her capacity to bear children: a few months earlier, her nursery had held two living daughters, though it now was sadly empty. By April 1687, she was once more pregnant and hopeful—until she miscarried in late October. This fetus was male, a circumstance that made the queen's announcement of her own pregnancy in November hard to bear, especially when Catholics at court began predicting that Maria would have a son, who would not only supersede Mary and Anne in the succession but assure a continuing line of Catholic monarchs.

Over the course of the next nine months, Anne frequently expressed doubts about the authenticity of Maria's pregnancy. In March 1688, for example, she wrote skeptically to her sister, using the code name "Mansell" for the king:

> I must tell you I cant help thinking Mansells wifes great bely is a little suspitious. 'tis true indeed she is very big, but she looks better than ever she did, which is not usial, for people when thay are so far gon for the most part look very ill.... Her being so positive it will be a son, and the principles of that religeon being such that they will stick at nothing be it never so wicked if it will promote theire interest, gives one some cause to fear there may be foul play intended.[101]

Anne's behavior during this period has struck many as devious.[102] In this letter, however, her desire to spread doubt about the pregnancy shades into denial. The narrative of the future that she cherished, in which her own Protestant progeny would carry on the Stuart line, was coming apart. When she wrote this letter, the princess believed she was pregnant once more, but that pregnancy terminated in a serious illness in April, when she "miscarried of the embrio she was pregnant with; but for two nights before she seemed in danger of death."[103] Some of her own servants told her uncle Clarendon that Anne "had only had a false conception,"[104] and under the circumstances, it is certainly possible that she had an episode of pseudocyesis or "hysterical pregnancy." Among the common causes of this disease is a strong desire to be pregnant, which Anne certainly had.[105] Unfortunately, substantial evidence of her inner state is lacking for this period, as her surviving correspondence with Sarah Churchill includes no letters written between 1686 and 1691. Other observers, however, speak of the princess's "rage" at the queen's pregnancy; her mental strain was evidently visible.[106]

As soon as she was able to travel, Anne and George departed for Bath; they were therefore absent from London when Maria delivered a son on 10 June 1688, a month before her doctors had predicted she would give birth. The sudden, unexpected birth of the prince contributed to public doubts about his authenticity. Princess Mary later complained that Anne had made an irreparable error in not being present for the birth, while others believed she had deliberately stayed away, avoiding being a witness so that she could continue to cast doubt upon the legitimacy of the child. At an even simpler level, however, Anne had sufficient reasons to want to be away from the court after the physical and mental trauma of the previous year, and it is possible that she chose to go to Bath because it was the place where Maria had become pregnant the previous fall.[107]

With his usual poor timing, James increased the frustration of his subjects as Maria's time drew near by ordering his Declaration of Indulgence to be read in every parish church in the nation. As most of his subjects were still illiterate, the Church provided the monarch with an efficient way to communicate to his people. Charles II, when seeking support for his dissolution of the Oxford Parliament in 1681, had ordered his *Declaration to all His Loving Subjects, Touching the Causes & Reasons That moved Him to Dissolve the Two last Parliaments* read from every pulpit, and James presumably believed he was doing something similar. The Church leaders, however, were reluctant to promulgate a statement diminishing their own authority and communicating the king's desire that his subjects embrace Catholicism. On 18 May, seven bishops presented James with a petition asking him to rescind the requirement that they read his Declaration; they included Francis Turner, who had preached the coronation sermon, and Thomas White, who had been a chaplain to Princess Anne. In the text of their letter, the bishops cast doubt on the legal decision that had upheld the king's dispensing power. On 8 June, just two days before his queen delivered a son, James angrily charged them with seditious libel and sent them to the Tower. At Bath, Anne witnessed a farewell sermon preached by another of the seven, Thomas Ken, who was departing for London, where he knew he would be imprisoned. "Her Royal Highness," according to one newsletter, "seemed much concerned at his present trouble."[108]

When she learned that Maria had given birth, Anne hurried back to London and remained there until late July. In the highly charged atmosphere created by the ongoing confrontation between the king and the Church, she was not alone in questioning the authenticity of the new Prince of Wales. Among the rumors that gained credence was the idea that a child born to another mother had been smuggled into the room in a warming pan. Others conceded that Maria had given birth, but maintained that the child had soon died and had then been replaced by an impostor. Still others doubted that James was the father, contending that Maria was pregnant by one of the many Roman Catholic priests at court; in this version of the story, Archbishop d'Adda was a favorite candidate. As Anne channeled her personal frustration at the prince's birth into expressions of doubt and suspicion, the authors of ballads and broadsides articulated their political frustration at the prospect of a Catholic succession in scurrilous and obscene verses. "An excelent new Balad caled the Prince of Darknes, showing how Nations may be set on fire by a warming pan" is a typical example of the vulgar poems in circulation at this time. The anonymous author learns from "one of the Chairmen" that the baby "was born overnight & was born the next day."

> But noe body knows from which parish it came
> & that is the reason it has not a Name
> Good Catholicks al were afraid it was dying
> There was such abundance of Sh:[itting] & Crying

Which is a good Token by which we may sweare
It is the Queens owne & the Kingdoms right Heir
Now if we should Happen to have a true lad
from the Veynes of soe wholesome a mother & dad
Twere Hard to determine which blood were the best
That of Southwark or the Bastard of Este
But Now we have cause for thanksgiving Indeed
There was noe other way for mending the Breed.[109]

Of course there were official gestures of thanksgiving. Behn provided another courtly panegyric, and the University of Cambridge published a book of Latin, Greek, and English poems on the prince. All these effusions, however, were perfunctory and uncertain. Even Dryden, whose *Britannia Rediviva* is the best poem written on this occasion, felt constrained to acknowledge the existence of rumors casting doubt on the child's legitimacy:

Fain would the Fiends have made a dubious birth,
Loth to confess the Godhead cloath'd in Earth.
But sickned after all their baffled lyes,
To find an Heir apparent of the Skyes.[110]

He also took note of the prince's illnesses, which gave hope to Anne and others distressed by the infant's existence. In one of her least attractive moments, the princess wrote to her sister in July expressing these hopes: "The Prince of Wales has been ill 3 or 4 days, & if he has been as bad as some people say, I believe it will not be long before he is an Angel in Heaven."[111] Dryden, recalling the three children Maria had lost before, prayed for the prince's survival:

Enough of early Saints one Womb has giv'n,
Enough encreas'd the Family of Heav'n:
Let them for his, and our Attonement go;
And reigning blest above, leave him to Rule below.[112]

The most revealing feature of *Britannia Rediviva,* however, is the address to the king with which it concludes. Mindful of the errors James was making, Dryden praises him for choosing "Justice" as his "Darling Attribute," a clear instance of the panegyric technique that Erasmus had wittily described as "exhorting to virtue under the pretext of praise."[113] By contrasting James's supposed love of justice with the actions of tyrants, the laureate was indirectly warning the king against the intemperate policies he was pursuing. Appropriating the vocabulary of the opposition, he speaks of "boundless pow'r, and arbitrary Lust," the very features of James's reign that had turned so many against him.

> Some Kings the name of conqu'rors have assum'd,
> Some to be Great, some to be Gods presum'd;
> But boundless pow'r, and arbitrary Lust
> Made Tyrants still abhor the Name of Just;
> They shun'd the praise this Godlike Virtue gives,
> And fear'd a title that reproach'd their Lives.[114]

In a concluding triplet, Dryden praises the idea of balance, in the kingdom and the world:

> Equal to all, you justly frown or smile,
> Nor Hopes, nor Fears your steady Hand beguile;
> Your self our Balance hold, the Worlds, our Isle.[115] }

According to the compressed syntax of these lines, James holds the balance of domestic politics, while England holds the balance of European politics. But in truth James had seriously unbalanced the domestic situation by attempting to unite Catholics and Dissenters against the established church, and he was so pre-occupied with domestic strife that he had not exerted himself in the ongoing quarrel between Louis XIV and the rest of Europe.

On 17 July, Anne and George attended the official fireworks celebrating the birth of the prince; the displays included "the figure of a Woman (bigger than the Life) representing *Plenty* and *Peace,* adorn'd with all the usual Ensigns of *Plenty* and *Peace,* wrought all in Fireworks, wreaths Cornucopia's, *&c.*," and "a Woman much bigger than the Life, a Coronet on her Head, adorn'd with the proper Emblems of *Firmness,* or *Stability of Empire,* and on every quarter of the Stage Fireworks of different kinds."[116] Attended by thousands, these pyrotechnics were "very fine," according to Evelyn, "& had cost some thousands of pounds about the pyramids & statues &c.: but were spent too soone, for so long a preparation."[117] Many of those present, not least Anne, would have been aware of the contrast between this carefully staged event and the spontaneous bonfires with which Londoners had greeted the acquittal of the seven bishops on 30 June. Once again, James appears to have believed (or hoped) that he could counter a genuine out-pouring of political energy with a well-prepared allegorical performance. As with other royal allegories, however, some features of the display invited skepticism. The idea of representing such permanent values as peace, plenty, firmness, and

empire in ephemeral explosions was fanciful at best. Some doubt about the efficacy of the occasion may lurk behind Evelyn's complaint that the fireworks were
"spent too soone."

§

For many in the English establishment, the birth of the prince, coming as it did in the
midst of an ugly confrontation between king and Church, suggested the limits of a
policy of passive obedience. On the day the bishops were acquitted, seven leading
men, including the Bishop of London and the Earls of Danby, Devonshire, and
Shrewsbury, dispatched a letter to William of Orange inviting him to intervene. As
Behn tactlessly pointed out in her poem on the birth of the prince, William had cause
to be distressed because the birth increased his distance from the English throne:

> Methinks I hear the *Belgick LION* Roar
> And Lash his *Angry Tail* against the Shore.
> Inrag'd to hear a *PRINCE OF WALES* is *Born*:
> Whose *BROWS* his *Boasted Laurels* shall Adorn.[118]

In public, however, William and Mary behaved appropriately, ordering prayers
for the prince to be said in their chapel. But as William contemplated the situation, he evidently concluded that his opportunity to act was at hand, and began
to make serious plans for an invasion. Not least among his motives was the prospect of enlisting the English army and the English economy in his lifelong
struggle against the French. In *Britannia Rediviva,* Dryden had fondly imagined
"our Isle" holding the balance of power in the world, and William saw an opportunity to make that wish a military reality. Neither the poet nor the would-be
king could have known that the ultimate achievement of that goal would come in
the reign of Queen Anne.

The princess was probably aware of the invasion plans by the time she and
George left for Tunbridge Wells on 24 July, a week after the fireworks.[119] On 27
July, John and Sarah Churchill, who were up to their ears in the conspiracy, conveyed their estate at Sandridge to a trustee, a device intended to protect their
children's inheritance in case the invasion failed;[120] the missing letters that passed
between Anne and Sarah during this period, doubtless destroyed by Sarah as a
precaution, probably alluded in one way or another to William's plans. On 21
August, observers at court learned that the Denmarks were extending their stay in
Tunbridge Wells for another month; by the time they returned on 17 September,
there were news reports of a huge Dutch fleet preparing to sail for England.[121]
Although James was slow to believe that his son-in-law would invade his realm, he
eventually took both military and political action. But it was too late. To a greater

extent than he would ever have believed, the officer corps of his army was riddled with men ready to defect to the Prince of Orange. And when he tried to reverse most of his domestic initiatives of the past year, dismissing many Catholic office-holders and promising to summon a Parliament, the changes, which might otherwise have been welcome, were seen as a panicky attempt to win support in the face of an invasion. Nor could the king entirely reform his own stubbornness: on 15 October, he attended the long-delayed christening of his son in the Catholic chapel. The pope, represented by d'Adda, was the godfather, and Catharine of Braganza, widow of Charles II, was the godmother. "The Catholic court was fine," the newswriters reported, "and the show great."[122] Even as he prepared to fight for his crown, James still failed to grasp the extent to which this kind of "show" gave offense to many of his subjects.

When William landed at Torbay on 5 November, he brought with him an army of fifteen thousand men; unlike Monmouth's improbable attempt, this invasion was carefully planned and widely supported. During the debate over Catholic army officers in James's last Parliament, the Whig politician Thomas Wharton had written mock-Irish words to a catchy jig called *Lilliburlero,* and as support for William spread, people of all ranks were singing and whistling that tune, which became a musical signal of opposition to the Crown. Although none of the parties ever told the whole truth about their plans, the actions taken in November by Prince George, John Churchill, Sarah Churchill, and Princess Anne were evidently coordinated. Other players, such as Bishop Compton, were also well prepared; there was nothing improvised about Compton's arrival with the Earl of Dorset to collect Anne, Sarah, and Barbara Berkeley from the back stairs of Whitehall, or about the progress to the North that they subsequently undertook. By 2 December, Compton and the Earl of Devonshire were writing to William from Nottingham to report having "raised a force of about a thousand horse"—a formidable bodyguard for Princess Anne.[123] By the time Anne reached Oxford, her army had grown to more than five thousand. Bishop Compton, who was evidently enjoying a reprise of his earlier role as a military officer, led a symbolic entry into the city "at the head of a noble troop of gentlemen, . . . riding in a purple cloak, martial habit, pistols before him, and his sword drawn." There was no danger whatsoever that James's army, which had returned to London in disarray, would oppose Compton's forces, whose function was now theatrical and symbolic, as was the elaborate welcome staged by the university. Prince George, who was rejoining his wife in Oxford, also knew how to play his part; the newsletters reported that he "received her Royal Highness at Christ Church quadrangle, with all possible demonstrations of love and affection; and they will be to-morrow at Windsor."[124]

While Anne was pursuing her symbolic progress, her hapless father, who had already sent his wife and infant son to safety in France, made his first attempt to join them, only to be intercepted by some English sailors and sent back to London. On December 18, the day before his daughter returned from her journey, he left London for the last time, sailing to Rochester under guard, though he soon escaped and made his way to St. Germain. According to an anecdote first published in 1734, Sarah and Anne took this occasion to make an ostentatious appearance at the theatre:

> While the poor old King was...exposed to the Mercy of the Elements, and an actual Prisoner under a Guard of *Dutchmen,* that very Moment, his Daughter *Denmark,* with her great Favourite, both covered with Orange Ribbonds, in her Father's own Coaches, and attended by his Guards, went triumphant to the *Play-House.*[125]

Though highly circumstantial, this tale is inaccurate in at least one detail, as James sailed for Rochester a day before his daughter returned to London. An appearance by the princess and Lady Churchill at the theatre in symbolic dress, however, is just the kind of gesture that those planning the coup might have wished to include in the script. During his short reign, James had frequently attended plays;[126] Anne's presence at the theatre was thus a way of claiming royal status as a patroness of drama. If the princess was technically a member of the audience on this occasion, she was also playing a role, as she had done fourteen years earlier in *Calisto* and seven years earlier in *Mithridates.*

In one important area, however, the script appears to have been incomplete: there was no agreement about the endgame. Even Sarah, the most convinced Whig in Anne's circle, later claimed to have believed that William's invasion would have the effect of forcing James to respect the laws and traditions of England and that William would return to Holland once this goal was accomplished.[127] When James fled to France, the confusion about what to do increased. Some favored a regency; others wished to crown Mary. When William made it clear that he wanted the crown for himself and threatened to return to Holland if he were not put in power, the Convention assembled to settle the state acceded to his wishes. Inventing a convenient pretext, they declared the throne vacant by ruling that James's departure amounted to an abdication. The "abdication" was a fiction, as James still regarded himself as king and would soon invade Ireland to press his claim, but it served the purpose at hand. With all parties tacitly agreeing to ignore the Prince of Wales, the legal succession should have run from Mary (James's eldest daughter) to Anne (his younger daughter) to William (in line because he was a grandson of Charles I, not because of his marriage). But William, now widely regarded as the savior of the nation, was in a position to reject this arrangement, and the Convention ultimately crowned him jointly with his wife, stipulating that he would continue to rule if she died, and settling the succession thereafter on his children by Mary (nonexistent and unlikely), followed by Anne and her children, followed by any children William might have by a second wife.

When the dust had cleared, Anne was in a better position than she might have been if James had continued to rule, but in a worse position than she had reason to expect. There is no direct evidence of how she felt about this outcome. Sir John Reresby later claimed that the Earl of Scarsdale, who was a Gentleman of the Bedchamber to George, told him that "the Princess of Denmarke was very sensible what a mistake she had committed to leave her father to come into the Prince, who was now endeavouring to invade her right and to gett priority of sucession before her."[128] Anne might well have expressed such thoughts, but she did not act on them. Her first biographer, Abel Boyer, is probably correct in giving Sarah Churchill credit for persuading the princess to support the Revolution Settlement:

> Though all concurr'd in lodging the Administration of Affairs in the Hands of the Prince of *Orange,* yet various were their Opinions as to the Title they should bestow on him; some being for making him *Regent* or *Protector,* and others, *King.* Nay, the latter appear'd divided into Three Parties, some maintaining, that the Princess of *Orange,* as next Heir, ought to be crowned alone, and the Prince to manage Affairs, as King only in the Right of his Consort; others being for making his Highness King singly; and the Majority for advancing both him and his Royal Consort to the Throne. This last Scheme being, in great Measure, derogatory to the Princess *Anne* of *Denmark*'s Title to the Crown, next after her Sister, 'twas justly apprehended that her Royal Highness, who had a considerable Party in both Houses, would hardly have consented to it: But, however, this Obstacle was soon after removed; her Royal Highness being prevail'd with (chiefly by the Persuasion of Lady *Churchill)* to prefer the Publick Good, and the Security of the Protestant Religion, before her private Interest.[129]

Although a decision about whether to dispute the succession was obviously of greater weight than a decision about the fate of an impertinent musician, Anne's letter about Edward Greeting is relevant evidence here, suggesting the validity of Boyer's account. "I will ever obey my deare Lady Churchills commands," Anne had written, "since I am sure you will never desire anything but what is reasonable." At this critical juncture, Anne's need to please her favorite was again a powerful motive, and Sarah, a more natural politician than the princess, quickly recognized that Anne's options were limited. Her own account suggests what she might have said to her royal mistress on this occasion: "had I been in her place," writes Sarah, "I should have thought it more for my honour to be easy in this matter than to shew an impatience to get possession of a crown that had been wrested from my father." For Anne, with her lifelong concern for honorable behavior, this argument may have carried some weight, especially when Sarah enlisted the prominent clergyman John Tillotson, later Archbishop of Canterbury, to persuade the princess of the "*expediency of the settlement proposed, as things were then situated.*"[130] For Tillotson, Lady Marlborough, and the nation, the patched-together settlement of 1689, despite its dubious legality, ultimately seemed more reasonable than any other alternative. Its consequences, however, would haunt Queen Anne throughout her reign, as the child born in 1688, evidently a legitimate son of James and Maria, continued to represent the claims of tradition for many of her subjects.

The one surviving anecdote describing Anne's behavior on 13 February 1689, when William and Mary were proclaimed, is curious but inconclusive. Speaking on behalf of the Convention, George Savile, Marquess of Halifax, formally asked the new monarchs to accept the crown at a ceremony in the Whitehall Banqueting House, a symbolic site that allowed William to emphasize his connections to the Stuarts. In a room decorated with paintings by Rubens celebrating the reign of James I, great-grandfather to both William and Mary, the new royal couple took their seats in chairs of state beneath a symbolic canopy. Most of those in the room were standing, but Anne, as a princess, had the right to be seated in the presence of the new monarchs. The servants, however, placed her tabouret (a formal stool used on such occasions) too close to Mary's chair, so that it was under the canopy of state, and Anne refused to be seated until the stool was moved.[131] This punctilious behavior was in keeping with her lifelong attention to protocol and etiquette, but perhaps it was also a small way of distancing herself from the Revolution Settlement. Although she had shared a canopy "supported by *Africans*" with her sister some fourteen years earlier in *Calisto,* she was careful not to share this canopy.

As she watched the coronation a few months later, Anne's emotions were doubtless mixed. Although she had been instrumental in bringing about the change in government, she had also made a significant sacrifice in acceding to the wishes of the Convention. In acting to preserve the established church, she had followed one of her most fundamental allegiances, but in order to do so, she had shirked her duties as a daughter and a subject. For all the enthusiasm with which the nation was greeting its new monarchs, the old king was still an active threat; he had landed in Ireland on 12 March and was now at the head of a formidable army there. As she had been in 1685, Anne was now in the later stages of a real pregnancy, and she knew that the hopes of the nation were focused on her. A living child, especially a son, would prove an emotional and political counterweight to the infant now at St. Germain and would remind her sister and the nation of her own importance in enabling a Protestant succession. As the choir again urged the congregation to "pray for the peace of Jerusalem," Anne might well have prayed for a healthy son.

CHAPTER 4

SHE REIGNS WITHOUT A CROWN

24 July 1695

Precocious and delicate, William Duke of Gloucester, beloved son of Princess Anne, reviewed his troop of youthful soldiers. It was his sixth birthday, and a group of older boys, "armed with wooden swords and muskets, wearing red grenadiers caps," had gathered to perform military drills in his honor. The little duke's own costume included a long basket-hilted sword like those worn by the Scottish dragoons who served his uncle and namesake, King William III. On this important day, as on the birthdays of the king and his parents, Gloucester proudly fired a salute "by discharging seven guns he had, viz. four iron ones, given him at Tunbridge, and two others, bought at Windsor, and a very fine one made by order of Prince Rupert, which the governor of Windsor-castle gave him, besides his small guns; all these were discharged six times round."

Jenkin Lewis, Gloucester's Welsh body servant, provides these details in his touching memoir of the duke's royal childhood. When William was four, says Lewis, his private army had twenty-two boys; by the time he was five, it had grown to ninety. "The boys were ordered to come on holidays, and in the afternoon on Saturdays, when they were exercised by the Duke very often" at Campden House, his home in Kensington, chosen by his mother for its healthy air.[1] For his sixth birthday, at least part of this army would have assembled at Windsor, where Gloucester was spending the summer with his parents.[2] Four older boys "had leave to wait upon the Duke from Eaton school, when he would have a little battle fought in St. George's Hall; whither he had his musquets, pikes, great swords, and artillery carried, being a dozen or fifteen in number."[3] These companions, selected with care as role models, included a son of Sarah Churchill and two sons of Frances Bathurst (née Apsley), to whom Anne had written passionate letters as a girl. By appointing the sons of her own childhood playmates as attendants for her precious boy, Anne was modeling his childhood on hers, though Gloucester's up-bringing as a sole surviving male was necessarily different from Anne's as a younger daughter.

On the day before the birthday, Hugh Boscawen, at sixteen the oldest of the Eton playmates, took the lead role in hunting a stag that the Ranger of Windsor Park had presented to Gloucester as a gift. Although the duke was too young to ride on horseback, he put on boots and spurs and followed the mounted hunters in his coach. Lewis, who was present, reports that Boscawen "took great pains with all who hunted to have the wounded deer driven toward the Duke's coach . . . in order that he might see most of the sport." When the animal's throat was cut, Samuel Masham, a page to Prince George, "came sideways, after dipping his hand in the blood, and on a sudden besmeared the Duke's face; who was a little sur-prised!" Despite the shock, the boy overcame his revulsion and made sure that his mother shared the experience: "being told it was customary at first seeing a deer killed, he had his face besmeared all over; and then he besmeared me, and his boys; with which we went home; and when he came opposite to the Princess's a-partment, he ordered us to hallow loud, by way of triumph."[4]

Anne, who remained an avid huntress, was also unable to ride—in her case because she was now too heavy to mount. Her current practice was to follow the chase in an open carriage, and Windsor Forest, with its wide pathways, was well suited to this sport. Seeing her son initiated into the rites of hunting, however su-perficially, would have pleased her greatly, especially in light of the health prob-lems he had experienced. Although advanced in mental attainments, the child had been backward in developing physical competence. He was so slow in learning to walk that his father lost patience and beat him, and his head was enormous, appar-ently because he suffered from hydrocephalus. "His hat," says the faithful Lewis, "was big enough for most men," and it was "difficult to fit his head with a peruke." Anne's maternal concern for her child was visible: "if he tottered whenever he walked in her presence, it threw her into a violent perspiration, thro' fear." In seek-ing a remedy for her son's uncertain balance, she turned again to her own child-hood training. When she "thought it high time to have him taught to walk regu-larly, so by degrees to dance," she brought her old French dancing master, Jeremiah Gohory, out of retirement to teach him, and the lessons were apparently effective. Lewis records that the duke "was perfectly easy and graceful, made an elegant bow," and took part in amateur theatricals, as his mother had done before him: "In little attempts toward acting plays in the family, for his entertainment, the Duke would act the part of a Prince himself, prettily and gracefully."[5]

In keeping with Anne's desire to expose her son to courtly arts, the birthday celebration in 1695 included a new piece of music composed for the occasion by Henry Purcell.[6] As "Composer in ordinary," Purcell's primary responsibility was to the reigning monarch, but he also offered many services to Princess Anne, who was more knowledgeable about music than her father or her sister—not to mention her tone-deaf brother-in-law. Not all of this music has survived. Recent research has identified some tantalizing fragments as the remains of an ode Purcell composed to celebrate the birth of Gloucester in 1689;[7] he may also have written other birthday pieces, now lost, for the beloved son of his musical patroness. Perhaps the music for Gloucester's sixth birthday escaped destruction because it turned out to be the composer's last substantial work. He died just four months after the little duke's birthday, and his widow recognized decades of patronage by dedicating a posthumous collection of his works for the harpsichord "To Her Royal Highness the Princess of Denmark," praising Anne for her "Generous Encouragement of my deceasd Husbands Performances in Musick."[8]

At first blush, the anonymous text for the birthday ode looks completely conventional, but some details reflect the political situation of 1695. Celebrating "this pleasing, shining, Wond'rous Day" when "the Sun has all his Summer's Glories on," the poet declares that it has "brighter Splendour far / From a little rising Star." Twenty years earlier, John Crowne had called Gloucester's mother "a little Star" in *Calisto*; still active in the 1690s, Crowne had seen two of his recent plays produced with music by Purcell and is thus a plausible candidate for the authorship of this ode.[9] Although poets writing court odes inevitably engaged in flattery, the superlatives in this birthday ode are especially excessive. By calling Gloucester a "Prince of Glorious Race descended," the poet creates a pretext for a pair of stanzas praising the royal parents for their courage and beauty. Although he gives the father only three lines, he exaggerates the Prince of Denmark's military career to the point of absurdity:

> The Father's Brave as e're was Dane,
> Whose Thund'ring Sword has thousands slain
> And made him o're half Europe Reign.[10]

As the younger son of the king of a small country and the often-forgotten consort of the heir to the English throne, Prince George could hardly be said to reign over half of Europe. For the last six years, King William had been expending British men and money in an effort to thwart Louis XIV's efforts to dominate the

Continent, yet even the French did not control half of Europe. Facts, however, had never dissuaded Crowne from flattery. His praise of the Dukes of York and Monmouth in *Calisto* had been similarly superlative:

> Two Heroes of his own Celestial Race
> Are sent; the one to Triumph o're the Seas,
> And all the watery Divinities.
> The other, Monsters of the Land to quell,
>   And make the Nymphs in safety dwell.[11]

In the earlier example, the poet's hyperbolical praise of James was presumably an attempt to efface the fact that the Test Act of 1673 had forced him to resign his military posts. In the later example, the praise of George's "Thund'ring Sword" may be an attempt to salve the wounds inflicted on his military pride by his arrogant in-laws. In 1690, when Gloucester was one year old, Prince George had traveled to Ireland at his own expense in order to take part in King William's campaign against James II, whose forces then controlled most of that kingdom. As earnest of his seriousness, he dismissed his Groom of the Stole and Master of the Horse when they declined to accompany him, but once he arrived in Ireland, he found himself completely ignored by the king, who refused to offer his brother-in-law a place in the royal coach. This disrespect continued after William's decisive victory at the Battle of the Boyne, which might have been an occasion for better manners, and even after a cannonball aimed at William's tent killed two of George's horses. A year later, the prince made plans to embark with the English fleet for the summer's campaign against the French, but at the last minute, when his baggage was already stowed on the chosen ship, Queen Mary ordered him "not to hazard himself on board the fleet."[12] With the Protestant succession dependent on the frail infant Gloucester, Mary's stated desire to protect a man capable of begetting more heirs was plausible, but she was also unwilling for her sister's husband to gain glory or attention at a time when her own husband's clout as a monarch depended upon his success in war.

By now, George's dreams of military glory were fading; he had suffered from asthma for years and was ill enough in June to be "blooded and blistred."[13] The poet nonetheless believed he would appreciate being praised for the courage he had shown in his youth. The composer, perhaps remembering how he had used John Gostling's bass voice to celebrate the prince's martial prowess in his music for the wedding, set the lines in praise of George's bravery as a bass aria, emphasizing "Thund'ring" and "thousands" through repetition and rhythmic stress.

The bass singer on this occasion, "Mr. Woodeson," did not have Gostling's low range, though the vocal compass of this passage is still nearly two octaves. But

Mus. Ex. 4.1: Henry Purcell, excerpt from *Who can from Joy Refrain?* (1695).

if Purcell placed his usual technical demands on his soloist, he was cautious in his harmonic language, avoiding the expressive dissonances of the wedding music. There is something almost perfunctory about this setting, as if Purcell were going through the motions, perhaps because he was aware that George's "Thund'ring Sword" was a thing of the past, now chiefly invoked as an inspiration to his son.

To praise George as a military hero was nonetheless risky in light of King William's frustrations in the Nine Years' War, and the stanza in which the poet paid court to Anne might easily be read as praising the princess at the expense of the king:

> The Graces in his Mother Shine
> Of all the Beauties, Saints, and Queens
> And Martyrs of her Line.
> She's great, Let Fortune Smile or Frown,
> Her Virtues make all Hearts her own:
> She reigns without a Crown.

Extolling royal persons for their ancestry was a predictable gesture, but at this moment even conventional language took on fresh meaning. As everyone knew, William's relation to the "Line" of Stuart monarchs was less direct than Anne's; both were grandchildren of the "Martyr" Charles I, but Anne was the daughter of a king. The reference to "Beauties, Saints, and Queens" was also poignant: some six months before this birthday party, Queen Mary had died of the smallpox, and the poems on her death repeatedly invoked her as saintly and beautiful. Although the royal sisters had actually been estranged at the time of Mary's death, the poet evidently hoped that some of the sentimental affection felt for her dead sister might now be transferred to Anne. No longer protected by his consort, William was increasingly unpopular. The high taxes, standing army, and dourly ascetic court of the frequently absent king left many longing for the "Graces" they remembered from some previous Stuart monarchs, especially Charles II. This stanza's conclusion—"She reigns without a Crown"—reflects the impatience of those who looked forward to Anne's accession. But it was at best tactless and at worst dangerous: to suggest that anyone might reign without a crown was to return to the rhetoric that had surrounded the Duke of Monmouth during the Exclusion Crisis.[14]

Perhaps aware that this line might be offensive to the king's supporters, Purcell set it only once and surrounded it with two longer settings of the previous line—"Her Virtues make all Hearts her own"—a safer expression of Anne's growing popularity. He devotes eleven measures to the line about Anne's virtues, stretching it out with extensive melismatic treatments of the word *all*, disposes of the line about reigning without a crown in only six measures, then returns to the words of the penultimate line for another eighteen measures. The musical setting thus alters the rhetoric of the poem, moving what had been a climactic and cadential line in the poem into a much less prominent position. "Composer in ordinary" to Charles II, James II, and William III, Purcell had recently written touching music for Queen Mary's funeral. He had good reasons to look forward to the accession of Anne, who knew more about music than her predecessors, but he had far too much tact to crown her prematurely.

In deference to Gloucester's obsession with warfare, the poet devoted the second half of his ode to predictions of the duke's success in battle:

Mus. Ex. 4.2: Henry Purcell, excerpt from *Who can from Joy Refrain?* (1695).

> Sound the Trumpet, and beat the Warlike Drumms:
> The Prince will be with Laurells Crown'd,
> Before his Manhood Comes.

The conventional imagery of trumpets and drums had specific resonance for Gloucester. A few years earlier, when his army of boys performed their exercises for the king and queen, the king "took particular notice of one, six years old, by name William Gardner, remarkable for beating the drum, almost equal to the ablest drummer: to him the King gave two pieces of gold." And when one of Gloucester's servants drank himself to death, the boy requested a man named Docker as a replacement; this preference, says Lewis, "proceeded from Docker's sounding the trumpet."[15] Fortunately for Purcell, Docker was not the only person at Windsor who could sound the trumpet. The small wind band in residence at the court of Prince George and Princess Anne included John Shore, the most gifted member of a family of trumpeters, and Purcell wrote brilliant solos for Shore in this part of the ode, probably hoping to please the little duke.

If Prince George, with considerable poetic license, was said to reign over half of Europe, his fragile son was expected to conquer the world:

> If now he burns with noble Flame,
> When Grown, what will he doe?
> From Pole to Pole he'l stretch his Fame
> And all the World subdue.

In a setting featuring Shore's trumpet, Purcell gave these lines to two boy sopranos, singers not much older than Gloucester, using matching melismatic figures to express the hope that the boy duke would *grow* to adulthood and *stretch* his fame.

Mus. Ex. 4.3: Henry Purcell, excerpt from *Who can from Joy Refrain?* (1695).

Mus. Ex. 4.4: Henry Purcell, excerpt from *Who can from Joy Refrain?* (1695).

Though couched in poetic and musical hyperbole, these fanciful predictions of world conquest were not without political implications for the current situation. At this very moment, William III was engaged in the siege of Namur, one of the most costly actions of the Nine Years' War. After heavy losses on both sides, the fortress would capitulate on 4 September 1695, but that welcome success did not change the essential character of the war, in which Dutch and English forces struggled against the French in Flanders, expending thousands of men without a decisive result. The dream of a king who could subdue the world was an understandable response to the current stalemate, but it was no more realistic than Gloucester's childish belief that his army of boys was prepared for actual combat.

In his closing stanza, the poet used an allegory of rivers to express a fantasy of world domination:

> Then Thames shall be Queen
> Of Tyber and Seine,
> Of Nilus, of Indus, and Ganges
> And, without forreign aid,
> Our Fleets be obey'd
> Wherever the Wide Ocean Ranges.

The trope of the Thames or the port of London as a queen had already appeared in the closing stanzas of *Annus Mirabilis,* the prologue to *Ariane,* and the prologue to *Calisto,* which placed particular emphasis on the bogus claim that Charles II would "Command (as all his Right allow) / The Empire of the Main."[16] If Crowne was indeed the author of this ode, he would have had a vivid memory of Moll Davis's performance as the river Thames in his earlier masque, receiving the tributes of the four continents. In the current climate, however, the hope for a queen who could achieve naval dominance "without forreign aid" might easily be read as another covert criticism of the current regime. William's navy had suffered some serious defeats during the past five years, and many were displeased with the king's dependence on the Dutch alliance in his struggles with the French.

§

It is not now possible to know whether Princess Anne and Prince George noticed all the political implications of this ode or sensed Purcell's efforts to soften some of its content. But celebrations of Gloucester's birthday were always political. To mark another year of his life was to focus on a future reign for which his parents fervently prayed. The ode's rhetorical question—"When Grown, what will he doe?"—was an expression of the widespread hope that this delicate child, who represented the best chance for a Protestant Stuart succession, would outgrow his frailties and succeed to the throne. From the moment of his birth, Gloucester's survival was vital for the nation and his mother, whose efforts to produce another child continued to prove fruitless. Decades later, Abel Boyer claimed that the boy's "auspicious Birth contributed much to dissipate the distant Fears of a *Popish* Successor";[17] at the time, however, those fears were hardly "distant." When Princess Anne delivered her long-awaited son on 24 July 1689, the Catholic Prince of Wales was thriving in St. Germain, and James II's army in Ireland, already in control of Dublin and much of the South, was besieging the city of Derry. If Derry fell, the Catholic army planned to use northern Ireland as a base for an invasion of Scotland, with the reconquest of England as its eventual goal. News that the siege had been relieved by English naval forces reached London ten days after the birth of Gloucester. In her diary, Queen Mary linked the raising of the siege and the survival of the child as "marcks of God's favour,"[18] but it would take several more years and direct intervention from William to put down the Irish revolt.

Aware that their position was strengthened by the birth of Anne's son, the new monarchs took a keen interest in him. When Bishop Compton baptized the baby on 27 July, the king stood godfather, along with the Earl of Dorset, who was officially representing the King of Denmark, Prince George's elder brother. For Anne, this constellation of sponsors had political and personal significance. Her son could claim two kings as his godfathers, while she herself could enjoy sharing this joyous occasion with Dorset and Compton, who had helped her make her midnight escape from Whitehall in the early days of the Revolution. "Some Days after" the christening, Boyer continues, "'twas moved in the House of Commons, to advance her Royal Highness's Revenue from Thirty Thousand to Seventy Thousand Pounds."[19] When the issue was finally settled in December, the increase to Anne's income was £50,000, giving her a total income of £80,000. Her struggle to gain that independent income pitted her against her sister Mary, who opposed any additional grant to the Denmarks; this quarrel was among the many disagreements that led the sisters to become permanently estranged in 1692.

Although there had actually been parliamentary discussions of an establishment for Anne as early as the previous March, Boyer's juxtaposition of the birth of an heir and the voting of an income shrewdly underscores the value a grateful nation placed on Anne's success in bearing a son. Even Queen Mary, in the years between her rupture with Anne and her death, was careful to invite the boy duke to visit her on her birthdays.

From the very beginning, however, the child's survival was in doubt. Jenkin Lewis attributes his delicate constitution to the stress his mother underwent during her pregnancy:

> He was a very weakly child; and most people believed he would not live long: which is the less to be wondered at, as the Princess was breeding with him when, constrained by necessity, she took the painful journey [to the North], in the gloomy month of November, with dejected spirits and an aching heart.[20]

Slipping down the back stairs to avoid confronting her father may have been traumatic for Anne, but witnesses who saw her a few days later in Nottingham described her as "wonderful pleasant and cheerful."[21] With Sarah at her side, she appears to have treated her progress to the North as a grand adventure, and she was at a very early stage of her pregnancy in December 1688. Little William's poor health, like that of his short-lived siblings, was probably genetic in origin.[22] As Lewis tells the story, there were frequent changes of wet-nurses in the first few months of Gloucester's life, during which he had convulsive fits that his doctors were unable to control:

> The Duke being given over by the physicians, all encouragement was offered for anyone who could find a remedy for convulsion fits. Among the country women that attended, Mrs. Pack, the wife of a Quaker, came from Kingston-Wick, with a young child in her arms of a month old, to speak of a remedy which had restored her children. As she sat in the presence room, Prince George of Denmark happened to pass by; and observing her to be a strong, healthy woman, he ordered her to go to bed to the young prince, who soon sucked her, and mended that night, continuing well whilst she suckled him.[23]

This pattern of serious illness, despair, and miraculous recovery would be repeated frequently during Gloucester's life; Anne's letters record her constant concern about his health. In 1692, for example, she considered taking him with her to Bath, but finally chose not to do so: "I had better be from him five or six weeks," she concluded, "then run the hazard of his meeting with any accident that one may have cause to repent of ones whole life."[24] Later in the same year, she acknowledged his unusual appearance: "my boy," she wrote to Sarah, "continues yet very well & looks better I think then ever he did in his life, I meane more healthy for tho I love him very well I cant brag of his beauty."[25] Even in carefully posed portraits, such as one made by Kneller in 1691, the boy's large head is apparent.

John Smith, *William, Duke of Gloucester*, mezzotint after Sir Godfrey Kneller (1691).

During the years of Gloucester's boyhood, Anne fretted constantly over his health while enduring four more unsuccessful pregnancies: a daughter, born 14 October 1690, lived for just two hours; a second son, George, born 17 April 1692, lived only minutes; and there were miscarriages on 23 March 1693 and 21 January 1694.[26] Although she was still in her twenties, these nearly continuous pregnancies accelerated the process by which Anne became an invalid; she often complained of being "on the rack" with physical pain.[27] When Purcell's opera *The Fairy Queen* came on stage in 1692, not long after one of these failed deliveries, Anne wrote to Sarah complaining that she was too lame and feverish to go to the theatre:

> I fancy now you are in Town you will be tempted to see the Opera which I shall not wonder at for I should be so too if I were able to stir but when that will be God knows for my feavor is not quite gone & I am still soo Lame I cannot goe without limping.[28]

For Anne, who had enjoyed daily riding and vigorous dancing a few years earlier, these nagging ailments were troublesome; they fed her jealousy of those more able to get around. In the same letter, the princess urged her favorite not to go to the opera with their mutual friend Barbara Berkeley, of whom she was becoming increasingly jealous:

> I hope Mrs freeman has noe thoughts of going to the Opera with Mrs. Hill [a code name for Barbara], & will have a care of engageing herselfe so much into her Company, for if you give way to that it is a thing that will insensible grow upon you; therefore give me Leave once more to beg for your own sake as well as poor Mrs. Morleys that you have as little to do with that Enchantress as possible, & pray pardon me for saying this.

The shows called operas in this period typically featured elaborate sets and magical themes: Charles Davenant's *Circe,* with an enchantress as its title character, was revived in June 1689 and performed at court in November 1690; Dryden and Purcell's *King Arthur,* featuring rival enchanters and thrilling illusions, opened in June 1691, with additional performances during the winter season. Anne was attempting a witticism by casting Barbara as an operatic "Enchantress," but her humor does not conceal her pain at the thought of Sarah's spending time in her rival's company.

Barbara's fortunes had changed since the Revolution. With the birth of the little duke of Gloucester, she resumed her position as governess to Anne's children; and in 1690, her husband, already Master of the Horse to the princess,

Sir Godfrey Kneller, *Barbara,Viscountess Fitzharding and Sarah, Duchess of Marlborough* (1691).

inherited an Irish title, becoming Viscount Fitzharding. Although the new Lady Fitzharding had been close to Anne and Sarah since all three were girls, Anne now found her company difficult:

> Ever since I came to this place Lady Fitzharding has bin the Spleenatick-
> est out of humour creature that ever was seen when she has bin with me,
> tho to all others she has bin very easy, but it does not att all afflict me, nor
> nothing can as long as my deare deare Mrs Freeman continues kind, her
> friendship being one of the things I value most which I would not loos to
> be Empress of the World.[29]

Although Anne characteristically protests that Barbara's ill humor "does not att all afflict me," her language, including the wonderful coinage "Spleenatickest," reveals that she was irritated, and with cause. Barbara was not only a rival for the attentions of Sarah, but a troublemaker in Anne's increasingly difficult relations with Queen Mary. Her sister Elizabeth Villiers had been William's mistress since 1680, so she enjoyed easy access to the new court, and it soon became evident to both Anne and Sarah that their childhood companion was conveying informa-tion about private conversations in the Cockpit to the new monarchs. When Sarah nonetheless continued to visit her old friend, Anne lost patience, dismiss-ing Barbara as "a jade" and declaring that "none of her family weare ever good for any thing."[30]

In another letter to Sarah, Anne reported observing a flirtation between her husband and Elizabeth Lawrence, the second wife of Edward Griffith, the prince's Secretary.[31] Griffith owed his court position to his connection with the Marlbor-oughs. His first wife was Sarah's sister Barbara Jenyns, who died in 1679, and Sarah continued to refer to him as "my Brother" for decades. The new Mrs. Griffith, young and vivacious, was a talented mimic; "at my request," wrote Anne to Sarah, she "mimiked you & severall others; Lady Fretchevill she dos much the best but for your self she dos over act you."[32] Anne was less amused, however, when she began to suspect that Elizabeth was angling for her husband:

> As for the complaints I made of some mortifications I had upon me,
> M.M. [i.e., Mr. Morley, a code name for George] has bin the occasion of
> them being grown very coquett to duck [a nickname for Elizabeth
> Griffith] who I see likes it very well & I don't doubt would be very willing
> if there weare opertunity to be better acquainted. This is a thing I have
> seen coming a good while & have bin often going to tell my deare Mrs
> Freeman of it but still hoped it would not last, & now finding it dos con-
> tinue I confess seeing it as I do very often makes me very uneasy.[33]

If the date usually assigned to this letter is correct, this moment of "mortification" came when Anne was in the advanced stages of her sixteenth pregnancy. If she felt unattractive and awkward, those feelings may have contributed to her being "uneasy" about seeing George show interest in another woman.

Anne's next letter to Sarah makes it clear that Sarah had shrewdly pretended not to understand her friend's fears:

> Since you do not understand what I meane by one part of my last, I will
> not explain it, tho I must own some things have happen'd of late that have
> given me some mortifications, but the fresh assurances you give me has
> revived my drooping spiritts, & I realy beleeve one kind word from deare
> Mrs Freeman would save me if I weare gasping.[34]

Her frequent "drooping spiritts" during this period may help explain the intensity of Anne's need for Sarah's emotional support, which she took practical steps to secure. The post of Groom of the Stole carried an annual salary of £400, a substantial sum, but Anne soon sought to improve Sarah's compensation. In 1691, she offered her favorite an additional pension: "I have designed ever since my revenue was seteled to desire you to acsept of a thousand pound a yeare from the faithfullest of your servants."[35] The linking of the pension to the "settling" of the princess's revenue was her way of expressing her gratitude for Sarah's help in the political struggle over her finances, but she also made this generous grant in order to claim her friend's continuing, constant attention. The phrase she uses in closing—"the faithfullest of your servants"—betrays again her jealousy of Lady Fitzharding, or indeed of any other woman desiring Sarah's company. Only when speaking of Marlborough himself did Anne consent to be second in Sarah's affections, and even then, her expression is equivocal: "I hope that next to Ld Churchill I may claim the *first* place in your heart," she wrote not long after her own marriage. A deferential yet wistful letter from October 1692, which Marlborough was to carry to his wife, sounds the same note:

> Mr Freeman having bin so kind to give himself the trouble to com hither
> to night, I cant help writing by him tho I have hardly any thing to say &
> beleeve a letter from Mrs Morely will be less mist when he is with deare
> Mrs Freeman than at another time.[36]

§

Her declining physical health, her maternal worries about her sickly child, and her various jealousies loom large in Anne's correspondence during these years, but her most serious problem was her growing estrangement from the queen. In addition to the confrontational dispute over Anne's request to Parliament for a separate maintenance, the sisters quarreled over Anne's lodgings in Whitehall, which were expanded to make room for the establishment of the little Duke of Gloucester. Issues of status were also contentious, as Anne believed her husband deserved more honor and respect than the new monarchs were willing to show him. Political groups of various kinds sometimes sought to portray the growing rift between the sisters as partisan, but it was fundamentally a matter of taste and personality. "The Queen & I," wrote Anne to Sarah in 1691, "are of very different humours."[37] Although they had been taught by the same musicians and dancing masters, they now had quite different tastes in the arts, which played an important part in their quarrel, giving both sisters indirect ways of expressing their personal and political beliefs.

When Mary returned to England in 1689, she had not seen Anne for ten years. Although she expressed joy at finding her sister "going on well with her big belly," their differences soon became apparent. Mary, who had become accustomed to a quiet, pious life in Holland, found the religious services in the English court too formal and ostentatious for her taste:

> I found a great change in my life, from a strickt retirement where I led the life of a nun, I was come into a noisy world full of vanity; from having publick prayers four times a day, to have hardly leisure to go twice, and that in such a crowd, with so much formality and litle devotion, that I was surprised.

Flexing her muscles as queen, she immediately tried to reform the liturgical practices of the Chapel Royal, making them simpler, less ornate, less "popish," and this reform program brought her into conflict with Bishop Compton, Dean of the Chapel and Anne's lifelong spiritual advisor. In recounting her attempt to alter the customs surrounding Communion, Mary describes Compton, who was an implacable foe of Catholicism and a strong supporter of the Revolution, as an "unreasonable" advocate of traditions that she dismisses as "foolery":

> There was an old custom left since the time of Popery, that the kings should receive almost alone; this had been alwais observed, this I could not resolve to do, but told the Bishop of London, who I found unreasonable upon that, and would keep up the foolery, but at last I got the better, and the king being of my mind, we resolved to make it a matter of as litle state as possible.[38]

For Anne, who was accustomed to receiving the sacrament "almost alone," who took pleasure in pomp and ceremony, and who counted Compton among her most loyal adherents, the new queen's getting the better of the bishop on this issue was an unwelcome reminder of her own loss of status under the new regime.

Mary's reform program for the chapel also had unfortunate consequences for the history of English music. During the reign of James II, the monarch had worshiped in the splendidly decorated Catholic chapel, which had a separate musical establishment (largely foreign), while Anglican services, loyally attended by Princess Anne, continued at the Chapel Royal. During those years, Henry Purcell, who was the organist, pleased the princess by composing several "symphony anthems," works involving stringed instruments, soloists, and the choir. All too aware of her father's elaborate music in the Catholic chapel, Anne did not want the Anglican services to appear inferior.[39] So when Mary, early in 1689, issued a command banning instruments from the chapel and replacing sung prayers with a spoken liturgy, she was altering a practice Anne had worked hard to sustain. According to Purcell's most recent biographer, "the royal intervention marked the beginning of a sharp decline in the Chapel Royal—not only in the importance and rich scoring of the music itself but also in the morale of the musicians and hence, inevitably, in standards of performance."[40] As in the case of Mary's quarrel with Compton, this clipping of Purcell's wings was felt as an insult by Princess Anne, who regarded attacks on those who served her as personal affronts.

In place of the music that had previously graced the chapel came a second sermon, delivered on Sunday afternoon. Mary believed that this innovation "pleased… most sober people" and complained that her sister "affected to find fault with every thing was done, especially to laugh at afternoon Sermons."[41] Anne's laughter, however, was probably an attempt to seem unconcerned about a distressing attack on forms and rituals she had found comforting in trying times. Three years later, when Mary peevishly ordered the mayor of Bath not to show her sister the customary honor and respect with which she was used to being treated, including attending her at church, Anne dismissed the insult as "a thing to be laughed at."[42] But this was bravado. For the princess, who had provided a focal point for Anglican loyalists by defying her father's attempts to convert her and keeping up her attendance at the Chapel Royal, the new queen's reduction of the musical portion of the morning service was not a small matter. If she put on a brave face by treating the afternoon sermon as "a thing to be laughed at," she nonetheless experienced it as a "mortification."

Worse yet, the attitude of the new court toward music proved to be more than a matter of puritanical scruples about anthems. William and Mary now significantly reduced the size of the royal band, from thirty-nine to twenty-four,[43] and showed scant respect for Anne's favorite composer. According to an anecdote

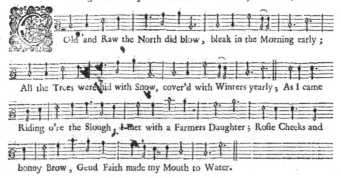

The Northern Ditty (1692).

passed down from John Gostling, he went one afternoon to sing for Queen Mary with Arabella Hunt, a soprano who had taken part in *Calisto*. The selections included some songs by Purcell, who accompanied the vocalists on the harpsichord, but "at length the queen beginning to grow tired, asked Mrs. Hunt if she could not sing the old Scots ballad 'Cold and Raw.' Mrs. Hunt answered yes, and sang it to her lute. Purcell was all the while sitting at the harpsichord unemployed, and not a little nettled at the queen's preference of a vulgar ballad to his music."[44] If Purcell was "nettled," he knew his duty, and in the birthday ode for 1692 he used "Cold and Raw" as a bass line for one of the arias.[45] Anne, who is mentioned in the same account as taking singing lessons from Arabella Hunt, would naturally have seen this episode as another instance of her sister's devaluing artists she prized—and thus as another "mortification."

"Cold and Raw" was printed in a broadside of 1692, which falsely advertised the tune as "New" and boasted—more accurately—that it was "much in Request at court." Unlike the many ballads celebrating erotic couplings, this one tells the story of a failed seduction. The speaker meets a farmer's daughter on her way to market and offers to buy all her barley if she will spend the night with him, but the young woman demurs, citing the danger of pregnancy, and when he admits that he is already married, she sends him home:

I told her *I* had wedded been
    Fourteen years and longer,

Else I'd chuse her for my Queen
   and tye the Knot yet stronger;
She bid me then no farther rome
   But mannage my Wedlock fairly;
And keep my purse for poor Spouse at home
   For some other shall have her *Barley.*

When Mary asked to hear this ballad, she had been married to William for four-teen years.[46] Though prudish and dignified, she had known since childhood that "men are always wery of their wifes and look for mistresses as sone as thay can get them."[47] She was certainly aware of her husband's liaison with Elizabeth Villiers, and by now she would have heard the rumors linking William sexually with his lifelong friend Hans Willem Bentinck, whose wife, another of the Villiers sisters, had died in 1688.[48] Queen Mary's fondness for "Cold and Raw" may have been grounded in the hope that the next person William tried to seduce would prove to be like the self-possessed and upright farmer's daughter in the ballad and send her husband back to his "poor Spouse at home."

At just the same moment, Anne was experiencing her spasms of jealousy about Sarah Churchill's relationship with Lady Fitzharding. In another letter on this topic, she begged Sarah not to see "the Lady," apologizing for her jealousy by citing a popular song:

> I feare deare Mrs Freeman will think me very impertinent for saying all
> this but if she will but remember what the song says (to be too jealous is
> the fault of every tender lover) I hope she will pardon me & believe her
> faithfull Morely can never be guilty of any other fault.[49]

The song Anne quotes, evidently expecting Sarah to know it, was the first item in *The Banquet of Musick, or, A Collection of the newest and best songs sung at court and at publick theatres* (1688), a popular songbook published by John Playford.[50] In contrast to "Cold and Raw," with its exemplary narrative, this lyric is an intense expression of passion:

> Forgive me, if your Looks, I thought,
> Did once some Change discover;
> To be too Jealous, is the fault
> Of ev'ry tender Lover.
> My truth those kind Reproaches show,
> Which you blame so severely;
> A sign, alas! you little know,
> What 'tis to love sincerely.

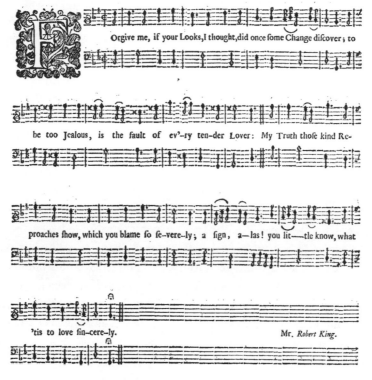

Orgive me, if your Looks, I thought, did once some Change discover; to

be too Jealous, is the fault of ev'-ry ten-der Lover: My Truth those kind Re-

proaches show, which you blame so se-vere-ly; a sign, a—las! you lit——tle know, what

'tis to love sin-cere-ly.   Mr. *Robert King.*

"Forgive me" from *The Banquet of Musick* (1688).

The Torment of a long Despair,
I did in silence smother;
But 'tis a pain I cannot bear,
To think, you love another.
My Fate depends alone on you,
I am but what you make me;
Divinely blest, if you prove true,
Undone, if you forsake me.

Both songs develop the theme of infidelity, and on that issue both royal sisters now had reasons to be jealous of the Villiers sisters, with whom they had been reared in Richmond. But the contrast in style is telling: the old ballad favored by Mary treats both the seduction and its refusal in pragmatic terms, exemplified by the offer of money for barley; the modern song preferred by Anne focuses entirely on the interior emotions of the speaker. By invoking this song, Anne was trying to send Sarah a message she might have found difficult to express in her own words: she knew that her jealousy was excessive, but looked on that jealousy as proof of her devotion to her favorite. There is a similarly striking contrast between the tunes to which these songs were sung. "Cold and Raw," a simple ballad, was already centuries old at this time. Frequently used for dancing, it was pressed into service to accommodate many different sets of words. "Forgive me," by contrast, was a sophisticated new composition by Robert King, now listed with Purcell among the royal composers. His urbane, modern theatre song, which shows the influence of French and Italian music, is quite unlike the rough-and-ready Scottish ballad tune that Mary prized. Even in the songs to which they turned as ways of assuaging their feelings, the tastes of Anne and Mary point in strikingly different directions.

§

Thanks to her courage in resisting her father's attempts to convert her, Princess Anne enjoyed widespread popularity. The army of mounted men that rallied around her in 1688 was proof of the affection she had earned by her stubborn adherence to Protestantism. Queen Mary, by contrast, was less familiar to her subjects, having spent the previous ten years in Holland, and the difficulties she experienced in the early months of her reign made her jealous of her sister's popular following. In her diary, she describes this period as a series of trials sent to her by God:

> I composed a prayer suitable to the present time, to which I add dayly as I see occasion. While I was thus endeavouring to settle my mind again, I met with many mortifications, but, I bless God, all turned to my souls good. I found my self here very much neglected, little respected, censured of all, commended by none. This was a great trouble at first, but when I considerd the thing right, I saw it was from the Lord, and I resolved to bear patiently whatever he should lay upon me. I wanted to be humbled, and I was it sufficiently. T'is hard to flesh and blood to bear neglect, especially coming as I did from a place where I was valued too much.[51]

This passage immediately follows Mary's account of her struggle with Compton over the liturgy, a contest of wills in which the queen prevailed. Her claim to be "much neglected, little respected, censured of all, commended by none," with its neatly parallel constructions and internal rhyme, is suspiciously rhetorical; it springs from the same part of her mind that had imagined herself as the tragic heroine Sophonisba when a girlhood companion was more attentive to her sister.[52]

Curiously enough, it was in the theatre that Mary suffered the most painful and public mortification of her first year on the throne. On 28 May 1689, some six weeks after her coronation, the queen went to the playhouse at Dorset Garden with her maids. Apparently aware that *The Spanish Fryar* had been banned for its jibes at priests during her father's reign, she ordered Dryden's "Protestant play" to be acted, but the Tory message of the play's serious plot, with its strong support for the legitimate succession, made her afternoon in the theatre extremely uncomfortable. Daniel Finch, Earl of Nottingham set down a very specific account, which leaves little doubt about the queen's embarrassment:

> Some unhappy expressions, among which these that follow, put her in some disorder, and forced her to hold up her fan, and often look behind her and call for her palatine, and hood, and any thing she could next think of, while those who were in the pit before her turned their heads over their shoulders, and all in general directed their looks toward her, whenever their fancy led them to make any application of what was said. In one place, where the queen of Arragon is going to church in procession, 'tis said by a spectator, Very good, she usurps the throne, keeps the old king in prison, and at the same time is praying for a blessing on her army.—And when said, That 'tis observed at court who weeps and who wears black for good king Sancho's death; 'tis said, Who is that, that can flatter a court like this? Can I sooth tyranny, seem pleas'd to see my royal master murthered; his crown usurped; a distaff in the throne: and what title has this queen but lawless force; and force must pull her down.—— Twenty more things are said, which may be wrested to what they were never designed; but however the observations then made, furnished the town with talk, till something else happened.[53]

As Nottingham points out, these lines, written and acted some eight years earlier, were "never designed" to apply to the Revolution of 1688, but disgruntled opponents of the Revolution, including the play's author, would have enjoyed noticing how closely such lines now seemed to fit the case of Mary, whose visible piety had not prevented her from betraying her father.

A second anecdote in the same letter affords further evidence of the difficulties Mary was suffering. The next time a play was "ordered to be acted," writes Nottingham, the queen sought "other diversion" by visiting a famous fortune-teller who had been predicting the restoration of her father, and this adventure resulted in public criticism from the king:

> The queen went to one Mrs. Wise's, a famous woman for telling fortunes, but could not prevail with her to tell any thing.... And besides a private reprimand given, the king gave one in public, saying to the queen that he heard she dined at a bawdy-house, and desired the next time she went he might go too. She said she had done nothing but what the late queen had

done. He asked her, if she meant to make her her example. More was said on this occasion than ever was known before, but it was borne with all the submission of a good wife, who leaves all to the direction of the k——, and diverts herself with walking six or seven miles a day, and looking after her buildings, making of fringes, and such like innocent things; and does not meddle in government, though she has a better title to do it than the late queen had.[54]

If Mary really sought to excuse herself by mentioning Maria of Modena, she gave William an irresistible opening for his cruel and demeaning remarks, evidently uttered when others were present to witness his witticisms and her discomfort. Although Nottingham served the new monarchs as one of their two secretaries of state from 1689 until 1693, his sneering attitude toward Mary is audible in his ironic praise of the queen for "walking six or seven miles a day," an activity not normally associated with court ladies, let alone queens. There may even be an implied contrast with Princess Anne, who stood godmother to Nottingham's son in early 1691;[55] her diversions at this time did not include long walks or the making of fringes. Nottingham's assertion that Mary "does not meddle in government," however, would soon prove false, as she became the effective head of government when William left England to lead his troops in wars abroad. Those appointed to advise her, including Nottingham himself, soon learned that Mary could be unbending and authoritative when she thought it necessary.

The embarrassment in the theatre, the rebuke from her husband, and the disapproval of her habits expressed by Nottingham and others were quite different forms of mortification, each of which exacerbated Mary's unease in her new role. Despite widespread support for the Revolution, an increasingly vocal minority, now called "Jacobites," continued to question the legitimacy of the new monarchs; their overt attacks on the regime were a constant irritant. On 18 November 1689, for example,

one Mr. Gray (who pretends to be a clergy man of the church of England, and chaplain to the late bishop of Chester, tho thought really to be a papist) was brought to the court of the kings bench to receive the judgment of the court, being convicted of making and publishing a most villanous libell upon the king and queen and their government, entituled, The Coronation Ballad: he was ordered to stand in the pillory for an hour at Westminster Hall gate, and at the Exchange the next day, to pay 100 marks fine, and be committed till all is done.[56]

The ballad in question insults William as "a dainty fine King," a man "not qualified for his wife," and a homosexual:

> He is not qualified for his wife,
> Because of the cruel midwife's knife,
> Yet buggering of Benting doth please to the life,
>   A dainty fine King indeed.

"Benting" here is the balladeer's rough spelling for Hans Willem Bentinck, who was rewarded for his many services by being created Earl of Portland just before the coronation. Those who promoted the rumor that the two men were lovers, a charge frequently repeated in Jacobite propaganda, often pointed to Mary's failure to produce children. Whatever the queen believed or knew about her husband's private life, it cannot have been pleasant to be reminded of that failure. Worse yet, the ballad directly attacked her as well:

> O' th' father's side she had honor we grant,
> But duty to parents she sadly doth want,
> Which makes her a fiend instead of a saint
>   A dainty fine Queen indeed.[57]

Ralph Gray, whom the "court of the kings bench" sent to the pillory for writing this poem, had been chaplain to Thomas Cartwright, Bishop of Chester, who preached a Tory sermon before Anne in 1682 and dedicated the published text to the princess, referring to her grandfather as a "*Glorious Martyr*" and complimenting her for displaying "an eminent share of his *Piety*."[58] Cartwright's dogged loyalty to the Stuarts gained him a bishop's seat but later forced him into exile with James II; he died in Ireland some four days after the coronation and was thus unable to protect his associate. By punishing Gray, the new monarchs were sending a warning to anyone else inclined to poke fun at their regime. They may not have known about Anne's previous association with Gray's patron Cartwright, but they were surely displeased when they learned that she sometimes referred to William as "the monster" or "Mr. Caliban."[59]

§

With his chief patron dead, Gray was unable to save himself from the pillory, but Dryden, despite having lost his court positions, still enjoyed the support of powerful patrons. The Earl of Dorset, who had helped the Bishop of London spirit Anne away from Whitehall in 1688, was now Lord Chamberlain, a post he received in recognition of his active support of the Revolution. In that capacity, he had already performed the unpleasant task of removing his friend Dryden from his offices as Poet Laureate and Historiographer Royal, though he generously softened the blow with a gift of money.[60] When Dryden resumed writing plays to support himself, he glanced ironically at recent events, not only in self-deprecating prologues and epilogues, but in the plays themselves. Although it was Dorset's duty to examine all plays to make sure they were not politically subversive, he was evidently willing to look the other way in the case of Dryden. Though sometimes censored or delayed, the former Laureate's plays written after the Revolution were all performed, despite the Jacobite innuendo with which the old poet slyly larded them.

In December 1689, a year after the Revolution and a few weeks after Gray stood in the pillory, the United Company presented *Don Sebastian, King of Portugal*, Dryden's first play since the Revolution. A contemporary witness, Roger Morrice, reported that "the Queene and the Prince of Denmarke were at the Playhouse to see Mr. Dreyden's new Play."[61] Anne (for once) was not pregnant at this time, so she probably also saw the play. The real Don Sebastian (1554–1578) was last seen charging his horse into enemy lines in a battle against the Moroccans. Because his body was never recovered, some Portuguese fondly believed that he might one day return to claim his kingdom, and an impostor briefly took advantage of that hope. In Dryden's version, Sebastian appears as a prisoner of war in the Moroccan marketplace, along with his bride Almeyda, "Queen of Barbary." The Moroccan emperor, Muley-Moloch, is a usurper, and his court is a tangle of plots and conspiracies; no one is trustworthy. Issues of succession, legitimacy, and power are central, and if the play does not offer a transparent "parallel" to recent political events, Dryden clearly had those events in mind when he composed it. His preface to the published play informs the reader that the text as first written and acted was "insupportably too long" and explains that "above twelve hunder'd lines" were cut in subsequent performances. Although Dryden describes the omitted lines as "the most poetical parts, which are Descriptions, Images, Similitudes, and Moral Sentences,"[62] the actor-manager Thomas Betterton, whom the poet praises for "judiciously" pruning his play, evidently suppressed some material open to dangerous political interpretations. Morrice says that the text was "very much Curtled before it was suffered to be Acted," which sounds as if the pruning was indeed political.

Dryden published the complete text in January, "and thereby restor'd it, to that clearness of conception, and (if I may dare to say it) that lustre, and masculine vigour in which it was first written."[63] For those still hoping that James II might be "restor'd," the old poet's verb was significant, and for readers of all parties, his preface was an invitation to discover what they had missed in the truncated version. In the first scene, for example, Dorax, "a Noble Portuguese now a Renegade" taunts Benducar, the "Chief Minister and Favourite to the Emperor," using language that might have struck some readers as an attack on the "masculine vigour" of the new king:

Bend. Now Dorax!
Dorax. Well, *Benducar!*
Bend. Bare *Benducar!*
Dor. Thou woudst have Titles, take 'em then, Chief Minister,
    First Hangman of the State.
Bend. Some call me Favourite.
Dorax. What's that, his Minion?
    Thou art too old to be a Catamite!

Dryden presumably surmised that supporters of the Revolution, for whom William was officially the virtuous champion of the Protestant religion, the brave military scourge of the French, and the devoted husband of Mary, would be unable to object to this gratuitous allusion, since to do so would lend credence to rumors alleging that their new monarch was fond of "Catamites."

The poet also included some comic jabs at other targets: when whipped by a Moroccan slave-driver, a Portuguese prisoner remarks that "the Doctrine of Non-Resistance is never practis'd thoroughly but when a Man can't help himself."[64] This joke glances at the Anglican teaching that any rebellion against a monarch was a sin, so that even unlawful and tyrannical commands from a monarch required passive obedience. In Dryden's view, such clergymen as Compton had violated that principle by rebelling actively against James and were now invoking the very doctrine they had ignored by requiring an oath of allegiance to a monarch many regarded as a usurper. The nine bishops who refused to take that oath, now called "non-jurors," included several with strong ties to Anne.[65] Even without such overtly political lines, the truncated version of the play seen on stage had at its core a subtle, complex exploration of the currently urgent question of loyalty, which had been a fundamental problem for Mary, Anne, and many others during the troubled reign of James II and the ensuing revolution.

As the play begins, Benducar, a scheming villain, is preparing to use Muley-Zedan, the jealous younger brother of the emperor, to further his own aims. The advice Benducar gives his dupe would have struck many in the audience as applicable to those who had flattered James while actively plotting his downfall:

Be still, and learn the soothing Arts of Court;
Adore his fortune, mix with flattering Crowds,
And when they praise him most, be you the loudest;
. . . .
The shadow of a discontent wou'd ruin us;
We must be safe before we can be great.

Boasting of his closeness to the emperor, Benducar admits to taking advantage of his master's trust:

> So often try'd, and ever found so true,
> Has given me trust, and trust has given me means
> Once to be false for all.[66]

Even those who supported the Revolution were often uneasy about the abuse of trust: many disapproved of John Churchill, who had served James II as a Gentleman of the Bedchamber and a Brigadier General while secretly aiding William's invasion plans. Gilbert Burnet, himself a strong supporter of the Revolution, recorded the criticisms circulating at the time:

> Churchill has been much censured; for as he had risen in the king's service through several degrees up to be a favourite, so a kindness which had begun upon the king's commerce with his sister was now so well fixed, that no man had more of personal favour and had found greater effects of it than he had. His coming into this design had the appearance of treachery and ingratitude, which has brought him under much reproach.[67]

Churchill had dined with the king on the very night he deserted him, an act that bore an uncomfortable resemblance to the behavior of Judas at the Last Supper, yet the letter the general left behind when he rode off to join William spoke eloquently of his conscience and his religion:

> I hope the great advantages I injoy under your majesty, which I can never expect in any other change of goverment, may reasonabley convince your majesty & the world that I am acted by a higher principle, when I offer that violence to my inclenation duty & intrest as to desert your majesty at a time when your affaires seeme to challenge the strictest obedience from all your subjects, much more from one who lyes under the greatest personable obligations imaginable, to your majesty. This, Sir, cou'd proceed from nothing but the inviolable dectates of my consceince & necessary concarn for my religion (which no good man can oppose), & with which I am instructed nothing ought to come in competition.[68]

The Revolution of 1688 was an important moment in the shift from a definition of loyalty emphasizing personal obligations to one emphasizing dictates of conscience, but that shift was gradual and difficult, fraught with inconsistencies

and contradictions. The peers of the realm, civil servants, army officers, clergymen, and others who decided to support or accept William and Mary as monarchs had come to believe that their loyalty to the Protestant religion trumped
their loyalty to any man, including a sacred monarch, yet many were caught between their need to defend cherished forms of religious, philosophical, or political belief and their respect for the older sense of honor to which Dryden's
Dorax appeals when Benducar attempts to enlist him in the conspiracy against
the emperor:

> He trusts us both; mark that, shall we betray him?
> A Master who reposes Life and Empire
> On our fidelity: I grant he is a Tyrant,
> That hated name my nature most abhors;
>
> . . . .
> But, while he trusts me, 'twere so base a part
> To fawn and yet betray, I shou'd be hiss'd
> And whoop'd in Hell for that Ingratitude.
>
> . . . .
> Is not the bread thou eat'st, the Robe thou wear'st,
> Thy Wealth, and Honours, all the pure indulgence
> Of him thou wou'dst destroy?
> And wou'd his Creature, nay his Friend betray him?
> Why then, no Bond is left on human kind:
> Distrusts, debates, immortal strifes ensue;
> Children may murder Parents, Wives their Husbands;
> All must be Rapine, Wars, and Desolation,
> When trust and gratitude no longer bind.

When Dorax utters this ringing speech in defense of the traditional definition of
loyalty, the audience already knows that he himself has abandoned his master Don
Sebastian, gone over to the other side, and turned Muslim. Benducar immediately
reminds him of this inconsistency:

> Well have you argued in your own defence:
> You, who have burst asunder all those bonds,
> And turn'd a Rebel to your Native Prince.[69]

In exchanges like these, Dryden was making dramatic art from the richly
human dilemmas he was witnessing all around him. Betterton, recognizing the
possibilities of the role, chose to play Dorax himself, so the best and most

experienced actor in the company was playing a tortured turncoat. It cannot have been an entirely comfortable experience for Queen Mary and her party to witness this drama, and it is to their credit—and Dorset's—that the play was allowed to proceed. Although Dryden's religion had cost him his court positions, his literary gift was a national treasure, and the premiere of a new play from his pen—even one that gave its audience moments of discomfort—was an important occasion.

In arguing for his belief that one must maintain loyalty to one's master, even if he proves a tyrant, Dorax draws on Robert Filmer's influential treatise *Patriarcha*, which equates the ties binding subjects to kings with those binding children to parents and wives to husbands. Mary and Anne had recently faced a choice between loyalty to their monarch and loyalty to their religion, which presented itself as a choice between loyalty to a Catholic father who was failing badly as a king and loyalty to a Protestant husband who chose to oppose that Catholic king. Like her royal sister and her friend John Churchill, Princess Anne chose to desert James II; like them, she prevaricated about her motives. But she was an uncertain and incompetent liar: during the early months of 1688, while continuing to go through the motions of dutiful service to James and Maria, she complained to Mary that it was "very uneasy to me to be with people that every moment of one's life one must be dissembling with, & put on a face of joy, when one's heart has more cause to ake."[70] She was especially uncomfortable playing this double role because she was fundamentally sympathetic to those feudal values of honor and loyalty that she was about to set aside in order to help her sister dethrone her father.

In the letter she left for Maria Beatrice as she slipped down the back stairs, Anne spoke openly of the conflict between duty to a father and duty to a husband, and described herself as having chosen her husband over her father, while claiming that both she and George were acting to "preserve" James:

> I am confident the Pr[ince] did not leave the K[ing] with any other design, than to use all possible means for his [i.e. James's] preservation; so I hope you will do me the Justice to Believe that I am uncapable of following him for any other End. Never was anyone in such an unhappy Condition, so divided between Duty & Affection to a Father, & an Husband; & therefore I know not what I must do, but to follow one to preserve the other.[71]

The implication of the first sentence is that Prince George, by defecting to the invading army, can discourage violence against James and help bring about a peaceful settlement; the implication of the last is that the princess will help preserve her father by going to her husband. Anne was not alone in hoping that the desertions would prompt the king to negotiate with William, call a Parliament, and back away from his autocratic stance, but her claim to be confused and conflicted was dishonest. Just one week earlier, she had written to William wishing him "good success in this so just an undertaking" and assuring him that "the Prince will soon be with you,... who I am sure will do you all the Service that lies in his power."[72] She had said nothing at all in that letter about her "duty and affection" to her father. There is a qualitative difference, however, between Anne's transparent, vulnerable, frightened lies and the courtly bravado of Churchill, who did not hesitate to speak of the "inviolable dectates of my consceince" as he deserted his king.

There is also a telling difference between Anne's description of her choice in the midst of the crisis and Mary's first long entry in her diary, a carefully constructed statement written well after the fact, which portrays her as troubled by the family conflict but resigned to God's will:

> The melanckolly prospect for me, to see my husband and father so far engaged against each other took off all the satisfaction I could have in this world, and made me find by experience it was not the place of rest or content. The sad exemple of my father shewd sufficiently it was not greatness could secure me; which exemple touched me so much the more by the nearness of the concern I had every way in it.
>
> On the other side I saw my husband in a prosperous way and blessed God for it, and was sorry I could not so much rejoyce as his wife ought; neither was I so sad as became the daughter of a distressed king. I bless my God [who] decided between the daughter and the wife and shewd me, when Religion was at a stake I should know no man after the flesh, but wait the Lords leisure and trust his goodness for the event.[73]

Mary also expresses nostalgia for the "strickt retirement" of her years in Holland, "where I led the life of a nun," and defends herself by invoking biblical language about carnal knowledge, as if her last month in Holland, where she waited for the summons to come to England and accept the crown, had actually been a period of resigned submission to God, a turning away from the flesh. Yet her subsequent actions as queen, especially during the periods when William was away pursuing military campaigns, were hardly those of a retired and passive woman, piously waiting for God's will. In 1693, for example, she refused clemency to William Anderton, a thirty-year-old printer with three small children, allowing him to be hanged for having allegedly printed a Jacobite pamphlet. By taking this cruel action, Mary was insisting on power as a way of retaining power, a position Dryden dramatized in a conversation between his usurping emperor, Muley-Moloch, and the scheming Benducar, who warns his master against secret enemies:

> *Benducar.* A secret Party still remains, that lurks
>   Like Embers rak'd in ashes—wanting but
>   A breath to blow aside th'involving dust,
>   And then they blaze abroad.
> *Emperor.* They must be trampled out.
> *Benducar.* But first be known.
> *Emperor.* Torture shall force it from 'em.
> *Benducar.* You wou'd not put a Nation to the rack?
> *Emperor.* Yes, the whole World; so I be safe, I care not.[74]

With fifty thousand Englishmen now abroad, the existence of a Jacobite party was hardly a secret, and many who served William and Mary hedged their bets by keeping up a correspondence with the exiled court at St. Germain. Under these circumstances, with rumors of conspiracy swirling constantly around them, the new monarchs felt compelled to punish such critics as Gray and Anderton. Although they had gained the throne because of James's tyrannical behavior, the policies by which they sought to retain it made them vulnerable to being called tyrants themselves. Dryden exaggerates this uncompromising philosophy of rule when his emperor speaks of his right to claim the woman for whom he lusts:

> What's Royalty but pow'r to please my self?
> And if I dare not, then am I the Slave,
> And my own Slaves the Sovereigns,—'tis resolv'd,
> Weak Princes flatter when they want the pow'r
> To curb their People.[75]

Despite the cautionary example of her father, whose insistence on being obeyed in all things had cost him his throne, and despite the contractual arrangement by which she came to the throne, Mary often insisted on the power and respect traditionally accorded sacred monarchs—and not merely in the case of the unfortunate printer. "I am the Queen," she declared at the height of her quarrel with Anne, "and I will be obeyed."[76]

§

When *Don Sebastian* came on stage in December 1689, James II was comfortably in control of most of Ireland, and William was preparing to take a large army there to oppose him, leaving England vulnerable to a French attack. Under the circumstances, both sisters recognized the need to keep up the appearance of solidarity and civility, though their differences in temperament and taste made that task increasingly difficult. On the first Sunday in March 1690, Anne received Communion in her own private chapel, an act Mary describes as "so unusuall a thing, that all the world toock notice of it," especially when Anne later came to their shared dining table, excusing her absence from the Chapel Royal by claiming to have felt ill. Although Mary thought Anne's claim of illness was fraudulent, the princess might well have been suffering from morning sickness; she delivered a short-lived daughter on 14 October 1690, and was thus probably pregnant in March.[77] From her sister's point of view, Anne's absenting herself from the court's corporate worship looked like an indication of her displeasure at the changes Mary had made in the liturgy and a further expression of the desire for a separate establishment that had led her to seek her own allowance from Parliament. A month later, when the queen was ill, Anne came to her and (in Mary's words) "asckt both the king and I to pardon what was past, and desired we would forget it."[78] The sisters repeated this pattern of estrangement and reconciliation several more times before their final break.

When their husbands sailed for Ireland in June, the queen and the princess made a show of moving in together at Whitehall, but this arrangement evidently suited neither of them. In her diary entry for this period, Mary complains of feeling entirely isolated:

> I found my self now at White Hall as in a new world, deprived of all that was dear to me in the person of my husband, left among those that were perfect strangers to me: my sister of a humour so reserved, I could have litle comfort from her; the great Council of a strange composition, the Cabinet Council not much better.[79]

This is a highly revealing passage. William had often treated Mary with contempt, as in his cruel remarks about her visit to the fortune-teller, yet she describes him here as "all that was dear to me." Although she had been back in England for eighteen months, the queen still thought of the inhabitants of the court as "perfect strangers." Her complaint that Anne is "reserved" accords well with Sarah's analysis of "the different characters and humours of the two sisters," written fifty years later: "Queen Mary grew weary of anybody who would not talk a great deal; and the Princess was so silent that she rarely spoke more than was necessary to answer a question."[80] Mary's description of her quiet sister as one from whom she could have "litle comfort" may seem cold, but it is mild compared to her systematic belittling of the ministers William left in place to help her, which follows immediately. The "Great Council," whose composition she considers "strange," was the Privy Council, a large group holding formal, minuted meetings; the "Cabinet Council," in this reign and the next, was a smaller body that functioned as an executive committee, whose members Mary proceeds to anatomize. Carmarthen, to whom she acknowledges "great obligations," is "of a temper I can never like"; Dorset is "too lazy to give himself the trouble of bussiness, so of little use"; Nottingham is "suspected by most as not true to the government." And so down the list, with her greatest contempt reserved for the council member closest to her sister: "I will say nothing of Lord Marlborough, because t'is he I could say the most of & can never deserve either trust or esteem."[81]

Trusting no one, Mary had a summer of terror and joy. The French fleet scored an impressive victory at the battle of Beachy Head on 30 June, leading to fears of an invasion. "I knew there was nothing for me to trust to humanly speacking, when the king was gone," wrote the queen. "And certainly, if any rising had happend upon the apeering of the French fleet, or had they landed after owrs was beaten, I had been in a very bad condition."[82] But the French only managed to burn one village, and within two weeks came the news of William's decisive victory over James at the Battle of the Boyne in Ireland—tidings doubly welcome to both sisters. Their husbands were safe, though William had sustained a wound, and there was now less immediate fear of retribution from a restored and resentful father.[83] Despite these reasons to rejoice, the queen and the princess did not celebrate the victory together. While Mary was in London attending to the summer's many crises, Anne went off to Tunbridge Wells, where she saw bonfires marking the victory in Ireland. One witness reported that "the Princesse never appeared till yesterday at church, & this morning she came & dranke ye Waters at the Well. There is so much crowding to see her, that I have not as yet seen her, so well as I shall do." Even from a distance, he noticed that "she seems to be much fatter than she was,"[84] perhaps not knowing that the princess was pregnant.

Such public demonstrations of interest in her sister piqued Mary's jealousy, and William's insulting treatment of Prince George during the campaign gave Anne a new reason for resentment. Nonetheless, the sisters made a joint appearance on 20 August at Blackheath, where they saw "about 6,000 men all drawn up 'in battalia,' and the Queen was pleased to give them 200 guineas to drink her health." In September, a few days after his return, William "went to pay a visit to the Princess of Denmark…accompanied by a great number of people with large acclamations of joy."[85] Making a conciliatory gesture of her own, Anne named the short-lived daughter she delivered on 14 October Mary, in honor of the queen. During this autumn, Anne and her court could take pleasure in Marlborough's successes during a whirlwind campaign in Ireland, though she lost a trusted friend when the Duke of Grafton died of wounds received at the siege of Cork. On Anne's next birthday, 6 February 1691, "the queen, prince and princesse, play'd publicly at cards at the cockpitt; and afterwards they danced country dances at Whitehall."[86] The king had already left for the Continent, where he was preparing for the summer's campaign against the French, and Mary admitted in her diary that she had decided to appear in public as a way of dramatizing her confidence in her husband's safety:

> For at the kings first going, to let the world see the difference I made between that journey & those wherein his person was exposed, I went once or twice to the play, I played every night at Comet or Basset; my sisters birthday I had dancing in my drawing room, & such things I did and would not leave them off for these troubles.[87]

Anne, too, sometimes appeared in public. On 9 April, for example, she attended "a Consort of Vocal and Instrumental Musick" at York Buildings, advertised as given "by the Command, and for the Entertainment, of her Royal Highness the Princess of Denmark."[88] The next day, both sisters suffered material losses when a fire destroyed large portions of Whitehall Palace. Although the fire began in the part of the building now reserved for the Duke of Gloucester and his servants, there does not appear to have been any retribution or backbiting. In May, however, came Mary's order forbidding Prince George to sail with the fleet, a bitter blow to his pride. Convinced that her sister was conspiring with the Jacobites, the queen described George's volunteering to serve in the navy as "a design of growing popular":

> This was very grievous to me to thinck my sister should be concerned in such things; yet t'was plain there was a design of growing popular by the princes resolution of going to sea without asking leave, only telling the king he intended it, which I had order to hinder, and when perswasions would not do, was obliged to send word by Lord Nottingham he should not, which was desired by them as much as avoided by me, that they might have a pretence to raile, and so in discontent go to Tunbridge.[89]

As Mary's discussion of her own motives for theatregoing and card-playing reveals, she was careful to "let the world know" how she wished to be perceived, and in this suspicious account of the behavior of her in-laws, she invented similar motives for their actions, assuming that they wished to create "a pretence to raile," an excuse for complaining. She was unable to believe that the prince might simply have wanted to serve his adopted nation in its wars against the hated French.

In August, both George and Anne wrote formally to the king to ask that he reward the Earl of Marlborough by making him a Knight of the Garter, a request that went unheeded. William's distrust of the Marlboroughs was evidently stronger than his gratitude for Churchill's swift and efficient conquests in Ireland during the autumn of 1690 and his outstanding tactical leadership on the

Continent during the summer of 1691. The winter was filled with plots and rumors, with many, including the Marlboroughs and the Denmarks, suspected of being in contact with the exiled court at St. Germain.[90] Finally, with everyone edgy and nervous, the veneer of courtly civility came off. On the evening of 9 January 1692, there was a heated quarrel between the royal sisters, and the next day William suddenly turned on Marlborough, stripping him of all his offices and banishing him from court. The diarist John Evelyn took the occasion to describe the unfortunate earl as "disgraced; & by none pittied, being also the first who betrayed and forsooke his Master K: James, who advanced him."[91] Evelyn's sneering language is a real-world example of the contempt Dryden's fictional Dorax had described as an inevitable consequence of betraying one's master: "'twere so base a part / To fawn and yet betray, I shou'd be hiss'd / And whoop'd in Hell for that Ingratitude."

Mary had long disliked Lady Marlborough, whom she (correctly) blamed for Anne's success in gaining her financial settlement from Parliament, and she seized this moment to insist that Anne part with her favorite. Her icily formal letter declaring that "Lady Marlborough must not continue with you" arrived on 5 February, the day before Anne's twenty-seventh birthday. In her immediate reply, Anne begged her sister to "recall your severe command," questioned Mary's motives, and insisted on her right to retain the beloved Sarah:

> And I must as freely own, that as I think this proceeding can be for no other intent than to give me a very sensible mortification, so there is no misery that I cannot readily resolve to suffer, rather than the thought of parting with her.[92]

Despite her own keen interest in protocol and propriety, the princess dares to dispute the queen's claim that it would be improper for her to appear at court attended by a woman whose husband was in disgrace, and goes on to allege that her sister's real purpose is to give her "a very sensible mortification," to cause her pain and put her in her place. Now in the later stages of another pregnancy, Anne faced this crisis at a time when she was especially vulnerable. In claiming that "there is no misery that I cannot readily resolve to suffer," she appropriates the language of martyrdom to express her willingness to suffer for her principles, though in this case the principles were not religious or political but personal.

Mary's response was decisive: she ordered the Marlboroughs to leave their lodgings in the Cockpit, overriding Anne's authority as the owner of that section of the palace. But if the queen thought her sister would capitulate, she underestimated Anne's stated resolve to suffer any misery rather than part with Sarah. Instead of dismissing her favorite, the princess left the palace, moving first to Sion

House, which the Duke of Somerset gallantly offered to her, then to Berkeley House in Piccadilly, which she occupied as a renter starting in October 1692. Both these locations brought her closer to Campden House in Kensington, which she had already rented as a healthy residence for her fragile son.

Mary, who was at least as stubborn as Anne, kept up the pressure. She stripped the prince and princess of the guards who had previously attended them, and this deprivation was more than symbolic: shortly after Anne moved to Sion House, her unguarded coach was stopped by thieves, and she herself was reportedly robbed.[93] When someone told Anne that there might be an opportunity for reconciliation that would not require her to dismiss Lady Marlborough permanently, she sent Lady Fitzharding to tell the queen, "*she should be very ready to give* HER MAJESTY *any satisfaction of that sort.*" But Anne had been sadly misinformed, as Lady Marlborough herself explains: "Upon the delivery of this message, the QUEEN fell into a great passion, and said, *her sister had not mistaken her, for she never would see her, upon any other terms, than parting with me, not for a time, but for ever,* adding, *that she was a* QUEEN *and would be obeyed.*"[94] In an imperious personal action, the queen appeared at Anne's bedside on 17 April, just hours after the princess had delivered a stillborn son, to demand once more that she dismiss Lady Marlborough. Unable to bully Anne into submission, even in her weakened state, Mary forbade her courtiers to visit her sister, with the result that only "two or three Jacobite ladies" visited the princess.[95] Though doubtless grateful for those who braved the queen's displeasure to maintain their friendships with her, Anne accepted her quieter social life with equanimity, maintaining her dignity and her separate quarters. Hopeful newswriters frequently reported rumors of a reconciliation, but Mary also refused to relent in any way, and the painful estrangement between the sisters continued until the queen's death.

§

Although she seethed at her sister, Anne was not entirely distressed at the simplification of her life that resulted from her leaving the court. Immediately after she left Whitehall for Sion House, observers referred to her newly empty court as "melancholy,"[96] but the princess, naturally shy and reticent, did not always long for the limelight. In her most revealing letter from this period, written on 19 March 1692, she rejects an offer from Sarah to abandon her employment as Groom of the Stole, an act that would have allowed Anne to resume her life at court. Assuring Sarah that she has consulted with Prince George, who she says is in complete agreement, she considers the possibility that her parliamentary grant might be reduced as a result of the standoff with her sister but measures that inconvenience against the advantages she has gained by leaving the court, such as escaping officious flatterers:

Can you think either of us so wretched that for the sake of twenty thousand pound, and to be tormented from morning to night with flattering
knaves and fools, we would forsake those we have such obligations to,
and that we are sertin we are the occassion of all theire misfortunes?[97]

Three years later, when Mary's death had brought about a partial reconciliation
with William, Anne again had a court full of visitors and complained to Sarah
about how exhausting it was to deal with the press of fawning courtiers:

I have undergon more fatigue to day in heareing & asking a thousand impertinent questions, for two hours together, then I did yesterday in my
journey, which makes me allready think of Mr Cowleys Country Mouse,
& I shall wish very often for ye Summer if I may enjoy some happy days
with deare Mrs Freeman at St Albans, but wherever I am & whatever happens to me, I will live & dye your faithfull passionett Morley.[98]

As in the case of the popular song about jealousy, Anne expresses her emotions indirectly by alluding to a text she expects Sarah to know. The poet Abraham
Cowley (1618–1667) was among the authors Sarah had been reading as part of a
program of self-education undertaken in these years.[99] He had written memorably on the classical theme of retirement, particularly in his *Several discourses by
way of Essays, in Verse and Prose* (1668). In the poem to which Anne alludes here,
a paraphrase based on Horace, "a good substantial Country-Mouse: / Frugal, and
grave, and careful of the main," provides rural hospitality for a "City Mouse well
coated, sleek, and gay," who offers to return the favor:

Your bounty and civility (said he)
Which I'm surpriz'd in these rude parts to see,
Shews that the Gods have given you a mind
Too noble for the fate which here you find.
Why should a Soul, so virtuous, and so great,
Lose itself thus in an Obscure retreat?
Let savage Beasts lodg in a Country Den,
You should see Towns, and Manners know, and men
And taste the generous Lux'ury of the Court,
Where all the Mice of quality resort.[100]

The city mouse's question—"Why should a Soul, so virtuous and so great, / Lose
itself thus in an Obscure retreat?"—was one Anne heard often during the years of
her self-imposed exile from court. But as the tale continues, it shows the dangers

inherent in courtly luxury. Cowley turns Horace's Rome into London: when the country mouse makes his visit to a lord's house, the two mice hide behind a curtain, which Cowley wittily describes as a tapestry from the Mortlake workshop in Surrey, set up by Anne's grandfather Charles I to supply artistic hangings for the court. As the guests at a lordly feast leave the table to dance at a ball, the mice venture forth to consume their leavings, and at first the "delicious bits" and "fat varieties" of city food strike the rural visitor as cause for gratitude, not only to his sophisticated host but to the gods, whom he thanks "for his Life's happy change," but joyful consumption turns to disaster when the servants and dogs arrive:

> Loe, in the midst of a well-fraited Pye,
> They both at last glutted and wanton lye.
> When see the sad Reverse of prosperous fate,
> And what fierce storms on mortal glories wait.
> With hideous noise, down the rude servants come,
> Six dogs before run barking into th' room;
> The wretched gluttons fly with wild affright,
> And hate the fulness which retards their flight.

For Anne, who was now too obese to walk comfortably, this was a cautionary tale on several levels. There was a part of her that genuinely desired the retirement and simplicity requested in the country mouse's concluding prayer:

> Give me again, *ye gods,* my Cave and wood;
> With peace, let tares and acorns be my food.

But as Cowley had also pointed out, it is often those most used to affluence, company, and attention who express the desire for simplicity, retirement, and obscurity. Queen Mary, who now seemed so insistent on her royal status, had initially responded to her newfound prominence by complaining of the "great change" in her life and referring nostalgically to her quiet days in Holland. But the queen soon recognized that a crowd of admirers was a necessary sign of her power. In appealing to Parliament for sufficient funds to maintain a court of her own, Anne was also insisting on being properly attended. When she went to take the waters at Tunbridge in the summer of 1690, a witness reported that "Her old chaplain Dr. Younger, Sr Cha: Scarborgh, Dr. & Mrs Wentworth & another or two of her usuall maides of honour attend her."[101] Even a small entourage of this kind would still have included coaches, horses, and a large number of servants.

Cowley was alert to these ironies. In his essay "Of Solitude," he quotes the Roman politician Scipio, who "found more satisfaction to his mind, and more

improvement of it by Solitude than by Company." Drawing on Scipio and Montaigne, the poet shrewdly exposes the tense and troubled relations between ambition and retirement, greatness and obscurity:

> This would be no wonder if it were as truly as it is colourably and wittily
> said by Monsieur *de Montagne,* That Ambition it self might teach us to
> love Solitude; there's nothing does so much hate to have Companions.
> 'Tis true, it loves to have its Elbows free, it detests to have Company on
> either side, but it delights above all things in a Train behind, aye, and
> Ushers too before it. But the greatest part of men are so far from the
> opinion of that noble *Roman,* that if they chance at any time to be
> without company, they'r like a becalmed Ship, they never move but by
> the wind of other mens breath, and have no Oars of their own to steer
> withal.[102]

Despite high-minded protests on both sides, the quarrel between Anne and Mary
came down to the fact that Mary was unwilling to treat Anne as "Company on
either side" and wanted her to be a subservient member of the "Train behind."
Worse yet, the queen enacted her assertion of primacy not only by stripping Anne
of her guards and forbidding great ladies to frequent her court, but by attempting
to separate her sister from the company of Sarah, the companion who had so often
provided the wind to fill the sails of the indecisive princess.

Forced by her sister into a quiet life that she might more readily have embraced had she chosen it freely for herself, Anne found it easier to express outrage
at William than at Mary, though it is clear from the surviving record that Mary was
the perpetrator and sustainer of the quarrel. When Anne spoke of Mary, her tone
was often one of regret, as in this letter from late 1691:

> The Queen & I are of very different humours, and if it were to save my
> soul I can't well make my court to any body I have not a very great incli-
> nation for; as she is my sister, if ever it weare possible to lye in my power
> to serve her, I should be readyer to do it then any body.[103]

But when she spoke of William, especially after the dismissal of Marlborough,
there was no such tenderness:

> Can you believe we would ever truckle to that monster who from the first
> moment of his coming has used us at that rate as we are sensible he has
> don, and that all the world can wittnes, that will not lett there interest
> weigh more with them then theire reason. But suppose I did submitt,

and that the King could change his nature so much as to use me with humanity, how would all reasonable people despise me, how would that Dutch abortive laugh at me and please himself with haveing got the better and which is more, how would my conscience reproch me, for haveing sacrificed it, my honor reputation and all the substantiall comforts of this life for transitory interest, which even to those who make it theire idol, can never aford any reale satisfaction, much less to a vertuous mind. No, my dear Mrs. Freeman, never beleeve your faithfull Mrs. Morley will ever submitt. She can wait with patience for a sun shine day, and if she does not live to see it yet she hopes England will flourish againe.[104]

Energized by her outrage, Anne forgets that she has praised the advantages of retirement earlier in this letter and ends by overtly expressing her hope of someday succeeding to the crown. The "sun shine day" for which she says she can "wait with patience" would eventually come, and as she surely knew, it would bring with it the necessity of being "tormented from morning to night with flattering knaves and fools."

§

Lame and feverish after her labor, and with every reason to feel unwelcome, Anne did not attend the birthday celebrations for her sister at the end of April 1692, which included an ode by Purcell. In the text, by the rakish old poet Charles Sedley, the speaker wonders why Venus, goddess of love, has bestowed such beauty on Mary, whose reforms of courtly behavior have made her not only a rival beauty, but an active enemy to love:

> Love's Goddess sure was blind this Day
>   Thus to adorn her greatest Foe,
> And Love's Artillery betray,
>   To one that would her Realm o'rethrow.
>
> Those Eyes, that form that lofty Meen,
>   Who could for Vertue's Camp design?
> Defensive Arms shou'd there be seen;
>   No sharp, no pointed Weapons shine.[105]

The notion of female beauty as weaponry was conventional, but as this ode was being sung, James II was preparing to invade his former kingdom, with thousands of soldiers standing ready to board a fleet of French ships. The overthrow of the realm was a real danger. Jacobites were expecting the former monarch with the next favorable wind, and fear of betrayal was a large factor in Mary's hostility to her sister and the Marlboroughs. At some level, Sedley was displacing current political fears into the harmless world of Greek mythology and courtly compliment, but the choice of military imagery at this tense moment was an odd one.

As the ode continues, Sedley uses the imagery of war to express the idea that Mary's "blest Example" will rid the nation of immorality:

> May her blest Example chase
>   Vice in troops out of the Land,
> Flying from her awful Face,
>   Like pale Ghosts when Day's at Hand.

Imagining Mary's exemplary virtue as having the power to dispel the allegorical "troops" of vice is a fanciful, baroque conceit, but if James had succeeded in landing real troops, it would have taken more than his daughter's "awful Face" to drive them away. Although the ode appears to endorse Mary's program to reform the manners of her subjects, which included disciplining young courtiers for swearing and forbidding hackney coaches to operate on Sundays, the poet's name, which was not concealed, was reason enough to doubt his sincerity.[106] Sedley had been a riotous companion of the second Earl of Rochester in his youth and had once been fined for public nudity after a drunken revel. Although he had aged, there was no reason to believe that he was now an earnest supporter of Mary's puritanical rules. It was this very stanza, ostensibly endorsing the queen's reforms, for which Purcell used "Cold and Raw" as a bass line. The whole ballad tune is played alone before the vocal part enters, as if the composer wanted to be absolutely certain that the queen would recognize his deferential compliment. He may have had the last laugh, however, as the tale of the farmer's chaste daughter fits all too well with Sedley's praise of the prudish Mary's drive to banish vice. Beloved by his contemporaries for his witty settings of obscene catches, the composer, like the poet, was probably disingenuous in his praise of moral reform.

A few days after Mary's birthday celebration, Prince George "asked leave of the queen in councill to goe for Denmark with his princesse for 2 or 3 years,"[107] a request the queen predictably ignored; and on 4 May the Earl of Marlborough, accused of treason by a professional informer and expert forger, was sent to the Tower, where he remained until the end of the parliamentary term on 15 June. Although the papers that led to his imprisonment were soon exposed as fraudulent, he needed to file a writ of habeas corpus and provide £6,000 in bail in order to gain his freedom, and the queen punished those who lent him the money by striking them off her list of Privy Counselors. Meanwhile, decisive English naval victories at Barfleur and La Hogue (19–23 May) put an end to the fear of a

French invasion, but did nothing to improve relations between the sisters. Although Anne considered making a formal visit to the queen to offer congratulations for the victory at sea, Mary let her know that she would not be welcome, and when the princess made her vacation visit to Bath in August, the queen warned the mayor that he was not to show her the courtesy of escorting her to church.[108]

When Anne returned from Bath in October 1692, the Denmarks took up residence at Berkeley House and began to attend St. James's Church in Piccadilly, but even their churchgoing had political implications. St. James's was a relatively new church (consecrated in 1684) and had recently gained possession of the splendid organ made for James II's Roman Catholic chapel in 1686 by the distinguished builder Renatus Harris, with an ornate wooden case carved by Grinling Gibbons. When William and Mary dismantled the "popish chapel," this fine instrument languished unplayed, so in 1691, the vestry of St. James's asked Queen Mary to let them have it. She granted their petition, but it was her sister Anne who provided 20 guineas to defray the cost of moving the organ. After testing by Henry Purcell and John Blow, the instrument received further improvements in its new home.[109] In light of Queen Mary's downgrading of music in the Chapel Royal, Anne's support of the music at St. James's was a pointed assertion of her own tastes. The rector of St. James's had become a bishop during the summer of 1692, so Anne's friend Henry Compton, Bishop of London, appointed Peter Birch, a High Church preacher whose opinions about the liturgy were in keeping with those of the princess. Queen Mary, who had already clashed with Compton, immediately intervened in this process, appointing her own more Whiggish candidate, William Wake, and the struggle eventually came to trial.[110] Mary took notice of her sister's choice of church by telling Birch that he was not to "lay the text upon her cushion, or take any more notice of her than of other people."[111] To his credit, the embattled rector refused to obey these instructions without a written order, and Mary declined to express her petty revenge in writing, though she pursued her goal of appointing Wake for the next three years. It was only after her death that Wake secured his appointment, winning a close vote in the House of Lords.

Birch was not alone in insisting on Anne's right to be respected in her new neighborhood. Ephemeral publications also expressed sympathy for the beleaguered princess. There was a tradition that the bellmen who walked the streets and rang the hours after dark would recite poems on important days, and Thomas Bamber, bellman in the parish of St. Giles, had recently printed some of his verses, including short poems on the birthdays of Queen Mary and Princess Anne. His poem on Anne, a clumsy effusion in ballad meter, praises her loyalty to the Church of England during the reign of her Catholic father:

As on this Day a Princess mild,
Into the World was Born,
Who with her Pious Actions doth
This Sinful Land adorn:
She in the worst of Times did stand,
When we thought she had fell
By the Contrivance and the Rage
Of Cruel *Jezabel*.

A Copy of Verses…by Thomas Bamber, Bellman (1692), detail.

Modeling his work on the old metrical psalms, the bellman remembers the reign of James II as "the worst of Times" and casts Maria Beatrice as the "Cruel *Jezabel*." Though mild and pious, Anne appears as a courageous and steadfast adherent to the Protestant faith.

As soon as Anne moved into Berkeley House, an anonymous poem from "The Night-Bell-Man of Pickadilly to the Princess of Denmark" began to circulate in manuscript, but this poem was clearly not the work of an actual bellman. The politically sophisticated poet, writing in pentameter couplets and using a much more subtle rhetoric than Bamber's, was adopting a convenient disguise. He begins by welcoming the princess to her new neighborhood:

> Welcome great *Princess* to this lovely Place,
> Where injur'd *Loyalty* must hide its Face;
> Your praise each day by every Man is sung,
> And in the Night by me shall e'er be rung.
> God bless your *Queen*, and yet I may moreover,
> Own you *our Queen* in *Berkly-Street* and *Dover*.
> May your great Prince, and you, live numerous years!
> That's the Subject of all our Loyal Prayers.[112]

Sarah, who had a lifelong interest in lampoons and satires, probably made sure her mistress saw these verses, knowing that Anne would find some comfort in the poet's sympathetic concern for her "injur'd *Loyalty*." Although Mary believed that her sister was trying to form a political party, the main force driving Anne's resistance to the queen was her dogged loyalty to Sarah, which Mary construed as disloyalty to herself and the government. The poet gets at this issue obliquely by describing Anne as a subject of Mary ("your *Queen*") but also as a queen in her own right, at least in her new location ("*our Queen* in *Berkly-Street*"). The rhetoric of possessives continues in the next couplet: "all our Loyal Prayers" ask long life for "your great Prince, and you." If taken literally, the last line implies that the poet's friends in Berkeley Street are saying no prayers for William and Mary, but hoping and praying for Anne's eventual accession.

Increasingly anxious about such praise of the Denmarks, the court probably made an attempt to discover the author of these lines, correctly interpreting them as politically subversive. In the printed broadside, eleven numbered paragraphs in prose, headed "My Lord Nottingham's order to Mr Dives late Clerk of the Council upon notice of the aforesaid verses," appear below the poem. These commands, which instruct the clerk to seek incriminating papers in the clothing and even the bell of the bellman, purport to show the Secretary of State trying to trace the origins of the poem. Though clearly a spoof, they were written by someone familiar with the queen's petulant commands to the mayor of Bath and the rector of St. James's church.[113] In 1692, it was evidently dangerous to speak of Anne as a queen, even in Berkeley Street. When Purcell, in 1695, took care not to emphasize the idea that Anne might reign "without a Crown," he may have been mindful of the court's determination to track down those who had expressed the same sentiments a few years earlier.

§

The ten years between Anne's departure from Whitehall and her succession to the throne were the most peaceful of her life. During the first three years (1692–1694), her complete absence from court gave her the freedom to spend as much time as she wanted with her son and to pursue her interests in music, theatre, and painting. On 14 July 1692, for example, she organized a fleet of barges to carry her party to Dorset Garden for a performance of Purcell's opera *The Fairy Queen*, which she had been too ill to attend a few weeks earlier.[114] Eight months later, she mentioned another play in a hasty note to Sarah: "I am com this minute from seeing ye old Batchelor & am going presently to Camden house."[115] *The Old Bachelor*, a popular comedy by the gifted young playwright William Congreve, enhanced with extensive incidental music by Purcell, opened in March 1693, and Anne, freed from official duties and officious flatterers, was able to see the play in the afternoon and go on to Campden House before her four-year-old's bedtime. She also found time to pose with her son for a touching portrait painted by Sir Godfrey Kneller (color plate 11). Although careful to include an ancient temple and soldier in the background as a compliment to Gloucester's military ambitions, the artist focuses on the domestic. He accentuates the strong family resemblance between mother and son by using a similar palette for their clothing, and depicts Anne's embrace as both tender and protective. As her arms enfold her fragile heir, her defiant gaze challenges any viewer to find fault with her. The portrait is a visual counterpart to a letter Anne wrote to Sarah from Berkeley House a year after the break with the queen: "I am so far of being weary of my way of living or repenting of the least of my actions since this time twelve month, that weare the yeare to run over againe I would tread the same steps."[116]

The princess was an avid and knowledgeable consumer of the visual arts during this period. Writing to Sarah, probably in 1693, she reports on a visit to "the picture drawers in leister fields":

> There was but a few pictures of people I know but those weare very like & the work me thinks looks more like flesh & blood then Sr Godfrey Nellars. He is to draw ye Prince & if that proves well I shall be tempted to desire my dear Mrs Freeman would once more give her selfe the trouble to sitt for her picture.[117]

The artist in question was probably the Swedish painter Michael Dahl, who had a studio in Leicester Fields during this period, and who later painted Queen Anne and Prince George. Anne's assessment of his work as superior to that of Kneller, who was the most expensive and prominent artist then at work in London, is earnest of her willingness to make independent judgments as a connoisseur. In the event, however, Dahl's work disappointed her, as she explains in a later letter:

> I am very glad Mr Closterman has begun deare Mrs Freemans childrens picturcs so well.... & the other man I once desired you to sitt to not proveing successful in that he begun of my boy nor that he has don of ye Prince, I can only depend upon this man to do one that is like.[118]

John Closterman, another important painter, later quarreled bitterly with Sarah over his group portrait of her children, though the works referred to here may be individual portraits. Anne's interest in painting was not confined to these living artists; she also sought out older works, including one with special meaning for her, described in her next letter to Sarah:

> I forgot to tell you in my last, that I had seen my mothers picture, & beleeve tis a very good one, tho I do not remember enough of her to know whether it is like her or no, but it is very like one the King had, which every body said was so.[119]

In the case of music, Anne was more than a consumer: she was actively practicing two instruments. A surviving manuscript, misleadingly labeled "Princes Ans Lutebook," bears witness to this activity; it is a collection of popular songs arranged in tablature for the five-course guitar, the instrument Anne had studied as a girl and evidently continued to play. Among the selections are eighteen pieces by Purcell, including excerpts from *King Arthur* (1691) and *The Fairy Queen* (1692). Whoever compiled this book was serving the princess by making transcriptions that allowed her to play music she had recently heard and liked, and the dates of some of the compositions show that she was playing from this score during the 1690s.[120] She also continued to play the harpsichord. In dedicating a posthumous collection of Purcell's keyboard pieces to the princess, his widow thanked Anne for her "Generous Encouragement of my deceas'd Husband's Performances in Musick, together with the great Honour your Highness has don that Science in your Choice of that Instrument, for which the following Compositions were made."[121] Frances Purcell's reference to Anne's choice of instrument can only mean that she knew Anne played the harpsichord, and there is additional evidence that the princess continued to take harpsichord lessons. In a letter written from Bath in 1692, she asked Sir Benjamin Bathurst, Comptroller of her House-hold, to "pay Mr. Baptist the money I desired you."[122] "Mr. Baptist" was probably Giovanni Baptista Draghi, who had been the organist in James II's Catholic chapel, playing the instrument now installed at St. James's Church; he had also composed the music for Dryden's St. Cecilia ode of 1687. As Anne remembered when grant-ing him a pension, Draghi had been one of her musical instructors in her youth; this letter suggests that the lessons continued.[123] Sir John Hawkins, writing late in the eighteenth century, says that Anne "had a spinnet, the loudest and perhaps the finest that ever was heard, of which she was very fond."[124] According to the anec-dote about Mary's taste in ballads, Anne was also taking voice lessons from Ara-bella Hunt,[125] which would help explain her interest in hearing professional singers: Draghi brought a recently arrived Italian singer to perform for her at the end of 1692, evidently hoping that royal patronage would help his protégé gain attention.[126] Also associated with Anne's small court at Berkeley House was an excellent young English singer, Annabella Dives, to whom *Orpheus Britannicus,* a posthumous collection of Purcell's songs, was dedicated in 1698. As the dedica-tion notes, Annabella, who married the old playwright and courtier Robert Howard in early 1693, took music lessons from Purcell and paid for the tablet that marks his grave in Westminster Abbey.[127]

In turning to art and music for solace and amusement during her absence from official functions, Anne was following the advice of Cowley, who had recom-mended acquiring knowledge of the arts as one way to deal with "little Intervals of accidental Solitude":

> If any man be so unlearned as to want entertainment...it is truly a great shame both to his Parents and Himself, for a very small portion of any Ingenious Art will stop up all those gaps of our Time, either Musique, or Painting, or Designing, or Chymistry, or History, or Gardening, or twenty other things will do it usefully and pleasantly.[128]

Despite the criticism made of Anne's education, both by her contemporaries and by modern scholars, her parents saw to it that she had instruction in music, paint-ing, dancing, and French; her artistic interests, acquired at an early age, now helped her maintain her mental health. In advocating a good education as a way to deal with "accidental solitude" Cowley makes no distinction between the arts ("Musique, or Painting"), the sciences ("Chymistry"), or the traditional humani-ties ("History"). Even gardening qualifies as a useful branch of learning, worthy of a place in the list of arts and sciences. Sarah Churchill, who had grown up in the same court as Anne, with an education similarly focused on the arts, was now pur-suing ambitious schemes of gardening in St. Albans; in an effort to improve the gaps of her own education, she was also avidly reading history and philosophy. Her brother-in-law Edward Griffith, in a letter probably written in 1694, playfully expresses his hope of "being Mounteign's rival in your Solitude."[129]

Anne was also reading in her solitude,[130] and there is reason to believe that she was sympathetic to a powerful critique of female education that appeared during her absence from court. In July 1694, Mary Astell published her *Serious Proposal to the Ladies,* in which she lamented the waste of female brain power resulting from the limited education available to women, developing her argument by making effective use of metaphors drawn from gardening:

> The Soil is rich and would, if well cultivated, produce a noble Harvest, if then the Unskilful Managers not only permit, but incourage noxious Weeds, tho' we shall suffer by their Neglect, yet they ought not in justice to blame any but themselves, if they reap the Fruit of their own Folly.[131]

In order to cultivate the rich soil of female talent, Astell proposes that women found their own educational institutions:

> Now as to the Proposal, it is to erect a *Monastery,* or if you will (to avoid giving offence to the scrupulous and injudicious, by names which tho' innocent in themselves, have been abus'd by superstitious Practices,) we will call it a *Religious Retirement*, and such as shall have a double aspect, being not only a Retreat from the World for those who desire that advantage, but likewise, an Institution and previous discipline, to fit us to do the greatest good in it.[132]

For the ladies choosing this retirement, Astell outlines an educational program "neither...too troublesome nor out of the reach of a Female Virtuoso," requiring "no more languages than are necessary to acquaint her with useful Authors. Nor need she trouble her self in turning over a huge number of Books, but take care to understand and digest a few well-chosen and good ones. Let her but obtain right ideas, and...thoroughly to understand Christianity as profess'd by the *Church* of *England*, will be sufficient to confirm her in the truth."[133]

It is not difficult to imagine this project appealing to Anne, especially during her own period of retirement, and according to George Ballard, who wrote a collection of biographies of eminent women in the middle of the eighteenth century, the princess considered funding Astell's proposed academy:

> The scheme given in her proposal, seemed so reasonable, and wrought so far upon a certain great lady, that she had designed to give ten thousand

pounds toward erecting a sort of college for the education and improvement of the female sex: and as a retreat for these ladies who nauseating the
parade of the world, might here find a happy recess from the noise and
hurry of it. But this design coming to the ears of Bishop Burnet, he immediately went to that lady, and so powerfully remonstrated against it, telling
her it would look like preparing a way for *Popish Orders*, that it would be
reputed a *Nunnery*, &c. that he utterly frustrated that noble design.[134]

This anecdote, first appearing in print nearly forty years after Anne's death, looks
somewhat suspicious. £10,000 (at least £2 million in today's money) would have
been one-eighth of Anne's annual income, a prohibitively large amount for her to
provide when she was paying high rents for her own lodgings and for Gloucester's.
She also had excellent reasons to be skeptical about the Whiggish Bishop Burnet,
who was close to William and Mary. Ballard's source for his information, however,
was the pioneering Anglo-Saxon scholar Elizabeth Elstob, who was personally acquainted with Astell, and neither Astell nor Elstob had any reason to fabricate
such a story.[135] If the proposed amount of money grew in Ballard's retelling, it is
hardly preposterous to imagine that Anne, at a moment when she was enjoying
her retirement from court life, might well have wished to support Astell's proposal
to provide a productive retirement for intellectual ladies. And if Burnet was not
the kind of clergyman to whom Anne would give easy assent, a warning against
anything looking like popery, whether from him or another, might have been sufficient to dissuade her.

In 1697, Astell dedicated a later, expanded edition of *A Serious Proposal* to
Princess Anne, directly appealing to her in print for support:

> And when I consider you Madam as a Princess who is sensible that the
> Chief Prerogative of the Great is the Power they have of doing more
> Good than those in an Inferior Station can, I see no cause to fear that
> your Royal Highness will deny Encouragement to that which has no
> other Design than the Bettering of the World, especially the most ne-
> glected part of it as to all Real Improvement, the Ladies.[136]

If Ballard's account is correct in its general outlines, we may read Astell's rhetoric
here as expressing her continuing hope that Anne will provide some financial "Encouragement," while defending her project from Burnet's aspersions: she can see
"no cause to fear" that Anne will withhold support, especially as her plan has "no
other Design than the Bettering of the World," certainly not a covert design to prepare the way for Catholic nunneries.

By the time of this second edition, Queen Mary was dead, but she was very much alive when Astell first published the *Serious Proposal*, and it is therefore worth asking why Astell turned to Anne, presumably believing that the queen was less likely to support her cause. Mary had been a reader of plays and a gifted dancer in her youth, but unlike her sister, she was now paying little attention to the arts or to the kind of intellectual improvement Astell was advocating. Instead, she alternated between intense political activity, her duty during William's frequent absences, and domestic handicraft. When William was abroad, the queen assumed the mantle of monarchy, ruling with considerable force, but when the king was in residence, she spent much of her time making fringes, an activity that occupied both hands with repetitive labor: as one hand looped the thread, the other passed a shuttle through the loop. According to contemporary reports, the maids of honor joined in this work, and it soon became a fashionable craze.[137] Keeping her fingers busy with fringe-making may have been intrinsically satisfying to Mary, and because the motions required quickly became automatic, the work allowed the constant flow of conversation she seems to have needed. But in light of her ongoing concern with how the world might regard her activities, her choice of handwork as a leisure activity bears further scrutiny. Her retreat from the exercise of power into the practice of "knotting," a stylized, conventionally feminine domestic activity, was a convenient way of appearing to be a meek and subservient spouse, the role she so carefully constructs for herself in her diary. A contemporary discussing Mary's handwork reportedly praised her for "resolving as much as in her lay to strike at the very root of vice and idleness";[138] she may have been trying to set a good example by her digital industry.

The potential for humor in the knotting craze was not lost on the poets. A witty squib attributed to Sedley compares Mary's fringe-making to the devotional activities of her stepmother:

> Bless'd we! who from such Queens are freed,
> Who by vain Superstition led,
> Are always telling Beads;
> But here's a Queen, now, thanks to God,
> Who, when she rides in Coach abroad,
> Is always knotting Threads.[139]

And a popular song, certainly by Sedley and deftly set by Purcell, depicts the plight of a pining lover unable to get the attention of his sweetheart, which is entirely focused on "knotting":

Hears not my *Phillis,* how the Birds
Their feather'd Mates salute?
They tell their Passion in their Words;
Must I alone be mute?
Phillis, *without Frown or Smile,*
Sat and knotted all the while.

. . . .

Must then your faithful Swain expire,
And not one Look obtain,
Which he, to sooth his fond Desire,
Might pleasingly explain?
Phillis, *without Frown or Smile,*
Sat and knotted all the while.[140]

For Phillis, knotting is a convenient way to fend off the unwelcome advances of the poem's speaker, but from his point of view, her obsession with her handwork has flattened out all her emotions: not only is she unable to smile in encouragement of her faithful swain; she cannot even frown to discourage him. Although this is hardly a political poem, it is possible to hear in Sedley's lines his awareness that Queen Mary's alternation between engaged governmental activity and mind-numbing craftwork had rendered her deaf to some kinds of emotion. The queen had no children and no female favorite; her relations with her husband were formal, and he was frequently absent pursuing his military campaigns. By filling her days with the chatter of conversation and the repetitive motions of the knotting shuttle, she was avoiding having to confront the essential emptiness of her life. The shy and reticent Anne, by contrast, was spending her time in caring for her son, in expressing her deep affection for Sarah, in reading Mr. Cowley's poems and Mrs. Astell's proposals, and in perfecting her skills as a musician—not because she ever expected to perform in public, but because being able to play Mr. Purcell's latest tunes on her guitar or her harpsichord allowed her to possess his music, with its richly human range of emotional expression, in a way that Mary, though nominally the royal mistress he served, could not claim.

§

Because Anne's life during this period was so private, the historical record is thin. Luttrell reports her miscarriages on 23 March 1693 and 21 January 1694, but says little else about her during these years. On her twenty-ninth birthday, 6 February 1694, she was well enough to watch her five-year-old son drill his troops in Hyde Park. "The officers," writes Luttrell, "have hatts and feathers, and the soldiers all red caps and 4 little drakes for cannon."[141] The court, however, took no notice.

Although Gloucester had been "carried to the queen in a rich dresse" on his fourth birthday in 1693,[142] there is no record of a similar visit in 1694. Anne's continuing concern for Gloucester's health led her to spend the summer of 1694 in Twickenham, even further from the unhealthy air of London, and the distance may have rendered a visit to Whitehall impractical. Rumors that the princess and the queen would soon be reconciled, though fairly frequent, always proved groundless.

By the autumn of 1694, Anne once again believed she was pregnant, but this ultimately proved to be another of her false pregnancies.[143] Although the princess was frequently "indisposed," the queen appeared to be in robust health. Her growing corpulence, noted by some lampooners, would not have struck her contemporaries as a sign of illness.[144] So everyone was surprised when she fell ill in December 1694, and when she showed the unmistakable symptoms of the smallpox, there was widespread alarm. Princess Anne, who had recovered from the same disease in 1677, sent at once to the queen *"to desire that* HER MAJESTY *would believe she was extremely concerned for her illness: adding, that if* HER MAJESTY *would allow her the happiness of waiting on her, she would, notwithstanding the condition she was in, run any hazard for that satisfaction."* The reply was a letter from Elizabeth, Countess of Derby, Groom of the Stole to the queen, which was handed to the lady Anne had dispatched with her own message. After thanking Anne and noting the importance of keeping the queen quiet, Lady Derby added a postscript asking that the messenger "present my humble duty to the PRINCESS." From this civil phrase, a violation of Mary's wish that her attendants shun her sister, Sarah accurately inferred that the queen was dying.[145]

With her mother long dead and her father unreachable in France, the loss of her sister left Anne more isolated than ever before. The fragile Gloucester, who had another frightening illness in the spring of 1695, was now the only relative by blood to whom she could cling, and regrets about her long dispute with Mary probably intensified and complicated her grief. Mary died on 28 December 1694, but the preparations for her funeral were so complex that it was not held until March. Anne was to have been chief mourner but excused herself, explaining that she was too ill to attend.[146] In absenting herself from the service, she missed experiencing the comforts of the Anglican burial service and hearing some moving new music composed for the occasion by Purcell.[147] Although the princess believed she was in the later stages of a pregnancy, she had attended two coronations while actually pregnant, so her decision to remain in seclusion probably reflected some considerations beyond her physical health. In light of the unresolved estrangement, Anne may have thought her sincerity as a mourner would be doubted if she appeared in public at the funeral, and there were plenty of courtiers and ballad-mongers prepared to make cynical reflections. Her decision to mourn in private was a tactful one, ensuring that the sad and solemn occasion would remain entirely focused on Mary.

Although she avoided the funeral, Anne wrote immediately to the king expressing her sympathy, and there was a tearful meeting at which they both expressed
their sorrow. Jenkin Lewis, who helped carry the princess upstairs in her sedan
chair, provides an eyewitness account:

> She told his Majesty, in faultering accents, that she was truly sorry for his
> loss! Who replied, he was much concerned for hers: both were equally
> affected, and could scarcely refrain from tears, or speak distinctly. The
> King then handed the Princess in, who staid with him three quarters of
> an hour.[148]

In addition to sharing Anne's grief, William was alert to the political importance
of improving his relations with the person next in line to his shaky throne. "He
was well aware," writes Sarah with her usual cynicism, "that every body who had a
mind to shew they did not care for him, would certainly do it by making their
court to her."[149] Although his motives were probably mixed, the king took concrete steps to heal the rift. He restored Anne's guards, arranged for St. James's
Palace to be prepared for her occupancy, and paid frequent visits to her at Berkeley House during the spring of 1695. He even made a point of coming from Kensington to the Chapel Royal to hear Henry Compton preach, visiting Anne on his
way back home. Taking note of these warmer relations, newswriters reported
rumors that Prince George and the Earl of Marlborough would join the king
during the upcoming campaign, though in the event, neither did so.[150]

In May, William sailed off to Flanders for the summer's fighting, which would
include the taking of Namur, his greatest success during the long, inconclusive
Nine Years' War. Although Prince George did not go with him, William made sure
that George's son Gloucester received news of the campaign. Lewis tells us that
"Major General Churchill and some other general officers of the army came to
wait upon the Duke" before embarking. General Churchill was John's younger
brother Charles, formerly page to Prince George, and the other generals probably
included his friend Henry Belasyse, whom Lewis later mentions in connection
with the duke.[151] Although Churchill and Belasyse were not present at Namur,
they contributed to the success of the siege by staging a crucial delaying action
that successfully confused the French as to William's true plans.[152] Gloucester,
who followed such movements avidly, knew that every available soldier was
needed in Flanders, so when the king sent "two troops of the earl of Oxford's regiment ... to attend the prince and princesse during their stay at Windsor,"[153] the
boy was in a position to appreciate what that order meant. While sending troops
to Windsor was a symbol of the respect with which William now wished the Denmarks to be treated, it is also pleasant to think that even in the heat of the campaign

for Namur, the king remembered the birthday of the royal heir and dispatched some adult soldiers to Windsor in order to delight his small, frail namesake.[154]

When Namur finally fell, Gloucester planned to celebrate with another cannonade, but his mother intervened. "The Duke was very joyous," writes Lewis, "and ordered his guns should be fired six times round; and was for imitating the siege, had not the Princess, whose tender care of him and fears prompted her to give orders that no gun-powder, or squibs of any kind, should be let off near the Duke."[155] Anne's "tender care" had not caused her to forbid the firing of Gloucester's cannon on his recent birthday or on any other festive occasion, so this explanation is dubious; Lewis's clumsy syntax betrays his strained effort to find an excuse for an embarrassing act. There were spectacular fireworks in London on 8 September, the day set aside for public thanksgiving, so Anne's command forbidding "gun-powder, or squibs of any kind" at Windsor might well have been thought a deliberate refusal to participate in the celebration. Her reluctance to have the victory saluted, even by her darling son, is further evidence that the truce between the in-laws, which both parties kept up for the sake of appearances, was actually shaky.

Well-meaning courtiers did their best to promote improved relations. "Three lords, whose judgment all the world valued," writes Sarah Churchill, advised the princess to write a formal letter congratulating the king on his victory, but the letter, once written and dispatched, "served no other purpose but to give the King an opportunity of shewing his brutal disregard for the writer; for he never returned any answer to it, nor so much as a civil message."[156] Sarah's husband, eager to avoid friction between the king and the heir apparent, gave William a chance to repair his omission by sending him a second copy of Anne's letter, tactfully pointing out that a packet boat filled with mail had been lost around the time of the first, but William ignored this message as well. Perhaps the king's "brutal disregard" for the princess was a response to a perceived insult. If someone attached to the ceremonial troops at Windsor informed the monarch that his sister-in-law had stilled their guns, William might have concluded that her quashing of the victory salute, especially when she knew how much it would please her son, showed her true opinion of his military efforts.[157]

§

When the Denmarks returned from Windsor in the fall of 1695, their status had changed significantly. Although courtiers were still wearing mourning for the queen, there were now fewer barriers to the expression of popular affection for the princess. Anne and George returned to Berkeley House, and Gloucester returned to Campden House, where the king came to visit on 12 October, just two days after returning from the Continent. William's prompt attention to his successor and her family reflects his awareness of their political significance; he came to Campden House again on 17 October, at the beginning of a royal progress to Newmarket for the horse races, and once more on 16 November, shortly after his return to London.

On his third visit, the king came bearing gifts:

> Thursday evening the king gave a visit to the prince and princesse of Denmark, and invited them to reside at St. James's house; and at the same time gave the garter (vacant by the death of the earl of Strafford) to the duke of Glocester; who, it is said, will have a patent for that title, a family establish'd for him, and an house for his highnesses court.[158]

Although these offers were welcome signs of respect, each one had some worrying aspect for Anne. Moving to St. James's meant living on a grander scale, and she was quick to invite the Churchills to occupy some choice rooms with a view of the park. But it also meant losing the independence she had enjoyed in her years at Berkeley House and exposing her asthmatic husband and frail son to the smoke and stench of Westminster. Several months later, on 6 February 1696, Anne held her birthday ball at Berkeley House.[159] The king, who also suffered from asthma, had always avoided Whitehall, remaining at Kensington Palace as much as possible; and the only palace Anne loved, as her practice once crowned would show, was Windsor. It was there, in St. George's Chapel, that Gloucester was installed as a Knight of the Garter on his seventh birthday, an event Anne marked by having him painted in his Garter robes, attended by the youngest of the Bathurst brothers.

The honor given to Gloucester, however, was also a reminder of the king's refusal to provide a Garter for Marlborough, despite requests from Anne and George. Grateful as she was for the early recognition of her son, the princess might have preferred that this vacancy go to the husband of her favorite. The plan to establish a "family" for Gloucester, which meant taking him out of the hands of women and appointing a male governor, was emotionally and politically difficult as well: Anne had every reason to expect that the king would take charge of the appointments to the duke's new court, ignoring her maternal prerogatives and insisting on his precedence, and when the household was established, there was indeed a bitter quarrel over its staff.

William and Anne complained about each other in private, but their royal training had taught them how to behave on state occasions, and they both had reasons to keep up appearances. Mary's death had left the king without the air of legitimacy she provided as a person in the normal succession, and it was therefore in his interest to present a public façade of friendship with his sister-in-law. Anne, too, had little to gain from a quarrel; her long estrangement from her sister had

John Smith, *William Duke of Gloucester; Benjamin Bathurst*, mezzotint
after Thomas Murray (1697).

taught her the cost of falling out with those in power. In the slightly displaced world of artistic expressions, however, those praising the princess often did so at the king's expense—presumably because they believed such gestures would please her. Although its allegorical text requires some decoding, "Lovely Albina," an anonymous poem that Purcell set to music sometime between Anne's return to London on 27 September and his own death on 21 November,[160] exemplifies this process:

> Lovely Albina's come ashore,
> To enter her just claim
> Ten times more charming than before,
> To her immortal fame.
> The Belgic lion, as he's brave,
> This beauty will relieve;
> For nothing but a mean blind slave
> Can live and let her grieve.

By calling Anne "Albina," the poet links her to the legendary Albina, a princess who supposedly came to England from Syria with her thirty-three sisters and gave birth to a race of giants.[161] The poetic name "Albion" came from this mythical princess, and some might still remember Dryden's opera *Albion and Albanius,* staged just ten years earlier, which had claimed these names for the Stuarts.[162] Calling Anne "Albina" was a way of insisting on her Englishness, a quality lacking in William, who appears here not as the King of England but as the "Belgic lion." In one of several contemporaneous poems employing that phrase, the alcoholic satirist Richard Ames reminded his readers of the Revolution:

> When all our Hopes to lowest Ebb were brought,
>> The Great *Nassau,* that Son of Fame,
>> Like mighty *Belgick Lyon* came
> And quickly chas'd these Rav'nous Beasts of Prey
>> From *Albion's* happy Clifts away,
> Dispell'd the Mists of night, and show'd us perfect day.[163]

By picturing lovely Albina coming ashore to enter her just claim, the author of the song text provides an alternative to the official mythology that pictured William coming ashore to rescue England from popery and arbitrary government.

At this moment, Albina's "just claim" was not merely Anne's claim to the public honors she had been denied after quarreling with Mary, or her claim to the throne, which some thought a better one than William's. The immediate and specific reference was to her claim to the income from 95,649 acres of land in Ireland formerly owned by her father, recently and brazenly granted by William to his mistress Elizabeth Villiers.[164] This grant, made public in May after William had sailed for the Continent, was in the news again in the fall: "the lord deputy and council" of Ireland, wrote Luttrell, "have sent to our lords justices several bills to be approved of before they passe into acts," including one "to confirm his majesties grants to the earls of Athlone and Romney, Mrs. Villiers, &c."[165] Anne, who expected to inherit these lands from her father, was still protesting this action in 1697 and certainly concerned about it in 1695. The poet was evidently close enough to her court to know of this concern. Back in the public eye after her period of exile from court, Anne is "Ten times more charming than before"—a compliment to her and a pointed reminder of her popularity, which made William intensely jealous. In keeping with the long tradition of mythical lions protecting vulnerable women, the princess appears as a helpless beauty in need of protection from "The Belgic lion," who can only be the king. Rhetorically limiting William's options, the author assures us that the lion, as proof of his bravery, *will* honor the beauty's just claim. If he fails to do so, he will cast doubt upon his reputation for courage, and if he lets her go on grieving, he will be "a mean blind slave," a remarkably insulting phrase with which to threaten a sitting monarch who had no intention of honoring Anne's "just claim" to her Irish lands.

Purcell's music for these dangerous words betrays the same caution about political messages observable in the recent birthday ode for Gloucester. All of the adjectives praising Anne—"lovely," "charming," "immortal"—call forth florid, melismatic passages; the composer stretches the first four lines of the poem across sixteen bars, then immediately repeats that whole section. Lost in the midst of this cheerful, celebratory music is the purpose of Albina's coming ashore: "To enter her just claim," stated just once, takes only a bar and a half. After the repeat, Purcell modulates to the relative minor and introduces the "Belgic lion," repeating the word *brave* six times, twice on the highest note of the song. Where the poet had treated the lion's bravery as a quality that would be proven by his relieving the needs of the beauty, the composer simply and repeatedly asserts the bravery as a defining quality of the lion; the repetition is so insistent that it is possible to hear it as ironic. The most embarrassing phrase—"mean, blind slave"—is set plainly and in the singer's lowest register, then immediately pushed out of our ears by a long melisma on "live," which leads in turn to a touching, almost recitative setting of "let her grieve," in which an expressive chromatic bass line moves the song to the parallel minor.[166]

This song has three main ideas, each with its own musical material: the charming beauty of Albina, the martial bravery of the lion, and the sorrow that will ensue if the beauty is left to grieve. All three are present in the poem, but

Mus. Ex. 4.5: Henry Purcell, "*Lovely Albina*" (1695).

Purcell has done his best to soften or obscure the political argument by which the poet *links* those ideas, the assertion that William's ignoring the just claims of his sister-in-law will invalidate his reputation as a brave, heroic lion, revealing him as a "mean blind slave."

The occasion for which Purcell's setting of these words was composed remains uncertain. The poem's rhetoric resembles that of a royal "welcome song," and it might plausibly have been performed for the princess and her court to celebrate her return to London from Windsor. If Anne traveled from Windsor by barge, as her uncle Charles II had often done, her arrival by water would explain the reference to her coming ashore.[167] Unlike previous monarchs, William did not insist on having a musical welcome when he returned from his military campaigns or his visits to the country; he never read poetry, listened to music, or attended the theatre. By commissioning a small welcome song of her own, Anne would have been behaving like a monarch and reminding attentive listeners of the cultural traditions followed by her Stuart forbears.[168] Alternatively, a performance could have been part of the ceremony on one of William's three autumn visits to Campden House, the last of which came just five days before the composer died.[169] In that case, however, it might have seemed odd to welcome the king with a song addressed to the princess, and there would have been the further risk that someone in the royal party, despite Purcell's efforts, might realize that the text of the song was less than complimentary. Another attractive hypothesis is that the song was prepared for a performance on the occasion of Anne's return to St. James's Palace, where she took up residence at about this time. A set of "privy stairs" led directly from the Thames to Whitehall, so Anne might have arrived in a way that would justify the reference to coming ashore, though she would then have needed a sedan chair to travel on to St. James's. A fourth possibility is that this song might have been performed to welcome Anne as she "came ashore" to a performance at the Dorset Garden Theatre, which was normally entered from the water.[170] Yet even if there was no public performance at all, any song by Mr. Purcell was likely to pass into circulation, and the composer's death made the song especially attractive to publishers; it appeared in two different printings early in 1696.[171] Although the king had no interest in music, publication might again have offered suspicious courtiers an opportunity to ferret out the subversive implications of the text, though no one appears to have raised a protest. Anne, however, might have hoped that some who saw the song in print would recognize it as a calculated insult to the monarch, realize that his disdain for the arts made him incapable of recognizing its allegorical message, and thus think less of him for being ignorant of poetry and music—arts that Anne cherished, understood, and would promote as queen.

CHAPTER 5

SWEET REMEMBRANCE SHALL REMAIN

1 August 1700

Moored at the edge of the Thames, the royal barges lay silent in the darkness. Even the watermen, notoriously fond of drink and foul of mouth, were subdued as they waited to convey a small coffin to Westminster. Originally, they had expected to row all the way to Windsor Castle, where William, Duke of Gloucester, a few days after his eleventh birthday, had died from a brief and violent illness. But the summer had been hot, the river was shallow, and the night was pitch dark, so John Churchill, Earl of Marlborough, who took charge of the arrangements as Gloucester's governor, thought it safer to transport the coffin by coach, transferring it to a barge downstream at Thistleworth, where the water was deeper. It was after midnight when the small procession came into view: first the duke's own coach, the very one in which he had followed the hunt as an eager six-year-old, then three other coaches escorted by "a Party of the Earl of *Oxford*'s Regiment of Horse," the soldiers the boy had so often admired. Marlborough and one trusted servant rode with the body; a few more "gentleman servants" and a handful of officials occupied the remaining coaches. Gilbert Burnet, Bishop of Salisbury, who had been Gloucester's preceptor, was present, as were Samuel Pratt and Richard Willis, two other clergymen who had served as his tutors. And because this funeral, though private, was still a royal event, two officials from the College of Arms, the "Somerset Herald" and the "Portcullis Pursuivant," attended the body in its journey from Windsor to Westminster. Samuel Stebbing, the Somerset Herald, set down an eyewitness account of their progress:

> The Proceeding from the *Castle*, was Privately through the *Park* (lighted by Flambeaux) to *Old Windsor*, and so through *Stains* to *Bedfont*, Guarded by a Party of the Earl of *Oxford*'s Regiment of Horse; where being Reliev'd by another Party of the same Regiment, they went on by *Hounslow* to *Thistleworth*, and arriving there at past Twelve in the Night, it was thought more adviseable by the Governor, *&c.* considering the Body was well fix'd in the Coach, as also the Delay and Trouble in the Removing of it, to discharge the Barges, and carry it on by Land; which was accordingly done.[1]

In deciding to proceed by land, Marlborough departed from the instructions given him by the Lords Justices, nine leading officials who took charge of the government when King William was abroad. Meeting in London, these men had decided to model the proceedings on the funeral of Anne's short-lived brother James, Duke of Cambridge, who died at Twickenham in 1667. In two letters to Marlborough, Robert Yard, Secretary to the Lords Justices, indicated their intention to dispatch three of the king's barges to Windsor; if necessary, he added, Marlborough might also commandeer the barges belonging to the Prince and Princess of Denmark.[2] Aware of Princess Anne's concern for propriety and ceremony, the Lords Justices presumably believed she would take some comfort in having the cortège proceed by water. She would not have remembered the funeral of her brother, who died when she was two, but she had probably heard descriptions of the black-draped barge that brought the body of Queen Elizabeth back to Whitehall after her death at Richmond in 1603.[3] Despite her devastating loss, it was in character for Anne to expect her cherished son to receive honors befitting a monarch; it was also in character for Marlborough, ever the practical tactician, to decide that no one would notice the royal barge on a starless night and to take the simpler expedient of proceeding by land. Shrewdly, he kept that decision quiet: Luttrell, like other newswriters, reported that "the corps of the duke of Glocester was brought from Windsor in one of his majesties barges," and it was not until 1707 that Stebbing quietly published the true story.[4] It is distinctly possible that Anne never knew about the change of plans.

During the next week, the body lay in state in the prince's apartments in Whitehall, in a room "adorn'd with Three Dozen of Taffeta-Scocheons of His Highness's Arms, intermix'd with small Stars of the Order of the *Garter*," an appropriate detail because Gloucester had become a Garter Knight some four years earlier. In an effort to control the crowds, the guards would only admit those wearing mourning, and they took elaborate precautions to keep curious onlookers away from the private funeral service on 9 August, as Luttrell reports:

> In the evening the lords justices were at the duke of Glocesters interment, which was performed with great order by 9 at night: the guards, consisting of 400 men, made a lane from the house of lords to the east door of Westminster Abbey to keep off the mobb, and every other man had a flambeau lighted [in] his hand, which made it visible to the spectators: there were the bishops of London, Winchester, Salisbury, lords Normanby, Godolphin, and many others of the nobility, with all the yeomen of the guards, the heralds at armes, &c.[5]

Moving down the lane created by the torch-bearing guards, the noble mourners "proceeded to the *Abbey-Church*, where the Dean and Choir of *Westminster* stood with Wax-Lights in their Hands, and fell into the Proceeding between the Earl of *Marlborough* His Highness's Governor, and *Clarenceux* King of Arms, and passing down the south-Isle by the West-end of the Choir, went up the North-side to King *Henry* the Seventh's Chapel, whilst an Anthem proper for the Occasion was Sung." Although Stebbing does not specify a composer or a text, Purcell's funeral music for Queen Mary, which the choir had sung at the composer's own burial in 1695, would have been readily available and known to some of the performers. Whatever the choice of repertoire, performing at this service was a poignant duty for the boy choristers, who were close in age to the deceased. As the brief service ended, "the White-Staff Officers," those holding important posts in Gloucester's court, "breaking their White-Staves, threw them into the Vault," formally signifying the end of their duties, and the chief mourners, all Knights of the Garter, wearing "Long Cloaks, and…their Collars of the Order," left the abbey.[6]

§

Princess Anne would certainly have approved of these solemn and dignified rites, but she did not participate, remaining secluded at Windsor with Sarah Churchill, who had hurried from St. Albans to be at her side. Not until 26 November did the Denmarks return to London, though the princess's absence from public view did not deter poets and clergymen from publishing sermons, elegies, and letters of consolation addressed to her. Both universities issued substantial collections of poems by students and faculty mourning this royal death, as they had done when Mary died some five years earlier; the boys of Westminster School, who had not produced a volume on Mary's death, published one for Gloucester containing forty poems.

Most of the verse in these three collections is in Latin, though each presents a few poems in Greek, Hebrew, and other learned tongues.[7] As the choice of languages suggests, the poets were usually more concerned to display erudition than to express grief. At least five elegies, however, were written by boys who actually knew Gloucester, and these more personal poems give us precious glimpses into his world. Addressing his comrades in the duke's boy army, Allen Bathurst, now a sixteen-year-old undergraduate at Oxford, writes movingly about his years as a playmate of the dead boy. Bathurst's father was Anne's Household Treasurer, his mother was her girlhood favorite Frances Apsley, and he himself had been one of the four Eton students given leave to play soldiers with Gloucester at Windsor in 1695. Skillfully deploying the details of ancient military funerals—trailing pikes rattling on a stony path, trumpets hoarsely proclaiming grief, arms flung onto a pyre, and a weeping, riderless horse—he pictures Gloucester, "his cheeks aflame with anger," barking out short commands to his cohorts and showing reluctance to order a retreat, even in a sham battle.[8] Remarkably enough, Kneller's last portrait of Gloucester (color plate 12), depicting him in armor in a pose derived from portraits of his royal uncle, shows his cheeks suffused with color.[9] In his closing lines, Bathurst imagines the thought of their lost leader kindling a martial spirit in his surviving companions, whose trophies will adorn his memory. If their tears now bear witness to the honor due to the boy, their glorious deeds in the future will prove what honor is due to the man.[10] Implicit in the rhetorical contrast between boy and man is the sad knowledge that now there would be no man, no warrior-king, burning with noble flame, prepared to subdue the world.

In his highly competent poem, Bathurst names two other childhood companions of the duke, urging them to join him in mourning their comrade's death. He tells Lionel Sackville, son of the poetic Earl of Dorset, to tune his father's lyre, and Sackville, now styled Lord Buckhurst, promptly did so: his Latin poem dedicating the volume to the king is the first entry in the Westminster collection.[11] Protesting his youthful inexperience and turning some elegant compliments to the monarch, Buckhurst introduces his fellow poets without saying anything substantive or personal about the dead boy, though he was doubly connected to Gloucester's mother as the son of Dorset and the nephew of Bishop Compton; his father and his uncle had helped Anne escape from Whitehall while pregnant with the child who became the Duke of Gloucester.

Although Buckhurst was evidently a member of Gloucester's boy army, he does not appear to have been as close to the duke as the other boy Bathurst names: John, Lord Churchill, Sarah's eldest son. Born in 1687, Jack Churchill was another of the Eton boys who had leave to play with Gloucester in 1695. Lewis gives touching details of their early friendship, based on the shared belief that they would join King William in fighting the French:

My Lord Churchill was a bold-spirited youth, and not above two or three years older than the Duke, when he was admitted by him a

Lieutenant-General.... Mrs. Wanley asked his Lordship, if he would go with the Duke? who answered, briskly, "Yes, I will!"—"What if you are killed?" said she. "I do not care!" which the Duke hearing, took a secret delight in him from that moment. My Lord admired the Duke's Highland sword, which was readily bestowed on his Lordship, by the Duke, although he was very fond of it, saying, he would bespeak another.[12]

Already a "Lieutenant-General" in the boy army, young Churchill secured a salaried post as Master of the Horse in Gloucester's small court in 1698, at the age of eleven.[13] When that court dissolved after the death of Gloucester, the Churchills sent their son to Cambridge, where he arrived in time to contribute a Latin poem to the university's memorial collection. The editors recognized his personal connection to the dead prince by printing his poem at the very beginning of the volume.[14] Although it has only six lines, Churchill's elegy is personal and moving. He directly addresses his mother's friend Anne, asking why she should have to suffer such evil, a question the princess might well have asked herself at this time. His opening phrase, "Infelix Mater," identifies the queen as an "unfortunate mother," and from this day forward, Anne would sign all her letters to Sarah as "your poor unfortunate faithfull Morly." In his closing turn, young Churchill says that anyone wanting to bring solace to the destitute mother will lack it himself, an elegant but clear acknowledgment of his own grief.[15]

Churchill's strong personal response to the loss of the duke was apparent to his contemporaries. Bathurst asks him to mix praises with his sharp grief, as if the exercise of panegyric might mitigate his sorrow; and James Sandys, a Westminster scholar whose father was Gentleman-Usher to Princess Anne, addresses his entire consolatory poem to young Churchill, treating him as a bereaved member of Gloucester's family.[16] Sandys praises Churchill's attention to Gloucester, whether they rode to hounds or studied their books, and pictures a grieving Anne watching Churchill on horseback and thinking how his hands and face resemble those of her lost child.[17] In his closing lines, he draws on Virgil and Homer to imagine Gloucester and Churchill as adults falling heroically in battle:

> But if as a man he had fallen, surrounded by foes and arms,
> Struck by a French or German hand,
> You would never have wept for the fate of dead Gloucester alone;
> The same urn would have sufficed for two.[18]

Like Virgil's Nisus avenging his comrade Euryalus, Churchill would have died avenging Gloucester; their ashes could then have been mingled in the same urn, like those of Homer's Achilles and Patroclus. Sandys had no way to know that his

lines would become more poignant when Jack Churchill, like his friend Gloucester, missed his chance for a glorious death in combat, succumbing to the smallpox
in 1703.

Like Sandys and Bathurst, William Burnet, the eldest son of Gloucester's preceptor, mourned for the duke by combining personal reminiscences with classical
allusions. In the long Latin poem he contributed to the Cambridge collection,[19]
Burnet mentions serving meals to the duke as part of a band of comrades, a function later assumed by his younger brother.[20] He remembers leaving for Cambridge
in 1698 (at the age of ten) and hearing Gloucester promise to follow him. When
seeking consolation from reading, he is overwhelmed by recalling how much
Gloucester loved the same books. Significantly, he refers to his dead friend as Ascanius, son of Aeneas and chief of an army of boys, revealing that one of the books
they both treasured was Virgil's *Aeneid*. In his most dramatic passage, Burnet re-
counts a recurring dream in which his ghostly comrade appears in the night and
tells him to learn manly virtue from his example. The language used by the ghost
comes directly from Aeneas's advice to Ascanius before the final battle in the
epic.[21] If the duke resembled the brave boy Ascanius during his life, in death he
has become Aeneas, an adult hero and role model. In addition to winning the
affection of his boyhood companions, Gloucester had begun to win their respect.

§

For his comrades, his royal namesake, his parents, and the nation, the loss of
Gloucester was more painful because his health had become less precarious as he
grew older. Although untreated hydrocephalus has a 50 to 60 percent death rate,
the gravest danger is in infancy, and a patient's odds of survival go up dramatically
as he becomes older. None of the five Latin poems by boys within Gloucester's
circle alludes to his being ill or feeble; several of them make it clear that he had
learned to ride a horse, despite the problems with balance typical of hydroce-
phalic children.[22] In his detailed account of Gloucester's activities between 1695
and 1697, Jenkin Lewis reports no serious illnesses, only a bloodshot eye in the
spring of 1696, which his doctors attempted to cure by blistering his back and
giving him medicine that he stubbornly refused to swallow. Beaten by his father,
the duke finally took the draught, but his eye did not improve. His mother, no
stranger to eye ailments, "went herself to Bloomsbury, to consult Dr. Richley, a
very old man, famous for curing complaints in the eyes, who gave the Princess a
small bottle of liquid, to be put on the eyelid with a feather, or small camel's hair
brush, which cured him in a very short time," earning the doctor 50 guineas from
a grateful Anne.[23]

Although it reminds us of the appalling state of medicine, this episode is hardly
comparable to the frequent life-threatening illnesses that plagued Gloucester's early

life. His balance and vigor appear to have improved significantly in his later years. Lewis records his continuing delight in fighting "sham battles" and informs us that the duke learned to box and to fence, took daily walks, and was apparently eager for physical activity:

> June 1696. The Duke accompanied his Royal Parents to Windsor, where he walked in the Park every morning; and perceiving a dry ditch sur- round that part of the Castle toward the Park, said, "I must use myself to go into such motes and places;" and upon being prevented, he laid him- self upon the brink and would have rolled down, but was stopt. However, he asked his father's permission afterwards, who granted it.[24]

Lewis, as usual, is circumspect, but his clear implication is that Anne prevented her son from rolling down the embankment. She had already forbidden his servants to fence with him, though promising to "have him taught regularly," and she was gen- erally cautious about his engaging in strenuous activity. Prince George, by contrast, though willing to use a switch to punish his son, was content to let him explore the moat. Details of Gloucester's life after 1697 are less plentiful because Jenkin Lewis left his service in October of that year, but the remaining evidence suggests that the hopes now pinned on the duke were not unreasonable. "He had gone through much weakness, and some years of ill health," writes Bishop Burnet, who took charge of his education in 1698, "but we hoped the dangerous time was over."[25]

Despite his uneasy relationship with Princess Anne, King William was clearly among those who hoped the boy would outgrow his ailments. As he remarked to a German duchess who inquired about Gloucester's health, he had been a delicate child himself—but had survived to adulthood.[26] Perhaps identifying with his frail, precocious namesake, the childless monarch was evidently fond of the boy. On William's first visit to Campden House in the fall of 1695, "when the Duke saluted him in the same way the officers of the Guards salute the Royal Family, with his pike, . . . the King was well enough pleased," and when Gloucester came to collect his Garter in January 1696, the king himself tied it on, a signal honor.[27] Al- though he was probably aware of the continuing friction between his mother and his uncle, Gloucester's admiration for the warrior-king was authentic, and he made frequent gestures of loyalty, especially after William narrowly evaded a Jaco- bite plot against his life. In February 1696, a group of about twenty men devised a serious and plausible plan to assassinate the king on his way back from his weekly hunt, but one of their comrades betrayed them, and William, warned of the danger, stayed in Kensington. As the authorities rounded up the conspirators, many of whom proved to be members of James II's guard who had quietly entered England, horror at the revelations prompted both Houses of Parliament and many town corporations to sign "Associations," pledges to support William and avenge his death should he be slain.[28] Not to be outdone by the adults around him, Gloucester wrote his own version:

> I, your Majesty's most dutiful subject, had rather lose my life in your Majesty's cause, than in any man's else: and I hope it will not be long ere you conquer France.
>
> GLOSTER

He also dictated a pledge to be signed by the members of the boy army, who promised to stand by the king "as long as we have a drop of blood."[29] Few of the protestations of loyalty that poured into Whitehall at this time can have been as gratifying.

Although he was in Flanders at the time of Gloucester's formal installation as a Garter Knight, King William paid the expenses for the midday meal and would have heard reports of Gloucester's dignified behavior at the solemn ceremony, which took place at Windsor on his seventh birthday (24 July 1696).[30] In contrast to the previous summer's intense campaign, climaxed by the victory at Namur, the action in 1696 was sluggish and evasive, as both sides were financially exhausted and seeking opportunities for negotiation. In the next year, 1697, Hans Willem Bentinck, Earl of Portland, William's boyhood friend and faithful companion, privately worked out the terms of a settlement with Marshal Boufflers of France, who had commanded the defense of Namur. The result was the Treaty of Ryswick, which William and Louis signed in September. Although Louis would soon renege on his promises, he now agreed to return most of the land he had gained in the previous decade and formally recognized William as the King of England. James II, however, remained at St. Germain, despite vague assurances that Louis might ask him to relocate to Rome or Avignon.

With the nation finally at peace, there were rumors that William would give Gloucester nominal command of a real regiment, but Parliament, mindful of the costs of the war, opposed the king's plans for a large standing army and moved to demobilize most of the soldiers who had served in the Nine Years' War. The plan for Gloucester to command his own regiment was probably a casualty of this political struggle.[31] In 1698, William established a separate court for his nephew, with Marlborough as his governor, Bishop Burnet as his preceptor, and a complete "family" of instructors and servants.[32] Although his mother and his uncle quarreled over the composition and funding of this small court, its very existence was a critical step toward establishing Gloucester as the eventual heir to the throne. Reports of the boy's activities in newsletters of 1699 point in the same direction. In March he joined the king and his parents in observing the trial of two noblemen who had murdered a captain in a tavern brawl, thus learning something about the state of criminal justice. In April, along with his mother and his uncle, he made a gift to "the poor Vaudois," Waldensian Protestants who had been persecuted for their religion. William ostentatiously contributed £2000 to this cause, Anne gave £500, and Gloucester gave £300. In order to make such a contribution, even if someone else made all the arrangements, the duke had to have funds officially at his disposal. In June, when William left to spend the summer in Holland, he "appointed a horse guard of 6 gentlemen to attend the duke of Glocester" and required foreign ambassadors who visited England in his absence to "have audience" with his young nephew. In November, Gloucester joined his father and the king in reviewing a muster of troops in Hyde Park. The soldiers, three troops of horse guards commanded by noblemen with close ties to the king, were "newly accoutred from top to toe," and despite the parliamentary opposition to standing armies, the boy duke had every reason to expect that a day would come when he could take command of such a splendid troop. A few weeks later, on Queen Elizabeth's birthday, he "fired all his guns," as he had always done on important days.[33]

Before leaving England for his summer trip to Holland in 1700, William "was pleased to give the late queens lodgings at Kensington to the duke of Glocester, that he may have him under his protection."[34] The king was clearly planning to groom the boy for his eventual accession to the throne, as he showed by offering his namesake the space once occupied by his queen. From the Revolution forward, Hans Willem Bentinck, Earl of Portland, had occupied chambers adjoining William's, but in a recent remodeling of Kensington Palace, the king had ordered a new set of doors connecting his own chambers to those of Arnold Joost van Keppel, a strikingly handsome younger Dutchman.[35] As this innovation suggests, Keppel, created Earl of Albemarle in 1697, had now succeeded Portland as William's closest companion, and William's need for companionship had increased with the loss of his wife. As he looked forward to Gloucester's growth into manhood, the king would have seen an opportunity to train his nephew in arms and diplomacy, treating the young man as a surrogate son. But less than a month after William issued the order assigning the late queen's lodgings to Gloucester, the boy was dead, and the king's response looks like authentic grief. He kept to his chambers for several days and wrote a simple, unaffected letter to Anne:

> I do not believe it necessary to use many words to tell you of the surprise and sorrow with which I learned of the death of the Duke of Gloucester. It is so great a loss for me and for all England that my heart is pierced with affliction. I assure you that on this occasion and on any other I shall be glad to give you any marks of my friendship.[36]

A few days later, however, William failed to provide a mark of friendship that would have meant much to Anne. The princess wrote formally to the court of her cousin Louis XIV, informing them of her loss, with the expectation that they would politely go into mourning, but when the earl of Manchester, William's ambassador to France, sought to deliver the letters, he was informed that the French court would only receive them if they were first notified of the death by the king, who made no such gesture, despite polite efforts by Manchester.[37] If William felt "surprise and sorrow" at the loss of Gloucester, those emotions did not prevent him from insisting on his monarchial prerogatives.

§

Like the king, the princess had begun to believe that Gloucester would grow to adulthood, and many of the boy's activities in the last four years of his life gave her pride and pleasure, compensating in some measure for the grim series of reproductive failures that she continued to suffer. In light of her lifelong passion for propriety, she would have found her son's behavior when given the Order of the Garter early in 1696 deeply satisfying. According to Lewis, Bishop Burnet "came to tell the Duke, that he should have the Garter within two days; and asked him, if the thoughts of it did not make him glad? 'I am gladder of the King's favour to me,' he said, without being prompted to it." No one needed to whisper this decorous answer into the ear of the six-year-old because Anne had designed his upbringing to produce a boy who could make just such a response. Two days later, when his father took him to receive the Garter, "he behaved himself so well, as to be commended by all present. The next day the Marquis of Normanby came to see him, and highly commended his behaviour; which, he said, could not have been better if he had been thirty years old."[38] The man now called Normanby was Anne's old beau John Sheffield, Earl of Mulgrave; praise for her son's maturity from this particular courtier would have been especially welcome, and imagining the boy as a thirty-year-old took on more importance in light of Anne's continuing inability to produce another heir. On 18 February, six weeks after this episode and three days after William learned about the assassination plot, the princess miscarried. Despite her strained relations with the king, news of a conspiracy that might have placed her on the throne quite suddenly, thrusting upon her the responsibility for calming a nation plunged into turmoil, was obviously frightening. Any relief she might have felt when the plot proved unsuccessful came with the sobering knowledge that her father had allowed his supporters to plan the murder of her brother-in-law. There is no way to know when the princess learned about the plot, which became public knowledge on 22 February, but if she was informed at the time of the first discoveries, it is possible that the emotional stress of this moment hastened her miscarriage.

When summer came, the little duke joined the adult Garter Knights for his solemn investiture at Windsor. Lewis's account is rich in detail:

> He behaved himself extremely well during the ceremony, and walked in procession with the Knights' Companions, &c. from St. George's Chapel to the Castle. The King had ordered an elegant entertainment at his own expence: tables were spread in St. George's Hall for the Princess and company; and others in the King's Guard-chamber for the Knights, who dined in their robes. The Duke sat down a while, and eat with his companions, when he desired them to excuse him for leaving them; he then retired to rest for two or three hours, and afterwards took the air. In the evening, the same noble personages, with many of the nobility besides, were magnificently entertained by the Prince and Princess of Denmark. There was also a ball, and a new ode, performed in honour of the Duke's birth-day; with ringing of bells, illuminations, bonfires, and other expressions of joy.[39]

Gloucester's being seated with the other Garter Knights, including his father, meant that he dined in a different room from his mother and her party, a significant turning point in his personal and official life. His excusing himself for an afternoon nap need not mean that he was weak or ill; any seven-year-old would have been exhausted by the formal ceremonies and the huge meal. The adults might also have wanted a rest between the "elegant entertainment" provided by the king and the "magnificent" festivities of the evening, hosted by Anne and George, which included an ode composed by Purcell's younger brother Daniel.[40] Though pregnant once more, the princess probably led out the dance at the ball. Four weeks later, on 20 and 21 September 1696, she delivered two dead fetuses—one male, the other female.

Despite this disappointment, Anne danced again at the king's birthday ball in November, for which she was the official hostess. A woman who was present reports that the monarch was "extremely out of humour,"[41] though she does not guess at a reason. Whatever the motive, William's grumpy behavior undermined Anne's good-faith effort to keep up a façade of courtly behavior. The differences between the tastes of the king and those of his apparent heir were now painfully evident to artists as well as courtiers. A week after the birthday, Anne attended an unusual performance at Lincoln's Inn Fields: *The Anatomist*, a three-act farce by Edward Ravenscroft, into which the players interpolated a musical entertainment in four scenes called *The Loves of Mars and Venus*, written by the Huguenot journalist Peter Motteux and set to music by the Moravian composer Gottfried Finger and the Englishman John Eccles. A special prologue welcoming the princess to the theatre, written by Motteux and spoken by Anne's old voice teacher Elizabeth Barry, thanked her for her royal patronage, glancing obliquely at the king's disregard for drama:

> More blest than Day, be this auspicious Night!
> When with Your Presence we indulge our Sight.
> Our solitary Stage no longer grieves:
> The Sight of Princes still from Fate reprieves.
> So, when the glorious Ev'ning-Star does rise,
> Her glittering Train attends, and fills the circling Skies.
> Thus we at need on Heav'n and You depend:
> Our Wishes rise, and the kind Beams descend.
> Oh! That we here cou'd oft'ner thus be blest!
> But mighty Joys too seldom are possest.
> With gloomy Looks we did your Absence mourn,
> And only liv'd in hopes of your Return.
> In pity grant our Sports one kindly Ray!
> We by your Presence live, and by your Smiles the Play.[42]

With Mary dead and William disdainful, Anne had become the theatre's only hope for the "Sight of Princes," but her poor health, lack of mobility, and pre-occupation with her son meant that she could not often bless the players with her presence.[43] Implicit in Motteux's elegant praise is his hope that once on the throne, Anne will gratify his wishes, and those of his fellow artists, by allowing the "kind Beams" of her patronage to "descend" on them.

On Anne's next birthday, 6 February 1697, the king thoughtfully honored her interest in the theatre by bringing the actors to court for a special performance of Congreve's *Love for Love* at Whitehall. Anne had definitely seen Congreve's earlier comedy, *The Old Bachelor,* when it opened in 1693;[44] she had probably seen *Love for Love* when it opened in 1695. If William gave her the opportunity to name the play for this occasion, which seems likely, her choosing Congreve's sparkling comedy for the honor of being performed at court would account for the play-wright's decision to dedicate *The Mourning Bride,* his only tragedy, "to Her Royal Highness, the Princess." Although he had written poems in praise of William, some of Congreve's language in this dedication appears to elevate Anne, the patroness of the arts, above the reigning monarch. After speaking of the praise of royalty as a duty, Congreve pays the princess a series of elegant and telling compliments:

> That high Station, which, by your Birth You hold above the People, exacts from every one, as a Duty, whatever Honours they are capable of paying to Your Royal Highness: But that more exalted Place, to which Your

> Vertues have rais'd You, above the rest of Princes, makes the Tribute of our Admiration and Praise, rather a choice more immediately preventing that Duty.... For they who are at that distance from Original Greatness, as to be depriv'd of the Happiness of Contemplating the Perfections and real Excellencies of Your Royal Highness's Person in Your Court; may yet behold some small Sketches and Imagings of the Vertues [of] Your Mind, abstracted and represented in the Theatre.[45]

This extravagant language is typical of dedications, but there are some remarkable assertions lurking beneath the heavy layer of perfume. If Anne's virtues have raised her "above the rest of Princes," they have presumably raised her above William. Though artists like Congreve routinely praise royalty as a duty, they readily choose to pay tribute to Anne—with the strong implication that their praise for William is merely a duty. The theatre may represent Anne's virtues for those not able to see them in her court, and because only a few fortunate people can contemplate her perfections in the small court at St. James's, the "Imagings" of those perfections in plays will have to suffice until Anne reigns over a larger court.

The court performance of *Love for Love* took place on the afternoon of Anne's birthday, and in the evening the Denmarks hosted a ball at St. James's, where Jenkin Lewis witnessed a curious interaction between Anne, William, and Gloucester:

> The Princess had ordered [Gloucester] a suit of cloaths against her birthday, the button holes and buttons of which were set with diamonds; many of which the King had given the Princess, some time after the Queen's death, upon the reconciliation's taking place: the King had also presented the Duke with a George on horseback, the order for which was eight hundred pounds, its real value seven hundred pounds. Upon which occasion, thus equipped, he appeared at St. James's in honour of the day; where the King also visited the Princess; when, after the compliments had passed, he told the Duke he was very fine: the Princess said, "Much the finer for you, sir;" and desired the Duke to thank his Majesty; but he expressed his gratitude by a bow only, as the Princess could not prevail upon him to speak then, which he most likely would, had he been left to himself without being prompted to it. The jewels that he wore upon this occasion were said to be worth four thousand pounds.[46]

It had been a generous gesture on William's part to give Queen Mary's jewels to her sister after her death, but Anne did not like to wear jewelry, least of all her sister's jewelry, so she decided to use the diamonds to adorn her son's new suit. She may have felt upstaged, however, by the king's direct gift to Gloucester, a statuette of St. George to wear on his collar as a sign of his membership in the Order

of the Garter. Anne's quick response to the king's kind compliment was deliberately ambiguous. In saying that her son was "much the finer" thanks to William,
she might have been referring to the George, the recycled diamonds, or both. Her
seizing the opportunity to speak was probably the result of some fear on her part
that the king might question the use she had made of his earlier present. By giving
a quick and polite response, Anne was hoping to prevent the king from being "out
of humour," but she inadvertently offended Gloucester, who clearly felt old
enough to speak for himself "without being prompted," as he had done a year earlier in the conversation with Burnet. Among his mother's attributes, the boy had
inherited an adequate share of pride.

In addition to the play and the ball, the birthday celebration probably included
an ode set by Anne's old harpsichord teacher Giovanni Baptista Draghi, and the
princess took steps to see that the composer realized a reward for his efforts: his
music, now lost, was performed for a paying audience on 24 February at York Buildings, "by her Royal Highness's Command," a phrase implying that the princess was
present, and repeated once more a week later, accommodating music-lovers unable
to find a seat at the first royal concert.[47] On 25 March, however, Anne miscarried
again, prompting the Denmarks to change their summer pattern. This year, they decided to spend ten weeks at Tunbridge Wells, probably because the princess thought
the waters might help her conceive a healthy child. In light of her interest in music,
the news that "a new and approved consort of music" was being organized to play at
"Tunbridge Wells in the music-room upon the Walks from June 24th" was welcome.[48] Some of these musicians probably took part in the performance of the ode
for Gloucester's eighth birthday in July, set to music by John Blow.

In this charming work, the anonymous poet took note of the new location by
shaping the ode as an English pastoral. The singers of the first chorus claim to
speak for the tutelary deities of Tunbridge:

> The nymphs of the wells
> And the nymphs of the hills
> Which preside ore the waters and aire
> Depute us to pay
> The duties of the day
> And to offer their usual care.[49]

Two Druids, sung by a bass and a countertenor, appear and offer prayers that the
duke may have a long and fruitful life. In keeping with the legendary connection
between Druids and oaks, the text presents the boy as a "Royall Oake":

> 1st Druid [bass]:
> Blest be this morn, blest be the hand

Which planted in the British land
The Royall Oake, which this day bears
The full account of twice four years.
This plant, the noblest of the grove
Is worthy of the care of Jove.

2nd Druid [countertenor]:
Be Jove propitious to our Isle
And bless the aire and bless the soile.
Bless on till some may live and see
A Thriving plant, a stately tree.
Bless till it bears a lofty head
Into branches Royall spread.

The "Royall Oake," however, was more than a fanciful piece of Celtic coloring. By invoking this image, the anonymous poet was downplaying Gloucester's connection to his uncle (by marriage) the king, and linking him strongly to his great-uncle (by blood) Charles II, who never tired of telling the story of his miraculous preservation after the disastrous Battle of Worcester, when he hid in the so-called "royal oak" in Boscobel Park. The use of the word *propitious* in conjunction with *Jove* and *Royall Oake* suggests a specific source: Dryden's poem on Charles II's coronation, conveniently reprinted in 1695,[50] which uses all those words in close proximity. Written in 1661, Dryden's poem takes note of the fact that the restored monarch was considering marrying either a Spanish or a Portuguese princess, which gave the poet an opportunity for a sly sexual joke:

Both *Indies* (Rivalls in your bed) provide
With Gold or Jewels to adorn your Bride.
This to a mighty King presents rich ore,
While that with Incense does a God implore.
Two Kingdomes wait your doom, and, as you choose,
This must receive a Crown, or that must loose.
Thus from your Royal Oke, like Jove's of old,
Are answers sought and destinies fore-told:
Propitious Oracles are beg'd with vows,
And Crowns that grow upon the sacred boughs.[51]

This passage begins with yet another image of exotic lands presenting treasures to adorn a bride, with the twist that the East and West Indies appear here as rivals in Charles's bed, which had already welcomed numerous real mistresses. Dryden further complicates this imagery by bringing in an allusion to the Greek oracle of Dodona, where worshipers sought prophetic guidance from a mighty oak tree sacred to Zeus. By connecting the oak of Dodona to the royal oak of Charles's recent history, the poet compliments his monarch but leaves ample room for a libertine reading, in which the prophetic oak, source of oracles and crowns, is the royal phallus.

"The Nymphs of the Wells," a fanciful poem for a child, makes no such display of sexual sophistication, yet the later poet was clearly expressing the hope that Gloucester, unlike his great-uncle Charles, would sire some legitimate heirs. It was obvious to sober observers that the king would remain childless, despite occasional rumors that he might marry a European princess, and Anne's heroic efforts to produce another heir were proving fruitless; she would miscarry again in early December. With hope for the succession focused on the eight-year-old Gloucester, courtiers were necessarily beginning to imagine a future in which he might spread into royal branches. Within a few weeks of the performance of this ode, King William, who was hunting in Germany with his friend Georg Wilhelm, Duke of Zell, reportedly discussed a possible match between the Duke of Gloucester and Sophia Dorothea, Princess of Hanover, the ten-year-old daughter of the future George I.[52] Our source for this anecdote, the philosopher Gottfried Leibniz, says that Gloucester later wrote a complimentary letter to the princess telling her that he hoped to meet her when he came over to hunt with the king in the country near Zell.[53] If this story is true, Gloucester would presumably have written his letter in French, the preferred language of the Hanoverian court, perhaps with the help of his mother, whose French was excellent.

§

There was considerable precedent for thinking of royal children as future parents. Little Princess Mary was not yet eight when she appeared as Clorin in *The Faithful Shepherdess* in 1670, yet one purpose of that performance, emphasized by Dryden's witty epilogue, was to remind the court that she and her youthful companions would soon be sexual beings. Five years later, Crowne's *Calisto,* harping insincerely on the theme of innocence, presented Mary (and Anne) as potential objects of courtship. Although Mary was not yet thirteen, political discussions of her marriage had been going on for years by the time she acted Calisto. But while Crowne drew on an erotic myth from Ovid to portray the princesses as "beauteous nymphs," the writers who imagined Gloucester founding a royal line invoked the heroic epic of Virgil.

Like other privileged boys, the duke had early training in Latin, the language that gave men access to the rich traditions of Roman history and legend. Jenkin Lewis tells us that "he learnt the use of the globes, mathematicks, and Latin" from Samuel Pratt, the clergyman who taught him daily lessons. During the summer Anne's court spent at Tunbridge Wells, Pratt "made a pentagon, with out-works, in a wood near the Wells, for the Duke's improvement and entertainment," infuriating Lewis, who regarded military games as his own province;[54] yet Roman history and literature, the subjects Pratt was hired to teach, contained plenty of material to feed Gloucester's interest in martial matters. The classical figure who provided the most obvious parallel to the duke was Ascanius, the son and heir of Aeneas, who leads cavalry maneuvers by an army of Trojan boys in the fifth book of the *Aeneid*. In 1696, Basil Kennett, a scholar at Corpus Christi College in Oxford, dedicated his book on Roman antiquities to Gloucester, explicitly referring to this episode and its imitation by later Roman youths:

> There is one custom, which I am apt to fansie YOUR HIGHNESS will read with particular Pleasure; I mean, SIR, the *TROJAN GAME;* a Martial Exercise, perform'd by the Youth of the first Quality in *Rome*, under such a Captain as Your self: And deriving its Original from young *Ascanius,* whom I need not fear to mention as your Precedent, since YOU have already honour'd Him with your Imitation.... It was celebrated by Companies of Boys neatly dress'd, and furnish'd with little Arms and Weapons, who muster'd in the publick *Circo.* They were taken, for the most part, out of the noblest Families; and the Captain of them had the honourable Title of *Princeps Juventutis;* being sometimes the next Heir to the Empire; and seldom less than the son of a principal Senator. This Custom is so very remarkable that it would be an unpardonable Omission not to give the whole Account of it in *Virgil'*s own Words; especially because the Poet using all his Art and Beauties on this Subject, as a compliment to *Augustus* (a great Admirer of the Sport) has left us a most Divine Description.[55]

He then proceeds to quote some fifty lines of Virgil's Latin, followed by a competent but wooden translation into English couplets.

Other books dedicated to Gloucester at this time include a Latin grammar, a French dictionary, a set of Indian fables, lengthy accounts of Greek poets and Roman emperors, and even a scandalous exposé identifying the "true mother" of his rival the Prince of Wales.[56] There is no evidence that the boy read all of these volumes, but according to Lewis, he did read Kennett's history, "which he explained to me one day while Mr. Prat was at prayers, who had left [the book] upon his glass book-case, as the Duke did not always like to be confined to prayers."[57] The appealing picture of Gloucester explaining Roman antiquities to his servant while playing hooky from prayers makes it clear that he knew what it meant to be compared to Ascanius, the boy through whom the Caesars claimed descent from Aeneas. In the same year, the anonymous author of the text for the ode sung at his

Garter installation called him "The Darling hope of our rejoyceing Troy" and asked "Apollo's darling sons" to "Praise Anna for Ascanius to the skies."[58] William Burnet's poem in Gloucester's memory, addressing him as Ascanius, suggests that this identification was part of the mythology shared by the privileged boys in Gloucester's army.

Reinforced by a visual image, the idea of the boy duke as Ascanius reached a wider public when John Dryden's translation of Virgil appeared in 1697. Each subscriber who had paid five guineas in advance received a "large-paper" copy in which he could see his name and coat of arms attached to one of the 101 engravings that

Illustration from Dryden's *Virgil* (1697).

adorned the splendid folio. The king, again displaying his disdain for the arts, did not subscribe, even though Jacob Tonson, the publisher, attempted to flatter him by having the illustrations retouched to give Aeneas a hooked nose like William's.[59] Princess Anne, Prince George, and the Duke of Gloucester were therefore the highest ranking subscribers, and the poet and publisher, attentive to Gloucester's military interests, seized the opportunity to put their young patron's name on the illustration of Ascanius and his mounted army of boys.[60] Turning to his own page in Dryden's splendid rendering of Virgil, Gloucester could take delight in the picture and the vigorous description of the maneuvers:

> Th 'unfledg'd Commanders and their Martial Train,
> First make the Circuit of the sandy Plain
> Around their Sires: and at th 'appointed Sign,
> Drawn up in beauteous Order form a Line:
> . . . .
> In Troop to Troop oppos'd, and Line to Line.
> They meet, they wheel, they throw their Darts afar
> With harmless Rage, and well-dissembled War.[61]

The proud parents watching their sons on horseback, depicted in the foreground of the engraving, include Ascanius's father Aeneas, but not his mother, Creüsa, lost years earlier in the flames of Troy. In Dryden's version, however, the lines describing the spectators take into account the feelings a mother in such a position might have for her son. The applauding parents in the Latin original rejoice when they recognize the features of their ancestors in the anxious faces of their children; Dryden, making additions to the text as usual, multiplies the emotions on both sides:

> The pleas'd Spectators peals of shouts renew;
> And all the Parents in the Children view;
> Their Make, their Motions, and their sprightly Grace,
> And hopes and fears alternate in their face.[62]

For Virgil, the family resemblance lies in facial features, but Dryden expands the one word *ora* ("faces") into a whole line describing the shape, motions, and "sprightly Grace" of the beloved boys—a line Anne might have read as expressing the widespread hope that her awkward and fragile baby would continue to grow into a graceful young man.[63] Where Virgil uses one adjective, *pavidos,* to describe the fearful faces of the boys, anxious to please their parents by properly executing their drill, Dryden expands again, speaking of "hopes and fears alternate in their face." The translator's syntax is deliberately ambiguous: if *alternate* is an adjective, the parents see hopes and fears alternating in the faces of the boys, who are hoping to do well but fearful of failing; but if *alternate* is a verb, it makes just as much sense for the spectators to be feeling hope and fear—hope that the family lines they can discern in their offspring will continue but fear that some dreadful accident will prevent that longed-for future. Aeneas's Trojan band, after all, is a saving remnant from a defeated city, wandering the ancient world in search of a new home. This exhibition of mounted drill takes place as part of the funeral games for Anchises, father of Aeneas and grandfather of Ascanius, who has died without seeing the end of their quest; it comes just before the Trojan women, misled by a meddling goddess, try to burn the ships and end the journey. The Trojan parents have reasons to look on their children with nostalgia for the past, hope for the future, and fear of failure—emotions Princess Anne now felt for her son. If she no longer experienced the "violent perspiration" Lewis observed when she watched a younger Gloucester tottering as he tried to walk, she was still concerned for his safety.[64] Now that the boy could ride, her feelings when she saw him on horseback would have included pride as she recognized his Stuart features, hope as she pictured a future mounted king, and also, inevitably, the terrible fear that he might fall.

For *The Works of Virgil,* the Jacobite poet and his Whig publisher solicited subscribers from a wide range of political, religious, and cultural persuasions, believing that all political factions could unite to support a translation of a Roman classic by an Englishman. They also paid careful attention to the matching of patrons and pictures, seeking whenever possible to pay appropriate compliments to the 5-guinea subscribers.[65] The details of the matching are often intriguing in their political complexity. At the beginning of the volume, the plates prefixed to the first three *Pastorals* are dedicated to three high-ranking officials in the king's court—the Lord Chancellor, the Lord Privy Seal, and the Earl of Dorset, who resigned as Lord Chamberlain a few months before the publication—but the plate illustrating the fourth *Pastoral* bears the name and arms of Dorset's son (and Gloucester's friend) Lionel, Lord Buckhurst, aged nine. Virgil's poem celebrates a son born to a Roman consul after a great military victory; allegorical readers had long interpreted it as an inspired, unconscious prophecy of the birth of Christ. Dryden takes note of this reading in the "argument" prefixed to his translation; the illustration, which shows a mother with an infant in her arms, resembles traditional paintings of the Presentation in the Temple. Assigning this plate to Buckhurst marked him out as a promising son in both Roman and Christian terms, and allowed his plate to follow his father's, a gracious gesture to Dryden's lifelong patron Dorset.

That much Tonson would have understood, but Dryden had other more private reasons for this dedication. Despite its special history in Christian allegory, Virgil's pastoral was nonetheless a poem for the birthday of a prominent person's son, and thus the ultimate ancestor of "The Nymphs of the Wells" and the other birthday odes for Gloucester. Long before planning a complete Virgil, Dryden had made a translation of this poem, which he published in 1684, during Princess Anne's first pregnancy.[66] The hopeful lines the Laureate had written in 1684, mapping Virgil's prediction of a golden age onto the nation's hope for progeny from the teenaged princess, appeared unaltered in 1697:

> The last great Age foretold by sacred Rhymes,
> Renews its finish'd Course, *Saturnian* times
> Rowl round again, and mighty years, begun
> From their first Orb, in radiant Circles run.
> The base degenerate Iron-off-spring ends;
> A golden Progeny from Heav'n descends.[67]

For Dryden, who had once imagined Anne as the source of "golden Progeny," it was now possible to think of Gloucester as the promised savior who would end the "base degenerate" iron age of William and restore a Stuart dynasty with values closer to the poet's—including respect and patronage for the arts. Assigning this plate to Gloucester himself would have been too obvious a gesture in that direction, and of course the picture of Ascanius and his boy cavalry cried out for Gloucester's name, but little Lord Buckhurst, in addition to being a precocious poet and actor,[68] was a member of Gloucester's boy army, and thus, for these purposes, a useful stand-in.

As an unrepentant Catholic Jacobite, Dryden had long nourished the hope that James II would be restored, and that the Prince of Wales, whose birth he had celebrated in 1688, would become the successor. His letter of 17 February 1697, requesting the Earl of Chesterfield's permission to dedicate the *Georgics* to him, records the diminishing of that hope:

> My Translation of Virgil is already in the Press and I can not possibly deferr the publication of it any Longer than Midsummer Term at farthes[t]. I have hinder'd it thus long in hopes of his return, for whom, and for my Conscience I have sufferd, that I might have layd my Authour at his feet: But now finding that Gods time for ending our miseries is not yet, I have been advis'd to make three severall Dedications, of the Eclogues, the Georgics, and the Eneis.[69]

At the time of this letter, a year after the revelation of the assassination plot, Dryden knew that James II's cause was lost, and by the time the book appeared, with the terms of the Treaty of Ryswick already settled, hopes for a second restoration had all but vanished. Under the circumstances, and gratefully aware that the small court of the Denmarks had purchased at least four 5-guinea copies of *The Works of Virgil*,[70] Dryden might well have begun to consider what patronage might be available when James's daughter Anne became queen. Some such thinking may lie behind the decision to dedicate the first illustration of the *Aeneis* to Prince George and the second to Princess Anne. George's plate shows Aeneas in a violent storm, praying to the gods to save his men from drowning; Dryden thus identifies the prince with heroism in much the way Purcell had done through martial music. Anne's plate shows the shipwrecked Trojans making camp near Carthage, an image of calm domestic tranquility after a challenging storm, readable as a prediction of better times to come in her reign. Interpreted in this way, the plate was an analogue to the Virgilian prophecy of "*Saturnian* times... and mighty years" succeeding the "base degenerate Iron" age of the present. By associating Anne, George, and Gloucester with Virgil's heroic and patriotic epic, Dryden was offering them meaningful compliments, as well as drawing everyone's attention to the absence of a plate for the king.

Again allying himself with those opposed to William and friendly to Anne, Dryden dedicated the *Aeneis* to John Sheffield, Marquess of Normanby, who had lost his place on the Privy Council for refusing to sign the "Association" after the assassination plot. Describing Virgil as a subtle court poet, Dryden told Normanby that his Roman model "dext'rously...mannag'd both the Prince and People, so as to displease neither, and to do good to both; which is the part of a Wise and an Honest Man."[71] Despite his gestures of partisanship, some more overt than others, Virgil's translator was also dexterous in managing his readership. He rejoiced when readers whose politics were unlike his own appreciated his translation: "My Virgil succeeds in the World beyond its desert or my Expectations," he wrote to his sons; "It has pleasd God to raise up many friends to me amongst my Enemyes."[72] But he also took pleasure in communicating to multiple audiences on multiple levels, and readers alert to the ever-shifting patterns of alliance in court politics might have detected a growing interest on Dryden's part in engaging the attention of Anne's court. Like his much younger friend and collaborator Purcell, however, the old poet did not live to see the new reign: he died on 1 May 1700, three months before Gloucester's death and two years before Anne's accession. His hope for better treatment at her hands, however, was prescient. Early in Anne's reign, Lady Elizabeth Dryden, the poet's widow, sought "arrears due to her husband John Dryden dec[ease]d as poet Laureate and Historiographer to K Chas 2. and K. Jas. 2. being 150 £." The queen attended the meetings of her Treasury Board, and the answer to Lady Dryden's petition reflects her will: "pay her 50. £ at a time till the 150. £ is paid."[73]

§

As a princess whose life was played out under public scrutiny, Anne often had to maintain relations with people representing quite contrasting political views, "so as to displease neither, and to do good to both." During her father's brief reign, she complained about the difficulty of maintaining civil relations with her imperious stepmother; now, for the sake of her beloved son, she was constrained to keep up appearances with William, whom she privately regarded as a monster. Dryden, with his gift for ambiguity, could enjoy playing a double game; as a poet, and especially as a translator, he made the most of his opportunities for concealment, indirection, and implication. Anne, by contrast, knew that she needed to be submissive and complimentary in her dealings with William, but found it impossible to do so sincerely. She took no pleasure in feigning emotions she did not feel, and her attempts at disguise were often inept.

The princess's efforts to undo the loss of her Irish lands provide poignant examples. Although displeased with William for giving all those acres to his former mistress, she did not strike a public pose of injured outrage. The anonymous poet who wrote the lyrics for "Lovely Albina" in 1695 evidently believed that Anne would prefer an artful, indirect, and allegorical expression of her "just claim," and when she raised the issue herself in 1697, she politely pretended to believe that William had given away the land without knowing that it belonged to her:

> The occasion of my giving your Majesty the trouble of this letter, proceeds from my having been informed that a grant which your Majesty made some years since of the Irish estate which was the late King my fathers when Duke of York, and then settled upon his children after his death, is now designed to bee confirmed by Act of Parliament. I am apt to believe your Majesty has not been informed of this estate's being thus settled and have therefore taken the liberty to speak to my Lord Chamberlain to put a stop to any further steps upon this bill till I had acquainted your Majesty with it.
>
> I beg leave to assure your Majesty that I doe it with the greatest respect and duty imaginable, and with the greatest sense of your kindnesse to me, who shall always be very far from enterposing to hinder the Effects of your Majesty's bounty and favour in any case, and I am confydent your Majesty is soe well persuaded of this, that being now made acquainted in what manner this estate has been long since settled, your Majesty will have the goodness to lett the grant rest upon its own strength, and not give it your countenance for a Conformation by Act of Parliament.

I have been extreamly much concerned to hear your Majesty has been indisposed, and doe heartily wish you good health and a successfull summer.[74]

Without a richer context, or even a reliable date, it is difficult to understand this letter, apparently the only direct communication from Anne to William on this question. The surviving copy is in Sarah Churchill's hand, with an endorsement describing it as "only one Instance to show how watchful the Duke of Marlborough and I were of all the princesses Concerns"—a phrase implying that the Marlboroughs had a hand in drafting the letter.[75] But neither Anne nor her friends can have expected William to regard anything in the letter as sincere. It was hardly an instance of "the greatest respect and duty imaginable" for the princess to ask Robert Spencer, Earl of Sunderland, William's new Lord Chamberlain, to "put a stop" to the process by which a royal grant was being confirmed. And in trying to stop that process, she was doing exactly what she claimed she would never do: interposing "to hinder the Effects of [his] Majesty's bounty and favour" to Elizabeth Villiers, Countess of Orkney, whom she pointedly leaves unnamed. By asking William to "lett the grant rest upon its own strength" she shows her awareness of the growing parliamentary opposition to the grants of Irish land with which he had rewarded several of his favorites. The "country Whigs," the same group that successfully reduced the size of William's army, would soon attempt to reclaim those lands and apply their income to the large national debt incurred by the Nine Years' War. Anne's asking William not to interfere with the legislative process may have been her indirect way of telling him that she expected Parliament to overturn his earlier action. Although some of its layers of irony and innuendo remain opaque, this apparently polite letter does not conceal Anne's irritation. In light of their recent experience with the congratulatory letter to the king about Namur, neither Sarah nor Anne should have been surprised when William left it unanswered.

Although this direct approach to the king bore no fruit, Anne made other efforts to undo the Irish grant, many of them recorded in letters surviving in her own hand. On 16 October 1697, she wrote to Sir Benjamin Bathurst from Windsor, hoping he could help her procure a copy of the bill confirming William's grant. Afraid to ask directly, she recommended a bit of quiet bribery:

This is to desire you would get me a copy of an Irish bill that is now before the Councill here, which is intituled the Bill of Outlawrys, & ye best way to do it will be to employ some body without naming me, to give a giney or two to one of the Clerks of the Councill for it, which is a thing Ime told they will refuse no body, & pray do this as soon as you can possibly.[76]

As she prepared to oppose the king's disposal of her property, Anne was trying to stay in the background, but just one week later, she was ready to take a more direct approach:

> I think it will be best for you to go to the attorney generall from me, & tell him I desire a coppy of ye Bill of outlawrys not knowing but that I may be conserned in it.[77]

Even here, however, there is an attempt at evasion, as the princess pretends not to know the contents of the bill, with which she was all too familiar.

Yet despite her plans to oppose the king in this matter, Anne was still determined to appear conscientious in her role as his official hostess. On 20 October, between these two letters to Bathurst, she wrote to Sarah seeking advice about how to celebrate William's birthday on 4 November:

> I writt yesterday to ask your opinion what must be don on the birth day, being unwilling to depend on my own in any thing, espesialy at this time being much more inclined to have a play, but I doubt that will not be soe well liked because a ball is reckoned a thing of more respect, & I think I have heard the King dos not care for plays; one very good pretence there is for a play, which is the shortness of the time for peoples learning to dance, and that it must be putt upon if I excuse a ball, without doubt there are people that will find fault with mantos, for one must expect every new thing will be disliked at first, the generality of the world disapproving of every fashion they do not bring up themselves.[78]

In this letter, Anne carefully weighs the possible responses of various parties to the birthday plans. She would prefer to import a dramatic production from one of the theatres, as William had done for her last birthday, but she knows she needs a "pretence" for doing so. For some who share her detailed knowledge of protocol, "a ball is reckoned a thing of more respect," but if there is to be a ball, people must learn to dance the special figures required. There is also the question of dress: the letter continues with a long discussion about whether manteaus rather than gowns would be acceptable attire for the ladies, with Anne recording her surprise that Lady Fitzharding, still evidently a thorn in her side, disapproves of manteaus. As they engaged in the icily polite discussion of proper dress reported in this letter, both parties were uncomfortably aware that Lady Fitzharding was Barbara *Villiers* Berkeley, and that the Countess of Orkney, designated recipient of the Irish estate that Anne hoped to reclaim, was Elizabeth *Villiers* Hamilton, Barbara's sister. In dealing with the sister who was still serving as governess to the Duke of Gloucester,

Anne could not help remembering and resenting the sister whose attentions to the king had been so richly rewarded.

At the time of this letter, William expected to return to England in time to make a grand entry on his birthday, triumphantly brandishing the freshly signed peace treaty, but adverse winds delayed him, and his return to London, complete with arches, odes, and celebrations of the peace, did not occur until 16 November. As Anne wondered whether a play would be well liked or a ball thought more respectful, she cannot have forgotten that the king had been "extremely out of humour" on his last birthday. Whether he was present or not, the powerful people in attendance were sure to be opinionated about her performance as the hostess, reading some meaning into the clothing she wore and the dances she led. As she says about the manteaus, "Without doubt there are people that will find fault," and she knew from experience how broadly true that observation was. Pregnant, lame, and generally unwell, she now faced the challenge of hosting yet another party for a monarch she had many reasons to dislike. Yet she found one humorous outlet for her frustration in feigning ignorance about the king's disdain for the arts: her seemingly innocent phrase—"I think I have heard the King dos not care for plays"—is a wicked piece of irony designed for Sarah's amusement, though it might seem perfectly harmless if the letter fell into the wrong hands.[79]

In her next letter, Anne reports her continuing efforts to find dancers and worries about what her husband will be expected to do when the king arrives:

> There are soe few dancers that I believe if there weare never soe much time to prepare for a Ball one could hardly pick up enough to make one, but since it is only to make a Noise I will be sure to send to as many as I can think of to get themselves in a readiness. This report of the Kings being to com in Ceremony thorow the City gives the Prince some uneas-yness about what he is to do, for we are told heare every body is to waite on his Majesty a horse back, and he desires to know if there be any such thing, and what preparation he must make for this Triumph.[80]

Again, Anne's diction reveals a layer of private irony: in her opinion, the stalemate with which the Nine Years' War had ended was hardly an occasion for a Roman "Triumph," though this joke, like the earlier reference to the king's taste in drama, was subtle and easily deniable. By the time she returned to Windsor on 24 October, after spending a day or two in London, she had probably learned that the king would be absent on his birthday. With evident relief, she abandoned the idea of a ball:

> I am pretty well after my Journey, and hope keeping quiet these three or four days will enable me to beare the fatigue of the Birthday, which tho

there be no ball will be a great one, for one who is a creeple and inclined soe much to vaypours as I am.[81]

Although the king was becalmed on the Continent, the celebrations went forward, and when he arrived on 16 November, there was a grand cavalcade. Prince George, who had ridden to Greenwich to meet the returning monarch, gained a place of honor next to William and the Earl of Albemarle in the royal coach, "attended by the privy council, the great officers of the household, nobility, bishops, judges, &c." The procession, led by "horse granadeers," trumpeters, and drummers, included eighty coaches, each with six horses; Princess Anne watched the show from a house near the Royal Exchange. Three weeks later, she suffered another miscarriage.[82]

§

Among incentives for the princess to maintain civil relations with the king was the ongoing process of setting up a court for Gloucester. As early as November 1695, the king had promised that the boy would have "a family establish'd for him, and an house for his highnesses court,"[83] but the process was slow, in part because William was always reluctant to spend money. For the princess, having her son "taken out of women's hands" was an opportunity to rid herself of the irritating presence of Lady Fitzharding, his governess, who would now be replaced by a male governor. Not surprisingly, Anne wanted Marlborough appointed to that position, and in April 1697 she received a letter from Sarah (now lost) that made her believe she would have her wish. Her reply is ecstatic:

> What ever may happen to me now, I shall be very easy about my Son, if I should live long it will be a great pleasure to see him in such good hands, & if I weare to dye never soe soon it would be an unexpresible satisfaction to leave him in them, & could you see my hart you would find more sense of your kindness, & more passion & faithfullnes in it to deare Mrs Freeman, then other ways tis possible for you to believe.[84]

Anne's joy was premature, as William did not actually name Marlborough to the post until December, and then only after failing to persuade his friend Charles Talbot, Duke of Shrewsbury, to serve.[85] The king also coupled the appointment of Marlborough with one far less attractive to Anne, naming Bishop Burnet—a Scot, a Whig, and a busybody—as Gloucester's preceptor. With this pair of appointments, William presumably believed he was creating some kind of balance; he was certainly reminding Anne, who disliked Burnet, that he was the king. According to Burnet's own account, however, the princess was personally gracious and encouraging to him:

> All my endeavours to decline this [appointment] were without effect; the king would trust that care only to me, and the princess gave me such encouragement, that I resolved not only to submit to this, which seemed to come from a direction of Providence, but to give my self wholly up to it.[86]

At a time when political divisions were hardening along party lines, Anne sought to build personal relations of obligation and trust, even when dealing with a highly partisan man whose appointment she had opposed. As queen, she would frequently act on the same principles.

With the two chief officers in place, the next step was funding. When Parliament convened on 3 December 1697, the members moved rapidly to reduce the size of the army, ignoring William's argument that he needed troops in readiness for future conflicts, but they were much more generous when they came to the king's "Civil List." In actions taken on 21 and 22 December, they increased that amount from £600,000 to £700,000 without requiring an itemized budget. Among expenses Parliament considered in making the increase was a promised annual payment of £50,000 to Maria Beatrice, James II's queen, in return for which James's exiled court was supposed to move to Italy; Portland and Boufflers had privately made this odd arrangement while negotiating the Treaty of Ryswick.[87] Few in Parliament can have expected that such payments would actually be made, and none ever were, but real costs were certain to be incurred in establishing a court for the presumed eventual heir to the throne, an expense William deliberately overestimated. "The KING," writes Sarah, "insinuated to such members of the parliament, as he knew were desirous to have the DUKE handsomely settled, that it would require near 50,000 *l.* a year, . . . but, when his HIGHNESS's family was settled, would give him no more than 15,000 *l.* a year."[88] Sarah's outrage probably led her to exaggerate the scale of William's deceit. As many would remember, the king had opposed the parliamentary grant of £50,000 to Princess Anne in 1689. Sarah herself reports his wondering then how Anne could spend £30,000;[89] so it might have seemed odd for him now to estimate the expenses of Gloucester's miniature court at £50,000. When the financier and poet Charles Montagu presented the government's case in the Commons, he mentioned a figure of £25,000 pounds for Gloucester's court,[90] and on 23 December, the day after the bill passed, Luttrell reported that the king was planning to allot "20,000*l.* yearly to the Duke of Gloucester, to keep a court with"[91]—a figure soon trimmed to £15,000. Sarah's point holds good, even if one of her numbers is inflated: the king clearly requested more money for Gloucester than he was willing to allocate, and he proved reluctant to release even those limited funds. According to Sarah, "he refused to advance one quarter, though it was absolutely wanted to buy plate and furniture: so that the PRINCESS was forced to be at that expence herself."[92]

Early in January, most of Whitehall Palace was destroyed by a devastating fire that consumed priceless artworks, including Bernini's bust of Charles I, yet William, while promising to rebuild the palace "much finer than before," did not forget his plans for Gloucester. "The officers of the household for the duke of Gloucester are for the most part settled, and an apartment is assign'd for his highnesse in the pallace of St. James,"[93] wrote Luttrell on 6 January, one day after the fire burned itself out. The decision to give the new court space in St. James's may reflect the sudden lack of appropriate space in Whitehall. As she prepared to see the rearing of her child taken over by men, Anne could derive some comfort from having Gloucester's new court in her own palace.

Although there was space and money available, William waited six more months before making the appointments to Gloucester's court official. Perhaps he was preoccupied by relocating his ministers after the fire; perhaps, as Sarah's sneering account alleges, he took the opportunity to receive the increase in the Civil List without beginning to make expenditures. Yet Anne does not appear to have protested this delay, perhaps because the king had promised her the opportunity to name most of the other servants, as Sarah's narrative explains:

> The KING (influenced, I suppose, in this particular, by MY LORD SUNDER-
> LAND) sent the PRINCESS word, that, though he intended to put in all the
> preceptors, he would leave it to her to chuse the rest of the servants
> except one, who was to be the deputy governor and gentleman of the
> duke's bed-chamber, (which was MR. SAYERS.)
>   This message was so humane, and of so different an air from any
> thing the PRINCESS had been used to, that it gave her an extreme pleasure;
> and she immediately set herself to provide proper persons, and of the
> most consideration, for the several places.[94]

Anne had a lifelong interest in surrounding herself with compatible servants, and often rewarded those closest to her by giving their friends and relatives positions in her court. In April 1697, for example, she promised to give Abigail Hill, an orphaned relative whom Sarah Churchill had been supporting, a position as a bedchamber woman "whenever Bust dies," a reference to Ellen Bust, who had served her in that capacity for decades and was now in poor health.[95] Her choices for Gloucester's court reflect the same attention to family connections and old obligations. She chose Hugh Boscawen, the youth who had steered the stag hunt toward

Gloucester's coach, as one of the Grooms of the Bedchamber; he was the nephew of her trusted friend Sidney Godolphin, whose son was now engaged to marry Sarah's daughter Harriet. For Sarah's son Jack, a close friend of Gloucester, Anne reserved an important position as Master of the Horse, assisted as Equerry by Peter Wentworth, son of her girlhood friend Isabella (née Apsley). She found room for Alice Hill, Abigail's younger sister, among the laundresses; and in a gracious gesture dramatizing her willingness to make the best of an appointment she had opposed, she placed Bishop Burnet's younger son Gilbert among the Pages of Honor.[96]

Despite Anne's keen interest in the arts, the small allowance for Gloucester's new court limited fresh expenditures in that area. The list of his official servants does not even include a salaried dancing master, though we know he took lessons from Jeremiah Gohory. Nor does the official list name any musicians, though other evidence points to the presence of at least one string player in the duke's court. Jenkin Lewis tells us that "Mr. Powell" provided music for the puppet shows that Gloucester enjoyed in his childhood; this man was probably Charles Powell, a violinist in King William's "Private Musick," who died in April 1700. In June 1701, an advertisement for a concert to benefit Powell's widow and her seven children described him as "late servant to his Majesty, and his late Highness the Duke of Gloucester." The last phrase was not an empty flourish. When Powell died, just a few months before Gloucester's own death, the duke made a formal request that a place among the royal musicians be held for Powell's son George, and his promise was honored. Although George was too young at the time to take up professional employment, the man sworn into his place explained in 1703 that he held it "in trust and for the sole benefit and advantage of the said Elizabeth & George Powell."[97] As in the case of the furniture and silverware, Anne probably bore the expenses associated with having her son instructed in music and dancing, courtly accomplishments that meant far more to her than to the king. In providing for his violinist's family, Gloucester was following the example of his mother, who consistently remembered and rewarded her past servants.

§

King William, by contrast, was reluctant to spend money on his own court or anyone else's; his grief at Gloucester's death did not prevent him from immediately terminating all the servants in the duke's small court.[98] Throughout his reign, especially after the death of Mary, actors and musicians struggled to survive, as forms of direct and indirect patronage they had enjoyed under previous monarchs disappeared. The generous and worldly Earl of Dorset became Lord Chamberlain after the Revolution, and in 1695, he helped Thomas Betterton and some other veteran actors secede from the United Company, establishing a new theatre in Lincoln's Inn Fields that restored theatrical competition to London. But in January 1696, Dorset's office issued an order requiring both theatre companies to submit their scripts to Charles Killigrew, Master of the Revels, who was told to be diligent in "Correcting all Obsenitys & other Scandalous matters & such as any ways Offend against ye Laws of God Good Manners or the Knowne Statutes of this Kingdome."[99] It is exceedingly unlikely that the impetus for this directive came from Dorset himself; he was evidently following orders originating in the court, though he probably knew that this edict, like similar initiatives in the past, would prove ineffectual. Killigrew, accurately described as "incompetent and lackadaisical,"[100] was not a diligent censor.

During the next theatrical season, Dorset gave up his post, and the Earl of Sunderland, who replaced him on 20 April 1697, immediately demanded that all new scripts be submitted to his secretary for censorship, complaining that "many of the new Plays Acted by both Companies of his Majesty's Comedians are scandalously lew'd and Prophane, and contain Reflections against his Majesty's Government."[101] Although plays of this period were generally less salacious than those of the 1670s, they were often irreverent. *The Provok'd Wife*, a witty comedy by John Vanbrugh, came onstage not long before Sunderland's edict, which it may have triggered. In a tavern scene, a character called "Lord Rake" sings a song in praise of "Liberty of Conscience," one of the principles of the Revolution, but instead of commending that principle for allowing freedom of worship for Protestant Dissenters, Lord Rake celebrates it for allowing him to worship wine and women:

> What a Pother of late
> Have they kept in the State
>   About setting our Consciences free?
> A Bottle has more
> Dispensations in Store
>   Than the King and the State can decree.
>
> When my Head's full of Wine,
> I o'erflow with Design,
>   And know no *Penal Laws* that can curb me.
> What e'er I devise,
> Seems good in my Eyes,
>   And Religion ne'er dares to disturb me.
>
> No sawcy Remorse
> Intrudes in my Course,
>   Nor impertinent Notions of Evil:
> So there's Claret in store,
> In Peace I've my Whore,
>   And in Peace I jog on to the Devil.

His companion, Sir John Brute, applauds, declaring that he "wou'd not give a Fig for a Song, that is not full of Sin and Impudence."[102] Charles II, who was always tolerant of wit, even at his own expense, would doubtless have applauded this high-spirited scene, but for the humorless William, this kind of writing was "scandalously lew'd and Prophane," and its passing shots at "the King and the State" were "Reflections against his Majesty's Government."

The next spring, concerns about pamphlets questioning the doctrine of the Trinity prompted an address from the House of Commons to the king, urging him to crack down on blasphemy, so William duly issued a proclamation "For Preventing and Punishing Immorality and Prophaneness" (24 February 1698). Although this edict took specific aim at books promoting unorthodox ideas about religion, it evidently encouraged the prudish clergyman Jeremy Collier to publish a book-length attack aimed specifically at the theatre. Appropriating a phrase from the royal proclamation, Collier issued his *Short View of the Immorality and Profaneness of the English Stage* in late March, attacking Vanbrugh, Dryden, and Congreve, among others.

In May, emboldened by Collier's attack, "The Grand Jury for the County of *Middlesex*, . . . being made sensible of his Majestys pious intentions, for suppressing Prophaneness and Immorality, . . . observing that such Vices are much encreased by the more than ordinary Licentiousness used by the Poets, that supply the Play-Houses in this County, with very prophane and lewd Comedies," brought charges against the playwrights William Congreve and Thomas D'Urfey, specifically citing passages from *The Double Dealer* and *Don Quixote*, and extended their charges to include the booksellers Jacob Tonson and Samuel Briscoe, who had printed those plays.[103] This indictment was no more effective than the earlier proclamations, as no criminal charges ensued, but it was a further reflection of antitheatrical sentiment, and the threat to the livelihood of poets, actors, and printers was worrying. Unwisely, both Congreve and Vanbrugh published replies to Collier, who answered in due course, keeping the controversy alive.

In past reigns, puritanical opponents of the theatre had had to contend with monarchs who enjoyed the drama; now they believed they had support from the king himself in their campaign to curtail or suppress dramatic performances. Under these circumstances, the playwrights, actors, and musicians who felt that their livelihood was threatened were eager to have continued support from Princess Anne. Two of those named in the Middlesex case could already claim her as a patroness. In the absence of support from the monarch, Tonson had made the most of Anne's subscription to Dryden's *Virgil*; and in 1697, after William began issuing orders for theatrical reform, Congreve's *Love for Love,* a play specifically attacked by Collier as obscene, had a court performance on the princess's birthday. As they sought to answer Collier's charges, both men had reason to hope the princess might protect them, and even more reason to look forward to her accession.

In the spring of 1698, just as the Collier controversy was gathering steam, Anne attended a performance of *Caligula*, a dark and violent tragedy by John Crowne. Her presence was so significant that the company at Drury Lane, not content to present a special spoken prologue like the one Motteux had written for *The Loves of Mars and Venus,* commissioned two new songs for the occasion, one composed by the bass Richard Leveridge and performed by Mary Lindsey, a popular mezzo, the other composed by Daniel Purcell and sung by an unnamed boy. The printed scores pointedly describe Leveridge's song as "made for the Entertainment of her *Royall Highness* the PRINCESS in the *Tragedy* of *Calligula,*" and Purcell's as "A Song in CAL-IGULA…Sung before her Royall highness by the Boy."[104] Although Crowne's play includes a "short Entertainment of Musick and Dancing" in act 5, the new songs were probably performed between the acts, with the singers addressing themselves directly to Anne. The players evidently chose to use these songs as a way of honoring the princess because they were well aware of her fondness for music.

The text for Daniel Purcell's song comes from a poem first printed anonymously in 1697 and now known to be by Ambrose Philips, who was a Cambridge undergraduate when *Caligula* was acted.[105] In Philips's lyric, a lover singing to his lute "Beneath the Covert of a Grove" breaks a string, which makes him mindful of his own mortality; the text has no obvious connection to the play or to Princess Anne. The anonymous text for Leveridge's song, by contrast, presents a female speaker asserting her power and independence, as the princess was doing by attending the theatre at a time when it was under attack. The singer begins by deploring her failure to move the man she loves:

> Tho' over all Mankind beside
> My Conquering beauty Reignes,
> From him I Love, when I meet disdain,
> A killing damp comes ore my Pride,
> I'm fair & young in Vain.

The trope of female beauty as a conquering force that reigns over mankind was of course entirely conventional, but it is nonetheless significant that Leveridge chose a text beginning with that trope for a song designed to welcome the princess to the theatre. Although her lover's disdain gives a "killing damp" to her pride, the conquering beauty does not yield to melancholy. Instead, she confidently concludes that her value is not dependent on the approval of this one foolish lover:

> No, let him wander where he will,
> I shall have Youth & beauty Still:
> Beauty, that can charme a Iove,

And no fault but Constant Love.
From my arms then let him fly,
Shall I Languish pine & Dye:
No, no, no, no, not I.

In choosing this text, which shares some language with songs by Aphra Behn,[106] Leveridge may have been hinting at a parallel between the proud defiance of the woman in the song and Anne's insistence on her own autonomy, which she was displaying by coming to this performance.

The theatre was now a principal source of revenue for many musicians, as William had scaled back the size of the royal band and allowed the salaries of his remaining musicians to fall into arrears. Under these straitened circumstances, the eight musicians who held salaried positions in the court of the Denmarks had reason to be grateful for their employment, and the composers, singers, and instrumentalists employed in musical dramas had reason to be grateful for Anne's support, as the zeal of the reformers threatened them as well. Although Collier had principally directed his attack against playwrights, he included one passage complaining about theatre music, calling the tunes

> generally Airy and Galliardizing . . . contriv'd on purpose to excite a sportive Humour, and spread a Gaity upon the Spirits. To banish all Gravity and Scruple, and lay Thinking and Reflection asleep. This sort of Music warms the Passions, and unlocks the Fancy, and makes it open to Pleasure like a Flower to the Sun. It helps a Luscious Sentence to slide, drowns the Discords of *Atheism,* and keeps off the Aversions of Conscience.[107]

With this kind of accusation hanging over their heads, the theatre musicians had excellent reason to look forward to the succession of a music-loving monarch.

On 18 February 1699, the king issued yet another order for the reformation of the stage, repeating the formula Collier had used for his title and complaining that his previous edicts had been ineffective:

> His MAJESTY being informed, That notwithstanding an Order made the 4th of *June 1697,* by the *Earl* of *Sunderland,* then Lord Chamberlain of His Majesty's Houshold, to prevent the Prophaneness and Immorality of the Stage; several Plays have lately been Acted, containing Expressions contrary to Religion, and good Manners: . . . These are therefore to signify His Majesty's Pleasure, That you do not hereafter presume to Act any thing in any Play contrary to Religion or good Manners, as you shall answer it at your utmost Peril.[108]

Although the players often improvised suggestive dialogue, it is difficult to find much that is "contrary to Religion or good Manners" in the printed texts of the plays produced during this season. The two most popular new productions were fanciful operas. Betterton's company at Lincoln's Inn Fields offered *Rinaldo and Armida,* with a text by John Dennis and music by John Eccles, who would succeed the aged Nicholas Staggins as Master of the King's Music in 1700.[109] Drury Lane countered with *The Island Princess,* with a text by Motteux and music by Leveridge, Daniel Purcell, and Jeremiah Clarke.[110] Neither libretto has much literary merit or contains anything likely to attract the ire of the government or the censor. By this time, the issuing of royal decrees insisting that the stage must be reformed had begun to look like an empty routine, and fortunately for the theatre companies, the decrees rarely led to meaningful action. If William had really wished to make censorship more systematic, he might have started by replacing Charles Killigrew as Master of the Revels, but Killigrew retained his post throughout this reign and into the next.

Still, there was a striking contrast between William's personal indifference and official hostility toward the theatre and Anne's continuing interest. On 29 April 1699, the princess attended a special showing of a favorite opera, an event reported in the *Post Boy,* one of the newspapers that sprang up after the lapse of the Licensing Act in 1695: "Her Royal Highness is this day pleased to see the Opera, call'd The Island Princess, Performed at the Theatre Royal by her own Command." A command performance of this kind was an extra payday for everyone involved in the production, and another reason for musicians to look forward eagerly to Anne's accession.

§

Despite their many disagreements, both William and Anne understood the importance of maintaining the public drama of royal activities. After his own chapel was destroyed by the Whitehall fire, William began attending services at Anne's chapel in St. James's, and asked "to have the privilege of seeing company in the drawing-room before church."[111] The witness reporting this last request adds that it "must be complied with," insinuating that the princess might have preferred not to comply, but there is no evidence that Anne resisted William's presence on Sundays. Indeed, they appear to have made a point of attending services together, as we know because that practice sparked one strange incident. On 3 April 1698, as the king was escorting the princess into her chapel, one of her household officers "took up near the communion table a screwed pistol, loaden with 2 bullets, supposed to be brought thither on some ill design."[112] While it is just possible that the person who left the pistol in the chapel intended to use it, it is more likely that this weapon was a symbolic warning from a disgruntled Jacobite. By leaving the pistol in the chapel where the king and his immediate successor were both worshiping, this terrorist was reminding them of their vulnerability. By placing it under the Communion table, he was pointing toward a key difference between Anglican and Roman Catholic worship, perhaps in the hope that altars like those in James II's "Popish chapel," recently consumed by fire, might someday return to England. And by loading the pistol with two bullets, he was attempting to frighten both William and Anne, though neither appears to have paid much heed. William left the next day for the horse races at Newmarket, accompanied by Prince George, who evidently believed his wife was safe.

The investigation of this episode quickly began to resemble a comic opera. Some in attendance remembered "two strange-looking men...who, contrary to the usual custom, had seated themselves among the ladies."[113] A woman who said she knew the man who had left the weapon in the chapel refused to reveal his name, claiming that he was her lover; when questioned more closely, she spoke of having seen the Archbishop of Canterbury at the chapel service, though Thomas Tenison, who had held that post since 1695, was certainly not present on this occasion. An innocent glover from Hereford who had come in hopes of catching a glimpse of the princess was seized, "upon the information of some of the women, that they had seen him there the Sunday before, and he knelt down near to the form where the pistol was found."[114] As Count Tallard, the French ambassador, wrote to a colleague, "this is a very strange business."[115] Significantly, Tallard's main concern now was to keep suspicion away from the French government, which had recently made peace with England. The contrast with the situation two years earlier, when a serious assassination attempt was timed to precede a French invasion, is telling.

Among Tallard's reasons for wanting to avoid suspicion in the matter of the pistol was his need to avoid any disturbance of the secret negotiations between Louis and William about how to divide the Spanish Empire when its disabled and erratic king died. Tallard, in London, was representing France in this delicate process. The Spanish king, Carlos II, was a Habsburg, and the Austrian branch of that family headed by Leopold I—who held the titles of Holy Roman Emperor, King of Hungary, and King of Bohemia—hoped to inherit the vast, if declining, riches of the Spanish Empire. So, too, did the French, whose last two kings had married Spanish princesses, though both had signed documents renouncing any claim to the Spanish throne. Neither the Dutch nor the English had a claim to Spain, but they rightly feared the prospect that France, already the dominant power in Europe, would become far too powerful if she gained a significant portion of Spain's possessions. In a secret treaty signed in October 1698, William and Louis partitioned the Spanish Empire: the Electoral Prince of Bavaria, Leopold's grandson, was to become King of Spain, while the Duchy of Milan (currently a Spanish possession) went to the

Archduke Charles, Leopold's younger son; the Dauphin, Louis's eldest son, was to receive the kingdoms of Naples and Sicily. This agreement, the First Partition Treaty, was doomed to fail. Not only did Leopold refuse to accept any division of the Spanish Empire, but the Electoral Prince, a promising boy at the time of the treaty, died at the age of seven in February 1699. The second Partition Treaty, signed by the French, the English, and the Dutch in March 1700, was also destined to fail, as neither the Habsburg emperor nor the Spanish aristocracy would consent to any partition of the empire. This diplomatic failure set in motion the forces that led to the full-scale war of Queen Anne's reign, in which Tallard himself, as the French commander at Blenheim, would be defeated and taken prisoner.

A few weeks after the discovery of the pistol, on 28 April 1698, Harriet Churchill, Sarah's eldest daughter, married Francis Godolphin, Sidney Godolphin's only son. The princess had known about this match since the previous autumn, when she wrote to Lady Marlborough offering a substantial dowry for the bride:

> I must again tell my deare Mrs. Freeman that I am mighty glad the Marriage advances and think she has all the reason in the world to be fond of it; I am ashamed to say how litle I can contribute towards it, but since Millions could not express the sincere kindness I have for you, I hope deare Mrs. Freeman will accept of 10000£, a poor offering from such a faithfull hart as mine. You may command it whenever you please, it being in the Prince's keeping, and I hope tho I can not express my self as I would that you are soe just as to beleeve there is not a hart that is more passionatly and truly my deare Mrs. Freemans than your faithfull Morleys.

> Pray get me a bottle of orange flower water for I am in great distress for some at present, and in a very litle while shall want some tea.[116]

Anne's gift, which she denigrates as "a poor offering" here and a "mite" in another letter, was one-eighth of her annual income, offered at a time when her finances were under the added strain of providing for those aspects of Gloucester's court that the king refused to fund. Aware of these and other expenses, and mindful that their second daughter might soon be married as well, the Marlboroughs decided to accept only half of the offered sum. Anne was telling the truth in declaring her heart to be "passionately and truly" devoted to Sarah, and she would soon appoint Harriet Godolphin as a Lady of the Bedchamber. But as the postscript asking for orange-water shows, her devotion to her longtime favorite did not prevent her from expecting continued faithful service from her Groom of the Stole.

At the time of the wedding, Anne's situation was better than it had been in many previous years. The destruction of Whitehall had made St. James's Palace more important. A month after the fire, the princess hosted a birthday celebration there,[117] and on 24 February she announced plans for a weekly ball at St. James's on Mondays, presumably an effort on her part to be more active as an official hostess. Even when his palace was intact, William was not eager to give balls, but he does not appear to have objected to the princess's efforts to give regular balls of her own, which brought her into frequent contact with important figures. On 3 May, for example, there was a ball at the palace "by order of the princesse of Denmark, ... where were present the Suedish ambassador and his lady, count Tallards son, and many of our nobility."[118] Although Anne's personal dealings with William continued to be difficult, he had shown some official respect for her family by inviting Prince George to ride in his coach when he entered the City after signing the peace, by including the prince in his entourage when going to Newmarket, by granting Marlborough the top position in Gloucester's court, and by promising Anne that she could choose the duke's servants.

Yet the king remained imperious and unpredictable. In June, shortly before departing for the Continent, he confirmed Marlborough and Burnet as Gloucester's governor and preceptor—then suddenly claimed the right to make all the other appointments to Gloucester's court, ignoring his earlier promise to Anne and leaving her in the embarrassing situation of having promised salaried places to people who might not be appointed after all. "In the mean time," writes Sarah,

> the KING was in no haste to finish the affair of the DUKE's establishment; and a little before he left England to go make the campaign, told MY LORD MARLBOROUGH, (who was now restored to the army, and was to be governor to the DUKE OF GLOUCESTER) that he would send a list, from abroad, of the servants he would have in the duke's family, not in the least regarding the former message, he had sent to the PRINCESS; which my lord observing, took the liberty to put HIS MAJESTY in mind of it, adding that the PRINCESS, upon the credit of that message, had engaged her promises to several persons; and that, not to be able to perform those promises, would be so great a mortification, as he hoped his majesty would not give her, at a time, when any thing of trouble might do her prejudice, she being then with child. Hereupon the KING fell into a great passion, and said, *she should not be* QUEEN *before her time, and he would make the list of what servants the* DUKE *should have.*[119]

Marlborough's brave attempt to reason with his angry king shows great insight into Anne's character: for one who depended upon the loyalty of her servants and who returned that loyalty in large measure, "not to be able to perform those promises" she had made would indeed have been "a mortification." In this crisis, her loyal servants the Marlboroughs served their mistress well. Anne's outraged letter on the subject makes it clear that her friends advised her not to lodge a protest with William lest his position harden. "Tho I submit to this Brutal usage," writes Anne, "because my freinds think it fitt (whos Judgment I shall ever prefer before my own), my hart is touched to that degree as is not to be exprest."[120] While Anne fumed, Marlborough persuaded William's favorite, the Earl of Albemarle, to engage in some delicate diplomacy, with the result that Anne's original list was ultimately "approved, with very few alterations."[121]

At the same moment, Anne was also having to face some unpleasant facts about Sir Benjamin Bathurst, who had been her Household Treasurer since her marriage in 1683. Bathurst owed his position to his standing as the husband of Anne's girlhood favorite Frances Apsley, but he had used his power to amass a personal fortune. Sarah Churchill, who had a nose for financial corruption, started warning Anne early about his devious practices. In April 1697, Anne told Sarah that she had come across a bill confirming Sarah's suspicion that Bathurst was asking tradesmen dealing with the court of the Denmarks for kickbacks.[122] Later in the same year, they corresponded about a piece of dishonest bookkeeping that was very costly to Anne. During the early 1690s, counterfeiting and "clipping" had so devalued silver coins that the golden guinea saw its value rise as high as 30 shillings. A complete recoinage, organized and managed by Charles Montagu, restored confidence in the pound, with the result that the value of the guinea was fixed at 21 shillings. Bathurst, however, went on making up his accounts at the inflated exchange rate. Although Anne, with Sarah's help, put a stop to this practice, she could not bring herself to dismiss her dishonest Treasurer, perhaps because his family was so intertwined with hers. Allen and Peter Bathurst had long been Gloucester's companions in military games, and if Anne now referred to Frances as "the Nag's Head" in her letters to Sarah, she had not forgotten how close they had been as girls. Now, in June 1698, she discovered that her Treasurer had been selling some of the lower positions in her court, asking those appointed as cooks and menial servants to pay large bribes to secure their positions.[123] Coming as it did on the heels of Anne's disappointment about the staff positions in Gloucester's new court, this news was dispiriting.

§

In July, the princess assembled her various physicians to discuss her plan to spend the summer as usual at Windsor. Although some advised against it "for fear she should miscarry, being bigg with child," she decided to make the journey, and there were no immediate consequences. Her determination to carry this child to term may account for the apparent absence of a formal birthday celebration for Gloucester this summer. On 13 September, however, the princess was reported "ill of the gout," and on 15 September, she was "let blood twice." The result was all too familiar: soon after being bled, she "miscarried of a son."[124] In the face of this disappointment, even the welcome news that the king would honor most of her appointments to Gloucester's court was small comfort. Still, Anne continued her efforts to produce another heir: in June 1699, she conceived again, and that pregnancy continued until January 1700.

His mother's inability to bear another child increased the significance of Gloucester and his court. In contrast to the previous summer, when Anne's advanced pregnancy was the focus of attention at Windsor, the summer of 1699 featured splendid festivities for the duke's tenth birthday, reported as "a great concourse of nobility and gentry...at Windsor; the entertainment very magnificent...the like scarce known before."[125] The king, however, was not among the revelers. Following his normal practice in the summer, he was taking the opportunity "to breathe a little" at Het Loo, his summer palace in the Netherlands. For those who were tired of foreign rule, William's absence confirmed the growing suspicion that he disliked being in England;[126] the celebration at Windsor was a rehearsal for the day when the native-born princess would reign as queen. Yet the only record we have of Anne's response to the festivities is not political but aesthetic. Always appreciative of skill in dancing, she noticed that young Jack Churchill had been practicing his steps, and wrote immediately to his mother:

> Your son danced a Minuet last night which upon my word he performed very well, & I do realy beleeve in time he will make a fine dancer, therefore I hope you will encourage him in it.[127]

Implicit in her praise of young Churchill is Anne's hope that her own son, who had tottered while walking when younger, might now be encouraged to emulate his friend by dancing at court balls.

A few weeks after the birthday came the news that George's elder brother, King Christian V of Denmark, had died after a hunting accident. The occasion required the Denmarks to put their entire court into "deep mourning," maintaining black clothing and drapery for several months. William knew these conventions well, having recently insisted on a prolonged period of mourning for his queen.[128] On this occasion, however, the king was intolerant of Prince George's need to honor his dead brother. As the royal birthday in November approached, Anne dutifully made plans for an evening ball in William's honor at St. James's,[129] but she also drew upon her detailed knowledge of protocol and precedent to request that George be exempted from the normal practice of appearing on the birthday in colorful new clothes. As her emissary, she shrewdly chose the Duke of Albemarle, who had been effective in the controversy over Gloucester's servants, but this time William's favorite could not change his master's mind:

> The PRINCESS, knowing that it had been the custom in former reigns, to wait upon the KING, on a birth-day, without coloured clothes, when the mourning was very deep, found means to get my LORD ALBEMARLE to ask the KING's leave, that the prince might be admitted, in his mourning, to wish his majesty joy. The answer was, *That the KING would not see him, unless he came in colours,* and the PRINCE was persuaded to comply, though he did it with great uneasiness.[130]

Again, William was unpredictable. Less than two weeks after embarrassing his brother-in-law by insisting that he come to the birthday party "in colours," the king asked his Parliament to make good on a substantial debt owed to George. Part of the financial structure put in place to support the Denmarks when they married in 1683 had been the prince's income from mortgages he held on some substantial tracts of land in his native Denmark. In 1689, however, King William persuaded Prince George to sign those lands over to the Duke of Holstein, who wanted them as a condition of joining William's alliance against the French.[131] At the time, the king promised restitution, but ten years had now passed without the prince's receiving a penny. For reasons that remain inscrutable,[132] William now proposed to Parliament that George be repaid in full. In the ensuing debate, the Tory Edward Seymour took the occasion to complain that the king had not contributed to the court of the Duke of Gloucester at the level expected when Parliament passed the increase in the Civil List three years earlier; "the remainder," he pointed out, "might be applied to the Prince's debt." The courtier and sometime poet John Howe joined the chorus, proposing that Parliament "requite the Prince's generosity...by a present in land of equal value" and suggesting that they might "take the Duke of York's estate from my Lady Orkney, and give it to the Prince and Princess." The discussion then turned to the issue of whether Gilbert Burnet was "unfit to be about the Duke of Gloucester," a question that actually came to a vote, with the bishop retaining his place by a margin of forty votes.[133] Parliament then referred the original motion for repaying the prince's debt in cash to a committee, where it languished for another two months.

In another context, Anne might have been pleased to have William's selfish actions about the Irish land and her son's establishment held up to parliamentary scrutiny, but the prospect of finally regaining over £85,000 in principal and interest was a good reason to wish that her friends in Parliament might save these criticisms of the monarch for another time. While the king and the princess waited for a decision, which was delayed by a lengthy and heated discussion of all the king's Irish grants, court life continued. Although New Year's Day marked the end of a century, William postponed the usual festivities for a week and combined them with an early celebration of Anne's birthday, which was moved up by a month because she expected to deliver a child in February. If Sarah had commented on this decision, she would probably have sneered at William's motives, presuming that he combined the two parties to save money. But Sarah was preoccupied: on 2 January her second daughter Anne, the princess's namesake and a great beauty, married Sunderland's son Charles Spencer, who was a radical Whig. In another instance of her tendency to honor personal commitments over ideology, Princess Anne ignored the groom's politics and provided £5,000 for Anne Churchill, as she had done in 1698 for her sister Harriet.

When the princess miscarried on 24 January, just two weeks before her birthday, the midwives thought she was "within six weeks of her time."[134] Undaunted, and of course unaware that this pregnancy would prove to be her last, she held a hastily organized celebration on her actual birthday, for which John Blow and an anonymous poet provided an ode. Similarities between the text for this ode, beginning "Come, bring the song," and the text for "The nymphs of the wells," Blow's song for Gloucester's birthday in 1697, suggest that his poetic collaborator was the same on both occasions. As in the previous ode, the poet mentions Druids and expresses the hope that Anne will have more descendants by using the imagery of branching plants. Gloucester, personified as a "Royall Oke" in the previous ode, is here "the promising branch which grows / On fair sabrinas banks," while Anne appears as a "generous frutefull Vine":

> Long may the heavens shine
> on this generous frutefull Vine.
> may she flourish many years
> free from Blasting Frights and cares,
> and bring forth more such frute
> as glad Glovernia bears.[135]

In speaking of "such frute / As glad Glovernia Bears," the poet is again imagining Gloucester as a future parent. If both text and music were composed on short notice, as seems likely, the poet was hoping to reassure Anne after her most recent disappointment. Perhaps he was even blaming her misfortune on some unspecified "Blasting Fright." But as the poet, the composer, and the crowd of courtiers who heard this ode surely knew, this was Anne's thirty-fifth birthday. It had been more than ten years since her last live birth, and her chances of bearing another child were going steadily down. She did not conceive again.

On 14 February, a grumpy and divided Parliament finally passed the bill repaying George for his Danish lands. The next day, Anne wrote to Sarah expressing her gratitude to Marlborough, who had worked hard to secure the bill's passage, for "what was don last night concerning the princes business."[136] This is her last surviving letter to Sarah until the beginning of her reign in 1702. Letters from Lady Marlborough to Lady Bathurst written during June 1700 show Sarah relaying Anne's wishes about the appointments of some servants at Windsor and make it clear that the flow of correspondence between the princess and her favorite continued.[137] We catch fleeting glimpses of Anne in newsletters over the next few months—dining in public with the other court ladies in April, making a gift to the poor in May, and decamping as usual to Windsor for the summer—but the accidental disappearance of her personal correspondence makes it difficult to assess her emotional condition.[138]

Although Gloucester's eleventh birthday was not as significant a milestone as his tenth, Anne at last had the satisfaction of seeing him dance during the festivities.[139] Two days later, the boy felt ill, and it was soon clear that he was in serious danger. Some thought his illness was brought on by being overheated at the party; others mentioned his having eaten fruit. Modern medical experts who have studied the very full autopsy prepared by the royal physicians conclude that his disease was an "acute...bacterial infection of the upper and lower respiratory tracts culminating in pneumonia."[140] In a world without antibiotics, such conditions were often fatal, and Anne evidently recognized the signs of impending death. According to Bishop Burnet, the princess attended her dying son "with great tenderness, but with a grave composedness, that amazed all who saw it. She bore his death with a resignation and piety, that were indeed very singular."[141]

Despite her remarkable sense of propriety, which did not desert her in this crisis, Anne was clearly devastated. During the first few weeks, she had herself carried into the garden daily for fresh air, and by the middle of August she had "ordered the day on which the duke of Glocester died to be annually kept as a day of mourning in her family."[142] She was ill herself in September but recovered in time to make a visit to the Marlboroughs at St. Albans in October. In a larger sense, however, Anne never recovered from the event she later called "my great misfortune of loosing my dear child."[143] The loss was both personal and political, as the death of Gloucester undermined Anne's hope that her progeny would sustain the Stuart line. Politicians of all persuasions responded immediately to the sudden absence of a successor: Jacobites began intriguing on behalf of the Prince of Wales, James II's Catholic son, who was a healthy but Catholic boy of twelve in France; others urged William to marry again, though he had shown no inclination to do so in the five years since Mary's death; the king himself, already on the Continent, went to visit Sophia, Electress of Hanover, who was the nearest Protestant aspirant to the throne. Ministerial and parliamentary discussions of the succession began as soon as William returned to England, and in the spring of 1701 a divided Parliament achieved a moment of consensus by passing the Act of Settlement, which stipulated that the crown would pass to the next Protestant heir after William, Anne, and the "heirs of their bodies," of whom none now existed or were likely to exist. The Act specifically named the Hanoverians, descendants of James I's daughter Elizabeth, who had married a German prince, and it was that line that succeeded, despite intrigues and machinations that continued throughout Anne's reign.

Several of those who addressed condolences to the princess on the death of Gloucester treated his death as ending any hope for a direct succession to Anne. In the dedicatory epistle to a treatise called *The Consolation of Death*, for example, Richard Burridge wished her long life but omitted any mention of future progeny:

> Matchless Lady of Piety! Your royal self being the only hopes great *Brittain* has now left to make her happy, I pray the Almighty King of Kings may lengthen your life with a *Nestorian* age, that by your resplendent Vertues we may be guided to those everlasting Mansions, where the blessed Duke now sits crowned with immortality.[144]

Burridge was correct in assuming that Anne would not conceive again, but the queen did not abandon hope. As late as 1703, she wrote to the Duchess of Marlborough describing her continuing efforts to become pregnant:

> I intend to morrow (an it please god) to take physick in order to drink the Spaw waters, which my Doctors have adviced me to & I have a great inclination for them my self, hopeing they may make my Lady Charlotte return, for unless I can compass that it is to be feared my vaypours will rather grow upon me than decrease, & I can never have any manner of hopes of ye unexpressible Blessing of another Child, for tho I do not flatter my self with the thought of it, I would leave no reasonable thing undon that might be a means toward it.[145]

For years Anne had written to Sarah about her menstrual cycles, using "a visit from Lady Charlotte" as a code, and the use of that phrase here (though partially blotted in the manuscript) expresses the hope that drinking the waters would restore some regularity to her cycle, which had become erratic.[146] Anne's determination to "leave no reasonable thing undon" in her quest to conceive again is remarkable, but her choice of words suggests that she was beginning to realize that the "Blessing of another Child" was not only "unexpressible" but unattainable.

§

Early in 1708, six years into Anne's reign, Ambrose Philips published four pastorals in a miscellany of poems by university wits. In the ten years since Princess Anne heard his song on mortality performed at *Caligula*, Philips had been a Cambridge don, then an army officer, then a prisoner of war in Spain. His pastorals appeared after he escaped from captivity and made his way back to England. In the next year, 1709, the London publisher Jacob Tonson began his annual miscellany with Philips's pastorals, now expanded to six in number.

The second pastoral in the group of four, which became the third in the group of six, is a poem of mourning called "Albino." After an introductory passage pointing to Virgil's praise of Augustus and Spenser's praise of Queen Elizabeth, Philips claims a similar relationship to his Queen:

> Since...Swains at ease through *ANNA*'s Goodness live;
> Like them will I my slender Musick raise,
> And cause the vocal Vallies speak her Praise.[147]

From this introduction, we might expect a poem in praise of Anne's reign, but what follows is a poem in memory of the Duke of Gloucester. Philips introduces a pair of "Country Swains" who retire to a mossy cave and give vent to melancholy thoughts about the death of "young *Albino*":

> Revolving now the solemn Day they find,
> When young *Albino* died: his Image dear
> Bedews their Cheeks with many a trickling Tear;
> To Tears they add the Tribute of their Verse:
> These *Angelot*, those *Palin* did rehearse.
> *Angelot*. Thus yearly circling by-past Times return;
> And yearly thus *Albino*'s Fate we mourn:
> *Albino*'s Fate was early; short his Stay:
> How sweet the Rose! How speedy the Decay!

Philips deliberately gives Angelot a speech reworking a pregnant moment in the fifth book of Virgil's *Aeneid,* when the Trojans return to Sicily one year after the burial of Aeneas's aged father Anchises, and Aeneas marks the anniversary by announcing funeral games. This passage would have been prominent in the minds of Philips and other poets because Dryden had quoted it, in Latin, as the epigraph for his last book, *Fables Ancient and Modern* (1700), and had translated it memorably in his *Aeneis* (1697), a book Gloucester read and treasured:

> The shining Circle of the Year has fill'd,
> Since first this Isle my Father's Ashes held:
> And now the rising Day renews the Year,

> (A Day for ever sad, for ever dear,)
> This wou'd I celebrate with Annual Games,
> With Gifts on Altars pil'd, and holy Flames.[148]

Compared to the sonorous cadences of Dryden, Philips's verse is "slender Musick" indeed, but the allusion is a potent one: as the pious Aeneas marks the day of his father's death as "A Day for ever sad, for ever dear," so Anne commanded yearly observance of the anniversary of Gloucester's death. The emotional difference between the death of a parent, old and full of years, and the death of a promising child adds to the poignancy of the Virgilian allusion. As Angelot later says, those grieving for Albino can only imagine his manhood:

> How all our Hopes are fled like Morning Dew!
> And we but in our Thoughts thy Manhood view.

Some readers might also have remembered that the episode of the boy cavalry, the one whose illustration bore the Duke of Gloucester's name in Dryden's folio, is part of the funeral games described in the same book of the *Aeneid*. Angelot points in that direction by remembering Gloucester's passion for military exercises, but alluding to ancient arms:

> Who now shall teach the pointed Spear to throw,
> To whirl the Sling, and bend the stubborn Bow?

In using the resonance of Virgil's epic and imagining the duke wielding classical weapons, Philips was proceeding in his English poem along lines laid down by those who had mourned Gloucester in Latin in the academic collections of 1700. When he brings the queen herself onstage, however, the generic model is not epic but tragedy:

> The pious Mother comes, with Grief opprest:
> Ye conscious Trees and Fountains can attest,
> With what sad Accents and what moving Cries
> She fill'd the Grove, and importun'd the Skies,
> And ev'ry Star upbraided with his Death,
> When in her childless Arms, devoid of Breath,
> She clasp'd her Son: Nor did the Nymph for this
> Place in her Darling's Welfare all her Bliss,
> And teach him young the Sylvan Crook to wield,
> And rule the peaceful Empire of the Field.[149]

By the time this poem appeared in print, Philips had become friendly with the prominent poet and dramatist Joseph Addison and the Anglo-Irish clergyman and satirist Jonathan Swift. His own opinions were Whiggish, but he maintained relationships with men of both parties because he was hoping to secure government patronage. Under those circumstances, it might have appeared risky for him to describe the queen, minimally distanced by the conventions of pastoral, as if she were a tragic heroine upbraiding the stars. But Philips was sure-handed in managing the tone of his poem, introducing the second shepherd, Palin, for a conclusion designed to comfort and praise the monarch:

> *Palin.* No more, mistaken *Angelot*, complain;
> *Albino* lives, and all our Tears are vain:
> And now the royal Nymph, who bore him, deigns
> To bless the Fields, and rule the simple Swains;
> While from above propitious he looks down.
> For this the convex Skies no longer frown,
> The Planets shine indulgent on our Isle,
> And rural Pleasures round about us smile:
>
> . . . .
>
> To thee these Honours yearly will we pay,
> When we our shearing Feast and Harvest keep,
> To speed the Plow, and bless our thriving Sheep.
> While Mallow Kids and Endive Lambs persue,
> While Bees love Thyme, and Locusts sip the Dew,
> While Birds delight in Woods their Notes to strain,
> Thy Name and sweet Remembrance shall remain.

There is no written record of Anne's having read this poem, but it is an intriguing circumstance that one year after it appeared in the Oxford miscellany, Ambrose Philips was posted to Copenhagen as Secretary to Daniel Pulteney, Envoy-Extraordinary to the Danish court. And although Swift thought Philips had run "Party-mad" in his devotion to the Whigs, it was Philips who wrote the words for Anne's birthday ode for 1713, set by no less a composer than George Frideric Handel.[150]

CHAPTER 6

ENTIRELY ENGLISH

28 August 1702

An hour after sunset, the royal coaches came into sight, and the waiting performers moved to their stations. The mayor and citizens of Bath had not forgotten their embarrassment in 1692, when Queen Mary ordered them to snub her sister. A decade later, with Anne at last on the throne, they were determined to make her visit memorable. A "splendid Train" of local horsemen greeted the royal party, providing an escort for their coaches, and as the cavalcade approached the city, the queen encountered

> a Great Company of Citizens cloathed like *Granadiers,* and after them about 200 Virgins in two Companies richly attir'd, many of them Apparell'd like Amazons with *Bows* and *Arrows,* and some with Guilt Scepters and Ensigns of the *Regalia* in their *Hands,* all of them with a set of Dancers who danced by the side of *Her* Majesties Coach as she pass'd along.[1]

The details of this pageant, carefully recorded in a pamphlet called *The Queen's Famous Progress,* reflected the policies and preferences of the new queen, who had ascended the throne just six months earlier. The "Citizens cloathed like *Granadiers*" were honoring the troops engaged in the War of the Spanish Succession, an

effort led by Anne, who declared war on France within three months of her accession. The real grenadiers, men chosen for their size and courage, were in Flanders with the Earl of Marlborough, now Captain-General of the English and
Dutch land forces, trying to lure the French into a full-scale battle. Although
his Dutch allies, fearful of losses, limited his options during this first campaign,
Marlborough would nonetheless seize three fortresses along the river Meuse
during Anne's vacation in Bath. He had already shown more willingness to
engage the French than had been common in the slow, grinding war of sieges
that King William had waged in the 1690s. Accustomed as they were to a king
who joined his troops in the field, some Englishmen resisted the idea of a
queen as supreme commander, expressing their unease in a bad joke: "Her
Majesty...declaring War against *France*, it was whisper'd that *Lewis* XIV.
should thereupon joakingly say, *It's a sign I grow old when the Ladies declare War
against me.*"[2] The decision to dress the company of virgins at Bath as Amazons,
the fierce female warriors of Greek mythology, was an answer to these doubts,
and this female monarch would have unprecedented success in her quest "to
reduce the exorbitant Power of *France*."[3] The scepters and ensigns in the hands
of the other virgins were reminders of Anne's splendid coronation on St.
George's Day (23 April), an occasion notable for minute attention to tradition.
Balancing these political icons with a recognition of the queen's personal artistic
tastes, the citizens had also trained "a set of dancers" to move in synchrony by
the side of her coach.

The queen's first reason for coming to Bath was medical: Prince George's
asthma had flared up badly in early August, and the royal physicians believed the
Bath waters would be helpful to him and to his wife. But in staging this visit as a
royal "progress," Anne was also claiming the mantle of Queen Elizabeth, whose
subjects had often greeted her with allegorical pageants during her grand progresses through her realms, including one to Bath in 1574. On her return journey,
as she "passed over the *Downs* in *Wiltshire*," Anne encountered a pastoral tableau
like those enacted in the court theatricals of her youth, with the crucial difference
that the entertainers were genuine shepherds and spinners, not trained performers
in costume:

> A great Number of Shepherds from all parts of the Country, all dress'd
> in their long coarse white Cloaks, with their *Crooks, Shepherds Scrips*
> and *Tar-boxes*, playing all the way they march'd upon their Pipes of
> *Reeds*, humbly present[ed] themselves to her Majesty; who was
> pleased to hear their Country Songs and *Musick*...after which a great
> Number of *Spinners* with their *Spinning-Wheels*, presented themselves

before her Majesty, and were favourably received, and tasted *very liber-ally* of her *Majestys Bounty*.[4]

Like Elizabeth, the new queen bestowed her royal touch on those suffering from scrofula, "a great many coming thither upon that Account, who being viewed by Her Majesty's Physitian, such as was found afflicted with that Distemper received *Tickets* according to the usual Custome, and was admitted, and touched by Her Majesty."[5] In reviving this ancient ritual, Anne was pointedly embracing older tra-ditions and rejecting the practice of William, who scoffed at the ceremony and never touched his subjects. In December, she announced that she was appropriat-ing Elizabeth's motto, "semper eadem" (always the same), as her own, to be used "wheresoever there shall be occasion to Embroider, Grave, Carve, or Paint her Majesty's Royal Arms."[6]

The messages of loyalty and love that the citizens of Bath and Wiltshire expressed in dumb show echoed those delivered in prose and verse during the queen's visit to Oxford University, where she stayed overnight on her way to Bath. When she "entred her Lodgings," there were formal speeches in English and Latin, concluding with a poem composed and spoken by Simon Harcourt, an eighteen-year-old youth now moving from the Inns of Court to Christ Church, most likely chosen for this honor because his father had become Solicitor General in June. The elder Harcourt was among those members of the queen's entourage who received honorary degrees on this occasion; he was therefore present to hear his son declaim this poem:

> When haughty Monarchs their proud State expose,
> And Majesty an awful Greatness shows,
> Their Subjects, Madam, with amazement seized,
> Gaze at the Pomp, rather surpriz'd than pleas'd.
> But your more gentle Influence imparts
> Wonder at once, and Pleasure to our Hearts.
> Where e're you come Joy shines in ev'ry Face,
> Such winning Goodness, such an easy Grace,
> Through all your Realms diffusive Kindness pours,
> That ev'ry ENGLISH Heart's entirely yours.[7]

Drawing on conventional gender values, the poet contrasts the queen's "gentle Influence," "winning Goodness," and "easy Grace" with the pride of those "haughty Monarchs," presumably male, who amaze and surprise their subjects. By leaving the haughty kings unspecified and plural, he allows multiple readings: the most obvious example was Louis XIV, Anne's opponent in the current war, but the queen might also have thought of King William, whose pride she had often deplored, while others might have remembered James II, whose imperious stance had cost him his crown. The reference to "ev'ry ENGLISH Heart," by contrast, is an unambiguous and overt allusion to the most notable phrase in Anne's first speech to her Parliament, delivered on 11 March 1702, three days after William's death:

> It shall be My constant Endeavour, to make you the best Return for that
> Duty and Affection you have expressed to Me, by a careful and diligent
> Administration for the Good of all My Subjects: And, as I know My own
> Heart to be entirely *English*, I can very sincerely assure you, there is not
> any Thing you can expect, or desire from Me, which I shall not be ready
> to do for the Happiness and Prosperity of *England*; and you shall always
> find Me a strict and religious Observer of My Word.[8]

Anne's decision to declare her heart "entirely *English*" was her way of differentiating herself from the foreign-born king who preceded her, and young Harcourt would later show sympathy for the Jacobite cause, a movement fueled in part by fear of foreigners. In this poem, however, he recalls Anne's reception in Oxford after she fled from Whitehall and her father in 1688; if his language is cautious, there is no apparent disapproval of the Revolution:

> These happy Walls by Royal Bounty plac'd,
> Often with Royal Presence have been Grac'd.
> Here Kings to ease the Cares attend a Crown,
> Preferr'd the Muses Lawrels to their Own.
> And here You once enjoy'd a safe Retreat,
> From Noise and Envy free: To this lov'd Seat,
> To be a Guest, You then did condescend,
> Which now, its happy Guardian, You defend.

Mindful of James's interference in university elections, and of William's disinterest in all things artistic and intellectual, Harcourt suggests that the proper role of the monarch is to provide "Royal Bounty" to the university, preferring the laurels of poetry to those of power. After finding Oxford "a safe Retreat" in times of trouble, Queen Anne has now become the university's "happy Guardian," defending it from all threats.

The idea of Anne as the defender of traditional and patriotic values, including those of the university, appears again in the verses she heard when she sat down to supper, spoken by Heneage Finch, a nineteen-year-old undergraduate whose father was the Member of Parliament for the university. In Finch's poem, the new queen "frees us from Alarms, / Secures our Quiet, and directs our Arms"; those now singing her praises will soon volunteer to defend her:

> Our *Muses* hear the Battles from afar,
> And sing the Triumphs, and enjoy the War.
> This now, but soon the quivering *Spear* they'l weild,
> And lead the shouting *Squadrons* to the field.
> They'l serve that Princess whom before they sung
> Defend that QUEEN beneath whose Eye they sprung.
> > So spreading Oaks from lovely WINDSOR born,
> > Shall shelter BRITAIN, which they now adorn
> > With swelling Sails o're distant Seas they'l go,
> > And guard that Goddess by whose Care they grow.

Although Finch is evidently thinking of himself and other student poets, he actually says that the Muses, those female inspirers of art now nurtured by a queen sympathetic to poetry, will go to war to defend her. As they wield "the quivering *Spear,*" the Muses begin to resemble the virgin Amazons who would greet the royal party at Bath. In a similar transformation, the oaks Anne cherishes in her beloved forest at Windsor will repay her care by becoming the wooden ships of the British navy.[9] Three more student poems, lost but probably similar, greeted the music-loving queen at the Sheldonian Theatre, where she heard "a Consort of *Vocal* and *Instrumental* Musick."

In one sense, these celebrations of the queen in pageantry, dance, poetry, and music were broadly patriotic demonstrations of loyalty to a new monarch ruling in a time of war. Alert observers, however, could find partisan messages embedded in these panegyric exercises. On 2 July, the queen had dissolved the Parliament she inherited from William, and "Elections for the ensuing Parliament," as Abel Boyer explains, were proceeding "with great Warmth and Contention, though with visible Advantage on the Side of the *Church,* or *Tory-Party,* which was, in great Measure, owing to the Countenance and Encouragement they receiv'd from the Court."[10] The poems Anne heard in Oxford, written by the sons of Tory politicians, reflect their party's confidence. In most of his poem, young Harcourt is attentive to political balance, but his emphasis on Anne's claim to be "entirely *English,*" a phrase suggested by her uncle Laurence Hyde, the Tory Earl of Rochester, has partisan resonance. According to Boyer, "many were highly offended at this Expression in her Speech, *That her Heart was* ENTIRELY ENGLISH; which was a glaring Insinuation, That the late King's Heart was not so."[11] Harcourt appropriates the controversial slogan in order to praise the queen for her "winning Goodness," which has so thoroughly impressed her subjects that "ev'ry ENG-LISH Heart's entirely yours." Lurking not far beneath the gracious compliment, however, is the partisan implication that loyalty to the queen and the nation will naturally entail support for Tory positions.

When young Mr. Finch describes his queen directing English arms in the war, he deliberately praises the British navy, which would be far less successful than the army in its operations of summer and early fall:

> ENGLAND before its ruin'd Trade deplor'd,
> A mourning Victor, and disputed Lord.
> Now moulding Fleets in *Gallick* Harbours ly,
> Whilst *British Ships* their double World defy.

In August 1702, this vision of naval victory was a fantasy, but it also served a political purpose. Finch's father, a Tory Member of Parliament, would have recognized the nod to the navy as an endorsement of the position held by Rochester, who had vigorously contended that England should not be drawn into an expensive land war on the Continent but should confine her efforts to the seas. Choosing Marlborough's advice instead, the queen had rejected this view, as the younger Finch had ample reason to know, so he was careful to balance his naval imagery with the lines on quivering spears and shouting squadrons, a mythologically displaced acknowledgment of the ongoing land war, before moving back to the seas with his conceit about the oak trees. In seeking a balance between attention to the army and the navy, young Finch was following the lead of his prominent uncle Daniel Finch, Earl of Nottingham, a High Church Tory who had become one of Anne's two Secretaries of State on 2 May. On 14 August, just two weeks before the queen's visit to Oxford, Nottingham had written to Anthonie Heinsius, the Grand Pensionary of Holland, expressing his belief that "no Warr can be of great Dammage to France, but that which is prosecuted...by a Fleet, and an Army accompanying it."[12]

Although they entertained the queen with "Country Songs and Musick" rather than freshly composed poems, the male shepherds and female spinners in the pastoral pageant in Wiltshire were also making a political point. Forty percent of English exports at this time consisted of woolen cloth, which filled the hold of many an outgoing ship, but Louis XIV had now blocked imports of English cloth to France, Spain, the Spanish Empire in South America, the Spanish Netherlands, and the entire Mediterranean Sea, with all its ports. For the Whigs, as for moderate Tories and the queen herself, securing and protecting foreign markets for English cloth was "a chief incentive for taking up arms."[13] If a French prince became King of Spain, these world markets might be permanently closed to English

woolens, and the results would be disastrous for everyone involved in the manufacture of cloth. Anne's largesse to the musical shepherds and spinners, some
"20 or 30 Guineas" according to the pamphleteer, was an expression of her determination to protect their livelihood. When she addressed her new Parliament on
21 October, she made a particular point of describing the manufacture of wool as
an industry "of great Consequence to the whole Kingdom." "On my Part," she
pledged, "nothing shall be omitted for its Encouragement."[14]

On her way home to London from Bath, Anne spent the night at the home of
Charles Seymour, Duke of Somerset, the same man who had gallantly lent her his
London house when she quarreled with her sister in 1692. Mindful of his personal
loyalty, the queen allowed "the proud Duke," a moderate Whig whom William
had made President of the Privy Council on 20 January 1702, to continue in his
post; he reciprocated by supporting her war policies, and she made him her
Master of the Horse in July. When Anne reached the village of Marlborough,
where Somerset had his estate, the scholars of the local free school greeted her
with yet another pastoral pageant. In a memorized speech, a boy pretending to be
Virgil's shepherd Tityrus offered the queen a crown of oak leaves:

> Welcom, great Guardian of our Flocks,
> From roaming Wolfe, and cunning Fox,
> What fitter offering can we make,
> For us to give, or you to take,
> Than Royal Oak, that sacred Tree
> To Jove and your great Family?

Another boy identified as Thyrsis asked her to

> Accept our Chaplets, Crooks, and Reeds,
> Our Artless Songs and Rural Weeds.[15]

Anne had good reason to doubt that any song delivered in her presence could
be truly "Artless." To be praised as the "great Guardian of our Flocks" again suggested her support for the woolen trade, though it was difficult to know whether
the wolf and the fox were foreign or domestic predators. The imagery of the oak
tree, however, pointed in a different direction. Since 1662, the English had celebrated Royal Oak Day (29 May) as the anniversary of Charles II's escape after the
Battle of Worcester. By calling the oak "sacred...to your great Family," the poet
who wrote these lines for the schoolboys to recite was emphasizing Anne's identity as a Stuart. Yet the queen was all too aware that she had no heir to continue her
line in that "great Family." Indeed, she might have sadly remembered the emphasis

placed on the royal oak by the "Druids" who sang their birthday song for Glouces-ter at Tunbridge Wells just five years earlier.[16] Worse yet, a rival claimant was alive and well in France, and Louis XIV had helped push the English toward the current war by recognizing the thirteen-year-old Pretender as "James III" when Anne's father died in September 1701. Many resented this act, which was a brazen viola-tion of treaties Louis had signed with William, but a significant percentage of Anne's subjects regarded the boy in St. Germain as the rightful heir. Indeed, Jaco-bites opposed to the Hanoverian succession would later appropriate the imagery of oak leaves to express their loyalty to the Stuart line.[17]

With pamphlets and newspapers now offering opinion, gossip, and slander on a daily basis, Whigs were already accusing all Tories of being closet Jacobites, while Tories in turn accused all Whigs of being closet republicans. Readers of all persuasions, including the queen herself, were learning to be alert to covert and ambiguous messages. Allegorical pageants featuring shepherds, spinners, or Ama-zons might deploy the matter of myth in the service of politics, and a poem imag-ining the oaks of Windsor as the planks of ships might also express the passions of a party.

§

From the moment she became queen, Anne displayed not only a competent un-derstanding of domestic and international affairs but a sophisticated grasp of the artful modes of indirect political discourse that greeted her during this royal prog-ress. On the day of William's death, 8 March 1702, Bishop Burnet drove at speed from Kensington to St. James's Palace, expecting to gain favor by being the first to congratulate the new queen, but Anne, attentive as always to "giving people their due Ranks,"[18] refused to see him. She knew perfectly well that the responsibility for informing her of the king's death belonged to the Gentleman of the Bed-chamber currently on duty at his court, on this occasion Algernon Capel, second Earl of Essex. Even though Anne had no strong connection to Essex, the son of a Whig conspirator honored as a martyr by his party, she allowed him to deliver the official notification. By insisting on following the rules, the new queen was send-ing several important messages. She was letting Burnet know that his previous service as Gloucester's tutor did not give him the right to perform duties that were not his, and by receiving the news from Essex, an even more rabid Whig than Burnet, she was placing protocol above party, as she would frequently do during her reign. She was also demonstrating her intent to treat William's establishment with appropriate respect—a practice she extended to the king's most menial ser-vants. "Her majestie," reported Luttrell on 12 May, "will not begin to keep house as queen till the 1st of July" and "has declared that all the money which till then comes in upon the civil list shal goe towards paying the arrears due to the late kings servants." By the time she opened her court at Windsor "in great splendor and magnificence," she had "ordered all the servants of the late king to be paid half a years salary"—a policy quite unlike William's peremptory termination of Gloucester's staff in 1700.[19] The idea of the monarch as repository and keeper of tradition was personally comfortable to the new queen and politically calculated to quiet those who might question her right to the throne or advocate an altered succession after her reign.

Late in life, an embittered Sarah claimed that "Lord Godolphin had conducted the Queen with the care and tenderness of a father or a guardian through a state of helpless ignorance."[20] While Godolphin was genuinely attentive to the princess and did much to instruct her, Sarah's claim that Anne was helplessly ignorant is manifestly false. In her confident, sure-handed actions as her reign began, Anne was not a puppet mechanically following instructions but a monarch who had prepared herself to rule. The years just before her accession are the least well-documented in her adult life, but the glimpses we catch of her do not suggest "helpless ignorance." Mourning for her son and then for her father, she kept a low profile for long periods, but she was evidently attentive to political developments.

For the first six months after the death of Gloucester, Anne was virtually absent from public view, remaining secluded at Windsor until October 1700 and further delaying her return to London by visiting the Marlboroughs at St. Albans. When the king staged his usual birthday party on 4 November, the royal court "appeared very gay and splendid, . . . having laid aside their Mourning," but the bereaved prince and princess, unwilling to abandon their black clothes, were absent. Not until 31 January 1701, six full months after their son's death, did they visit the king.[21] In her retirement, however, Anne was quietly preparing for the "sun shine day" she had imagined in 1692. According to René Saunière de L'Hermitage, who supplied the Dutch government with frequent dispatches from London, the princess undertook a program of serious reading after Gloucester's death;[22] the politician Robert Harley, in a personal summary of his career, remembered "often attending on the Princess Anne by her command" in 1700.[23] When she asked him to "attend" her, the princess was making sure that she was briefed on current politics, both foreign and domestic, and in Harley she had an unusually well-placed informant.

In her youth, Anne had watched her uncle and her father prorogue and dismiss their Parliaments, ruling for long periods without a sitting legislature. The Triennial Act of 1694 eliminated that possibility, requiring general elections and meetings of Parliament at least every three years.[24] In practice, Parliament met yearly during William's reign, and elections were also frequent; the partisan and fractious Parliaments of the king's later years were often hostile toward his standing army, his ministers, and his Dutch favorites. Harley, who entered Parliament in 1689, was skilled at adapting to the shifting alliances that characterized this period: as the leader of the "country Whigs," he successfully forced a massive demobilization after the Treaty of Ryswick in 1697, and when various groups in Parliament began to realign themselves, he moved closer to such Tories as Rochester (Anne's uncle) and Godolphin (long her trusted friend). When the general election of January 1701 gave the Tories a majority in the Commons, Harley became Speaker of the House.

The new Parliament had its first meeting on 6 February 1701, which happened to be Anne's birthday.[25] In keeping with her continued desire for retirement, the princess spent the day at Windsor, not St. James's, and the newspapers reported that "divers of the Nobility went to Windsor to Congratulate her Royal Highness."[26] This was most likely the occasion on which Anne heard a birthday ode set to music by the composer Jeremiah Clarke, who appears to have become her harpsichord teacher in this period, as Purcell was dead and Draghi disabled by gout. The vocal soloist most prominently featured in this birthday music, the high tenor Richard Elford, sang in the choir at St. Paul's Cathedral, where Clarke was now one of the organists.[27] In addition to four solo singers and the usual strings, the music includes parts for kettledrums, a trumpet, a pair of oboes, and a pair of recorders—all instruments available from Prince George's small military band, which normally traveled to Windsor with the Denmarks.[28] The vocal soloists probably covered the four parts necessary for the choral sections, though the choir of St. George's Chapel might have been available if Clarke wanted larger forces.

The anonymous text tells us much about the image Anne wished to project to her friends and supporters at this time. The poet begins with seasonal imagery, imagining Anne transforming a cold winter day into spring:

> Let Nature smile, let all be gay;
> Tis royal royal Anna's day.
> Now Spring revive, roll on ye Spheres;
> She with delight our Souls employs,
> From this bless'd day, she dates her years,
> And we our lasting joys.[29]

The first person plurals, as so often in court poetry, define a particular group: the "we" who date "our lasting joys" from Anne's birth are presumably those most faithful to "royal royal Anna" and most eager for her accession. In return for their loyalty, the princess *employs* their souls with delight, and that odd verb begins to make sense when the poet invokes the patronage that flows from the knowledgeable princess, here explicitly called a "Patroness of Arts":

> Pay your homage chearful hearts,
> Greet the Patroness of Arts.
> With song your tribute to her bring,
> Who best inspires you how to sing;
> None better claims your lays than she
> Whose very soul is Harmony.
> O happy those whose art can feast
> So just, and so refined a taste.

This entire section is a solo for Elford, who had left his post in the choir of Durham cathedral in 1699 to come to London and try his fortune as a singer in the theatres. When his awkward stage presence put an end to that dream, he found employment in the choir at St. Paul's and later in the choirs of Westminster Abbey, St. George's Chapel, and the Chapel Royal. Anne evidently played a role in recommending him for some of these posts; he was her favorite singer for the rest of her life.[30] The "chearful hearts" addressed in this stanza are clearly the performers, fortunate to be offering their art as a feast for a princess who had the ears and the training to savor it and looking forward to improved patronage in her reign. In Elford's case, such expectations were justified: Anne heard him frequently at court while on the throne, took him along during her summer progress to Bath in 1703, and granted him an annual pension of £100 beginning in 1705.

Although no contemporary writer tells us why Anne admired Elford, the organist and composer William Croft praised him as "being in a peculiar Manner eminent for giving such a due Energy and proper Emphasis to the *Words* of his *Musick*."[31] Elford's excellence in expressing the words may have been one reason for his appeal to a woman who had "a softness of voice, and sweetness in the pronunciation, that added much life to all she spoke."[32] In this birthday ode, Clarke gave Elford a touching and delicate aria expressing the hope that Anne might bear another child. After an innocent string ritornello in B-flat major, the vocalist enters in d minor; Clarke's wistful expression of the hope for more heirs to Anne's virtues thus delicately acknowledges her sorrow for the lost Gloucester.[33] The contrast with earlier birthday odes, in which composers saluted Gloucester with martial fanfares, is striking.

Despite her continuing grief, Anne clung to her hope for another child. She had been pregnant until a few weeks before her last birthday, and she was just turning thirty-six. As late as 1705, when the queen was forty, poets were

Mus. Ex. 6.1: Jeremiah Clarke, excerpt from *Let Nature Smile,*
birthday ode for Princess Anne (1701?).

still asking heaven to give her a son.[34] The text for this aria, however, expresses that hope as an obligation:

> In her brave offspring still she'll live,
> Nor must she bless our age alone;
> But to succeeding ages give,
> Heirs to her virtues, and the throne.

The syntax actually says that Anne *must* produce "heirs to her virtues and the throne," a construction betraying the urgency felt by those for whom all of the possible successors were unattractive options.

§

Five days after this ode was performed, King William addressed the new Parliament, urging them to take steps to settle the succession "in the Protestant line";[35] a few weeks later, Daniel Defoe published *The Succession to the Crown of England Considered*, an anonymous pamphlet in his characteristically blunt style. A Dissenting businessman with enormous energy and talent, Defoe would be both troublesome and helpful to Anne during her reign; even at this relatively early moment in his career, there were few public controversies about which he could remain silent. "The Death of the Duke of *Gloucester*," he writes, "may very justly be accounted a Misfortune to the Nation, . . . By putting us to the trouble of looking about the World for a Successor."[36] Dismissing as unlikely the possibility that Anne or William might produce a child,[37] Defoe carefully lists all of those with claims to the throne, beginning with Anne's first cousin Anne-Marie, with whom she had shared a nursery during her childhood visit to France. His description of this claimant is genealogically accurate and politically pointed:

> *Anna Maria*, Dutchess of *Savoy*, Daughter to the present Duke of *Orleans*, by *Henrietta*, eldest Daughter to King *Charles* the First, being without doubt the nearest of Kin to the Crown of *England*, as standing in the same Degree by the Female Line, as the Princess *Ann* by the Male.

After offering similar descriptions of several other Continental princesses descended from James I, Defoe brusquely points out that "all these *Claimants* are *Roman Catholicks*" and therefore barred from the succession by acts of Parliament passed after the Revolution.[38] "The next in course, and the First *Protestant Heir*" he continues, "is that Excellent Princess *Sophia*, . . . Dutchess and Electoress Dowager of *Hannover*, Grand-Daughter to King *James* the First, and who is still living." Although she was seventy years old, the Electress was the candidate favored by the king, and the one most likely to be named when the new Parliament took up the question of the succession. Defoe's description of her as an "Excellent Princess" leads the reader to expect him to support the Hanoverian succession, especially when he declares "the House of *Hannover*...the only line which with an undisputed Right of *Descent* stands fair to Claim the *Crown* of *England*." It is therefore strange and surprising to find him making a passionate argument for a candidate with a highly disputed descent: James Scott, Earl of Dalkeith, son of the executed Duke of Monmouth.

Like many of his fellow Dissenters, Defoe had joined Monmouth's army during his ill-fated invasion in 1685; he evidently retained his belief that Monmouth was a legitimate son of Charles II. Warming to his task, he speaks of the duke and his progeny in mythic language:

> Here would be an *English King*, born among us, that wou'd Claim an Interest in our *Hearts* as well as *Crown*; a King whose Value wou'd be raised upon *the Foundation of his Father's Merit*, and be *illustrated by his Own*.

> A *Phoenix*, rais'd out of the *Ashes of his Father*, who Sacrificed his *Life*, to save the *People* his Son wou'd *govern*.

In Defoe's enthusiastic fantasy, the dead Duke of Monmouth becomes a savior, sacrificing his life for the sake of his people. His son, imagined as a phoenix, will fulfill his lost father's dream of kingship and magically solve the looming problems of the nation: "All the *Pretences* of Foreigners, Claims of *Princes*, and the Prospect of a long and bloody War, would *cease* and *vanish*."[39] The language about "the *Pretences* of Foreigners" is astonishing, coming as it does from a man who had often defended King William against xenophobic attacks, and the claim that the succession of Dalkeith will remove the threat of war with France is even more puzzling. Yet Defoe was by no means the only writer to fall prey to internal contradictions when considering the succession. The future queen and her closest advisors would also prove to be ambivalent, uncertain, and contradictory in their feelings and statements about this highly emotional issue.

Although there is no hard evidence that Anne read Defoe's pamphlet, Harley would have kept her up to date. A month after Gloucester's death, he heard an alarming rumor from the knowledgeable civil servant John Ellis: "They are laying wagers at St. Germains that they shall be called home before Christmas by the Parliament."[40] Although believing that James II and his family would be "called home" was a Jacobite pipedream, the Prince of Wales had many supporters and advocates. In November 1700, the Earl of Manchester, William's ambassador to Paris, reported the arrival of an emissary to St. Germain supposedly "sent over by Sir C[hristopher] M[usgrave, a prominent Tory,] and other Parliament-Men, with Proposals, in order to get the succession settled upon the pretended Prince of *Wales* on certain conditions."[41] The "conditions" probably included having the boy change his religion, thus avoiding the parliamentary exclusion of Roman Catholics.[42] Inevitably, such talk revived the old story that the prince was an impostor: William Fuller, who made a small career of "revealing" the boy's "true parentage," was actively publishing pamphlets during this period, and a poem appearing late in 1701 retold the legend of the warming pan in lurid detail.[43] Discussions of other claimants also alleged conspiracies and secrets. Defoe's proposal to name the Earl of Dalkeith would have required proving that the Duke of Monmouth was legitimate, thus reviving the belief that Charles II had willfully concealed an early marriage. An answer to his proposal made much of the fact that Dalkeith was married to Henrietta Hyde, daughter of Anne's uncle Laurence, Earl of Rochester, "who has had the Honour of seeing a Sisters Daughter [i.e., Mary] Crown'd Queen of *Great Britain* and *Ireland*, [and] would not be backward in contributing his best Endeavours to advance his own [daughter] to the same dignity."[44] The preposterous idea that Rochester, a Tory ideologue, would promote the succession of the son of Monmouth, a beheaded rebel beloved by radical Whigs, may suggest how ready Englishmen were to entertain conspiracy theories about the succession.

Some of the Catholic claimants barred by Parliament also sought recognition. A month after Defoe's pamphlet appeared, the Duchess of Savoy, Anne's first cousin, dispatched a formal message to Parliament arguing her case. Though "well informed, that there is an Act of Parliament already past, which excludes all the Princes of the Catholick Religion," she declared her title "indisputable," claiming to have "so great an Idea of the Wisdom and Justice of the King and Parliament, that she has no cause to fear, that they will do any thing prejudicial to Her and her Children."[45] There were also rumors that Anne-Marie might allow her infant son, the Prince of Piedmont, to come to England and be reared as a Protestant, thus qualifying him for the crown. Faced with all these conflicting claims, William was acting prudently in urging Parliament to settle the succession, and Harley worked hard to bring about the passage of the Act of Settlement (June 1701), which named the Hanoverians as heirs to the throne if neither Anne nor William produced a child.

Curiously enough, the most striking theatrical event of the season, staged at Dorset Garden in performances culminating on 3 June, was a short opera dramatizing a difficult choice. Congreve's libretto for *The Judgment of Paris* had been set to music by four different composers—Daniel Purcell, John Eccles, Gottfried Finger, and John Weldon—and all four versions were given complete performances, so that the audience had an opportunity to make its own judgment about whose music was best.[46] Contemplating the three beautiful goddesses contending for the golden apple, Congreve's Paris sings a couplet applicable to the current puzzle about the succession:

> Distracted I turn, but I cannot decide,
> So equal a Title sure never was try'd.[47]

In the fantasy world of myth and opera, Paris can reject the crowns offered by Juno and the military triumphs offered by Pallas, choosing Venus because she promises to give him the beautiful Helen. In the real world of parliamentary and courtly politics, more practical concerns proved dominant. Anne accepted and officially supported the Act of Settlement, though her feelings toward the Electress Sophia, who had once sneered at her mother's "mediocre family," were not warm. To the end of her life, however, she resisted proposals that either the Electress or her son Georg Ludwig be brought to England to live. In 1701, she was not alone in considering a child of hers by far the best solution to the failing succession; the absence of other attractive options helps explain why poets addressing her as princess and later as queen continued to express that hope.

Despite her keen interest in music, the princess does not appear to have attended the "Prize Music" event. Although she had emerged from mourning for her birthday, she was still spending most of her time in seclusion, and the birthday poet worked hard to make a virtue of her retirement:

> The Sun can warm us with his rays,
> Tho' he conceal his face;
> So the bright object may retreat
> Yet still impart the heat:
> Nor is her bounty less admired
> United with her power;
> While she's unseen, and most retired
> Warm blessings still they shower.

In treating bounty and power as royal attributes separable from the physical being of the princess, the poet draws on the old political theory of the monarch's two bodies, the belief that the monarch has not only a mortal, physical body, but an enduring, mystical body that serves as the earthly manifestation of sacred sovereignty. In this case, the grieving mother Anne has withdrawn her physical body from public view, but even when the princess herself is "unseen," her bounty and power, metaphorically separated from her person in this stanza, can still shower warm blessings on her subjects. Because the sacred monarch could claim mythic status, those displeased with past regimes had often expressed their views by attacking the royal ministers. As far back as the Long Parliament, some of those pressing for change had insisted that they were not fighting against Charles I himself but against his "evil counselors." Willfully ignoring the fact that these men had been appointed by the king and were carrying out his wishes, the Long Parliament proceeded to blame, attack, and even execute some of them while claiming to be loyal subjects acting in the king's best interest.

Such tactics were still being deployed in the Parliament of 1701, in which the Tories, bent on partisan revenge, used their new power to attack the leaders of the "Junto," men who had worked closely with King William while the Whigs were in ascendancy. By narrow majorities, the Commons voted in April to impeach John Lord Somers, Edward Russell (Earl of Orford), Charles Montagu (recently ennobled as Baron Halifax), and Hans Willem Bentinck (Earl of Portland). All four men had made enemies during their years in power, but the attack on Portland was particularly bold and unquestionably personal, as Bentinck had been William's intimate friend since boyhood—a friend, many believed, to the king's physical body as well as his mythical body.

Harley took a leading role in the impeachment process, convening the Commons as a "committee of the whole" in order to participate in the debate himself. The impeachments he supported were acts of partisan revenge and expressions of an old parliamentary resentment at not being consulted in matters of foreign policy. All of the ministers under attack had played important roles in negotiating the First and Second Partition Treaties, which William had kept secret from his Parliament. As the House debated the impeachments, details of both treaties began to emerge, made no less disturbing by the fact that they had failed to achieve their goals. Although Louis XIV had signed the Second Partition Treaty on 25 March 1700, he chose to ignore it just seven months later, when King Carlos II of Spain, feeble-minded and physically frail, finally died (21 October/1 November 1700), leaving his whole empire to Philip, Duke of Anjou, grandson of the French king. By accepting Carlos II's will, Louis broke the promises he had made to Portland and the other English ministers when he agreed to a "Partition" of Spanish holdings. This high-handed action came in concert with a military coup: in February 1701, with the permission of the man he had recognized as the new King of Spain, Louis sent French troops to occupy the forts in the Spanish Netherlands that had previously housed Dutch garrisons. In the face of these peremptory actions, the resentment the Tories and country Whigs felt toward the king and his past ministers soon gave way to a resentment of France that unified all parties.

One comic moment in the debate over the secret treaties reveals the growing awareness that separating the sacred monarch from his fallible ministers was a fiction. On 29 March, John Howe, a constant gadfly in this Parliament, compared the First Partition Treaty to "a combination of three robbers to rob the fourth"; when challenged for his language, he defended himself by alleging that "he reflected only upon the ministry," repeating the pious formula that "kings can do no harm." This was too much for Sir William Strickland, a Whig supporter of the Junto. "If Kings can do no wrong," he retorted, "then we have injuriously expelled K[ing] J[ames]; if his councellors are to blame, then are we more in fault for they are councellors now."[48] One particular target of Strickland's scorn was Anne's friend Sidney Godolphin, who had served James II in the Treasury before the Revolution and had taken up the same post under William III. It may not, however, be irrelevant that Strickland, Godolphin, and Howe were all breeders of racehorses and therefore rivals on the turf as well as in politics. Although the impeachments could have led to very serious consequences for those accused, the witty character of the debate suggests that men on both sides realized that convictions were unlikely. In a gesture of artistic bravado, Halifax organized the "Prize Music" competition while the impeachment was hanging over his head. As both Howe and Strickland probably expected, the House of Lords, irritated by the Commons' attacks on four of its members, acquitted two of the Junto ministers and dismissed the charges against the other two. Yet when Anne came to the throne, less than a year later, she promptly removed all four men from her Privy Council, along with their close associate Thomas Wharton. Loyalty to Godolphin and Harley was one motive for this decision, but the queen was also eager to separate herself from Portland, as she demonstrated by granting his lucrative position as Ranger of Windsor Great Park to Sarah Churchill, thus replacing William's foreign favorite with her own native-born favorite. Anne may also have taken some pleasure in naming a female Ranger; Sarah remains the only woman to have held the post.

Although William spoke English adequately and quickly became adept at dealing with Parliament, he could not overcome the xenophobic antagonism many felt toward his Dutch associates. Partisan fervor and resentment of secret negotiations were powerful motives driving the parliamentary attempt to impeach Portland in 1701, but hatred of foreigners, a persistent strain in English culture, was also at work. With government censorship greatly weakened by the lapse of the Licensing Act (1695), writers felt free to express such ugly sentiments. In a dreadful poem called *The Foreigners,* published within a few days of Gloucester's death, the radical pamphleteer John Tutchin describes Holland and its people in bitterly racist language:

> A Land much differing from all other Soils,
> Forc'd from the Sea, and buttress'd up with Piles.
> . . . .
> Its Natives void of Honesty and Grace,
> A Boorish, rude, and an inhumane Race;

> From Nature's Excrement their Life is drawn,
> And born in Bogs, and nourish'd up from Spawn.

Tutchin goes on to attack "*Bentir*," a thinly disguised version of Hans Willem Bentinck, Earl of Portland, as a man "Of mean Descent, yet insolently proud, / Shun'd by the Great, and hated by the Crowd." Arnold Joost van Keppel, Earl of Albemarle, William's younger Dutch favorite, appears as "*Keppech*,"

> the Imperious Chit of State,
> Mounted to Grandeur by the usual Course
> Of Whoring, Pimping, or a Crime that's worse;
> Of Foreign Birth, and undescended too,
> Yet he, like *Bentir*, mighty Feats can do.

By alluding coyly to "a Crime that's worse," Tutchin repeats the charge that William's favorites were his homosexual lovers. He should not have been surprised when he was taken into custody on suspicion of "seditious libel." Not only had he attacked the king's favorites in a particularly vulgar way, but in addressing the issue of the succession, he had come close to arguing for the abolition of monarchy:

> When no Successor to the Crown's in sight,
> The Crown is certainly the Peoples Right.
> If Kings are made the People to enthral,
> We had much better have no King at all.[49]

Remarkably enough, Tutchin eventually escaped prosecution because he had (ever so slightly) disguised the names of those he attacked.[50]

The Foreigners would be deservedly forgotten were it not for the fact that it prompted several answers, including *The True-Born Englishman*, the poem that made Defoe famous. Boldly attacking a racial definition of nationality, Defoe pointed out that the English population was a mixture of tribal strains from various parts of the world:

> Thus from a Mixture of all Kinds began,
> That Het'rogeneous Thing, *An Englishman*:
> In eager Rapes, and furious Lust begot,
> Betwixt a Painted *Britton* and a *Scot*:
> Whose gend'ring Offspring quickly learnt to bow,
> And yoke their Heifers to the *Roman* Plough:

> From whence a Mongrel half-bred Race there came,
> With neither Name nor Nation, Speech or Fame.
>
> . . . .
>
> This Nauseous Brood directly did contain
> The well-extracted Blood of *Englishmen*.[51]

When Anne said her heart was "entirely *English*" in 1702, she was rejecting the correct but embarrassing view of nationality put forward by Defoe. Although she treated the foreigners who attended her court with exemplary civility and gave generous support to foreign painters and composers, her sneering references to William as "Mr. Caliban" or "that Dutch abortive" come uncomfortably close to Tutchin's characterization of the Dutch as "an inhumane Race." As poets praising her frequently pointed out, Anne was "a native QUEEN,"[52] and she consciously sought opportunities to remind her subjects that she had been born in the realm she ruled.

§

The attempt to impeach the Junto ministers for their diplomatic activities in the past lost traction as Parliament realized that the French occupation of the Spanish Netherlands required action in the present. When the citizens of Kent petitioned Parliament in May 1701, asking the members to aid the king in meeting the threat from France, the House of Commons imprisoned the men who delivered the petition, yet toward the end of its contentious session, Parliament voted generous bills of supply in preparation for what many now realized was a likely war. Buoyed up by this belated support yet recognizing his own physical weakness, William appointed Marlborough as commander-in-chief of the small English force sent to aid the Dutch, and as his plenipotentiary for the negotiations with the Dutch, the Habsburg Emperor, and the various smaller powers that joined the Grand Alliance opposing Louis in 1702. Although evidently failing in his health, the king made his usual summer visit to the Netherlands, hunting, hosting visitors, and inspecting the troops while leaving the administrative work to Marlborough.

The well-preserved correspondence between Marlborough and Godolphin during this period shows them working in concert to keep the princess informed. In his first letter to his wife after landing at the Hague, Marlborough asked Sarah to "asure the Prince and Princesse of their having a faithfull servant here."[53] A few weeks later, he mailed Godolphin a copy of the treaty he had negotiated with the Habsburg Emperor. Although the king had recently made a show of providing Parliament with documents related to earlier treaty negotiations, he wanted the terms of this new pact kept confidential, but Marlborough, who was well aware of

William's poor health, specifically instructed Godolphin to "shoe the treaty to the Prince and Princess, and make my excuse to him for my not writing."[54] Both men were trying to give the future queen the knowledge she would need to rule effectively, and they evidently found her eager to acquire it.

In September, Sarah Churchill joined her husband in Holland, where she remained for two months, giving Anne an even more personal source of information about the men now forging international alliances. It is especially unfortunate that their correspondence for this period has not survived, as it might have shed light on Anne's response to the next cataclysmic event in her life: the death of her father. Expected since March, when he suffered a serious stroke, James II's death on 5/16 September 1701 was emotionally complex for the princess and politically complex for England, especially because Louis XIV promptly broke the promises he had made in the Treaty of Ryswick, ignored the advice of his ministers, and recognized the young Prince of Wales as "James III." An outraged William broke off diplomatic relations, expelling Count Tallard, the French envoy to England, and ordering the Earl of Manchester, "his Ambassador Extraordinary at the court of France, to come from thence immediately without taking his Audience of Leave."[55] It was impossible for Anne to take an objective, dispassionate, strategic view of these developments. The man now shouldering diplomatic and military responsibility for the coming war was the husband of the person she loved most in all the world; the heir whose death had thrown the succession into doubt was her cherished son; the Electress of Hanover and all of the others with claims to the throne were her cousins; the exiled king whose death had triggered renewed hostility toward France was her father; and the boy now recognized as "James III" by King Louis was her half-brother, as she had probably begun to admit to herself by now. Like the princess, all of those hoping to avoid bringing in another foreign monarch were now dependent on her damaged and unreliable body.

In these trying circumstances, her father's death was sure to stir up contradictory feelings in Anne, and her visible response to his death was sure to attract public scrutiny. She now felt pressure from all sides. Within two weeks, she received a pointed letter from her stepmother, Maria Beatrice, urging her to support the claims of the Prince of Wales:

> I think myself indispensably obliged to differ [defer] no longer the acquainting you with a message, which the best of men as well as the best of Fathers left with me for you; some few days before his death, he bid me find meanes to let you know that he forgave you all that's past from the bottom of his heart, and pray'd to God to do so too, that he gave you his last blessing and pray'd to God to convert your heart and confirm you in the resolution of repaireing to his Son the wrongs done to himself.[56]

This account of James forgiving her on his deathbed was not designed to provide Anne with comfort or closure. In Maria's version of the story, the dying king asks God to forgive his daughter, a gesture confirming the belief that she had committed a grave sin in helping her sister depose him. Maria was obviously hoping to provoke feelings of guilt that would lead Anne to accept the claims of "James III." She may have based her language about Anne's "resolution" to do so on a letter Anne is alleged to have sent to her father in 1696, in which she supposedly asked his permission to accept the crown when William died and expressed "a readiness to make restitution when opertunitys should serue."[57] Even Jacobite sources, however, provide only a paraphrase of this letter, which may be a forgery. If it were true, as these sources also claim, that "the Princess of Denmark had all along kept up a fair correspondence with the King, full of assurances of duty and repentance,"[58] surely James's secretaries would have saved these useful and important letters. None survive.

In any case, it would not have been an unusual rhetorical gesture for Maria to refer to a "resolution of repaireing wrongs" as a way of suggesting that Anne should now make a commitment to support the prince, much in the way that Dryden, hoping to persuade James II to reconsider his rash policies in 1688, praised him for his balance and justice, virtues the poet believed the king had abandoned and hoped he would reclaim in the future.[59] Maria does not say that James "pray'd to God to…confirm you in *your* resolution," which would clearly be a reference to a resolution made and acknowledged by Anne, but that he "pray'd to God to convert your heart and confirm you in *the* resolution," as if the resolution would be a consequence of the conversion. As Maria probably knew, the prayer that Anne would "repair" her wrongs to her father was as unlikely to be answered as the prayer for her conversion to Catholicism. Even before the birth of the child Maria called the Prince of Wales, Princess Anne had expressed doubts about his authenticity. If she were now to acknowledge that he was James II's legitimate son and heir, it would be incumbent upon her to abandon her own claim to the crown and allow the boy to succeed immediately. To do that, however, would be contrary to Parliament's acts barring Roman Catholics from succeeding to the throne,[60] contrary to Anne's firm Protestant faith, and contrary to her determination to become queen in her own right.

Yet Anne was also clearly uncomfortable with William's gestures embracing the Hanoverians, now officially designated as her successors if she remained childless. Moving to dramatize the Act of Settlement, the king had already sent Charles Gerard, Earl of Macclesfield, on a formal embassy to Hanover, where he presented the Electress with a copy of the new law and invested her son Georg Ludwig with the "Habit and Ensigns" of the Order of the Garter. English newspapers gave frequent full accounts of this embassy, and reported that Georg and his uncle, the aged but vigorous Duke of Zell, would soon visit William at Het Loo; thanks to "some Difficulties about the Ceremonial," Georg Ludwig did not make the journey but sent his son Georg August (the future George II), who was now the "Electoral Prince of Hanover."[61] On 13 September, while Anne was still absorbing the initial shock of her father's death, William was reported to have "ordered lodgings to be prepared at St. James for the electoral prince of Hanover, who comes over hither next month." Newspaper accounts explained that William was bringing the young prince with him when he returned to England so "that he may learn the English Constitution."[62]

For Georg August, who spoke no English, such a visit might have been valuable training, but for Anne, who had already begun to hang her apartments with mourning for her father, the news that a possible successor was to visit London and be housed in her palace cannot have been welcome, and she evidently found a way to persuade the king to postpone this project. According to a letter written by Leibniz in 1714, Anne told William she was pregnant and therefore unable to act as hostess.[63] Those accepting this account have always assumed that Anne was telling a convenient lie,[64] but it is far from impossible that she believed she was with child. In the emotional throes of dealing with her father's death, the French king's duplicity, and the consequences of the Act of Settlement, Anne might easily have missed a period and made the hopeful inference that she had conceived. In that case, it would be important to avoid the stress of a state visit, and the visit might even be pointless, as a surviving child would block the Hanoverian succession.

The continuing tension between the king and the princess now found expression in a disagreement about the protocol for mourning James II. In this struggle, Anne's loyal servants sought to control her visible actions lest they cause political trouble. Aware of Anne's punctiliousness about forms and ceremonies, Marlborough and Godolphin knew that her most likely response to the loss of her father— even though she had played a role in the coup that deposed him, and even though she had no intention of heeding Maria's pleas for support—would be to put her court into full mourning, an observance that required hanging black draperies in her apartments in St. James's Palace. They also knew that the king, who insisted on being informed of such actions before they were taken, would probably choose a lower level of observance in mourning for his father-in-law, especially in light of the French king's provocative action in recognizing the Prince of Wales.

Both expectations were correct. A news item dated 15 September reported that Anne's servants had "begun to hang the Appartments at St. James's Pallace with Mourning,"[65] and on the same day, Marlborough wrote to Godolphin, urging him to advise Anne against going into deep mourning:

> I understand by my Lord Albemarle, who is always soe kind to lett me
> know anything that he thinkes may be for the Princesses service, that the

King is very desirous the Princess should mourn for her father, as she thinkes proper; but at the same time he thinkes there should be noe derections for mourning till he had been acquainted with itt, soe that if the Princess should have forgote to desire Lord Chamberlain to write to the King from her, I desire you will give my humble duty to her, and desire that she will doe itt.[66]

As he had done a few years earlier in the controversy over appointments to Gloucester's court, Marlborough sought out Albemarle, with whom he had kept up good relations, in order to ascertain the king's opinions. In generously pretending that Anne might have "forgote" to inform the Lord Chamberlain of her directions for deep mourning, her loyal friend was giving her a chance to avoid friction with the king, although he knew perfectly well that Anne was unlikely to ask permission from the current Lord Chamberlain, Edward Villiers, Earl of Jersey, the brother of the Villiers sisters with whom she had spent her childhood. She had known him all her life and appreciated his excellent manners, but she had also once urged Sarah to "remember none of [that] family weare ever good for any thing."[67]

Though fully aware of Anne's personal reasons for ordering full mourning, Marlborough feared the political consequences and urged his friend Godolphin to intervene:

I beg she will not give derections for the putting St. Jeamses in mourning, if she has any thoughts to doe itt, till Lord Chamberlain has acquainted the King.... If the Princesses mourning be not already putt on, I hope you will think it reasonable to prevaile with her not to doe itt, till she hears from the king, which may prevent the malice of a party that may be but to[o] much inclined to doe her ill offices in England. I speake as a faithfull servant, and doe from my hart wish this may come before she has putt on her mourning.

When he speaks of "the malice of a party," Marlborough is reminding Godolphin (and thus Anne) that suspicious Whigs might interpret her going into deep mourning for her father as a sign that she actually supported the Jacobite succession. The very next day, he wrote again, with even more specific instructions:

I should not have troubled you againe this post, had not the King just now toke notice to mee of the mourning, and commanded mee to write to the Princess to lett her know that he should mourn for King Jamse, but that he intended to put himself, his coaches and liv[erie]s in mourning but not his apartments, and that he desired the Princess would doe the same, by which he meant she should not putt St. Jamses in mourning; soe that if she had thoughts of itt, you see it can't bee. Soe that you will be pleased to give my humble duty to her Highness, and that I beg she will give you leave to turn this business soe as that it may well be taken of the King, and consequently doe her Highness good in England. For if after this she should putt her house in mourning, for God sake think what an outcry itt would make in England.[68]

Although Anne had already set about putting her court into full mourning, the king chose not to hang mourning in his lodgings, though he and his servants would wear black clothing and ride in coaches covered with black. This disagreement replayed in a higher key the earlier episodes concerning Prince George's prolonged mourning for his brother and Anne's unauthorized letter to the French court announcing the death of Gloucester. In all three instances, William insisted on his kingly prerogatives, reminding Anne once more that she was not to be "Queen before her time." In this last instance, however, Marlborough was alerting Anne to the growing importance of public opinion: by refusing to conform to the king's practice, she risked provoking a troublesome "outcry." In expecting her future subjects to accept her going into full mourning as the private act of a daughter, something entirely separate from her official acceptance of the Hanoverian succession, which was the public act of a future monarch, Anne was enacting her faith in the outmoded doctrine of the monarch's two bodies. The worldly Marlborough was reminding her of the demise of that doctrine: her private acts were now inevitably public.

Godolphin, who was possessed of infinite tact, clearly found a way of telling Anne that she should conform to the king's preference while assuring her of his sympathy for her position. His letter has disappeared, but her reply survives:

I can not lett your servant goe back without returning my thanks for the letter he brought me, & assureing you it is a very great satisfaction to me to find you agree with Mrs Morley conserning the ill natured cruel proceedings of Mr Caliban, which vexes me more then you can imagin, & I am out of all patience when I think I must do soe monsterous a thing as not to put my lodgings in mourning for my Father, I hope if you can get a coppy of the will Ld Manchester says he will send over, you will be soe kind as to let me see it, & ever believe me your faithfull servant.[69]

In Anne's interpretation of events, William has once again given proof of being a subhuman Caliban and has used his power to make her do a "monsterous thing."

Yet even while expressing her outrage, the princess exhibits strong interest in ac-quiring factual knowledge. Vexed though she was, she did not forget the impor-tance of seeing the late king's will, which was important to her not only as his daughter but as the future queen.

While Maria, William, Marlborough, and Godolphin were giving Anne in-structions about how she should act in response to James's death, at least one poet was telling her how she should feel. Among the poetic elegies provoked by the old king's demise—some serious, some gloating—appeared *The Generous Muse*, a poem plausibly attributed to the High Church Tory William Pittis, who had the nerve to dedicate his work, on its title page, "To Her *Royal Highness*" and to preface it with a page of verses addressed "To the Princess":

> MADAM,
> Tho' Grief, like Yours, so great appears,
> As not to need Addition to Your Tears,
> Which at a Father's Tomb You justly shed,
> And having *Wept* him living, *Mourn* him dead;
> Yet would the pious Muse the favour crave,
> At least to scatter Roses round his Grave,
> To speak her Sorrows, and reveal her care,
> And pay her *Praises* since he's past her *Pray'r*.[70]

Although he published this poem anonymously and distanced himself from its making by speaking as a "pious Muse," Pittis was not bashful about approaching famous people. Two years earlier, he had written (and signed) a poem on the death of the Earl of Abingdon addressed to Dryden, whom he asked to compose an elegy on his former patron. In his preface, Pittis informed the reader that he had sent the manuscript to Dryden and profited by corrections made by the old poet.[71] It is therefore not unlikely that he also sent this poem to its dedicatee. If so, we can only imagine how Anne might have responded to the poet's asking her permission to scatter roses around her father's grave, presuming to tell the world that her grief was great, and offering a highly ambiguous description of her tears,

> Which at a Father's Tomb You justly shed,
> And having *Wept* him living, *Mourn* him dead.

As a daughter, Anne might "justly" shed tears for her dead father; few of any party would have denied her that right. But when Pittis says that she "*Wept* him living," he opens the dangerous question of Anne's feelings about her father in the years since the Revolution. Did she weep for her father's rash actions while king, the very actions that led her to support William's invasion, or did she shed tears of regret for having supported the man she now thought monstrous, weeping for the cruel fate of her deposed and living father? As the day when Anne would succeed to the throne drew closer, the question of her feelings about the Stuart court in St. Germain, compressed by Pittis into one slippery line, became more urgent, as Marlborough and Godolphin recognized when they warned her that formal mourning might cause "an outcry."

When Pittis returns to the subject of Anne's grief in the body of his poem, this time in the third person, the political ambiguity increases:

> Amidst the rest, and with superior Grace,
> ANNA bedews with Tears her Royal Face,
> And almost weeps the Period of her Race.
> Scarce has the Year its Annual Circle run,
> In which the childless Parent mourn'd her Son,
> But a fresh Cause provokes Her dutious Sighs,
> And forces Streams to trickle from her Eyes.
> Oft would She, when alive, lament his Fate,
> And grieve in secret for his falling State
> Ask Heav'n to have his Suff'rings in its view,
> Just to her *Father*, and her *Country* too.

Pittis quotes Virgil's description of the death of Priam in Latin as his epigraph, and in this account of the "Annual Circle" of Anne's last year he borrows language from Dryden's splendid rendering of another Virgilian passage, in which Aeneas announces funeral games in honor of his father Anchises, speaking of the "shining Circle of the Year" and the marking of his father's death day "with Annual Games."[72] The language and imagery are obviously similar, but the situation is poignantly different. Aeneas, who has left a burning Troy with his father on his back, leading his son by the hand, is an exemplar of familial and political continuity. A year after the old man's death, he can enact his mourning through ritual games in which his son plays a leading role. Under his leadership and through his progeny, a defeated Trojan remnant will fulfill its destiny by founding the Roman Empire. Anne, by contrast, had decreed that the day of her son's death would be an annual day of mourning and presumably observed that day on its first return in 1701. Within a month, however, she had lost her father as well and was now cut off from both the previous generation and the following one. If unable to produce another child, she would witness the end of the Stuart line, here called "the Period of her Race." For any reader who noticed it, the allusion to Dryden's Virgil emphasized the stark disparities between Anne, who was in danger of ending her family's dynasty, and Aeneas, who made possible a glorious future for his descendants.

Those noticing the borrowings from Dryden might also remember the politics of the old poet, who had died in the previous year. For readers who shared Dryden's Jacobite beliefs, the notion that Anne often "grieve[d] in secret" for her father's "falling State" might suggest the hope that she regretted her actions in 1688 and would soon move to endorse "James III." For these readers, a daughter who lamented her father's fate and asked heaven to relieve his sufferings would surely, in the words of Maria's letter, "repair to his Son the wrongs done to himself." Other readers, however, might imagine Anne grieving and praying for her father without abandoning "Revolution principles." Much depends on how one reads the line describing Anne as "Just to her *Father*, and her *Country* too." Her desire to put on deep mourning was proof enough of her determination to be just to her father; the difficult question she was now facing was how to be just to her country. In the next stanza, Pittis retreats from the Jacobite position toward which he appeared to be moving and looks forward to Anne's "glorious Reign," urging her to produce "Young *British* Kings":

> Oh! Could She but our suppliant Tears receive,
> And think how *Albion* weeps to see her Grieve,
> Vouchsafe to be reminded of the Throne, ⎫
> Senates decree shall one day be her own,   ⎬
> And that our Hopes are fix'd on her alone. ⎭
> How that she owes us yet a glorious Reign,
> Young *British* Kings to Rule the *British* Main:
> Hearing our Pray'rs she'd our lost Hopes restore,
> And shew the *Daughter* less, and *Princess* more.

When the speaker declares that "our Hopes are fix'd on her alone," he parts company with those advocating the immediate succession of "James III" and joins those hoping that Anne will manage to produce an heir, but the verb he chooses is ominous. In Pittis's formulation, Anne should recognize that "she *owes* us" a glorious reign and multiple heirs. Even a poet who presumably thought he was writing a sympathetic and complimentary poem could not help emphasizing Anne's obligations.

§

Despite frequent rumors that they were about to return to St. James's, the Denmarks spent the entire autumn of 1701 at Windsor. Early in October, they moved from the drafty castle to a house outside the gates owned by Godolphin, where they planned to stay for a month.[73] The Earl of Manchester, recalled from his embassy in France, visited them there on 17 October, presumably bringing along the will Anne had wanted to see and providing the princess with a well-informed report on recent events in France.[74] When the king came to visit his successor on 13 November, nine days after he landed in England, she was still at Windsor.[75] He was evidently willing to brave her disapproval, as he was issuing writs for a new Parliament, hoping that the election would bring him a majority of Whigs inclined to support the coming war. Anne's close friend Godolphin, who had urged the king to continue with his existing Parliament and his largely Tory ministry, had been visiting her at Windsor on 9 November when William informed the Cabinet of his intention to dissolve Parliament. As soon as he heard the news, Godolphin hurried back to town and resigned from the Treasury,[76] yet William came to Windsor himself just three days after accepting Godolphin's resignation and paid another call on Anne a week later, when she was reported to be "so ill of the Gout that she cannot stir."[77] In light of the long history of friction between William and Anne, his attention to her at this moment probably reflects his awareness of his own failing health and his determination to do his part in making her ready to succeed him.

Marlborough, who stayed behind at the Hague until early December, continued to fret about Anne's public image. On 7 November, he wrote to Godolphin expressing concern about a report that the Earl of Sandwich and his wife Elizabeth were planning a trip to France: "Lord and Lady Sandwiche's journey," he wrote, "makes a noyse here to the disadvantage of the Princess. If it should doe soe in England, methinkes something should be done to avoyde itt, if possible."[78] With diplomatic relations with France broken off and treaties leading to war being signed, it would have raised eyebrows for any English aristocrat to go to France, and a visit there by this couple would surely have made a noise. Edward Montagu, Earl of Sandwich, was Master of the Horse to Prince George of Denmark; his Countess, the witty and musical daughter of the rake and poet John Wilmot, second Earl of Rochester, was a good friend of Anne's—and a lifelong Jacobite. Although the trip they were planning might have been innocent enough, as the Countess had previously spent some years in France and was close to the composer Charles Dieupart, Marlborough was worried that the Earl and his French-speaking Countess might appear to be private emissaries from Anne to the court at St. Germain.[79] His advice apparently had results; there is no historical record of a visit to France by the Sandwiches in 1701 or 1702.

Thanks in part to Godolphin's efforts on behalf of Tory candidates, the election did not bring William the Whig majority for which he was hoping. When the new Parliament assembled on 30 December, Harley was elected Speaker once more, defeating the court's candidate by four votes. Conscious that his

Parliament was almost evenly divided between the parties, the king addressed them on 31 December, urging them to set aside their partisan battles and unite behind the war effort:

> I hope you are come together determined to avoid all Manner of Disputes and Differences, and resolved to act with a general and hearty Concurrence for promoting the common Cause; which alone can make this a happy Session.
>
> I should think it as great a Blessing as could befall *England,* if I could observe you as much inclined to lay aside those unhappy fatal Animosities, which divide and weaken you, as I am disposed to make all My Subjects safe and easy as to any, even the highest, Offences committed against Me.[80]

William's slippery rhetoric here appears to say that it would be a great blessing if the parties would lay aside their animosities and that he means to set a good example by forgiving the offenses his subjects have committed against him. For those who knew that Lord Somers, one of the four Whig lords impeached by the last Parliament, had drafted this speech for the king, the reference to offenses committed against the king might appear to point particularly at the Commons' boldness in impeaching his past ministers, while the promise to "make all My Subjects safe and easy" looked like a pledge to work constructively with Harley and the Tories. Yet by describing the attacks on his ministers as "Offences committed against *Me,*" the king disallowed the old convention of separating the sacred monarch from his fallible counselors. For William, that myth was no more plausible than the belief that those touched by the monarch would miraculously recover from scrofula. He never forgot that he had been invited to invade the realm he ruled and had thus enacted a theory of government quite unlike the ancient faith in the divine right of kings.

As the artists serving Anne were aware of her fondness for traditional tropes of monarchial splendor, the artists serving William were conscious of his more modern concept of kingship. New Year's Day was traditionally a time for an ode in praise of the king, written by the Poet Laureate and set by the Master of the King's Music. On this occasion, however, Nahum Tate addressed his *Ode upon the Assembling of the New Parliament, Sung before his Majesty on New-Years-Day,* directly to the legislators. The text begins with a sense of urgency and crisis. "Wake *Britain,* 'tis high Time to Wake," warns Tate, in a martial aria that John Eccles set for Richard Elford, beginning his music with the notes of a bugle call. To "Mr. Cook," a bass, fell the task of describing the imminent threat by singing a minor-key aria depicting France as a Spenserian dragon:

> Behold the Dragon, GALLICK Pow'r,
>   With wide Extended Wings,
>   Baleful Eyes and Brandisht Stings,
>   Watching his expected Hour,
> States and Empires to Devour.

In this hour of need, Tate does not present the king as a dragon-slaying hero, a role in which poets and artists had often cast him, but urges Parliament to play that role collectively. While praising the members as an "August ASSEMBLY" of "Great PATRIOTS," the poet implores them to put aside party strife and save the nation:

> Hail August ASSEMBLY, hail!
> Fortune's Doubtful Ballance stands,
> Poiz'd in your Deciding Hands,
> 'Tis You, Great PATRIOTS, You must turn the Scale.

One of William's ministers may well have suggested to Tate that he cast the themes of the king's speech into verse. The poem closely parallels the address, and the concluding "GRAND CHORUS" invokes the ideal of a balanced government, celebrating the benefits of union between the king and his Parliament:

> While *Britain*'s Great Monarch and Senate Unite
> For Religion Law Safety Fame Freedom and Right,
> With Success may the Glorious Assembly be Crown'd,
> And this Happy *Year* thro' all Ages Renown'd.[81]

By crowding six abstract nouns into his second line, the poet suggests a cornucopia of benefits to be derived from cooperation between the "Great Monarch" and his "Senate." But the jolly anapestic rhythm and some of the words come from Tate's earlier libretto for Henry Purcell's opera *Dido and Aeneas*, performed at a girls' school during the reign of James II and recently revived at Lincoln's Inn Fields as a set of "entertainments" inserted into a production of *Measure for Measure*. In the opera, a highly condensed version of the fourth book of the *Aeneid*, the chorus eagerly antici-pates a marriage between the Carthaginian queen Dido and the Trojan hero Aeneas:

> When Monarchs unite, how happy their State,
> They Triumph at once o'er their Foes and their Fate.[82]

Working in haste, as his ode was to be performed the day after William addressed the new Parliament, Tate was saving time by recycling some elements of his
earlier chorus, yet the disparities between the opera and the ode are numerous and
striking. The operatic chorus expresses the hope that Aeneas and Dido will jointly
lead Carthage to greatness, but neither character achieves the happiness they predict: Aeneas's imperial destiny will force him to abandon his great love and sail on
to Italy, and Dido's passion for her Trojan guest will soon destroy her. Because the
story was so familiar, those who heard Purcell's cheerful music for this chorus were
likely to be conscious of these ironies. In Tate's recycled version, the widowed William unites in political marriage with his "Senate," and the poet breathlessly lists
"Religion Law Safety Fame Freedom and Right" as the fruits of their union. Yet the
absence of real offspring from the marriage of William and Mary had helped to pre-
cipitate the current crisis, and the relations between William and his parliaments
during the past thirteen years had often been strained. The music Eccles wrote for
this chorus does not survive, so we cannot know whether he followed Purcell's lead
and provided dancelike music in triple time. But even if they did not notice the
verbal (and possibly musical) echoes of *Dido and Aeneas,* those hearing Tate's ode,
especially those aware of the king's precarious health, might well have wondered
what kind of renown "this Happy *Year*" would actually have.

Although her favorite singer was featured, Princess Anne did not hear the
performance. She returned to St. James's on 9 December, and the nobility took
note of her presence with formal visits of welcome on 10 and 11 December. Years
later, Sarah Churchill cynically alleged that those visiting the princess had done
so "more in opposition to KING WILLIAM, than from any real respect for the
PRINCESS OF DENMARK. And the winter before she came to the crown, they had
in the same spirit of opposition to the KING, and in prospect of his death, paid her
more than usual civilities and attendance."[83] The historical record, however, suggests that relations between the princess and the king continued to be civil. Anne
and George dined with William at Kensington on 26 December, after which the
king went to Windsor in order to spend 28 December, the anniversary of Mary's
death, in solitude. When he returned to the capital on 30 December, his inbound
coaches probably passed the outbound coaches of Anne, who went back to
Windsor on the same day, remaining there for three days and thus missing both
the opening of Parliament and the New Year's celebration.[84] If there is any truth
to Sarah's claim that the Tories were using Anne's court as a center of opposition,
it is to Anne's credit that she stayed out of William's way at this juncture, keeping
up the polite dance of formal visits but allowing him to be the center of attention
as Parliament opened.

§

The assassination plot of 1696, the most elaborate of several plans to kill King William, took advantage of his fondness for hunting, so it is ironic that the incident that actually precipitated his death took place while he was "hunting a stagg near Kingston upon Thames" on 21 February 1702. According to Luttrell's first report, "his horse fell with him and broke his collar bone; which was soon after sett, and [he] is now pretty well again, and is expected in [a] few dayes at the house of peers to passe what bills are ready."[85] Missing from this account is the fact that the fracture came apart again while the injured king's coach traversed the bumpy road to Kensington, so that the bone had to be set a second time. The shock to his weakened system was severe, and William did not appear again in public, though he sent a message to Parliament urging them to take up the question of political union with Scotland. On 24 February, Prince George and Princess Anne visited the ailing monarch on their way to making another short stay at Windsor, but they may not yet have known that his illness was grave.[86] Over the next few days, he became feverish, and his lungs, ravaged by a lifetime of asthma, began showing signs of pneumonia. As late as 6 March, he was reported to be improving, but by the next day it was obvious to his doctors that he was dying. During his final hours, the Earl of Jersey, Lord Chamberlain to the king, was "writing and sending perpetually to give an account" to the princess as the monarch's "breath grew shorter and shorter."[87] While Sarah, our only source for this story, expresses horror at this "odious" action, Jersey's frequent reports gave Anne the chance to prepare herself for the challenges ahead and may help explain her retaining him in office as her own reign began.

The transition to the new reign was remarkably smooth, in part because Parliament, in the wake of the assassination plot of 1696, had passed a law keeping itself in session in the event of the king's death. When William expired, at eight o'clock on Sunday morning, 8 March, both Houses of Parliament were called to Westminster, while the members of the Privy Council met with Anne at St. James's. Gifted with a melodious voice and trained for her role by theatrical experience, the queen charmed everyone by the way she delivered her formal and previously scripted remarks. Bishop Burnet, despite having his own officious actions repulsed on the same day, describes Anne's first meeting with her Privy Council with admiration:

> Upon the king's death, the privy council came in a body to wait on the new queen: she received them with a well considered speech.... She pronounced this, as she did all her other speeches, with great weight and authority, and with a softness of voice, and sweetness in the pronunciation, that added much life to all she spoke. These her first expressions were heard with great and just acknowledgments: both houses of parliament

met that day, and made addresses to her, full of respect and duty: she answered both very favourably, and she received all that came to her in so gracious a manner, that they went from her highly satisfied with her goodness, and her obliging deportment; for she hearkened with attention to every thing that was said to her.[88]

In a note on this passage, Arthur Onslow, who became Speaker of the House under George II, echoes Burnet's praise: "I have heard the queen speak from the throne," he writes. "I never saw an audience more affected: it was a sort of charm."

These accolades, coming as they do from men whose ideology was much unlike the queen's, stand in opposition to Sarah's dismissive notion that Anne ascended the throne in "a state of helpless ignorance." She may not have possessed the intricate knowledge of finance that Godolphin had acquired in decades of experience or the comprehensive command of military strategy that Marlborough brought to the battlefield, but she was able to make those who came into her presence believe that she "hearkened with attention" to their words, and when she herself spoke, "it was a sort of *charm*"—a word derived from the Latin *carmen*, meaning "song." The "female accomplishments" of Anne's early education—singing, acting, dancing, and guitar playing—contributed significantly to her ability to rise to this momentous occasion.

As tradition demanded, heralds proclaimed the new monarch at St. James's, Charing Cross, the Temple Bar, and the Royal Exchange during the afternoon, with a trumpet fanfare in each location. Despite her obesity and her chronic illnesses, Anne was attentive to ritual, expectation, and appearance. Godolphin, calling her "very unwieldy and lame," asked Harley whether she might forgo the expected journey to Parliament and expressed doubt about whether she had any robes,[89] but he seriously underestimated her. When she went to Parliament on 11 March, the queen wore the heavy crown of England over a red velvet cap, a long, red velvet robe lined with ermine and trimmed with gold, a statuette of St. George on a gold chain around her neck, and her blue Garter ribbon on her left arm (color plate 14). Count Wratislaw, the imperial ambassador who set down these details, believed that she had modeled her costume on a portrait of Queen Elizabeth (color plate 13).[90]

The strongly favorable first impression made by the queen was not merely a matter of her stage presence. In the actions taken in the first few months of her reign, she paid close attention to tact and balance. When she went to address Parliament, "The earl of Marlborough carried the sword before her, and his lady accompanied her majestie in the coach,"[91] confirming the expectations of those who feared that the Marlboroughs would be dangerously powerful during Anne's reign. But when she awarded Marlborough a Garter two days later, she paired him with

Wriothesley Russell, second Earl of Bedford, a son of the Whig advocate of Exclusion beheaded in the wake of the Rye House Plot in 1683. In choosing her trusted friend for this important honor, Anne was satisfying a wish that had been frustrated when William ignored her letters urging him to award Marlborough the Garter; in choosing Bedford, she was offering an olive branch to those who had opposed her uncle and her father in the struggles of the 1680s and taking a concrete step toward the lessening of party strife that William had advocated in his last speech to Parliament.

On 26 March, the queen issued the first of her many proclamations "For the Encouragement of Piety and Virtue, and for the Preventing and Punishing of Vice, Prophaneness, and Immorality." Although the tone of this document and some of its language resembled similar proclamations issued by William, Anne took particular aim at those who neglected Sunday services:

> And we do hereby strictly Enjoyn and Prohibit all Our Loving Subjects, or what Degree of Quality soever, from Playing on the Lords Day at Dice, Cards, or any other Game whatsoever, either in Publick or Private Houses,...and do hereby Require and Command them and every of them Decently and Reverently to Attend the Worship of God on Every Lords Day....And we do strictly Charge and Command all Our judges, Mayors, Sheriffs, Justices, of the Peace, and all other Our Officers...that they take Effectual Care to prevent all Persons Keeping Taverns, Chocolate-Houses, Coffee-Houses, or other Publick Houses whatsoever, from Selling Wine, Chocolate, Coffee, Ale, Beer, or other Liquors...in the Time of Divine Service on the Lords Day.[92]

For those who had admired her godly sister Mary, including many puritanical Dissenters, this official endorsement of virtue was welcome, but by particularly emphasizing the importance of "Attend[ing] the Worship of God on Every Lords Day," Anne was reminding her subjects of her devotion to the established church.

Notably absent from the list of places to be suppressed were the theatres, an omission that did not go unnoticed. The radical Dissenter John Tutchin, already notorious as the author of *The Foreigners,* was now publishing a paper called the *Observator,* written as a comic dialogue between "Country-man" and "Observator." "Country-man" reports that many people

> are much Angry at the Queen's Proclamation against *Vice, Prophaness* and *Debauchery,* especially the *Vintners,* and more especially their *Wives,* some of which, had the Profits of the *Sundays* Claret to buy 'em

Pinns; ... and the Beaus, who sit at Home on *Sundays*, and Play at Picquet and *Back-Gammon*, are under dreadful Apprehensions of a Thundering Prohibition of Stage-Playing.

"Observator" replies with a strong condemnation of the theatre but explains that Anne will not close the playhouses for fear of being thought a "Presbyterian":

That would Pin the Basket. For those Nurseries of *Vice*, the *Play-Houses*, do more Mischief to the Souls of Young People, to their Parents Estates, and their own Fortunes, than ... all the other Means of Lewdness practised in that Town: But should her Majestie issue such a Proclamation, she would be presently Branded for a Presbyterian, as was Her Pious and Vertuous Sister, the late Queen *Mary* of Blessed Memory, for no other Reason, than that she was not a common Frequenter of Play-houses.[93]

William's edicts against vice had encouraged Jeremy Collier and others to attack the theatres, and as recently as 16 February, the actors in Thomas Betterton's company at Lincoln's Inn Fields had been tried and fined for "Profane, Vicious, & immoral Expressions."[94] As they had hoped she might, the new queen quietly protected the actors from legal harassment—not because she feared being thought a prude, as Tutchin suggested, but because she genuinely appreciated drama. When Betterton and his colleagues sent her a petition complaining that they were being prosecuted for performing plays already duly licensed by the Lord Chamberlain's office, Anne "was graciously pleas'd to order a stop to the said prosecution."[95] Not only was she active in protecting the actors, but when they came to court to perform in her presence, she paid them at a rate more than double that offered by earlier monarchs.[96] Again there was a principle of balance. The frequent injunctions about gaming and drinking were sure to please those who shared Anne's concerns about vice, and she held her own ministers to a high moral standard, but as she had already shown by attending the theatres when they were under attack, the new queen did not share the Puritan view of the drama as sinful or dangerous.

An anonymous poet claiming to speak for the Church of England emphasized the distinction between the native Anne and the foreign William:

A Native QUEEN in all her pomp appears
To crown our Hopes and dissipate our Fears.[97]

On 31 March, Luttrell reported the new queen's determination to be more active than her predecessor in shaping the leadership of the Church: "Tis said her majestie will herself dispose of all ecclesiastical preferments belonging to the Crown as they become vacant, and not leave it to the archbishop of Canterbury and 5 other bishops, as the late king did."[98] Anne's first opportunity to exercise this reclaimed power came when the aged Bishop of Carlisle died on 12 April, and she tried to use it to heal another old wound. The famous clergyman Thomas Ken, whom Anne had often heard preach during her father's reign, had lost his position as Bishop of Bath and Wells in 1691 when he refused to take the oaths of allegiance to William and Mary. Anne's plan was to move the man who had replaced him to Carlisle and persuade Bishop Ken to resume his old seat. The saintly Ken, old and unwilling to recant, politely declined, and Anne was content to award him a generous pension. As the elevation of Bedford to the Garter was a gesture to the Whigs, the attempt to reinstall Ken was a gesture to the non-jurors.

The most dramatic display of all was Anne's decision to forgo £100,000 of the money from the Civil List due to her as queen. On 30 March, after Parliament voted to award her the same revenue they had allotted to King William,

> her majestie came to the house of lords and past the civil list bill: and after made a speech, thankt them for the revenue they had setled upon her, and promised to give 100,000*l*. out of it this year for the publick service. Upon which the commons voted an addresse of thanks for her majesties unparalell'd goodnesse in contributing out of her own revenue to the ease and releif of her subjects.[99]

Beyond its generosity, Anne's action is clear evidence of her close attention to parliamentary history. She was mindful of her own bitter struggle with her sister about an income to support her small court as Princess in 1689, in which she had successfully appealed to Parliament. She was also well aware that William had gained an increase of £100,000 for himself in 1697 by claiming that he would need to provide an annual stipend for Maria Beatrice, which was never paid, and support a court for Gloucester, which he briefly funded at a much lower level than predicted. Thanks to Harley's frequent visits, she would also have known that members opposed to the ministry in William's later Parliaments had frequently brought these matters to the floor, most insistently on 2 May 1701, when John Howe proposed reducing William's Civil List income from £700,000 to £600,000—and succeeded in having the measure passed by the House of Commons. Later in the month, after some complex maneuvers by Harley, the Commons approved a compromise leaving William with about £600,000 a year for the next five years but allowing him to retain his title to the full £700,000.[100]

Fully aware of this history, Anne told Parliament that "while her Subjects remain'd under the Burden of such great Taxes, she would straighten her self in her own Expences, rather than not contribute all she could to their Ease and Relief,"[101] thus freely granting what William's enemies had sought to confiscate from him by legislative action. Godolphin, who was in on the secret, knew that William had left large unpaid debts and was worried that some member might move to reduce Anne's income before she had a chance to make her own grand gesture. Ten days before the passage of the bill, he promised Sarah that he would "use all my endeavours to convince people that that matter ought to be left entirely to the Queen, and that whatever shall bee thought fitt to bee done of that kind, the grace of it might wholly be owing to her Majesty."[102] He was evidently successful, and Anne played the role of the bountiful monarch perfectly. While she duly noted the importance of maintaining "the Honour and Dignity of the Crown," she believed she could manage with the remaining funds, and by appointing Sarah as Groom of the Stole, Mistress of the Robes, and Keeper of the Privy Purse, she put her personal expenses under the eye of a shrewd and careful manager. In practice, however, revenues fell off during her reign and never reached the expected level.[103]

§

Despite the many times he had angered her, including the recent disagreement over mourning for her father, the new queen punctiliously ordered full-scale mourning for William, taking a brief journey to Windsor so that her apartments in St. James's could be hung with black drapes. In her remarks to the Privy Council and Parliament, she spoke carefully and respectfully of the loss the nation had suffered, and promised to fulfill the dead king's wishes in opposing the French and seeking union with Scotland. A committee of seven lords appointed to plan William's funeral decided on a private ceremony on the night of 12 April, at which Prince George dutifully served as chief mourner. With an expensive war about to begin, the lords were content to honor the king's desire to be buried next to Queen Mary "without any pomp."[104]

Once William was laid to rest, attention turned to the preparations for the coronation, which gave the new monarch an opportunity to display her fondness for tradition. She chose St. George's Day (23 April), which had been the coronation day for her uncle Charles II and her father James II, and meticulously followed all the prescribed rituals, including those omitted in 1685. The order of service closely resembles that followed in 1689, with small adjustments reflecting the gender of the new monarch, and almost all of the music appears to have been the same as well.[105] The most substantial addition was a specific oath rejecting Roman Catholic doctrines, which the Members of Parliament had already been constrained to take.[106]

Among the participants were many who had served the queen during her years as princess. The list of "Officers, Gentlemen, & children of her Majestys

Chappell Royall at Whitehall who attend ye Coronation" includes the bass John Gostling and the countertenor William Turner, both of whom had performed at Anne's wedding in 1683, as well as the composer John Blow, who had written music for Gloucester's birthday in 1697 and Anne's birthday in 1700.[107] Turner composed one of the two new pieces of music sung at this coronation, a setting of parts of Psalm 21 beginning "The Queen shall rejoyce."[108] The man chosen to preach the coronation sermon was John Sharp, Archbishop of York, who had been the princess's ally in the struggle to preserve the Church of England during her father's reign, incurring James's wrath by preaching against those who made convenient conversions to Rome. On this occasion, he was careful to include a reference to that period, praising Anne's "Firmness to the *English* Church, and *English* Interest, in the most difficult times."[109] The queen's immediate female attendants included Lady Marlborough and her two married daughters, both now Ladies of the Bedchamber. A Pindaric ode written for the occasion describes the Marlborough ladies as exemplary in beauty and morals:

> MARLBOROUGH and her lovely Race
> > The Triumphs Grace,
> Wou'd Nature fresh Supplies of *Beauties* make,
> > From them she must the Model take,
> > Such were the Nymphs when Angels deign'd
> > To mix with Mortals here below,
> > Such the Seraphick Sons Inflam'd,
> > But no such Guilt their Souls have Stain'd,
> Their Fame's as White as Flakes of falling Snow.[110]

This self-consciously baroque poem, imitating Cowley and Dryden, is a representative sample of the poems on the coronation, many of which were Pindaric odes. In choosing an old-fashioned form associated with sublimity and excess, the poets were providing a literary analogue to the splendid costumes and jewels on display during the ceremony.

Anne's weight and gout made it hard for her to walk, so she followed the procession down the blue carpet stretching from Westminster Hall to Westminster Abbey in an open chair. Four strong yeomen of the guard carried the chair with its heavy occupant, and sixteen noblemen supported the royal canopy. When she reached the Abbey doors, however, the queen alighted and walked down the aisle to the altar; she was willing to endure the pain for the sake of propriety, and in order to be closer to her subjects, whom she greeted "with obligeing Lookes and bows." The last phrase comes from an eyewitness account of the coronation set down by Celia Fiennes, a curious and observant young woman who kept a detailed

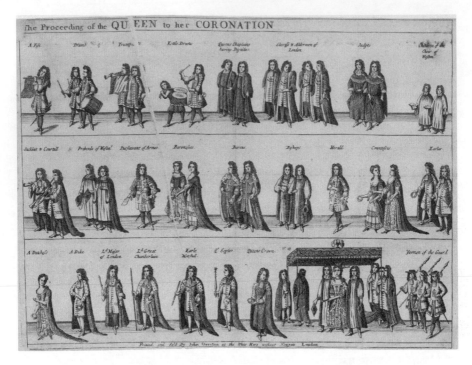

The Proceeding of the Queen to her Coronation (1702).

journal of her travels. The survival of this narrative is fortunate, because there is no detailed pictorial record of this coronation comparable to the one produced by Sandford for the ceremonies in 1685, though one crude popular print of the procession survives. Fiennes gives a particularly full description of the queen's appearance:

> I saw her thus; her Cannopy was Large[,] bore by the sixteen, and she because of Lameness of the Gout had an Elbow Chaire of Crimson velvet with a Low back, by which meanes her mantle and Robe was Cast over it and bore by the Lord Master of the Robes and the first Dutchess, with 4 maiden Ladies, Earles Daughters on Each side Richly Dress'd in Cloth of Gold or Silver, Laced, with Long traines, Richly Dressed in fine Linnen, and jewells in their hair, and Embroider'd on their Gowns. The Queens traine was 6 yards Long, the Mantle suitable of Crimson velvet with Earmine as the other of the nobility, only the rowes of powdering Exceeded, being six rowes of powdering. Her Robe under was of Gold tissue, very Rich Embroydery of jewelry about it, her peticoate the same of Gold tissue with gold and silver lace, between Rowes of Diamonds Embroyder'd, her Linnen fine.... Her head was well dress'd with Diamonds

mixed in the haire which at the Least motion Brill'd and flamed.... Thus
to the quire doore she Came, then Leaveing the Cannopy—(the Chaire
she Left at the Abby doore—) she is conducted to the Alter which was
finely deck'd with Gold tissue Carpet and fine Linnen, on the top all
the plaite of the abby sett, the velvet Cushions to place the Crown and
all the regallias on.

In describing the actual moment when Anne was crowned, Fiennes is well enough
informed to know that the splendid crown was essentially a stage prop, "made on
purpose for this Cerimony,"

vastly Rich in Diamonds, the borders and the Globe part very thick sett
with vast diamonds, the Cross on the top with all diamonds which flamed
at the Least motion, this is worth a vast summe, but being made for this
Cerimony and pulled to pieces againe, its only soe much for the hire of
such Jewells that made it.[111]

Sarah Churchill's scrupulous accounts as Mistress of the Robes show a payment
of £100 to Sir Francis Child, a prominent goldsmith and recent Lord Mayor,
"For the loan of Jewells for her Maties use at the Coronation," a fee about
which the queen later complained, though she also made a considerable outlay
for clothing in the year 1702, much of it attributable to expenses incurred at
the coronation. In Anne's first year on the throne, Sarah paid £357.6.4 to
"Mr Elliot—laceman," £686 to "Mr Alexander—mercer," and a stunning £1200
to "Mr Brown—furrier."[112]

The queen's announced resolve to "straighten her self in her own Expences"
evidently did not apply to the coronation, an occasion on which it was crucial to
display "the Honour and Dignity of the Crown." Surviving records show the purchase of new liveries for the trumpeters and drummers, including new banners to
hang from the trumpets. Even humble and necessary items were elaborate: the
Lord Chamberlain, alert to the length of the ceremonies, ordered "two large
Closestools ... For Her Majesties Service in Westminster Abbey and Westminster
Hall," and the maker's bill describes these conveniences as "covered with crimson
Velvet & trimmed with gold arras Lace, gilt Nayles and Locks with double pewter
pans to each and Leather Cases."[113] Participants expected the traditional gratu-
ities: when the mounted champion appeared at the elaborate meal served after the
ceremony to defend Anne's claim against any challenger, "she drank to him out of
a gold bowl, ... which he after had as his fee," and the "Gentlemen Ushers" who
attended her "claime[d] as their ffee for that service, the Gold Tabby which covered
the Throne in Westminster Abby which at the two last Coronations was allowed

John Croker, *Coronation medal for Queen Anne* (1702).

them."[114] Foreign ministers received gold medals, and some lucky spectators caught the silver medals that were "Cast about by the treasurer of the household" during the singing of the anthems.[115]

In addition to being an example of the queen's largesse, the medals presented her in a classical context. The allegorical scene on the back side depicts Anne as Pallas Athena, the goddess born fully armed from the head of Zeus, hurling thunderbolts at a grotesque, Hydra-like monster. In the male myth the artist adapted, Herakles, a son of Zeus, fights with the Lernean Hydra, which has nine heads; each time he cuts off a head, two more spring up in its place. The monster Anne is about to defeat, brandishing stones and clubs in its four arms, has eight serpent heads on its body and two human heads on its neck. As the inscription states, the queen is "Vice-regent of the Thunderer"; her bolts will make short work of both kinds of heads. For a queen who would declare war shortly after the coronation, this image was a way of appropriating the heroic, military role her society normally coded as male. It was a visual version of the claim Queen Elizabeth had made so memorably in her speech to the troops at Tilbury in 1588: "I know I have the bodie, but of a weak and feeble woman, but I have the heart and Stomach of a King, and of a King of *England* too."[116] The monarch's two bodies supposedly transcended the limitations of gender, and this tradition enabled the depiction of Anne as a slayer of monsters. Although Tate's New Year ode had recently portrayed "Gallick Power" as a fearsome dragon, the monster on this medal, with its vulgar faces and crude weapons, makes no sense as an image of Louis XIV, who presided over the most elegant court and the most centralized government in Europe. In showing Anne defeating an enemy with many heads, John Croker was more likely thinking of political and religious factionalism in the queen's own realm.[117]

If the classical iconography of the medal cast Anne as a heroic figure, the Christian iconography of Archbishop Sharp's sermon emphasized her female, nurturing aspects. His text was Isaiah 49, specifically the verse promising that "Kings shall be thy Nursing-Fathers, and their Queens thy Nursing Mothers." The original prophecy in which this verse appears, addressed to the Hebrew people in captivity in Babylon, promises deliverance and a glorious restoration. Though now defeated and enslaved, the nation will live to return to its homeland, where its people will multiply so rapidly that there will be no room for them:

> The children which thou shalt have, after thou hast lost the other, shall say again in thine ears, The place is too strait for me: give place to me that I may dwell. Then shalt thou say in thine heart, Who hath begotten me these, seeing I have lost my children, and am desolate, a captive, and removing to and fro? and who hath brought up these? Behold, I was left alone; these, where had they been? Thus saith the Lord GOD, Behold, I will lift up mine hand to the Gentiles, and set up my standard to the people: and they shall bring thy sons in their arms, and thy daughters shall be carried upon their shoulders. And kings shall be thy nursing fathers, and their queens thy nursing mothers: they shall bow down to thee with their face toward the earth, and lick up the dust of thy feet.

Although Sharp quotes only the last verse of this passage, which presents the kings and queens of the Gentiles as servants to a restored and powerful Israel, the religious queen was probably aware of the larger context, which was emotionally and politically relevant to her situation as a woman who had lost her children, and who daily prayed that God would grant her new progeny.

In keeping with centuries of Christian interpretation, Sharp treats this Old Testament prophecy as an allegory for the growth of the Christian religion:

> This Chapter out of which I have taken my Text, hath always been understood to be, and it certainly is, a Prophecy of our Lord *Jesus Christ*, and of the Propagation of his *Religion*, and the spreading of his *Church* throughout the World. And it teacheth us, That though the Beginnings of the *Religion*, this *Church* of *Christ*, were very small and inconsiderable; yet in due time a vast number of *Nations* and *Peoples* should be brought in to it: So that *Kings* and *Queens* should submit their *Scepters* to that of *Jesus Christ*, and become *Nursing-Fathers* and *Nursing-Mothers* to his *Church* and *People*.

On this reading, earthly kings and queens must submit to the Church, an idea many in Sharp's audience would have associated with the feared power of Rome, so the preacher smoothly redefines the servile role of Isaiah's kings and queens as implying "a wonderful *Trust* reposed in Princes; and a wonderful Care, and Solicitude, and Tenderness required of them on the behalf of their *subjects*." Among his examples of British monarchs who have displayed such care, Elizabeth is prominent: "Her Reign alone will let us see, that it was not without great reason, that in my Text *Queens* are joyn'd as equal Sharers with *Kings*, in making up the *Blessing* which is here promis'd to GOD's People." Identifying Anne as "such another QUEEN," Sharp is now ready to praise her for the instances of motherly care already apparent in her reign, including her zeal for the coming war, her generous gift to the Treasury, her support for the Protestant succession, and her proclamation against vice. He concludes that God "hath given us in *Her* another *Nursing-Mother* to his *Church* and *People*; and one who will make good that Character."[118] In the allegory of the scriptural passage and the sermon, Anne was expected to act the part of a nursing mother to the Church and the nation, but many members of the congregation also shared her hope that she would again be a mother to an actual child. The choice of text for the sermon, whether made by Sharp or by Anne herself, pointed in that direction, and was reinforced by a new anthem composed for the occasion by Jeremiah Clarke, effectively setting the verse describing queens as nursing mothers.[119]

Alert to the significance of ceremony, Anne's subjects were aware of the differences between her coronation and those that preceded it. When Fiennes describes the ceremonial meal, she provides a comparative history of canopies:

> The queen being Come up to her table which was a great rise of stepps she was seated on her throne which was under a fine Cannopy. When

> King James was Crown'd he sate soe: at his Left hand sate his Queen under another Cannopy, but King William and Queen Mary being both principalls sate under one Large Cannopy on one Large throne, but our present Queen should have sate alone as she did in the upper End under the Cannopy, but she sent and did invite Prince George her Consort to dine with her. So he Came and at her request tooke his seate at her Left hand without the Cannopy.[120]

Anne's management of the canopy is another instance of the balancing act she was performing in the opening months of her reign. In keeping with her lifelong attention to forms and ceremonies, she quite properly sat alone on her throne under the royal canopy, enacting the role of the sacred monarch. In her private identity as a wife, however, she invited her husband to join her, but was careful to see that his chair remained outside the canopy, just as she had once insisted on having her own stool moved outside a canopy covering William and Mary.[121]

§

Anne's desire to secure appropriate recognition for her husband, touchingly played out in the coronation rituals, posed a problem for those helping her to prepare for the coming war. Within days of her accession, she appointed Marlborough as "Captain-General" of English land forces and dispatched him to Holland to reassure her allies, but she also asked him to persuade the Dutch to appoint Prince George as their new Stadholder, the title William had held in the Netherlands, and wrote to her allies herself urging them to choose her husband as their leader. Marlborough dutifully "endeavoured to incline thes pepell to desire the honor of having the Prince to command their arme as well as the English," as he wrote to Godolphin in a letter evidently designed to be shown to the queen. "The difficulty of this matter," he continued, "is that not only every province, but every town must consent before the States can make an offer."[122] As a description of the cumbersome political machinery of the Dutch republic, this is accurate enough, but of course the real difficulty was that the Dutch were fully aware of the royal consort's limitations. Not only was George in poor health, but he was sorely lacking in military or administrative experience. He had not seen military action since attempting to join William in the Irish campaign of 1690, and while he had served on the Privy Council and the central Cabinet during William's reign, he had not taken an active role in the making of policy. The Dutch were therefore unwilling to comply with Anne's request, though reluctant to offend her; they left her letter unanswered. Marlborough had better success in convincing the Allies to agree to an additional clause binding all of them to oppose "the pretended Prince of Wales." The diplomats representing the Habsburg Emperor, who was a Roman Catholic and a strong believer in divine right monarchy, were understandably troubled by the term "pretended," but some clever casuistry by the Emperor's Jesuit confessor allowed him to make the agreement, without which he would not have been able to declare war on his lifelong enemy Louis XIV.[123] By the time Marlborough returned to England to attend William's funeral and Anne's coronation, the Allies had signed all the necessary treaties and privately chosen 4/15 May as the date for a joint declaration of war.

On 14 April, recognizing the meaning of the Dutch silence, the queen took action herself, appointing her husband "Generalissimo of all her Forces, both by Sea and Land."[124] In practice, this grand title proved symbolic at best. As Lord High Admiral, a position to which the queen appointed him on 21 May, the Prince chaired a council directing the affairs of the navy, working closely with Admiral George Churchill, Marlborough's younger brother, but Marlborough continued to make all the important decisions about English forces on land, and when he returned to the Netherlands for the summer campaign, the Dutch made him commander of the allied forces, the position Anne had wanted for her husband, though they significantly limited his power by stipulating that his Dutch deputies could decide to withhold their troops from any action of which they disapproved.

As the date for declaring war drew near, the queen convened her Privy Council, to which she had added a number of new members, including her lifelong religious advisor Henry Compton, Bishop of London, and her old beau John Sheffield, now Marquess of Normanby, whom she named Lord Privy Seal. Surveying these and other changes, Abel Boyer concluded that the queen was revealing "her Inclination to favour the *High-Church* or *Tory Party*, preferably to the *Low-Church* Men, or *Whigs*,"[125] but those who thought that Tory policies would automatically prevail were sorely mistaken. The meeting of 2 May was a decisive showdown between Anne's uncle Rochester and her loyal friend Marlborough. The Privy Council Register blandly records the queen's decision, "with the Advice of her Privy Councill," to inform the Commons and Lords of her intention "to Issue her Royal Declaration of War,"[126] but Boyer, who evidently had good sources within the council, gives a revealing summary of the debate omitted from the official record:

> It having been moved in Council to declare War against France and Spain, the Earl of *Rochester*, and some other Members, represented the Inconveniencies that might attend such a step; urging, that it was safer for the *English* to act only as *Auxiliaries:* But the Earl of *Marlborough* maintain'd, on the contrary, that it not only became the Honour of the Crown and Nation, to make good the late King's Engagements, but that *France* could never be reduced within due Bounds, unless the *English* entered as Principals in the Quarrel. This Opinion being supported by the

Dukes of *Somerset* and *Devonshire*, the Earl of *Pembroke*, and some others, the Majority of that illustrious Assembly gave into it, and thereupon her Majesty order'd a Declaration of War to be drawn up.[127]

In arguing against the expense and danger of a land war on the Continent, Rochester was articulating the views of the most conservative wing of the Tory party: country squires exhausted by the heavy taxes levied for William's wars and therefore content to let the navy protect and further English interests. Having served the last three kings in important capacities, he expected his niece to heed his advice, but Marlborough, who was far closer to Anne, presented arguments against isolationism that proved persuasive not only to the monarch, but to her Cabinet. By claiming that honor obligated the queen and the nation "to make good the late King's Engagements," he enlisted the support of those who had admired and served King William; coming just twenty days after the funeral, this reminder of the dead man's dream of defeating France gained emotional force. By alleging that the other allies would not be able to defeat the French on their own, he tapped into nationalistic pride; no member of the Privy Council would have dared raise doubts about the bravery and skill of English soldiers. Although we do not know what arguments they added, the men who spoke in support of Marlborough included the current President of the council (Somerset), the past and future President (Pembroke), and one of the principal organizers of the mounted bodyguard that escorted and protected Anne in the early days of the Revolution of 1688 (Devonshire). Somerset and Devonshire were Whigs, and Pembroke a moderate Tory. [128]

The Lords and Commons were unanimous in supporting Anne's decision, and on 4 May the queen had the satisfaction of drawing a ceremonial sword, handing it to Prince George as her Generalissimo, and hearing her declaration of war read by "the Heralds at Arms, attended by the Serjeants at Mace, Trumpets and Kettle Drums."[129] Two days later, in an act that would prove essential for the successful prosecution of the war, she appointed Godolphin Lord Treasurer, effectively making him her prime minister.

§

Despite the determination of the queen, her Captain-General, and her new Lord Treasurer, the opening campaign was frustrating and slow. The first of many delays occurred when Marlborough, impatient to sail for the Continent, had to wait more than a week for favorable winds. To Sarah, who accompanied her husband to Margate, the queen wrote a long letter on 19 May that reveals her state of mind at this moment. Taking a patient view of the immediate situation, Anne notes that Marlborough has been ill and hopes the delay will allow him to recover; she mentions the arrival of an embassy from the Dutch as another reason for equanimity about

the contrary winds. Turning to domestic matters, she writes at length about the disposition of lucrative places in the government, a process that had begun with her
alterations in the Privy Council and was now continuing to positions at a lower level.
She notes, for example, that Sir Christopher Musgrave, a leading Tory who was expecting a reward, has proved unwilling to take a post under Prince George in the
Admiralty, insisting instead on a position that would require displacing a Whig. This
narrow and vindictive attitude was all too typical among Anne's Tory supporters,
but the queen had a larger mind: "whatever he dos in that matter," she writes to
Sarah, "you may be sure that care will be taken of the other person." In the event, the
person displaced when Musgrave became a Teller of the Exchequer was Guy Palmes,
a Whig who was friendly with the Marlboroughs, and the queen was as good as her
word, awarding Palmes a pension of £1,000 per year in August.[130]

Her sympathy, however, did not extend to the Earl of Portland, who had recently asked Godolphin to repay a loan of £10,000 that he claimed to have "layd
out by the King's order."[131] Anne, who had no intention of repaying the alleged
loan, takes evident pleasure in sharing with Sarah the details of a recent interview:

> Lord and Lady Portland took there leave of me this morning. She
> I thought looked a little grave, but he was in one of his gracious ways, and
> I fancy is fool enough to think his unreasonable demands will some time
> or other be complyed with, but if they weare never soe just, and that one
> had mony to throw away, I think he should be one of the last to be consi-
> derd. Mentioning this worthy person putts me in mind of asking deare
> Mrs Freeman a question which I should have don some time ago, and
> that is if you would not have the Lodg for your life.

Writing with the wicked irony of a novelist, Anne understates the discomfort of
Lady Portland ("She I thought looked a little grave"), attributes the Earl's gracious
manners to his foolish hope that his loan would be repaid, and sarcastically refers
to him as "this worthy person" in a sentence repeating her offer of one of his posts
to Sarah. The "Lodg," which would be Sarah's main residence for the next several
years, was among the perquisites of the Ranger of Windsor Park, a position Anne
had taken away from Portland to bestow upon her favorite.

In keeping with her lifelong concern about those serving her, Anne was evidently monitoring the distribution of offices with care, but she was also attentive
to the state of her various royal properties. As the letter draws to a close, she takes
time to complain about the state of the gardens at Kensington:

> I went to Kensington to walk in the garden, which would be a very pretty
> place if it weare well kept but nothing can be wors. It is a great deal of pity

and indeed a great shame that there should be no better use made of soe great an alowance, for I have bin told the King alowed four hundred pound a yeer for that one garden.[132]

Mindful of her popular decision to forgo £100,000 of income from the Civil List, Anne deplores William's failure to receive value for money in his gardens. By sharing these details with Sarah, who had greatly improved her own gardens at St. Albans, she may have been reminding the Keeper of her Privy Purse that they would both need to hold their employees accountable. But there is also some subtle irony at work here: when Anne says, "*I have bin told* the King alowed four hundred pound a yeer for that one garden," she is displaying the same mock-ignorance she had used when she told Sarah, in 1697, "*I think I have heard* the King dos not care for plays."[133] In both cases, the sly humor emphasizes William's inattention to the arts, among which Anne certainly included gardening. In her view, it was not only a "pity," a waste of money and effort, for the gardens to be in disarray, but a "shame." The hated Portland, who prided himself on his knowledge of gardening, had been Superintendent of the Royal Gardens under William, so Anne's disapproval of the state of the gardens at Kensington is of a piece with her general disdain for her predecessor's favorite. Although she had voluntarily put herself on a tighter budget, she had promised her Parliament to maintain "the Honour and Dignity of the Crown," and she was determined to ensure that her gardens were "well kept." A few days after sending this letter, the queen asked Henry Wise to take over the gardens at Kensington Palace, displacing William's Dutch gardener. Over the next several years she spent more than £26,000 on the gardens at Kensington, commissioning Wise to lay out a large baroque "parterre garden." An orangery built there, probably designed by Nicholas Hawksmoor, became one of her favorite places for summer dining.[134]

Although she was continuing William's policies by prosecuting the war, the queen was clearly moving away from his practices by paying closer attention to the Church and the arts—and by encouraging the Tories. A week after sending this letter, with Marlborough now safe at the Hague, Anne gave what proved to be her last speech to the Parliament she had inherited from William. Her conclusion, while repeating the conventional hope for legislative unanimity that the king had expressed the previous December, gave unmistakable evidence of her preference for "the Church party." "I shall always Wish," said Anne,

> That no Difference of Opinion, among those that are Equally Affected to My Service, may be the Occasion of Heats and Animosities among themselves. I shall be very Careful to preserve and Maintain the Act of Toleration, and to Set the Minds of all My People at Quiet; My Own Principles

must always keep me intirely Firm to the Interests and Religion of the Church of *England*, and will Incline Me to Countenance those who have the truest Zeal to Support it.[135]

It was this signal of support from the Crown that gave her Tory ministers and their poetic sons the confidence displayed in the poems with which they greeted the queen at Oxford in August. Although the Lord Keeper prorogued Parliament until 7 July after this declaration, few can have expected that there would actually be a summer meeting, and on 2 July the queen dissolved her Parliament and issued writs for an August election.

Anne may have delayed dissolving the English Parliament in order to resolve some issues with the Scottish Parliament, which met in June. She was publicly committed to an act uniting England with Scotland, an initiative William had recommended in his final days, and she recognized that allowing the Scots to name their own monarch, as they had done for centuries, would add to the confusion surrounding the already problematic succession. As a Stuart, Anne was a direct descendant of James VI of Scotland, who became James I of England in 1603. As everyone knew, however, she had no living issue, and her half-brother in France, if one accepted his parentage as legitimate, was also a Stuart, and therefore a more attractive successor to many Scots than the Hanoverians designated to succeed by the English Parliament, which had passed the Act of Settlement in 1701 without bothering to consult with the Scottish Parliament. The Pretender, however, was a Roman Catholic, and Catholics were an even smaller minority in Scotland than in England. The established Church of Scotland, the Kirk, was Calvinist in doctrine and Presbyterian in government, with elders elected by each congregation and a general assembly voting policies for the whole church—a much more "republican" model than the hierarchical organization of the Church of England, with its powerful archbishops and bishops. Episcopalian clergy, however, served in many Scottish parishes and cherished the hope that a united church would bring bishops back to Scotland. Though deeply divided among themselves, Scots of all persuasions felt considerable antagonism toward England, thanks to a long history of conflict, yet they recognized that an Act of Union might finally give their impoverished country a larger share of the lucrative foreign trade enjoyed by their southern neighbors. Both countries thus had reasons to explore a closer bond.

When the Scottish Parliament convened, however, those opposed to Union seized the initiative. There had been no elections in Scotland since the Revolution because King William, content with the support of the strongly Presbyterian and Whig majority elected to the Scottish Convention Parliament of 1689, chose to continue the same Parliament throughout his reign. Though required by law to meet within twenty days of the death of the monarch, the Scottish Parliament did not assemble until 9 June, three full months after William's death, and a group of dissidents led by James, Fourth Duke of Hamilton, took advantage of the delay to contend that the meeting was illegal and that new elections should be held at once. They dramatized their position by marching out of the Parliament House in a body and reconvening in a nearby tavern. The remaining members heard a letter from the queen, read by James Douglas, Duke of Queensberry, her High-Commissioner to Scotland, and continued to meet in regular sessions. On 25 June, this reduced Scottish Parliament passed acts recognizing Anne as their monarch and agreeing to negotiations toward a possible Union. One week later, Anne dissolved the English Parliament. Hamilton and his allies, however, sent an address of their own to the queen, continuing their protests against the legality of actions taken by the "Rump" Scottish Parliament. With characteristic civility, Anne allowed their envoy to pay her a formal visit; with characteristic firmness, she refused to receive or read the address he was bearing. As a result, the resolutions passed by the disputed Parliament took effect, and commissioners for both sides began their negotiations in November.[136]

§

When Anne left for Bath in August, accompanied by a large entourage including Godolphin and the Duchess of Marlborough, there had been no significant progress in the war. The "200 Virgins Apparell'd like Amazons" who greeted her coach were expressing hope for military success but not yet celebrating substantial victories. During the queen's vacation, however, news arrived of Marlborough's success in capturing Venloo, Stevensweert, and Ruremonde—three fortresses along the river Meuse—and shortly after her return to London he captured the city of Liège, depriving the French of the ability to move men and supplies along a significant waterway. From Marlborough's own point of view, the campaign was disappointing, as he missed several opportunities to force a decisive battle with the French army under advantageous conditions; on each of these occasions, the Dutch generals serving under him invoked their prerogative and held back their troops. There was also bad news from Germany, where Maximilian Emanuel, the Elector of Bavaria, ambitious and thoroughly dishonest, suddenly changed sides in September, throwing in his lot with Louis and capturing the city of Ulm. In England, however, Marlborough's series of small victories was welcome. A letter printed in the *Daily Courant* in early October, allegedly written by a wounded officer, is typical:

> I will not pretend to determine what Influence this Success of our Arms
> is owing to; but it is certain that this one Campaign has gain'd more Glory
> to England and Advantage to the Allies than the whole last War; and both

these might probably have been still much greater, if our General had been at liberty to pursue his own Methods without Controul.[137]

A poet celebrating 1702 as an *annus mirabilis* expressed a similar thought in verse and gave the queen full credit for her general's victories:

Late tho' you fill'd the Sacred Throne, yet more
In Months were done than were in Years before:
Nor sooner did you there ascend, than shine
With Robes Cœlestial, and with *Guards Divine*:
They with your Gen'rals on your Errands went,
Fought under them your *Cause*, as from you sent:

. . . .

In all Attacks, where clashing Armour bray'd,
They led the Van, and First your Foes dismay'd.[138]

Although praised in similar terms in this poem and elsewhere, naval operations designed to secure control of the Mediterranean were much less successful than the infantry campaign. Admiral Rooke, whose mission was to take the strategically located Spanish port of Cadiz, decided that it was too well fortified to be captured from the sea. Instead, he landed a detachment of marines under the command of the Duke of Ormond at Fort St. Catherine, well north of the city, with orders to make their way south and take Cadiz. Flushed with some initial successes, the soldiers pillaged the town of Port St. Mary, lost momentum, and at last abandoned the campaign. Luckily for Rooke, who was sailing home with nothing to show for his efforts, an English chaplain stumbled onto the news that the Spanish treasure fleet, loaded with South American silver and escorted by a fleet of French warships, had put in at Vigo Bay. Seizing the moment, Rooke's ships broke the boom protecting the harbor while Ormond's marines attacked the fort that overlooked it. Although the Spanish quickly sent most of the silver inland, the English destroyed or disabled fifteen French ships, three Spanish galleons, and thirteen merchant vessels. Rooke returned to London claiming a great victory, but the new King of Spain, grandson of the King of France, actually received almost all of his shipment of silver, and English speculators who owned an interest in the merchant vessels sunk in the action suffered significant losses. According to Isaac Newton, Anne's Master of the Mint, the silver seized in this battle was worth only £14,000.[139]

While rightly concerned about the naval campaign, especially as news of the engagement at Vigo did not reach England until late October, the queen was elated by the success of the army, and many in her new Parliament expected her to make some reference to Marlborough's victories when she addressed them on 21 October. But Anne, who was planning elaborate rewards for Marlborough, cunningly forced her legislators to take the lead in praising her Captain-General. In a speech drafted by Godolphin, she stressed the need for "such Supplies,...as may be necessary for the Encouragement of Our Allies, and the Prosecuting of the War, where it shall most sensibly affect our Enemies, and be most Effectual for Disappointing the Boundless Ambition of France," omitting any specific mention of Marlborough's campaign. The only engagement to which she referred by name was the disaster at Cadiz:

> I cannot without much Trouble take Notice to you of the Disappointment We have had at *Cadiz:* I have not yet had a Particular Account of that Enterprize; nor of all the Difficulties our Forces may have met with there; But I have had such a Representation of Disorders and Abuses committed at *Port St. Mary's,* as hath obliged Me to give Directions for the Strictest Examination of that Matter.[140]

In the face of Anne's surprising reticence, the Houses of Parliament vied with one another in emphasizing the success of the land campaign. The Lords took "Leave, on this Occasion, to congratulate the prosperous and glorious Success with which it has pleased GOD to bless Your Majesty's Arms, in Conjunction with Your Allies, under the Command of the Earl of *Marlborough*,"[141] while the Commons spoke of "the wonderful Progress of your Majesty's Arms under the Conduct of the Earl of Marlborough."[142] As Godolphin pointed out in a letter to Sarah, having such praise articulated by the Houses of Parliament afforded "better grace" for the queen "than if she had done it herself."[143] Armed with these parliamentary addresses praising Marlborough, Anne now felt confident that she could make him a duke and provide for him financially; she immediately wrote to the countess informing her of those plans. Sarah, who was wary of the expense and formality of becoming a duchess, later claimed that she let this letter drop from her hand, "and was for some minutes like one that had received the news of the Death of one of their dear friends,"[144] but Marlborough, hopeful that the higher title might give him more leverage with the Dutch and his other allies, agreed to become a duke.

Curiously enough, the first of this Parliament's many partisan divisions concerned the wording of the praise for Marlborough in the "loyal address" from the Commons:

> On the 24th, the Commons waited also upon the Queen with a loyal and affectionate Address, wherein, among other Things, they said, *That ... the vigorous Support of her Allies, and the wonderful Progress of her Arms, under*

the Conduct of the Earl of Marlborough, *had signally* RETRIEVED *the an-cient Honour and Glory of the* English *Nation.* It is observable that the Word RETRIEVED occasioned a great Debate in the House of Commons, several Members alledging, that it implied a Reflection on the late King's Memory, and therefore they insisted to have the word MAINTAIN'D put instead of it: But upon a Division, One Hundred and Eighty Voices were for the First, and Eighty only for the latter: Which shew'd, that the *Tory* Party had a vast Majority in the House.[145]

Because men normally stood for Parliament without overtly announcing their party affiliations, this division about which verb to use was the first clear indication of the size of the Tory majority. Although Anne would soon have differences with her chosen party, she began this session with the belief that she would enjoy solid support for her most important projects; the retention of the tougher verb, which was indeed designed to make a distinction between her successes and William's failures, was gratifying.

The queen's new confidence shows in her next letter to Sarah Churchill, written a few days after her speech. It was a reasonable guess that Sarah, though distressed at the outcome of the election, would take pleasure in having her husband's military prowess recognized, and Anne seized the moment to urge her fiercely partisan friend to temper her support for the Whigs.

I am very glad to find by my dear Mrs Freemans letter that I was bless'd with yesterday, that she liked my speech, but I can't help being extremely concern'd that you are so partial to the Whigs, because I wou'd never have you, & your poor unfortunate faithfull Morley differ in opinion in the least thing. What I said when I writ last on this subject does not proceed from any inclination to the other party, but I know the principles of the Church of England, & I know those of the Whigs, & it is that, & no other reason, which makes me think as I do of the last, and upon my word my dear Mrs Freeman, you are mightily mistaken in your notion of a true Whig, for the character you give them does not in the least belong to them, but to the Church.[146]

In no previous letter does Anne so directly contradict her friend. For her to tell Sarah that she was "mightily mistaken" was a distinct departure from the deferential stance of past years, in which she had often promised to "obey my deare Lady Churchills commands since I am sure you will never desire anything but what is reasonable."[147] With her army succeeding, her people grateful, and her Parliament dominated by the "Church party," Anne was finally prepared to assert herself in her most important personal relationship. She had rewarded the Churchills lavishly for their years of support and was now preparing an even larger prize for them, so this looked like a moment when she might balance those substantive demonstrations of love with a forthright declaration of her political principles. In the manuscript that preserves this letter, it is followed immediately by Sarah's outraged account of Anne's meeting secretly with the Tory Robert Harley and taking his advice—events that occurred much later in her reign. The sequence of pages suggests that Sarah recognized this early letter as a pivotal moment and associated it with later episodes in which Anne demonstrated her fondness for the Tories. The importance of the letter, however, lies not in Sarah's stubborn response but in Anne's determination to retrieve the honor and glory of the Crown. Armed with the "Scepters and Ensigns" of queenly power, the attendant nymph had become an Amazon.

CHAPTER 7

DOMINION OVER THE MIGHTY

7 September 1704

Exactly four weeks after receiving the news of Marlborough's glorious victory at Blenheim, Queen Anne traveled to the City for a service of thanksgiving. Although the preparations had been hurried, the ceremonies were splendid. St. Paul's Cathedral stood imposing but unfinished on Ludgate Hill, its great dome still swathed in scaffolding, but Christopher Wren had taken time away from his work on the building to fashion a throne for the queen at the west end, facing the altar and visible to most of the congregation. Richard Sherlock, Dean of St. Paul's, prepared a sermon comparing the recent engagement to "the Miraculous Victories of the *Jews* over their Enemies, when God visibly fought their Battels for them."[1] John Blow, Composer to the Chapel Royal, wrote three substantial new verse anthems in time to teach them to the vocal soloists and the choir. Tailors, seamstresses, and grooms worked hard to dress the court party for the grand cavalcade. Even the horses, as Luttrell reports, were "curiously deck't":

> This being the thanksgiving day for the victory over the French and Bavarians, her majestie was complimented by the whole court at St. James's; about 10, the cavalcade began, the streets being lin'd with the trained bands, and the several companies in their livery gowns, the balconies hung with tapistry and crowded with spectators. First the foot

guards march'd to make way; next followed a great many coaches, with 6 horses, of the nobility; among them the archbishop of Canterbury, the lord keeper, the lord treasurer, the lord president, the lord chamberlain, Mr. secretary Harley, &c.; the duke of Ormond rode alone in one of the queens coaches, and the duke of Somerset, master of the horse, on horseback: her majestie was drawn in a coach and 8 horses, having the prince on her left, the dutchesse of Marlborough and the lady Fretchvill riding forwards, the horses curiously deck't with white and red ribbons, made up like roses, and guarded by the earl of Albemarles troop richly accoutred.[2]

The diarist John Evelyn, eighty-three but still alert to detail, noticed that the Duchess of Marlborough wore "a very plaine garment," a choice presumably made to avoid upstaging the monarch, who was "full of Jewells." Luttrell, not notably sensitive to high art, described the music for the service as "very curious," but Evelyn, a sophisticated connoisseur, praised the "Musick composed by the best Masters of that art, to accompany the Church musique & Anthems." The choir performed the *Te Deum* and the *Jubilate Deo*, probably using Henry Purcell's grand settings of these traditional hymns of victory, joyous works with prominent trumpet parts written in 1694.[3] Hearing these sacred anthems may have influenced Evelyn's language about the weather, in which he echoed a line from Purcell's secular music: "After an exceeding wet & stormy day," he wrote, "succeeded one of the most serene & Calmest bright-days, as had been all the yeare."[4] Somewhere in the old man's mind lay a memory of Purcell's setting of the words *serene and calm* in the last act of Dryden's patriotic opera *King Arthur*, first performed in 1691 and frequently revived thereafter.[5] After Arthur defeats the Saxon prince Oswald in single combat, the enchanter Merlin "waves his Wand; the Scene changes, and discovers the *British* Ocean in a storm." Æolus, god of winds, appears "in a Cloud above" and sings a command to his servants:

> Ye Blust'ring Brethren of the Skies,
> Whose Breath has ruffl'd all the Watry Plain,
>   Retire, and let *Britannia* Rise,
> In Triumph o'er the Main.
>   Serene and Calm, and void of fear,
>   The Queen of Islands must appear.[6]

Purcell's imaginative setting uses rapid scales in the strings to represent the blustering winds, then sustained peaceful chords as the winds retire and "The Scene opens, and discovers a calm Sea, to the end of the House. An Island arises,

fear   The Queen of   Is - lands   must ap - pear.   Se-rene   and

calm, _____   ___   se - rene   and   calm _____

___   and void of   fear   The Queen of   Is - lands   must ap - pear.

Mus. Ex. 7.1: Henry Purcell, "Serene and calm," aria from *King Arthur* (1691), Act 5.

to a soft Tune; *Britannia* seated in the Island, with Fishermen at her Feet." The ensuing aria, accompanied by sweet sonorities in the recorder parts, repeats the words *Serene and calm* six times.[7]

By describing a wet and stormy Wednesday giving way to a serene and calm Thursday, Evelyn was associating the service of thanksgiving with this operatic transformation and its vision of a peaceful, female "Queen of Islands." As poets quickly realized, the iconography employed in Dryden's opera, with its celebration of Britannia as an island queen embodying harmony and stability, was particularly suitable for Anne. In a song performed for the royal birthday in 1703, set as a bass solo by John Eccles, Peter Motteux moved Dryden's internal rhyme between "serene" and "Queen" to a more prominent position and equated Anne with Britannia:

> Firm as a Rock above the Ocean seen
> Unmov'd she sits Majestick and serene
> Like her Britannia's self among the Isles a Queen.

After establishing Anne as firm, unmoved, majestic, and serene, Motteux provides a more active alternative, this time drawing on classical mythology:

> Our Pallas thus appears in Arms
> But to secure the worlds repose
> She sheilds its Friends and quells its Foes
> And Aws at once and charms.

In imagining the queen as "Our Pallas...in Arms," Motteux remembers the portrait of Anne as Pallas on her coronation medal, quelling her domestic foes (see image in chapter 6). Even here, however, he is reluctant to present the queen as truly violent; his emphasis falls on her capacity to secure repose and shield her allies, to awe and charm both friends and enemies.

> In vain at Sea in vain at Land
> Her Pow'r her genius they withstand,
> Whole Fleets whole Countries conquer'd find
> Wise conduct with her valour Joyn'd,
> And Crowns that Female heads disclaim
> Now totter at a Female name.[8]

When he speaks of Anne's "Pow'r," Motteux pairs it with her "genius"; when he speaks of her "valour," he pairs it with her "Wise conduct." His closing compliment gives the "Female name" of Britain's queen the power to alarm those countries whose laws prevent women from ruling—most obviously the France of Louis XIV.

In the sermon delivered at the thanksgiving service, Richard Sherlock moves away from this cautious and balanced view, making a conscious effort to link the queen more directly with military might, to present her not as "Unmov'd" and "serene," but as the active scourge of her foes. Quoting verses from ten different Psalms and the first book of Samuel,[9] Sherlock highlights passages in which King David exults in the crushing defeat of his enemies:

> The Psalmist attributes all great and wonderful Successes to...the Wonders of Providence, and there are none greater than the wonderful Events

of War; such intire Victories as *David* describes, *Psal.* 18.37, &c. *I have persued mine Enemies, and overtaken them, neither did I turn again till they were consumed; I have wounded them, that they were not able to rise: They are fallen under my Feet.*

This quoted verse is indeed appropriate for a celebration of Blenheim, where the allied forces under Marlborough pursued the retreating French with devastating results, but in order to apply David's psalm to Anne, the preacher has to engage in an awkward act of ventriloquism, imagining what Marlborough might now say to his queen:

And your renowned Captain General, the Duke of *Marlborough*, whose Name will live in Story, may address your Majesty in the words of the Psalmist, *I have persued your Enemies, and overtaken them, neither did I turn back, till they were consumed. I have wounded them, that they are not able to rise, they are fallen under your Majesties Feet.*

The biblical David—warrior, king, and poet—could fight his own battles and sing his own hymns of thanks and exultation, while Anne depended on others to fight her battles and celebrate her victories. Sherlock's rewriting of the psalm elides the distinction between the queen and her agents: Marlborough has pursued, over-taken, and wounded the defeated French, but they have somehow fallen beneath Anne's feet. To believe this fantasy, even within the context of a celebratory sermon, required suppressing the inconvenient fact that Anne's feet were so swol-len by gout that she could not walk from her coach to Wren's throne and had to be carried into St. Paul's "in an open chair" in order to hear these words of praise.[10]

If Marlborough's "Name will live in Story," Sherlock continues, Anne's victory "will...shine in the *English* Story, and equal you to the greatest Heroes of your Race!" Again, the claim that Anne will be "equal...to the greatest Heroes" dresses the queen in the borrowed robes of male commanders. Perhaps recognizing that problem, Sherlock now shifts to a different example—not David or Marlborough but Queen Elizabeth, whose mantle Anne had already claimed by adopting "semper eadem" as her motto:

It is in vain for any Prince to affect an Universal Empire while an *English Queen* sits upon the Throne. *Queen Elizabeth*, of blessed memory, gave such a fatal blow to the *Spanish* Monarchy, in the height of all their pride and glory, as they could never recover to this day; and we hope *France* will as long and as sensibly feel the power of your Majesty's Arms.

Conveniently for Sherlock's purposes, Elizabeth had actually come to a thanksgiving service at the old St. Paul's after the wreck of the Spanish Armada in 1588, a parallel that was all the more striking as none of the intervening male monarchs had attended such services.[11] But the resemblance to Elizabeth claimed by Anne and repeated by many was far from perfect, not least because Elizabeth was officially the "maiden Queen," while Anne, as everyone knew, was a wife and had been a mother. Avoiding such awkward details, Sherlock links Elizabeth and Anne by employing a more general and complimentary ideology of gender. According to this equation, "a proud insulting Monarch"—certainly referring to a male ruler and specifically suggesting Louis—will run the risk of being humbled whenever "an *English Queen* sits upon the Throne."[12]

Here the preacher's patriotism shades into gallant compliment, a pose frequently struck by male writers praising Anne. In a poem published early in 1703, for example, one "W.H." claims that the island of Britain has a "Female Shape," which supposedly accounts for the success of its "Female Governments." If one tries to imagine the geographical shape of the island as female, the figure appears to be pregnant, and in praising the queen, the poet urges all men to show "Respect to Womankind":

> Our Mother-Isle a Female Shape presents,
> And best succeeds in Female Governments.
>
> . . . .
> Thus now, O Sacred QUEEN! Men read in You, ⎫
> How Justly, how Inviolably due ⎬
> Is all Respect to Womankind they Shew. ⎭
> You Conquer more with charming Voice and Smiles,
> Than twenty Kings in Military Toils.[13]

The detail of the "charming Voice" is specific to Anne, but the idea that women conquer men through beauty and personal magnetism comes from a thoroughly exhausted Petrarchan tradition treating attractive female features as weapons. The poem's title, *Thura Britannica*, translates as "British incense," and the poet, like the later preacher, is shrouding some inconvenient political realities under a heavy layer of perfume.

§

In preparing the music for the service, John Blow also faced the task of praising a sedentary female monarch for her army's success. Unlike Sherlock, who put together his own eclectic set of biblical passages, Blow was attentive to the order of service published in advance for use in all churches in the kingdom, which listed proper psalms and lessons for this occasion:

¶ Proper Psalms are, LXXV, LXXVI, CXLIV.

¶ Proper Lessons.
{
The First, Judges V. ver. 1. to ver. 22.
Te Deum
The Second, Revel[ation] XIX. The first 6 verses.
Jubilate Deo[14]
}

This rubric stipulates that the hymn *Te Deum Laudamus* be sung after the first lesson, and that Psalm 100, *Jubilate Deo,* be sung after the second. Both were expected at celebrations of military victories, and Blow appears to have had sufficient instrumental forces to perform Purcell's justly famous settings.[15] An occasion of this importance, however, required new music as well. Despite having little time, Blow produced three verse anthems designed to feature the best available vocal soloists, accompanied by the cathedral organ. The celebrated bass John Gostling, who was still active, was probably the bass soloist, and all three anthems have prominent parts for two high male singers, one of whom was probably Richard Elford, Anne's favorite. Brief sections for full choir vary the texture without giving Blow's boy sopranos too much music to learn.

Two of these new anthems draw their texts from the psalms and lessons designated in the printed *Form of Prayer. Blessed be the Lord, my strength* follows the first eleven verses of Psalm 144, and *Awake, awake, utter a song* takes its text from Judges 5, an ancient song in which the prophetess Deborah, the only female judge in the history of Israel, rejoices in the victory of her general Barak over the Philistines. As a married noncombatant who ruled her nation, Deborah was a much closer biblical analogue for Anne than the martial David, whose psalms Sherlock selected but was then constrained to rewrite—and a much closer historical analogue than Queen Elizabeth, whose power depended in part on remaining unmarried. In the story as told in the Bible, "Deborah, a prophetess, the wife of Lapidoth,...sent and called Barak...and said unto him, Hath not the LORD God of Israel commanded, saying, Go and draw toward mount Tabor, and take with thee ten thousand men?" (Judges 4:4–6). She urges Barak to attack the enemy and promises him that God will grant him victory. Blow's anthem allowed attentive listeners to imagine Anne as Deborah, encouraging her general and prophesying the downfall of the mighty. Better yet, one detail in the song's description of the battle perfectly matched the events at Blenheim: "The river of Kishon," sings the prophetess, "swept them away," and at the end of the recent battle, at least two thousand French cavalrymen had drowned in the Danube, pushed into the river by the advancing allies.[16]

The person who stipulated that the "First Lesson" would end with verse 22 of Judges 5 was deliberately suppressing another part of this biblical story. After the battle, an actively heroic woman named Jael kills the enemy commander Sisera by driving a stake through his temple as he sleeps in her tent. Deborah's song of triumph includes a passage in praise of Jael, but the "First Lesson" for September 7 comes to an end before reaching that part of the song (verses 24–27). As edited, the "Proper Lesson" encouraged worshipers in St. Paul's and throughout the nation to focus on the calm and prophetic Deborah as a model for Anne, without being distracted by the more active and violent story of Jael.

Blow constructs the text for his anthem by carefully rearranging material from the recommended chapter. He begins with verse 12 but omits the names of both Deborah and Barak, so that the command to awake and utter a song becomes more general. He next sets verses 2–5 and 11, which praise the mighty works of God, then moves forward to a section describing the battle, which he once again reorders (19, 22, 21) so as to end with the verse about the river. After a lengthy imitative treatment of the rushing river, he reaches back to verse 13, from which he takes Deborah's boast that "the Lord made me to have dominion over the mighty," then forward to verse 31, which was not officially a part of the lesson, but which prays that all the Lord's enemies will similarly perish. By selecting and reordering his text, the composer gives Anne credit for the drowning of the foe but without ludicrously casting the invalid queen as a heroic actor. Although there is no definitive proof that Blow himself was responsible for this rearrangement of the biblical text, the musical texture changes at each of the places where the singing text departs from the order of the biblical text. After one soloist declaims the story of the river, for example, the other joins him to celebrate Deborah's "dominion over the mighty" in a canonic duet involving several hair-raising dissonances, after which the first singer, again alone and safely back in triadic harmonies, delivers the prophecy.

Queen Anne's capacity to appreciate this harmonically advanced music, which a puzzled Luttrell thought "very curious," set her apart from her immediate predecessor, as did her determination to appear in public for services of thanksgiving in Wren's grand cathedral. After the Peace of Ryswick in 1697, the dean and choir prepared a thanksgiving service at St. Paul's, expecting King William to attend it; they were disappointed when he chose instead to go to private prayers at Whitehall.[17] Anne, by contrast, took part in many public services of thanksgiving during her reign and displayed a keen interest in their liturgical details. On 2 November 1702, ten days before the first such service, she informed the Archbishop of Canterbury that she wished "to see the form of prayer for the Thanksgiving Day before it was sent to the press,"[18] and in 1708, she personally

Mus. Ex. 7.2: John Blow, excerpt from *Awake, awake, utter a song* (1704).

chose the words for an anthem composed by William Croft.[19] A monarch who took such specific interest in the details of these similar services might well have stipulated that the "proper lessons" in 1704 include the story of Deborah, a woman who gained "dominion over the mighty" through her moral and spiritual force. She might even have found a way to let Mr. Blow know that she would

appreciate an anthem celebrating that ancient female ruler. The careful trunca-
tion of the lesson from Judges 5 also suggests that someone, quite possibly Anne
herself, wanted to keep the focus on Deborah by omitting the story of Jael.

At least one clergyman preaching on this occasion developed the intended
allegory. In a sermon delivered in Rochester cathedral, John Grant pointed to the
parallels by declaring the modern versions of Deborah and Barak too obvious to
name:

> I need not tell you who the Pious and *Glorious Deborah* is, who under
> God has been the Publick Saviour and Deliverer or our *Israel*. I need not
> tell you who the *Brave and Valiant Barak*...is, who with so much Glory
> and Conduct has fought our Battels.

But instead of omitting the slaying of Sisera by Jael, as suggested by the *Form of
Prayer,* Grant took the opportunity to develop the absence of a parallel into another compliment to Marlborough:

> And tho the Ancient *Sisera*...fled from the Field of Battel, and was
> ignominiously slain by a Woman;...the present *Sisera*,...instead of an
> Ignominious Death, is taken Prisoner of War, and his Life is given unto
> him: And tho anciently Prisoners were chain'd to the Wheels of the Vic-
> tor's Chariot, yet the great Humanity of our *Barak*, permits his Prisoner
> *Sisera* the Favour and Honour of Riding in his own Chariot with him.[20]

The famous note that Marlborough scribbled to his wife at the battle's conclusion,
giving his "duty to the Queen" and informing her of his "glorious victory," mentions the fact that "Monsieur Tallard and two other generals are in my coach."[21]
Thanks to Sarah, this message was in print within hours of being received and was
thus familiar to those hearing Grant's sermon. Although the Song of Deborah was
beautifully suited to this celebratory occasion, even Grant, who used the recommended text, could not resist the opportunity to add his clever conceit contrasting Marlborough with Jael, while Sherlock decided to ignore the prescribed text
altogether—perhaps because of some conscious or unconscious unease about
female heads of state. Only the composer Blow embraced the recommended text
wholeheartedly and directed its praise exclusively toward his queen.

As a prophet and ruler, Deborah offered a model of female heroism quite different from Pallas or Elizabeth. To praise Anne as an avatar of Deborah required
neither an awkward retooling of male heroic myth nor a display of gallant male
compliment entailing some measure of unspoken condescension. For just those
reasons, women writers of this period recognized the power of Deborah's story.

In an important poem defending her right to compose poetry, probably written before 1690, Anne Kingsmill Finch cites the prophetess as an enabling model:

> A Woman here, leads fainting Israel on,
> She fights, she wins, she tryumphs with a song,
> Devout, Majestick, for the subject fit,
> And far above her arms, exalts her witt,
> Then, to the peacefull, shady Palm withdraws,
> And rules the rescu'd Nation, with her Laws.[22]

There is no evidence that Queen Anne had seen this poem, which remained in manuscript throughout the poet's life, yet Finch perfectly captures the appeal of Deborah as a prototype for a female ruler. The prophetess "leads fainting Israel on" not with a spear but with the force of her compelling voice, and Anne knew exactly what it meant to lead the fainthearted: she had frequently had to face down men in her own Cabinet who opposed fighting the French on land. Enacting her leadership in poetry and music, Deborah "tryumphs with a song," and Anne paid close attention to the music performed at her thanksgiving services, believing that works like Blow's gave artistic expression to God's providential care for her country. By being "Devout," Deborah becomes "Majestick," and Anne had recently displayed her own religious faith by making a major financial grant to the poor clergy. In one of Finch's most interesting phrases, Deborah is "for the subject fit," and Anne, from the moment she took the throne, had sought to fit her actions to the needs of her subjects. Exalting her wit above her arms, Deborah encourages her generals, but finds her own place as a lawgiver seated beneath a "peacefull, shady Palm." Though fully committed to Marlborough's campaign and vindicated by his victories, Anne longed to rule her "rescu'd Nation" in peace, "Serene and Calm" like Dryden's vision of Britannia.

§

Tranquility, however, proved elusive for the queen in the years leading up to Blenheim. Her campaigns abroad, though sometimes glorious, were always expensive and risky, while partisan and denominational struggles continued to trouble her at home. The parliamentary session that opened in October 1702 began in a promising fashion, with all parties applauding the recent successes in the war, yet even those victories quickly took on partisan resonance as the Tories placed excessive emphasis on the naval campaign, using Ormond and Rooke as counterweights to the popular Marlborough, whose efforts to avoid the rage of party were doomed to fail—not least because of the passionate Whiggery of his wife. In November, faced with a resolution from the House of Commons thanking both Ormond and

Marlborough, Anne had to write a reassuring note to Sarah: "I never looked upon the Sea fight as a victory, and I think what has bin said upon it, as rediculous as any body can do."[23] In seeking to reward her favorite general and protect her husband, she confronted the limits of her monarchial power. Having deftly maneuvered both Houses of Parliament into making addresses to her that explicitly praised the *"wonderful Progress of her Arms, under the Conduct of the Earl of* Marlborough,"[24] she confidently announced that she was making him a duke and awarding him an annual pension of £5,000 during her life. Yet when she asked her legislature to extend that grant to Marlborough's heirs, they demurred, begging leave "humbly to lay before your Majesty the Apprehensions they have, of making a Precedent for the future Alienations of the Revenue of the Crown, which has been so much reduced by the exorbitant Grants of the last Reign."[25] The rhetoric of this address gently reminds Anne of William's "exorbitant Grants" to his favorites while smoothly thanking her for her "unparalleled Grace and Goodness" in devoting some of her income to the nation, but it did not mollify the monarch, who was probably aware that her uncle Laurence Hyde, Earl of Rochester, was actively working behind the scenes to prevent the grant to Marlborough's descendants.[26] Complaining that her generosity had been "maliciously hindred in the parliament," Anne wrote to Sarah, asking "my dear Mrs Freeman & Mr Freeman…to accept of two thousand pound a year out of the privy purse, besides the grant of the five." "This can draw no envy," she added, "for no body need know it."[27]

The queen had better results when she asked Parliament to provide for her husband in case she predeceased him. Mindful of Prince George's chronic asthma, the Commons voted the royal consort a generous grant of £100,000 a year, cynically (and correctly) expecting that it was unlikely to be paid, but the bill ran into trouble in the House of Lords because of a technicality concerning the rights of naturalized citizens. Thanks to quiet lobbying by Marlborough, it eventually passed by a narrow margin, but the suspicious relations between the two Houses were now evident to all. The newly elected Tories enjoyed an overwhelming majority in the House of Commons, but the appointive House of Lords was more closely divided. Thanks to the turmoil in church and state following the Revolution, William had made numerous appointments during his reign, and his choices of peers and bishops, not surprisingly, had included many Whigs.

The contentious debates concerning the most substantive domestic issue of this session underscored the differences between the two chambers. Flushed with their success in the recent elections, the Tory majority in the Commons now pressed for passage of a bill forbidding the practice of "Occasional Conformity," which had been widespread under William. For the past fourteen years, Dissenting Protestants had been able to practice their religion openly, thanks to the Act of Toleration (1689), but they remained unable to attend the universities or hold political office. In order to become eligible for political positions, some men who normally worshiped in Independent or Presbyterian chapels took the sacrament once or twice a year in the established church, "conforming" to the law and successfully entering the political arena; two such men had become Lord Mayors of London during the 1690s. For "High Tories" like Nottingham, this practice was irritating, not least because Dissenters were typically Whigs. The proposed bill, clearly designed to keep Dissenters out of public life, imposed huge fines and loss of office on any public official who attended a Nonconforming religious service.

Loyal as ever to the Church of England, Anne embraced this initiative, presumably persuaded that the established church, whose attendance and collections had fallen off in recent years, was indeed "in danger." In May, signaling her hope for a Tory Parliament, she had declared herself "Incline[d]...to Countenance those who have the truest Zeal to Support...the Church of *England*,"[28] and some High Church zealots immediately came forward to assail the Dissenters and warn of dire dangers to the Church. Within weeks of the queen's speech, Henry Sacheverell, a Tory preacher based in Oxford, published a shrill pamphlet associating modern Dissenters with the Puritans of the Civil War period. Born in 1674, Sacheverell had no personal memories of the Interregnum, yet he urges his case against Occasional Conformity with a pointed description of "the Late, Wretched, Times of *Confusion*, which...made *Rebels* of One part of the Nation, made Downright *Atheists* of the Other, and Prov'd as much the Subversion of *Christianity*, as of Our Government, and Constitution." Those with "any True Allegiance for Our *Sovereign*," he writes, "must Watch against These Crafty, Faithless, and Insidious Persons, who can *Creep* to Our Altars, and Partake of Our Sacraments, that They may be *Qualify'd*, more Secretly and Powerfully to Undermine Us." From this paranoid perspective, the Dissenters, far from being fellow Protestants with a few minor differences in theological belief and liturgical practice, are "Open and Avow'd Enem[ies] to our *Communion*;...Against Whom, every Man, that Wishes Its Welfare, ought to Hang out the *Bloody Flag,* and *Banner* of Defiance."[29]

Such violent rhetoric, now backed by a powerful majority in the House of Commons, was naturally alarming to Dissenters, especially to those who had cherished hope for even greater levels of acceptance. But Occasional Conformity was also abhorrent to many devout Dissenters, whose vivid memories of having their conventicles raided and destroyed made them bitterly hostile to the church their more supple brethren sometimes attended. As early as 1698, Daniel Defoe had chided Sir Humphrey Edwin, the Dissenting Lord Mayor, for attending services of both denominations. "*He who Dissents from an Establish'd Church on any account, but from a real Principle of Conscience, is a Politick, not a Religious Dissenter,*" wrote Defoe. "But if I shall thus Dissent, and yet at the same time Conform; by Conforming I deny my Dissent being lawful, or by my Dissenting I damn my Conforming as sinful."[30] This uncompromising position drew Defoe into a printed exchange with a Nonconformist minister who held more ecumenical views, but their pamphlets were of interest only within the Dissenting community.[31]

When the bill prohibiting Occasional Conformity came before Parliament, however, Defoe saw it as a first step toward renewed persecution on a national scale. Sacheverell had already spoken of "Hang[ing] out the *Bloody Flag*," and an anonymous pamphleteer (possibly Sacheverell again) now had the audacity to claim that the punishments proposed were acts of kindness. As St. Paul had "executed...his wrath against" sinners "with a kind intention of preserving them from greater Evil, and an everlasting Vengeance," the Church's punitive methods, which "discourage our Dissenting Brethren from the dreadful Sin of Schism," will contribute to "their immortal Happiness and Salvation."[32] Concerned to alert his fellow Dissenters to the danger, Defoe chose an artful and devious method to expose the excessive and violent hatred behind the new bill. He timed his action carefully. On 28 November, the Commons passed the bill and sent it to the Lords, who acknowledged receipt of the bill on 2 December. On 1 December, with interest in the bill at its peak, booksellers began to vend a pamphlet called *The Shortest-Way with the Dissenters; or Proposals for the Establishment of the Church*. As in many works of controversy, the title page lists no author and no publisher. The writer, who appears to be the kind of zealot now called a "High-Flyer," makes Sacheverell look moderate. Dismissing as pointless the "light foolish handling" of the Dissenters "by Mulcts, Fines, &c.," he boldly proposes a permanent solution:

> They that will go to Church to be chosen Sheriffs and Mayors, would go to forty Churches rather than be Hang'd.... If one severe Law were made, and punctually executed, that who ever was found at a Conventicle, shou'd be Banish'd the Nation, and the Preacher be Hang'd, we shou'd soon see an end of the Tale, they wou'd all come to Church; and one Age would make us all One again.[33]

It took some time for this work to be recognized as parodic, and even longer for it to be traced to Defoe. Those who first commented on *The Shortest-Way* believed that it was the work of a partisan High Church clergyman, and while modern readers have often expressed surprise that this exaggerated hoax was not immediately recognized as satiric or fraudulent, the idea of a death penalty for embracing a Nonconforming faith was actually all too familiar. During the Popish Plot hysteria of 1679–1680, at least nine Jesuits had been executed, as had a number of unfortunate Catholic laymen. After Louis XIV's revocation of the Edict of Nantes in 1685, numerous French Protestants had suffered death at the hands of a government bent on enforcing religious uniformity, and over four hundred thousand Huguenots had emigrated to other countries, including Great Britain, where they joined the Dissenting community. Bishop Burnet, who led the opposition to the bill in the House of Lords, claimed that "all who pleaded for the bill, did in words declare for the continuance of the toleration, yet the sharpness with which they treated the dissenters in all their speeches, shewed as if they designed their extirpation."[34] By inventing a speaker who explicitly proposes the hanging of Dissenting clergymen, Defoe was suggesting that the most passionate Tories were indeed determined to eliminate their opponents, and that the proposed bill was the first step toward a program of savage persecution.[35]

For Nottingham, the most important politician behind the bill, Defoe's mimicry was intolerable; using the investigative powers he enjoyed as Secretary of State, the Earl successfully discovered who had written the pamphlet and doggedly pursued the author, who promptly went into hiding, evading the authorities for five months.[36] In order to justify his pursuit of Defoe, Nottingham might well have shown Anne the passage in which the imaginary speaker recommends that the queen herself take the lead in destroying the Dissenters:

> THE Queen has promis'd them, to continue them in their tolerated Liberty; and has told us she will be a religious observer of her Word.
>
> WHAT her Majesty will do we cannot help, but what, as the Head of the Church, she ought to do, is another Case: Her Majesty has promised to Protect and Defend the Church of England, and if she cannot effectually do that without the Destruction of the Dissenters, she must of course dispence with one Promise to comply with another.[37]

Directly quoting her past speeches while implying that she has failed in her role as head of the Church, the invented speaker urges the queen to act like the absolutist monarch she was currently opposing on the battlefield. The outrage Anne felt at such preposterous advice gained force because her support for the bill against Occasional Conformity, offered in the hope of helping her beloved church, had already put her in an embarrassing position. She now found it necessary to send Prince George to cast his vote for the bill in the Lords, knowing full well that her husband, who maintained a Lutheran chapel in keeping with his Danish upbringing, was himself an occasional conformist. Her two most trusted advisors, Marlborough and Godolphin, felt similar pressure from the queen and dutifully cast their votes as she wished, but the controversy over this bill nonetheless contributed to the growing rift separating these men from Rochester, Nottingham, and the other High-Flying Tories.

The Lords eventually conditioned their approval on amendments unacceptable to the Commons; when the committee appointed to resolve their differences was unable to do so, the bill was lost. Although the laws remained unchanged, the debate exposed some raw nerves. As Sacheverell's inflammatory rhetoric showed, religious hatred in England was not restricted to pope-baiting. Memories of the Civil War and class-based struggles also found expression in hostility toward the Dissenters, and there were politicians ready to use this religious hostility for their own highly secular ends. Defoe's sly counterfeit, which eventually landed him in jail, fooled many readers because the views he dramatized were not far removed from those actually held by the most passionate advocates of the bill; it embarrassed the queen, who treasured tranquility and consensus, by associating her with those harsh and divisive views. The bill, however, would reappear in several subsequent Parliaments. As Anne's friend William Legge noted, "it was afterwards frequently taken up to inflame parties and distress the court, as opportunities offered themselves to either side."[38]

Anne's actions in the wake of this debacle are revealing. She had every reason to expect determined opposition to the bill from the Dissenters, including the counterfeiting pamphleteer Defoe, but she was surprised and distressed when the Whig bishops in the Lords, especially Burnet, spoke strongly against it. If Defoe's wicked hoax, suggesting that supporters of the bill were bloodthirsty bigots, insulted the queen by holding her ministers up to public ridicule, Burnet's smooth oratory felt like personal disloyalty, especially in light of Anne's kind behavior toward him when he served as Gloucester's preceptor. Leaving Nottingham to hunt down Defoe, she took out her resentment on Burnet by ordering that his lodgings in St. James's Palace be turned over to her old friend Henry Compton, Bishop of London, who had supported the bill.[39] At the same time, however, she exerted her control over one of the strongest advocates of the controversial measure: her uncle the Earl of Rochester. Aware that Rochester had worked against the grants to Marlborough and Prince George, and displeased with his continued opposition to her war policies, she ordered him to go to Ireland and take up his position there as Lord Lieutenant. When he demurred, she replaced him and removed him from the Privy Council. Although her friend Sarah habitually saw the world in strongly partisan terms and stubbornly tried to win the queen over to a more tolerant view of the Whigs, Anne had already begun to realize that differences of opinion *within* the parties might prove as troublesome to her as those *between* the parties. Godolphin and Rochester were both Tories, but they disagreed about many issues, both foreign and domestic; there were similar disparities between the views of a traditional grandee like Somerset and those of a radical republican like Sarah's son-in-law Charles Spencer, now Earl of Sunderland, though both were nominally Whigs. In grasping those differences and acting upon them, the queen showed her evolving understanding of the complexities of modern partisan politics. Her growing sophistication, however, did not weaken her nostalgia for tradition: her fundamental conception of loyalty was still more personal than ideological.

§

While these distressing dramas were being played out in the political arena, Queen Anne celebrated the first New Year's Day of her reign, a day traditionally marked by an ode in praise of the monarch. Among the servants she had inherited from William were his Master of the Music, John Eccles, and his Poet Laureate, Nahum Tate, who collaborated on the expected musical work. At the beginning of the reign, the music publisher John Walsh had launched a periodical called the *Monthly Mask of Vocal Music,* which gave the musical public access to songs recently performed in the theatres and at court, including this New Year's ode. Although Tate's last New Year's ode for William had addressed the Members of Parliament, his first for Anne entirely suppresses domestic politics. In an aria sung by Richard Elford, with a trumpet obbligato probably played by John Shore, Tate and Eccles picture "*Britain's ANNA*" bringing peace to "*Europe's* Sighing Plains":

> Sound thy loudest Trumpet, Fame,
> The Joyful Jubilee Proclaim,
> Through *Europe's* Sighing Plains,
>   And Nations long Opprest;
> Tell 'em *Britain's ANNA* Reigns,
> *Britannia's ANNA* Reigns, and *Europe* shall have Rest.[40]

As practiced in ancient Israel, the jubilee, which occurred every fifty years, included the freeing of slaves and the returning of property to its original owners. In keeping with that tradition, Tate predicts that "*Britain's ANNA*" will liberate peoples and lands "Opprest" and enslaved by the absolutist monarch Louis. For readers applying the formula of a jubilee every fifty years, there were other intriguing possibilities. Anne's coronation had occurred exactly fifty-one years after the coronation of Charles II. Calling the first New Year of her reign a "Joyful Jubilee" was a way of implying that the crown had now returned to the Stuarts, its rightful owners.

In this new reign the royal birthday, another occasion for formal celebration, would always come a scant five weeks after New Year's Day, a circumstance requiring poets and composers to produce the two required odes on a tight schedule. Showing his awareness of that challenge, Tate begins his poem with the Muses asking the goddess of Spring to make a premature appearance, bringing flowers

"To Crown the Day that Crowns the Year." The goddess, however, explains that she will not appear until the queen's birthday:

> Like You (the Goddess Thus Replies)
> This Young Auspicious Day I prize,
> But One more Blest is drawing near;
> Till Then, my Infant-Sweets must sleep,
> And I my fragrant Glories keep
> For ANNA's Royal Day; 'tis That which Crowns the Year.

As Tate surely knew, preparations for the birthday were already under way; on 2 January, Luttrell reported the passage of "a privy seal…for paying out of the exchequer 20,000*l.* to the duke of Somerset, master of the horse for the queens liveries, &c. against her majesties birthday the 6th of February."[41] The Laureate probably also knew that his colleague Eccles was getting around the need for a second new composition by refurbishing a birthday ode he had composed for William but never used, adapting it to serve for Anne's birthday. The original librettist, Peter Motteux, added some new material, including the lines describing Anne as "Majestick and serene…among the Isles a Queen," but recycled most of the original, making minimal adjustments. "From this happy day we date, / William's birth and Europe's joys," for example, became "From this happy day we date, / Anna's birth And Britain's joys."[42]

When the royal birthday arrived, Abel Boyer reported that "there had not been such a Magnificent Appearance at Court for Twenty Years past."[43] Diplomats and peers always purchased elaborate new clothing for the monarch's birthday, and on the first such occasion of a new reign, the expenditures were especially lavish. Establishing the pattern she would follow on most of her future birthdays, the queen heard morning prayer in her Chapel Royal, then received formal compliments from the nobility.[44] Later in the morning, probably unaware of its original form, she heard the ode by Motteux and Eccles, performed by musicians from the Chapel Royal, including Elford. "At Noon," the newspapers reported, "all the Tower Guns were discharged,"[45] the first of a number of public displays of joy occurring in concert with the private entertainments enjoyed by the nobility. The queen dined, played cards in her drawing room, and heard a second performance in the evening, an "Entertainment of Musick" with words by the minor poet Thomas Wall and music by John Abell, a well-known Scottish singer who had spent ten years serving the exiled James II at St. Germain. Again avoiding domestic politics, this musical masque celebrates "the Success of Her Majesty's Arms by Sea and Land," with "Performers Representing *Fame, Pallas, Victory, Triumph,* and *Britain.*"[46] As the queen's guests took part in "a magnificent Ball…with other Diversions suitable to the Solemnity of the Day," the common people saw "a Fine Firework…lighted in the Artillery-Ground, representing the Letters A. R. and P. G. and likewise VIVAT REGINA.… The Streets of London and Westminster were Illuminated, and there appeared all other Demonstrations of Publick Joy, that a Loyal People could shew to a Gracious Princess."[47] Some of those "Demonstrations of Publick Joy" were alcoholic, as John Tutchin reported in his *Observator,* which marked the birthday with some terrible poems linking Anne as closely as possible to William and praying that she would favor the Whigs. "May no curst *Tory* to her Councils creep / Nor have Command by *Land,* or on the *Deep,*" wrote Tutchin's "Country-man," excusing his wretched verses by explaining that he wrote them with a hangover from the birthday, having spent the previous evening in "the Tavern, where we Drank the Queens Health so long that my Head-Ak'd so the next Morning, I was not able to go to Church in the Forenoon."[48]

Five days later, those not invited to St. James's reportedly had an opportunity to hear the birthday ode by Motteux and Eccles performed at Lincoln's Inn Fields, as part of a mixed bill featuring *Acis and Galatea,* a masque written in 1700 by the same poet and composer.[49] Within the year, John Walsh had printed scores for both the New Year's song and the birthday song, enabling amateur musicians to own the new pieces composed for the queen.[50] As far back as 1697, Anne had arranged for a birthday ode by Draghi to have a commercial performance "by her Royal Highness's Command";[51] while there is no reason to think that she specifically instructed her Master of the Music to seek a wider audience for the odes of 1703, he would not have done so if he thought she wanted them kept within the walls of the palace. Here as in so many other areas, Anne appears to have lived in two time frames: her fondness for the panegyric imagery embodied in odes and masques is in keeping with her interest in the traditional trappings of monarchy, but her acquiescence in the wider distribution of the New Year's and birthday music shows a surprisingly modern desire to include more of her subjects in these celebrations, thus building political support. After her disappointments during the first few months of the current Parliament, the queen was freshly aware of how much she needed that support.

Thanks to the use of the reworked ode by Motteux, Tate did not have to produce two court odes in rapid succession this year, so he turned his attention to another kind of panegyric. The painter John Closterman, winner of the commission to paint the new monarch for the Guildhall, had finally completed his painting, a formal portrait showing the queen with the allegorical figures of Justice and Prudence, who appeared on pedestals adorned with the arms of the City of London. The painting has unfortunately disappeared, but a surviving study in oils and an engraving made from the original give some idea of the central figure.

Studio of John Closterman, study for *Queen Anne* (c. 1702).

Seizing this opportunity, Tate composed his *Portrait-Royal*, an elaborate poem "upon Her Majesty's Picture Set up in Guild-Hall...Drawn by Mr. Closterman." Dedicated to Prince George and published shortly before the anniversary of Anne's accession,[52] this substantial work was the Laureate's way of showing the royal couple that he could write something longer and more complex than the short conventional verses required for the New Year's and birthday celebrations. Adapting the old tradition of poems telling painters how to depict important

Anna D. G. Angliæ Scotiæ Fra. et Hib. Regina.

John Faber, Jr., *Queen Anne*, mezzotint after John Closterman (c. 1725–1756).

persons or battles, and borrowing ideas from some recent poems on the sister arts, including Dryden's great poem to Sir Godfrey Kneller, Tate writes most of his poem in the voice of the Muse of Poetry, who confesses herself outdone by the work of the painter:

> How starv'd our Rhet'rick, and our Style how faint
> To Pictur'd Passion, and Pathetick Paint!
> To those warm Colours, which I here behold,
> My Tropes are Flat, my Metaphors all Cold:
> Wit's sprightly Air is lost; her Varnish flies,

And all the Light'ning of her Fancy dies.
PAINTING Alone presents Victorious Bright, ⎤
With radiant Glories of resistless Light,   ⎬
To Sally, seize, and Captivate the Sight.   ⎦
Your's is the Wreath of Fame by Conquest due, ⎤
And all my vanquish'd Pride can now pursue,   ⎬
Triumphant Dame, must be henceforth to Copy You. ⎦

In this fascinating passage, the female Muses stand in for Tate and Closterman, the actual male artists. In order to praise the "Pathetick Paint" of her rival,
Poetry dismisses the tropes and metaphors of her own art, though she wittily appropriates "Varnish," an important element in the painter's craft, as a metaphor for
language. In directly praising Painting, she describes the other Muse as a "Triumphant Dame" who can "Sally, seize, and Captivate" like Marlborough's grenadiers.
By displacing both actual combat and the lively rivalry between painters and poets
into the imagined world of the female Muses, Tate prepares the way for his poem's
central topic: the grandeur of the queen. In reply to the enthusiastic praise offered
her by Poetry, the Muse of Painting ascribes her success to the glorious qualities
of her subject:

Your Panegyrick Paint's too richly spread;
The Stroke's too Bold:—if my Performance please,
And with unusual Charms Beholders seize,
'Twas Fortune, and I must ascribe it All
To the Unparalel'd ORIGINAL
The QUEEN, the Prosp'rous QUEEN—
So much the Darling of Propitious Fates,
Success upon her very Shadow Waits.

According to this passage, even a work of art as fine as Closterman's portrait is
merely a "Shadow" of the queen, though that shadow possesses "unusual Charms."

Addressing a "gazing Throng" whose sudden appearance Tate must awkwardly excuse in a footnote, the Muse of Poetry now asks the Britons to "Feast
[their] Eyes on This Design, / Where Art's Confed'rate Pow'rs and Forces join."
Newspaper accounts of the ongoing war typically described the English and
Dutch forces as the "Confederate Powers," and these lines, published as all eyes
turned toward the next phase of the war, conflate the artistic skills of Anne's favored artist with the military and diplomatic skills of her favored general. In a
later catalogue of British worthies, Tate gives a prominent place to "Triumphant
MARLBOROUGH, . . . Who could, with double Fame— / The Soldier's and the

Statesman's Part sustain." Despite the effusive praise given to the Muse of Paint-
ing, the Muse of Poetry has now taken over the poem. In order to delineate the
"Complicated Glories" of Anne's face, she develops literary allusions to the fierce
Amazons of the classical world and the calm, yet effective Deborah of the Old
Testament:

> Whom would not that Majestick Awe confound?
> Who would not wish to see such Mildness Crown'd?
> With Amazonian Terror Arm'd, yet Calm
> As Deborah beneath her Grove of Palm.[53]

The devout queen knew her Bible well, but it is possible that Tate's allusion to
Deborah in this poem influenced her choice of scriptural passages for the Blenheim celebration some eighteen months later. Although Anne normally sought to
produce "Awe" in her subjects by a public image emphasizing "Mildness," she was
also capable of "Amazonian Terror." On 30 March 1703, for example, Luttrell
reported that "Mr. Gough, who keeps the Thatch't House tavern by St. James's,
is ordered to be prosecuted by the attorney general for suffering gameing in his
house upon Sundays." There were evidently some teeth in Anne's proclamations against vice. Even more revealing is a report on prisoner exchanges in
early April: "the marquesse d' Galicioner might have been released for the
Dutch consuls daughter at Leghorn, taken by the French; but he scrupling at
first to be exchanged for a woman, her majestie has now refused him her liberty."[54] As the French prisoner discovered, Anne had little patience with those
who underrated women, either as participants in an exchange or as monarchs.
Nor was she afraid to exercise critical judgment in artistic matters. At the Treasury meeting on 19 May, one of the petitions was from Sir Godfrey Kneller,
"praying payment of £570 due to him for drawing several pictures of Her Majesty and the late King." Anne's response was icy: "Her Majesty does not care for
the picture of £350; the others are to be paid for." The "picture of £350" was
Kneller's large portrait of William on horseback, so the queen's decision may
have been personal as well as aesthetic.[55] The day after this meeting, Defoe,
who had hidden from the authorities for months, was finally captured. Imprisoned for "seditious libel," he, too, felt the queen's wrath: despite his guilty plea,
his submissive letters, and his offer to serve her in the army, she concluded that
his "Confession...amounts to nothing" and saw to it that the pamphleteer
stood in the pillory and returned to prison.[56]

Tate's poem on the portrait is uneven and at times obscure, but his attempts
to find appropriate metaphors for a female monarch are fascinating. Tropes previously used for the personified London or Thames, treating the city or the river as

a "Maiden Queen" courted by the world, reappear as ways to praise an actual ruling queen. Speaking through the Muse, Tate describes the phallic scepter engaging in an erotic courtship of the queen's hand and breast:

> See how th'Imperial Emblem of Command,
> The Royal Sceptre, Courts her Sacred Hand;
> And Leans his Golden Honours on her Breast.

The orb of command becomes a cherished child, cradled by the nurturing queen:

> The giddy Globe Rouls to her Side for Rest:
> There, like a Cradled Infant, Safe from Harm,
> And Rock'd Asleep on her Protecting Arm.[57]

Though Anne's adolescent days of courtship and flirtation had ended long ago, the scepter, personifying "Command," still seeks her as a mate; though her actual infants were all now dead, the world itself has become her "Cradled Infant." If these metaphors seem far-fetched, even "metaphysical," they do at least show Tate trying hard to accommodate the discourse of monarchial power to the fact of a female ruler.

§

In what looks like an awkward attempt to ingratiate himself personally with the monarch, Tate also includes some lines recalling the death of Gloucester: "When ALBION's Self Convulsive Passion felt, / When Marbles Wept, and Flinty Rockes did melt."[58] In the very month in which she received this poem, Queen Anne had reason to recall that loss with terrible intensity. Young Jack Churchill, Gloucester's friend and Sarah's darling son, was now a handsome youth of seventeen addressed as the Marquess of Blandford. Still enrolled at Cambridge, he was planning to leave the university in March in order to accompany his father on the next campaign. But as the day of his longed-for adventure drew near, Blandford fell violently ill with what proved to be smallpox. Sarah hurried to his bedside, and Anne sent her own doctors after her. The letters surviving from this agonizing period make for painful reading; they show Anne desperately hoping that her beloved Sarah would not suffer the same terrible loss she had recently experienced. "I am mightily vexed," she wrote on 18 February,

> that the Doctors have bin soe long upon the road, for not one minute should be lost in you dear childs condition, and I wish the messenger that carys the medicins my dear Mrs Freeman sends for could fly, that nothing

may be wanting the moment there is any occasion. I can't help being in a little better hart than I was when I wrote this morning, becaus I have bin told since, that tho bloody water is a very ill Symtom, yet severall have don well that has had it. I pray God from the Bottom of my soul that Ld Blanford may be one of that number. I shall be all impatience till I heare again, and shall end this with assuring my deare Mrs Freeman that her poor unfortunate faithful Morly is on the rack for you, and beging you would have a care of your dear dear self.[59]

The end came two days later, and Marlborough, who arrived in time to be present at his beloved son's death, took his distraught wife home to St. Albans. He was under orders to proceed to Holland the next week, so the couple had a very limited time in which to grieve together. Although Anne sent daily letters asking permission to visit, Sarah clung to John, and even pushed Godolphin to allow her to accompany her husband to Europe, a request he politely declined.[60]

From Anne's point of view, Sarah's devastating loss was an opportunity for commiseration, and she was evidently frustrated by being kept at a distance. "Tho hearing from you is allways an unexpressible satisfaction and would be soe now especially," she writes on 22 February, "yet I know soe well what you feel, that I am not soe unreasonable to expect a letter till it is more easy to you to writt than I beleeve it is at this time."[61] A day later, with Sarah making preparations to come to London, she strikes a note of resignation that does not entirely hide her petulance:

> It would have bin a great satisfaction to your poor unfortunate faithfull Morly if you would have given me leave to have com to St Albans, for the unfortunate ought to com to the unfortunate, but since you will not have me, I must content my self as well as I can, till I have the happiness of seeing you heare.[62]

But if the queen believed that their shared experience of losing a cherished son would restore the closeness she had once enjoyed with Sarah, she was sorely mistaken. By May, she was writing to Sarah about the state of their relationship with genuine alarm:

> I came from London yesterday with a very heavy hart, to see my deare Mrs Freeman look in soe much trouble, and find her soe formall and cold to her poor unfortunat faithfull Morly, oh how is it possible then when one sees such a change to forbeare asking the cause, for Christ Jesus sake tell me whats the matter, lay all the faults you think me guilty of before me, that I may vindicate my self and not lye under your displeasure.[63]

The petitions the queen received daily from soldiers, widows, and criminals under sentence of death often employed language similar to the final phrases used here. "But my Lord," wrote Defoe to Nottingham after being revealed as the author of *The Shortest-Way*, "if after this I should still have the Misfortune to remain under her Majesties Displeasure, I am then her Most Humble Peticoner, that she will please to Remitt the rigor of Prosecution."[64] By asking to vindicate herself and begging not to "lye under your displeasure," Anne was treating Sarah as if her favorite were the monarch and she were a humble petitioner.

Gossips at the time were quick to compare the two women, contrasting Anne's calm resignation with Sarah's histrionic grieving: "We hear the Duchess of Marlborough bears not her affliction like her mistress," wrote Anne Pye, wife of a prominent parliamentarian, to her cousin Abigail, wife of Robert Harley, "if report be true that it has near touched her head."[65] Neither of the two surviving poems on the death of Blandford, however, compares or links the two women. One poet focuses mainly on Anne, the other exclusively on Sarah. An anonymous Latin elegy on the young man's death, probably the work of a Cambridge student, makes much of the queen's grief: "We see the Queen of *Albion* bemoaning your fate," writes the poet, "and her sacred cheeks made wet with tears." He even imagines Anne saying that Gloucester has demanded Blandford as his companion in the Elysian Fields, where they live now as a happy pair.[66] Although the real Anne never goes that far in her letters to Sarah, her insistence that she knows how Sarah feels and her inclusion of Sarah among the ranks of the "unfortunate" are attempts to claim a kinship in grief and loss. Sarah's resistance to those attempts suggests that she saw her own loss as different from Anne's, a view confirmed by the other poem on Blandford's death, a lengthy pastoral by William Congreve called *The Tears of Amaryllis for Amyntas*.

Although he had written no new plays since *The Way of the World* (1700), Congreve was a prominent figure in London and a leading member of the Kit-Cat Club, a largely Whig association of literary men including Joseph Addison, Richard Steele, John Vanbrugh, and Jacob Tonson. Sarah's daughters were among the beauties toasted when the Kit-Cats assembled for drink and social chat, but the duchess disapproved of Congreve's friendship with her married but flirtatious daughter Harriet. His hope to overcome her suspicions may have been one of the poet's reasons for making Sarah's personal plight the focus of his work. Despite having previously dedicated a play to Anne, Congreve never once alludes to the queen or the Duke of Gloucester in this poem. His emphasis falls on the beauty and despair of the bereft Amaryllis:

> 'Twas then that Amaryllis, Heav'nly Fair,
> Wounded with Grief, and wild with her Despair,

Forsook her Myrtle Bow'r and Rosie Bed,
To tell the Winds her Woes, and mourn *Amyntas* dead.

As the poem begins, we might suppose that the "Heav'nly Fair" Amaryllis is the mistress of Amyntas, or possibly his sister, but Congreve quickly makes it clear that she is his mother:

No Voice, no whisp'ring Sigh, no murm'ring Groan,
Presum'd to mingle with a Mother's Moan;
Her Cries alone her Anguish could express,
All other Mourning would have made it less.

The insistence here that only Amaryllis, weeping alone, can express her anguish, that "All other Mourning" would diminish her grief, dramatizes in mythical terms Sarah's refusal to allow Anne to join her in mingled sorrow. In the speech Congreve writes for Amaryllis, she insists that her loss is unique:

Have I not Cause, ye cruel Pow'rs, to mourn?
Lives there like me another Wretch forlorn?
Tell me, thou Sun that round the World dost shine,
Hast thou beheld another Loss like mine?

The queen probably saw this poem, which was dedicated to Godolphin and circulated widely in manuscript before being printed in July. If she noticed these lines, she might well have responded that she herself was "another Wretch forlorn," that she had indeed experienced "another Loss" like Sarah's. Her favorite's refusal to acknowledge the similarity of their losses, reinforced by Congreve's smooth pastoral, was wounding.

Effectively answering those gossips who interpreted Sarah's grief as insanity and compared her unfavorably to the queen, *The Tears of Amaryllis* presents the duchess as a beauty made more attractive by her sorrow. There were many such figures in recent literature. Congreve's only tragedy, the play he dedicated to Princess Anne in 1697, was called *The Mourning Bride,* and the actress Anne Bracegirdle, who played the inconsolable Almeria, often played beautiful women racked with grief. Mournful ladies were also attractive to painters: a portrait long attributed to John Riley, now thought to be by John Closterman, shows Anne Morrice, a celebrated beauty, in mourning for her husband, with her left arm resting on a funeral urn. The dolphin fountain that she touches with her right hand represents the hope of resurrection, but the somber palette and gloomy landscape insist upon an aesthetic of grief (color plate 15).[67] A few years after Congreve's poem for

Sarah, his friend Joseph Addison would codify his culture's linking of beauty and sorrow in his famous series of essays on "The Pleasures of the Imagination":

> There is yet another Circumstance which recommends a Description more than all the rest, and that is, if it represents to us such Objects as are apt to raise a secret Ferment in the Mind of the Reader, and to work, with Violence, upon his Passions. For, in this Case, we are at once warmed, and enlightened, so that the Pleasure becomes more Universal, and is several ways qualified to entertain us. Thus, in Painting, it is pleasant to look on the Picture of any Face, where the Resemblance is hit, but the Pleasure increases, if it be the Picture of a Face that is beautiful, and is still greater, if the Beauty be softened with an Air of Melancholy or Sorrow.[68]

As he pondered how to address the duchess, who was only forty-two and still a striking beauty, Congreve saw an opportunity to treat her bereavement as an instance of this trope. Hoping to please her by emphasizing her youthful appearance, he paid special attention to her hair:

> Her loosely flowing Hair, all radiant bright,
> O'er-spread the dewy Grass like Streams of Light:
> As if the Sun had of his Beams been shorn,
> And cast to Earth the Glories he had worn.
> A Sight so lovely sad, such deep Distress
> No Tongue can tell, no Pencil can express.[69]

The language comparing Sarah's tresses to the beams "shorn" from the sun and "cast to Earth" is more than complimentary; Congreve delicately alludes to a dramatic episode in the marriage of the Churchills, a story he had probably heard from their daughter Harriet. During the later years of William's rule, John invited to dinner a Tory lord particularly hated by his passionately Whiggish wife. He told Sarah about the unwanted guest while she was at her dressing-table, and she expressed her anger by cutting off most of her hair and throwing it at him.[70] Conflating this anecdote with the classical motif of mourners rending their hair, Congreve depicts his Amaryllis as "A Sight so lovely sad" that she is beyond the expressive capacities of a poet's "Tongue" or a painter's "Pencil."

§

Aware that her sympathetic mistress would not insist that she remain in constant attendance at court during this period of mourning, Sarah could give herself time to play the role of the melancholy beauty, but neither the duke nor the queen had such leisure. Marlborough sailed for the Continent on 5 March and immediately set about preparing for the next phase of the campaign, in which he would contend once more with the incompetence and caution of his allies. In one letter to Godolphin, he reports seeing a "very great procession" in Cologne and admits that "the thoughts how pleased poor Lord Churchill [i.e., Blandford] would have been with such a sight, has added very much to my uneasiness. . . . I doe wish from my soul I could think less of him."[71] In a letter to his wife written on the same day, he gives more details of the same procession but suppresses any mention of his grief, speaking instead of his hope that she might be with child, an expectation prompted by an interruption in Sarah's menstrual cycle, presumably caused by the stress of her grief.

The queen, though writing daily to her beloved Sarah, was also mindful of her official duties. One week after Blandford's death, she donned her formal robes in order to prorogue her Parliament, in a speech thanking them "for the great Supplies with which you enable Me to carry on the War" and the "Readiness you have shewn in the Provision made for the Prince." Without directly mentioning the controversial bill against Occasional Conformity, she reaffirmed her hope that "such of [my Subjects] as have the Misfortune to dissent from the Church of *England* will rest secure and satisfied in the Act of Toleration, which I am firmly resolved to maintain," while insisting once more on her own support for the established church:

> I shall always make it My own particular Care, to encourage and maintain this Church, as by Law established, and every the least Member of it, in all their just Rights and Privileges; and, upon all Occasions of Promotions to any Ecclesiastical Dignity, I shall have a very just Regard to such as are eminent and remarkable for their Piety, Learning, and constant Zeal for the Church; that, by this and all other Methods which shall be thought proper, I may transmit it securely settled to Posterity.[72]

Perhaps because of her constant ill-health, Anne now returned frequently to the idea of leaving her church, her nation, and her family "securely settled." In a letter to Sarah, written on the very day she delivered this speech, she used similar language in speaking of Prince George: "The Parliament is at last up, and now that the Princes bill is past, when ever it pleases God to take me out of this world, I shall dye in quiet, which I should not have don if I had left him unseteld."[73] Still, she remained painfully aware that her lack of living progeny left the succession dangerously "unseteld." When Sarah told her that an almanac had predicted another royal pregnancy, she responded wistfully: "I have heard of the Almanack you mention, and should be very glad what it says may com to pass, that I may be soe happy when I dye as to leave my poor Country seteld upon a lasting foundation, I am sure nothing shall be wanting on my part towards it."[74] And when Sarah, still missing her period, concluded in July that she was pregnant, Anne expressed her own joy by declaring herself willing to die:

> I can not express how glad I am of the good news you send me of your deare self, upon my word. Since my great misfortune of loosing my dear child, I have not known soe much real satisfaction in any thing that has happened as this pleasing news has given me, and I shall now be very well contented to leave my dear Mrs Freeman behind me, which otherways would have bin an unexpressible mortification to me.[75]

As long as she remained in this world and on the throne, however, Anne needed Sarah—not only for her company, but for her service as Groom of the Stole and Keeper of the Privy Purse. She was therefore alarmed when Sarah, late in May, proposed giving up those posts, evidently suggesting that her husband was also ready to retire, though that was not the case. Marlborough had written to his wife on 13 May, gently chiding her for her partisan passions and accurately predicting that he himself would eventually be a victim of party politics:

> I am very sorry to see by all your letters that the factions continue soe extreamly angry. As for myself I doe assure you, I shal meadle with nether partys, having noe privat ends of my own, but whielst I am in the world endeavour to serve her Majesty the best I can. I know by this methode whichever party is upermust will be angry with mee, so that at last the Queen will be obligd by them to let mee retir.[76]

It is a remarkable instance of Sarah's capacity to see the world through her own eyes that she construed and reported this letter as expressing an active desire to retire. Having just captured Bonn after a difficult siege, Marlborough was writing in the midst of a campaign that required all of his skills. In writing to Sarah, he often expresses his desire to "live quietly" with her at St. Albans, and in writing to Godolphin, he expresses weariness and frustration with his Dutch allies, but in both cases he always affirms his determination to serve the queen. He was not preparing to step down.

The queen, however, had heard from Sarah that both of the Marlboroughs were ready to resign their posts. Faced with an apparent crisis, she mustered all her eloquence to insist upon their continued service:

> The thoughts that both my dear Mrs Freeman and Mr Freeman seem to have of retyering, gives me no small uneasyness, and therfore I must say

something on that subject. It is no wonder at all people in your posts should be weary of the world who are soe continually troubled with all the harry and impertinencys of it, but give me leave to say you should a litle consider your faithfull freinds and poor Country, which must be ruined if ever you should putt your melancholy thoughts in execution. As for your poor unfortunate faithfull Morly she could not bear it, for if ever you should forsake me, I would have nothing more to do with the world, but make another abdycation, for what is a Crown, when the support of it is gon? I never will forsake your dear self, Mr Freeman nor Mr Montgomery, but allways be your constant faithfull Servant, and we four must never part, till death mows us down with his impartiall hand.[77]

Mindful of her own recent expressions of weariness with the world and impatience with its "impertinencys," Anne expresses some sympathy for the harried Churchills, but she also signals her belief that Sarah's "melancholy thoughts" have come from immoderate grief. By describing the possible retirement as "putt[ing] your melancholy thoughts in execution," she treats it as if it were an act of suicide and asks her favorite to concentrate instead on her "faithfull freinds and poor Country." Painting a dismal picture of her forsaken self, she dangles the idea that she might abdicate, fully aware of what a disaster that might prove for her friends. In order to encourage Sarah to continue in her service, she describes herself as "your constant faithfull Servant" and promises never to forsake the Churchills or Godolphin, who was "Mr. Montgomery" in the code employed by "Mrs. Freeman" and "Mrs. Morley." Scholars commenting on this letter have often puzzled over Anne's failure to mention her husband, Prince George, who was sometimes "Mr. Morley." But no one has ever noticed that the final phrase comes from a translation of Horace by the poet Abraham Cowley, whom Anne had loved from her youth and quoted in earlier letters:

> We look on Men, and wonder at such odds
>   'Twixt things that were the same by Birth;
> We look on Kings as Giants of the Earth,
> These Giants are but Pigmeys to the Gods.
>   The humblest Bush and proudest Oak,
> Are but of equal proof against the Thunder-stroke.
> Beauty, and Strength, and Wit, and Wealth, and Power
>   Have their short flourishing hour;
>   And love to see themselves, and smile,
> And joy in their Preeminence a while;
>   Even so in the same Land,

Poor Weeds, rich Corn, gay Flowers together stand;
Alas, Death Mowes down all with an impartial Hand.[78]

Quoting from memory and clearly expecting Sarah to recognize that she was quoting a poem they both knew, Anne brings into play a memorable expression of the fragility of all human lives, including those of kings and queens. Sarah's beauty, Marlborough's strength, Congreve's wit, Godolphin's wealth, and Anne's own power might "joy in their Preeminence a while," but their hour of flourishing would inevitably be short. Death had mown down Anne's cherished son, and now Sarah's. It threatened John daily on the battlefield and would soon claim Prince George. The queen's own health, wrecked by her heroic efforts to produce an heir, was at best precarious. Yet in seeking a way to express the complex feelings called forth by this situation, Anne sensed the limits of her own style and turned to her beloved "Mr. Cowley."

In choosing to conclude her personal and heartfelt plea with a classical allusion, Anne was hoping that the power of poetry and tradition might induce Sarah to abandon the fashionable modern pose of the melancholy beauty and embrace the Stoicism of Horace, linked strongly in her mind to patriotism and duty. Both women had passed through the kind of education typically available to affluent girls, preparing them for such activities as acting in *Calisto,* but preventing them from reading Latin literature in the original. Anne's appropriation of Horace (by way of Cowley) was an attempt to claim the view of emotion her society had traditionally coded as male, in which "moral sentiment" was "a bond between elite males deeply *but reticently* involved in one another's humiliations and triumphs of self-discipline."[79] The queen's innate reticence, a fundamental part of her personality, made her uneasy in the presence of Sarah's more histrionic expressions of emotion, though her own expressions of love for her favorite, set down in her private correspondence, are often quite passionate. Indeed, Anne may have originally been drawn to Sarah because she saw in her beautiful, high-strung favorite a wider range of emotional expression than she could readily call forth from herself. Still, Sarah's prolonged and intense expressions of grief for her recent loss embarrassed Anne, as did her partisan fervor for the Whigs, which was a growing source of friction between them.

The conflict played out at this moment in the personal relations between the queen and her favorite, with Sarah embracing the role of the mourning beauty and Anne insisting on self-discipline and loyalty, is a particular instance of their culture's complex, inconsistent, and shifting attitude toward human emotions. Although differing theories of emotion do not correspond in any simple way to political parties or artistic styles, they played a significant role in the way both politics and the arts developed under Anne. Though few were now alive who personally remembered the Civil War and the Interregnum, one influential narrative excoriated the Puritan and Parliamentarian forces of the seventeenth century as "fanatics" and "enthusiasts" whose emotional zeal had murdered a monarch and thrown a nation into chaos. The First Earl of Clarendon's *History of the Rebellion*, written in the early 1670s but now appearing in print for the first time, was a particularly trenchant version of this way of reading the previous century's turmoil. According to Anne's uncle Rochester, who was editing his father's work for publication, modern Whigs, including Sarah, were lineal descendants of these passionate rebels. Thanks to his stubborn opposition to the land war and his high-handed disdain for the Marlboroughs, Rochester had incurred Anne's wrath and lost his official positions, but her movement away from such Tory extremists did not make the queen any more attentive to Sarah's fervent pleas on behalf of her Whig associates. Suspicious of the Whigs as hotheaded revolutionaries, Anne continued to favor moderate Tories. Godolphin—patient, unflappable, competent, loyal, and traditional in his manners—was ideally suited to serve her, as was Marlborough, who was sincerely "sorry to see...that the factions continue soe extreamly angry." Both men evidently had emotional lives: John's love for Sarah, touchingly expressed in his letters, was deep and strong, while Godolphin had been so devastated by his wife's death in childbirth in 1678 that he never remarried, though he cherished tender feelings for Sarah and (more dangerously) for Maria Beatrice, James II's widow, whom he had served as a young man. Anne, who had genuine insight into other people's emotions, knew all of this, but she depended on her Captain-General and her Lord Treasurer to leave their passions at the door when serving the Crown. Sarah's inability to do so was slowly eroding their cherished relationship; indeed, the shrillness of her advocacy was actually increasing the queen's aversion to the Whigs.

A similar conflict about the expression of emotion appears in writings about the arts in this period. Poets and playwrights had long been smugly confident that literature, with its capacity to appeal to the rational mind, was superior to painting and music, which they regarded as less intellectual, more emotional, and more "feminine" than poetry. Dryden's influential "Parallel of Poetry and Painting" (1695) provides a typical formulation of this prejudice with respect to painting:

> The Authour of this Book...tells you almost in the first lines of it, that the *chief end of Painting is to please the Eyes: and 'tis one great End of Poetry to please the Mind.* Thus far the Parallel of the Arts holds true: with this difference, That the principal end of Painting is to please; and the chief design of Poetry is to instruct. In this the latter seems to have the advantage of the former.[80]

The "advantage" Dryden claims for poetry is intellectual and moral. Poetry, he insists, has the capacity to "instruct," while painting can only "please." His preface to his opera *Albion and Albanius* (1685) offers a parallel instance of the same prejudice, this time applied to music:

> The recitative part of the *Opera* requires a more masculine Beauty of expression and sound: the other, which (for want of a proper *English* Word) I must call *The Songish Part,* must abound in the softness and variety of Numbers: its principal Intention, being to please the Hearing, rather than to gratify the understanding.[81]

By referring to the more lyrical parts of the opera as "the other" and naming them with a deliberately awkward coinage, *"The Songish Part,"* Dryden makes arias, duets, and choruses appear to be imported commodities for which there is no "proper *English* word." It is remarkable that a poet with Dryden's lyrical gifts should have been so threatened by the emotive power of music that he would single out for praise the recitative, that part of opera in which the music, by becoming subordinate to the text, loses much of its power to move us.

In the seventeen years since the premiere of *Albion and Albanius,* consumers of the arts had become much more interested in what Addison would call "Objects ... apt to raise a secret Ferment in the Mind of the Reader, and to work, with Violence, upon his Passions." Interest in the musical expression of feelings had grown steadily, as had interest in collecting or commissioning paintings. Tate's poem on the royal portrait, in keeping with this trend, praises painting for its "Charms that can inspire / Promethean Flame," while expressing real anxiety about poetry's capacity to touch the emotions of its readers, as the poet contrasts his "starv'd Rhet'rick" and "Flat Tropes" with the "Pictur'd Passion" and "Pathetick Paint" of the visual artist. Though he held the office of Poet Laureate, Tate was aware that he lacked Dryden's skill and stature, but the issue was not merely a matter of individual talent. Writers of all kinds were increasingly conscious of the public's willingness to pay substantial prices for paintings—or to hear famous musicians perform. The preeminence of the word was evidently under threat. In the theatres, actors and managers were experiencing doubts about whether spoken drama could draw sufficient crowds to sustain them, as is evident from their advertisements, most of which highlight musical attractions. On May 28, 1703, for example, less than a week after Anne's letter to Sarah, Drury Lane advertised a performance of a comedy by Richard Steele called *The Funeral, or, Grief A-la-Mode.* Like most newspaper advertisements of the period, this one does not list the actors in the cast but provides specific names and details about the music,

In which will be perform'd several New Sonatas by the Famous Gas-
perini; particularly one for a Violin and Flute compos'd by him, but the
Flute part perform'd by Mr Paisible. And Entertainments of Singing by
Mr Leveridge, Mrs Campion, and others. With several Dances, particularly *Tollett's Ground*, by Mr Weaver and Mrs Lucas; and another Dance
between Mr Laferry and Mrs Bignall. And a comical Epilogue spoken by
Mr Pinkeman.[82]

The most sensational new performer of the 1702–1703 theatrical season
was an Italian singer, Margherita de L'Epine, who received "Twenty Guyneas
for one days Singing in the play call'd the Fickle Shepherdess" on 27 May.[83] This
was a huge fee for a single appearance, about half of what some of the actors received as a yearly salary, and de L'Epine evidently collected similar amounts
when she sang privately in the homes of her aristocratic fans. Small wonder,
then, that the entrepreneurial playwright John Vanbrugh, now also working as
an architect, chose this moment to assemble a large group of wealthy backers
who promised in June "to pay one hundred Guineas each, towards the building
a new Theatre in or near the Haymarket,"[84] a venue purpose-built for operatic
productions. Although later attacks on the Italian operas staged by Handel in
the new theatre would treat this art form as foreign, Catholic, sexually ambiguous, and inimical to British values, Vanbrugh's group, many of them members
of the Kit-Cat Club, consisted mainly of wealthy Whigs, including the Duke of
Somerset, Anne's Master of the Horse, and the Duke of Devonshire, her Lord
Steward.

Although they were Whigs, Somerset and Devonshire were hardly the *"Rank
Republicans"* about whom Sarah thought Anne "had been told strange frightfull
things." Devonshire had spoken in the House of Lords against the bill prohibiting
Occasional Conformity, but he had also hired the Catholic artist Verrio to paint
baroque ceilings for his spectacular mansion at Chatsworth. His support for opera
was not at odds with his taste in other matters, nor (in his mind) with his politics.
Even the Tories, who officially embraced traditional values including self-discipline
and reticence, and who therefore often expressed unease about emotion and
pleasure, nonetheless proved susceptible to the supposedly dangerous charms of
operatic music. The Tory hero Ormond, now Lord Lieutenant of Ireland, was on
Vanbrugh's list of investors in the opera house, and the sternly traditional Earl of
Nottingham, Anne's Tory Secretary of State and Defoe's relentless pursuer, soon
became a fan and promoter of Margherita de l'Epine. He probably first heard her
when the queen, now far too lame to attend the public theatre, summoned de
L'Epine to court on 28 April, ordering Sarah, as Keeper of the Privy Purse, to pay
her 30 guineas for singing.[85] A few months later, after performing with Richard

Elford at Tunbridge Wells, de L'Epine made a long visit to Nottingham's country estate, where she probably became his mistress.

§

When she prorogued her Parliament on 27 February 1703, the queen announced that its deliberations would resume on 22 April, but a series of further prorogations and a long visit to Bath in the summer and fall meant that Parliament did not reassemble until November. Meanwhile, Anne took some steps designed to weaken the Whig majority in the Lords. On 8 March, she marked the anniversary of her accession with bonfires, fireworks, and a mustering of the horse guards, and on 9 March, she added five new members to the House of Lords. Three of these were moderate Tories, men likely to support the policies of Godolphin and Marlborough, though the queen, as usual, had personal reasons for each appointment. The prominent lawyer Heneage Finch was the father of the student poet who had welcomed her to Oxford the previous summer; Anne would have remembered with gratitude his spirited defense of the seven bishops tried for seditious libel during her father's reign. John Granville was the younger son of the recently deceased Earl of Bath, whose experiences with King William closely paralleled Anne's. While Princess Anne was trying to recover her Irish lands, Bath was exhausting his resources in fruitless lawsuits seeking to recover his hereditary title as Earl of Albemarle, which William had brazenly awarded to his young Dutch favorite Joost van Keppel. Overwhelmed by the debts of his father's estate, Bath's eldest son committed suicide in 1701, a few weeks after his father's death, so the queen had every reason to show some sympathy toward the surviving son.[86] The third new Baron, Sir John Leveson-Gower, had led the fight to impeach the Earl of Portland, William's older favorite, in 1701, and the queen was still hostile to Portland. She would soon take legal action accusing him of fraud and seeking to reclaim for her Treasury some £91,000 he had obtained from the late king.[87]

Urged to make these appointments by Godolphin, Anne understood that adding new Tory peers to the House of Lords might affect some votes taken there, but personal connections and resentments were a part of her thought process whenever she made appointments, and the other promotions she made at this time were demonstrations of her interest in appearing to be above the rage of party. Mindful of her recent dismissal of Rochester, she extended an olive branch to the High Tories by creating another new peer from their branch of the party,[88] and by elevating her old beau John Sheffield, Marquess of Normanby and Lord Privy Seal, to the title of Duke of Buckinghamshire. Fully aware that Buckingham was making trouble for Marlborough and openly feuding with Sarah, the queen balanced his promotion by ennobling John Hervey, an outspoken Whig who was a personal friend and client of the Marlboroughs. In taking this action, she infuriated the other new peers but allowed her favorite to fulfill an old promise, perhaps remembering how distraught she had been when King William prevented her from keeping promises she had made to those chosen to serve in Gloucester's court. Although she had embraced a pragmatic political goal, in this case reducing the size of the Whig majority in the Lords, Anne was willing to undercut that effort in order to acknowledge such personal connections and obligations. She also wished to remind all parties of her queenly prerogatives.

While Parliament was in recess, Anne and her ministers undertook some important diplomatic efforts. A year of patient work by the gifted father-and-son diplomats John and Paul Methuen had at last persuaded the King of Portugal, previously a client of the French king, to support the claims of the Archduke Charles of Austria, the candidate for the Spanish throne supported by the English and their allies. The two nations signed a military treaty in Lisbon on 5/16 May, giving the British navy a safe port in Lisbon from which to launch the expected assault on Spain as well as ready access to the Mediterranean. In return, the Portuguese hoped for help from the Allies in recovering some lands long under dispute with Spain; they demanded that the Archduke come to the Iberian peninsula to press his claim in person, with the English, the Dutch, and the Habsburg Emperor all sending ground troops to defend Portugal and help Charles gain the throne.[89]

Shortly after the signing of the military agreement, a senior Portuguese diplomat came to London, where he enjoyed a special evening at the theatre, with a musical program that survives in an advertisement for an old play called *The Villain,* presented by the company at Lincoln's Inn Fields:

> For the Entertainment of his Excellency Don *Luiz da Cunha*, Envoy Extraordinary from the King of *Portugal* to Her Majesty the Queen of *Great Britain*... will be reviv'd a Play call'd *The Villain*. With several Entertainments of Singing, particularly that celebrated Trumpet Song compos'd by the late Famous Mr *Henry Purcell*, beginning at *The Fife and Harmony of War*. With several Italian Trumpet Sonatas being intirely new.[90]

Once again, the actors go unnamed while the musical performers get top billing. The decision to perform Purcell's "celebrated Trumpet Song" on this occasion looks like a signal of the court's hope for success in a new theatre of war, though the text for that song, written by the Whig clergyman Nicholas Brady for the St. Cecilia's Day celebration of 1692, is by no means a straightforward celebration of martial glory. In Brady's ode, military music, like all earthly music, must yield to the angelic strains of Cecilia's organ:

> The Fife and all the Harmony of War,
> In vain attempt the Passions to alarm,
> Which thy commanding Sounds compose and charm.[91]

In these odd lines, war supposedly has "Harmony," while the sacred organ issues "commanding Sounds" that calm those passions the fife has sought to alarm. Purcell's D major setting, with a prominent trumpet part and a rattling drum line, makes some small gestures in the direction of Brady's ironies, providing melting minor harmonies at "compose and charm." Still, it would be very odd indeed if the intent of this revival were ironic; it is far more likely that the person responsible for choosing this selection remembered the martial character of the song but not its more subtle details.

This slightly ambiguous artistic celebration of the treaty is in keeping with its cautious reception by Anne's administration. The opportunity to land troops safely on the Iberian peninsula was welcome, and a related commercial treaty, finally signed in December 1703, proved advantageous for both sides, with the English gaining a market for their cloth and the Portuguese gaining a market for their wines. Marlborough and Godolphin, however, soon realized that Leopold I, the Habsburg Emperor, would not contribute the troops he was supposed to send to the Iberian theatre as part of that pact, though he did send his son to meet with the Allies and prepare to enter Spain. In need of every battalion he could muster in the current theatre, Marlborough fretted about finding the promised troops for Portugal, but he dutifully called on the young man in Düsseldorf in October, inviting him to visit England over the winter.[92]

It was also too early to know what good might come of the other major diplomatic development of 1703. The devious and unreliable Duke of Savoy, Victor Amadeus, ruled a small but strategically significant territory including Turin (his capital), Nice (his major seaport), and the mountain homes of the "poor Vaudois," the French-speaking Protestants whose persecution had often troubled the English. One of the duke's daughters was the wife of Philip, Duke of Anjou, whom Louis XIV had recognized as the new King of Spain, giving Victor Amadeus a powerful motive for supporting the French. The duke's own wife, however, was Queen Anne's first cousin Anne-Marie, with whom she had shared a nursery as an infant. As Defoe had acknowledged in his pamphlet on the succession back in 1700, the House of Savoy had a strong claim to the English throne.[93] Sensing an opportunity, Anne's ministers dispatched a fleet to Nice in the summer of 1703, demonstrating their ability to keep good lines of supply and communication open to the Savoy; at the same time, Godolphin dangled the promise of substantial cash subsidies. In October, the French king got wind of these discussions and disarmed all the Savoyards then serving in his army. Infuriated by Louis's action, Victor Amadeus imprisoned the French emissaries in his own territory and publicly joined the English, the Dutch, and the Habsburg Empire in an expanded alliance against the French. At a family level, this change of sides put the duke into an alliance with his kinsman Prince Eugene, a Savoyard who was the commander of

Leopold's imperial army. In 1697, a few months after gaining this command, Eugene had won a decisive battle against the Turks, ending their threat to overrun Vienna, and in the first two years of the War of the Spanish Succession, he had won a series of important victories against French armies in Italy, actions extensively reported and admired in England. Eugene shared with Marlborough an impatience with sieges and a willingness to fight battles. They were natural comrades in arms.

§

Though pleased by these diplomatic gains, Anne continued to struggle with her northern kingdom. The commissioners appointed to discuss a scheme for uniting England and Scotland met frequently during the winter of 1702–1703, and the queen took a keen interest in their meetings. Early in the process, she sent the group a message saying that the heads of an eventual agreement should be obvious to all, and on 14 December 1702, she actually attended a meeting in order to urge the two sides to find common ground. There was a moment in January 1703 when the commissioners appeared to have achieved a workable solution. Despite their ancient pride, the Scots agreed to merge the two parliaments, a concession that seemed likely to guarantee a Protestant succession and a single monarch, while the English—even more remarkably—agreed to grant their northern neighbors full access to their own markets. The problems came when the Scots asked for access to colonial trade, and in order to avoid resolving that problem, the English commissioners began staying away from the meetings, which could not proceed without a quorum. Still hoping to move the negotiations forward, Anne redrafted the rules, reducing the number of men required on each side from thirteen to seven, but a solution remained elusive. On 3 February 1703, the queen adjourned the commission, instructing them to meet again in October. The huge elephant folio that was to record the minutes of the meetings seeking Union has fifty-two of its pages filled in; the rest, sadly, are blank.[94]

Mindful that the upcoming general election in Scotland was likely to produce a Parliament hostile toward England and deeply divided, the queen then issued two proclamations designed to win support from her Scottish subjects. On 4 February, she wrote a carefully worded letter to her Scottish Privy Council encouraging the bickering clergy to find a mode of coexistence. "We...recommend to your Care," she wrote, "the Church now establish'd by Law, in its superior and inferior Judicatures, such as Sessions, Presbyteries, Synods, and General Assemblies." By naming its various levels of representative governance, the queen left no doubt that she would leave the Presbyterian Kirk and its traditional structure intact. In the next sentence, she even described the Episcopal clergy, members of her own faith, as "Dissenters": "We are informed, that there are many *Dissenters* within that Kingdom, who, albeit they differ from the establish'd Church in Opinion, as to Church Government and Form, yet are of the *Protestant Reformed Religion*, some of which are in Possession of Benefices." Her instructions to these unhappy Episcopalians are remarkable, especially when considered in light of her recent support of the bill against Occasional Conformity.

> It is our Royal Pleasure, that they should be directed to live suitably to the *Reformed Religion*, which they profess, submissively to our Laws, decently and regularly with Relation to the Church establish'd by Law, as good Christians and Subjects; and in so doing, that they be protected in the peaceable Exercise of their *Religion*, and in their Persons and Estates, according to the Laws of the Kingdom: And we recommend to the Clergy of the establish'd Discipline [i.e., the Presbyterians], their living in Brotherly Love and Communion with such *Dissenters*.[95]

With her usual attention to balance, the queen now made a gesture of forgiveness to another group of Scottish subjects. On 16 March, she offered a general indemnity for all acts of "treason," "laese majesty," or "liesing makings" committed by Scots.[96] Behind the legal jargon lay a desire to allow the many Scottish Jacobites who had followed her father into exile, including some who had served his court at St. Germain, to return home from France without fear of reprisal. Many took advantage of the amnesty, though Anne's hope that her generosity would ensure their future loyalty went unfulfilled.

Once more, Anne sought to offer something for each side: for the Scottish Whigs, virtually all of whom were Presbyterians, she provided a firm indication of support for their beloved Kirk; for the Tories, many of whom were Jacobites, she offered an opportunity for reunion with friends and relatives trapped in hostile France. She would therefore have been particularly gratified by any expression of praise for both gestures, and David Symson, the son of a Scottish Episcopal clergyman turned printer, promptly published *A poem on Her Sacred Majesty Queen Anne, Occasioned by Her Majesty's Gracious Letter to Her Honourable Privy Council; and Her Act of Indemnity to all Her good Subjects of the Kingdom of Scotland*. In this substantial poem in couplets, evidently modeled on Dryden's court panegyrics, Symson couches his praise for the queen in language designed to influence the deliberations of the new Scottish Parliament. His opening lines, though highly conventional, send some important signals:

> Hail Sacred Princess! Hail *Great Britain's* Glory!
> Hail Mirror of this Age, and future Story!
> Hail Matchless Princess, for illustrious Birth!
> Hail, thrice again more matchless for great Worth!

Not until 1707, when the Union with Scotland finally succeeded, would the two realms be formally called *Great Britain*, but Symson shows his support for the eventual Union by hailing his queen as the glory of that imagined realm. His second line gestures explicitly toward future historians, who will honor Anne for uniting her kingdoms. She is "Matchless" for her "illustrious Birth," a reminder of her direct descent from Scottish kings, but much more matchless for her inherent "Worth," most recently demonstrated in her kind and considerate proclamations.

Symson's first example of Anne's merciful nature is not political, but aesthetic:

> Greatness is oftimes Good; looks ov'r a Crime;
> Then pardon a rude Muse's Loyal Rhyme.

A "modesty trope" of this kind was so conventional as to be virtually required in such poems, but Symson manages to make it more pointed by rhyming "Crime" with "Rhyme." A queen who could forgive the artistic flaws of his heartfelt verse could also forgive the serious crimes of the Scottish Jacobites, as she had just offered to do in her proclamation of indemnity. With the exception of Anne's vengeful father, the Stuart kings had often been celebrated for their merciful nature. Dryden had written memorably of Charles II's clemency at the time of the Restoration, and many believed that Charles I's willingness to forgive his enemies had hastened his tragic end. Symson invokes this history when urging Anne to control the "factious Rabble," whom he describes as a many-headed Hydra like the one depicted on her coronation medal:

> A factious Rabble does but make a Sport
> At Crown and Scepter when the Sword's too short.
> Your Sacred Grandsire knew the *Hydra* well,
> Rarely describes their Looks and masked Zeal.
> He pity'd, pardon'd, and gave all they sought,
> Till to the Block His Royal Head was brought.
> But may Your Sword be Terror, Blood and Flame
> To all who slight Authority's Great Name.

While reminding Anne of the danger of offering too much mercy, Symson nonetheless imagines "the Pious, ag'd & wise" lifting up their hands to praise another merciful Stuart:

> O Sacred Branch of the *Old Family*,
> Fill'd with your God-like Grandsirs Clemency!
> Blest be the Time that ever You were born,
> Thus to relieve th' afflicted and forlorn.

As a female monarch, Anne adds nurturing care to her family's tradition of mercy; she is both "God-like" and maternal:

> Freedom and Ease to grant, as dear as Light,
> After so long, and such a gloomy Night!
>   And ev'n to pardon the Delinquent too,
> Is very great: No more can Mercy do.
> Heav'n offers Mercy for *Repent* and *Mourn:*
> So you do too, to such as will return
> Unto their Duty, which those that despise
> I think they'r neither Good, nor Just, nor Wise.
>   And this your care, that we should love each other,
> Proves you the tender-hearted Nursing Mother.

Alluding to the Old Testament text chosen for Anne's coronation—"Kings shall be thy Nursing-Fathers, and their Queens thy Nursing Mothers"—Symson stresses Anne's motherly care for all her subjects. In this metaphorical world, the Presbyterians and Episcopalians, urged by the queen to live in "*Brotherly* Love and Communion," are like squabbling siblings, calmed and reconciled by a mother who instructs them to "love each other." Though "tender-hearted," this maternal figure can also exert authority, and Symson points in that direction by criticizing "those that despise" her mercy. He was probably aware that Anne's proclamation of indemnity would have a time limit: on 27 July, she issued *A proclamation Against such as have gone to or stayed in France since Her Majesties Gracious Indemnity*, directed against those who had presumed "at their own hand to return into this Kingdom, where they may prosecute their evil and wicked practices," and requiring anyone now wishing to return to obtain special leave from the queen or the Scottish Privy Council.

In a section supposedly spoken by a "Grave Divine," Symson mentions Achitophel, Absalom, and other rebels against King David, again recalling Dryden, and predicts that "Ruine will fall on such as do combine / To ruin and destroy this antient Line." In praying for a lasting bond between the queen and her people, he alludes to two female figures from the Old Testament:

> May we you, as the *Jews* did *Esther*, love;
> And may you to us like *Deborah* prove.[97]

The clumsy word order and clunky meter of these lines may help explain why Symson sought royal mercy for his "rude Muse," but the allusions are telling. Using her feminine beauty but taking great personal risk, Esther saved her people from genocide; though not a close analogue for Anne, she provides an attractive pretext for Symson's prayer that the Scots may love their queen. His parallel prayer that Anne will prove to be another Deborah strengthens the themes of justice and mercy. Like Tate's reference to Deborah in his poem on the royal portrait, this allusion may have influenced Anne's choice of texts for the Blenheim thanksgiving service. The queen was not in the habit of recording what she read, but there is one intriguing piece of evidence suggesting that she read this poem: in 1708, a year after the Union between England and Scotland finally took place, she made David Symson her Historiographer Royal for Scotland.

Despite Anne's hopes and Symson's fervent praise, the Scottish Parliament that assembled in May proved to be dominated by voices opposed to the queen's policies. Acting as her Commissioner, the Duke of Queensberry sought passage of a Toleration Act protecting the rights of the remaining Episcopal clergy, who had petitioned the queen in March, seeking her "Royal Bounty and Indulgence."[98] Rejecting this gesture toward ecumenicism, the Parliament passed instead an "Act for securing the true Protestant religion and presbyterian government," which stipulated that "Our sovereign lady....perpetually confirms...the government of the church by kirk sessions, presbyteries, provincial synods and general assemblies, as agreeable to the word of God and the only government of Christ's church within this kingdom."[99] The Parliament also constrained Anne to agree that anyone ruling after her would not have the power to make war without the consent of a future Scottish Parliament. Worse yet, the Scots spent much of the summer constructing an "Act of Security" in which they threatened to name their own monarch if Anne died without issue, "unless there be such conditions of government enacted this sessions as may secure the honour and independency of the crown of the kingdom, the frequency, freedom, and power of parliaments, and the religion, liberty, and trade of the nation from the English or any foreign influence."[100] Needing Scottish troops, funds, and support in the current war, Anne gave her assent to the acts confirming the system of church government and limiting the war-making powers of future monarchs, but she asked for more time to study the Act of Security, hoping the delay might provide opportunities for further negotiation. To Sarah, who had evidently urged her to force the Scots to accept the Hanoverian succession, she wrote a lengthy reply that shows how deeply she understood the importance of seeking a long-term Union rather than a short-term concession:

> I have read and heard read all the accounts that are com from Scotland, and am very sory to see things go soe ill there. The disaffected people heare have no doubt a good understanding with those there, and will allways help to make distractions in both kingdoms. I must beg my dear Mrs Freemans pardon for differing with her in that matter as to the

succession, for sertainly if the union can ever be compassed, there would be no occassion of nameing a successour, for then we should be one people and the endeavouring to make any settlement now would in my poor opinnion putt an end to the union, which every body that wishes well to theire country must own would be a great happyness to both nations.[101]

The queen was also aware of another way to avoid a prolonged squabble about the Scottish succession: producing an heir. In the same month, June 1703, she wrote to Sarah announcing her intention to "take physick in order to drink the Spaw waters,…hopeing they may make my Lady Charlotte return,"[102] and her trip to Bath, where she stayed from mid-August until early October, was a return to a place whose waters were thought conducive to conception.

§

The queen's entourage at Bath was evidently large. Writing in August to Sarah, who was still at Windsor, Anne reported that the town was full and lodgings hard to pro-cure,[103] a difficulty that may partially explain why Sarah did not arrive until 9 Sep-tember. Having now discovered that her supposed pregnancy was an illusion, the duchess was physically unwell and emotionally peevish; her husband, writing from his military encampment, was "sorry to find…that the Bath is soe disagreable to you" and afraid that Sarah's mood would "hinder the watters from doing you good."[104] Godolphin, a less volatile companion, dutifully accompanied the queen to Bath and kept up his usual stream of work and correspondence before going off to Newmarket for the horse races. In addition to the waters, Anne's attendants found other holiday amusements on offer. A group of actors from London, hoping to draw an audience in the slack summer season, rented a tennis court in order to present plays during the royal visit, but it is unlikely that the queen visited their makeshift theatre; the mineral waters did nothing to relieve her gout, which was now so bad that she could not walk without using two canes. Her favorite singer, Richard Elford, who traveled to Bath as part of the court party, presumably sang for her in private and at church; and her chaplain Richard Duke, who had written a skillful poem on her marriage in 1683, came along to attend to her spiritual needs.

Thanks to "her Majesties Special Command," we have the complete text of a sermon Duke delivered before the queen at Bath on 29 August, carefully calibrat-ing his message to suit her situation. Preaching on "the Imitation of Christ," Duke emphasizes the ethical duties of Christians and casts doubt upon those who describe their faith in emotional language:

The Love of God, in Us, is the immediate and genuine Effect of Faith, and Generally proportionable to the Light of Our Belief is the Warmth of

Our Affection. But the Love of God which was in Christ, as it flow'd from a much Nobler Principle; so questionless it rose [to] a much greater height, and left infinitely below it all that was ever call'd by that Name among the Sons of Men. But yet we find nothing in it like those Transports of Passion, those Extravagant Raptures and Exstacies which some Warm and Fanciful People pretend to.

For Anne and the others who heard this homily, the language about "Extravagant Raptures and Exstacies" was immediately palpable as a reference to the Dissenters, some of whose services featured "Transports of Passion." In the next sentence, Duke is equally careful to distinguish true faith from "those Wild Expressions, those Unwarrantable, if not Impious Flights, that Mystical Writers affect and delight in, of being *swallow'd up, and United by Love to the Divine Essence, and Transfus'd into God*"— language his hearers would readily decode as a reference to such Catholic mystics as St. Bernard and St. Teresa, both of whom frequently used similar expressions.

Dismissing Dissent and Catholicism as similar modes of enthusiasm,[105] Duke celebrates a dutiful and sober Anglican practice in worship and life as the true imitation of Christ, whom he describes as submissive to religious and civil authority, rigorous in regulating his own passions:

> If we consider Our Lord's Example in his Outward Expressions of Religion and the Ceremonial part of God's Worship, as it was then in use in the *Jewish* Church, we shall find nothing in his Behaviour but Obedience and Conformity.... Nor was our Saviour's Obedience to the Civil Government under which He liv'd, less remarkable, or Instructive.... And as He pay'd to God and the Powers ordain'd by Him the most Entire Obedience, so He Exercis'd over Himself the most Absolute Command. The Regulating of Our Passions aright is the Ground of all, or most of the Duties relating to Ourselves; and Our Saviour was undoubtedly the most perfect Master of These that ever the World knew.[106]

As Duke surely knew, this is a grossly distorted account of Jesus, who actually enraged the Pharisees and disturbed the Roman authorities—not least by casting the money changers out of the Temple in a notable display of passion. In choosing to present "Our Saviour" as an obedient and unruffled conformist, a "perfect Master" of his emotions, Duke was clearly seeking to please his queen, who was made uneasy not only by religious and civil dissent but by Sarah's unwillingness to regulate her passions.

Anne saw to it that her chaplain's sermon got printed, but if she cherished any hope that it might encourage her subjects to embrace "Obedience and

Conformity," she was disappointed. The news from the fractious Scottish Parliament, still in session when she arrived in Bath, was depressing: in retaliation for her refusal to consent to the Act of Security, the members refused to release the money necessary to pay the Scottish troops under Marlborough's command. In contrast to the previous year's vacation, when allied victories along the Meuse provided occasions for rejoicing, the news of the war was mixed and muted. Marlborough had spent the whole summer in a campaign of feints and sieges, as his cautious Dutch allies again prevented him from forcing the battle he wanted. The lack of any notable success beyond the surrender of Bonn played into the hands of Rochester, Nottingham, and the other opponents of the land war. Although the English Parliament, which had been prorogued several more times, would not assemble until November, partisan maneuvers were already under way. Writing to his wife on 11 October, Marlborough hoped that Anne "may hear noe more of the gout all this winter, for if my intelligence be good, she will have but to[o] much trouble given her by [Parliament]."[107]

A week later, the Earl of Rochester, now leading the High Tory opposition to the ministry, published the second volume of his father's *History of the Rebellion*, with a long dedication to the queen that was actually a polemic against Whigs and Dissenters. Although her uncle formally presented her with the volume, Anne took no notice of his dedication until tipped off by Sarah, who evidently found it offensive. Anne's response, apparently written before she looked at the dedication, shows that she knew exactly what to expect:

> Sir B. Bathurst sent me Ld Clarendons history last week, but haveing not quite made an end of the first part, I did not unpack it, but I shall have the Curiosity to see this extraordinary dedication, which I should never have looked for in the Second part of a book, and methinks it is very wonderful, that people that dont want sense in some things, should be soe rediculous as to shew theire vanity.[108]

When Anne confesses that she has not quite finished the first volume, in which Clarendon takes 557 pages to describe in minute detail the parliamentary clashes leading up to the beginning of hostilities in the English Civil War, she is humorously indicating her skepticism about the usefulness of this history; it is even possible that "haveing not quite made an end" is a sly euphemism for "not having bothered to read." She also remarks on Rochester's odd decision to offer her a dedication in the *second* volume of a three-volume work, as well as his vanity in assuming the role of a literary editor.

These knowing remarks suggest that once she opened the package, the queen had no difficulty recognizing that the oily gestures of respect and fealty in her uncle's dedication were actually condescending admonitions. The rhetorical slippage begins in the opening sentences:

> To Your Majesty is most humbly Dedicated this Second Part of the *History of the Rebellion and Civil Wars*, written by *Edward* Earl of *Clarendon*. For to whom so naturally can the works of this Author, treating of the times of Your Royal Grandfather, be address'd, as to Your self; now wearing, with Lustre and Glory, that Crown, which, in those unhappy days, was treated with so much contempt and barbarity, and laid low even to the Dust?

The implication is that Anne will lose the luster and glory of her crown, and may even see it laid low in the dust, if she fails to embrace his High Tory principles. Glancing at his own recent dismissal, Rochester suggests that the book may serve as a counselor, even though Anne is no longer willing to hear directly from her troublesome relative:

> This History may lie upon Your Table unenvied, and Your Majesty may pass hours and days in the perusal of it, when possibly, they who shall be most useful in Your Service, may be reflected on for aiming too much at influencing Your Actions, and engrossing Your Time.

In an even more obnoxious passage, Rochester suggests that the wisdom of his father's book may make amends for the limitations of Anne's education:

> And seeing no Prince can be endued in a moment with a perfect experience in the conduct of Affairs, whatever knowledge may be useful to Your Majesties Government, if it may have been concealed from You in the Circumstances of Your private Life, in this History it may be the most effectually supplied; where Your Majesty will find the true constitution of Your Government, both in Church and State, plainly laid before You, as well as the Mistakes that were committed in the management of both.

The implication here is that Anne is hopelessly ignorant and can only learn how to rule by considering and avoiding the mistakes made by Charles I. Describing his father as "a Prophet as well as an Historian," Rochester then departs entirely from the stated purpose of his dedication to complain about some alleged excesses of current Whigs and Dissenters:

> That this Remark may not look froward or angry, with great submission to Your Majesty, it may be consider'd, what can be the meaning of the

several Seminaries, and as it were Universities, set up in divers parts of
the Kingdom, by more than ordinary Industry, contrary to Law, supported by large contributions; where the Youth is bred up in Principles
directly contrary to Monarchical and Episcopal Government? what can
be the meaning of the constant Solemnizing by some Men, the Anniversary of that dismal thirtieth of *January,* in scandalous and opprobrious
feasting and jesting, which the Law of the Land hath commanded to be
perpetually observ'd in fasting and humiliation?[109]

Barred by law from attending Oxford or Cambridge, Dissenters had indeed established schools for their children, including the excellent academy at Stoke
Newington where Defoe had his education, but it was a paranoid fantasy to imagine that the main purpose of these schools was political indoctrination. The
complaint about "scandalous and opprobrious feasting and jesting" is even more
far-fetched, resting as it does on patently fictional accounts of the alleged activities of the "Calves-Head Club," enemies of monarchy who supposedly feasted on
the head of a calf and drank toasts to Cromwell on the anniversary of Charles I's
execution.[110]

Dignified as usual, the queen made no formal response to this patronizing
dedication, whose shrill and partisan tone confirmed what she already knew. Her
government was about to be attacked by the High Tories on one side and the
Whigs on the other. With no significant victories on land or sea to report, the
queen highlighted her recent diplomatic gains in her speech opening the new session of Parliament on 9 November 1703. "I hope," she said,

> I have improved the Confidence you reposed in Me last Year, to your Sat-
> isfaction, and the Advantage of us and our Allies, by the Treaty with the
> King of *Portugal,* and the Declaration of the Duke of *Savoy;* which, in
> great Measure, may be imputed to the Chearfulness with which you sup-
> ported Me in this War, and the Assurance with which you trusted Me in
> the Conduct of it: And we cannot sufficiently acknowledge the Good-
> ness of Almighty God, who is pleased to afford us so fair a Prospect, as we
> now have, of bringing it to a glorious and speedy Conclusion.

She continued by imploring her legislators to "avoid any Heats or Divisions, that
may disappoint me of that Satisfaction, and give Encouragement to the common
Enemies of our Church and State."[111] The Commons and the Lords played their
part in the formal dance by making flattering addresses to the queen in gratitude
for her speech, including assurances that they would avoid "Heats or Divisions,"
but within days the Tories in the Commons were launching an investigation of

military expenditures and preparing to introduce a slightly softened version of their beloved bill against Occasional Conformity. A devastating hurricane on 26 November, which ripped up thousands of ancient trees, killed a bishop and his wife in their bed, and sank fifteen warships at sea provided another occasion for a show of unity. The Commons asked the queen to "give Direction for repairing this Loss, and for building such capital Ships, as her Majesty shall think fit," promising to "make good that Expence" and to provide support for the families of the fifteen hundred seamen lost in the storm.[112] For her part, the queen ordered "a General and Publick Fast...to implore God Almighty's Blessing and Favour, and that it would please him to pardon the crying Sins of this Nation, which have drawn down this fatal Judgment."[113] She did not specify what "crying Sins" she had in mind, but when the day of fasting came, her chaplain Samuel Pratt, formerly Gloucester's tutor, preached a sermon deploring "our own unreasonable and shameful Animosities, Divisions, and Dissentions among our selves" and exhorting his hearers "To a Chearful and Religious Performance of all the Obligations which in Love and Duty are owing to our most Gracious SOVEREIGN."[114]

By 19 January 1704, when Pratt preached this sermon, the "Animosities, Divisions, and Dissentions" between the two Houses of Parliament were evident to all. Once more the Commons had passed the bill against Occasional Conformity; once more the Lords had thwarted their will, this time by voting the bill down on its second reading. Queen Anne, though protesting to Sarah that she saw "nothing like persecution in this Bill,"[115] did not insist that Prince George attend the Lords on this occasion. She had begun to recognize the malicious motives of the pious supporters of the bill and was planning a more positive act of her own in support of the Church. Still, she would not have been pleased by reports that one of the Whig Lords who voted against the bill on 14 December "came that Evening, to a Musick Meeting Erected at the Play-house, by the Subscriptions of his Faction; with a Roll of Paper or Parchment tied up like a Bill in his hand, which in the Face of all the Audience he threw Scornfully upon the Publick Stage, and told'em *there was the Occasional Conformity Bill for'em*; which was immediately made the Subject of the insipid Drollery, of all the Fools that applauded that Action."[116] The "Musick Meeting" in question was one of a series of subscription concerts organized by the Whig dukes of Devonshire and Somerset, both members of the queen's Privy Council and investors in Vanbrugh's future opera house. Most of these featured a young British singer, Catherine Tofts, though she was unable to sing on this particular evening because of a cold. Tory music-lovers attended similar concerts at York Buildings, organized by the Earl of Nottingham, Anne's Secretary of State, and featuring the sensational Italian soprano Margherita de L'Epine.[117]

Even more troubling was the parliamentary response to reports of a Jacobite plot in Scotland. Like most plots of this period, this one was largely the creation of a troublesome liar, in this case Simon Fraser, a convicted rapist who had managed to convince the court in exile that he could deliver an army of Highlanders to effect the restoration of "James III." Taking advantage of Anne's amnesty, Fraser then returned to Scotland, forged some documents that appeared to incriminate the leaders of the Opposition in the Scottish Parliament, and delivered the whole suspicious package to the Duke of Queensberry, Anne's High-Commissioner for Scotland. But when Anne called both Houses of the English Parliament together on 17 December to inform them that she had "Unquestionable Informations of very Ill Practices and Designs carried on in *Scotland*, by Emissaries from *France*,"[118] the House of Lords, still dominated by Whigs, decided to launch its own investigation, taking into custody some witnesses whom Nottingham, as Secretary of State, regarded as his own. The rhetoric surrounding this struggle left no doubt that the Whig grandees in the Lords were unwilling to trust Nottingham to make a thorough and impartial investigation of the "Scotch Plot" because they suspected the queen's Secretary of being a Jacobite himself. Although the identity of the recipient remains unknown, a short note written by the queen at this moment, probably addressed to one or more of those troublesome Whig lords, gives strong evidence of her own irritation:

> Her Majesty having so lately acquainted you that she had communicated to you all the particulars relating to the design against Scotland which could yet be made publick, without prejudice to the service, her Majesty did not expect to be pressed upon that matter before it was scarcely possible that the state of it could be altered.[119]

§

In the midst of this unpleasant controversy, Anne had to play hostess for a formal visit by the Archduke Charles, now referred to throughout the alliance as the "King of Spain" or "Charles III of Spain." Marlborough, who had already met the young man, and Somerset, in keeping with his ceremonial role as Master of the Horse, collected Charles at Spithead on Christmas Day and transported him to Windsor, spending a night en route at Petworth, Somerset's splendid estate in Sussex. Prince George, dispatched by his wife to meet them there, arrived after a harrowing journey in which his coach overturned on the muddy roads.[120] Perhaps because Charles was only eighteen and not yet married, the ceremonies surrounding his visit to Windsor included rituals of courtship and gallantry:

> The Queen receiv'd him with great Demonstrations of Respect and Affection. After he had made his compliment to her Majesty, acknowledging

his great Obligations to her for her generous Protection and Assistance, He led her Majesty into her Bed Chamber, where the Queen presented about forty Ladies of the first Quality to his Majesty, who saluted them all with a Kiss.... He supp'd that Night with the Queen, who gave his Majesty the Right Hand at Table, which he with great Difficulty admitted, the Prince sitting at the End of the Table on the Queen's side....After Supper his Catholick Majesty would not be satisfied, till after great Compliments, he had prevail'd with the Dutchess of *Marlborough* to give him the Napkin, which he held to her Majesty when she wash'd. And in returning the same to her Grace, his Majesty put his Diamond Ring in it, as a mark of his great Esteem for that Lady.[121]

Determined to convince the young Habsburg that her court was as genteel and cultured as any in Europe, Anne also offered her guest an "Afternoon...spent in Entertainments of Musick, and other Diversions, the court making the most splendid Appearance that ever was known in *England*." Not content with her own salaried musicians, the queen hired eight prominent theatrical singers and instrumentalists for this performance, and paid them lavishly from the Privy Purse. Only two of these special artists, the bass Richard Leveridge and the soprano Catherine Tofts, were British; the rest were German, Italian, or French. Six of them received 30 guineas each; Margherita de L'Epine and the composer Jakob Greber, whose music she frequently performed, received 40 guineas each.[122]

If Boyer's account and the parallel stories in the newspapers were the only surviving narratives of this royal visit, we might suppose that the English put aside their party squabbles in order to present an elegant and courtly show of unity for the young king. But this was not so. On 4 January 1704, a few days after the concert at Windsor, there was another subscription concert at the Drury Lane Theatre, with a special prologue and epilogue by the Whig poet Arthur Maynwaring, later a close associate of the Duchess of Marlborough.[123] The epilogue shows how quickly the events of the royal visit had taken on a partisan valence, as Maynwaring maps partisan passions onto the growing rivalry between Tofts and de L'Epine, the two sopranos featured at Windsor.

Maynwaring begins his "Epilogue to the Ladies" by complimenting the women in the box seats, treating their attendance at the concert as an act of patriotism:

> With Joy we see this Circle of the Fair,
> Since the late Trial of the tuneful Pair:
> Your Country's Friends, you love the Native Strains
> Of Musick here, where *England*'s Genius reigns.
> In other Walls tho' Harmony be found,

> You know 'tis foreign, and disdain the Sound:
> Who haunt New Consorts, Faction wou'd create,
> And are Dissenters in *Apollo*'s State:
> They shun our Stages where he keeps his Court,
> And to some gloomy Meeting-house resort:
> While you with Duty own his rightful Cause,
> And guard this Place, Establish'd by his Laws.[124]

By referring to the command performance for Charles III as "the late Trial of the tuneful Pair," Maynwaring recasts the recent concert at Windsor as a contest between the two sopranos, which was certainly not Anne's intent in inviting both of them to sing. By praising the ladies in the theatre for supporting "the Native Strains / Of Musick," he recasts an artistic preference as a political one. The Whigs were always eager to smear the Tories as supporters of foreign, Catholic artists, a useful step toward implying that all of them were supporters of a foreign, Catholic king; applauding loudly for the native-born Protestant Tofts was a convenient way to express these sentiments. Maynwaring, however, ironically reverses the usual terms of abuse, calling the supporters of the Italian artist "Dissenters in *Apollo*'s State" and humorously deriding their musical venue as a "gloomy Meeting-house" while praising the theatre as "Establish'd" by law like the Church of England. This twisted metaphor turns the Tories into a version of the very people they had been trying to suppress through the act against Occasional Conformity.

The epilogue continues in a much less partisan fashion, suggesting that the praise and admiration of beautiful English ladies will help the young king secure his new kingdom:

> That blooming Hero, you at Court admir'd,
> In Arms must Triumph, by your Praises fir'd:
> Success is yours, and Victory inclines
> Still to that Side on which your Favour shines:
> *Mars* will himself conduct our future Wars,
> When ev'ry *Venus* for this Prince declares.

Maynwaring imagines Charles in the future, "Grac'd with a Crown, which *Anne* alone cou'd give," remembering the forty English ladies he had kissed in her bedchamber:

> That warm Idea he must still retain:
> And think, tho' Seated on the Throne of *Spain*,

Tho' with the Treasure of both *Indies* Crown'd,
He left a brighter Empire than he found.

The fanciful rhetoric of these lines, linking eroticism and empire, continues the tradition of Dryden's court panegyrics,[125] but this strain of patriotic compliment to British beauty clashes awkwardly with the sharply partisan argument of the opening lines. Despite Anne's frequent pleas for unity, partisan fervor would infect all aspects of British culture for the remainder of her reign. Even music, supposedly an art without explicit content, became highly political, with performers and composers claimed and supported by one party or another. In the shadowy world of lampoon and rumor, the rivalry between Tofts and de L'Epine took on a sexual dimension: Tofts had grown up in the home of the Whig Bishop Gilbert Burnet, who employed her father, and some scandal-mongers claimed that Burnet had tried to debauch the singer when she was only sixteen; similar stories, considerably more plausible, described de L'Epine as the mistress of Nottingham.[126] The competition turned ugly when a woman employed as a servant by Tofts pelted de L'Epine with oranges during a public performance in February 1704, apparently as a way of expressing disapproval of her singing in Italian.[127]

After the huge effort expended on the royal visit, the New Year's celebration for 1704 appears to have been something of an afterthought, and only one stanza of the ode survives, its text not even a complete sentence.[128] For the birthday, however, there was a full-scale celebration, held on Monday, 7 February, because the actual birthday fell on a Sunday. In the morning, the queen heard a substantial ode with music by Eccles, and in the evening she attended a performance of Dryden's *All for Love*, starring actors from both theatre companies and adorned with musical interludes between the acts, including two songs by her beloved Purcell. Like the earlier concert for the visiting king, this dramatic performance prompted highly partisan commentary. Anne had recently issued one of her periodic orders "for the regulation of the Stage," complaining that "many of the Old as well as New Plays are still acted without due Care taken to leave out such Expressions as are contrary to Religion & Good Manners,"[129] and the radical Whig John Tutchin, a lifelong opponent of the theatre, seized upon this proclamation to claim that the players had been impudent in choosing Dryden's play:

> When her Majesty, to Divert the Court, Order'd them to Act before Her, and as any Body might suppose, to see how Innocent they were in their Behaviour; they took care to show themselves by Acting things which Angred Her very much, and some say did it on purpose.[130]

There is no reason to credit Tutchin's claim that Anne was displeased by the performance. John Downes, a theatre prompter who recorded his memories of hundreds of productions, reports that the court was "very well pleas'd" on this occasion,[131] and Anne quickly invited the players back to act at court on Prince George's birthday and on the anniversary of her coronation. There is good evidence that she usually selected the plays performed before her,[132] and it is hardly surprising to find her asking Thomas Betterton and Elizabeth Barry, actors she had known since her childhood, to perform a well-known tragedy by Dryden, whom she had also long admired. First staged in 1677, Dryden's play is generally refined and chaste in its language, though it does depict the tragic consequences of Antony's adulterous passion for Cleopatra, which gave Tutchin the opening he wanted:

> They say he was so Drowned in his Sordid *Lust*, and Doted so much upon her, that he quitted his *Army* … and made his Retreat to the Arms of this Syren; and through the height of Intollerable *Stupidity*, gave himself over to *Love* and *Despair*; and this they call *Losing all for Love*; and then add, That so to do, is *the World well lost*. The English of the Story is this, That he who Sacrifices all his *Fortunes*, and his *Life*, to the Embraces of a *Whore*, loses the *World well*.

Replying to Tutchin's angry sputtering, the author of a rival paper with a Tory bias, *Heraclitus Ridens,* pointed out that the *Observator*'s criticism of the play chosen for the birthday was likely to spill over onto the monarch: "he do's not so much aim at pulling down the Play-house, as he does at rendring the Queen Odious to the People."[133]

As she had done since the start of her reign, Anne was actually seeking to calm such partisan passions, thus rendering herself attractive to all her subjects. The poet Matthew Prior, chosen to write a special prologue for the dramatic performance on this birthday, emphasized her efforts to secure the love of her people:

> Entire and sure the Monarch's Rule must Prove,
> Who founds her Greatness on her Subjects Love;
> Who does our Homage for our Good require,
> And orders that which we should first desire.
> Our vanquish'd Wills, that Pleasing Force obey,
> Her Goodness takes our Liberty away,
> And Haughty BRITAIN yields to Arbitrary Sway.[134]

Wittily appropriating the commonplaces of Whig rhetoric—love of "Liberty" and fear of "Arbitrary Sway"—the poet identifies Anne's "Goodness," her moral integrity, as a "Pleasing Force" that will vanquish any opposition. The Earl of Jersey, Anne's Tory Lord Chamberlain, had employed Prior as his secretary in France in the 1690s and presumably tapped him to write these verses. When he was a boy working in his uncle's tavern, Prior had impressed the Earl of Dorset, who found him reading Horace in Latin; at Dorset's expense, the talented lad attended Westminster School, where he became friends with Charles Montagu, yet despite his humble origins and his Whig connections, he was now a Tory. His rhetoric in this prologue, however, is urbane and cool, quite unlike the strident partisan language of the newspapers. Recognizing his capacity to reconcile rival views, Anne would later employ him on a vital diplomatic mission.

Confirming Prior's praise of her "Goodness," the queen used the occasion of her birthday to announce a significant gift to her church. She had long been aware of the pitiable state of those clergymen serving in parishes whose "livings" produced very little income, and she was embarrassed that taxation by the Crown increased the poverty of the lower clergy. When Henry VIII broke with Rome in 1535, he redirected to himself two taxes previously paid to the pope: the "first fruits," which were originally the entire first year's income received by a priest in a new parish, and the "tenths," originally a tenth of each subsequent year's income. Over time, the Crown had reduced these heavy taxes and fixed them at set amounts, but they remained a burden on men unable to pay them. Queen Anne's Bounty, her birthday present to the Church, forgave the many unpaid debts owed her under the old law, excused clergy serving parishes with annual incomes of less than £50 from ever paying the taxes again, and placed the income collected from richer parishes into a fund for increasing the stipends paid to those ministering to the nation's poorest parishes.

In pressing for the bill against Occasional Conformity, the High Tories had claimed to be protecting the Church from danger by weakening its supposed enemies. Queen Anne's Bounty, by contrast, sought to strengthen the Church by providing assistance to its least well-rewarded servants. The Tory program was evidently partisan, while the Queen's Bounty extended to men of all parties. Most remarkable of all was the fact that the idea for such tax relief originated with the Whig Bishop Gilbert Burnet, who had proposed a similar program to King William in the late 1690s. It is a striking instance of Anne's generosity that in pursuing a lofty goal, she was willing to embrace a proposal first made by a man who had frequently irritated her. According to Burnet, "The queen was pleased to let it be known, that the first motion of this matter came from me."[135] The egotistical bishop evidently regarded Anne's recognition of his role in suggesting this relief as personal praise, but there was probably some shrewd political calculation involved as well. The lower clergy were predominantly Tory, and the queen's direct support for the poorest of them was likely to soften their

John Croker, *Medal commemorating Queen Anne's Bounty* (1704).

disappointment with her for failing to press harder for the bill against Occasional Conformity. The bishops, by contrast, were mainly Whigs, but any disappointment they might have felt at the long-term redistribution of resources from wealthy livings (including their sees) to poorer parishes (usually served by Tories) would be difficult to express in light of the fact that their hero Burnet was the originator of the plan.

The result was everything Anne might have wished. Both Houses of Parliament quickly endorsed the plan, pious addresses of thanks poured in from various cathedrals, a silver medal commemorating the bounty linked the queen's piety to that of Augustus Caesar, and one pamphleteer explicitly described her action as a way of reconciling both sides in the debate about Occasional Conformity:

> For those Gentlemen who were traduced for designing only some private
> Interest, or State-end, in promoting the *Bill against Occasional Conformity,*

have shewn, by their disinterested Zeal for this *Act for the Poor Clergy*, that they meant the Advantage of the *Established Church* by the other, whether they judged right, or no, as to the Time and Consequences of it; which I will not pretend to determine. And such as did not think fit to concur with their Friends in the former Measures, but were hearty for this last Act, have given us sufficient reason to believe, that they also wish well to the true Interest of Religion, and the Established Church, tho' they did not judge, that a Bill against *Occasional Conformity* was, at this juncture, seasonable or proper.[136]

Warming to his task, the anonymous writer refers to the Tories as "Gentlemen who were traduced" for having political motives, while describing the Whigs as those who "did not think fit to concur with their Friends." As he surely knew, he was not describing reality. Nottingham's motives for "promoting the *Bill against Occasional Conformity*" were manifestly partisan, and Burnet's vehement opposition was far from being a disagreement among "Friends."

Despite Anne's determination to dampen it, party spirit remained intense, even within her deliberately bipartisan ministry. Although she had already dismissed her troublesome uncle Rochester, the remaining High Tories among her serving ministers were increasingly at odds with Godolphin and Marlborough, who pressed her to make further changes. In April, the Earl of Nottingham, the most powerful Tory in the government, fatally overplayed his hand. Claiming that the queen would govern more effectively if her entire Cabinet came from one party, he insisted that she dismiss the Duke of Somerset and the Archbishop of Canterbury.[137] Somerset had recently angered Nottingham by taking a leading role in the Lords' investigation of the "Scotch Plot," while Thomas Tenison, the Archbishop, had opposed the bill against Occasional Conformity. In making his partisan demand for their ouster, however, Nottingham failed to reckon with Anne's personal loyalties. Somerset had given Princess Anne a place to live when she quarreled with her sister in 1691, a favor she never forgot, and he had excellent courtly manners, which had recently impressed no less a person than the Holy Roman Emperor, who "wrote a letter to the duke of Somerset, to thank him for the civilities he shewed to his son, the king of Spain; and sent him several rich presents, particularly 6 fine Hungarian horses."[138] The duke was also an important backer of a project of great interest to the queen, the opera house now being built by Vanbrugh; on 18 April, "his Grace Charles Duke of Somerset" laid the cornerstone for the new building.[139] His Duchess was one of Anne's most trusted Ladies of the Bedchamber, praised by Whigs and Tories alike for her "dignity at court, . . . great respect to the queen and civility to all others."[140] In asking Anne to part company with the Somersets, Nottingham showed how little he understood her values. So, too, with the clergy. The queen was much closer to John Sharp, Archbishop of York, than she was to Tenison, but the Archbishop of Canterbury was the head of her Church and thus a figure toward whom she felt reverence and respect. Anne's refusal to reshape her Cabinet along High Tory lines inevitably led to Nottingham's resignation, and she took the opportunity to replace two of his allies at the same time. Edward Villiers, Earl of Jersey and Lord Chamberlain, lost his position in this shakeup, as did Sir Edward Seymour, Comptroller of the Household. A few days after their resignations, Sir Benjamin Bathurst, husband of Anne's girlhood favorite Frances, died, creating another vacancy. Conscious of Bathurst's corrupt dealings as her Household Treasurer before she came to the throne, Anne had parked him in the lesser place of Cofferer, a lucrative post to which she now appointed Francis Godolphin, son of her Treasurer and son-in-law of Sarah Churchill. The job of Lord Chamberlain went to Henry Grey, Earl of Kent, who was certainly recommended by Sarah and widely rumored to have won her support by deliberately losing a vast sum to her at cards. Politically insignificant and ridiculed for his body odor, Kent evidently knew how to throw a party: on the evening of 25 May, he "treated her majestie and the court upon the river Thames, where were near 1000 barges and boats, with all sorts of musick and eatables."[141]

The most important new appointment brought Robert Harley, Speaker of the House and Anne's trusted confidante since 1700, into her Cabinet as Secretary of State for the Northern Department, replacing Nottingham. Like his friends Godolphin and Marlborough, Harley was now a moderate Tory, more loyal to the queen than to any party. In a partisan poem lamenting the changes in the Cabinet, an anonymous High Church writer took some comfort in his appointment:

> For my lov'd *Nottingham*'s Retreat
>   I comfortless should Weep,
> Did *Harley* not possess his Seat,
> A Patriot truly Good and Great,
>   And of Experience deep.[142]

Harley's deep experience, however, included an education in Dissenting schools and a parliamentary debut as a "country Whig." During his years as Speaker of the House he had been an Occasional Conformist, quietly attending a Presbyterian conventicle as well as services in the established church.[143] His views were much less rigid than Nottingham's, and he maintained personal connections with people across the entire political spectrum, including Daniel Defoe. In the fall of 1703, Harley had worked quietly with Godolphin to launder £150 of Secret Service money in order to pay Defoe's bail and get him released from Newgate, gaining the writer's lifelong gratitude. In his new position, he put Defoe to work gathering intelligence in England and Scotland and even persuaded Anne to pardon him.[144] The contrast with Nottingham, who took personal umbrage at Defoe's clever irony and pursued him with vindictive zeal, is telling.

§

With the English Parliament prorogued and a new administration in place, public attention turned to the war, and the campaign of 1704 offered far more excitement than the frustrating and inconsequential actions of 1703. As Marlborough recognized, the alliance between the Bavarians and the French threatened to cut off the Emperor in Vienna from the states in central and northern Germany that formed part of his empire. Combined French and Bavarian forces already controlled much of the Danube, and there was a real danger that Vienna itself, also threatened from the east by a Hungarian revolt, could fall, assuring France of dominance in Europe. Aided by a written order from his queen, Marlborough told his Dutch allies that he intended to march his English troops east from Maestricht through Bonn, which had fallen the precious summer, to Coblenz, where the Moselle joins the Rhine. He did not tell them how much further he actually planned to march. Observing his motions, the French began to prepare for a campaign along the Moselle, but Marlborough did not turn south there. Instead, he continued moving east, now threatening to turn south down the Rhine, invading Alsace from the north. Hanoverian and Prussian troops joined his column in Coblenz; Danes and more Prussians fell into line at Ladenburg. The duke expected the French to follow his movements, and as his growing army made its daring march, a substantial French force moved in the same direction along parallel lines to the south. Eventually it became clear that Marlborough was moving toward Bavaria itself, where imperial troops under the formidable Prince Eugene could join him. On 31 May/10 June, the two commanders met for the first time, and on 22 June/ 2 July, Marlborough won a costly victory, overwhelming a fortress overlooking the Danube at Schellenberg with the help of imperial troops commanded by the German prince Ludwig of Baden. The allied army sustained six thousand casualties, including fifteen hundred killed in action, but its general gained a bridgehead on the Danube and placed his army between the French and Vienna.[145]

Even before this battle, an alarmed Marshall Tallard had been moving through the Black Forest to reinforce the Bavarians. Prince Eugene, whose troops were stationed between Tallard and Marlborough, kept his comrade well informed of the progress of the French column. Despite Marlborough's decision to force a battle at Schellenberg, the French were still expecting a more conventional campaign of sieges, and may have been encouraged in that belief by Marlborough's laying siege to the small town of Rain during July. Tallard and his officers appear to have been genuinely surprised when the combined forces of Marlborough and Eugene appeared on the hills above their defensive position at Blenheim (properly Blindheim), a small town on the Danube. The battle of 2/13 August was bloody and decisive. Thousands died, including many forced into the river and drowned by the allied advance; twenty-eight French regiments surrendered, losing their flags and artillery; the Holy Roman Empire, saved by this victory, would not be threatened again in the long remaining course of the war. The grateful Emperor made Marlborough a prince, awarding him (with Anne's permission) the small principality of Mindelheim, not far from the site of his great victory.

In an era of countermarches and sieges, a battle of this nature was astonishing, and it inspired an unprecedented number of poems and paintings. More than a century later, the American poet Joel Barlow was still turning to Blenheim as a telling example of the military sublime. "In a general engagement," he wrote in 1825,

> the shock of modern armies is, beyond comparison, more magnificent, more sonorous and more discoloring to the face of nature, than the ancient could have been; and is consequently susceptible of more pomp and variety of description. Our heaven and earth are not only shaken and tormented with greater noise, but filled and suffocated with fire and smoke. If Homer, with his Grecian tongue and all its dialects, had had the battle of Blenheim to describe, the world would have possessed a picture and a piece of music which now it will never possess. The description would have astonished all ages, and enriched every language into which it might have been translated.[146]

In an effort to describe the noise and shock of modern warfare, Barlow imagines Homer writing a poetic account of Blenheim, which would be not only a poem but "a picture and a piece of music." Although Marlborough would later participate in such mythmaking by commissioning a splendid tapestry depicting the battle, his message on the day itself, a note scribbled with a lead pencil and dispatched to his wife, is laconic:

> I have not time to say more, but to beg you will give my duty to the queen, and let her know her army has had a glorious victory. Monsieur Tallard and two other generals are in my coach, and I am following the rest. The bearer, my aide de camp Collonel Parkes, will give her an account of what has passed. I shal doe it in a day or two by another more at large.[147]

Riding fast and aided by favorable winds, Parke delivered Marlborough's note to the duchess on 10 August. Pausing briefly to make a copy for the newspapers,

Sarah sent him on to Windsor, where he found the queen. Generous as always, Anne honored the exhausted messenger's request for a reward—a miniature portrait of herself, set in diamonds—and added 1,000 guineas in cash. Devout in victory, she "ordered the bishops to draw up a form of prayer for a thanksgiving to be used throughout England and Wales,"[148] setting in motion the preparations for the grand service at St. Paul's. At this moment, Deborah's claim that "the Lord made me to have dominion over the mighty" would have had special resonance for Anne. Her army had inflicted a stunning defeat on the hated French, and she had reason to hope that this unprecedented success would make it more difficult for her domestic foes to question her policies. For the pious queen, the amazing events now echoing across Europe were a fulfillment of a song celebrating the power of her prayers, written by her Laureate, set by her Master of the Music, and sung to her by Mr. Elford on her last birthday:

> Her Powerfull Foes she thus Alarms,
> She makes their Mighty Hosts to yeild,
> With Devotion's Stronger Charms,
> And in her Closet wins the Feild.[149]

CHAPTER 8

WHAT FRUITS FROM OUR DIVISIONS SPRING

6 February 1707

"Richly habited," as the occasion required, "the Nobility of both Sexes" settled into their seats for a court performance of Giovanni Bononcini's opera *Camilla*.[1] Many of them had seen it before, either on the Continent, where it had been a staple of the Italian repertory since 1696, or at the Drury Lane Theatre, which had presented numerous performances sung in English during the last ten months. Their queen, however, hobbled by gout and distracted by business, had not yet seen this popular opera, so she asked the singers and instrumentalists to bring it to St. James's for her birthday. Because the festivities also included a new ode by Tate and Eccles and a new dance in honor of the long-awaited Union of England and Scotland, the players presented a shortened version of *Camilla*, but they also invited a newly arrived sensation, the castrato Valentini, to sing some solos in Italian before and after the main piece.[2]

This was the third consecutive birthday at which Anne heard an opera. In 1705, the Drury Lane company presented *Arsinoe, Queen of Cyprus,* with a libretto adapted from an Italian source, new music by the English composer Thomas Clayton, and the popular soprano Catherine Tofts in the title role. In 1706, singers from both theatre companies honored the queen with *England's Glory,* a short opera written specifically for the occasion by the German composer James Kremberg. *Camilla,* the opera chosen for 1707, originated in Italy, as did *Arsinoe,* but this time the company had imported the original music as well as the libretto. Established in Europe for most of the previous century, opera was finally gaining a foothold in London, and the queen's sponsorship was a significant endorsement of the new form.

Like many operas of its era, *Camilla* draws loosely on the epic tradition. In Virgil's *Aeneid,* Camilla is a brave female warrior who leads her Volscian cavalry in support of the Rutulian prince Turnus in his war against Aeneas and the invading Trojans. Turnus is jealous as well as patriotic; he has lost his fiancée Lavinia because Latinus, king of the Latins, has decided to seal a pact with the Trojans by marrying her to the widowed Aeneas. Poignantly described by Virgil, Camilla's death in battle reminds us of the terrible human cost of establishing an empire, but no such sorrow darkens Bononcini's opera. Although characters called Turnus, Lavinia, Latinus, and Camilla appear in Silvio Stampiglia's libretto—and in the English translation sung in London—there is no Aeneas, and no one dies. In this version, Camilla appears disguised as a shepherdess named Dorinda, concealing her true identity because Latinus has usurped her father's throne. Her first aria, sung this afternoon by Catherine Tofts, laments her loss of power and status.

If the queen remembered performing as a dancing shepherdess in *Calisto* or telling Sarah that she would "rather live in a Cottage with you then Reinge Empresse of the world without you,"[3] the spectacle of royalty "in Disgrace" would have been a poignant one for her, and the princess in disguise soon displays her heroic character. As she concludes her aria, a party of hunters invades the "sweet Vallies" where she herds her flocks, and one of them wounds and enrages a wild boar. Bravely slaying the dangerous beast, Camilla wins the gratitude and love of the frightened Prenesto, who turns out to be the son of her enemy Latinus and the brother of Lavinia. The brave Volscian captain Metius arrives too late to be of aid to Prenesto but promptly falls in love with the irresistible Camilla. When the scenery changes to an interior apartment, we meet Turnus, who is utterly unlike his heroic Virgilian prototype. Sung in Italy by a castrato and in England by the countertenor Francis Hughes, this Turnus has disguised himself as a Moorish slave in order to gain access to Lavinia, sung in this production by Joanna Maria Lindelheim, who was called "the Baroness" in theatrical advertisements. Although the threat of tribal violence among the Latins, Rutulians, and Volscians hovers over much of the opera, the plot turns on misunderstanding, conspiracy, and jealousy among the lovers. While Prenesto and Metius woo Camilla, Turnus promises to aid her cause and shows signs of desiring her person, prompting a jealous outburst from Lavinia. Camilla, while wondering which of her admirers can best help her regain her throne, admits her passionate love for her political enemy Prenesto. After many reversals and against all odds, Camilla ultimately weds Prenesto, and Lavinia weds Turnus. The magnanimous princess declines to take vengeance

Mus. Ex. 8.1: Giovanni Bononcini, aria from Act 1 of *Camilla* (1696, 1706).

on the usurper Latinus, and this happy ending brings the previously hostile tribes together.

Although the English version of *Camilla* followed Stampiglia's plotline and used most of Bononcini's original arias,[4] the Drury Lane company made adjustments to adapt the opera to the tastes of their audience. The translated libretto, apparently the work of several hands,[5] shortened all the recitatives—the sung conversations that still seemed strange to English ears—and these editorial changes made Bononcini's recitative music unusable, so Christopher Rich, the manager of Drury Lane, hired the cellist and antiquary Nicola Haym to compose new music for the English recitatives.[6] The adaptors also emphasized a comic subplot in which Camilla's servant Linco woos Lavinia's superannuated maid Tullia.[7] The comic scenes featuring these characters—sung in London by the popular bass Richard Leveridge and the veteran mezzo Mary Lindsey—probably seemed less strange to the audience than the serious plot, as there was a long tradition of comic "dialogue songs" performed in English theatres by singers impersonating quarreling couples.[8] Thus adapted, *Camilla* proved to be a sustaining show for Drury Lane, with eleven performances in the season of 1705–1706 and twenty-three more in the season of 1706–1707.[9]

Despite its origins in an earnest Renaissance attempt to revive Greek tragedy, opera had now become a vehicle for star singers, as poets reluctantly recognized. In 1691, five years before the premiere of *Camilla* in Naples, the Italian librettist Giuseppe Salvadori issued these cogent "warnings for librettists unfamiliar with music":

> Modern composers are men of power whose textual changes it is useless to resist. A prudent librettist familiarizes himself with the talents of the singers who will perform his work, and he collaborates wherever possible with the composer. Since arias are what the public most desires, it is senseless to emulate those who try to include in their works as many as three or four scenes devoid of arias.... Lengthy scenes should be avoided, as should aria texts whose accented syllables involve vowels other than "a" and "o."[10]

These were essentially the principles followed by Stampigilia and by those who translated, adapted, and arranged *Camilla* for the production in London. Similar considerations shaped the version presented at court in 1707, which shortened the opera once more by compressing or eliminating recitatives, cutting eighteen whole scenes and one-third of the arias.[11] The court *Camilla* moves from aria to aria with a minimum of explanation or motivation. Instead of engaging in sung dialogue with Prenesto and "Dorinda," as he does in the Drury Lane production, Metius makes his first entrance with an aria proclaiming his love for the beautiful shepherdess, which would have made no sense at all to anyone unfamiliar with the more complete version. Lavinia's jealousy has no apparent cause, as the scene in which Turnus appears to woo Camilla has vanished entirely. The person who truncated the opera for the birthday performance was obviously less interested in presenting a plausible story than in including the arias that had proved most popular in the commercial production.[12]

Thanks in part to Dryden's popular translation, many members of the audience at court would have had some knowledge of Virgil's *Aeneid*. If they had measured *Camilla* against the *Aeneid*, with its costly violence, selfless heroism, and moral complexity, the opera would have looked like a ludicrous parody. It is therefore worth asking why English audiences, notoriously resistive to through-sung opera during the previous century, were now willing to accept the conventions of an art form so completely dominated by music that its plots routinely debased their epic sources. A growing interest in music for its own sake, which the queen certainly shared, was part of the story, but in order to place the belated vogue for opera in England within a larger cultural frame, we should recognize that opera begins to flourish as epic itself becomes untenable. Dryden and Pope, the leading English poets of Anne's lifetime, translated classical epic into English and wrote successful mock-epics, yet neither composed an original epic poem. Perhaps they were reluctant to attempt writing epic because they recognized that the heroic principles and beliefs underlying the epic were moribund. Marlborough was a skillful general, but as poets seeking to celebrate his victories discovered, the language of epic heroism had become problematic in a world where Virgil's Turnus could appear as a countertenor disguised as an African, and where major battles had become occasions for partisan satires rather than Homeric similes.

In light of her lifelong interest in music and her recent patronage of opera, the queen's inviting the singers and musicians to present their current hit at court for her birthday was not surprising, but in choosing a piece created by a poet and composer with no connection to the English Crown, she passed up an opportunity to use the performance for explicit political purposes. That choice was certainly available. On this very day, Lieutenant-General Richard Ingoldsby, the British commandant in Ghent, celebrated Anne's birthday by presenting an elaborate military parade, a fireworks display, and a new, highly topical opera:

> From the place where the Fire-works were perform'd, the General went to the Play-house, where he had taken all the Boxes for the Ladies, and they were Entertain'd with a new Opera called the *Battle of Ramellies*, in honor of his Grace the Duke of Marlborough, in which were perform'd several Songs, &c. in praise of her Majesty and her Glorious Reign.[13]

In this opera, for which the French libretto survives, Anne appears as the goddess Pallas, surrounded by a chorus of singing Amazons.[14] If a general serving on foreign soil could commission an opera praising Marlborough's victory in the most important battle of 1706, the queen could have done something similar in her capital. *England's Glory*, the piece performed in the previous year, had consisted entirely of "Songs...in praise of her Majesty and her Glorious Reign," with a large role for Bellona, the goddess of war, who also appears in *La Bataille de Ramelie*. *Camilla* was obviously very different. Perhaps Anne chose this work, with its concluding reconciliation between jealous lovers and warring tribes, because she was proud of the imminent Union with Scotland, celebrated on this day with "a new Dance compos'd by Mr Isaac." Perhaps she identified with the heroine, wooed by ambitious rivals as she herself was constantly importuned by ambitious politicians seeking her favor. Perhaps she simply hoped that a fluffy, tuneful entertainment would encourage her courtiers to lay aside their partisan bickering for at least one evening.[15]

§

Despite the queen's pronounced distaste for them, partisan struggles had been a constant in the years since Blenheim. In her letter congratulating Marlborough on his victory, dispatched on 11 August 1704, Anne made the hopeful prediction that it would have positive domestic consequences: "Soe Glorious a victory," she wrote, "will not only humble our enemyes abroad, but contribute very much to the putting a stop to the ill desinges of those at home."[16] Ten weeks later, when she opened the annual session of Parliament, the process of turning the battles of the summer into opportunities for partisan propaganda was well under way, with poems and pamphlets reinforcing the positions of leading politicians. Once more, Anne tried to call for unity. "The Great and Remarkable Success with which God hath Blessed Our Arms in this Summer," she said, "has stir'd up Our good Subjects in all Parts of the Kingdom, to Express their Unanimous Joy and Satisfaction."[17] By emphasizing the similarity of the many prose addresses of congratulation she had received since Blenheim, the queen was urging her legislators to seek the accord she had seen in her other "good Subjects."

But if joy was more or less unanimous, its expression was not. Again those reluctant to celebrate conquests on land inflated the importance of naval operations. Shortly before the battle in Bavaria, Admiral George Rooke had captured Gibraltar; two days after Anne's letter to Marlborough, he fought an inconclusive naval engagement with a French fleet sent to retake the fort and declared victory when his adversaries withdrew overnight. As Parliament began its session, the Lords pleased the queen with an address applauding Marlborough's success, but the House of Commons showed its continuing Tory bias by pairing his accomplishments with those of Rooke. Like these parliamentary addresses, topical poems contradicted Anne's wistful prediction that victory would silence her critics. Eight separately printed poems on the summer's campaigns appeared between the Battle of Blenheim and the opening of Parliament, and at least thirty more would follow in the ensuing months, most expressing some partisan bias. Several Tory poets pointedly chose to celebrate Rooke's "victory" rather than Marlborough's, while Whig poets made a point of studiously omitting any reference to naval warfare. A few included both events, a compromise that Sarah and others considered insulting.

Even drinking songs could have partisan valence. A "Trumpet Song on the Duke of Marlborough," for example, printed in the *Monthly Mask of Music* for August 1704 with music composed by Richard Elford, begins with these lyrics:

> Come let a Cheerful Glass go Round,
> to Englands brave Retriever,
> let all our Cares in this be Drown'd;
> Curse on the unbeliever.

Pale Envy yeilds to his desert,
United Whig and Tory,
are both agreed to bear a part,
in Ecchoing of his Glory.[18]

Despite the claim that "Whig and Tory" will unite in praise of the victory, it was possible to detect the party allegiance of the anonymous poet. Back in 1702, the first great division of this Parliament had been about whether to commend Marlborough for having "retrieved" or "maintained" the "ancient Honour and Glory of the English Nation," with the Whig minority arguing in vain that the idea of his having retrieved England's honor was an insult to King William. By calling the general "Englands brave Retriever," the anonymous poet betrays his Tory sympathies.

Defoe provides a more complex and extended example of partisan verse. His elaborate *Hymn to Victory,* one of the first poems on Blenheim to appear, was available for purchase on 29 August, less than three weeks after news of the battle reached England. In a Pindaric ode addressed to the goddess Victory, the poet blames political corruption for Victory's absence in recent decades and claims that Anne's recent changes in her ministry have enabled Victory to return. The notion that the queen had made Marlborough's success at Blenheim possible by removing a few High Tories from her Cabinet was preposterous, but it gave Defoe an excuse for an extended attack on Nottingham, who had forced him to stand in the pillory one year earlier:

The fatal Blast confounded all their Powers,
Blew R[ocheste]r and S[eymou]r out of Doors;
And N[ottingha]m, when his Supporters fell,
Alas, what Pen the fatal News can tell!
Sunk Soul-less, down the mighty Bubble sate,
    Like the meer Tool of State:
And he that us'd his Honour like his Whore,
Was just as Senceless now, as Useless long before.[19]

According to this vituperative account, Nottingham is not only "Soul-less," "Senceless," and "Useless" but a dishonorable whoremonger. In *The Dyet of Poland* (1705), Defoe amplified the last charge, identifying the minister's mistress as Margherita de l'Epine. "Charm'd with Foreign *Margueritta*'s Song," this fictional version of Nottingham neglects his official business, and his singing mistress acquires a prominence that properly belongs to the queen:

Whole Fleets attend the *Minstrels* softer Notes
By her the Statesman *steers*, the Members *votes*.[20]

By linking the fleet to de L'Epine's soft notes, Defoe glances wickedly at Nottingham's advocacy of a "blue water" policy, and he had a personal motive for this line of attack: in 1703, while hiding from the authorities in the wake of *The Shortest-Way*, he had sent his wife to plead his case with Nottingham, who apparently took the opportunity to ask Mary Defoe for sexual favors.[21] Infuriated by the earl's high-handed attempt to take advantage of his wife, the poet now seized the opportunity to satirize him for his affair with the opera star.

For Defoe as for many others, the great victory at Blenheim was an occasion demanding a poem, but he did not feel compelled to restrict his poem to the battle. In addition to settling a personal score with Nottingham, the *Hymn to Victory* rewrites parliamentary history, representing the queen, who had been more or less neutral in the most recent debate about Occasional Conformity, as working actively to defeat the bill. Only when the attempt to persecute the poet and his fellow Dissenters fails does Victory deign to return:

> The Royal Blast the Party overtakes,
>   The deep Contrivance breaks.
> The Queen, to Peace the Willing Land perswades,
> And with that Word their deep Design invades:
> The Willing Lords close with the Royal Word,
> And damn'd the Bill as cruel and absurd.
>
>   'Twas now that VICTORY return'd:
> The flame of Civil Strife too long had burn'd.
> The Queen too plainly saw the vile Design:
>   Her Majesty blew up the Mine.
> . . . .
> The Queen at Home a greater Conquest gains,
> Greater than this on the *Bavarian* Plains.[22]

As Defoe surely knew, it was absurd to claim that Anne's studied silence during the debates about the Occasional Conformity bill of 1703 was a greater conquest than the Battle of Blenheim. Like other panegyrists of the period, however, he was not under oath. The genre of panegyric had always licensed flattery, and now it licensed partisan fervor. By praising Anne for a position she had not publicly taken, Defoe was probably hoping to influence her actions when the bill came up again, and while there is no evidence that the queen had read this poem, she did nothing to support the third Occasional Conformity bill, which passed the House of Commons once more in November 1704, and she bitterly opposed the Tory attempt to "tack" the bill to the Land Tax. The aim of the "Tack" was to force the Lords and the queen to accept the bill in order to fund the ongoing war, thus circumventing their aristocratic and monarchial prerogatives. Thanks to the determined efforts of Harley, the Tack went down to defeat on 28 November by a vote of 251 to 134.[23] Marlborough, still on the Continent, wrote to Godolphin expressing his relief:

> I see the pains that has been taken to carry the Tack. If thay had succeded it is what must have disturbed everything, for not onely in England, but here also, thay would have been so out of heart, that thay would have advanced no monys, so that all our preparations must have stod stile. I hope [Nottingham] and [Rochester] did not know these fatal consequences when thay were so earnest for itt, for it is most certaine no greater services could be done to France.[24]

The duke was being generous in hoping that the disgruntled Tory leaders had acted from ignorance rather than malice, but Godolphin, with unusual bitterness, told Sarah that he would never consider anyone who voted for the Tack worthy to hold a place in the government.[25] The queen, resentful of any attempt to reduce her power, came to share this vindictive spirit, and bent her efforts toward seeing the Tackers defeated in the next election.

Working against the Tackers, however, necessitated working with the Whigs, and while Anne and her Treasurer hoped to find moderate allies within that party, men who would grasp the importance of maintaining the queen's prerogatives, Sarah tactlessly seized this moment to contend that Anne was entirely wrong in her opinions of the two parties. Weary of being badgered, the queen wrote a letter on 17 November in which she insisted on her own consistency ("I have the same opinnion of whig and tory, that ever I had") but acknowledged the need to make individual judgments ("there are good and ill people of both sorts, and I can see the faults of the one as well as the other").[26] Not at all content with this concession, Sarah replied with a pointed lecture on political history, probably designed to counteract the Tory account of the Civil War that Anne's uncle Rochester had dedicated to her. In a letter written on 20 November, which survives because she kept two copies, the duchess expresses her belief that "Dear Mrs Morley...has sucked in with her milk a great abhorance of what they call'd in those days wiggs, or round heads,"

> and I don't at all wonder at it, I will allow they had cloven feet, or what you please, tho there is nothing more certain, then that you never heard the whole truth of that story,...but I that have read every booke little, and great, that has been writ upon that subject, can assure you the extream weakness of that unfortunate King [Charles I], contributed as much to his misfortunes, as all the malice of those ill men, nay I will venture

to say more, that it had not been possible for them to have hurt him, if he had not been govern'd by almost as bad people, without knowing it, the Queen Mother who had absolute power over him, not being only a french woman (which was misfortune enough) but a very ill woman, and his chief manager of his affairs my Lord Bristol, tis well known dyed a Roman Catholick.[27]

Caught up in the passion of her politics, Sarah bullies the queen by claiming to have done extensive historical reading, implying that Anne is ignorant. She apparently forgets that she is accusing Anne's own grandfather of "extream weakness" while calling her French grandmother, whom the little princess had known as a child, "a very ill woman." It was probably this letter that prompted Anne to complain of "Lady Marlborough's unkindness" to Godolphin. "I can't hope as you do," wrote the queen, "that she will ever be easy with me againe, I quite despaire of it now, which is no small mortification to me."[28]

The intensity of her partisanship, which made Sarah insensitive to her friend's feelings, also made her receptive to Defoe's sharply partisan poems, even though they came from a Dissenting milieu quite unlike her own. In May 1705, Charles Montagu, Baron Halifax, a Whig and a poet, wrote to the duchess in praise of the *Hymn to Victory* and *The Double Welcome,* a poem on Marlborough's return to England. Enclosing Defoe's works in his letter, he told her that the poet "might deserve encouragement.... The Verses have some turns in them that are pretty, and are very respectfull to the Queen."[29] Understanding perfectly what Halifax meant by "encouragement," Sarah dispatched 100 guineas to Defoe, though she told neither the queen nor her husband that she had done so.

The other side had its extremists as well. The High Church Tory William Pittis had already published several "answers" to works by Defoe, moving through his rival's poems and pamphlets a sentence at a time and offering Tory refutations. Now he matched the Pindaric *Hymn to Victory* with a Pindaric *Hymn to Neptune* singing the praises of Admiral Rooke. Like Defoe, Pittis ranges beyond the immediate occasion, commending his hero for the action at Gibraltar but reaching back to the 1690s to defend him against those who had criticized his conduct in previous campaigns, notably William Colepepper, who was Defoe's attorney. While attempting to sound confident in his belief that the nation will ultimately recognize Rooke's worth, Pittis sounds desperate and shrill, and his incompetence at Pindaric verse does not help his cause:

> No, 'tis in vain, not all their Factious Arts,
>   Made use of to debauch our hearts,
>   And draw us from the just Esteem

> Of such an Man, and such a Theme,
> 　　Shall be of any force;
> The Muse does all their Practices despise,
> 　　Their little Tricks, and Whiggish Lyes,
> 　　　　Unshaken in their Course:
> And up the mighty Name she'll bear,
> Above the Stars, and fix it there,
> Where Envy cannot rise.[30]

Not long after the publication of this execrable poem, Pittis suffered the same dis-grace his antagonist had experienced in 1703: by the late fall of 1705, when he published *A Hymn to Confinement,* he was in prison, and in April 1706, he stood in the pillory as a punishment for his part in defending a notorious pamphlet called *The Memorial of the Church of England,* which enraged the queen by claiming that she had failed to protect the Church from its enemies.[31] Although his poem on Rooke appears to have made no public splash, it cannot have helped Pittis's cause when he ran into trouble with the authorities a few months later. Rooke, who was in poor health and lacked support among Anne's ministers, lost his post as Admiral of the Fleet in January 1705, when Anne replaced him with Sir Cloudesley Shov-ell, who was much more acceptable to the Whigs.

§

With the memory of his own imprisonment still fresh, it is remarkable that Defoe should have taken the risk of writing strongly partisan poems, especially while dependent for his employment on Robert Harley, the government's chief advo-cate for "moderation." Nor could Defoe assume that busy ministers like Harley had no time for poetry. Like other important politicians, Harley was keenly inter-ested in the poetic responses to the summer's campaign and eager to promote poems friendly to his cause. Working with his associate Henry St. John, now Sec-retary at War, he sought out an Oxford poet with Tory opinions, John Philips, and offered him £100 to compose *Bleinheim,* a poem in Miltonic blank verse *Inscrib'd to the Right Honourable Robert Harley.*[32] In addition to the monetary reward, which they drew from Secret Service funds, the ministers invited their chosen poet to write his verses at St. John's comfortable country house. Although he de-voted the bulk of his poem to a grisly description of the battle on the shores of the Danube, Philips was careful to include a section celebrating Rooke's victory at Gibraltar. His poem begins with a direct address to his patron Harley:

> From low and abject Themes the Grov'ling Muse
> Now mounts Aerial, to sing of Arms

Triumphant, and emblaze the Martial Acts
Of *Britain*'s Heroe; may the Verse not sink
Beneath His Merits, but detain a while
Thy Ear, O HARLEY, (thô thy Country's Weal
Depends on Thee, thô Mighty *ANNE* requires
Thy hourly Counsels) since with ev'ry Art
Thy self adorn'd, the mean Essays of Youth
Thou wilt not damp, but guide, wherever found,
The willing Genius to the Muses Seat:
Therefore Thee first, and last, the Muse shall Sing.

In this passage, Marlborough appears in the third person and without a proper name, as "*Britain*'s Heroe," while Harley is named, addressed in the second person, praised as indispensable to the queen, and flattered as a sophisticated connoisseur of poetry.

When Philips gets around to addressing Marlborough, he does so in lines that praise Anne for choosing him as her general, a gesture more or less required in such poems:

... Great *ANNE*, weighing th'Events of War
Momentous, in Her prudent Heart, Thee chose,
Thee, CHURCHILL, to direct in nice Extreams
Her banner'd Legions.

As the passage continues, however, Philips veers away from Marlborough to applaud "GODOLPHIN, Wise, and Just," for keeping the troops well fed in "other Climes, where diff'rent Food and Soil/Portend Distempers."

He, of the Royal Store
Splendidly frugal, sits whole Nights devoid
Of sweet Repose, Industrious to procure
The Soldiers Ease; to Regions far remote
His Care extends, and to the *British* Host
Makes ravag'd Countries plenteous as their own.[33]

Godolphin's close attention to military supplies was not a common topic in the popular press, though his correspondence with Marlborough frequently addresses the need for shoes, clothing, and food for men and horses. Harley and St. John, familiar with this aspect of the war from their ministerial service, probably provided Philips with details of the Treasurer's industry in his post, and Godolphin allegedly sent a "present" to the poet.[34]

There is a more definite record of Godolphin's direct involvement in commissioning the best known poem on Blenheim, *The Campaign* by Joseph Addison. According to Thomas Tickell, a fellow Kit-Cat who edited Addison's complete works, "the Lord-Treasurer *Godolphin*, who was a fine judge of Poetry, had a sight of this work, when it was only carried on as far as the applauded simile of the *Angel*; and approved the Poem, by bestowing on the Author…the place of Commissioner of Appeals."[35] Eustace Budgell, writing more than a decade after Tickell, gives a more elaborate account in which Godolphin asks Halifax to recommend a poet "whose Pen was capable of doing justice to the Action."[36] At first, the Whig Lord demurs, complaining that poets are never adequately rewarded, but when reassured by Godolphin that a proper reward will be forthcoming, he names Addison. There are reasons to doubt the historical accuracy of Budgell's account, which continues by picturing an astonished Addison receiving a visit from the Chancellor of the Exchequer in his "indifferent" lodgings. Still, the idea that Halifax might have recommended Addison is highly plausible: both men were Kit-Cats, and Addison had dedicated a Latin poem on the Peace of Ryswick to Charles Montagu in 1697, before his patron's elevation to the House of Lords as Baron Halifax. Despite his willingness to commend Defoe to Sarah, Halifax might logically have thought of Addison when choosing a poet for Godolphin. Unlike the shrill and combative Defoe, Addison had a history of cordial relations with men across the whole political spectrum: he had been intimate with the Jacobite Catholic Dryden in the 1690s, and his closest friend during his undergraduate years at Oxford was Henry Sacheverell, already notorious as a fervent High Church preacher.[37] From Halifax's point of view, and eventually from Godolphin's, the smooth and clubbable Addison was a perfect choice to write an official poem on Blenheim, a writer likely to keep his poem focused on Marlborough and victory, thus promoting the elusive unity the queen was seeking.

At first blush, however, it seems odd that Godolphin would have turned to Halifax for advice on this matter. Although the two men had served together in the Treasury during William's reign, Godolphin supported Harley's attempt to impeach Halifax and the other leaders of the Whig Junto in 1701, and they had remained on opposite sides in more recent years. At this point, however, Godolphin needed to cultivate some Whig support for the government as a counterweight to the intransigent High Church Tories. Perhaps he deliberately requested poetic advice from Halifax as a way of opening a dialogue, hoping that the younger man might be flattered by having his judgment sought in a field where he had some pretensions to expertise. For both men, a conversation about choosing an appropriate poet to celebrate a recent victory might have been easier to start than a conversation directly confronting their past political differences. And even if Budgell's account of Halifax as the recommender of Addison is a fond fabrication,

Godolphin was consciously extending an olive branch to the Whig Junto by asking the Kit-Cat Addison to compose a poem on Blenheim and rewarding him not with a one-time gift but with a permanent, salaried position made vacant by the recent death of the Whig philosopher John Locke. His patronage of Addison is an example of the way powerful people during Anne's reign, including the queen herself, used aesthetic choices to send subtle political messages. It was one of the earliest signs of Godolphin's moving away from the High Tories and beginning to work with the Whigs.

Neither of the eighteenth-century accounts of Addison's being commissioned to write *The Campaign* stipulates a date, but it is most likely that he finished the poem in the autumn, and that his patrons timed its publication to coincide with Marlborough's return on 14 December. Godolphin's poetic discussions with Addison (and possibly with Halifax) would therefore have taken place not long before Halifax helped the Treasurer out of a tight place. On 29 November, the day after the defeat of the Tack in the Commons, the queen herself, "with the dutchesse of Marlborough and the lady Fretcheville," came to the House of Lords, and sent a signal of her growing warmth toward moderate Whigs by allowing the Duke of Somerset, the most prominent Whig in her Cabinet, to escort her to the throne.[38] But if Anne expected her presence to restrain the partisan passions of the Lords, she was disappointed, as Nottingham and Rochester chose this day to launch a determined attack on their former colleague Godolphin, assailing him for having advised the queen to give her assent to the Scottish Act of Security, a decision made a few days before Blenheim, when the need for Scottish money and troops appeared to give her no real choice. Rising to the occasion, Halifax made a proposal designed to compel the Scots to enter into serious negotiations toward Union, thus easing the pressure on Godolphin. In the Act of Security, the Scottish Parliament had stipulated that it would name its own monarch when Anne died, unless England granted it full and free access to trade. To this attempt at political blackmail, Halifax proposed an equally tough response, suggesting that "Scotsmen should not enjoy the privileges of Englishmen...until an Union be had, or the Succession settled as in England."[39] Other Whigs suggested additional measures preventing the Scots from exporting cattle and linen to England, and the threat of being treated as aliens and losing vital elements of trade eventually brought the Scots to the table, making possible one of Anne's greatest achievements. Cold, hard calculation on the part of the Whig leadership was doubtless a part of their decision to rescue Godolphin at this moment, but his generosity toward Addison may well have helped make this rapprochement possible.

On a first reading, Addison's poem appears to be a nonpartisan historical narrative, following Marlborough from the Moselle to the Rhine to the Danube,[40] yet some aspects of *The Campaign* reveal the Whig beliefs of its author, who praises

Britain as a nation where men may rise by merit, describing Marlborough as a shining example of this progressive system:

> Thrice Happy BRITAIN, from the Kingdoms rent,
> To sit the Guardian of the Continent!
> That sees her Bravest Son advanc'd so high,
> And flourishing so near her Prince's Eye;
> Thy Fav'rites grow not up by Fortune's sport,
> Or from the Crimes, or Follies of a Court;
> On the firm Basis of Desert they rise,
> From long-try'd Faith, and Friendship's Holy Ties:
> Their Sov'raign's well-distinguish'd Smiles they share,
> Her Ornaments in Peace, her Strength in War,
> The Nation thanks them with a Publick Voice,
> By Show'rs of Blessings Heaven approves their Choice;
> Envy it self is dumb, in Wonder lost,
> And Factions strive who shall applaud 'em most.[41]

According to these lines, Britain has a long tradition of allowing men to rise "On the firm Basis of Desert," and Marlborough, though not born into an aristocratic family, has established a legitimate claim to Anne's favor by winning the decisive victory at Blenheim. One implicit comparison, then, sees Britain, with its relatively fluid class structure, as superior to France, with its hierarchical obsession with titles and family. To locate Britain's strength in its nascent meritocracy, however, was to embrace a view of society guided by Whig principles. When Addison claims that royal favorites, including Marlborough, have *not* gained their status "from the Crimes, or Follies of a Court," he risks having his reader remember that young John Churchill owed his early advancement to his sister Arabella's position as the mistress of the Duke of York (later James II). Jacobites had never forgiven Churchill for betraying his master in 1688, and many Tories continued to regard him with suspicion, but this was not a moment at which they might usefully bring up this part of his history. High Tory poets had nothing to fall back upon but the weak expedient of praising George Rooke, as Addison notes by proclaiming that "Envy it self is dumb," while more moderate Tories had no choice but to join in the chorus of praise, as "Factions strive who shall applaud 'em most."

  Although we do not know whether Addison and Philips had seen each other's poems before releasing their works to the press, the intriguing parallels between the poems make possible a comparison of the partisan beliefs of those who wrote and commissioned them.[42] Addison's apostrophe to "Thrice Happy BRITAIN," for example, bears a curious resemblance to Philips's address to "Thrice Happy *Albion*":

Thrice Happy *Albion!* from the World disjoin'd
By Heav'n Propitious, Blissful Seat of Peace!
Learn from Thy Neighbour's Miseries to Prize
Thy Welfare; Crown'd with Nature's Choicest Gift
Remote Thou hear'st the Dire Effect of War
Depopulation, void alone of Fear,
And Peril, whilst the Dismal Symphony
Of Drums and Clarions other Realms annoys.[43]

Both poets notice Britain's position as an island, "rent" (Addison) or "disjoined" (Philips) from the rest of Europe, but where Addison sees Britain as separate from other nations because of its willingness to let men rise by merit, Philips sees it as protected from invasion and "Depopulation" by the Channel—an odd point to make in a poem ostensibly celebrating a daring march that had taken a British army deep into Bavaria. This passage is also susceptible to a partisan reading, as Harley and St. John, Philips's immediate patrons, were already looking for a way to conclude the expensive war so that England might once more be a "Blissful Seat of Peace."

Though chosen by the queen's chief ministers to celebrate a great victory, and therefore envied by other poets, both Philips and Addison evidently had difficulties in finding a compelling poetic idiom for praising military heroism. The Poet Laureate, Nahum Tate, who had already cast doubt on the efficacy of poetry in his verses on the royal portrait, delayed his own poem on Blenheim until 18 January and devoted much of it to a self-conscious dialogue with his muse concerning the difficulty of writing on this topic,

A Task that does the Mystick Talent crave
To rage with Order, and with Reason rave.[44]

As these lines suggest, poets writing on Blenheim were conscious that the scale and importance of the battle required invoking the sublime, perhaps by raging and raving, but also aware that the impressive strategic planning undertaken by the victor constrained them to honor order and reason. In a world where opera threatened the legitimate theatre, grand gestures of rage ran the risk of seeming absurd or comic. In a world where protecting and extending trade was a powerful and "rational" cause for war, the conventions of chivalric epic—knights in armor, personal honor, single combat—had begun to ring hollow. Milton, the last great epic poet, had been at pains to distinguish his moral purposes from those of chivalric poets, declaring that he was

Not sedulous by Nature to indite
Wars, hitherto the only Argument

> Heroic deem'd, chief maistry to dissect
> With long and tedious havoc fabl'd Knights
> In Battles feign'd; the better fortitude
> Of Patience and Heroic Martyrdom
> Unsung.

In the "War in Heaven" episode in *Paradise Lost*, the poet dramatized his disdain for chivalric poetry by describing the satanic forces inventing gunpowder and cannon. As the loyal angels march forward in their knightly armor, they encounter "deep throated Engins…disgorging foule / Thir devilish glut." A hail of iron globes from the cannon reduces the loyal angels to an impersonal heap of tangled metal:

> Whom they hit, none on thir feet might stand,
> Though standing else as Rocks, but down they fell
> By thousands, Angel on Arch-Angel roll'd.[45]

These lines satirically enact the threat to traditional ideas of heroism posed by artillery. Reduced to faceless thousands, the angels lose their heroic individuality, and the hierarchy collapses as angels and archangels roll together in the same humiliating heap. A radical opponent of monarchy and privilege, Milton served as Latin Secretary to Oliver Cromwell and stoutly defended the beheading of Charles I. His attack on chivalry quite consciously includes an attack on the related notions of rank and privilege. Yet John Philips, a Tory from a non-juring family, was so impressed by the grandeur of Milton's language that he embraced the radical republican as his poetic model, closely imitating Milton in all his works.

In *Bleinheim,* Philips comes perilously close to unintended comedy in trying to make language borrowed from the "War in Heaven" work as a factual description of a modern battle:

> …Now from each Van
> The brazen Instruments of Death discharge
> Horrible Flames, and turbid streaming Clouds
> Of Smoak sulphureous; intermix't with these
> Large globous Irons fly, of dreadful Hiss,
> Singeing the Air, and from long Distance bring
> Surprizing Slaughter; on each side they fly
> By Chains connex't, and with destructive Sweep
> Behead whole Troops at once; the hairy Scalps
> Are whirl'd aloof, while numerous Trunks bestrow

> Th'ensanguin'd Field; with latent Mischief stor'd
> Show'rs of Granadoes rain, by sudden Burst
> Disploding murd'rous Bowels, fragments of Steel,
> And Stones, and Glass, and nitrous Grain adust.

French cannons aimed at the invading English ground troops fired grape shot and primitive grenades, but "chain shot," which Philips appears to describe here, was naval ordnance, prized for its capacity to shred sails. Moreover, it was fundamentally the superiority of the British and imperial cavalry forces that won the battle, which Philips describes not as an organized, concerted action but as a series of heroic vignettes. Aiming for the sublime, he often risks bathos. When he describes Marlborough narrowly escaping death, for example, he transforms a strategist into a hero in the mold of Achilles or Roland:

> With Aim direct the levell'd Bullet flew,
> But miss'd her Scope (for Destiny withstood
> Th'approaching Wound) and guiltless Plough'd her Way
> Beneath His Courser; round His Sacred Head
> The glowing Balls play innocent, while He
> With dire impetuous Sway deals Fatal Blows
> Amongst the scatter'd *Gauls.*[46]

Although he has veered away from earlier opportunities to write in praise of Marlborough, glancing at the general on his way to praising Harley and Godolphin, Philips now deploys the hyperbolic language of myth and religion. This Marlborough has a "Sacred Head" that goes miraculously untouched by "glowing Balls." Himself a combatant, he "deals Fatal Blows" to the enemy.

Addison also admired *Paradise Lost* and would help establish Milton's reputation by writing some highly influential essays on his work in the *Spectator.* Yet he drew a quite different lesson from Milton's critique of chivalric poetry—and perhaps from the cautionary example of Philips. Wary of the traditional devices of heroic verse, Addison sought to celebrate military victory in more realistic terms. His Marlborough is a strategist, planning and executing a campaign covering many miles and lasting many months. The general's victories do not arise from the "dire impetuous Sway" of his own right arm, but from organization, discipline, and determination, all evident in Addison's account of the attack on the fortress at Schellenberg, which describes actual infantry formations:

> Thick'ning their Ranks, and wedg'd in firm Array,
> The close compacted *Britons* win their way;

> In vain the Cannon, their throng'd War defac't
> With Tracks of Death, and laid the Battel waste;
> Still pressing forward to the Fight, they broke
> Through Flames of Sulphur, and a Night of Smoke,
> 'Till slaughter'd Legions fill'd the Trench below,
> And bore their fierce Avengers to the Foe.[47]

Despite the formal diction and the witty conceit that imagines the dead men carrying their avengers to the foe, these prim couplets offer an accurate narrative of Marlborough's tactics. As the "close compacted *Britons*" pressed forward in their tight formation, dead bodies filled the trench that protected the fortress, allowing those arriving from the rear to walk over them in order to cross the moat and disable the enemy cannon. When he sent his highly disciplined troops to attack in this way, the general knew they would sustain significant casualties but expected their numbers and persistence to win the day.

Addison clearly recognized that to write about war in this way was to break with the long tradition of epic and chivalric poetry, which had focused on the heroic deeds of individuals, not the effectiveness of massed forces. At the end of the poem, he applauds his hero for needing no "spurious Rays," no "borrow'd Blaze" of bogus mythology—and thus congratulates himself for avoiding poetic fiction:

> When Actions, unadorn'd, are faint and weak,
> Cities and Countries must be taught to speak;
> Gods may descend in Factions from the Skies,
> And Rivers from their Oozy Beds arise;
> Fiction may deck the Truth with spurious Rays,
> And round the Heroe cast a borrow'd Blaze.
> Marlbro's Exploits appear divinely bright,
> And proudly shine in their own Native Light;
> Rais'd of themselves, their genuine Charms they boast,
> And those who Paint 'em truest Praise e'm most.[48]

The poetic devices Addison scorns—personification of cities and countries, pagan gods descending from the heavens, rivers arising "from their Oozy Beds"—were those employed for centuries in courtly panegyrics and masques. In *Calisto,* for example, Crowne had included the continents as singing characters, personified London as Augusta, cast a royal mistress as the river Thames, and brought Jupiter, Juno, Mercury, and Diana onstage. Anne's birthday opera for 1706, *England's Glory,* shows the persistence of such devices; its singing characters include Bellona, Ceres, Britannia, Europe, Asia, Africa, America, Neptune, and Atlas. Addison's assertion that poets employ the mythological tropes of panegyric in order to inflate actions that are actually "faint and weak" is an implicit criticism of this tradition and reflects his Whig principles. Already praised for rising to prominence "on the firm Basis of Desert," Addison's Marlborough has achieved victories that need no classical or Miltonic allusions to gain the nation's respect. The poet, who was also a self-made man, is being true to modern heroism (and to Whig beliefs) by painting the general's exploits as accurately as he can.

Eight years later, the same Addison would warn Alexander Pope against using mythological imagery to celebrate the Peace of Utrecht, a treaty negotiated by a Tory administration headed by Harley and St. John. Ignoring the older poet's advice, Pope included Ceres, Britannia, and Neptune in *Windsor-Forest* and used "old Father *Thames*," arising "from his Oozy Bed," to deliver the poem's closing lines in praise of the treaty.[49] His decision to retain and reanimate the mythological language of courtly poetry may reflect his close connection with the Tory ministers and his desire to please Queen Anne, but at an even more basic level it reflects his aesthetic resistance to the Whig disdain for mythology. Poetry is not journalism, and Addison himself used figurative language effectively in *The Campaign*. Tickell tells us that Godolphin decided to hire Addison on the basis of "the applauded simile of the *Angel*," a complex passage depicting Marlborough in the midst of the battle:

'Twas then great MARLBRO's mighty Soul was prov'd,
That, in the Shock of Charging Hosts unmov'd,
Amidst Confusion, Horror, and Despair,
Examin'd all the Dreadful Scenes of War;
In peaceful Thought the Field of Death survey'd,
To fainting Squadrons sent the timely Aid,
Inspir'd repuls'd Battalions to engage,
And taught the doubtful Battel where to rage.
So when an Angel by Divine Command,
With rising Tempests shakes a guilty Land,
Such as of late o'er pale *Britannia* past,
Calm and Serene he drives the furious Blast;
And, pleas'd th' Almighty's Orders to perform,
Rides in the Whirl-wind, and directs the Storm.[50]

"Unmov'd" amid the slaughter, this hero examines, surveys, sends, inspires, and teaches—all verbs of deliberate, measured action. He does not, like Philips's hero, deal fatal blows himself, exhibiting instead what Milton had called "the better fortitude / Of Patience." The famous simile, however, compares the general to an angel executing a "Divine Command," so that Marlborough relates to Anne as the angel of the storm relates to God. Moreover, the angel in the simile is punishing "a guilty Land," and lest we think of France as the only nation deserving the wrath of God, Addison specifically invokes the great hurricane of 1703, which the queen herself had described as punishment for the "crying Sins of this Nation." "Calm and Serene" as he executes God's will, the angel represents a morally idealized version of Marlborough, carrying out the will of a queen habitually described as "Serene and Calm."[51] In this simile, Addison found one possible solution to the problem of depicting heroism in the modern world. The Marlborough represented by the angel is not an angry Achilles, indiscriminately slaughtering his foes, not a chivalric knight aggrandizing his own honor, and certainly not an opera singer reducing heroism to virtuosity. He is the calm and efficient messenger of a higher power. If Anne read only one of the many poems on Blenheim, she probably read this one.

§

After numerous advance notices in the *Diverting Post,* a new periodical devoted to the arts, Addison's poem appeared for sale on 14 December, the very day on which the Duke of Marlborough returned to England.[52] The account of the formalities surrounding the duke's arrival in the same newspaper treats the event as if it were a piece of theatre and juxtaposes the formal expressions of gratitude with news from the actual theatres:

> On *Thursday* last in the Afternoon, his Grace the Duke of *Marlborough* was introduced into the Presence of the Queen, by the Prince of *Denmark:* Her Majesty was pleased to receive him with particular Marks of Distinction; and thank'd him for his signal Services to the Allies in general, and this Nation in particular. Yesterday the Lord-Keeper in an Eloquent Oration, thank'd the Duke of *Marlborough* in the Name of the House of Lords, for his great Services Abroad. One and Twenty Commissioners appointed by the House of Commons waited upon his Grace, to return the Thanks of the House, upon the same occasion. The Lord *Mount Harman,* Eldest Son to the Earl of *Montague,* is to be Married in a few Days to the Daughter of the Duke of *Marlborough.* This Day, at the Theatre Royal in *Drury-Lane,* Mrs. *Cross,* Famous for Singing and Acting in the last Reign, Sings a New Dialogue with Mr. *Leveridge....* Mr. *Clayton's* Opera, which is set in the *Italian* manner is to be performed there. Madam *De La Valle,* a Person Eminent for Dancing,... has performed twice with great Applause.[53]

If we imagine this narrative of Marlborough's visit to the queen as the conclusion of an opera, we have all the usual elements: Prince George, a secondary character, introduces the hero in recitative; the queen and the Lord Keeper sing their arias of gratitude; a chorus of "One and Twenty Commissioners" expresses the joy of the nation. No operatic finale would be complete without a wedding, so this scene includes an announcement of the forthcoming wedding of Marlborough's daughter Mary. It was therefore natural for the newswriter to move on to mention "Mr. *Clayton's* Opera" *Arsinoe,* which opened a month later, with "an Epithalamium Song" in its final scene. Described on its title page as "An OPERA After the *Italian* MANNER: All Sung," *Arsinoe* was the first through-sung opera presented in London since *Albion and Albanius* in 1685. Although the *Diverting Post* had reported earlier that it would open at Vanbrugh's large new theatre in the Haymarket, the production actually premiered at Drury Lane—perhaps because there had been so many difficulties and delays in the construction of the new building, perhaps because the composer had inherited some shares in Drury Lane from his father, perhaps because Christopher Rich, the manager of the rival company, alertly saw an opportunity for profit, and certainly because Charles Dieupart, who played the harpsichord in the eventual production, helped the composer organize a subscription, selling hundreds of tickets in advance in order to guarantee at least three performances.[54] This process was presumably easier because there had been a successful subscription for a series of concerts in the previous season starring Catherine Tofts, who was to sing the title role in *Arsinoe.* The opera opened for subscribers on 16 January and played to large houses throughout the spring. Confirming her keen interest in opera, Anne asked the players to bring *Arsinoe* to court on her birthday (6 February 1705).

The queen was also attentive to the progress of Vanbrugh's new theatre. A manuscript note attached to a newsletter printed in August 1704, which gives architectural details and optimistically predicts the building's completion by Christmas, claims that the monarch has made a major financial contribution:

> Mr Vanbrookes Play house in the Haymarket is Roofeing and will be finisht by Christmas, being the largest in Europe. It is 60 foot wide, 132 long and 50 foot high. The walles in the foundation 7 foot thick. It is built by subscription and 3000 Guineas already subscribed by the Dukes of Devon-[shire], Somerset, etc. and it's said the Queen gave 1000 Guineas towards it.[55]

Although the anonymous author is well informed about the dimensions of the building and the particulars of the fund-raising scheme, it is unlikely that Anne provided financial support on anything like the scale imagined in this report.[56] It is even less likely that she attended, as "an audience of one," a concert in the unfinished building sometime in November, as some have inferred from a garbled advertisement in the *Diverting Post.*[57] But it is certain that she issued, on the very day that Marlborough returned to England, a "License for a New Company of Comedians," in which she gave Vanbrugh and Congreve, two prominent Kit-Cats, control over the theatre company currently occupying Lincoln's Inn Fields:

> Whereas We have thought fitt for the better reforming the Abuses, and Immorality of the Stage That a New Company of Comedians should be Establish'd for our Service, under stricter Government and Regulations than have been formerly. We therefore reposing especiall trust, and confidence in Our Trusty and Welbeloved John Vanbrugh and William Congreve Esqrs for the due Execution, and performance of this our Will and Pleasure, do Give and Grant unto them the said John Vanbrugh, and William Congreve full power and Authority to form, constitute, and Establish for Us, a Company of Comedians with full and free License to Act and Represent in any Convenient Place, during Our Pleasure all Comedies, Tragedys Plays, Interludes Operas, and to perform all other Theatricall and Musicall Entertainments whatsoever and to settle such Rules and Orders for the good Government of the said Company, as the Chamberlain of our Household shall from time to time direct and approve of Given at our Court at St James this 14th day of December in the third Year of Our Reign.[58]

The pious language about "reforming the Abuses, and Immorality of the Stage" was ironic, as Jeremy Collier, the self-proclaimed expert on the "immorality and profaneness of the English stage," had repeatedly attacked both Congreve and Vanbrugh for their allegedly smutty comedies. The purpose of the proclamation, however, is clear enough: the actors currently performing at the small and inadequate theatre in Lincoln's Inn Fields were ready to move to the splendid new building as soon as it was finished. Betterton, who had been the leader of this troupe since its secession from the United Company in 1695, was nearly seventy years old and thus amenable to giving up the burdens of management. Vanbrugh, who had raised the money to erect the theatre and designed the structure himself, would now be in charge, with the assistance of his good friend Congreve. If Godolphin was signaling his rapprochement with the Whigs by sponsoring Addison's poem, deliberately published on the day of Marlborough's triumphant return, it is certainly possible that Anne was sending a similar signal by issuing her theatrical order empowering Vanbrugh and Congreve on the same momentous day. As she had shown by sponsoring a lavish musical entertainment for the "King of Spain" a year earlier, the queen wanted London to be as sophisticated and advanced in its culture as other European capitals, and the prospect of a theatre larger than any on the Continent, presenting operas as well as spoken plays, was a promising step toward this goal. As she knew, most of Vanbrugh's wealthy investors came from the group of estab-

James Thornhill, *Queen Anne's Patronage of the Arts* (1704).

lishment Whigs whose support Godolphin was now enlisting. What better day for the queen to issue his license than the day marked by the arrival of the general who had rescued Europe from French domination?

Vanbrugh made a direct bid for royal support by naming his venue the Queen's Theatre and by commissioning a ceiling painting depicting "Queen Anne's Patronage of the Arts," for which a sketch by the decorative artist James Thornhill survives. Thornhill was to become the leading decorative painter of the era, adorning such important spaces as the dome of St. Paul's Cathedral, the queen's bedroom at Hampton Court, and the hall ceiling in Blenheim Palace. At this time, however, he was just emerging from apprenticeship; his first documented commission was painting the scenery for *Arsinoe*. If Thornhill actually painted the ceiling of the Queen's Theatre, which is not at all certain, his work did not have a long life.[59] The grand barrel vault that Vanbrugh had designed made spoken dialogue hard to hear, and shortly after the theatre opened, it closed again for extensive renovations, which included lowering the ceiling. The sketch, however, provides fascinating evidence about what the young artist thought might please Queen Anne. Rather than attempting an actual depiction of the now obese monarch, Thornhill presents her as Pallas Athena, holding a spear and a shield inscribed "AR" (for Anna Regina) and surrounded by the icons of the British monarchy: the lion, the unicorn, the crown, and the star associated with the Order of the Garter.[60] In the semicircular frieze, with three circular spaces to accommodate the chandeliers, he places one set of painting implements, one dramatic mask, and at least six musical instruments; the prominence of music here is in line with Vanbrugh's operatic dreams. Directly above Athena, illuminated by bright light, sits the figure of Apollo, surrounded by the nine Muses, to whom Thornhill, mindful of the absence of a Muse of painting in the ancient scheme, has added a tenth with a palette and brushes. An eleventh Muse, measuring the globe with a square and a ruler, represents Geography, an appropriate figure for an expanding empire, as is Navigation, the bearded male figure to Apollo's left, who holds a cross staff, a device used for measuring the height of the sun from the deck of a ship.[61] The ominous figure of Time, holding his iconic sickle, may be Thornhill's way of encouraging Anne to continue and increase her patronage of the arts, reminding her of the aphorism that art endures while life is short. The queen, however, did not need a reminder of her own mortality. It was she, after all, who had recently quoted Cowley's lines on death who "Mowes down all with an impartial Hand," and her court would spend this whole winter in mourning. On 31 October 1704, they began to wear black in honor of "the duchesse of Holstein, sister to Prince George," and after briefly donning colored clothing for the royal birthday in February, they went into mourning again for Anne's cousin the Queen of Prussia, daughter of the Electress Sophia.[62]

§

On 15 December, the day after Anne's theatrical order, Marlborough attended the House of Lords, where he cast his vote against a second reading of the bill prohibiting Occasional Conformity. Nottingham and Rochester were among the diehard Tories who lodged a protest against the vote, despite the presence of their disapproving queen. Although Anne's hope for parliamentary concord was evidently doomed, the string of patriotic celebrations continued. On 30 December, in a grand ceremony at Windsor attended by "abundance of the nobility and gentry,"[63] Godolphin became a Knight Companion in the Order of the Garter. A poem on his installation follows the lead of a news story in the unreliable *Diverting Post,* announcing that "their Graces the Dukes of *Northumberland* and *Marlborough*" were to act as Anne's proxies:[64]

> He that has wisely fix'd a Monarch's Throne,
> Should be in Honour's Seat installed by none,
> But by a Monarch's Champion, and a Monarch's Son. }

The "Monarch's Son," was George Fitzroy, Duke of Northumberland, the youngest of Charles II's illegitimate sons by the Countess of Castlemaine. Though handsome and charming, Northumberland owed his eminence entirely to his somewhat

Plate 1

Sir Peter Lely, *Queen Anne, when a Child*
(c. 1667–68).

Plate 2

Sir Peter Lely, *Queen Anne, when a Child*. Detail.

Plate 3
Sir Peter Lely,
Mary II when Princess
(c. 1672).

Plate 4 Pierre Mignard, *Louise Kéroualle,
Duchess of Portsmouth* (1682).

Plate 5 Pierre Mignard, *The Marquise de
Seignelay and Two of her Sons* (1691).

Plate 6 Peter Paul Rubens, Oil sketch for *Peace Embracing Plenty* (1633–34).

Plate 7
Studio of
Sir Peter Lely,
Moll Davis
(c. 1668).

Plate 8
Benedetto Gennari,
Annunciation
(1686).

Plate 9
Anne Killigrew, *Venus Attired
by the Three Graces*
(c. 1683).

Plate 10
Anne Killigrew, *Venus Attired
by the Three Graces*, Detail.

Plate 11
Studio of Sir Godfrey
Kneller, *Princess Anne
with William Duke of
Gloucester* (c. 1694).

Plate 12
Studio of
Sir Godfrey Kneller,
William, Duke of Gloucester
(c. 1699).

Plate 13 Anonymous English artist, *"Coronation Portrait" of Queen Elizabeth I,* (c. 1600).

Plate 14 Studio of Sir Godfrey Kneller, *Portrait of Queen Anne* (c. 1705).

Plate 15 John Riley (or John Closterman), *Anne Morrice* (c. 1692).

Plate 16 Sir Godfrey Kneller, *John Duke of Marlborough* (1706).

Plate 17 Godfrey Kneller, *Queen Anne presenting the plans of Blenheim to military Merit* (1708).

Plate 18
Sir Godfrey Kneller,
John, Duke of Marlborough
(1712).

WHAT FRUITS FROM OUR DIVISIONS SPRING ❧ 395

tainted birth, in contrast to the "Monarch's Champion," Marlborough, who had achieved his current distinction on what Addison called "the firm Basis of Desert." Pairing these two men gave the anonymous poet an opportunity to use a device Dryden had perfected in his Virgilian translations: a triplet where the context leads the reader to expect a couplet, with a six-foot "alexandrine" at the end. In this instance, the "Monarch's Throne" in which Godolphin has "fix'd" the queen finds its echo in the "Honour's Seat" he now occupies at Windsor, with the "Monarch's Champion" and the "Monarch's Son" providing balance in the long last line. Unfortunately, the poet was probably mistaken in identifying Marlborough as a formal participant in the Garter installation. According to Boyer's very full account, Northumberland's associate in installing Godolphin was actually the Earl of Pembroke, President of Anne's Privy Council.[65] The only other Garter Knight whom Boyer specifically identifies as present was the Duke of Buckingham, whose decision to attend this celebration is curious, as Godolphin was now actively seeking to remove him from the Cabinet. In late March, as Marlborough was leaving for the Continent, Anne dismissed her old beau from his position as Lord Privy Seal and replaced him with John Holles, Duke of Newcastle, a wealthy, moderate Whig recommended by Robert Harley—and an investor in Vanbrugh's new theatre.

Two days after the Garter ceremony, the queen heard the expected New Year's ode. In Tate's verses for this occasion, evidently written for several singers,[66] the infant New Year complains there is nothing left for him because 1704, the year just concluded, has spent the whole fund of glory and praise; "old Time" consoles the whining New Year by assuring him that he will witness more great deeds. The concerns expressed in this clumsy ode proved justified: the military campaign of 1705 did not make gains remotely comparable to those achieved in 1704. At this point, however, the nation was more interested in celebrating past victories than in imagining the future. Two days after the queen heard the New Year's song, she watched as Marlborough led a grand parade carrying the 34 standards and 128 colors captured from French regiments at Blenheim from the Tower to St. James's and on through St. James's Park to Westminster Hall, "the Hautboys playing the Tune of, *Let the Soldiers Rejoyce*"—a piece by her beloved Mr. Purcell. From the lodgings in St. James's occupied by the Fitzhardings, whose windows opened onto the Mall, Anne had an excellent view of this colorful procession and heard "40 Guns in the Park being twice fired at the same time,"[67] a salute quite likely to make her remember the Duke of Gloucester, who had been so fond of firing his cannon on such occasions. On 6 January, the Lord Mayor played host for a splendid dinner in honor of Marlborough and his senior officers, with an ode by Peter Motteux, set to music by the organist and composer John Weldon and sung by the chapel tenor Richard Elford and the theatrical bass Richard Leveridge.[68]

Events like the New Year's observance, the parade, and the banquet were supposed to be unalloyed expressions of patriotic joy, but for some of Anne's subjects, these celebrations were irresistible opportunities for covert political discourse. As a Huguenot refugee, Motteux gravitated toward the Whigs,[69] and the climactic duet in his ode develops the Whig belief that military successes, by opening new markets for world trade, will make Britain prosperous:

> Ocean, proud to Share the Blessing,
> Happy Town, thou'rt now possessing,
> Turns the ready Stream, to See
> Thee in the Worthies blest, the Worthies blest in Thee.
> See, see, the Sword, the Trident, and the Gown,
> Joyn with the Nerve of War, the Wealthy, Willing Town.

The "Wealthy, Willing Town," represented on this occasion by its mayor and aldermen, believed that the government's massive expenditure on the war was a sound investment, sure to be repaid in increasing trade with the wider world. Motteux gives artful expression to these views by personifying the Ocean, which sees the army, the navy, and the Church joined to the City by "the Nerve of War." There are several points of contact between this poetic allegory and Thornhill's sketch for the theatre ceiling, with its addition of Navigation and Geography to the representatives of the arts.

The day after the Lord Mayor's banquet, the Vice-Chancellor of Oxford University presented the queen with a printed copy of the orations and poems in Latin declaimed at the university's New Year celebration in the Sheldonian Theatre, which expressed views of heroism, patriotism, and the current war quite unlike those sung for the duke in the City.[70] As someone who knew Latin probably pointed out to Anne, fully half the poems in the volume were tributes to Admiral Rooke, whom she was preparing to dismiss on 6 January. In an ill-considered address, the Vice-Chancellor treated Blenheim and Gibraltar as equivalents, and the monarch "return'd a dry Answer."[71] She probably never knew that the Oxford volume included a Latin poem in praise of Marlborough by Gilbert Burnet, Jr., the bishop's youngest son, who had served in Gloucester's court as a little boy and devoted a section of his poem to expressing his honor and love for Anne's much-lamented son. Professional poets also enlisted the ghosts of Gloucester and Blandford, the lost heirs of the queen and the Marlboroughs, to help them celebrate the recent victory. In Philips's *Bleinheim*, which finally appeared on 2 January, the ghosts of the French soldiers slain on the field "roam / Erroneous, and disconsolate" in an underworld imagined in classical terms,

> when lo! They see,
> Thrô the Dun Mist, in Blooming Beauty fresh,
> Two Lovely Youths, that Amicably walkt
> O'er Verdant Meads; ... One, to Empire Born,
> Egregious Prince, whose Manly Childhood shew'd
> His mingled Parents, and portended Joy
> Unspeakable; Thou, His Associate Dear...
> Shouldst CHURCHILL be! But Heav'n severe cut short
> Their springing Years.[72]

When they recognize Blandford as the son of "their Great Subduer," the French ghosts flee in fear. In a similar passage, the Irish poet Edmund Arwaker alters the mythic geography to place the lost boys in heaven, looking down on the battlefield and "stooping" like birds of prey to join the fight:

> Mean time *Marcellus* scorning to survey
> His Parents Arms confess a doubtful Fray[,]
> The Golden Gate of *Saphire* Heav'n unbars,
> Stoops to the Conflict, and forsakes the Stars.
> *Alexis* from the Clouds his Prince attends,
> Both valiant Youths, Hereditary Friends.
> O Death! How has thou blasted in their Spring
> A blossom'd Hero and a blooming King![73]

Neither poet would have included such a passage if he feared it would give offense. Both of them evidently believed that there might be some comfort for their monarch and her favorite in imagining how thrilled their sons would have been by a victory on the scale of Blenheim.

Although the Marlboroughs now seemed fated to have no male heirs, Parliament provided for their descendants by making permanent the grant of £5,000 a year that they had previously limited to the queen's lifetime. On 11 January, the Commons "humbly desir'd her Majesty, That she would be Graciously pleas'd to consider of some proper Means to perpetuate the Memory of the great Services perform'd by [Marlborough]."[74] Anne made a show of taking some time to consider her response, then announced that she was "inclined" to grant the duke and his heirs the royal manor of Woodstock. This plan had evidently been under discussion before these formal steps; years later, the architect Vanbrugh remembered meeting Marlborough at the theatre in December and beginning to discuss with him the project that became Blenheim Palace.[75] All the pieces fell quickly into place: the Commons gave their assent and found the required funds; the duke made two trips to study the site before leaving for his summer campaign on the Continent; the architect constructed a wooden model, which Anne and George examined and approved; and on 19 June, at "about six o'clock in the evening," Vanbrugh laid the first stone at Blenheim, described by a witness as "finely polished, about 18 inches over," with an inscription commemorating the battle "inlayed with Pewter.... 7 Gentlemen gave it a stroke with a Hammer, and threw down each of them a Guinea." The celebration that followed, in marked stylistic contrast to the operas for which the architect had designed his new theatre, was a country revel featuring "three Morris Dances, one of Young Fellows, one of Maidens, and the other of Old Beldames." In the Town Hall, "plenty of Sack, Claret, Cakes, etc., were prepared for the Gentry and better sort; and under the Cross eight Barrels of Ale, with abundance of Cakes, were placed for the Common People."[76] The country folk had cause for rejoicing, as the construction project and the grand house it created would both be sources of employment; by August, some thirteen hundred men were at work on the site.[77] Yet Vanbrugh's problems as a theatre manager, which were apparent long before this ceremony, may well have been a consequence of his becoming preoccupied with architectural work. His first great baroque building, Castle Howard, was under construction in Yorkshire, and now he needed to devote significant time to planning and executing Blenheim Palace.

In joining to confirm the grant to Marlborough, Parliament achieved a rare moment of unity in the midst of a bitter struggle. For much of this session, both houses were preoccupied with a disagreement over a disputed election in Aylesbury, a quarrel that began in 1702 when a Tory official refused to allow a working man to cast his vote. This dispute about the franchise, which had bubbled up intermittently during the last two sessions of Parliament, now degenerated into a war between the two houses, with the House of Commons imprisoning for "breach of privilege" a group of Aylesbury men who had taken their case to court, and the House of Lords supporting the prisoners' petition for habeas corpus. The legal and parliamentary maneuvers undertaken in this overblown controversy eventually paralyzed the legislature. Even more troubling to the queen were frequent complaints about "mismanagements in the admiralty," including one tactlessly presented to her on the eve of her birthday.[78] Embarrassed by the implied criticism of her husband, who remained the titular head of the admiralty, Anne put a stop to both discussions in mid-March by proroguing, then dismissing her Parliament. The Triennial Act required new elections, which followed in due course.

§

This year's royal birthday came between the flurry of celebrations marking Marlborough's brief stay in England and the queen's exasperated prorogation of her fractious legislature. It was her fortieth, however, and the official *Gazette* reported "an extraordinary Appearance at Court of the Nobility and Gentry, as well for their number as the Magnificence of their Habits."[79] The main event in the day's entertainment was the opera *Arsinoe*, which was still a new sensation. The first three performances had been largely for the subscribers, so many of the "Nobility and Gentry" at St. James's got their first opportunity to experience "Mr. Clayton's opera" at the queen's birthday celebration. No contemporary witness tells us whether Thornhill's sets came to court with the production, but there is every reason to believe that the creators and performers of *Arsinoe*, thrilled by the opportunity to perform at court, did all they could to make this production memorable. Persuading English audiences to accept through-sung opera was a challenge, and the royal birthday was a golden opportunity to present an opera for a captive audience of important people.

Until this moment, an "opera" in England had normally been a spoken play with elaborate musical scenes. The best of these works enjoyed a long afterlife; musical programs of the period, including the subscription concerts funded by the nobility, frequently featured excerpts from Dryden and Purcell's *King Arthur* (1691).[80] In an English "dramatic opera" or "semiopera" of this kind, speaking actors carried the main plot, but in order to mount a fully sung opera with recitatives, Clayton needed a full cast of top-quality singers, and very few such voices were available, which probably explains the adjustments Peter Motteux made when translating Tommaso Stanzani's libretto. By eliminating one major character and cutting numerous scenes, Motteux was able to reduce the cast to three male and three female singers, yet Clayton's self-serving preface to the published libretto says nothing at all about his collaborator's helpful alterations:

> The Stile of this Musick is to express the Passions, which is the Soul of Musick: And though the Voices are not equal to the *Italian*, yet I have engag'd the Best that were to be found in *England*; and I have not been wanting, to the utmost of my Diligence, in the Instructing of them.
>
> The Musick being Recitative, may not, at first, meet with that General Acceptation, as is to be hop'd for from the Audience's being better acquainted with it: But if this Attempt shall, by pleasing the Nobility and Gentry, be a Means of bringing this manner of Musick to be us'd in my Native Country, I shall think all my Study and Pains very well employ'd.[81]

As Clayton evidently knew, gestures of modesty were an expected feature of prefaces, but instead of expressing humility about his music, he risks insulting his singers by calling them "not equal to the *Italian*," and underestimates his hearers by insinuating that it will take them time to become "better acquainted" with recitative—a gesture that seems especially strange in light of the fact that a subscription raised from "the Nobility and Gentry" had made the production possible. This is a remarkable show of pride from a composer whose music is not only vastly inferior to Purcell's, but not nearly as tuneful as the works of the Italian composers to whom he claims to have dedicated his "Study and Pains."[82] Clayton implies that he has found a musical way "to express the Passions," and the plot of this opera, like that of the later *Camilla*, features swirling passions among the main characters, with the queen and others falling hopelessly in love, an important male character in disguise for most of the drama, a conspiracy against a ruling monarch, an attempted suicide, and a comic subplot involving the servants. For a composer who could actually express the passions, there were some good opportunities, and Petronio Franceschini, the original composer, had exploited some of them.[83] But Clayton, despite having studied in Italy, was a much weaker composer than those on whom he modeled his work.

Mindful of the English company's limitations, Motteux cut the first two scenes of the Italian *Arsinoe*, which required elaborate machinery, a ghost, and a male chorus.[84] His opera begins with a reworked version of Stanzani's third scene, a moonlit garden in which the hero Ormondo, sung by the countertenor Francis Hughes, seeks his beloved Dorisbe but instead encounters the beautiful Arsinoe, who is sleeping outside. As he gazes in wonder at the queen, whose identity is unknown to him, a masked assassin enters, drawing a bow to kill her. Ormondo bravely prevents the murder, while his servant Delbo, an ancestor of Mozart's Papageno, quails in terror. Motteux condensed this scene from a much longer version in the Italian libretto, presumably hoping that rapid action and frequent changes of speaker would engage the audience. Clayton's setting, however, is rhythmically wooden and harmonically inept.[85]

The airs in the opera, many of which became popular enough to appear in the *Monthly Mask of Vocal Music*, are better than this incompetent recitative, but not much better. It is hard to escape the conclusion that *Arsinoe* succeeded in spite of its music. It was a novelty, with new sets and a popular star in the title role, and it gave audiences some idea of what an opera might be like. By the time Clayton mounted his next opera, *Rosamond*, with an original English libretto by Addison, his limitations as a composer had become obvious—not least because the audience had heard Bononcini's music for *Camilla*.

Despite Clayton's shortcomings, Congreve and Vanbrugh knew they had missed an opportunity. Tapped to write the prologue for the court performance of *Arsinoe*, Congreve could hardly avoid considering how the royal interest shown in the opera might have helped his new company. On 3 February, he wrote wearily to a friend, "I know not when the house will open, nor what we shall begin withal; but I believe with no opera. There is nothing settled yet."[86] Three days later, he was

Mus. Ex. 8.2: Thomas Clayton, recitative from Act 1 of *Arsinoe* (1705).

presumably present at St. James's to hear someone recite his elegant and courtly prologue, which makes no direct reference to the opera being presented by the rival company. Instead, the poet promises that his "Happy Muse, to this high Scene preferr'd / Hereafter shall in Loftier Strains be heard." Obliquely answering Collier and other prudish critics, he predicts that the muse will "Sing of Virtue and Heroick Fame."

> Happy her future Days! Which are design'd
> Alone to Paint the Beauties of the Mind.
> By Just Originals to draw with Care,
> And Copy from the Court a Faultless Fair:
> Such Labours with Success her Hopes may crown,
> And shame to Manners an incorrigible Town.

Although Congreve appears to be promising to reform the stage, he is also delivering a concealed compliment to Harriet Godolphin, Sarah Churchill's daughter, whom he regarded as a "Faultless Fair" and who would have been present at court in her function as a Lady-in-Waiting to the queen.[87] He goes on to picture the muse wondering which of the virtuous "Originals" to draw, until her gaze falls upon the queen, whose "Inimitable Worth" awes the muse and whose auspicious birth, remembered on this day, has led inevitably to "Foreign Conquest," "Domestick Peace," and even "the Battel won at BLENHEIM's Glorious Field."[88]

Smarting from their missed opportunity to mount *Arsinoe*, Vanbrugh and Congreve now decided to stage a real Italian opera for their long-awaited opening, which took place on Monday, 9 April, the day after Easter. Their timing was disastrous. Congreve's prediction that they would *not* begin with an opera, made as recently as February, suggests that the new piece, *Gli amori d'Ergasto*, with music by Jakob (or "Giacomo") Greber, was put together very quickly—but not quickly enough to take advantage of a town filled with possible supporters. When Anne prorogued Parliament on 14 March, a move widely understood as a prelude to dismissing them and calling elections, many members of both houses departed for the country. Marlborough sailed for the Continent on 29 March, so there were no army officers to join the audience. Worse yet, the court itself celebrated the end of the parliamentary session by planning an extended holiday trip to Newmarket, which was to include a formal visit to Cambridge. The queen left on 10 April, the morning after the first performance of Greber's opera; many of her courtiers had left earlier to prepare the way.[89] Perhaps because it had a short and unsuccessful run, this pastoral opera has left very sketchy records. Like the later *Camilla*, it featured shepherdesses and a wild boar, as we know from the bilingual word-book printed by Tonson, but the music has disappeared and the cast is unknown. "It lasted but 5 Days," according to Downes the prompter, "and they being lik'd but indifferently by the Gentry; they in a little time marcht back to their own Country."[90] The reference to the audience as "the Gentry" is telling. Clayton, in his preface to *Arsinoe*, had expressed his hope of "pleasing the Nobility and Gentry," and the government *Gazette* had used the same phrase to describe the guests who heard his opera at Anne's birthday party. Downes is thus laconically recording the absence of the nobility from the Haymarket premiere, which was surely a disappointment to the hapless new managers.

Accompanied by many members of "the Nobility," the queen attended the races at Newmarket, where a horse owned by the Duke of Somerset won the "Queen's Plate" on 12 April.[91] On the day of the race, a delegation from Cambridge invited her to make a formal visit to the university, which had evidently been part of the plan from the start. In contrast to Tory Oxford, whose leaders had recently annoyed her, Cambridge had a Whig Chancellor, the same Duke of Somerset, who had left London on 5 April to prepare for the royal visit.[92] Like the commissioning of a poem on Blenheim from Addison, this royal progress to the university was an indirect but effective way for Godolphin "to announce the ministry's intentions to the electorate."[93] Godolphin's son Francis, the husband of Sarah's daughter Harriet, had recently received his M.A. from Cambridge, and his father was planning to put him forward as a candidate for Parliament, hoping to defeat one of the two Tackers who represented Cambridge University. By promoting court candidates like his son, the Lord Treasurer intended to strengthen that part of the Tory party that had not supported the Tackers, and while he was also willing to work with the Whigs to defeat the Tackers, he was not hoping for a Whig landslide.[94] The queen's personal animus against the Tackers remained sharp, but she was by no means ready to cede control of the government to the Whigs, whom she still mistrusted.

When Anne arrived in Cambridge, on Monday, 16 April, she enjoyed a splendid reception: "The Ways were all along strowed with Flowers: the Bells rung, and the Conduits run with Wine."[95] Somerset greeted her with a formal speech expressing "The deep Sense the University had of the great Honour her Majesty was pleased to do them, by her Royal Presence," and William Ayloffe, the University Orator, who had written a poem on Anne's wedding back in 1683, "made her a Speech full of Loyalty and Obedience." As was usual during a royal visit, "Degrees in the several Faculties were, by her Majesty's especial Grace, conferred upon Persons of high Nobility, and distinguishing Merit." The list of "Noble Persons admitted Doctors in Law" on this occasion includes sixteen Whig lords, half of whom were investors in Vanbrugh's opera house: Devonshire, Grafton, Bolton, Hartington, Kent, Kingston, Wharton, and Halifax appear on both lists. Although they were entitled to free admission as investors, it is highly unlikely that these Whig grandees managed to attend *Gli amori d'Ergasto* before traveling to Newmarket and Cambridge, where they had the opportunity to receive academic honors and make plans for the upcoming election. In addition to granting these honorary degrees, Anne knighted three Cambridge scholars, including Isaac Newton, who was her Master of the Mint. Although the queen had some knowledge of Newton's mathematical prowess, having previously named him as mathematics instructor to the Duke of Gloucester, her motive for knighting him now was political: Halifax, who had long been close to Newton, and who was having an affair with the mathematician's niece, had persuaded him to stand as a candidate in the upcoming election.[96]

The dinner itself took place at Trinity College, with the queen "upon a Throne erected five Foot high for that purpose; and four large Tables, with 50 Covers each, were prepared for the Nobility and Gentry." Student poets had written verses for the occasion, but the manuscript preserving their poems tells us that "they were none of 'em spoke, but given about at the tables where the Noblemen sate."[97] Between courses, the queen and her party would thus have had the opportunity to read copies of a poem comparing her favorably to Henry VIII and Edward III, the founders of Trinity:

> The mighty Dead the ffounders of this Place,
> Monarch's and happy Heroes of thy race,
> Harry and Edward, joyous shou'd be shewn
> Scourges of France, and Types of thy Renown.
> Each shou'd confess a Queen's superiour Reign
> Cressy shou'd yield to Blenheim's fatal plain
> And Marlbro' last compleat ye glorious Scene.

According to these flattering lines, the queen is "superiour" to her royal predecessors, and the victory at Blenheim is greater than the Battle of Crécy, a crushing defeat inflicted on the French by Edward III in 1346.

Not content to invoke the past in order to praise the present, the student poet concludes by predicting a glorious future:

> So may thy Marlbro' still fresh Lawrels bring,
> And his next Triumph shew a Captive King.
> May Branches still like these thy Train support,
> And Churchills yet unborn adorn thy Court;
> Ages of Bliss may thy Great Consort live
> And Joys uninterrupted take and give:
> And last these Blessings to confirm and crown
> Let Him and Heaven conspire to give a Son.

In order to gain "fresh Lawrels," the heroic duke, who has already captured the commander-in-chief of the French army, will now have to capture Louis XIV, and in order to "confirm and crown" the blessings of this reign, both Sarah (forty-four) and Anne (now forty) will have to give birth again. In gesturing toward the "Branches" from Churchill's stock who support the queen's train, the poet presumably refers to Marlborough's daughters, two of whom were among her Ladies of the Bedchamber, and by hoping for "Churchills yet unborn," he flatters the duchess, who still looked younger than her age, and alludes delicately to Lord Blandford, who had died in his rooms at King's College just two years earlier and would thus have been remembered by many current Cambridge students. But Sarah was not present. Her grief for Blandford was still too intense for her to contemplate returning to the place of his death,[98] and the election gave her an opportunity for political activity. Admiral George Churchill, Marlborough's brother, had long been a Tory MP for St. Albans and was sure to be returned, but the second representative of the town, John Gape, had actually voted for the Tack. After seeing Marlborough off at the seaside, the duchess went to St. Albans to gather support for Henry Killigrew, a moderate Tory Admiral whom the court had put forward in hopes of defeating Gape.[99]

§

After the visit to Cambridge, Anne spent a few more days at Newmarket, returning to London in time to celebrate the third anniversary of her coronation (23 April), which she marked by issuing her official proclamation calling for a new Parliament. Although the anniversary was normally an occasion for rituals of joy, this year there was urgent concern about a recent execution in Scotland. Thomas Green, a young English sailor returning from a trading voyage to India, had brought his leaky ship into harbor in Edinburgh the previous July, only to have his whole crew arrested and charged with murdering a Scottish captain whose ship had gone missing in Madagascar. This arrest was evidently a reprisal for the seizing of a Scottish merchant ship in London some six months earlier at the instigation of the East India Company, who were unwilling to allow a vessel flying Scots colors to participate in the lucrative trade to the East Indies. Although the case against Green was vague and weak, he became a scapegoat for the deep resentment felt by many Scots toward the English, a feeling exacerbated by the recent actions of the English Parliament. The queen, who was aware of the trial, had dispatched a reprieve to Edinburgh before going to Newmarket, but mob justice prevailed, and Green was hanged, with two of his officers, on 11 April.[100] On the evening of 23 April, which Anne might have hoped to devote to celebrations, she held instead "a great council at St. James's," at which "the case of captain Green, . . . was warmly debated, but came to no resolution."[101]

This tantalizing summary by Luttrell is the only surviving record of the discussion of this case in Anne's Privy Council.[102] From the description of the debate as "warm," we may infer that some of those participating shared the views of an anonymous English poet who now excoriated Scotland as "a greedy, dark, degenerate place of Sin" and expressed his outrage "That English Blood shou'd be a Sacrifice, / To please a Scabby Land's plebeian Eyes."[103] Although he devotes most of his pages to condescending and racist condemnations of the Scots, this poet also stresses the importance of domestic unity:

> *Tory* at *Whigg*, and *Whigg* at *Tory* rails;
> (Fume in their Heads, and Firebrands at their Tails)
> Biggots with Fiery Zealots disagree,
> And the Devil dances to the Harmony.

. . . .

Thus while they are pretending to withstand
The Pow'r of *France*, they lend a helping hand.[104]

The poet does not seem to have recognized that if partisan and religious discord within England strengthened the hand of France, then strife with Scotland did so as well, especially as there was reason to fear that the Scots might someday name the Pretender as their monarch. The queen, however, grasped this truth and evidently concluded that it would be unwise to allow the case of Green to undo the larger process leading to a discussion of Union. She did what she could for the remaining members of the crew, who were quietly released in October, but she did not allow Green's death to terminate the process that now looked likely to produce face-to-face negotiations on the question of Union. In the address she sent to the Scots Parliament, which was preparing to meet in June, she emphasized the importance of achieving Union and studiously omitted any reference to the unfortunate Captain Green.

A few weeks later, there was another notable discussion in the Privy Council, this one concerning international relations and royal protocol. On 12 May, the queen received formal notification of the death of the Emperor Leopold in Vienna, an event that reminded some of her advisors that Leopold had not gone into mourning when William died in 1701:

> It being debated in Council, Whether the Queen, and the Court, should go into Mourning for the late Emperor, the Majority of the Board gave their Opinions against it, because the Emperors of *Germany,* assuming too great a Superiority over the other Crown'd Heads of *Europe,* had hitherto refus'd to mourn for the Monarchs of *Great Britain;* But Count *de Gallas* having promised in his Master's Name, that the Emperor would for the future, go into Mourning for the Kings and Queens of *England,* Her Majesty did the same for the late Emperour.[105]

By honoring the Habsburg Emperor, which was her instinctive preference, Anne believed she was securing his family's promise to honor her when her own time came, and there were also good political reasons for her decision to override her advisors and go into mourning once more. The dead man was the father of Charles III, who was now in Portugal, supported by British troops as he actively sought the Spanish throne. Leopold's elder son Joseph, the new Emperor, had given assurances that all the promises his father had made to the Allies would remain in force, so it would be unwise to risk offending him by appearing to disregard his father's death. But this was also the same Queen Anne who had, as Sarah puts it, "the greatest memory that ever was, especially for such things as are all forms, & ceremonys, giving people their due Ranks at Processions & their proper Places at Balls, & having the right order at Installments & funerals."[106] At a personal level, she still remembered her outrage when William stopped her from putting her apartments into mourning for her father in 1701. Such decisions were now hers to make, and by refusing to accede to the majority, she was reminding her courtiers, most of them up to their elbows in a hotly contested election, that she retained some personal prerogatives as queen and would not hesitate to use them.

Yet if Anne believed she had sent a signal of her autonomy by insisting on putting her court into mourning, she soon had to face the fact that even the world of "forms, & ceremonys" had now become an arena for partisan action. In a letter to the Duchess of Marlborough, written on 15 May, Halifax reports a conversation with Godolphin in which the Lord Treasurer appeared to invite the Whigs to "propose somebody to be employ'd" in conveying Anne's condolences to the Emperor:

> He spoke to Me of sending some Man of Quality to Vienna, in such a manner, as if He would have had us propose somebody to be employ'd in that Compliment. I was not prepared to offer one, and that discourse fell. I have since thought that if there was a disposition to make Ld Sunderland Secretary, the employing Him on such an Embassy, for three or four months, might properly introduce him into the method of the businesse, the Queen would be better acquainted with Him, and soe would soften by degrees.[107]

When asked to propose a poet for Blenheim some eight months earlier, Halifax had allegedly named the moderate and civilized Addison, but when asked to propose an envoy to Vienna, he now named a keen partisan. Charles Spencer, Earl of Sunderland, despite his status as the scion of a noble family and his marriage to Marlborough's daughter Anne, was an outspoken opponent of monarchy and privilege who had deeply irritated the queen by opposing the grant to Prince George in 1702. As a price for their support of the war, the leading Whigs were now pressing to have him appointed as one of the two Secretaries of State, replacing Sir Charles Hedges, a moderate Tory who had been Secretary of State for the Southern Division since Anne came to the throne. Anticipating resistance, Halifax proposes putting Sunderland forward for a short-term post as Anne's special envoy to Vienna, in the hope that her opposition to him will "soften by degrees." Godolphin evidently embraced this plan, and Anne, after a struggle, acceded. "I have no thought or desire to have you join yourself to any one party," she wrote wearily to Godolphin. "All I wish is to be kept out of the power of both."[108]

408 of QUEEN ANNE

In light of her resistance to appointing him, Anne's gracious civility toward Sunderland is remarkable. In a lengthy letter written on 17 June, she asks him to seek "an Accommodation" between the new Emperor and his rebellious subjects in Hungary:

> We have to that purpose given you a Commission to interpose as well with the present Emperor to receive his Subjects to mercy, as with the Malecontents in Hungary to have recourse to it, and to lay down their Arms, and to soften things on both Sides as much as possibly may be, in order to the bringing them to an Agreement.[109]

Anne is unlikely to have known that Halifax, in pushing for this appointment, had hoped that her opposition to Sunderland would "*soften* by degrees," so it is striking to see her hoping that Sunderland himself can "*soften* things on both Sides" in distant Vienna.

By the time the queen wrote this letter, it was clear that she had not succeeded in her plan to punish the Tackers, over half of whom had retained their seats in the election. Godolphin was embarrassed and displeased when his son and Sir Isaac Newton lost the contest at Cambridge; Sarah was outraged when Henry Killigrew lost by three votes to John Gape, the incumbent Tacker at St. Albans, though a later challenge in the House of Commons overturned the results. The Whig party as a whole had made significant gains, some of them at the expense of the moderate Tories favored by the queen and the Treasurer, and now they were clamoring for a share of government posts. Godolphin was attempting to placate them by engineering Sunderland's appointment as the envoy to Vienna and by installing Addison, whose administrative talents he had recognized, as an Undersecretary of State, working for Charles Hedges.[110] But these measures did not "soften" Whig demands for more important offices. Pressure was growing on the queen to replace the aged and incompetent Nathan Wright, who had been her Lord Keeper since her accession. Many important ecclesiastical appointments came through the office of the Lord Keeper, so the queen was especially nervous about letting that post fall into the hands of a Whig. "I wish you may find the restless Spirits of both parties quiet when you com back," she wrote to Marlborough on 12 June, "but I mightely feare it, every thing, in my poor opinnion, haveing a mellencoly prospect."

The principal topic of this letter, however, is a different kind of disappointment. Marlborough had begun this year's campaign with the hope of invading France by way of the Moselle, but Prince Ludwig of Baden, who had been a useful ally in the Rhine campaign the previous summer, now complained of an infected toe, the result of a minor wound that went untreated, and failed to arrive with a large contingent of promised troops. With insufficient forces for the thrust into France, Marlborough moved back to the Low Countries, where he had to work hard to protect his previous gains. Understanding his "vexsation & uneasyness," Anne reassures him that "some thing or other will happen to make you very well satisfyed with your self before this campagne is at an end,"[111] and there was indeed one moment of glory: on 6/17 July, the allied troops succeeded in breaking through the Line of Brabant, a formidable series of fortifications the French had constructed across a seventy-mile stretch of land between Antwerp and Namur. Once past this line, the duke had several opportunities for full-scale battles he believed he could win, but the Dutch again refused to allow their troops to participate. Marlborough's frustration is evident in his letters, but he would have to wait until 1706 to exploit the advantage he had gained in breaking the lines.

The queen, however, lost no time in making the most of this small victory. When the news reached London, she proclaimed a national day of thanksgiving to take place on 23 August and proceeded to St. Paul's in a parade designed to look as grand as the previous year's. "The Streets through which Her Majesty passed," says the *Gazette*, "were lined from *St. James's* as far as *Temple-Bar* by the Militia of *Westminster*; from thence to St. *Paul's* they were railed and hung with blue Cloth, the City Trained-Bands lining both sides."[112] This account may be true, but the person responsible for writing it copied it word for word from the account of the thanksgiving for Blenheim on 7 September 1704; the government, which controlled the *Gazette*, apparently wanted to treat the two victories as comparable. Some of those involved in the ceremony, however, acknowledged the disparity. The clergyman appointed to deliver the sermon—Richard Willis, a royal chaplain who had been among Gloucester's tutors—chose not to focus on celebrating the military success. Instead, he preached on the theme of national unity, using a passage from Isaiah as a pretext for urging concord between Dissenters and Anglicans. When Willis finally reaches the battle, on the fifteenth of his sixteen pages, his praise is muted at best:

> When we met here the last Year, it was to celebrate One of the most Signal Victories that this, or almost any Age has seen; That which we are now to praise GOD for at present, has not indeed so much of the dreadful Parade of Blood and Slaughter, but seems to be the Effect of as Wise Counsel, and as much Bravery as the other.

Glancing at the frustrations of the campaign, Willis even refers to the "fatal Mistakes which do too often attend the best formed Confederacies."[113] Although Anne was in agreement with the moderate position her chaplain took in discussing religious politics, she might have hoped he would display more enthusiasm for the occasion. The anthem composed by Jeremiah Clarke would have been more

Mus. Ex. 8.3: Jeremiah Clarke, excerpt from *I Will Love Thee, O Lord* (1705).

to her liking, especially as she was trying to make the most of a small victory. Clarke took as his text some verses from an exultant psalm of triumph:

> I will follow upon mine enemies, and overtake them: neither will I turn again till I have destroyed them. I will smite them, that they shall not be able to stand: but fall under my feet. They shall cry, but there shall be none to help them: yea, even unto the Lord shall they cry, but he shall not hear them.[114]

His setting of the last verse, expressing the desolation of the defeated, is especially effective. No record of the queen's response to this anthem survives, but someone asked Clarke to compose the music for the next New Year's Day ode, a task normally assigned to John Eccles as Master of the Music.[115]

§

The parade of coaches bringing members of the government and royal household to St. Paul's ended with a "Coach of State drawn by Eight Horses" in which spectators could glimpse the queen and three other people: "his Royal Highness, the Dutchess of Marlborough Groom of the Stole, and the Countess of Sunderland, being the Lady of the Bed-Chamber in waiting."[116] Although the Ladies of the Bedchamber waited on the queen in a regular rotation, some observers might have attached significance to the fact that Lady Sunderland, whose husband was in Vienna pursuing the embassy to which Anne had reluctantly appointed him, was present in the royal coach with her mother. What almost no one knew was that the queen and her longtime favorite were at odds. For a period of eight months, stretching from their bitter exchange over party politics in late November 1704 to a pair of letters written in August 1705, only one short letter from Anne to Sarah survives.[117] Because some letters are evidently missing, we do not know the details of their increasing estrangement, but clearly all was not well. Although they put up a brave public show for the thanksgiving service, Sarah went off to Tunbridge Wells as soon as it was over, and Anne returned to Windsor. The duchess had agreed to accompany the queen to Winchester for a hunting vacation at the end of August, but she was now beginning to realize that Anne had become close to Abigail Hill, who had been serving her for years as a bedchamber woman. In addition to being quietly attentive to Anne's needs, Abigail was a devout churchwoman and could play the harpsichord; she was well suited to her role. On 3 August, Anne wrote to Sarah explaining her reluctance to take on another bedchamber woman, although there was a vacancy: "sein[g] that Hill dos al Feildings business," she writes, "I am soe much better served, that I find no want of another." When afflicted by gout, she continues, she is "forced to be help'd to do every thing," and would be embarrassed to be served in this way by a newcomer.[118]

Anne's acknowledgment of her growing intimacy with Abigail, however inadvertent, appears to have enraged Sarah, for the queen's next letter, written on 10 August, strikes a note of despair: "and oh may you be convinced before I am *layde in my cold grave*," she writes, "how litle your poor unfortunat faithfull Morly has deserved to be unkindly thought of by her dear dear Mrs Freeman."[119] In dramatizing her belief that she has been unjustly accused, Anne draws once more on her early reading of melodramatic plays. Her source here is Nathaniel Lee's *Sophonisba*, the very tragedy her sister Mary had quoted to express her feelings of jealousy toward Anne and Frances Apsley when all of them were girls.[120] Near the end of the play, Sophonisba responds to the threat of being captured by the Romans by wishing she were dead:

> Alas my Lord 'twere better I were dead,
> *In my cold grave* safe from these troubles *laid*.

When Massanissa promises to defend her faithfully, a vow he will prove unable to keep, Sophonisba insists on the uniqueness of her love for him:

> Some surfeit with their love as on a feast.
> And then they loath when once they're satiated,
> But you'le remember me when I am dead.
> From these dear eyes to endless shades remov'd,
> None e're will love you sure, as I have lov'd.[121]

As she had earlier quoted from Horace (and Cowley) in order to insist that Sarah must continue to serve her, Anne now quotes from Lee in order to cast herself as the faithful heroine, surrounded by hostile forces and misunderstood by the one she loves best.

Ironically, it was just at this moment that someone in the Tory camp, probably the physician and controversialist Joseph Browne, published a fiction purporting to show that Sarah had complete control over Anne.[122] *The Secret History of Queen Zarah,* which appeared in September, gives a voyeuristic account of Sarah's early life in which she exploits her beauty to seduce John Churchill and her conniving mother manipulates him into marrying her. Browne's main complaint, however is that the Duchess has gained unlimited power from her official positions. Sarah appears as "Zarah," Anne as "Albania":

> The Government of the Kingdom was in a manner in her Hands, and whoever expected Favours or Rewards must apply themselves to *Zarah*, by whom all was granted, as the Pipe that convey'd the Royal Bounty to the Subject;…for it may be said without Exaggerating upon the Subject too much, *Albania* took the Crown from her own Head to put it on *Zarah's*.[123]

Although being described as a piece of plumbing through which royal bounty flowed was surely infuriating, even Sarah knew better than to acknowledge such an attack by answering it. In order to defend herself, she would have had to admit that her influence over the queen, generally overestimated by her friends as well as her enemies, was now on the wane, and this was not a moment when it suited her to make that admission. Anonymous scribblers were not alone in expressing hostility toward the duchess at this time. When Sarah visited Woodstock after returning from Winchester, she discovered that the Tory aristocrats in Oxfordshire were not prepared to welcome their new neighbors. Montagu Venables-Bertie, Earl of Abingdon, recently removed from his position as Lord Lieutenant of Oxfordshire to make way for Marlborough, had long been the sponsor of an annual horse race at Woodstock. In a gesture that Sarah was sure to interpret as a snub, he now moved the race to another location near Oxford. When she attempted to continue the old tradition by staging a race at Woodstock and offering a prize, the local nobility declined to attend, and "only a parcel of Whiggish, Mobbish People appear'd." The antiquary Thomas Hearne, a High Church Tory, is our source for this evidently biased account, and we know from other witnesses that a horse owned by Lord Wharton won the race, so there were certainly some titled people in attendance.[124] Still, the setting up of two rival horse races shows that party sentiment was particularly intense in the wake of the elections just concluded. Abingdon's wife, who had served with Sarah and her daughters as a Lady of the Bedchamber, resigned her position later in the fall,[125] and when the Commons looked into the contested election in St. Albans, there was testimony suggesting that the duchess had intervened there in a high-handed way, even claiming to speak for the queen. Henry Killigrew gained his seat, but Sarah had to endure some withering comments on the floor of Parliament.[126]

Although the parliamentary session that began on 25 October had some awkward moments for her favorite, it was quite satisfactory for Anne. When she returned to London to prepare for the session, the queen bowed to the inevitable, agreeing to appoint William Cowper, a skilled and respected young lawyer, as Lord Keeper, though she forced him to cut his hair and wear a wig lest anyone should think she had "given the seals to a boy," and arranged to retain monarchial control of some ecclesiastical livings normally in the gift of the Lord Keeper.[127] Although Cowper and his Whig associates lavished praise on Sarah for the role she had played in bringing about this change, the duchess knew that she had further damaged her tattered friendship with the queen by prodding her to make it.[128] For her part, the queen probably calculated that making a major Whig appointment several weeks before the opening of Parliament would help assure a smooth beginning to the session. Good news from her forces in Spain was also helpful: with some support from local Catalonian rebels, forces commanded by the colorful and erratic Earl of Peterborough had managed to take Barcelona; Charles III entered the city in triumph on 3/14 October. Even the Scots, whose parliamentary session over the summer had been stormy, were now prepared for serious discussions of the Union. Anne could thus open Parliament on a positive note, and she took the occasion to deliver a stinging rebuke to those responsible for High Tory propaganda claiming that the Church was "in danger": "I am willing to hope," said the queen, that

> not One of My Subjects can really entertain a Doubt of My Affection to the Church, or so much as suspect, that it will not be My chief Care to support it, and leave it secure after Me; and therefore we may be certain, that they, who go about to insinuate Things of this Nature, must be Mine and the Kingdom's Enemies, and can only mean to cover Designs, which they dare not publicly own, by endeavouring to distract us with unreasonable and groundless Distrusts and Jealousies.[129]

Describing Nottingham, Rochester, and Buckingham as having "Designs, which they dare not publicly own" was as close as Anne ever came to Sarah's sweeping accusation that all Tories were Jacobites at heart.

By the time she delivered this speech, the queen knew that the Tory party was planning to nominate William Bromley of Oxford as their candidate for Speaker. By putting forward an unrepentant Tacker, indeed the very man who had proposed the Occasional Conformity bill in each of the last three years, the Tories were showing that they were far more united than she had hoped they would be. Godolphin and Harley set about collecting a few dozen votes from "moderate Tories," mainly employees of the court, with the result that John Smith, the Whig candidate, narrowly secured election, which proved a reliable signal of the direction in which Parliament would now move. There was no renewed attempt to pass a law against Occasional Conformity, and the Commons took an important step toward the Union by rescinding the harsh measures enacted against the Scots in the previous year. When the Tories attempted to embarrass the queen by introducing a motion compelling her to invite the Electress Sophia to reside in England, the Whigs countered with a sensible Regency Act, laying out procedures to be followed when the queen passed on.[130] Anne was so relieved by the defeat of the Tory proposal that she apparently wrote to Sarah expressing gratitude to the Whigs. In a letter known only from Sarah's printed account, the queen predicts that "dear MRS. FREEMAN and I shall not disagree as we have formerly done; for I am sensible of the services those people have done me that you have a good opinion of, and will countenance them, and am thoroughly convinced of the malice and insolence of *them*, that you have always been speaking against."[131]

Unwilling to accept defeat, Anne's troublesome uncle Rochester delivered an ill-considered speech alleging "that the church of England was in danger from the Scotch act of security; the not having the Hanover family here; and the losse of the occasional bill."[132] The result was a resolution by both Houses firmly rejecting those ideas; on 12 December, it was

> Resolved, by the Lords Spiritual and Temporal and in Parliament assembled, That the Church of *England* as by Law established, which was rescued from the extremest Danger by King *William* the Third, of Glorious Memory, is now, by God's Blessing, under the happy Reign of Her Majesty, in a most safe and flourishing Condition; and that whoever goes about to suggest and insinuate, that the Church is in Danger under Her Majesty's Administration, is an Enemy to the Queen, the Church, and the Kingdom.[133]

In the opening session of Anne's first Parliament, in 1702, the resolution of the Commons praising Marlborough for having "*retrieved* the ancient Honour and Glory of the English Nation" had implied a gratuitous Tory insult to the memory of King William. As they declared the Church to be "flourishing," the Whigs were now careful to remind their colleagues that their hero William had "*rescued* [it] from the extremest Danger." Both verbs would appear again in public discourse.

§

The Whigs were now in a better position than at any time so far in Anne's reign. Their majority in the Lords was reliable, and although they lacked a clear majority in the Commons, they had gained the advantage of the Speaker's chair. They did not, however, have anything like control of the government, which remained in the hands of Godolphin, Marlborough, and Harley. Thanks to such experienced leaders as Somers and Halifax, the Whigs were capable of impressive party discipline, but they were still, like all political parties, a loose confederation of people with different aims, class backgrounds, and ideological beliefs. A party that contained such sophisticated connoisseurs as Somerset and Devonshire was also the natural home of Huguenot refugees and self-made merchants. Writers associated with the Whig cause ranged from Addison, a clergyman's son with an Oxford M.A. and a talent for Latin poetry, to Defoe, a Dissenting pamphleteer with an eye for the main chance. We should not be surprised that there was no consistent Whig position on the arts. Vanbrugh, a solid Whig, had built his new opera house in the hope of bringing English musical tastes in line with those prevailing on the Continent, but his fellow Whig Defoe, taking advantage of the fact that the site of the theatre had formerly been a stable, attacked it in an unusually nasty poem. "Apollo spoke the Word," he wrote, "And straight arose a Playhouse from a T[urd]."[134] The Greek god Apollo, the reigning figure in Thornhill's sketch for the theatre ceiling, is as much a target for Defoe's scatology as the architect Vanbrugh—and here we encounter again the Whig unease about mythology that

Addison expresses more elegantly in the closing lines of *The Campaign*. Committed by their ideology to seeing history as a struggle between liberty and oppression, Whigs necessarily had a bad conscience about using the arbitrary and capricious Greek gods to represent positive values, including the power of beauty.

Some of this uncertainty appears in *Liberty, A Poem,* a curious work first published during the early sessions of Anne's new Parliament. The anonymous author quotes on his title page, in Latin, the famous passage in which Virgil makes a gracious compliment to Greek aesthetic and intellectual accomplishments while defining conquest and diplomacy as Roman arts. Dryden had given these lines a memorable turn in English:

> Let others better mold the running Mass
> Of Mettals, and inform the breathing Brass;
> And soften into Flesh a Marble Face;
> Plead better at the Bar; describe the Skies,
> And when the Stars descend, and when they rise.
> But, *Rome,* 'tis thine alone, with awful sway,
> To rule Mankind; and make the World obey:
> Disposing Peace, and War, thy own Majestick Way.
> To tame the Proud, the fetter'd Slave to free;
> These are Imperial Arts, and worthy thee.[135]

Here Roman political administration becomes an art form comparable to the sculpture, oratory, and astronomy at which the Greeks had excelled. In his *Letter from Italy,* a poem he addressed to Halifax in 1701, Addison had already reworked these lines, with Italy now cast as the superior artistic culture and Britain as the master of international politics:

> Others with Towring Piles may please the sight,
> And in their proud aspiring Domes delight;
> A nicer Touch to the stretcht Canvas give,
> Or teach their animated *Rocks* to live:
> 'Tis *Britain's* Care to watch o're *Europe's* Fate,
> And hold in Balance each contending State.
> To threaten bold presumptuous Kings with War,
> And answer her afflicted Neighbour's Pray'r.[136]

The poet of *Liberty* has similar aims. He begins with an apostrophe to the "Beauteous Goddess" Liberty, a "Harmonious Pow'r / Whose happy Influence Mankind adore." Liberty, of course, was not a Greek goddess but an abstraction turned into a deity by the ancient Romans.[137] Drawing on the widespread belief that ancient Norse and Germanic societies were more egalitarian than those of the Mediterranean, the English poet wonders why Liberty chiefly resides in "frozen Climes" and considers it

> Strange! That those Regions (where the Friendly Sun,
> And lavish Nature all their Pride have shown)
> By a severer Fate should be opprest;
> Nor taste the Joys of *Liberty* We boast.

The prime example, of course, is Italy, and the author, perhaps a young man recently returned from a grand tour, devotes several pages to an enthusiastic account of Italian architecture, sculpture, painting, and music, naming Michelangelo, Bernini, Correggio, and Corelli, among others. Despite the raptures he expresses when describing the Italian arts, his political principles will not allow him to enjoy them:

> For *Tyranny* through all *Italia* reigns.
> Condemn'd by Fate, no other Choice they have;
> But only to be *Priest*, or to be *Slave*.

Fired by his disapproval of popery and arbitrary government, the poet now demeans the very arts he has just praised:

> What are the Sumptuous *Palaces* they boast,
> But well-built stately Prisons at the most?
> Their Beauteous *Sculpture*'s but an Art design'd
> The poor unthinking Multitude to blind.
> Their *Paintings* too the *Priesthood*'s Cheats describe,
> To make Men Bigots, and enrich the *pamper'd Tribe.*
> *Musick* has Charms, 'tis true; but what avail
> Her Charms, unless o're Reason to prevail?

As a counterweight, he offers British (indeed Whiggish) political virtues:

> We envy not such Arts; but boast our own,
> Our *Learning* and our *Laws*———
> For to inform the Mind, the Soul to arm
> With Courage, which no Dangers can alarm;
> To give Ambition Bounds when in Success,
> And lend a pitious Ear to Virtue in Distress;

> To guard our Liberties from Lawless Force,
> And curb Usurpers in their Dangerous Course;
> To answer each Insulted Nation's Pray'rs;
> These are our *British* Arts, these are our Gen'rous Cares.[138]

After this turn, it is a short step to lines in praise of "*Right Reason*," William III, the Whig Duke of Devonshire, and the queen. Yet it is surely significant that the poet's facility with couplets breaks down just at the point where he claims not to envy Italian art. Any Englishman who had heard Corelli's music and Clayton's, or who had compared Correggio's painting to that of Godfrey Kneller (himself an imported artist) would be more than justified in envying the accomplishments of Italian art. But when the poet tries to counter the seductive arts of Italy with the desperate claim that we "boast our own," he cannot find a rhyme. One obvious word to have rhymed with "our own" might have been "throne," but the Whig context, elevating "Learning" and "Laws" in order to praise the civic virtues of a whole people, makes that rhyme impossible. Unwittingly, this earnest yet contradictory poem dramatizes the difficulty of forging a Whig aesthetic.

Poets writing for court occasions, who had inherited an expected set of Royalist tropes and conventions, now faced problems of their own. Some of the mythic allusions that had appeared in royal poetry for centuries were beginning to seem either overblown or empty; many of them might now imply allegiance to a Tory ideology that had been called into question by recent political events. The Poet Laureate, Nahum Tate, had already expressed doubts about his own art in his poems on the royal portrait and the victory at Blenheim; we may track his increasing discomfort in his text for the New Year's song for 1 January 1706, which was more elaborate than any of the previous New Year's odes for this queen. Taking full advantage of his opportunity to be heard at court, Jeremiah Clarke scored his music for four-part strings, two recorders, five named vocal soloists, and full choir, and Tate dutifully supplied a longer poem than usual, but a poem full of contradictions and disjunctions. He sets out to ask a personified "Harmony" to celebrate the New Year, but his questioning rhetoric implies that Harmony no longer enjoys the power it once had:

> O Harmony where's now thy Pow'r,
>   That made the Forrest move,
> And list'ning Spheres approve
>   The Musick of thy bow'r?
>
> To bid the New-Born SEASON Joy,
>   Thy Former Charms Renew;
> Generous Musick, All employ
>   All, All, and All too Few.

The syntax of the last two lines is confused and confusing. Tate probably means to say that even if "All" Anne's subjects "employ…Generous Musick," they will be "too Few" to give adequate expression to her greatness. Still, a more general and ominous sense of inadequacy hangs over these lines.

When Tate turns to direct praise of the queen and Prince George, he is reduced to borrowing from Shakespeare:

> O for a Muse of Fire
> And more than Mortal Quire
> To Sing the Royal pair
> Whose Prudent, Pious, Prosp'rous Care
> Such Glorious Hopes Inspire.

The original speaker of that first line, the Chorus in *Henry V*, is asking for the poetic power needed to celebrate the martial victories of a courageous king. Here the same fiery muse is supposed to celebrate a notably sedentary royal couple for their "Prudent, Pious, Prosp'rous Care" of the nation, but these solid, practical virtues hardly required a "Muse of Fire" to praise them. Clarke's setting shows that he recognized the problem: he devotes eighteen bars to the first three lines, which he then repeats, disposes of "Prudent, Pious, Prosp'rous Care" in two measures, and gives the next sixteen bars to an extended treatment of "Glorious Hopes."[139]

Developing his wish for a "more than Mortal Quire," Tate continues by declaring "Mortal Harmony" inadequate to celebrate Anne's triumphs:

> Charming Themes, but ah! in Vain,
> Shall Mortal Harmony Essay
> The Triumphs of our *ANNA*'s Reign,
> And Glories of the Day.

Clarke omitted this stanza, perhaps considering it less than complimentary to his composition and the excellent musicians who would perform it. Yet Tate is unlikely to have meant to slight his colleagues in the choir of the Chapel Royal. He was simply employing one of the worn-out tropes of royal panegyric, in which human arts are always inadequate to express the glories of the monarch. At a more personal level, this conventional "modesty trope" also expresses Tate's struggle to find a plausible idiom for courtly praise. When he honors the mythic tradition, as he does by describing the New Year as "Tryumphant in it's Morn,…Like *Hercules* for Wonders Born," he encounters the same difficulties John Philips had faced in applying the language of heroic epic to modern events: 1706 would be a year of wonders in the ongoing war, but those triumphs would come from organization

Mus. Ex. 8.4: Jeremiah Clarke, excerpt from *O Harmony where's now thy Pow'r?* (1706).

and strategy, not from a club-wielding champion like Hercules. Yet when Tate alludes more realistically to the present, as he does by praising Parliament for "Supplying with Treasures / Thy National Wants, / And Doubling their Gifts by *Dispatch* in their Grants," he compromises the elevated tone of his ode.

Clarke, who appears to have had good taste, omitted the bathetic lines on parliamentary grants, but he did write music for Tate's final "Grand Chorus," in which martial imagery, largely absent from the rest of the ode, makes a sudden and awkward appearance:

> Let us Try, Let us Try, in so Glorious a Cause,
> Tis Noble to Dare, and we Fall with Applause:
> >Sound, sound an Alarm,
> >While our Courage is Warm:
> >>Let us Try, Let us Try
> Tis Glory to Conquer, and Honour to Die.[140]

Although these lines are entirely conventional, they have no thematic connection with the rest of the poem and appear to have been tacked on at the last minute. We have no knowledge of the process by which Tate and Clarke put this ode together, but one explanation might be that they added this ending after learning of the imminent arrival of the Duke of Marlborough, who finally reached London late on the night of 30 December after an exhausting trip to Berlin and Vienna, where he had been shoring up the alliance for the next year's campaign. His entourage included Sunderland, who had now concluded his mission to the Emperor, and Charles Talbot, Duke of Shrewsbury, a close friend of Godolphin and Marlborough who had been prominent in William's government. Shrewsbury was returning to England after a long sojourn in Italy, bringing with him his new Italian wife, Adelaide Roffeni, who was a notable music-lover. The performance of Tate and Clarke's ode would have been the first opportunity for the new Duchess of Shrewsbury to appear at court, where her foreign manners caused a stir.[141]

As printed, Tate's text reads like a set of excerpts from several different poems, and Clarke's selective setting makes the final product even more scrappy and disconnected. Clearly determined to escape these problems, the anonymous librettist for *England's Glory,* the short opera created specifically for Anne's birthday in 1706, achieves a degree of unity by avoiding concrete references to actual events. Sung entirely by mythological figures, this courtly opera is a throwback to the fanciful world of the early Stuart masque. The first singer to appear is Bellona, correctly identified in the printed text as the "Goddess of War," but she does not mention Marlborough or the European campaign, singing instead in praise of the "rural Blessings" of Britannia. The closest Bellona comes to mentioning warfare is a line in praise of England's "Lofty Forests," which yield "vast Fleets, and stately Building." When Britannia herself begins to sing, she urges the "Natives of this Isle" to rejoice at the "*Saturnian* Pleasures" of Anne's reign, but only in the most general terms:

> Bright *ANNA* bids your Troubles cease,
> And now in War procures you Peace.[142]
>> Arts and Arms Her Favours nourish;
>> Musick, Wit, and Learning flourish.
>> Tides of Wealth by Her are flowing;
>> Virtue, Trade, and Empire growing;
>> Fame abroad our Triumphs sounding,
>> And Content at Home abounding.

According to the logic of these lines, the queen supports music, wit, learning, and virtue, but the emphasis here falls on wealth, trade, and empire. In a sequence evidently modeled on Crowne's *Calisto,* the four continents appear with their gifts: Europe, hailing the "victorious Nation," lays a sword at Britannia's feet; Asia pays tribute with "Spices, Pearls, and Gums"; Africa offers "all her Slaves in Chains"; and America "Opens her latent Mines."[143] Such dreams of empire, long a feature of the masque tradition, were not necessarily partisan, but the next scene would surely have struck some of the birthday revelers as a piece of Tory propaganda. In a prospect reminiscent of Dryden's *Albion and Albanius,* "*Neptune* arises in a Chariot, drawn by Sea-Horses, where a remote View of the *Brittish* Fleet terminates the Sight." His aria celebrates the navy and names the current enemies:

> View *Neptune's* arose
> In spight of thy Foes,
>   His Trident and Mace to surrender.
> The Rule of the Main
> Thy Flags shall maintain,
>   And thy Ships ride the Ocean's Defender.
> Not *Spain,* or proud *France*
> Shall dare to advance,
>   When Broadsides begin their loud rattle;
> But like Cowards turn Tail,
> Or with Terror strike Sail,
>   And yield you the Triumph of Battel.

In this naval fantasy, British ships defeat their immediate enemies and go on to conquer the world, a prophecy given concrete form when Atlas appears and lays the globe at Anne's feet. An elaborate stage effect, shown as a frontispiece in the printed libretto, concludes the opera: the globe "opens and divides into three equal Parts," with emblems representing the battles of Blenheim, Gibraltar, and Barcelona, events the librettist has been careful *not* to name, as a rejoicing chorus enjoins obedience to the queen's benign dominion:

> In Dances and Songs let Obedience be shown,
> Since all the whole Earth now submits to Her Throne;
> And *Britain's* become great Fortune's chief Minion,
> T'extend o'er the Globe Her much lov'd Dominion.[144]

In light of the poet's strong emphasis on naval power and his striking failure to include any parallel reference to the war on land, it is hard to avoid the inference that Tory patronage of some kind is at work here. The prompter Downes, in a somewhat garbled account of this occasion, names Margherita de l'Epine first in a list of singers taking part in the birthday. She probably appeared as Bellona, the largest female role, and as satiric squibs linking her with Nottingham attest, she remained the darling of Tory music-lovers.[145] Although the libretto requires seven female singers, Catherine Tofts, the soprano favored by the Whigs, did not take part.

Frontispiece to *England's Glory* (1706).

For the Tory librettist of *England's Glory*, "Obedience" is paramount, and the reigning monarch shows her worth by supporting "Musick, Wit, and Learning," but for the Whig poet of *Liberty*, the true "*British* Arts" are "guard[ing] our Liberties" and "curb[ing] Usurpers." Both poets, however, connect the Virgilian prophecy of empire to the queen. In his Latin epigraph, the Whig poet makes one crucial alteration, substituting *Regina* for *Romane*, so that the revised passage advises Anne to rule her subject peoples with wisdom. In Bellona's final aria, the Tory librettist gives Heaven credit for acting on Anne's behalf, again in language derived from Virgil:

Behold how Heav'n asserts Her Cause!
Subdues proud Pow'rs, and gives them Laws.[146]

Like the Bible, the *Aeneid* was not the property of either party, and Virgil's prophecy of Roman empire was open to both Whig and Tory readings. As these examples show, the relationship between partisan ideology and aesthetic choice was not always predictable or consistent. In theory, Whig artists may have hoped to develop a modern mode of expression freed from the shackles of myth and convention, but in practice they were unlikely to jettison such foundational texts as the *Aeneid*, preferring to reinterpret tradition for their own purposes. The nostalgia of Tory artists is sometimes astonishing: there is hardly a line in *England's Glory* that would have been out of place in an early Stuart masque. Yet someone involved in the production thought it important to inscribe the names of recent battles on the pyramid that arises in the closing scene.[147] Even poets whose work was not marked by partisanship struggled to achieve consistency. The incoherence of Tate's New Year's ode, for example, springs from his inability to reconcile traditional myths with recent legislative actions, and people far more gifted than Tate were just as inconsistent: Sir Isaac Newton, whose *Opticks* (1704) was a remarkable step forward, pointing toward modern physics, spent decades poring over the prophetic books of the Old Testament and trying to work out a scheme of biblical chronology.

§

The foreign and native singers who performed Kremberg's lost music for *England's Glory* had a very busy spring, as the theatre companies competed strenuously with operas in various styles. Vanbrugh had spent the previous summer trying to forestall such competition by proposing that the two companies form a new United Company under his control, but he was unable to bully Christopher Rich into submission, so competition continued. His partner Congreve, fearing that the costs of competition would prove ruinous, removed himself from the management of the Haymarket theatre in December, leaving Vanbrugh to run the company on his own,[148] and Vanbrugh, still pursuing his operatic dreams, poured money and energy into musical productions. On 21 February, in the remodeled Queen's Theatre, he presented *The British Enchanters*, a "tragedy" by George Granville with instrumental music by the virtuoso violinist William Corbett and songs by John Eccles and Bartholomew Isaack.[149] Written a decade earlier, this was an English semiopera heavily influenced by Dryden's *King Arthur*, which Drury Lane revived to run against it. Staged by Betterton, who had vast experience with this kind of show, *The British Enchanters* was much more successful than Vanbrugh's next project, another through-sung pastoral opera from Italy. Unlike *Gli amori d'Ergasto*, the previous season's disaster, *The Temple of Love*, first staged on 7 March, had an English text translated by Motteux to fit the original Italian music, but it was even less successful than its predecessor, with only two recorded performances. This failure became even more painful for Vanbrugh when Bononcini's *Camilla,* which his rival Christopher Rich presented on 30 March, turned out to be so popular. Yet Vanbrugh continued his heavy investment in the scenes, machines, and music required for operas, mounting an unprecedented third operatic production on 5 April: Thomas D'Urfey's *Wonders in the Sun; or, The Kingdom of the Birds,* a comic semiopera in the vein of Aristophanes. D'Urfey burlesques the myth of Orpheus and Eurydice, who appear as a modern couple bored with married life, and pokes fun at both political parties, who appear as groups of birds called "High-Flyers" and "Low-Flyers." Despite its up-to-date topical humor, this production was another failure, with only five known performances.[150]

There was much at stake in the competition between the two licensed theatres, and Vanbrugh continued to float proposals to combine the companies. Congreve drew the obvious analogy to the Scottish negotiations, telling a friend in April that he had "heard there is to be a Union of the two houses as well as Kingdoms."[151] The Drury Lane company, however, basking in the success of *Camilla,* had no interest in theatrical union. In the original epilogue for *Camilla,* printed as the work of the actor Richard Estcourt but actually composed by the Whig poet Arthur Maynwaring, the actress Anne Oldfield celebrates the benefits of theatrical competition, which she compares to partisan competition in the state:

> And see what Fruits from Our Divisions spring;
> Both Houses now *Italian* Musick Sing.
> The Fair can only tell, which pleases best;
> For Ladies always have the nicest Tast.
> But this We know, had that dire Union been,
> You ne'er in *England* had *Camilla* seen.
> They would some *Masque* have shewn, or *Country Farce;*
> *Paris's Judgment,* or the *Loves* of *Mars:*
> But since the *Stage*'s Freedom you Restore,
> And we no more dread Arbitrary Power,
> To please this Audience, we'll no Charges spare,
> But chearfully maintain a Vigorous War.
>
> . . . .
> Our Stage is thus, an Emblem of the State,
> With Mildness Rul'd, by Opposition Great.[152]

Although Vanbrugh's Whig credentials were impeccable, Maynwaring tries hard to associate him with "Arbitrary Power," which he links in turn to the musical "masques" popular before the advent of Italian opera. *The Loves of Mars and Venus,* which Princess Anne had attended in 1696, was a short musical entertainment with a script by Motteux and music by John Eccles and Gottfried Finger—two of the four composers who set Congreve's libretto for *The Judgment of Paris* in the celebrated contest of 1701. Both were still in the repertory of the rival company.[153] The up-to-date *Camilla*, on this reading, could only have come to England as a result of freedom and competition. Despite the claims this epilogue makes for competition, it was financially ruinous, and in August the two theatres agreed to limit it by restricting the Queen's Theatre to spoken plays, with some of the actors from Drury Lane moving there to perform them, while Drury Lane was to have a monopoly on operas. As Congreve pointed out, the facilities were "misapplied" by this arrangement, as Vanbrugh had designed the Haymarket with operas in mind.[154]

When he celebrates the fruits that spring from "our Divisions," Maynwaring engages ideas that reach well beyond theatrical competition: in gardening, "division" multiplied the number of plants, allowing them to yield more fruit; in music, "division" was the much-admired ornamentation of vocal lines, in which a gifted singer divided long notes into improvised melodic fragments; and in Parliament, a "division" took place when the members filed through lobbies to have their votes recorded. According to the Whig ideology driving this epilogue, political divisions are a healthy sign of liberty: the nation is "by Opposition Great." Unlike France, with its autocratic monarch, England is "With Mildness Rul'd"—a conventional compliment to Anne but also an approving description of the limited, constitutional monarchy installed in 1689. The queen, however, was weary of partisan divisions; her own beliefs were closer to those dramatized by a character called "Moderation" who appears in D'Urfey's mock-opera, singing a comic song poking fun at both parties and urging them, in a repeated refrain, "Agree, ye rash *Britains*, agree."[155]

Pushing hard for an agreement between her two kingdoms, Anne prorogued the English Parliament (19 March), dispatched Marlborough to begin the campaign (10 April), and turned her energies toward the long-delayed negotiations for Union between England and Scotland. William Cowper had now won her confidence, not only by cutting his hair but by refusing the New Year's gifts traditionally made to the Lord Keeper by the legal establishment, "looking upon it to be an ill custome."[156] He took a leading role among the English commissioners Anne appointed to conduct these critical negotiations, a group including her chief ministers, two archbishops, and a number of prominent Whigs, including Sunderland. In his opening speech, delivered on 16 April, Cowper declared that his colleagues were "fully Resolv'd... to Act, as if we were already United in Interest, and had nothing left to consider but what Settlements and Provisions are most likely to conduce to the common Safety and Happiness of this whole Island of *Great-Britain*."[157] As in the abortive negotiations held during the winter of 1702–1703, the English side initially emphasized the need for a joint Parliament and a single succession, while the Scots insisted on free trade, including trade with the "Plantations." This

H. Vale, *The Relief of Barcelona* (c. 1706).

time, however, both sides were more determined to find common ground, and committees soon set about planning the details of a joint system of taxes and trade regulations.

Less than a month after these talks began, the commissioners, the queen, and the citizens of both nations heard astonishing news from the Continent. In March, the French had besieged Barcelona with a large army, and Marlborough was not alone in being concerned that Charles III, who had chosen to remain in the city, was vulnerable to capture, especially because Peterborough had moved his ground forces toward Valencia. But when Admiral John Leake, sailing at top speed from Lisbon, appeared with a large fleet on 30 April/11 May, the French hastily abandoned the siege. The news of this action arrived in England more or less simultaneously with the news that Marlborough had decisively defeated the French and the Bavarians at the battle of Ramillies (12/23 May). Over the next ten days, Louvain, Brussels Ghent, Bruges, Antwerp, and many other fortified towns surrendered to the confederate armies. For the first time since Louis had seized them in 1701, the fortresses of the "Spanish Netherlands" could now serve as a buffer zone protecting the Dutch from the French. For those with personal experience of the Nine Years' War, most of it fought in this disputed territory, Marlborough's recovery of these crucial objectives was miraculous.

In addition to exultant accounts in the newspapers, there was at least one theatrical recognition of the victory. On 23 May, at a performance of *Camilla,* the audience heard a new prologue gallantly giving the English ladies credit for Marl-borough's triumph:

> Ladies, to you our Gratitude we pay
> For the late Triumphs of a glorious Day;
> Urg'd by your Charms our Troops their Foes subdue,
> And well may Conquer, when inspir'd by You.

According to the poet, the French have lost the battle because they have "no such Beauties" and because they are "wretched Slaves":

> But how shou'd wretched Slaves so long oppress'd
> By Lawless Power, with no such Beauties bless'd[,]
> Contend with Brittains; for their Freedom arm'd
> And with the thoughts of this fair Circle warm'd.

Once more, the Whiggish rhetoric of slavery and freedom makes its appearance, and the poet sends a further coded message of his party affiliation when he an-nounces that "'Tis almost Treason not to shew your Joy."

> When British Arms, in this surprising Reign,
> Such Towns retake, such early Conquests gain,
> Shall any dare to breath in English Air
> Whose dismall looks their Secret spleen declare.[158]

The in-joke here is the word *dismall,* which had long been a nickname for the dour and swarthy Earl of Nottingham. Marlborough and Godolphin had often com-plained to each other about Nottingham's tendency to downplay even the greatest victories in the land campaign, and the day after this prologue was spoken, Godol-phin mailed it to Halifax, who was in the Hague on a diplomatic mission, with an amusing cover letter:

> I shall not trouble you with one Word upon the progress of the D. of
> Marlbro's successes, because you will hear them so much quicker from
> the Hague, but the effect of them yesterday at the last representation of
> *Camilla,* which you will see in the paper enclosed, will I make no ques-
> tion be very agreeable to you.[159]

For Godolphin and Halifax, former rivals now working together against Notting-ham and the other High Tories, sharing works of literature was an indirect but highly effective form of communication. When writing about important figures, Godolphin and Marlborough used numerical codes, as did Anne and Sarah, but on this occasion, Godolphin could pass along a joke at the expense of "Dismal" by sending Halifax this apparently innocuous prologue; Addison, who was serving as a secretary to Halifax on this mission, probably shared in the laughter.

On 21 May, while Marlborough was still consolidating his gains in Flanders, Anne proclaimed 27 June as a day of thanksgiving for this "Signal and Glorious Victory in *Brabant,* over the *French* Army" and for the "great Successes in *Catalonia,* and other Parts of Spain."[160] She then came in person to the meeting of the commissioners for the Union, gave a short speech encouraging them to bring their treaty "to a happy Conclusion, with as much dispatch as the nature of it will admit," and departed for Windsor, leaving them to their work. On 26 June, back in town for the service of thanksgiving, she returned to the Cockpit "to see what further Progress you have made in this Treaty, and to press a speedy Conclusion of it."[161] In their capacities as Privy Councilors or members of the House of Lords, most of the commissioners for England were in attendance at the service of thanksgiving in St. Paul's the next day, at which they heard another fine anthem by Jeremiah Clarke, sung by the men and boys of the Chapel Royal; those with different tastes in music and religion had an opportunity to hear a *Te Deum* at the private chapel of the imperial ambassador, "admirably well performed by the best *Italian,* and other Musicians in Town," and followed by a dinner and a ball.[162]

The preacher at St. Paul's, famous for his sonorous voice and balanced rhetoric, was George Stanhope, Dean of Canterbury Cathedral. His praise of Marlborough, while doubtless pleasing to Anne and Sarah, includes some coded language aimed at pleasing both parties. "To His marvelous Application and Victorious Name," says Stanhope, "we owe an honourable Revulsion in the *Spanish Netherlands,* almost as speedy, as that infamous one made some Years ago by Treachery and Surprise; A Country, wont to be gotten by Inches, but Now retrieved, (rescued rather) in the beginning of one glorious Campaign." The talk of getting land "by Inches" refers unmistakably to the Nine Years' War, with Marlborough's astonishing speed contrasting with William's slow progress. Once more the loaded term *retrieved* appears, alluding to the parliamentary address that had used that term to contrast Marlborough's early successes with William's failures, but the preacher quickly offers *rescued* as an alternative, probably remembering the more recent resolution honoring William for having "*rescued* [the Church] from extremest Danger." When he speaks of the pious queen, Stanhope treats her as God's agent, who has "brought down from Heaven such signal and accumulated Successes, as seem to declare her, of all the Princes of the Earth, the Person, whom God delights to honour." Next to God, Anne is "the Cause and Instrument of All our publick Blessings," but Stanhope claims that her deeds speak for themselves.

"Let Others seek out mercenary Historians, dexterous in eloquent Flattery to write their Annals," he says. "Hers ask no Art or Ornament"—a gesture not unlike Addison's concluding lines in *The Campaign,* where Marlborough's feats are said to shine on their own, without the "borrowed blaze" of mythology.[163]

The queen's Poet Laureate, Master of the Music, and Composer to the Chapel Royal, who had been working overtime in recent years to provide artful ornaments to celebrate her accomplishments, might well have been puzzled by this claim, and when Godfrey Kneller painted an oil sketch for a mounted portrait of Marlborough, "soon after the Battle of Ramilies," he showed the duke accompanied by Hercules and crowned by Victory, his horse trampling Discord and a shield with Louis XIV's crest. Freed from her manacles, a woman in ermine, probably representing the Spanish Netherlands, offers him a miniature citadel (color plate 16).[164] The prominent poets who responded to this most recent victory chose similarly allegorical modes, eschewing Addison's call for chastened, realistic narrative. The Tory Matthew Prior celebrated Ramillies with an ode closely modeled on Horace and cast in English Spenserian stanzas, complete with archaic Elizabethan diction; the Whig William Congreve wrote a Pindaric ode, which he personally presented to the queen.[165] Neither paid much attention to details of the battle, preferring to work through myth and allusion. Prior imagines a towering sculpture of Anne as a fit memorial of the victory:

> Let *Europe* sav'd the Column high erect,
> Than *Trajan*'s higher, or than *Antonine*'s;
> Where sembling Art may carve the fair Effect,
> And full Atchievement of Thy great Designs.
> In a calm Heav'n, and a serener Air,
> Sublime, the *Queen* shall on the Summit stand,
> From Danger far, as far remov'd from Fear,
> And pointing down to Earth her dread Command.
> All Winds, all Storms that threaten Human Woe,
> Shall sink beneath her Feet, and spend their Rage below.[166]

Once more, the queen is serene and calm, but in this vision she is also sublime. The winds and storms that had signaled the sublime in Addison's simile of the avenging angel now "sink beneath her Feet, and spend their Rage below." It is reasonable to ask why these poems, like most of the other poems on Ramillies, float serenely above the battle itself like the imagined queen on her column, disdaining narration of strategic details. Perhaps the poets, like others reading about the engagement, were shocked by the scale of the slaughter. It was a cavalry battle larger than any yet recorded, and Marlborough took full advantage of having larger mounted forces than his enemies. The French army, which entered the battle some sixty thousand strong, lost more than thirteen thousand men in one day, while the victorious allies lost about thirty-six hundred. Faced with death on that unprecedented scale, artists of all parties retreated to the safe ground of myth.

§

As Anne made her way to St. Paul's in the traditional parade, one familiar figure was missing from her coach. Prince George, reported ill on the day after the presentation of *England's Glory,* had not yet fully recovered and therefore avoided the fatiguing ceremonies. Hoping to nurse him back to health, the queen spent much of this summer at Windsor, but on 23 July she returned to St. James's for the forty-fifth meeting of the commissioners for the Union, at which both sides presented her with the articles of agreement they had hammered out over the last several months. Cowper, perhaps overwhelmed by the significance of this occasion, forgot the speech he had planned to deliver from memory and had to read it from his notes,[167] but he was careful to give Anne due credit for her earlier interventions: "Your MAJESTY's Royal Presence, and seasonable Admonition to us at the fittest Junctures," he declared, "were…a very great Encouragement and Assistance to us in the Difficulties we met with." The process, of course, was not over, as both Parliaments needed to ratify the agreements, and Anne made a point of expressing her wish "That my Servants of *Scotland* may lose no time in going down to propose it to My Subjects of that Kingdom."[168]

The Scottish Parliament was not scheduled to meet until October, and Anne might therefore have hoped for a few peaceful months at Windsor. Throughout this summer, however, she had to deal with renewed pressure to make Sunderland a Secretary of State. Godolphin, who had now embraced this plan, tried to mollify the queen by proposing that Sir Charles Hedges, who had served her since the beginning of her reign, be given a lucrative post as a judge of the Prerogative Court of Canterbury when the incumbent, who was ill, resigned or died. Anne, who was always loyal to those who served her, replied unhappily on 30 August:

'Tis a great hardship to persuade any body to part with a place they are in possession of in hopes of another that is not yet vacant.…All I desire is my liberty in incouraging & employing all those that concur faithfully in my service, whether they are called Whigs, or Torys, not to bee tyd to one, nor the other. If I should bee soe unfortunate as to fall into the hands of either, I shall look upon my self, tho I have the name of queen, to bee in reality but their slave, which as it will be my personall ruin so it will bee the destroying of the Government.[169]

Though clearly distraught, Anne retains her wit, employing for her own purposes the rhetoric of liberty and slavery, which was habitual in the discourse of the Whigs. In her version, a monarch who "falls into the hands of either" party becomes a slave; "liberty" is the ability to choose one's own servants regardless of party. Nonetheless, just before convening the English Parliament, she bowed to the inevitable and appointed Sunderland.

When the Scottish Parliament met in Edinburgh in October, the commissioners for the Union faced the passionate and eloquent opposition of Andrew Fletcher of Saltoun, a formidable Scots patriot, as well as widespread popular antagonism, expressed in written addresses to the legislature and public disturbances in the streets. Dr. John Arbuthnot, who was serving as one of Prince George's physicians, did what he could to help by publishing a "sermon" appealing to his fellow Scots. "A gracious Queen of the Ancient Line of our own Monarchs," he wrote, "desire[s] nothing more than that the People from whom she derives her Blood, should enjoy the same Liberty and Plenty with others whom Providence has called Her to Govern."[170] Defoe, who had some credibility in Scottish circles because of his Presbyterian faith, spent months in Edinburgh working to gain support for the Union. Although the public debate was fierce, the Scottish Parliament began to move slowly through the draft accords, approving them a section at a time by comfortable majorities. Anne delayed convening the English Parliament in the hope that the Scottish consideration of the Union might be complete, but the Scots were still in session when the English met on 3 December 1706. Marlborough had arrived in England on 16 November and could thus be present to receive the thanks of his peers. There was also good news from Italy, where Prince Eugene had won a significant victory over the French in September, saving the Duke of Savoy's kingdom by relieving Turin, which had been besieged since May. Even the news from Spain was promising, though Peterborough had so thoroughly alienated Charles III that the young king missed a crucial chance to march into Madrid, which he might easily have done because his rival Philip had retreated to France after the debacle at Barcelona.

The mood in London was celebratory. On 19 December, Marlborough led another parade featuring captured French standards, which Anne watched again from the Fitzhardings' window. This time the flags went to the Guildhall, and the Lord Mayor hosted a splendid dinner at Vintner's Hall for the commander and his general staff, with musical entertainment provided once more by Elford and Leveridge, singing a new ode set by Weldon. The text was by the irrepressible satirist Thomas D'Urfey, who recognized Godolphin's presence by casting his words as a lighthearted dialogue between Mars and Mammon. While Mars celebrates Marlborough's triumphs at Ramillies, Mammon takes credit for Eugene's victory at Turin:

> Beyond the *Alpine* Mounts of Snow,
> Far as the Banks of ancient *Po*,
> The Cordial Coyn was sent, O happy Chance,
> To heal their Fainting Troops, and send a Plague to *France*.[171]

Although such praise was welcome, Godolphin knew perfectly well that the £50,000 advance he had provided for Eugene at the beginning of the campaign had not been a "happy Chance." Aware of the acute danger to the kingdom of Savoy, the Treasurer dispatched those funds without waiting for the Dutch to pay their share, and his decision paid off.[172] The next day, 20 December, a concert at York Buildings featured "a particular Piece of new Musick compos'd by Mr Jer[emiah] Clark, on her Majesty's happy Success under his Grace the Duke of Marlborough the last Campaign."[173]

On the final day of the year, the queen invited both Houses of Parliament to join her at another thanksgiving service at St. Paul's. Although this was the third such event in sixteen months, the two previous services had taken place during the summer, when Parliament was not in session. In light of the ongoing process of moving the two kingdoms toward Union, it can hardly be an accident that the preacher on this festive occasion was Bishop Burnet, an assimilated Scot, who shrewdly chose as his text a verse praising the good ruler: "He shall judge the poor of the People, he shall defend the Children of the Needy, and shall break in pieces the Oppressor." Although this passage ends with a phrase that might easily be applied to military victories, it begins by emphasizing the charity of the monarch, and when Burnet, at the end of his homily, speaks explicitly of the queen, his emphasis falls on her piety and her nurturing care for her subjects, with the longed-for Union in a climactic position:

> What may not yet be expected from a Queen that offers up the Praise of all the wonders of her Reign to that God under whose Protection she humbly puts her self, and whom she so solemnly and constantly worships? Who seems to have no other relish of the Greatness of Power, but as it puts her in a Capacity of doing much Good Abroad as well as at Home. Her Reign has been hitherto one continued Flood of Prosperity, without any Ebb of Mixture of Misfortunes. We see in it likewise a course of noble Projects, for the Good & the Happiness of Her People, well begun and steadily carried on. Her first care was to rescue her Clergy from Poverty, and its consequences, Ignorance and Contempt. With what zeal has she for some Years pursued the Designs of Uniting her Kingdoms into one Body, as well as all her Subjects into one Mind? Oh when shall both be happily effected![174]

Prince George missed this service, "being unable to endure the fatigue,"[175] and Anne postponed the New Year's celebration until 6 January 1707, when she heard an ode by Tate and Eccles. Although the music has disappeared, Tate's text is shorter and much more cohesive than his effort for 1706. The grand chorus, like Burnet's sermon, stresses the importance of the Union:

> Valour may the Foe Disarm,
> But UNION is the Lasting Charm,
>   Of ev'ry Bliss, The Golden Chain,
> Our *ANNA*'s Royal Gift, and Glory of her Reign.[176]

Ten days later, by a vote of 110 to 69, the Scottish Parliament ratified the Treaty of Union. The debate in the English Parliament would last until 4 March,

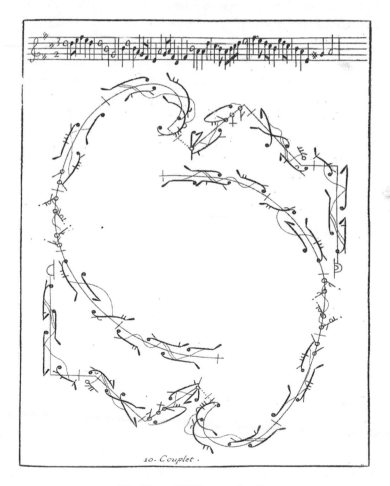

The Union (1707), couplet 10.

with Nottingham, Rochester, and Buckingham playing their now familiar roles as protesters against the will of the majority. Yet Anne, who frequently attended the deliberations in the House of Lords, approved a performance of "The Union," a new dance with choreography by "Mr. Isaac" and music by James Paisible, as part of her birthday celebration on 6 February. Addressing themselves to the royal presence, in this case the queen on a throne at the end of the ballroom, the performing couple danced to two contrasting tunes, a slow and courtly *loure* and a lively Scottish hornpipe, in a performance artfully demonstrating the process of union between male and female genders, courtly and popular styles, fast and slow tempi—and by extension the English and Scottish peoples.[177] All of their steps and gestures had specific meanings for the knowledgeable monarch, trained in such formal dances from her childhood, and even for those in attendance who lacked her level of expertise, it was clear that the queen was celebrating the Union now as a way of indicating her disdain for those who still dared to oppose it. If *Camilla,* heard earlier in the day, was chosen for its popularity and charm, "The Union" was courtly art with a clear political purpose. Though irritated with the Tories who sought in vain to block her project, Anne had not embraced a full-blown Whig ideology. Maynwaring, celebrating theatrical competition, might celebrate the fruits that supposedly sprang from "division," but Anne believed that the Union she had worked so hard to achieve would bear abundant fruits, a sentiment eloquently expressed in one of the many sermons celebrating the agreement when it finally came to pass:

> Be thankful, I say, for this *Union,* and the prospect it gives of Excellent Fruits. *Union* is from GOD, and the Root of multitudes of Blessings to Nation; even as Division and Dissension is the Root from whence many Evils Spring up.[178]

CHAPTER 9

THE BREATH OF OUR NOSTRILS

7 March 1710

The empty throne was the only unoccupied seat in Westminster Hall, the enormous room where Queen Anne had eaten her coronation banquet and where Charles I had stood trial for his life. Now another trial had captured so much public interest that Parliament had asked Christopher Wren to construct new scaffolds to seat the spectators.[1] On this, the eighth day of the proceedings, more than two thousand people, clutching their hard-won tickets, had crammed into the "noble *Gothic* Building"[2] to hear the defendant speak on his own behalf. The queen herself was present, not on her throne but in a special box with the Ladies of her Bedchamber, behind a curtain that marked her presence as "incognito," although everyone knew she was there and wondered what she thought of the man on trial.

The defendant was Dr. Henry Sacheverell, an Oxford don who had incurred the wrath of the Whig majority in Parliament by delivering a sermon on *The Perils of False Brethren* in St. Paul's Cathedral on 5 November 1709. Those preaching at services commemorating the Gunpowder Plot typically warned their flocks against papist plotters and celebrated William's landing at Torbay on the same date, so it was especially insulting when Sacheverell took the occasion to attack the Dissenters as the gravest danger to the Church and to call into question Revolution principles dear to the hearts of the Whigs. His High-Flying Tory sermon, delivered with intense emotion, provided a rallying point for his party; over one hundred thousand copies were in print within a few weeks. Angry and insulted, the Junto Whigs decided to make Sacheverell an example by impeaching him and having him tried in the House of Lords—a decision they would come to regret.[3] By the time the trial began, the partisan sentiments it aroused in supporters and opponents of "the Doctor" had become so intense that shouting mobs greeted Sacheverell's coach and surrounded the queen's sedan chair as they made their way to the trial. Those inside the hall were also fervent partisans: one Tory lady, after offering a piece of cold chicken to the gentleman seated beside her, took it back when she learned that he was opposed to Sacheverell.[4] Expressions of support for the man on trial turned violent on the night of 1 March, when a mob burned several Dissenting houses of worship, including the chapel served by Daniel Burgess, the leading Presbyterian preacher in London.

An indifferent scholar and intemperate drinker, Sacheverell was an unlikely figure to bring down a government, yet his trial provided the occasion for a stylized but substantial debate on unresolved issues originating in the Revolution of 1688, if not before. The preacher's insistence on the traditional Anglican doctrine of nonresistance appeared to vindicate the practice of the non-jurors, who had scrupulously refused to swear allegiance to William; his hostility to the Dissenters called into question the much-cherished Toleration, which allowed Presbyterians and Baptists to attend their chapels without harassment, but also permitted freethinkers to dispense with attendance at any religious services. In the popular imagination, especially in the country, the Whigs were associated with religious skepticism. As they now held control of Parliament and the ministry, High-Flying Tories like Sacheverell were not alone in having fears that the Church was "in danger."

The legal talent involved in this trial was impressive. Attorney General James Montagu, the younger brother of Lord Halifax, led the prosecution, and the senior defense attorney was Sir Simon Harcourt, who had been Anne's Attorney General until 1708, when a failed political coup forced his resignation. Although he was seriously ill, Harcourt held his audience's attention for nearly two hours, thanks to his "soft, beautifully-modulated voice." Before mentioning "the strength, the justness and the beauty of [his] expression,"[5] one diarist praised "the cadences" of his speech—a detail that may remind us that Anne and her contemporaries were keenly sensitive to prose rhythm. English prose had borrowed from Latin three effective ways of ending a sentence or clause: the *cursus planus* ("hélp and defénd us"); *cursus tardus* ("góverned and sánctified"); and *cursus velox* ("púnished for òur offénces").[6] Frequent in the *Book of Common Prayer*, from which these examples come, such elegant "closes" came to be expected in formal oratory, so much so that speakers who lacked the ear to create them attracted ridicule.

Although the Whig politician Charles Townshend "spoke materially, with argument and knowledge," he "failed to please," says a friendly witness, because "his diction was not only inelegant, but frequently ungrammatical, always vulgar; *his cadences false,* his voice unharmonious, and his action ungraceful."[7] Harcourt, by contrast, with his modulated voice and careful attention to cadence, was able to capture the admiration of those opposed to the content of his speech.

Though given to extremes of diction and imagery in his sermons, Sacheverell possessed a voice that a prominent Whig divine would praise as "audible without Noise or any *harsh grating Accent* to impress the Close of a Sentence upon the Ears of the Congregation."[8] His ability to deliver a cadence with appropriate musical emphasis contributed to the power of his speech in his own defense. Many witnesses report that women, including some inclined to condemn him, wept at the defendant's eloquence, and the managers of the prosecution sought an adjournment rather than proceeding to rebuttal on the same day. Although some thought his words had been written or edited by others, Sacheverell spoke, according to the diarist, "with a fine accent and the most agreeable voice that ever I heard."[9] We may gain a faint idea of how the beleaguered preacher employed his vocal instrument by considering one sentence from his peroration, in which he refutes those accusing him of Jacobitism by proclaiming his loyalty to the queen and the Protestant succession:

> It is my sincere and hearty Prayer, that God would prolong the Life of her most Sacred Majesty, whose Exemplary Goodness and Piety give us the best hopes we have, of averting that Vengeance, which is due to the Wickedness of the Age we live in; that he would bless her Counsels at Home, and her Arms abroad, and make Her Reign exceed that of her renown'd Predecessor Queen *Elizabeth,* in Length as well as Glory; but when the Inheritrix of the Blessed Martyr's Crown and Piety; when She, the Desire of our Eyes, and the Breath of our Nostrils, shall, full of Years and Honour, be gathered to Her Fathers, and exchange her Temporal for an Immortal Crown, (since we are depriv'd of that Prince Her Royal Offspring, whose Loss no true Lover of his Country, and of the Royal Family, can reflect upon, without a bleeding Heart; and whom God, in his Anger, took from us, because we were unworthy of so inestimable a Blessing) I earnestly beseech God, in defect of future Issue from Her Majesty, to perpetuate the Succession of the Crown, as it is Establish'd in the most Illustrious House of *Hanover,* which I look upon as, next to his Providence, the best Guard we have against Popery and Arbitrary Power; the best Security of our Church, and of the Constitution of our Government, which is the Glory and Happiness of our Nation, and the Envy of all others.[10]

In order to deliver such a long sentence effectively, Sacheverell needed great breath control, and Maynwaring mentions "the Strength of his Lungs" as one reason for his effect on his audience.[11] He also needed to signal suspended syntax by varying the pitch of his voice, so that he could deliver the touching parenthesis on the death of Gloucester without allowing his hearers to lose the syntactic thread connecting Anne's "exchang[ing] her Temporal for an Immortal Crown" with his "beseech[ing] God…to perpetuate the Succession." Attention to cadence, both in composition and delivery, was a part of this technique. Consider the rhythm of the passage just before the parenthesis:

> when Shé, | the Desíre | of our Éyes, | and the Bréath of our Nóstrils, |
> sháll, | full of Yéars | and Hónour |, be gáthered to Her Fáthers, |
> and exchánge | her Témporal | fór an Immórtal Crówn

Each phrase here has five main stresses, like a line of English poetry; each divides into subphrases of gradually increasing length. "Bréath of our Nóstrils," the astonishing metaphor Sacheverell uses to make the queen the principle of life for her people, is a simple *cursus planus,* and "gáthered to Her Fáthers," a phrase he borrows from Scripture, is an extended *cursus planus.* The absence of a similar falling close in the last phrase is a signal that the sense will be carried on, through the long parenthesis, until the sentence ends with "Énvy of all óthers," another perfect cadence.

As these details will suggest, the Sacheverell trial was a sensational piece of theatre, its performers admired for their eloquence as much as for their arguments. The popularity of the trial even forced adjustments in the schedule of the professional opera company, as Richard Steele pointed out in his popular newspaper the *Tatler:*

> All Persons who employ themselves in Publick, are still interrupted in the Course of their Affairs: And it seems, the admired Cavalier *Nicolini* himself is commanded by the Ladies, who at present employ their Time with great Assiduity in the Care of the Nation, to put off his Day till he shall receive their Commands and Notice, that they are at Leisure for Diversions.[12]

A performance for the benefit of the famous Italian castrato Nicolini, which was an important and lucrative part of his contract with the opera company, had twice been delayed because the audience was less likely to come to the opera in the evening when attending the trial required them to rise very early in the morning. By pointing to that fact, the *Tatler* implies that "the Ladies" have been drawn to the trial not by their "Care of the Nation," but by the musical power of Sacheverell's rhythmic composition and beautiful voice. They have forsaken the virtuoso singing of a foreign castrato for the sonorous speaking of a virile English clergyman.

§

Like other satirical references to Italian opera in the *Tatler,* this passage has its origins in the failure of a serious attempt to mount a self-consciously English opera. In March 1707, just three years before the Sacheverell trial, music-lovers had their first chance to hear *Rosamond,* an opera with an original libretto by Steele's friend and collaborator Joseph Addison, who was serving as Undersecretary to the controversial Earl of Sunderland. This was not only an English project but a Whig project: the author presented a manuscript copy to the Duchess of Marlborough, to whom he dedicated the printed play, and the scenery included a "Plan of Blenheim *Castle*" seen in a dream and described by a singing angel:

> Behold the glorious Pile ascending!
> Columns swelling, Arches bending,
> Domes in awful Pomp arising,
> Art in curious Strokes surprizing,
> Foes in figur'd Fights contending,
> Behold the glorious Pile ascending![13]

Unlike *Arsinoe* and *Camilla,* set in Cyprus and Latium, *Rosamond* does not take place in the ancient Mediterranean, home of the gods and heroes whose dominance in poetry the Whigs were trying to escape. Instead, in a gesture toward patriotism, folk tales, and the dedicatee, Addison chose a plot from medieval Britain. According to a legend frequently retold in histories, poems, and ballads, King Henry II had a beautiful Welsh mistress named Rosamond Clifford, whom he visited at a lodge in Woodstock Park—the very piece of land Anne had recently granted to the Marlboroughs. The oldest ballad recounting this tale, sung to a tune called "Flying Fame," begins with an efficient exposition:

> When as King Henrie rul'd this land,
>   the second of that name,
> (Besides the Queene) he dearly lov'd
>   a faire and princely Dame.[14]

In order to confront her rival, Queen Eleanor of Aquitaine has to find her way through a labyrinth designed to frustrate intruders, so she takes advantage of a "trustie Knight" left behind to guard the king's mistress, from whom she seizes by force a "Clew of twined Threed" that leads her to Rosamond's room. Once inside, she gives the young woman a choice between being stabbed or drinking a bowl of poison, and Rosamond chooses the poison. In keeping with the improbable happy endings of *Arsinoe* and *Camilla,* Addison altered the story: in his opera, Sir Trusty, whose name obviously comes from the ballad, also drinks the poison, but it puts both him and Rosamond into a swoon. The king sees a vision of England's future glories, culminating in Blenheim Palace, and patches up a reconciliation with the queen; the mistress, once she awakens, enters a convent.

This plot provided opportunities for arias expressing love, jealousy, terror, and forgiveness, yet its English provenance may have been its most important attraction for Addison. When describing his travels in Italy a few years earlier, the poet had laughed at the disjunction between the "rough old *Romans*" who were the usual heroes of Italian operas and the "squeaking Eunuchs" who played them,[15] but the dramatic conventions he had mocked were now coming to England. A few days after the premiere of *Rosamond,* the castrato Valentini appeared as Turnus in a performance of *Camilla* at the same theatre, singing in Italian while the other performers sang in English. In April, Valentini would play the role of Orontes, a heroic general, in *Thomyris, Queen of Scythia,* a "Medley Opera" that Motteux constructed by writing new words to some well-known arias by Alessandro Scarlatti, composer of over one hundred operas, and Giovanni Bononcini, whose music had sustained *Camilla* for the last two seasons.[16] Nicolini, more celebrated and more expensive than Valentini, would make his first London appearance in 1708, in *Pyrrhus and Demetrius,* another heroic tale with music by Scarlatti: he sang Pyrrhus, Valentini sang Demetrius, and Margherita de l'Epine sang the male role of Marius. With Catherine Tofts and Joanna Maria Lindelheim in the female roles, *Pyrrhus and Demetrius* was still being performed at the time of the Sacheverell trial. Believing that the confusion of genders common in Italian performance practice undermined the whole idea of ancient heroism, Addison sought to avoid it by basing his plot on an English legend, and by having no part for a castrato. His Henry II, however, was a countertenor, Francis Hughes, who had been displaced from the role of Turnus in *Camilla* by Valentini; his Rosamond, supposedly a fair Welsh beauty, was the Italian soprano Maria Gallia. Creating an English opera on an English theme was not a simple task, yet Addison was evidently determined to employ an English composer. Thomas Clayton, whose *Arsinoe* was still in the repertory of the Drury Lane company, undertook the music, and by January 1707 the work was sufficiently advanced for Christopher Rich to make a confident reference to "Mr Claytons Opera call'd *Rosamond*" as a forthcoming production.[17]

As with previous operas, there was a subscription, which sold sufficient tickets to fill the house for the first performance (4 March 1707) and to reserve "The Front Boxes, the two Side Boxes, and the Pit" for two more (15 March and

22 March).[18] These three evenings, however, were the only performances *Rosamond* would ever have. The failure embittered Addison against opera, destroyed Clayton's career, and discouraged other English poets and composers from attempting to start a native tradition in opera. It is therefore worth trying to determine what went so dreadfully wrong. It was not a case of bad timing, which had contributed to the failure of *Gli amori d'Ergasto* in 1705. The premiere of *Rosamond* took place on 4 March, the day on which the House of Lords ratified the Union with Scotland, and London remained full of fashionable people for the rest of the spring. Notable public events included the grand celebration of the Union on 6 March (with a concert featuring Italian singers),[19] the arrival of a large delegation of Scottish nobles in April, and another thanksgiving service at St. Paul's on 1 May. Nor is there any reason to think that the singers were incompetent. Catherine Tofts, who sang Queen Eleanor, gave six more performances as Camilla before the season ended and took a leading role in *Thomyris*. Francis Hughes, who sang King Henry, performed as a soloist in summer concerts connected with the horse races at Nottingham, singing "a Collection of Songs taken out of the Operas of *Camilla, Thomyris,* and *Arsinoe*."[20] Party politics, which play a small part in Addison's libretto, do not appear to have contributed to the opera's failure either: it was a Whig opera produced at a time when the Whigs were riding high. The responsibility for the failure of *Rosamond* falls squarely on the shoulders of Addison and Clayton.

From the start, Clayton has taken most of the blame. The anonymous author of the one positive notice that the opera received, in a short-lived periodical called the *Muses Mercury,* expressed doubt about the quality of the music, grudgingly preferring *Rosamond* to *Arsinoe* because of its superior libretto:

> It has been disputed whether the Musick is as good as that of *Arsinoe*; but, without entering into Comparisons, it must be confess'd, that the Airs of *Rosamund* are fine, the Passions touch'd; and there being such a vast difference between the Merit of the Poems, the Dispute, 'tis probable, when decided, will be determin'd in Favour of *Rosamund*.[21]

In 1709, when one would have thought the carcass of *Rosamond* far too dead to be worth kicking, an anonymous critic called the music "abominable," describing it as

> nothing but a continuation of the *Bassi arpeggiati* (as the *Italians* term it) without any other design than to Promise much, and Perform nothing. Having begun ill in the very first Air, … he goes on in the same manner; and though nothing is said to be more fertile than Error, this Author's Genius is so narrow, as not to be able to vary upon that.[22]

Mus. Ex. 9.1: Thomas Clayton, aria from Act 1 of *Rosamond* (1707).

None of Clayton's recitative for *Rosamond* survives, but his musical short-comings are apparent in the forty-two "Songs" from the opera that John Walsh published just after the premiere. As Rosamond waits impatiently for Henry to return from the wars, she sings a primitive da capo aria.[23] In the A section, the voice outlines an f minor triad, but the frequent repetition of tight little four-note groups in the bass line gives the impression of energy without much direction, especially as the whole first phrase is immediately repeated; in the B section, the voice repeats a new phrase sequentially at the interval of a rising fourth, but on the third repetition Clayton abandons the sequence and the melody meanders back down, missing another opportunity for musical expression. The final phrase outlines the tonic triad once more and ends with a long descending scale. The da capo takes us back to the beginning, where we hear the first phrase two more times.

This empty aria, weak in melodic invention, is typical of Clayton's work, yet Addison also bears some responsibility, locally and generally, for the shortcomings of *Rosamond*. In this very aria, he repeats the word *fly* four times, and if he had any knowledge of compositional practice, he should have expected that word, with its awkward opening consonants, to be repeated insistently in the music. The phrase "Arms my Monarch" contains a knotty consonant cluster (*rmsm*) that Gallia, who was not even a native speaker, would surely have found difficult to negotiate quickly in sixteenth notes at a "brisk" tempo. Here and throughout the libretto, Addison often writes smoother poetry in the sections designed for recitative than in those designed for arias. Just before Rosamond launches into her impatient aria, he gives her these limpid lines:

> In vain the Spring my Senses greets
> In all her Colours, all her Sweets;
>   To me the Rose
>   No longer glows,
>   Every Plant
>   Has lost its Scent:
> The vernal Blooms of various Hue,
> The Blossoms fresh with Morning Dew,
> . . . .
> (Nature's softest, sweetest Store)
> Charm my tortur'd Soul no more.[24]

In this passage, Addison presumably means to express a despondent and melancholy mood before the character moves toward anger and frustration in her aria, but there is little evidence in either section that he has considered what it might be like to set or sing his words. There were probably cuts; if Clayton had actually set all the lines Addison wrote for recitative, the opera would have been very long indeed.

In his remarks on the operas he heard at Venice, Addison breezily declares that "The Poetry of 'em is generally as exquisitely ill, as the Musick is good." He may not have grasped (or appreciated) the extent to which Italian librettists had subordinated their art to the art of the composer, but as his speculations continue, he backs away from this sweeping judgment, admitting that the Italian language and its poetic traditions enable librettists to maintain decorum:

> The *Italian* Opera seldom sinks into a Poorness of Language, but, amidst all the Meanness and Familiarity of the Thoughts, has something beautiful and sonorous in the Expression.... The *English* and *French*, that always use the same Words in Verse as in ordinary Conversation, are forc'd to raise their Language with Metaphors and Figures, or by the Pompousness of the whole Phrase, to wear off any Littleness that appears in the particular Parts that compose it.[25]

When his turn came to compose an operatic libretto, Addison did not succeed in avoiding "Littleness." His expressions of emotion are conventional and stylized, and when he tries to sound elevated, his diction drifts toward the excess of Dryden's heroic plays. Worse yet, his decision to imitate *Arsinoe* and *Camilla* by including a comic subplot starring Richard Leveridge and Mary Lindsey as an unhappy couple guaranteed some "Meanness and Familiarity." Sir Trusty, Leveridge's character, calls his wife "ugly and old, / And a villainous Scold"; she retorts by calling him "a Rustick." In an attempt at political humor, Addison gives Sir Trusty some lines bemoaning the hard fate of those "who serve in the State":

> Yet this is the Lot
> Of him that has got
> Fair *Rosamond*'s Bow'r,
> With the Clew in his Pow'r,
> And is Courted by all,
> Both the great and the small,
> As principal Pimp to the mighty King *Harry*.[26]

One wonders what kind of recitative Clayton provided for that final line, where the vulgar word *pimp* completely destroys any hope of operatic decorum.

In addition to these local failures of tone, *Rosamond* was open to allegorical interpretations that risked offending the very patrons the poet sought to please. The mighty Harry, returning from the wars, was sure to suggest Marlborough, especially when the messenger announcing his arrival runs through the usual military clichés:

> From purple Fields with Slaughter spread,
> From Rivers choak'd with Heaps of Dead,
> From glorious and immortal Toils,
> Loaden with Honour, rich with Spoils,
> Great *Henry* comes! Prepare thy Bow'r
> To lodge the mighty Conquerour.[27]

The trope of a river "choak'd with Heaps of Dead" originates in an episode in the *Iliad,* but the theatre audience in 1707 was more likely to remember recent poems on Blenheim, including Addison's, which used similar language to describe the French cavalry drowned in the Danube.[28] Unlike Henry, however, the duke returned from his conquests to the arms of his wife, who would have been expected to attend a performance as the dedicatee of the printed libretto. If she came to the opera, Sarah heard a prologue hammering home the identification between King Henry and her husband,[29] yet Addison does not appear to have considered how she might respond to a story that showed its hero in the arms of a mistress. A few years earlier, the duchess had become suspicious of her husband and accused him of unfaithfulness; the person who appears to have been responsible for planting suspicions in Sarah's mind was her son-in-law, the Earl of Sunderland, now Addison's employer.[30] While it is not at all clear what Addison knew about this private matter, he should surely have considered what kinds of parallels between his characters and his patrons the audience might imagine.

There is good evidence to support the belief that *Rosamond,* with its nostalgia for the English past, was also part of a campaign to save the picturesque ruins at Woodstock.[31] If so, it again risked offending the Duchess of Marlborough, who would spend the next five years urging Vanbrugh to tear down those ruins. And while it seems quite unlikely that Addison knew much about Sarah's jealous rage when she discovered Abigail Hill's closeness to Queen Anne, he might nonetheless have considered how the powerful duchess to whom he had "humbly inscrib'd" his opera might respond to Queen Eleanor's jealous rage at being supplanted in the king's affections.[32] His inattention to aesthetic and social decorum in *Rosamond* is all the more remarkable because he had been so careful about tact and balance in *The Campaign* and would soon write, in the *Tatler* and the *Spectator,* essays that remain models of precision and politesse. Perhaps it was his fundamental distrust of the genre of opera that undermined Addison's effort to create a viable English opera. Believing that sung drama was inherently absurd, he inevitably committed absurdities of his own, from which the composer was unable to rescue him.

Thanks to "fifteen or sixteen Airs that were really good,"[33] *Thomyris,* the cobbled-together pasticcio starring de l'Epine and Valentini, raised a subscription of £1,200 and sustained seven performances between 1 April and the end of the season. Addison found an opportunity to express his irritation by writing an anonymous prologue for *Phædra and Hippolytus,* a spoken tragedy by Edmund Smith that had a short run at the Queen's Theatre while *Thomyris* was succeeding at Drury Lane. In this prologue lie the seeds of his later attacks on Handel in the *Spectator*:

> Long has a Race of Heroes fill'd the Stage,
> That rant by Note, and through the Gamut rage;
> In Songs, and Airs express their martial Fire,
> Combate in Trills, and in a Feuge expire;
> While lull'd by Sound, and undisturb'd by Wit,
> Calm and Serene you indolently sit;
> And from the dull Fatigue of Thinking free,
> Hear the facetious Fiddles Repartie:
> Our Home-spun Authors must forsake the Field,
> And *Shakespear* to the soft *Scarlatti* yield.

According to the logic of these lines, music is by definition unmanly, and a hero who rages "through the Gamut" or expires "in a Feuge" cannot really be heroic. Although Addison enjoys attacking the musicians, his real target is the audience, who have abandoned the English hero Shakespeare, forcing him to yield to the "soft *Scarlatti.*" Appropriating and undermining a phrase long used to praise the queen, the poet calls the indolent theatregoers "Calm and Serene" as they wallow complacently in musical pleasure, freed "from the dull Fatigue of Thinking." Enjoying the music of singers who are physically emasculated, those attending the opera become spiritually and politically emasculated. Addison's friend Steele, who supported him in his attacks on opera, took up this theme in 1709, when there was talk of peace, suggesting that "Opera's... have already inclin'd us to Thoughts of Peace, and if tolerated, must infallibly dispirit us from carrying on the War."[34] In the "rearguard action" the two friends fought against Italian opera,[35] poking fun at the sad fate of the castrati was a frequent tactic, already apparent in the pointed and nasty prologue of 1707:

> Had Valentini, musically coy,
> Shun'd *Phædra*'s Arms, and scorn'd the proffer'd Joy,
> It had not mov'd your Wonder to have seen
> An Eunuch fly from an enamour'd Queen:

How would it please, should she in *English* speak,
And could *Hippolitus* reply in Greek?[36]

The juxtapositions here are intentional. Addison wants to imply that having a dialogue sung in two languages is as unnatural as creating an adult male soprano through surgery. He had good reasons for concealing his authorship, as his own disappointment at the failure of *Rosamond* is all too apparent in this bitter little poem.

§

On 1 May 1707, some ten days after Addison's prologue was spoken, both theatres were dark as the nation observed a day of thanksgiving for the Union. The choir at St. Paul's sang the *Te Deum* as they would have for a military victory, and there was a "Union Anthem" jointly composed by John Blow, Jeremiah Clarke, and William Croft.[37] In a tedious and pedantic sermon, William Talbot, Bishop of Oxford, wrestled with the fact that Great Britain would now have two established churches, Anglican in England and Presbyterian in Scotland, and stressed the importance of "dissent[ing] with Modesty and Sobriety":

If these would not *judge* the other, nor the other *despise* these, this is, for ought I see, as great an Union in Judgment and Opinion, as can be expected, 'till that blessed Scene shall open, of *a new Heaven and a new Earth,…wherein will dwell light and knowledge as well as righteousness.*[38]

The poets were more enthusiastic, none more so than Charles Darby, a clergyman who predicted that the Union would be remembered longer than Marlborough's battles:

For no Oblivion shall this UNION blot:
Should *Ramellies,* and *Blenheim* be forgot.

In his most touching passage, Darby describes the joining of Anne's kingdoms as a substitute for the child she could not have:

May You to many happy Years arrive,
To see your *Britain* by this UNION thrive.
And if an Off-spring Heav'n should You deny,
Be this your Child, and Royal Progeny.[39]

The Queen soon showed how much she valued the Union. On 3 May she promoted Cowper, who had been the chief negotiator among the English commissioners, from Lord Keeper to Lord Chancellor; Pembroke, who had also been helpful, became Lord Lieutenant of Ireland on 30 April; Nottingham, Rochester, and Buckingham, who had persisted in their doomed opposition to the Union, were left out of the first Privy Council of Great Britain, which now included the leading Scots lords.

Before the new Privy Council met, however, word reached London of a disastrous battle in Spain. At the beginning of this year's campaign, the administration had replaced the Earl of Peterborough, victor at Barcelona in 1705, because of his disrespect for Charles III, his disregard for orders, and his inflated sense of his own importance.[40] The new commander in Spain was the Huguenot refugee Henri de Ruvigny, Earl of Galway, who immediately encountered his own difficulties with the would-be king and unwisely consented to a plan in which their forces divided, with a group headed by Charles III marching off to hold Catalonia while Galway's group moved toward Madrid. Waiting for him at Almanza on 14/25 April was a large French and Spanish army commanded by the Duke of Berwick, who was James II's son by Arabella Churchill (and thus Anne's half-brother and Marlborough's nephew). Born and raised in France, Berwick was an experienced and skilled commander, and on this occasion his forces significantly outnumbered Galway's. The result was a crushing defeat, in which the Allies lost at least four thousand men killed or wounded, with three thousand taken prisoner. French losses were also significant—estimates vary from two to five thousand—but this setback indefinitely postponed allied plans for establishing Charles III in the capital.

A few weeks later, a French army under Marshall Villars made themselves masters of Bavaria, overrunning the elaborate network of defenses erected by Prince Ludwig of Baden, who had died in January as a consequence of his infected toe. "The fruits of the victory at Blenheim," wrote a disappointed Luttrell, "were lost in one night without opposition."[41] Bavaria lay undefended because the emperor had commandeered German troops in order to stage an invasion of Naples, which was a Spanish possession. An imperial army of fifteen thousand entered Naples unopposed in July and proclaimed Charles III, but their presence there weakened allied efforts elsewhere. Marlborough, defending his gains of the previous summer while trying in vain to provoke another battle in the Low Countries, strongly backed a planned assault on the port of Toulon by imperial and Savoyard forces under the command of Prince Eugene, with naval support provided by the British fleet under Sir Cloudesley Shovell. Attacking the French on their own soil, he reasoned, would force them to withdraw forces from Spain and Germany. Toulon, however, was well defended by the time the allied forces were in place, and Eugene lacked the numerical superiority he would have had with the troops sent to Naples, so the planned attack became a siege, which was eventually abandoned in August.

As this summary will suggest, 1707 was the worst summer for the Allies since the beginning of the war. It was also a very difficult summer for the queen. Her husband's health continued to be precarious, and her relations with the Duchess of Marlborough, which had been stormy for most of 1706, took a decided turn for the worse. Mindful of Sarah's jealous nature, the queen had not been candid with her about the growing importance of Abigail Hill. During the spring of 1707, Anne learned of a romantic attachment between Abigail and Samuel Masham, who had long served Prince George—first as a page, then as an equerry, and now as a Groom of the Bedchamber. It was he who "besmeared" the young Duke of Gloucester with blood at the boy's first stag hunt, an event the queen had probably not forgotten.[42] When Abigail married Samuel in the chambers of George's physician John Arbuthnot, the queen honored the couple with her presence and took concrete steps to support them. On 1 May, the day of the thanksgiving for the Union, Luttrell reported that "the lord Windsor's regiment of horse is taken from him, and given to col. Massam,...one of the grooms of the bedchamber to the prince,"[43] and on 11 June, the queen herself signed a receipt for 2,000 guineas from the Privy Purse, which was evidently her wedding present to Abigail.[44] As Sarah was the Keeper of the Privy Purse, Anne should have known that a withdrawal of that size would attract her suspicions, and on 17 June, the duchess apparently said something that prompted a nervous response:

> By what my dear Mrs Freeman said a litle before she went from me this evening, I can not help fearing she may have heard some new Lye of her poor unfortunat faithfull Morly, and therefore I beg you to open your dear hart, hide nothing, but tell me every the least thing that gives you any hard thoughts of me, that I may justify my self, which I am sure I can do, never haveing don any thing willingly to deserve your displeasure. I would have made this request when I parted from you, but I found my hart and eyes growing soe full, I durst not atempt it, being sure if I had, I should not have bin fitt to have seen any body. For the same reason I desire an answer to this in writting, and that for Jesus sake as soon as it is possible, for I am on the rack and can not bear liveing as we do now, being with the same sincere tender passion that I ever was my dear deare Mrs Freemans and shall be soe inviolably to my last moment.[45]

The contradictions within this letter are striking. Although she herself has held back information, Anne asks Sarah to open her heart, but because the crisis has reduced her to tears, she modifies her request for candor by asking to have Sarah's thoughts in writing. Although she is "on the rack," a phrase she normally uses in speaking of physical pain, the queen does not make any sort of confession, and Sarah would not learn the truth about Abigail's marriage until September.

At this point, however, Sarah's concerns about Abigail were more political than personal. She was aware that her cousin was also related to Robert Harley, and suspected (rightly) that the bedchamber woman was arranging to give the secretary personal access to the queen. The queen's stubborn insistence on naming her own candidates to two vacant bishoprics, an exercise of her personal preroga-tive that came close to destroying Godolphin's administration, convinced the duchess that Harley was encouraging Anne to disregard her chief ministers. In light of their support for the war and the Union, Sarah's Whig friends expected to have a say in the disposal of valuable offices in the Church as well as in the govern-ment and the military, and Godolphin, who needed Whig support in Parliament, was trying to work with them. Anne's intransigence baffled and outraged her Treasurer and the Whig leadership, as the men she intended to appoint as bishops were Tories, whose presence in the House of Lords would weaken the Whig ma-jority. Wharton actually told Godolphin that he thought the Treasurer was play-ing a double game, promising to deliver these positions to Whig candidates, then allowing the queen to appoint Tories, but Sarah vigorously promoted her con-spiracy theory, insisting that the favored Abigail was giving the devious Harley special access to the monarch, which he was using in turn to forward a Tory agenda.[46] According to one eighteenth-century account, these meetings took place "under the colour of concerts of music, at which the queen herself is also said to have been present."[47] While written long after the event, this narrative pres-ents a plausible picture, with Harley ostensibly coming into the queen's apart-ments to hear private concerts, then taking advantage of the opportunity to chat about politics with Anne.

Yet neither the notion of Godolphin as a double agent nor the notion of Harley as the secret force behind the queen gives sufficient weight to Anne's own powers of will. While it was undoubtedly true that his kinship with Abigail gave Harley opportunities to converse with the queen, her motives in the tussle over the bishoprics were not necessarily partisan. She had strong personal opinions about clergymen and favored those whose theological views were close to her own. John Sharp, Archbishop of York, whom she now trusted more than any other bishop, enjoyed ready access to her, and she took his advice seriously. As an expe-rienced connoisseur of pulpit rhetoric, the queen also judged clergymen by their eloquence, a fact insufficiently considered by both eighteenth-century politicians and modern historians.

The candidates put forward by the Whig Leadership were Samuel Freeman, Dean of Peterborough, and Charles Trimnell, Prebendary of Norwich. Both were on the list of Chaplains in Ordinary to the queen, but if they ever preached before her, she did not order their sermons printed. Freeman, who was nearing the end of a fairly modest career, had published nothing since his funeral sermon for William Russell, Duke of Bedford in 1700, a strongly Whig performance in which he referred to the dead man's son, executed in 1683 for his alleged complicity in the Rye House Plot, as "a Martyr." A section on the old duke's virtues is a fair sample of Freeman's disorderly syntax:

> I need not mention that mighty Zeal He had for the Protestant Religion, for the Interest of his Country, its Laws and Liberties; and his never-to-be-shaken Faith and Affection to our invincible Monarch, who generously, in spight of all Hazards and Oppositions, came over for the Rescue and Deliverance of them. They are too flaming to be hid.[48]

Using the tired Ciceronian device of listing someone's qualities while pretending that he "need not mention" them, Freeman appears to be starting a list of the objects of Bedford's "Zeal": "*for* the Protestant Religion, *for* the Interest of his Country"—until he awkwardly breaks that promising sequence and meanders off into a relative clause in praise of William III. By the time we reach the end of the sentence, there is no obvious referent for its final word, "them," by which Freeman presumably means to indicate "Laws and Liberties." The grammatical confusion increases when the next sentence begins with "They," which cannot possibly refer to "Laws and Liberties" and is probably meant as a reference to Bedford's "Zeal,... Faith, and Affection." Though not as incompetent as Freeman's, the prose of Charles Trimnell, the other Whig candidate, is also loosely strung together. In the sermon he preached at Norwich on the thanksgiving day for Blenheim, Trimnell spent more time praising the memory of William III than celebrating the present queen and ascribed Marlborough's greatest victory to the "Infatuation" of the French:

> For if we may do it without detracting from them, who have deserv'd so well at our hands; we cannot but observe, that there seems to have been an Infatuation from Heaven let down upon the minds of our Enemies, in their not having disturbed our coming up to them, thro' a vain confidence of their being superiour to us.[49]

In addition to displaying an odd reluctance to name the man of the hour, this clotted, wordy prose lacks any principle of symmetry or balance.

The contrast between the awkwardly suspended style of these men and the rhetoric employed by Anne's candidates is striking. One of the men she proposed to make a bishop, Offspring Blackall, preached before her at St. James's on

17 November 1706, describing in balanced cadences some troubles Anne knew all too well:

> There is indeed no State or Condition of Life free from Trouble, and it is impossible that while we live in a miserable and naughty World we should meet with nothing in it to vex us. He that is above Contempt is the Object of Envy; and he that is not affronted to his Face may be slander'd behind his Back; and he that is too great to be crush'd and trampled upon by others, may yet suffer as great Mischief by secret Treachery; and he that is powerful enough to resist Violence, may not be wary enough to avoid a Snare....For the Rich Man as well as the Poor may have unkind Relations, undutiful Children, false Friends, or unfaithful Servants; The Rich as well as the Poor may be disappointed in his Designs, may be robb'd and spoil'd of what he has, may have a Body very sickly and infirm, and may suffer the sharpest Pains: And all these, and many more such like Evils, which no Man is by any Wealth or Dignity exempted from, are Trials of our Patience, as well as those which are more peculiarly incident to Poverty.[50]

Every sentence in this paragraph has a clear syntactic principle, carried through with admirable balance. The second is especially fine:

He that is above Contempt	is the Object of Envy;
he that is not affronted...	may be slander'd;
he that is too great...	may yet suffer;
he that is powerful enough...	may not be wary enough.

The queen heard these eloquent words in her Chapel Royal a few weeks before being forced to appoint Lord Sunderland as a Secretary of State, a concession she had resisted for over a year—and a painful instance of Blackall's theme. Though her "State or Condition of Life" was monarchial, she was plagued with trouble; though blessed with wealth, she was "sickly and infirm"; her beloved Sarah, who had pressed her to make that distasteful appointment, seemed more and more to be an "unfaithful Servant," perhaps even a "false Friend." Despite some remarkable successes abroad and at home, the queen knew what it meant to be "disappointed in [her] Designs." The preacher's recognition that troubles could vex the rich as well as the poor therefore struck a chord in her heart, and allowed her to hope for the promised blessing: "Blessed are the poor in spirit, for theirs is the Kingdom of Heaven." Politically, Blackall was the kind of moderate Tory with whom Anne was comfortable, a supporter of the Revolution of 1688 without being a believer in a contract theory of government. Her preference for him, however, may have had more to do with his pulpit style than with his partisan allegiance.

The other man Anne wished to promote, William Dawes, was a poet and a baronet as well as a clergyman. He had preached before her, also in November, on *The danger of talking much, and wisdom of the contrary*, a text sure to please the notoriously taciturn queen. "When once they are engag'd in talk," says Dawes, people "very often let fly at random, and foolishly blirt out every thing, that comes uppermost; how much soever it may tend, to the dishonour of God, the prejudice of their neighbour, or the eternal ruin of their own precious and immortal Souls." His list of "ways of offending with our Tongues" sounds for all the world like a catalogue of the kinds of speech Anne had heard and deplored in her court, her Privy Council, and her Parliament:

> There are so many several ways of offending with our Tongues, both against God and against Man: by prophan and atheistical, lewd and irreligious, light and scoffing Discourses: by reproach and scandal, by slander and detraction, by false defamations and uncharitable truths, by lying and equivocation, by court and flattery, by bragging and boasting, by murmuring and complaining, by arrogancy and positiveness, &c.

Dawes gives his lists their musical shape by employing doublets, often pairing a word of Saxon origin and a word of Latin origin ("lewd and irreligious," "lying and equivocation"), a device familiar to the queen from its frequent use in the *Book of Common Prayer* ("sins and offences," "alms and oblations"). Cautioning his hearers against a range of spoken offenses, Dawes lays special stress on the importance of discretion "when you happen to be ingag'd in discoursing upon Subjects of, more than ordinary, moment and importance,"

> such as, for instance, the venerable Mysteries of our Religion, the Characters of our Governours, the Conduct of our Superiours, &c. These are nice and sacred Subjects, by no means rashly or irreverently to be treated; here we shall be in great danger, without our utmost care, of lashing out into things, which are too high for us: here our mistakes and misrepresentations will be of the most fatal and mischievous consequence: here our duty exacts from us, all the respect, tenderness and waryness, all the humility, modesty and charity, that we can possibly put on.[51]

Assailed on every side by those who felt free to cast aspersions on the conduct of their superiors, the queen wanted her subjects to speak of her with "respect, tenderness and waryness." She hoped they would avoid not only "false defamations" but even "uncharitable truths." Perhaps she believed she might encourage such behavior by appointing as bishops the men who had preached these sympathetic, judicious, and eloquent sermons before her.

§

In April 1707, Anne privately promised Blackall and Dawes that they would become the Bishops of Exeter and Chester, and in June the Whigs, who had expected Godolphin to deliver those sees to Freeman and Trimnell, issued a threat they believed would force the queen to rescind her promises: if they were denied these appointments, they told Godolphin, they would launch an investigation into the conduct of the admiralty, thus exposing the queen's husband and Marlborough's brother George to public scrutiny. To everyone's amazement, the queen held firm. The Whigs blinked first, offering to allow Blackall to take up his see in return for control over all future appointments, but again the queen refused to compromise. If Sarah had remembered Princess Anne's "mortification" when William prevented her from keeping her promises about appointments to Gloucester's court, she might have understood one reason for Queen Anne's firmness. If she had considered the fact that Charles Trimnell, the candidate pushed hardest by the Whigs, had been the tutor of her son-in-law Sunderland, she might have understood another. But neither the troubled favorite nor her party was able to credit Anne herself with having this much backbone, so they laid the blame on Harley. On 17 July, the duchess met with the queen in a room off the Long Gallery at Windsor, where she evidently accused her mistress of following the advice of Harley and Abigail. In a letter sent the next day, Anne said "something in answer to . . . the suspicions you seem'd to have concerning your Cousin Hill, who is very far from being an occasion of feeding Mrs. Morley in her passion, as you are pleased to call it, she never medling with anything."[52] The last phrase is crucial: by alleging that Abigail never meddles with anything, Anne denies the central tenet of Sarah's conspiracy theory and implicitly rebukes Sarah for her own obsessive meddling.

Once this personal confrontation had failed, the Whig leadership decided to try to force Harley out of the government; the August meeting at which they reached this decision took place at Sunderland's home in Althorp. Understandably alarmed, Godolphin enlisted Marlborough to help persuade the queen to compromise with the Whigs. In his letter to the duke, sent on 16 August, he accepted Sarah's theory that Anne had been manipulated by Abigail and Harley:

> I reckon one great occasion to Mrs. Morley's obstinacy, and of the uneasyness she gives herself and others, especially about the clergy, proceeds from an inclination of talking more freely than usually to [Mrs. Masham].

And this is layd hold of, and improved by [Harley] upon all such matters, if not upon others, to insinuate his own notions.[53]

But when Marlborough himself wrote to Anne, telling her that she would need to make a choice between following Harley's advice or Godolphin's, the queen insisted once more on taking responsibility for her own decisions:

I can not think my haveing nomi[na]ted Sir William Daws and Dr Blackall to be Bishops is any breach, they being worthy men, & all the Clamour that is raised against them proceeds only from the Malice of [the Whigs], which you would see very plainly, if you weare heare. I know this is otherways represented to you, & I beleeve you have bin told as I have, that these two persons weare recommended to me by [Harley], which is soe far from being true, that he knew nothing of it till it was the talk of the town; I do assure you these men weare my own choice, they are sertinly very fit for the Station I design them, & indeed, I think my self obligd to fill the Bishops Bench with those that will be a creditt to it, & to the church.[54]

Harley also solemnly denied having recommended Blackall and Dawes, although both his friends and his enemies believed he was behind the queen's intransigence. With the government assailed by both parties, he was now in a position to assemble support from a group of "moderates," present the queen with an allegedly nonpartisan administration, and claim a leading role for himself.[55] Although his actions during the autumn and winter remain difficult to trace, there is evidence that he was having secret conversations with the Dukes of Newcastle and Somerset, wealthy Whig magnates who already held important court positions as Lord Privy Seal and Master of the Horse;[56] he probably also spoke with the new Duke of Devonshire, who had succeeded his father as Lord Steward when the old man died in September. By bringing these men into conversation with some Tory officeholders—including Henry St. John, the Secretary at War; Sir Simon Harcourt, Anne's Attorney General; and Sir Thomas Mansell, her Comptroller of the Household—Harley evidently hoped to fashion a new, "nonpartisan" ministry. Secretive and sly, he nonetheless kept up a steady stream of correspondence with Godolphin and Marlborough, professing continued loyalty and concern.

Himself a lifelong advocate of nonpartisan ministries, Godolphin was frantically trying to keep his government afloat, still hoping that the Whig Junto could protect him from the High Tories. To that end, he wrote frankly to the queen on 11 September imploring her to give ground on the bishoprics in order to secure continued support for the war. Expressing himself with real urgency, he reminded her that the bad results of the summer's campaign would make her administration vulnerable when the new Parliament met:

> What *colour of reason* can incline your Majesty to discourage and dissatisfy those whose principles and interest lead them on with so much warmth and zeal to carry you through the difficulties of this war, and have already given you so many unquestionable proofs of their preferring your Majesty's interest and the support of your Government, above all others? and what appearance will it have, what reflexion will it not cause in the world that all these weighty things together can not stand in the ballance with this single point, whether Dr. Blackall at this time bee made a Bishop, or a Dean, or a prebend?[57]

As earnest of his seriousness, he asked to be allowed to retire, a request the queen immediately rejected. "Whoever of the whigs," she wrote the next day, "thinks I am to be Heckter'd or frighted into a complyance tho I am a woman, are mightily mistaken in me, I thank God I have a Sould above that, and I am too much conserned for my reputation to do any thing to forfet it, as this would."[58] Like Elizabeth at Tilbury, Anne uses the conventional notion of female weakness as a foil for her assertion of strength. In thanking God for her soul, she proclaims her belief in her own character, as she had done as a girl of fourteen, facing the tensions of the Popish Plot yet declaring to Lady Apsley: "I have a good heart thank God or els it would have bin down long ago."[59] In refusing to forfeit her reputation, she rejects the weakest part of Godolphin's letter, in which he treats her concern about breaking her word as an "imaginary" objection.[60]

Although it clearly *did* matter to Anne whether Blackall became a bishop, Godolphin saw his appointment as far less important than the coming attack in Parliament, of which there were already signals in the press. Sounding for all the world like the Tory Nottingham, the radical Whig journalist John Tutchin gave an early foretaste of the planned assault on the admiralty in the *Observator* for 10 September. "Our wise and prudent Ancestors," he wrote,

> ever thought the Sea-Security the best; the Navy was always in the Hands of Such as had a Sea-Genius, and knew right well the Management.... [H]ad we made our Fleet our chief Concern in assisting King *Charles,* and pay'd our Quota for Land-Service, we might ere now, have destroy'd most of the Enemies Ships.[61]

Poor and obscure, Tutchin was vulnerable, and shortly after this issue was published, thugs whose employer remains unknown beat him so severely that he died.

No such tactics would be available to the government in defending itself against the great men of both parties now calling it to account in Parliament. On 25 September, Godolphin wrote grimly to Harley, speaking of "the great clamours which I hear are preparing against the management of our sea affairs, which must needs be very disagreeable to the Queen and particularly uneasy to the Prince; in short, I expect to see the whole government torn to pieces, with no friends to support it."[62]

In a show of unconcern, the queen went off to see the races at Newmarket, where a fast horse owned by Godolphin won two prizes.[63] While she was away, Samuel Freeman, one of the Whig candidates for a bishopric, succumbed to disease, but his death did nothing to reduce the pressure on the government. Writing to Sarah at the end of the month, Anne pointedly repeated a phrase from her Lord Treasurer's letter: "If I have not answered all my dear Mrs Freemans letters," she wrote,

> I beg she would not impute it to any thing but the aprehensions I was in of saying what might add to the ill impressions she has of me, for tho I beleeve we are both of the same oppinion in the main, I have the misfortune that I cannot agree with her exactly in every thing, and therefore what I say is not thought to have the least *colour of reason* in it, which make[s] me realy not care to enter into particulars.

In the discourse of politics and philosophy, *color of reason* normally indicated a specious argument that its speaker knew to be specious. When Godolphin asked Anne "what colour of reason" might incline her to baulk the will of the Whigs, he was implying that she had no plausible excuse for her action. But Anne's basic reason for appointing Blackall and Dawes was not a matter of party: it was a deep and sincere belief in the intellectual and spiritual superiority of her candidates. When she laments that what she says "is not thought to have the least colour of reason in it," she is wittily appropriating Godolphin's phrase to express her exasperation at not being taken seriously. She goes on to assure the duchess that she has no intention of allowing her Treasurer or her Captain-General to retire:

> Can dear Mrs Freeman think that I can be soe stupid, as not to be sensible of the great Services that Mr. Fre[eman] and Mr. Mont[gomery] has don me, nor of the great misfortune it would be if they should quit my service, no sure you cannot beleeve me to be soe void of sense and gratitude.[64]

On the day she wrote this letter, Anne approved the choice of a Speaker in her new House of Commons and adjourned them for a week. Writing to the teenaged poet Alexander Pope, the old comic dramatist William Wycherley described this first Parliament of Great Britain, with its colorful cast of characters, as welcome theatrical entertainment: "there is likely to be so much Comedy, acted, by the two great Play-Houses of the Nation the House of Lords, and that of the Commons, that me-thinks all People should come to Town but for their diversion."[65] Among Wycherley's reasons for hoping to be amused by the legislature was the sad state of the two real theatres, paralyzed by mismanagement, rivalry, and confusion; the productions on offer this fall were mainly tired reruns.[66] As Godolphin knew, however, this session of Parliament would prove to be anything but comic, and a recent tragedy made the situation even worse: Sir Cloudesley Shovell might have been able to provide some helpful support for the beleaguered naval office, but on his way home from Toulon his ship struck the rocks near Scilly in a dense fog; all hands perished.[67]

The House of Commons made an initial show of unity, with a new Scots member seconding the nomination of John Smith as Speaker and a unanimous House voting to continue him in the chair. A week later, the queen gave her expected speech, acknowledging the setbacks of the previous summer while holding out the hope that the Union would strengthen the nation. On 15 November, however, the Commons heard a petition from "several Merchants of London," complaining of insufficient protection and great losses to French privateers, and on 19 November, they asked "Doctor Trimnell," the disappointed Whig candidate for a vacant bishopric, to preach before them on 14 January, "the Day appointed by her Majesty's proclamation for a general Fast and Humiliation."[68] For Godolphin and Marlborough, humiliation quite unlike that imagined in the queen's devout proclamation looked imminent, as the dreaded attack on the government proved even more intense in the House of Lords. The Commons had unanimously thanked the queen for her address, but when the time came for the Lords to consider a response to her speech, Wharton and Somers, leaders of the Whig Junto, spoke of "the great decay of trade and scarcity of money" and "the ill condition and late mismanagement of the Navy." Encouraged by this display of resistance to the government, Buckingham and Rochester, the leaders of the High Tories, opposed consideration of an address to the queen until the Lords had discussed "the State of the Nation." Both houses launched investigations into naval affairs, and John Thompson, Baron Haversham, who always enjoyed opportunities to embarrass the establishment, confirmed Godolphin's fears that his government would be "torn to pieces" by bluntly calling for a new administration: "My lord," he said, "I take the root of all our misfortunes to be in the ministry; and without a change of the ministry, in my opinion, no other remedy will be effectual."[69]

On the night of 5 December, Harley made his move, asking for a secret meeting with Godolphin and Marlborough, at which he revealed his plan to create an

alliance of moderate Whigs—including Newcastle, Somerset, and Devonshire—
and moderate Tories loyal to himself. This plan, greeted with more enthusiasm by
Marlborough than by Godolphin, was supposed to keep the revolt in check, but the
High Tories continued their attack. On 19 December, in the presence of the queen,
"there was a long and memorable debate in the House of Lords, in relation to the
Affairs of Spain," with several speeches in praise of Peterborough, the former commander, designed to reflect upon the government that had sacked him. Haversham,
sneering at Galway, said that it was "no wonder our Affairs in *Spain* went so ill, since
the Management of them had been entrusted to a Foreigner." This campaign to
embarrass the administration included the carefully timed publication of *Camillus*,
a long poem by Aaron Hill, Peterborough's secretary, extolling his employer as an
"Injur'd Hero."[70] Rochester, who had always opposed the operations in the Low
Countries, attempted to undermine Marlborough's military authority by proposing "that we should stand on the Defensive in *Flanders*, and send from thence 15 or
20,000 Men into *Catalonia*," an insulting remark that the duke, fresh from a frustrating summer, answered "with some Warmth," listing all the reasons why his
forces needed to be strengthened. Revealing the results of the diplomatic efforts he
had undertaken at the end of the summer's campaign, Marlborough put an end to
the debate by assuring his colleagues that "Measures had been already concerted
with the Emperor for the forming an army of 40,000 men . . . for sending powerful
succours to King *Charles*," and by suggesting that Prince Eugene might take command of that force.[71] Reassured by Marlborough, the Lords now voted their long-
delayed address to the queen. This time, the Junto Whigs, who had joined the
attack on the government just one month earlier, did not support the High Tories.
Although the disappointments of the previous summer had emboldened Rochester and his allies, Marlborough's record of success gave him considerable authority.

In the same month, the duke took the trouble to use his prestige in a different
arena, interceding with the queen on Vanbrugh's behalf to support a new arrangement designating the theatre in the Haymarket as the only venue for operas. "At
last," writes Vanbrugh,

> I got the Duke of Marlborough to put an end to the Playhouse Factions,
> by engaging the Queen to exert her Authority, by means of which, the
> Actors are all put under the Patent at Coventgarden House [i.e., Drury
> Lane theatre], And the Operas are Establish'd at the Haymarket, to the
> generall likeing of the whole towne; And both go on in a very Successfull
> manner; without disturbing one an Other.[72]

Although he had finally achieved the goal he was seeking when he built the theatre, the struggling impresario still faced daunting challenges, as the Italian opera

singers he hoped to import were ruinously expensive. In the same letter, he claims that the powerful duke is supporting his appeal for an annual subsidy of £1,000 from the queen, but this was probably wishful thinking, as Anne did not make the requested grant. The cost of the war was probably among her reasons for avoiding financial involvement in the opera house. While providing a generous supply of money, the Lords and Commons agreed on 22 December that "no peace can be honourable or safe, for your majesty or your allies if Spain, the West Indies, or any part of the Spanish monarchy be suffered to remain under the power of the House of Bourbon."[73] This unanimous resolution received immediate assent from the queen, who knew, as her legislators did not, that Charles III was about to sign a trade agreement giving British merchants huge opportunities for profit.[74] She could not, however, risk having critics claim that the high taxes levied to support a war on several fronts were actually paying for operas, and in time the idea that there could be "no peace without Spain" would make it difficult for her to bring the long war to an end.

§

Although Anne's Parliament still wished to continue the war, her subjects were growing weary. In his New Year's ode for 1708, the Poet Laureate wrote wistfully of his hope for peace.

> Then shall the Drum and Trumpet sleep,
>   The Weary World have Rest;
> The Seas Pacific Silence keep,
> Calm as their Guardian *GEORGE*'s Brest.
>
> Nor in those Halcyon Days of Peace
> Shall Glorious *ANNA*'s Triumphs cease;
>
>   *Grand Chorus.*
>   New Wonders of Glory
>   Unrival'd in Story,
> New Scenes of Applause, shall her Annals Adorn,
> With a Harvest of Blessings for Ages Unborn.[75]

Tate's reference to Prince George as the guardian of the seas, coming at a time when the admiralty was under severe pressure from parliamentary committees, is earnest of his loyalty, though the weak pun on *Pacific* is a failure of taste. Poems in praise of this queen had often given her credit for Marlborough's victories, and this very ode mentions Blenheim and Ramillies while trying—not very successfully—to find something to praise in the previous summer's campaign.[76] The poet is much more comfortable imagining the queen as freed at last from warfare, offering "a Harvest of Blessings" to future ages.

The immediate challenge, however, was finding domestic peace. On 7 January, Anne officially appointed Blackall and Dawes to their new sees; thanks to another vacancy, she was able to make Trimnell a bishop at the same time. But the end of the struggle over the bishoprics did not end the jockeying for position among the leaders of both parties. Harley was continuing his efforts to serve as a power broker, and had frequent contact with Godolphin, Marlborough, and the queen during December. On New Year's Eve, however, an impoverished clerk in his office, William Gregg, was caught selling state secrets to French agents, and the Secretary suddenly looked both sloppy and vulnerable. Questioned by a committee from the Privy Council,[77] Gregg made a full confession on 3 January 1708, pleaded guilty at his trial on 19 January, and suffered the grisly punishments for treason in April, maintaining to the end that he had acted alone, though *The Traytor's Reward, or Mr. William Greg's Sorrowful Lamentation,* a crude broadside ballad published during the trial, put a different story into his mouth:

> From those whom I served,
> Small Comforts have I
> For now i'm discover'd
> they leave me to dye;
> Which makes it appear,
> It is true by m[y] Fate,
> the treason they Love,
> But the traytor they hate.[78]

The anonymous balladeer was not alone in believing (or hoping) that Harley would be brought down by Gregg's treason, as he might well have been in an earlier era, when guilt by association destroyed those on the far fringes of the Popish Plot and the Rye House Plot. These were different times, however, and by calmly going about his business, Harley retained his head, his office, and the opportunity to continue his plotting for a few more weeks. His enemies would assert for years that the conspiracy extended beyond the corrupt clerk, and even those who discounted such theories were distressed by the careless procedures in Harley's office, which had made it easy for Gregg to copy secret documents. Suspicions of ministerial incompetence increased on 29 January when St. John was forced to admit, on the floor of the House of Commons, that only 8,660 British soldiers out of the 29,595 men designated for Spain by the previous year's Parliament had actually fought at the Battle of Almanza. The queen and her administration were eventually able to account for the missing men, who had either gone to Catalonia with King Charles, stayed in Portugal, or died of disease, but the discrepancy initially seemed staggering.

Though undermined by Gregg's perfidy and tainted by St. John's revelations, Harley persisted in trying to take control of the government. The detailed development and chronology of his attempted coup may never be perfectly known, but there is a modern consensus, which rests on contemporary testimony from four witnesses: Bishop Burnet, a lifelong collector of secret history; James Montagu, the queen's Solicitor General and the younger brother of Halifax; Joseph Addison, employed in Sunderland's office and therefore well informed about administrative matters; and Addison's friend Jonathan Swift, who had come to London in November with the Earl of Pembroke, Lord Lieutenant of Ireland, in hope of persuading Godolphin to extend Queen Anne's Bounty to the Anglican Church of Ireland. Although they differ about some details, all four men agree that the Secretary "was at the centre of a conspiracy aimed at removing many leading Cabinet ministers; three of the four versions make it clear that the Tories were to be the beneficiaries of the intended changes; while two of the four plainly suggest that Harley was aiming to head the new administration himself."[79] Harley had reason to hope that Marlborough, who had long deplored the rancor of the two parties, would fall in with his scheme for a "nonpartisan" administration, and he may at first have intended to work with Godolphin as well. At some point, however, he decided to supplant Godolphin and claim the prime ministerial role for himself. When the Treasurer learned of this duplicity, he was naturally appalled, especially when Harley wrote to him protesting his innocence. "I have received your letter," Godolphin replied on 30 January, "and am very sorry for what has happened to lose the good opinion I had so much inclination to have of you, but I cannot help seeing and hearing, nor believing my senses. I am very far from having deserved it from you. God forgive you!"[80]

As Addison remarked, Harley's scheme "came to Light before its time,"[81] but the plan for an altered administration was attractive to the queen, who had long desired to free herself from the shackles of party. Had Marlborough been willing to sacrifice Godolphin, the outcome would almost certainly have been different, and even after he decided to back his old friend, Anne did not immediately fold her hand. The denouement was remarkably dramatic. On Friday, 6 February, the queen received the compliments of the nobility on her birthday at Kensington. For the first time since her reign began, she did not come to St. James's, nor did she offer a play, an opera, or a ball. Although she was supposedly "lame and indisposed,"[82] the crisis in her government was probably the real reason for her unprecedented indifference to the rituals normally observed on this occasion. On her birthday, when she might have been enjoying an opera, Anne sent Henry St. John to tell Marlborough that she was ready to part company with Godolphin; the duke replied that night, stating clearly that neither he nor Godolphin would serve with Harley.[83] On Saturday, 7 February, the House of Lords met, and the administration suffered an embarrassing defeat: by five votes, the Lords joined the Commons in abolishing the Scottish Privy Council, a body the Treasurer and the queen had found useful, effective 1 May 1708.[84] On Sunday, 8 February, just before a scheduled Cabinet meeting at Kensington, Anne's three oldest supporters offered their resignations in person. General James Stanhope, a veteran of the Spanish campaign, took note of the words exchanged, and Sir John Cropley passed along his narrative in a letter to the Earl of Shaftesbury:

> I must tel you some parts of the Dialogue.
> Ld Trea[surer] told the Q[ueen] he came to resign the staff, that serving her longer with one so perfidious as Mr H[arley] was impossible. She replied, in respect of his long service she would give him til to-morrow to consider then he should doe as he pleas'd, with all she could find enough glad of that staff.
> Then came Lady Duchess with great Duty and Submission, that she had served her ever with affec[tion] & tenderness. Her utmost had been her duty and she had been faythfull in it. The reply is said to be, you shall consider of this til tomorrow, then if you desire it, you shall have my leave to retire as you desire. I shall then advise you to go to your Little house in St Albans and there stay till Bleinheim house is ready for your Grace.
> Then enterd the Duke prepard with his utmost address. He told her he had ever served her with obedience and fidelity, that [he] had used that sword he must now resign her to her honour & advantage, that he must lament he came in competition with so vile a creature as H[arley], that his fidelity and Duty should continue so long as his breath. That it was his Duty to be speedy in resigning his commands that she might put the sword into some other hand immediately, and it was allso his Duty to tell her he fear'd the Dutch would immediately on the news make a peace very ruinous for England. And then, my Lord, says she, will you resign me your sword. Let me tell you, says [she], your service I have rewarded to the utmost of my power, and if you do, my lord, resign your sword, let me tell you, you run it through my heart. She went to the council, beging him to follow, he refusing, so the scene ended.[85]

For those who witnessed it, this performance was a better drama than the play or opera they had missed at the birthday. Self-consciously enacting a stylized "scene" with the structure of a fairy tale, the three suppliants approached the throne in sequence, playing their roles with at least as much attention to the audience as to each other. If she had been "lame and indisposed" on Friday, the queen was evidently in full possession of herself on Sunday. Her responses to the proposed resignations, as remembered by Stanhope, are both eloquent and shrewd. She gives Godolphin more time, hoping that he will find a way to be part of the new administration, but warns him that she can find others eager to serve in his stead. She pointedly informs Sarah that forsaking her service will mean giving up her spacious lodgings in St. James's Palace, and that she will have to stay in her "Little house in St Albans" until she can move into Blenheim—an example of the monarch's largesse to her favorite's family but a massive project that will take years to complete. To Marlborough, whose speech is the most gallant and selfless of the three, she makes an emotional appeal, telling him that he will be destroying her by his resignation. The conclusion of her speech scans as two lines of blank verse:

> And if you do, my lord, resign your sword,
> Let me tell you, you run it through my heart.

As so often at moments of crisis, Anne is remembering tragic drama, specifically Nathaniel Lee's *Sophonisba*. When urged by his generals to abandon Sophonisba, King Massanissa describes his torment in similar terms:

> You'd have me shake her off and live; I'd know
> Whether this Flesh you wear you can forego,
> And be the same. Here through my Bosom run
> Your Sword; and when the bloody Deed is done,
> When your Steel smoaks with my Heart's reeking Gore,
> Bid me be well as e'er I was before.[86]

In the face of this dramatic appeal, it took the kind of confidence that had sustained him in combat for the duke to refuse to follow his monarch into the council chamber. Did he know that when she arrived there, the Duke of Somerset would rise from the table and declare himself unwilling to discuss the conduct of the war in the absence of the general? For the queen, whose obligations to Somerset began when he lent her his house in 1692, his principled stand was a clear sign that Harley would not prove acceptable to the moderate center, especially when Pembroke, who retained the presidency of the Privy Council while serving the queen in Ireland, took the same position. In order to supplant Godolphin, Harley would have needed the unflinching support of such moderates as Somerset and Pembroke. Instead, the other Privy Counselors whom he had courted—Devonshire, Newcastle, and Lord Chancellor Cowper—all threatened to resign. When news of the pending changes reached Parliament the next day, the Commons pointedly refused to debate the bill of supply, which was on the agenda, and the Lords appointed a committee to look into the Gregg affair, thus threatening Harley with possible impeachment.

On February 11, Harley resigned, taking with him St. John, Harcourt, and Thomas Mansell. Mrs. Masham, who was the queen's personal servant, remained in her place, much to the irritation of Sarah and others who blamed her for everything that had transpired. Godolphin and Marlborough resumed their positions, though Godolphin now felt renewed pressure to come to an accommodation with the Whigs. The idea of a nonpartisan administration—a temporary political convenience for Harley but a lifelong cherished dream for Anne—was dead. When Harley returned to power in 1710, he would do so on a wave of highly partisan support. Not until 1738, when a much older St. John wrote his influential essay on "The Idea of a Patriot King," would anyone seriously question the inevitability of government by party.[87]

§

The settling of this administrative crisis did not end the embarrassing parliamentary investigation into past mismanagement in Spain and at sea, and a new threat from abroad produced some highly partisan responses. By late February, it was clear that a French fleet, with James Francis Edward Stuart himself on board, was assembling at Dunkirk to attempt an invasion of Scotland. Efficient in this crisis, the queen dispatched Admiral George Byng with a large fleet to attempt to prevent the French from leaving port, while Marlborough summoned ten battalions home from Flanders to defend their native island. The House of Commons immediately drafted a "Humble Address...beseech[ing] your Majesty that you will be pleased to take particular Care of your royal Person" and assuring her that they were "fully and unanimously resolved to stand by and assist her Majesty with their Lives and Fortunes,"[88] but the Lords seized the occasion to express their contempt for Harley:

> We hope Your Majesty will always have a just Detestation of those Persons, who, at a Time when this hellish Attempt was a-foot, and so near breaking out, were using their Endeavours to misrepresent the Actions of Your best Subjects, and create Jealousies in Your Majesty of those who had always served You most eminently and faithfully. And we beseech Your Majesty not to give so just a Cause of Uneasiness to Your People, as to suffer any such hereafter to have Access to Your Royal Person .... We most humbly offer it to Your Majesty, as our Opinion, that Your Majesty should principally depend upon and encourage those who have been ever since the Revolution most steady and firm to the Interest of the late King, and of Your Majesty during Your happy Reign.[89]

Addresses of this kind were published, so the public as well as the queen had the opportunity to recognize Harley and St. John as "those persons…using their Endeavours to misrepresent the Actions of Your best subjects."[90] Marlborough and Godolphin were evidently "those who had always served You most eminently and faithfully," and Mrs. Masham was guilty of giving the wrong people "Access to Your Royal Person." The final sentence, with its allusions to "the Revolution" and "the late King," is not the "humble offer" it purports to be, but a strong adjuration to the queen, urging her to employ and promote the Whigs. Anne's reply is a masterpiece of understatement: "As I cannot but wish there were not the least Occasion of Distinction among My Subjects," she writes, reiterating her distaste for partisan strife, "so I must always place My chief Dependance upon those who have given such repeated Proofs of the greatest Warmth and Concern for the Support of the Revolution, Security of My Person, and of the Protestant Succession"[91]—a paraphrase that pointedly omits "the late King."

Though dignified in her formal pronouncements and efficient in marshaling her forces, the queen may have been emotionally labile at this time. Thomas Birch, writing long after Anne's death, alleged that she displayed "Compassion and Concern" for the Pretender:

> In 1708 when the Attempt was made on Scotland, Sir George Byng had no Instructions as to the Person of the Pretender. When this Particular was taken into Consideration the Council broke up in Confusion. For when some mentioned Methods of Dispatch the moving Appearance of her flowing Tears, prevented all further Deliberation.[92]

No contemporary witness reports any such outburst, although it supposedly took place at a Privy Council meeting. Lady Hervey, a friend of the Marlboroughs who was in London at this time, says that the queen "looked a good deal out of humour" on 13 March, though "she was very gracious to me." If there was a display of emotion, it need not have been prompted by sisterly feelings toward the young man, whose legitimacy Anne had often doubted. Her own proclamation, made on 6 March, describes "the said pretended Prince" as "Attainted of High Treason"—an outlaw and a traitor whose landing in her realms would mark him for death.[93] Sarah's memory of Anne's emotional state is much more plausible than Birch's dubious tale: "When the Nation was allarm'd with the *Pretender*'s attempt to land in *Scotland*," she writes, "the *Queen* herself had terrible impressions about his coming in a forcible manner, & shew'd the greatest signs of fear & concern about the matter."[94]

As it developed, the invasion was never a serious threat. Thanks to the wind, which kept Byng at a distance, the French were able to embark, but once they passed Yorkshire, for reasons that remain mysterious, they overshot their mark by a hundred miles and had to turn south from Aberdeen toward Edinburgh, where they hoped for a friendly reception. They lost valuable time, and with it the opportunity to land the Pretender and his troops, for as soon as they had anchored in the Firth of Forth, Byng's fleet, now numbering at least thirty ships, came into sight. As the smaller French fleet attempted to escape, Byng caught up with one vessel and captured it; scattered by the pursuit and the weather, the rest of the enemy ships limped ignominiously back to Dunkirk.[95] By the end of March, Marlborough was able to cross the Channel and begin the summer's campaign.

His duchess, however, did not make her usual journey to Margate to bid him farewell. Obsessed with Abigail Masham's imagined power over the queen and apparently passing through a period of strained relations with the duke, Sarah went to Windsor Lodge at the end of March, after having paid herself £12,000 from the Privy Purse, a sum she presumably calculated as her due because Anne had offered her £2,000 a year from that source in 1702.[96] From Windsor, she sent the queen a serious offer to resign her court posts, pointedly reminding Anne of her promise that they would go to her daughters—and thus *not* to Abigail. "If your Majesty thinks fitt to dispose of my employments according to the solemn assurances you have been pleased to give me," she wrote on 31 March, "you shall meet with all the submission and acknowledgements imaginable." "As to the conclusion of your letter," replied Anne on the same day, "I can never hearken to it as long as you live, and if I should outlive you, your faithfull Morly will remember her promises."[97] Encouraged to stay in her positions by the Whig wit Arthur Maynwaring, now serving as her secretary,[98] Sarah returned to court in April, apparently in a much better humor, and quietly restored the money to the Privy Purse.

"As soon as the fright of the invasion is pretty well over," wrote Godolphin to Marlborough at the Hague, "the enemy begins to pluck up a spiritt again."[99] Needless to say, "the enemy" he mentions is not the French but the parliamentary opponents of his battered administration. Tory complaints about failures in Spain and inadequate recruitment for the army continued, and there were ominous leaks from the committee investigating Gregg's treason, consisting entirely of Whig Lords. Now that Harley was gone, the Junto expected more posts in the government, as they had made clear in the recent address, and Godolphin, acutely aware of how much he owed them, was supporting their request to bring Lord Somers into the Privy Council as its President—an appointment that was odious to Anne. He was disappointed when Marlborough, who had spoken of making a brief trip back to England to help settle these issues, went instead to Hanover to persuade the future George I to embrace the allied plans for this year's campaign. The execution of Gregg and the dissolution of Parliament, both of which took place in late April, provided no more than a brief respite, as the attention of the political nation turned to the elections.

Among Sarah's reasons for recovering her spirits at this time was the pleasure she took in collaborating with Maynwaring on a series of anonymous publications. For a woman who wished she "had been so happy as to have been a Man,"[100] Maynwaring's willingness to take her writing seriously was intoxicating, and he knew just how to flatter her. In an exchange about "Dr. Tillotson's sermons," he calls the famous preacher "the best writer that ever was in our language, I mean for the style." "Your having read him so much," he tells her, "may be one reason why you allways write so clearly, & properly, & with such natural expressions, in which you excel every Body." One of her recent letters, he claims, has "one part that is written exactly after Montain's manner, so much has your G[race] profited by those few Books which you say you have read!"[101] The most presentable piece resulting from the drafts the duchess and her secretary exchanged this spring was a treatise on the upcoming election, *Advice to the Electors of Great Britain*.[102] Into this four-page pamphlet, Sarah poured the intense party feeling she had so often expressed in her letters to Anne. If the resulting prose is not at the level of Tillotson or Montaigne, it is clear and direct. "The true Principle of the Tories," she writes,

> is to profess Passive Obedience and Non-Resistance, to set up an Establishment opposite to Liberty, void of Property, and destructive of all the ends of human Society .... The true Principle of the Whigs is to maintain the Religion, Liberty and Property of their Country; and to have a just Concern for the common Good and Welfare of their Fellow-Subjects.

She continues by accusing the Tories of complicity in the attempted invasion and a cover-up of the Gregg affair:

> But if the next should prove a Tory-Parliament, will they make this Enquiry, as they ought to do, when 'tis certain it will fall heavy on some of their own Friends? Will they discover who gave the Invitation, that are certainly themselves the Inviting Party? Will they look into the bottom of *Gregg*'s Treason? ... Be assured, Gentlemen, no such Enquiries as these can be expected from such a Parliament.

Nothing Anne had said or written to Sarah in the previous decades had shaken her visceral belief that all Tories were secret Jacobites. By partially rewriting a phrase from the queen's recent answer to the Lords, she attempts to portray the monarch as fully supporting her position:

You have the best of all Authorities to direct you at your next Elections, even Her Majesty's own, who in her most gracious Answer to the Address of the Lords, professes that *Her chief Dependance is upon those who on all Occasions have express'd their Zeal for the Support of the Revolution.* You see therefore what Men Her Majesty recommends to you.[103]

Anne had spoken of "repeated Proofs of the greatest Warmth and Concern" but not of "Zeal," and she had begun her sentence by wishing that "there were not the least Occasion of Distinction among My Subjects," a plea for nonpartisan support that Sarah pointedly omits.

The duchess proudly sent *Advice to the Electors* to her husband in Flanders, who read it twice and praised it. She did not tell him what now seems virtually certain: that she had also helped Maynwaring write *A New Ballad, To the Tune of Fair Rosamond,* a parody of the old ballad that Addison had consulted in putting together his failed opera, with Anne cast in the role of King Henry and Abigail in the role of his mistress:

When as Q[ueen] A[nne] of great Renown
   Great Britain's Scepter sway'd,
Besides the Church, she dearly lov'd
   A Dirty Chamber-Maid.[104]

O! *Abi[gail]* that was her Name,
   She starch'd and stitch'd full well,
But how she pierc'd this Royal Heart,
   No Mortal Man can tell.

However for sweet Service done,
   And Causes of great Weight,
Her Royal Mistress made her, Oh!
   A Minister of State.

Her Secretary she was not,
   Because she could not write;
But had the Conduct and the Care
   Of some dark Deeds at Night.

The Important Pass of the Back-Stairs
   Was put into her Hand;
And up she brought the greatest R[ogue]
   Grew in this fruitful Land.[105]

Disguising their work as a product of the lower-class world of crudely composed and cheaply printed broadsides gave the authors license to be vulgar and vituperative, but perceptive readers soon realized that this work was more complex than most broadsides. As the object of the queen's passion, Abigail plays the role of Rosamond, but as the keeper of the key to the back stairs, she also plays the role of Sir Trusty, the "principal Pimp" to the monarch. For prurient readers, the "dark Deeds at Night" would be lesbian lovemaking, but that deliberately ambiguous phrase works equally well as a description of the dark consultations between Harley and the queen about changes in the ministry, supposedly conducted "under the colour of concerts of music." The authors equate sexual and political corruption as "dark Deeds" made possible by a "Dirty Chamber-Maid." Addison, sending it to a friend in April, described it as "a Print that is thought to be well-written," and added his opinion about its authorship: "I fancy it is Manwarings."[106]

The strongest internal evidence for Sarah's involvement in the composition of this work comes when Abigail asks Harley for advice about her relationship with the duchess:

> From Shreds and Dirt in low Degree,
>   From Scorn in piteous State,
> A Dutchess bountiful has made
>   Of me a Lady Great.
>
> Some Favours she has heap'd upon
>   This undeserving Head,
> That for to ease me, from their Weight,
>   Good God, that she were dead!
>
> Oh! Let me then some means find out;
>   This Teazing Debt to pay:
> I think, quoth he, to get her Place,
>   Would be the only way.[107]

In her letters to the queen, Sarah harps on her own role in rescuing Abigail from poverty and recommending her for a post at court, while accusing her rival of seeking to supplant her, not only in Anne's affections but in her official positions. The ballad effectively airs these complaints by showing Mrs. Masham describing herself as "undeserving" and embracing Harley's suggestion that she replace her benefactor. Sarah's campaign to promote the circulation of this song is also suggestive external evidence for her having helped to write it. In July, she wrote a lighthearted letter to Lady Mary Cowper, the wife of the Lord Chancellor, offering to sing two ballads against Abigail, of which this was certainly one: "I wish

I may have the honour of waiting upon you when you are in Hertfordshire," says Sarah, "and that you will allow me to sing with you, for indeed I think I am much improv'd, at least in the two Ballads of the Battle of Abigal. I can sing them most rarely."[108]

Like other young ladies trained at court, the duchess had probably had some singing lessons, and she had been friendly in the 1690s with Annabella Dives Howard, who was an excellent singer and a patroness of Purcell, yet her offer to sing these ballads herself, accompanied as it is by a claim to have been practicing, is striking. Maynwaring, who could play the harpsichord and liked to sing, may have encouraged Sarah to renew her interest in music at this time, and she often attended the operas that her architect Vanbrugh was producing at the Queen's Theatre. We know that she heard *Thomyris* on 20 April because Maynwaring was afraid that her sometime friend Halifax would take the occasion to pester her about his brother James, the Solicitor General, who coveted the higher post of Attorney General and thought that Sarah could help him gain it.[109] This operatic performance was one of the last given in a troubled season. Desperately short of repertoire and unable to come to terms with new foreign singers, Vanbrugh now realized that there was no way to gain the profits he had once dreamed of realizing from his purpose-built opera house. In May, he sold the business to the impresario Owen Swiney, whom he accurately describes in a letter to the Earl of Manchester: "He has a good deal of money in his Pocket; that he got before by the Acting Company; And is willing to Venture it upon the Singers."[110] Picking up the negotiations where Vanbrugh had left off, Swiney finally persuaded Nicolini to come to London for the next season, while Vanbrugh, who was enjoying a rare moment of approval from his troublesome client, joined the duchess at Woodstock in May to confer about the building.[111]

Although she was pretty clearly involved in the composition and circulation of the song about Abigail, Sarah nonetheless presented it to the queen as an anonymous street ballad, one that should concern the monarch as evidence that her public image was tarnished. Anne was indeed concerned about her reputation, but instead of fretting about ballads describing her fondness for Mrs. Masham, she wrote to Godolphin expressing the fear that her estrangement from Sarah would be noticed at court:

> You know I have often had the misfortune of falling under the Dutchess of Marlboroughs displeasure, & now after several reconciliations she is againe relapsed into her cold unkind way, & by a letter she writt to me on Munday, I find she has taken a resolution not to com to me when I am alone, & fancys no body will take notice of the change. She may impose upon some simple people, but how can she emagin she can, on any that

has a grain of Sense, can she think the D[uchess] of Somerset & my Lady
Fitz[harding] who are two of the most observeing, pryeing, Ladys in
England, wont find out that she never coms neare me, nor looks on me as
she used to do, nor that the tateling vice, will not in a little time make us
the Jest of the town? . . . I beg you would never mention any thing on the
subject that I have bin writing on before the Prince, because I have not
told him how unkind Mrs Freeman is to me, nor he shall never know it if
I can help it.[112]

"The tateling vice" is Anne's knowing way of describing Thomas Coke, who had
become Vice-Chamberlain of her household in 1706, and who was "a great Lover
of Musique And promoter of Operas."[113] Her remarks on the two "pryeing Ladys"
rest on decades of experience. The postscript, however, is the most touching feature of this letter. Although she is perfectly aware that court gossips will be quick to
notice her estrangement from the duchess, Anne hopes to shield her husband from
this knowledge lest it give him pain. Her determination that "he shall never know
it" betrays her awareness that the prince's current illness was likely to be his last.

§

The behavior of the duchess toward the queen in the summer of 1708 is puzzling
because she had so many reasons to be pleased with the current state of affairs:
Harley was out of office and out of London, living quietly in the country; the Whigs
had made substantial gains in the election; and on 30 June/11 July, the Duke of
Marlborough had won another great victory at the Battle of Oudenarde. Marlbor-
ough's ambitious battle plan for the summer envisioned three separate thrusts into
France, with Prince Eugene leading an army down the Moselle and the Duke of
Savoy making an incursion from the south while Marlborough himself moved into
France from the Low Countries. Obviously, this three-pronged attack would
require large forces and careful coordination; the duke went to Hanover in April
in order to secure troops from the Elector to help make up Eugene's army.
Although they did not tell the future George I, Marlborough and Eugene had a
backup plan in readiness, in which Eugene would join his army to Marlborough's.
As matters developed, Eugene did not gather sufficient men in time for an attack
down the Moselle, but thanks to disputes between the French generals, he had
just enough time to bring part of his troops into conjunction with Marlborough's,
and when the French forced the issue by capturing Ghent and Brussels, the confederates, who were in danger of losing a safe path to the sea, forced a battle at
Oudenarde. Although battlefield casualties were similar, with each side losing
about three thousand soldiers, the Allies took seven thousand French prisoners
and ended the day as masters of the field. Soon, Marlborough was laying siege to

Lisle, the second largest city in France, a difficult action that would take many months to complete, as he had to move his troops frequently in order to prevent the French from raising the siege and in order to secure his threatened lines of supply. Not until the very end of the year did the citadel at Lisle surrender, and even then Marlborough remained in the field, hoping to protect his gains and force the French to make peace on favorable terms.

As soon as she received news of the victory at Oudenarde, Anne wrote warmly to Sarah congratulating her on her husband's latest triumph,[114] but Sarah continued to criticize Anne's personal life. In a cruel and dishonest letter written on 24 July 1708, she posed as a loyal friend, keeping the isolated queen informed about scabrous attacks. "I found plainly," she writes,

> when I had the honour to shew your Majesty the two Ballads, that you never see any of them but from me, tho the town and country are full of them, and therefore I take the liberty to send you this, for tis no more to bee expected that your Majesty's new favourite should shew you any of these things of which she her self is generally the subject, then that she should inform you right of any other matter, and tho your Majesty was pleased to desire me not to speak any more of her, which I know to bee her own request, and what would bee of great advantage to all her designs if she could obtain it, yet I most humbly beg pardon if I can not obay that command, the rather because I remember you said at the same time that of all things in this world, you valued most your reputation, which I confess surprised me very much that your Majesty should so soon mention that word after having discovered so great a passion for such a woman, for sure there can be noe great reputation in a thing so strainge and unaccountable, to say no more of it, nor can I think the having noe inclination for any but of ones own sex is enough to maintain such a character as I wish may still be yours, but to the preserving a great reputation, general greatnesses are certainly necessary, such as justice and wisdome and constancy, and I hope your Majesty will forgive me if I can not think it was very just to disgrace your faithfull servants for the sake of some that had betray'd you nor very wise to disoblige all the honest part of the nation for a few inconsiderable people of ill principles, and noe interest, nor if I may bee allow'd to say so, was it any great proof of your Majesty's former constancy to leave Lord Marlborough and me for Mr Harley, and a woman that I took out of a garret.[115]

According to this account, there has already been a face-to-face meeting at which Sarah has shown two ballads to the queen, including the one she probably helped

Maynwaring write.[116] Anne has responded by revealing her "great passion" for Abigail while still insisting that she values her reputation. The headlong speed of Sarah's writing here is telling: phrases and clauses come tumbling out of her in an unbroken stream, and she makes no attempt to achieve the balance and order Maynwaring had praised in her more formal prose.

Any explanation for Sarah's deceitful actions and abusive language must necessarily be speculative, but her claim to be a disinterested friend concerned for the queen's reputation is evidently bogus, and her reference to same-sex love as "a thing so strainge and unaccountable" is hard to reconcile with the history of her own relationship with Anne, which some observers did not hesitate to describe as passionate, or with the evidence that she herself had close relationships with other women. Anne's jealousy when she feared that Sarah would go to the opera with Barbara Berkeley, Lady Fitzharding, back in 1692, was based on a perception of closeness,[117] and one lampoon from that period implies that Lady Fitzharding was among those who played the "Man's part" in lesbian lovemaking.[118] In 1693, Sarah received a series of flirtatious and suggestive letters from Annabella Dives Howard, the beautiful young singer, who was evidently smitten with her. "Doe you walk about in your short nightgound," asks Annabella in one letter, and in the next, requesting a visit in the country, she claims to have "a short nightgound that must keep company with yours," signing herself "your sincear admirer." Below her signature, she writes a curious postscript: "That sounds like a lover."[119] We are unlikely to recover evidence that Sarah had physical relations with Anne, Barbara, Annabella, or any other woman, but she was no stranger to affectionate feelings among women, and personal jealousy played a part in her outrage at the ascendancy of Abigail Masham.

Like the *New Ballad*, however, Sarah's letter to Anne juxtaposes sexual failures with political failures, as Sarah moves breathlessly from worrying about the queen's personal reputation to speaking of the necessity for "general greatnesses, . . . such as justice and wisdome and constancy."[120] The broadside she enclosed in this letter, *A New Song to the Tune of Lilly burlaro* (1708),[121] was a highly political screed accusing Harley and Masham of treason, which refers to Abigail as "a Bitch with a Broom" and shows her meeting with a "Triumvirate" consisting of Harley, St. John, and Harcourt:

> This Triumvirate
>   With *Abigail* sate,
> Who boldly pronounc'd
>   On the strength of Debate,
> No more the poor Church
>   Shou'd be left in the Lurch

> And none but true Tories
>   Bear rule in the State
>
> . . . .
>
> To finish the Plan
>   'Twas cunningly laid,
> That *France* in the Nick
>   Shou'd *Scotland* invade;
> That *Perkin* shou'd come
>   With Trumpet and Drum
> And try of what Metal
>   That Council was made.[122]

Like the Lords' address to the queen about the invasion and *Advice to the Electors*, these crude verses posit a connection between Harley's failed plot to bring in Tory ministers and the Pretender's failed invasion.

Though not as sophisticated a writer as Maynwaring, the balladeer responsible for *A New Song* senses the difficulty of holding an allegedly ignorant chambermaid responsible for an international conspiracy:

> 'Tis Nonsense to dream
>   That a Bitch with a Broom
> Cou'd ever contrive
>   T' have laid such a Scheme.

The explanation he offers, however, is obscure and implausible:

> But that *Roger* of *York*,
>   For so pious a Work
> Her Parts had improv'd
>   By cutting of Phlegm.

Thanks to her chronically red nose, Abigail was often slandered as a heavy drinker, and strong drink, in the pseudomedical parlance of the times, was said to "cut the phlegm." The historical Archbishop Roger of York (1115–1181) was an associate of Henry II and an enemy of Thomas Becket, but the balladeer probably means to draw John Sharp, the current Tory Archbishop of York and a favorite of the queen, into his net of vituperation.[123] Neither the influence of Sharp nor that of strong drink, however, is any kind of explanation for the powers credited to Abigail in these ballads, and Sarah might have thought twice before mailing this one to the queen.[124]

§

By the time she sent the letter enclosing the ballad, the duchess already knew that she would be attending the queen at a thanksgiving service on 19 August to mark the victory at Oudenarde and the foiling of the Pretender's invasion. This was the seventh such service at St. Paul's since the beginning of Anne's reign, and there was clearly a risk that such repeated celebrations might come to seem routine. The poets who had celebrated Blenheim and Ramillies were silent: there is no poem on Oudenarde by Addison, Prior, or Congreve, and most of the effusions that found their way into print were anonymous. The longest and best of these poems laments the heavy losses on both sides:

> Now *Death* in all its gloomy Pomp appears,
> One Hour destroys the Work of many Years.
> Horrors and Fate in wild Confusion fly,
> And missive Bullets wound the tender Sky.
> Forsaken Horses wand'ring o'er the Plain,
> Contemn the Bit, their gen'rous Riders slain.
> Relenting Gods the bloody Action view,
> And mourn the Ills ambitious Wars persue.
> Whilst thus both Parties urge the horrid Fight,
> Thick Clouds of Smoke make an uncertain Night.
> The weary'd War successive Troops supply,
> Which march upon their Fellows as they die.
> To neither Side impartial Conquest flies,
> Griev'd one must win, when both deserve the Prize.[125]

The first line in this effective passage deforms the opening line of one of the joyous poems on Anne's coronation—"A Native QUEEN in all her pomp appears"—with Death ominously replacing the monarch.[126] In the "wild Confusion" of battle, even the "tender Sky" is vulnerable; the horses, missing their riders, are "Forsaken," and the gods "mourn the Ills" they have caused. Reworking the account of Schellenberg in *The Campaign,* in which Addison portrayed the dead soldiers underfoot as active agents who "bore their fierce Avengers to the Foe," this poet unsparingly shows the soldiers at Oudenarde "march[ing] upon their Fellows as they die." The final line, with its surprising acknowledgment of bravery on both sides, contrasts sharply with the victory poems of the previous six years, which had usually demeaned the enemy as cowardly.

Anne made a personal contribution to the service by giving the composer William Croft a specific text to set, in which she showed her awareness that her subjects were becoming war weary. Avoiding the psalms in which David exults in victory, which had featured prominently in earlier services, the queen gave her royal composer a carefully shortened version of Psalm 34, where the emphasis falls on praising the Lord for his protecting grace:

> I will alway give thanks unto the Lord:
> his praise shall ever be in my mouth.
> My soul shall make her boast in the Lord:
> the humble shall hear thereof, and be glad.
> O praise the Lord with me: and let us magnifie his name together.
> I sought the Lord, and he heard me: yea he delivered me out of all my fear.
> The angel of the Lord tarrieth round about them that fear him: and delivereth them.
> O taste and see how gracious the Lord my strength is:
> blessed is the man that putteth his trust in him.
> I will alway give thanks unto the Lord.
> Hallelujah.

Honoring his queen's commands, Croft responded with a substantial anthem in several contrasting sections, with a prominent part for Richard Elford.[127]

The preacher chosen for the occasion, William Fleetwood, also avoided the martial themes of previous services and cautioned his hearers against always expecting victory:

> The Year, the People think, is quite lost, that does not bring the *Queen* to this good Place, to render up her Thanks to God for some great *Victory*. That, to be sure, is the Desire of Her's and all our Hearts. But wise Men mingle with their Zeal, and Prayers, the Consideration of the Uncertainties of War; ... and thank God heartily for what Success he gives, but are not over-much surprized, nor grow impatient at their Disappointments.[128]

Fleetwood's main text, taken from the prophet Ezekiel, urges the children of Israel to consider the Lord's favors to them as reasons to repent: "*Not for your sakes do I this, saith the Lord God, be it known unto you: Be asham'd and confounded for your own ways, O House of Israel.*" Applying this verse to the current situation, the preacher bravely points out that Marlborough's victories are not a reward to the nation for good behavior:

> Tho' God never punishes a Nation, but when it deserves it at his Hands, yet he often blesses a Nation when it does not deserve it.... The Sense of

these undeserved Favours should work upon Mens Hearts, and stir them up the rather to Repentance.[129]

Anne had recently made the moderate Whig Fleetwood a bishop; although the Whigs persisted in interpreting all her ecclesiastical appointments in partisan terms, her promotion of this thoughtful and eloquent clergyman, like those of Blackall and Dawes, probably reflected her admiration for his preaching style.

At the six previous thanksgiving services, the queen and her favorite had been careful to make an appropriately dignified appearance, with Sarah riding in the royal coach and attending her royal mistress as she entered the cathedral, but this time there was a noisy quarrel. The resentments felt on both sides, which had been building up for years, exploded over an issue concerning the queen's costume, which was Sarah's responsibility in her capacity as Mistress of the Robes. According to a letter she wrote just after the event, the duchess had carefully laid out Anne's jewels and was surprised and hurt when the queen refused to wear them. At some point, probably after they left the coach and entered the church, Sarah told the queen to be quiet, a command that Anne deeply resented. After this heated exchange, it may have been difficult for Anne to attend closely to either the anthem or the sermon, though both the composer and the preacher had worked hard to please her. The only primary evidence we have about the quarrel is Sarah's letter of the next day, which survives as a long unsent draft, and a shorter but no less angry version that she sent to the queen and later printed. Her narrative, given here from the longer draft, deserves careful scrutiny:

> I cannot help sending your Majesty this letter to shew how exactly Lord Marlborough agrees with me in [my] opinion, that he has now noe interest with you, tho when I said so in the ~~church~~ coach, you were pleased to say it was untrue.... I have but one request to make, that you will please either to order your affairs that he may writt me a letter quite contrary to this, or else that you will give me leave to tell him that hee has quite lost his interest with you, and that you are in the possession of Mrs Abigal, and are resolved to make the best of her and her interest, for tis certain you must come very soon to one of these two resolutions. I beleive Ld. Marlborough will be surprised that when you had allow'd me to put your jewells in a way that I thought you would like, and that it had cost me so many hours to doe them, Abigal could make you refuse to wear them, in so shocking a manner, because that was a sort of power she had not thought fitt to exercise before. I will leave you to make your own reflections upon it, only that I must needs observe, that Your Majesty

chose a very wrong day to mortify me upon, when you were just going to return thanks for a victory obtained by Lord Marlborough.[130]

Unable to let tempers cool, Sarah invokes her victorious husband at every turn. Without his permission, she encloses a letter he has written to her, in which he supposedly says that he "has noe interest" with the queen. The relevant passage in Marlborough's letter actually says that the Queen "is noways *governed* by anything I can say or do," which is not quite the same as saying that he has no interest with her.[131] Sarah goes on to predict that the duke will be "surprised" to hear about the quarrel over the jewels, as if Anne should be afraid of her tattling to him about her treatment of his wife. And she ends the paragraph by complaining about the impropriety of the queen's publicly scolding her on a day devoted to celebrating a victory achieved by her husband, as if the triumph were his alone, not the queen's or the nation's.

Sarah's insistence on Marlborough's importance suggests some sense of vulnerability on her part. Although we must infer what actually happened from her angry and self-serving account, it is fascinating that the immediate cause of the quarrel was a disagreement about how the queen should appear in public. Being "covered with jewels" was a traditional mark of the court lady: in 1675, when they were girls appearing in *Calisto,* both Anne and Sarah had worn costumes adorned with jewels; in 1683, Prince George had given his bride expensive jewelry to wear at her wedding; in 1702, when Anne came to Westminster to be crowned, in a costume arranged by Sarah, "Her head was well dress'd with Diamonds mixed in the haire which at the Least motion Brill'd and flamed"; and in 1704, at the thanksgiving for Blenheim, John Evelyn had noticed that the queen was "full of Jewels," with the duchess in a plainer garment at her side. Sarah thus had every reason to believe that Anne would once again wish to adorn herself with jewels for this public occasion. When she says that the duke will be "surprised to hear that...Abigal could *make you refuse* to wear them, in so shocking a manner," she implies that Abigail actually advised the queen against wearing the jewels, presumably in Sarah's presence. Yet in light of the fact that Sarah and her Whig associates had long exaggerated and feared what they thought Mrs. Masham could make the queen do, it is also possible that Anne herself declined to wear the heavy jewels on a hot day in August and that Sarah leapt to the conclusion that Abigail was to blame. In a letter about her costume for an earlier thanksgiving service, Anne reminds Sarah that "heavy cloths are soe uneasy to me...tho at the same time I have a mind to be fine to[o]," and proposes "diamond buttonholes" as a way to be "fine" without being overwhelmed.[132] We shall never know exactly what transpired this time, but we may be certain that Sarah felt she was being supplanted in another important aspect of her service to the queen, who she believed was now turning to Abigail not only for solace and companionship but for advice about her public image. Issues of class lie behind the outrage: though the duchess herself was from the minor gentry and had risen to her current title and eminence through beauty, wit, and political acumen, she imperiously rejected the notion that "a Bitch with a Broom" might tell a monarch what to wear—though the woman whose influence she so urgently deplored was in fact her own first cousin.

Anne was deeply offended—not only by the letter but by being silenced in the cathedral by one who was, after all, a royal servant. Her reply is dignified, cold, and furious:

> After the commands you gave me on the thanksgiving day of not an-
> swering you, I shou'd not have troubled you with these lines but to return
> the Duke of Marlboroughs letter safe into your hands, and for the same
> reason do not say any thing to that nor to yours which enclosed it.[133]

Undaunted, Sarah wrote back at length, protesting that she had told the queen to be quiet for fear of being overheard and enclosing yet another letter from Marl-borough. She received no reply, but on 31 August, less than two weeks after the terrible row at St. Paul's, Anne granted a fifty-year lease on a prime piece of land near St. James's Palace to trustees for the duchess, at an annual rent of 5 shil-lings.[134] Although she had repeatedly refused Sarah's offers to retire and had once pointedly reminded her that doing so would mean going to her "little house at St. Albans," she now gave Sarah the opportunity to build a house of her own that would provide her with a London residence if she ceased to serve the queen and therefore had to vacate her lodgings in the palace. Anne's action was a remarkable piece of generosity but also an acknowledgment that her estrangement from Sarah was likely to be permanent. It is sad to record that at this point Sarah began making large withdrawals from the Privy Purse, which were entered as loans but never marked as repaid.[135] The money she borrowed presumably paid for the construc-tion of the new house, but neither gratitude for the grant of land nor guilt about the payments she was making to herself dissuaded Sarah from urging Anne to abandon Abigail and do the will of the Whig Junto. When the two women met at Windsor on 9 September they quarreled again, and Sarah set down the main points of disagreement in a strange document called "Heads of the conversation with Mrs. Morley," devoted mainly to alleging that "nobody [is] countenanced or trusted by her but who is some way or other influenced by Mr. Harley," who "never had a good reputation in the world, but is much worse thought of since hee is out of her service."[136]

§

The death of a mutual friend, which might have been another occasion for a reconciliation, had no apparent effect on the continuing quarrel. Maynwaring, who visited Lady Fitzharding in London on the day of Sarah's meeting with Anne, wrote to Sarah reporting that "my Lady has someway hurt her foot, so as to make work for a surgeon; & she is afraid she shall not be at Windsor this week....I really think now she woud rather be with you than any Body."[137] The foot was soon much worse, and the duchess hurried to London for a last visit with her friend, but arrived too late. The day after Barbara's death, Sarah wrote to Godolphin about the disposition of her late friend's lodgings at St. James's, and the Treasurer replied that he could not yet give her an answer, "the Queen being gon a hunting this fine morning."[138] Evidently neither woman was much affected by the loss. When Luttrell reported Lady Fitzharding's death, he described her as "greatly beloved by her majestie" and remembered that Anne had provided her girlhood friend with a substantial pension "for her faithful services to the Duke of Glocester." The next day, however, he reported a rumor that "Mrs. Masham" would have the place of "mall keeper of St. James's Park, worth 500*l*. per ann., vacant by the death of the lady Fitzharding."[139]

The old poet Elkanah Settle, perhaps hoping for a reward from her husband, bestirred himself to write a substantial elegy on the viscountess, reminding his readers that her mother, Frances Villiers, had been governess to Queen Mary and Queen Anne when they were children, as Barbara in turn became governess to Anne's unfortunate children. In a curiously metaphysical passage, Settle imagines the queen's three palaces bending their heads to grieve for her friend:

> Yes proud St. *James,* Thou select Orb of Power,
> Commanding *ANNA*'s darling Soveraign Bower,
> To this long sleeping HEAD all bending low,
> How must thy Royal drooping Turrets bow.
> Nay sad *Whitehall,* once Majesty's bright Throne,
> Now a dark Pile of Ruefull Dust alone,
> With hideous Desolation overgrown,
> Alas, to mourn the Fair *FITZHARDING* Dead,
> Shrinking yet low'r in His long Dusty Bed,
> E'vn with new Ashes strews his ruinous Head.
> But what hast thou the wailing *Windsor* lost?
> To pay the Funeral Tribute which thou owest,
> Ev'n thy *Imperial* British *Standart* wave,
> A *mourning Flag* o'er thy *FITZHARDING*'s Grave.[140]

Conflating Queen Anne with her palaces, the poet depicts St. James's drooping its turrets in grief. By asking Windsor Castle to wave its "*Imperial* British *Standart*" as a "mourning flag," he draws military imagery into the process of grief; the standard now flown over Windsor was the Union Jack, newly adopted by British land forces after the Union of 1707. But it is the image of Whitehall, burned in 1697 and still not fully rebuilt, that is the most remarkable here: mourning for Lady Fitzharding, the palace "strews his ruinous Head" with ashes, an image drawn from the grief enacted by Achilles in the *Iliad* when he learns of the death of Patroclus. Settle, who had written a popular play on the fall of Troy, would have known this passage in the translation by George Chapman:

> With both his hands he rent
> The blacke mould from the forced earth, and pour'd it on his head;
> Smear'd all his lovely face; his weeds (divinely fashioned)
> All filde and mangl'd; and himselfe, he threw upon the shore;
> Lay, as laid out for funerall. Then tumbl'd round, and tore
> His gracious curles.[141]

Filtered through the architectural personification of the charred Whitehall, language originating in the violent grief of an epic hero for his bosom friend now helps the poet imagine Anne's grief for a friend of her girlhood. Settle presumably did not know that his queen, jealous of Barbara's closeness to Sarah, had often spoken disparagingly of her.

A more significant death, however, was near at hand: Prince George was losing his battle with asthma. Even the welcome news that the town of Lisle had surrendered to the Allies, which Anne gratefully received from Sir Richard Temple on 18 October, could not long distract her from nursing her husband, described by Godolphin as "languishing...for above a month."[142] As the end drew near, even Sarah rallied to Anne's side, though not without lodging one more complaint:

> Tho the last time I had the honour to waitt upon your Majesty your usage of me was such as was scarce possible for me to imagin, or for any body else to beleive, yet I can not hear of so great a misfortune & affliction to you, as the condition which the Prince is in, without comming to pay my duty in inquiring after your health, & to see if in any perticular whatsoever my service can either be agreeable or usefull to you, for which satisfaction I would doe more then I will trouble your majesty to read att this time.[143]

Lady Marlborough wrote these words at Windsor on 26 October, took coach that night, and put her note into the hands of a serving-woman at Kensington on October 27, as we know from her later detailed account of this sad time.[144] Early in the afternoon of 28 October, with his wife at his side, George expired. With some difficulty, Sarah persuaded Anne to go with her to St. James's, "saying she might goe away privately in my coach, with the curtains down, & see nobody," but the queen remained concerned about the treatment of her husband's body. On the way to St. James's, she asked the duchess to "send to my Lord Treasurer & beg of him to take care & examine whether there was room in some vault, to burry the Prince in at Westminster, & to leave room for her too." In her narrative, Sarah calls this request "a very extraordinary thought" and expresses surprise that Anne ate regular meals while nursing George and grieving for him. She also questions the queen's response to an officious act on her own part: as soon as George died, Sarah removed his portrait from Anne's rooms, so that Anne had to write to her after the funeral, "begging you once more for God sake to lett the Dear picture you have of mine, be putt into my Bedchamber for I can not be with out it any longer."[145] On the manuscript of this letter is a note scrawled by Sarah, explaining that she removed the picture "because I thought she loved him, & *if she had been like other people* 'tis terrible to see a picture while the afliction is just upon one."[146]

For the duchess, who had grieved long and hard for her son in 1703, refusing to eat or sleep and embracing the role of the melancholy beauty, being *like other people* meant being like her; she was clearly unable to understand the very different way Anne experienced and expressed grief. Despite their years of closeness, the two women had contrasting temperaments, perhaps related to contrasts in their upbringing. Anne had lost several siblings as a small child and had experienced the deaths of her grandmother and her aunt during her early visit to France, followed by the death of her own mother when she was only six; as an adult she had lived through the loss of her sister and of all her own children. Her training as an heir to the throne, with its emphasis on formality and dignity, was also a factor, and she evidently found the process of planning George's funeral therapeutic, though Sarah utterly failed to grasp that fact. "Before the Prince was buryed," writes the duchess, "she passed a good deal of time looking into presidents [i.e., precedents] that she might order how it should be performed." The records of the committee appointed to plan the funeral include two complete lists of the order in which the mourners should proceed into the Abbey, in which it is clear that there has been careful consideration of the protocols dictating that "Barons eldest Sons," for example, should precede "Earls younger sons."[147] Although she did not attend the committee's meetings, the queen was clearly involved in making these plans. Sarah, however, thought Anne's interest in such matters was "unusual, & not very decent, but she naturally loved all forms and ceremonys, & remembered more of them that I could ever doe."

The duchess also misinterpreted a touching note Anne wrote to her requesting particular precautions when the heavy corpse of her husband was moved from

Kensington to the Painted Chamber at Westminster, where he lay in state for a few days before his private funeral. "I Scratched twice at dear Mrs Freemans door," writes Anne politely,

> as soon as Ld Treasurer went from me, in hopes to have spoke one word more to him before he was gon, but no body heareing me, I writt this not careing to send what I had to say by word of mouth, which was to desire him that when he sends his orders to Kensington that I desired, he would give directions there may be a great many yeomen of the Guards to cary the Princes dear body that it may not be lett fall, the Great Stairs being very Steep & Slipery.[148]

Failing to catch the note of pathos, Sarah describes this message as "a little note at which I could not help smiling," expressing disbelief that the queen would be concerned that "the dear Prince's body should be shoke as he was carryd out of some room, though she had gon long jumbling journeys with him to the Bath, when he must feel it, and when he was gasping for breath." What Sarah did not know, but Anne probably remembered, was that these very stairs had been damaged when Queen Mary's body was carried out of Kensington Palace in 1695; an order for "mending the steps of the grt Stairs that was broke in carrying the Q's body down" suggests that the yeomen dropped the coffin, a memory that would certainly have given Anne reason to fear a similar mishap.[149]

"I did see the teares in her eyes two or three times after his death," continues Sarah, "and, I beleive, she fancyd she loved him, and she was certainly more concernd for him than she was for the fate of Gloucester; but her nature was hard and she was not apt to cry." If she had seen the diplomatic correspondence Anne undertook after George's death, Sarah might have gained more insight into Anne's ways of expressing grief, which were quite unlike her own. In a letter to the Dutch government, for example, the queen expresses her desire to remain silent and withdrawn, while acknowledging the powerful sense of duty that makes complete withdrawal impossible:

> This dreadful misfortune burdens us with a sadness so intense that we would willingly remain in profound silence, if the close ties which we have with your State did not oblige us to communicate everything that happens to us, by the will of God, be it good or evil.[150]

And to the King of Denmark, George's nephew, she writes in her own hand, significantly dropping the royal "we":

As he had been quite indisposed for some time, the anticipation of this disaster should have prepared me to bear it with more fortitude. But I find myself obliged to admit to your Majesty that the loss of such a husband, who loved me so passionately and so constantly, is too burdensome to bear as well as I should.[151]

Even here, writing informally to a member of her husband's family, Anne expresses her sense of duty: she *should* have been prepared, and she *should* now find a way to bear her burden of grief. She was certainly a dutiful correspondent, as her letter book for this period shows: not only did she write announcing George's death to all the important courts in Europe, but she wrote different notes to the members of each royal family and answered the messages of condolence she received in reply.

Settle's use of Achilles's extravagant ritual of self-abasement as a model for Anne's imagined grief for Lady Fitzharding could not have been more wrong, yet one of the anonymous poets who addressed her on the occasion of her consort's death understood her formal nature far better than Settle—or Sarah. In an elevated Pindaric ode, this writer asks Anne to consider her kingdoms, even as she grapples with her grief:

> Yet, Monarch, spare an useless Grief,
>   That Grief might well be spared as vain,
>   Which to thy Wound brings no Relief,
>   But thro' thy Realms diffuses Pain.[152]

Despite her grief, Anne did her best to remain attentive to her monarchial duties. She wept the first time she was asked to sign admiralty documents that had previously gone to George, but she took on the burden of overseeing that troubled department, and while she felt unable to open Parliament on 16 November, deputing that task to a commission including the Chancellor and the Treasurer, she attended a meeting of her Privy Council on 25 November, less than a month after losing her husband. As the parliamentary session began, the queen surrendered to months of pressure from the Whigs and redistributed some important offices. The Earl of Pembroke, a court Tory acceptable to the Whigs, became Lord High Admiral, returning to a position he had held under King William, and two Junto Whigs whom Anne deeply distrusted kissed her hand for his other offices: Lord Wharton became Lord Lieutenant of Ireland, and Lord Somers became President of the Privy Council, taking his seat at the first meeting Anne attended after the death of George.[153] The timing of these appointments might have encouraged Sarah and others obsessed by the influence of Abigail and Harley to reconsider their theories. Abigail continued to enjoy Anne's favor, and Harley had been elected to a seat in the Commons, which brought him back to London from his self-imposed exile in the country, presumably renewing his backstairs access to the queen. Despite his presence, however, the queen was cooperating with the Junto, perhaps because another line of communication reminding the queen of Tory views—one probably more important than the back stairs—had closed when Prince George died. Marlborough's brother George Churchill, a convinced, un-shakeable Tory, had been Prince George's closest friend and his right-hand man in the office of the admiralty. After the Whig success in the last elections, he was al-ready vulnerable, and Marlborough had written a serious letter to him on 31 August advising him to resign.[154] With the death of the prince, Admiral Churchill lost his post and with it his ability to communicate Tory positions to the queen through the sympathetic conduit of her husband. The appointments of Somers and Wharton, which the queen had resisted for at least six months, followed immediately.

§

The court went into in deep mourning. When the queen asked her Groom of the Stole to procure a purple quilt and three purple pillows for her bed, she cau-tioned Sarah against allowing any shiny buttons on the dark fabric,[155] but when the grieving widow first received female company in her bedroom, the duchess "was the only one that had powder in her hair or a patch on her face," an early signal of her impatience with the rituals of mourning.[156] Among the men allowed to visit Anne was her old spiritual advisor Henry Compton, Bishop of London, who reportedly came to see her every day.[157] She had fires made in two small rooms that the prince had occupied and sat there alone for hours. The ever-suspicious Sarah thought she had chosen these spaces because there was "a door that opened upon his back Stairs which went down to Mrs. Mashams Lodgings" and wondered why Anne would wish to read or pray in a closet "full of his tools which he worked with." As with the portrait, the duchess thought it was "natural" to avoid reminders of someone who had just died, but the queen clearly derived some comfort from seeing the woodworking implements her husband had used to build model ships. With characteristic generosity, she pensioned off all his ser-vants, including the eight oboists in his private military band, "provided they keep no publick houses."[158]

In recognition of the prince's death, the theatres closed for six weeks, de-laying the long-awaited debut of Nicolini, who sang in *Pyrrhus and Demetrius* on 14 December, when both houses reopened. Despite the official mourning, some well-connected people found opportunities to hear Nicolini before he performed in public, as we know from a letter written on 10 December by Lady Isabella

Wentworth, née Apsley, whose family had long been closely connected to Queen Anne:

> Yesterday I had lyke to have been ketched in a trap, your Brother Wentworth had almost parswaded me to have gon last night to hear the fyne muisick, the famous Etallion sing att the rehersall of the Operer, which he assured me it was soe dark none could see me. Indeed musick was the greatist temtation I could have, but I was afraid he deceaved me, soe betty only went with his wife and him; and I rejoysed I did not, for thear was a vast deal of company and good light—but the Dutchis of Molbery had got the Etallian to sing and he sent an excuse, but the Dutchis of Shrosberry made him com, brought him in her coach but Mrs Taufs huft and would not sing because he had first put it ofe; though she was thear yet she would not, but went away. I wish the house would al joyne to humble her and not receav her again. This man out dus Sefashoe, they say that has hard both.[159]

Though sorry to have missed hearing "the famous Etallion," Lady Wentworth was glad to avoid been seen at a quasi-public amusement during a time of mourning, though Sarah ("the Dutchis of Molbery") does not appear to have had such scruples. As a native speaker of Italian, the Duchess of Shrewsbury was evidently effective in persuading her compatriot to keep his promises, but Catherine Tofts, jealous at being upstaged, refused to sing. When Lady Wentworth reports that Nicolini "out does Sefashoe," she presumably refers to "Siface," a castrato of a previous generation whom she had probably heard perform at the Catholic chapel of James II when she was a Lady-in-Waiting to Maria Beatrice.[160]

Remarkably enough, the popularity of Nicolini now had a palpable effect on parliamentary politics. The disappointed Whig candidate in the borough of Westminster, Sir Henry Dutton Colt, filed a petition against the Tory Thomas Medlicott, alleging (with considerable evidence) that there had been irregularities in his election. Confident that the large Whig majority would carry the day, some thirty-five Whig MPs went to hear the second public performance of *Pyrrhus and Demetrius* on Saturday night, 18 December, and "Mr. Medlycot's friends," who had "stuck close to a man," took the opportunity to push through a vote seating their candidate. We owe this story to Addison, who goes on to say that the opera fans "have been so reproached by their party for this piece of negligence, that it will have a good effect upon 'em for the remaining part of the parliament."[161] Still smarting from the failure of *Rosamond*, Addison could not miss an occasion for expressing his hostility toward the Italian opera, and when he went to Dublin as secretary to Lord Wharton in May, he took along Thomas

Clayton, his collaborator on the failed English opera, who staged "Entertainments of that kind" in Dublin Castle.[162]

Like many majority parties, the Whigs were overconfident. There were persistent rumors that the freethinkers among them intended to repeal the Test Act, thus opening the door for Dissenters (or even atheists) to hold political office. One disgruntled Tory reported their saying they were "under no obligations to any man for their new preferments, that they forced what is done for them,"[163] an unwise claim to make in the reign of a queen who preferred to think of herself as graciously offering positions to those who served her, even when she had been constrained to do so by political realities. With administrative and legislative power firmly in their hands, the Whigs might have chosen to be particularly attentive to the feelings of their mourning queen. Instead, they made a political move that offended her in both style and substance. With her usual attention to liturgical detail, the widowed queen had requested that the prayers made for her on the anniversary of her accession omit the usual petition asking that she be blessed with children. Using this as a pretext, some young Whigs in the House of Commons proposed an address urging her "to have such indulgence to the hearty desires of her subjects as to entertain thoughts of a second marriage"—not because they thought there was any prospect that Anne would marry or conceive again but in order to prevent the Tory minority from introducing another bill inviting members of the House of Hanover to take up residence in England.[164] Everyone, including Anne, understood the political logic behind the address, but the language in which it was couched was unnecessarily embarrassing, so much so that some Tories thought it was a deliberate joke, and a very bad one. In the original formulation, Parliament would have asked the queen to "indulge the hearty desires of her subjects" as if she were a barmaid in a roomful of randy drinkers, and to "entertain thoughts of a second marriage" as if she were a wealthy widow being courted in a stage play. Someone even published a broadside called *The Hasty Widow, or The Sooner the Better,* a title Anne's servant Peter Wentworth recognized as "impudent."[165] Cooler heads prevailed, and the language that officially went forward to the queen was more polite, asking her not "to decline the Thoughts of a second Marriage."[166] Beneath the bemused dignity of Anne's carefully worded reply, we may detect her hurt feelings: "the Provision I have made for the Protestant Succession," she wrote, "will always be a proof how much I have at My Heart the future Happinesse of the Kingdom: the Subject of this Addresse is of such a Nature, that, I am persuaded, you do not expect a particular Answer."[167]

As part of her mourning, Anne canceled the usual New Year's song and announced that her birthday this year would be a sober affair without a play or a ball, but on 6 January 1709, mindful of the success of the long and bitter campaign, she issued a proclamation for a public thanksgiving on 17 February, "for the taking of

Lisle, and the reduction of Ghent and Bruges." Despite several letters from Godolphin urging him to come home in time for the celebration, Marlborough remained in Europe. Not yet ready for a public appearance at St. Paul's, the mourning queen marked the day in her chapel at St. James's, where Thomas Manningham, her current favorite among her chaplains, took note of the oddity of "keeping a Day of Thanksgiving in a Mourning Chappel." Choosing a double-edged text from Ecclesiastes—"*In the Day of Prosperity, be joyful; but in the Day of Adversity, consider*"—he applied it not only to the grieving widow but to the war itself. In his general remarks on war, and in his specific description of the complex and costly campaign of the autumn and winter, the preacher gives full weight to the cost of victory:

> *War,* tho' we have Success in it, is so direful a *Calamity;* and we must pass over, at least in our Minds, such Heaps of Slaughter and Ruin, before we can think of Rejoycing: That the *Day of Adversity,* do what we can, will mingle it self with our *Day of Prosperity.* ... The famous Siege of *Lisle,* tho' slowly, yet effectually carry'd on, and ending at last with all the Glory that belongs to such a *Master-Piece* of War, is the most remarkable Scene that enters in this Day's *Prosperity.* Tho' it were often interrupted, by calling off great Detachements for sudden Excursions, and for sure Convoys, yet it was still warmly renew'd, and might have been soon dispatch'd by an unchristian Waste of Lives, had nothing but Destruction and false Honour, been the inspiring Principle.[168]

As with the celebration of Oudenarde some six months earlier, the drift away from unalloyed rejoicing is clear. Manningham actually refers to "the Duty of being *joyful,*" a heading under which he includes "express[ing] our Thanksgiving to God in *Psalms, and Hymns, and spiritual Songs*" but also "tak[ing] Care to remove our Sins, and our Quarrels."[169]

Sarah, who was present, does not appear to have taken that last adjuration to heart, as her quarrels with the queen continued, but she told Mary Cowper that the music, which she heard in the bright, clear acoustic of the Tudor chapel in St. James's, was "much better I believe than any that has ever been yet heard at any of the Operas."[170] In light of the duchess's keen interest in Nicolini, this is a fascinating appreciation of the music written for the service by William Croft, which included new settings of the *Te Deum* and the *Jubilate* with orchestral accompaniment, the first such settings by any English composer since 1696. In addition to strings, Croft used two trumpets and a solo oboe, which has important obbligato parts in several arias. Perhaps he included the oboe as a tribute to Prince George, who had evidently loved the sound of that instrument.[171] As vocal soloists, Croft had at his disposal not only Richard Elford, the queen's longtime favorite, but the countertenor Francis Hughes, who had been replaced in all his operatic roles by imported castrati and had therefore joined the Chapel Royal. In the anthem, his first since the death of his teacher Blow, Croft matches Manningham's sermon in recognizing both adversity and prosperity and in treating prosperity as an occasion

Mus. Ex. 9.2: William Croft, excerpt from *Sing unto the Lord* (1709).

not only for rejoicing but for showing gratitude by living holier lives. In one particularly effective juxtaposition, the words "Leave us not, neither forsake us, O God," set for full choir in the haunting tradition of Purcell, lead immediately to more hopeful music for three soloists. "So we that are thy people," they sing in a brighter idiom, "and the sheep of thy pasture, shall give thee thanks for ever, and will always be shewing forth thy truth." In the trio section, we may hear Croft beginning to move toward the diatonic clarity of the baroque style, which is also audible in his orchestrally accompanied music for this occasion. He had evidently learned something from the Italian music on offer at the opera house.

§

The weather was bitter cold. Frost had begun on Christmas Day, and for weeks there was heavy snow in much of England. The winter was even more severe in France, where widespread hunger gave rise to the belief that Louis XIV would soon be forced to sue for peace. On 15 January 1709, Samuel Buckley, editor of the *Daily Courant*, published a "rough Draught of a Scheme for the lasting Peace of Europe"; Anne's Privy Councillors, offended that a mere journalist should presume to discuss this subject, reportedly had him arrested.[172] Yet despite the solemn promises they had made to one other about negotiating as a united force, various parties on the allied side, including Marlborough, were already engaged in secret communications with French agents.[173] Although many expected the duke to bring terms of peace with him when he returned to England after an absence of nearly a year, his purpose for this brief visit was to consult with the Cabinet and the queen about negotiations that had not yet officially begun.[174] The victorious general reached the English coast in the final days of February and attended the House of Lords on 2 March, accepting congratulations on the campaign and hearing the final version of an address to the queen about terms of peace:

> We...most humbly beseech Your Majesty,...that the *French* King may be obliged to own Your Majesty's Title and the Protestant Succession, as it is established by the Laws of *Great Britain*; and that Your Allies be engaged to become Guarantees of the same.
>
> And that Your Majesty would take effectual Methods, that the Pretender shall be removed out of the *French* Dominions; and not suffered to return, to disturb Your Majesty, Your Heirs, or Successors in the Protestant Line: And that, for the Security of Your Majesty's Dominions, the Preservation of Trade, and the general Benefit of the Allies, Your Majesty will be graciously pleased that Care may be taken, that the Fortifications and Harbour of *Dunkirk* may be demolished and destroyed.[175]

Except for the clause about demolishing Dunkirk, which was added by the House of Commons, this address deliberately omits specific demands about territory; significantly, Parliament did not repeat its desire that the entire Spanish Empire be ceded to Charles III, nor did it enter into details about which fortresses in the Spanish Netherlands might be part of the "Barrier" demanded by the Dutch as a protection against future French invasions. The Whig managers evidently wanted the queen's representatives at the bargaining table to have some flexibility.

Marlborough had good reason to be pleased with the vagueness of this address, and on the evening of 2 March he had an opportunity to celebrate: the first performance of the new opera *Clotilda*, a pasticcio featuring Nicolini, Valentini, Tofts, and de l'Epine, with music by eight different Italian composers. We do not know whether the duke and his duchess were in attendance at the premiere, but they were surely present on 17 March, when the company presented *Camilla* in honor of Marlborough, as we know from a letter written to his nephew by Charles Dering, Auditor General to the Lords Justices of Ireland:

> I am growing in love very fast with operas, which I own I did not relish at first, and we have now three—namely Pyrrhus and Demetrius, Camilla, and now Clotilda—and this very day Camilla is acted expressly for Lord Marlborough. Our famous Nicolini got 800 guineas for his day [i.e., his benefit performance, which took place on 19 January], and it is thought Mrs Tofts, whose turn it is on Tuesday next, will get a vast deal. She was only sunday last at the Duke of Somerset's, where there was about thirty gentlemen, and every kiss was a guinea. Some took three, others four, others five kisses at that rate, but none less than one. A pretty trade, if it would only last all the year.[176]

Dering's admission that he now enjoys an art form he "did not relish at first" is significant. Despite Addison's sneers, audiences were evidently becoming more comfortable with the conventions of operatic form, and the quality of singing had improved since the days of *Arsinoe*. The estimate of Nicolini's profits from his benefit is probably exaggerated, but if Somerset's Whig friends were willing to pay a guinea (at least £210 in today's money) for a single kiss from their favorite singer, Dering was not the only theatregoer falling in love with opera. Swiney had a very successful season. With the weather at last turning mild, the public elated by the prospect of peace, and the town still full for the meetings of Parliament, which sat until late April, March was a perfect time to offer a new opera, but there were no comparable opportunities for the "Bayliffs, Wardens and Assistants of the Company of Silk Weavers," as Anne's subjects were still wearing black. In a series of petitions, the weavers "besought Her Majesty to take the sad Condition of the poore Manufacturers of Silk in Her Royal Consideration," and on 27 March the queen,

> having Compassion for so many Families who are likely to fall into Want...was Graciously pleased hereby to Declare, That she does not Require or Expect, that any of Her Subjects (except only Her own Servants and such as have Access to Her Royal Person) should Continue to observe the present Mourning.[177]

Her own mourning, however, would last for two full years.

During Marlborough's short visit, the news reached England that Louis XIV, with his subjects starving, had dispatched an experienced diplomat, Pierre Rouillé, to meet with two Dutch negotiators at a village called Moerdijk. Although this action confirmed the widespread belief that famine would force the French to seek terms, it underscored the danger that the Dutch, who had achieved most of their goals for the war, might make a separate peace. At the end of March, Marlborough headed back to Holland, where he successfully insisted that the Dutch send Rouillé home. Although he believed this move would force Louis to send another emissary to negotiate officially with all of the allies, the duke was prepared to start another military campaign if the French could not be brought to terms at the table. Not only had he stayed in the field well into the winter to secure a strong position, but he had worked with Prince Eugene to raise a huge army for the next campaign. At home, the Whig Parliament had passed a strong bill of supply, and the Treasury had secured a substantial loan from the Bank of England financed by offering shares to the public, which sold out within hours on 22 February.[178]

Marlborough was thus ready for either peace or war, and there are strong reasons to believe he expected further hostilities. During this brief visit, or possibly during his even shorter visit in April, he asked Queen Anne to make him Captain-General for life. Prince George had held the (largely symbolic) title of "generalissimo," and his death may have prompted the duke to make this extraordinary request. A letter from Maynwaring to Sarah, written on 6 December 1708, shows that the Marlborough circle was actively discussing this matter shortly after the death of the prince. "Some Addition of Honour being onely intended, and not of wealth," writes Maynwaring, "I know at present but two ways of doing that; either by some new Increase of his Titles, or by some publick Record of his Actions." Suggesting caution lest new titles provoke envy, he proposes "something like a Roman Pillar or Triumphal Arch."[179] The queen may also have hoped to satisfy Marlborough's need for an "Addition of Honour" by artistic means. According to a manuscript in the hand of the artist, she commissioned Sir Godfrey Kneller "in the Year 1708,...to design a Large Picture Twelve foot high and Eight foot broad for the upper end of the Long Gallery at Blenheim." Although "State Differences happening betwixt the Queen & the Duke of Marlborough" prevented Kneller from executing the planned painting, he made a lively oil sketch (color plate 17) and later remembered that

> the Duke of Marlbrough (who was then present) desired that no person should be represented by the life Except the Queens Majesty. But that the whole Picture should be Allegoricall.... The Queen is represented by the Figure of Generosity holding in her Left hand her Scepter with the Eye of Providence on the Top resting on a Lyon, with a Globe of the World under his Paw, the Emblem of Power & Strength. With the Right hand she presents to a Warlike Vigorous Figure representing Military Merritt.

Other allegorical figures include Architecture, Victory, Mars, Hercules, History, Plenty, Apollo, and "three Boys holding a Serpent in a Circle the Emblem of Eternity."[180]

Despite the apparent modesty of his request for an allegorical painting rather than a portrait to the life, the duke persisted in seeking a life appointment in the real world. Records of his discussions with the queen are scanty, and his motives remain unclear.[181] He may have been looking for leverage in working with allied military commanders and bargaining with the French: if he held a life appointment, everyone would know that it was pointless to wait for better terms from a different English leader. He may also have hoped to outflank his political enemies at home, who were seeking to undermine the Captain-General as a first step toward seeking peace. The queen, however, demurred, recognizing that his request raised grave constitutional issues, and early in May she sent him a signal of her unwillingness to abandon monarchial influence over the military. Major General George MacCartney, a veteran of the debacle at Almanza, had made a drunken assault on his housekeeper, the widow of a clergyman; his victim complained to the Bishop of London and eventually charged MacCartney with rape. Despite attempts to intercede by Godolphin and Somerset, who shared Marlborough's sympathy for his military associate, Anne sacked MacCartney from all his positions, even though that decision meant abandoning a planned invasion of French Canada, which he was expected to command. As a woman, an advocate of public morality, and a loyal daughter of the Church, she was on solid ground; as queen, she was demonstrating her power over all her subjects, including her Captain-General.[182]

The other sign that Marlborough expected the war to continue was a sally of wit, reported in the first issue of the *Tatler* (12 April 1709):

> The late Offers concerning Peace, were made in the Style of Persons who think themselves upon equal Terms: but the Allies have so just a Sense of their present Advantages, that they will not admit of a Treaty, except *France* offers what is more suitable to her present Condition. At the same Time we make preparations, as if we were alarm'd by a greater Force than that which we are carrying into the Field. Thus this Point seems now to be argued Sword in Hand; which was what a Great General alluded to, when being ask'd the Names of those who were to be Plenipotentiaries for the ensuing Peace; answer'd, with a serious Air, *There are about an Hundred thousand of us.*[183]

The newspaper in which this paragraph appeared would soon distinguish itself from its competitors by the range of topics it explored and the quality of its prose. Written by Richard Steele with help from Swift and Addison, it was nominally the work of an old astrologer called "Isaac Bickerstaff," a persona Swift had used to play a wicked joke on the freethinking almanac-maker John Partridge. As "Bickerstaff," Swift published a set of prophecies for the year 1708, including the claim that "Partridge the Almanac-maker...will infallibly dye upon the 29th of March next, about Eleven at Night, of a raging fever." When March arrived, he published a pamphlet claiming that his prediction had been fulfilled; although the real Partridge protested that he was alive, the joke ruined his business.[184] Steele needed a pseudonym because he held a salaried post as the compiler of the *London Gazette*, the dull, official paper recording the government's version of the news; the previous association of "Bickerstaff" with a satirical jest allowed him to make a distinction between men of wit, to whom his paper meant to appeal, and those obsessed with "Transactions of State":

> Tho' the other Papers which are publish'd for the Use of the good People of *England* have certainly very wholesom Effects, and are laudable in their Particular Kinds, they do not seem to come up to the Main Design of such Narrations, which, I humbly presume, should be principally intended for the Use of Politick Persons, who are so publick-spirited, as to neglect their own Affairs to look into Transactions of State. Now these Gentlemen, for the most Part, being Persons of strong Zeal and weak Intellects, It is both a Charitable and Necessary Work to offer something, whereby such worthy, and well-affected Members of the Commonwealth may be instructed, after their Reading, *what to think*: Which shall be the End and Purpose of this my Paper....I resolve also to have something which may be of Entertainment to the Fair Sex, in Honour of whom I have invented the Title of this Paper.

Most of the newspapers already in business were devoted entirely to politics, especially foreign affairs; their writers were willing to print rumors in the absence of verifiable fact and in most cases shaded the news toward the ideology of one party or another. In attempting to separate his enterprise from theirs, Steele slyly claims that the "Politick Persons" for whom newspapers are "principally intended"—certainly avid consumers of news in the coffeehouses, but surely some Members of Parliament as well—are "Persons of strong Zeal and weak Intellects" and thus in need of being "instructed…*what to think.*" At the risk of insulting potential readers, he implies that too much concentration on politics will weaken one's intellect, though it may strengthen one's zeal. The audience he is defining will appreciate this kind of wit, even at its own expense, and will want to read about topics other than politics. Significantly, that audience will include members of "the fair Sex," whom he treats with gallantry and bemused humor.

The stories in the first issue, distributed free on 12 April, demonstrate the paper's intended range. Steele begins with an experiment in prose fiction, a lively account of "the deplorable Condition of a very pretty Gentleman" who has fallen in love with a lady he saw from a window, whom he can neither find nor forget. With an eye to future sales, he promises his readers that this story will be continued in later issues. He then reviews a special performance of Congreve's *Love for Love* at Drury Lane, staged for the benefit of Thomas Betterton (now seventy-three), who played the youthful gallant Valentine, the part he had performed at Anne's birthday celebration in 1697. Keeping up the Bickerstaff joke, Steele takes a parting shot at Partridge, who had again published an almanac for 1709. "I have in another Place…sufficiently convinc'd this Man that he is dead," he writes, "and if he has any Shame, I don't doubt but that by this Time he owns it to all his Acquaintance."

> I shall, as I see occasion, proceed to confute other dead Men, who pretend to be in Being, that they are actually deceased. I therefore give all Men fair Warning to mend their Manners, for I shall from Time to Time print Bills of Mortality; and I beg the Pardon of all such who shall be nam'd therein, if they who are good for Nothing shall find themselves in the Number of the Deceased.

By warning his contemporaries that they should "mend their Manners," Steele sends another important signal: the *Tatler*'s critical eye would survey not only politics and the arts but social behavior as well. Sandwiched between these amusing tidbits is a short summary of news from the Continent including Marlborough's remark about the one hundred thousand plenipotentiaries, a scoop suggesting that the author has intimate knowledge of the great and powerful.

§

For the next six weeks, it looked as if the one hundred thousand plenipotentiaries might not be necessary. Apparently serious about seeking peace, the French king dispatched the Marquis de Torcy, his most important diplomat, to meet with the Allies at the Hague, and Marlborough urged the Whig Junto to appoint another plenipotentiary to join him at the table, presumably because he did not wish to be held solely responsible for the outcome. They considered Halifax, who demurred, and Sunderland, whom they deemed inappropriate, before settling on a younger man: Charles, Viscount Townshend. By the time Torcy arrived in the Netherlands, on 23 April/4 May, Marlborough was back in England for a very short visit, during which he took a quick trip to Woodstock with Sarah and Godolphin to assess the progress of Blenheim Palace. When he returned to Holland on 2/13 May, he brought Townshend with him.[185]

Although there were passing references in the press to Townshend's appointment,[186] it does not appear to have been widely known at first. On 6 May, when Marlborough and Townshend were already overseas, Ralph Bridges, Chaplain to the Bishop of London, wrote to his uncle Sir William Trumbull, Secretary of State during William's reign, complimenting the old man by telling him that *he* was being considered as a plenipotentiary:

> I beleive you've grown so out of Love with London, that you woud not come thither for a place at Court, or to be Plenipotentiary at the next treaty of Peace. To that Post you've bin advanc't for this week past, both in the discourse and wishes of the City and Westminster and the Town; tho' our Freind Pope's seeming complement to you be a serious Truth, To all the world illustriously are lost, yet I don't know how it comes to pass (such is the inconstancy of mens opinions) Sir Will[iam] Trumbull's name has bin tost about from mouth to mouth, as the only commoner in England, fit to manage the important affair, Peace.[187]

The phrase Bridges quotes from "our Freind Pope" comes from Alexander Pope's *Pastorals,* his first appearance in print, published on 2 May in the annual miscellany from Jacob Tonson's shop. Addressing Trumbull, with whom he often went riding, the young poet had written two elegant couplets complimenting the old statesman on his retirement:

> *You*, that too Wise for Pride, too Good for Pow'r
> Enjoy the Glory to be Great no more,
> And carrying with you all the World can boast,
> To all the World Illustriously are lost![188]

Even in this tiny excerpt, Pope's management of poetic rhetoric is precocious. The admirably modest Trumbull is "too Wise" to indulge in pride and thus "too Good" to hold power in an age Pope delicately implies is corrupt. While others, such as Marlborough, "Enjoy the Glory to be Great," Trumbull is content to have left such things in the past; being "Great no more" has a glory of its own. In a clever Ovidian "turn," the phrase *all the World* appears in two consecutive lines, with its grammatical function deftly altered in the second. As Bridges recognized, Pope's subtle oxymoron calling Trumbull both "Illustrious" and "lost" functions as a compliment, but in his eagerness to deliver his own compliment to his kinsman, the clergyman overlooked (perhaps deliberately) the fact that a Whig administration was unlikely to entrust a critical negotiation to a retired Tory soon to be seventy years old.

As the negotiations began, Torcy seemed earnest in his desire for an agreement; he yielded to all the points the House of Lords had raised in its address and to most of the Dutch proposals about the Barrier. With France now suing for peace, there were further demands from the Habsburg Empire, Portugal, and the Savoy, some of them difficult for Torcy to swallow. Eventually a document got hammered out, and on 21 May, Horatio Walpole, who was serving Townshend as his secretary, arrived in London "with the preliminaries for a general peace; Sunday evening [22 May] they were read before the queen in council, and afterwards sign'd by her majestie,…and Monday morning sent back by him to the Hague."[189] On Tuesday, 24 May, the Duchess of Marlborough laid the cornerstone of her new house in London, optimistically inscribing it with the words "anno pacifico" (the year of peace).[190] She had engaged Sir Christopher Wren to design the building, and thanks to a new and improved lease from the queen, she now had two more acres of land on which to build; her friend the Duke of Shrewsbury, himself a notable patron of architecture, consulted with her about the design.[191] On the very same day, however, the *Post Boy* advertised a novel of scandal that would prove distressing to Sarah: *Secret Memoirs and Manners of Several Persons of Quality of Both Sexes, from the New Atalantis, an Island in the Mediterranean*. In this loosely strung-together collection of sexual and political tales from the 1690s and earlier, eventually known to be the work of Delarivier Manley, the Marlboroughs and their friends make frequent unsavory appearances. Manley repeats the tired stories of young John Churchill's affair with the Countess of Castlemaine, his sister's affair with the Duke of York, and his betrayal of his master at the Revolution, but she also describes the Duke of Shrewsbury as sexually involved with both Sarah and her friend Annabella Howard, who is depicted as shocked to learn that he is returning to England with a foreign wife.[192] For anyone uncertain about which famous people lurked beneath such names as "Jeanatin" and "Fortunatus," the bookseller could furnish a separately printed "key." A second edition was needed by July, and in September the *Tatler* mentioned the *Memoirs* as a book much read at court.[193] With her keen interest in ballads and lampoons, Sarah cannot have ignored this work, but she is unlikely to have called it to the attention of Queen Anne, whom Manley treats with respect and discretion.

When Manley's novel first appeared, however, public attention was still focused on the expected peace. In its issue for the same week, the *British Apollo,* a periodical combining personal advice with coverage of the arts, offered an anonymous "Poem on the Prospect of a Peace" in which the writer complimented the queen on her success:

> A wondrous *Convert* you have made of *France,*
> Who to your *Measures* now is pleas'd to *Dance.*[194]

This playful couplet imagines the Protestant queen converting the Catholic king, an impossible but heartwarming fantasy, and teaching him to move in time with her tune, a recognition of her continuing interest in the dance. Torcy's mission to Versailles, however, did not have the outcome expected by this optimistic poet. Article 37 in the list of "preliminaries" was a demand that Philip, Duke of Anjou, abandon his pretensions to the throne of Spain and that Louis XIV, his grandfather, compel him to do so. As the Grand Dauphin, son of Louis and father of Philip, angrily pointed out, this clause could force the French king to go to war against his own grandson, who had established himself in Madrid and enjoyed the support of many important Spaniards. Appealing to the patriotism of his subjects, Louis refused to sign and ordered his troops to prepare for another summer of combat.

The English public, fondly believing that France had no remaining resources, expected the allied army to march unopposed to Paris, but Marlborough and Eugene, who knew better, began the campaign by besieging Tournai, a necessary step before moving south. Much of the struggle took place underground, with sappers mining and countermining in tunnels under the fortress, which finally surrendered at the end of August. The French commander Villars, who had been unable to relieve the siege, deployed his army to prevent a further allied advance, using woods and trenches to protect his position. Undaunted by his strong defenses, which included newly felled trees with their branches sharpened to block assaults on the trenches, Marlborough and Eugene attacked. The Battle of Malplaquet (31 August/11 September) was the bloodiest engagement of the entire war, and an eerie anticipation of the costly trench warfare that would take place on the same ground just over two hundred years later. "It is now in our power to have what peace we please,"[195] an exhausted Marlborough wrote to Godolphin at the end of the battle, but his losses (20,500 killed and wounded) were greater than those sustained by the French (12,500). The allies broke through the formidable French defenses, but the remaining French troops retired in good order, even though Villars was gravely wounded and carried from the field unconscious. Despite the victor's hopes, the shocking carnage did not increase the chances for peace. Neither this battle nor the successful siege of Mons, which capitulated on 9/20 October, prompted a serious poetic response; commenting on how many battles the duke had won, Maynwaring described his fellow poets as depleted: "our English wits," he wrote to Sarah, "will have a great difficulty in finding any new praises to give him."[196] The writers of popular songs, however, were equal to the occasion; one musical "catch" compared the French to "Conys in burrows," applauding the English as "ferretts."[197]

§

While Marlborough was carrying out these operations, his diplomatic colleague Townshend was at work on the Anglo-Dutch Barrier Treaty, signed on 18/29 October, which promised the Dutch that once the war was over, their troops would garrison a large number of towns and citadels in the southern Netherlands, thus protecting them from future French invasions. Marlborough, who thought the terms too generous, refused to sign. As the campaign drew to a close, he wrote to the queen renewing his request to be made Captain-General for life. In a departure from his usual tact, he now joined his duchess in complaining about the influence of Abigail Masham: "I was asured last winter," he wrote, "that Mrs. Masham [h]as asured Mr. Harley and some of his wretches, that let my services or success's bee what they would, from thence forward I should receive noe incouragement from your Majesty, which she was very confydent must oblige me to retire." He did not yet know that his wife was staging a series of quarrelsome meetings with Anne at Windsor: when Abigail went to Kensington to give birth to her second child, Sarah used her absence to complain again about her influence. By the time the queen replied to Marlborough's letter, she was able to thank and congratulate her general for "the good news of the surrender of Mons," but when she finally responded to his request for promotion, she again declined his entreaty and directly contradicted his assertion that she was following Mrs. Masham's advice: "What I said," she insisted, "was my own thoughts, not thinking it for your service nor mine to do a thing of that Nature."[198] She also wrote a long letter to Sarah, which was so specific in its complaints about her "teasing and tormenting" behavior that the duchess destroyed it, replying in turn with "a voluminous headlong narrative" of her own, in which she used copies of Anne's earlier letters to her to argue that it was she who had been mistreated.[199]

Shortly before Marlborough returned to England, the Junto finally compelled the queen to replace Admiral Pembroke, the last remaining Tory in her Cabinet, with the Whig Earl of Orford, whom she distrusted and disliked. When Parliament opened on 15 November, the Whigs used their overwhelming majority to pass bills of supply with unprecedented speed, but there were beginning to be some signs of a Tory reaction, fueled in part by the appalling losses at Malplaquet. A few days after the opening of Parliament, Delarivier Manley issued part 2 of *The New Atalantis;* the curious and prurient who bought this sequel got a potent dose of Tory propaganda along with the sexual gossip they were seeking. There are flattering portraits of Harley and Peterborough, but the Duchess of Marlborough, who appears as "Madam *de Caria,*" is part of a ménage à trois including Godolphin and her husband and shamelessly exploits her high standing with "the Princess *Olimpia*" by selling offices:

> The Marchioness cou'd set no Bounds to her Acquisitions, because her Desires were unlimitted; she was starving in the midst of Plenty; she enjoy'd not any thing, though she was in Possession of all things. *True* Merit was what she never consider'd, neither did she *reward* or *raise* without a *Bribe;* the *meanest* as well as the *greatest* Offices had a settled Price, yet sometimes were they to be dispos'd of to the highest Bidder.

On the next page, Manley introduces "a new and rising Favourite," obviously Mrs. Masham:

> *Hilaria,* for so was she call'd, had a Soul fitted for *Grandeur;* a capacious Repository for the Confidence of *Royal Favour.* She lov'd and understood Letters, introduc'd, nay, applauded the Ingenious, and did always her endeavour to make them taste of the Royal Bounty: ... She not only *wore,* but *lov'd,* the Holy awful *Robe* of *Religion,* with tender Pity and Concern to those, who seem'd to squander away their precious looser Hours, unthoughtful of a future State.[200]

By picturing "Hilaria" as a patroness of "Ingenious" writers, Manley rejects the false claim that Abigail was illiterate, prominent in the ballad Sarah may have helped to write. The Whig establishment might have been well advised to ignore Mrs. Manley, but Sunderland, perhaps encouraged by his mother-in-law, quickly issued a warrant for the author, printer, and publishers of *The New Atlantis,* and Manley spent a week in jail before being "admitted to bail."[201] The attendant publicity probably increased the sales of her novel. On 5 November, the day of Manley's release from prison, Henry Sacheverell preached his inflammatory sermon, which was available in print by 25 November; a second edition in quarto and a huge third edition in octavo appeared on 1 December. Like the novelist, the preacher soon found himself in custody; the decision to impeach him, a much more extreme course of action than trying him in a normal court, was to prove disastrous for the Whig cause.

In the midst of all this ferment, on 22 November, came the thanksgiving service for the year's campaign. Although Luttrell reported a rumor that she would go to St. Paul's,[202] the queen again attended her own chapel, and she took the unprecedented step of writing out, in her own hand, a prayer to be used in the service. This touching document provides telling evidence about her own state of mind and her view of the war:

> O most Glorious God the Lord of Heaven and earth, wee thy miserable and most unworthy Creatures, presume to draw nigh unto thee, on this Solemn day with the profoundest adoration and Humility offering unto thee the Sacrafice of thanksgiveing and telling out thy works with gladness. Thou art the God that dost wonders, and hast declared thy power among the people. Thou hast given us the Blessings of health and plenty and peace at home, and hast also vouchsafed us thrô the whole course of this yeare many Signall and glorious Successes abroad which we this day Commemoratte with joyful hearts.[203]

For Manningham, a year earlier, thanksgiving had been a "Duty"; now Anne calls it a "Sacrafice," made "with the profoundest adoration and Humility" by the Lord's "miserable and most unworthy Creatures." Solemnity is more prominent than joy in this prayer, as it was in other parts of the service. Croft set his anthem to a text casting doubt on military might: "Some put their trust in Chariots," reads one verse, "and some in Horses: but we will remember the name of the Lord our God."[204] White Kennett, a prominent Whig clergyman, preached on the story of Jesus cleansing the ten lepers. Remembering Christ's compassion toward these outcasts, he urged his hearers to have

> Bowels of Tenderness and Kindness toward those, who have suffer'd any Loss or Harm, in the Glorious Defence of their QUEEN and Country. ...And of those who have fall'n in any Day of Battle, we ought to Regard their Disconsolate Widows, and to Encourage their Children not to degenerate, and to plant some of their own *Laurels* on their Graves.[205]

For the queen and her court, this was a muted thanksgiving, with an emphasis on suffering and sacrifice, but for William Collier, an enterprising shareholder in the Drury Lane theatre company, the "day of publick rejoyceing" was an opportunity. At the end of the last theatrical season, the Earl of Kent, Anne's Lord Chamberlain, had lost patience with Christopher Rich, the manager of Drury Lane; in retaliation for Rich's repeated refusals to live up to his contracts with his leading players, Kent ordered the Drury Lane company not to act. When they tried to open in September, he sent his secretary, Sir John Stanley, to shut them down. Owen Swiney, who was producing the operas starring Nicolini, alertly hired several of the leading actors and began to present spoken plays in alternation with the operas at the Haymarket, leaving the remaining actors without work or income. Collier somehow persuaded Kent to grant him a license to operate a new company at Drury Lane, with a starting date of 23 November. "On or about the 22d day of the said month," says Collier's later account,

> it being a day of publick rejoyceing he ordered a Bonefire to be made before the Playhouse Door and gave the Players money to Drink your Majesties health & the then Lord Chamberlains and to rejoyce for the victory which was that day Commemorated, &...he came that Evening to the Playhouse & showed the Players Sir John Stanley's Letter and told them they might act as soon as they pleased.

Christopher Rich, however, told a very different story, alleging that his rival

> came with a Corporal & divers soldiers armed with swords & Musquett in a riotous & violent manner broke open the Doors of the said Theatre & turnd out Mr Rich's servants who were then in the quiet possession of the same.[206]

The Lord Chamberlain's inability to arrange a change of theatre management in a more dignified fashion may have been among Anne's reasons for replacing him a few months later.

The queen was now more isolated than she had ever been, both politically and personally. Confident in their control of Parliament and the Cabinet, the Whigs showed how little they valued the monarch by usurping functions she thought her own, including Church appointments and court protocol. In a legislative replay of the earlier bishoprics crisis, the House of Commons sent her an address urging her to reward Benjamin Hoadley, a highly partisan Whig clergyman who was close to Sarah Churchill; Anne sent for his books and let it be known that she planned to read them before taking any action. A month later, the House "ordered a bill to be brought in to limit the time for public mournings, that the silk manufacture may not be lost,"[207] another encroachment on the queen, who would have remembered not only her recent gracious gesture to the silk weavers but her struggle with William about mourning for her father.

Surrounded by partisan Whigs, Godolphin, who had functioned so effectively in earlier mixed ministries, was unable to protect the queen from such disrespectful acts. In her personal life, Anne was mourning for George and approaching the end of another relationship that had sustained her for decades but had now become a constant irritant, as the Duchess of Marlborough continued to criticize her at every opportunity. The duke, who had usually been more reasonable than his wife, was now pressing demands on her that seemed entirely unreasonable, and joining his wife in blaming her faithful Abigail for everything they disliked. David Hamilton, a Scottish physician who specialized in female complaints, recognized that Anne's emotional stress was affecting her health, and on 9 December he asked Godolphin to refrain from bringing her papers that she would find distressing. The Treasurer did his best to comply, but it was impossible to protect the queen from the turmoil around her.[208] Even the thanksgiving service, which she had sought to keep focused on "profoundest adoration and humility," included an attempt to influence her treatment of Marlborough. In recounting the story of the twelve lepers, Kennett reminded the congregation that the one man who returned to thank his healer was a Samaritan, which gave him an opportunity to develop the theme of ingratitude:

> When the Jews themselves would not see the Power of GOD, a very Stranger did behold it, and adore it. So possibly, when by GOD's Help, any wonderful Actions are perform'd by a GREAT MAN: If some of the Nation to which He belongeth, could be content to diminish, and detract from his Merits; yet Foreigners and Strangers shall judge impartially, and give the due Abundant Honour.[209]

It was true that Marlborough, whose prestige was now being undermined at home, enjoyed honor and respect from many of his European allies and comrades; the congregation at St. James's would have had no doubt about who was meant by "a GREAT MAN."

But if Kennett imagined that the queen would be influenced by the message he was sending, he was soon disappointed. On 10 January, the Earl of Essex died, and Anne took it upon herself to give the regiment he had commanded to John Hill, Abigail's younger brother. Marlborough correctly regarded Hill as useless and was deeply affronted by this incursion of royal preference into military matters. Absenting himself from the meetings of the House of Lords and the Cabinet, he went off to the country, and some of his strongest supporters, including Maynwaring and Sunderland, began to float the idea of a parliamentary address to the queen asking her to dismiss Mrs. Masham. Even Sarah realized that this was a terrible idea: although Anne had undercut Marlborough's authority by making a military appointment without consulting him, it was even more disrespectful for the legislature to concern itself with the monarch's personal servants. At the urging of Godolphin, Somers, and Cowper, Anne "deferred" Hill's appointment, awarding him a handsome pension instead, and another uneasy truce was patched up, but it was now clear to all that the hegemony of the Marlboroughs was at an end. On 6 February, "'Twas observed that the Dutchess of M_____ did not make her appearance at Chappel with the Qveen [on] her Birth day, which most of the Ladys of the Bed Chamber did."[210] On 15 February, in the midst of the preparations for the Sacheverell trial, the Commons took the unprecedented step of asking the queen "to send the Duke of *Marlborough* forthwith into *Holland*, where his Presence is absolutely necessary...to procure a safe and honourable Peace for her Majesty, and her Allies." Prompted by Marlborough himself, this address required a reply, and Godolphin drafted some language in which Anne would praise the duke as "God Almighty's chief instrument of my glory," but the queen insisted on revisions: "I am so sensible of the Necessity of the Duke of *Marlborough*'s Presence in *Holland* at this critical Juncture," she wrote, "that I have already given the necessary Directions for his immediate Departure," thus rejecting the idea that she needed a parliamentary reminder, "and I am very glad to find, by this Address, that you concur with me in a just Sense of the Duke of *Marlborough*'s eminent Services," a deliberately bland formula.[211]

Anne also managed to delay sending this reply to Parliament until after Marlborough's departure, thus signaling her continuing irritation. When she thought that the Commons might actually ask her to part with Abigail, she was much more direct, sending for some legislators, including Maynwaring, and "declar[ing] with great spirit and courage against it."[212] Although she retained "a just Sense of the Duke of *Marlborough*'s eminent Services," she was looking for new opportunities to assert herself. For all these reasons, her attitude toward Sacheverell evidently softened during his trial. "After the impeachment was brought up to the lords," writes Bishop Burnet, "she said to me, that it was a bad sermon, and that he deserved well to be punished for it."[213] The queen may well have made some such remark to the Whig bishop at the beginning of the trial, but she later told Abigail Masham, who was urging her to "let people know her mind in the matter," that "she did not meddle one way or other," and she told Dr. Hamilton that "there ought to be a punishment but a mild one, least the mobb appearing of his side, shoud occasion great commotions[,] and that his Impeachment had been better lett alone."[214] By 7 March, when the doctor rose to speak, Anne had become receptive to the language in which he proclaimed his respect for her, which was not only sonorous but immediately applicable to her current plight. If the House of Commons had thought of their queen as "the Desire of our Eyes, and the Breath of our Nostrils," they would not have presumed to tell her when to send Marlborough to

Holland—and they certainly would not have considered telling her to sack her most cherished servant. As she struggled to retain the prestige and power of the Crown, and as she heard, with feelings that were surely mixed, an eloquent clergyman articulating traditional views of monarchy in the very room where her grandfather had been condemned to death, Anne had reason to feel that she was "the Inheritrix of the Blessed Martyr's Crown and Piety."

TO FIX A LASTING
PEACE ON EARTH

6 February 1713

With fresh excitement, the men and boys of the Chapel Royal prepared to sing, as they had so often done on the birthday of their beloved queen.[1] On the last two royal birthdays, they had performed odes by English composers, only to be upstaged by the singers from the opera company, who had the advantage of music by George Frideric Handel, the gifted German composer whose Italian operas had made such a strong impression in London. Now they were about to perform a work specifically written for them by Mr. Handel. Clearly aware of the queen's musical preferences, the composer had provided extended solos for Richard Elford, as well as movements featuring the countertenor Francis Hughes and the basses Samuel Weely and Bernard Gates,[2] but he had also written solos for two women. For the all-male Chapel choir, in which boys sang the soprano parts, performing with women was unprecedented during this reign,[3] yet these new soloists were excellent. The contralto Jane Barbier was a regular performer in the operas at the Haymarket, often taking male roles; the soprano Anastasia Robinson, daughter of an English painter, had studied music with William Croft, Composer to the Chapel Royal. Someone, however, had told Handel that the queen especially enjoyed hearing Elford, so he quickly rearranged an aria he had written for Mrs. Barbier to be sung instead by the choir's star singer, leaving her only a pair of duets with Mrs. Robinson.[4]

In recent years, both Croft and Eccles had sought to emulate the Italian music now popular in the opera house, but in this birthday ode, Handel showed his respect for English traditions. The opening aria, featuring Elford, had a trumpet obbligato for John Shore, a versatile and inventive musician who had served the queen and her late husband for years, often working with Elford.[5] At thanksgiving services during Anne's reign, Shore and Elford would often have performed the prominent parts for high tenor and trumpet in Henry Purcell's *Te Deum* and *Jubilate*, so Handel was honoring the traditions of the Chapel Royal by using them as soloists, and by composing a canon between the voice and the trumpet that imitates Purcell's compositional practice.[6]

The text Handel set was not by Nahum Tate, who normally provided words for birthday odes, but by the Whig poet Ambrose Philips, whose *Pastorals* had included a touching poem in memory of Gloucester.[7] His carefully constructed ode has seven stanzas, each ending with the same couplet:

> The Day that gave great Anna Birth,
> Who fix'd a lasting Peace on Earth.

Handel set each of Philips's stanzas as a solo or duet, leading immediately to a choral setting of the repeated couplet; he showed the range and variety of his compositional invention not only by varying the settings of the verses, but by constructing seven different settings for the refrain. Previous birthday poets had sometimes

Mus. Ex. 10.1: George Frideric Handel, aria from *Eternal Source of Light Divine* (1713).

hoped or predicted that Anne would rule a nation at peace in the future, but Philips describes the peace as already accomplished. Negotiations in Utrecht, which had been in progress for over a year, were now in their final stages, and the Tory ministry that had sought to make peace enjoyed widespread support. As a Whig writing for a birthday celebration at a court now dominated by Tories, Philips therefore needed to work cautiously. His first four stanzas employ a familiar pastoral idiom, appealing to the sun ("Eternal Source of Light divine"), the "winged Race" of birds, the "Flocks and Herds," and the "rolling streams" of the English countryside to celebrate the monarch, but in the last three stanzas, he moves from this generalized vision of rural peace to some more specific details. Aware of the queen's many ailments, he pictures a personified Health bringing her "new life":

> Kind Health descends on downy Wings,
>   Angels conduct her on the Way,
> T 'our glorious Queen, new Life she brings,
>   And swells our joys upon this Day.

With the succession still a touchy issue, those eager for political stability had reason to pray that the queen's fragile health would mend, and Handel's setting, a gently rocking *siciliana* for the two female singers, gives lyrical support to this prayer. The hope that "kind Health" might descend to aid the monarch was safely nonpartisan, enabling Philips to deplore "blasted Faction" as he moved toward a final stanza in praise of the peace treaty, which Handel set grandly as a double chorus:

> United Nations shall combine,
>   To distant Climes the Sound convey,
> That Anna's Actions are divine,
>   And this the most important Day.
> The Day that gave great Anna Birth,
> Who fix'd a lasting Peace on Earth.[8]

As Philips indirectly suggests by imagining the sound of Anne's glory extending to "distant Climes," the Treaty of Utrecht (31 March/11 April 1713) would give English merchants and colonists access to new possessions and new economic opportunities in Africa, America, and the Caribbean. Like all such agreements, it was cobbled together by a process of compromise and deal-making, but Philips was not alone in treating it as the result of "divine" action by the queen. Although Pope's famous version of this trope is much better poetry, it is ultimately similar in content:

> At length great *ANNA* said—Let Discord cease!
> She said, the World obey'd, and all was *Peace*![9]

§

In the spring of 1710, however, peace still seemed far away. Between late February and early April, French plenipotentiaries engaged in three rounds of negotiations with the Dutch and the English at Geertruidenberg, seeking to settle the remaining issues, but as early as 28 February/11 March, Marlborough had concluded that "the only good step wee can make towards a peace is to gett early into the field." "The chief designe of France," he told Godolphin, "is to cause a devission amongst the Allyes,"[10] though article 37, the requirement that Louis compel his grandson to abandon Spain, remained the most obvious barrier to peace. In insisting on that article, Marlborough and Townshend were following the directions of the Whig ministry, which was still "interested only in total victory, whatever the cost." They had not yet realized that the queen was moving toward Robert Harley's belief that "peace with France was both possible and urgently necessary."[11]

Marlborough's large-scale strategy was simple: by pushing further and further into France, he hoped to force the French to make peace on humiliating terms, including giving up Spain and its empire, and many of his colleagues in the government agreed. Personal glory, however, was also a motive. A letter dispatched to Sarah on 8/19 March includes a detailed report on "the hangings now makeing att Bruxelles,"[12] a series of tapestries depicting "The Famous Victories of the Duke of Marlborough," most of which may still be seen at Blenheim Palace. His associates knew that the duke had invested a considerable amount of money to commission this permanent visible record of his triumphs: two days after the slaughter at Malplaquet, Count Sinzendorff, the representative of the Habsburg Empire at the Hague, had written jovially to Marlborough describing the battle as "a good addition to the tapestries";[13] and a woven representation of Malplaquet duly appeared, showing the trenches and woods that made the French position so difficult to assault. The Dutch had lost three thousand men in one hour attempting to assault those lines, and the designer of the tapestry, perhaps in recognition of the terrible cost of this victory, did not show Marlborough's face in this panel, as he had been careful to do in those depicting Blenheim, Ramillies, and Oudenarde.[14] Although the last tapestry was to be a depiction of peace, there was a part of Marlborough that still wanted to add new panels to the series.

Even before Malplaquet, the Whig physician Richard Blackmore had published a poem to John Vanderbank, a Huguenot weaver in London, offering him instructions for depicting Marlborough on fabric. In keeping with Addison's insistence that Marlborough's heroism needed no mythological elaboration, Blackmore asks the weaver to be realistic and modern:

In every Piece let Art and Labour shine;
Let Glorious Deeds the *Briton*'s Palace crown,
Not those of antient Heroes, but his own;

Judocus de Vos, *The Battle of Malplaquet* (1711).

In the bright Series of his Story show
What *Albion*, what Mankind to *Marlbro'* owe.[15]

Blackmore could not have known that Marlborough had already ordered a set of tapestries depicting the victories of Alexander the Great, an "antient Hero" with whom he identified, nor could he have known that Marlborough had asked Kneller to make his large painting for Blenheim an allegory,[16] yet the hangings now at Blenheim exemplify the realism advocated by the poet, carefully reproducing the geographical sites of Marlborough's battles, the movements of the troops, and the faces of his generals. There are no mythological figures.

Richard Steele found the whole idea of celebrating battles in hangings amusing, and quickly exploited Blackmore's poem in a witty *Tatler*:

Waller and *Denham* had worn out the Expedient of *Advice to a Painter*: This Author … directs his Genius to the Loom, and will have a new Set of Hangings, in Honour of the last Year in *Flanders*. I must own to you, I approve extremely this Invention, and it might be improv'd for the Benefit of Manufactury: As, suppose an Ingenious Gentleman should write a Poem of Advice to a Calico Printer: Do you think there is a Girl in *England*, that would wear any Thing but *The Taking of* Lisle, or *The Battle of* Oudenarde?[17]

Neither Steele nor Blackmore nor Marlborough could have guessed that by 1711, ladies in England, rather than wearing garments depicting the duke's famous victories, would be carrying fans depicting Sacheverell as the hero of a Tory allegory. On one such fan, the mounted men on the left, their faces turned toward the viewer, are the Duke of Ormond, who eventually replaced Marlborough as Captain-General, and the arch-Tacker William Bromley, who became Speaker of the House late in 1710. Holding Anne's portrait at the top of the fan is an angel whose sword has just deflected a cannonball fired from a boat steered by the pope, while the angel on the other side of the portrait drops a bishop's mitre onto the head of Sacheverell. King David, playing a large harp on the far right, appears as the poet of peace. There is a striking contrast between the relatively realistic Blenheim tapestries and the unabashedly mythical Sacheverell fan, in which Anglican martyrs rise from their graves and heroes slay hydras and dragons.[18]

The process by which a Whig government supporting the war gave way to a Tory government seeking peace was complex, and some of the backstage maneuvers may never be known. Sacheverell's trial, however, was an important impetus.

A historical emblematical fan (1711).

Marlborough sent Sarah his report on the tapestries on the day after Sacheverell's compelling speech, taking a hopeful view encouraged by her earlier letters: "I see you think the tryale of Sacheverelle has been very well managed, which I am extreame glad of, for in time it must have a good effect all over England." At the bottom of the same page, however, he acknowledged "many disagreable accounts com[ing] from England" telling of "the inclinations of the people for Sacheverelle, which dose great hurt." Godolphin, who had initially favored the impeachment, now wished "it never had began, for it has occasioned a very great ferment." As the Lords discussed the verdict and the punishment, the Treasurer became aware of some important defections. He now believed that the Duke of Somerset, long a pillar of Whig moderation, was "entirely linked with the opposite party, upon the foot of knowing the Queen's inclinations."[19] Somerset's duchess, a daughter of the vastly wealthy Percy family and a Lady of the Bedchamber, had insisted on standing when she was "in waiting" at the trial, a display of punctilious attention to courtly protocol that irritated Sarah, who had asked permission to sit.[20] While Somerset cautiously absented himself on the day of the all-important vote, some other Whigs not part of the Junto, including the Duke of Shrewsbury, voted for Sacheverell's acquittal. The vote was close, and the punishment imposed was light: "all this bustle and fatigue," wrote Godolphin, "ends in no more but a suspension for 3 years from the pulpit, and burning his sermons at the old Exchange,"[21] as if that symbolic act would keep them out of circulation. A motion to ban the doctor from taking "any dignity or preferment in the church" during the same three years failed by one vote, an outcome allowing one of his wealthy backers to offer him a well-endowed parish.

Two days after the verdict, the Queen's Theatre finally presented the long-delayed premiere of *L'Idaspe fidele,* or *Hydaspes,* a new opera brought to London by Nicolini, with music by Francesco Mancini, sets painted by an artist transported from Venice, and no less than three castrati in the cast. Nicolini himself appeared in the title role, "taking the Habit of a Moor" as Valentini had done as Turnus in *Camilla.* The idea of disguising a castrato as an African, thus making him "exotic" in both gender and race, appears to have had some appeal to the audience; in another of his satirical glances at the opera, Steele describes a "coquet" who will "never have done upon the *Opera.* One while she would break out upon, *That hideous King!* Then upon the charming Black-moor! Then, *Oh that dear Lion!*"[22] There was indeed a part for a lion, with whom the "charming Black-moor" Hydaspes fought a battle. "Mr. Lawrence," a tenor who played a minor role, was the only native-born singer, but he sang in Italian like the rest of the cast; the bilingual word-book, giving Italian and English on facing pages, would have been necessary for anyone hoping to follow the plot. It begins with an untranslated Italian dedication from Nicolini to Henry Grey, Earl of Kent, praising him for his "Justice, Virtue, and Prudence."[23]

Nicolini evidently did not know that Anne was preparing to dismiss her Lord Chamberlain.

Neither did Godolphin. The queen's decision to replace Kent, softening the blow by making him a duke, was the first move in a process that eventually led to a completely new ministry. Those seeking to explain the steps she now took have usually given full credit (or blame) to Robert Harley, who was doubtless working behind the scenes, but Anne had motives of her own. On 29 March, the third peace conference at Geertruidenberg ended without an agreement, and Marlborough and Eugene joined their armies in the field. Although there would not be another Malplaquet, bloodshed was sure to continue; the successful siege of Douai, the first major action in this campaign, cost Marlborough over eight thousand men. On 5 April, Allen Bathurst, the wealthy son of the queen's girlhood favorite and her old Household Treasurer, presented her with a loyal "address" from the Tory gentlemen of Gloucestershire, who assured their monarch that

> we now are, and always shall be, ready to sacrifice our Lives and Fortunes,
> in Defence of Your Majesty's most Sacred Person, *Prerogative*, and *Government*...against all *Republican, Traiterous, Factious*, and *Schismatical*
> Opposers at Home, and all open and profess'd Enemy's Abroad.[24]

The adjectives used for Anne's domestic enemies point unmistakably toward the Whigs, including some now serving in her government. On the very day she received this address, the queen prorogued her Parliament for ten days, promising to summon them again if there were a concrete peace proposal to consider, which she knew was unlikely. Among the laws to which she gave her assent before the prorogation was the "An Act for the Encouragement of Learning, by Vesting the Copies of Printed Books in the Authors or Purchasers of Copies," the first English law protecting the rights of authors, and a lasting legacy of the last Whig Parliament of her reign. "I could heartily wish," she said in her speech, "that Men would study to be quiet, and do their own Business."[25]

The Duchess of Marlborough was not studying to be quiet. On the next day, 6 April, she forced the queen to endure a face-to-face meeting at Kensington. She had been seeking this confrontation for some time, hoping to press Anne about the bundle of papers she had submitted to justify her conduct, which included copies of their earlier correspondence and excerpts from spiritual tracts selected to prick the queen's conscience. Anne had avoided answering that voluminous "letter" and had already postponed this meeting several times.[26] Although their interview actually occurred on Maundy Thursday, Sarah titles her narrative, which is our only source, "the account of a conversation with the Queen upon good friday 1710." Consciously or unconsciously, the duchess was casting herself as an innocent victim, sacrificed for the sins of others. The meeting was tense and unpleasant, with Anne insisting that "there is nothing you can have to say but you may write it" and Sarah seeking to clear herself from lies that she believed the Duchess of Somerset was telling about her. To each request, Anne repeated the same formulaic phrase: "I shall make you noe answer to any thing you say." Sarah's narrative of the ending is chilling: "I made my chursey, saying I was confydent she would suffer in this world, or the next for so much inhumanity, & to that she answerd, that would bee to her self."[27]

These cannot have been easy words for either woman to hear; ten months later, Anne remembered Sarah's threat, repeating it to Dr. Hamilton and remarking "that it was very hard passing a Sentence upon any body, for that was a thing, between God and themselves."[28] Yet the finality of this scene appears to have liberated the queen. Eight days later, with an unsuspecting Godolphin off watching the races at Newmarket, she demanded the seals and staff from Kent and made the Duke of Shrewsbury her new Lord Chamberlain. It was a cunning gambit. Shrewsbury, who had signed the letter inviting William to intervene in 1688, was nominally a Whig, and had long been friendly with Marlborough and Godolphin; his appointment to a post with duties concerning the household and the theatre did not look likely to alter foreign or domestic policy. He had, however, voted for the acquittal of Sacheverell, and he was known to be friendly with Harley. If Anne had appointed someone like Buckingham to this post, the outcry would have been immediate and intense, but by appointing a man with friends in both parties, she gained room to maneuver. Although they feared that this appointment was a harbinger of more sweeping changes, some of the Whig ministers thought they might gain stability by forming an alliance with the new Lord Chamberlain, a plan that Sarah correctly dismissed as unworkable. When Maynwaring, a chief promoter of the ill-fated address urging the dismissal of Abigail, asked Sarah to remind the queen that she had opposed that initiative, the duchess replied with a witty allusion: "I suppose she will not imagin that like Duke Trinkolow I can make a rebellion by my self."[29] Among the changes Dryden and William Davenant had made in rewriting Shakespeare's *Tempest* for Restoration tastes was an expansion of the subplot featuring the drunken sailors, with two new characters and some broad political humor ridiculing the republican ideas circulating during the Interregnum. When Stephano, Mustacho, and Ventoso inform their friend Trincalo that they have appointed themselves as the duke and viceroys of the island, he objects: "I say this Island shall be under *Trincalo*, or it shall be a Common-wealth." Swords are drawn, but the self-appointed Duke Stephano avoids bloodshed. "My Subjects are but few," he declares: "let him make a rebellion / By himself."[30] Drury Lane mounted this version of *The Tempest* several times during the spring of 1710, including a benefit performance for Cave Underhill, the actor who had first played Trincalo in 1667.[31] By identifying with a stage buffoon, Sarah was wryly acknowledging that she no longer wielded significant political power.

§

As it happened, Shrewsbury's first official act as Lord Chamberlain was welcoming a group of exotic visitors. On 19 April, four "Indian Kings"—Mohawk chiefs from northern New York—arrived at St. James's Palace, where Shrewsbury introduced them to the queen. In a speech made through an interpreter, the chiefs begged Queen Anne to send some of her "children" to help them invade and capture French Canada. Those hoping to mount such a campaign had been disappointed

Anonymous print after Jan Verelst, *The true Effiges of the four Indian kings* (1710).

in 1709, when Anne sacked MacCartney, the designated commander, and sent the ships prepared to sail for North America to Portugal instead. She received her strange visitors graciously and defrayed the cost of their being painted by Jan Verelst, but she did not immediately promise military aid. During the next two weeks, the "Four Kings" saw London, and London saw them. They attended a performance of *Macbeth,* at which the audience, not content with being told that they were in the box seats, insisted that they be seated on stage. They were invited to an opera, a concert, a swordfight, and a bear-baiting, as well as a puppet show depicting the Battle of Malplaquet, though it is not certain which of these entertainments they actually witnessed. A Dublin newspaper reported that they would be baptized, with Anne herself as their godmother. Although this fantasy did not come true, the chiefs heard Bishop Compton preach in St. James's chapel before starting their long journey back to Boston.[32] By the time they departed, the queen had decided to honor their request; the ship on which they sailed was part of a convoy of "about Eighteen Sail," including "a Bomb-Ship and Tender, and several Transports, with *British* Officers, a Regiment of Marines, Provisions and Stores of War."[33]

With no progress in the peace talks and the military campaign not yet in full swing, the "Indian Kings" were newsworthy; they became the subject of pictorial representations, poems, and essays, including a thoughtful piece in the *Tatler.* As the casual racism of theatrical and operatic scenes featuring "Blackamoors" might suggest, Steele's contemporaries assumed that Europeans were inherently superior to other races and cultures. The dignified comportment of the Amerindian chiefs, however, had made an impression, which Steele chose to develop in an essay posing fundamental questions about "honor and titles." Like many *Tatlers,* this one takes the form of a conversation. "Timoleon," a transparently fictional character, gives a "handsome discourse" on the origin of honorific titles:

> In those ages which first degenerated from simplicity of life and natural justice, the wise among them thought it necessary to inspire men with the love of virtue, by giving those who adhered to the interests of innocence and truth some distinguishing name to raise them above the common level of mankind.

Although he introduces it in a relative clause, Steele is promoting the idea that history is a "degenerat[ion] from simplicity of life and natural justice" rather than a taming of barbarism by civilization; he is treating the "state of nature" as a primitive ideal, not a Hobbesian world of nasty and brutish violence. "Urbanus" responds with a story about the "Indian Kings," who had taken lodgings at the home of an upholsterer in King Street:

These just and generous Princes, who act according to the Dictates of natural Justice, thought it proper to confer some Dignity upon their Landlord before they left his House. One of them had been sick during his Residence there, and having never before been in a Bed, had a very great Veneration for him who made that Engine of Repose, so useful and so necessary in his Distress. It was consulted among the Four Princes, by what Name to dignify his great Merit and Services. The Emperor of the *Mohocks* and the other Three Kings stood up, and in that Posture recounted the Civilities they had received, and particularly repeated the Care which was taken of their Sick Brother. This, in their Imagination, who are used to know the Injuries of Weather, and the Vicissitudes of Cold and Heat, gave them very great Impressions of a skilful Upholsterer, whose Furniture was so well contrived for their Protection on such occasions. It is with these less instructed (I will not say less knowing) People, the Manner of doing Honour, to impose some Name significant of the Qualities of the Person they distinguish, and the good Offices received from him. It was therefore resolved to call their Landlord *Cadaroque,* which is the Name of the strongest Fort in their Part of the World.

Steele invites his readers to admire the Mohawks, "who act according to the Dictates of natural Justice." If they are "less instructed" than Europeans, they are not "less knowing," and their decision to give their landlord a new name honoring his skill in furniture-making sheds an oblique light on the obsession with titles and honors in the "civilized" world, recently exemplified by Marlborough's demand to be Captain-General for life. As a demonstration of the perils of being "instructed," a third speaker, "Minucio," interrupts with questions reflecting his "constant Suspicion as to State-Affairs."

Will any Man, continued he, perswade me, that this was not, from the Beginning to the End a concerted Affair? Who can convince the World that Four Kings shall come over here, and lie at the Two Crowns and Cushion, and one of them fall sick, and the Place be called *King-street,* and all this by meer Accident? No, no: To a Man of very small Penetration, it appears that *Tee Yee Neen Ho Ga Row,* Emperor of the *Mohocks,* was prepared for this Adventure before-hand.[34]

For Minucio, nothing can be coincidental; his paranoid conviction that there are hidden plots beneath the names of streets and houses contrasts unfavorably with the innocent and noble behavior of the "Four Kings."

Suspicious attitudes like those of Minucio were the norm in Queen Anne's world. Unable to believe that the French might genuinely want peace, Marlborough was certain that they had remained at the bargaining table in order to delay his preparations for war and encourage dissension among the Allies. Unable to believe that Anne might simply prefer to have courtly rituals and theatrical performances managed by the urbane and sophisticated Shrewsbury rather than the limited and smelly Kent, Godolphin complained that her decision would be interpreted as the beginning of a wholesale change of ministry, which would alarm her allies abroad and his bankers in the City. The Tory addresses pledging loyalty to the Crown were a way of urging the queen to hold new elections, while the Whig addresses blaming "Papists and Jacobites" for the mob violence during the Sacheverell trial were designed to persuade her to maintain her present Parliament. Although the conventions of the "loyal address" demanded some degree of indirection and decorum, anonymous poets could offer direct and pointed advice to the queen, as one did on 12 May, attacking her ministers as "a Vile Brood of Men,"

> Rebels to Monarchy, Sworn Foes to God,
> Serpents and Vipers that wou'd drink thy Blood.
> Whose Principles took off thy Grandsire's Head, ⎫
> And from whose Rage thy Unhappy Father fled, ⎬
> Forc'd in a Foreign Land to Beg his Bread. ⎭
> And can'st thou warm these Snakes within thy Breast?
> Are they alone to be with Favours Blest?[35]

Appropriating the official imagery making Anne the "nursing mother" of her country, the poet warns her against nursing vipers. Not content to identify her Whig ministers with the parliamentary rebels who beheaded her grandfather, he also laments the fate of her father. Minucio would readily have identified him a Jacobite.

Written language, whether prose or poetry, was not the only medium for the expression of partisan passions. In June and July, Sacheverell staged a slow "progress" to the West, taking seven weeks to travel from Oxford to his lucrative new living, conduct one service there (without a sermon), and return. During his journey, town corporations and wealthy men provided him with meals and lodging, and many of the places through which he passed "manifested the great Esteem they had for the Dr. by the Ringing of Bells Bonfires & other Demonstrations of Joy." At Coventry, "above 500 horse & more than double the Number of foot" met him at the city gates.[36] Like Monmouth's politically charged "progress" in 1680, this symbolic journey was an appropriation of a royal practice, and while Sacheverell

528 ~ QUEEN ANNE

was not dramatizing a claim to the crown, his supporters, including the armed men at Coventry, expected their actions to have an influence on the queen. Opponents of Sacheverell, noticing the coverage of his progress in French newspapers, accused him of giving aid and comfort to the enemy.[37] Like Steele's Minucio, these correspondents see dark conspiracies everywhere: if the writers of the Parisian newspapers mention Sacheverell in their reports from England, they must be suggesting to their readers that there will soon be a new English government more friendly to France.

Every action the queen took at this time was subject to such determined interpretation, so when she demanded the resignation of Sunderland from his position as Secretary of State on 14 June, she should not have expected her subjects to regard her action as a simple transaction between two people, as if she were a Mohawk chieftain operating "according to the dictates of natural justice." Looking back on this period, Swift gave due weight to Anne's personal distaste for Sunderland (and perhaps for Kent): "It is most certain," he wrote, "that when the Queen first began to change her servants, it was not from a dislike of things but of persons, and those persons were a very small number."[38] At the time, however, those responding to this forced resignation saw its implications as much larger. Sunderland, who made no secret of his radical ideas, was the closest thing to a "Republican" in Anne's ministry; his removal delighted the resurgent Tories, especially when Anne replaced him with William Legge, Earl of Dartmouth, who had voted to acquit Sacheverell. Because Sunderland was married to the daughter of the Marlboroughs, those who had long deplored the influence of that powerful couple could see his removal as Anne's public declaration of her break with Sarah and a further assertion of her authority over the duke, a process she had already begun by refusing to approve a list of military promotions from which he had omitted Mrs. Masham's husband and brother.

Not surprisingly, Marlborough objected. "I am sorry Lord Sunderland is not agreable to the Queen," he wrote to Godolphin on 9 June,

> But his being at this time singled out, has no other reason but that of being my son-in-law. When this appears in its treu light, I am very confident every man in England will be sensible that my enemys have prevailled to have this done, in order to make it impossible for me with honour to continue at the head of this glorious army, that has throw the whole corse of this warr, been blessed by God with surprising successes.

It is remarkable that Marlborough, who was skilled at perceiving the intentions of those he opposed on the battlefield and the motives of those with whom he negotiated treaties, should have been so blinded by considerations of honor and glory that he believed his "enemys" (presumably meaning Harley) had "prevailled" upon the queen to replace his son-in-law for "no other reason" than to dishonor him. His earlier letters to the duchess about Sunderland make it abundantly clear that he knew about the younger man's political ideas and recognized his bad manners. By this time, however, Marlborough was focusing on the image he would present to history, in written narrative and woven tapestry, as an honorable general at the head of a "glorious army." "When you have read this letter to the Queen," he told his old friend, "I desire you will keep it for my justefycation after my death."[39]

The queen's answer survives in a holograph letter to Godolphin. "It is true indeed," she writes,

> that the turning a Son in Law out of his office may be a mortification to the D: of Mar: but must the fate of Europe depend on that, & must he be gratefyed in all his desires, & I not in soe reasonable a thing as parting with a man who I took into my Service with all the uneasyness emaginable & who's behaviour to me has bin Soe ever Since, & who I must add is I believe obnoxious to all people exsept a few.[40]

Remembering her own mortifications in the 1690s, Anne understands that she has done something hurtful, but she rejects the notion that one small change in her domestic ministry will alter "the fate of Europe."[41] By questioning whether her commander had to be "gratefyed in all his desires," she slyly equates his lust for glory with baser appetites. Count Fortunatus, the fictional version of Marlborough in Mrs. Manley's *New Atalantis,* uses similar language in offering his friend Germanicus a chance to sleep with the Dutchess De L'inconstant. "'Tis the Law of *Nature,*" says the cynical Fortunatus, "the pursuit is pleasing, and a Man owes himself the Satisfaction of gratifying those Desires that are importunate, and important to him."[42] By associating Marlborough's hope to retain his honor with the gratification of fleshly desires, Anne is able to argue that she is being "reasonable" in parting with Sunderland, whose behavior has been "obnoxious to all people exsept a few"—and not one of the Junto Whigs came forward to defend their colleague. Marlborough, who had hoped they would "strugle with all their might and power," wondered how they could "remain tamly quiet."[43] He may not yet have realized that his Whig associates, who were trying to retain their own positions, were unwilling to risk irritating the queen by supporting a colleague they had often found difficult.

The most common inference drawn from the replacement of Sunderland was that there would be many more changes in the ministry, as well as new elections, so the queen made determined attempts to quiet such speculation. Within hours of taking the seals from Sunderland, she met with four Directors of the Bank of England and "was pleased to declare to them, that she had no thoughts of making any other removal." Three days later, she gave similar assurances to "the Imperial, Prussian, Dutch, and other foreign ministers."[44] On 15 June, she appointed the Whig Speaker of the House to the Privy Council; when she asked her physician "what the people said," he "told her, that from her making Sir Richard Onslow one of the Council, it look'd as if she would keep a ballance."[45] She also sent Halifax, another man with contacts in both parties, to join Townshend at the Hague as a second plenipotentiary, and when Henry Hesketh, an aging Tory clergyman, "preach't before the queen a very high flying sermon, far exceeding that of Dr. Sacheverel," he found himself "forbid preaching any more in the royal chappel."[46]

At this point, Anne may well have been sincere in claiming that she planned no further ministerial changes and did not intend to dismiss her Parliament. Even Harley, with his lifelong preference for mixed government, was still apparently hoping to "graft the Whiggs on the bulk of the Church Party," and thus not eager for parliamentary elections.[47] The Whigs, however, now made a serious strategic error by encouraging the Allies to write to the queen warning her against making more changes in her government. Anne correctly surmised that this irritating foreign interference was stage-managed, and at a Cabinet meeting on 2 July, she "ordered (her self) an answer to be wrotte by Mr. Boyle to Lord Townshend to acquaint the States that she was verry much surprissed at so extraordinary a prosseeding but that nothing should lessen her affections to the States, but as it was the first of this kind, she hoped it would be the last."[48] When he learned of this episode, the Tory leader Bromley declared that the queen's answer was "worthy of Q. Elizabeth."[49] Her irritation with the Junto accelerated the drift toward the Tories: on 11 July, Luttrell reported that three prominent Tories would soon replace three Whigs in the posts of Comptroller of the Household, Chancellor of the Exchequer, and Treasurer of the Navy. Although those changes did not occur immediately, the next few months saw many new appointments, including one affecting a writer: Dartmouth's appointment as Secretary of State left a vacancy on the Board of Trade, to which the queen appointed the Tory poet Matthew Prior, who had served as a secretary to diplomatic missions during William's reign.[50] He was to play a significant role in the peace process.

§

For Steele, a convinced Whig who used the persona of Bickerstaff to feign political neutrality, the removal of Sunderland and the appointment of Prior should have been clear signals that his government employment as the "Gazeteer" was in jeopardy, but instead of retreating into safe observations of manners, the *Tatler* warned its readers to beware the machinations of Harley. Steele had often printed letters from readers—occasionally real, more frequently fictional—and in early July he published a letter signed by "John Downes," the longtime prompter of the old Duke's Company, which purported to discuss the politics of theatrical management. As everyone knew, the theatre companies had been in turmoil. It had been less than a year since William Collier's violent takeover of Drury Lane, after which he had appointed as his manager a young poet named Aaron Hill, formerly secretary to the Earl of Peterborough. Inexperienced and egotistical, Hill immediately alienated the actors, who staged a riot in early June. Unsuspecting readers might therefore have read the letter by "Downes" as another chapter in this troubled history, but those with a little of the "penetration" exemplified by Steele's "Minucio" would quickly have realized that it was an allegory retelling the recent career of Robert Harley:

> It cannot be unknown to the Nobility and Gentry, That a Gentleman of the Inns of Court, and a deep Intriguer, had some Time since worked himself into the sole Management and Direction of the Theatre. Nor is it less notorious, That his restless Ambition, and subtle Machinations, did manifestly tend to the Extirpation of the good old *British* Actors, and the Introduction of foreign Pretenders; such as Harlequins, *French* Dancers, and *Roman* Singers; which, tho' they impoverish'd the Proprietors, and imposed on the Audience, were for some Time tolerated, by Reason of his dextrous Insinuations, which prevailed upon a few deluded Women, especially the Vizard Masks, to believe, that the Stage was in Danger. But his Schemes were soon exposed, and the Great Ones that supported him withdrawing their Favour, he made his *Exit,* and remained for a Season in Obscurity.

Although the reference to "*Roman* Singers" is in keeping with other attacks on Italian opera in the *Tatler,* the purpose here is to identify the Tories with "foreign Pretenders," a reference to the invasion attempt of 1708, and with efforts to convince the public that "the Stage was in Danger," a transparent rewriting of the Tory insistence that the Church was "in Danger." The plotter's "Season in Obscurity" corresponds to Harley's year away from court after the failure of his attempted coup, and as the allegory continues, we learn that he has continued his schemes:

> During this Retreat the Machivilian was not idle, but secretly fomented Divisions, and wrought over to his Side some of the inferior Actors, reserving a Trap Door to himself, to which only he had a Key.

Alert readers would understand this sentence as referring to Harley's successful courtship of such men as Somerset and Shrewsbury, with the "Trap Door" standing for his backstairs access to the queen and the "Key" for Abigail Masham. Yet despite his "calling in the most eminent Strollers from all Parts of the Kingdom," the theatrical plotter does not have enough trained actors to mount a play:

> When he comes to cast the Parts there is so great a Confusion amongst them for Want of proper Actors, that for my Part I am wholly discouraged. The Play with which they design to open is, *The Duke and no Duke;* and they are so put to it, That the Master himself is to act the Conjurer, and they have no one for the General but honest *George Powell.*[51]

The main point here is that the Tories have no one to put into important positions but the older men who had occupied those posts at the beginning of the reign. Taking advantage of the fact that there really was an old farce by Tate called *The Duke and No Duke,* the writer points to one of the biggest problems facing an incoming Tory administration: how to deal with the popular and successful Duke of Marlborough. Even if Harley can fool the queen and the nation with his conjuring tricks, "they have no one for the General but honest *George Powell,*" an actor notorious for excesses of drink and rage, recently arrested for attempting to stab Aaron Hill. As Steele would certainly have remembered, the tall, handsome Powell had played Alexander the Great in several plays and had appeared as Mars to speak a prologue in praise of Marlborough on the opening night of Addison's ill-fated *Rosamond.*[52] For those following the allegory, the implication was that the new administration had no substantial candidate to replace the Captain-General, and might just as well appoint an actor who looked the part.

Like Steele's attacks on Italian opera, the letter from "Downes" was a witty argument for a lost cause. The Tories were steadily gaining power, and Whig officeholders, including Steele, would not long remain in place. The most significant change came in early August. As the government he had served with tireless energy began to collapse around him, Godolphin's tact and discretion deserted him, and in late July he said something at a Cabinet meeting that offended the queen. Yielding to Harley, who had been prodding her to dismiss her Treasurer for months, she agreed to put the Treasury into commission and wrote a sad little letter to "Mr. Montgomery" on 8 August:

> The uneasiness which you have showed for some time has given me very much trouble, though I have borne it; and had your behaviour continued the same it was for a few years after my coming to the crown, I could have no dispute with myself what to do. But the many unkind returns I have received since, especially what you said to me personally before the Lords, makes it impossible for me to continue you any longer in my service; but I will give you a pension of four thousand a year, and I desire

that, instead of bringing the staff to me, you will break it, which I believe will be easier to us both.[53]

Uneasiness in this period was a medical term for anxiety or depression; the queen's sensitive physician begins his history of her decline "with an *uneasiness* which her Majesty appeared to have, about the beginning of December, 1709," and blames her physical ailments on "a Succession of disquiets."[54] In the letter to Godolphin, Anne complains that his uneasiness "has given me very much trouble, though I have borne it," as if his depression were a communicable disease. Chiding him for his "unkind returns," she asks him not to visit her personally to surrender his staff, which would have been the normal procedure, but to break it, as the household officers did at the end of a royal funeral. Dutifully throwing his sign of office into the fire, Godolphin, who was sixty-five and exhausted, began to descend into the physical decline that would soon bring on his death.

Aware that the dismissal of Godolphin would be controversial, Anne kept herself informed about responses to the political changes she was making. On 16 August Dr. Hamilton brought her a copy of an anonymous Whig broadside called *Queries*, consisting entirely of questions her new ministers might find hard to answer, including these:

> Whether any Instance was ever known till now, of a Treasurer being remov'd without the least Fault pretended; who in all the time of this expensive War has by Wonderful Ability and Reputation kept down the interest of Money to Six *per Cent*. And who in the Management of above Forty Millions is not suspected by his Enemies to have diverted one Penny to his own private Use....
>
> Whether the new Commissioners could have sat two Days in the Treasury, if they had not been supported by the late Ministers; who press'd all their Friends to supply the Necessities of the War, and all the Foreign Ministers to prevent the breaking of our Alliance?[55]

Both of these points were legitimate: no one had seriously impugned Godolphin's integrity, and he had stayed in town to help assure a smooth transition to the new commission, notably by urging the City bankers to continue their loans to the government. Her royal status kept the queen at some distance from the rough-and-tumble discourse of the streets, but she was clearly using Hamilton to find out how her actions were perceived by her subjects, and in discussing the anonymous pamphlets he brought to her, she sometimes corrected his guesses as to their authorship.[56]

On 5 September, Dr. Samuel Garth, a physician and a Kit-Cat, published a sympathetic poem to the fallen Treasurer, in which he praised Godolphin for his hard work and integrity:

> So much the Publick to your Prudence owes,
> You think no Labours long for our Repose:
> Such Conduct, such Integrity are shown,
> There are no Coffers empty, but your Own.

He also takes note of Godolphin's willingness to reward talented men, perhaps remembering his generous support of his friend Addison:

> From mean Dependance Merit you retrieve,
> Unask'd you offer, and unseen you give.

Garth's best lines, however, are those praising the former Prime Minister for his patient and selfless work with those who succeeded him:

> But now some Star, sinister to our Pray'rs,
> Contrives new Schemes, and calls you from Affairs:
> No Anguish in your Looks, or Cares appear,
> But how to teach th'Unpractis'd Crew to steer.

As Garth's lines suggest, the fallen Treasurer remained publicly dignified and helpful during the transition: on the day after receiving Anne's letter of dismissal, he wrote to Marlborough describing his circumstances as "a little discouraging" but declaring that he would not "neglect doing what is best for the whole."[57] Like many physicians, Garth was suspected of atheism; when he delivered the Latin oration at Dryden's funeral in 1700, some complained that its allusions to pagan gods were inappropriate for a Christian burial in Westminster Abbey. In describing Godolphin's fall, however, Garth unmistakably invokes the Christian idea of sacrifice; his last couplet draws upon the prophecies of the "suffering servant" in Isaiah and Christ's prayers for those who executed him:

> Thus, like a Victim, no Constraint you need,
> To expiate their Offence by whom you bleed.[58]

Sarah had attempted to claim the role of a sacrificial victim by placing her final conversation with the queen on Good Friday, but Godolphin's claim to this role was stronger than hers. By casting Godolphin as a Christ-like martyr, Garth might even be suggesting that Queen Anne, whom he never mentions, has played the role of Pontius Pilate, weakly doing the will of the crowd while knowing that her victim was innocent. Matthew Prior promptly published a systematic deconstruction of Garth's grammar and imagery in a Tory journal called the *Examiner*. Avoiding the serious implications of the lines on sacrifice, he rallied the doctor for using the word *bleed*, with its medical connotations. Yet the very fact that a Tory writer bothered to attack this poem at length suggests that some parts of it hit home.[59]

The change of administration that followed Godolphin's removal was rapid and somewhat disorderly. Harley, who was evidently the leading member of the Treasury commission, became Chancellor of the Exchequer, but he was not able to control all the changes that ensued. The dissolution of Parliament, announced on 21 September, prompted a wave of ministerial resignations. Cowper resigned as Lord Chancellor, although Harley and Anne both begged him to stay, and was briefly replaced by a commission before Harcourt, first reinstated as Attorney General, became Lord Keeper. St. John followed a similar path, first reclaiming his old position as Secretary at War, then getting the position he wanted as Secretary of State, a promotion Harley initially opposed. Somerset, appalled by the dissolution, absented himself from meetings of the Cabinet in protest, though he retained his position as Master of the Horse. To the public, the most shocking changes of all were those restoring two old Tories who had served Anne at the opening of her reign but opposed her bitterly since leaving office: Rochester replaced Somers as President of the Privy Council, and Buckingham replaced Devonshire as Lord Steward. There were even rumors that Nottingham would rejoin the government, but Anne refused to allow the return of "Dismal," whom she personally disliked.[60] Sarah and a few other optimists hoped the divisions between the self-proclaimed moderate Harley and the passionate High-Flyers might help the Whig cause in the elections, but the feelings unleashed by the Sacheverell affair led to a decisive Tory victory, which made it almost impossible for Harley to pursue his goal of a mixed or moderate administration.

Writing years later, St. John spoke frankly of the attitudes the Tories brought with them as they took power:

> I am afraid that we came to Court in the same dispositions as all parties have done; that the principal spring of our actions was to have the government of the state in our hands; that our principal views were the conservation of this power, great employments to ourselves, and great opportunities of rewarding those who had helped to raise us, and of hurting those who stood in opposition to us. It is, however, true that with these considerations of private and party interest there were others intermingled, which had for their object the public good of the nation, at least what we took to be such.[61]

In an age of obscene lampoons, coded allegories, and vigorous satires, a political sea change of this kind provided plenty of material for writers, but the Tory interest in "hurting those who stood in opposition to us" directly threatened the employment of writers who had been dependent on Whig patronage. Like his friend Steele, Addison had gained his current post from a Junto lord; he was still in Dublin with Wharton when Godolphin fell from power. When the Lord Lieutenant left Ireland at the end of August, intending to "wait upon her majestie to give her an account of the affairs of that kingdom,"[62] his secretary sailed with him, aware of the uncertainty of his master's continued employment—and his own. Soon Addison was actively writing for the *Whig Examiner,* a short-lived attempt to answer each number of the Tory *Examiner,* and on 14 September he countered Prior's attack on Garth with a similarly detailed critique of a poem by Prior on the Sphinx.[63] Jonathan Swift, still seeking to persuade the government to extend Queen Anne's Bounty to the Church of Ireland, was also on Wharton's yacht when it left Dublin, and because he wrote daily to "Stella" (his beloved Esther Johnson in Dublin), we have a lively and detailed account of how he experienced this period of sudden political change. On 22 October, Swift told Stella that Steele had "lost his place of *Gazetteer,* three hundred pounds a year, for writing a *Tatler,* some months ago, against Mr. *Harley.*"[64] Although Steele had disguised the attack on Harley as a letter on the theatre signed by Downes and later denied that he had written it, his wit cost him his job, though he retained a government sinecure in the Stamp Office. In the same month, Ormond reclaimed his old position as Lord Lieutenant for Ireland, replacing Wharton, and Addison lost his post as secretary. The demise of Steele's *Tatler,* which issued its last number in January 1711, and the launching of the *Spectator,* which Addison and Steele began to publish in March, were consequences of the political changes that had removed both men from their salaried jobs.

Their old friend Swift, however, embraced the change. Once settled in London, he visited Godolphin, with whom he had previously spoken about relief for the Irish clergy. "My Lord Treasurer," he told Stella, "received me with a great deal of coldness, which has enraged me so, I am almost vowing revenge."[65] Although Swift courteously (or perhaps ironically) gave him his old title, Godolphin was no longer in a position to help and had understandably lost interest in the issue. Swift's "revenge" was a nasty lampoon, *The Virtues of Sid Hamet the Magician's Rod*, appearing in mid-October. Cervantes had assured his readers that the "original author" of *Don Quixote* was a Moor called Sid Hamet Benengeli, which conveniently allowed Swift to give the fallen Treasurer a demeaning version of his first name; Godolphin appears throughout the poem as "Sid." Emphasizing the shame Godolphin experienced when told to break his staff of office, Swift constructs his whole poem as a set of variations on the theme of the rod. In the book of Exodus, the rod of Moses becomes a snake when he lays it on the ground, but Godolphin's rod becomes "an all-devouring Asp" when he picks it up. He can ride it like a witch's broomstick or use it like a diviner's rod to find "Golden Mines"; like the "*Rod* of *Hermes*," the Treasurer's staff can close the eyes of lesser men, including "a *British* Senate"; it can catch fish while preserving the bait, draw a conjuring circle, or blossom into "Golden Boughs, and Golden Fruit." Two more vulgar connections, the rod as a phallus and the rod as an instrument of punishment, lurk everywhere in the poem, finally coming to the fore in the closing lines:

> Dear *Sid*, then why wer't thou so mad
> To break thy *Rod* like naughty Lad?
> You should have kiss'd it in your Distress,
> And then return'd it to *your Mistress*,
> Or made it a *Newmarket* Switch,
> And not a *Rod* for thy own Breech.
> But since old *Sid* has broken this,
> His next may be a *Rod in Piss*.[66]

In the idiom of the streets, a "rod in piss," sometimes more politely called a "rod in pickle," was a punishment not yet exacted, but sure to come. Although this cruel poem celebrates her dismissal of the Treasurer, Swift's picture of the queen as a schoolmistress beating a "naughty Lad" was hardly a gesture of respect. Shortly after this squib was published, its author had the pleasure of hearing Peterborough read it aloud in the presence of Prior, each man suggesting that the other had written it.[67] Flattered by the Tories and grateful to Harley for promising rapid action to extend Queen Anne's Bounty to the Irish clergy, Swift changed his party allegiance; by November he had become the chief writer for the *Examiner*.

§

News of domestic politics, including the landslide victory of the Tories in the elections, held the attention of the reading public during the summer and autumn months of 1710, but there was also news from abroad. In northern France, where Marlborough and Eugene again had large and superior forces, both sides were careful to avoid a repeat of the carnage at Malplaquet, and the campaign was conducted as a series of sieges. After capturing Douai, which surrendered on 15/26 May, the allied generals moved on to Béthune, which surrendered on 18/29 August, followed by St. Venant on 19/30 September. In Spain, General Stanhope won a cavalry engagement at Almenara on 16/27 July, in which he personally slew the rival commander in close combat, then a larger battle at Saragossa on 8/19 August. Cast down by the dismissal of Godolphin, Marlborough took heart when he learned of the second victory. "This news is so good," he wrote to Sarah, that I againe begine to think we may yett have a good peace."[68] Harley was also pleased: "I look upon the country as conquerd once more," he wrote on 16 September, "& if we don't take pains to manage it away it wil bring a Peace."[69] A medal struck to celebrate the victory at Almenara shows Stanhope with sword in hand, cutting down the rival general like the hero of a chivalric epic, and a ballad urging the Electors of Westminster to choose him for Parliament, sung "To the Tune of *Fair Rosamund,*" affects archaic diction in telling his story, especially in an imagined dialogue between the general and Charles III:

> Brave *Stanhope,* (saith the King) I know
>   Thy Valour to be great:
> It's fit thy Empress be obey'd,
>   Go, act what seemeth meet.[70]

John Croker, *Medal commemorating the Battle of Almenara* (1710).

Although many in Britain now felt that the disgrace of Almanza had been avenged, Stanhope's gains proved temporary. Charles III entered Madrid on 17/28 September but discovered that his rival had won the affection of his people, especially in the capital; he abandoned the city on 31 October/11 November. At home, the general's heroism was not sufficient to secure his election to Parliament as a Whig for Westminster, which displayed the same Tory passions as the rest of the country.

Placing particular emphasis on the victories in Spain, the queen issued a proclamation on 28 September declaring 7 November a day of thanksgiving. By the time the service was held, there was news of two more successes: in North America, the expedition prompted by the visit of the "Indian Kings" besieged and captured the Canadian fortress at Port Royal in late September, and on October 29/November 9 a fourth French fortress, Aire, surrendered to Marlborough. Although some had expected her to return to St. Paul's, the queen, still dressed in mourning, attended the thanksgiving service at St. James's, surrounded by her new Tory ministers.[71] The celebration in the royal chapel included another performance of William Croft's settings of the *Te Deum* and the *Jubilate* with instruments, the music that had impressed Sarah when first performed, but the duchess was not in attendance.[72] The text for the new anthem Croft composed expressly for this service responds to the altered political climate, carefully balancing the celebration of victory with the desire for peace.[73] The anthem opens with verses from Psalm 98, a traditional hymn of triumph:

> O Sing unto the Lord a new Song: for he hath done marvellous things.
> With his own right hand, and with his holy arm: hath he gotten himself
> the victory.

A verse from Psalm 118 picks up the theme of the Lord's right hand:

> The right hand of the Lord hath the preeminence; the right hand of the Lord
> bringeth mighty things to pass.

Hearing these verses, many would have thought of General Stanhope's strong right arm at Almenara. Those eager for peace, however, might have responded more warmly to the concluding words of the anthem, verses borrowed from Psalms 28 and 29:

> O save thy people; O give thy blessing unto thine Inheritance, feed them,
> and set them up for ever.

> The Lord shall give strength unto his people: the Lord shall give his people the blessing of peace.[74]

Harley and his associates, now actively exploring ways to achieve "the blessing of peace," evidently believed that an end to the war would "set them up for ever."

George Stanhope, a distant cousin of the victorious general, gave the sermon, in which he compared the current campaign in France to the victories of Henry V, though coyly noting that "our Arms have not yet penetrated so far into the Enemies Country, as at some times heretofore." Turning to Spain, he declined to name his cousin, suggesting that "Another, in my Place, might with more Decency, enlarge his Praise," but he also declared that "the Disasters of Almanza" had been "not only *retrieved,* but amply revenged at Almanira and Saragossa," awarding to General Stanhope the potent verb that Anne's first Parliament had voted to use for Marlborough. The most striking feature of this sermon, however, is the preacher's emphasis on the cost of war and the desirability of peace. "Many Instances in Scripture," he says, "teach us, that men do not only provoke, but prolong, their own Miseries." His prime example is "*a tedious and bloody War,*" inevitably "attended *with miserable Calamities.*"

> The lamentable Effusion of the Blood of our Brethren and Fellow-Subjects, The Numbers of Widows and Orphans, the Discouragement and Decay of Commerce, caused by it, entail Grief and Poverty upon Private Families: And the Publick suffers many ways to a very great Degree.

Aware that such sermons were always published, the new Tory ministry would have especially appreciated Stanhope's concluding prayer for "A Peace, that may be safe, advantageous, and honourable; a Security to Us, our Allies, and our Posterity,"[75] yet the secret negotiations already under way, set in motion by Harley before the dismissal of Godolphin, involved a dishonorable betrayal of the Allies. The Abbé Gaultier, chaplain to Tallard before the war, was now the priest for the private Roman Catholic chapel of the Habsburg embassy in London—and a longtime French spy. Among his congregants was the Catholic wife of Edward Villiers, Earl of Jersey, known to Anne since her childhood and once her Lord Chamberlain. With Harley's blessing, Jersey and Gaultier began to discuss proposals for peace in the summer of 1710, and Gaultier reported the substance of their talks to Torcy in Paris. The parties agreed to pursue a separate peace between England and France, with the English receiving "great commercial advantages in Europe and America" and the Dutch getting far less than had been promised in the Barrier Treaty of 1709. The Duke of Anjou was to retain Spain and its colonial possessions, and Jersey also indicated—with or without the permission of

Harley—that it might be possible to restore James Francis Edward after Anne's death. In one of the most shocking letters surviving from these negotiations, written shortly after Stanhope's victories in Spain, Gaultier informs Torcy that Jersey has told him they will have to wait for the fortunes of war to change in Spain before proceeding with the plan to cede the Spanish Empire to the Bourbons.[76] As Harley took part in the celebration of Stanhope's victories in Anne's chapel, he might still have believed that a strong military position in Spain could "bring a Peace," as he had written in September, but he was also aware that his agent in the secret peace talks was hoping for a different outcome in the next engagement. Jersey got his wish on 28 November/8 December, when a French army sent to Spain won a decisive victory at Brihuega; cut off from his Austrian allies and surrounded by a superior force, Stanhope was taken prisoner, along with many of his troops. As soon as the news reached England, Harley sent Gaultier to France to discuss peace terms with Torcy.

Two days before the disaster in Spain, and a month before the news reached England, the queen made her speech at the opening of Parliament, echoing the themes of the thanksgiving service:

> The carrying on the War in all its Parts, but particularly in *Spain*, with the utmost Vigour, is the likeliest Means, with God's Blessing, to procure a safe and honourable Peace for us, and all our Allies, whose Support, and Interest, I have truly at heart....I am sensibly touched with what my People suffer by this long and expensive War, to which, when it shall please God to put an End, the flourishing Condition of my Subjects shall be as much my Care, as their Safety is at Present.[77]

Harley, now Prime Minister in all but name, presumably wrote this speech. To read the script he coolly provided for the queen while secretly arranging to jettison his allies is to appreciate the accuracy of the *Tatler*'s account of him as a "Machivilian." His tentacles reached far and deep, as shown by an *Examiner* written by Swift and published just before the meeting of Parliament. With a Tory majority of 153—many of them young, zealous, and Jacobitical—this would be the first Parliament in Anne's reign *not* to vote thanks to the Duke of Marlborough, and Swift's essay was designed to justify that snub. "Let us examine," he writes, "how the Services of our General have been rewarded."

> The Lands of *Woodstock*, may, I believe, be reckoned worth 40000*l*. On the building of *Blenheim* Castle 200000*l*. have been already expended, tho' it be not yet near finish'd. The Grant of 5000*l. per An.* on the Post-Office, is richly worth 100000*l*. His Principality in *Germany* may be computed at

30000*l*. Pictures, Jewels, and other Gifts from Foreign Princes, 60000*l*. The Grant at the *Pall-mall*, the Rangership, *&c.* for want of more certain Knowledge, may be called 10000*l*. His own, and his Dutchess's Employments at five Years Value, reckoning only the known and avow'd Sallaries, are very low-rated at 100000*l*. Here is a good deal above half a Million of Money.

From Sarah's point of view, it was quite unfair of Swift to include the principality of Mindelheim and the miscellaneous gifts from other allies in this reckoning; it was also arbitrary of him to multiply by twenty the annual grant made to Marlborough by the queen and to multiply by five the various salaries she and her husband enjoyed. All of this, however, paled in comparison to a truly wicked paragraph on "those who sometimes happen to *pay themselves*":

> A Lady of my Acquaintance, appropriated twenty six Pounds a Year out of her Allowance, for certain uses, which her Woman received, and was to pay to the Lady or her Order, as it was called for. But, after eight Years, it appeared upon the strictest Calculation, that the Woman had paid but four Pound a Year, and sunk two and twenty for her own Pocket; 'tis but supposing instead of twenty six Pound, twenty six thousand, and by that you may judge what the Pretensions of *Modern Merit* are, where it happens to be its own Paymaster.[78]

Swift could have pointed to public sources for the various grants he enumerated in reaching his total of "above half a Million," but he would have needed insider information to know that Sarah had now borrowed about £22,000 from the Privy Purse, which had an annual budget of £26,000. Although everything about the Privy Purse was supposed to be safe from public scrutiny, someone had slipped Swift these numbers, and Harley seems a likely suspect.[79]

Sarah, who had always prided herself on keeping scrupulous accounts, was outraged. "To be printed & cryd about the country for a common cheat, & pickpockit is too much for human nature to bear," she wrote to Dr. Hamilton, proposing to defend herself by printing letters from the queen "acknowledg[ing] my care & frugality in her servise."[80] The duchess had kept most of Anne's letters, while insisting that Anne burn hers, and this was not the first time she had threatened to make some or all of those letters public. In discussing this blackmail attempt with Dr. Hamilton, the queen worried that some of her promises to her favorite, such as her declaration *"That she wish'd never to see heaven, if ever she parted from her,"* would reflect badly on her if printed. Hamilton, trying to maintain his "Integrity both to the Queen and to the Duchess," said he "would endeavour if possible, to obtain [the letters] from the Duchess."[81] He did not succeed. Stung by Swift's making her questionable financial dealings public, Sarah now suggested that Anne's questionable sexual behavior would soon be made public. In a letter to Hamilton, written on 6 December and clearly intended to be read to Anne, she said it was

> certain that the town & country are very full of prints that do Mrs Morley great hurt, because she has given so much ground for such papers, & I hear there is some lately come out which they said were not fit for me to see, by which I guess they are upon a subject that you may remember I complain'd of to you, & really it troubl'd me very much, upon my own account as well as others, because it was very disagreeable, & what I know to be a lye, but something of that disagreeable turn there was in an odious ballad to the tune of fair Rosamond, printed a good while agoe, in which the Queen gives an account of Mr Harleys & Mrs Mashams base designs against all those that had brought them to court, & ridiculed her very justly, but that which I hated was the disrespect to the Queen and the disagreeable expressions of the dark deeds of the night.[82]

By referring to rumors of the queen's lesbian passions as "very disagreeable, & what I know to be a lye," Sarah disassociates herself from those rumors, which she had actually done much to spread, and when she says that she "hated ... the disrespect to the Queen" in the "odious ballad," she is trusting that Hamilton has no knowledge of her own involvement in helping Maynwaring write it and promoting its circulation.[83] The queen's response, as recorded by Hamilton on 8 December, was remarkably mild: "The Duchess wrote free," said the queen, noting that "the Du[chess] of Somerset never told a lie of her."[84] Still, fear of public exposure was certainly one of Anne's reasons for leaving Sarah in possession of her court employments, at least for the time being, even though the former favorite was no longer taking her turn "in waiting."

On 12 December, the duchess came to London to arrange new clothing for the monarch, who was to come out of mourning on Christmas Day. Although the Mistress of the Robes would normally have visited the queen to see how the new clothes fit, Anne refused to meet with Sarah, and because Marlborough House was still under construction, the duchess made arrangements to move into apartments in Montagu House, the London residence of her youngest daughter Mary. By planning to vacate her lodgings in St. James's, she acknowledged that her service to the queen was coming to an end. She also missed the Christmas celebrations at St. James's, where "the Court was extream magnificent. But the wonted Rejoycings of these Holy-Days were much apal'd, by the il News that came in the

Day before from *Spain*."[85] Anne responded to the news of Brihuega by writing a spirited letter to the Emperor in Vienna asking him to send "help from Italy, where you had forces in readiness to support your brother's cause at this most disastrous time." Though written for her in Latin by St. John, this letter bears the marks of the queen's irritation, especially when she tartly reminds the Emperor that he has "hitherto contributed almost nothing to the Spanish War."[86] Her Parliament proceeded to spend much of the winter discussing the entire history of the war in Spain, again investigating the reasons why Galway had not had sufficient troops at Almanza in 1707 and casting aspersions on Stanhope, who was a prisoner of war and unable to defend himself.

A few days after Anne learned of Stanhope's defeat, an exhausted Marlborough returned to England. On 1 December, presumably remembering the struggles of the previous winter, the queen had complained to Dr. Hamilton that the duke had become "illnatur'd" and "could not forbear swearing in her Presence," but now he was "very humble, and submissive," and she was "sorry to see him so broken." Motivated by the belief that he could achieve a complete defeat of the French in one more campaign, the duke bent his efforts toward retaining his command. Anne had "no thought of putting him out,"[87] but she was determined to end her official relationship with his wife. Marlborough made one last attempt to preserve appearances by persuading the duchess to write a letter of apology to the queen, who received it on 17 January but remained insistent on having Sarah resign. On 18 January, the duke personally delivered Sarah's gold key of office to his monarch. Before he returned to his troops in Holland, Dr. Hamilton, impressed with Marlborough's self-control during the difficult weeks he had passed in England, "told him, some gave him as Great, or greater Character, for that Victory over himself under the Provocations, than for all his other victories."[88]

When she closed the books on her service as Keeper of the Privy Purse, Sarah collected an additional £18,000 (£3.6 million in modern money)—a figure reflecting Anne's offer to her of £2,000 per year from the Privy Purse, made in 1702 and not then claimed. Her ability to publish embarrassing letters gave the duchess some leverage over the queen, but Anne may also have agreed to this final settlement as compensation for her unwillingness to keep her old promise to give Sarah's places to her daughters. Following her current preferences rather than her old pledges, Anne made Abigail Masham the Keeper of the Privy Purse, awarding the courtly positions of Groom of the Stole and Mistress of the Robes to the Duchess of Somerset. In a conversation with Dr. Hamilton, she expressed her withering opinions of Sarah's offspring:

> The one [Lady Sunderland] is cunning and dangerous to be in the Familly, the other [Lady Godolphin] Silly and Imprudent, and lost her

Reputation, and Montague was just like her Mother (One would not say this to them). Besides I have put out [Lady Sunderland's] husband and that wont look well to have her have Her Places.[89]

In this unguarded moment, the queen forgot that her sister Mary had been acting on the same principle in 1692 when she insisted that Lady Marlborough, whose husband had been put out of his places, must leave the service of Princess Anne.

§

The new and old Members of Parliament who came up to London for the winter found that there had been yet another shuffle in the management of the theatres. After a pitiful effort to open in October, both theatres closed again in confusion for a month. On 6 November, Lord Chamberlain Shrewsbury issued an edict giving the leading actors permission to present spoken drama at Drury Lane under the supervision of Owen Swiney, who had previously managed the opera company, and putting the opera company at the Haymarket under the supervision of William Collier, who had previously managed Drury Lane. New singers began to arrive, and Collier once again subcontracted day-to-day operations to the irrepressible Aaron Hill. A revival of *L'Idaspe fidele* on 22 November featured the basso Giuseppe Boschi in a role previously sung by a castrato, and on 6 December Boschi's wife, the contralto Francesca Vanini, appeared in a revival of *Pyrrhus and Demetrius,* in which she sang an aria by George Frideric Handel, who was almost certainly in London by this time. Fresh from several years in Italy, Handel had accepted an appointment as Kapellmeister to the Elector of Hanover in July but had immediately taken leave to travel, eventually making his way to England. The Boschis already knew him, having performed in his opera *Agrippina* in Italy, and the soprano Elisabetta Pilotta Schiavonetti, who was also employed by the Hanoverian court, may have come to London with Handel or at his urging; she also appeared in *L'Idaspe.* The energetic Hill had enlarged the stage again, and two new operas were in preparation: *Etearco,* with music by Bononcini, and *Rinaldo,* with music by Handel.[90]

As he made arrangements for the queen's birthday on 6 February, the first proper birthday celebration since Prince George's death and his first as Lord Chamberlain, Shrewsbury was necessarily aware of the excitement surrounding these recent arrivals, especially Handel. Having spent several years in Italy and acquired an Italian wife, the duke was more familiar than most with the quality of opera on offer in Rome and Venice. When the birthday arrived, with everyone splendidly attired, there was a new ode by Tate and Eccles, featuring Richard Elford as usual, but with an English text "*Set after the* Italian *Manner,* [which] *requir'd the* Recitativo-Parts *to be writ in Blank Verse, closing (for the most Part) with a Dissylable, the Rest in* Roundo-Metres, *or* Da-Capo's, *as the* Italians *call them.*"⁹¹ Although Eccles's setting has disappeared, he evidently tried hard to emulate the vogue for Italian music and persuaded Tate to give him a text that he could set in an up-to-date style. The dramatic entertainment, the first presented at the queen's birthday since *Camilla* in 1707, was *The Jew of Venice,* an old play by the Tory politician George Granville, who had become Secretary at War when St. John became Secretary of State. When first produced in 1700, Granville's revision of Shakespeare's *Merchant of Venice* had included a masque with music by Eccles, but on this occasion, the scene in which Bassanio offers an entertainment for his guests provided an opportunity to present "excellent Musick by the famous Mr. *Hendel,* a Retainer to the Court of *Hanover,* in the Quality of Director of his Electoral Highness's Chapple, and sung by Signior *Cavaliero Nicolini Grimaldi,* and the other Celebrated Voices of the *Italian* Opera: With which Her Majesty was extreamly well pleas'd."⁹² We do not know what pieces by Handel were included in this concert, but it is a reasonable guess that the performance included some arias from *Rinaldo,* which was to have its premiere in less than three weeks, on 24 February. For the singers and the composer, the opportunity to give the noble courtiers and their bejeweled wives a preview of coming attractions would have been welcome.

Although the invalid queen had no opportunity to experience the visual splendor of *Rinaldo* on stage, the performance at court allowed her to appreciate the excellence of the singers and of Handel's music, which was better than anything heard in London since the death of her beloved Mr. Purcell. In choosing selections for this important occasion, Handel and his colleagues would have been sure to give Nicolini an opportunity to display his agility, but they might also have hoped the queen would appreciate the beauty of Almirena's aria of resignation and despair, "Lascia, ch'io pianga," a melody that originated, like much of the music in *Rinaldo,* in an earlier work by Handel. In 1705, before he turned twenty, Handel had scored *Almira,* a long and complex libretto in German based on an Italian original. In a scene resembling the pageants of the continents in *Calisto* and *England's Glory,* though considerably more elaborate, characters representing Europe, Africa, and Asia make grand entries in their chariots, each accompanied by his own onstage band; the fact that neither Italy nor Germany had significant trade with the New World presumably accounts for the absence of America. When the prince representing Asia appears, in a chariot drawn by lions, his attendants perform an "Asian dance." Lacking any real knowledge of Asian music, the young composer provided the most "exotic" form he could manage for this entry: a sarabande, a slow and sensuous dance originating in South America, banned in Spain for its alleged obscenity in 1583.⁹³ It was a cleaned-up and domesticated sarabande, though still accompanied by castanets, that little Princess Anne and

her sister had danced with the other ladies in *Calisto* in 1675, and by 1705 sara-
bandes were frequent in instrumental and vocal music all over Europe. Handel's
"Asiatic dance" follows the usual rhythmic pattern but gives early evidence of his
gift for memorable melody.

Mus. Ex. 10.3: George Frideric Handel, "Sarabande——Tanz von Asiatern,"
from *Almira* (1705), Act 3, no. 52.

Between 1705 and 1711, however, Handel had gained experience and sophistication as a composer. In 1707, while in Rome, he reworked this dance as an aria
for an oratorio, and by the time he had revised it once more, as an aria for the
kidnapped Almirena in *Rinaldo*, the result was a work with greatly increased emotional power. Though essentially the same as the early dance, the A section of
"Lascia, ch'io piange" gains much from the expressive qualities of the human voice
and from the richer scoring, but in place of the original B section, with its predictable harmonic motion, Handel has composed something truly striking, with
much more daring harmonies and expressive downward leaps in the vocal part.
Perhaps it was this piece, among others, with which the queen was "extreamly well
pleas'd."

Although the birthday celebrations would have kept her busy all day, the
queen found time at some point to sign a letter to Robert Hunter, the Governor of

🔊 Mus. Ex. 10.4: George Frideric Handel, aria from *Rinaldo* (1711), Act 2, no. 22.

New York, endorsing a project vigorously promoted by Henry St. John. The British vision of the world emphatically did include America, and Anne's letter announces her determination "to attempt the Recovery of Our…Country of Canada and Island of Newfoundland." Encouraged by the capture of Port Royal, those supporting this scheme proposed to increase British holdings in North America by sending a fleet up the St. Lawrence to Quebec, while infantry troops led by Native American guides reached the same goal by land. As Quebec was then a fort defended by a small garrison, the plan seemed plausible, and St. John made it more attractive to Anne by promising to give command of the land forces to Brigadier John Hill, Abigail's overpromoted brother. The letter is brutally clear about the commercial motives for the proposed invasion:

> There being no European nation besides Great Britain and France who have any footing or Settlements in North America, by driving out the French from thence, the several Indian Nations will be under Our Subjection and Our Subjects will enjoy the whole Trade of Furr and Peltry, which they purchase with the Woollen Manufacture of this Kingdom, and with Guns, Powder, Shott, Knives, Scissars, Beads & Toys.[94]

Although they had asked for her aid, being under Anne's "Subjection" was probably not what the "Indian Kings" had been seeking in their visit during the previous spring.

§

Thanks in part to the efforts of Aaron Hill, the premiere of *Rinaldo* on 24 February was a more complete and satisfying theatrical experience than any operatic performance yet staged in London. In his preface to the printed word-book, which gives English and Italian on facing pages, Hill takes credit for the overall shape of the production:

> *The Deficiencies I found, or thought I found, in such Italian* OPERA's *as have hitherto been introduc'd among us, were,* First; *that they had been compos'd for Tastes and Voices, different from those who were to sing and hear them on the* English *Stage; And* Secondly, *That wanting the Machines and Decorations, which bestow so great a Beauty on their Appearance, they have been heard and seen to very considerable Disadvantage.*[95]

By all accounts, the "Machines and Decorations" were spectacular. There were fountains onstage with real water, a flock of live birds, and tricky illusionistic transformations. After the evil enchantress Armida kidnaps Rinaldo's beloved Almirena, the hero sails in a boat to the enchanted palace of Armida, who *"changes her self into the Likeness of* Almirena." When Rinaldo embraces her, she *"reassumes her proper Shape,"*[96] and this instantaneous change of identity, a complex stage illusion, is repeated twice. Some in the London audience might have recognized Armida's transformation as a more elaborate version of a scene in Dryden's semiopera *King Arthur* (1691) where the evil Grimbald appears disguised as the beautiful Emmeline, Arthur's beloved, and is revealed in his true monstrous shape only at the last minute. By drawing his plot from Tasso's *Gerusalemme Liberata,* Hill was using an Italian source, but because chivalric epics from Italy had long been models for the writers of English heroic plays and semioperas, many of the episodes would have seemed familiar. In his essay "Of Heroique Plays" (1672), Dryden had claimed Ariosto as a general source for heroic drama; in his opera *King Arthur* (1691), he had borrowed an entire scene involving an enchanted grove from *Orlando Furioso.* The English version of the libretto for *Rinaldo,* advertised as a translation of the Italian version by Giacomo Rossi but probably written first, contains many verbal echoes of *King Arthur.*[97] Thanks to Hill's attention to English traditions and his efforts to appeal to English theatrical tastes, *Rinaldo,* though sung entirely in Italian, may not have seemed as "foreign" as its predecessors. It also featured the strongest collection of operatic voices yet assembled in London.

Presumably aware that Handel's music had gained Anne's approval at the birthday performance, Hill did all he could to claim the monarch as a patroness, dedicating the bilingual libretto to her in terms that give her credit for supporting all the arts, but especially music:

> Among the numerous Arts and Sciences, which now distinguish the Best of Nations under the Best of Queens; Musick, the most engaging of the Train, appears in Charms we never saw her wear till lately; when the Universal Glory of your Majesty's Illustrious Name drew hither the most celebrated Masters from Every Part of *Europe.*

Anne's reputation as a music-lover may have reached other parts of Europe, but it was the promise of compensation that had brought the "celebrated Masters" to London, and the opera company was again finding it difficult to pay the bills. On 3 March, the date of the third performance, Hill suddenly lost his job. As he later told the story,

> William Collier...under Colour of a pretended Lycence or Order from the said Lord Chamberlaine in a Violent manner entered upon the said House, turn'd out Your Orator's Treasurer and other servants which were Intrusted with the Receiving and distributing the publick money received

from the Audience and put new ones in their places, took possession of all the Cloathes Scenes ffurniture and other Goods And set himselfe up for sole Master and director of the Theatre Royall.[98]

Hill may have thought that Collier's order from the Lord Chamberlain was "pretended," but Shrewsbury was definitely concerned: on 5 March, having learned that many involved in the production had not been paid, he asked Collier to give him a complete account of receipts and disbursals and insisted on authorizing all future payments. Despite these financial and managerial difficulties, *Rinaldo* had fifteen performances in this season; *Etearco,* the other new opera, had only seven.

A week after the opening of *Rinaldo,* Addison and Steele launched the *Spectator,* a daily paper with essays on a wide variety of subjects. The political turmoil that had cost them their government posts had not abated: the "October Club," a group of "young gentlemen of estates that has never been in Parliament before," were telling "every body what they designe, to have every Whig turn'd out."[99] While Harley resisted the wholesale purge these young zealots were calling for, changes continued. On 27 February the Whig Charles Townshend was recalled from his diplomatic position at the Hague and replaced by the Tory Thomas Wentworth, Lord Raby, formerly Anne's ambassador to Berlin. Thanks to the kindness of Jonathan Swift, the post of secretary to Raby's mission went to William Harrison, a Whig poet who had continued the *Tatler* after Steele gave it up.[100] This was not the only case in which Swift took "pains to recommend the whig wits to the favour and mercy of the ministers,"[101] but Addison and Steele, not wishing to depend on such uncertain favors and mercies, began their new journal by insisting on their neutrality, assuming the persona of "Mr. Spectator," an invisible onlooker who listens carefully, speaks seldom, and appears (if silently) in the theatres, the Royal Exchange, and the coffeehouses frequented by politicians, clergymen, lawyers, scholars, and writers. "I live in the World," he claims,

> rather as a Spectator of Mankind, than as one of the Species; by which means I have made my self a Speculative Statesman, Soldier, Merchant and Artizan, without ever medling with any Practical Part in life.... I never espoused any Party with Violence, and am resolved to observe an exact Neutrality between the Whigs and Tories, unless I shall be forc'd to declare my self by the Hostilities of either side.[102]

For the most part, the authors of the *Spectator* held to their resolution of political neutrality, but as early as the fifth issue (6 March) they abandoned any pretence of neutrality about opera. "Its only design," writes Addison, echoing his anonymous prologue of 1707, "is to gratify the Senses, and keep up an indolent Attention in the

Audience."[103] He mocks "*Nicolini* exposed to a Tempest in Robes of Ermin, and sailing in an open Boat upon a Sea of Paste-Board," pokes fun at the live birds and fountains, and ridicules the formal Italian of the librettist's preface. Not even Tasso escapes his scorn, as he "agree[s] with Monsieur *Boileau*, that one Verse in *Virgil*, is worth all the *Clincant* or Tinsel of Tasso."[104] Amused by his graceful raillery, the reader may not immediately notice that "Mr. Spectator" is entirely silent about the music, taking note of Rossi's claim that Handel composed it in a fortnight but saying nothing at all about its quality. Even Addison probably recognized that Handel had gifts beyond anything dreamt of by Thomas Clayton,[105] but if he remained unwilling to praise Handel's music, his opinion of the new composer was not a function of party politics. Handel's employer, the Elector of Hanover, had excellent reasons to be friendlier with the English Whigs than with the Tories, but the composer's English patrons and critics came from all religious and political persuasions. Remarkably enough, Handel's advocates and detractors appear to have judged his music on aesthetic grounds rather than blindly following party allegiance.[106] The contrast with such earlier developments as the rival subscription concerts featuring Margherita de L'Epine for Tory audiences and Catherine Tofts for the Whigs is telling.

Two days after the appearance of this witty *Spectator*, the court was again in its finery to celebrate the ninth anniversary of Queen Anne's accession to the throne, but Harley had more on his mind than the celebration. Since the beginning of the war, various English ministers—including Marlborough, Godolphin, and St. John—had been in contact with a colorful French rogue named Antoine de Guiscard, who had collected money from the English for helping to plan a projected invasion of Normandy and other schemes involving internal revolts by French dissidents.[107] Unable to collect a promised pension, Guiscard had now become a double agent, as Harley discovered by intercepting letters he had sent to the French court. Arrested at three o'clock in the afternoon on 8 March, Guiscard was brought to Whitehall to be interrogated by a group of ministers. When St. John denied his request for a private conference, he suddenly stabbed Harley with a penknife. As it happened, the Prime Minister was wearing formal dress in honor of the anniversary of the accession, including a heavy coat and a brocaded waistcoat; slowed by passing through these garments, the blade of the cheap knife broke when it struck his breastbone, but Guiscard struck a second blow with the broken blade before St. John and Ormond drew their swords and wounded him, after which the guards burst in and subdued Guiscard, beating him soundly in the process.[108] He died in prison some nine days later, and his jailors did a good business exhibiting his body, which they crudely preserved in a barrel full of salt water, and identifying the wounds made by his various assailants; horrified by this tasteless practice, the queen ordered his burial.[109]

This absurd and violent little drama provided opportunities for writers. Delarivier Manley hurried into print with a "true narrative" of the stabbing; an anonymous poet imagined a dialogue in hell between Guiscard and the traitor William Gregg; and Matthew Prior published a poem addressed to Harley, correctly predicting that the attack would increase the Prime Minister's fame and popularity:

> The barb'rous Rage that durst attempt thy Life,
> HARLEY, Great Counsellor, extends thy Fame:
> And the sharp Point of cruel *Guiscard*'s Knife
> In Brass and Marble carves thy Deathless Name.[110]

Five years earlier, in his poem to the queen on Ramillies, Prior had proposed a towering monument "Where sembling Art may carve the fair Effect, / And full Atchievement of Thy great Designs," but the imagery of carving in this later work is wittier and darker. Instead of carving a wound into Harley's flesh that will lead to his death, the Frenchman has unintentionally carved his enemy's name into a "Deathless" monument. The most alarming feature of this whole episode, however, was kept from public knowledge. Guiscard had been urgently seeking a private meeting with Anne herself in the days before his arrest, and though many accounts state that he was denied access, Lord Dartmouth, who was in a position to know, later acknowledged that the queen received Guiscard alone on the night of 7 March, with only one attendant "in the outer room" and another "within call…who was commonly asleep."[111] If his testimony is true, Anne was not only distraught by the attack on her most trusted minister, but mindful of the danger in which she had placed herself, which may explain why she immediately became ill, running a fever and taking quinine for the "ague." She did not recover until 20 March.

When she regained her health, Anne informed her council of the plan to invade Quebec; Harley sent her a message on the day after his stabbing begging her not to pursue this scheme, but because he was unable to protest in person, the preparations went forward.[112] His absence, which lasted from 8 March until 27 April, had other serious consequences. St. John, who had been kept in ignorance of the secret peace negotiations, now grasped the opportunity to take charge of them; although he had come into politics as a protégé of Harley, they were now effectively rivals, struggling for preeminence. In the hotly contested election for Directors of the Bank of England in April, the Whigs defeated a slate of Tory candidates offered by Harley, who was not well enough to lobby for them. If a gossipy correspondent can be believed, the Duchess of Marlborough used the opera house as a venue for demonstrating her support for the Whig candidates:

> Upon the last election of the Governors of the Bank, she appeared herself
> to bribe the electors for the persons chosen, who were most of them
> Whigs to her taste, but not knowing how it would go, the night before,

she was at the opera, and had there a list brought her of the candidates' names; those she disliked were scratched out and others nominated, and carried it by her management. Immediately after this she had an intimation given her that her conduct displeased the Q[ueen], to which she answered she did not care, for that she would print all the letters that had passed between them since the Revolution.[113]

Sacheverell, who spent £500 to become a voting shareholder, was reportedly insulted when he came to cast his vote in what proved to be a losing cause.[114]

The only significant positive initiative in this troubled spring was a plan to erect an architectural monument—one more to Queen Anne's taste than Prior's imagined tower. The population of London had grown rapidly in the previous decade, and there were not nearly enough parish churches to serve the people, a fact that may have increased attendance at Dissenting chapels. The Convocation of Bishops and Clergy called attention to the need for new churches, and Anne pointedly urged her Parliament to begin "the great and necessary Work of Building more Churches within the Bills of Mortality,…which may be so much to the Advantage of the Protestant Religion, and the firmer Establishment of the Church of *England*."[115] This ambitious project did not reach its goal of building fifty new churches, but it did result in important new buildings designed by Nicholas Hawksmoor, James Gibbs, and Thomas Archer. Anne, who famously showed Archer her idea for St. John's Smith Square by turning her footstool upside down, took a keen personal interest in these new buildings. The money for the churches was to come from increasing the tax on coal, which had been levied decades earlier to pay for the reconstruction of St. Paul's Cathedral, now nearly finished. The enthusiasm with which the queen and her Tory Parliament embraced the project, however, probably stemmed from their belief that the Treasury would soon be free of the huge burdens imposed on it by the war. Swift, who never missed an opportunity to cast aspersions on the Marlboroughs, used the occasion of the bill to remind his readers of the cost of Blenheim Palace:

> I have computed, that Fifty Churches may be built by a Medium, at Six Thousand Pound for a Church; which is somewhat *under* the Price of a *Subject's Palace:* Yet perhaps the Care of above Two Hundred Thousand Souls, with the Benefit of their Prayers for the Prosperity of their Queen and Country, may be almost put in the Balance with the Domestick Convenience, or even Magnificence of any *Subject* whatsoever.[116]

Two important deaths in April provided new incentives to make peace. On 3/14 April, the Grand Dauphin, son of Louis XIV and father of Philip, Duke of Anjou, the French claimant to the Spanish throne, succumbed to the smallpox.

Joseph Skelton, *St. John's Smith Square* (1814).

Thanks to the peculiar logic of the French law of succession, this death placed Philip further from the French throne than he had been before, as his older brother Louis, Duke of Burgundy, now became the Grand Dauphin, with the succession passing from him to his own children. Three days later, on 6/17 April, the Emperor Joseph died of the same disease in Vienna; his death meant that his younger brother, whom the Allies had recognized as "Charles III of Spain," would now become Charles VI, the Habsburg Emperor. The fear of seeing France in possession of the Spanish Empire had been a strong initial motive for the war, but if the Allies persisted in the idea that there could be "no peace without Spain," the Holy Roman Empire might now become far too large and powerful for comfort. The news of Joseph's death appeared in London newspapers on 19 April, and on 26 April Anne presented her Cabinet with peace proposals supposedly made by Torcy and ordered a copy sent to Heinsius in Holland. These proposals, presented as originating in France, were in fact Torcy's responses to a set of proposals made by Harley through Jersey and carried to France by Gaultier; it is unlikely that Anne was aware of the subterfuge.

§

Even after the queen revealed them to her Cabinet, the peace negotiations remained secret, but many observers now expected a treaty. Two days after news of the Emperor's death reached London, Addison opened his *Spectator* essay with a reference to the likelihood of peace and the inevitable influx of French fashions that would follow the lifting of the long embargo:

> There is nothing which I more desire than a safe and honourable Peace, tho' at the same time I am very apprehensive of many ill Consequences that may attend it. I do not mean in regard to our Politicks, but to our Manners. What an Inundation of Ribbons and Brocades will break in upon us? What Peals of Laughter and Impertinence shall we be exposed to? For the Prevention of these great Evils, I could heartily wish that there was an Act of Parliament for Prohibiting the Importation of *French* Fopperies.

With their party out of power, Addison and Steele had gained great popularity by eschewing "Politicks" for witty and observant discussions of "Manners," but these two topics could no more be kept apart than could politics and the arts. In humorously proposing "an Act of Parliament for Prohibiting the Importation of *French* Fopperies," Addison echoes the language of the "Act of Parliament prohibiting the Importation of *French* Wines," symbolically repealed in March 1711 by a Parliament anticipating peace.[117] In the next paragraph, he illustrates the dangers of "*French* Fopperies" by remembering a time when Englishwomen employed French servants:

> I remember the time when some of our well-bred Country Women kept their *Valet de Chambre,* because forsooth, a Man was much more handy about them than one of their own Sex. I my self have seem one of these Male *Abigails* tripping about the Room with a Looking-Glass in his hand, and combing his Lady's Hair a whole Morning together. Whether or no there was any Truth in the Story of a Lady's being got with Child by one of these her Hand-maids I cannot tell, but I think at present the whole Race of them is extinct in our own Country.[118]

The time invoked is the reign of Charles II, before the series of wars against the French interrupted commerce between the two countries, and Addison draws a sneering picture of the effeminate French valets who once served English ladies while pruriently suggesting that at least one such valet was capable of getting his mistress with child. Not quite buried in this flurry of satirical wit is the reference to "one of these Male *Abigails*." "Abigail," like "Betty," had long been a generic term for a maid,[119] but Whiggish readers might have seen its use here as glancing at Abigail Masham and drawing the queen's favorite into the general critique of sexual impropriety as a particularly dangerous instance of French foppery. Despite his pledge of neutrality, "Mr. Spectator" could not easily observe the foibles of society without crossing the invisible line into politics.

Attendance at particular operatic performances could also be a political statement, as we learn from a letter sent by Lady Hervey to her husband, the Whig lord ennobled by the queen in 1703 as a favor to Sarah:

> I have been mightily sollicited for the Opera for the benefit of Pilota, who has a great interest made against her because she came from Hanover, and has so many Whigg friends, in which number she reckons me, and has been to see me, so I have taken a ticket and now promist to go, being out of hopes of being better entertained. Yesterday I dind with Lady Dalkeith, and she and Lady Katt: supd with me after the Opera, which was as full as ever I saw it at a subscription, but that was by way of party, in order to get it empty on Saturday.[120]

There was indeed a performance of *L'Idaspe fidele* on Saturday, 28 April, as a benefit for Elisabetta Pilotta Schiavonetti, who sang under her maiden name, and a very well-attended performance of *Rinaldo* on Wednesday, 25 April.[121] If the Tories who were trying to hold down attendance at Pilotta's benefit were truly inimical to her "because she came from Hanover," they could only express their opposition by attending an opera composed by another employee of the Hanoverian court, in which Pilotta herself sang a major role. Although the original project to construct an opera house had been largely a Whig and Kit-Cat venture, some disgruntled Whigs now took pleasure in a puppet show poking fun at the opera. Martin Powell, a puppeteer from Bath, had been presenting shows in Covent Garden for several years, and according to a letter datable to May 1711,

> he has turned his ordinary show into an opera in ridicule of *Hydaspes,* in which Punch most heroically kills a pig and sings *Io Pean* in Italian music, this has affronted Nicolino and he threatens to tread the stage no more. But what will most suprise you is that this folly prevailed so much that it was acted six weeks by subscription at a crown a ticket. Mr. Walpole and Mr. Mackertny were managers, received the tickets at the door, and suffered no Tory to mix with them in this extraordinary pleasure.[122]

"Mr. Walpole" is presumably Robert Walpole, who had lost his position as Treasurer of the Navy Office in January 1711, and "Mr. Mackertny" is probably General George MacCartney, who was forced to sell his regiment after drinking confusion to the Tory ministry in December 1710. Both had excellent reason to promote an amusing event that might allow their defeated party to regroup. But if they were actually trying to keep out the Tories, as this correspondent claims, they failed. Mary Delany, born into the Jacobite Granville family, remembered seeing the same show as a little girl and sitting on the lap of St. John himself.[123]

Despite the continued influence of party politics on the practice of the arts, the period between the death of the Emperor in April and the revelation of the preliminary peace proposals in October witnessed the emergence of some fresh ideas about artistic creation—more abstract and less obviously partisan than some of those circulating earlier. A widely shared hope for an end to the long war, not yet undermined by disagreements about the terms of peace, helped these ideas flourish. The *Spectator*, with its declared policy of neutrality, was instructing a wide and various audience in the development of good taste as a species of good manners. Despite his occasional lapses into partisan humor, Addison could move from the specific to the general with remarkable speed, and if his strictures on contemporary follies sometimes betray his partisan loyalties, his ruminations on culture show his desire to transcend a merely partisan discourse. In another early *Spectator*, he pokes fun at two of his usual targets, the opera and the French, on his way to setting up some larger principles about the function of the arts:

> I remember the last Opera I saw in that merry Nation [France], was the *Rape of Proserpine*, where *Pluto*, to make the more tempting Figure, puts himself in a French *Equipage*, and brings *Ascalaphus* along with him as his *Valet de Chambre*. This is what we call Folly and Impertinency; but what the French look upon as Gay and Polite.
>
> I shall add no more to what I have here offer'd than that Musick, Architecture and Painting, as well as Poetry and Oratory, are to deduce their Laws and Rules from the General Sense and Taste of Mankind, and not from the Principles of those Arts themselves; or in other Words, the Taste is not to conform to the Art, but the Art to the Taste. Musick is not designed to please only Chromatick Ears, but all that are capable of distinguishing harsh from disagreeable Notes. A Man of an ordinary Ear is a Judge whether a Passion is expressed in proper Sounds, and whether the Melody of those Sounds be more or less pleasing.[124]

The satirical criticism of the French tendency to present mythological figures as modern courtiers is amusing and pointed, but this particular example helps Addison develop some much broader thoughts about the relations between creative artists and their audiences. By setting up "the General Sense and Taste of Mankind" and the "Man of an ordinary Ear" as the tests of artistic success, he draws on the same egalitarian beliefs that made his fellow Whigs advocate wider suffrage in the political realm. His fear of an art that follows its own principles runs parallel to his fear of centralized and autocratic power, an evil exemplified, for the Whigs, by France. Yet if this essay, like the later series on the "Pleasures of the Imagination," is feeling its way toward what might broadly be called a Whig aesthetic, it is not a partisan document.

Alexander Pope also took pains to avoid the appearance of partisanship at this time, and for good reasons. As a Roman Catholic, he was under immediate suspicion as a likely Jacobite, and the tuberculosis of the spine that had made him a twisted hunchback left him open to cruel comments about deformed minds in deformed bodies. He was therefore careful to avoid being identified with either party, maintaining good relations with both Addison and Swift. Pope's *Essay on Criticism*, published on 15 May, was the most remarkable literary production of 1711, but in laying down some general principles for criticism in finely crafted couplets, the author, who was only twenty-three, risked offending older men who had been considering these issues long before he was born. Necessarily aware of the power of prejudice, he speaks with precocious wisdom of the difficulty of forming proper judgments:

> 'Tis with our Judgments as our Watches, none
> Go just alike, yet each believes his own.

Like Addison and Steele observing "manners," Pope chooses a safe example, and a current one, as pocket watches were a relatively new and expensive innovation. He was surely aware, however, that party politics could be at least as powerful as defective clockwork in making each of us "believe his own." As he develops the theme of human limitation, he employs a series of metaphors drawn from the world of power and politics:

> Nature to all things fix'd the Limits fit,
> And wisely curb'd proud Man's pretending Wit:
> As on the *Land* while *here* the *Ocean* gains,
> In *other Parts* it leaves wide sandy Plains;
> Thus in the *Soul* while *Memory* prevails,
> The solid Pow'r of *Understanding* fails;
> Where Beams of warm *Imagination* play,
> The *Memory*'s soft Figures melt away.
> One *Science* only will one *Genius* fit;
> So *vast* is Art, so *narrow* Human Wit;
> Not only bounded to *peculiar Arts*,
> But oft in *those*, confin'd to *single Parts*.

> Like Kings we lose the Conquests gain'd before,
> By vain Ambition still to make them more:
> Each might his *sev'ral Province* well command,
> Wou'd all but stoop to what they *understand*.[125]

Pope's main point is that different minds have different strengths: one person may have a well-trained memory but a deficient understanding; another may enjoy a creative imagination without being able to remember useful details; even a genius can only know one branch of knowledge. In describing the limits of our minds, however, the poet uses language familiar to readers of newspapers. When he illustrates the dangers of trying to acquire too much knowledge by comparing restless minds to kings who "lose the Conquests gain'd before, / By vain Ambition still to make them more," he invites his readers to imagine the boundaries disputed in recent European warfare as metaphors for our mental boundaries. When he explains that Nature has "wisely curb'd proud Man's pretending Wit," he allows his readers to remember the recent curbing of the Pretender's attempt to invade Scotland, though many in the Catholic circle of his family still cherished the hope of a Stuart restoration. None of this language, however, is overtly partisan. Pope has not banished politics from his poem. Instead, he has treated politics generically rather than specifically, using political imagery to illustrate the aesthetic, psychological, and moral principles that form his true subject. Although he emphasizes our limited capacity to appreciate art ("So *vast* is Art, so *narrow* Human Wit"), Pope does not embrace Addison's belief that works of art should therefore conform to the taste of ordinary men. His deep respect for tradition, authority, and genius influenced his views on art, as Addison's passion for liberty influenced his, but with the possibility of peace now in sight, there was less reason to put party labels on such aesthetic or philosophical differences. In a gracious later *Spectator,* Addison praised Pope's poem as "a Master-piece in its kind" and wished that its "Author, who is very justly esteemed among the best Judges," had been able to write his poem without specifically criticizing some of his fellow writers.[126]

The third Earl of Shaftesbury, grandson of the fiery Whig leader of the 1680s, published his *Characteristicks* in the summer of 1711, as he was sailing to Italy in a vain attempt to recover his health. The roots of the aesthetic philosophy he develops in this influential work lie in the Whig reverence for Liberty, but it is not a narrowly partisan treatise. Although the Whig minority in Parliament was fearful of the Tory ministry's efforts to secure a peace, Shaftesbury celebrates peace as a necessary condition for artistic production: "'Tis with us at present," he writes, "as with the *Roman* People in those early Days, when they wanted only repose from Arms to apply themselves to the Improvement of Arts and Studys." A part of this improvement will be self-knowledge, urgently needed by writers, but made more difficult by the struggle between Appetite and Reason, here comically presented as the leaders of "Partys":

> For APPETITE, which is the elder Brother to REASON, being the Lad of stronger Growth, is sure, on every contest, to take the advantage of drawing all to his own side....When by a certain powerful Figure of inward Rhetorick, the Mind *apostrophizes* its own FANCYS,...it will soon happen that Two form'd Partys will erect themselves *within*.... Those on the side of the elder Brother APPETITE, are strangely subtile and insinuating. They have always the Faculty to speak by Nods and Winks. By this practice they conceal half their meaning, and like Modern Politicians pass for deeply wise, and adorn themselves with the finest Pretexts and most specious Glosses imaginable; till being confronted with their Fellows of a plainer Language and Expression, they are forc'd to quit their mysterious Manner, and discover themselves mere *Sophisters* and Impostors, who have not the least to do with the Party of REASON and *good Sense.*

There was a long tradition of personifying parts of the mind in conflict, reaching back to the *Pyschomachia* of Prudentius, but Shaftesbury reflects his own time in treating Appetite and Reason not as warriors but as "Modern Politicians" who "speak by Nods and Winks" and "conceal half their meaning"—language that might suggest the devious and secretive Harley. In pamphlet wars and public debates, one side often claimed to represent reason and good sense while accusing the opposition of being motivated by greed or appetite. The Tory offensive against the Duke of Marlborough, for example, developed and maintained by Swift's *Examiners*, contended that he had prolonged the war unreasonably for his own personal gain. While Shaftesbury's allegory of the forces within our minds as politicians gains immediacy and resonance from these connections to contemporary practice, his real topic, like Pope's, is the importance of understanding the internal struggles of our own psychology, a necessity for writers of all kinds:

> But the Case of *Authors*, in particular, being, as we apprehend, the most urgent; we shall apply our Rule in the first place to these Gentlemen, whom it so highly imports to know themselves, and understand the natural *Strength* and *Powers*, as well as the *Weaknesses* of a human Mind. For without this Understanding, the *Historian*'s Judgment will be very defective; the *Politician*'s Views very narrow, and chimerical, and the *Poet*'s Brain, however stock'd with Fiction, will be but poorly furnish'd.[127]

Like Addison, with his faith in the judgment of the ordinary man, Shaftesbury has due respect for "the natural *Strength* and *Powers*" of the mind, but like Pope, he also recognizes its "*Weaknesses*." Whether they present themselves as historians, politicians, or poets, authors will not be able to write effectively if they do not know their own strengths and weaknesses, and the "narrow, and chimerical" views of politicians are a specific instance of what happens when authors lack this self-knowledge.

All three of these writers make gestures linking literature with the other arts. Addison includes "Musick, Architecture and Painting" in the list of arts that must "deduce their Laws and Rules from the General Sense and Taste of Mankind." Pope, in a memorable triplet, uses music to exemplify the aspects of all the arts that cannot be reduced to rules:

> *Musick* resembles *Poetry*, in each
> Are *nameless Graces* which no Methods teach,
> And which a *Master-Hand* alone can reach.[128]

And Shaftesbury, in a passage that would prove influential in the next century, links the arts with Truth:

> For all *Beauty* is TRUTH. *True* Features make the Beauty of a Face; and true Proportions the Beauty of Architecture; as *true* Measures that of Harmony and Musick. In Poetry, which is all Fable, *Truth* still is the Perfection.

There was of course a long tradition of discourse about the "Sister Arts," but what makes these passages especially poignant is their shared desire for a world in which writers might be judged as composers and painters were. Handel had supporters (including Shaftesbury's son) and detractors (including Addison), but he was not the property, or the bugbear, of one political party. Visual artists were also less subject to partisan pressures than writers. The Academy of Painting and Drawing, the first such organization in British history, held its organizing meeting on 18 October 1711, less than a week after explosive revelations in the press sparked a heated debate about the peace process, yet their plans for setting up a "place for drawing, a large room, ground floor, in the great house the middle of great Queen street near Lincolns Inn fields," proceeded without any disturbance from politics. Sir Godfrey Kneller, who was elected president, had painted portraits of all the Kit-Cats and moved in a generally Whig orbit, but the other founding members included the portrait artist Michael Dahl (a Swedish Roman Catholic much employed by the queen), the architect James Gibbs (a Scottish Roman Catholic favored by Tories and Jacobites), the decorative painter James Thornhill (an English gentleman closely associated with Vanbrugh and Halifax), and the theatre manager Owen Swiney; the journalist Richard Steele joined in 1712.[129] Despite its wide range of religious and political allegiances, the Academy flourished.

§

While some writers longed for a less partisan discourse about the arts, others continued to devote their talents to spirited arguments on behalf of one party or another. Swift, who was a born controversialist, published his last *Examiner* on 14 June before handing the paper over to Delarivier Manley. "The main Design I had in writing these Papers," he declared in his penultimate issue, "is fully executed. A great Majority of the Nation is at length thorowly convinced, that the Qu—— proceeded with the highest Wisdom, in changing Her Ministry and Parliament."[130] A week later, he appropriated military imagery in order to congratulate himself on having defeated his enemies:

> When a General has conquer'd an Army, and reduced a Country to Obedience, he often finds it necessary to send out small Bodies, in order to take in petty Castles and Forts, and beat little straggling Parties, which are otherwise, apt to make Head and infest the Neighbourhood: This Case exactly resembles mine; I count the main Body of the *Whigs* entirely subdu'd; at least, 'till they appear with new Reinforcements, I shall reckon them as such; and therefore do now find my self at leisure to *Examine* inferior Abuses.[131]

Not content with abusing Marlborough, which he had done consistently and effectively for the past six months, Swift now playfully claimed the general's identity as a conqueror. Maynwaring, who was physically ill but keeping up a vigorous debate with Swift in a Whig journal called the *Medley,* responded by describing his opponent as a madman in Bedlam:

> Now you have him again, in the beginning of his Paper, fancying himself *a General, who has conquer'd an Army,... and routed the main Body of the Whigs:* That is to say, all who love the Revolution, the Toleration, the Protestant Succession, Liberty, Trade and Mony.... Does not all this put one in mind of some Inhabitants of a certain Place, who are often heard making War alone in their dark Rooms?[132]

This, too, was an act of appropriation, as the "Digression concerning Madness" in Swift's own *Tale of a Tub,* reprinted with additions in 1710, had comically recommended turning madmen into military officers:

Is any Student tearing his Straw in piece-meal, Swearing and Blasphem-
ing, biting his Grate, foaming at the Mouth, and emptying his Pispot in
the Spectator's Faces? Let the Right Worshipful, the *Commissioners of
Inspection,* give him a Regiment of Dragoons, and send him into *Flanders*
among the *Rest.*[133]

Although they clearly enjoyed demeaning their opponents and displaying their
wit, both men were careful to remind their readers of their fundamental ideological positions. Swift remembers to defend the queen's "Wisdom, in changing Her
Ministry and Parliament," and Maynwaring manages to condense Whig principles
into a list of six abstract nouns: "the Revolution, the Toleration, the Protestant
Succession, Liberty, Trade and Mony."

Partisan struggles remained intense, and many of the events of the spring and
summer exemplified Pope's contention that "we lose the Conquests gain'd before, /
By vain Ambition still to make them more." The House of Commons proved quite
refractory in Harley's absence. The zealous young Tories of the October Club
were frustrated by his failure to embrace their objectives, which were very much
in keeping with St. John's later description of their desire for "great employments
to ourselves, and great opportunities of... hurting those who stood in opposition
to us."[134] Left to their own devices, the club would have wished "to punish the
'misdemeanours' of the late ministry, to remove every possible Whig from the
Queen's service,... to resume into public hands the lands granted to private subjects in England by the Crown in the reign of William III,... [and] to push the
claims of its own members to office."[135] Neither Harley nor Anne, however, was
inclined to remove loyal and competent servants of the Crown from their positions for no other reason than their party affiliation, and St. John, whose views
were closer to those of the October Club, had difficulty keeping his colleagues in
check. In March, when he proved unable to prevent them from defeating an important tax on leather, Peter Wentworth remarked that "several Politi[ci]ans that
cou'd not endure Mr. Harley say they see now there's no man the Court imploys
has address enough to manage the House of Commons but him."[136]

A few days before Harley returned to Parliament, his brother Edward, the Auditor of the Exchequer, informed the Commons that Godolphin had left £35 million unaccounted for—a charge soon shown to be false. Harley himself celebrated
his return by unveiling a scheme to deal with the national debt by establishing a
"South Sea Company," which would buy up the debt in return for a monopoly on
commerce between Britain and South America. Those embracing his plan correctly assumed that the coming peace would give Britain exclusive control of the
lucrative slave trade, but alert and concerned parties in Amsterdam recognized
that any such plan would inevitably require "making a partition of the dominions

of Spain" and would probably deny Dutch merchants equal access to the South Sea trade.[137] Both inferences were correct. In seeking to demonstrate that a Tory administration could manage the debt, Harley had inadvertently made it possible for others to trace the outlines of his secret plan for peace. As Steele had suggested in his *Tatler* on theatrical history, the Tories still lacked an adequate supply of ministerial talent: when Anne's proud uncle, the Earl of Rochester, died suddenly on 4 May, forcing another reshuffle of the Cabinet, her old beau Buckingham became President of the Privy Council. Harley was evidently more comfortable with old Tory noblemen than with the young ideologues of the October Club, and Anne was more comfortable with Harley than with any other minister. Later in the same month, she made him Lord Treasurer, and on 29 May, the date of Charles II's birthday and Restoration, she ennobled him as Earl of Oxford. By moving to the House of Lords, however, the new Prime Minister lost the opportunity to control and manage debate in the lower house. Two days after he took his seat in the Lords, the vindictive Commons issued a lengthy, hectoring address to the queen, implicitly criticizing her for her moderation.

> Your Majesty had, from the Beginning of your auspicious Reign, expressed a true Christian Moderation, by Promises of Lenity and Protection to all your peaceable Subjects, and of Countenance and Favour to those, who should most recommend themselves by their Zeal for the established Government in Church and State; but these Ministers framed to themselves wild and unwarrantable Schemes of balancing Parties, and, under a false Pretence of Temper and Moderation, did really encourage Faction.[138]

Although aimed at the defeated Whigs, this language can hardly have pleased Harley, who had a long history of devising "Schemes of balancing Parties," and who now found the zeal of the High Tories as problematic for his ministry as the opposition of the Whig minority.

Anne prorogued her Parliament on 12 June and decamped to Windsor, where she enjoyed at least a month of good health, hunting frequently in her open calash. Duties of state, however, intruded upon her summer. When the Whig Duke of Newcastle, who had been Lord Privy Seal since 1707, died in a hunting accident in July, Harley pressed the queen to give his post to the Earl of Jersey, another former minister whom she distrusted, correctly suspecting him of being a Jacobite. After Jersey wrote a formal letter declaring his support for the Protestant succession, she reluctantly agreed to the appointment, but he died on the very day on which he was to take office. She replaced him with John Robinson, a career diplomat and clergyman who was already Bishop of Bristol and who became her plenipotentiary at Utrecht in January 1712, joining Lord Raby, whom she ennobled as Earl of Strafford in June 1711. St. John's cherished expedition to Quebec, which finally got under way in August, proved a dismal failure, as Hovenden Walker, the naval commander, lost his way in the mouth of the St. Lawrence and wrecked eight transports on the rocks, drowning seven hundred soldiers; hearing the news, the ground troops heading north through the forests turned back, and the remains of the fleet came home with nothing to show for their efforts. Before the embarrassing news of this debacle reached London, there was a victory in France, where the troops defending their homeland had established a long and impressive line of defensive earthworks, which they proudly named the "ne plus ultra." Marlborough's army was smaller than in previous years: St. John had commandeered five of his battalions for the expedition to Quebec, and the new Emperor had sent Prince Eugene and his troops to defend the Rhine against an imagined threat from the Bavarians. Despite these disadvantages, the general saw an opportunity for one last display of strategic skill. Massing his Dutch and English troops as if preparing to give battle, the duke drew the French forces to the west, then outran them in a daring forced march to the east and walked through the "ne plus ultra" without losing a single man. Once past the line of defense, he besieged and took the town of Bouchain, the last significant fortress blocking his path to Paris, and marked this final success by commissioning three new tapestries for the "Famous Victories."

Although he had exposed the "vain Ambition" of the enemy by circumventing their lines, Marlborough's own ambition to march to the capital would never be fulfilled. In July, before these maneuvers began, Anne had secretly sent Matthew Prior to Paris to begin the next stage of negotiations for a peace treaty. Conscious of the importance of noble birth to Continental courts, she had resisted sending Prior abroad as her representative because of his "meane extraction,"[139] but Harley, who appreciated Prior's fluent French, supple mind, and previous experience as a secretary to the Duke of Portland and the Earl of Jersey, persuaded her to make use of him, and Prior held his ground in meetings with the formidable Torcy, who dispatched Nicolas Mesnager, an expert on commerce, to England for further discussions with the Cabinet. An alert customs official, however, spotted Prior when he landed in England in the company of Gaultier and Mesnager; the envoy was detained, and by the time orders had been sent for his release, the news that an Englishman had been in France on a secret mission was spreading. The Duke of Somerset, who was attending Anne in Windsor as her Master of the Horse, had pointedly stayed away from Cabinet meetings since the dissolution of Parliament in the previous year; at a meeting on 12 August, however, he tried to claim his seat, presumably in order to find out more about the rumored peace. Perhaps remembering the pivotal role Somerset had played in defeating the attempted coup of

1708, and certainly unwilling to share the details of the delicate negotiations, Harley and his colleagues broke up the meeting.[140]

With the not-quite-secret talks now continuing in England, mainly at Prior's house in London, the government could not easily make official statements. "The rumour of Mr Prior's journey into France," wrote St. John to Peterborough on 18 September, "and of several other particulars concerning a negociation of peace, has been every where propagated with great industry.... I confess my opinion is, that to take any pains either to deny or to own it, is below the character of the Queen."[141] Three days later, Harley jotted down a note regarding a "new treaty of commerce: As to Assiento the French nor no other nation to be allowed to sell blacks or partake in this."[142] With this and other lucrative "advantages" nearly in their grasp, the ministers needed to do something to deflect the rumor-mongers. Once again, they turned to a professional writer. *A New Journey to Paris,* an account of Prior's mission thinly disguised as the work of a French servant, sold out two editions in a few days. The real author was Swift, and the detailed description of the main character leaves no doubt about his identity:

> Monsieur P— has signalized himself, both as an eminent Poet, and Man of Business; ... He was Secretary to the *English* Ambassy, at the Treaty of *Reswick*; and afterwards, to my Lords the Counts of *P—d* and *J—y*; and, in the Absence of the latter, manag'd, for some time, the Affairs of *England* at our Court by himself.

According to the narrator, supposedly a Frenchman hired to assist "Monsieur P—," the Englishman met with "Monsieur *de la Bastide*," a French agent, for several days in Boulogne, then traveled to Paris, where he had an audience with the king. From scraps of conversation that he overhears, the narrator surmises that Prior has insisted on advantageous terms for a peace. At one point, he listens through "a thin Wainscot" as *De la Bastide* (presumably Torcy) complains to his companion:

> *Good God! Were ever such Demands made to a great Monarch, unless you were at the Gates of his Metropolis? For the Love of God, Monsieur P— relax something, if your Instructions will permit you, else I shall despair of any good Success in our Negotiation? Is it not enough that our King will abandon his Grandson, but he must lend his own Arm to pull him out of the Throne?*[143]

Readers of Swift's alleged "translation" were evidently supposed to believe that Prior had continued to insist on article 37 of the failed preliminaries of 1709, which constrained Louis to force his grandson Philip to abandon the throne of

Spain. By putting out this misleading version of the negotiations, Swift gave Oxford and St. John time to pursue their talks with Mesnager, which were proceeding on the understanding that Philip would remain King of Spain. Although he took great pleasure in the commercial success of this narrative, the author was probably no more aware of the true state of affairs than his readers. Taking advantage of their propagandist's "vain Ambition," the ministers flattered him and dined with him but fed him only a few of their secrets. Had Swift known that they were also discussing the restoration of the Pretender, he would have been appalled.

§

By using a clever poet as his emissary and a gifted prose satirist as his propagandist, Harley achieved his immediate goal: on 27 September, the representatives of France and Great Britain signed the preliminaries of their separate peace. On 13 October, however, the Whig *Daily Courant,* which had received a copy from the imperial diplomat Count Gallas, published the terms for all to see. Instead of promising to remove his grandson from the throne of Spain, the French king now agreed to take "all just and reasonable Measures for hindering that the Crowns of France and Spain may never be united on the head of the same Prince."[144] A firestorm of protest ensued, which the government attempted to stop by arresting booksellers and publishers, and by preventing a pope-burning planned for Queen Elizabeth's birthday, but it was impossible to silence those who generally objected to a separate peace and specifically objected to the abandonment of the pledge that there would be "no peace without Spain." Anne expelled Gallas from her court in retaliation for his embarrassing leak, but he stayed in London and met frequently with Whig opponents of the peace, as did Willem Buys, the Dutch envoy.

When Marlborough returned from Bouchain on 17 November, opponents of the peace rallied around him, and he brought along another formidable figure. Baron von Bothmar, representing the Elector of Hanover, came armed with a "Memorial" from Georg Ludwig expressing strong opposition to the peace proposals. To many, Marlborough was still a hero, and his personal prestige was a factor in the debate about the peace. *He's Wellcome Home,* a broadside cast as "A Dialogue between John and Sarah," speaks for those who still honored the duke; it begins with a couplet borrowing much of its language from an aria in *Rosamond:*

> Wellcome Home, from Wars Alarms,
> Wellcome to my Longing Arms:
> . . . .
> Spight of Lyes, and *Tory Malice,*
> Hither thou art Wellcome always.
> Let ungrateful People Rail,

Falshood never shall prevail.
All good *Men* will do thee right,
Injur'd now by Party Spight;
Tho' thy Service they up braid,
Grumbling at the Sums they've paid:
Odiums ne'er shall blast thy Fame,
Honour still attends thy Name.[145]

Aware of the controversy, Anne had been apprehensive for months about the opening of Parliament, realizing that "something must be said in my Speech of the Peace."[146] With the meeting now imminent, both sides were careful to time their blasts. In *The Conduct of the Allies*, published anonymously on 27 November, Swift made the case for the new treaty. He did his best to assume a calm and reasonable voice, less shrill and vituperative than the persona he had used for the *Examiner*, and his pamphlet reached a wide audience, selling eleven thousand copies in a month. His methods of argument, however, could hardly be called fair. He begins by declaring that there can be only three motives for opposing the peace: personal greed, party advantage, or ignorance:

> *I lay it down for a Maxim, That no reasonable Man, whether* Whig *or* Tory *(since it is necessary to use those foolish Terms) can be of Opinion for continuing the War, upon the Foot it now is unless he be a Gainer by it, or hopes it may occasion some new Turn of Affairs at home, to the Advantage of his Party; or lastly, unless he be very ignorant of the Kingdom's Condition, and by what Means we have been reduced to it.*

By establishing this premise, Swift excuses himself from having to answer the opinions of those who might wish to continue the war for any other reason. In keeping with his title, he complains mightily about the failure of the Allies to contribute their fair share of money and men to the war. Ignoring the huge sacrifices made by the Dutch army and the enormous debt incurred by the States-General, he declares that "they never once furnished their Quota either of Ships or Men." His critique of the Habsburg Empire, which had indeed fallen short of its promises, quickly focuses on the gift of the principality of Mindelheim to Marlborough: "They computed easily, that it would cost them less to make large Presents to one single Person, than to pay an Army." Warming to his task, Swift continues a theme already established in his *Examiners*, accusing Marlborough of having "an unanswerable Love of Wealth, which his best Friends allow to be his predominant Passion," and dismissing the victories of the last ten years as pointless exercises in personal glory and greed:

Getting into the Enemy's Lines, passing Rivers, and taking Towns, may be Actions attended with many glorious Circumstances: But when all this brings no real solid Advantage to us, when it hath no other End than to enlarge the Territories of the *Dutch,* and encrease the Fame and Wealth of our *General,* I conclude, however it comes about, that Things are not as they should be.

Reflecting on the large burden of debt incurred by ten years of war, the Irish parson describes the nation in language derived from the parable of the prodigal son, who "took his journey into a far country, and there wasted his substance with riotous living":[147]

And as we have wasted our Strength and vital Substance in this profuse manner, so we have shamefully misapplied it to Ends at least very different from those for which we undertook the War, and often to effect others which after a Peace we may severely repent.[148]

After ten years of celebrations encouraging the nation to identify itself with King David, triumphing over his foes with the help of the Lord, Swift needed all his rhetorical skill to persuade his countrymen to identify with the prodigal son, who has wasted his inheritance and must now repent.

Hoping that Swift's arguments would be fresh in the minds of the members and the public, the ministry delayed publication of this powerful pamphlet until the day on which the session was to open, but a last-minute decision to prorogue Parliament for one more week gave the Whig opposition an opportunity to fire the last round in its musket. The day after Swift's pamphlet was published, the Elector's "Memorial" was handed to a clerk in St. John's office, and on 5 December, two days before the delayed opening of Parliament, it appeared in the *Daily Courant.* In a stirring conclusion, the Elector declared that the peace proposals were contrary to the will of God:

The Almighty has blessed the Arms of the Queen and of Her Allies, with so many Triumphs over their powerful Enemy; ... and it cannot be his Pleasure that an Enemy so exhausted, and vanquished as he has been on all Occasions, should at last carry his Designs by this War, and get out of it by a Peace Glorious to Him, to the Ruine of the Victorious Allies, and to the Destruction of the Liberty of all Europe.[149]

Hearing that the man most likely to be their next king opposed the proposals gave many pause, including the queen, whose ministers had not told her about Georg

Ludwig's "Memorial," and who first read it when the Duchess of Somerset showed it to her in print. Attempts to cast doubt on the authenticity of the document did little to weaken its force.

In this atmosphere of tension and distrust, the queen opened Parliament with a speech written by her ministers, though possibly modified by the orator herself.[150] "I have called you together," she began,

> As soon as the Public Affairs would permit: And I am glad that I can now tell you, that, notwithstanding the Arts of those who delight in War, both Place and Time are appointed for opening the Treaty of a General Peace.

The friends and supporters of the Duke of Marlborough, who was present, would surely have regarded Anne's reference to "the Arts of those who delight in War" as a rebuke, but when challenged by her Whig physician, the queen described her phrase as "the words of the Common Prayer."[151] She was thinking of these verses from the Psalter:

> For thy temple's sake at Jerusalem: so shall kings bring presents unto thee.
>
> When the company of the spear-men, and multitude of the mighty are scattered abroad among the beasts of the people, so that they humbly bring pieces of silver: and when he hath scattered the people that delight in war.[152]

In the psalm, "the people that delight in war" are clearly the defeated enemy, but there is no reference to their "Arts," a loaded word that still often suggested devious practices. Thanks to that word, the queen's phrase was readily readable as a criticism of those on her own side who still advocated continuing the war—including a general who regarded the well-executed campaign he had just concluded as analogous to a work of art. Before commissioning the "Famous Victories" series, Marlborough had purchased a set of tapestries called *The Art of War*, with generic scenes including *La Marche, La Bataille, La Siege*, and two panels depicting *Pillage*; his old antagonist the Elector of Bavaria had commissioned the original designs, and William III had also owned a set.[153] By questioning "the Arts of those who delight in War," Anne was now suggesting that the arts of all such men were inimical to peace.

This phrase was not the only ambiguous aspect of the royal speech. Though understandably wary, the Dutch had now offered to host the talks at Utrecht, so Anne's declaration that "both Place and Time are appointed" was true. Her next paragraph, however, was manifestly false:

Our Allies (especially *The States General*), whose Interest I look upon as inseparable from My own, have, by their ready Concurrence, expressed their entire Confidence in Me; and I have no Reason to doubt, but that My own Subjects are assured of My particular Care of them.

It was cruel of Oxford to ask Anne to speak these words to a Parliament now fully aware that there was no "ready Concurrence" with the peace plans in Vienna or Hanover. She was probably much more comfortable when reminding the "Lords and Gentlemen" of the benefits of peace:

> I shall endeavour, that, after a War which has cost so much Blood and Treasure, you may find your Interest in Trade and Commerce improved and enlarged by a Peace, with all other Advantages which a tender and affectionate Sovereign can procure for a dutiful and loyal People.... Such a Peace will give new Life to our Foreign Trade, and I shall do My utmost to improve that happy Opportunity to encourage our Home Manufactures; which will tend to the easing of My Subjects in that excessive Charge they now lie under in maintaining the Poor, and to correct and redress such Abuses as may have crept into any Part of the Administration during so long a War.[154]

Bidding for bipartisan support, Anne holds out the hope of improved trade and commerce, a gesture toward Whig interests, while appealing to the Tories by offering to lower taxes and "correct and redress...Abuses," an invitation they would soon take up by investigating the wartime financial practices of the Duke of Marlborough.

In the House of Lords, however, the response to the queen's speech was a disaster for the ministry. The Earl of Nottingham, pointedly left out when the Tories reclaimed the top offices, had made an unlikely alliance with the Whig Junto, and when the usual motion was made "That an humble Address be prepared, to return Her Majesty the humble Thanks of this House, for Her Majesty's most Gracious Speech from the Throne," he rose to offer an amendment asking that the address "represent it to Her Majesty, as the humble Opinion and Advice of this House, That no Peace can be safe or honourable to *Great Britain* or *Europe,* if *Spain* and *The West Indies* are to be allotted to any Branch of the House of *Bourbon*." A similar amendment in the Commons was promptly defeated by a lopsided vote (232 to 106),[155] but in the Lords, after a long debate, "Dismal" and his new Whig allies passed his amendment by a margin of one vote; a procedural attempt to overturn the decision went down to defeat on the next day. Anne's response to this unwelcome address was laconic. "My Lords," she wrote, "I take the Thanks you give Me kindly." Her specific response to Nottingham's amendment employs three consecutive subjunctive verbs—*should, could,* and *would*: "I should be sorry any one could think I would not do My utmost, to recover *Spain* and *The West-Indies* from the House of *Bourbon*."[156] One possible reading of this evasive sentence, which looks like the work of Oxford, is that the queen and her ministers had now decided that Spain would probably stay in the hands of the Duke of Anjou, but did not yet want to take responsibility for that decision.

Nottingham had driven a hard bargain for serving the cause of his former enemies, and on 15 December, the bill came due when he offered "An Act for preserving the Protestant Religion, by better securing the Church of *England* as by Law established," which was a somewhat toned-down version of the bills against Occasional Conformity that had proved so divisive early in Anne's reign. Seconded by the notoriously irreligious Wharton, this measure promptly passed both houses, causing more discomfort for Oxford, who had been reared in a Dissenting household. A controversy about the Scottish peers was also divisive: Anne had given her kinsman James Hamilton, already fourth Duke of Hamilton in Scotland, an additional title as Duke of Brandon in England, but when he proposed to take his seat among the English peers, they voted that "no Patent of Honour, granted to any Peer of *Great Britain,* who was a Peer of *Scotland* at the Time of the Union, can entitle such Peer to sit and vote in Parliament,"[157] a ruling not likely to preserve positive feelings about the Union. The Commons then proceeded with its investigation of Marlborough and Robert Walpole. Like previous generals, Marlborough had received a 2.5 percent rebate on the wages of foreign soldiers under his command, which he had used to fund the "secret service," his extensive and effective intelligence network, but because there was no systematic accounting for these funds, his enemies, urged on by Swift, could easily claim that much of the money had gone into his own pockets. He had also received a rebate on the contracts for providing his troops with bread, another practice common at the time, giving his enemies an additional opening. Walpole's practices with respect to "Forage Contracts" also attracted scrutiny, and the commissioners appointed to look into all these matters made a full and pointed report on 21 December, which the Commons agreed to take up again after the Christmas recess.[158] The adjournment of both Houses on 22 December gave the ministry some badly needed breathing space, though not enough; the Commons planned to reconvene on 14 January, but the Lords, where the foes of the ministry were hoping to push their own agenda, voted to reconvene on 2 January.

§

During the recess, Oxford persuaded the queen to dismiss Marlborough from all his positions, ending a friendship that dated back to her teens. The ostensible reason was that he should not continue as Captain-General while under investiga-tion by the Commons, but the real reason was his opposition to the peace treaty that the ministry was determined to complete. As she had done in the case of Godolphin, Anne delivered the news in writing, but her letter to the duke does not survive, as he threw it angrily into the fire, though he was sufficiently master of himself to write a dignified response.[159] Characteristically, Marlborough also chose to express his response to being dismissed in a visual medium. Early in 1712, he asked Kneller to paint his portrait, and the sympathetic artist produced a somber, standing image of the cashiered general, erect in his armor, with a seated figure of Britannia weeping in the background and a "drooping" eagle overhead (color plate 18). According to James Brydges, Duke of Chandos, who later owned this painting, these figures were creations of "sr Godfrey Kneller's Fancy," but it is also possible that Marlborough, who had given Kneller instructions about at least one earlier allegorical painting, had a hand in suggesting the picture's content.[160]

Among the scores of broadsides and pamphlets prompted by the fall of Marl-borough was a one-page squib purporting to be a letter from Louis XIV to the Arch-bishop of Paris commanding that a *Te Deum* be sung in Notre Dame to celebrate "the surrender and demolishing of the strong important Fortress of *Marl—gh*,"

> hitherto thought impregnable, being so well fortify'd both by Nature and Art, and which, for ten Years together, has baffled our utmost Efforts. And since immense Sums profer'd could never corrupt the Honesty, nu-merous Armies terrify the Bravery, the Conduct of our most experienc'd Generals never surprize the Vigilance of the Governor; therefore we have been forc'd to pursue *other Measures*, and at length have the Comfort of seeing the Disappointment of such as *delight in War*. . . . We must with all Justice acknowledge this great Success to be owing, next under God, to our Trusty and Well-beloved Councellors the President *d'Harlay*, Marshal *d'Harcourt*, and Count *d'St. Johns*.[161]

By treating Marlborough as a fortress, a move oddly reminiscent of the way the Indian kings had complimented their landlord, the anonymous author gains some rhetorical space in which to praise the fallen general for his honesty, which was currently being impugned in the House of Commons; by having the French king thank the Tory ministers, whose names he lists in pseudo-French forms, he im-plies that they are traitors. His italics call attention to his appropriation of "such as *delight in War*," the controversial phrase from the queen's speech, thus laying some of the blame on her as well.

There were also publications by Marlborough's exultant foes, including a novella called *The perquisite-Monger: or the rise and fall of ingratitude. Being one of the stories,*

*which the monks of Godstow were formerly wont to divert fair Rosamond with…Made
Publick from an Original Manuscript lately found in the Ruines of Woodstock-Bower.*
Like the Whig author of the ballad welcoming Marlborough home, the Tory
author of this story evidently remembered Addison's opera; the prose style and
the episodes featured suggest the pen of Delarivier Manley. In this transparent fiction, ostensibly set in Persia, "Artemidorus," the Marlborough figure, amasses a
great fortune by corruption, and when finally called to account has "nothing to
have recourse to by way of Defence, but his old way of calling Bribes Perquisites."
"Annastasia," the queen, has

> a Soul too susceptible of Tenderness not to try to save the life of a
> Person that had for many Years been highly regarded by her, and there-
> fore remov'd him from all his Places, to make him the less Obnoxious
> to Displeasure and Envy. But the Cries of the Oppressed were so loud,
> and the Exchequer so low, that she was forc'd unwillingly at last to give
> him up to their Resentment, who…dragg'd him to a Stately Edifice
> which had been built in Memory of a Victory obtain'd by him, (which
> if prosecuted might have ended the War at once) and from thence tum-
> bled him down Headlong, as a Warning for all such as abuse the Favours
> of Princes.

The bloodthirsty fantasy of Marlborough thrown from the roof of Blenheim
Palace enacts the resentment some now felt toward him, though the author is accurate in taking note of the "Tenderness" of the queen, who had recently described
herself as "a tender and affectionate Sovereign" toward all her people. The picture
of a helpless ruler, "forc'd unwillingly at last to give him up to their Resentment,"
again suggests the story of Pilate.

In the midst of all this noisy controversy, Addison published a series of three
thoughtful *Spectators* on the "Desire of Fame." Although he based these papers on
an essay he had drafted much earlier,[162] publishing them now was a way of offering
a philosophical response to the spectacle being enacted in the public arena. Holding to his pledge of neutrality and mentioning no names, Addison invited his readers to ponder ambition, greatness, and the perils of celebrity; if some readers
thought of Marlborough as a current example, they were free to do so, though by
no means constrained. The first essay begins by conceding that "Desire of Fame"
motivates many human accomplishments:

> It was necessary for the World, that Arts should be invented and im-
> proved, Books written and transmitted to Posterity, Nations conquered
> and civilized: Now since the proper and genuine Motives to these and

the like great Actions, would only influence vertuous Minds; there would be but small Improvements in the World, were there not some common Principle of Action working equally with all Men. And such a Principle is Ambition or a Desire of Fame.

The first sentence recalls the Virgilian passage Addison had used in his *Letter from Italy* a decade earlier, in which the Latin poet presents conquest and administration as Roman "arts"; the order in which Addison lists these "great Actions," with the invention of the arts and the writing of books mentioned before the conquering and civilizing of nations, reflects his own priorities. Only a virtuous few would undertake any of these tasks for "proper and genuine Motives," so a benign deity has provided ambition as a goad to "all Men." Yet despite its usefulness in spurring us on to write, invent, and conquer, ambition is fraught with danger:

> Desire of Fame naturally betrays the Ambitious Man into such Indecencies as are a lessening to his Reputation. . . . For tho' his Actions are never so Glorious, they lose their Lustre when they are drawn at large, and set to show by his own Hand; and as the World is more apt to find fault than to commend, the Boast will probably be censured when the great Action that occasioned it is forgotten.[163]

In late December 1711, some readers were likely to apply this general description of "the Ambitious Man" to Marlborough, who had pushed hard to be made Captain-General for life, a request that Anne and others thought "Indecent," and had ordered his "Famous Victories" "drawn at large" in the series of Flemish tapestries. Although he had been submissive to the queen and civil to her Tory ministers before embarking on the campaign of 1711, the duke had successfully insisted on continued government payments toward the construction of Blenheim Palace. His pride in his accomplishments, like that of any person with an "extraordinary Reputation," was thus bound to draw "a Multitude of Eyes upon him," including some who would be "pleased when they have taken him in the worst and most disadvantageous Light."

> There are many who find a Pleasure in contradicting the common Reports of Fame, and in spreading abroad the Weaknesses of an exalted Character. They publish their ill-natured Discoveries with a secret Pride, and applaud themselves for the Singularity of their Judgment which has searched deeper than others, detected what the rest of the World have over-looked, and found a Flaw in what the Generality of Mankind admires.

Such writers, continues Addison, will find readers eager to learn about the flaws of the famous:

> A Satyr or a Libel on one of the common Stamp, never meets with that Reception and Approbation among its Readers, as what is aimed at a Person whose Merit places him upon an Eminence, and gives him a more conspicuous Figure among Men.[164]

Satirists, however, could also be ambitious, and Swift, who had been one of Marlborough's most tenacious critics, could not enjoy victory without crowing. Concerned that the Duchess of Somerset, now Groom of the Stole to the queen, might plant Whiggish ideas in the mind of the sovereign, he wrote "The Windsor Prophecy," which he claimed to have translated from a moldy parchment found by a gravedigger. In this piece, which appeared in print on 24 December, Swift revived an old slander alleging that the duchess had been complicit in the murder of Thomas Thynne, to whom she was married in her teens. Referring to her as "Carrots" because of her red hair, he advised the queen to dismiss her and stay close to Abigail Masham:

> Root out these *Carrots*, O Thou, whose *Name*
> Is backwards and forwards always the same; [Anna]
> And keep close to Thee always that *Name*,
> Which backwards and forwards is allmost the same. [Masham]
> And *Englond* wouldst thou be happy still,
> Bury those *Carrots* under a *Hill.*[165]

Although Mrs. Masham herself warned Swift not to publish it, the "Windsor Prophecy" was printed and widely read; its publication proved offensive to the queen, who later refused to offer Swift preferment in the Church of England.[166] Swift's ambition to have his wit appreciated thus ruined his ambition to become an English dean or bishop. His fate exemplifies the moralistic conclusion of Addison's third essay, which warns against seeking praise in the human sphere:

> From what has been already observed, I think we may make a natural Conclusion, that it is the greatest Folly to seek the Praise or Approbation of any Being, besides the Supream, and that for these two Reasons, because no other Being can make a right Judgment of us, and esteem us according to our Merits; and because we can procure no considerable Benefit or Advantage from the Esteem and Approbation of any other

Being.... And as the Supreme Being is the only proper Judge of our Perfections, so is he the only fit Rewarder of them.[167]

Published on Christmas Day, this pious advice to the ambitious was theolog-
ically sound, but it is hard to imagine that the thought of a future reward in heaven
was much consolation to Marlborough, especially when he learned that the queen
was creating twelve new peers in order to give the peace party a working majority
in the House of Lords. Named on 31 December 1711, the new Lords included
Samuel Masham, who was a replacement for a nominee who declined the honor.
They were all in attendance when the House of Lords reconvened on 2 January
1712, and immediately showed their power by voting for an adjournment until
14 January. The New Year's celebration at court, recorded in a private letter,[168]
escaped the notice of the newswriters, who were understandably focused on the
dismissal of Marlborough, the creation of the new peers, and the impending visit
of Prince Eugene, who was coming to London in an attempt to persuade the
queen and the ministry of the continuing need for military action. Although the
ministry did all it could to discourage and obstruct Eugene's planned visit, he arrived on 5 January and dutifully called on the queen the next day. His presence
placed Anne in a difficult position: she always wished to welcome foreigners of
royal birth in a way that would show the sophistication of her court to maximum
advantage, but she knew that Eugene would gravitate toward the Marlboroughs,
who were now living within sight of St. James's Palace. On 9 January, the two
famous soldiers went together to the opera house. Handel had returned to Hanover, and the company's latest show was *Antioco,* a pasticcio with music by
Francesco Gasparini, in which Nicolini sang one-third of the arias; those curious
to catch sight of the prince swelled the house, and the management alertly decided to give more performances during the period of his visit. Eugene heard
Nicolini again the next evening, when the star castrato sang at a supper given by
the Duchess of Shrewsbury.[169] His days and nights were filled with social events;
Boyer lists twenty-two nobles who "vied with one another, who should best regale
and entertain his highness." Although he was frequently at Marlborough House,
the prince also made a point of cultivating the Tory Duke of Ormond, Marlborough's successor as Captain-General. When Eugene's nephew, a young man of
twenty who was part of his entourage, died from the smallpox, Ormond kindly
made a place available in the Butler family vault at Westminster Abbey.[170]

Despite his charm and his willingness to court both parties, Eugene could not
persuade the government to fall in with his proposals for an aggressive campaign.
On 17 January, Anne dismissed the old Duke of Somerset, the last Whig in her cabinet, and late that night a vindictive Tory majority sent Robert Walpole, the most
effective advocate for the Whigs in the House of Commons, to the Tower for "high

Breach of Trust." The queen was happy to accept the resignations of all three of Marlborough's daughters, who gave up their positions as Ladies of the Bedchamber, but she was greatly relieved when Somerset allowed his wife to remain in her service as Groom of the Stole. The duchess's sympathetic company and perfect manners were far more important to Anne than the party loyalties of her husband. With her family removed from court and her party balked by the new peers, the Duchess of Marlborough created a stir by floating the idea of having a ball at Marlborough House on 6 February, which was Anne's birthday, but the duke, unwilling to be accused of setting up a court in opposition to the queen's, put a stop to that plan. On her birthday, Anne enjoyed another special performance by the stars of the opera company, led by Nicolini, and presented Prince Eugene with a sword whose golden hilt was encrusted with jewels. This ornate and expensive gift, said to be worth £400, was an appropriate expression of the queen's attitude toward the Savoyard soldier. By giving him a weapon, she honored his courage, his many successes in battle, and his service to the allied cause; but because this particular sword was actually a work of art, better suited for a drawing room than for the battlefield, she was also signaling her desire for peace. A poem celebrating the prince's visit explained the double message the queen was sending through her gift:

> Behold the Sword, which *ANNE* a Present made;
> The Hilt's to grace a Peace, a War the Blade!
> When thro' the habitable Orb did live
> One Greater to receive, or One so Great to give?[171]

The poet, who compliments the Duke of Marlborough as well as the prince and the queen, may have underestimated Anne's determination to end the war.

Peace remained elusive. When the official negotiations opened at Utrecht, the French surprised everyone by proposing to award the Spanish Netherlands to their ally the Elector of Bavaria and demanding the restoration of most of the fortresses captured by Marlborough during the past ten years. Faced with these preposterous terms, Oxford and St. John instructed Strafford and Bishop Robinson to stall for time while they pursued their secret communications with Torcy. An even greater difficulty arose when Louis, Duke of Burgundy, who had been the Grand Dauphin for less than a year, died during an epidemic of the measles, which also claimed his wife and his eldest son. The surviving son, who was also infected, was only two years old. With the succession imperiled, Louis XIV's solemn assurances that he would prevent the union of the crowns of France and Spain began to look shaky, as Philip, Duke of Anjou, who was already ruling Spain as "Felipe V," would be the successor to the French crown if the child died. Saved by a

Mus. Ex. 10.5: Francesco Gasparini, aria from *Ambleto* (1712).

governess who refused to let the doctors bleed him, the little boy lived to become Louis XV, but no responsible diplomat could have depended on that outcome in 1712. St. John expressed the concern of the ministry in a letter written on 4 March to the queen's plenipotentiaries: "The deaths of the father and eldest son, which only leave a child of two years old between Philip and the crown of France, make it absolutely necessary to have this matter settled without loss of time."[172] In letters to Torcy, Anne's ministers immediately proposed two schemes for adjusting the peace terms to reflect these new uncertainties: either Philip should renounce any claim to the French throne, or he should hand over Spain and its empire to Victor Amadeus, Duke of Savoy, an outcome that would have allowed Oxford to silence those who had accurately accused him of betraying the principle calling for "no peace without Spain."[173] As these private negotiations proceeded, the House of Commons launched a public attack on the Barrier Treaty of 1709, accusing Townshend of having exceeded his instructions when he negotiated it and thus confirming Dutch fears that it would not be honored.

Eugene prolonged his visit until after the celebration of the anniversary of Anne's accession to the throne (8 March), which he also attended. He would thus have been able to hear another new opera, *Ambleto,* which had its premiere on 27 February. The librettist, Apostolo Zeno, retold the story of Hamlet, which he took from the Danish historian Saxo Grammaticus rather than Shakespeare; half of the music in the London production was by Gasparini, the original composer, though the use of arias by other composers, including Handel, made it a kind of pasticcio. Nicolini sang Hamlet, and Margherita de L'Epine took the male role of "Valdemar, General of the King's Army." Premiered in Italy in 1705, *Ambleto* could not possibly have been intended as a commentary on the British politics of 1712, yet one of Valdemar's arias, with a text ostensibly celebrating peace but set to highly martial music, is emblematic of the prevailing confusion about war and peace.[174] The florid melismatic passages setting the word *pace* would make much more sense for *guerra,* but opera-lovers, who came to hear such passages brilliantly executed by the star singers, probably did not care.

§

In the artificial world of *opera seria*, in which a woman could play a general and a castrato could sometimes play a woman, peace and war were as interchangeable as genders. In the real world, however, the issue of whether to pursue war, peace, or both was urgent. On 9 April, Ormond set sail for the Hague; the British troops under his command and the Dutch and German forces under Eugene significantly outnumbered the French, and Marlborough had left them in a position to move further into French territory. There is every reason to believe that Ormond expected to wage a serious campaign; a broadside toast to the queen and her new commander urged him on while belittling Marlborough and the Dutch:

> Oh! May he still Faithful, still Generous and True,
> His Mistresses En'mies and *Britain*'s subdue.
> May he always press forward in search of a Peace,
> (For a Town in a Year will not make the War cease)
> And instead of a Siege for the *Hollander*s Profit,
> (For they only make their Advantages of it)
> To the Gates of fam'd *Paris* the following Campaign,
> Advance and demand the Delivery of Spain;
> To shew *France* how soon he can finish the Strife
> The ne'er could be ended by a *General for Life*.[175]

Oxford and St. John, however, were hoping to work out a peace agreement before expending more blood and money and were particularly anxious to *prevent* further allied advances into France, lest a decisive victory allow the Dutch to claim their share of the commercial advantages the British were to receive in the agreements now pending. On 9 May, they learned that the French king had asked his grandson Philip to make a choice between the two expedients they had offered: he must either renounce his claim to France or hand over Spain to the Duke of Savoy. In light of this knowledge, which showed that Louis was determined to make peace, they sought Anne's permission to issue commands to Ormond enjoining him to "avoid engaging in any siege, or hazarding a battle." In the letter informing Ormond of this "positive command," St. John claimed that "the Queen cannot think with patience of sacrificing men, when there is a fair prospect of attaining her purpose another way; and besides, she will not suffer herself to be exposed to the reproach of having retarded, by the events of the campaign, a negociation which might otherwise have been as good as concluded in a few days."[176] In their later attempts to defend themselves, both Oxford and St. John would claim that this notorious "restraining order" was the queen's own idea, which seems unlikely. It was probably true, however, that she could no longer "think with patience of sacrificing men."

On 17 May, expecting to conclude a separate peace as soon as Philip chose his crown, St. John wrote to Thomas Harley, Oxford's cousin, informing him that "her Majesty is fully determined to let all negociations sleep in Holland."

> The rule prescribed to my Lord Privy Seal for his conduct, till farther orders, is, that he absolutely decline treating with the Ministers of the States, either on the subject of the amendments to the barrier-treaty, or of the general plan of peace, or on any other subject whatsoever.[177]

Although they believed peace was imminent, Oxford and St. John can hardly have imagined that their orders tying the hands of both their commanding general and their chief negotiators would long remain secret. It was immediately obvious to Eugene that Ormond was avoiding discussions of attacking the French, and on 28 May, Halifax, who had learned of these delays, asked the House of Lords "To address Her Majesty, That She would be pleased to send Orders to Her General, to act, in Concert with Her Allies, offensively against *France*, in order to obtain a safe and honourable Peace." Marlborough, Godolphin, and Nottingham were present to support this motion and disappointed when the House rejected it by a margin of sixty-eight to forty, a vote reflecting a growing acceptance of the inevitability and desirability of peace. The debate was a bitter one. Oxford lied to his colleagues, alleging that no separate peace was "ever intended" and that such a peace—which he had been actively seeking for two years—would be "base, knavish and villainous." He also claimed that Ormond had been given permission to engage in a siege, which was not true. When Marlborough rose to contest the idea that one could begin a siege without being prepared for a battle, John, Earl of Poulett, a close associate of

Oxford, accused him of placing his officers in danger "in order to fill his pockets by disposing of their commissions"—a slander to which the duke responded by challenging the younger man to a duel. After Poulett's terrified wife sent several urgent letters to Dartmouth, the queen told Marlborough to desist.[178]

On 6 June, Anne herself came before her Parliament to outline the terms of peace. Philip had surprised his grandfather and the English ministers by choosing to stay in Spain and agreeing to renounce any future claim to the throne of France; his making that choice prompted the queen to make a public statement. She began her address by reminding the "Lords and Gentlemen" that "the making Peace and War is the undoubted Prerogative of the Crown" and that there had been many "Obstructions, artfully contrived, to hinder this great and good Work." Once again, the ambiguous language did not specify whether the artful contrivers of obstacles were foreign or domestic. She then proceeded to the main points. France was to acknowledge "the Protestant Succession, as by Law established, in the House of *Hanover*, in the strongest Terms," including the removal of the Pretender from its dominions. The crowns of France and Spain would remain separate:

> *France*, at last, is brought to offer, that the Duke of *Anjou* shall, for himself
> and his Descendants, renounce for ever all Claim to the Crown of *France*;
> and . . . the Succession to the Crown of *France* is to be declared, after the
> Death of the present Dauphin and his Sons, to be in the Duke of *Berry*
> and his Sons, in the Duke of *Orleans* and his Sons, and so on to the rest of
> the House of *Bourbon*.

Describing the "Treaty of Commerce" as still in progress, she was able to announce that Britain would acquire undisputed possession of St. Christopher, Newfoundland, Nova Scotia, Gibraltar, Port Mahon, and Minorca, significantly improving access to trade in the Mediterranean and the New World; the harbor at Dunkirk, long a safe haven for French privateers, was to be demolished. In addition to gaining full access to "the Trade to *Spain* and to *The West Indies*," Britain would have a monopoly on the slave trade:

> The Part which we have borne in the Prosecution of this War entitling us
> to some Distinction in the Terms of Peace, I have insisted, and obtained,
> that the Assiento, or Contract for furnishing *The Spanish West Indies* with
> Negroes, shall be made with us, for the Term of Thirty Years, in the same
> Manner as it has been enjoyed by the *French* for Ten Years past.

Anne also provided some details of future borders and barriers but acknowledged that she had not yet settled the demands of her allies:

I have not taken upon Me to determine the Interest of Our Confederates: These must be adjusted in the Congress at *Utrecht*, where My best Endeavours shall be employed, as they have hitherto constantly been, to procure to every One of them, all just and reasonable Satisfaction.[179]

There are some slippery expressions in this speech, which was presumably the work of Oxford. The claim that France had been "brought to offer" Philip's renunciation was false, as the proposal that he choose between the crown of Spain and the possibility of succeeding to the crown of France had come from the British side. The notion that Anne had "constantly" employed her "best Endeavours" at Utrecht was obviously fraudulent. Parliamentary opinion, however, had moved strongly toward peace, and both Houses adjourned on 21 June without further fireworks.

In the public arena, however, the debate about the peace continued. Each of the events of the past year—Prior's secret mission to France, the leaking of the preliminaries, Nottingham's unlikely alliance with the Whigs, the dismissal of Marlborough, the accusations of profiteering leveled at Marlborough and Walpole, Eugene's extended visit, and the embarrassing "restraining order"—had called forth pamphlets, poems, ballads, prophecies, and sermons. By one reliable count, there were 748 political pamphlets published in 1712,[180] not counting the many newspapers devoting all or most of their space to political matters. Among measures passed by this Parliament was the Stamp Act, taxing newspapers and separately printed pamphlets, presented as a way to raise revenue but probably also aimed at critics of the ministry. It went into effect on 1 August, and by one careful count, newspaper circulation in the following year dropped from fifty thousand to thirty thousand, with many periodicals changing their publication schedules or formats, and some going out of business.[181] Even the popular *Spectator,* which was forced to double its price in order to pay the tax, ceased publication in December 1712. It is therefore worth noticing that during this spring, well before the imposition of the tax, some writers voluntarily turned away from the public fray. Ambrose Philips translated Racine's *Andromaque* as *The Distrest Mother* and saw it produced to considerable acclaim in March; the story of Andromache, widow of Hector, struggling to protect her son was a reminder of the human cost of all wars but offered no immediate parallel to the current war. Although he made a small partisan gesture by dedicating his tragedy to Marlborough's youngest daughter, Philips did not hesitate to describe the French dramatist as "a very great Master, whose Writings are deservedly admired in all Parts of *Europe.*" In his preface, he makes a distinction between "two Manners of Style; the one simple, natural and easie; the other swelling, forced, and unnatural." "The true Sublime," he continues, "does not lie in strained Metaphors and the Pomp of

Words; but rises out of noble Sentiments and strong Images of Nature."[182] Although the context is theatrical, the political screeds of the past few months had afforded many examples of swelling and straining, and by choosing to tell Andromache's story in "simple, natural and easie" language, Philips was trying to rise above the discourse of Grub Street.

Alexander Pope published his first, short version of *The Rape of the Lock* in a poetical miscellany issued in May by the bookseller Bernard Lintot. Although this two-canto version is much less elaborate than the revised five-canto poem of 1714, its mockery of heroism is effective, as in these lines depicting a comic battle between well-dressed lords and ladies:

> To arms, to arms! the bold *Thalestris* cries,
> And swift as Lightning to the Combate flies.
> All side in Parties, and begin th' Attack;
> Fans clap, Silks russle, and tough Whalebones crack;
> Heroes and Heroins Shouts confus'dly rise,
> And base, and treble Voices strike the Skies.
> No common Weapons in their Hands are found,
> Like Gods they fight, nor dread a mortal Wound.[183]

Like politicians, the characters "side in Parties"; like opera singers, they have "base, and treble Voices"; like the gods of ancient myth, they need not "dread a mortal Wound." Displaced to an elegant tea party at Hampton Court, "Combate" no longer seems serious, and the dispute over a lock of hair, which had actually divided two prominent families, casts an oblique light upon the long dispute over the Spanish succession—and all the other "trivial Things" from which "Mighty Contests" arise. Acute in his observation of social rituals, Pope allows his readers to ponder the connections between petty human squabbles and the fate of nations, but he does not insist that they do so.

On 17 May, the Queen's Theatre presented *Calypso and Telemachus,* the first through-sung opera in English since *Rosamond,* with a libretto by the Whig writer John Hughes and music by John Ernest Galliard, who had been one of the oboists in Prince George's military band. Hughes had a much better understanding of the dimensions required for an opera libretto than did Addison, and Galliard's music, though not as inventive as Handel's, was considerably better than Clayton's.[184] The singers included Jane Barbier as Telemachus and Margherita de l'Epine as Calypso; the popular bass Richard Leveridge sang Proteus. Like Philips's play, this opera had a French source, *Les Aventures de Télémaque* by Archbishop Fénelon, who had been the tutor of the recently deceased Duke of Burgundy. With peace in the air, the composer and librettist apparently felt safe in adapting a novel by a

French priest for their harmless mythological drama. Although Nicolini did not take part, he evidently made an effort to support this production, which took place just before his departure from England, and it is pleasant to record the fact that Addison responded graciously. "I am very sorry to find," he wrote on 14 June,

> that we are likely to lose the greatest Performer in Dramatick Musick that is now living, or that perhaps ever appeared upon a Stage. I need not acquaint my Reader, that I am speaking of *Signior Nicolini*. The Town is highly obliged to that Excellent Artist, for having shewn us the *Italian* Musick in its Perfection, as well as for that generous Approbation he lately gave to an Opera of our own Country, in which the Composer endeavoured to do Justice to the Beauty of the Words, by following that Noble Example, which has been set him by the greatest Foreign Masters in that Art.[185]

Nicolini's departure was a disaster for the opera, which had limped through the season without a new work by Handel, who was in Hanover. The Duke of Marlborough, perhaps prompted by his opera-loving wife, sent a message to the Elector on 23 May asking him to allow Handel to return, and the composer was back in London by 21 October, with a short, pastoral opera (*Il Pastor Fido*) and a new, five-act opera to a libretto adapted by Nicola Haym from a French source (*Teseo*). But even these new works could not draw an audience like those that had come to hear Nicolini, and Owen Swiney, who had once again undertaken the management of the company, fled to the Continent in January 1713, unable to pay his debts.[186]

On 21 June, the day of the parliamentary adjournment, Addison published the first of a series of eleven linked *Spectators* on "The Pleasures of the Imagination." Like the series on ambition, these essays were worked up from an earlier draft, yet his decision to publish them just at this juncture is curious. Halifax, Addison's friend, patron, and fellow Kit-Cat, had introduced the address deploring the "restraining order" just two weeks earlier, and there were surely Whigs who hoped that "Mr. Spectator" might now attack the ministry rather than meandering off into aesthetic philosophy. Properly understood, however, these famous essays outline a view of aesthetics grounded in a progressive political ideology, although they make no reference at all to current events. Addison begins by declaring that "Our Sight is the most perfect and most delightful of our Senses."

> It fills the Mind with the largest Variety of Ideas, converses with its Objects at the greatest Distance, and continues the longest in Action without being tired or satiated with its proper Enjoyments. The Sense of Feeling

can indeed give us a Notion of Extension, Shape, and all other Ideas that enter at the Eye, except Colours; but at the same time it is very much streightned and confined in its Operations, to the number, bulk, and distance of its particular Objects. Our Sight seems designed to supply all these Defects, and may be considered as a more delicate and diffusive kind of Touch, that spreads it self over an infinite Multitude of Bodies, comprehends the largest Figures, and brings into our reach some of the most remote Parts of the Universe.

In Addison's mind, the human desire for exploration and variety is natural and universal, and finds its aesthetic counterpart in the sense of sight. In the economic and political sphere, exploration could readily turn into exploitation; the promise of mercantile opportunities making it possible for British ships to "reach some of the most remote Parts" of the world was one reason why Whig opposition to the Peace was losing its fervor. Addison, however, celebrates "Enjoyments" of a more abstract kind: as sight is "more delicate and diffusive" than touch, so the Imagination, a power derived from sight, can satisfy our need for variety and astonishment without our needing to board an actual vessel or bring home exotic goods. To see something beautiful is, in effect, to possess it:

> A Man of a Polite Imagination is let into a great many Pleasures, that the Vulgar are not capable of receiving. He can converse with a Picture, and find an agreeable Companion in a Statue. He meets with a secret Refreshment in a Description, and often feels a greater Satisfaction in the Prospect of Fields and Meadows, than another does in the Possession. It gives him, indeed, a kind of Property in every thing he sees, and makes the most rude uncultivated Parts of Nature administer to his Pleasures: So that he looks upon the World, as it were in another Light, and discovers in it a Multitude of Charms, that conceal themselves from the generality of Mankind.[187]

The claim that a "Man of Polite Imagination...feels a greater Satisfaction in the Prospect of Fields and Meadows, than another does in the Possession" glances obliquely at the Tory emphasis on landholding, lately hardened into law by the Qualification Bill, a parliamentary act requiring each member of the House of Commons to own land yielding at least £300 annually,[188] but again, Addison is recasting the particular quarrels of his contemporaries as more general aesthetic principles. In his philosophical system, possession is broadly analogous to touch, so that the owner of land holds it in his grasp, while pleasure is broadly analogous to sight, so that the man enjoying a prospect of someone else's fields has an aesthetic experience that may be more satisfying than mere ownership. The last move in this sequence promotes the ideas in the mind above those things that we actually see with our eyes, especially when those ideas are prompted by literature:

> Words, when well chosen, have so great a Force in them, that a Description often gives us more lively Ideas than the Sight of Things themselves. The Reader finds a Scene drawn in stronger Colours, and painted more to the Life in his Imagination, by the help of Words, than by an actual Survey of the Scene which they describe. In this case the Poet seems to get the better of Nature; he takes, indeed, the Landskip after her, but gives it more vigorous Touches, heightens its Beauty, and so enlivens the whole Piece, that the Images which flow from the Objects themselves appear weak and faint, in Comparison of those that come from the Expressions.[189]

By offering the possibility that a poet may "get the better of Nature," Addison holds out the hope that gifted writers may transcend the particulars of their own times. As he knew from personal experience, the political parties had become important patrons. His willingness to write *The Campaign* in 1704 had gained him a series of salaried positions, and his sometime friend Prior was receiving similar rewards from the party now in power. Yet by turning away from the immediate political moment to contemplate the function of the imagination, Addison was dreaming of a world in which writing well would be its own reward. The last paper in the series, which celebrates "morality, criticism, and other speculations abstracted from matter," suggests his aim:

> The pleasures of the imagination are not wholly confined to such particular authors as are conversant in material objects, but are often to be met with among the polite masters of morality, criticism, and other speculations abstracted from matter, who, though they do not directly treat of the visible parts of Nature, often draw from them their similitudes, metaphors, and allegories.[190]

As "polite" moralists and philosophers draw similitudes and allegories from Nature, though they do not directly describe it, Addison constructs his aesthetic philosophy by drawing similitudes and allegories from politics, but without directly participating in the shrill and discordant babble he heard all around him.

§

As soon as Parliament adjourned, Ormond detached his troops from the allied army, though the foreign mercenaries who were part of his army chose to stay behind and fight for Eugene at half pay. By all reports, the British troops now ordered to retreat felt shame and disappointment, which became worse when the Dutch garrisons of Bouchain and Douai refused to open their gates to their former allies. At the same time, Brigadier Hill occupied Dunkirk with a small British force, a concession promised by Torcy as a reward for Ormond's withdrawal from the field, which was described by the British and French as a two-month "cessation of arms." The Dutch were appalled and wrote remonstrances to the queen, which they also published. Anne's answer, presumably scripted for her by her ministers, was unapologetic. "It will be your own fault," she informed them, "if all our Measures about War or Peace be not taken in concert with your State."

> The Earl of Strafford will be with you in a few days, with full Instructions concerning our Intentions. Our Ministers will be dispos'd and authoriz'd to do all that's incumbent on us to renew an entire Confidence with you, and to prevent, for the future, such Misunderstandings as have been fomented with so much Artifice, and so little Foundation.
>
> But we cannot pass over in Silence our great Surprize, to see your Letter of the 5th Instant, N.S. was printed and publish'd almost as soon as we received it from the Hands of your Minister; a Proceeding which is equally contrary to good Politicks and Decency.[191]

Once more those opposing the peace process stand accused of "Artifice," and the protest against the printing of the Dutch letter, described here as "an Appeal to the People, rather than an Address to the Sovereign," reflects Oxford's lifelong fondness for secrecy, though of course this reply was also printed. Anne ennobled St. John on 7 July, but he did not become an earl as he had hoped and requested; mindful of his reputation for sexual adventures, of which she strongly disapproved, she made him Viscount Bolingbroke, and Oxford did nothing to dissuade her. The disparity of rank increased the growing rivalry between the two chief ministers, which became worse when Oxford, but not Bolingbroke, received a Garter in the fall.

The allies soon had a very serious reason to be distressed with the British. On 13/24 July, Marshall Villars brought the full force of his army to bear upon a detachment of Dutch and German troops under the command of the Earl of Albemarle at Denain. Outnumbered and overwhelmed, Albemarle's troops attempted to retreat across the river Scheldt, where Eugene's main force was stationed, but the bridge they were using collapsed, and many drowned. Albemarle was among those taken prisoner. A London newspaper published a dispatch from the Hague describing the defeat as one of "the dismal Effects of the Separation of our Army from the Troops of Great Britain,"[192] but Torcy wrote to Bolingbroke with a very different view: "the Queen of Great Britain," he declared, "begins to be avenged for the little regard paid by her allies to her wise counsels." Bolingbroke read this letter to Anne and reported her response to the French diplomat:

> The Queen cannot but be greatly affected that the shedding of blood, and the miseries of war, should still continue, at a time when it depends upon her allies to restore the repose of Europe; she hopes the advantage gained by his Majesty's forces will contribute to conquer an obstinacy unexampled.[193]

The first part of this report rings true: Anne would have remembered kindnesses done to her by the Duke of Albemarle when he was William's young favorite, and she was certainly weary of bloodshed. The hope that such misfortunes would compel the Dutch to accept a peace dictated by the French and the British, however, was the policy being pursued by her ministers, and Bolingbroke was probably disingenuous in claiming that Anne herself had explicitly expressed that hope.

The public embarrassment about Denain did not prevent the queen from sending Bolingbroke to Paris for further talks with Torcy in August. His trip to the French capital, accompanied not only by the diplomat and poet Prior but by the French priest Gaultier, alerted the suspicions of those who feared that one aspect of the coming peace would be a Stuart restoration—especially when reports reached London that the queen's Secretary of State had been at the opera on a night when the Pretender was also in the audience. A Dutch newspaper reported that Bolingbroke, who had been offered the king's box, vacated it when James Francis Edward arrived and was "placed in a box over against him." Although there was no claim that the two men had spoken to one another, their presence in the same space, compounded by Bolingbroke's polite yielding of his seat, set off an alarm. Anne told Dr. Hamilton that her minister "ought to have gone Out Immediatly."[194] There were also rumors that Bolingbroke had met with Maria Beatrice and that the Pretender was "taking upon him the Tittle of Duke of *Gloucester*."[195] When Bolingbroke returned, he discovered that Oxford had asked Dartmouth, in his capacity as Secretary of State for the southern department, to take over relations with France. A period of dissension within the cabinet ensued, and the Hanoverian agent in London reported that the queen wept after one stormy meeting.[196] It eventually became obvious that Bolingbroke, who knew much more about the history of the negotiations than Dartmouth, would have to continue to manage them.

As her current ministers struggled, bickered, and waited for the Dutch to cooperate, Anne received sad news about a previous minister. Sidney Godolphin, who was visiting the Marlboroughs at St. Albans, died from an attack of kidney stones on 15 September. The queen expressed her concern to Dartmouth, who delivered the news, asking him to use his influence with the press "to hinder... scurrilities coming out upon him."[197] In expressing this fear of unfair attacks, she was probably remembering Swift's cruel lampoon of two years earlier. Censorship, as both Whig and Tory ministries had discovered, was unlikely to be effective, but Bolingbroke's Stamp Tax, which charged a penny for every sheet of paper used, had slowed the flood of printed matter, and Godolphin's death went unmarked by pamphlets of praise or blame. With his old friend gone and his gains of the last year nullified by the French, who followed their victory at Denain by recapturing Bouchain, Marlborough decided to return to the Continent, where he still enjoyed the esteem of his colleagues. The awarding of a Garter to his enemy Lord Poulett and the appointment of Jack Hill to the Privy Council were irritating signs of his loss of influence in England. He left on 30 November, and his duchess followed him in February. "We four must never part," Anne had written to Sarah in 1703, but their parting was now permanent, with Godolphin in the grave and the Marlboroughs on the Continent, where they would remain until the queen's own death.

Neither Anne nor her ministers wanted to face a Parliament until they could present the final terms of a peace, and Oxford successfully opposed Bolingbroke's proposal to dismiss this Parliament and hold new elections, so the queen issued eleven consecutive prorogations, keeping her legislature from meeting until April 1713. Everyone expected peace, but the negotiations in Utrecht stalled for months because of a squabble between the servants of the French negotiator Mesnager and those of Count Rechteren, one of the Dutch participants.[198] Still confident of a peace, Anne decided to appoint an ambassador-extraordinary to France and chose the Scottish Duke of Hamilton, to whom she had awarded a Garter along with Oxford. On 13 November, she wrote to Oxford, asking that Hamilton be urged to begin his journey,[199] but on 15 November, her emissary was killed in a bloody duel in Hyde Park, in which his antagonist, Marlborough's friend Lord Mohun, also died. General MacCartney, the rapist whom Anne had sacked in 1709, was Mohun's second, and some reports blamed him for Hamilton's death; he fled the country immediately after the fray. Despite Steele's eloquent essays against dueling, the combination of alcohol, swords, and an exaggerated code of honor continued to cause such losses with alarming frequency. Without making a public comment on Hamilton's death, the queen asked Shrewsbury to take his place in Paris.

On 18 December, facing reality, the Dutch agreed to join the English in a treaty with France. Patient work behind the scenes had granted them an adequate barrier, though they would control fewer fortresses than had been promised in the agreement of 1709. In early January, negotiators for Spain and Portugal reached an amicable agreement, and later in the month, the representatives of the Habsburg Empire and the Savoy reportedly "came into the Queen's measures." By mid-January, Anne had commissioned Handel to write a new *Te Deum* and *Jubilate* for the thanksgiving service that would mark the end of the war; with the opera company in disarray after Owen Swiney's sudden departure, he was happy to take on a task for the court, even though it involved celebrating a treaty that his employer, the Elector of Hanover, continued to oppose.[200] In February, diplomats from all the countries involved in the peace talks at Utrecht took part in a grand celebration of Anne's birthday. As the queen slept calmly in London, hoping that she had "fix'd a lasting Peace on Earth," the ministers in Holland celebrated in style:

> Most of the Ministers, with their Ladies, the *English* Gentlemen, and other Persons of Quality, din'd at the Lord Privy-Seal's House: In the Evening, the Earl of *Strafford* gave a splendid Ball and Masquerade, at which were present above Five Hundred Persons of Distinction; who were afterwards entertain'd by his Excellency at Supper; and the Diversions lasted 'till Five a-Clock in the Morning.

CHAPTER 11

ALL A NATION
COULD REQUIRE

24 August 1714

Attired in solemn black garments, the participants in the funeral procession entered Westminster Hall by their designated doors and went to their proper rooms to await the ceremony. A notice from the Earl Marshall, printed in the *Post Man*, had given them precise instructions:

> The Lords, the Peeresses, and Lords Sons, the Privy Councellors and Judges are to meet in the House of Lords at 6 in the Evening: the Maides of Honour and Bed-Chamber Women, are to assemble in the Robing Room adjoyning the Lobby next the Painted Chamber, as all others concerned are to do in the said Painted Chamber, and none are to have admittance into the Prince's Chamber, Westminster Abbey, or King Henry VII's Chappel, before the Entrance of the Solemn Procession, except such as by reason of their particular Services must attend there.[1]

Following orders issued by the Privy Council on 17 August, Queen Anne's body had been brought from Kensington the night before, "in a Hearse covered with purple velvet," the same kind of cloth she had worn in France at the age of five when her uncle insisted that she put on formal mourning for her Aunt Minette. The bills for the funeral, carefully compiled by the Lord Chamberlain's office, show that the coach maker provided a large new vehicle for this event, made entirely of oak; in addition to the velvet cloth attached to the hearse by one thousand darkened nails, the Lord Chamberlain paid for "Twenty three Yards of purple Velvet to cover the Coffins of her late Majesty" and "Sixty Six Yards of Refine purple Cloth...for covering & hooding the Eight Flanders Horses." "John Pincke Herald painter" received £31 "for painting Escutcheons and the Royal Hearse Chariot." The Prince's Chamber, where the body awaited burial, was "hung with purple Cloath, and the Floor covered with Purple Bays," while the "Passage from the Princes Chamber to the Palace Yard" was lined with "a Ring of black Cloath," through which the coffin would be carried by the Yeomen of the Guard, one hundred of whom received new mourning liveries for this occasion. As Serjeant-Trumpeter, John Shore signed the receipt for mourning cloth issued to the sixteen trumpeters and four kettle-drummers who marched in the procession; as Master of the Children, William Croft signed for the new clothing made for the choirboys.[2]

For those who arrived at Westminster Hall on time, the wait was long, as the ceremonies did not begin until ten o'clock in the evening:

> Being called out in Order by the Officers of Arms, they proceeded about Ten of the Clock thro' the Princes Chamber into the Palace Yard, and thence unto the South-East Door of the Abbey, one of the great Guns at the Tower firing every Minute, until Her Majesty was Interred. The Royal Corps was borne under a canopy of Purple Velvet, preceded by a great Number of Her late Majesty's Servants, the Judges, Privy-Councellers, the Lords Spiritual and Temporal, and the Great Officers. Her Grace the Dutchess of Ormond (in the absence of the Duchess of Somerset, who was Indisposed) was chief Mourner, supported by the Dukes of Somerset and Richmond in long Cloaks, wearing their Collars of the Order, her Train borne by two Duchesses, assisted by the King's Vice Chamberlain, and follow'd by two other Duchesses, at the head of Fourteen Countesses as Assistants, all in long Veils of black Crape; and after them the Ladies of the Bedchamber and the Maids of Honour in like Veils; then the Bedchamber Women, and the Gentlemen Pensioners closed the Proceeding.

> At the Entrance into the Church the Dean, Prebends and Choir received the Royal Body with an Anthem, and marching before Norrow King of Arms, who carried the Crown and Cusheon, they proceeded singing into King Henry the Seventh's Chapel, where being arrived the Body was deposited on Tressels, while the Service of the Church was performed by the Bishop of Rochester, Dean of Westminster, and afterwards Interr'd in the same Vault with their late Majesties King Charles the Second, King William and Queen Mary, and his Royal Highness Prince George of Denmark.[3]

The crown being carried by the ceremonial officer, which would be deposited in the vault with the body, was actually made of tin, then covered with gold paint—one small economy in a funeral that cost £10,579.8s.8d (well over £2 million in modern money). The queen had neglected to sign her own will and thus officially died intestate, but in keeping with her lifelong interest in "all forms, & ceremonys, ... & having the right order at Installments & funerals,"[4] she left directions for the treatment of her earthly remains. On the day of her death, 1 August 1714, the Privy Council instructed the Lord Chamberlain to "cause Notice to be given to the Sworn Physicians in Ordinary and Extraordinary to Her late Majesty as also to the Serjeant Surgeon and to Mr. Blundele who usually attended Her Majesty in her Illness, That they attend and be present at the Opening of the said Body, *it having been so directed by Her Majesty in her Life time.*"[5] Always mindful of her most humble attendants, Anne had also made sure that Shrewsbury would draw up a list of "such Inferior Servants...as are not in a Condition to put themselves into Morning," so that they would not incur a ruinous expense. Remembering the days she had devoted to planning the details of her husband's funeral, she established that ceremony as a model for her own. Shrewsbury was to "issue his Warrants...and give such further Directions as may be needfull, pursuant to what was done at the Funerale of His Royall Highness Prince George of Denmark."[6] We do not know what anthem Croft chose, but Anne presumably trusted him to select appropriate music. Because the choir had to sing while marching into the chapel, the anthem could not have been too complex; aware of the queen's own musical training and taste, Croft might well have used one of the anthems that Purcell had written for her sister's funeral.

There were some details, however, that were now beyond Anne's control. Originally scheduled for Sunday, 22 August, her funeral was postponed for two days on orders from George I, proclaimed king on the day of Anne's death but still en route from Hanover. The officiating clergyman, Francis Atterbury, was widely (and correctly) regarded as a Jacobite, and would probably not have been Anne's first choice, though it was his right as Dean of Westminster to perform the service.[7] The Chief Mourner was not the person she had chosen, but a substitute, and there was a further historical irony: when asked to serve as Chief Mourner at the grand public funeral of her sister Mary in 1695, Princess Anne had declared herself indisposed, and Elizabeth Seymour, Duchess of Somerset, had served in her stead; this time, the duchess herself was unable to serve, and Mary, Duchess of Ormond, who had been a Lady of the Bedchamber throughout the reign, took her place. Two of Sarah Churchill's daughters, who had resigned their posts in the same group two years earlier, were among the participants in the funeral, though their mother, who had returned to London within days of the queen's death, was not present. The Marlboroughs had begun their return from self-imposed exile before Anne died; they arrived in London on 4 August, and Peter Wentworth remarked upon "the insulting manner" in which they "enter'd the town...met with a train of coachs and a troop of Militia with drums and trump[et]s,"[8] though he was honest enough to report that the duke was embarrassed by this display, coming as it did at a time when the nation was in mourning.

Although such major poets as Pope, Congreve, and Prior remained silent, there were numerous poems on the death of the queen. In a pastoral dialogue, an anonymous "Gentlewoman" celebrated the many virtues of the dead monarch, particularly praising her for showing that women were capable of ruling nations:

> Too long her Sex under Reproach has lain,
> And felt a general (oft a just) Disdain:
> But She redeems their Fame; in Her we find
> What Excellence there is in Womankind:
> And to her Sex this lasting Honour brings,
> That they are capable of highest things.[9]

Lewis Theobald, lawyer and poet, imagined the devout and musical queen joining the heavenly choir:

> But now more Glorious, She, in Bliss above
> Reigns in the Presence of Eternal Love;
> With Angels mix'd, she tunes her Heav'nly Voice;
> Adores the Throne; and her Chast Sp'rit employs
> In *Hallelujah's* and Undying Joys![10]

Purbeck Turner, a theatrical singer, published a Pindaric ode in which he claimed that poetry could assuage the nation's grief:

> In vain we give the Tribute of our Eyes;
> T'Express so great a Loss a Deluge can't suffice.
> By Magic Sounds as DAVID's Lyre
> (Sounds that could gentle Thoughts inspire)
> Did frantick SAUL's wild Rage controul,
> And tun'd the Frenzy of his Soul;
> In alternate Measures so,
> As wavy Passions ebb and flow,
> While we pay Tribute to Her Herse,
> We calm our raging Grief, and sooth our Cares with Verse.[11]

§

It was perhaps a blessing that the queen was unable to read these earnest but inept effusions. She was, however, very much alive when Alexander Pope published *Windsor-Forest* (7 March 1713), the finest and most subtle poem on public affairs to appear during her reign. Pope had begun to compose this poem in 1707, as a companion piece to his *Pastorals;* in 1712, at the request of George Granville, he expanded and revised it to make it into a poem in praise of the Peace of Utrecht. Granville, now Lord Lansdowne, was one of the twelve new peers Anne had created to assure the peace, and in 1712, he had moved from the office of Secretary at War to that of Comptroller of the Household; when Hugh Cholmondeley, the Treasurer of the Household, raised objections to the peace treaties in April, Anne removed him and promoted Lansdowne into his post. As Lansdowne enjoyed some access to the queen, it is reasonable to suppose that he would have given his royal mistress a copy of Pope's poem on the peace, which draws on the long tradition of Stuart iconography.[12]

Before *Windsor-Forest* appeared, the best known poetic treatment of the treaty was Thomas Tickell's *Poem, to His Excellency the Lord Privy-Seal, on the Prospect of Peace,* published on 28 October 1712, puffed by Addison in the *Spectator,* and already in its fourth edition. It is a long, awkward performance, in which the poet tries hard to paper over all forms of controversy. Louis XIV, whose troops had been victorious in the campaign of 1712, recapturing all the towns taken by Marlborough in 1711, appears as a suppliant begging a magnanimous Anne for peace:

> To *Britain's* QUEEN the sceptred Suppliant bends,
> To Her his Crowns and Infant Race commends,
> Who grieves Her Fame with Christian Blood to buy,
> Nor asks for Glory at a Price so high.[13]

The "suspension of arms," already the subject of a bitter debate in the House of Lords, becomes an act of grace by the queen, accepted with joy by her soldiers.

> At Her Decree the War suspended stands,
> And *Britain's* Heroes hold their lifted Hands,
> Their open Brows no threat'ning Frowns disguise,
> But gentler Passions sparkle in their Eyes.[14]

As Tickell surely knew, the British troops had been vocally reluctant to desert their comrades and bitterly disappointed to miss opportunities for plunder in France; here and elsewhere, the poet seems determined to put the best possible face on events, blithely disregarding truths that were widely known. Although both Tickell and Pope invite bipartisan support for the peace, they employ very different strategies for doing so. Tickell's main device is the catalogue: a section on military heroes names Marlborough, of late the hero of the Whigs, along with Peterborough and Ormond, the favorites of the Tories; a section on poets jumbles together such Whigs as Congreve, Garth, Ambrose Philips, and William Harrison with the Tory partisan Prior and the Tory sympathizer Pope. By listing in close proximity men associated with both parties, Tickell writes as if a common enterprise, whether war or poetry, might completely efface ideological differences; from reading his poem, one would never guess that the issue of the peace had been acutely divisive. Pope's strategy is much more abstract. While Tickell names or transparently alludes to scores of living figures, Pope names only three living people: Granville, Queen Anne, and Sir William Trumbull. In his allegorical vision, historical and mythological figures do most of the work required to draw disparate groups together to celebrate the peace. Properly understood, Pope's poem acknowledges the ideological forces that caused the war, as well as those now bringing about the peace, but instead of discussing those issues in partisan terms, the poet transforms them into myth and allegory.

He begins with a direct address to the woodlands surrounding Anne's favorite residence:

> Thy Forests, *Windsor!* and thy green Retreats,
> At once the Monarch's and the Muse's Seats,
> Invite my Lays. Be present, Sylvan Maids!
> Unlock your Springs, and open all your Shades.

For the current monarch, who loved to follow the hunt in an open calash down the wide avenues of Windsor Forest, the "green Retreats" of her parkland were a respite from the press of business and the troublesome rivalries of her ministers, though because the castle was one of her royal "Seats," some aspects of government moved with her when she went there. For the poet, who cherished his family's home at Binfield in a wooded area some seven miles from Windsor, the forest was the natural haunt of the Muses, those "Sylvan Maids" whose presence he requests in the opening lines. As Pope indicates by referring to "Springs" and "Shades," the forest landscape combines potentially discordant elements into a pleasing whole:

> Here Hills and Vales, the Woodland and the Plain,
> Here Earth and Water, seem to strive again;
> Not *Chaos*-like together crush'd and bruis'd,
> But as the World, harmoniously confus'd:

> Where Order in Variety we see,
> And where, tho' all things differ, all agree.

Unlike Tickell, whose catalogues of soldiers and poets had arbitrarily "crush'd and bruis'd" men of different parties together into one chaotic list, Pope acknowledges that Nature must work to make harmony from seeming strife. Hills and vales, woodlands and plains, earth and water "seem to strive" because they are genuinely different, but in Windsor Forest, presided over by the reconciling force of the queen, they all agree. Although it is perfectly possible to read these lines as a direct description of Nature, they are open to several allegorical readings: in the world of politics and diplomacy, forging agreements among differing parties or nations requires the moral force of a sacred monarch; in the world of art, Pope's couplets enact an analogous process, with the potentially discordant elements harnessed into harmony by form and syntax.

As he celebrates the English landscape in language drawn from painting ("russet Plains," "blueish Hills," "Purple Dies"), Pope gestures toward the spice-bearing trees of the tropics, though clearly preferring his own surroundings:

> Let *India* boast her Plants, nor envy we
> The weeping Amber or the balmy Tree,
> While by our Oaks the precious Loads are born,
> And Realms commanded which those Trees adorn.

This witty conceit, appearing some thirty lines into the poem, is the first moment when the reader may sense the presence of the Treaty of Utrecht, which opened the Southern Hemisphere to British trade. In the world created by the peace, the oaks of Windsor Forest, transformed into the planks of sturdy merchant ships, will bring back "precious Loads" from the East and West Indies; in a prophetic vision of empire, the ships of the British navy, guarding this lucrative commerce, will "command" those distant realms. Britons therefore need not envy the plants that flourish in warmer climes, nor need they feel inferior to "proud *Olympus*," where the gods of ancient Greece assembled. As the poet surveys the landscape, he sees some of those deities transplanted to England, along with one important new god:

> See *Pan* with Flocks, with Fruits *Pomona* crown'd,
> Here blushing *Flora* paints th' enamel'd Ground,
> Here *Ceres'* Gifts in waving Prospect stand,
> And nodding tempt the joyful Reaper's Hand;
> Rich Industry sits smiling on the plains,
> And Peace and Plenty tell, a STUART reigns.

If Pan, Pomona, Flora, and Ceres represent the agrarian values held dear by Tory squires, "Rich Industry" represents the entrepreneurial spirit of the Whigs. By reminding his readers that Anne is a Stuart, Pope expresses nostalgia for the line of monarchs now reaching its end. These lines, like many others in his poem, reflect the mythological tradition of the Stuart masque, not least in invoking "Peace and Plenty," who appear as characters in many of Jonson's masques and take singing parts in Crowne's *Calisto*. Aware that suspicious readers might catch a faint whiff of Jacobite sentiment, the poet continues with an account of William the Conqueror and other past tyrants, praises "Succeeding Monarchs" who "heard the subjects cries," and issues an apparent endorsement of the Revolution by invoking Liberty, the favorite goddess of the Whigs:

> Fair *Liberty, Britannia*'s Goddess, rears
> Her chearful Head, and leads the golden Years.

In a country blessed with liberty, hunting is not only a sport for kings, but a pastime for "vig'rous Swains." As Pope describes the capture of partridges with the help of dogs and nets, he uses the military conquest of a town as a metaphor:

> Secure they trust th' unfaithful Field, beset,
> Till hov'ring o'er 'em sweeps the swelling Net.
> Thus (if small Things we may with great compare)
> When *Albion* sends her eager Sons to War,
> Some thoughtless Town, with Ease and Plenty blest,
> Near, and more near, the closing Lines invest;
> Sudden they seize th' amaz'd, defenceless Prize,
> And high in Air *Britannia*'s standard flies.

For writers who had celebrated Marlborough's victories during the previous decade, the investing of towns by lines and trenches was the main topic, with hunting occasionally employed as a metaphor. Pope's reversal of this process was a way of banishing war from his poem as Anne had banished it from Europe. In Windsor Forest, a landscape embodying the benefits of peace, military skills will be practiced only in hunting, with arms displaced from the battlefield to the royal preserve and the shrill trumpets of war replaced by the "chearful Horns" of the hunt:

> The shady Empire shall retain no Trace
> Of War or Blood, but in the Sylvan Chace,
> The Trumpets sleep, while chearful Horns are blown,
> And Arms employ'd on Birds and Beasts alone.

Although no one expected Anne to join her troops in battle, she was an avid huntress, so the poet naturally invokes Diana, goddess of the hunt, while gallantly preferring his queen to the classical deity:

> Let old *Arcadia* boast her ample Plain,
> Th' immortal Huntress, and her Virgin Train;
> Nor envy, *Windsor!* since thy Shades have seen
> As bright a Goddess, and as chast a Queen.

Pope then proceeds to tell at length a pseudo-Ovidian fable in which the rural
nymph Lodona, one of the virginal attendants of Diana, attracts the lustful attention of Pan. As the god pursues her, so close that his breath "Pants on her neck,
and fans her parting hair," the endangered virgin calls on the gods:

> "Let me, O let me, to the Shades repair,
> "My native Shades—there weep, and murmur there."

The nymph's prayer is answered as she turns into the river Loddon, a minor tribu-
tary of the Thames:

> She said, and melting as in Tears she lay,
> In a soft, silver Stream dissolv'd away.
> The silver Stream her Virgin Coldness keeps,
> For ever murmurs, and for ever weeps.

Pope's invented metamorphosis most closely resembles an Ovidian episode in
which a nymph becomes the fountain Arethusa, but if Queen Anne read this
poem, her most immediate reference point might have been the similar myth of
Calisto, saved from disgrace by becoming a constellation. Although Pope was a
voracious reader of older literature, it seems unlikely that he would have come
across Crowne's *Calisto,* a court masque presented almost forty years earlier and
printed only once. Yet *Windsor-Forest,* with its deep nostalgia for myth and allegory, has more in common with Stuart masques than with the political poetry of
its own time. At the climax of the poem, Pope depicts Anne intervening decisively
to alter the course of history:

> She saw her Sons with purple Deaths expire,
> Her sacred Domes involv'd in rolling Fire,
> A dreadful series of Intestine Wars,
> Inglorious Triumphs, and dishonest Scars.

>   At length great *ANNA* said—Let Discord cease!
>   She said, the World obey'd, and all was *Peace*!

Like an earlier Stuart monarch dismissing the noisy antimasquers and initiating a glorious baroque vision of peace and plenty, "great *Anna*" undoes the damage caused by the Plague, the Great Fire, and the English Civil Wars. Punctuation connects the line describing "Inglorious Triumphs, and dishonest Scars" to the "Intestine Wars" of the previous century, but readers who were so inclined were free to apply its adjectives to the more recent wars now coming to an end.

As soon as Anne has spoken her command, "Old Father *Thames*" appears to deliver a prophecy of peace and prosperity resembling but surpassing similar scenes in *Annus Mirabilis, Ariane, Calisto, Albion and Albanius*, and *England's Glory*.

>   The Time shall come, when free as Seas or Wind
>   Unbounded *Thames* shall flow for all Mankind,
>   Whole Nations enter with each swelling Tyde,
>   And Seas but join the Regions they divide;
>   Earth's distant Ends our Glory shall behold,
>   And the new World launch forth to seek the Old.
>   Then Ships of uncouth Form shall stem the Tyde,
>   And Feather'd People croud my wealthy Side,
>   And naked Youths and painted Chiefs admire
>   Our Speech, our Colour, and our strange Attire![15]

Although they frequently invoked Liberty as a sacred principle, the Whigs of Pope's world linked freedom closely to property and profit. For Tickell, whose version of this trope is typical, liberty is freedom to pursue commerce without being molested: "Fearless our Merchant now may fetch his Gain, / And roam securely o'er the boundless Main."[16] Pope offers something far more radical, a vision of an unbounded river that "shall flow for all Mankind." The exotic people he imagines coming to London are not captives brought in chains to the center of empire, not opera singers disguised as "charming Black-moors," but willing travelers like the four Mohawk chiefs. Londoners had gawked at the "Indian Kings" in 1710, and Tickell, despite their gentle behavior, had depicted them as frightening savages, "Chiefs who full Bowls of hostile Blood had quaff'd, / Fam'd for the Javelin, and invenom'd Shaft."[17] Pope, by contrast, imagines future visitors from distant lands feeling free to marvel at the strange attire and foreign speech of their English hosts. Although Anne had proudly announced to her Parliament the gaining of the Asiento, which would allow English ships to transport up to five thousand African slaves to South America for each of the next thirty years, Pope's vision of peace includes the end of slavery:

Oh stretch thy reign, fair *Peace!* from Shore to Shore,
'Till Conquest cease, and Slav'ry be no more:
'Till the freed *Indians* in their native Groves
Reap their own Fruits, and woo their Sable Loves.

Unlike the African slave in Mignard's portrait of the royal mistress (color plate 4), dressed in European finery to deliver the treasures of empire to her owner, Pope's "freed *Indians*" will be at liberty to follow the customs of their own culture, living in their own land.

A reader who understood the political imagination behind Pope's prophecy and recognized the confident mastery of its poetic expression would have been unconvinced by his modest conclusion, in which he pretends to be a simple poet of Nature:

My humble Muse, in unambitious Strains,
Paints the green Forests and the flow'ry Plains,
Where Peace descending bids her Olives spring,
And scatters Blessings from her Dove-like wing.[18]

This final vision of painted forests brings us back to the landscape of the opening. The "Dove-like" personification of Peace superficially resembles the "Kind Health" of Philips's birthday ode, who "descends on downy Wings" to bring "New Life" to the ailing queen, but Pope is more likely to have been remembering Milton, who invokes the Holy Spirit in its "dove-like" form in the opening lines of *Paradise Lost*:

Instruct me, for Thou know'st; Thou from the first
Wast present, and with mighty wings outspread
Dove-like satst brooding on the vast Abyss
And mad'st it pregnant.[19]

In Pope's transforming hands, the earthly, human, frail Queen Anne, badly in need of "Kind Health," becomes the sacred, allegorical, majestic being he calls "great *Anna*," an avatar of the Holy Spirit. The widow bereft of all her children becomes a nursing mother, "brooding on the vast Abyss" and possessing the inseminating power to make it pregnant, a parent who can both engender and deliver peace. The mortal who would die some seventeen months after the publication of Pope's poem becomes a mythical and immortal figure like "Old Father *Thames*," embodying the lasting peace she had worked so hard to achieve.

§

Sophisticated readers appreciated Pope's poem. The philosopher George Berkeley, to whom the poet presented a copy, called it "a very ingenious new Poem upon Windsor Forest,"[20] and Swift, who was now friendly with Pope, endorsed it in a characteristically imperative way: "Mr. *Pope* has published a fine poem, called *Windsor Forest,*" he wrote to Stella. "Read it."[21] Tickell's sprawling poem of the previous fall, however, evidently outsold Pope's, reaching a sixth edition in 1714. Artists of every kind saw the peace as an opportunity. On 5 March, two days before the publication of *Windsor-Forest,* and again on 7 March, the day of its publication, there were full-scale dress rehearsals of Handel's new *Te Deum* and *Jubilate* in St. Paul's Cathedral, attended by "Persons of Quality of both Sexes." On 19 March, "abundance of the Nobility and Gentry were present" to hear a third rehearsal, this one in Inigo Jones's Banqueting House at Whitehall, with an admission fee of half a guinea. Handel had worked carefully on this piece, most of which seems to have been freshly composed, although he drew on earlier works for some parts of the *Jubilate.* He provided solos for Elford, Hughes, Weely, and Gates, as he had done in his birthday song for the queen, and honored English traditions by modeling some of his movements on Purcell's well-known settings of the same canticles. The scale of this work, however, is much larger than Purcell's, as the composer took note of the huge space where it was to be performed and the monumental event it was to celebrate, setting much of the text for full chorus and seeking grand and impressive effects.[22]

Handel's decision to feature the chorus, singing its collective praise, may reflect a desire for national unity in support of the peace, which was widespread. On 27 March, for example, Berkeley "breakfasted with Mr Addison at Dr Swift's lodging" and made an optimistic inference from the civil relations between writers of different political persuasions. Swift's "coming in whilst I was there," he wrote, "and the good temper he shewed, was construed by me as a sign of an approaching coalition of parties." In the same letter, Berkeley reports on a project of Steele's for entertainments at York House, "to consist of the finest pieces of Eloquence translated from the Greek & Latin Authors…accompanied with the best Musick suited to raise those passions that are proper to the occasion." "He talks as if he would engage my Lord Treasurer in his project," Berkeley explains, "designing that it shall comprehend both Whigs & Tories."[23] Two days after this hopeful breakfast, Dr. Sacheverell, whose three-year prohibition from preaching had expired, "preach'd the first Time at his Church of St. Saviours Southwark, where a prodigious multitude of People throng'd to hear, or, at least, to see him." Abel Boyer complained that the High Church hero, by preaching on "the *Duty of Praying for our Enemies,*" was claiming a "Parallel between his Sufferings and those of our *Blessed Saviour,*" which was "the greatest Piece of Arrogance any Man can be guilty of."[24] Yet even Sacheverell was making a show of conciliation by choosing this text and by describing *"our Enemy himself"* as "our *Brother*, and consequently intitl'd to our *Affection* and *Prayers*. For his Enmity can never deprive him of his Humanity, or efface the Image of God stampt on his Person."[25]

On 31 March, the Peace of Utrecht was finally signed, and on 9 April the queen addressed her Parliament. Swift was elated at being shown the speech in advance and having a chance to "correct" it, but his hopes for preferment in the Church of England would soon come to nought with his appointment as Dean of St. Patrick's Cathedral, Dublin, a post he could not decently refuse, but which he regarded as a form of banishment. We do not know which parts of the speech Swift edited, but its studied vagueness suggests that the main hand was Oxford's. "I have deferred opening the Session until now," said the queen,

> being desirous to communicate to you, at your First Meeting, the Success of this important Affair. It is therefore with great Pleasure I tell you, the Treaty is signed; and, in a few Days, the Ratifications will be exchanged. The Negociation has been drawn into so great a Length, that all our Allies have had sufficient Opportunity to adjust their several Interests.

The deliberately obscure phrase claiming that the Allies "have had sufficient Opportunity to adjust their several Interests" masks a significant failure. Although one of the treaty's provisions gave the Habsburg Empire possession of the lands formerly called the Spanish Netherlands, the representatives of the Emperor did not sign the treaty, nor did those of the Hanoverian court, and both these parties indicated their willingness to continue the war.[26] Georg Ludwig, who knew that his Kapellmeister had composed new music celebrating the peace, signaled his displeasure by abruptly terminating Handel's contract "in a way which [the composer] found particularly mortifying."[27] In Catalonia, forces loyal to "Carlos III" kept up a doomed resistance to "Felipe V." Avoiding any reference to these disappointments, the queen urged her legislature to check the "unparalleled Licentiousness" her subjects were showing by "publishing seditious and scandalous Libels,…blaspheming every Thing sacred, and propagating Opinions tending to the Overthrow of all Religion and Government." As this request suggests, the Stamp Act of the previous year had slowed but not stopped the publication of pamphlets embarrassing to the ministry, including some that were critical of the peace. Mindful of the recent deaths of Mohun and Hamilton, Anne also asked Parliament to find "some speedy and effectual Remedy" for "the impious Practice of Dueling."[28]

Hoping that the occasion would help his sales, Pope's publisher brought out a second edition of *Windsor-Forest* on the day of the queen's speech, but this "edition" was actually the unsold sheets of the first edition with a new title page.[29] The attention of the town had now turned decisively to the theatre. Addison, who had not previously written a play, had completed a high-minded tragedy on the death of Cato of Utica, a Roman republican who committed suicide rather than yield to the monarchical ambitions of Julius Caesar, and the premiere attracted keen anticipation. Accordingly to Berkeley, "the front boxes were all bespoke for nine days, a fortnight before the play was acted,"[30] a remarkable advance sale for any new play. The Master of the Queen's Music, John Eccles, who had not composed theatre music for years, wrote the act music.[31] *Cato* had a long initial run and proved to be the most influential English play of the eighteenth century; it played a central role in shaping sentimental liberalism and provided the American revolutionaries of the 1770s with stirring phrases. It is not, however, an allegorical account of the War of the Spanish Succession, the Peace of Utrecht, or the partisan maneuvers of the previous decade. Like Addison's most thoughtful essays in the *Spectator*, this tragedy raises important moral questions about political life but poses those questions in general rather than specific terms. As one honest witness wrote at the time, "'Tis certain 'tis the best Tragedy I ever read, but I can not think there is any view toward party in it, which makes it the more valuable."[32] That truth, however, did not stop both political parties from trying to use this popular drama to promote their own beliefs and policies.

In a stiff and formal exposition, Portius, one of Cato's sons, informs his brother Marcus that the civil war is ending, and that Caesar has prevailed:

> Already *Cæsar*
> Has ravaged more than half the Globe, and sees
> Mankind grown thin by his destructive Sword:
> Should he go further, Numbers would be wanting
> To form new Battels, and support his Crimes.
> Ye Gods, what Havock does Ambition make
> Among your Works!

This speech is dramatically awkward, as Marcus already knows these facts, but it gives Addison a chance to return to the theme of ambition, which he had already developed in his *Spectators* for December 1711. Like those reading his essays, those watching his play were free to apply his critique of ambition as they saw fit. If Whig partisans thought most immediately of Louis XIV as an example of destructive ambition and rejoiced that the war now ending had reduced "the exorbitant Power of *France*,"[33] their Tory counterparts were free to think of Marlborough as a version of the ambitious Caesar, eager "to form new Battels." Neither man, however, fit neatly into the mold of Caesar establishing himself as emperor on the ashes of the Roman republic, and any reading identifying particular figures in this play with specific living figures required foregrounding some parts of the plot and ignoring others.

Addison's comments on political oratory, though quite pointed, also resist application to particular persons. As two treacherous plotters discuss an impending meeting of the Utican Senate, Syphax warns Sempronius that "*Cato* has piercing Eyes, and will discern / Our Frauds, unless they're cover'd thick with Art," language recalling Anne's recent references to "the arts of those who delight in war" and to the "Obstructions, artfully contrived, to hinder" her efforts at peace. Sempronius, scorning "cold Hypocrisie," explains his oratorical strategy:

> I'll conceal
> My Thoughts in Passion ('tis the surest way;)
> I'll bellow out for Rome and for my Country,
> And mouth at *Cæsar* till I shake the Senate.
> Your cold Hypocrisie's a stale Device,
> A worn-out Trick: Wouldst thou be thought in Earnest?
> Cloath thy feign'd Zeal in Rage, in Fire, in Fury!

Although these lines were certainly applicable to recent debates in the British Parliament, neither party had a monopoly on covering its frauds with art, or on concealing its thoughts by clothing them in rage and fury. If suspicious Whigs were sure that the Tory rhetoric in praise of peace concealed a devious plan to bring in the Pretender, Tories were certain that the celebration of traditional liberties in Whig speech-making concealed a desire to be rid of all monarchs. Depending on their particular political allegiances, those hearing this exchange were free to think of Halifax, Nottingham, St. John, Harcourt, Walpole, or any other noted speaker on the floor of either House.

Addison's positive celebration of moral and political virtues was as widely applicable as his critical commentary on ambition and deceit. In lines derived from the touchstone passage on Roman arts in the *Aeneid,* the noble Juba, an African ally of Cato, celebrates the civilizing power of Rome:

> A Roman Soul is bent on higher Views:
> To civilize the rude unpolish'd World,
> And lay it under the Restraint of Laws;
> To make Man mild and sociable to Man;
> To cultivate the wild licentious Savage
> With Wisdom, Discipline, and lib'ral Arts;
> Th'Embellishments of Life: Virtues like these,
> Make Human Nature shine, reform the Soul,
> And break our fierce Barbarians into Men.

By putting these noble sentiments into the mouth of an African while exposing many of the Roman figures in his play as duplicitous schemers, Addison implies that "fierce Barbarians," when cultivated by "Wisdom, Discipline, and lib'ral Arts," may learn to be more virtuous than those who claim the mission of civilizing the "rude unpolish'd World." This speech has points of contact with Steele's admiring account of the four Indian kings and the utopian conclusion of Pope's *Windsor-Forest*, but again its ideas resist a specifically partisan label. Although the Treaty of Utrecht would enable a significant expansion of Britain's imperial reach, Addison is both enthusiastic and cautious about the prospect of empire.

In the play's most striking scene, Liberty becomes a source of the sublime as Cato celebrates the sacrifice of his son, who has fallen defending Roman freedom:

> How beautiful is death, when earn'd by virtue!
> Who would not be that youth? what pity is it
> That we can die but once to serve our country!
> . . . .
> Why mourn you thus? Let not a private Loss
> Afflict your Hearts. 'tis Rome requires our Tears.
> The Mistress of the World, the Seat of Empire,
> The Nurse of Heroes, the Delight of Gods,
> That humbled the proud Tyrants of the Earth,
> And set the Nations free, Rome is no more.
> O Liberty! O Virtue! O my Country![34]

There proved to be lasting power in the idea that a death suffered in the defense of patriotic ideals was beautiful, yet some of the phrases Cato uses to describe the Rome for which he mourns were applicable, at least obliquely, to the queen. The idea of a personified, female Rome as the "Nurse of Heroes" recalls the coronation rhetoric making Anne the "nursing mother" of her nation; as she surveyed an expanding empire, she could also be considered the "Mistress of the World"; despite her gender, many of the poems on her victories claimed that she had "humbled the proud Tyrants of the Earth," notably the French king. Yet by transferring language and imagery often used for his living, triumphant queen to a republic imagined as dying, Addison again complicates the political and moral valence of his play. While stimulating the audience to think about the connections between liberty, virtue, beauty, and death, the author is evidently trying to forestall any simple-minded application of his lines to the present.

The initial reception of this play, however, exemplifies the tendency of English audiences in this period to interpret philosophical, moral, and even aesthetic ideas by imposing upon them the terms of partisan politics. Addison was visibly nervous before the premiere, presumably concerned about whether his play would succeed on its own merits, but also fearful of an overly partisan response. Berkeley's account has the normally abstemious author fortifying himself by drinking champagne and burgundy in his box,[35] and Pope describes how he "sweated behind the scenes with concern to find their applause proceeded more [from] the hand than the head." We have a multitude of witnesses to this process. "The word Liberty," wrote John Johnson to his brother Maurice, "never failes of a Whigg Clap but more especially in one Place where Cato laments the Loss of Rome & Liberty more than that of his son who lyes dead before him."[36] Although Addison was a Kit-Cat and a Whig, he was surely hoping for a response to his play that was more serious than automatic applause when hearing a particular word. Pope, who wrote an elegant prologue praising the play for its presentation of "Virtue confess'd in human shape," found himself "clapped into a stanch Whig sore against his will, at almost every two lines." He is one of several spectators who describe the efforts of the Tory ministry to claim the play for themselves. "All the foolish industry possible," he wrote to his friend John Caryll, "has been used to make it a party play."

> I believe you have heard that after the applauses of the opposite faction, my Lord Bullingbrooke, sent for Booth who played Cato, into the box, between one of the acts and presented him with 50 guineas; in acknowledgment (as he expressed it) for his defending the cause of liberty so well against a *perpetuall dictator*. the Whigs are unwilling to be distanced this way, as 'tis said, and therefore design a present to the said Cato very speedily; in the meantime they are getting ready as good a sentence as the former on their side.[37]

Bolingbroke's staged remark about the perpetual dictator was an attempt to enforce a reading of the play in which Caesar's victories in the Roman civil wars would be equated with Marlborough's attempt to be appointed Captain-General for life, and the Whigs felt compelled to answer—not only with a purse of their own but with an equivalent sally of wit. The debate about which party owned the play extended well beyond the playhouse. Christopher Wandesford, Viscount Castlecomer, a Whig MP, tells a personal story concerning the attempts of both parties to claim the play, the leading actor, and the author:

> There was a good whimsical passage happen'd to me at Court last Sunday....In the apartments I met Mr Harcourt my Ld. Chancellor's son, & rallying with him in asking him how he like'd our play. Your play, My Lord, 'tis ours says he, or at least you will allow Cato to belong to us,

by reason Mr Booth is one of us. Very good, quoth I, take him, i god's name, you purchased him at your rate of 54 guineas, which Ld. Bulling-broke collected among you young gentlemen at the play the other night. At that rate my Lord says he, if your friends will give him 60, you may bring [him] over. Upon which I observed that it was by no mean's worth our while; & further added they might make the best of their player, since we had our Poet, & bribe him if you can. And this Sr. was our gay inter-view, & this is a specimen of our current humour, who shall have the honour of the play.[38]

§

With exchanges of this sort taking place in her own apartments, Anne was neces-sarily aware of the popularity of Addison's play and the battle to control its interpre-tation. The partisan passions enacted by claques in the playhouse were harbingers of serious problems in her Parliament. An attempt to extend the malt tax to Scot-land, breaking a promise made at the time of the Union, encountered serious oppo-sition and led to a motion in the Lords to dissolve the Union, which failed by only four votes on 1 June; and on 18 June the ministry lost a crucial vote in the House of Commons, where it normally enjoyed a comfortable majority. As queen, Anne was free to sign the Treaty of Utrecht without consulting Parliament, but the com-mercial treaties with France required parliamentary consent. Codifying the general understanding worked out by Bolingbroke and Mesnager, Arthur Moore, a Com-missioner of Trade and now a Director of the South Sea Company, had drafted these agreements, which included clauses removing the existing tariffs on French goods. Extending "most favored nation" status to France looked like a threat to ex-isting trade partnerships and to British industries that had long enjoyed protection; a Whig campaign of addresses from Portuguese merchants and weavers of English woolens, among many others, attracted sufficient Tory support to sink the treaties. Shrewsbury, who had the difficult task of trying to explain these developments in Paris, advised Oxford to press forward. "Mankind is so changeable a creature," he observed,

> that if this session you find the Parliament disposed to give a sanction to the peace never defer it to another, for though to unbiassed men this will always appear the most advantageous and necessary peace England ever concluded yet no man can foresee what turn faction, interest, malice, envy &c. may at one time give to the best of actions.[39]

If the grand thanksgiving long expected at St. Paul's had taken place on schedule, it would have occurred two days before this setback for the government.

In a proclamation of 18 May, the queen had set 16 June as the day of thanksgiving, and the *Form of Prayer* for the service was actually printed with that date. On 8 June, however, claiming that the time was "too short, for making the Preparations necessary for so great a Solemnity," she postponed the ceremony until 7 July.[40] The choir and orchestra were presumably ready, having had one more rehearsal in May, and the others involved in the proceedings, veterans of numerous earlier thanksgiving services, surely knew what to do. There is no primary evidence showing Anne's real reason for the postponement. Her uncertain health is a possibility, but she may also have hoped that her legislators would find some common ground or that the Habsburg Emperor would finally ratify the peace, providing an additional reason for rejoicing. On 3 July, she reiterated her intention "to go to *St. Paul's* Church, as has been accustomed at former Times,"[41] but just two days later, she decided against attending the service. Her letter to Oxford announcing that decision, written on 5 July, betrays her unease at opting out of a ceremony celebrating her victory in the long war and her success in making peace. The Treasurer, who was also ill, had missed their usual Sunday meeting, though he would manage to attend the ceremony on Tuesday. "I am very sorry," wrote the queen,

> you continue so much indisposed and therefore concludeing I shall not have the satisfaction of seeing you to-day I give you this trouble to enquire after your health and to lett you know that I find myself soe much tyerd with the little fatigue of yesterday that it will be impossible for one to undertake that of going to St. Paul's; but however I think both Houses should go thither and I will perform my devotions at St. James's and be contented without a sermon. It is really very uneasy to me that I cannot go, which I hope all my friends beleeve. I think it will be best to declare this to-night, but would not make it publick till I had first acquainted you with it.[42]

The "little fatigue of yesterday" was an elaborate visit from the Duc D'Aumont, the new French ambassador, who came with a large entourage and delivered formal compliments from Louis XIV to his cousin the queen, whose "Indisposition" made her unable to rise from her throne when the ambassador entered. Although this was officially his "public entry," D'Aumont had been in London since 30 December 1712, and had already caused plenty of trouble. He entertained important people on a lavish scale and was rumored to be selling French wine from his house, which burned down under suspicious circumstances; wilder speculation had him bringing the Pretender with him in disguise for secret meetings with the queen; and he was relentlessly hostile toward the Duke of Marlborough, despite the fact that Marlborough was no longer in England. As Anne probably knew, D'Aumont had recently sponsored a short opera called *Lucio Cornelio Silla,* with music by Handel, which appears to have had at least one private perfor-mance.[43] Its libretto, published in Italian with no accompanying translation, has a dedication to D'Aumont from Rossi, the librettist of *Rinaldo,* dated 2 June, 1713, which may have been the date of the performance, unless the masked ball for six hundred people hosted by D'Aumont at Somerset House on 21 May was the occa-sion.[44] As the opera begins, the Roman general Silla, sung by a castrato and presented as crass, cruel, and relentlessly lustful, enters Rome with an army and declares himself "perpetual dictator."[45] In light of the recent use of that phrase by Bolingbroke in connection with *Cato,* this strange little opera looks like a crude allegorical attack on Marlborough, especially as its convoluted plot, in a departure from history, ends with Silla voluntarily resigning all his positions and going off to live in private. If word of Handel's involvement in this performance reached the Elector, it gave him another good reason for sacking his Kapellmeister.

In addition to his embarrassing social activities, D'Aumont's agenda included pressing Anne to spare further demolitions at Dunkirk, a concession she could not easily make in the current political climate. Peace had not notably lessened the pressures on the queen, whose exhaustion after D'Aumont's visit may not have been entirely physical. She ends her letter to Oxford by asking for help in dealing with another parliamentary matter: "I must desire you to think of an answer for me to give the House of Commons' address about the Pretender," she writes, al-luding to a measure urging her to demand that James Francis Edward, who was residing in the Duchy of Lorraine, be expelled from his refuge there. Anne's insist-ence that "it is really very uneasy to me that I cannot go" sounds as if she is trying to convince herself that her decision not to go to the cathedral is appropriate, and she goes on to express the hope that she will be believed, at least by her friends. She was not, of course, believed by everyone. Dame Sarah Cowper, mother of the former Lord Chancellor, referred in her diary to the performance of "the Church Opera...at the Cathedral of St. Paul. Why or wherefore the Queen was not pre-sent, Whither she cou'd not or wou'd not, is hard to know," she continued, "for Court secrets are better kept than ever."[46] Lady Cowper was among many Whigs, including Members of Parliament, who deliberately stayed away from the service, and Anne's announcement that she would attend a shorter service in her own chapel was probably a way of making sure that no one interpreted her staying away from St. Paul's as a repudiation of the peace she had worked so hard to achieve. Dr. Hamilton reports that he "advised Her not to go to Pauls, least she suffer'd in Her Health, but rather to St. James's, and that would satisfy the People, and not injure her." He may have been genuinely concerned for the queen's well-being, but it is worth noting that this sentence comes at the end of a paragraph complaining about Oxford's failure to pay the royal servants, including Hamilton himself, from which the Whig doctor draws the conclusion that Anne is "forced, by Indisposition and returns of disquiet to trust others."[47] Knowing that she trusted him, he may have advised her against attending the service in order to deprive his Tory enemies of her presence at the celebration of their cherished treaty.

As the queen had requested, the ceremony went forward as if she were present. There was the usual grand parade, led by "the Speaker of the House of Commons,"

> his Coach being followed by near 200 others of the Members of that Honourable House, who were richly dress'd upon this Occasion. After them came the Judges in their proper Habits, then the Barons, Bishops, Viscounts, Earls, Marquisses, and Dukes, all in their Robes; the Lord President, Lord-Treasurer, and Lord-Chancellor closing the Procession, which was very solemn and magnificent.[48]

The cavalcade passed by a huge children's choir specially organized for this occasion:

> About Four Thousand Charity-Children (Boys and Girls) new-cloath'd, were placed upon a Machine in the Strand, which was in Length above 600 Foot and had in Bredth Eight Ranges of Seats one above another, whereby all the Children appear'd in full View,...singing Hymns of Prayer and Praise to God for Her Majesty.

Although they missed their expected chance to see the queen, the children sang a hymn begging God to grant her health and praising her as "A Nursing Mother to thy Fold."[49] Once inside, the worshipers heard Handel's splendid canticles, a newly composed thanksgiving anthem by Croft, and a sermon by George Hooper, Bishop of Bath and Wells. Like the charity children, the bishop was expecting his efforts to be heard by the monarch, on whom he lavished his compliments:

> That hearty Care of Her Majesty for the Publick Good, that large Wisdom and steady Resolution, which have been Blessed by the Almighty to procure us this Peace: may, we hope, by the same Divine Assistance Restore to us Quiet at Home, and Overcome all Oppositions against It.

Reminding his congregation of Anne's place in history, Hooper described the war as a task she had inherited from King William; with the war now over, she would be free to follow the pattern of Queen Elizabeth:

> The Heavy War, which was demised to Her Majesty with the Crown, and has since required the continual Application of Her whole Reign; is now

happily ended. And she is at Leisure to set about the Work, she has long desired to take in hand: to regulate Her Domestick Affairs, and re-invigorate Her Laws; to advance true Piety and Virtue, Fidelity and honest Industry; and like the Queen her glorious Predecessor (whose Example she does her the Honour to follow) to put Her Kingdom into a Course and Train of Peace and Plenty, that may convey them to future Generations.

As a fresh beginning, Hooper argued, this thanksgiving was actually a new coronation:

> The Festival is, as it were, that of a New Inauguration: She has been now Crown'd with Peace: and, for a new Æra, a Reign of Peace is henceforth Commencing; as glorious, we hope, for the Advantages it will bring Her Subjects; as the other, the Martial one, for the Resistance and Repulses it gave a mighty Enemy. And at this Her Coronation, we Her Subjects are likewise to repeat our Professions of Allegiance, and our Wishes for many Years.[50]

Although she did not hear it delivered, Anne evidently read Hooper's sermon. On 22 July, she told Dr. Hamilton that "She heard there were some Whig Lords who heard, and liked the Thanksgiving Sermon," adding her personal opinion that "it was no Party One."

In a similar conversation two days earlier, Hamilton informed the queen of some critical responses to the speech she had given in closing the parliamentary session on 16 July: some unspecified "People," he told her, objected to the speech "for not having said one word of the Family of Hanover in it, and…the Nobility were offended at being call'd from their differing from the Ministry, Factious."[51] The speech was unusually direct. Alluding to the Commons' failure to pass the commercial treaty, the queen suggested that they did not understand its potential benefits: "I hope," she said, "at the next Meeting, the Affair of Commerce will be so well understood, that the advantageous Conditions I have obtained from *France* will be made effectual for the Benefit of our Trade." By referring to herself as obtaining these conditions from the former enemy, the queen laid personal claim to the treaty, and she used the same formula when urging the Lords to support her:

> I recommend it to you all, to make My Subjects truly sensible what they gain by the Peace; and that you will endeavour to dissipate those groundless Jealousies which have been so industriously fomented amongst us; that our unhappy Divisions may not weaken, and in some Sort endanger, the Advantages I have obtained for My Kingdoms.[52]

Such language was, as Bishop Burnet complained, unusual. "The sharpness with which she expressed herself," he wrote, "was singular, and not very well suited to her dignity or her sex." In an even more misogynistic passage, the Bishop treats his queen as an ignorant woman: "it seemed strange, that the queen, who did not understand matters of trade, should pass such a censure on both houses, for their not understanding the affair of commerce."[53] Anne's exasperation with her legislature may well reflect her awareness that they underestimated her.

The Bishop of London, a far more sympathetic clergyman, was not present to hear this speech, nor was he able to attend the earlier service in his own cathedral. At six o'clock in the evening on 7 July, as the celebration at St. Paul's was drawing to a close, Henry Compton, an important presence in Anne's life since her childhood, died at his home in Fulham at the age of eighty. His death opened up an important bishopric, to which Anne promoted John Robinson, Bishop of Bristol, rewarding him for his diplomatic services at Utrecht. Because Robinson was ready to give up his other position as Lord Privy Seal, which had been filled by a commission during his absence overseas, there was a struggle between Bolingbroke and Oxford about how to redistribute the places in the Cabinet, with Bolingbroke hoping to bring in High Tories loyal to him and eager for office. Oxford, however, outflanked his rival, and the new Cabinet, announced from the court at Windsor on 17 August, strengthened the Treasurer's hand: Dartmouth, who had found his post as Secretary of State a burden, became Lord Privy Seal. William Bromley replaced Dartmouth, and there was a further shuffle of responsibilities among the secretaries, with Bromley given the northern division, including most of the important diplomatic correspondence, and Bolingbroke shunted off to the southern division. The office of a third secretary for Scotland, vacant for the last several years, was reestablished and given to John Erskine, Earl of Mar, long a friend of Oxford's.[54] On the same day, the queen issued writs summoning a new Parliament, and the election process commenced. When she asked Dr. Hamilton "what they talk'd about the Changes," meaning the alterations in the Cabinet, he replied that "they were so busy about the Elections, that they talk'd of Nothing Else."[55]

The queen passed a quiet autumn at Windsor, but the maneuvers of her ministers continued. Shrewsbury returned from Paris for a brief stay before taking up his duties as Lord Lieutenant of Ireland, and Bolingbroke enlisted him as an ally, hoping, as the French ambassador put it, "to balance the power of the Earl of Oxford."[56] Seeking support within the queen's own bedchamber, Bolingbroke also made a determined approach to Lady Masham, suggesting that part of the queen's quarter share in the profits of the Asiento might be made over to her favorite, a substantial bribe that appears to have won her support. Shares were also designated for Bolingbroke himself and his associate Arthur Moore, but Oxford refused to take a share for himself.[57] Bolingbroke made his approach to Lady Masham while Oxford was absent from court for the wedding of his son Edward, who married Lady Henrietta Holles, daughter of the late Duke of Newcastle, on 31 August. Among the arrangements the Lord Treasurer had made in securing this lucrative marriage for his son was an understanding that the queen would revive the title made extinct by the late duke's accidental death, naming Edward Harley as Duke of Newcastle. When he mentioned this to Anne on 16 September, however, she refused it "with Seeming Resentment."[58] Aware that he had committed a "never enough to be lamented folly,"[59] Oxford lapsed into a depression exacerbated by heavy drinking and made yet worse by the death of his favorite daughter on 20 November. There was no comfort for him in the sweeping Tory victory in the elections, which brought more country zealots and Scottish Jacobites into Parliament. As soon as the new Parliament was elected, Anne prorogued it, and prorogations continued until mid-February. We catch one happy glimpse of her retired life at Windsor in a record ordering that John Eccles be paid "traveling charges" for himself and twenty-two of the queen's musicians, "being commanded to perform the Te Deum at Windsor on the 19 of November 1713."[60] If the piece performed was the new setting by Handel, as seems likely, the queen liked what she heard: on 28 December she issued a warrant granting Handel an annual pension of £200.[61]

§

With the war over, the peace made, and the sovereign's health precarious, the most pressing issue was the succession, and despite their pious public statements in support of the Hanoverian succession, both of the queen's chief ministers were now in communication with the Pretender. Oxford, again using Gaultier as a conduit, was pressing the young man to convert to the Church of England—and went so far as to draft a statement for him to use if he did so.[62] Typically, however, the Treasurer hedged his bets, writing a friendly letter to Marlborough on Christmas Day and paying him £10,557 of his arrears.[63] With his usual circumspection, Oxford would surely have concealed both of these initiatives from Jonathan Swift, who was present at Windsor during the autumn months, having taken leave from his Irish deanery to return to England in the hope that Oxford or Bolingbroke might help him gain a more desirable position. It is thus a very curious circumstance that Swift chose this moment to offer Alexander Pope 20 guineas to change his religion. The first letter we have from Pope to Swift, dated 8 December 1713, is a comic rejection of what was probably a lighthearted proposal from his older friend, who was now actively soliciting subscriptions for Pope's proposed translation of Homer. Pope begins with a shocking parallel, noting that Swift's offer "is almost as many Pieces of Gold as an Apostle could get of Silver from the Priests of old, on a much more valuable Consideration." Then he lights on the idea of multiplying his profits by getting prominent people of both parties to contribute to a fund for his conversion, as they were contributing to support his work on the *Iliad*:

> I believe it will be better worth my while to propose a Change of my Faith by Subscription than a Translation of Homer. And to convince you how well disposed I am to the Reformation, I shall be content if you can prevail with my Lord Treasurer, and the Ministry, to rise to the same Sum, each of them, on this pious Account, as my Lord Halifax has done on the prophane one.... I know they have the Truth of Religion so much at Heart, that they would certainly give more to have one good Subject translated from Popery to the Church of England, than twenty heathenish Authors out of any unknown Tongue into ours.

Pope's remarkable talents as a poet were apparent to those who had read his published work, and it was reasonable to hope that a translation of Homer by this gifted writer might attract the same kind of broad-based support that Dryden had enjoyed when working on his Virgil. But at a moment when fears of a Catholic monarch were widespread, Pope's religion was a factor. George Berkeley, while clearly appreciative of Pope's gifts, refers to him as "a Tory, and even a Papist" in his letter describing the premiere of *Cato*. It is thus a telling detail that the one subscriber Pope names in this letter is the Whig Lord Halifax, who had exemplified the kind of nonpartisan support Swift was now busily soliciting for his friend by subscribing for ten sets of the *Iliad* at 6 guineas each. An encounter with a possible subscriber unwilling to support a translation by a "Papist" may lie behind Swift's gruff suggestion that Pope take a bribe to convert. By making his offer, Swift insinuated that Pope was not truly devout in his religion, a stance like that assumed by Oxford when he reminded the Pretender of the rewards he might gain by becoming a nominal Anglican. In both cases, however, the man who was pressed to convert felt deep loyalty to his parents, who had suffered for their religion, and therefore refused the proffered rewards.[64]

In Pope's case, the refusal is charming and comic. He agrees to give up many points of Catholic doctrine but protests against having to abandon prayers for the dead, a ploy that allows him to estimate the cost of saving the souls of some dead writers:

> Old Dryden, tho' a Roman Catholick, was a Poet; and 'tis revealed in the Visions of some ancient Saints, that no Poet was ever saved under some Hundreds of Masses. I cannot set his Delivery from Purgatory at less than Fifty Pounds sterling.... Walsh was not only a Socinian, but (what you will own is harder to be saved) a Whig. He cannot modestly be rated at less than a Hundred.

In addition to the dead, there are living men who must be saved, with prices for each. Among others, Pope names Charles Jervas (the artist with whom he had studied painting), John Gay ("an unhappy Youth, that writes Pastorals during the Time of Divine Service"), and "One more whose Salvation I insist upon,"

> but indeed it may prove of so much greater Charge than all the rest, that I will only lay the Case before you and the Ministry, and leave to their Prudence and Generosity what Summ they shall think fit to bestow upon it. The person I mean is Dr Swift, a dignified Clergyman, but one, who, by his own Confession, has composed more Libels than Sermons. If it be true, what I have heard often affirmed by innocent People, that too much Wit is dangerous to Salvation, this unfortunate Gentleman must certainly be damned to all Eternity. But I hope his long Experience in the World, and frequent Conversation with Great Men, will cause him (as it has some others) to have less and less Wit every day. Be it as it will, I should not think my own Soul deserved to be saved, if I did not endeavour to save his; for I have all the Obligations in Nature to him. He has brought me into better Company than I cared for, made me merrier when I was sick, than I had a mind to be, and put me upon making Poems on Purpose that he might alter them, &c....At this rate it is impossible Dr Swift should be ever out of my Debt, as matters stand already; and for the future he may expect daily more Obligations from his most Faithful, Affectionate Humble Servant. A. Pope.[65]

By suggesting that the "Great Men" whose conversation is sapping Swift's wit should settle on a generous sum to save the soul of their most effective propagandist, Pope shows his awareness of Swift's disappointment at being "exiled" to Dublin and indirectly expresses sympathy with his friend's hopes for a better reward. Neither Pope nor Swift, however, appears to have realized how much offense the queen had taken at "The Windsor Prophecy." At the time of Swift's appointment to St. Patrick's, Anne was at pains to tell Dr. Hamilton that she had not promoted him, as "all the Deanerys in Ireland were of the Lord Lieutenants gift, and the Bishopricks of hers."[66] Unwilling to be thought responsible for his gaining the Irish post, she had no intention of giving him an English one.

Pope's affectionate and appreciative conclusion, thanking Swift for his help and his friendship, allows him to avoid making a direct negative response to Swift's proposal, but the Pretender had no such option. His refusal to convert significantly reduced the options now open to Oxford and Bolingbroke, and a life-threatening illness that struck the queen on Christmas Eve underscored the urgency of the government's dilemma. If the leading ministers continued to support the Hanoverian succession, which was of course their public position, the queen's death would end their power, as the Hanoverians were certain to prefer the Whigs. But if they worked, covertly or overtly, on behalf of a Stuart succession, they would be putting their lives at risk, and James Francis Edward's unwillingness to change his faith significantly reduced their chances of persuading Parliament and the nation to accept him. The queen's recovery from her serious illness was a relief, but only a temporary one.

Anne was well enough in early February to host what would prove to be her last birthday celebration, held at Windsor. Boyer reports "a great Appearance of Foreign Ministers, Nobility and Gentry, sumptuously Drest, who about Two a Clock in the Afternoon, paid their Compliments to her Majesty; And, at Night, there was a Ball and a splendid Entertainment in the Castle."[67] William Croft, who had taken his doctorate at Oxford a few days after the summer thanksgiving, presenting another ode on the Peace as his doctoral "exercise," provided a birthday song featuring Elford, Gates, and Weely.[68] The anonymous text is clumsy; Anne appears as "great Clorona,"[69] the "parent of this cheerful Isle," and "the brightest morning star." In a short aria for Gates, the poet compares the rejoicing at her birth to the rejoicing at the Nativity in Israel and heaven.

§

Comparing the ailing, lame, obese queen to the Christ child was poetically preposterous, and this was an especially odd year to make such a gesture, as the queen had been thought likely to die on Christmas Day. The awkward simile, however, may well reflect the poet's sense that only Anne could save the nation from chaos and civil war, a belief shared by many in attendance at the birthday. Most of Croft's setting, including this bass aria, is in the cheerful, celebratory key of D major, but the final chorus, with a text inviting all to "rejoyce in verse sublime" begins and ends in the parallel minor key. At some level, Croft probably recognized that there would be no more such parties for "the brightest morning Star, the Queen."

Singers from the Italian opera company may again have provided part of the "splendid Entertainment" in the evening: the Queen's Theatre, which normally presented an opera on Saturday evening, gave no performance on Saturday, 6 February, a circumstance suggesting that the star singers had gone to Windsor to entertain the queen.[70] As there had been at many previous birthdays, there was a new dance designed by Mr. Isaac the choreographer, dedicated to Harriet Godolphin, the fifteen-year-old granddaughter of the deceased Lord Treasurer and the Marlboroughs, who was now one of the queen's Ladies of the Bedchamber, and who may have even performed the new dance with a partner.[71] The decision to feature and print a dance called *The Godolphin* was a delicate and healing gesture toward a past ministry and past friends, but in London the political demonstrations marking the royal birthday were more overt:

> The *Whiggs*, particularly the HANOVER CLUB, signalized, on this Occasion, their Zeal and Affection to her Majesty's Government, and the *Protestant*

🔊 Mus. Ex. 11.1: William Croft, aria from *Prepare, ye Sons of Art* (1714).

Succession in the most Illustrious House of *Hanover,* by causing the Effigies of the *Devil,* the *Pope,* and the *Pretender* to be carried in Solemn Procession from *Charing Cross* to the *Royal-Exchange,* and so back to *Charing Cross,* and afterwards burnt at this last Place.

Three drummers who fell in with the crowd and beat time for the marchers found themselves clapped into jail for their trouble, as Tory officials were not amused.[72]

§

On 16 February, ten days after the royal birthday, the newly elected Parliament met and chose as its Speaker Sir Thomas Hanmer, a Tory who had voted with the Whigs against the Commerce Treaty. Among those appearing in the House of Commons for the first time that day was Richard Steele, who had thrown off his nonpartisan mask and was now publishing an unabashedly Whig journal called the *Englishman*. On 19 January, expanding on themes developed in the *Englishman,* he had published *The Crisis,* a long separate pamphlet that sold widely and appeared in a French translation on the Continent. This combative treatise is the literary equivalent of a pope-burning. Steele begins by reminding his readers of the benefits they were enjoying as a result of the Revolution of 1688:

> We are, by all the Laws of God and Man, enstated in a Condition of enjoy-ing Religion, Life, Liberty, and Property, rescued from the most imminent Danger of having them all for ever depend upon the Arbitrary Power of a Popish Prince. We should have been chained down in this abject Condi-tion in the Reign of the late King *James,* had not God Almighty in Mercy given us the late happy Revolution, by that glorious Instrument of his Providence the great and memorable King *WILLIAM.*

He then recites the entire Bill of Rights enacted in 1689 and all the laws passed since to ensure and protect the Protestant succession. Turning to the recent war, he praises the Duke of Marlborough at length, listing all his major battles and most of his sieges, deplores the "Suspension of Arms" and the subsequent rout at Denain, and contends that the Peace of Utrecht has left France in a strong position:

> I shall not presume to enter into an examination of the Articles of Peace between us and *France*; but there can be no Crime in affirming, (if it be a Truth) that the House of *Bourbon* is at this Juncture become more formi-dable, and bids fairer for an Universal Monarchy, and to engross the whole Trade of *Europe*, than it did before the War.

After casting doubt on the authenticity of the Pretender's birth, Steele reminds his readers of the persecution of Protestants under Mary Tudor and revives once more the most paranoid fears of what might happen under a Catholic ruler:

> Our Bishops and Clergy must all lose their Spiritual Preferments, or submit to all Antichristian Tyranny: And should they submit to every thing, they must notwithstanding part from their Wives and Children, which, according to the Church of *Rome*, are Harlots and Spurious. The Laiety, possessed of Lands that formerly belonged to the Roman Catholick

Clergy, must resign their Estates, and perhaps be made accountable for the Profits received.[73]

There was no real prospect that those living on lands that had last belonged to the Roman Catholic Church in 1534 would lose them, but Steele was an experienced and persuasive controversialist, and Defoe, writing to Harley, worried that he would now "set up to make speeches in the House and print them,"

> that the malice of the party may be gratified and the Ministry be bullied in as public a manner as possible. If, my lord, the virulent writings of this man may not be voted seditious none ever may, and if thereupon he may be expelled it would suppress and discourage the party and break all their new measures.[74]

Remarkably enough, this was the plan that Oxford now embraced, and plans for a Tory measure to expel Steele for sedition were evidently in place before the House of Commons met for business. In the meantime, the ministry procured an answer to his popular pamphlet: on 23 February, *The Publick Spirit of the Whigs* appeared, certainly by Swift but published anonymously. It is an odd performance, concentrating much of its fire on supposed failings in Steele's prose style and rhetoric. When Swift does undertake to contradict Steele's arguments, he is forced into some odd contortions, the strangest of which comes in his discussion of the suspension of arms. Steele had reminded his readers that "the *British*, in the midst of the Enemies Garrisons, withdrew themselves from their Confederates,"[75] a simple truth that Swift boldly contradicts:

> The Fact is directly otherwise; For the *British* Troops were most infamously deserted by the Confederates, after all that could be urged by the Duke of *Ormond,* and the Earl of *Strafford,* to press the Confederate Generals not to forsake them. The Duke was directed to avoid engaging in any Action till he had further Orders, because an Account of the King of *Spain's* Renunciation was every day expected: This the *Imperialists* and *Dutch* knew well enough, and therefore proposed to the Duke in that very Juncture to engage the *French,* for no other Reason but to render Desperate all the QUEEN's Measures towards a Peace.

Even those who had voted down Halifax's attempt to undo the suspension of arms in the summer of 1712 had not dared to accuse the Allies of deserting the British. This answer to his old friend Steele was the last task Swift undertook on behalf of the Tory ministers, whose inability to work together made him rightly fear that they were courting disaster. At the end of his piece, he wearily describes it as "the most disgustful Task that ever I undertook: I could with more ease have written *Three* dull Pamphlets, than remark'd upon the Falshoods and Absurdities of *One*."[76] Steele's alleged "Falshoods and Absurdities" were surely not Swift's only reason to feel disgust. Avoiding further apologetics for the ministry, he took comfort in genial evenings with his friends Pope and Gay, hosted by Dr. Arbuthnot in his rooms at St. James's, and joined on occasion by the Lord Treasurer himself, who enjoyed their witty banter.[77]

Among the reasons why the ministry feared Steele's dangerous eloquence was his advocacy of a plan to invite the Electoral Prince of Hanover (the future George II) to take his seat in the Lords as the Duke of Cambridge. From a Whig point of view, having at least one prominent member of the Hanoverian family in residence in England would discourage a coup on behalf of the Pretender if the queen should die, providing those loyal to the Protestant succession with a clear rallying point. The queen herself had resisted earlier proposals of this kind from both parties and now looked on this prospect with unconcealed horror. On 26 February, a few days before she was to give her opening speech, she summoned the Duke of Kent and told him "she hoped, he would always join her ministers in all the affairs that might be debated in parliament." Unsatisfied by his bland reply, she sent him off for a two-hour conference with Oxford. The Hanoverian envoy Georg Schütz, to whom we owe this information, reports that Oxford spoke "ambiguously as usual" but strenuously opposed the idea of bringing over "some one of the family of Lunenburg." Such a move, said Oxford, "would be to place her coffin before her Majesty's eyes; and...those who had any respect and friendship for her, could never propose a thing that was so disagreeable to her."[78] Although Oxford had motives of his own for opposing bringing over the Electoral Prince, he was correct about the queen's intense feelings on this topic. When she addressed her Parliament on 2 March, Anne began by emphasizing her recovery, a point she was also making by appearing in person. "My Lords, and Gentlemen," she began,

> The Joy which has been generally expressed on My Recovery from My late Indisposition, and on My coming to this City, I esteem as a Return to that tender Affection which I have always had for My People.

Referring to rumors of her death, which had briefly reduced the value of bank stocks, she returned to a theme she had often emphasized, the need to control the press:

> I wish that effectual Care had been taken, as I have often desired, to suppress those seditious Papers and factious Rumours, by which designing Men have been able to sink Credit, and the Innocent have suffered.

Although there is no reason to doubt her sincerity about the ill effects of "factious Rumours," she was probably more concerned about "seditious Papers" questioning her devotion to the Protestant succession, treating such critiques with undisguised scorn:

> There are some who are arrived to that Height of Malice, as to insinuate, that the Protestant Succession in the House of *Hanover* is in Danger under My Government.
> Those who go about thus to distract the Minds of Men with imaginary Dangers, can only mean to disturb the present Tranquillity, and bring real Mischiefs upon us.
> After all I have done to secure our Religion and your Liberties, and to transmit both safe to Posterity, I cannot mention these Proceedings without some Degree of Warmth; and I must hope you will all agree with Me, that Attempts to weaken My Authority, or to render the Possession of the Crown uneasy to Me, can never be proper Means to strengthen the Protestant Succession.[79]

No one hearing this speech can have doubted that Anne's reference to "Attempts to weaken My Authority, or to render the Possession of the Crown uneasy to Me" was aimed at those proposing an invitation to the Duke of Cambridge.

Shortly after this speech, the aged Poet Laureate published *A Congratulatory Poem, on her Majesties Happy Recovery, and Return to Meet her Parliament.* We do not know whether Tate undertook this project on his own or at the prompting of the ministry. Much of his deliberately old-fashioned poem, which imitates Spenser and revels in myth, describes the terror felt by the Muses, Britannia, Augusta, the Thames, and the rural swains when they hear that the queen is ill. When Anne recovers, the musical instruments the Muse has abandoned play themselves:

> Her Pipe (for on the Ground her Pipe was flung,
> And high, to Winds expos'd, her Harp was hung.)
> Her Pipe Leapt up and Play'd, (she knew not How)
> Her Harp Loud-Answer'd, from a dancing Bough,
> The Message *Zephyr* Whisper'd to her Shell,
> Melodiously Resounding *All is Well.*

When the recovered queen appears on her throne, "Like *Juno* Awful, as *Aurora* Mild," Tate describes her presence as angelic and her famous speaking voice as capable of dispelling discord:

But Doubly Blest who saw and heard her *Speak!*
They heard the Spheres, and saw the Morning break:
A Presence so Angelic as could Charm
And Malecontents of all their Rage disarm;
Accents that Storms of Discord could Dispel,
While Softer They than shedding *Roses* fell.[80]

The most powerful classical precedent for the idea that words might dispel "Storms of Discord" was the first simile in the *Aeneid,* in which Virgil establishes a contrast between piety and *furor,* his word for the dark and irrational passions that fueled Roman violence. The main narrative describes Neptune calming a storm that has scattered Aeneas's fleet, which Virgil amplifies by comparing the god controlling the winds to a Roman citizen controlling a street mob. Dryden's translation of 1697 would have been familiar to many at this time:

As when in Tumults rise th'ignoble Crowd
Mad are their Motions, and their Tongues are loud;
And Stones and Brands in rattling Vollies fly,
And all the rustick Arms that Fury can supply.
If then some grave and pious Man appear,
They hush their Noise and lend a list'ning Ear;
He sooths with sober Words their angry Mood,
And quenches their innate Desire of Blood.[81]

By describing Anne's words as falling "Softer...than shedding *Roses,*" Tate appropriates the power of this famous passage while making it more applicable to a female ruler. His vision of an angelic and charming queen, disarming the malcontents with words like rose petals, is in keeping with Anne's insistence on the "tender Affection" she felt for her people, but nonetheless odd as a description of a speech in which she forthrightly rebuked those eager to establish a Hanoverian court on English soil.

Remarkably enough, Steele had drawn on Virgil's simile in explicating the history of political authority. In the preface to *The Crisis,* he uses a man calming a mob to illustrate the origins of power:

I Never saw an unruly Crowd of People cool by Degrees into Temper, but it gave me an Idea of the Original of Power and the Nature of Civil Institutions. One particular Man has usually in those Cases, from the Dignity of his Appearance, or other Qualities known or imagined by the Multitude, been received into sudden Favour and Authority; the Occasion of their Difference has been represented to him, and the Matter referred to his Decision.[82]

Recognizing Steele's source, Swift takes him to task for turning Virgil's simile into a fact:

> This Paragraph of Mr. *St—le's*, which he sets down as an Observation of his own, is a miserable mangled Translation of Six Verses out of that famous Poet.... *Virgil*, who liv'd but a little after the Ruin of the *Roman* Republick, where Seditions often happened, and the Force of Oratory was great among the People, made use of a Simile, which Mr. *S—le* turns into a Fact, after such a manner, as if he had seen it an hundred Times; and builds upon it a System of the Origin of Government.[83]

Pedantic and inattentive in writing his answer, Swift actually underestimates Steele's radicalism. If Steele had actually built "a System of the Origin of Government" on Virgil's lines, he would have expressed some respect for authority, but his explication of the borrowed image shows no respect at all for the idea of sacred power that Tate develops in his delicate picture of the queen scattering her calming petals. "Absolute unlimited Power in one Person," writes Steele, "seems to have been the first and natural Recourse of Mankind from Disorder and Rapine; and such a Government must be acknowledged to be better than no Government at all." A better system, he goes on to explain, is Liberty, defined as "the Happiness of Men living under Laws of their own making by their personal Consent, or that of their Representatives."[84] It was opinions like these that persuaded the ministry to seek Steele's expulsion from the House of Commons. They succeeded in their effort, but not before he had spoken in his own defense "for almost three hours, ... his memory and astonishing fluency faltering only occasionally and then reviving quickly under the promptings of his great friend Addison, who sat at his elbow armed with sheaves of notes."[85] Both sides, however, could make use of the queen's complaints about seditious writings: in the House of Lords, where the Whigs retained more strength, Wharton managed to get *The Publick Spirit of the Whigs* condemned as seditious, though his call for the prosecution of the writer failed when no one came forward to identify Swift.

The expulsion of Steele put an end to the plan for a parliamentary address urging the queen to invite the Duke of Cambridge to England, but Baron Schütz did not believe he needed parliamentary action. On 12 April, he went to Simon Harcourt, now Lord Chancellor, and demanded in Sophia's name a "writ of summons" for the Electoral Prince, in effect an invitation to take his seat in the House of Lords. As a matter of protocol, this request was difficult to ignore, as Anne had granted the title to the prince as a courteous gesture in 1706. Reporting on the Cabinet meeting at which this matter was discussed, Oxford wrote to his cousin Thomas Harley, who was the British envoy in Hanover: "I never saw her Majesty so much moved in my life. She looked upon it that she is treated with scorn and contempt, and she will not believe that he could have any orders for it, but must be imposed upon by the advice of some angry people here."[86] Harcourt duly issued the writ, but his covering letter to Schütz emphasizes the queen's displeasure,[87] and Anne herself acted firmly against the offending envoy, declaring him *persona non grata* and forcing him to leave her realms. She followed up in May with a letter of her own to the Electoral Prince's father in which she treats this proposal as an affront to her sovereignty:

> I…freely own to you, that I cannot imagine, that a prince who possesses the knowledge and penetration of your Electoral Highness, can ever contribute to such an attempt; and that I believe you are too just to allow, that any infringement shall be made on my sovereignty which you would not choose should be made on your own. I am firmly persuaded, that you would not suffer the smallest diminution of your authority: I am no less delicate, in that respect; and I am determined to oppose a project so contrary to my royal authority, however fatal the consequences may be.

This letter is more than a protest by a queen determined to retain her dignity; it is a warning to George about his own future sovereignty. By telling her likely successor that she is sure he "would not suffer the smallest diminution of [his] authority," Anne is advising him to cling to his royal prerogatives, aware that the enthusiasm with which the Whigs supported the Hanoverian succession masked their belief that a foreign monarch might easily be turned into a ceremonial figurehead, leaving the politicians free to run the country. While reminding the Elector that she has given, "on all occasions, proofs of my desire that your family should succeed to my crowns," Anne nonetheless insists that "it is not possible to derogate from the dignity and prerogatives of the prince who wears the crown, without making a dangerous breach on the rights of the successors."[88] She thus claims that by keeping his son out of her realms, she is protecting his future rights, and there is no reason to doubt that she believed she was telling the truth.

In the event, no one from Hanover attempted to cross the Channel, and on 29 May/8 June the old Electress died suddenly, at the age of eighty-three, leaving her vigorous son as the presumptive heir. Before her death, the Electress attempted to excuse herself for her part in the debacle about the writ, alleging that Schütz had misinterpreted her instructions. If anyone in England was to blame, it was surely the Whigs, who met frequently with Schütz and stayed in communication with the

Hanoverian court and the Duke of Marlborough.[89] Oxford's enemies within his own ministry, however, contrived to blame him for the entire episode, although he appears to have sympathized with the queen's concerns. According to a memoir written by his brother Edward, the Auditor of the Exchequer, "Lord Bolingbroke and Lady Masham took this occasion to insinuate [to the Queen] that this was a contrivance of the Treasurer's, to which perhaps she might be the more induced because Mr. Thomas Harley was then her Envoy at Hanover; whereas in truth it was by means of the Treasurer, and Mr. Harley's conduct there, that the Prince's coming over was prevented."[90] Although Oxford had already tried to resign in March, an initiative rebuffed by the queen, he was still in possession of a working majority in the Cabinet and a lifetime of experience in managing the legislature. When his opponents put forward a "Schism Bill" aimed at preventing the Dissenters from establishing their own schools, they thought they had created "a mine dug to blow up the White Staff," as Defoe colorfully put it.[91] If Oxford opposed the bill, he could be vilified as an enemy to the Church, which would do him no good with the queen, but if he supported it, he would be turning against the very schools in which he had been reared. But the man now often called "the Dragon" was still slippery: he allowed the bill to pass the Commons, then had it loaded with so many amendments in the Lords that it was effectively "castrated." In the Cabinet, he forced through a proclamation offering a reward for the Pretender, an embarrassment to Bolingbroke and his Jacobite supporters. The queen offered £5,000 from her Privy Purse, and the Commons increased the prize to £100,000.

§

These victories proved to be the last in Oxford's long career. Bolingbroke was working tirelessly to undermine his onetime mentor and had enlisted the support of Lady Masham and the Duchess of Somerset; he was also in touch with the Duke of Marlborough, who was planning to return to England once Parliament was prorogued. Although her health was precarious at best, the queen recognized that she would soon have to part with one of her quarreling ministers, and a parliamentary investigation of the treaty of commerce with Spain forced her to take Bolingbroke's side. On 8 July, a clerk from the Board of Trade admitted to the House of Lords "That he saw a Paper, in *French*, of an Indulto[92] to the Queen, from the King of *Spain*, of certain Reservations out of the Assiento Contract; and, by an Endorsement which he wrote thereon, a Grant was made to Mr. *Moor*, from the Queen, of the Advantages therein mentioned."[93] Now that the Lords knew that Anne had made over a part of her quarter to Arthur Moore, there was every reason to believe that the parallel grants to Lady Masham and Lord Bolingbroke would come to light if this investigation were allowed to proceed. Rousing herself into action, the queen came to the Lords on 9 July and put an end to this session of

Parliament, expressing her hope to meet with them "early in the winter." She had saved Bolingbroke from public exposure, though saving Lady Masham may have been a more powerful motive. She had also defended once more the royal prerogative that she often perceived as threatened. Her response to the Lords' request that she make over the entire Asiento to public use, read in the House before she arrived, is polite but stony: "As to the Particulars desired, Her Majesty will dispose of them as She shall judge best for Her Service."[94]

Although she was now determined to take the white staff away from Oxford, the queen was not prepared to give it to Bolingbroke. Desperate to be rid of his rival, Bolingbroke took the expedient of proposing that the Treasury be put into commission but immediately had difficulty putting together a plausible group of men to serve. His last attempt at such a list included some with no appropriate experience and others widely thought to be Jacobites. When she made up her mind to dismiss Oxford, Anne told her Cabinet that "he neglected all business, that he was seldom to be understood, that when he did explain himself she could not depend upon the truth of what he said; that he never came to her at the time appointed, that he often came drunk, that lastly to crown all he behav'd himself toward her with ill manner, indecency, & disrespect."[95] The man who recorded these remarks, Erasmus Lewis, was loyal to Oxford and had no reason to exaggerate these criticisms, which were Anne's way of communicating her belief that Oxford's exhaustion, depression, and alcoholism had made a change necessary. Once more, the queen had to part with a long-serving minister, though this time she did so in a face-to-face meeting at Kensington on the evening of Tuesday, 27 July. When the Cabinet, meeting later that night, failed to come to any resolution about how to manage her affairs, she went to her bedroom in "violent Agitation."[96] Dutiful to a fault, she had attended more Cabinet meetings than any previous monarch, and the failure of this one weighed heavily upon her.

By the next day, it was apparent to all that the queen was seriously ill, though she attended another inconclusive meeting. There was no meeting on Thursday, as the queen was too ill to take part, and on Friday morning, 30 July, she had "two very violent convulsions,"[97] almost certainly signs of a stroke. When Lord Chancellor Harcourt entered her room, he thought she was already dead, but finding signs of life, he now did his duty as her senior minister and took charge. The best account we have of what followed was narrated by Harcourt to Sir John Evelyn, grandson of the famous diarist, whose sister was married to Harcourt's son:

> As soon as he [Harcourt] recover'd himself he desired the Lords to follow him immediately into ye Council Chamber, saying he had something of moment to propose to them, and when they were assembled he spoke to them after this Manner.

I believe my Lords you are all sensible of the dangerous condition the Queen is in. But perhaps you don't consider, that if it shou'd please God to take away her Majesty before she has appointed a Ld Treasurer, the nation must want a *Ld Justice*,[98] & what might be of fatal consequence [must want] one to issue money upon any emergency that might happen, besides the ordinary payments necessary for carrying on ye Government. And Therefore I desire you will command me instantly to recommend one to her Majesty, & I think th[e] D[uke] of Shrewsbury['s] abilities, his service to her Majesty, & Zeal for the succession are so well known, that none is fitter for so great a trust.

We can only imagine how Bolingbroke, who was on the verge of claiming power for himself and probably preparing to attempt a Jacobite coup, received this speech. Knowing that he lacked sufficient support to oppose Harcourt's centrist plan, he kept silent, but he surely knew that a significant opportunity had slipped away. By proposing to empower the Duke of Shrewsbury, who had only returned from Ireland in June, and who had not decisively taken sides in the struggle between Oxford and Bolingbroke, Harcourt was asking his colleagues to put their trust in the traditional aristocracy. Anne had elevated Oxford and Bolingbroke to peerages, but Shrewsbury, the heir of the ancient Talbot family, was a born aristocrat, sensitive like his queen to traditional values, forms, and hierarchies. Anne's last conscious act was placing the fate of her kingdoms in his hands:

The Lords unanimously agreing to his Choice, finding by the Physitians that the Queen was come to her senses again, [Harcourt] forthwith went into ye roome, attended by the Ld President, Ld Bolingbroke, Ld Steward, Ld Privy Seal, & told her Majesty he desired in ye name of & by the direction of her whole Council, that she wou'd for ye good of her Kingdome immediately make ye D[uke] Shrewsbury, Ld High Treasurer of Great Britain, & command him to prepare his Patent. She answer'd if they desired it, she wou'd, & taking the White staff of ye Ld Chamberlain out of Ld Chancelor's hand, she return'd it to ye D[uke] Shrewsbury as Ld Treasurer.[99]

After making this final gesture, Anne sank into a coma, and expired peacefully at 7:45 on Sunday morning, 1 August 1714. Under Shrewsbury's direction, her Privy Council called up the guard, closed the ports, and dispatched James Craggs, a trusted messenger, to summon the Elector of Hanover. For the next six weeks, a group of regents previously nominated by George I ruled England; their choice of Addison as their secretary was one of many signs that the future government would be in the hands of the Whigs. In addition to his new title as Lord Treasurer, Shrewsbury remained Lord Chamberlain and was thus responsible for the funeral arrangements, in which he scrupulously followed the wishes of the dead queen, making only those alterations required by protocol. The White-Staff officers, for example, did not break their staves and throw them into the vault, as the arrangements for the succession stipulated that they were to remain in office until the new king signified his pleasure. Many of the bequests stipulated by the unsigned will were also carried out, including the delivery of the queen's beloved harpsichord to William Croft, in his capacity as "master of the children of the Chapel Royal."[100]

Lewis Theobald, whose poem on Anne's death was one of the first tributes published, was not a distinguished poet; indeed, it would later be his fate to appear as the Prince of Dunces in Pope's first version of *The Dunciad*. In one couplet, however, he managed a compact and accurate tribute to Queen Anne:

> O! She was All a Nation could require
> To satisfie its Hope, or large Desire.[101]

Desire was a traditional part of the rhetoric surrounding female monarchs, and if Anne did not encourage that imagery as Elizabeth had done by remaining unmarried, she had a deep understanding of the erotic dimensions of her relationship to the nation and ultimately succeeded in redirecting those tender feelings toward an image of the queen as the "nursing mother" of her country. The struggle over the succession that effectively finished her life was a struggle between two kinds of hope—the hope for a Protestant constitutional monarch, serving as a figurehead for an increasingly democratic government, and the hope for a sacred and hereditary monarch, embodying an increasingly nostalgic view of national identity. As the events of the queen's last months had shown, these two hopes could not simultaneously be satisfied, and Anne's own ambivalence about the succession reveals her as caught between them. Yet despite the external conflicts she strove to resolve and the internal sorrows of her difficult life, she had an acute sense of what her nation required of her as queen. In her unfailing attention to administrative detail and courtly ritual, religious devotion and artistic excellence, she strove throughout her life and reign to be "All a Nation could require."

ACKNOWLEDGMENTS

I have incurred many debts during the six years spent writing this book. A fellowship from the American Council of Learned Societies, which I held in 2008, enabled me to spend a semester in London, pursuing research and writing the first several chapters. In 2009, Boston University named me as one of its William Fairfield Warren Professors, and the research funds associated with that chair have helped to defray the costs of my research travel, as well as paying the musicians who recorded the musical examples and the permission fees associated with the illustrations. During the 2012–13 academic year, I held two fellowships, one from the National Endowment for the Humanities, the other from the Guggenheim Foundation. I am grateful to both those foundations and to Virginia Sapiro, dean of the Boston University College of Arts and Sciences, who enabled me to take the leave funded by these grants, which made possible some seven months of sustained research and writing in London. My colleague Bonnie Costello stepped into my administrative position and ably directed the Boston University Center for the Humanities in my absence. Christine Loken-Kim, the senior administrator, provided continuity for the Center and helped to support my work while I was abroad.

It is a particular pleasure to thank librarians, without whom no scholar of the humanities would be able to function. I have received invaluable assistance from the staff of the British Library, especially those working in the Manuscripts Library and the Music Collection, and from librarians at the National Archives at Kew, the University of Nottingham Library, the Lambeth Palace Library, the Bodleian Library, the Cambridge University Library, and the libraries of St. John's College, Cambridge, and Christ Church College, Oxford. At home, I received steady support from the staff of the Boston University Library, especially Linda Carr and Holly Mockovak, and from the administration and staff of the Boston Athenæum. In the increasingly electronic world of information, we also need help from computer experts: Mike Mallon of the Boston University College of Arts and Sciences Computing Services Group kept my machines working smoothly, even when doing so required servicing them from across the ocean.

Let me also celebrate the community of scholars, and especially the community of those who share my interest in Queen Anne and her period. Bill Speck answered a query from a stranger seeking knowledge about Prince George of Denmark and became a warm supporter of the project, providing invaluable guidance. Frances Harris steered me to manuscripts I might not otherwise have found and demonstrated that at least one person could learn to read Sarah Churchill's headlong scrawl. Olive Baldwin and Thelma Wilson generously shared their unparalleled knowledge of singers active during Anne's life, as well as their friendship and marmalade. Among others who have answered queries, checked items in distant libraries, and read parts (or all) of the manuscript are Misty Anderson, Paula Backscheider, Anna Battigelli, Robert Bucholz, Donald Burrows, Bill Carroll, Arianne Chernock, Bonnie Costello, Alan Downie, Ophelia Field, the late Edward Gregg, Paul Hammond, Ellen Harris, Ruth Herman, Martin Holmes, Joseph Hone, David Hopkins, James Hume, Robert D. Hume, Richard Johns, Claudia Kairoff, Margaret Laurie, Rebecca Martin, Thomas McGeary, Kathryn McKee, Janet McMullin, Judith Milhous, Jessica Munns, Erin Murphy, Estelle Murphy, Juan Christian Pellicer, Naomi Percival, Andrew Pinnock, Curtis Price, Michael Prince, Bruce Redford, Cedric D. Reverand II, Sir Christopher Ricks, Pat Rogers, George Rousseau, Jim Siemon, David Taylor, James Grantham Turner, Claudine Van Hensbergen, David van Leer, Melissa Schoenberger, Aaron Shapiro, Frederick Tarrant, Sandra Tuppen, Andrew Walkling, Howard Weinbrot, Amanda Eubanks Winkler, and Bruce Wood.

Because music was important to Queen Anne, I was determined from the outset to provide performances of the musical examples, many of which have never been recorded. My colleague Peter Sykes played keyboard instruments on every one of those examples and served as my contractor in gathering the superb musicians who recorded the excerpts. I am grateful to him and to Roberto Toledo and Frank Cunningham, who were the audio engineers. The names of all the musicians appear in the list of musical examples, but I want to express particular gratitude to Teresa Wakim, whose beautiful singing made the recording sessions so satisfying for me and her colleagues.

The staff of Oxford University Press has provided steady and highly professional help in converting my manuscript into a handsome book. I am particularly grateful to Martha Ramsey, Marc Schneider, Rebecca Hecht, and the incomparable Nancy Toff.

My personal obligations are the most difficult to describe in this small space. I have been blessed with moral and emotional support from Linda Gregerson and Steven Mullaney, Bernard and Florence Hunt, Duncan and Juliet Fraser, Arthur and Helen Paxton, Chris and Ellen Lovell, David Kopp, Robert E. Sullivan, and Judith Serkin. My father, Albert C. Winn, did not live to see this book completed, but he read two early chapters with interest and commented on them shrewdly. My sister, Grace W. Ellis, who took responsibility for caring for our father in his final years, still found time to read my work and visit me in London. My remarkable children, Ellen and Philip, continue to give me boundless joy and now increasingly provide me with wisdom; I salute them. All of these people and many others know about the personal miracle I experienced while working on this book: the return of Lucy Chapman, the lost love of my youth, who became my wife in 2009. I have found peace and solace in the music of her violin and the melody of her voice; she has cheerfully endured scholarly conferences and academic dinners and arranged a leave from New England Conservatory in order to come with me to London. She has read every word of this book at least twice, and her comments have made it better. Her help with this project, however, is but one tiny portion of the boundless support she has given me. I dedicate it to her with gratitude and love.

J.A.W.

ABBREVIATIONS USED IN THE NOTES

Boyer, *Annals*	Boyer, Abel. *History of Queen Anne, Digested into Annals.* 11 vols. 1703–14.
Boyer, *History*	Boyer, Abel. *The History of the Life & Reign of Queen Anne. Illustrated with all the Medals Struck in this Reign.* 1722.
Burnet, *History*	Burnet, Gilbert. *Bishop Burnet's History of his own Time: with Notes by the Earls of Dartmouth and Hardwicke, Speaker Onslow, and Dean Swift.* 6 vols. Oxford: Oxford University Press, 1833.
Conduct	Churchill, Sarah, Duchess of Marlborough. *An Account of the Conduct of the Duchess Dowager of Marlborough.* 1742.
CSP Dom.	*Calendar of State Papers, Domestic Series. Charles II* (1660–85). 28 vols. 1860–1939. *James II* (1685–88). 3 vols. 1960–72. *William and Mary* (1688–1702). 11 vols. 1895–1937. *Anne* (1702–14). 2 vols. 1916–24, covering 1702–4 only. *Descriptive List of Secretaries of State: State Papers Domestic, Anne.* 3 vols. List and Index Society, vols. 258–260. 1995.
CTB	*Calendar of Treasury Books.* 32 vols. 1904–62.
Dryden, *Works*	*The Works of John Dryden,* ed. Edward Niles Hooker, H. T. Swedenberg, et al. 20 vols. Berkeley: University of California Press, 1956–2000.
English Post	*English Post with News Foreign and Domestick.*
Gregg, *Queen Anne*	Gregg, Edward. *Queen Anne.* Routledge & Kegan Paul, 1980.
Harris, *Passion*	Harris, Frances. *A Passion for Government: The Life of Sarah, Duchess of Marlborough.* Oxford: Clarendon Press, 1991.
HC	Sandford, Francis. *The History of the Coronation of…James the Second.* 1687.
HMC	*Reports of the Historical Manuscripts Commission:* III, VII, VIII, IX, XI, XII, *Bath, Buccleuch, Downshire, Egmont, Hastings, Laing, Le Fleming, Ormonde, Portland, Rutland, Various Collections.*

JHC   *Journals of the House of Commons.*
JHL   *Journals of the House of Lords.*
LDI   Brown, Beatrice Curtis, ed. *The Letters and Diplomatic Instructions of Queen Anne.*
               New York: Funk and Wagnalls, 1968.
Lewis   Lewis, Jenkin. *Memoirs of Prince William Henry, Duke of Gloucester.* 1789.
LS2MH   Milhous, Judith, and Robert D. Hume, comps. and eds. *The London Stage 1660–*
               1800, Part 2: 1700–1729, Draft of the Calendar for Volume I, 1700–1711. Available at
               Professor Hume's website: www.personal.psu.edu/users/h/b/hb1/London%20
               Stage%202001/.
LTQ   Bathurst, Benjamin, ed. *Letters of Two Queens.* Holden, 1924.
Luttrell   Luttrell, Narcissus. *A Brief Historical Relation of State Affairs, from September 1678*
               to April 1714. 6 vols. Oxford: Oxford University Press, 1857.
MGC   Snyder, Henry L., ed. *The Marlborough-Godolphin Correspondence.* 3 vols.
               Oxford: Clarendon, 1975.
MQE Memoirs   Mary, Queen of England. *Memoirs of Mary, Queen of England.* Ed. R. Doebner.
               Leipzig: Veit & Comp., 1886.
NGDM   *The New Grove Dictionary of Music and Musicians.* 2nd ed. Ed. Stanley Sadie. Mac-
               millan, 2001.
ODNB   *Oxford Dictionary of National Biography.* Oxford: Oxford University Press, 2004.
Post Man   *Post Man and the Historical Account.*
RECM   Ashbee, Andrew. *Records of English Court Music.* 9 vols. Snodland, Kent:
               A. Ashbee, 1986–96.
Term Catalogue Arber, Edward, ed. *The Term Catalogues, 1668–1709, With a Number for Easter*
               Term, 1711 A.D. A Contemporary Bibliography of English Literature in the Reigns of
               Charles II, James II, William and Mary, and Anne. 3 vols. Edward Arber, 1903/
               1905/ 1906.
Wing   Wing, Donald. *A Short-Title Catalogue of Books Printed in England, Scotland, Ire-*
               land, Wales, and British America and of the English Books Printed in Other Countries,
               1641–1700, 2nd ed., rev. and enl. 3 vols. New York: Index Committee of the
               Modern Language Association of America, 1972–88.

NOTES

Place of publication is London unless otherwise noted.

PREFACE

1. *The Works of Alexander Pope*, ed. Whitwell Elwin, 9 vols. (John Murray, 1871–79), I, 331.
2. For a spirited argument against those who have underestimated Queen Anne, see Robert Bucholz, "The 'Stomach of a Queen,' or Size Matters: Gender, Body Image, and the Historical Reputation of Queen Anne," in *Queens and Power in Medieval and Early Modern England*, ed. Carole Levin and Robert Bucholz (Lincoln: University of Nebraska Press, 2009), 242–272.
3. See especially Winton Dean and John Merrill Knapp, *Handel's Operas, 1704–1726* (Oxford: Clarendon Press, 1987).
4. See Neville Connell, *Anne: The Last Stuart Monarch* (Butterworth, 1937); David B. Green, *Queen Anne* (Collins, 1970); and especially Edward Gregg, *Queen Anne* (Routledge & Kegan Paul, 1980). Anne Somerset's *Queen Anne: The Politics of Passion* (HarperPress, 2012) appeared when I was in the final phases of preparing my own book, and I have not consulted it.

CHAPTER 1

1. John Crowne, *Calisto: or, The Chaste Nimph* (1675), sig. a4r–v. I have silently reversed the italics used by seventeenth-century printers to indicate lines set to music, and expanded the names of speakers for clarity. My account of *Calisto* draws extensively on Eleanor Boswell (Murrie), *The Restoration Court Stage, with a Particular Account of the Production of Calisto* (Cambridge, Mass.: Harvard University Press, 1932), and Andrew Walkling, "Masque and Politics at the Restoration Court: John Crowne's 'Calisto,'" *Early Music* 24 (1996): 27–74. See also the extended analyses in Harriette Andreadis, *Sappho in Early Modern England* (Chicago: University of Chicago Press, 2001), 155–176; Valerie Traub, *The Renaissance of*

Lesbianism in Early Modern England (Cambridge: Cambridge University Press, 2002), 229–275; and especially Frances Harris, *Transformations of Love* (Oxford: Oxford University Press, 2002), 214–233.

2. An entry in *The Bulstrode Papers,* ed. A. W. Thibaudeau (Privately printed, 1897), dated 8 February 1675, reports that "the Great Maske ... will be publiquely acted on Tuesday 7 night next, by which time her Royal Highnesse will be able to be present, being already, thankes be to God, in pritty good health" (277). As Walkling has proved by a careful sifting of the evidence, the premiere actually took place on 22 February, a week later than previous scholars had assumed; see "Masque and Politics," 28–30. The "Bulstrode papers" are manuscript newsletters sent from London to Richard Bulstrode, a convert to Catholicism who was on the Continent. Those responsible for writing the newsletters were very well informed about the court of the Duke of York. Only one volume, covering the years 1667–1675, was ever printed. The original manuscripts, which run through 1689, are now in the Harry C. Ransom Center at the University of Texas. In 2012, the collection was completely reorganized and recatalogued; in citing unpublished newsletters from this collection, I follow the new unique MS numbers.

3. "I did see the young Duchess, a little child in hanging sleeves, dance most finely, so as almost to ravish me, her airs were so good—taught by a Frenchman that did heretofore teach the King and all the King's children and the Queen-Mother herself, who doth still dance well." *The Diary of Samuel Pepys,* ed. Robert Latham and William Matthews, 11 vols. (Berkeley: University of California Press, 1970–83), IX, 507 (2 April 1669). In the first of the many editions of *Angliæ Notitia: Or The Present State of England* (1669), Edward Chamberlayne lists a "Dancing-Master" and a "Singing-Master" among the "Servants belonging to the Lady *Mary*" (325). The edition of 1673 names these servants as "Monsieur Gohory" and "Monsieur *Robart.*" A "French Tutor" and a "Musitian" also appear in this edition (237). After Mary's marriage, the same servants appear in the list associated with Princess Anne, a circumstance suggesting that they had long taught both young ladies. An early letter in Mary's hand confirms this practice: "While I danced with Mr. Gory my sister writt; she went to dance in hast and left her letter for me to seal." *LTQ,* 64; this collection prints Bathurst's very accurate transcriptions of originals now in the British Library: GB-Lbl Loan 57/69 and 57/71.

4. *HMC,* VIII, i, 280. The order is dated "January 24, 1667," which I take to be Old Style, i.e., 1668. The man appointed was evidently the Anthony Robert or Roberts who had served Queen Henrietta Maria, was admitted to the king's music for viols and voices in 1662 and made his will on 24 June 1677, giving his age as "fourscore." The will, written in French and proved on 25 August 1679, provides money for Catholic masses in his memory. See *RECM,* I, 38; 172–173.

5. *HMC,* XII, vii, 70. The entry for 6 April 1670, in *The London Stage, 1660–1800,* pt. 1, *1660–1700,* ed. William van Lennep (Carbondale: Southern Illinois University Press, 1965), 169, cites a parallel passage in the manuscript diary of Richard Boyle, Earl of Burlington, that identifies the play and verifies Mary's participation: "I saw Lady Mary, daughter of the Duke of York, and many young ladies act The Faithful Shepherdess very finely." Anne, who was only five, cannot have been a participant, as she was in France. Mary's playing the title role of Clorin would account for her signing her letters to Frances Apsley as "Mary Clorine." See *LTQ,* 38, 39, 43, etc.

6. The Royal Collection dates this painting "c. 1672." Andrew Walkling has suggested that it may be a few years later, in which case it could have some connection to *Calisto*; see "Masque and Politics," 50.

7. *Sociable Letters* (1664), 50–51. I have analyzed this passage in greater detail in *"When Beauty Fires the Blood": Love and the Arts in the Age of Dryden* (Ann Arbor: University of Michigan Press, 1992), 138–140.

8. *The Meditations of Lady Elizabeth Delaval, Written between 1662 and 1671,* ed. Douglas G. Greene, *Publications of the Surtees Society,* vol. 190 (Gateshead: Northumberland Press, 1978), 123.

9. *MQE Memoirs,* 5. In quoting from this source, I have occasionally and silently corrected errors in transcription and spellings that might be confusing. I provide a fuller account of this episode in chapter 3 below.

10. For some fascinating details, see Jennifer Thorp and Ken Pierce, "Three English Chaconnes of the Early Eighteenth Century," *Dance History* 3 (1994): 3–16.

11. For a detailed argument attributing this poem to Dryden, see "John Dryden, Court Theatricals, and the 'Epilogue to the faithfull Shepheardess,'" *Restoration* 32 (2008): 45–54.

12. "*Epilogue,* spoken by the Lady *Mary Mordont,* before the King and Queen, at Court, to the faithfull Shepheardess," in *Covent-Garden Drolery* (1672), 86, correcting one obvious misprint ("chose" for "choose" in line 2).

13. Crowne, *Calisto,* sig. a4v.

14. A strong indication that some of the young ladies were aware of the implications of Crowne's text comes in a letter from Margaret Blagge, who played Diana, to Mary Evelyn, wife of the diarist John Evelyn. Referring to the revised version acted in April, which is the basis for the printed text, Margaret Blagge says that "the alterations are many, the ladys not disposed to act some of them." GB-Lbl Add. MS 78307, fol. 60. Although Crowne's preface informs us that the lines in Pindaric verse are "what I left of the old Play uncorrected, as not needing Emendation" (sig. a3r), identifying the lines in couplets as those he had revised, the process of revision was probably continuous, and it is impossible to know precisely which lines were spoken in February and which were added for the April revival.

15. See Agnes Strickland, *Lives of the Queens of England,* 8 vols. (Bell, 1885), VII, 3. Strickland describes York House as "the ancient dower palace of the queens of England at Twickenham," but it was actually built in the 1630s. Though filled with intriguing details, Strickland's influential work is factually unreliable and strongly reflects her political beliefs. Acutely problematic for the modern scholar is her tendency to give fragmentary and often inaccurate footnotes for materials quoted from primary sources. I have therefore made it a practice not to quote such passages at second hand, preferring to track them wherever possible to the actual source.

16. Judith Hook, *The Baroque Age in England* (Thames and Hudson, 1976), 41.

17. Princess Anne arrived in France on 5 July 1668, and returned to England on 23 July 1670. See Gregg, *Queen Anne,* 6–9. As a result of this long childhood stay, her spoken French was, by all reports, excellent throughout her life.

18. Julia Mary Cartwright, *Madame: A Life of Henrietta, Daughter of Charles I* (Seeley and Co., 1900), 373. Although there is presumably a primary source for this anecdote, Cartwright gives neither a bibliography nor notes.

19. *Bulstrode Papers,* 191, 211.

20. Letter from Rachael, Lady Russell to William, Lord Russell, her husband, printed in *Some Account of the Life of Rachael Wriothesley, Lady Russell,* ed. Mary Berry (Longman, Hurst, Rees, Orme, and Brown, 1820), 170. The date given for this letter, "September 23, 1672," cannot be correct; it must have been written in 1673.

21. See Beth S. Neman, "Crowne, John (*bap.* 1641, *d.* 1712)," in *ODNB*.

22. Crowne, *Calisto,* sig. a1r–v.

23. Crowne, *Calisto,* 6–7.

24. See Harris, *Passion,* 16–17.

25. *LTQ,* 51.

26. On Lady Sussex and Ralph Montagu, see S. M. Wynne, "Palmer, Barbara, Countess of Castle-maine and *Suo Jure* Duchess of Cleveland (bap. 1640, d. 1709)," in *ODNB.* On Lady Sussex and the Duchess of Mazarin fencing in their nightgowns in St. James's Park, see *HMC,* XII, v, 34.

27. *LTQ,* 37–38. References to "Mrs. Jenings" (Sarah Jenyns) and "lady hambelton" (her older sister Frances Jenyns, maid of honor to the first duchess, who married George Hamilton in 1666) place this letter after 1673, when Sarah Jenyns came to court, and before 1677, when both Sarah and Princess Mary were married. According to S. M. Wynne, "Myddelton, Jane (bap. 1646, d. 1692)," in *ODNB,* Eleanor Needham appears to have become Monmouth's mistress about 1674. Her departure from court, the event reported in this letter, is also mentioned in *Bulstrode Papers,* 311; 17 August 1675: "Her R. H. has very ill luck with her maids of honour, for another of them called Mrs Needham, having managed an intrigue of love with his Grace the D. of Monmouth a little too grossly, has forsaken her service & is retir'd, nobody knows whither nor how."

28. *Letters of Sarah, Duchess of Marlborough* (John Murray, 1875), 37.

29. For detailed lists of the performers based on primary documents, see Walkling, "Masque and Politics," tables 2–5.

30. For a good summary of the scanty information on Staggins, see Watkins Shaw, "Staggins, Nicholas," in *NGDM.* The surviving songs from *Calisto,* preserved only as melodies, are in GB-Lbl Add. MS 19759. The instrumental pieces are in US-NYp Drexel 3849.

31. See Robert Strizich, "Corbetta, Francesco," in *NGDM.* Corbetta was listed among important musicians in London by an Italian visitor in 1668; see *Lorenzo Magalotti at the Court of Charles II,* ed. and trans. W. Knowles Middleton (Waterloo, Ontario: Wilfred Laurier University Press, 1980), 151. A surviving establishment book for the Duke of York's household, dating from 1677 to 1678, lists Corbetta among Anne's household servants. GB-Lbl Add. MS 18958, fol. 8v.

32. See Boswell, *The Restoration Court Stage,* 154–155.

33. This entry would also have given Henrietta Wentworth and Sarah Jenyns, who were presumably among the "Princesses and the other Ladies" on stage as dancers earlier in the Prologue, time to change into different costumes in order to appear as Mercury and Jupiter in the first scene of the spoken drama. On Wren and Streeter, see Boswell, *The Restoration Court Stage,* 200–214.

34. George Stradling, *A Sermon Preached before the King at White-Hall, Jan. 30. 1674/5* (1675), 33. For a survey of later sermons on this occasion, see Howard D. Weinbrot, "The Thirtieth of January Sermon: Swift, Johnson, Sterne, and the Evolution of Culture," *Eighteenth-Century Life* 34 (2009): 29–55.

35. In the text underlay for musical example 1.1, I have used the spellings of Crowne's printed text rather than those of the MS. A later hand has labeled this tune as a "catch"; the internal repeat signs and the replacement of an expected rest by an untexted eighth note in bar 5 may be instructions for a performance in canon. Crowne's preface, however, makes it clear that Moll Davis sang this song as a solo in the original performance.

36. Crowne, *Calisto,* sig. b1r.

37. Boswell, *The Restoration Court Stage,* 226.

38. See Robert D. Hume, "The Economics of Culture in London, 1660–1740," *Huntington Library Quarterly* 69 (2006): 487–533, here citing 501.

39. *Angliæ Notitia* (1669), 296, 298–299.

40. In *Coelum Brittanicum*, one of the last Stuart masques, Mercury speaks for the court, declaring that "we advance / Such vertues only as admit excesse, / Brave bounteous Acts, Regall Magnificence." *The Poems of Thomas Carew,* ed. Rhodes Dunlap (Oxford: Clarendon, 1949), 170. Although Charles II greatly reduced the scale of royal dining in 1664, Chamberlayne, evidently fond of his statistics about royal consumption, was reluctant to give up this passage. When he reprinted it in 1671, he added a qualifying phrase locating the display of plenty "in the last Kings Reign before the troubles" (207). For a very full and informative account of Charles II's public dining, see Anna Keay, *The Magnificent Monarch* (Continuum, 2008), 135–142.

41. See Harris, *Transformations of Love,* 105.

42. See Anthony Hamilton, *Memoirs of the Life of Count de Grammont…, Translated from the French by Mr. [Abel] Boyer* (1714), 299: "The D[uchess] was the *highest Feeder* of any Woman in *England:* And that being an *unforbidden* Pleasure, she indulg'd herself in it, to make up other *Self-Denials:* And, indeed,'twas a most edifying Sight to see her eat!" Roger Coke appears to have been the first writer to blame Anne's obesity on her mother. See *A Detection of the Court and State of England… The fourth edition. Continued thro' the Reigns of King William and Queen Mary, and to the Death of Queen Anne,* 3 vols. (1719), III, 481–482: "her Body growing extreamly fat and unwieldy, she disused [hunting] and other Diversions that might have been conducive to her Health, and which, perhaps, might have been longer preserv'd, if she had not eat so much, an Unhappiness deriv'd to her *ex traduce,* not from her Father, who was abstemious enough, but from her Mother; and not supp'd so much Chocolate: I say, she was grown monstrously fat."

43. Charles II to Henriette, Duchess of Orleans, 9 February 1663, quoted in Boswell, *The Restoration Court Stage,* 136: "ici nous avons eu le projet d'organiser une mascarade et nous en avions assez bein dessiné le plan général, mais il n'y a pas eu moyen d'en venir à bout, n'ayant pas ici un seul homme en état de faire une entrée supportable."

44. The reference to Monmouth's minuet appears in the complete version, but not in the program libretto, *The Prologue to Calistho [sic], With the Chorus's Between the Acts* (1675), which refers only to the dance by the nymphs. The program libretto prints lyrics for *The Song to the Minouet,* but places them out of order, at the end of the prologue. All of this evidence suggests that the minuet was a late addition to the masque.

45. See Eric Walter White, *A History of English Opera* (Faber, 1983), 21–22. On Maria's interest in music, see Margaret Mabbett, "Italian Musicians in Restoration England (1660–90)," *Music and Letters* 67 (1986): 237–247, and Edward T. Corp, "The Exiled Court of James II and James III: A Centre of Italian Music in France, 1689–1712," *Journal of the Royal Musical Association* 120 (1995): 216–231.

46. In his preface, Crowne says that the play "was to be written, learnt, practiced, and performed, in less time than was necessary for the writing alone" (*Calisto,* sig. a1v). Some of the costumes, as Walkling has shown, were ordered in September 1674, which suggests that the original plan was to perform the masque at Christmastime, the traditional season for Stuart court masques. Preparing the music and dancing, however, took longer than planned, and the birth of Maria's daughter Catherine Laura on 9 January 1675 led to further delays.

47. For a detailed account, see R. Hutton, "The Making of the Secret Treaty of Dover," *Historical Journal* 29 (1986): 297–318.

48. See J. S. Clarke, *The Life of James the Second, Collected out of Memoirs writ of his own Hand*, 2 vols. (Longman, Hurst, Rees, etc., 1816), I, 442–444, 448–451.

49. See Mark Govier, "The Royal Society, Slavery, and the Island of Jamaica: 1660–1700," *Notes and Records of the Royal Society* 53 (1999): 203–217. There is contemporaneous evidence of the king's strong interest in the slave trade: "The planters and inhabitants of Barbadoes…are indebted to the Royall Company at least £40,000 for negroes, and have been soe many yeares, which his Majestye findes to bee a great want of justice in those islands, and is thinking how to remedy it for the future, as alsoe to set a rule for a faire rate for blackes, to bee furnished there for the support of the Royall Company, but resolving to support that trade soe as the charter of that Company shall not bee invaded." *Bulstrode Papers*, 99; 13 May 1669.

50. See Kenneth Gordon Davies, *The Royal African Company* (New York: Octagon Books, 1975), 65, 74. James invested £3,000 in 1672 and sold his stock in 1689; he realized profits of £6,210, a 12 percent annual return. "In June 1677 he was voted a purse of 500 guineas for extraordinary services" (156).

51. See David Ogg, *England in the Reign of Charles II*, 2 vols. (Oxford: Clarendon Press, 1934; rev. ed. 1955), I, 351.

52. *The Diary of John Evelyn*, ed. E. S. De Beer, 6 vols. (Oxford: Clarendon Press, 1955), III, 607.

53. *Bulstrode Papers*, 214; 5 January 1672.

54. See John Harold Wilson, *A Rake and His Times* (New York: Farrar, Straus, and Young, 1954), 208.

55. See Peter Holman, "Grabu, Luis," in *NGDM*.

56. As Davies has shown, dividends in the company reached their highest levels in history during "the months immediately preceding the Franco-Dutch treaty of Nymwegen in 1678." As he concludes, "Charles' foreign policy, dishonourable, furtive and vacillating as it was, proved no bad thing for trade" (*The Royal African Company*, 63). See also P. E. H. Hair and Robin Law, "The English in Africa to 1700," in *The Origins of Empire*, ed. Nicholas Canny (Oxford: Oxford University Press, 1998), 241–263, especially 257.

57. *JHC*, IX, 281.

58. Letter by Bianca Barbazzi; GB-Lbl Add. MS 53816, fols. 114–116; Evelyn, *Diary*, IV, 30. Some scholars, including De Beer, have supposed that Evelyn actually saw the French opera *Ariane*. Others have speculated that he saw an opera by Giovanni Baptista Draghi, sung in Italian by members of the "King's Italian Musick," a private group of singers who had been in London since the 1660s. Recent study of the manuscript of *L'Erismena*, first reported by J. Stevens Cox and now owned by Oxford University, supports the possibility that it was performed at court, and the emerging scholarly consensus points to the early 1670s as the most likely date for this anonymous manuscript. New College, Oxford hosted an international conference on the opera in 2010; see David Stuart and Greg Skidmore, "Cavalli's *Erismena*," *Early Music* 38 (2010): 482–483.

59. For useful details and a complete text, see John Buttrey, "New Light on Robert Cambert in London, and His *Ballet et Musique*," *Early Music* 23 (1995): 199–220.

60. *Ariadne, or The marriage of Bacchus* (1674), sig. B1v.

61. *Ariadne*, sig. B4v. This is an English translation printed for the audience. The French text, which was actually sung, makes a little more sense:

> Nimphe, tes soins officieus,
> Ont eû de ce Grand Roi, leur juste récompence:

Et l'on a veû sans repugnance,

Ses Peuples recevoir ton Enfant precieus:

Mais tu dois ton bonheur aux charmes de ses Yeux.

Ces Yeux Seuls, triumphant de notre resistance,

Par une douce violence,

Font des Adorateurs de tous ses Envieuz. (*Ariane, ou le marriage de Bacchus* [1674], sig. B2v)

62. Perhaps Dryden remembered this moment in *Calisto* when he wrote the scornful passage in *Absalom and Achitophel* referring to Monmouth's quasi-royal "progresses" to the West of England, stage-managed journeys in which he was greeted by bands of young men in allegorical costumes:

Thus, in a Pageant Show, a Plot is made;

And Peace it self is War in Masquerade. (ll. 751–752)

All citations of Dryden follow Dryden, *Works*, with poems cited by line number, plays by act, scene, and line, and prose by volume no. and page.

63. Crowne, *Calisto,* sig. b1r–v.

64. Crowne, *Calisto,* sig. a2r.

65. Claudian, *De Consulatu Stilichonis,* III, 136, in *Claudian,* 2 vols. (Cambridge, Mass.: Harvard University Press, 1922).

66. *Annus Mirabilis* (1667), stanzas 297–298.

67. *Crowne, Calisto,* sig. a4r–v.

68. Crowne's remarks in the preface suggest that he did assign parts to the singing professionals: "I have in the *Prologue* represented the River *Thames* by a Woman, and Europe by a Man, contrary to all Authority and Antiquity. . . . I know of no Sexes in Lands and Rivers, nor of any Laws in Poetry, but the fundamental one to please; they who do that, follow the highest Authority, and agree with the best Antiquity. The principal part of the *Prologue* being the River, my business was not to consider how the Latin Poets painted it, but how . . . to have the Part sung best to delight the Court; and the graceful motions and admirable singing of Mrs. *Davis,* did sufficiently prove the discretion of my choice" (*Calisto,* sig. A2v–A3r).

69. *Diary,* VIII, 83 (25 February 1667).

70. Crowne, *Calisto,* sig. A4v–b1r.

71. See Traub, *The Renaissance of Lesbianism,* 217: "The association of the clitoris with immoderate desire, and of clitoral hypertrophy with the putative tribadism of African women, crops up in the medical works of classical and medieval Arabic authors, and is one source of early modern accounts."

72. For an analysis of this masque as "both an elucidation of the nature of blackness and a celebration of empire," see Kim F. Hall, *Things of Darkness: Economies of Race and Gender in Early Modern England* (Ithaca: Cornell University Press, 1995), 128–140, here quoting 133.

73. *The Workes of Benjamin Jonson* (1616), 894, silently normalizing *i* and *j, u* and *v.* Like Crowne, the French authors of *Ariane* were apparently aware of the "great concave shell, like mother of pearle," in which the daughters of Niger had appeared in *The Masque of Blacknesse* some seventy years earlier. Their stage directions call for "a Great Shel as it were of Mother of Pearl, bearing 3. *Nimphs*" (*Ariadne,* sig. B1v).

74. GB-Lna LC 9/274, fol. 290, printed in Boswell, *The Restoration Court Stage,* 334. For a very full account of the iconography of pearls in this period, see Eddy de Jongh, "Pearls of Virtue and Pearls of Vice," *Simiolus* 8 (1975–76): 69–97.

75. Jonson also mentions this myth, though he rejects it as an explanation of African blackness. In a long speech, the river Niger blames "Poore brain-sicke men, stil'd *Poets*" for

> Letting their loose, and winged fictions flie
> To infect all clymates, yea our puritie;
> As of one PHAETON, that fir'd the world. (*Workes*, 896)

76. Crowne, *Calisto*, 81.

77. Moll Davis, Mary Knight, and Charlotte Butler, who sang Thames, Peace, and Plenty in the prologue, also appeared as shepherdesses in the pastoral interludes, but Butler was the only one who also appeared in the "Entry of *Africans*." She did not sing in the April revival, in which she was replaced by Arabella Hunt. See Walkling, "Masque and Politics," 35, 38.

78. See, for example, Ben Jonson, *Part of the Kings Entertainment in Passing to his Coronation* (1604), which describes Peace as follows: "The first and principall person in the Temple, was IRENE, Or *Peace*,…her attyre white, semined with starres, her haire loose and large: a wreathe of olive on her head, on her shoulder a silver dove: in her left hand, shee held forth an olive branch, with a handfull of ripe eares, in the other a crowne of lawrell, as notes of victorie and plentie" (*Workes*, 853). Compare the costume ordered for Peace in *Calisto*: "a habitt of silver tabby covered all over with silver and gold lace…1 feather, 33 falls, white…an olive branch…an olive cap." GB-Lna LC 9/274, fols. 268, 293, 271, printed in Boswell, *The Restoration Court Stage*, 306–307.

79. Crowne, *Calisto*, sig. a4r–v, emphasis mine.

80. The entire passage is as follows:

> *Momus.* All, all, of a piece throughout;
> Pointing to *Diana.* Thy Chase had a Beast in View;
> to *Mars.* Thy Wars brought nothing about;
> to *Venus.* Thy Lovers were all untrue.
> *Janus.* 'Tis well an Old Age is out,
> *Chronos.* And time to begin a New. (ll. 86–91)

For a full account of the music by Daniel Purcell, see Kathryn Lowerre, *Music and Musicians on the London Stage, 1695–1705* (Farnham, Surrey: Ashgate, 2009), 257–258.

81. Alexander Pope, *Windsor-Forest*, ll. 41–42. All citations of Pope follow *The Twickenham Edition of the Works of Alexander Pope*, ed. John Butt et al. (Methuen, 1950–67). Pope, who had been studying painting during the period in which he wrote this poem, was well aware of the Rubens ceiling. For a full discussion, see Pat Rogers, *The Symbolic Design of "Windsor-Forest"* (Newark: University of Delaware Press, 2004), 56–62.

82. Crowne, *Calisto*, sig. b2r.

83. Crowne, *Calisto*, 3.

84. See the letter of 30 December 1673, from Lord Conway to Arthur Capel, Earl of Essex: "The Dutchesse of Modena [Maria Beatrice's mother] is gone away this morning in great wrath and displeasure with most of the Lady's of our Court, and the Duke hath already made his visitts to Mrs. Churchill." *Essex Papers, Volume I, 1672–79*, ed. Osmund Airy (Camden Society, 1890), 159. This volume actually ends in 1675.

85. Crowne, *Calisto*, 26.

86. *LTQ*, 49. Mary, who signs herself "Mary Clorine," refers to Frances Apsley frequently as "my dear husband," though she sometimes also addresses her as "Aurelia." Frances cannot have played Mary's "husband" in *The Faithful Shepherdess*, as the play begins with the burial of Clo-

rin's beloved, but in light of the frequency with which these letters draw on court theatricals, I would think it likely that they were cast as husband and wife in some other play. So, too, with the name "Aurelia." Characters named Aurelia appear in Massinger's *Maid of Honour,* Cowley's *Cutter of Coleman Street,* Etherege's *Love in a Tub,* and Dryden's *Evening's Love*—all plays the princesses and their ladies might have seen in the theatre and later acted out, formally or informally. Anne, whose letters begin somewhat later, calls herself "Ziphares" and Frances "Semandra"—names drawn from Nathaniel Lee's *Mithridates* (1678), which was acted on two different occasions by court ladies. See the fuller discussion in chapter 2.

87. The article on Thomas Betterton in *Biographia Britannica: or, The lives of the most eminent persons who have flourished in Great Britain and Ireland…,* 7 vols. (1747–66), claims that Thomas and Mary Betterton, leading actors from the Duke's Company, coached the young ladies: "The same year [1675] a Pastoral of Mr Crowne's was represented at Court, called *Calisto, or The Chaste Nymph,* which was written at the desire of Queen Catherine, and the Ladies Mary and Anne, daughters to the Duke of York,…performed parts in it. On this occasion, Mr Betterton instructed the noble Actors, and supplied the part of Prompter, and Mrs Betterton gave lessons to the young Princesses, in grateful remembrance of which, Queen Anne settled a pension of one hundred pounds a year upon her" (II, 772). Frequently repeated and often erroneously attributed to Colley Cibber, to whose *Apology* it was added in two nineteenth-century editions, this account first appeared long after the events it purports to describe. Queen Catharine, not notable for her interest in the theatre, is far less likely to have requested this drama than the duchess, whose stepdaughters were featured. The Bettertons would have been very busy at this time preparing for the production of *Psyche,* an opera by Thomas Shadwell that opened a few weeks after the premiere of *Calisto.* They may have instructed the princesses, but Crowne's extensive revisions between the performance in February and the performance in April suggest that he was also involved in the progress of the rehearsals. My thanks to Andrew Walkling for helping me track this anecdote to its ultimate source. Queen Anne did in fact order a pension for Mary Betterton on 20 January 1711, shortly after the death of her husband, though there is no evidence that she did so with a memory of *Calisto* specifically in mind. See GB-Lna AO 15/23, fol. 199, and *CTB,* XXV, 142.

88. Crowne, *Calisto,* 7.
89. *LTQ,* 54–55.
90. Nathaniel Lee, *Sophonisba* (1676), in *The Works of Nathaniel Lee,* ed. Thomas B. Stroup and Arthur L. Cooke, 2 vols. (New Brunswick: Scarecrow Press, 1954), act 3, scene 4, 47–50. All citations of Lee from this edition.
91. Lee, *Sophonisba,* act 3, scene 4, 191–196.
92. Crowne, *Calisto,* 20.
93. Buggery Act of 1533 (25 Hen. VIII c. 6).
94. There are instances of the word "tribade" in Elizabethan times. Although the derivation suggests a simple meaning, "one who achieves sexual gratification by rubbing," the term came to refer more specifically to a woman who supposedly used an enlarged clitoris to penetrate another woman. See Andreadis, *Sappho in Early Modern England,* 4–6, and Traub, *The Renaissance of Lesbianism,* especially 160: "tribadism referred primarily to an extreme of female erotic transgression…not only anatomical but moral monstrosity." The first entries for *lesbian* and *sapphist* in the *OED* date from the 1890s.
95. On an Elizabethan instance of the depiction of Peace and Justice as a pair of naked embracing women, see Traub, *The Renaissance of Lesbianism,* 158–164.
96. *LTQ,* 51.

97. Dryden, *The Indian Emperour,* act 2, scene 2, 26–27; 66–71.

98. Dryden, *The Indian Emperour,* act 2, scene 2, 40.

99. *Bulstrode Papers,* 311; 17 August 1675.

100. Crowne, *Calisto,* 20.

101. Katherine Philips, "To my Lady Elizabeth Boyle," in *Poems by the most deservedly admired Mrs. Katherine Philips, the matchless Orinda* (1667), 107.

102. For a shrewd account of the transformation of Philips into "what men wanted in a woman writer," see Paula R. Backscheider, *Spectacular Politics* (Baltimore: Johns Hopkins University Press, 1993), 74–80. As we now know from careful studies of Philips's manuscripts, Cotterell reordered the poems for the printed edition, thus effacing the narratives of female friendship implicit in the poet's own ordering. See Carol Barash, *English Women's Poetry, 1649–1714* (Oxford: Clarendon Press, 1996), especially 68–74, and Peter Beal, *In Praise of Scribes* (Oxford: Clarendon Press, 1998), 147–179. On *preciosité* and Platonic love, see Erica Veevers, *Images of Love and Religion: Queen Henrietta Maria and Court Entertainments* (Cambridge: Cambridge University Press, 1989), especially 56–64.

103. Evelyn, *Diary,* III, 505. See *The London Stage,* pt. 1, 128–129, and the very full account by Beal, *In Praise of Scribes,* 179–191.

104. "A Friend," in Philips, *Poems,* 94–95.

105. See Harriette Andreadis, "Re-configuring Early Modern Friendship: Katherine Philips and Homoerotic Desire," *Studies in English Literature* 46 (2006): 523–542.

106. "To Mrs. Mary Awbrey," in Philips, *Poems,* 70–71. For a thoughtful sifting of the modern controversy over how to read the homoerotic language of Philips's poems, see Elizabeth Susan Wahl, *Invisible Relations: Representations of Female Intimacy in the Age of Enlightenment* (Stanford: Stanford University Press, 1999), 130–170.

107. *LTQ,* 50, 54.

108. Crowne, *Calisto,* 20.

109. For a vulgar example, see the broadside ballad titled *The male and female husband: or, A strange and wonderful relation how a midwife living at St. Albans, being brought to bed of an hermophrodite, brought it up in womans apparel, and carryed it with her as her deputy to be assisting at the labours of several women, going under the name of Mary Jewit: and how at last a discovery of it was made by it lying with a maid, and getting her with-child, whom the said hermophrodite was thereupon obliged to marry: with a particular account of the trades and imployments it was put to during its minority. With several pleasant passages that happened. To the tune of, What shall I do, shall I dye for love, &c.* (n.d.) (Wing M313).

110. Hamilton, *Memoirs,* 234. The French text refers to "Mrs. H—t" as "Mademoiselle Hobart." David Roberts, in *The Ladies* (Oxford: Clarendon Press, 1989), 111, was the first to suggest the relevance of this record to *Calisto.* He says that Mrs. Hobart was dismissed from her post as mother of the maids because of her fondness for women and implies that this dismissal occurred shortly before *Calisto.* But this is a misunderstanding of Hamilton, who refers to Mrs. Hobart as "the Senior of the Community" in this group of maids (230; the French text has "doyenne"), and who elsewhere refers to her interest in "the Niece of the *Mother of the Maids*" (234). As other documents show, Lucy Wise was the mother of the maids at this time. Although Hamilton rarely gives dates, this alleged episode clearly occurred in the early 1660s, long before *Calisto.*

111. See Emma Donoghue, "Imagined More Than Women: Lesbians as Hermaphrodites, 1671–1766," *Women's History Review* 2 (1993): 199–216, especially 209.

112. Hamilton, *Memoirs*, 235.

113. See *Angliæ Notitia* (1669), 321. A "Mrs. Hubert" is named as a maid of honour to the duchess in an early household book (GB-Cul Add. MS 7091, 20): "There was due to Mrs. Hubert one of the Mayds of honour to her R: H: the Duchess of Yorke for her salary or allowance of 20l. p. ann. according to his R: Highness's establishmt: for one yeare and a halfe ended the 24th of June 1662: The sum of £30:00." My thanks to Paul Hammond for transcribing this MS. Frances Harris has suggested that the elusive "Mrs. Hobart" was Frances Hobart, author of a surviving manuscript letter on the death of the first duchess; see *Transformations of Love*, 125–126. This woman, born in Norfolk in 1644, was the daughter of Sir Nathaniel Hobart and his wife Anne, née Leake. She does not appear to have married. In her letter, dated 5 April [1671], she asks her uncle to advance her £10 so that she can buy mourning: "without your assistance I cannot avoid being ridiculous or singular which is a thing I perfectly hate." GB-Lbl Microfilm 636/24 (Verney MSS). Her interest in *not* appearing to be "singular" is fascinating in light of Hamilton's claims about her sexual *"Singularity."* Frances Hobart's family called her "Frank," which was not uncommon as a pet name for Frances in the seventeenth century. The use of that name for both men and women is another indication of the fluidity of gender in this period. See Margaret M. Verney, *Memoirs of the Verney Family from the Restoration to the Revolution* (Longmans, Green, and Co., 1899), 51, 69.

114. Although Hamilton's account of this episode has often been quoted by modern scholars as primary evidence, "one can easily discern the formal narrative or theatrical conventions underlying Hamilton's account; …one may even argue that the story is nothing more than a tale fabricated from court gossip" (Wahl, *Invisible Relations*, 216).

115. See *Court Satires of the Restoration*, ed. John Harold Wilson (Columbus: Ohio State University Press, 1976), 3 and notes, recording one instance as early as 1663. This sense of the word *flat* remains unremarked by the *OED*.

116. *LTQ*, 39.

117. *A New Ballad: To the Tune of Fair Rosamond* (1708). For a much fuller discussion of this work in its context, see chapter 9 below.

118. "[In the Isle of Brittain]," in *The Works of John Wilmot, Earl of Rochester*, ed. Harold Love (Oxford: Oxford University Press, 1999), 85–86.

119. Rochester wrote a prologue for a court performance of Elkanah Settle's play *The Empress of Morocco* in the spring of 1673. In an account of Crowne's career published in 1721, John Dennis alleged that Rochester contrived to have Crowne chosen to write *Calisto* and that he did so because of his hostility to Dryden. See "Some Passages in the Life of Mr. John Crown," in *The Critical Works of John Dennis*, ed. Edward Niles Hooker, 2 vols. (Baltimore: Johns Hopkins University Press, 1939–43), II, 404–406. I have suggested some reasons to doubt this often-repeated story in *John Dryden and His World* (New Haven: Yale University Press, 1987), 245, 271 and notes.

120. Crowne, *Calisto*, 81–82.

121. *Diary of Dr. Edward Lake*, ed. George Percy Elliotte (Camden Society, 1846), 5.

CHAPTER 2

1. Letter to the Earl of Huntingdon, 15 July [1683]; *HMC Hastings*, II, 174.

2. Letter of Thomas Clarges, 30 July 1683; *HMC Laing*, I, 434. The prince evidently gave his bride these jewels in time for her to wear them at the wedding, as a correspondent writing to Sir

Richard Bulstrode on 27 July reported: "I believe Lady Anne will be marryed to Pr. George very soone (perhaps to morrow) & I'me told His Presents (which are very noble) are tendered to her this day." US-Aus PFORZ-MS-1459.

3. Quoted phrases from the account of the wedding in the *London Gazette,* 26–30 July 1683. See also Edgar Sheppard, *Memorials of St. James's Palace,* 2 vols. (Longmans, Green, and Co., 1894), II, 67.

4. In *Royal Welcome Songs,* pt. 1 (Kent: Novello, 2000), Bruce Wood notes that "the date of [the] performance remains a matter for conjecture" and suggests that "From Hardy Climes" was performed "shortly after July 19, 1683," when Prince George arrived to make his addresses to the princess. *The Works of Henry Purcell,* XV, xi. The autograph manuscript of this piece (GB-Lbl R.M. 20.h.8), however, is headed "A Song that was perform'd to Prince George upon his Marriage with the Lady Ann," and I take "upon his Marriage" to point toward a performance closer to the time of the actual wedding. The poem, addressed to George, refers to Anne's "beauties" as "The wonders you have since possess'd," and on 19 July, George had not yet "possess'd" Anne; this text would therefore have made more sense on 29 July. On 18 July, the day before George arrived, the royal musicians performed a new anthem by John Blow, rapidly composed and rehearsed in the wake of the trial of the Rye House plotters; it would have been impracticable for them to learn two substantial new works at the same time. For all these reasons, I believe 29 July is the most likely date for the performance. A morning performance would fit the pattern of New Year's Day celebrations and royal birthdays, in which the new ode was typically performed in the morning.

5. GB-Lna LC 5/140, fols. 309, 384; LC 5/142, fol. 119, transcribed and printed in *RECM,* I, 126, 131–132, 173.

6. The National Portrait Gallery dates this painting "probably 1695," i.e., the year of Purcell's death, but as David Piper points out, "the sitter's youthful appearance suggests a date early in the 1680s." *A Catalogue of the Seventeenth-Century Portraits in the National Portrait Gallery* (Cambridge: Cambridge University Press, 1963), 291.

7. Textual quotations follow *Royal Welcome Songs,* pt. 1, ed. Wood, which prints serviceable texts of the mainly anonymous poems Purcell set.

8. See the fuller discussion in chapter 1.

9. G[ideon] Pierreville, *The Present State of Denmark* (1683), 39.

10. The doubled D in the vocal part, which accurately reproduces the manuscript, provides an alternative for a bass singer lacking Gostling's low range. Bruce Wood has called my attention to a parallel case in the symphony song *If Ever I More Riches Did Desire,* where Purcell added a cue-size low D and marked it "Gostling."

11. On 21 March, James wrote from Newmarket to Charlotte Lee, Countess of Litchfield, who was the daughter of Charles II by the Countess of Castlemaine: "the Dutchesse and my Daughter have been several tymes abroad to take the aire on horse back, and twice to see the cock-fighting." "Some familiar Letters of Charles II. and James Duke of York addressed to their daughter and niece, the Countess of Litchfield; transcribed and edited by Harold Arthur, Viscount Dillon," *Archæologia* 58 (1902): 153–188, here quoting 177. See also Anne's letter to Frances Apsley Bathurst, written on the same day: "this place affords no news but of Races & cock matches which you don't care for" (*LTQ,* 159).

12. A letter of 29 March, 1683, by John Verney sheds light on the activities of the court ladies at the time of the fire: "I heare the Queen & Duchess are not Cater-Cosins, the latter having at Newmarket given the Country Ladyes leave to come to her in mantos, her Court was every night full, & the Qu: sate alone. So when the Fire happed, the Duchess & Lady Anne went to the

Queen's dore to attend her, but she sent them out word she would be private. Then they went to Ld Suffolks whither the Qu' &c. being alsoe to goe, said she should fill the house her selfe, soe the Duchess &c removed to Rochester's"; Margaret M. Verney, *Memoirs of the Verney Family from the Restoration to the Revolution* (Longmans, Green, and Co., 1899), 270.

13. For a judicious account, see Ronald Hutton, *Charles the Second* (Oxford: Clarendon Press, 1989), 420–421. As Hutton points out, "it soon became obvious that two plots had been discovered, the murder project, discussed by former Cromwellians from London of insignificant social and political rank, and a scheme to overpower the Guards and seize custody of the King, mooted by leading Whigs" (421).

14. Save for the omission of one phrase, the text as set by Blow is identical to that given in the Psalter of the 1662 edition of the *Book of Common Prayer*.

15. *HMC*, III, 289.

16. Luttrell, I, 257. See also the letter from Leoline Jenkins, Secretary of State, to Philip Stanhope, second Earl of Chesterfield, dated "Windsor, May, 1683," and printed in *Letters of Philip, Second Earl of Chesterfield* (E. Lloyd and Son, 1829), 244. This reports an audience in which Christian von Lente, the Danish ambassador, formally proposed the match, with the result that the king granted Prince George "leave to make his application to the princess." A letter of 4 May from Sunderland to Jenkins uses very similar language. See the *CSP Dom., Charles II, January–June 1683*, 230. Details of the financial arrangements are reported in a letter from the Duke of Ormond to the Earl of Arran, *HMC Ormonde*, n.s., VII, 22, in which Ormond concludes that "it is thought the Prince will make haste to be possessed of so good a fortune."

17. *LTQ*, 165.

18. On George and Anne at the theatre, see *CSP Dom., July–December 1683*, 201, a newsletter to John Squier of Newcastle dated 24 July: "Yesterday her Royal Highness, Prince George and the Lady Anne were at a play and sat in one box." On the very day of the wedding, 28 July, James, Duke of York, wrote to his niece: "the Dutchesse, Lady Anne, and Prince George are gone to the play, and I am sent for to attend his Majesty" ("Some familiar Letters," 179). I infer that the prince and princess played cards from a surviving letter from George to Lady Belasyse, written from Windsor, which mentions his losses at "Bassette," which he played in the apartment of "Lady Anne." See *HMC*, IX, ii, 458. Lady Belasyse (née Susan Armyne) was the widow of Sir Henry Belasyse, killed in a duel in 1667. James, Duke of York, briefly courted her after the death of his first duchess and made her a Lady of the Bedchamber to Maria Beatrice; see *Angliæ Notitia: Or The Present State of England* (1676, 1677, 1679, 1682). Her father-in-law, John Belasyse, was one of the five Catholic lords impeached in 1678 and at this time still imprisoned in the Tower. The date given for the letter in *HMC*, 3 May 1683, cannot be correct. There is no other record suggesting that George was in England in that year before his much-trumpeted arrival in July. And like the correspondent who wrote to the Earl of Huntingdon on 15 July [1683] (*HMC Hastings*, II, 174), George mentions an impending trip to Paris by the Countess of Pembroke. If the letter was written in July, sometime during the nine days of the official courtship, the interest George expresses in "the Italian players whom we expect here about the 20th of this month" presents a new problem. He did not arrive in England until 19 July, which makes that reference impossible. I believe this letter was actually written in August, which is the most plausible month in terms of its contents. I have been unable to locate the manuscript, but I surmise that "Aug" was misread as "May." Other records show that Charles II was arranging for Italian comedians to perform at Windsor in August; see *The London Stage, 1660–1800*, pt. 1, *1660–1700*, ed. William van Lennep (Carbondale: Southern Illinois University Press, 1965), 319–320.

19. *Hymenæus Cantabrigiensis* (Cambridge, 1683), sig. P2r. This volume appears in the Term Catalogue for November, but its publication can be dated to late September, thanks to a surviving letter from the bishop of Oxford to Secretary Jenkins. "You were very obliging in your advertisement of the compliment the University of Cambridge has now paid to the marriage of Prince George and Lady Anne. What is done by them now at the end of September was solemnly performed by us at the beginning of last July, where we had a just poem repeated in the full theatre in honour of that alliance, a copy whereof, if you please, shall be sent you." *CSP Dom., July–December 1683*, 414.

20. *Hymenæus Cantabrigiensis*, sig. R1v.

21. *Hymenæus Cantabrigiensis*, sig. P4v.

22. Henri Misson, *Memoires et observations faites par un Voyageur en Angleterre* (Paris, 1698), trans. John Ozell as *M. Misson's memoirs and observations in his travels over England* (1719), 352–353.

23. "Some familiar Letters," 179.

24. *Hymenæus Cantabrigiensis*, sig. R2r–v.

25. Dryden, *Absalom and Achitophel*, 5–10.

26. *Royal Welcome Songs*, pt. 1, xxx.

27. *Royal Welcome Songs*, pt. 1, xxix.

28. Letter of Thomas Clarges, 30 July 1683; *HMC Laing*, I, 434.

29. "The Dionysian connexions to fertility and sacrifice are not wholly inappropriate in the depiction of a young woman approaching marriageable age." David A.H.B. Taylor, "A Rediscovered Portrait of Queen Anne, When a Child, by Sir Peter Lely," *Burlington Magazine* 145 (2003): 501–504, here quoting 504. Mr. Taylor's article includes a splendid color reproduction of the original painting.

30. Crowne, *Calisto*, 82.

31. *Memoirs of the Verney Family*, 236.

32. The fullest study remains J. P. Kenyon, *The Popish Plot* (New York: St. Martin's Press, 1972). Hutton's account (*Charles the Second,* chap. 13), on which I depend here, is clear and helpful.

33. GB-Lna, PC 2/66, fols. 392–411.

34. Luttrell, I, 1.

35. Henry Arundell, third Baron Arundell, was the brother of Katherine Cornwallis; John Belasyse was the father-in-law of Susan, Lady Belasyse.

36. See Andrew Barclay, "The Rise of Edward Colman," *Historical Journal* 42 (1999): 109–131. The MS newsletters preserved by Richard Bulstrode include 235 letters sent between 9 April 1675 and 26 September 1678 from a newsletter office organized by Colman; a note dated 31 August 1675 asks Bulstrode to address his letters "à Monsr Colman, Sece de S.A.R. Madame la Duchesse D'Yorc"; *The Bulstrode Papers,* ed. A. W. Thibaudeau (Privately printed, 1897), 313.

37. GB-Lbl Add. MS 75401, unfoliated.

38. Katherine was the widow of Francis Cornwallis (d. 1667), first cousin to Frederick Cornwallis (1610–1662), Treasurer of the King's Household at the time of the Restoration. For their marriage, but not their progeny, see the helpful pedigree of the Cornwallis family in *The Private Correspondence of Jane Lady Cornwallis, 1613–1644,* ed. Richard Griffin, Baron Braybrooke (S. & J. Bentley, Wilson & Fley, 1842), xlvi. Katherine appears among Maria's "Bed-chamber Women" in *Angliæ Notitia,* and in the establishment book for the Duke of York's household for 1677–78, with a salary of £150 a year; GB-Lbl Add. MS 18958, fol. 7r. A later note in the same MS records an additional pension of £200 granted to her by the duchess in October 1680 (fol. 13r). The entry is struck through, with an *x* in the margin. She appears again among the Bedchamber Women in the establishment book for 1682, with a salary of £150; GB-Lbl Add. MS

38863, fol. 4v. For details about her daughters, see the fascinating letter to Mrs. Cramlington from Mary Cornwallis, written after Cicely's death and dated 22 December 1725; H. J. Coleridge, *St. Mary's Convent, Micklegate Bar, York* (Burns and Oates, 1887), 133–134. Mary identifies her father as "Francis Cornwallis, not brother, but cousin german to my Lord Cornwallis, the first who was made Lord at the Restoration of King Charles the 2nd" and her mother as "daughter to my Lord Arundell at Wardour Castle." She explains that her two elder sisters, Betty and Blanche, were born in Norfolk, whereas she and Cicely were born in London. At the time of her writing, there were "but two left, my Sister Betty at Rouen and her sinful sister in the world," i.e., Mary herself.

39. For details, see Henry Foley, *Records of the English Province of the Society of Jesus*, 7 vols. (Burns and Oates, 1877–1883), V, 746–750. Father Pracid used "Cornwallis" as an alias. In her deposition, Cicely gave her age as twenty-one and stated that her father had died "11 years ago June." She identified her mother as a "retainer to the Duchess of York" and stated that she herself "lived in London with her mother till about 3 months past," which would place her departure at about the time of the first revelations of the Popish Plot. For information on the Hammersmith convent, see Edward Walford, *Old and New London*, VI, *The Southern Suburbs* (Cassell, 1893), 529–548.

40. GB-Lbl Add. MS 61426, fols. 172–174. The statement attributed to the king is partially obliterated in the manuscript.

41. See Arthur Irwin Dasent, *The History of St. James's Square* (MacMillan, 1895), especially the map showing the original inhabitants of the square, 22. Moll Davis lived next door to Arabella Churchill on the other side.

42. Harris, *Passion*, 23–25.

43. Hutton, *Charles the Second*, 361–368.

44. Letter from Sir Robert Southwell to James, first Duke of Ormond, 8 March 1679; *HMC Ormonde*, n.s., IV, 497–498. Southwell goes on to note that "some that took close and accurate notice wondered much to see so little sorrow in *iu* [the king] and *pq* [Queen Catharine]."

45. The editor of *The London Stage*, pt. 1 places this performance "between January 1677/8 and August 1679" (267). He also suggests February 1678 as the most plausible date for the first performance of *Mithridates* in the commercial theatre. The play was licensed for publication on 28 March 1678; the date of its actual appearance in print was certainly later. In practical terms, the court ladies could not easily have mounted a production between the publication of the text and Anne's going to spend the summer at Windsor. After the departure of the duke and duchess for Brussels on 3 March 1679, however, Anne and her ladies would have been in London for at least three months with little to do. The first letter in which Anne refers to Frances as Semandra is dated "Windsor June the 18th"; Bathurst suggests 1679 as the most likely year. The most revealing letter in this connection is that from Anne to Frances dated "Bruxsells October the 3d," which can only have been written in 1679, in which Anne refers to some other participants: "Pray tell my honourd Mothere faire Monima I would have writt to her but that I have not time now but will next post; my Brothere presents his service to you & says he hass writt severall times." Bathurst makes the plausible suggestion that Frances Apsley's older sister Isabella, now Lady Wentworth, may have played the part of Monima. As he also suggests, Anne's "Brothere" would be the lady who played Pharnaces. This lady was clearly with Anne in Brussels, and though we have no record of those who accompanied her, I should think Mary Cornwallis a likely candidate. There is a similar reference in a letter dated "Windsor May the 12," which Bathurst places in 1680: "I desired my Brother to lett you know why I did not write to you by him." See *LTQ*, 102–103, 112–115.

In a forthcoming book, Andrew Walkling argues that the private performance by the ladies took place *before* the first performance in a commercial theatre; his suggested date is "late 1677 or early 1678, during the Christmas/Carnival season, and prior to the Drury Lane production that is believed to have appeared sometime in February or March." My thanks to Professor Walkling for allowing me to see his argument in advance of its publication. The existence of a manuscript of this play whose provenance was one of the English nunneries in France is also intriguing. See A. L. McLeod, "The Douai Ms. of Lee's 'Mithridates,'" *Notes and Queries*, n.s., 7 (1960): 69–70. This manuscript, dated 1695, does not follow printed editions, omits several lines and one scene, and occasionally adjusts the text, for example, by replacing "right a ravish'd maid" with "right a harmless maid." In light of the fact that three of the Cornwallis sisters became nuns, it seems at least possible that this manuscript was copied from a text used in the private performance.

46.   Burnet, *History*, V, 2. The anecdote is not in Burnet's original text but in a note by William Legge, Earl of Dartmouth, son of George Legge, Master of the Horse to the Duke of York. "While the duke was in exile in Brussels and Edinburgh, [the elder] Legge was one of his chief correspondents, informing him of political developments in London." J. D. Davies, "Legge, George, First Baron Dartmouth (c.1647–1691)," in *ODNB*. If George Legge is the ultimate source of this anecdote, he was in the right place at the right time.

47.   My suspicion that Maria would not have allowed Anne to act a male role, reinforced by the fact that the princess apparently played Semandra in the production in Edinburgh in November 1681, at which Maria was present, is another reason to place this first performance *after* the departure of the Yorks for the Continent.

48.   In *Works of Nathaniel Lee*, ed. Thomas B. Stroup and Arthur L. Cooke, 2 vols. (New Brunswick: Scarecrow Press, 1954), I, 294. All citations from this edition. The editors do not comment on this odd line. Walkling interprets it as meaning that Lee was asked to write a play for the court ladies, perhaps as a follow-up to Crowne's *Calisto*, and that the commercial production came later, a plausible theory. More simply, however, Lee may be saying that he wrote the play to appeal to the ladies in the audience.

49.   *Mithridates*, act 1, scene 1, 252–257.

50.   *Mithridates*, act 1, scene 1, 185–194.

51.   See Ezechiel Spanheim, *Relation de la Cour de France*, ed. Émile Bourgeois (Paris: Picard et Fils, 1900), appendix, *Relation de la Cour d'Angleterre*, 594. There is contemporaneous evidence that such a match was being discussed before George's visit to London in December 1680. A newsletter addressed to Sir Richard Bulstrode, dated 23 February 1679 [i.e., 1680], reports: "There is a discourse, that the Bishop of Osnabrug's Son is comeing hither, in his returne from Italy, & some Courtiers will talke of a Match between him & ye Lady Anne." US-Aus PFORZ-MS-1133. George's father, Ernst August, held the title of prince-bishop of Osnabrück.

52.   GB-Lbl Add. MS 61414, fol. 13.

53.   Compare Evelyn's famous account of Charles in the final month of his life: "the King, sitting & toying with his Concubines Portsmouth, Cleaveland, & Mazarine: &c: A french boy singing love songs, in that glorious Gallery,…a sceane of uttmost vanity." *The Diary of John Evelyn*, ed. E. S. De Beer, 6 vols. (Oxford: Clarendon Press, 1955), IV, 413.

54.   *Mithridates*, act 3, scene 2, 365–372; 481–487; 531–535; 593–595.

55.   *LTQ*, 108. Anne's self-assessment is confirmed by Lord Dartmouth in his comment on her being trained in speaking by Elizabeth Barry. After noting that "it was a real pleasure to hear" Anne speak, he adds that "she had a bashfulness that made it very uneasy to herself to say much in public" (Burnet, *History*, V, 2n).

56. *Mithridates,* act 3, scene 2, 614–619; act 4, scene 1, 528–603.

57. Discussed more fully later in this chapter.

58. See chapter 1 above.

59. *The Diary of Sir David Hamilton, 1709–1714,* ed. Philip Roberts (Oxford: Clarendon, 1975), 44.

60. Hutton, *Charles the Second,* 377–378.

61. Harris, *Passion,* 27–28.

62. *LTQ,* 106–107.

63. *LTQ,* 112. There were evidently two sisters with this surname; in an earlier letter, Anne mentions writing long letters "to miss & Mrs. Watts" (*LTQ,* 104).

64. I have used Old Style or English dating throughout this episode, even though dates on the Continent were eleven days ahead, as Anne evidently dates her letters using the English calendar.

65. See Margaret Toynbee, "A Further Note on an Early Correspondence of Queen Mary of Modena," *Notes and Queries* 193 (1948): 292–295.

66. See Craig M. Rustici, "Gender, Disguise, and Usurpation: 'The Female Prelate' and the Popish Successor," *Modern Philology* 98 (2000): 271–298. For details of the pope-burning, see 271–272 and notes.

67. See Tim Harris, "Scott [Crofts], James, Duke of Monmouth and First Duke of Buccleuch (1649–1685)," in *ODNB.*

68. *A True Narrative of the Duke of Monmouth's Late Journey into the West* (1680), 3.

69. Charles II was attentive to this ceremony: "From the Restoration to his death he touched somewhere in the region of 100,000 people; with an English population of a little under five million, that figure amounts to 2 per cent of the entire population"; Anna Keay, *The Magnificent Monarch* (Continuum, 2008), 118. William III, by contrast, scoffed at the ritual as a superstition and never performed it.

70. See *The London Stage,* pt. 1, 284. Nell Gwyn, the popular actress turned royal mistress, suffered a similar insult in April, "affronted by a person who came into the pitt and called her whore" (Luttrell, I, 34–35).

71. *The Female Prelate* (1680), act 3, p. 30. My citations follow the first edition.

72. Rustici, "Gender, Disguise, and Usurpation," 273.

73. John Harold Wilson, "Theatre Notes from the Newdigate Newsletters," *Theatre Notebook* 15 (1961): 79–84, here quoting 80. *Macbeth,* in the version adapted by William Davenant, was a frequent item in the repertoire of the Duke's Company and a vehicle for Thomas Betterton, the star actor of the Company. Although the duchess would have achieved her goal of "disobliging" Settle no matter what play was performed, I should think it at least possible that she requested *Macbeth* on this occasion.

74. See *LTQ,* 109.

75. *The Female Prelate,* act 3, p. 26.

76. *HMC,* XII, ix, 100.

77. See Georg's letter to his mother (in French), 31 December 1680 [O.S.], GB-Lbl King's MS 140, fol. 113r.

78. Newsletter addressed to Sir Richard Bulstrode, US-Aus PFORZ-MS-1219.

79. "Il Principe d'Hannover è fatto Cave della Giarretiera, ma non parlasi più del suo matrimonio con la Principessa Anna, la quale n'era in sostanza innamorata." Abbé Ronchi's letter from Edinburgh, dated 12 February 1681 [N.S.], as printed in Emilia Rowles, Marchesa Campana de Cavelli, *Les Derniers Stuarts,* 2 vols. (Paris: Didier, 1871), I, 371.

80. There are only two substantive pieces of primary evidence about this episode: Georg's letter to his mother describing his visit to London, which records his being allowed to kiss the princess, and Ronchi's letter, presumably based on news or rumors that had reached him from London. But the lack of hard evidence has not prevented historians from offering speculation as fact. According to Gilbert Burnet, "the Prince of Hanover had come over...to make addresses to her: but he was scarce got hither, when he received orders from his father not to proceed in that design" (*History*, II, 380). This appears to be a conflation of two events. As Ragnhild Hatton, George I's biographer, has explained, Georg's father was in Italy at this time, and serious discussions of the plan to marry Georg to his first cousin did not begin until 1682. See Hatton, *George I, Elector and King* (Cambridge, Mass.: Harvard University Press, 1978), 40. Numerous narratives from the eighteenth century forward state as fact the theory that Georg himself or his family rejected Anne, causing her to be hostile toward him in later life. Evidence of this alleged hostility, however, is limited. Edward Gregg, Anne's distinguished biographer, dismisses the idea that the House of Hanover abandoned the plan and concludes that "Charles II and the Duke of York, not the Hanoverian court, vetoed the marriage"; Gregg, *Queen Anne*, 24. See his fuller argument in an earlier article, "Was Queen Anne a Jacobite?," *History* 62 (1972): 358–375. Others claim that Anne herself resisted Georg's advances; see for example David G. Chandler, *Marlborough as Military Commander* (New York: Scribner, 1973), who states that "Anne with difficulty fended off George as a suitor for her hand" (125–126) but offers no documentary evidence for this claim. William of Orange was also an interested party, and Agnes Strickland, though offering no evidence, argues that he worked to prevent the match: "If George of Hanover married Anne of York, and the princess of Orange died first, without offspring (as she actually did), William of Orange would have had to give way before their prior claims on the succession; to prevent which he set at work a three-fold series of intrigues, in the household of his sister-in-law, at the court of Hanover, and at that of Zell"; Strickland, *Lives of the Queens of England*, 8 vols. (Bell, 1885), VII, 78. Modern scholars, however, with convincing documentary evidence, have shown that William was in fact friendly to the match; see Hatton, *George I*, 39 and notes.

81. "L'on coupa avant hier la tête à Milord Stafort, cela ne fit pas plus de bruit, que si on l'avoit coupée à un poulet." GB-Lbl King's MS 140, fol. 113v.

82. *The Tryal of William Viscount Stafford for High Treason* (1680/81), 5.

83. Charles Blount, *Appeal from the Country to the City* (1679), 29.

84. Dryden, *The Spanish Fryar*, act 1, scene 1, 65–70.

85. Dryden, *The Spanish Fryar*, act 5, scene 2, 431–432.

86. When critics pointed out that Dryden, as usual, had stolen much of his plot from earlier sources, Charles supposedly exclaimed, "God's fish! steal me such another play any of you, and I'll frequent it as much as I do the Spanish Fryar." This anecdote was first printed in *Biographia Dramatica*, ed. Stephen Jones, 3 vols. (Longman, Hurst, etc., 1812), III, 292. It does not appear in the edition of 1764, edited by David Erskine Baker, or in the edition of 1782, edited by Isaac Reed.

87. For a detailed account of the episode, see my *John Dryden and His World* (New Haven: Yale University Press, 1987), 325–329 and notes.

88. According to Edward Gregg, "it was even suggested, albeit without significant results, that Lady Anne should be named heir, as the candidate of national unity, being of undoubted legitimacy and unscarred by marriage to a foreign prince and by residence abroad" (*Queen Anne*, 19–20).

89. See David Ogg, *England in the Reign of Charles II*, 2 vols. (Oxford: Clarendon Press, 1934; rev. ed. 1955), II, 616; K.H.D. Haley, *The First Earl of Shaftesbury* (Oxford: Clarendon Press, 1968), 631–632; Bryan Bevan, *Nell Gwyn* (Robert Hale, 1969), 136–137.

90. *The Earl of Shaftsbury's Expedient for Settling the Nation, Discoursed with His Majesty in the House of Peers at Oxford, Mar. 24th 1680/1* (1681), 5–7.

91. See H. C. Foxcroft, ed., *A Supplement to Burnet's History of my own Time* (Oxford: Clarendon Press, 1832), 106.

92. Luttrell, I, 103.

93. James to the Countess of Litchfield, 26 November 1681; "Some familiar Letters," 161–162.

94. *CSP Dom., 1680/81*, 407.

95. Harris, *Passion*, 30.

96. "Some familiar Letters," 161, 164.

97. "Some familiar Letters," 161. For details, see William van Lennep, "The Smock Alley Players of Dublin," *ELH* 13 (1946): 216–222.

98. Sir John Lauder of Fountainhall, *Historical Observes of Memorable Occurrents* (Edinburgh, 1840), 51.

99. "Some familiar Letters," 162.

100. As van Lennep explains, W. R. Chetwood, who is the oldest authority for the claim that Ashbury coached Anne in this role, says that the performance took place "in the Banqueting-House, Whitehall." Chetwood, *A General History of the Stage* (1749), 84 and note. But there is no other evidence to support the idea of a London performance. Because there is firm evidence that Ashbury and Anne were both in Edinburgh in 1681, and firm evidence of a performance of *Mithridates* there, van Lennep reasonably concludes that Ashbury's instruction took place in Scotland. See "The Smock Alley Players," 220 and note.

101. *LTQ*, 138.

102. Thomas Cartwright, *A sermon preached at Holy-Rood House, January 30, 1681/2, before Her Highness the Lady Anne* (Edinburgh, 1682), sigs. A2r–B1r.

103. Luttrell, I, 171.

104. See Harold Love, "The Wreck of the *Gloucester*," *Musical Times* 125 (1984): 194–195, and *RECM*, I, 200; II, 2. Greeting was the "Thomas Greeton" first named as a "Musitian" to Princess Mary in the 1673 edition of *Angliæ Notitia*.

105. According to R. O. Bucholz, there were some eleven hundred "places" at the court of Charles II, and three hundred more at the court of the Duke and Duchess of York. *The Augustan Court: Queen Anne and the Decline of Court Culture* (Stanford: Stanford University Press, 1993), 12–13.

106. Kingsmill appears among Maria's maids of honor in the establishment book for the court of the Duke and Duchess of York dated 29 September 1682 (GB-Lbl Add. MS 38863, fol. 5r), and in the similar list printed in *Angliæ Notitia* (1684). For details of her literary activities and a new attribution, see James A. Winn, "'A Versifying Maid of Honour': Anne Finch and the Libretto for *Venus and Adonis*," *Review of English Studies*, n.s., 59 (2008): 67–85.

107. Although frequently described as a maid of honor, Killigrew does not appear on any surviving official list. She may have been appointed after the completion of the establishment book of 1682, but she does not appear in *Angliæ Notitia* for either 1682 or 1684. She was evidently resident at court; her father, Henry Killigrew, was almoner to the duke, and appears on the list of his pensioners. GB-Lbl Add. MS 38863, fol. 2r. Agnes Strickland lists both Kingsmill and Killigrew among six alleged maids of honor to Maria (*Lives of the Queens of England*, IV, 307) citing Gregorio Leti, but in fact Leti lists neither. He lists only "Quattro Dame d'honore,"

Catherine Sedley, Catherine Watts, Frances Walsingham, and Catherine Frazier. *Del Teatro Brittanico*, 2 vols. (1683), II, 691.

108. "La Prencipessa Anna tiene ancora vna Corte decente, con più di 30. Persone tutte Salariate, particolarmente buon numero di Maestri per ogni sorte di nobile professione. La Signora Vicontessa Hyde è la sua Gouernatrice, che ne hà sempre tenuto particular cura." Leti, *Del Teatro Brittanico*, II, 692.

109. *HMC*, VII, 98. On 5 October 1682, the Bulstrode newsletters reported the earl's dismissal: "My Lord Mulgrave is disgraced and forbid the Court; and all his employments are disposed of." More than a month later, the writer was still unable or unwilling to state the cause: "Whitehall November 10, 1682. In my last I told you of the disgrace of the Earle of Mulgrave,…which I can now confirme, but cannot tell you the cause of it, that remaining still a secret." US-Aus PFORZ-MS-1383, 1392. Luttrell, in a reference under the heading "November," but without a specific date, says that Mulgrave "is fallen into his majesties displeasure (by pretending courtship, as is said, to the Lady Ann, daughter to his royall highnesse)" (I, 236). A manuscript poem on Mulgrave's fall, preserved in the Portland MSS, compares him to Lucifer and Nimrod:

> So falls our Courtier now, to pride a prey,
> And falls too, with as much reproach as they.
> And justly.
> That with nauseous Courtship durst defile
> The Sweetest Choicest beauty of our Isle:
> That he was proud wee knew; but now we see.
> (Like Janus, looking at Eternity)
> Both what he was and what he meant to be.
> Stern was his Look and sturdy was his gate,
> He walk'd and talk'd and wou'd have F____'d in State.
> Disdain and scorn sat perching on his brow;
> But (Presto!) where is all that greatness now?
> Why Vanish'd, fled, disolv'd to empty Air,
> Fine ornaments indeed to cheat the Fair!
> And which is yet the strangest thing of all
> He has not got one friend to mourn his fall. (GB-NO Portland MS Pw V 45/3)

Though banished from Whitehall, Mulgrave was not, as many sources state, punished by being sent to Tangiers in a leaky boat. That episode occurred in 1680, long before his flirtation with the princess.

110. A manuscript diary preserved in the Portland MSS gives some details of the child's illness and death. When she began to have convulsions, her father was at Newmarket with the king, and a special messenger was dispatched to summon him home. "Last Sunday night," writes the diarist on 10 October, "the Lady Charlotte Maria the Duke of Yorks youngest daughter was very magnificently interred amongst the Royall ffamily in Westm.r Abby since which time the Duchesse has been much indisposed so that his highnesse continues att St. Jamess till her recovery and then designes for Newmarkett againe." GB-NO Portland MS Pw V 95, fol. 6r.

111. "The Dream," in *The Works of John Sheffield…Duke of Buckingham*, 2 vols. (1723), I, 30–32. Queen Anne made Sheffield Duke of Buckingham in 1703. Alexander Pope was the editor of his posthumous works, which were suppressed on their first appearance because of several Jacobitical passages in the prose. There were many subsequent editions.

112. "An Allusion to Horace," ll. 61–66, in *The Works of John Wilmot, Earl of Rochester,* ed. Harold Love (Oxford: Oxford University Press, 1999), 72.

113. "The Convert," in *The Works of Buckingham,* I, 60–61.

114. For a list of Kirk's reputed lovers, see above, chapter 1.

115. *LTQ,* 154.

116. "Whitehall August 20, 1683. The Earle of Mulgrave has kissed the King's and Dukes hand, and does now make his Court very constantly.... August 24. My Lord Mulgrave has waited againe as Gentleman of the Bedchamber to the King." US-Aus PFORZ-MS-1466, 1467.

117. The crucial record here is a dispatch from the French ambassador Paul Barillon, dated 9/19 November 1682: "On a chassé de Saint Gesmes la fille d'une femme de chamber de Meadame la Duchesse d' York, nommeé Meistris Cornouwalis. Elle estoit fort bien avec la Princesse Anne. Cela fait soupçonner qu'il y a en quelque intelligence entre elle et Milord Meaugraf, et que cette fille estoit la confidante. Le fonds de tout cela n'est pas encore bien eclairez, mais la disgrace de Meilord Meaugraf est complette autant qu'elle le peut etre on ce pays cy." GB-Lna PRO 31/3/153, fol. 72v.

118. Letter from Princess Mary to Lady Bathurst, 23 February 1683 (*LTQ,* 158). "The persone you there mention" has sometimes been thought to refer to Mulgrave, but the term "friendship" and the reference to "such time as *she* was forbid" make it clear that Mary is writing (somewhat guardedly) about Mary Cornwallis.

119. In his notes to Burnet's *History* (II, 91), William Legge claims that Sarah used Bishop Compton in order to get rid of Mary Cornwallis so that "she should have the entire confidence to herself." As Frances Harris has pointed out, however, Legge, whose father was jealous of John Churchill's close relationship with the Duke of York, is not a reliable witness. See *Passion,* 32–33 and notes.

120. GB-Lbl Add. MS 61426, fol. 5.

121. GB-Lbl Add. MS 61426, fol. 172.

122. GB-Lbl Add. MS 61414, fol. 10, editorially dated [1683?]. In this and subsequent citations, "editorial dates" are those penciled into the manuscripts by British Library staff.

123. *CSP Dom., Charles II, January–June 1683,* 296, 311.

124. The earliest extant letters from Anne to Sarah all appear to concern this appointment; see GB-Lbl Add. MS 61414, fols. 1–6.

125. *CSP Dom., October 1683–April 1684,* 182; *CSP Dom., July 1684–February 1685,* 293; *HMC Buccleuch,* II, 209.

Chapter 3

1. *HC,* caption to the illustration following 104.

2. GB-Lbl King's MS 140, fol. 48r: "Les Soldats du Regiment des Gardes ayant des habits neufs, et dans un equipage fort leste, étoient ranges en haye des 2. côtés de la ruë."

3. *HC,* 33.

4. See above, chapter 1, note 18.

5. Luttrell, I, 286; 30 October 1683.

6. Luttrell, I, 335. Lely had died in 1680, and Charles II, not atypically, had left the post unfilled until June 1684, when he appointed Verrio.

7. On Verrio's work for Charles, of which fragments survive, see Cécile Brett, "Antonio Verrio (c1636–1707): His Career and Surviving Work," *British Art Journal* 10 (2009–10): 4–17. When he became king, James gave the "Queen's Chapel" at St. James's Palace, built for Henrietta Maria by Inigo Jones, to his queen and worshiped there with her until his new chapel

opened in December 1686. Princess Anne continued to worship in the Anglican Chapel Royal. See the entry for March 1685 in the *Memoirs of Sir John Reresby*, ed. Andrew Browning, rev. Mary K. Geiter and W. A. Speck (Royal Historical Society, 1991), 356: "It was now out of doubt that the King was a papist, for he went publiquly to mass, but ordered the chappell at Whitehall to be kept in the same order as formerly, wher the Princesse of Denmark went daily. The King repaired to the Queens private chappell." In *HMC Rutland,* II, 109, there is a puzzling entry dated 2 June [1686], claiming that "Her [Anne's] chappell at Whithall is taken away to have masse said there, and all the chapplings dismissed." The writer, evidently recording a rumor, was misinformed: Anglican services continued in the Chapel Royal throughout the reign. See, for example, the letter of 21 October 1687, from the Lord Chamberlain, at this time Anne's former suitor the Earl of Mulgrave, to Nicholas Staggins, Master of the King's Music: "Whereas you have neglected to give Order to the Violins to attend at the Chappell at White-hall where Her Royal Highnesse the Princesse Ann of Denmarke is present. These are there-fore to give notice to them that they give theire attendance there upon Sunday next & soe continue to doe so as formerly they did." GB-Lna LC 5/148, fol. 31, printed in *RECM,* II, 15–16. My thanks to Peter Leech for helpful correspondence about the various chapels.

8. *HC*, sig. c1r.
9. According to a petition from Sandford, "His Matie giving special directions to be very minute & particular therein, the History became Enlarged from 12 sheets to 37 sheets, besides the addition of more Sculps than were proposed." He goes on to beg for additional compensation. GB-Lbl Harleian MS 6815, fol. 167r. As Matthias Range notes, citing a penciled annotation on GB-Ob G.2.8.Jur., it appears that only one hundred copies of Sandford's book were printed, with a retail cost of £100—a huge sum for a book. See *Music and Ceremonial at British Corona-tions from James I to Elizabeth II* (Cambridge: Cambridge University Press, 2012), 62–63.
10. *HC*, 6.
11. *HC*, 4.
12. Range, *Music and Ceremonial*, 65–66.
13. Francis Turner, *A Sermon Preached before Their Majesties K. James II and Q. Mary at their Coro-nation* (1685), 18–20.
14. *HC*, 89.
15. GB-Lbl King's MS 140, fol. 53r: "La Reine alla voir la Princesse de Danemarc dans la logue qu'on avoit faite, au dessus de celle des Ministres publies, pour S. A. qui y étoit incognito, S. M. resta quelque tems a parler avec elle et avec le Prince de Danemarc, d'où Elle S'en retourna precedent le Roi dans le même ordre, à la grande Sale de Westmunster."
16. Luttrell, I, 345.
17. GB-Lbl Add. MS 61426, fol. 33.
18. Bruce Wood discovered this anthem in Ely Cathedral MS 6, where it is attributed to Blow; see "A Coronation Anthem Lost and Found," *Musical Times* 118 (1977): 466–468. In his very full account of all the music used at the coronation (*Music and Ceremonial*, 67–93), Range supports the manuscript attribution to Blow, discounting Sandford's printed statement that the anthem was "composed by Mr. *Hen. Purcell*." On stylistic grounds, I believe the music is Pur-cell's. Until Wood's discovery, it had been thought that the anthem sung at the coronation was another setting by Purcell of the same text, composed in about 1683 for the Chapel Royal, but this work is much more intimate in scale and less well suited to a grand occasion. Significantly, the setting of the same phrase in this earlier anthem is even more dissonant, with the disso-nance again at its most intense on the word "peace."

🔊 Mus. Ex. 3.2: Henry Purcell, excerpt from *I was glad* (1683).

In the wake of the Exclusion Crisis, there was at least as much reason to pray for peace in 1683 as in 1685.

19. *The Diary of John Evelyn*, ed. E. S. De Beer, 6 vols. (Oxford: Clarendon Press, 1955), II, 292–293 (11 April 1689).

20. For the longer list of bishops, see GB-Lbl Harleian MS 6815, fol. 170r. For a list of bishops in attendance in 1685, see *HC*, 73. Handwritten annotations in one of the British Library copies of Sandford's account (shelfmark 604.i.19) note that in addition to the nine names printed there, five other bishops marched in 1685, one in his post as dean of Westminster, and two each supporting the king and queen; another was present at Westminster Hall but physically unable to walk in the procession. The annotator also lists nine absent bishops.

21. GB-Lbl Harleian MS 6815, f. 170v. Although the last number in each column appears to be a total, in neither case is it an accurate sum. The columns add up to ninety-two and seventy-seven, respectively.

22. GB-Lbl Add. MS 61422, fol. 199.

23. The order of service, which was adjusted by Bishop Compton, is printed in full in *Three Coronation Orders*, ed. J. William Legg (Henry Bradshaw Society, 1900), 15–36. In his learned introduction, Legg also provides a useful chart comparing the order of service for William and Mary with that used by James II; see xiv. The rare broadside partially shown in the text here is not listed in the *English Short Title Catalogue*. The only copy known to me is tipped into the Boston Athenæum's copy of *HC*.

24. "The coronation came on; that was to be all vanity, yet the Bishop of London spoke seriously of it and shewd me it ought to be an act of devotion and accordingly they made some very good

alterations in the Office.... One thing was to be done which I was much against, it was receiving the Sacrament; this all I could say they would have it, because it had been left out by my father, and worldly considerations prevailing it was done; but I confess my self much to blame in the matter, and never had any thing so much troubled me as that did; for there was so much pomp and vanity in all the ceremony that left little time for devotion." *MQE Memoirs*, 12. As Melinda Zook has pointed out, "Mary's image as a passive wife to William was...a product of her own making. She crafted her 'memoirs' (descriptions of the years between 1689 and 1693, written at the end of year in one or two sittings) within the conventional ideas of womanhood in the late seventeenth century—passive, obedient, pious—and, unlike most of her other personal papers, she did not burn them when she became ill. The 'memoirs' represent Mary as she wished to be remembered and need to be balanced against other sources that often describe the Queen as firm, assertive, and once convinced, unwavering." See "The Shocking Death of Mary II: Gender & Political Crisis in Late Stuart England," *British Scholar* 1 (2008): 21–36, here quoting 23.

25. "'Tis well known how frequently [I may say constantly] she joyn'd in the Worship of God with the *Dutch* and *French* Churches, tho' their Constitution and Order are very different from those of the Church of *England*. I have been a witness of the Kindness and Respect, with which she treated *English* Dissenting Ministers, and was present when she thank'd one of that quality, for a Practical Book of Divinity, which he had publish'd, and had been put into her Hands." *The Royal Diary* (1705), 7 (brackets original).

26. *MQE Memoirs*, 4–5.

27. Gilbert Burnet, *A Sermon Preached at the Coronation of William III. and Mary II* (1689), 5. Burnet's text, quoted here as printed in his sermon, is 2 Samuel 23:3; Turner's text, quoted from *A Sermon Preached before Their Majesties,* is 1 Chronicles 29:23. Unless otherwise noted, all biblical quotations are KJV.

28. *England's Royal Renown, in the Coronation...* (1685).

29. GB-Lbl Add. MS 75384, fol. 168r. The holographs of the letters Princess Anne wrote to Princess Mary during the reign of James II no longer exist. I follow the manuscript versions preserved in GB-Lbl Add. MS 75384, most of which are printed (in somewhat modernized versions) in *LDI,* 16–43.

30. Charles Sackville, Earl of Dorset, patron of poets and himself an amateur poet, had married Henry Compton's niece Mary in 1685, so the two men had a family alliance as well as a shared distaste for the rule of James II.

31. *HC,* 88.

32. *The Form of the Intended Coronation Oath* (1688).

33. *JHL,* XVII, 68.

34. For a full-scale exposition of the latter view, see Steve Pincus, *1688: The First Modern Revolution* (New Haven: Yale University Press, 2009).

35. GB-Lbl Add. MS 75384, fol. 167v; compare *LDI,* 16.

36. *Pindarick Poem on the Coronation,* in *The Works of Aphra Behn,* ed. Janet Todd, 6 vols. (Pickering and Chatto, 1992), I, 200–221, ll. 6–7, 25, 27, 32–36, 230–247.

37. *Venus and Adonis,* following the collation of manuscripts provided by Andrew Walkling in "Court, Culture, and Politics in Restoration England: Charles II, James II, and the Performance of Baroque Monarchy," Ph.D. diss. (Cornell University, 1997), II, 604. The description of Killigrew as "Accomplisht" is from the title of Dryden's ode in her memory.

38. On the painting, see C. H. Collins Baker, "Notes on Pictures in the Royal Collections— XXIV—Anne Killigrew," *Burlington Magazine* 28 (1915): 112–116. The original canvas, which has recently been cleaned, now hangs at the Falmouth Art Gallery in Cornwall.

39. Alexander Pope, *The Rape of the Lock*, I, 133; II, 21–22. Maureen Duffy was the first modern scholar to point out the influence of Behn's poem on Pope's; see *The Passionate Shepherdess* (Cape, 1977), 237.

40. *Spectator* 253 (30 October 1712). This and all citations from *The Spectator*, ed. Donald F. Bond, 5 vols. (Oxford: Clarendon Press, 1965). Addison had almost certainly seen a draft of Pope's poem.

41. For a very full study, see Abigail Williams, *Poetry and the Creation of a Whig Literary Culture, 1681–1714* (Oxford: Oxford University Press, 2005).

42. Behn, *Pindarick Poem*, ll. 260–266.

43. See Andrew Barclay, "Sedley, Catharine, Suo Jure Countess of Dorchester, and Countess of Portmore (1657–1717)," in *ODNB*.

44. *The Proceeding to the Coronation of their Majesties King William and Queen Mary* (shown in an illustration earlier in this chapter) confirms that this custom was preserved, even in 1689.

45. GB-Lbl Add. MS 63759, fol. 48r; for a similar letter from Graham to the Earl of Sunderland, see *HMC*, VII, i, 288–290.

46. Shadwell's model was the *tragédie-ballet* by Molière produced in 1671, with musical scenes by Lully, not the later opera adapted from that play in 1678. Matthew Locke wrote the music for *Psyche*, which is extant and has been printed in *Dramatic Music, with the Music by Humfrey, Banister, Reggio and Hart for "The Tempest,"* ed. Michael Tilmouth, *Musica Britannica*, vol. 51 (Stainer and Bell, 1986). John Banister, listed as music master (i.e., harpsichord teacher) to Princess Anne in 1677, wrote the music for *Circe;* his settings of act 1 survive in manuscripts at the Royal College of Music and the Fitzwilliam Museum, Cambridge.

47. See Sandra Tuppen, "Shrovetide Dancing: Balls and Masques at Whitehall under Charles II," *Court Historian* 15 (2010): 157–169.

48. Dryden, *Works*, XV, 3.

49. For an excellent account of the visual iconography of this opera, see Paul Hammond, "Dryden's *Albion and Albanius:* The Apotheosis of Charles II," in *The Court Masque*, ed. David Lindley (Manchester: Manchester University Press, 1984), 169–183.

50. Dryden, *Works*, I, 48.

51. *Albion and Albanius*, act 1, scene 1, 72.

52. With Bryan White's permission, I have added a necessary flat to the third quarter-note in the fourth viola part in the last complete bar quoted in this excerpt.

53. *Albion and Albanius*, act 3, scene 1, stage direction.

54. *HMC*, XII, v, ii, 85; John Harold Wilson, the first modern scholar to call attention to this record, gives the date as 24 May; "More Theatre Notes from the Newdigate Newsletters," *Theatre Notebook* 16 (1962), 59. But the actual date was 29 May, which was the king's birthday and the anniversary of his restoration.

55. Boyer, *Annals*, IX, 335. Boyer later condensed his *Annals*, which he had published annually, into a comprehensive account: Boyer, *History*. The *History* includes some political details that Boyer might have been reluctant to publish during Anne's lifetime, while the *Annals* include some details of court life that he deleted from the *History*. For details of the performance in 1711, see chapter 10 below. "Nicolini" (properly Nicolo Grimaldi) was the leading singer in the opera company at the time.

56. *A True Narrative of the Duke of Monmouth's Late Journey into the West* (1680), 3.

57. See especially the letters preserved in the Middleton Papers, GB-Lbl Add. MS 41803.

58. *The Declaration of James, Duke of Monmouth* (1685), 2–3.

59. "I see plainly," Churchill wrote to Clarendon, "that the troble is mine, and that the honor will be anothers: however my life shall be freely exposed for the Kings service." *The Correspondence of Henry Hyde, Earl of Clarendon*, 2 vols. (Colburn, 1828), I, 141.

60. Luttrell, I, 360.

61. See Maurice Lee, Jr., *The Heiresses of Buccleuch* (East Lothian: Tuckwell Press, 1996), 1–3, 117–118.

62. GB-Lbl Add. MS 61414, fols. 21, 23.

63. Reresby, *Memoirs*, 385.

64. Luttrell, I, 364.

65. Reresby, *Memoirs*, 405.

66. *The Ellis Correspondence*, ed. G. A. Ellis, 2 vols. (Colburn, 1829), I, 3.

67. See musical example 3.4.

68. *Ellis Correspondence*, I, 136–137. After the Revolution, *An exact account of the whole proceedings against the Right Reverend Father in God, Henry, Lord Bishop of London, before the Lord Chancellor and the other ecclesiastical commissioners* (1688) appeared in print. Compton was probably responsible for this pamphlet, which quotes in full the documents he was prevented from reading at the hearing.

69. John Michael Wright, *An Account of his Excellence Roger Earl of Castlemaine's Embassy, From his Sacred Majesty James the IId.... To His Holiness Innocent XI* (1688), 1.

70. Wright, *Castlemaine's Embassy*, 71–73.

71. S. E. Plank, "Monmouth in Italy: *L'Ambitione Debellata*," *Musical Times* 132 (1991): 280–284.

72. See W. J. Lawrence, "The French Opera in London: A Riddle of 1686," *Times Literary Supplement* (28 March 1936): 268. There is no surviving English word-book.

73. My paraphrase of the stage direction for act 4, scene 2, and the recitative sung by Echion in act 4, scene 3. *Cadmus et Hermione...Partition Génerale* (Paris, 1719), 135, 138. This was the first printing of the music; the libretto, verbally identical in this scene, was printed in 1673.

74. Peregrine Bertie, in a letter to the Countess of Rutland, *HMC*, XII, v, ii, 104.

75. Thomas Jevon, *The Devil of a Wife* (1686), sig. A4r.

76. GB-Lbl Add. MS 75384, fol. 167r; compare *LDI*, 28.

77. *Ellis Correspondence*, I, 92.

78. *HMC Rutland*, II, 109. This is the same letter that erroneously reports that Anne's chapel is being taken away; see note 7 above.

79. Luttrell, I, 377.

80. Sarah's first daughter, born in 1679, lived just two years, but the daughters born in 1681, 1683, 1688, and 1689 all lived to adulthood.

81. GB-Lbl Add. MS 61414, fol. 106. Thomas Wentworth, who was among the Pages of Honor to the queen, may have been the person insulted by Greeting. See GB-Lbl Add. MS 38863, fol. 5r.

82. GB-Lbl Add. MS 61426, fols. 5–6.

83. GB-Lbl Add. MS 61414, fol. 167.

84. *Ellis Correspondence*, I, 153–154; 167–168.

85. Evelyn, *Diary*, IV, 534–535 (5 January 1687); IV, 537 (30 January 1687). The castrato Evelyn heard, Giovanni Francesco Grossi, was called "Siface." See also Evelyn's account of his performance at a private salon arranged by Pepys (IV, 547; 19 April 1687).

86. *The Letters of John Dryden*, ed. Charles E. Ward (Durham: Duke University Press, 1942), 27. For Etherege's pension, see GB-Lbl Add. MS 38863, fol. 4.

87. *Letters of Rachel, Lady Russell*, 2 vols. (Longman, Brown, Green, and Longmans, 1853), I, 212.

88. GB-Lbl Add. MS 75384, fol. 168v; compare *LDI*, 30–31.

89. Writing to Mary in March, Anne complains about this decision: "The satisfaction I propos'd to myself of seeing you this spring has been deny'd me." GB-Lbl Add. MS 75384, fol. 165 r–v.

90. See the diary of Younger's friend Thomas Smith, a valuable source for details of this episode, printed in John Rouse Bloxam, *Magdalen College and King James II, 1686–1688* (Oxford: Oxford Historical Society, 1886), 3.

91. GB-Lbl Add. MS 75384, fol. 168r; compare *LDI*, 29–30.

92. *English Historical Documents, 1660–1714*, ed. Andrew Browning (Eyre and Spottiswoode, 1953), 399–400.

93. Luttrell, I, 397–398.

94. Evelyn, *Diary*, IV, 545 (25 March 1687).

95. Barillon to Louis XIV, 3 April 1687; printed in Emilia Rowles, Marchesa Campana de Cavelli, *Les Derniers Stuarts*, 2 vols. (Paris: Didier, 1871), II, 130.

96. GB-Lbl Add. MS 75384, fol. 169r; compare *LDI*, 32.

97. See the letter of Father Petre, quoted (without a reference) in Edwin and Marion Sharpe Grew, *The Court of William III* (Mills and Boon, 1910), 194: "Luther was never more earnest than this Prince."

98. *Autobiography of Sir John Bramston* (Camden Society, 1845), 280–281.

99. *Diary of Thomas Cartwright* (Westminster: Camden Society, 1843), 67. For Cartwright's sermon dedicated to Anne in 1682, see chapter 3 above.

100. Count Terriesi to the Grand Duke of Tuscany, 21 November/1 December 1687, translated and quoted in Martin Haile, *Queen Mary of Modena: Her Life and Letters* (Dent, 1905), 172.

101. GB-Lbl Add. MS 75384, fol. 173r; compare *LDI*, 34.

102. Edward Gregg, a generally sympathetic biographer, calls her "the major perpetrator, and perhaps the originator, of the calumny that her stepmother's pregnancy was false." *Queen Anne*, 53. While she did express doubt about the pregnancy, Anne can scarcely be called the "originator" of the doubts about the birth, as she was not present at the delivery.

103. *Ellis Correspondence*, I, 345–346.

104. *Correspondence of Henry Hyde, Earl of Clarendon*, II, 169.

105. For a shrewd discussion of this possibility, see Gregg, *Queen Anne*, 53.

106. Sarah, who was meticulous about saving Anne's letters from other periods, presumably destroyed these letters because they contained evidence of planning for the Revolution of 1688. On Anne's mental state, see Terriesi to the grand duke, 23 December/2 January 1687/8, in Haile, *Queen Mary of Modena*, 173.

107. For Mary's disapproval of Anne's absence, see *Lettres et Mémoires de Marie Reine D'Angleterre*, ed. Comtesse de Bentinck (La Haye: Nijhoff, 1880), 73. Boyer, following Burnet, claims that James urged his daughter to go to Bath, telling her that "He was sure the Waters and the Bathing had been so beneficial to the Queen, that he could not doubt but that they would do her a great deal of good" (Boyer, *History*, 3; compare Burnet, *History*, III, 249). For an example of doubts about the birth of the prince, see the long letter dated 13 June 1688, usually attributed to James Johnstone, in GB-Lbl Add. MS 13545, fols. 70–79: "The generality of people conclude all is a trick; because they say, the reckoning is changed, the Princess sent away, none of the Clarendon Family, nor the Dutch Ambassadour sent for" (fol. 74r).

108. *HMC Portland*, III, 409. A few months earlier, on 1 April, Anne had heard Bishop Ken preach in London. John Evelyn's notes are sufficient proof of the political urgency of the message: "The Princesse being come, The Bishop preached on 7: Mich[ah] 8.9.10: Describing the Calamity of the Reformed Church of Judah, under the Babylonish persecution, for her sinns;…That yet by Gods providence from this Captive desolate state as Juda emerged; So should the now Reformed Church, where ever persecuted & Insulted over:…This he preached

with his accustom'd action, zeale & Energie, so as people flock'd from all quarters to heare him." *Diary*, IV, 577–578 (1 April 1688).

109. GB-Lbl Add. MS 27402, fol. 168.

110. *Britannia Rediviva*, ll. 122–125. Dryden's own footnote to this passage, "*Alluding to the Temptations in the Wilderness*," seems deliberately misleading, as if he did not quite want to acknowledge his reference to what an earlier footnote calls "*the Commonwealth Party*."

111. GB-Lbl Add. MS 75384, fol. 169v; compare *LDI*, 38.

112. *Britannia Rediviva*, ll. 165–168.

113. From a letter by Erasmus to the orator of the University of Louvain, as translated by Francis Morgan Nichols in *The Epistles of Erasmus*, 3 vols. (Longmans, 1901), I, 366.

114. *Britannia Rediviva*, ll. 239–244.

115. *Britannia Rediviva*, ll. 359–361.

116. *England's Triumphs for the Prince of Wales* (1688).

117. *Diary* IV, 591 (17 July 1688); compare Luttrell, I, 451.

118. *Works*, ed. Todd, I, 298, ll. 45–48.

119. Luttrell, I, 452.

120. Harris, *Passion*, 46. For an extended argument to the effect that Churchill was the leading conspirator, see Stephen Saunders Webb, *Lord Churchill's Coup* (New York: Knopf, 1995).

121. *Ellis Correspondence*, II, 135.

122. *Ellis Correspondence*, II, 254.

123. *CSP Dom., James II, 1687–89*, documents 2050, 2051 (372, 373).

124. *Ellis Correspondence*, II, 368–369.

125. Beville Higgons, *A Short View of English History* (1734), 304–305. This anecdote does not appear in the earlier edition of 1727, which is a suspicious circumstance, nor is there any other evidence of theatrical performances during the Revolution turmoil.

126. James and his court "attended a higher proportion of the plays given in London during his reign than any other later Stuart monarch, including his theater-loving brother." R. O. Bucholz, *The Augustan Court: Queen Anne and the Decline of Court Culture* (Stanford: Stanford University Press, 1993), 25.

127. "But I do solemnly protest, that, if there be truth in any mortal, I was so very simple a creature, that I never once dreamt of his being king. Having never *read*, nor employed my time in any thing but playing at cards; and, having no ambition my self, I imagined that the PRINCE OF ORANGE's sole design was to provide for the safety of his own country, by obliging KING JAMES to keep the laws of ours; and that he would go back as soon as he had made us all happy." *Conduct*, 20. Frances Harris (*Passion*, 53) accepts this explanation, though the self-deprecating remark about playing cards looks overstated, and the claim to have "no ambition my self" is evidently false. For a clear account of the history of the printed version of *Conduct*, see Harris, "Accounts of the Conduct of Sarah, Duchess of Marlborough, 1704–1742," *British Library Journal* (1982): 7–35.

128. Reresby, *Memoirs*, 551 (2 February 1689).

129. Boyer, *History*, 5.

130. *Conduct*, 22–23.

131. Agnes Strickland, *Lives of the Queens of England*, 8 vols. (Bell, 1885), VII, 198, citing the "MSS. of [John] Anstis, Garter king at arms." Anstis, an "indefatigable antiquarian,…left a mass of unpublished papers,…now held in the British Library, the Bodleian Library, and All Souls, Oxford." See Stuart Handley, "Anstis, John (1669–1744)," in *ODNB*. I have not been able to locate the particular MS containing this anecdote.

CHAPTER 4

1. Lewis, 14, 53, 16.
2. Anne owned a small house in Windsor, described by John Macky in *A Journey Through England* (1714): "Over against the Bridge which leads to the upper Court, is a neat little Palace, that joins to the Park, which this Queen purchased when She was Princess of *Denmark,* and lived in it, when in Disgrace with King *William* [i.e., during the period from January 1692 until Mary's death in December of 1694]. The Green-House and Garden are very Fine, and Her Majesty Retires often hither from the Castle, when she would be free from Company. The Duke of St. *Albans,* Natural Son to King *Charles* the Second, by Mrs. *Guyn,* hath also a Palace here, which was built by his Mother" (27). By 1695, having come to a partial reconciliation with William, Anne was again able to use Windsor Castle, but as this record suggests, she remained fond of the house adjoining Windsor Great Park. As early as 1685, she had been interested in the adjacent house, then used by Charles II's mistress Nell Gwyn. In a letter editorially dated [?3 August 1685], she tells Sarah: "I like what you advise me about Nellys hous very well but I will not trouble the King about anything more now because I shall not be at Windsor this yeare except he should alter his resolution about going to Winchester." GB-Lbl Add. MS 61414, fol. 31.
3. Lewis, 9, 14, 16, 61. Lewis names "Mr. Boscawen, and my Lord Churchill, with the two Mr. Bathursts." Hugh Boscawen, the oldest at about sixteen, was the nephew of Anne's close friend Sidney Godolphin; his mother, Godolphin's sister Jael, was friendly with Sarah Churchill, whose darling son John, now nine years old, was another member of the group. The two young Bathursts were Allen and Peter, sons of Anne's Household Treasurer Benjamin and his wife Frances. A third son, Benjamin, born in 1693, was too young to be a playmate at this time, but a painting made in 1697, when he was four, shows him as Gloucester's attendant (see the illustration later in this chapter, John Smith, *William Duke of Gloucester; Benjamin Bathurst,* mezzotint after Thomas Murray, 1697).
4. Lewis, 68–69.
5. Lewis, 12, 76, 29, 50.
6. For a detailed description, see Olive Baldwin and Thelma Wilson, "Who Can from Joy Refraine? Purcell's Birthday Song for the Duke of Gloucester," *Musical Times* 122 (1981): 596–599.
7. This work was once thought to be for James II, but as Bryan White has shown, it was intended for the infant Gloucester. See "Music for a 'Brave Livlylike Boy': The Duke of Gloucester, Purcell, and 'The Noise of Foreign Wars,'" *Musical Times* 148 (2007): 75–83.
8. Dedication to *A choice collection of lessons for the harpsichord or spinnet composed by ye late Mr. Henry Purcell* (1696).
9. Purcell wrote music for Crowne's tragedy *Regulus* (1692) and his comedy *The Married Beau* (1694), and Crowne was receiving an annual pension of £50, which his contemporaries believed Princess Anne had requested. See Neman, "Crowne, John," in *ODNB.* The pension, described simply as "bounty," dates from 18 June 1695; *CTB,* X, 1386.
10. All citations of words and music follow *A Song for the Duke of Gloucester's Birthday, 1695,* ed. Ian Spink (Kent: Novello, 1990), in *The Works of Henry Purcell,* IV. In the edition of 1891, W. H. Cummings suggested that Nahum Tate, who became poet laureate when Shadwell died in 1692, was the author of the poem, a speculation endorsed by Baldwin and Wilson. Spink is more circumspect, and because I believe the ode is less than complimentary to the monarch, I also doubt that Tate was responsible.

11. John Crowne, *Calisto: or, The Chaste Nimph* (1675), sig. b1r.

12. For the dismissal of George's servants, see Luttrell, II, 51 (2 June 1690); for the loss of the horses, see II, 94 (17 August 1690); for William's disrespectful treatment of George, see *Conduct*, 38, where Sarah speaks of George's "remembrance of the extreme ill usage he had met with, when, at a great expence, he attended HIS MAJESTY into Ireland. For the KING would not suffer HIS ROYAL HIGHNESS to go in the coach with him: An affront never put upon a person of that rank before." For Mary's order preventing George from sailing, see Luttrell, II, 225 (May 1691).

13. Luttrell, III, 488; 20 June 1695.

14. There is a curious parallel between this line and a passage from *Azaria and Hushai* (1681), a poem by Samuel Pordage written as a riposte to Dryden's *Absalom and Achitophel*. The Shaftesbury figure in this poem gives the Monmouth figure sound advice, cautioning him against claiming the crown. Like the anonymous poem for Gloucester's birthday, this passage mentions the smiles of Fortune and contains the phrase "without a crown":

> *Tho Fortune seems to smile*, and egg you on,
> Let Vertue be your Rule and Guide alone.
> Thus David for his Guide his Vertue took;
> Nor was by Fortune's proffer'd Kindness shook.
> His Vertue and his Loyalty did save
> King Saul, when Fortune brought him to his Cave.
> And if that I may to you Counsel give,
> You should *without a Crown* for ever live,
> Rather than get it by the Peoples Lust,
> Or purchase it by ways that are unjust. (17, emphasis mine)

15. Lewis, 14, 31. William Gardner evidently developed the talents he showed as a boy. He appears on the list of drummers to Queen Anne in the Establishment Book listing all royal servants as of 1703 (GB-Lbl Add. MS 69962, fol. 21). As late as 1710, he appears in the Privy Purse accounts, on a list of pensioners and servants receiving New Year's gifts, where he is touchingly described as "William gardiner ye Duke of glo: drummer" and allowed 2 guineas (GB-Lbl Add. MS 61420, fol. 48).

16. Crowne, *Calisto*, sig. b1v.

17. Boyer, *History*, 5.

18. *MQE Memoirs*, 15; compare Luttrell, I, 566 (3 August 1689).

19. *History*, 5. Boyer is evidently referring to the motion made on 9 August to make a provision of £40,000 for the princess, with a proviso that the £30,000 settled on her by her father would remain in place. For an earlier motion on 26 March 1689 (no amount given), the proposals of 9 August, and the action taken on 18 December, granting her an additional £50,000, see *JHC*, X.

20. Lewis, 4.

21. *Correspondence of the Family of Hatton, Being Chiefly Letters Addressed to Christopher, First Viscount Hatton, 1601–1704*, ed. Edward Maunde Thompson, 2 vols. (Camden Society, 1878), II, 118–119.

22. In his well-documented biography, Neville Connell provides a helpful and complete list of Anne's pregnancies, miscarriages, and stillbirths (*Anne: The Last Stuart Monarch* [Butterworth, 1937], app. 2, 275–280) and argues that her lack of success in bearing children was the result of "hereditary syphilis." In a more professional medical analysis, Frederick Holmes has

argued persuasively that her "chronic non-deforming arthritis [makes] it very likely that the Queen had lupus erythematosus associated with the antiphospholipid antibody, a known spoiler of pregnancies." See G.E.F. Holmes and F.F. Holmes, "William Henry, Duke of Gloucester (1689–1700), Son of Queen Anne (1665–1714), Could Have Ruled Great Britain," *Journal of Medical Biography* 16 (2008): 44–51, here quoting 44.

23. Lewis, 6–7.

24. GB-Lbl Add. MS 61415, fol. 13.

25. GB-Lbl Add. MS 61415, fol. 29.

26. Connell, *Anne,* app. 2.

27. See, for example, GB-Lbl Add. MS 61415, fol. 39, editorially dated [19 March 1693], four days before one of Anne's miscarriages.

28. GB-Lbl Add. MS 61414, fol. 141, editorially dated [c. 1691.] I believe a date of June 1692 is more likely. Sarah notes that Anne had a fever following her delivery of the short-lived child in April (*Conduct,* 73). *The Fairy Queen* opened on 2 May; Luttrell reports that the princess "is indisposed" on 23 June and "continues ill of feaver" on 30 June (II, 491, 497).

29. GB-Lbl Add. MS 61414, fol. 128, editorially dated [1691?].

30. GB-Lbl Add. MS 61414, fol. 169.

31. *Angliæ Notitia: Or The Present State of England* (1692), 182. When he sought a license to marry Elizabeth Lawrence on 1 March 1689, Griffith described himself as a gentleman widower of "about 37." The bride was a spinster "about 16." *Allegations for Marriage-Licenses Issued by the Vicar-General of the Archbishop of Canterbury, July 1687 to June 1694,* ed. George J. Armytage (Harleian Society, 1890), 97.

32. GB-Lbl Add. MS 61415, fol. 30. "Lady Fretchevill" is Anna, Viscountess Frescheville, who began serving Anne in 1686. See also Elizabeth's letter to Sarah in which she speaks of being "perfect in imitating you": "But since you have recommended me to the princess I must once more exercise my tallant." GB-Lbl Add. MS 61454, fol. 107. See also fol. 109, where Elizabeth refers to herself as "poor Duck" and signs herself "Duck." My thanks to the late Professor Edward Gregg for giving me a reference to this letter.

33. GB-Lbl Add. MS 61415, fol. 44, editorially dated [1692–93].

34. GB-Lbl Add. MS 61415, fol. 46. Both Anne and Sarah evidently remembered this episode, as we may discern from a very interesting letter to Elizabeth Griffith in which Sarah describes her efforts to help her brother-in-law at the time of Anne's accession: "The last occasion he had of any resentment against me (which I know he express'd very warmly) was when I had not interest to continue him in the secretary's place. I prevail'd with her majestie to add four hundred pound a year out of the privey purse to the green cloath [the office to which Griffith was appointed]. I did endeavour to have had him in the Bedchamber, because he desir'd it of me, but the queen refused it, & gave a reason for it which I could not tel him, but I know it to be so true, that if he had been my father I cou'd not have reply'd upon that subject" (GB-Lbl Add. MSS 61454, fol. 133). I infer that the "reason" Sarah could not share with Edward was the queen's fear that having the Griffiths in close proximity might revive Prince George's interest in Elizabeth.

35. GB-Lbl Add. MS 61414, fol. 114, editorially dated [early 1691]. Brown prints this letter (*LDI,* 50–51), dating it "About 1690," but omits a crucial phrase. The act of Parliament awarding an additional £50,000 annually to Anne was passed in December 1689, and a date of 1690 would therefore be plausible, except that Anne goes on to say: "tis now a year & very neare a quarter so that at midsummer there will be 1250: due to you." This would suggest a date of May or June 1691, with Anne counting the pension as beginning at Lady Day 1690.

36. GB-Lbl Add. MS 61414, fol. 15, editorially dated [c. 1683–84?], emphasis mine; GB-Lbl Add. MS 61415, fol. 28, editorially dated [?October 1692].

37. GB-Lbl Add. MS 61414, fol. 147.

38. *MQE Memoirs*, 11.

39. When Lord Chamberlain Mulgrave, in 1687, specifically ordered the "Violins to attend at the Chappell at Whitehall where Her Royal Highnesse the Princesse Ann of Denmarke is present," he was probably responding to a request from Anne herself. GB-Lna LC 5/148, fol. 31, printed in *RECM*, II, 15–16.

40. Bruce Wood, *Purcell: An Extraordinary Life* (ABRSM, 2009), 125–126.

41. *MQE Memoirs*, 16, 24.

42. GB-Lbl Add. MS 61415, fol. 17.

43. *RECM*, II, 28; II, 130.

44. Sir John Hawkins, *A General History of the Science and Practice of Music*, 5 vols. (1776), IV, 6.

45. See "Love's Goddess Sure was Blind," in *Birthday Odes for Queen Mary*, pt. 2, ed. Bruce Wood (Kent: Novello, 1998), in *The Works of Henry Purcell*, XXIV, 31–33.

46. I base this calculation on the fact that the birthday ode making use of "Cold and Raw" is the one for 1692; this incident must therefore have taken place in 1691 or early 1692.

47. *LTQ*, 51.

48. In light of the persistent rumors suggesting that William had male lovers, an entry in one of Thomas Birch's collections of anecdotal material may be relevant. In the course of a "Character of K. William," Birch describes the king as "incapable of Procreation" and adds that "Lady Or- kneys endearing offices, are supposed to have been—foeda Labiorum Ministeria," i.e., acts of fellatio. GB-Lbl Sloane MS 4224, fol. 87.

49. GB-Lbl Add. MS 61414, fol. 143.

50. The song was evidently popular. *The Union First Line Index of Manuscript Poetry*, maintained by the Folger Shakespeare Library (http://firstlines.folger.edu), records its appearance in four dif- ferent manuscripts and three separately printed broadsides.

51. 13.

52. See chapter 1 above.

53. Sir John Dalrymple, *Memoirs of Great Britain*, 2 vols. (1771–88), II, app., pt. 2, 78. The perfor- mance is on the Lord Chamberlain's list of plays attended by royalty: "The Queene a Box, and a Box for the Maids of Honor at the Spanish Fryer: £15" (GB-Lna LC 5/149, fol. 368).

54. Dalrymple, *Memoirs of Great Britain*, II, app., pt. 2, 79–80.

55. Luttrell, II, 174.

56. Luttrell, I, 606.

57. Ralph Gray, *The Coronation Ballad* (1689), in *Poems on Affairs of State*, ed. George deForest Lord, 7 vols. (New Haven: Yale University Press, 1963–75), V, ed. William J. Cameron, 40–45.

58. See chapter 2 above.

59. William Coxe, *Memoirs of John, Duke of Marlborough* (Longman, Hurst, Rees, Orme and Brown, 1918), 48n.

60. See my *John Dryden and His World* (New Haven: Yale University Press, 1987), 434–435. For a subsequent gift from Dorset to Dryden, see James A. Winn, "Dryden and Dorset in 1692: A New Record," *Philological Quarterly* 85 (2006): 391–397.

61. *The Entring Book of Roger Morrice 1677–1691*, ed. Mark Goldie, 6 vols. (Woodbridge, England: Boydell Press, 2007), V, 314.

62. Dryden, *Works*, XV, 65–66.

63. *Works*, XV, 66.

64. Dryden, *Don Sebastian,* act 1, scene 1, 65–69; 520–522.

65. The nonjuring bishops Turner, Ken, and Cartwright had all preached before Anne; see chapter 3 above.

66. Act 1, scene 1, 22–24; 27–28, 31–33.

67. H. C. Foxcroft, ed., *A Supplement to Burnet's History of my own Time* (Oxford: Clarendon Press, 1832), 291–292.

68. GB-Lbl Add. MS 61101, fols. 1–2. The version printed in Coxe, *Memoirs of Marlborough,* 22, in addition to correcting Marlborough's rough-and-ready spelling, makes substantive changes, including omitting the word "duty."

69. Act 2, scene 1, 288–291; 296–298; 303–311; 312–314. In the last passage, Dryden recycles some language from *The Medall* (1682), his satire on the first Earl of Shaftesbury:

> Pow'r was his aym: but, thrown from that pretence,
> The Wretch turn'd loyal in his own defence;
> And Malice reconcil'd him to his Prince. (ll. 50–53)

70. GB-Lbl Add. MS 75384, fol. 169v; compare *LDI,* 38.

71. GB-Lbl Lansdowne 1236, fol. 237.

72. GB-Lna SP 8/2, fol. 152. See also the letters sent to William from Nottingham by the Earl of Devonshire and the Bishop of London, reporting on the troops they had gathered to serve the princess, fols. 67–69.

73. *MQE Memoirs,* 3. For some insightful commentary on Mary's memoirs, which she did not destroy before her death, although she burned many other papers, see Melinda S. Zook, "The Shocking Death of Mary II: Gender & Political Crisis in Late Stuart England," *British Scholar* 1 (2008): 21–36.

74. Dryden, *Don Sebastian,* act 2, scene 1, 77–82.

75. Act 2, scene 1, 46–50.

76. *Conduct,* 101, quoted in full below.

77. Described as "two months premature," the infant lived only two hours. See Connell, *Anne,* app. 2.

78. *MQE Memoirs,* 24, 26.

79. *MQE Memoirs,* 29.

80. *Conduct,* 25.

81. *MQE Memoirs,* 29–30.

82. *MQE Memoirs,* 31.

83. Despite this defeat, James II remained unwilling to accept his exile as permanent; on 14 February 1691, for example, he wrote to Philip Cardinal Howard, complaining that some Catholic monarchs in Europe had joined William in opposing the ambitions of Louis XIV: "All the world sees the sad effects the Emperor's joyning with the P. of Orange has had in Hungary, and had not the King of Spaine and the D. of Savoy done the same, in all apearence before this I had been restored and Catholike religion established again, as it was in my tyme, in all my dominions." *Calendar of the Stuart Papers Belonging to His Majesty the King* (Mackie, 1902), I, 68. James's persistence in claiming that the Catholic religion had been "established" during his reign is astonishing, especially in light of the fact that his efforts on behalf of his fellow Catholics had cost him his throne.

84. US-Ws X.d. 473, MS letter of C[harles] T[wyden], dated "Tunbridge-Wells, July." The year is certainly 1690, as Twyden speaks of "the great victory in Ireland, which makes great joy, & to night is to be a great Bonefire, some pounds as I am told, being collected this Day for it."

85. *HMC Le Fleming*, 285, 291.

86. Luttrell, II, 172.

87. *MQE Memoirs*, 36.

88. Michael Tilmouth, "Calendar of References to Music in Newspapers Published in London and the Provinces (1660–1719)," *R.M.A. Research Chronicle* 1 (1961): ii–vii and 1–107, here citing 10. There were regular concerts at York Buildings beginning in the 1670s.

89. *MQE Memoirs*, 38.

90. The letter from Anne to her father, dated "December 1, 1691," and printed in J. S. Clarke, *The Life of James the Second, Collected out of Memoirs writ of his own Hand*, 2 vols. (Longman, Hurst, Rees, etc., 1816), II, 477, may be a forgery. It is not, as many have noted, written in her characteristic style, and it was supposedly not delivered until the summer of 1692, a suspicious circumstance. Gregg, who suggests that the letter was written at the instigation of Marlborough, argues that it was part of a "double policy" undertaken by Marlborough and Godolphin: "While actually undertaking every possible measure to prevent a Jacobite restoration, they continually held out false hopes to St Germain that the princess (and later the queen) secretly sympathized with the exiled Prince of Wales and would essay his restoration 'at the right time' (a time carefully left unspecified)." *Queen Anne*, 83.

91. *The Diary of John Evelyn*, ed. E. S. De Beer, 6 vols. (Oxford: Clarendon Press, 1955), V, 255.

92. Letter printed by Sarah in *Conduct*, 56.

93. Agnes Strickland, *Lives of the Queens of England*, 8 vols. (Bell, 1885), VII, 352. Proceeding as usual without footnotes, Miss Strickland reports the robbery and claims that it led to reflections on William and Mary: "This adventure was made the subject of many lampoons, and great odium was thrown on the king and queen, on account of the danger to which the heiress-presumptive was exposed, through their harshness." I have been unable to discover any such lampoons, though they may be lurking in manuscript collections.

94. *Conduct*, 101.

95. *Conduct*, 95. The queen reportedly told Laurence Hyde, Earl of Rochester (Anne's uncle), and Henry Compton, bishop of London (long her spiritual advisor), that they were not to visit the princess "till further order," but a few days after that report the earl and the bishop joined the Denmarks for dinner at the Marlboroughs' country estate in St. Albans. Luttrell, II, 521, 525.

96. *Correspondence of the Family of Hatton*, II, 177.

97. GB-Lbl Add. MS 75400 (not foliated), printed (in a somewhat edited form) in *LDI*, 60.

98. GB-Lbl Add. MS 61415, fol. 110. The editorial date is [1695?], and the content suggests 15 January 1695, the date of Anne's first public court at Berkeley House; see Harris, *Passion*, 76.

99. Harris, *Passion*, 58.

100. All citations of Cowley follow his *Several discourses by way of Essays, in Verse and Prose*, printed in *The Works of Mr. Abraham Cowley* (1668), many sections separately paginated, here citing 109–111.

101. US-Ws, X.d. 473. "Dr. Younger" is the clergyman John Younger, who was still Anne's chaplain; "Sr Cha: Scarborgh" is Sir Charles Scarburgh, a prominent scientist and physician who had served Charles II and James II and was now physician to Prince George; both are listed in *Angliæ Notitia* (1692), 182, 184. "Dr. & Mrs. Wentworth" are William Wentworth and his wife, Isabella (née Apsley), older sister of Anne's girlhood favorite, Frances Apsley. "Lady Apsley," the mother of Frances and Isabella, was a bedchamber woman to the first and second duchesses of York, listed in all the editions of *Angliæ Notitia* through 1677; in 1679, her daughter Isabella, listed as "Lady Wentworth," succeeded her in that post and continued to serve Maria after James II came to the throne; see *Angliæ Notitia* (1687), 202. A "Mrs. Wentworth" is listed

among Anne's maids of honor in *Angliæ Notitia* (1687), 182; she is more fully identified as "Mrs. Isabella Wentworth" in the edition of 1694, 275.

102. Cowley, *Works,* 91.

103. GB-Lbl Add. MS 61414, fol. 147.

104. GB-Lbl Add. MS 75400; compare *LDI*, 60–61.

105. *The Poetical and Dramatic Works of Sir Charles Sedley,* ed. Vivian de Sola Pinto, 2 vols. (Constable, 1928), here quoting I, 26.

106. Sedley published his verses with his name in the *Gentleman's Journal* for 2 May 1692, a few days after the performance of Purcell's music. Evidence for the date of the performance is contradictory. According to the headnote for the poem in the magazine, "The 30th of *April,* being Her Majesties Birth-day, was observ'd with all the usual Solemnity," but the title is "An Anniversary Ode sung before Her Majesty the 29th of *April."*

107. Luttrell, II, 438; 3 May 1692.

108. These instructions came in a letter to the mayor from the Earl of Nottingham; GB-Lbl Add. MS 61415, fol. 14. Mary evidently had her sister closely watched. A letter from Frances Bathurst to Sarah, dated from Kensington on 20 October [1692], reports that "Mr Boyle is struck out of the liste for the Ball on the Kings Birthday, by reason of his paying his Duty to the Princess at the Bath." GB-Lbl Add. MS 61455, fol. 4r.

109. See "St. James's Church, Piccadilly," in *Survey of London: Volumes 29 and 30: St James Westminster, Part 1,* ed. F.H.W. Sheppard (English Heritage, 1960), 31–55; and Andrew Freeman, "Organs Built for the Royal Palace of Whitehall," *Musical Times* 52 (1911): 521–523; 585–587.

110. Robert D. Cornwall, "Birch, Peter (1651/2–1710)," in *ODNB.*

111. *Conduct,* 100.

112. I follow the accidentals of the printed broadside. For a slightly different text, derived from manuscript copies, with much helpful commentary, see *Poems on Affairs of State,* V, ed. William J. Cameron, 339–344.

113. At just this time, Luttrell reports the court's concern: "A vindication of the princess of Denmark is printed, in which are severall reflections bordering on treason: search is made after the author and printer" (III, 16; 17 January 1693). No tract with such a title survives, and it is possible that Luttrell is referring to this very broadside.

114. See her letter to Sir Benjamin Bathurst asking him to "order half a dozen boats to be at the bridge at Whitehall…to carry me to the playhouse" (*LTQ,* 225) and her letter to Sarah complaining of being ill (GB-Lbl Add. MS 61414, fol. 141).

115. GB-Lbl Add. MS 61415, fol. 20. The editorial dating, [?1692], cannot be correct in light of the known opening date of Congreve's play.

116. GB-Lbl Add. MS 61415, fol. 37.

117. GB-Lbl Add. MS 61415, fol. 27.

118. GB-Lbl Add. MS 61415, fol. 74, editorially dated [?18 August 1693]. This letter is more easily datable than others, as it records Prince George's going into mourning for the death of his sister, who was queen of Sweden.

119. GB-Lbl Add. MS 61415, fol. 77, editorially dated [?25 August 1693]. I infer that the painting Anne saw was by Lely, who painted her mother several times, and that "the King" to whom she refers is her father, James II.

120. See the notice of this MS, now at the Gemeentemuseum in the Hague: Elizabeth C. D. Brown, "Announcement Regarding the 'Princess an Lutebook,'" *Lute Society of America Quarterly* 43:3 (September 2008): 38. As Brown explains, the pieces are in guitar tablature and have "unhelpful generic titles such as Chanson, Gigue, Gavote, Menuet, Trompete and Sarabande." She

has identified "18 pieces originally by Henry Purcell, as well as nine pieces published in Play-ford's *Dancing Master* collections." Significantly, "the dates of the identified pieces from the manuscript cluster in the early 1690's, when Anne was in her mid-twenties."

121. Dedication to *A choice collection of lessons*.

122. *LTQ*, 226.

123. *CTB*, XVII, 71; see also GB-Lna T 52/22, fol. 14; GB-Lna AO 15/21, fol. 34.

124. Hawkins, *General History*, IV, 427*n*.

125. Hawkins, *General History*, IV, 6. This claim gains plausibility from Anne's having granted a pension of £100 per annum to Arabella Hunt when she became queen; GB-Lna AO 15/21, fol. 29.

126. See the letter from John Baynard, dated 7 January 1692/3, GB-Lbl Sloane MS 1388, fols. 77r–78v: "We have arrived very lately a young Italian Gentlewoman who sings to admiration; as they say; & sung last Tuesday in York buildings at the Musick Meeting[,] where they received above 3 score & ten pounds on her account, and might have had as much more if there had been Room. Mr Baptist & his Partner there were at the Charge of bringing her from Italy with her father & Mother, which cost them about 150 *li*. She was carried to the Princess of Denmark last week to sing, by Mr Baptist, who like[d] her so well that she gave Baptist 20 Ginnies to dispose of; which he immediately gave all to her. But as nobody can please all, there are some of our English practical musicians, who have endeavoured to lessen her." This unidentified singer was presumably "the Italian lady" who appeared at York Buildings on 10 January, as mentioned in the *London Gazette*, 19 January 1693. Tilmouth's speculative identification of this singer as Margherita de L'Epine ("Calendar," 13) is not possible.

127. Luttrell, III, 45 (28 February 1693): "Sir Robert Howard, auditor of the exchequer, (aged 70,) on Sunday last married young Mrs. Dives, maid of honour to the princesse, aged about 18." Although Annabella Dives does not appear on any of the official lists of Anne's maids of honor, she was a celebrated beauty, and her father, the Secretary to the Privy Council, had died a few months earlier. Her service to Anne may have been unofficial and was probably brief. Frances Purcell's dedication "To the Honourable Lady Howard" speaks of "your Ladiship's extraordinary skill in Musick, beyond most of either Sex, and Your great Goodness to that dear Person, whom You have sometimes been pleased to honour with the Title of Your Master." *Orpheus Britannicus* (1698), ii.

128. Cowley, *Works*, 93.

129. GB-Lbl Add. MS 61454, fol. 128v, editorially dated [169_,] but from the sequence of surrounding letters, most likely written in 1694.

130. Her apt citation of "Mr Cowleys Country Mouse" (GB-Lbl Add. MS 61415, fol. 110) suggests as much.

131. *A Serious Proposal to the Ladies* (1694), 25–26.

132. *Serious Proposal*, 60–61.

133. *Serious Proposal*, 76–78.

134. George Ballard, *Memoirs of several ladies of Great Britain, who have been celebrated for their writings or skill in the learned languages arts and sciences* (Oxford, 1752), 146.

135. For a judicious account, quoting Elstob's letter to Ballard, see Florence M. Smith, *Mary Astell* (New York: Columbia University Press, 1916), 21–23.

136. Mary Astell, *A Serious Proposal to the Ladies in two Parts* (1697), sig. A2v.

137. Strickland, in *Lives of the Queens of England*, VII, 396, quotes a contemporary as saying that "her majesty did not disdain to busy her royal hands with making of fringes, or knotting, as it was then called. She was soon imitated, not only by her maids of honour, but by all ladies of

distinction throughout the kingdom, and so fashionable was labour of a sudden grown, that not only assembly-rooms and visiting rooms, but the streets, the roads—nay, the very playhouses were witnesses of their pretty industry." Strickland's footnote ascribes this passage to "Tindal," presumably the translator of Rapin's *History of England,* but these words do not appear in his work.

138. Strickland, *Lives of the Queens of England,* VII, 397. The footnote for this quotation directs us to "Tindal's Continuation," i.e., Nicholas Tindal, *The Continuation of Mr. Rapin de Thoyras's History of England, from the Revolution to the accession of King George II,* 4 vols. (1751). No such passage appears in Tindal's work.

139. Sedley, *Works,* ed. Pinto, II, 148, in a section of poems "ascribed to Sedley on Doubtful Authority."

140. *Works,* I, 34–35. For an informative discussion, see Olive Baldwin and Thelma Wilson, "Purcell's Knotting Song," *Musical Times* 128 (1987): 379–381.

141. Luttrell, III, 266. As Lewis's account of celebrations in 1695 shows, Gloucester's arsenal continued to grow. The "drake," a small cannon that could be carried behind a man on horseback, was a recent invention, first mentioned by Luttrell in another context in 1691.

142. Luttrell, III, 144.

143. For a sympathetic account by a contemporary, see Lewis, 43: "The Princess, from grief at the long separation that had subsisted between the Queen and her, laboured under an indisposition of the body, that made her believe she was with child, which she had much the appearance of, although it proved otherwise."

144. See, for example, this verse on Mary from an MS poem called "K. Wms Triumph," which specifically mentions the king's wound received at the Battle of the Boyne and must therefore have been written after the summer of 1690:

> That Royal Dame can only fill
> > Her Husbands Vacant Throne,
> For she's as big as three of him,
> > And bears two Queens in One. (GB-NO Portland MS Pw V 48/14, fols. 29–30).

145. *Conduct,* 105–106; compare GB-Lbl Add. MS 61415, fols. 105–106.

146. "The princesse is to be cheif mourner" reports Luttrell in his entry for 3 January 1695 (III, 421). All the accounts of the funeral, however, report that Elizabeth Seymour, Duchess of Somerset, was the chief mourner, a role she was supposed to fill again at Anne's own funeral in 1714.

147. There is an excellent recording of all the music performed at the funeral, newly edited and assembled by Bruce Wood, on Sony Classical, SK 66243.

148. Lewis, 42.

149. *Conduct,* 110–111.

150. Luttrell III, 427, 437, 439, 445, 455, 475.

151. Lewis, 44–45. In his description of the birthday celebration for 1695, Jenkins states that Gloucester "was well pleased to have his guns fired, while General Bellasis *fired*" (70). Belasyse cannot possibly have been present on 24 July; he was still active in the field, and did not move his troops into winter quarters until late September. Although we cannot now date it with exactitude, the generally reliable Lewis probably did remember some interaction between Gloucester and Belasyse, who had been known to Anne for some time. One of her letters to Mary before the Revolution mentions "Sr H: Bellasis" as a reliable courier. GB-Lbl Add. MS 75384, fol. 168r.

152. See John Childs, "Belasyse, Sir Henry (1648–1717)," in *ODNB*, and H. R. Knight, *Historical Records of the Buffs, East Kent Regiment, 3rd Foot, formerly designated the Holland Regiment and Prince George of Denmark's Regiment*, vol. I, 1572–1704 (Gale & Polden, 1905), 376–382.

153. Luttrell, III, 509; 6 August 1695.

154. These troops from the "Oxford Blues," now the Horse Guards, were not the only soldiers who came to Windsor. "The Duke," writes Lewis, "was highly pleased with Sir Henry Bellasis's regiment exercising in Windsor Park, and firing in platoons, commanded by Lieutenant-Colonel Tempest" (Lewis, 76–77). Tempest was commissioned as lieutenant-colonel to Belasyse on 1 March 1695. See *English Army Lists and Commission Registers, 1661–1704, vol. IV, 1694–1702* (Eyre & Spottiswoode, 1898), 91. Lewis's memory of Gloucester taking delight in their drills is likely to be accurate, but cannot be placed in the summer of 1695, as the regiment, which was active in the summer campaign, did not return to England until October. On 10 October, Luttrell reported that "Sir Henry Bellasis's regiment of fusileers is com hither to keep guard" (III, 536). Belasyse himself, however, was in Ghent, where he presided over the court-martial of the Danish General Johan Anton Ellenberg from 9 October until 25 October; see Knight, *Historical Records of the Buffs*, 381–382.

155. Lewis, 76.

156. *Conduct*, 113–114.

157. The congratulatory letter itself might also have made him suspicious. Anne speaks there of "the Satisfaction that I am sensible your Majesty must needs find in this great addition to the reputation of your arms," as if the war were being fought for the sake of mere "reputation," not (as William believed) to block the expansive ambitions of the French king. GB-Lbl Add. Ms. 61415, fol. 122.

158. Luttrell, III, 551.

159. "*Thursday* last being the Anniversary of the Birth of her Royal Highness the *Princess of Denmark*; in the morning she received the Compliments of the Nobility and Gentry on this Occasion, and at Night there was a fine Ball at *Berkley House*, His Majesty being present till 11 at Night; all the Court appeared there in a most glorious manner." *Post Boy*, 6–8 February 1696.

160. In *Orpheus Britannicus*, 133, this song is said to be "the last Song the Author sett before his Sickness." Two earlier printings describe it as "The last Song that Mr. Henry Purcell sett before he Dy'd," but Frances Purcell, who was in a position to know, gave that honor to "From rosy bowers."

161. For a very full account, see Tamar Drukker, "Thirty-Three Murderous Sisters: A Pre-Trojan Foundation Myth in the Middle English Prose *Brut* Chronicle," *Review of English Studies*, 54 (2003): 449–463.

162. A poem on the death of Mary by her chaplain, Henry Dove, addressed to Princess Anne and published in 1695, is titled *Albania*. There were two poems titled *Albina* issued in 1702: one on William's death, the other on Anne's coronation; these use "Albina" as a name for Anne. When Ambrose Philips recalled the death of Gloucester in his *Pastorals* (1708), he called the dead duke "Albino"; see the fuller discussion in chapter 5 below.

163. Richard Ames, *The Double Descent* (1692), 4. Aphra Behn had called William "the *Belgick LION*" in 1688, in her poem on the birth of James Francis Edward, quoted in chapter 3 above.

164. See Joseph Fisher, "The History of Landholding in Ireland," *Transactions of the Royal Historical Society* 5 (1877): 228–326. On 25 November 1695, Elizabeth married George Hamilton, a brigadier general and a hero of Namur; he was made Earl of Orkney some five weeks later.

165. Luttrell, III, 525; 14 September 1695.

166. As Margaret Laurie has pointed out to me in private correspondence, the figures attached to the bass line in *Orpheus Britannicus* lack the authority of the composer; some are certainly erroneous. The bass line as printed earlier in *Thesaurus Musicus*, V (1696), and in a single-sheet publication by Thomas Cross (also 1696) has no figures. The music of the final bars is unambiguously minor, but because the final note is unfigured, even in *Orpheus Britannicus*, the performers might decide to end the piece on a c minor triad, a C major triad, an open fifth, or an open octave. In private correspondence, Curtis Price has suggested to me that the song as we have it may be unfinished.

167. Compare, for example, "Swifter, Isis, swifter flow," composed by Purcell for Charles II in 1681, which contains such phrases as "Land him safely on her shore" and "See, see! It is the royal barge." *Royal Welcome Songs*, pt. 1, ed. Bruce Wood (Kent: Novello, 2000), in *The Works of Henry Purcell*, XV, xxvi.

168. As no contemporary records the length of Purcell's final illness, a late September date may not be inconsistent with his widow's claim that "Lovely Albina" was the last song he set "before his Sickness." He contributed quite a lot of music to *Bonduca*, a patriotic tragedy advertised in October (and probably on stage in September), and he wrote three more songs for *The Rival Sisters*, a comedy advertised in November (and probably on stage in October), but he had probably completed these theatrical pieces before Anne's return from Windsor at the end of September. There is no good reason to doubt Frances Purcell's testimony that "Lovely Albina" and "From rosy bowers," which was sung in Thomas D'Urfey's *Comical History of Don Quixote, Part III*, are his last two songs.

169. Presumably believing that his illness was brief, Maureen Duffy contends that "it must have been" for the visit on 16 November "that Purcell set the lines." See *Henry Purcell* (Fourth Estate, 1994), 263.

170. Olive Baldwin and Thelma Wilson have made this suggestion to me in private correspondence. There is a record of Anne traveling by barge to see *The Fairy Queen* in 1692 (*LTQ*, 225), and while there is no similar record of her attending the theatre during the autumn of 1695, she might have done so, though she was once again pregnant. Theatrical records for this period are scanty, and Dorset Garden was being used less often than previously, but there were evidently some productions there in the autumn of 1695, certainly including *Don Quixote, Part III*.

171. It appears in *Thesaurus Musicus*, V (advertised in the *Post Boy* on 22 February 1696), and in a single-sheet publication by Thomas Cross. One of these has been copied verbatim from the other, but it is not now possible to determine which appeared first.

Chapter 5

1. Samuel Stebbing, *A genealogical history of the kings and queens of England, and monarchs of Great Britain, &c.... First publish'd to the beginning of King Charles the Second's reign, by Francis Sandford, Esq; Lancaster Herald of Arms: and continued to this time,... by Samuel Stebbing, Esq; Somerset Herald* (1707), 863.

2. GB-Lbl Add. MS 61101, fols. 64–65. My thanks to Professor Robert Bucholz for helping me to identify Robert Yard. Detailed records of the funeral of James, Duke of Cambridge, do not appear to survive, but when his younger brother Edgar, also called the Duke of Cambridge, died in 1671, his remains came to the Abbey by barge; see *The Bulstrode Papers*, ed. A. W. Thibaudeau (Privately printed, 1897), 191; 13 June 1671.

3. See Ian W. Archer, "City and Court Connected: The Material Dimensions of Royal Ceremonial, ca. 1480–1625," *Huntington Library Quarterly* 71 (2008): 157–179.

4. Luttrell, IV, 673. Abel Boyer, who was employed at this time in the household of Sir Benjamin Bathurst, Anne's domestic Treasurer, repeats this error in his life of Anne—a fact suggesting that the truth was not widely known. The error has continued into most modern histories and biographies.

5. Luttrell, IV, 675–676. Most of those named here had close ties to Anne. The bishop of London was her spiritual advisor Henry Compton; the bishop of Salisbury was Gloucester's preceptor Gilbert Burnet; Normanby was Anne's old beau John Sheffield, Earl of Mulgrave. Sidney Godolphin had long been a close friend and advisor and was closely allied to the Marlboroughs; his son had recently married their daughter. Only Peter Mews, the eighty-one-year-old bishop of Winchester, had no known personal tie to Anne, though as a hero of the Battle of Sedgemoor and a moderate Tory, he was certainly in her political orbit.

6. Stebbing, *Genealogical history,* 863–864.

7. See *Exequiæ Desideratissimo Principi Gulielmo Glocestriæ Duci ab Oxoniensi Academia Solutæ* (Oxford, 1700), *Threnodia Academiæ Cantabriginesis in Immaturum Obitum Illustrissimi ac Desideratissimi Principi Gulielmi Ducis Glocestrensis* (Cambridge, 1700), and *Principi juventutis Gulielmo celsissimo Duci Glocestriæ præmaturâ morte abrepto Scholæ Westmonasteriensis alumni regii hæc carmina moerentes consecrant* (1700). The Cambridge volume includes an Arabic poem, and the Oxford volume includes two elegies in Anglo-Saxon.

8. "Dicite ut armorum servens simulacra ciebat, / Ludicra ut accensis arserit ira genis." *Exequiæ,* sig. G2r.

9. For the pose, compare the portrait of William, "possibly after William Wissing," in the National Portrait Gallery (NPG 580). Gloucester's tendency to blush is confirmed by Jenkin Lewis: "He told me one day, that he was no plain person, but a Prince. I gravely replied, he was like to be a great Prince; but if he did not behave as became a Prince, he would not be considered as of more consequence than another man; which, from a conviction of my having uttered what was true, made him blush" (78).

10. "Testentur lachrymæ, Puero quæ gloria præsens; / Quæque future viro, gloria vestra probet."

11. *Principi juventutis,* sig. A2r. The language of Buckhurst's poem echoes that of Bathurst, suggesting that he had read his friend's poem before composing his own.

12. Lewis, 51.

13. *Angliæ Notitia: Or The Present State of England* (1700), 521; Harris, *Passion,* 81. On 26 March 1698, Luttrell reported that the young Duke of Grafton, Anne's godson and cousin, "is made master of the horse to the duke of Glocester" (IV, 360), but all other records show young Churchill in the post, and Grafton embarked on a grand tour of the Continent later in 1698; see A. A. Hanham, "FitzRoy, Charles, Second Duke of Grafton (1683–1757)," in *ODNB.*

14. *Threnodia Academiæ,* sig. A1r. Churchill's contribution follows the opening poem by Thomas Greene, Master of Corpus Christi and Vice-Chancellor of the university. Not only is it the first poem by a student but it precedes contributions by such faculty luminaries as Richard Bentley, Master of Trinity, and Joshua Barnes, Regius Professor of Greek.

15. "Omnia luctus habet: Matri solatia ferre / Qui velit, afflictæ quæ ferat, ipse caret."

16. Bathurst's line is "Tuque acri laudes misce, *Churchille,* dolori." For "Ad Dominum Churchill," the poem by Sandys, see *Principi juventutis,* 45–46. According to G. F. Russell Barker, *The Record of Old Westminsters* (Chiswick Press, 1928), James Sandys was the son of "Henry Sandys of London." "Colonel Henry Sandys," listed among Anne's servants in *Angliæ Notitia* (1700), 519, was the "colonel Sands" who foiled an assassination attempt in April 1698. His father's presence at the court of the Denmarks would account for Sandys's intimate knowledge of Gloucester's activities with young Churchill.

17. "Ad Dominum Churchill," 46:

> Et jam, frænato dum tendis in arva caballo,
> Vinsoriæve colis limina nota domûs,
> *Anna* Tuos quàm sæpe pererrat lumine vultus,
> Quas Tecum quærit nectere sæpe moras?
> Et dicit láchrymis oculos perfusa nitentes,
> Sic Meus ille manus, sic tulit ora Puer.

18. "Ad Dominum Churchill," 46:

> Quod si Hostes inter cecidisset adultus & Arma,
> Percussus Gallâ, Teutonicâve manu:
> Non sic extincti Divisus fata Gloverni
> Flevisses, eadem ceperat urna Duos.

Translation mine. My thanks to my colleague Professor Patricia Johnson and to Mr. Tyler Travillian, a graduate student in the Department of Classics at Boston University, for assisting me in working out the complexities of all these neo-Latin poems.

19. See *Threnodia Academiæ*, sigs. G1r–G2v.

20. William's younger brother, Gilbert junior, served as a Page of Honor in Gloucester's court. See *Angliæ Notitia* (1700), 521.

21. "Disce Puer virtutem ex Me curamque virilem, / Fortunam ex aliis" (sig. G1r). Compare *Aeneid*, XII, 435–436: "disce, puer, uirtutem ex me uerumque laborem, / fortunam ex aliis."

22. Bathurst's reference to a horse weeping for his lost rider only makes sense if Gloucester could ride, and James Sandys's reference to Churchill and Gloucester riding to hounds provides confirmation. Jenkin Lewis reports a conversation between Gloucester and the king in October 1695 in which William asked his nephew "if he had any horses yet? 'Yes,' replied the Duke, 'I have one live one, and two dead ones;' meaning the wooden horses that were to draw him upon; at which the King laughed; which enraged the Duke, who, when the King retired, gave orders to bury them out of sight" (Lewis, 77). Having buried his wooden horses, Gloucester was eager to ride a real horse, and clearly did so. After the duke's death, Sir Benjamin Bathurst procured for his nephew "the ondly horse the duke of Glocester ever rid, which was very well qualified for such a young person" (*LTQ*, 236).

23. Lewis, 90, the only source for this episode. In their detailed article on Gloucester's medical biography, G.E.F. Holmes and F.F. Holmes refer to this illness as "an episode of conjunctivitis." See "William Henry, Duke of Gloucester (1689–1700), Son of Queen Anne (1665–1714), Could Have Ruled Great Britain," *Journal of Medical Biography* 16 (2008): 46. I should think it possible, however, that the boy's condition was papilledema, a swelling of the optic disc caused by intracranial pressure and a common symptom of hydrocephalus.

24. Lewis, 90–91.

25. Burnet, *History*, IV, 452.

26. "Oui, dit le Roy,…il est bien délicat. Il est vray que j'ay été aussi bien délicat, moy, et je vis encore." The primary source for this anecdote is a little-noticed letter (in French) from Leibniz to the Electoral Princess Caroline, dated 3 October 1714, in *Die Werke von Leibniz gemäss seinem handschriftlichen Nachlasse in der Königlichen Bibliothek zu Hannover*, ed. Onno Klopp, 11 vols. (Hanover, 1864–84), XI, 15–17.

27. Lewis, 77, 81.

28. For a very full account of the plot and its aftermath, see Jane Garrett, *The Triumphs of Providence* (Cambridge: Cambridge University Press, 1980).

29. Lewis, 86–87.

30. Lewis's account as printed in the eighteenth century dates this event 27 July, but this is probably a misreading of the manuscript. The detailed account in Luttrell makes it clear that the celebration took place on 24 July.

31. See Luttrell, IV, 451 (17 November 1698): "The king is hourly expected from Holland; 'tis said the duke of Wirtemberg comes over with his majestie for some arrears due to him, as also to surrender his commission of collonel of the Dutch regiment of foot guards to the duke of Gloucester." The generally reliable *English Army Lists and Commission Registers, 1661–1714* has no entry for Gloucester, nor can I find any other reference to his actually taking command of adult troops. William may have been hoping to give Gloucester command of a unit of the Dutch "Blue Guards," the troops that guarded St. James's. But the demobilization forced on him by Parliament scotched those plans. All the Blue Guards left England in 1699, and the only units allowed to continue in operation (a total army of just seven thousand) were units that had existed before 1680.

32. *Angliæ Notitia* (1700), 520, also names Willis as "Sub-Præceptor" and Pratt as "Almoner," a "Monsieur Persode" as "French instructor," and "_____ Newton" as "Mathematick Master." Although the compiler did not know his first name, there can be little doubt that Sir Isaac, who had become Master of the Mint in 1696, is indicated. There is no evidence to help us determine whether he actually taught lessons to Gloucester; his protégé David Gregory was appointed to the post in 1699, with the support of Newton and Burnet. See Anita Guerrini, "Gregory, David (1659–1708)," in *ODNB*.

33. Luttrell, IV, 499, 506, 523, 580, 585.

34. Luttrell, IV, 664; 6 July, 1700.

35. Henry Horwitz, *Parliament, Policy and Politics in the Reign of William III* (Manchester: Manchester University Press, 1977), 203.

36. Pierpont Morgan Library, Rulers of England, box XI, quoted in Gregg, *Queen Anne*, 427n21.

37. See Manchester's correspondence with Edward Griffith, secretary to the Prince of Denmark, James Vernon, and the Earl of Jersey, Lord Chamberlain to William, in Christian Cole, *Historical and Political Memoirs* (1735), 207–209.

38. Lewis, 80–81.

39. Lewis, 93.

40. There is a manuscript copy of the complete ode in GB-Ob MS Tenbury 1175, 1–21, where it is wrongly ascribed to Henry Purcell. The opening song, which calls on "Apollo's darling sons" to "tune [their] Celestial Strings" in praise of Gloucester, was engraved by Thomas Cross, and copies of the printed version survive in the Guildhall Library and in the library of the Royal College of Music. The heading provides clear evidence of the date: "A Song Sung by Mr *Robart* at the Instalment of his Highness the Duke of *Glocester* Set by Mr *Daniel Purcell* and exactly engrav'd by *Tho: Cross*." "Mr *Robart*" was Anthony Robart, Jr., son of Anne's childhood singing master.

41. Mary Fanshawe to Thomas Coke, *HMC*, XII, ii, 365.

42. *The anatomist, or, The sham doctor written by Mr. Ravenscroft; with The loves of Mars and Venus, a play set to music, written by Mr. Motteux* (1697), sig. a*.

43. It is unlikely that all of Princess Anne's visits to the theatre have left historical traces. Thanks to the belated printing of a special prologue addressing her as the "Sacred Patroness of Poetry," we know that she attended a performance of *Ibrahim*, a tragedy by Mary Pix, probably in May or

June 1696. No newspaper account took notice of this occasion, and there were probably other occasions when newswriters failed to note her attendance at a play. This prologue was first printed in Thomas D'Urfey's *Songs Complete Pleasant and Divertive* in 1719, five years after Anne's death; it appears, with useful notes, in Pierre Danchin, *The Prologues and Epilogues of the Restoration, 1660–1700, Part III* (Nancy: Presses Universitaires de Nancy, 1985), V, 288–290. My thanks to Kathryn Lowerre for helping me locate this record.

44. See chapter 4 above.

45. Congreve, *The Mourning Bride* (1697), sigs. A1r–A2r.

46. Lewis, 95–96.

47. Michael Tilmouth, "Calendar of References to Music in Newspapers Published in London and the Provinces (1660–1719)," *R.M.A. Research Chronicle* 1 (1961): 19. There is no specific record of a performance at court on the birthday, but as Olive Baldwin and Thelma Wilson have pointed out to me, such songs were normally performed in the morning or at midday, so a performance would not have conflicted with the play or the ball.

48. Tilmouth, "Calendar," 20.

49. GB-Lbl Add. MS 31452, fols. 54–68. This score, the only source for Blow's ode, was evidently written in haste, and the text underlay, which involves frequent repetitions of words and phrases, is inconsistent. My transcription of the poetic text is necessarily a reconstruction of what I infer the poet wrote. There is no independent source for the text. My thanks to Bruce Wood for confirming the attribution to Blow and identifying the scribe as the young William Croft.

50. The poem was freshly available as part of a multivolume set of Dryden's works issued by Tonson in 1695. See John Dryden, *The Fourth Volume of the Works of Mr. John Dryden. Containing, A poem upon the death of O. Cromwell. Poem on the return of K. Charles II. On the coronation of K. Charles II. A poem on the L. Chancellor Hide. Annus mirabilis. Mack Flecknoe. Absalom and Achitophel. The medal, a poem. Religious laici [sic], a poem. Elegy on the death of K. Charles II. The hind and panther. Poem on the birth of the Prince. Eleonora.*

51. Dryden, *To His Sacred Majesty,* ll. 123–132.

52. Georg Wilhelm (1624–1705) is now more commonly called the Duke of Brunswick-Lüneburg; Zell, a castle in lower Saxony, is now normally spelled "Celle." For the whole discussion, see the letter by Leibniz in *Werke von Leibniz,* ed. Klopp, XI, 15–17. Although he wrote this account years later, after the death of Queen Anne, Leibniz says that he was present at Zell during this visit, and his dating of the events as "a little after the Peace of Ryswick" is roughly correct. A news item dated "*From the Kings Camp at Cockleberg,* July 29," in the *Post Man* for 24–27 July 1697, reports that "3 of the K.'s Grooms were sent off towards *Loo* with some of his Majestys Horses, and 'tis said the King will go thither on *Friday* or *Saturday,* and from thence to *Zell,* to hunt there a month or six weeks.... His Majestys leaving the Camp in this juncture, is a strong argument that the Peace is as good as concluded." According to Leibniz, it was Eleanor, the French Huguenot wife of Georg Wilhelm, who spoke to William, urging him to settle the succession on the Electress of Hanover, her sister-in-law, and proposing a marriage between the Duke of Gloucester and "the Princess of Hanover," her granddaughter. Leibniz also claims to have encouraged Eleanor to speak to William because of her charm and grace.

53. "Et le Duc de Glocester fit faire un compliment à la Princesse d'Hanovre, et dire qu'il espéroit de la voir, en venant chasser avec le Roy dans le pays de Zell." *Werke von Leibniz,* ed. Klopp, XI, 17.

54. Lewis, 78, 97. Lewis complains that Pratt's construction of the fort "answered so well as to gain him much credit, by doing in fact what did not so properly belong to his office, or his cloth; and

thereby depriving another of the opportunity of being employed, who from his long and faithful attention to the Duke, would even have ventured his life in his service."

55. Basil Kennett, *Romae antiquae notitia* (1696), sig. A3r, 252–256.

56. See William Clare, *A compleat system of grammar, English and Latin…Dedicated to his Highness the Duke of Gloucester* (1699); Abel Boyer, *The royal dictionary in two parts, first, French and English, secondly, English and French…for the use of His Highness the Duke of Glocester* (1699); *The fables of Pilpay, a famous Indian phylosopher containing many useful rules for the conduct of humane life…address'd to His Highness the Duke of Gloucester* (1699); Basil Kennett, *The lives and characters of the ancient Grecian poets dedicated to His Highness the Duke of Glocester* (1697); Laurence Echard, *The Roman history from the settlement of the empire by Augustus Caesar to the removal of the imperial seat by Constantine the Great…for the Use of His Highness the Duke of Gloucester* (1698); and William Fuller, *La decouverte de la veritable mere du pretendu Prince de Galles, connüe par le nom de Marie Grey.…Dedié au Duc de Glocester* (1696).

57. Lewis, 92.

58. GB-Ob MS Tenbury 1175.

59. For commentary on the illustrations, see (among others) Steven Zwicker, *Politics and Language in Dryden's Poetry: The Arts of Disguise* (Princeton: Princeton University Press, 1984), 177–205, and Curtis Price, "Political Allegory in Late Seventeenth-Century English Opera," in *Music and Theatre: Essays in Honour of Winton Dean,* ed. Nigel Fortune (Cambridge: Cambridge University Press, 1987), 1–29, especially 13–16.

60. Gloucester's personal copy of this splendid book, recently sold by Christopher Edwards, eventually passed from Samuel Pratt, his tutor, to Heneage Finch, who inscribed it as follows: "Heneage Finch—February: 12: 1703/4. I receiv'd this Book as a Present from my Worthy Freind the Reverend Doctor Prat—Out of the Library of the late most Illustrious Prince William Duke of Glocester." I have not been able to determine whether the recipient was Heneage Finch, later Fourth Earl of Winchilsea, husband of the poet Anne Finch; Heneage Finch, MP for Oxford University and later first Earl of Aylesbury; or his son Heneage Finch, an Oxford undergraduate and a poet, later second Earl of Aylesbury. My thanks to Mr. Edwards for helpful correspondence.

61. Dryden, *Aeneis,* V, 753–756; 760–762. All citations of this translation from Dryden, *Works,* by book and line.

62. Dryden, *Aeneis,* V, 749–752.

63. Dryden had often used the rhyme between "face" and "grace." See *"When Beauty Fires the Blood,"* ll. 247, 339.

64. Lewis, 76.

65. For a detailed discussion, see John Barnard, "Dryden, Tonson, and the Patrons of *The Works of Virgil* (1697)," in *John Dryden: Tercentenary Essays,* ed. Paul Hammond and David Hopkins (Oxford: Oxford University Press, 2000), 174–239.

66. See Earl Miner, "Dryden's Messianic Eclogue," *Review of English Studies* 11(1960): 299–301. On the dating of this poem in relation to Anne's pregnancy, see my *John Dryden and His World* (New Haven: Yale University Press, 1987), 607*n*.

67. Dryden, *Fourth Eclogue,* ll. 5–10.

68. At Christmas 1695, a few weeks before his eighth birthday, Buckhurst spoke a prologue written by the poet and diplomat Matthew Prior, one of his father's protégés, for a performance of Dryden's *Cleomenes* given by the boys of Westminster. As the prologue makes clear, Buckhurst also took part in the play, acting the role of the young prince Cleonidas.

69. *The Letters of John Dryden*, ed. Charles E. Ward (Durham: Duke University Press, 1942), 85–86.

70. In addition to the prince, the princess, and the duke, Viscount Fitzharding, Master of the Horse to the princess and husband of Gloucester's governess, was a subscriber.

71. Dryden, *Works*, V, 283.

72. Dryden, *Letters*, 92.

73. GB-Lna T 29/13, fol. 212. I have been unable to find a record confirming that the promised payments were made. They do not appear in E 403/1046, the Exchequer Roll; T 30/2, 3 etc., summaries of royal income and expenses; T 52/22, Royal warrants; T 53/16, Warrants relating to the payment of money; or T 60/6, the Order Book. In a more public gesture, the queen chose Dryden's *All for Love* for a court performance on her birthday in 1704. See Olive Baldwin and Thelma Wilson, "Music in the Birthday Celebrations at Court in the Reign of Queen Anne: A Documentary Calendar," *A Handbook for Studies in 18th-Century English Music* 19 (2008): 1–24, here citing 6.

74. GB-Lbl Add. MS 61415, fol. 144, editorially dated [November 1697]. Gregg suggests 1 November 1697, which would place the letter close to Anne's letters seeking a copy of the bill in question, which can clearly be dated to October 1697. A date later in November, closer to the opening of Parliament, would fit nicely with her concern for William's health; on 25 November, Luttrell reported that the king had "some small fits of the gout in his knee" (IV, 310). But the phrase wishing William "a successfull summer" argues strongly against an autumn date. The spring of 1698 is too late: by that time, the Commons had already mounted an attack on all the king's Irish grants. Anne's wishing William success would fit much better with the summer of 1697, which was given over to peace talks. On 23 March 1697, William had "some symptoms of an ague" (Luttrell, IV, 200), and on 6 April another grant of Irish lands, this time to a male favorite, was in the news: "The new earl of Albemarle having gott a grant of 4000*l.* per ann. of the forfeited estates in Ireland, the said grant is sent thither to pass the seals in Dublin" (IV, 207); other Irish grants to Portland and Albemarle are mentioned on 24 April (IV, 215). On 20 April, Robert Spencer, Earl of Sunderland, became Lord Chamberlain, replacing Dorset. Although Anne had been bitterly opposed to Sunderland during her father's reign, he was now close to the Marlboroughs and seems a likely candidate for her to have approached with this request. According to Sarah, Sunderland "wholly managed" the official reconciliation between William and Anne after Mary's death, and "shewed himself a man of sense and breeding" (*Conduct*, 110–111). William sailed for Holland on 24 April 1697, and the Denmarks left for Tunbridge in June. I am therefore inclined to date this letter to the late spring of 1697.

75. GB-Lbl Add. MS 61415, fol. 145. This description, which continues with the admission that "this Letter had no effect upon King William," is not in Sarah's hand but in the hand of an amanuensis whose work appears frequently in this volume. It appears to have been dictated by Sarah. On the same cover, in Sarah's unmistakable scrawl, there is a further annotation: "Coppy of a letter from the Princesse to King William about the estate that was settled upon the D: of Yorke and his children which the King gave to Mrs. Villiers."

76. *LTQ*, 241. Brown, who prints these two letters, assigns them to 1699, which is not possible. The superscription—"Windsor. Saturday the 16th of October"—allows us to assign this letter confidently to 1697, a year in which 16 October fell on a Saturday. Another letter, undated but probably written earlier in the same year, asks Bathurst to "writt to some body of your acquaintance in Ireland in your name, to send you a coppy of the Act of Parliament in which that estate that is given to Lady Orkney was settled upon the King my father when Duke of York, but do not lett me be named in it" (*LTQ*, 242).

77. *LTQ*, 242, dated "Windsor fryday the 22 of October." The next day, in a letter dated "Windsor Saturday morning," Anne reports her action to Sarah: "I have writt to Sir Benjamin to go to the attorney generall about the Irish Bill." GB-Lbl Add. Ms 61415, fol. 139.

78. GB-Lbl Add. MS 61415, fols. 135–136. The editorial date, [1697], is correct. Although Gregg dates this letter 1696, it falls into sequence with other letters describing the plans for the birthday and mentioning Anne's delay in coming to London, which she also mentions in the datable letters to Bathurst.

79. Anne's caution about revealing too much in her letters is apparent in her letter to Sarah of 24 October: "I do not doubt but I shall be very well satisfied with what you have said in my name to the person you mention." GB-Lbl Add. MS 61415, fol. 143v). In light of her continuing campaign about the Irish estate, I should think it likely that the unnamed person to whom Sarah had spoken on Anne's behalf was Sunderland.

80. GB-Lbl Add. MS 61415, fol. 137.

81. GB-Lbl Add. MS 61415, fol. 143. In his entry for 4 November, Luttrell reports that "the princesse invited a great many persons of quality to a ball this night at St. James's" (IV, 301), but Anne's letter makes it clear that the celebration was merely a "drawing room" party. *The London Stage, 1660–1800*, pt. 1, *1660–1700*, ed. William van Lennep (Carbondale: Southern Illinois University Press, 1965) posits a performance at court of an entertainment by Peter Motteux, but there is no record of a payment for that performance, which is normally the case for plays at court, and the title page points to a different venue and date: *Europe's Revels for the Peace, and His Majesties Happy Return, a Musical Interlude Performed at the Theatre in Little Lincolns-Inn-Fields*.

82. Luttrell, IV, 304, 306–307, 316. The precise date of the miscarriage is not known; William paid Anne a call of condolence on 10 December; see *CSP Dom., 1697*, 508.

83. Luttrell, III, 551.

84. GB-Lbl Add. MS 61415, fol. 126.

85. James Vernon, *Letters Illustrative of the Reign of William III*, 2 vols. (Colburn, 1841), I, 443–445.

86. Burnet, *History*, IV, 386.

87. Horwitz, *Parliament, Policy and Politics*, 227.

88. *Conduct*, 116–117.

89. "For the late LORD GODOLPHIN had told me that the KING, on some meeting at the Treasury, speaking of the civil list, *wondered very much how the* PRINCESS *could spend* 30,000 l. *a year*, though it appeared afterward that some of his favourites had more" (*Conduct*, 32).

90. Horwitz, *Parliament, Policy and Politics*, 227.

91. Luttrell, IV, 323.

92. *Conduct*, 117.

93. Luttrell, IV, 328.

94. *Conduct*, 117.

95. GB-Lbl Add. MS 61415, fol. 32. By 1700, Abigail was listed as "Mother of the Maids," and she appears on the list of bedchamber women made at the time of Anne's accession as queen. See Frances Harris, "Masham [née Hill], Abigail, Lady Masham (1670?–1734)," in *ODNB*.

96. Most of these appointments are recorded in *Angliæ Notitia* (1700), 520–522.

97. See Lewis, 31, and the entry for "Powell, Charles," in Andrew Ashbee and David Lasocki, *Biographical Dictionary of English Court Musicians, 1485–1714* (Aldershot: Ashgate, 1998).

98. "Upon the news of the DUKE OF GLOUCESTER's death," writes Sarah, the king "sent orders, by the very first post, to have all his servants discarded.... It was by the contrivance of LORD MARLBOROUGH, assisted by LORD ALBEMARLE, that the servants received their salaries to the quarter-day after the DUKE died" (*Conduct*, 120). Anne's behavior after William's death provides a useful

contrast. On 12 May 1702, she announced that she would "not begin to keep house as queen till the 1st of July" and "declared that all the money which till then comes in upon the civil list shal goe towards paying the arrears due to the late kings servants." On 2 June, she "ordered all the servants of the late king to be paid half a years salary" (Luttrell, V, 172, 190).

99. GB-Lna LC 7/1, fol. 43.

100. Robert D. Hume, "Jeremy Collier and the Future of the London Theater in 1698," *Studies in Philology* 96 (1999): 480–511, here quoting 492. I am dependent on Hume's insightful article throughout this section and grateful to him for relevant private communications as well.

101. GB-Lna LC 5/152, fol. 19.

102. John Vanbrugh, *The Provok'd Wife* (1697), 36.

103. *Post Man*, 10–12 May 1698. See also Luttrell, IV, 379.

104. GB-Lg Mus G 313, no. 25. For the song by Leveridge, see Richard Leveridge, *Complete Songs*, ed. Olive Baldwin and Thelma Wilson (Stainer and Bell, 1997). My thanks to the editors for helpful correspondence about both items.

105. The poem is the first entry in *Poetical Miscellanies* (London and Cambridge, 1697), where it is titled "Mortality." This anonymous volume (Wing M2232A) is attributed to John Philips in Wing and in *Early English Books Online*, but as W. J. Cameron proved more than fifty years ago, it is the work of Ambrose Philips. See "Ten New Poems by Ambrose Philips (1674–1749)," *Notes & Queries* 102 (1957): 469–470. The same poem appeared again with minor revisions in Tonson's *Poetical Miscellanies. The Sixth Part* (1709), 282, where it is identified as "by the Same Hand" as the preceding poem, beginning "Why we love and why we hate," which Philips himself published in his *Pastorals, Epistles, Odes* (1648). See *The Poems of Ambrose Philips*, ed. M. G. Segar (Oxford: Blackwell, 1937).

106. The penultimate line of Leveridge's song—"Shall I Languish pine & Dye?"—is very close to a line in Behn's "Song. On her Loving Two Equally," first published in her *Poems on Several Occasions* (1684): "For both alike I languish, sigh, and die" (89). The speaker's complaint that her lover's disdain causes a "killing damp" resembles a speech in *The Town-Fopp* (1677):

> All gay I met him full of youthful heat,
> But like a damp, he dasht my kindled flame,
> And all his Reason was—he lov'd another. (40)

By the time *Caligula* was produced, Behn had been dead nine years, so what we have here is either a song text by someone imitating her style or an old song text that Leveridge found among her theatrical remains. It may be relevant that Leveridge composed another song with words known to be by Behn. In his collection for 1699, the song from *Caligula* is the first item; the third, which is similarly identified as being sung by "Mrs. Lindsey," is "Fly from his charming language, fly," based on a text found in Behn's *Selinda and Cloris*, an "entertainment at Court" that she printed in *Miscellany, being a collection of poems by several hands; together with Reflections on morality, or, Seneca unmasqued* (1685), 209.

107. Jeremy Collier, *A Short View of the Immorality and Prophaneness of the English Stage* (1698), 278.

108. *London Gazette*, 27 February 1698/99.

109. For his appointment, see GB-Lna LC 5/166, fol. 43, transcribed and printed in *RECM*, II, 67.

110. For much useful information about these productions, including important corrections of the dating proposed by *The London Stage*, pt. 1, see the introduction by Curtis A. Price and Robert D. Hume to their facsimile edition of *The Island Princess: British Library Add. MS 15318* (Tunbridge Wells: R. Macnutt, 1985).

111. *CSP Dom.*, 1698, 36.

112. Luttrell, IV, 363–364.

113. *Letters of William III. and Louis XIV. and their Ministers,* ed. Paul Grimplot (Longmans, 1848), 383.

114. Vernon, *Letters Illustrative of the Reign of William III,* II, 39–40, 48–49.

115. *Letters of William III. and Louis XIV.,* 408.

116. GB-Lbl Add. MS 61415, fols. 137v–138r.

117. We may infer that there was a birthday celebration from the fact that two musical odes written for the occasion were performed later in the spring. The *London Gazette* for 2 May 1698, advertises "the Song which was sung before Her Royal Highness, on Her Birth Day last; with other Variety of New Vocal and Instrumental Musick, Compos'd by Dr [William] Turner," to be performed "On Wednesday next, the 4th of May,…in York Buildings." The *Post Master* for 24 May 1698, advertises "a new Entertainment of Vocal and Instrumental Musick, with the Song which was sung to her Royal Highness on her Birthday. Composed by Mr Daniel Purcell." I owe both these references to Estelle Murphy, "The Fashioning of a Nation: The Court Ode in the Late Stuart Period," Ph.D. diss. (National University of Ireland, Cork, 2011). My thanks to Dr. Murphy for sharing her findings with me.

118. Luttrell, IV, 348, 375.

119. *Conduct,* 116–117. If the conversation between Marlborough and the king took place in June, as seems likely, Sarah is accurate in describing Anne as pregnant. Her only factual slip is her reference to William's going to "make the campaign." Thanks to the Peace of Ryswick, the king's journey to the Continent in the summer of 1698 did not involve combat.

120. GB-Lbl Add. MS 61415, fol. 149, editorially dated [15 June 1698].

121. *Conduct,* 119.

122. "I have bin looking upon my accounts this afternoon, & found a bill which I think is a confirmation of Sr Benjamins taking poundage of the trads people." GB-Lbl Add. MS 61415, fol. 124. Anne dates her letter "Tuesday the 6th of April," which makes the editorial date [?1697] virtually certain.

123. See GB-Lbl Add. MS 61415, fols. 151–152.

124. Luttrell, IV, 402, 426, 427.

125. Luttrell, IV, 540–541.

126. See Horwitz, *Parliament, Policy and Politics,* 259.

127. GB-Lbl Add. MS 61415, fol. 160r–v.

128. When the widowed king returned from the summer campaign in October 1695, more than eight months after Mary's death, most of his courtiers were still wearing mourning.

129. The *Post Boy* for 31 October–2 November reports "great preparations…for the Celebrating of his Majesty's Birth-Day, which is on Saturday next, at which time the Court will appear very Gay, there being to be a fine Ball at Night at *St. James*'s." The *Post Man* for 2–4 November reports that Anne and George are to dine with William at Kensington. GB-Lna LC 5/152, fol. 220, dated 23 October 1699, requests payment for John Colmark, Stephen le Fevre, Thomas Chevalier, John Aubert, Peter la Tour, and John Shore, five oboists and a trumpeter described as "Musitians to her Royal Highness the Princess Ann," for performing "att two Balls & a Play att Whitehall on his Majesty's Birthday." See also *Angliæ Notitia* (1700), 518, which lists the same musicians as servants of Prince George.

130. *Conduct,* 114.

131. The request to George and his agreement to give up the lands are minutely documented in correspondence between Nottingham, the prince, and Godolphin. See GB-Lbl Add. MS 61101, fols. 25–42.

132. Acknowledging the absence of any written evidence explaining "how the king was finally influenced to take steps to honour his debt," Gregg argues that "the growing power of the Tories in the country…must have been influential" (*Queen Anne*, 118). I see little evidence that William was influenced in other areas by "the growing power of the Tories," and if he was repaying Prince George as a favor to the Tories, why did they seize the occasion to attack Burnet? Horwitz believes that the request that Parliament settle the debt "can be read as another sign of William's desire to improve relations with the Princess" (*Parliament, Policy and Politics*, 261), but if the king wanted to improve his relations with Anne, why did he force George to give up his mourning? I find it intriguing that William's efforts to repay George began shortly after the death of Christian V and would offer the speculation that some private agreement with the Danish king had prevented William from paying off George, which he was now free to do.

133. Vernon, *Letters Illustrative of the Reign of William III*, II, 382, 386–388.

134. Luttrell, IV, 607.

135. GB-Ob Mus. C. 6, fol. 41. I give the text as printed by Rosamond McGuinness in *English Court Odes, 1660–1820* (Oxford: Clarendon Press, 1971), 55. A complete ode by Daniel Purcell, headed "Song on her Royall Highness Birth Day February: 6th 1699/1700," survives in GB-Lbl Add. MS 30934, fols. 36–57. The text makes reference to "the younger William," i.e., Gloucester. It seems unlikely that both odes were performed on 6 February 1700; perhaps one of them was sung at the delayed New Year's celebration, for which Daniel Purcell provided an ode addressed to the king. See McGuinness, 23, 54–56.

136. GB-Lbl Add. MS 61415, fol. 166.

137. See *LTQ*, 244–247.

138. Luttrell, IV, 636, 648.

139. See the letter from Robert Harley to Edward Harley, *HMC Portland*, III, 624.

140. Holmes and Holmes, "William Henry," 50. For the autopsy, see GB-Lbl Add. MS 61101, fols. 44–63.

141. *History*, IV, 452.

142. Luttrell, IV, 676.

143. This phrase comes in a letter of 9 July 1703, in which Anne was responding to a false report that Sarah was pregnant: "I can not express how glad I am of the good news you send me of your deare self, upon my word Since my great misfortune of loosing my dear child, I have not known soe much real satisfaction in any thing that has happened as this pleasing news has given me." GB-Lbl Add. MS 61416, fols. 122v–123r.

144. Richard Burridge, *The Consolation of Death* (1700), sig. A2r. Burridge apparently presented his treatise in person to the grieving princess. "The last time I troubled *Your* unbounded *Goodness* in this kind," he writes in the preface to a poem on her coronation, "was at *Windsor* Castle, on as *Sorrowful* an Occasion as this is *Joyful*; where You were graciously pleas'd to accept my small Treatise of *The Consolation of Death*, on a *Loss* that much afflicted England." *A congratulatory poem, on the coronation of Queen Ann* (1702), sig. A2r, reversing italics.

145. GB-Lbl Add. MS 61416, fols. 92v–93r.

146. Remarkably enough, Sir David Hamilton, her physician in her later years, reported an instance of the queen's menstruation on 11 February 1710, a month before her forty-fifth birthday: "Yea the Menses happened to her as if she had been but 20 years old." *The Diary of Sir David Hamilton, 1709–1714*, ed. Philip Roberts (Oxford: Clarendon, 1975), 6.

147. All quotations from Philips in this section follow the first printing of this pastoral, in *Oxford and Cambridge Miscellany Poems*, edited by Elijah Fenton, which was advertised for sale in early

January 1708. Philips revised this and his other poems before their printing in Tonson's miscellany, and again before publishing them himself in 1748.

148. Dryden, *Aeneis,* V, 61–76.

149. In the version printed by Tonson in 1709, Philips altered "her childless Arms" to "her widow'd arms." Anne was by then a widow, as George died in 1708.

150. See chapter 10 below.

Chapter 6

1. *The Queen's Famous Progress* (1702), 5.

2. John Lord Somers, *The true secret history of the lives and reigns of all the kings and queens of England, from King William the first, called the Conqueror, to the end of the reign of the late Queen Anne,* 2nd ed., 2 vols. (1730), II, 272–273. Many historians, beginning with Agnes Strickland, have reported this remark as one actually made by Louis XIV, but this source shows that it was a remark Englishmen imagined him making.

3. *JHL,* XVII, 64; entry for 8 March 1702.

4. *Queen's Famous Progress,* 7.

5. *Queen's Famous Progress,* 6.

6. *London Gazette,* 21–24 December 1702.

7. *Queen's Famous Progress,* 2–3.

8. *JHL,* XVII, 67–69; 11 March 1702.

9. Alexander Pope, now a boy of fourteen, would give the same conceit more memorable form in *Windsor-Forest* (1713), his great poem on the Peace of Utrecht. The speaker in this passage is the River Thames:

> Thy trees, fair *Windsor!* now shall leave their Woods,
> And half thy Forests rush into my Floods,
> Bear *Britain*'s Thunder, and her Cross display,
> To the bright Regions of the rising Day. (ll. 385–388)

Pope might easily have seen Finch's poem, as it was reprinted in *Poems on Affairs of State* (1703), a widely circulated volume.

10. *History,* 33.

11. *History,* 12.

12. Northamptonshire Record Office, Finch-Hatton MSS. 275, fols. 75–76, quoted in Henry Horwitz, *Revolution Politicks: The Career of Daniel Finch, Second Earl of Nottingham, 1647–1730* (Cambridge: Cambridge University Press, 1968), 168.

13. George Macaulay Trevelyan, *England under Queen Anne,* 3 vols. (Longmans, Green and Co., 1930–34), I, 96–98.

14. *JHL,* XVII, 156; 21 October 1702. In the same paragraph, the queen asks Parliament "to consider of some better and more effectual Method to prevent the exportation of Wool," by which she means the illegal smuggling of raw wool to France. The object of her policy was to support the spinning of English wool into cloth before its export.

15. *Queen's Famous Progress,* 7–8.

16. See chapter 5 above.

17. Pat Rogers, *The Symbolic Design of "Windsor-Forest"* (Newark: University of Delaware Press, 2004), 106–107.

18. Sarah's comment; GB-Lbl Add. MS 61422, fol. 199.

19. Luttrell, V, 172, 190. The lists of those receiving pensions during Anne's reign include many who had served her sister Mary; see GB-Lna AO 15/21, fols. 27–31.

20. *Private Correspondence of Sarah, Duchess of Marlborough*, 2 vols. (Henry Colburn, 1838), II, 125.

21. *Post Boy*, 2 November–5 November 1700; *English Post*, 31 January–3 February 1701.

22. GB-Lbl Add. MS 17677, XX, fol. 262: "dêpuis la mort du duc de Gloucester... elle se plaisoit beaucoup, estant souvent 3 ou 4 heures seule dans son cabinet à s'occuper de la lecture."

23. "Heads of a Memoriall for the E. of Oxford," Longleat, Portland Papers, X, fols. 131–134, quoted in Gregg, *Queen Anne*, 119. The details in Harley's letters to his brother Edward about the death of Gloucester, including the fact that "his little body turned green and yellow immediately," suggest that Harley was at Windsor at the time; see *HMC Portland*, III, 624. As Gregg suggests, Harley's frequent visits to Anne may have begun in 1699.

24. Meeting of Parliament Act 1694 (6 & 7 Will. & Mar. c. 2).

25. Harley was certainly aware of this fact; see the letter to him from Henry Guy, dated 26 December 1700: "To balance the ill omens you mention of February 6th, it is the princess' birthday." *HMC Portland*, III, 641. The letter Guy was answering does not survive, but Harley may well have mentioned that 6 February was the date of Charles II's death and thus the date of James II's accession.

26. *English Post*, 5 February–7 February 1701.

27. For helpful accounts of Clarke's career, see Watkins Shaw et al., "Clarke, Jeremiah (i)," in *NGDM*, and H. Diack Johnstone, "Clarke, Jeremiah (1673x5–1707)," in *ODNB*. In order to have featured Elford, who left Durham for London about 1699, this birthday ode must have been performed in 1699 or later. The references to Anne as "unseen, and most retired" and the absence of any specific mention of Gloucester point strongly to 1701.

28. The orchestration thus resembles that of Purcell's music for Gloucester's birthday in 1695, which was also performed at Windsor. The instruments referred to in the score as "Flauto primo" and "Flauto 2do" were almost certainly recorders, as transverse flutes did not come into common use in England until later. As the "flauti" play simultaneously with the pair of oboes, the same two players cannot have doubled, but there were at least five French oboists in the band that served Prince George at this time, and wind players in this period normally played several different instruments, so I would suppose that two other oboists from the band played the recorders. As Peter Holman has pointed out, the six sonatas published by the German composer Johann Gottfried Keller in 1699 "were dedicated to Princess Anne, and were probably composed for musicians in her service, including the trumpeter John Shore and the oboe and recorder players James Paisible and Peter La Tour." See "Keller, J. Gottfried," in *NGDM*. One of those sonatas calls for a pair of oboes *and* a pair of "flutes."

29. All citations of text and music follow GB-Lbl Add. MS 31812, fols. 32–43, a transcription made in 1828 by R. J. S. Stevens, who complains at the end of the score that "Jeremiah Clarke's copy was so mutilated and torn, that I was obliged to end my Copy, in the middle of this grand Chorus." The original has disappeared.

30. For information on Elford's career, see Olive Baldwin and Thelma Wilson, "Elford, Richard (bap. 1677, d. 1714)," in *ODNB*, and the entry on Elford in app. C of Donald Burrows, *Handel and the English Chapel Royal* (Oxford: Oxford University Press, 2005), 582. Burrows quotes the manuscript record of Elford's appointment at Windsor on 29 December 1701 (GB-WRch Chapter Acts V B 5, 177): "having been recommended by the Princess, and to have augmentation of £18 p[er] a[nnum]." In the transcription by Stevens, Elford's parts in this ode are marked "alto" and written in the alto clef, but the tessitura is that of a high tenor. "His name is in a tenor

partbook at Durham, and Eccles, Blow, Clarke, Weldon and Croft wrote for him in the high tenor range, as did Handel." Olive Baldwin and Thelma Wilson, "Elford, Richard," in *NGDM*.

31. William Croft, preface to *Musica Sacra, or Select Anthems in Score,* 2 vols. (1724), I, 4.

32. Burnet, *History*, V, 2.

33. In the transcription by Stevens, there are a few errors in the viola part, which I have silently corrected in order to make the harmonies plausible.

34. A student poet celebrating Anne's visit to Cambridge in April 1705 prayed for long life for George and a child for Anne. GB-Lbl Add. MS 4276, fols. 36–37.

35. *JHL*, XVI, 594; 11 February 1701.

36. *The Succession to the Crown of England Considered* (1701), 4. The attribution of this pamphlet to Defoe, accepted by Paula Backscheider and other modern scholars, is highly plausible. Not only is the writing characteristic of Defoe in manner and matter but one of the replies to this pamphlet, *Animadversions on the succession to the crown of England, consider'd. Publish'd by Captain D—by* (also 1701), refers to the author of *The Succession* as "The Gentleman who oblig'd his Countrymen sometime since with the True Born *Englishman*" (1).

37. "'Tis Evident, that if the Princess Ann has no more Children, and His Majesty should continue to decline Marrying, *both which are but too probable*, the Settlement of the Crown, as made by Consent of Parliament, is at a full Stop" (6).

38. This stipulation had become law with the passage of the Bill of Rights in 1689, which provided that "all and every person and persons that is, are or shall be reconciled to or shall hold communion with the See or Church of Rome, or shall profess the popish religion, or shall marry a papist, shall be excluded and be forever incapable to inherit, possess or enjoy the crown and government of this realm" (1 William and Mary, sess. 2, c. 2. 6 S. R. 142).

39. Defoe, *The Succession*, 12–14, 21, 28.

40. *HMC Portland*, III, 626.

41. Christian Cole, *Historical and Political Memoirs* (1735), 234–235.

42. "It may not be impossible," wrote an anonymous pamphleteer in April 1701, "that his Royal Highness, the Prince when he attains to Years of Discretion, may rather imitate King *Henry* the IV. of *France* (his great Grandfather) and exchange one Religion for another, and accept of Three Kingdoms into the Bargain, than follow the Example of his Pious Father (King *James* the Second) and lose Three Kingdoms for Religion." *The Rights of King and subjects briefly stated: or, Considerations about the royal succession, submitted to the Commons of England in Parliament* (1701), 8.

43. See *Mr. Fuller's answer to the Jacobites* (1700); *Mr. Fuller's letter to the Right Honourable the Lord Mayor* (1700); *Fullers non-recantation to the Jacobites* (1701); *A trip to Hamshire and Flanders: discovering the vile intrigues of the priests and Jesuits* (1701); and *The Prince of Wales: a Poem* (imprint date 1702 but advertised in November 1701).

44. *Animadversions*, 2–3.

45. *Post Man*, 8 April–10 April 1701.

46. The four different versions were performed separately on 21 March, 28 March, 11 April, and 6 May. At a special subscription performance on 3 May, all four versions were performed, and the audience (surprisingly) chose the youngest composer, Weldon, as the winner. For a good account, with musical examples, see Roger Fiske, *English Theatre Music in the Eighteenth Century*, 2nd edition (Oxford: Oxford University Press, 1986), 14–24.

47. Congreve, *The Judgment of Paris* (1701), 6.

48. *The Parliamentary Diary of Sir Richard Cocks, 1698–1702*, ed. D. W. Hayton (Oxford: Clarendon, 1996), 71.

49. John Tutchin, *The Foreigners* (1700), 6–10.
50. See J. A. Downie, "Tutchin, John (1660x64–1707)," in *ODNB*.
51. Daniel Defoe, *The True-Born Englishman* (1700), 20.
52. *The Church of England's Joy on the Happy Accession of her Most Sacred Majesty* (1702), 2.
53. *MGC*, 7.
54. *MGC*, 14.
55. *Post Boy*, 20–23 September, 1701.
56. Letter of 16/27 September 1701, as printed in J. S. Clarke, *The Life of James the Second, Collected out of Memoirs writ of his own Hand*, 2 vols. (Longman, Hurst, Rees, etc., 1816), 602 (normalizing *u* and *v*).
57. Clarke, *Life of James the Second*, 560.
58. James Macpherson, *Original papers; containing the secret history of Great Britain*, 2 vols. (Dublin, 1775), I, 256.
59. *Britannia Rediviva*, ll. 239–44.
60. 1 William and Mary, sess. 2, c. 2. 6 S. R. 142. The prohibition had been confirmed by the Act of Settlement of 1701 (12 and 13 William sess. 3, c. 2).
61. For the fullest account of Georg Ludwig's investiture, see the article headed "Hanover, August 26" [N.S.] in the *Post Boy* for October 4–October 7, 1701. Reports of Georg's plans to visit William at Loo were contradictory. "The Duke of Zell, and the Prince of Hanover, are expected next Week at Loo," says the *Post Boy* for 4–6 September 1701, but the *Flying Post* for 6–9 September explains that "the Elector of Hanover is not to come, because of some Difficulties about the Ceremonial." In an article dated "Loo, September 23" [N.S.], the *London Gazette* for 15–18 September reports the presence of the grandfather and grandson: "The King being accompanied with the Duke of Cell and the Electoral Prince of Hanover went the 21st instant to Dieren."
62. Luttrell, V, 90; *Flying Post*, 16–18 September 1701.
63. "Le Roy dit à la princesse Anne, qu'il seroit à propos de faire venir le Prince Electoral. La Princesse répondit qu'elle étoit grosse. Cette grossesse ne se trouva point; mais le Roy ne vécut guères après cela; autrement il auroit fait venir le Prince." Leibniz, *Die Werke von Leibniz gemäss seinem handschriftlichen Nachlasse in der Königlichen Bibliothek zu Hannover*, ed. Onno Klopp, 11 vols. (Hanover, 1864–84), XI, 17. Leibniz was close to the Electress Sophia, who was his source for this story. Although there is no surviving correspondence, diary entry, or newspaper account from 1701 to confirm it, Anne's telling William she was pregnant would presumably have been a private matter.
64. For allegations that Anne was lying, see Gregg, *Queen Anne*, 123, following the lead of Onno Klopp, *Der Fall des Hauses Stuart und die Succession des Hauses Hannover in Gross-Britannien und Irland*, 14 vols. (Vienna, 1875–88), IX, 454. Klopp's only source, quoted in a footnote, is Leibniz.
65. *English Post*, 12–15 September 1701.
66. *MGC*, 34.
67. GB-Lbl Add. MS 61414, fol. 169.
68. *MGC*, 35.
69. GB-Lbl Add. MS 28070, fol. 2. The original letter is dated "Windsor teusday night," which leaves the actual date uncertain. Snyder, in his notes to *MGC*, provides a bracketed date of 16 September, which seems too early in light of the known dates of Marlborough's letters; 23 September seems more likely. In its issue for 25–29 September, the *New State of Europe* reported that "Mr. *Aubery* the King's Coachmaker, is ordered to cover 11 Coaches with Black Cloth, *viz.* 5 for His Majesty, and 6 for the Prince and Princess of Denmark."

70. William Pittis, *The Generous Muse* (1701), 2nd ed. "corrected," sig. A1r, reversing italics. The British Library copy of this edition has a handwritten inscription at the end "for the Reverend Mr Archdeacon Yeates, Islington," whom I take to be Cornelius Yeates, who was an archdeacon of Wilts and a rector in Islington but seems more likely to have been the recipient of a copy of this poem than its author. The same poet greeted Anne's accession with *The Loyalist, a funeral poem in memory of William III* (28 April 1702), again addressed to Anne, and described as "by the author of *The Generous Muse*." Comparison of both these poems with *The Patriots* (6 January 1702), a poem in praise of Harley that refers to "my generous Muse" in its opening line, suggests that all three are by the same hand.

71. See the preface to *An epistolary poem to John Dryden, Esq. occasion'd by the much lamented death of the Right Honourable James, Earl of Abingdon* (1699).

72. Dryden, *Aeneis*, V, 61–76.

73. *New State of Europe*, 9–11 October 1701.

74. Luttrell, V, 100. The *Post Boy* for 16–18 October puts this visit on 18 October.

75. *Post Boy*, 11–13 November 1701.

76. Henry Horwitz, *Parliament, Policy and Politics in the Reign of William III* (Manchester: Manchester University Press, 1977), 297.

77. *New State of Europe*, 18–20 November 1701.

78. *MGC*, 46.

79. Dieupart's six suites, published in Amsterdam in 1701, are dedicated to the Countess of Sandwich. For Sarah's correspondence with and about the Sandwiches, see GB-Lbl Add. Ms. 61455, fols. 178, 180b, 183, 187–201b, 204–206b.

80. *JHL*, XVII, 6; 31 December 1701.

81. Nahum Tate, *An Ode upon the Assembling of the New Parliament* (1702), 1–4, reversing italics. Eccles's settings of three songs from this ode were printed in 1703; see *The Monthly Mask of Vocal Music, 1702–1711*, ed. Olive Baldwin and Thelma Wilson (Aldershot: Ashgate, 2007), 41–42.

82. *An Opera Perform'd at Mr. Josiah Priest's Boarding-School at Chelsey. By Young Gentlewomen. The Words Made by Mr. Nat. Tate. The Musick Composed by Mr. Henry Purcell* (1689?), 4, correcting one misprint: "on" for "o'er," which is the reading of GB-Ob Tenbury MS 1266 (5). In an important article, "Letter from Aleppo: Dating the Chelsea School Performance of Dido and Aeneas," *Early Music* 37 (2009): 417–428, Bryan White has shown conclusively that the first performance cannot have been later than July 1688 and most likely took place on 1 December 1687. White also casts doubt on the theory that this work, like Blow's *Venus and Adonis*, was performed at court before the school performance, though Andrew Pinnock, citing resemblances between Tate's prologue to the opera and the ceilings designed by Antonio Verrio at Windsor Castle, continues to argue that the opera was designed for court performance. See "*Deus ex machina*: A Royal Witness to the Court Origin of Purcell's *Dido and Aeneas*," *Early Music* 40 (2012): 265–278.

83. *Conduct*, 123–124.

84. See *Post Boy*, 6–9 December 1701, Luttrell, V, 118, *English Post*, 26–29 December 1701, 29–31 December.

85. Luttrell, V, 145.

86. *English Post*, 23–25 February 1702.

87. *Conduct*, 120–121.

88. *History*, V, 2.

89. Godolphin to Harley, 8 March 1702; *HMC Portland*, IV, 34.

90. Klopp, *Der Fall des Hauses Stuart und die Succession des Hauses Hannover,* X, 9, citing a report of 11 March 1702, by Johann Wenzel, Count Wratislaw, the representative in London of the Habsburg emperor Leopold.

91. Luttrell, V, 151.

92. *London Gazette,* 26–30 March 1702.

93. *Observator,* 6–10 March 1703. The characters are responding to Anne's reissuing of her original proclamation, which she did many times. Tutchin borrowed his title and dialogue form from a paper published by the Royalist Roger L'Estrange during the Exclusion Crisis. Part of the joke was that his political ideology was completely unlike that of the original *Observator.*

94. For full details, see *LS2MH,* 52–53. Unless otherwise noted, all performance dates and venues given hereafter for London theatres follow this source.

95. The undated petition, probably sent to the queen soon after her accession, is GB-Lna LC 7/3, fol. 166, printed in *A Register of English Theatrical Documents, 1660–1737,* ed. Judith Milhous and Robert D. Hume (Carbondale: Southern Illinois University Press, 1991), no. 1696. There is no surviving response, but a later petition, GB-Lna SP 34/36, fol. 114, noting that prosecutions have continued and begging for relief, says that the queen, responding to the earlier request, ordered a stop to the prosecution.

96. GB-Lbl 61420 (Privy Purse accounts), fol. 16, records payments to Thomas Betterton and Christopher Rich in 1704. See commentary in *LS2MH,* 170–171.

97. *The Church of England's Joy on the Happy Accession of her Most Sacred Majesty* (1702), 2.

98. Luttrell, V, 157.

99. Luttrell, V, 158.

100. Horwitz, *Parliament, Policy and Politics,* 289–290.

101. Boyer, *History,* 13.

102. *MGC,* 51.

103. R. O. Bucholz, *The Augustan Court: Queen Anne and the Decline of Court Culture* (Stanford: Stanford University Press, 1993), 57.

104. Luttrell, V, 150.

105. The service is printed in full in J. R.Planché, ed., *Regal records or A chronicle of the coronations of the queens regnant of England,* (Chapman and Hall, 1838), 111–143.

106. The oath recited by Anne was as follows: "I do solemnly and sincerely in the presence of God profess, testifie, and declare, that I do believe that in the sacrament of the Lord's Supper there is not any Transubstantiation of the elements of bread and wine into the body and blood of Christ, at or after the consecration thereof by any person whatsoever. That the invocation or adoration of the Virgin Mary, or any other saint, and the sacrifice of the mass, as they are now used in the Church of Rome, are superstitious and idolatrous. And I do solemnly, in the presence of God, profess, testify, and declare, that I do make this Declaration and every part thereof in the plain and ordinary sense of the words read to me as they are commonly understood by English Protestants" (Planché, *Regal records,* 119).

107. GB-Lna LC 2/15/1, fol. 34.

108. No list of composers survives, but Professor Bruce Wood has used the texts of the anthems to show that most of them were the same as those sung in 1689. He has identified two new works: the introit, *I was glad,* a setting by Francis Pigott, and the anthem sung at the acclamation, *The Queen shall rejoice,* a setting by Turner. See "John Blow's Anthems with Orchestra" (Ph.D. diss., University of Cambridge, 5 vols., 1976), V, 13.

109. John Sharp, *A Sermon Preach'd at the Coronation of Queen Anne* (1702), 18–19.

110. *Albion's Glory, a Pindarique Ode on the Royal Train that Attended the Happy Coronation of Her most Sacred Majesty* (1702), 4–5.

111. Celia Fiennes, *Through England on a Side Saddle* (Scribner and Welford, 1888), 255–257, normalizing *ye* to *the* and *wch* to *which*.

112. GB-Lbl Add. MS 61407 (Sarah's account book as Mistress of the Robes), fols. 23, 9. The total outlay for 1702 was £5520.11.11; for 1703, by contrast, it was £3151.19.8; see fols. 9, 26. For Anne's later claim that the charges for renting jewels were "very extravagant," see *CTB*, XVIII, 5.

113. GB-Lna LC 2/15/1, fols. 25, 9.

114. Luttrell, V, 166; GB-Lna LC 2/15/1, fol. 32.

115. GB-Lna LC 2/15/1, fol. 34; Fiennes, *Through England on a Side Saddle*, 257.

116. *Cabala* (1653), 260. For some intelligent commentary on the question of the speech's authenticity, see Frances Teague, "Queen Elizabeth in Her Speeches," in *Gloriana's Face*, ed. S. P. Cerasano and Marion Wynne-Davies (Detroit: Wayne State University Press, 1992), 63–78.

117. Abel Boyer, describing this medal in his life of Anne (1722), calls the Hydra "the Emblem of Rebellion, Sedition, Schism, Heresy, &c." *History*, 718.

118. John Sharp, *A Sermon Preach'd at the Coronation* (1702), 3, 4, 16, 21.

119. For a full description, with musical excerpts, see Matthias Range, *Music and Ceremonial at British Coronations from James I to Elizabeth II* (Cambridge: Cambridge University Press, 2012), 111–116.

120. Fiennes, *Through England on a Side Saddle*, 258.

121. See the conclusion of chapter 3 above.

122. *MGC*, 55.

123. Winston Churchill, *Marlborough; His Life and Times,* new ed., 2 vols. (Chicago: University of Chicago Press, 2002), I, 521.

124. Boyer, *History,* 14.

125. *History,* 14.

126. *Privy Council Register*, GB-Lna PC 2/79, fol. 111.

127. *History,* 14.

128. This was Thomas Herbert, eighth Earl of Pembroke, the younger brother of Philip, the seventh earl, mentioned earlier as the husband of the younger sister of Charles II's mistress Louise Kéroualle. Philip's violent life was a short one (1652–1683).

129. *Post Boy,* 2–5 May 1702.

130. See the report of Spencer Compton, printed in *HMC*, XI, 130: "I further humbly certify to your Lord[shi]p that her present Majesty was graciously pleased to grant by Letters Patent dated August 4th, 1702, £1000 per ann. out of the Post Office during her Majesty's pleasure to the said Guy Palmes in consideration of his losses in the said office of Teller." Although Snyder, in his notes to this letter in *MGC*, suggests that the reference to "the other person" may point to Lord Fitzharding, Fitzharding is named later in the letter, and it seems more likely that Anne is reassuring the Whiggish Sarah that she will take care of the person Musgrave is determined to displace.

131. Godolphin to Sarah, 16 May 1702, *MGC*, 58.

132. GB-Lbl Add. MS 61416, fols. 3–4. This letter is printed, with some errors and omissions, in *MGC*; my quotations follow the MS.

133. GB-Lbl Add. MS 61415, fol. 136.

134. For a full account see David B. Green, *Gardener to Queen Anne: Henry Wise and the Formal Garden* (Oxford: Oxford University Press, 1956). There were similar improvements at Windsor

and at Hampton Court. On the disputed attribution of the orangery, sometimes thought to be by Vanbrugh, see Kerry Downes, *Sir John Vanbrugh* (Sidgwick & Jackson, 1987), 291–295.

135. *London Gazette,* 25–28 May 1702.

136. Anne's letter urging the commissioners "to consider of the most effectual method for establishing an Union between the two Kingdoms" informs them that "The Heads of this Treaty are so obvious that Her Majesty dos not think it necessary to mention them." GB-Lbl Add. MS 29548, fol. 33.

137. *Daily Courant,* 6 October 1702.

138. *Anna in Anno Mirabili: Or, The Wonderful Year of 1702* (1702), 8.

139. See the important revisionist account by Henry Kamen, "The Destruction of the Spanish Silver Fleet at Vigo in 1702," *Bulletin of the Institute of Historical Research* 39 (1966): 165–173. The myth that Rooke and Ormond had captured vast wealth died hard; as recently as the 1930s, Winston Churchill was confidently stating that the raid had netted "a million sterling" for the treasury. *Marlborough,* I, 611.

140. *London Gazette* 19–22 October 1702. Anne wasted no time in pursuing the investigation. At the meeting of the Privy Council on 22 October, it was "Ordered ... that all the Judges of Her Majesty's Courts at Westminster do meet and consider of the most proper way and method of proceeding against & bring to condign Punishment such Persons as shall be found Guilty of the Disorders committed at Port St. Maries, in the late Expedition to Cadiz." *Privy Council Register,* GB-Lna PC 2/79, fols. 225–226. At the next meeting, on 30 October, she sought a further opinion from the judges as to "whether the Persons accused to the said Disorders, may not be brought to Tryall for the same by a Court Martiall on Board the Fleet upon the Sea before their Arrivall within this Realme" (fol. 230).

141. *JHL,* XVII, 158; 22 October 1702.

142. *JHC,* XIV, 9.

143. *MGC,* 138.

144. GB-Lbl Add. MS 61416, fol. 19; for Anne's letter to Sarah, see GB-Lbl Add. MS 75400, which is not foliated but in roughly chronological order.

145. Boyer, *History,* 34–35.

146. GB-Lbl Add. MS 61416, fol. 24.

147. GB-Lbl Add. MS 61414, fol. 106.

CHAPTER 7

1. Richard Sherlock, *A Sermon Preach'd before the Queen* (1704), 10.

2. Luttrell, V, 462–463. This account differs in some particulars from the longer description in the *London Gazette* of 7 September 1704.

3. The title page of a surviving printed score of these two works describes them as "Perform'd before the Queen, Lords, and Commons, at the Cathedral-Church of St. Paul, on the Thanksgiving-Day for the Glorious Successes of Her Majesty's Army the last Campaign." The British Library catalogue gives "[1707]" as a date for this printing, identified on its title page as "The Second Edition." There is no entry in the Term Catalogue for this work, or for the (presumably lost) first edition. Donald Burrows, in a helpful essay, considers it "remarkable that Purcell's 1694 setting was the one that was regularly performed, rather than that by John Blow, who was still alive and was the principal Chapel Royal composer." See Burrows, "Orchestras in the New Cathedral," in *St. Paul's: The Cathedral Church of London, 604–2004,* ed. Derek Keene et al. (New Haven: Yale University Press, 2004), 399–402, here quoting 401.

4. *The Diary of John Evelyn,* ed. E. S. De Beer, 6 vols. (Oxford: Clarendon Press, 1955), V, 578.

5. A reprint of the text in 1695 may point to a revival in the 1694–95 theatrical season, and there is a definite record of a revival in 1698; see *The London Stage, 1660–1800,* pt. 1, *1660–1700,* ed. William van Lennep (Carbondale: Southern Illinois University Press, 1965), 441, 491. *LS2MH* lists performances on 29 January, 1 February, and 8 April 1701; some of the music, though not this scene from act 5, was performed in concert on 4 January 1704.

6. *King Arthur,* act 5, scene 2, 90–95.

7. Although the phrase "serene and calm" sounds fairly ordinary, Dryden's song is the only use of that sequence of words between 1477 and 1702 recorded in the comprehensive Literature Online database (http://lion.chadwyck.com). Nicholas Rowe, who probably picked up the phrase from Dryden, used it in his play *The Ambitious Step-Mother* (1702), act 5, scene 2; Lady Mary Chudleigh used it in her poem "On the Death of his Highness the Duke of Gloucester," first printed in her *Poems on Several Occasions* (1703). During Anne's reign, however, many poets employed this phrase and its variants.

8. GB-Lbl Add. MS 31456. John Walsh printed most of the music in 1703 as *The SONGS and Symphonys Perform'd before Her MAJESTY…on her Birth Day. 1703*; this song also appears in *A Collection of Songs for One Two and Three Voices…Compos'd by Mr. John Eccles* (1704), 92–95, and the library at Lambeth Palace holds one surviving copy of a separately printed text without the music. All versions differ slightly in accidentals and substantives; my quotations follow the MS. For a side-by-side comparison of the various versions, see Estelle Murphy, "The Fashioning of a Nation: The Court Ode in the Late Stuart Period," Ph.D. diss. (National University of Ireland, Cork, 2011), chap. 5.

9. He quotes Psalms 18, 28, 29, 58, 68, 76, 78, 82, and 116, as well as 1 Samuel 2.

10. Luttrell, V, 262.

11. When Anne attended her first such service in November 1702 Luttrell alertly noted the parallel: "The queen goes to St. Paul's Cathedrall (the like done in queen Elizabeth's reign)" (V, 232).

12. Sherlock, *Sermon,* 7–9, 19.

13. W. H., *Thura Britannica* (imprint 1702 but advertised in the Term Catalogue for 1703), 2–3.

14. *A form of prayer and thanksgiving to almighty God: to be used on Thursday the seventh of September next, throughout the Kingdom of England, Dominion of Wales, and town of Berwick upon Tweed; for the late glorious victory obtained over the French and Bavarians at Bleinheim, near Hochstet, on Wednesday the second of August, by the Forces of Her Majesty and Her Allies, under the Command of the Duke of Marlborough. By Her Majesties special Command* (1704). Sherlock quotes briefly from Psalm 76, which is listed, but ignores all the other texts.

15. Despite the fact that Blow's new anthems require only the organ, save for one brief passage calling for a lute, there appear to have been instrumentalists as well as singers in attendance. The account of the service in the *London Gazette* informs us that "The Hymn *Te Deum,* with other Anthems, were admirably well performed by Her Majesty's Choir and Musick"; "Musick" used in that context must refer to instruments. The earlier service in November 1702 also involved orchestral players: "All this Ceremony being over, Service began, Anthems, and *Te Deum* was Sung, the Musick both Vocal and Instrumental being incomparable" (*Post Boy* 14 November 1702). Blow's decision to forgo instruments in his new anthems, like his decision to compose brief and easy parts for the boy choristers, probably reflects the short time available to prepare the new music.

16. "The French lost at least 38,000 men, many captured….Allied losses were between 12,000 and 15,000 killed and wounded." *The Treaties of the War of the Spanish Succession: An Historical and Critical Dictionary,* ed. Linda Frey and Marsha Frey (Westport, Conn.: Greenwood, 1995). Contemporaneous and modern estimates of casualties in the battles of this war vary wildly; for

consistency, I have followed the estimates given in this modern reference work for all major battles.

17. Donald Burrows, *Handel and the English Chapel Royal* (Oxford: Oxford University Press, 2005), 32.

18. Godolphin to Harley, *HMC Portland*, IV, 49.

19. See Croft's autograph note on the score: "The words of this Anthem were chose and given to me by Her Most Excellent Majesty Queen Anne, and performed att St. Pauls upon a Thanksgiving Day." GB-Lbl Add. MS 17847, fol. 5, quoted in Burrows, *Handel and the English Chapel Royal*, 36–37.

20. John Grant, *Deborah and Barak the Glorious Instruments of Israel's Deliverance* (1704), 5, 7. This sermon was available from the same bookseller who published Sherlock's sermon; the two appear as adjacent entries in the Term Catalogue.

21. *MGC*, 349. Tallard spent the next eight years as a prisoner of war in England, treated with respect but prevented from returning to the field.

22. "The Introduction," in *The Poems of Anne, Countess of Winchilsea*, ed. Myra Reynolds (Chicago: University of Chicago Press, 1903), 6. Although Finch chose not to print it in her one published volume of 1713, this poem is the first entry in two different manuscripts of her work, both of which appear to have passed through many hands.

23. GB-Lbl Add. MS 61416, fol. 192, dated by Anne "St. James's Teusday morning." The dating of this letter is disputed. The MS is editorially dated [?31 October 1704], and Frances Harris follows that date, describing the letter as written in the context of the victories at Blenheim and Gibraltar (*Passion*, 113). Gregg (*Queen Anne*, 165) and Snyder (*MGC*, 98n) both propose 10 November 1702, linking the letter to the similar question of whether the action at Vigo Bay was comparable to Marlborough's victories along the Meuse. I agree with Gregg and Snyder because the letter mentions Prince George's illness: "I give you a thousand thanks, for your kind thoughts of coming to town if the Prince had continued ill. . . . Thank God he is now soe very well againe that I shall not desire you to com upon that account." The prince was reported to be "dangerously ill" on 3 November 1702, and "much better on November 5" (Luttrell, V, 232–233). I have found no comparable record of an illness in the autumn of 1704. In his dispatch of 3 November 1704, L'Hermitage reports on a meeting of Anne's council, after which "Sa Majesté et Son Altesse Royal s'en font retournies diner à Kinsington." GB-Lbl Add. MS 17677 ZZ, fol. 458.

24. Boyer, *History*, 34.

25. *JHC*, XIV, 87; 18 December 1702.

26. See W. A. Speck, "Hyde, Laurence, First Earl of Rochester (*bap.* 1642, *d.* 1711)," in *ODNB*.

27. GB-Lbl Add. MS 61414, fol. 32, dated 16 December [1702]. The Marlboroughs did not accept Anne's offer at this time, though Sarah later claimed the money.

28. *London Gazette*, 25–28 May 1702.

29. Henry Sacheverell, *The political union. A discourse shewing the dependance of government on religion in general: and of the English monarchy on the Church of England in particular* (Oxford, 1702), 58, 61, 59. Though he printed this work as a "discourse," Sacheverell had delivered an earlier version as a sermon in Oxford.

30. Defoe, *An enquiry into the occasional conformity of Dissenters in cases of preferment with a preface to the Lord Mayor, occasioned by his carrying the sword to a conventicle* (1698), 12–13.

31. Defoe reprinted his *Enquiry* in 1701, with a new preface addressed to the moderate Presbyterian John Howe (not to be confused with the Tory gadfly and poet of the same name). Howe replied, and Defoe replied again. See Defoe, *An enquiry into the occasional conformity of dissenters. In cases of preferment. With a preface to Mr. How* (1701); Howe, *Some consideration of a*

preface to an enquiry, concerning the occasional conformity of dissenters (1701); and Defoe, *A letter to Mr. How, By Way of reply to his Considerations of the preface to an Enquiry into the Occasional Conformity of Dissenters* (1701).

32. *The Establishment of the Church, The Preservation of the State* (1702), 13.

33. *The Shortest-Way with the Dissenters: or Proposals for the Establishment of the Church* (1702), 21.

34. *History*, V, 51.

35. For some helpful commentary, see Ashley Marshall, "The Generic Context of Defoe's *The Shortest-Way with the Dissenters* and the Problem of Irony," *Review of English Studies* 61 (2010): 234–258.

36. By far the most thorough account of this entire episode is that given by Paula R. Backscheider, *Daniel Defoe: His Life* (Baltimore: Johns Hopkins University Press, 1989), 94–119. Maximillian Novak makes the intriguing suggestion that Anne "was apparently a close reader of *The Shortest Way.*" *Daniel Defoe, Master of Fictions* (New York: Oxford University Press, 2001), 189.

37. *The Shortest-Way*, 16.

38. See his note to Burnet, *History*, V, 49.

39. Luttrell, V, 257 (14 January 1703).

40. *The song for New-Years-Day, 1703. Perform'd before Her Majesty. Set by Mr. Eccles, Master of her Majesty's Musick. The words by Mr. Tate, Poet Laureat to her Majesty.* This publication gives only the text, which differs in minor details from the text underlay provided with the printed music; see *The Monthly Mask of Vocal Music, 1702–1711*, ed. Olive Baldwin and Thelma Wilson (Aldershot: Ashgate, 2007), 10–15.

41. Luttrell, V, 253.

42. GB-Lbl Add. MS 31456. For details, see Murphy, "The Fashioning of a Nation," chap. 5.

43. Boyer, *Annals*, I, 215.

44. See Olive Baldwin and Thelma Wilson, "Music in the Birthday Celebrations at Court in the Reign of Queen Anne: A Documentary Calendar," *A Handbook for Studies in 18th-Century English Music* 19 (2008): 1.

45. *English Post*, 5–8 February 1703.

46. *An ode for an entertainment of musick on Her Majesty's birth-day, and, the success of Her Majesty's arms by sea and land. The night performance before Her Majesty at St. James's. The words by Mr. Wall. Set to musick by Mr. Abell* (1703).

47. The initials represent "Anna Regina" and "Princeps Georgius."

48. *Observator*, 6–10 February 1703.

49. *LS2MH*, 89. Newspaper accounts differ, and it is possible that the court music on offer at the public theatre was the New Year's song rather than the birthday ode. As Olive Baldwin and Thelma Wilson have pointed out to me (private correspondence), the singers were probably not the ones who performed at court, as Chapel Royal singers did not normally appear in the public theatres.

50. As Estelle Murphy has pointed out in a private communication, the printed versions "were not suitable as performance texts" because too many musicians would have had to read from the same score. "It seems more likely," she adds, "that they were used as exemplars from which each performer could copy a part." Supporting her thesis is the fact that some surviving manuscript parts have clearly been copied from the printed scores.

51. Michael Tilmouth, "Calendar of References to Music in Newspapers Published in London and the Provinces (1660–1719)," *R.M.A. Research Chronicle* 1 (1961): 19.

52. The poem was advertised, apparently for the first time, in the *Post Man*, 27 February–2 March 1703.

53. Nahum Tate, *Portrait-Royal. A poem upon Her Majesty's picture set up in Guild-Hall; by order of the Lord Mayor and Court of Aldermen of the City of London* (1703), 4–6, 19.

54. Luttrell, V, 282, 285. The "marquesse d' Galicioner" is presumably the "Marquis de la Gallissioner" listed among other French prisoners in the appendix to the *Thirtieth Report of the Deputy Keeper of the Public Records* (1869), 326.

55. *CTB*, XVIII, 51. See Oliver Millar, *The Tudor, Stuart, and Early Georgian Pictures in the Collection of Her Majesty the Queen* (Phaidon, 1963), 143.

56. Godolphin's letter to Nottingham, GB-Lbl Add. MS 29589, fol. 46. Also relevant is Nottingham's letter to Godolphin of 22 July 1703, GB-Lbl Add. MS 29595, fol. 229. Neither specifically states that the queen was present when Defoe was interrogated, but both Backscheider and Maximillian Novak believe she was. See Backscheider, *Daniel Defoe,* 117; Novak, *Daniel Defoe, Master of Fictions,* 189.

57. Tate, *Portrait-Royal,* 8.

58. Tate, *Portrait-Royal,* 15.

59. GB-Lbl Add. MS 61416, fol. 42.

60. See *MGC,* 152 and notes.

61. GB-Lbl Add. MS 61416, fol. 50.

62. GB-Lbl Add. MS 61416, fol. 51.

63. GB-Lbl Add. MS 61416, fol. 64.

64. GB-Lna SP 34/2/27.

65. *HMC Portland,* IV, 59.

66. *Elegia in praematurum obitum nobilissimi, & maximae spei adolescentis Johannis, marchionis de Blancford* (1703):

> Vidium Albionis Dominam Tua Fata gementem,
> Et Lachrimis Sacras immaduisse Genas.
>
> . . . .
> Ille sibi comitem Superum te poscit in Aula.
> Chare Puer, lateri & semper adesse suo.
> Felices ambo Elysis.

67. See J. Douglas Stewart, "Closterman, John (1660–1711)," in *ODNB.* Stewart argues persuasively that this painting is the work of Closterman and comments helpfully on its iconography.

68. *Spectator* 418 (30 June 1712).

69. William Congreve, *The Tears of Amaryllis for Amyntas. A Pastoral* (1703), 2–3, 6–7.

70. Harris, *Passion,* 84.

71. *MGC,* 165.

72. *JHL* XVII, 321–322; 27 March 170.

73. GB-Lbl Add. MS 61416, fol. 53.

74. GB-Lbl Add. MS 61416, fol. 34, editorially dated [late 1702–3]. As almanacs often appeared around the New Year, a January date is plausible.

75. GB-Lbl Add. MS 61416, fol. 122.

76. *MGC,* 183.

77. GB-Lbl Add. MS 61416, fol. 70r–v, editorially dated [22 May 1703].

78. *Several discourses by way of Essays,* 125–126. This excerpt appears a mere fifteen pages after the passage on the country mouse alluded to in a much earlier letter; GB-Lbl Add. MS 61415, fol. 110.

79. Julie Ellison, *Cato's Tears* (Chicago: University of Chicago Press, 1999), 10, emphasis mine.

80. Dryden, *Works*, XX, 51. The "Parallel" is Dryden's preface to his translation of *De Arte Graphica*, a Latin poem on the graphic arts by the Frenchman Charles Alphonse Dufresnoy.

81. *Works*, XV, 3–4.

82. *LS2MH*, 102; the editors suggest that "Laferry" may actually be "La Forest," a known dancer. James Paisible, featured here as a flutist, had played in *Calisto* and served Queen Anne when she was princess; he was now married to Moll Davis, the former royal mistress who had a large singing role in *Calisto*.

83. De L'Epine signed a receipt acknowledging this payment, which she received from Elizabeth Barry, Anne's former vocal coach, who was now a sharer in the company at Lincoln's Inn Fields; see *LS2MH*, 102.

84. GB-NO, Portland MS Pw2.571, quoted in *LS2MH*, 103.

85. GB-Lbl Add. MS 62410, fol. 78: "£32 5s. Pd. as given to the Itallian woman for singing before the Queen."

86. See Victor Stater, "Grenville, John, First Earl of Bath (1628–1701)," in *ODNB*. In addition to making him Baron Granville, Anne gave him a salaried sinecure as "housekeeper of St. James's and ranger of St. James's park." Luttrell, V, 289.

87. See David Onnekink, *The Anglo-Dutch Favourite: The Career of Hans Willem Bentinck, 1st Earl of Portland (1649–1709)* (Farnham, Surrey: Ashgate, 2007), 249. Portland, backed by the testimony of two prominent goldsmiths, won the case.

88. Francis Seymour-Conway, whom she made first Baron Conway of Ragley, was the younger son of the second marriage of Sir Edward Seymour, a High Tory currently serving as Comptroller of the Queen's Household; in the next year, Conway would marry Rochester's daughter.

89. Formal Latin correspondence relevant to these treaties survives in GB-Lbl Add. MS 29548, fols. 25, 31, 35.

90. *Daily Courant*, 14 June 1703.

91. *Ode on St. Cecilia's Day 1692*, ed. Peter Dennison (Kent: Novello, 1978), in *The Works of Henry Purcell*, VIII, xvi.

92. See *MGC*, 247–254.

93. Defoe, *The Succession to the Crown of England Considered* (1701), 4.

94. GB-Lna SP 54/2, fols. 1–52. For a modern summary, see Allan I. Macinnes, *Union and Empire* (Cambridge: Cambridge University Press, 2007), 94–95.

95. Boyer, *History*, 53.

96. *By the Queen: A Proclamation of Indemnity* (Edinburgh, 1703).

97. *A poem on Her Sacred Majesty Queen Anne* (Edinburgh, 1703) 1, 4–6.

98. Boyer, *History*, 54.

99. *The Records of the Parliaments of Scotland to 1707*, ed. K. M. Brown et al. (St Andrews, 2007–12), 1703/5/189.

100. Luttrell, V, 321.

101. GB-Lbl Add. MS 61416, dated "Windsor Munday June the 7th" [1703], fols. 79v–80r. Anne's belief that the English Whigs were acting in collusion with the "Revolution Whigs" in Scotland was prescient. See *The London Diaries of William Nicolson, Bishop of Carlisle, 1702–1718*, ed. Clyve Jones and Geoffrey Holmes (Oxford: Clarendon, 1985), 211.

102. GB-Lbl Add. MS 61416, fols. 92v–93r.

103. GB-Lbl Add. MS 61416, fol. 132, letter dated "Bath munday August the 23." Elizabeth, Lady Hervey, who was also in Bath, told her husband on 14 August that "the town is extreamly full already." *Letter-Books of John Hervey, First Earl of Bristol*, 3 vols. (Wells: Ernest Jackson, 1894), I, 194.

104. *MGC,* 247.

105. Duke's position resembles the one Jonathan Swift develops in his hilarious satire *A Tale of a Tub,* published some eight months later. In Swift's fable of the three brothers, Peter, the imperious Papist, eventually bears a strong resemblance to Jack, the canting Calvinist, which Swift explains as a result of "the Phrenzy and the Spleen of both having the same Foundation." *A Tale of a Tub,* ed. A. C. Guthkelch and D. Nichol Smith (Oxford: Clarendon, 1920), 199.

106. Richard Duke, *Of the imitation of Christ* (1703), 10–12, 14–15.

107. *MGC,* 252.

108. GB-Lbl Add. MS 61416, fol. 141r–v, editorially dated [21 October 1703].

109. Edward Hyde, first Earl of Clarendon, *The history of the rebellion and civil wars in England, Volume the second* (Oxford, 1703), sigs. a1r–a2v; b1r–v.

110. Edward Ward's *Secret History of the Calves-Head Clubb* ran through three editions in 1703. For a judicious account, see Michele Orihel, "'Treacherous Memories' of Regicide: The Calves-Head Club in the Age of Anne," *Historian* 73 (2011): 435–462.

111. *JHL* XVII, 331; 9 November 1703.

112. *JHC,* XIV, 242; 1 December 1703.

113. Boyer, *History,* 100.

114. Samuel Pratt, *A Sermon Preach'd At the Savoy-Church on Wednesday the 19th of January, 1703/4.* (1704).

115. *Conduct,* 155.

116. *The Memorial of the Church of England* (1705), 49.

117. For a full account, see Olive Baldwin and Thelma Wilson, "The Subscription Music of 1703–04," *Musical Times* 153 (2012): 1–17.

118. *London Gazette,* 16–20 December 1703.

119. GB-Lbl Add. MS 29548, fol. 29. Although this note appears in a collection of letters addressed to Nottingham, it makes no sense as a letter from the queen to her Secretary of State and is more likely a draft of a message she intended to send to his enemies.

120. Boyer, *Annals,* II, app. 3, 11–12.

121. Boyer, *Annals,* II, 226–227.

122. GB-Lbl Add. MS 61420, fol. 13.

123. There were three printings of Maynwaring's poem. The first, a two-page broadside called *Prologue for the musick, Spoken on Tuesday, January the 4th, 1703* [i.e., 1704], has no headnote. The second, in *Poems on affairs of state, from 1640 to this present year 1704* (1704), has a headnote that has often been misinterpreted: "Epilogue to the Ladies, spoke by Mr. *Wilks* at the Musick-Meeting in *Drury-Lane,* where the *English* Woman [i.e. Tofts] sings. Written by Mr. *Manwaring* upon the occasion of their both singing before the Queen and K. of *Spain* at *Windsor.*" The third printing, in *The third part of Miscellany poems* (1716), repeats this headnote verbatim. Modern editors, including Pierre Danchin, have silently and inaccurately corrected "the Queen and K. of Spain" to read "The King and Queen of Spain," but Charles III was unmarried in 1703; "the Queen" refers to Anne. They have also interpreted the statement that Maynwaring wrote "upon the occasion" of the concert featuring de L'Epine and Tofts as meaning that he wrote this epilogue *for* that occasion, confidently stating that the epilogue was recited at court and repeated in the theatre. See *The Prologues and Epilogues of the Eighteenth Century, The First Part, 1701–1720* (Nancy: Presses Universitaires de Nancy, 1990), I, 170. It is obvious to me that the "Epilogue to the Ladies" cannot have been spoken at court in the form in which we have it. It refers quite specifically to the concert on 29 December 1703, as "the *late* Trial of the tuneful Pair" and directly addresses the Whig ladies attending the performance by Tofts

on 4 January 1704. None of this would have made any sense at Windsor on 29 December. With some adjustments in tenses, the second part, connecting the lovely ladies to the young man's hope to claim the Spanish crown, might have been spoken at court, though I doubt it.

124. "Epilogue to the Ladies," following the first printing, in *Prologue for the musick* (1704).

125. Compare the similar imagery in Dryden's poem "To His Sacred Majesty" (1661), ll. 123–132.

126. For a detailed account, see Olive Baldwin and Thelma Wilson, "The Harmonious Unfortunate: New Light on Catherine Tofts," *Cambridge Opera Journal* 22 (2011): 217–234.

127. Tofts wrote a letter to Christopher Rich, the manager of Drury Lane, apologizing and disclaiming responsibility. For details, see LS2MH, 144–146.

128. See "While Anna with Victorious Arms," which Eccles included in his *Collection of Songs for One Two and Three Voices*, 26–28.

129. GB-Lna LC 5/153, fol. 433, quoted in *LS2MH*, 139.

130. *Observator*, 16–19 February 1703/4.

131. *Roscius Anglicanus*, ed. Judith Milhous and Robert D. Hume (Society for Theatre Research, 1987), 97.

132. Writing in January 1707, the author of the *Muses Mercury* expresses surprise at the attacks on the theatre following in the footsteps of Jeremy Collier: "Indeed, who would imagine it needed any Vindication, when Her Majesty has vouchsaf'd to Favour it, and a New Theatre has been since Built under Her Auspices, and Honour'd with Her Royal Name. When she has since Commanded some of those Plays to be Acted at St James's, which were Insolently treated in the *Short Views*: And the Reverend Judges have order'd the same Comedies, or Plays of the same Character, to be represented before them at the Temple." "The Dispute about the Stage Reviv'd," *Muses Mercury*, January 1707, 23.

133. *Heraclitus Ridens*, 19–22 February 1703/4.

134. Prior, *Poems on Several Occasions* (1707), 43.

135. Burnet, *History*, V, 121.

136. *A just and impartial character of the clergy of the Church of England, occasioned by Her Majesty's most Gracious bounty to them, in giving Her whole revenue of first-fruits and tenths for the augmentation of poor livings* (1704), 22–23.

137. See Godolphin's letter to Sarah of 18 April, *MGC*, 280–281.

138. Luttrell, V, 423.

139. Kerry Downes, *Sir John Vanbrugh* (Sidgwick & Jackson, 1987), 255.

140. Burnet, *History*, VI, 34; Dartmouth's note.

141. Luttrell, V, 429.

142. *The Church of England's address to the members of her communion. Especially to such as have laid down their offices at this critical juncture, or those that are inclinable to do it* (1704), 9.

143. See the excellent brief biography of Harley by David W. Hayton in *The History of Parliament: The House of Commons 1690–1715*, ed. David W. Hayton, Eveline Cruickshanks, and Stuart Handley, 5 vols. (Cambridge: Cambridge University Press, 2002).

144. For full details, see Backscheider, *Daniel Defoe*, 122–125.

145. See the helpful map in Winston Churchill, *Marlborough; His Life and Times,* new ed., 2 vols. (Chicago: University of Chicago Press, 2002), I, 766. Churchill's detailed account of the campaign and battle remains unmatched; see I, 711–884.

146. Joel Barlow, *The Columbiad* (Washington: Joseph Milligan, 1825), xvi–xvii.

147. *MGC*, 349.

148. Luttrell, V, 455.

149. Eccles, *Collection of Songs for One Two and Three Voices*, 141.

CHAPTER 8

1. John Harold Wilson, "Theatre Notes from the Newdigate Newsletters," *Theatre Notebook* 15 (1961): 83. See the helpful account in Olive Baldwin and Thelma Wilson, "Music in the Birthday Celebrations at Court in the Reign of Queen Anne: A Documentary Calendar," *A Handbook for Studies in 18th-Century English Music* 19 (2008): 11–13.

2. Scholars have inferred the presence of "Valentini" (properly Valentino Urbani) on this occasion because of a later payment to him from the Privy Purse. Sarah's note requesting this payment, dated 25 June 1708, and endorsed by Urbani, orders the goldsmith John Coggs to pay 20 guineas to "Seig:n Valentino for his Share for the Opera that was Acted at Court on the Queens Birth day last was twelve month" (GB-Lbl Add. MS 61420, fol. 31); there is a similarly worded record of the same payment, dated 26 June, in a list of disbursements, fol. 84. It is just possible that Valentini sang the role of Turnus, which he is first advertised as performing at Drury Lane (in Italian) on 8 March 1707, but the part of Turnus in the court production is heavily cut, which argues against his taking it. Baldwin and Wilson conclude that he performed separately, as de l'Epine had done on an earlier occasion.

3. GB-Lbl Add. MS 61414, fol. 167.

4. The Drury Lane production "retained Bononcini's music for fifty-two of the fifty-four arias." Lowell Lindgren, "I Trionfi di Camilla," *Studi Musicali* 6 (1977): 89–160, here citing 114.

5. Nicola Haym's contract with Christopher Rich, helpfully printed as an appendix to the modern facsimile edition, Giovanni Bononcini, *Camilla: Royal College of Music MS 79*, ed. Lowell Lindgren (Stainer and Bell, 1990), says that Haym hired "a gentleman" to turn Stampiglia's libretto into English prose, and that Rich then hired "Mr. Northman" (not otherwise known) to turn the prose into verse. Owen Swiney (or McSwiney), who signed the preface to the English word-book, *Camilla, An Opera* (1706), was probably not the translator, as he was principally an impresario. Peter Motteux, who was involved in other operatic projects for Rich, may also have had a hand in this one.

6. Haym was among the musicians paid special fees for performing for the "King of Spain" in 1703. At this time, he was employed by Wriothesley Russell, second Earl of Bedford, whom Anne had elevated to the Garter in 1702 and who was among the supporters of Vanbrugh's theatre project.

7. Although this subplot was evidently present in the production of 1696 in Naples, the production of 1698 in Venice, for which a printed libretto survives, severely truncated it, converting the servants into noble companions and changing their names to Arbante and Elvira. See *Camilla, Regina de' Volsci* (Venice, 1698), and Lindgren, "I Trionfi," 110–113.

8. For a helpful summary, see Kathryn Lowerre, *Music and Musicians on the London Stage, 1695–1705* (Farnham, Surrey: Ashgate, 2009), 21–23.

9. It remained in repertoire until 1710, and was revived as late as the 1720s. Foreign singers who joined the cast, including Valentini (Turnus) and de l'Epine (Prenesto), evidently sang their parts in Italian, while the original performers continued to sing in English. See for example the advertisement in the *Daily Courant* for 6 December 1707, which stipulates that several of the performers will sing "in Italian" or "part in Italian." Tonson's later editions of the libretto also include some numbers in Italian. Later revivals were sung in English.

10. This useful summary of the concluding pages of Salvadori's *Poetica toscana all' use* (1691) comes from Robert Freeman's wide-ranging essay "Apostolo Zeno's Reform of the Libretto," *Journal of the American Musicological Society* 21 (1968): 321–341, here quoting 323.

11. See Lindgren's introduction to *Camilla: Royal College of Music MS 79*, xv. In a private communication, Baldwin and Wilson have expressed "serious doubts about the practicalities of the

very cut version of *Camilla* being performed at court." Vice-Chamberlain Coke's papers, GB-Lbl Add. MS 69968C, include a copy of the printed libretto, in the edition of 1706, with "a series of crossings out in the recitatives to produce a slightly shortened version," and it is possible that this version, rather than the radically shortened version preserved in the MS published in Lindgren's facsimile edition, was the one performed at court. It would, however, have taken much longer, and the court evidently monitored the timing of performances. *Heraclitus Ridens,* in the issue for 19–22 February 1703/4, explains the cuts made in the court performance of Dryden's *All for Love* by claiming that the court "would not allow more than Two Hours for the Representation, Entertainments of Singing and Dancing, &c."

12. The manuscript is in the hand of James Kremberg, who composed the (lost) music for *England's Glory,* the short opera performed for the queen's birthday the previous year. He may have made the cuts, though there is no firm evidence.

13. *Post Man,* 15–17 February 1707.

14. The opera was *La Bataille de Ramelie ou les Glorieuses Conquestes des Alliez,* sung to a libretto by Jean Jacques Quesnot de la Chesnée, a theatrical director who made his career in the Spanish Netherlands. The words were printed in Ghent in 1706, with a picture of Marlborough and a dedication to Adam de Cardonnel, his Huguenot secretary. A manuscript prologue survives among the Blenheim papers, GB-Lbl 61360, fols. 12–15. The scene is Mount Parnassus, and the singing characters are "La Poësie, La Musique, et Le Ballet."

15. In his birthday ode, sung earlier in the day, Nahum Tate mentions "MARLBRO's Conqu'ring Banners" and "EUROPE's Rescu'd Realms," but his main emphasis falls on "Mirth and Musick":

> 'Tis ANNA's Day, and all around
> Only Mirth and Musick sound,
> Mirth and Musick all the Noise,
> Shouts and Songs, and Laughing Joys. (*Muses Mercury,* February 1707, 28)

16. GB-Lbl Add. MS 61101, fol. 72. In referring to the "ill desinges" of her enemies at home, the queen echoed her own description of "Scotch Plot" of 1703 as a series of "very Ill Practices and Designs carried on in Scotland, by Emissaries from France." *London Gazette,* 16–20 December 1703.

17. *London Gazette,* 23–26 October 1704.

18. *The Monthly Mask of Vocal Music, 1702–1711,* ed. Olive Baldwin and Thelma Wilson (Aldershot: Ashgate, 2007), 74. The verses also appear, with minor variants, in the *Diverting Post* for 23–30 December 1704.

19. Defoe, *A Hymn to Victory* (1704), 17.

20. Defoe, *The Dyet of Poland* (1705), 9.

21. In a letter to Harley, Defoe describes his wife as "a woman whose fortunes I have Ruin'd, . . . and yet who in the worst of my afflictions when my Ld N. first Insulted her Then Tempted her, scorn'd So much as to Move me to Complye with him, and Rather Encourag'd me to Oppose him." *The Letters of Daniel Defoe,* ed. George Harris Healey (Oxford: Clarendon, 1955), 17.

22. *Hymn to Victory,* 19–20.

23. *JHC,* XIV, 437 (28 November 1704).

24. *MGC,* 409.

25. "We shall have a good majority, though perhaps not all who are in the Queen's Service and the Prince's; but in that case, there must bee no present resentment showen nor soe much as threatned, though I assure you when the session is over, I shall never think any man fitt to

continue in his employment, who gives his vote for this Tack." *MGC,* 405. In urging that "no present resentment" be shown, Godolphin was tactfully warning the passionate Sarah to wait patiently with him for the next election rather than further alienating MPs who had voted for the Tack but who might support the administration on some other issue.

26. GB-Lbl Add. MS 61416, fol. 193; letter dated "St James's Nov: the 17th" [1704].

27. GB-Lbl Add. MS 61416, fol. 195, letter dated "Windsor Parke no: the 20th 1704." Compare the fair copy, fols. 197–198.

28. GB-Lbl Add. MS 61118, fol. 1, editorially dated [25 November 1704?].

29. GB-Lbl Add. MS 61458, fols. 160–163. Henry L. Snyder called attention to these letters in "Daniel Defoe, the Duchess of Marlborough, and the 'Advice to the Electors of Great Britain,'" *Huntington Library Quarterly* 29 (1965): 53–62. See also Harris, *Passion,* 117.

30. William Pittis, *A Hymn to Neptune* (1705), 1–2.

31. *The Memorial* was burned by the hangman on 4 September 1705; Luttrell, V, 488. Robert Harley devoted considerable time and effort to trying to identify the authors. GB-Lbl Add. MS 70340 (unbound) contains extensive handwritten records of his examination of David Edwards, the printer, his wife Mary, and various other printers, porters, and messengers named by Edwards, who claimed that a masked woman had brought him the copy. For a judicious account of this entire episode, see J. A. Downie, *Robert Harley and the Press* (Cambridge: Cambridge University Press, 1979, chap. 4.

32. GB-Lna T 48/17, an account of secret-service funds kept by William Lowndes, Secretary of the Treasury, records a payment to John Philips of "One hundred Pounds, as Our Royall Bounty for writing a Poem in Blank Verse, on the Battle of Blenheim," endorsed by the queen and by Henry Boyle, Chancellor of the Exchequer, on 16 May 1705. See Juan Christian Pellicer, "Harleian Georgic from Tonson's Press: The Publication of John Philips's *Cyder,* 29 January 1708," *Library* 7 (2006): 185–198, here citing 193*n*41.

33. John Philips, *Bleinheim* (1705), 1–3. My quotations follow the first edition.

34. Proof for this claim is somewhat elusive. In his excellent article "Whig and Tory Panegyrics: Addison's *The Campaign* and Philips's Bleinheim Reconsidered," *Lumen* 26 (1997): 163–177, John D. Baird cites *The Poems of John Philips,* ed. M. G. Lloyd Thomas (Oxford, 1927), xxii. Thomas bases her claim on a footnote in the article on Philips in *Biographia Britannica,* V (1760), 3359*n*. The footnote in this reference work reprints a passage from a poem on the death of Philips by Edmund Smith, who refers to the dead poet as one whom Godolphin "owns"; an annotation at the side of that passage states that the Treasurer made "a present" to Philips. Smith's *Poem on the Death of Mr. John Philips* first appeared on 22 May 1710; neither the first edition nor any reprint before *Biographia Britannica* annotates the passage. The context is a riposte to Addison ("a haughty Bard") for supposedly criticizing Philips specifically and blank verse more generally. Curiously enough, Smith compares his dead friend to the operatic soprano Margherita de l'Epine:

> Thrice happy Youth whom nobel *Isis* crowns!
> Whom *Blackmore* censures, and *Godolphin* owns;
> So on the tuneful *Margarita*'s Tongue
> The list'ning Nymphs, and ravish'd Heroes hung;
> But Citts and Fops the Heav'n-born Musick blame,
> And bawl, and hiss, and damn her into Fame:
> Like her sweet Voice is thy harmonious Song,
> As high, as sweet, as easie, and as strong. (8–9)

35. *The Works of the Right Honourable Joseph Addison,* ed. Thomas Tickell, 4 vols. (1721), I, x–xi.

36. Eustace Budgell, *Memoirs of the life and character of the late Earl of Orrery, and of the family of the Boyles.* (1732), 150–153.

37. See Pat Rogers, "Addison, Joseph (1672–1719)," in *ODNB.*

38. Luttrell, V, 492; *The London Diaries of William Nicolson, Bishop of Carlisle, 1702–1718,* ed. Clyve Jones and Geoffrey Holmes (Oxford: Clarendon, 1985), 238.

39. Tindal, who annotates his account of the debate on 29 November with the names of speakers in the margin, credits "Lord *Halifax*" with this part of the proposal. Nicholas Tindal, *The Continuation of Mr. Rapin de Thoyras's History of England, from the Revolution to the accession of King George II,* 4 vols. (1751), III, 675. On 11 December, another session attended by the queen, these ideas became the Alien Act, which declared that no subject of Scotland would have "any of the Freedoms or Privileges of Englishmen, until such Time as a perfect and entire Union be settled between the Two Kingdoms, or the Succession to the Crown of Scotland shall be declared and settled, by Act of Parliament in Scotland, in the same Manner the same is settled in England." *JHL,* XVII, 596 (11 December 1704). By stipulating that all these acts would take effect on Christmas Day 1705, more than a year later, Parliament clearly showed that they were intended as threats.

40. In 1756, the literary critic Joseph Warton would refer sneeringly to *The Campaign* as "that gazette in rhyme." *An Essay on the Writings and Genius of Pope* (1756), 30.

41. Joseph Addison, *The Campaign* (1705), 2–3. My quotations follow the second edition.

42. The only hard facts here are the dates of publication: Addison on 14 December 1704, Philips on 2 January 1705. Perhaps influenced by those dates, eighteenth-century witnesses, including Dr. Johnson, usually described Philips's poem as a Tory "answer" to Addison's. As John Baird has pointed out, however, Philips was slow at composition, and his reference to hearing birds sing while writing his poem at St. John's estate suggests that he began his work in the autumn. Baird speculates that Addison may have been "answering" Philips, though there is no proof that either poet saw the other's work in manuscript. More recently, Nicholas von Maltzahn has insisted that "Philips's answer in *Bleinheim* was closely to rewrite Addison into Miltonian verse, a process we can trace from section to section of the poem, and often from line to line." See "The War in Heaven and the Miltonic Sublime," in *A Nation Transformed: England after the Restoration,* ed. Alan Houston and Steve Pincus (Cambridge: Cambridge University Press, 2001), 154–179. In an excellent recent dissertation on Philips, Juan Christian Pellicer makes the useful point that "all Addison needed to know, if we are to account for *The Campaign* as a response to Philips, was that his Christ Church rival was writing a panegyric in formal imitative style, with *The Iliad* as a primary model and *Paradise Lost* VI as a strong secondary model." He concludes that "the marked differences between the poems—in structure, narrative event, and authorial method or approach—make it difficult to see how either poem can be read as a mere reworking of the other." See "John Philips, 1676–1709: Life, Works and Reception," Ph.D. diss. (University of Oslo, 2002), chap. 3.

43. *Bleinheim,* 17–18.

44. Nahum Tate, *The Triumph* (1705), 8.

45. *Paradise Lost,* IX, 27–33; V, 586–594, in *Milton: Complete Poems and Major Prose,* ed. Merritt Y. Hughes (Indianapolis: Bobbs-Merrill, 1957).

46. *Bleinheim,* 7–9.

47. *The Campaign,* 7–8.

48. *The Campaign,* 22–23.

49. For Addison's warning, see *Spectator* 253; for a fuller discussion of *Windsor-Forest*, see chapter 11 below. The juxtaposition of the river god with the queen's declaration of peace is particularly striking:

> At length great *ANNA* said—Let Discord cease!
> She said, the World obey'd, and all was *Peace!*
>   In that blest Moment, from his Oozy Bed
>   Old Father *Thames* advanc'd his rev'rend Head. (*Windsor-Forest*, ll. 325–328)

50. *The Campaign*, 14.

51. See the discussion of this phrase in chapter 7.

52. In its very first, issue, published on 28 October 1704, the *Diverting Post* begins the advance publicity: "We hear that shortly will be publish'd a Poem upon the Signal Battel of Blenheim; wrote by Joseph Addison Esq; and Printed by Jacob Tonson: It's believ'd that this Piece will be perform'd with that Spirit and Fire, even to reach the Glory of that Celebrated Action, in its highest and most exalted Perfection." The next issue (oddly dated 28 October–2 November) has "An Imitation of the Sixth Ode of Horace…Apply'd to…the Duke of Marlborough….by Capt. R[ichard] S[teele]," which begins with another advertisement for his friend's forthcoming poem:

> Should Addison's Immortal Verse,
> Thy Fame in Arms, great Prince, Rehearse,
> With Anna's Lightning you'd appear,
> And glitter o'er again in War.

The issue of 4–11 November notes Addison's appointment to "the Place of Mr. John Lock lately Deceas'd," again mentioning the forthcoming poem, which is advertised once more in the issue of 2–9 December.

53. *Diverting Post*, 9–16 December 1704.

54. According to the *Diverting Post* of 28 October 1704, there were two operas in preparation: "The Play-House in the Hay-Market (the Architect being John Vanbrugh Esq;) built by the Subscription Money of most of our Nobility, is almost finish'd, in the mean time two Opera's translated from the Italian by good Hands are setting to Musick, one by Mr. Daniel Purcel, which is called Orlando Furioso, and the other by Mr. Clayton, both Opera's are to be perform'd by the best Artists eminent both for Vocal and Instrumental Musick at the Opening of the House." For some intelligent commentary, see Thomas McGeary, "Thomas Clayton and the introduction of Italian Opera to England," *Philological Quarterly* 77 (1998): 171–185. Nothing ever came of the alleged opera by Daniel Purcell, although there is a later reference to it in the *Muses Mercury* (January 1707, 11).

55. Manuscript attached to the printed issue of the *Post Man* for 29–31 August 1704, William Andrews Clark Memorial Library, University of California, Los Angeles; printed in J. D. Alsop, "The Quarrel between Sir John Vanbrugh and George Powell," *Restoration and Eighteenth Century Theatre Research*, n.s., 5 (1990): 28–29.

56. According to Graham Barlow, the building when finished "measured approximately 124' long and 55' wide with a further 12' 0" for a promenade corridor and a partition wall at all levels that ran the width of the building. From basement to eaves the height was 52' 6"." See "Vanbrugh's Queen's Theatre in the Haymarket, 1703–9," *Early Music* 17 (1989): 515–521, here quoting 516. No other document of the period confirms the queen's alleged contribution. Although records

of disbursements from the Privy Purse are not complete, a payment on this scale would have been hard to keep quiet, and as Robert D. Hume and Judith Milhous have pointed out to me in private correspondence, Vanbrugh would also have wanted his supporters to know that the queen had contributed.

57.　The belief that Anne attended a concert performance in the not-yet-complete theatre rests on one dubious piece of evidence, a notice in the *Diverting Post* of 25 November–2 December 1704:

> Segniora Sconiance, a Famous Italian Singer, who lately came from those Parts, had a few Days since the Honour to Sing before Her Majesty with great Applause, upon the First Opening of the THEATRE in the Hay Market, erected by the Contribution of the Nobility. She is to Sing several Italian Songs, never Sung in this Kingdom before, Compos'd by the most Celebrated of the Modern Italian Masters.

There are many reasons to regard this notice skeptically. The *Diverting Post* often predicted events that did not occur. In the issue for 28 October–4 November for example, the newspaper announced a forthcoming opera: "Amadis de Gaul, an Opera in French, Set to Musick by Baptista de Lully, and translated into English by the Honorable G. Granville Esq; now set to Musick by Mr. Eccles: The Parts are all dispos'd, and will speedily be perform'd at the New Theatre in little Lincoln's-Inn-Fields." No such opera was ever performed. Queen Anne *never* attended a theatrical or musical performance during her reign, other than those that came to her at court, so her going to Haymarket would have been unusual and newsworthy, the kind of event Luttrell and other diarists, as well as the many newspapers now active, would have reported. "Seignora Sconiance" is not otherwise known in England or Italy, an odd circumstance for a "Famous *Italian* Singer."

The notice itself is evidently garbled, as its verb tenses make no sense as printed. Two small corrections in punctuation, however, give us a more plausible narrative, thus:

> Segniora Sconiance, a Famous Italian Singer, who lately came from those Parts, had a few Days since the Honour to Sing before Her Majesty with great Applause[. U]pon the First Opening of the THEATRE in the Hay Market, erected by the Contribution of the Nobility[,] She is to Sing several Italian Songs, never Sung in this Kingdom before, Compos'd by the most Celebrated of the Modern Italian Masters.

On this reading, Segniora Sconiance had sung privately for the queen at court some time not long before the newspaper was printed. Plenty of such instances clearly occurred, as we know from frequent payments to performers from the Privy Purse. The ad goes on to note that Sconiance will be featured when the Haymarket opens, an event the writer probably thought would happen sooner than it did. On what I take to be two misprints in hastily set type, scholars have erected an edifice. Ophelia Field, in *The Kit-Cat Club: Friends Who Imagined a Nation* (HarperCollins, 2008), 138, fancifully describes the queen arriving at the theatre, seeing her picture on the ceiling, and being attended, as an "audience of one," by servants in "scarlet livery." This is completely implausible.

58.　GB-Lna LC 5/154, fol. 35.

59.　There is no contemporary record of Thornhill's having executed the painting, nor does any contemporary make mention of its being altered or destroyed when the ceiling was lowered.

60.　Thornhill may have remembered that the queen had appeared as Pallas on her coronation medal; he cannot have known that de la Chesnée would bring her onstage as Pallas in *La Bataille de Ramelie,* which had not yet been written.

61. My thanks to my colleague Rebecca Martin, and to Richard Johns, curator at the Royal Museums, Greenwich, for help with the iconography of this sketch.

62. Luttrell, V, 481, 516–517. Princess Frederica Amalia of Denmark died on 19/30 October 1704; Sophia Charlotte of Hanover died on 10/21 January 1705.

63. Luttrell, V, 503.

64. *Diverting Post*, 23–30 December 1704.

65. *Annals*, III, 187.

66. Eccles's music is lost, but a change of pronouns in the text suggests that a different singer enters after the first four lines, with a third singing the part of "old Time":

> [1st singer:]
> From Fates dark Cell to Empire call'd,
> Ah how forlorn must I appear,
> Succeeding to the Glorious Year,
> That has the Mart of Fame forestall'd.
> [2nd singer:]
> Conquest, Triumph, ev'ry Blessing
> Nothing left for thy possessing,
> War's Wreath from Thee untimely torn,
>   Of all bereft,
>   No Garland left
>   Thy Cradle to adorn.
> [1st singer:]
> Ah wo! wo! wo! That ever I was born!
> [3d singer:]
> Cease, Oh Cease, (old Time replies)
>   My Darling Infant Cease thy Cries,
> Thy Predecessor we must own
>   Past Ages to have far outshone,
> But still for Thee to shine, Fame's spacious Orb has room:
> Great are the Blessings past, but greater Thine to come.

Nahum Tate, "The ODE for *New-Year's Day*, Perform'd to Musick before Her MAJESTY *January the First, 1705*," printed as an addendum to *The Triumph* (1705), 26–27. In keeping with past practice, these opening lines would have been a duet for Elford and another tenor, in which case Old Time would have been a bass.

67. *Daily Courant*, 4 January 1705; *Annals* III, 188.

68. As with the New Year's ode, the music is lost. The rare broadsheet that prints the text—*Words Sung at the Entertainment given by the Right Honorable Sir* Owen Buckingham, *Lord Mayor ... Written by Mr* Motteux. *Set to Musick by Mr* Weldon (1705)—prints the names of "Mr *Leveridge*" and "Mr *Elford*" next to the verses each man sang.

69. The first volume of his influential periodical the *Gentleman's Journal* (1692–94) is dedicated to Devonshire, the second to Halifax.

70. Boyer, *Annals*, III, 188.

71. Boyer, *History*, 169. In his more cautious account in the *Annals,* published while Anne was still alive, Boyer says that some at court were displeased but that the queen herself was civil. Nicholas Tindal, who follows Boyer closely, emends "dry Answer" to "cold answer." *Continuation*, III, 677.

72. *Bleinheim*, 13–14.

73. *The Birth-Night, A Pastoral. By Mr. Arwaker*, i.e. Edmund Arwaker the Younger (1705), 9.
74. *Annals*, III, 190.
75. The source is a deposition in one of Vanbrugh's later lawsuits with Sarah, in which he says "That abt Xmas 1704 he meeting casually with the Duke at the Playhouse in Drury Lane the Duke told him he designed to build a house in Woodstock Park." GB-Lbl Add. MS 38056, fol. 101.
76. *Post Man*, 28–30 June 1705. Oxfordshire was famous for Morris dancing, and the performers would have been in practice, as Whitsunday, the most important annual occasion for Morris dancing, had fallen on 27 May, a few weeks earlier.
77. Luttrell, V, 578.
78. Luttrell, V, 516.
79. *London Gazette*, 4–7 February 1705. Because Anne's birthday fell on Ash Wednesday, it was celebrated one day early, on 5 February.
80. The concert on 4 January 1704, at Drury Lane, featuring Catherine Tofts, included performances of "The Frost Musick: From *King Arthur*" and "The Sacrifice: From *King Arthur*"—two large-scale scenes requiring orchestra, soloists, and chorus. A benefit performance for the actress Anne Oldfield on 28 March included a reprise of "The Sacrifice." "Mr Leveridge, Mr Hughs, [and] Mrs Lindsey," all of whom had roles in *Arsinoe*, performed "The Frost Musick" on 30 April 1705. See *LS2MH*, 137, 157, 225.
81. *Arsinoe, Queen of Cyprus, An Opera* (1705), sig. A1r.
82. In a fuller statement about his training and aims, the preface to *The Passion of Sappho and the Feast of Alexander* (1711), Clayton describes his travels: "I was at the Trouble and Charge to go into *Italy* to consult the greatest Masters in [music], and by the study of Dead Authours, and Instruction of the greatest living, in some Years time I attained to so much Skill, as to take upon me, at my Return, to introduce the *Italian* Method of composing Musick upon our *English* Stage" (sig. A2r). Thomas McGeary, in his article cited above (n. 54), was the first modern scholar to call attention to this preface.
83. Two complete manuscript scores of the Italian opera survive, in the same hand, said to be that of the composer, in the the Biblioteca Nazionale Marziana in Venice: MSS It. IV, 392 and 393. One of these corresponds closely to a printed libretto, *Arsinoe drama per musica da recitarsi nel Teatro di S. Angelo l'anno 1678* (Venice, 1678); the other begins with a long prologue, presumably the one printed in *Prologo ed intermedi dell'Arsinoe da rappresentarsi nel Teatro Formagliari l'anno 1677* (Bologna, 1677). The manuscripts have been digitized and are available at the website of the Venetian libraries: http://polovea.sebina.it/SebinaOpac/Opac. The Venice edition of the libretto is available at the website of the Bibliothek des Deutschen Historischen Instituts in Rom: http://daten.digitale-sammlungen.de/~db/0004/bsb00048312/images/index.html. I have not seen the Bologna edition.
84. I assume here that his source was the printed libretto of the production in Venice; if he was working with the version produced in Bologna, he cut the entire prologue.
85. See GB-Lbl Egerton MS 3664, fol. 5r. This elegantly written score includes all the recitatives as well as instrumental parts not reproduced in the various printed collections of songs from *Arsinoe*. The printed versions often transpose the arias into keys that would be easier for amateur singers, whereas the keys and clefs used in the MS score accord well with our knowledge of the ranges and voice types of the singers who performed the work in 1705.
86. *William Congreve: Letters and Documents,* ed. John C. Hodges (New York: Harcourt Brace and World, 1964), 35.
87. Harriet later became Congreve's mistress and bore him a daughter, to whom he left most of his estate.

88. *Prologue to the Court; On the Queen's Birth-Day, 1704* (1705). First printed without the author's name, the poem appears in *The Works of Mr. William Congreve* (1717). The Old Style date has misled some scholars, but the reference to Blenheim in the final line means that the prologue cannot possibly have been spoken in 1704.

89. See, for example, an entry in the records of the Lord Steward, dated 26 March 1705: "Wee find there will be a great resort of Persons of all Qualityes this meeting at Newmarkett, and do apprehend the Harbinger may meet with some difficulty in accomodating Her Majesty's Officers and Servants with convenient Lodgings." GB-Lna LS 13/175, fol. 23v.

90. Edward Downes, *Roscius Anglicanus*, ed. Judith Milhous and Robert D. Hume (Society for Theatre Research, 1987), 98–99. Downes calls the performers "a new set of Singers, Arriv'd from Italy; (the worst that e're came from thence)." Skeptical modern scholars have suggested that Greber used some Italian singers who were already resident in London. See *LS2MH*, 220–221.

91. Luttrell, V, 539–540.

92. Luttrell, V, 537.

93. W. A. Speck, *Tory & Whig: The Struggle in the Constituencies, 1701–1715* (Macmillan, 1968), 100.

94. Writing to Sarah on April 9/30, Marlborough expressed the views he shared with Godolphin and Anne, knowing full well that his partisan wife was of a different mind: "You nor nobody living can wish more for the having a good Parliament then I do, but we may differ in our notions. I will own to you very freely mine, which is that I think at this time it is for the Queen's Service and the good of England, that the choyce might be such as that neither party might have a great majority, so that her Majesty might be able to influence what might be good for the common cause." *MGC*, 423.

95. All quoted descriptions of the visit follow Boyer, *Annals*, IV, 11–13.

96. See Richard S. Westfall, "Newton, Sir Isaac (1642–1727)," in *ODNB*.

97. For this phrase and the quoted poem, see the letter from John Maulyverer to the Reverend Mr. Thomas Dwyer in Leeds, GB-Lbl Add. MS 4276, fols. 36–37.

98. The evidence here is a touching letter to Sarah from Dr. Francis Hare, who had been Blandford's tutor and became Marlborough's aide. Apparently Francis Godolphin, Sarah's son-in-law, brought Dr. Hare to dinner, where his unexpected presence upset Sarah. He apologizes to her "for suffering you to be surprised by a sight, which could but raise a fresh remembrance of what I am too sensible can never be forgot." *Private Correspondence of Sarah, Duchess of Marlborough*, 2 vols. (Henry Colburn, 1838), I, 6; letter dated "Chelsea College, January 4, 1704–5."

99. Killigrew was the older brother of the poet and painter Anne Killigrew and is mentioned in Dryden's ode. According to a piece of gossip recorded by Pepys, he was among the many lovers of the Countess of Castlemaine; see *The Tangier Papers of Samuel Pepys*, ed. Edwin Chappell (Navy Records Society, 1935), 211.

100. Trevelyan's stirring narrative of this episode is a tour de force; see George Macaulay Trevelyan, *England under Queen Anne*, 3 vols. (Longmans, Green and Co., 1930–34), II, 249–256. For a sober modern account, citing many primary sources, see Samuel Pyeatt Menefee, "Green, Thomas (1679/80–1705)," in *ODNB*.

101. Luttrell, V, 543.

102. The official record of this meeting in the *Privy Council Register*, GB-Lna PC 2/80, fols. 322–329, makes no mention of this debate. It was evidently the practice of the scribes keeping those records to set down only decisions officially taken, and according to Luttrell's sources, this discussion was inconclusive.

103. "An ELOGY upon the unmerited Deaths of Capt. Green, Mr. Madder, &c.," printed as a section of *A Trip Lately to Scotland* (1705).

104. *A Trip,* 1–2.

105. *Annals,* IV, 19.

106. GB-Lbl Add. MS 61422, fol. 199r.

107. GB-Lbl Add. MS 61458, fols. 63v–64r.

108. *HMC,* IX, ii, 472.

109. GB-Lna SP 104/203, fols. 44, 47. In this lengthy and detailed letter, the queen tells Sunderland to go first to the Hague, where he is to meet with Anthonie Heinsius, the grand pensionary of Holland, and with the Portuguese ambassador; next, he is to "proceed to the Place where you shall be informed Our Right Trusty and Right Entirely beloved Cousin and Councellor John Duke of Marlborough then is and concert with him the necessary measures." Marlborough's correspondence shows that the two men met in Europe and continued to work together for the next several months.

110. Luttrell, V, 569 (3 1705): "It's said Jos. Addison, esq., one of the commissioners of appeals, will succeed Mr. Ellis, under secretary to sir Charles Hedges, secretary of state."

111. GB-Lbl Add. MS 61101, fol. 78.

112. *London Gazette,* 23–27 August 1705; compare 7–11 September 1704.

113. Richard Willis, *A Sermon Preach'd before the Queen* (1705), 15.

114. Psalm 18:37–38, 41; Clarke follows the text given in the Psalter of the 1662 edition of the *Book of Common Prayer.* This was one of the Psalms featured in Sherlock's sermon on Blenheim; see chapter 7 above. The title of the full anthem, *I Will Love Thee, O Lord,* is the first verse of Psalm 18. As Thomas J. Taylor explains in his helpful *Thematic Catalog of the Works of Jeremiah Clarke,* Detroit Studies in Music Bibliography, no. 35 (Detroit: Information Coordinators, 1977), Clarke wrote two completely different anthems beginning with this verse. The one composed for the celebration on 23 September 1705 is Taylor's no. 106, which survives in several manuscripts. My excerpt follows the version preserved in *The Gostling Manuscript,* ed. Franklin B. Zimmerman (Austin: University of Texas Press, 1977), an important collection compiled by the famous bass, whose note on the score is detailed and definitive: "Thanksgiving Anthem 23 September 1705 at St. Pauls, the Queen present, for the victory & success in fflanders, in passing the ffrench lines." The other anthem, Taylor's no. 105, is much better known, surviving in a number of early printed sources as well as numerous manuscripts, but its occasion remains uncertain.

115. Estelle Murphy makes the plausible suggestion that Eccles, who was busy composing the opera *Semele,* hired Clarke as a subcontractor to compose this New Year's ode; see Murphy, "The Fashioning of a Nation: The Court Ode in the Late Stuart Period," Ph.D. diss. (National University of Ireland, Cork, 2011), 68–71. Still, it would not have been difficult for the queen to communicate her interest in Clarke's music to Eccles or to Kent, the Lord Chamberlain.

116. *London Gazette,* 23–27 August 1705.

117. In that one letter, editorially dated [21 March 1705], the queen reports having reprieved a highwayman at Sarah's request and expresses joy at Harriet's recovery from a case of the smallpox. There is no compelling reason to believe that the two women failed to correspond during these months, and no explanation for Sarah's failure to preserve Anne's letters. I would speculate, however, that letters in this period were less frequent than formerly.

118. GB-Lbl Add. MS 61416, fol. 205: "I own what you propose of my takeing another bedchamber woman seems very reasonable, but as the saying is, Charety begins at home, & sein[g] that Hill dos al Feildings business, I am soe much better served, that I find no want of another, & besides the reasons you think makes me not care to add to my number, the uneasyness it would be to me to have a stranger about me when I have the gout & am forced to be help'd to do every

thing, is a very powerful one to hinder me from it." In her annotations on this letter, and on letters from the two previous years, Sarah constructs a narrative in which Anne has supposedly become enamored of Abigail but is unwilling to tell Sarah. By blaming Abigail for the breakdown of her own relationship with the queen, Sarah is able to avoid confronting her own part in that breakdown.

119. GB-Lbl Add. MS 61416, fols. 207r–208v.

120. See chapter 1 above.

121. Lee, *Sophonisba*, act 4, scene 1, 207–208; 230–234, emphasis mine. Another possible source is Congreve's play *The Old Batchelor* (1693), which Anne saw in its first run. Laetitia, acting the part of the abandoned woman, complains to Fondlove: "No no, you are weary of me, that's it—That's all, you would get another Wife—Another fond Fool, to break her Heart—Well, be as cruel as you can to me, I'le pray for you; and when I am dead with grief, may you have one that will love you as well as I have done: I shall be contented to lie at peace in my cold Grave—Since it will please you" (p. 35). I suspect Congreve was parodying Lee.

122. For an excellent account, see J. A. Downie, "What if Delarivier Manley Did *Not* Write *The Secret History of Queen Zarah?*" *The Library* 5 (2004): 247–264.

123. *The Secret History of Queen Zarah* (1705), 100.

124. "The lord Wharton's horse won the duke of Marlboroughs plate at Woodstock race." Luttrell V, 595 (25 September 1705). Hearne made his entry in 1706: "Upon the Turning out from Court of the Earl of Abbingdon, the Earl remov'd the Horse-Race, which us'd to be yearly, for a Plate which he gave, at Woodstock, to Port-Meadow by Oxford. Upon which the Dutchess of Marlborough continu'd it beginning last year, when only a parcel of Whiggish, Mobbish People appear'd. And this Year, a Plate being given by her of 50 libs, 'twas run for on the Eleventh of Sept. when but one Horse run viz. that of ye Ld. Kingston: so that there was no manner of sport, & 'tis thought the Dutchess of Marlborough, an insatiable covetous proud Woman will hav the Plate again as a present from that Lord, who is a most Rank Whig. Very few Gentry were at this Appearance, & of the Nobility only Ld. Wharton, Duke of Richmond, and one or two more of that Party: & to grace all the Bp. Of Sarum [Burnet] with his Lady, waited upon the Dutchess. Next day was a Race at Oxon in the said Meadow, where was a great Appearance of Nobility &c." *Remarks and Collections*, ed. C. E. Doble, 11 vols. (Oxford: Oxford Historical Society, 1885–1921), I, 287, normalizing abbreviations.

125. Luttrell, V, 609; 9 November 1705.

126. *JHC*, XV (1803), 38.

127. On Cowper's hair, see John Campbell, *The Lives of the Lord Chancellors* (John Murray, 1846), IV, 294*n*. On Anne's retention of the livings, see her letter to Sarah, dated "Windsor, July the 17th" [1706?], GB-Lbl Add. MS 61417, fol. 17r–v: "I have a very good opinnion of him, & would depend uppon his recommendation on any occasion sooner then on most peoples, but as to this particular, I think the Crown can never have too many liveings at its disposal, and therefore tho there may be some trouble in it, it is a power I can never think reasonable to part with, and I hope those that com after me will be of the same mind."

128. Harris, *Passion*, 120–121.

129. *JHC*, XV, 7.

130. *JHL*, XVIII, 19.

131. *Conduct*, 159–160. "Book B" of the Althorp Papers, now GB-Lbl Add. MS 75400, contains many of the letters that Sarah prints in the *Conduct*, including the one she quotes on the page before this one. For some reason, it does not include this letter, which one would have expected Sarah to cherish, as it is the closest Anne ever came to agreeing with her about party politics.

132. Luttrell, V, 621.

133. *JHL*, XVIII, 45.

134. "On the Playhouse in the Haymarket," *Review of the Affairs of France*, 3 May 1705; this squib, printed as a riposte to Garth's prologue for the opening night, is presumably Defoe's, though unsigned.

135. *Aeneis*, VI, 1168–1177.

136. Addison, "A Letter from Italy." This poem was printed in 1703, then reprinted as the first item in Tonson's *Miscellany* for 1704, the edition followed here.

137. For a fuller discussion, see James A. Winn, *The Poetry of War* (Cambridge: Cambridge University Press, 2008), chap. 6.

138. *Liberty, A Poem* (1705), 3–4, 7–8.

139. GB-Ob MS Mus. C. 6, fols. 17v–19r. I have also consulted GB-Lbl Add. MS 31813, fols. 95–96, a nineteenth-century score constructed from single parts by R.J.S. Stevens. My text underlay follows the accidentals of Tate's printed text rather than those of either MS.

140. Nahum Tate, *The song for New-Year's-Day, 1706. Perform'd to musick before Her Majesty, at St. James's* (1706), 1–4. There are only two known copies; fortunately the one from the Folger Shakespeare Library is available as a digital scan, at the Library's website: http://luna.folger.edu/luna/servlet/detail/FOLGERCM1~6~6~637748~142613:The-song-for-New-Year-s-Day,-1706.

141. In a letter dated 8 January 1706, Sir William Simpson describes the duchess as "extremely affected in her carriage, so full of gaiety and motion that it would not be borne with in a mad-amoiselle of 18 at Paris"; in an undated letter, probably from about the same time, the Duchess of Marlborough complains about her "entertaining everybody aloud, thrusting out her disagreeable breasts with such strange motions." See Stuart Handley, "Talbot, Charles, Duke of Shrewsbury (1660–1718)," in *ODNB*.

142. The poet appears to have known a five-part madrigal by the Elizabethan composer Thomas Weelkes, "Harke all yee lovely saints above" (in *Balletts and madrigals to five voyces with one to 6. voyces* [1598]), which includes these lines:

> See, see your Mistris bids you cease,
> And welcome love, with loves increase,
> *Diana* hath procurd your peace. (VIII, normalizing *u* and *v*)

143. In their very full discussion of *England's Glory*, Olive Baldwin and Thelma Wilson offer Tate and Motteux as possible librettists. See "*England's Glory* and the Celebrations at Court for Queen Anne's Birthday in 1706," *Theatre Notebook* 62 (2008): 7–19, here citing 11. To my ears, the verse is too smooth to be Tate's and the political perspective too Tory to be Motteux's. Crowne was still alive, though reportedly ill, and still receiving a royal pension. In light of the many verbal echoes of *Calisto* and his other plays, he deserves consideration as a candidate for the authorship of this libretto.

144. *England's Glory* (1706), 2, 4–5.

145. See Baldwin and Wilson, "*England's Glory*," 16.

146. Compare Virgil, *Aeneid*, VI, 851–853:

> tu regere imperio populos, Romane, memento;
> hae tibi erunt artes; pacisque imponere morem,
> parcere subiectis, et debellare superbos.

147. This stage effect was evidently added late in the planning for the performance. GB-Lbl Add. MS 61701, included among the Blenheim Papers, is a manuscript pamphlet, titled "Britannia's

Happiness," which appears to be an earlier draft of the libretto for *England's Glory*. The title page describes the work as "Most humbly dedicated To All the Lady's and Lords Of Her Majesty's Court, Compos'd For Severall Voices and all Sorts of Instruments By James Kremberg Composer." The text is very close to the printed version, but the entries of Atlas and Neptune at the end come in a different order, and the ending, like that of an early Stuart masque, calls for a series of dances, probably cut because they would have required Bellona, Ceres, and Britannia to dance. In the final version, the effect of the globe becoming a pyramid concludes the masque.

148. *William Congreve: Letters and Documents*, 38; 15 December 1705.

149. See *The Monthly Mask of Vocal Music*, notes to songs 136–139.

150. For lists of performance dates and details of all these productions, see *LS2MH*, 271–300.

151. *William Congreve: Letters and Documents*, 40; 30 April 1706.

152. *Camilla, Regina de' Volsci* (Venice, 1698), 39. For the attribution, see Henry L. Snyder, "Prologues and Epilogues of Arthur Maynwaring," *Philological Quarterly* 50 (1971): 610–619.

153. Vanbrugh staged a revival of *The Judgment of Paris*, in the version set by Eccles, on 11 March, a few weeks before *Camilla* opened; he had presented *The Loves of Mars and Venus* in the previous season; see *LS2MH*, 224, 286.

154. Congreve, letter of 10 September 1706, in *William Congreve: Letters and Documents*, 143.

155. Thomas D'Urfey, *Wonders in the Sun* (1706), 41–42.

156. Luttrell, VI, 2. For a fuller account, see Campbell, *Lives of the Lord Chancellors*, IV, 296–299.

157. Boyer, *Annals* V, 14.

158. GB-Lbl Add. MS 61630, fol. 6. Arthur Maynwaring is a likely candidate for the authorship of this prologue, which is preserved in the Blenheim Papers and closely resembles his "Epilogue to the Ladies," spoken at Drury Lane in early 1704. The earlier piece makes a similar appeal to a "Circle of the Fair" and imagines that Charles III "In Arms must Triumph, by your Praises fir'd."

159. New York Public Library Drexel MS 1986, fol. 128v, quoted in *LS2MH*, 298.

160. *Annals*, V, 140.

161. *Annals*, V, 32, 62.

162. Clarke's anthem was *The Lord is my Strength*, Taylor's no. 119; for the Catholic service, see *Annals*, V, 154.

163. George Stanhope, *A Sermon Preach'd before the Queen* (1706), 12–13.

164. The quoted phrase is from an inscription on the lining canvas; for useful commentary, see J. Douglas Stewart, *Sir Godfrey Kneller* (National Portrait Gallery, 1971), 68.

165. "I have written an ode which I presented to the Queen, who received it very graciously." *William Congreve: Letters and Documents*, 43.

166. Matthew Prior, *An Ode Humbly Inscrib'd to the Queen* (1706), 15.

167. Neville Connell, *Anne: The Last Stuart Monarch* (Butterworth, 1937), 163.

168. Boyer, *Annals*, V, 74–75.

169. GB-Lbl Add. MS 61118, fols. 6–7.

170. John Arbuthnot, *A sermon preach'd to the people, at the Mercat-Cross of Edinburgh, on the subject of the union* (Edinburgh, 1706), 1.

171. The only known printed copy of D'Urfey's ode as originally published is in GB-Lbl Add. MS 61360, fols. 42–43. D'Urfey reprinted the poem in several later collections. He also wrote, on the same occasion, a long, more serious ode called *The Trophies*. For the parade and ceremonies, see Boyer, *Annals*, V, 397.

172. See Roy A. Sundstrom, *Sidney Godolphin, Servant of the State* (Newark: University of Delaware Press, 1992), 173–174.

173. *Daily Courant,* 19 December 1706. The music does not survive, but I suspect the text is that printed in the *Muses Mercury* (January 1707, 7) as "*SONG.* For the Performance of Musick at *York-Buildings* on the Thanksgiving-Day, *December* the 31*st*, 1706. By *Nahum Tate* Esq; Her Majesty's Poet Laureat." That poem answers to the description in the advertisement, and it seems unlikely that there were two concerts within eleven days. The supposed concert on 31 December was not advertised.

174. Gilbert Burnet, *A Sermon Preach'd before the Queen and the Two Houses of Parliament* (1707), 14.

175. Luttrell, VI, 122.

176. *Muses Mercury,* January 1707, 9.

177. For a very full analysis, see Linda J. Tomko, "Issues of Nation in Isaac's 'The Union,'" *Dance Research* 15 (1997): 99–125. Like many others, Tomko believes that the performers were a Frenchman named Desbarques and an Englishwoman named Hester Santlow—dancers regularly featured in the theatre, who were advertised as performing this dance at a public concert in April. Olive Baldwin and Thelma Wilson, however, have argued persuasively that court balls were restricted to members of the nobility, and have suggested that Charles Lennox, Duke of Richmond, who is complimented by Mr. Isaac for having performed his dances at court in 1706, was probably one of the performers in 1707. As the son of Charles II by the Duchess of Portsmouth, Richmond would have had excellent training in dance from childhood.

178. John Bates, *Two* (United) *are better than One Alone* (1707), 29.

CHAPTER 9

1. For a reliable and very detailed narrative of the entire Sacheverell affair, on which my account depends, see Geoffrey Holmes, *The Trial of Doctor Sacheverell* (Eyre Methuen, 1973).

2. The phrase is Defoe's, in his *Tour through the Whole Island of Great Britain,* 4 vols., 7th ed. (1769), II, 142. He goes on to point out that from the outside, the building resembles a "great Barn of 300 feet long."

3. For Marlborough's alleged participation in discussions of how and where to try Sacheverell, for which Alexander Cunningham is our only source, see Holmes, *Trial,* 87–89, and the skeptical comments of Snyder, *MGC,* 1406. The only contemporary to claim that Queen Anne supported the impeachment was Bishop Burnet.

4. GB-Lbl Add. MS 47026, fols. 6v–7r. The lady was the widow of Admiral Rooke.

5. "Account of the Trial of Dr Sacheverell," in the Beinecke Library at Yale, US-NHub, Osborne MSS, box 21, no. 22, quoted in Holmes, *Trial,* 181.

6. For a clear exposition, see Norton Robert Tempest, *The Rhythm of English Prose* (Cambridge: Cambridge University Press, 1930).

7. *The Letters of Philip Dormer Stanhope, Fourth Earl of Chesterfield,* ed. Bonamy Dobrée, 6 vols. (Eyre and Spottiswoode, 1932), IV, 1454, emphasis mine.

8. [White Kennett], *A Visit to St. Saviour's* (1710), 16.

9. "Account of the Trial," quoted in Holmes, *Trial,* 200.

10. *The Speech of Henry Sacheverell* (1710), 12–13.

11. Arthur Maynwaring, *Four Letters to a Friend* (1710), 13: "With the strength of his Lungs and Action, he gain'd to such a degree the soft Hearts of his Female Friends, that I wonder he should continue to be in favour with any of the Men."

12. *Tatler,* no. 142 (7 March 1710). All quotations from this journal follow the text given in the *Tatler,* ed. Donald F. Bond, 3 vols. (Oxford: Clarendon, 1987).

13. Addison, *Rosamond* (1707), 28. This presentation manuscript, now at Harvard, US-CAh, MS Hyde 11, bears "April 2, 1706," as its date, but according to Brean Hammond, the date "is not entirely reliable since it is almost certainly a later addition." "Joseph Addison's Opera *Rosamond*: Britishness in the Early Eighteenth Century,"*ELH* 73 (2006): 601–629, here citing 625n16. Still, the anonymous author of *A Critical Discourse on Opera's and Musick in England* (1709) refers to "the celebrated *Rosamond,* with the Expectations of which the Town had been full for a Year together" (68). The *Discourse* was printed as an appendix to *A Comparison between the French and Italian Musick,* a translation of François Raguenet, *Parallèle des Italiens et des Français* (Paris, 1705).

14. The ballad first appears in the second edition of Thomas Deloney's *Strange Histories, or Songs and Sonnets of Kinges, Princes, Dukes, Lords, Ladyes, Knights and Gentlemen* (1612), the text followed here. It also appears in the many editions of *The Garland of Good Will* (1631, 1678, 1685, 1688, 1690, 1700). The tune is now better known as "Chevy Chase," which is the ballad Addison singles out for praise in *Spectator* 70.

15. "The Arguments are often taken from some celebrated Action of the ancient *Greeks* or *Romans,* which sometimes looks ridiculous enough, for who can endure to hear one of the rough old *Romans* squeaking thro' the Mouth of an Eunuch, especially when they may chuse a Subject out of Courts where Eunuchs are really Actors, or represent by 'em any of the soft *Asiatic* Monarchs?" Addison, *Remarks on Several Parts of Italy* (1705), 96–97.

16. Johann Jakob Heidegger, who would play an important part in the later development of opera in London, selected the arias for which Motteux supplied texts. See Judith Milhous, "Heidegger, Johann Jakob (1666–1749)," in *ODNB*.

17. *LS2MH,* 331.

18. *LS2MH,* 347, 349, 351.

19. *LS2MH,* 348.

20. *LS2MH,* 368. The omission of *Rosamond* speaks volumes.

21. *Muses Mercury* (February 1707), 52.

22. *A Critical Discourse on Opera's and Musick in England,* 68–69.

23. *Songs in the new Opera call'd Rosamond* (1707), 15. Extrapolating from the differences between the manuscript score of *Arsinoe* and the simplified published songs for the earlier opera, I should think it likely that this aria had a violin part as well.

24. *Rosamond,* 9.

25. *Remarks on Several Parts of Italy,* 98–100.

26. *Rosamond,* 7–8.

27. *Rosamond,* 11.

28. Compare *The Campaign,* 17:

> Mountains of Slain lye heap'd upon the Ground,
> Or midst the Roarings of the *Danube* drown'd.

29. The Duke of Marlborough was ill during the first week of March 1707, and there is no historical record showing whether the duchess or any of her daughters attended a performance of *Rosamond*. The prologue, apparently written by the Whig MP and poet William Walsh and spoken by the actor George Powell, costumed as Mars, addresses "the Fair," i.e., the women in the audience, and specifically compliments the duchess. Walsh makes the identification between Marlborough and Henry explicit and somewhat awkwardly insists on the marital "Vertue" of the Marlboroughs:

Cloy'd with Successes, and releas'd from Care,
Mars humbly now pays Homage to the Fair:
Tir'd with Command, with Pride he here obeys;
And at your Feet his sacred Lawrel lays.
The Victor, vanquish'd by your conquering Eyes,
If you but frown, in midst of Triumph dies.
For what avail the Glories of the Field;
What Joys can *Blenheim* or *Ramillia* yield;
What *Brussels, Ghent,* or every Hostile Town,
Or by his Fame, or by his Valour won,
If the coy Nymph, unmov'd by all his Pain,
Damp his warm Onsets with her cold Disdain?
At Intervals of War, in these fair Bow'rs,
Victorious *Henry* past his softest Hours:
Here he retir'd with *Rosamond* the Fair,
Who sooth'd her *Hero,* tir'd with Toils of War.
Tho Vertue now these statelier Mansions grace,
Valour and Beauty still shall rule this Place.
In that high Palace *Mars* shall keep his Court;
To these cool Shades, the Graces shall resort;
Each by their Lustre shall the World surprize,
The Greatest Hero, and the brightest Eyes. (*Muses Mercury* [March, 1707], 57–58)

The headnote explains that the Lord Chamberlain temporarily suspended the production because of an objection to the prologue: "The following Prologue was spoken by Mr *Powell,* who at that time had the Misfortune to lie under my Lord Chamberlain's Displeasure for other things. And my Lord not having then declar'd that Mr *Powell* might return to the Stage, the House was suspended; which gave rise to a Report, that it was for some Offence taken at the Prologue.... There have been some very delicate Persons, who are mighty scrupulous of Flattery, when it does not concern themselves, that objected against this Prologue at the speaking of it, as if the Complement was too gross. Tho here's no Person nam'd, and him whom we imagin it was design'd for is too great to have any thing too gross said of him: His Actions being so glorious, that whoever attempts to praise them, will find he want Words rather than abounds. For whatever is said here of the God of War, is immediately apply'd by the Audience to the Duke of *Marlborough:* And whatever is said of the Graces, is apply'd to the Ladies of that Family, of whose Beauty there can be as little said too much, as of my Lord's Glory." In light of all the reasons why Sarah might have taken offense at the prologue or the opera, I am not convinced that the temporary suspension ordered by Lord Chamberlain Kent, who owed his position to Sarah, really had to do with George Powell's alleged misbehavior.

30. By far the most judicious account of this episode is given by Harris, *Passion,* 107–108. John's letter to Sarah blaming Sunderland is printed in *MGC,* 272: "My heart is soe full, that if I doe not vent this truth it will breake, which is that I doe from my soul curse that hour in which I gave my poor dear child to a man that has made mee of all mankind the most unhappyest."

31. See Hammond, "Joseph Addison's Opera *Rosamond,*" 608–609.

32. In "Mocking the meat it feeds on: Representing Sarah Churchill's hystericks in Addison's *Rosamond,*" *Comparative Drama* 29 (1995): 270–285, Luis R. Gamez argues that the opera is "designed to allegorize Sarah's passionate, heroic struggle with conflicting feelings of jealousy and

conjugal devotion." He speculates that Addison learned of Sarah's "hysterica pathi" from Sunderland but does not explain why Addison would have risked his career by staging the duchess's private emotions as an opera.

33. *A Critical Discourse on Opera's and Musick in England,* 71. "In all the rest of the Opera's put together, except Camilla," the critic continues, "there is not one tollerable Air to be found."

34. *Tatler,* no. 4 (19 April 1709). These particular sentiments are attributed to "a Great Critick," almost certainly meaning John Dennis, but they are in keeping with Steele's own remarks earlier in the same paragraph, where he says that the news of a successful opera performance "is not very acceptable to us Friends of the Theatre; for the Stage being an Entertainment of the Reason and all our Faculties, this Way of being pleas'd with the Suspence of 'em for Three Hours together…seems to arise rather from the degeneracy of our Understanding, than an Improvement in our Diversions." This complaint about the absence of intellectual stimulation in opera is very much in keeping with Addison's earlier prologue.

35. See Olive Baldwin and Thelma Wilson, "Clayton, Thomas," in *NGDM.*

36. Edmund Smith, *Phædra and Hippolytus* (1707), sig. A3r. Not until the edition of 1719 was Addison named as the author.

37. The text for this anthem begins with the opening verse from Psalm 133, one of the psalms designated as "proper" for the service in *A Form of Prayer and Thanksgiving* (1707): "Behold, how good and joyful a thing it is; brethren to dwell together in unity." The complete text, a pastiche of biblical material, is printed in *Divine Harmony, or a New Collection of Select Anthems* (1712), 34–35. Most of the music is lost, but one section by Croft survives in the composer's own hand in GB-Lbl Add. MS 17847. Two of the three composers would never again write music for the queen: Clarke, disappointed in love, shot himself on 1 December 1707, and Blow, whose health was already failing, died on 1 October 1708, leaving Croft to occupy alone the post of Composer to the Chapel Royal.

38. William Talbot, *A Sermon Preach'd before the Queen* (1707), 7.

39. C[harles] D[arby], *The Union* (1707), 7.

40. For a damning list of questionable actions by Peterborough, including drawing large sums from the Treasury, see Sunderland's list of questions the queen wishes to have answered. GB-Lbl Add. MS 61498, fols. 70–71, editorially dated [c. 14 September 1707].

41. Luttrell, VI, 179.

42. See chapter 4 above.

43. Luttrell, VI, 166.

44. Preserved by Sarah, this document is in GB-Lbl Add. MS 61417, fol. 64.

45. GB-Lbl Add. MS 61417, fol. 65.

46. For a full and judicious account, see G. V. Bennett, "Robert Harley, the Godolphin Ministry, and the Bishoprics Crisis of 1707," *English Historical Review* 82 (1967): 726–746.

47. Alexander Cunningham, *The history of Great Britain: from the revolution in 1688, to the accession of George the First,* 2 vols. (1787), II, 76. A letter from Vanbrugh about hiring opera singers speaks of "bringing the Queen into a Scheme, now preparing by my Lord Chamberlain and Others, to have Concerts of Musick in the Summer at Windsor, twice a Week in the Appartment." *The Works of Sir John Vanbrugh,* ed. Bonamy Dobrée and Geoffrey Webb, 4 vols. (Nonesuch, 1927–28), IV, 20–21, quoted in full in *LS2MH,* 432.

48. Samuel Freeman, *A sermon preach'd at the funeral of His Grace William Duke of Bedford* (1700), 25.

49. Charles Trimnell, *A Sermon Preach'd in the Cathedral Church of Norwich* (1704), 17.

50. Offspring Blackall, *A Sermon Preach'd before the Queen* (1707), 10–11.

51. William Dawes, *A Sermon Preach'd before the Queen* (1707), 2–3, 16.

52. GB-Lbl Add. MS 61417, fol. 79.

53. *MGC*, 884.

54. GB-Lbl Add. MS 61101, fol. 97r–v. The queen uses a numerical code for names of some people and parties.

55. For a thorough account of Harley's activities, on which I have drawn extensively, see G. S. Holmes and W. A. Speck, "The Fall of Harley in 1708 Reconsidered," *English Historical Review* 80 (1965): 673–698.

56. Bennett, "Robert Harley," 740.

57. GB-Lbl Add. MS 61118, fols. 17–20, emphasis mine.

58. GB-Lbl Add. MS 52540, fol. 48v.

59. *LTQ*, 106–107.

60. GB-Lbl Add. MS 61118, fol. 17v: "The objection of breaking your word which your Majesty often mentioned, would bee a great, if it were a reall, objection, but in my humble opinion, you would not find it more than an imaginary one, if you would please to give your self the trouble of speaking of it." Godolphin's garbled rhetoric presumably means that if Anne would take the trouble to tell Blackall and Dawes that circumstances have changed, they would understand.

61. *Observator*, 10–13 September 1710.

62. GB-Lbl Add. MS 70021, fol. 61, where this letter, evidently from 1707, is wrongly dated "1703."

63. Luttrell, VI, 220.

64. GB-Lbl Add. MS 61417, fol. 52, letter dated "Kensington Octo ye 30th" [1706?]. As Anne's echo of Godolphin's letter shows, the year should be 1707.

65. *The Correspondence of Alexander Pope*, ed. George Sherburn, 5 vols. (Oxford: Clarendon, 1956), I, 30.

66. See the headnote to "Season of 1707–08" in *LS2MH*.

67. It is possible that Shovell survived the wreck, only to be murdered by a woman who wanted his emerald ring; see John B. Hattendorf, "Shovell, Sir Cloudesley (*bap.* 1650, *d.* 1707)," in *ODNB*.

68. *JHC*, XV, 404, 435. By the time Trimnell preached his sermon he had been made a bishop, and his remarks were gracious; see *A sermon preach'd before the Honourable House of Commons, at the Church of St. Margaret Westminster* (1708).

69. Boyer, *Annals*, VI, 252–253, 256.

70. The poem was published on 24 December. Despite his position, Hill describes his defense of Peterborough as "unsummon'd."

71. *Annals*, VI, 297–298. As Sir Winston Churchill points out, Marlborough's speech was disingenuous, and within days the emperor had refused to send Eugene to Spain. Churchill, *Marlborough; His Life and Times,* new ed., 2 vols. (Chicago: University of Chicago Press, 2002), II, 303–306.

72. Vanbrugh, *Works*, IV, 16–17, cited in *LS2MH*, 417. See the order from Lord Chamberlain Kent, dated 31 December 1707; GB-Lna LC 5/154, pp. 299–300, printed in full in *LS2MH*, 400–401. I should think it possible that Marlborough's involvement in theatrical politics was among the factors giving rise to rumors that the dancer Hester Santlow was his mistress. Modern scholars, including Santlow's biographer, are inclined to discount these claims. See Moira Goff, *The incomparable Hester Santlow* (Aldershot: Ashgate, 2007), 32.

73. *JHC*, XV, 481.

74. GB-Lna SP 104/129, printed in *LDI*, 204–206.

75. Tate, *The Song for the New-Year 1708, Set by Mr. Eccles* (1708). The music is lost.

76. The best Tate can manage is calling the campaign of 1707 "not less Renown'd" than those of earlier summers:

> Fresh Lawrels shall Adorn his Brow,
> Like those of *Blenheim*'s and *Ramillia*'s Plain;
> Nor less Renown'd his last Campaign;
> Fame and the *Flying* Foe must this allow,
> Their Troops He Conquer'd Then, their Heart and Courage Now.

77. See Sunderland's notes, GB-Lbl Add. MS 61490, fols. 102–103, editorially dated [31 December 1707].

78. *The Traytor's Reward* (1708). The original, very badly printed, reads "true by mo Fate."

79. Holmes and Speck, "Fall of Harley," 679.

80. *HMC Bath*, I, 190.

81. *The Letters of Joseph Addison*, ed. Walter Graham (Oxford: Clarendon, 1941), 95.

82. *The London Diaries of William Nicolson, Bishop of Carlisle, 1702–1718*, ed. Clyve Jones and Geoffrey Holmes (Oxford: Clarendon, 1985), 448–449.

83. GB-Lbl Add. MS 61101, fols. 109–110.

84. *JHC*, XV, 512; *JHL*, XVIII, 450–451; Godolphin and Marlborough were among those who officially protested against this action.

85. GB-Lna PRO 30/24/21/fols. 21–23, emphasis original. Printed, in a modernized transcription, in Holmes and Speck, "Fall of Harley," 695–696. Cropley appears to have been writing in haste, and may have been inebriated, as he set down this story after dining with Stanhope. In the last sentence of Anne's speech, he writes "regarded" where he surely meant "rewarded," and "run it through my heard," which Holmes and Speck transcribe as "head," though I think "heart" was the word intended.

86. Nathaniel Lee, *Sophonisba* (1676), in *Works of Nathaniel Lee*, ed. Thomas B. Stroup and Arthur L. Cooke, 2 vols. (New Brunswick: Scarecrow Press, 1954), act 2, scene 1, 33–38.

87. Significantly, this essay was not published until 1749, not long before St. John's death.

88. *JHC*, XV, 590.

89. *JHL*, XVIII, 507–508; session of 12 March 1708.

90. For one print version, see *Observator*, 13–17 March 1708.

91. *JHL*, XVIII, 511; session of 15 March 1708.

92. GB-Lbl Add. MS 4221, fol. 26. There are excellent reasons to discount this story, which has frequently been repeated as fact. The man who offers it was three years old at the time of the invasion and obviously had no firsthand knowledge of Anne; his account of her reign treats her as a closet Jacobite and "a Timorous Weak Woman." Lady Hervey reports two Council meetings at Kensington on 11 March, in response to a message from Byng informing Godolphin that he was pursuing the French fleet. *Letter-Books of John Hervey, First Earl of Bristol*, 3 vols. (Wells: Ernest Jackson, 1894), I, 231, 233. In his notes for the first of those meetings, GB-Lbl Add. MS 16498, fol. 139, Sunderland records instructions about embarking the troops from Ostend and sending two companies of dragoons to Nottingham but makes no reference to any discussion of the Pretender's person. According to Sunderland, the second meeting took place at Whitehall, and Anne appears to have remained at Kensington.

93. GB-Lna PC 2/82, fol. 9.

94. GB-Lbl Add. MS 61426, "Characters of Princes," fol. 109.

95. For a full account, see John S. Gibson, *Playing the Scottish Card: The Franco-Jacobite Invasion of 1708* (Edinburgh: Edinburgh University Press, 1988).

96. For a clear explanation of this puzzling episode, see Harris, *Passion*, 143.
97. GB-Lbl Add. MS 61417, fols. 130, 133.
98. See, for example, his letter to her of 7 April, in which he states that it is "absolutely necessary that your Grace return to Court." GB-Lbl Add. MS 61459, fols. 20v–21r.
99. *MCG*, 944.
100. *Letters of Sarah, Duchess of Marlborough* (John Murray, 1875), 37.
101. GB-Lbl Add. MS 61459, fol. 85.
102. Henry L. Snyder corrected an earlier attribution of this work in "Daniel Defoe, the Duchess of Marlborough, and the 'Advice to the Electors of Great Britain,'" *Huntington Library Quarterly* 29 (1965): 53–62, pointing out that there are surviving drafts in Sarah's hand, and in Maynwaring's. For further information about the close collaboration between the duchess and Maynwaring, see J. A. Downie, "Arthur Maynwaring and the Authorship of the *Advice to the Electors of Great Britain*: Some Additional Evidence," *British Journal for Eighteenth-Century Studies* 2 (1979): 163–166.
103. *Advice to the Electors of Great Britain* (1708), 1–3. In attributing these passages to Sarah, I follow a suggestion made by Robert D. Horn in *Marlborough: A Survey* (Folkestone: Garland, 1975), 263.
104. For information on the original ballad, beginning "When as King Henrie rul'd this land," see note 14 above.
105. For useful commentary on the date and authorship of this ballad, see *Poems on Affairs of State*, ed. George deForest Lord, 7 vols. (New Haven: Yale University Press, 1963–75), VII, ed. Frank H. Ellis, 306–308.
106. *Letters of Joseph Addison*, ed. Graham, 111.
107. *A New Ballad, To the Tune of Fair Rosamond* (1708).
108. Letter to Mary Cowper, 18 July 1708; Hertfordshire Record Office, Panshanger MSS D/EP F 228, fol. 27, cited by Rachel Weil in *Political Passions* (Manchester: University of Manchester Press, 1999), 223n2. According to Frank Ellis's notes in *Poems on Affairs of State*, VII, the same collection of documents continues with a printed copy of this ballad, with a manuscript note identifying it as "The Ballad the Dutchess of Marlborough mentions."
109. See Maynwaring's letter to Sarah, 22 April 1708: "If your Grace had any fresh trouble from Ld. Halifax after the opera, I wish I was not accesary to it." GB-Lbl Add. MS 61459, fol. 33v. For the performance, see *LS2MH*, 428. The queen did not wish to promote James Montagu because he had taken a leading role in the drive to abolish the Scottish Privy Council; she eventually had to relent and make the appointment. See also GB-Lbl Add. MS 61118, fols. 102–105, Halifax's letter to Godolphin seeking this post for his brother, and Sarah's annotation, fol. 105v: "Lord Hallifax 1708 about his brother hee seems to think hee has don great service with out any advantage, but he was upon all occasions the most interested man that I have known ill judging very false insolent & vaine, ill bred but he had wit & some other talents."
110. Vanbrugh to the Earl of Manchester, in Vanbrugh, *Works*, IV, 20–21, printed in full in *LS2MH*, 431–432. See also the very helpful summaries of the seasons of 1707–8 and 1708–9.
111. See Harris, *Passion*, 145.
112. GB-Lbl Add. MS 61118, fols. 25–26, editorially dated [?28 May 1708].
113. The description is Vanbrugh's, in the letter cited in note 110. It is possible that the queen is actually referring to Peregrine Bertie, who was Vice-Chamberlain until 1706, when he traded offices with Coke. In their letters, Godolphin and Marlborough continue to refer to Bertie as "the old vice."
114. GB-Lbl Add. MS 75400 (not foliated).
115. GB-Lbl Add. MS 61417, fol. 153 r–v.

116. Gregg confidently identifies the second ballad as "Verses upon Mr. Harley being Lord Treasurer," but Ellis suggests that it was "Masham Display'd," which is almost certainly by Maynwaring. The tune for this ballad, "The Dame of Honour," had been sung in D'Urfey's *Wonders in the Sun* two years earlier; it appears in Claude M. Simpson's useful collection *The British Broadside Ballad and Its Music* (New Brunswick: Rutgers University Press, 1966), 155, where it is said to be "attributed to G. B. Draghi on very doubtful evidence." Maynwaring's letter, however, suggests that he believed the tune had been composed by his friend the actor Richard Estcourt, who had published several songs, and who mounted, in this very spring, an operatic parody called *Prunella*. Estcourt typically wrote words to preexisting melodies, as shown by his entries in *The Monthly Mask of Vocal Music, 1702–1711*, ed. Olive Baldwin and Thelma Wilson (Aldershot: Ashgate, 2007). Although he probably did not compose this tune, Estcourt was Maynwaring's source for it. In a letter to Sarah, dated 22 April 1708, Maynwaring encloses an unnamed ballad, complaining that "Escourt's tune requires that the verses shou'd be made so hobbling that they are not to be endur'd without it." GB-Lbl Add. MS 61459, fol. 32. This is an accurate description of the words to "Masham Display'd," which are a rhythmic *contrafactum* of D'Urfey's original words, sung by a character called "Hospitality," an antiquated dame from the court of Queen Elizabeth. Durfey's song begins thus:

> Since now the World's turn'd upside down,
> > And all things chang'd in Nature,
> As if a doubt were newly grown,
> > We had the same Creator:
> Of Ancient Modes and former ways,
> > I'll teach ye, Sirs, the manner,
> In good Queen *Besses* Golden days:
> > When I was a Dame of Honour. (*Wonders in the Sun*, 23)

Maynwaring's ballad, echoing the theme of change, begins thus:

> All things are chang'd in Court and Town,
> > Since Sarah's happy days Sir,
> One who of late had Scarce a Gown,
> > now Queen and Kingdom Sway's Sir,... (*Poems on Affairs of State*, VII, 317–321).

An obscene riposte in the same meter, preserved in the Portland MSS, pictures Godolphin engaged in cunnilingus with Sarah:

> Oh! Were the same Volpone bound
> > His Head her Thighs betwixt Sir,
> To suck from thence his Notions sound,
> > And Savory Politicks Sir. (GB-NO Portland MS Pw V 529).

117. GB-Lbl Add. MS 61414, fol. 141. Anne reminded Sarah of this episode in a letter written in 1704, in which she referred to Lady Fitzharding as "Loupa," a name she and Sarah often used for her: "What you say to convince me of Loupas being false was not at all necessary, for if you remember when you adored her to that degree that it had almost broke my hart, I allways thought her a jade." GB-Lbl Add. MS 61416, fol. 176v.

118. See Ruth Herman, "Dark Deeds at Night," in *Queer People*, ed. Chris Mounsey and Caroline Gonda (Lewisburg: Bucknell University Press, 2007), 195–209, here citing 204. The lampoon in question appears in GB-Lbl Lansdowne MS 852, fols. 42–43, and in the Portland Papers at

the University of Nottingham, GB-NO Portland MS Pw V 48, fols. 130v–131, which I follow. It is part of a pair of poems on homosexual practices: "The Womens Complaint to Venus" (called "The Ladys Complaint" in the Lansdowne MS), which deplores the spread of buggery in William's court, and "Venus Reply" ("Venus's Answer"), which describes female homosexual practices quite graphically:

> Why Nymphs, these are pityfull Storyes,
>   But you are to blame,
> And have got a New Game
>   Call'd Flatts with a Swinging Clitoris.
>
> . . . .
>
> Your Frogmore Frolics discover
>   Some Reasons of Art [Lansdowne: "Some Ladys of Art"]
> Soe play the Mans Part
>   You care for No Masculine Lover.

A marginal note in the Portland MS glosses "Frogmore" as "Ld. Fitzharding's Seat near Windsor." Lady Fitzharding's husband had at this time sublet a house at Frogmore, near Windsor. See Jane Roberts, *Royal Landscape: The Gardens and Parks of Windsor* (New Haven: Yale University Press, 1997), 212–213.

119. GB-Lbl Add. MS 61455, fols. 140v, 142r, 143r. Mrs. Howard also refers to her letters to Sarah as "billie doux" (fol. 140r).

120. GB-Lbl Add. MS 61417, fols. 155v, 154v.

121. Although the ballad does not survive with the letter, two comments in the letter point unmistakably to this text. "I took her from a Broom, as the Ballad says very rightly," writes the duchess, while reminding the queen "that your Royal father was in a manner sang out of his kingdomes by this very tune of Lilly burlaro."

122. *A New Song to the Tune of Lilly burlaro* (1708).

123. See Frank Barlow, "Pont l'Évêque, Roger de (*c.*1115–1181)," in *ODNB*. An MS copy of this poem in the Portland MSS has important variants:

> But that Johnny of York
> For so pious a work
> Hir parts had Improved
> By curing the spleen (GB-NO Portland MS Pw V 536).

124. As part of her campaign to embarrass the queen, Sarah also sent her a copy of a prose pamphlet, possibly by Maynwaring, called *The Rival Dutchess; or, Court Incendiary in a Dialogue between Madam Maintenon, and Madam M[asham.]* Her letter enclosing this piece, editorially dated [mid. 1708], strikes a similar pose: "the book [is] not well writt att all, but I think that looks so much the worse, for it shows that the notion is universally spread among all sorts of people, it is a dialogue between madam maintenon and madam masham, in which she thanks her for her good endeavours to serve the king of France here and seems to have great hopes of her from her promising beginnings and her friendship with Mr Harley, and there is stuff not fitt to bee mention'd of passions between wemen." GB-Lbl Add. MS 61417, fol. 137.

125. *The Battel of Audenarde* (1708), advertised on 20 July.

126. *The Church of England's Joy on the Happy Accession of her Most Sacred Majesty* (1702), 2.

127. The anthem survives complete in GB-Lbl Add. MS 17847, fols. 5–13, a score identifying the soloists as "Mr. Elford," "Mr. Freeman," and "Mr. Gates." Croft printed it in his *Harmonia Sacra*

(1725), II, 12–25; I have given the text, which Anne adapted from the Prayerbook Psalter, as printed in *Divine Harmony*, 23–24.

128. William Fleetwood, *A Sermon Preach'd before the Queen* (1708), 16.

129. Fleetwood, *Sermon Preach'd before the Queen*, 1, 3–4.

130. GB-Lbl Add. MS 61417, fols. 161r, 162r–v. Other copies of this letter, and the version printed in *Conduct*, have been shortened and cleaned up, but the original preserves Sarah's initial outrage. The striking out of "church," replaced by "coach" as the place where the quarrel occurred, is curious, as the later versions restore "church."

131. *MGC*, 887.

132. GB-Lbl Add. MS 61417, fol. 3.

133. GB-Lbl Add. MS 61417, fol. 164.

134. *CTB*, XXII, 379–380.

135. For a full account, see Harris, *Passion*, 155–156.

136. GB-Lbl Add. MS 61417, fol. 170r.

137. GB-Lbl Add. MS 61459, fol. 93v.

138. *MGC*, 1110.

139. Luttrell, VI, 353–354. The rumor was false, as it was Lord Fitzharding, not his wife, who held the position of Keeper of the Mall; see *CTB*, XIX, 353; XXIII, 152. My thanks to Professor Robert Bucholz for helping me track down this record. For the pension, see *CTB*, XXII, 38, recording minutes of 20 August 1708: "[By the Queen's directions my Lord orders a privy seal for] 1000*l. per an* to Lady FitzHardinge ... during the joint lives of her Majesty & the said lady." In April, a grant of £600 per annum, which Barbara had received since 1703, was annulled (XXII, 213), probably because the queen was planning to increase the amount, but just possibly because "Loupa" had done something that offended her.

140. Elkanah Settle, *Memoriæ Fragranti* (1708), 9–10.

141. George Chapman, *The Iliads of Homer prince of poets* (1611), 254.

142. Boyer, *Annals*, VII, 245; *MGC*, 1140.

143. GB-Lbl Add. MS 61417, fol. 175r.

144. "An account of the closset where she saw Mrs Masham & of what passed at the Princes death." GB-Lbl Add. MS 61422, fols. 31–34. All quotations not otherwise noted in this section follow this narrative, later printed in *Private Correspondence of Sarah, Duchess of Marlborough*, 2 vols. (Henry Colburn, 1838), I, 410–416.

145. GB-Lbl Add. MS 61417, fol. 179.

146. GB-Lbl Add. MS 61417, fol. 180, emphasis mine.

147. GB-Lna PC 2/82, fols. 92–104.

148. GB-Lbl Add. MS 61417, fol. 178.

149. See the Kensington Palace "Pay Book" for January 1694/5, printed in *The Royal Palaces of Winchester, Whitehall, Kensington, and St. James's*, ed. A. T. Bolton and H. D. Hendry (Oxford: Wren Society, 1930), 169.

150. GB-Lna SP 104/209, fol. 135: "Le funeste Malheur Nous accable d'une douleur si vive que Nous demeurerions voluntiers dans un profond Silence, si les etroites Liaisons que Nous avons avec votre Etat, ne Nous obligevient a Vous communiquer tout ce qui Nous arrive par la volunté de Dieu soit bon, ou mauvais."

151. GB-Lna SP 104/209/fol. 141: "Comme il avoit eté fort indisposé depuis quelque tems, l'attente de ce malheur devoit m'avoir preparé á le supporter avec plus de fermeté. Mais je me trouve obligée d'avoüer a votre Majesté que la perte d'un tel Mari, qui m'a aimé si passionément et si constamment, m'est trop accablante pour la pouvoir bien soutenir." A marginal note explains

that the original letter, dispatched to Copenhagen, was "All in the Queen own handwriting." See also SP 104/4/fols. 77–78, Henry Boyle's letter to Daniel Pulteney, Anne's envoy to the Danish court, dated 29 October/9 November 1708: "I was in hopes to have sent you by this Post her Majesty's Letters to the Queen & Queen Dowager of Denmark but as she writes them all with her own hand I cannot have them till the next."

152. *An Ode to the Queen* (1708), 5.
153. GB-Lna PC/2/82/fol. 104.
154. *MGC*, 1083.
155. GB-Lbl Add. MS 61417, fol. 179.
156. Letter of 5 April 1709, from Peter Wentworth, equerry to Prince George, to his brother Thomas Wentworth, Lord Raby, Anne's ambassador to the Prussian court in Berlin. In *The Wentworth Letters, 1705–1739*, ed. James J. Cartwright (Wyman & Sons, 1883), 82.
157. Letter from Ralph Bridges to Sir William Trumbull, GB-Lbl Add. MS 72494, fol. 89v.
158. Luttrell, VI, 390. For the pensions to the oboists, see GB-Lna, AO 15/23, fol. 170. Sadly, these pensions were not paid in a timely fashion. On 26 October 1711, Anne wrote to Robert Harley, who had become Earl of Oxford and Lord Treasurer, asking whether "there could be money enough found to pay the Prince's servants two quarters of the five they are in arrears, some of them being in very bad circumstances." *HMC Bath*, I, 214.
159. Letter from Isabella, Lady Wentworth, to her son Thomas, Lord Raby, a diplomat in Berlin. *Wentworth Letters*, 66.
160. See above, chapter 3, n. 85.
161. *Letters of Joseph Addison*, ed. Graham, 124. See also Geoffrey Holmes, *British Politics in the Age of Anne* (Hambledon, 1987), 305–306.
162. Richard Steele, *Memoirs of … the Marquess of Wharton* (1715), 69.
163. John Earl Poulett to Sir William Trumbull, 10 December 1708; *HMC Downshire*, II, 8766.
164. *JHC*, XVI (1803), 69.
165. *Wentworth Letters*, 70. This wretchedly printed broadside survives in one copy, at the Henry E. Huntington Library in San Marino, California; it makes no direct reference to the queen. My thanks to Howard Weinbrot for sending me a copy of its contents.
166. "With Hearts full of the most profound Respect and Duty to your royal Person," wrote the committee charged with drafting the address, "we most humbly beseech Your Majesty, graciously to consider the universal Desires, and most humble Supplications, of your faithful Subjects, that your Majesty would not so far indulge Your just Grief, as to decline the Thoughts of a second Marriage." *JHL*, XVIII, 620.
167. *JHL*, XVIII, 623.
168. Thomas Manningham, *A Sermon Preach'd before the Queen* (1709), 3.
169. Manningham, *Sermon Preach'd before the Queen*, 11, 13.
170. Hertfordshire Record Office, Panshanger MSS D/EP F 228, fols. 26–27, cited by Harris, *Passion*, 153.
171. For Croft's settings of the *Te Deum* and the *Jubilate*, see *William Croft, Canticles and Anthems with Orchestra*, ed. Donald Burrows (Stainer and Bell, 2011), *Musica Britannica*, XCI.
172. *Daily Courant*, 15 January 1709. According to Luttrell, "The privy council have ordered Mr. Samuel Buckley, author of the Daily Courant, to be taken into custody, for writing in this day's Courant a project for a lasting peace,…which may give offence to some of our allies" (VI, 396). Although no such order appears in either the Privy Council Records or Sunderland's minutes of the Cabinet Council, these records do not purport to be complete, and some actions were evidently kept out of the written record.

173. Churchill, *Marlborough,* II, 494–504.

174. In a letter to Sir William Trumbull, dated 2 March 1709, Thomas Butler confidently stated that Marlborough was bringing "a scheme of peace agreed to by the Confederates." *HMC Downshire,* II, 870.

175. *JHL,* XVIII, 654.

176. *HMC Egmont,* II, 236, quoted in *LS2MH,* 474–475.

177. GB-Lna PC 2/82, fol. 144r.

178. *MGC,* 1231.

179. GB-Lbl Add. MS 61459, fols. 155–156. Maynwaring cautiously adds his belief that "any thing of this kind wou'd be propos'd with the best grace after a Peace; tho if it might be publickly discours'd of this winter, & especially if People might be Employ'd in making some Designs for it, it wou'd have an imediate good Effect, & a very great Air Abroad."

180. GB-Lbl Add. MS 61355, fols. 1–2. Kneller's memory failed him in one detail: the canvas is signed and dated "1708," but he says that "The Queen sent her Orders to me by the Duke of Shrewsbury (Then Lord Chamberlain)," and Shrewsbury did not become Chamberlain until 1710. Kneller's memory of consulting personally with Marlborough might place the commission and subsequent planning for the picture during Marlborough's visit to England in early 1709, which was still 1708 in the English calendar.

181. For a thorough and judicious account, see Henry L. Snyder, "The Duke of Marlborough's Request of his Captain-Generalcy for Life: A Re-examination," *Journal of the Society for Army Historical Research* 45 (1967): 67–83.

182. *MGC,* 1252.

183. *Tatler,* no. 1 (12 April 1709).

184. See John McTague, "'There Is No Such Man as Isaack Bickerstaff': Partridge, Pittis, and Jonathan Swift," *Eighteenth-Century Life* 35 (2011): 83–101. While Swift's reasons for "killing" Partridge certainly included his disdain for the radical community from which the almanac-maker came, Steele appears to have appropriated the name, presumably with Swift's permission, because it was already a well-known nom de plume.

185. Luttrell, VI, 433, 436.

186. See for example the *Post Boy* for 30 April–3 May: "London, May 3 . . . The Duke of Marlborough design'd to have layn last Night at Rochester, but his Grace has put off his Journey to this Morning at Four of the Clock, and will lie this Night at Margate. Horatio Walpole, Esq; goes with the Lord Visc. Townsend."

187. GB-Lbl Add. MS 72494, fol. 113.

188. Alexander Pope, *Pastorals,* "Spring," ll. 7–10.

189. Luttrell, VI, 444.

190. Hearne, *Remarks and Collections,* ed. C. E. Doble, 11 vols. (Oxford: Oxford Historical Society, 1885–1921), II, 204.

191. For details, see Harris, *Passion,* 154–155.

192. Manley, *Secret Memoirs* (1709), pt. 1, 134–136.

193. The second edition was advertised in the *Post Boy* for 9–11 July; Steele's reference is in *Tatler* 63 (3 September 1709).

194. *British Apollo,* 20 May–25 May 1709.

195. *MGC,* 1360.

196. GB-Lbl Add. MS 61460, fol. 15r.

197. "A Catch for 3. Voc. Made on the French by their loss of Mons," *Monthly Mask,* 289.

198. Both letters are printed in full in Snyder, "Duke of Marlborough's Request," 73–74.

199. Harris, *Passion,* 159–161.

200. *Secret Memoirs*, pt. 2, 145, 147.

201. According to the generally reliable manuscript newsletters of John Dyer, Sunderland personally examined "Mrs. Mangly abt her 2 Volumes of Books." GB-Lbl Add. MS 70420, unfoliated, letter of 8 November 1709.

202. Luttrell, VI, 496.

203. Anne's prayer is kept with "Queen Elizabeth's Prayer Book" in the Lambeth Palace Library, shelfmark (ZZ)1569.6. For a photograph, see Neville Connell, Anne: The Last Stuart Monarch (Butterworth, 1937), 208.

204. *Divine Harmony*, 26.

205. White Kennett, *Glory to God, and Gratitude to Benefactors. A Sermon Preach'd before the Queen* (1709), 8.

206. GB-Lbl Add. MS 20726, fols. 29v–30r, printed in *LS2MH*, 524.

207. Luttrell, VI, 529, 541.

208. *The Diary of Sir David Hamilton, 1709–1714,* ed. Philip Roberts (Oxford: Clarendon, 1975), 5–6.

209. Kennett, *Glory to God*, 17.

210. *Wentworth Letters,* 108. This letter also tells us that "there was a drawing room at night, but every body in as deep mourning as ever."

211. *JHC,* XVI, 316, 327; compare *MGC,* 1418–19; Gregg, *Queen Anne,* 304–305.

212. Hamilton, *Diary,* 72*n*16.

213. Burnet, *History,* V, 432.

214. *HMC Portland,* IV, 532; Hamilton, *Diary,* 6.

CHAPTER 10

1. The queen was not in good health, and Abel Boyer reports that she only appeared "in Publick" to play cards in the evening. *Quadriennium annæ postremum; or the political state of Great Britain,* 8 vols. (1718–19), V, 89. Some scholars have therefore supposed that Handel's piece was not performed, or that it was postponed until the birthday of 1714. Olive Baldwin and Thelma Wilson, "Music in the Birthday Celebrations at Court in the Reign of Queen Anne: A Documentary Calendar," *A Handbook for Studies in 18th-Century English Music* 19 (2008), 21–23, support the belief that Handel's music was sung in 1713, and I have argued for that view in "Style and Politics in the Philips-Handel Ode for Queen Anne's Birthday, 1713," *Music and Letters* 89 (2008): 547–561. In a private communication, Baldwin and Wilson point out that Anne could have heard the ode at a midday performance attended only by the higher nobility and ambassadors, which would not have been a "Publick" event.

2. Donald Burrows has argued persuasively that an undated anthem by Handel, *As pants the hart,* using a text by his friend Dr. Arbuthnot and naming Elford as a soloist, was Handel's first composition for the Chapel Royal. If this anthem antedates the birthday ode, it gave Handel valuable experience in exploring the capacities of the choir and its soloists. See Burrows, *Handel and the English Chapel Royal* (Oxford: Oxford University Press, 2005), chap. 3.

3. There is one instance of a female performer in a birthday ode in the previous reign: a "Mrs. Ayliff" sang in "Celebrate this Festival," Purcell's birthday song for Queen Mary in 1693. My thanks to Olive Baldwin and Thelma Wilson for alertly reminding me of this precedent.

4. There are two versions of this aria, both in B-flat major, in Handel's autograph score, GB-Lbl R.M. 20.g.2. The alterations in the vocal line reflect Handel's understanding of Elford's tessitura, and his revising the ode to provide one more solo for her favorite singer is evidence of his desire to please the queen—and another reason to believe that she heard his piece in 1713.

5. In 1704, for example, "Mr John Shore, the famous trumpetter, and Mr Elford" appeared at Winchester as featured soloists in "a Consort of Vocal and Instrumental Musick" on St. Cecilia's Day. *Diverting Post,* 18–25 November 1704. Shore was also active as a lutenist for the Chapel Royal, a post to which he was appointed in March 1707, the document noting that "he hath for some time duely performed upon ye Lute in Our Royall Chappels at St. James's and Windsor without any Consideration for ye same." See the entry for Shore in Ashbee and Lasocki, *Biographical Dictionary of Court Musicians.*

6. Burrows has noted the "obviously Purcellian ancestry" of this passage (*Handel and the English Chapel Royal,* 109); the beginning of Purcell's *Jubilate,* in the same key, has a similar canon between trumpet and tenor. The opening vocal line of Handel's piece also bears a close resemblance to a passage by Giovanni Baptista Draghi, a contemporary of Purcell and one of Princess Anne's music teachers. His setting of Dryden's "Song for St. Cecilia's Day, 1687," an influential piece, survives in five manuscripts, one of them in the hand of John Blow.

🔊 Mus. Ex. 10.2: Giovanni Baptista Draghi, excerpt from *Song for St. Cecilia's Day,* 1687.

For some commentary on the influence of Draghi's work on Purcell and Blow, see Bryan White's excellent introduction to his edition of the music, *"From Harmony, from Heav'nly Harmony,"* ed. Bryan White (Novello, 2010), 11–12.

7. For an argument supporting the attribution to Philips and some theories about how he got the opportunity to write words for this ode, see "Style and Politics," especially 549–553.

8. I quote the text from its first printing, in *The Performances of the Antient Music for the Season 1781* (1781), no. 6, pp. 6–8. The text underlay in Handel's MS obviously antedates this version, but it is not clearly lineated and involves numerous textual repetitions.

9. *Windsor-Forest,* 325–326.

10. *MGC,* 1426.

11. This compact summary of the opposed positions comes from an unpublished thesis by Geoffrey Holmes, "The Great Ministry," 3. A copy of this very useful work is on deposit at the Institute of Historical Research, University of London.

12. *MGC,* 1431, 1433.

13. GB-Lbl Add. MS 61216, fol. 46: "Voila une bonne adjonction pour la tapisserie."

14. Jeri Bapasola, *Threads of History: The Tapestries at Blenheim Palace* (Oxford: Alden, 2005), 87.

15. Richard Blackmore, *Instructions to Vander Bank* (1709), 3.

16. See color plate 17, and compare color plate 16, Kneller's painting of a mounted Marlborough with Hercules by his side and Victory crowning him.

17. *Tatler* 3 (16 April 1709).

18. For a full and detailed account of the allegory, see the description at the website of the British Museum, www.britishmuseum.org/research/collection_online/collection_bject_details.aspx?objectId=3070729&partId=1&searchText=Historical+fan+Sacheverell&page=1.

19. *MGC*, 1433, 1428, 1437.

20. See Gregg, *Queen Anne*, 299, and notes. Because the duke burned his wife's entire correspondence with the Queen, we have limited knowledge of this important relationship.

21. *MGC*, 1440.

22. *Tatler* 157 (11 April 1710).

23. Francesco Mancini, *L'Idaspe fidele* (1710), 2–3.

24. Boyer, *Annals*, IX, 159.

25. *JHL*, XIX, 145.

26. Shortly after receiving Sarah's huge letter, Anne wrote to her asking for "a hundred gines to be sent to Mr. Gueche for the cure of my eyes, and five hundred to be sent to my backstairs some time this week." "I have not yet had leasure to read all your paypers," she added, "but as soon as I have, I will writt you some answer." GB-Lbl Add. MS 61418, fol. 68, editorially dated [?7 November 1709].

27. GB-Lbl Add. MS 61422, fols. 72–77. The note dating the conversation to "good friday" (fol. 77v) is in the hand of one of Sarah's amanuenses, but the narrative is in her own hand.

28. *The Diary of Sir David Hamilton, 1709–1714,* ed. Philip Roberts (Oxford: Clarendon, 1975), 25.

29. GB-Lbl Add. MS 61461, fol. 24r. Harris usefully summarizes the context for this letter; *Passion*, 170–171.

30. *The Tempest, or The Enchanted Island,* act 2, scene 3, 131–144.

31. *LS2MH*, 547, 560, 571.

32. See the very full and amusing account in Richmond Pugh Bond, *Queen Anne's American Kings* (Oxford: Clarendon, 1952).

33. *Annals,* IX, 191.

34. *Tatler* 171 (13 May 1710).

35. *Advice to the Q—n* (1710).

36. Dyer's newsletters, GB-Lbl Add. MS 70421, fol. 131v, entry for 6 June 1710; fol. 138r, entry for 13 June.

37. According to a letter supposedly dispatched from the allied camp in late July, "We are very well informed by the Paris Gazett of Sacheverels progresse, where he lies every night, and who it is that treats him: why so inconsiderable a man should find so much room in that famous Gazet, unless it be to keep up the spirits of the people, and encourage them to hold out the war one year longer, I can't comprehend." Luttrell, VI, 608. The Paris *Gazette* made frequent mention of Sacheverell, as this correspondent claims. See *Recueil des Nouvelles* (Paris, 1710), 296, 333, etc.

38. Jonathan Swift, *An enquiry into the behaviour of the Queen's last ministry* (1765), 72. This and all quotations from Swift's prose follow the excellent texts available at the website of the Jonathan Swift Archive, http://jonathanswiftarchive.org.uk, a project related to the new Cambridge edition (in progress). Where the archive offers several texts, I have normally chosen the earliest edition.

39. *MGC*, 1522. On 18/29 June, having written a depressed and complaining letter to Godolphin, Marlborough again displayed his concern with his future reputation: "When you read this letter pray burn it, for my desire is that nobody should know my complaints, but that the world may continue in their error of thinking me a happy man; for I think it better to be envyed then pittyed." *MGC*, 1535.

40. GB-Lbl Add. MS 61118, fol. 37 (13 June 1710).

41. In this phrase, Anne may be remembering Godolphin's impassioned letter to her during the Bishoprics crisis, which begins with similar language: "The liberties of all Europe, the safety of your Majesty's person and of these kingdoms, the future preservation of the Protestant religion, the strength of your Government, and the glory of your reign, depend upon the success of the next session of Parliament." GB-Lbl Add. MS 61118, fol. 17.

42. Manley, *Secret Memoirs* (1709), part 1, 32–33. The *Key* identifies "Germanicus" as the court rake Henry Jermyn, Baron Dover; the duchess, of course, is Lady Castlemaine, who numbered both men among her lovers.

43. *MGC*, 1521, 1530.

44. Luttrell, VI, 594–595.

45. Hamilton, *Diary*, 11.

46. Luttrell, VI, 602.

47. GB-Lbl Add. MS 70333 (formerly BL Loan 29/10), section 19, memorandum headed "May 20, 1710." For a detailed argument to this effect, see Holmes, "The Great Ministry," 36–40.

48. Dartmouth's minutes of the cabinet meeting, *MGC*, 1548n4.

49. Levens MSS, Bromley to James Grahme, 16 July 1710, quoted in Holmes, "The Great Ministry," 44.

50. Luttrell, VI, 604.

51. *Tatler* 193 (4 July 1710).

52. See chapter 9, note 29, and Paula R. Backscheider, "Powell, George (1668?–1714)," in *ODNB*.

53. GB-Lbl Add. MS 6118, fol. 47 (Sarah's copy).

54. Hamilton, *Diary*, 4. In her letters to Sarah, Anne often express her desire that they might once again be *easy*. "If I thought any thing I could say would make us live *easyer* together," she wrote in reply to one of Sarah's long, critical letters, "I should be encouraged to writt as large a volum to you." GB-Lbl Add. MS 61417, fol. 108.

55. *Queries* (1710).

56. See, for example, the entry for 22 September 1710: "upon shewing her the *letter to the Examiner* and *the Essay upon Credit*, she said the Author was not *D'Avenant* but tho' she knew him, yet must not discover him" (*Diary*, 17). The first of these pamphlets was by St. John; the second, by Defoe.

57. *MGC*, 1597.

58. Samuel Garth, *A Poem to the Earl of Godolphin* (1710).

59. *Examiner*, 31 August–7 September 1710.

60. For a detailed account of these changes, see Holmes, "The Great Ministry," 12–13.

61. Henry St. John, Viscount Bolingbroke, *A letter to Sir William Windham* (1753), 20.

62. Luttrell, VI, 624, 627.

63. *The Whig Examiner*, no. 1, reprinted in *The medleys for the year 1711. To which are prefix'd, the five Whig-Examiners* (1712), 5–14.

64. Swift, *A Journal to Stella* (1768), 64.

65. *Journal to Stella*, 4.

66. *Poems on Affairs of State*, ed. George deForest Lord, 7 vols. (New Haven: Yale University Press, 1963–75), VII, ed. Frank H. Ellis, 473–479, here quoting 479.

67. Swift, *Journal to Stella*, 54.

68. *MGC*, 1612.

69. Harley to the Rev. Mr. William Stratford. GB-Lbl Add. MS 70419 (formerly BL Loan 29/171), section 4.

70. *The Glorious Warrior* (1710).

71. Swift, *Journal to Stella*, 82: "It was a *Thanksgiving-day*, and I was at *Court*, where the queen past us by with all *Tories* about her; not one *Whig*." On 28 September, Luttrell reported that the queen would go to St. Paul's; VI, 634. As Boyer explains, however, "it was reported, That the Queen did not go to the Cathedral of St. Paul…to avoid giving the Mob an Opportunity to assemble, and commit Riots." *Annals*, IX, 253. An advertisement in the *London Gazette* for 9 November, seeking information about some iron bolts that had been removed from timbers in the roof of St. Paul's, "gave a Handle for the Report of a Plot, to destroy the Queen and the Court, by the Fall of the Roof of the Cathedral…on the Thanksgiving Day," a further instance of the credence Anne's subjects gave to conspiracy theories. *Annals* IX, 255.

72. Compare Hamilton, *Diary*, 20 (8 November 1710): "The Queen unwilling to hear of any thing about the Duchess."

73. There is no evidence from which to determine whether Croft himself or one of the clergymen associated with the Chapel Royal put together the text for the anthem.

74. *Divine Harmony, or a New Collection of Select Anthems* (1712), 79–80.

75. George Stanhope, *A Sermon Preached Before the Queen* (1710), 20–22, 10, 16–17, 24.

76. G. M. Trevelyan, "The 'Jersey' Period of the Negotiations Leading to the Peace of Utrecht," *English Historical Review* 49 (1934): 100–105.

77. *JHC*, XVI, 403.

78. *Examiner*, 16–23 November 1710.

79. In a private communication, Frances Harris suggests that Abigail Masham, who would succeed Sarah as Keeper of the Privy Purse, and to whom cash for the use of the queen was often disbursed, may have been in a position to know about Sarah's loans to herself. In a memorandum complaining about the *Examiner*, Sarah writes a passage that confirms this theory: "Long before I came from Court the Q—n was intirely in the hands of my Enemyes, who knew all I said to Her, saw all my letters and had my accounts for great soms in their hands before the Queen gave the discharge." GB-Lbl Add. MS 61422, fol. 153r.

80. GB-Lbl Add. MS 61423, fols. 16v–17r.

81. Hamilton, *Diary*, 20 (30 November 1710).

82. GB-Lbl Add. MS 61423, fol. 36v. Although Sarah does not name the "prints that do Mrs Morley great hurt," Manley had just published two more volumes of thinly disguised scandal, *Memoirs of Europe, Towards the Close of the Eighth Century*, which appeared in November 1710. Although there are no references to the queen, there are accounts of Sapphic sex involving the mezzo-soprano Mary Lindsey and the wife of Thomas Wharton, as well as extended attacks on the Duke and Duchess of Marlborough. I should think it possible that Sarah's daughters told her these books were "not fit for [her] to see" and that she inferred that they contained scandalous matter about Anne.

83. "Her letter to Hamilton was an attempt to distance herself from a campaign of slander that she herself had instigated." Rachel Weil, *Political Passions* (Manchester: University of Manchester Press, 1999), 187.

84. Hamilton, *Diary*, 21. Hamilton's text has "Duke of Somerset," which I believe is a slip for "Duchess," as Sarah had frequently complained of being slandered by the Duchess of Somerset.
85. Boyer, *Quadriennium*, I, 53.
86. Letter of 26 December 1710, GB-Lna SP 104/214, fols. 133–135, translated and printed in *LDI*, 312–313.
87. All quoted phrases from Hamilton, *Diary*, 20, 23–24.
88. Hamilton, *Diary*, 30.
89. Hamilton, *Diary*, 23.
90. See the excellent introduction to the season of 1710–11 in *LS2MH*, 595–600.
91. *The song for Her Majesty's birth-day, February the 6th, 17110/11* [*sic*]. *Set by Mr. Eccles, master of musick to Her Majesty, the words by Mr. Tate* (1711).
92. Boyer, *Annals*, IX, 335, correcting one obvious misprint (*"Cavalierw"*). In a brilliant recent piece of detective work, Olive Baldwin and Thelma Wilson have argued that the performance by the Italian singers in 1711 was not a "dialogue" by Handel in praise of the queen, as erroneously reported by Boyer, but an interlude in the theatrical performance. See "Handel, Eccles and the Birthday Celebrations for Queen Anne in 1711," *Musical Times* 154 (2013): 77–84.
93. See Richard Hudson and Meredith Ellis Little, "Sarabande," in *NGDM*.
94. GB-Lna SP 44/213 (unfoliated), partially printed in *LDI*, 321–322.
95. Aaron Hill, *Rinaldo* (1711), unpaginated front matter.
96. *Rinaldo*, 35–37.
97. See Curtis Price, "English Traditions in Handel's *Rinaldo*," in *Handel Tercentenary Collection*, ed. Stanley Sadie and Anthony Hicks (London: Royal Musical Association, 1987), 120–135; and James A. Winn, "Heroic Song: A Proposal for a Revised History of English Theatre and Opera, 1656–1711," *Eighteenth-Century Studies* 30 (1997): 113–137.
98. From Hill's testimony in a lawsuit filed on 9 July 1711, printed in *LS2MH*, 622.
99. *The Wentworth Letters, 1705–1739*, ed. James J. Cartwright (Wyman & Sons, 1883), 156.
100. *Wentworth Letters*, 181, 188; Williams, *Poetry and the Creation of a Whig Literary Culture*, 151.
101. *Journal to Stella*, 274.
102. *Spectator* 1 (1 March 1711).
103. Edmund Smith, *Phædra and Hippolytus* (1707), sig. A3r.
104. *Spectator* 5 (6 March 1711).
105. Addison remained loyal to his collaborator: Clayton's "Entertainment of Musick" at York Buildings on 24 May, a concert performance of his settings of poems by Dryden and William Harrison, was prominently advertised in the *Spectator*.
106. "Handel was supported by the Stuart Queen Anne, by the Hanoverians, by Tories, Whigs, nonjurors and Jacobites, whether they were Anglican, Catholic, Lutheran or Jewish. He was also opposed by members of all these factions and faiths." David Hunter, "Handel among the Jacobites," *Music and Letters* 82 (2001): 543–556, here quoting 547.
107. For a detailed account of Guiscard's bizarre career, see Peter Jones, "Antoine de Guiscard, 'Abbe de la Bourlie,' 'Marquis de Guiscard,'" *British Library Journal* 8 (1982): 94–113.
108. For an amusing account of the myth that Harley was saved by an "embroidered" waistcoat, see Clyve Jones, "Robert Harley and the Myth of the Golden Thread: Family Piety, Journalism and the History of the Assassination Attempt of 8 March 1711," *Electronic British Library Journal* (2010), article 11.
109. *Quadriennium*, I, 236.

110. *A true narrative of what pass'd at the examination of the Marquis de Guiscard at the Cock-pit, the 8th of March 1710/11; Great news from the other world; or a new dialogue between the Marquis de Guiscard, and William Gregg; To the Right Honourable Mr. Harley, Wounded by Guiscard* (all 1711).

111. Burnet, *History*, VI, 39–40, Dartmouth's long note.

112. *HMC Portland*, V, 655.

113. Letter from [Arabella Pulteney?] to Mr. [John?] Molesworth; *HMC Various Collections*, VIII, 250. For further evidence of Sarah's activities during this election, see *Letter-Books of John Hervey, First Earl of Bristol*, 3 vols. (Wells: Ernest Jackson, 1894), I, 287.

114. *Quadriennium*, I, 261–265.

115. *JHC*, XVI, 567; 29 March 1711.

116. *Examiner* 43 (24 May 1711).

117. *Quadriennium*, I, 250–251. Despite the strict embargo imposed on her subjects, the queen drank French wine throughout the war. See the Lord Steward's records, GB-Lna, LS 13/175, especially fol. 56 r/v, which records a legal opinion about the queen importing French wine for her service and family, a ruling she sought after a boatload of such wine, purchased in Rotterdam by her agents, was seized by customs.

118. *Spectator* 45 (21 April 1711).

119. *OED*, s.v. "abigail."

120. *Letter-Books of John Hervey*, I, 301.

121. Receipts for *Rinaldo* on 25 April were £129 10s. 3d; those for *L'Idaspe fidele* on 28 April were £99 11s. 3d. *LS2MH*, 634. Although Pilotta's enemies secured a larger house on Wednesday, the audience on Saturday was more than respectable.

122. *HMC Various Collections*, VIII, 251. The editor summarizing this letter refers to "Mr. Porrel," which I take to be a misreading of "Mr. Powell."

123. "I also saw Powell's famous puppet show, in which Punch fought with a pig in burlesque, in imitation of Nicolini's battle with the lion. My Lord Bolingbroke was of the party, and made me sit upon his lap to see it. The rest of the company were my father, my uncle Granville, Sir John Stanley, Vice-Chamberlain Cooke, Mr. W. Collier, my mother and Lady Stanley, and Mrs. Betty Granville." *The autobiography and correspondence of Mary Granville, Mrs. Delany*, 3 vols. (R. Bentley, 1861), I, 16. My thanks to Olive Baldwin and Thelma Wilson for alerting me to this reference.

124. *Spectator* 29 (3 April 1711).

125. Pope, *An Essay on Criticism*, 9–10; 52–67.

126. *Spectator* 253; 20 December 1711. One of those glanced at in Pope's poem, the dramatist and critic John Dennis, replied with *Reflections, Critical and Satyrical, upon a late Rhapsody, call'd An Essay upon Criticism*, a pamphlet of some 32 pages attacking Pope's logic, versification, and person.

127. Anthony Ashley Cooper, Third Earl of Shaftesbury, *Characteristicks* (1711), 223.

128. *An Essay on Criticism*, 143–145.

129. GB-Lbl Add. MS 23082, fols. 33–35, transcribed and printed in *Vertue Notebooks* (Oxford: Oxford University Press, 1955), VI.

130. *Examiner*, 7 June 1711.

131. *Examiner*, 14 June 1711.

132. *Medley*, 11 June 1711.

133. Swift, *A Tale of a Tub*, ed. A. C. Guthkelch and D. Nichol Smith (Oxford: Clarendon, 1920), 176.

134. See n. 61 above.

135. Holmes, "The Great Ministry," 102.

136. *Wentworth Letters,* 189.

137. See the letter from John Drummond to Oxford, *HMC Portland,* V, 1.

138. *JHC,* XVI, 685; 31 May 1711.

139. *HMC Bath* I, 217.

140. Holmes, "The Great Ministry," 136–137.

141. Letter of 18 September 1711. In *Letters and Correspondence of Bolingbroke,* ed. Gilbert Parke, cited hereafter as *LCB,* 4 vols. (1798), I, 361.

142. GB-Lbl Add. MS 70332, formerly BL Loan 29/10, section 16.

143. *A New Journey to Paris, Together with some Secret Transactions between the Fr—h K—g, and an Eng—Gentleman ... Translated from the French* (1711), 5, 12.

144. *Daily Courant,* 13 October 1711.

145. *He's Wellcome Home* (1711); for the aria, see musical example 9.1. The ballad is anonymous; I suspect the hand of Maynwaring.

146. *HMC Bath,* I, 214; 26 October 1711.

147. Luke 15:13 KJV.

148. [Swift], *The Conduct of the Allies* (1711), ii, 45, 48, 60, 28, 26.

149. *Daily Courant,* 5 December 1711.

150. For correspondence about the preparation of the speech, see *HMC Bath,* I, 215, 217. St. John, Dartmouth, and Shrewsbury were evidently among those consulted, though I should think Oxford was the main author.

151. Hamilton, *Diary,* 32. Some aspects of Hamilton's entry are puzzling. He says that he "told the Queen that the first part of the Speech was objected against, as not being suitable to her Calm Temper, and that the French King had used the Expression to Cardinal Noailles in his letter." This only makes sense if the doctor misremembered the date of their conversation. No letter from Louis XIV to Cardinal Noailles, real or fictional, was in circulation on 10 December, the date of this diary entry. Anne dismissed Marlborough on 31 December, and in early January, there was a spoof publication purporting to be a directive from Louis to Cardinal Noailles, in which Louis supposedly rejoices at "the Disappointment of such as *delight in War*" (see n. 161 below). On 12 January, the *Daily Courant* reported that "the King has ordered the Cardinal de Noailles, our Archbishop, to institute publick Prayers, that God will please to favour his Majesty's Intentions or Designs, and grant to the Kingdom of France, and to all its Allies, an honourable and lasting Peace." No such letters or directives appear in the *Paris Gazette* or in the *Amsterdam Gazette,* a French-language publication that circulated widely. My thanks to Alan Downie and Melissa Schoenberger for helping me try to sort out this puzzling tangle.

152. *Book of Common Payer,* Psalm 68:29–30.

153. Bapasola, *Threads of History,* 33–38.

154. *JHL,* XIX, 335–336.

155. *JHC,* XVII, 2.

156. *JHL,* XIX, 336, 341.

157. *JHL,* XIX, 346.

158. *JHC,* XII, 15–18.

159. The holograph no longer exists. There are MS copies in GB-Lbl Add. MS 61101, fols. 178–184.

160. In the only modern account of this painting, J. Douglas Stewart quotes two relevant letters by the Duke of Chandos, one explaining the iconography, the other reporting on a copy made for the Duke of Berwick, Marlborough's nephew. Unfortunately, Stewart misdates both letters.

The one he dates as written on 2 January 1712, was actually written in January 1720; the other, which he implies was written in April 1712, dates from April 1720. See "Chandos, Marlborough and Kneller: Painting and 'Protest' in the Age of Queen Anne," *Bulletin of the National Gallery of Canada* 17 (1971): 24–32. The original letters are in the Huntington Library in San Marino, California: Stowe Ms 57, XVI, 435–436, dated "1719/20 January 2," and XVII, 52, dated "1720 April 12." My thanks to Howard Weinbrot for confirming these dates.

161. *The King of France's Letter to the Cardinal de Noailles, Archbishop of Paris* (1712).

162. The notebook containing these early drafts is thought to date from the 1690s, though there is no hard evidence. For a very full account, see J. D. Alsop, "Victorian Scholarship and the Addison Manuscript," *Harvard Library Bulletin* 8 (1997): 49–62.

163. *Spectator* 255 (23 December 1711).

164. *Spectator* 256 (24 December 1711).

165. [Swift], *The Windsor Prophecy* (1711).

166. Hamilton, *Diary,* 40, 43.

167. *Spectator* 257 (25 December 1711).

168. "This day being New Year's Day the lords and Ladies, &c. has been to wish her Majesty many happy new years, and I thank God the Queen was so well as to come out to receive the compliments of her good subjects." *Wentworth Letters,* 235; if there was an ode, it has vanished without a trace.

169. *Wentworth Letters,* 246.

170. Boyer, *History,* 536, 547.

171. *Prince Eugene's Welcome* (1712), 1.

172. *LCB,* II, 199.

173. There is a full outline of the "Savoy plan" in St. John's letter of 29 April to Torcy: "Her Majesty therefore proposes, that this Prince [Philip] do, with his family, immediately retire from Spain; that the Duke of Savoy, with his, repair thither, and take possession of that monarchy and the Indies; that King Philip enjoy the kingdom of Sicily, the hereditary states of his Royal Highness, with the Montserrat, Mantuan; and, in case he succeeds to the crown of France, that Sicily be ceded to the House of Austria, but that the other states remain to be in future considered as provinces of France. The Queen could wish this proposition should appear to come from his Most Christian Majesty, as an effect of his moderation, and a sacrifice he is willing to make, to extricate Europe from her present embarrassment, and to restore a general tranquility." *LCB,* II, 284 (in French), using the translation by the editor, 550.

174. The bilingual word-book for the opera offers this English version:

> No more the Trumpet sounds to Wars,
> The glitt'ring Sword no more appears:
> Vict'ry her Ensigns does display,
> Triumphant Peace shall crown the Day.
> The fatal Steel the Swains do wield,
> And safely wound the passive Field.
> Eternal Laurels they shall raise,
> Victorious *Denmark,* to thy Praise. (*Hamlet, An Opera* [1712], 12)

Our only source for the music is John Walsh's publication, *Songs in the Opera of Hamlet* (1712). Walsh often simplified and transposed the pieces he published, as we know from cases where we have both an autograph score and one of his collections. In this case, the obbligato part, which Walsh marks as for "Violin or Trumpet," includes a number of pitches not obtainable on the natural trumpet. In the performance recorded for this book, we have used both a trumpeter and a violin section.

175. *The Queen's and the Duke of Ormond's New Toast* (1712).

176. *LCB*, II, 319–321. Trevelyan blames St. John for these orders, more or less exonerating Oxford. George Macaulay Trevelyan, *England under Queen Anne*, 3 vols. (Longmans, Green and Co., 1930–34), III, 215–218. Later scholars, including B. W. Hill, have disagreed. See Holmes, "The Great Ministry," 206–207.

177. *LCB*, II, 327.

178. Boyer, *History*, 570–571.

179. *JHL*, XIX, 471–472.

180. Robert D. Horn in *Marlborough: A Survey* (Folkestone: Garland, 1975), 364.

181. The most comprehensive study is D. F. Foxon, "The Stamp Act of 1712," Sandars Lecture for 1978, typescript, GB-Lbl, Ac. 2660.m (32).

182. Ambrose Philips, preface to *The Distrest Mother* (1712), sig. A5r.

183. Pope, *The Rape of the Lock* (1712), II, 95–103.

184. Walsh published the music as *Songs in the Opera of Calypso & Telemachus* (1712); for an example of Galliard at his best, see "How shall I speak my secret pain," a touching minor-key aria with an oboe solo.

185. *Spectator* 405 (14 June 1712).

186. For documents related to Swiney's flight and the subsequent reorganization of the opera company, see Judith Milhous and Robert D. Hume, *Vice-Chamberlain Coke's Theatrical Papers, 1706–1715* (Carbondale: Southern Illinois University Press, 1982), 198–202.

187. *Spectator* 411 (21 June 1712).

188. This was the amount required for the representative of a borough. A knight of a shire was required to own land yielding £600. Trevelyan, *England under Queen Anne*, III, 108–110.

189. *Spectator* 416 (27 June 1712).

190. *Spectator* 421 (3 July 1712).

191. *Flying Post*, 28 June–1 July 1712.

192. *Post Boy*, 19–22 July 1712.

193. *LCB*, II, 442–443; 452, using the translations by the editor, II, 607, 611.

194. Hamilton, *Diary*, 43, 94.

195. Boyer, *Annals*, XI, 212.

196. Gregg, *Queen Anne*, 359 and notes. For a full account of the many issues dividing the Cabinet at this time, see Holmes, "The Great Ministry," 221–225.

197. Burnet, *History*, VI, 143–144; Dartmouth's note.

198. Boyer, *History*, 598.

199. *HMC Bath*, I, 223.

200. In a letter to the Elector dated 13 January 1713, Thomas Grote reports learning of the queen's commission to Handel from Bolingbroke. See Donald Burrows, "Handel and Hanover," in *Bach, Handel, Scarlatti: Tercentenary Essays*, ed. Peter Williams (Cambridge: Cambridge University Press, 1985), 35–59, here citing 42.

Chapter 11

1. *Post Man*, 21–24 August 1714.

2. All details and quoted phrases from GB-Lna LC2/18 (unfoliated), the Lord Chamberlain's papers concerning the funeral.

3. *London Gazette*, 24–28 August 1714.

4. GB-Lbl Add. MS 61422, fol. 199. The unsigned will is in GB-Lna SP 44/116.

5. GB-Lna LC2/18, emphasis mine. "Mr. Blundele" was a surgeon; my thanks to Robert Bucholz for help in identifying him.

6. GB-Lna LC2/18. See also Paul S. Fritz, "From 'Public' to 'Private': The Royal Funeral in England, 1500–1830," in *Studies in the Social History of Death*, ed. Joachim Whaley (Europa, 1981), 61–79.

7. According to Dartmouth, Anne expected Atterbury to be "as meddling and troublesome as the Bishop of Salisbury" but appointed him at Harcourt's urging, having refused to make Sacheverell a bishop. Burnet, *History*, VI, 165 (Dartmouth's note).

8. *The Wentworth Letters, 1705–1739*, ed. James J. Cartwright (Wyman & Sons, 1883), 410.

9. *An Elegy on the Death of her Sacred Majesty* (1714), 8.

10. *The Mausoleum* (1714), 21.

11. *A Pindarick Ode upon the Death of her Late Majesty Queen Anne* (1714), 6.

12. Like all students of this great poem, I am indebted to Pat Rogers, who has published two remarkable books approaching *Windsor-Forest* from different perspectives, *The Symbolic Design of "Windsor-Forest"* (Newark: University of Delaware Press, 2004), and *Pope and the Destiny of the Stuarts* (Oxford: Oxford University Press, 2005).

13. Tickell, *On the Prospect of Peace* (1713), 1.

14. Tickell, *On the Prospect of Peace*, 2.

15. Pope, *Windsor-Forest*, 1–4, 11–16, 29–32, 37–42, 91–92, 103–110, 371–374, 159–162, 201–206, 323–328, 397–406.

16. Tickell, *On the Prospect of Peace*, 9.

17. Tickell, *On the Prospect of Peace*, 9.

18. Pope, *Windsor-Forest*, 407–410, 427–430.

19. *Paradise Lost*, I, 19–22.

20. GB-Lbl Add. MS 47027, fol. 16v.

21. Swift, *A Journal to Stella* (1768), 334.

22. For an excellent account, see Donald Burrows, *Handel and the English Chapel Royal* (Oxford: Oxford University Press, 2005), 74–113.

23. GB-Lbl Add. MS 47027, fols. 20v–21r. The description of this "noble entertainment for persons of a refined taste" comes from an earlier letter (fol. 16). The language about raising the passions, which Thomas Clayton had often used in describing his own music, suggests that Clayton may have been involved in this scheme, which apparently did not bear fruit.

24. *Quadriennium annæ postremum; or the political state of Great Britain*, 8 vols. (1718–19), V, 172–173.

25. Sacheverell, *The Christian Triumph: Or, The Duty of Praying for our Enemies* (1713), 18.

26. Defending her speech to Dr. Hamilton on 11 April, Anne expressed her belief that "the Emperour would Certainly come in." By 5 May, however, she was telling him that "the Emperours, always stood out from coming in to a Peace." *The Diary of Sir David Hamilton, 1709–1714*, ed. Philip Roberts (Oxford: Clarendon, 1975), 53, 54.

27. Kreienberg's letter of 5 June 1713, Niedersächsiches Hauptstaatsarchiv Hanover, Dep. 103 Nr 148, quoted and translated in Donald Burrows, "Handel and Hanover," in *Bach, Handel, Scarlatti: Tercentenary Essays*, ed. Peter Williams (Cambridge: Cambridge University Press, 1985), 43–44.

28. *JHL*, XIX, 511–512. The bill against dueling died in committee before the end of this parliamentary session.

29. See R. H. Griffith, *Alexander Pope: A Bibliography*, 2 vols. (Austin: University of Texas Press, 1922, 1927), I, item 9.

30. GB-Lbl Add. MS 47027, fol. 26.

31. The *Post Boy* for 23–26 May 1713, advertises as "Just Published": "The Musick perform'd in the Tragedy of Cato in Parts for Violins, Trumpets and Hautboys: composed by Mr John Eccles." Sadly, no copies survive. My thanks to Olive Baldwin and Thelma Wilson for alerting me to this advertisement.

32. William Wogan to John Perceval, 30 April 1713; GB-Lbl Add. MS 47027, fol. 31.

33. Anne's own phrase, in her first address to Parliament on 8 March 1702; *JHL*, XVII, 64.

34. Addison, *Cato* (1713), 1, 7, 9, 53.

35. GB-Lbl Add. MS 47027, fol. 26.

36. *The Correspondence of the Spalding Gentlemen's Society 1710–1761*, ed. Diana and Michael Honeybone (Boydell and Brewer, 2010), 8.

37. Pope to John Caryll, 30 April 1713; *Correspondence of the Spalding Gentlemen's Society*, I, 175–176. John Gay provides similar testimony in a letter to Maurice Johnson: "Cato affords universal discourse, & is received with great applause. my Lord Oxford, Lord Chancellor and the Speaker of the House of Commons have bespoke the Box on the Stage for next Saturday.... [T]he Audience for several Nights clapp'd some Particular parts of the Play which they thought reflected upon the Tories ... but you see that the Ministry are so far from thinking it touches them, that the Treasurer and Chancellor will honour the Play with their Presence." *The Letters of John Gay*, ed. C. F. Burgess (Oxford: Clarendon Press, 1966), 3.

38. Letter of 28 April; GB-Lbl Add. MS 47027, fols. 58–59. "Mr Harcourt my Ld. Chancellor's son" is Simon Harcourt, who had written a poem welcoming the Queen to Oxford in 1702. See chapter 6 above.

39. *HMC Bath*, II, 234–235.

40. *Quadriennium*, V, 399.

41. *Quadriennium*, VI, 12.

42. *HMC Bath*, II, 235.

43. For a full account, see Duncan Chisholm, "Handel's 'Lucio Cornelio Silla': Its Problems and Context," *Early Music* 14 (1986): 64–70.

44. Boyer, *Quadriennium*, V, 341; *History*, 645.

45. Giacomo Rossi, *L. C. Silla* (1713), "Argomento," sig. b1: "di propria autorità Dittatore perpetuo."

46. HRO, Panshanger MS D/EP F35, quoted in Burrows, *Handel and the English Chapel Royal*, 82.

47. Hamilton, *Diary*, 56.

48. *Post Boy*, 7–9 July 1713.

49. *Post Boy*, 11–14 July 1713.

50. George Hooper, *A Sermon Preach'd before Both Houses of Parliament, in the Cathedral Church of St. Paul's* (1713), 20–21.

51. Hamilton, *Diary*, 57.

52. *JHL*, XIX, 615.

53. *History*, VI, 167.

54. For a full account of the process leading to these appointments, see Geoffrey Holmes, "The Great Ministry," unpublished thesis on deposit at the Institute of Historical Research, University of London, 282–285.

55. Hamilton, *Diary*, 58.

56. GB-Lna PRO 31/3/201, fol. 87, quoted and translated in Gregg, Queen Anne, 371.

57. According to evidence preserved in Macpherson, *Original Papers Containing the Secret History of Great Britain*, 2 vols. (Dublin, 1775), II, 635, the plan was to divide the queen's share into sixteen parts, with five going to Oxford, five to Bolingbroke, four to Lady Masham, and two to Arthur Moore. The whole plan eventually collapsed in the face of a parliamentary investigation.

58. Hamilton, *Diary,* 64.

59. *HMC Portland,* V, 466.

60. GB-Lna E 351/566, printed in *RECM,* II, 150.

61. GB-Lna T 52/25, p. 380.

62. Gregg, *Queen Anne,* 375–376 and notes.

63. GB-Lbl Add. MS 61125, fol. 143. The letter promises another £3296 and reassures Marlborough that as the meeting of Parliament draws near, "all those I converse with are resolved not to give your Grace the least disturbance." Oxford promises to let the duke know if that situation changes.

64. For an "Abstract" of the Pretender's letter, see MacPherson, *Original Papers,* II, 525–526. His closing paragraph begins with a reference to "my grandfather and father," who "had always a good opinion of the principles of the church of England, relating to monarchy."

65. *Correspondence of the Spalding Gentlemen's Society,* I, 200–201.

66. Hamilton, *Diary,* 54.

67. *Quadriennium,* VII, 184.

68. Baldwin and Wilson assign this ode, *Prepare, ye Sons of Art,* to the birthday of 1714 because of the dates of Weely's appointment and the MS reference to the composer as "Dr. Croft." "Music in the Birthday Celebrations at Court in the Reign of Queen Anne: A Documentary Calendar," *A Handbook for Studies in 18th-Century English Music* 19 (2008), 24. A score naming the soloists survives as GB-Lbl Add. MS 31455; there are parts, differing from the score in some respects, in GB-Lbl R.M. 24.d.5.

69. This odd name for Anne also appears in a song by D'Urfey, addressed to the Duchess of Marlborough during the period when she was in favor at court and set to a tune from *Camilla,* printed in *Pills to Purge Melancholy,* 2 vols. (1719), II, 123. The text for *Prepare, ye Sons of Art* survives only as text underlay in the score and may be incorrectly entered there.

70. See Olive Baldwin and Thelma Wilson, "Theatre Dancers at the Court of Queen Anne," *Court Historian* 15 (2010): 171–187. As Baldwin and Wilson point out, "the birthday entertainment at Windsor cannot have included a play, for on the night of the birthday the new and successful tragedy *Jane Shore* was acted at Drury Lane."

71. *The Godolphin. Mr. Isaac's New Dance, made for Her Majesty's Birthday.* (1714).

72. *Quadriennium,* VII, 184–185.

73. Steele, *The Crisis* (1714), 2, 31, 34.

74. *HMC Portland* V, 384.

75. *The Crisis,* 31.

76. Swift, *The Publick Spirit of the Whigs,* 2nd ed. (1714), 32, 43.

77. These meetings, of which only three can be given certain dates, gave rise to the story of the "Scriblerus Club," now shown to be largely the creation of later scholars. See Ashley Marshall's bracing article "The Myth of Scriblerus," *Journal for Eighteenth-Century Studies* 31 (2008): 77–99.

78. MacPherson, *Original Papers,* II, 574.

79. *JHL,* XIX, 625.

80. Tate, *A Congratulatory Poem* (1714), 7, 10.

81. Dryden, *Aeneis,* I, 213–220.

82. *The Crisis,* v.

83. *The Publick Spirit of the Whigs,* 16.

84. *The Crisis,* v, 1.

85. Holmes, "The Great Ministry," 342–343.

86. *HMC Portland* V, 417.

87. GB-Lbl Stowe MS 242, fol. 98.

88. MacPherson, *Original Papers,* II, 621.

89. See Marlborough's letter of 7/18 June, in which he alleges that "all the considerable Men of both sides…earnestly desired" the Electoral Prince to establish himself in England. GB-Lbl Stowe MS 242, fols. 121–22.

90. Stowe MS 242, fol. 130, in French, using the translation printed in *HMC Portland,* V, 662. See also her letter of the same day to the Electress Sophia, fols. 134–35, and Oxford's attempt to mollify the Electress, fols. 115–16.

91. Defoe, *Secret History of the White Staff, Part I* (1714), 17.

92. In this context, a grant or favor.

93. *JHL,* XIX, 755.

94. *JHL,* XIX, 758–759.

95. *The Correspondence of Jonathan Swift,* ed. Harold Williams, 5 vols. (Oxford: Clarendon, 1963), II, 86.

96. *Quadriennium,* VIII, 626. In the following account of the queen's last days, I follow Boyer and a very helpful article by Henry L. Snyder, "The Last Days of Queen Anne: The Account of Sir John Evelyn Examined," *Huntington Library Quarterly* 34 (1971): 261–276.

97. *HMC Downshire,* I, ii, 902.

98. In this context, a Lord Justice was one of those responsible for governing the country in the absence of a monarch. Harcourt's fear was that Oxford, not having yet been replaced, might try to reclaim his position among the Lords Justices.

99. Diary of Sir John Evelyn, quoted in Snyder, "Last Days," 269. Snyder argues persuasively against accounts claiming that the dramatic arrival of Somerset and Argyle to claim their seats on the Privy Council turned the tide, explaining that they probably did not reach Kensington until after the transfer of the staff to Shrewsbury.

100. Sir John Hawkins, *A General History of the Science and Practice of Music,* 5 vols. (1776), IV, 427*n*.

101. Theobald, *The Mausoleum,* 20.

BIBLIOGRAPHY

Place of publication is London unless otherwise noted.

MANUSCRIPT SOURCES

Venice: Biblioteca Nazionale Marziana
MSS It. IV 392 and 393.

Cambridge: Cambridge University Library (GB-Cul)
Add. MS 7091.

London: British Library (GB-Lbl)
Additional Manuscripts: 4221, 4238, 4276, 4478B, 5017, 5822, 5832, 5868, 6309, 6375, 7078, 12514, 13545, 14407, 15752, 15897, 15915, 16498, 17677GG, 17677XX, 17847, 17917, 18738, 18958, 19759, 20726, 23082, 24901, 27402, 28070, 29548, 29589, 30934, 31452, 31455, 31456, 31812, 31813, 33045, 34515, 38056, 38863, 41803, 47026, 47027, 52540, 53816, 61101, 61102, 61118, 61125, 61216, 61355, 61360, 61407, 61414, 61415, 61416, 61417, 61418, 61420, 61421, 61422, 61423, 61424, 61426, 61454, 61455, 61458, 61459, 61460, 61461, 61462, 61480B, 61490, 61498, 61630, 61701, 62410, 69962, 70021, 70332, 70333, 70340, 70419, 70420, 70421, 72494, 75384, 75388, 75389, 75390, 75400, 75401, 78307.
Egerton MS 3664.
Harleian MS 6815.
King's MS 140.
Lansdowne MSS 852, 1236.
Microfilm 636/24 (Verney MSS).
Royal Music Library: R.M. 20.g.2, R.M. 20.h.8, R.M. 24.d.5.
Sloane MSS 1388, 4224.
Stowe MS 242.

London: National Archives (GB-Lna)
AO 15/21, AO 15/23.
E 351/566, E 403/1046.
LC 2/15/1, LC 5/140, LC 5/142, LC 5/148, LC 5/149, LC 5/152, LC 5/154, LC 5/166, LC 7/1,
    LC 7/3, LC2/18 LC2/18.
LS 13/175.
PC 2/79, PC 2/80, PC 2/82.
PRO 30/24/21, PRO 31/3/153, PRO 31/3/201.
SP 8/2, SP 34/2/27, SP 34/36, SP 44/116, SP 44/213, SP 54/2, SP 104/4, SP 104/129, SP 104/203,
    SP 104/209, SP 104/214.
T 29/13, T 30/2, T 48/17, T 52/22, T52/25, T 53/16, T 60/6.

London: Guildhall Library (GB-Lg)
Mus G 313

Nottingham: Nottingham University Library (GB-NO)
Portland MSS: Pw V 45/3, Pw V 48/14, Pw V 529, Pw V 536, Pw V 95.

Oxford: Bodleian Library (GB-Ob)
MS Mus. C. 6.
MS Tenbury 1175.
MS Tenbury 1266 (5).

Austin, Texas: Harry Ransom Center (US-Aus)
PFORZ-MS-1133, 1219, 1383, 1392, 1459, 1466, 1467.

New York: New York Public Library (US-NYp)
Drexel 3849

Washington, D.C.: Folger Shakespeare Library (US-Ws)
X.d. 473.

Newspapers

British Apollo
Daily Courant
Diverting Post
*English Post with News Foreign and Domestick
    (English Post)*
Examiner
Flying Post
Gentleman's Journal
Heraclitus Ridens
London Gazette

Muses Mercury
New State of Europe
Observator
Post Boy
Post Man and the Historical Account (Post Man)
Post Master
Recueil des Nouvelles (Paris)
Review of the Affairs of France
Whig Examiner

Printed Primary Sources

A Form of Prayer and Thanksgiving. 1707.
*A form of prayer and thanksgiving to almighty God: to be used on Thursday the seventh of September
    next, throughout the Kingdom of England, Dominion of Wales, and town of Berwick upon Tweed; for
    the late glorious victory obtained over the French and Bavarians at Bleinheim, near Hochstet, on*

Wednesday the second of August, by the Forces of Her Majesty and Her Allies, under the Command of the Duke of Marlborough. By Her Majesties special Command. 1704.

A just and impartial character of the clergy of the Church of England, occasioned by Her Majesty's most Gracious bounty to them, in giving Her whole revenue of first-fruits and tenths for the augmentation of poor livings. 1704.

A New Ballad, To the Tune of Fair Rosamond. 1708.

A New Song to the Tune of Lilly burlaro. 1708.

A Pindarick Ode upon the Death of her Late Majesty Queen Anne. 1714.

A poem on Her Sacred Majesty Queen Anne. Edinburgh, 1703.

A Trip Lately to Scotland. 1705.

A True Narrative of the Duke of Monmouth's Late Journey into the West. 1680.

A true narrative of what pass'd at the examination of the Marquis de Guiscard at the Cock-pit, the 8th of March 1710/11. 1711.

Addison, Joseph. *The Campaign.* 1705.

Addison, Joseph. *Cato.* 1713.

Addison, Joseph. *The Letters of Joseph Addison.* Ed. Walter Graham. Oxford: Clarendon Press, 1941.

Addison, Joseph. *Remarks on Several Parts of Italy.* 1705.

Addison, Joseph. *Rosamond.* 1707.

Addison, Joseph. *The Works of the Right Honourable Joseph Addison.* Ed. Thomas Tickell. 4 vols. 1721.

Addison, Joseph, and Richard Steele. *The Spectator.* Ed. Donald F. Bond. 5 vols. Oxford: Clarendon Press, 1965.

Advice to the Q—n. 1710.

Airy, Osmund, ed. *Essex Papers, Volume I, 1672–79.* Westminster: Camden Society, 1890.

Albion's Glory, a Pindarique Ode on the Royal Train that Attended the Happy Coronation of Her most Sacred Majesty. 1702.

Ames, Richard. *The Double Descent.* 1692.

An Elegy on the Death of her Sacred Majesty. 1714.

An exact account of the whole proceedings against the Right Reverend Father in God, Henry, Lord Bishop of London, before the Lord Chancellor and the other ecclesiastical commissioners. 1688.

An Ode to the Queen. 1708.

Animadversions on the succession to the crown of England, consider'd. Publish'd by Captain D—by. 1701.

Anna in Anno Mirabili: Or, The Wonderful Year of 1702. 1702.

Arbuthnot, John. *A sermon preach'd to the people, at the Mercat-Cross of Edinburgh, on the subject of the union.* Edinburgh, 1706.

Ariadne, or The marriage of Bacchus. 1674.

Ariane, ou le marriage de Bacchus. 1674.

Armytage, George J., ed. *Allegations for Marriage-Licenses Issued by the Vicar-General of the Archbishop of Canterbury, July 1687 to June 1694.* Harleian Society, 1890.

Arthur, Harold, Viscount Dillon. "Some Familiar Letters of Charles II. and James Duke of York Addressed to Their Daughter and Niece, the Countess of Litchfield; Transcribed and Edited by Harold Arthur, Viscount Dillon." *Archæologia* 58 (1902): 153–188.

Arwaker, Edmund the Younger. *The Birth-Night, A Pastoral. By Mr. Arwaker.* 1705.

Ashbee, Andrew. *Records of English Court Music.* 9 vols. Snodland, Kent: A. Ashbee, 1986–96.

Astell, Mary. *A Serious Proposal to the Ladies.* 1694.

Astell, Mary. *A Serious Proposal to the Ladies in two Parts.* 1697.

Baldwin, Olive, and Thelma Wilson, eds. *The Monthly Mask of Vocal Music, 1702–1711.* Aldershot: Ashgate, 2007.

Ballard, George. *Memoirs of several ladies of Great Britain, who have been celebrated for their writings or skill in the learned languages arts and sciences.* Oxford, 1752.

Barlow, Joel. *The Columbiad.* Washington, D.C.: Joseph Milligan, 1825.

Bates, John. *Two (United) are better than One Alone.* 1707.

Bathurst, Benjamin, ed. *Letters of Two Queens.* Holden, 1924.

The Battel of Audenarde. 1708.

Behn, Aphra. *The Town-Fopp.* 1677.

Behn, Aphra. *Poems on Several Occasions.* 1684.

Behn, Aphra. *Miscellany, being a collection of poems by several hands; together with Reflections on morality, or, Seneca unmasqued.* 1685.

Behn, Aphra. *The Works of Aphra Behn.* Ed. Janet Todd. 6 vols. Pickering and Chatto, 1992.

Biographia Britannica: or, The lives of the most eminent persons who have flourished in Great Britain and Ireland. 7 vols. 1747–66.

Blackall, Offspring. *A Sermon Preach'd before the Queen.* 1707.

Blackmore, Richard. *Instructions to Vander Bank.* 1709.

Blount, Charles. *Appeal from the Country to the City.* 1679.

Blow, John. *John Blow, Anthems IV: Anthems with Instruments.* Ed. Bruce Wood. Stainer and Bell, 2002. *Musica Britannica,* vol. 79.

Blow, John. *Selected Verse Anthems.* Ed. Fredrick Tarrant. Middleton, Wis.: A-R Editions, 2009.

Bononcini, Giovanni. *Camilla: Royal College of Music MS 79.* Ed. Lowell Lindgren. Stainer and Bell. 1990.

Boyer, Abel. *The royal dictionary in two parts, first, French and English, secondly, English and French...for the use of His Highness the Duke of Glocester.* 1699.

Boyer, Abel. *History of Queen Anne, Digested into Annals.* 11 vols. 1703–14.

Boyer, Abel. *Quadriennium annæ postremum; or the political state of Great Britain.* 8 vols. 1718–19.

Boyer, Abel. *The History of the Life & Reign of Queen Anne. Illustrated with all the Medals Struck in this Reign.* 1722.

Bramston, John. *Autobiography of Sir John Bramston.* Westminster: Camden Society, 1845.

Brown, Beatrice Curtis, ed. *The Letters and Diplomatic Instructions of Queen Anne.* New York: Funk and Wagnalls, 1968.

Brown, K. M., et al. *The Records of the Parliaments of Scotland to 1707.* St. Andrews, 2007–12.

Browning, Andrew, ed. *English Historical Documents, 1660–1714.* Eyre and Spottiswoode, 1953.

Budgell, Eustace. *Memoirs of the life and character of the late Earl of Orrery, and of the family of the Boyles.* 1732.

Burnet, Gilbert. *A Sermon Preached at the Coronation of William III. and Mary II.* 1689.

Burnet, Gilbert. *A Sermon Preach'd before the Queen and the Two Houses of Parliament.* 1707.

Burnet, Gilbert. *Bishop Burnet's History of his own Time: with Notes by the Earls of Dartmouth and Hardwicke, Speaker Onslow, and Dean Swift.* 6 vols. Oxford: Oxford University Press, 1833.

Burridge, Richard. *The Consolation of Death* 1700.

Burridge, Richard. *A congratulatory poem, on the coronation of Queen Ann.* 1702.

By the Queen: A Proclamation of Indemnity. Edinburgh, 1703.

Cabala. 1653.

Calendar of State Papers, Domestic Series. Charles II (1660–85). 28 vols. 1860–1939.

Calendar of State Papers, Domestic Series. James II (1685–88). 3 vols. 1960–72.

Calendar of State Papers, Domestic Series. William and Mary (1688–1702). 11 vols. 1895–1937.

Calendar of State Papers, Domestic Series. Anne (1702–14). 2 vols. 1916–24. (Covering 1702–4 only).

Calendar of State Papers, Domestic Series. Descriptive List of Secretaries of State: State Papers Domestic, Anne. 3 vols. List and Index Society, vols. 258–260. 1995.

Calendar of the Stuart Papers Belonging to His Majesty the King. Mackie, 1902.

Calendar of Treasury Books. 32 vols. 1904–62.

Carew, Thomas. *The Poems of Thomas Carew.* Ed. Rhodes Dunlap. Oxford: Clarendon, 1949.

Cartwright, James J., ed. *The Wentworth Letters, 1705–1739.* Wyman & Sons, 1883.

Cartwright, Thomas. *A sermon preached at Holy-Rood House, January 30, 1681/2, before Her Highness the Lady Anne.* Edinburgh, 1682.

Cartwright, Thomas. *Diary of Thomas Cartwright.* Westminster: Camden Society, 1843.

Cavendish, Margaret. *Sociable Letters.* 1664.

Chamberlayne, Edward. *Angliæ Notitia: Or The Present State of England.* 1669, 1676, 1677, 1679, 1682, 1687, 1692, 1694, 1700.

Chapman, George. *The Iliads of Homer prince of poets.* 1611.

Chesnée, Jean Jacques Quesnot de la. *La Bataille de Ramelie ou les Glorieuses Conquestes des Alliez.* Ghent, 1706.

Chetwood, W. R. *A General History of the Stage.* 1749.

Chudleigh, Mary. *Poems on Several Occasions.* 1703.

The Church of England's address to the members of her communion. Especially to such as have laid down their offices at this critical juncture, or those that are inclinable to do it. 1704.

The Church of England's Joy on the Happy Accession of her Most Sacred Majesty. 1702.

Churchill, Sarah, Duchess of Marlborough. *An Account of the Conduct of the Duchess Dowager of Marlborough.* 1742.

Churchill, Sarah, Duchess of Marlborough. *Private Correspondence of Sarah, Duchess of Marlborough.* 2 vols. Henry Colburn, 1838.

Churchill, Sarah, Duchess of Marlborough. *Letters of Sarah, Duchess of Marlborough.* John Murray, 1875.

Clare, William. *A compleat system of grammar, English and Latin...Dedicated to his Highness the Duke of Gloucester.* 1699.

Clarke, J. S. *The Life of James the Second, Collected out of Memoirs writ of his own Hand.* 2 vols. Longman, Hurst, Rees, etc. 1816.

Claudian. *Claudian.* 2 vols. Cambridge, Mass.: Harvard University Press. 1922.

Clayton, Thomas. *Arsinoe, Queen of Cyprus, An Opera.* 1705.

Clayton, Thomas. *Songs in the new Opera call'd Rosamond.* 1707.

Clayton, Thomas. *The Passion of Sappho and the Feast of Alexander.* 1711.

Cocks, Richard. *The Parliamentary Diary of Sir Richard Cocks, 1698–1702.* Ed. D. W. Hayton. Oxford: Clarendon, 1996.

Coke, Roger. *A Detection of the Court and State of England...The fourth edition. Continued thro' the Reigns of King William and Queen Mary, and to the Death of Queen Anne.* 3 vols. 1719.

Cole, Christian. *Historical and Political Memoirs.* 1735.

Collier, Jeremy. *A Short View of the Immorality and Prophaneness of the English Stage.* 1698.

Congreve, William. *The Old Batchelor.* 1693.

Congreve, William. *The Mourning Bride.* 1697.

Congreve, William. *The Judgment of Paris.* 1701.

Congreve, William. *The Tears of Amaryllis for Amyntas. A Pastoral.* 1703.

Congreve, William. *Prologue to the Court; On the Queen's Birth-Day, 1704.* 1705.

Congreve, William. *The Works of Mr. William Congreve.* 1717.

Congreve, William. *William Congreve: Letters and Documents.* Ed. John C. Hodges. New York: Harcourt Brace and World, 1964.

Cooper, Anthony Ashley Third Earl of Shaftesbury. *Characteristicks*. 1711.

The Correspondence of the Spalding Gentlemen's Society 1710–1761. Ed. Diana and Michael Honeybone. Boydell and Brewer, 2010.

Covent-Garden Drolery. 1672.

Cowley, Abraham. *The Works of Mr. Abraham Cowley*. 1668.

[Croft, William.] *Divine Harmony, or a New Collection of Select Anthems*. 1712.

Croft, William. *Musica Sacra, or Select Anthems in Score*. 2 vols. 1724.

Croft, William. *Harmonia Sacra*. 1725.

Croft, William. *William Croft, Canticles and Anthems with Orchestra*. Ed. Donald Burrows. Stainer and Bell, 2011. Vol. 91 of *Musica Britannica*.

Crowne, John. *Calisto: or, The Chaste Nimph*. 1675.

Crowne, John. *The Prologue to Calistho* [sic], *With the Chorus's Between the Acts*. 1675.

Cunningham, Alexander. *The history of Great Britain: from the revolution in 1688, to the accession of George the First*. 2 vols. 1787.

Dalrymple, Sir John. *Memoirs of Great Britain*. 2 vols. 1771–88.

Danchin, Pierre, ed. *The Prologues and Epilogues of the Restoration, 1660–1700, Part III*. Nancy: Presses Universitaires de Nancy, 1985.

Danchin, Pierre, ed. *The Prologues and Epilogues of the Eighteenth Century, The First Part, 1701–1720*. Nancy: Presses Universitaires de Nancy, 1990.

D[arby], C[harles]. *The Union*. 1707.

Dawes, William. *A Sermon Preach'd before the Queen*. 1707.

The Declaration of James, Duke of Monmouth. 1685.

[Defoe, Daniel.] *The Succession to the Crown of England Considered*. 1701.

Defoe, Daniel. *An enquiry into the occasional conformity of Dissenters in cases of preferment with a preface to the Lord Mayor, occasioned by his carrying the sword to a conventicle*. 1698.

Defoe, Daniel. *The True-Born Englishman*. 1700.

Defoe, Daniel. *An enquiry into the occasional conformity of dissenters. In cases of preferment. With a preface to Mr. How*. 1701.

Defoe, Daniel. *A letter to Mr. How, By Way of reply to his Considerations of the preface to an Enquiry into the Occasional Conformity of Dissenters*. 1701.

Defoe, Daniel. *The Shortest-Way with the Dissenters: or Proposals for the Establishment of the Church*. 1702.

Defoe, Daniel. *A Hymn to Victory*. 1704.

Defoe, Daniel. *The Dyet of Poland*. 1705.

Defoe, Daniel. *Secret History of the White Staff, Part I*. 1714.

Defoe, Daniel. *Tour through the Whole Island of Great Britain*. 7th ed. 4 vols. 1769.

Defoe, Daniel. *The Letters of Daniel Defoe*. Ed. George Harris Healey. Oxford: Clarendon, 1955.

Delany, Mary. *The autobiography and correspondence of Mary Granville, Mrs. Delany*. 3 vols. R. Bentley, 1861.

Delaval, Elizabeth. *The Meditations of Lady Elizabeth Delaval, Written between 1662 and 1671*. Ed. Douglas G. Greene. *Publications of the Surtees Society*, vol. 190. Gateshead: Northumberland Press, 1978.

Deloney, Thomas. *Strange Histories, or Songs and Sonnets of Kinges, Princes, Dukes, Lords, Ladyes, Knights and Gentlemen*. 1612.

Dennis, John. *Reflections, Critical and Satyrical, upon a late Rhapsody, call'd An Essay upon Criticism*. 1711.

Dennis, John. *The Critical Works of John Dennis*. Ed. Edward Niles Hooker. 2 vols. Baltimore: Johns Hopkins Press, 1939–43.

Desiderius, Erasmus. *The Epistles of Erasmus.* Ed. Francis Morgan Nichols. 3 vols. Longmans, 1901.

Dove, Henry. *Albania.* 1695.

Downes, Edward. *Roscius Anglicanus.* Ed. Judith Milhous and Robert D. Hume. Society for Theatre Research, 1987.

Draghi, Giovanni Baptista. *"From Harmony, from Heav'nly Harmony."* Ed. Bryan White. Novello, 2010.

Dryden, John. *The Fourth Volume of the Works of Mr. John Dryden. Containing, A poem upon the death of O. Cromwell. Poem on the return of K. Charles II. On the coronation of K. Charles II. A poem on the L. Chancellor Hide. Annus mirabilis. Mack Flecknoe. Absalom and Achitophel. The medal, a poem. Religious laici [sic], a poem. Elegy on the death of K. Charles II. The hind and panther. Poem on the birth of the Prince. Eleonora.* 1695.

Dryden, John. *The Letters of John Dryden.* Ed. Charles E. Ward. Durham, N.C.: Duke University Press, 1942.

Dryden, John. *The Works of John Dryden.* Ed. Edward Niles Hooker, H. T. Swedenberg, et al. 20 vols. Berkeley: University of California Press, 1956–2000.

Duke, Richard. *Of the imitation of Christ.* 1703.

D'Urfey, Thomas. *Wonders in the Sun.* 1706.

D'Urfey, Thomas. *Pills to Purge Melancholy.* 2 vols. 1719.

D'Urfey, Thomas. *Songs Complete Pleasant and Divertive.* 1719.

The Earl of Shaftsbury's Expedient for Settling the Nation, Discoursed with His Majesty in the House of Peers at Oxford, March 24th 1680/1. 1681.

Eccles, John. *A Collection of Songs for One Two and Three Voices… Compos'd by Mr. John Eccles.* 1704.

Echard, Laurence. *The Roman history from the settlement of the empire by Augustus Caesar to the removal of the imperial seat by Constantine the Great… for the Use of His Highness the Duke of Gloucester.* 1698.

Elegia in praematurum obitum nobilissimi, & maximae spei adolescentis Johannis, marchionis de Blancford. 1703.

Ellis, G. A., ed. *The Ellis Correspondence.* 2 vols. Colburn, 1829.

England's Glory. 1706.

England's Royal Renown, in the Coronation. 1685.

England's Triumphs for the Prince of Wales. 1688.

The Establishment of the Church, The Preservation of the State. 1702.

Evelyn, John. *The Diary of John Evelyn.* Ed. E. S. De Beer. 6 vols. Oxford: Clarendon Press, 1955.

Exequiæ Desideratissimo Principi Gulielmo Glocestriæ Duci ab Oxoniensi Academia Solutæ. Oxford, 1700.

The fables of Pilpay, a famous Indian phylosopher containing many useful rules for the conduct of humane life… address'd to His Highness the Duke of Gloucester. 1699.

Fenton, Elijah, ed. *Oxford and Cambridge Miscellany Poems.* 1708.

Fiennes, Celia. *Through England on a Side Saddle.* Scribner and Welford, 1888.

Finch, Anne. *The Poems of Anne, Countess of Winchilsea.* Ed. Myra Reynolds. Chicago: University of Chicago Press, 1903.

Fleetwood, William. *A Sermon Preach'd before the Queen.* 1708.

Foley, Henry. *Records of the English Province of the Society of Jesus.* 7 vols. Burns and Oates, 1877–83.

The Form of the Intended Coronation Oath. 1688.

Foxcroft, H. C., ed. *A Supplement to Burnet's History of my own Time.* Oxford: Clarendon Press, 1832.

Freeman, Samuel. *A sermon preach'd at the funeral of His Grace William Duke of Bedford.* 1700.

Fuller, William. *La decouverte de la veritable mere du pretendu Prince de Galles, connüe par le nom de Marie Grey....Dedié au Duc de Glocester*. 1696.

Fuller, William. *Mr. Fuller's answer to the Jacobites*. 1700.

Fuller, William. *Mr. Fuller's letter to the Right Honourable the Lord Mayor*. 1700.

Fuller, William. *A trip to Hamshire and Flanders: discovering the vile intrigues of the priests and Jesuits*. 1701.

Fuller, William. *Fullers non-recantation to the Jacobites*. 1701.

Galliard, John Ernest. *Songs in the Opera of Calypso & Telemachus*. 1712.

The Garland of Good Will. 1631, 1678, 1685, 1688, 1690, 1700.

Garth, Samuel. *A Poem to the Earl of Godolphin*. 1710.

Gasparini, Francesco. *Songs in the Opera of Hamlet*. 1712.

Gay, John. *The Letters of John Gay*. Ed. C. F. Burgess. Oxford: Clarendon Press, 1966.

The Glorious Warrior. 1710.

Grant, John. *Deborah and Barak the Glorious Instruments of Israel's Deliverance*. 1704.

Great news from the other world; or a new dialogue between the Marquis de Guiscard, and William Gregg. 1711.

Griffin, Richard, Baron Braybrooke, ed. *The Private Correspondence of Jane Lady Cornwallis, 1613–1644*. S. & J. Bentley, Wilson & Fley, 1842.

Grimplot, Paul, ed. *Letters of William III. and Louis XIV. and their Ministers*. Longmans, 1848.

H., W. *Thura Britannica*. 1702.

Hamilton, Anthony. *Memoirs of the Life of Count de Grammont...., Translated from the French by Mr. [Abel] Boyer*. 1714.

Hamilton, David. *The Diary of Sir David Hamilton, 1709–1714*. Ed. Philip Roberts. Oxford: Clarendon, 1975.

Handel, George Frideric. *Ode for the Birthday of Queen Anne* (1713). Ed. Walther Siegmund-Schultze. Kassel: Bärenreiter, 1962. *Hallische Handel-Ausgabe*, ser. 1, vol. 6.

Handel, George Frideric. *Rinaldo* (1711). Ed. David R. B. Kimball. Kassel: Bärenreiter, 1993. *Hallische Handel-Ausgabe*, Series 2, vol. 4.

Handel, George Frideric. *Almira* (1705). Ed. Dorothea Schröder. Kassel: Bärenreiter, 1994. *Hallische Handel-Ausgabe*, Series 2, vol. 1.

Hawkins, Sir John. *A General History of the Science and Practice of Music*. 5 vols. 1776.

Hearne, Thomas. *Remarks and Collections*. Ed. C. E. Doble. 11 vols. Oxford: Oxford Historical Society, 1885–1921.

He's Wellcome Home. 1711.

Higgons, Beville. *A Short View of English History*. 1734.

Hill, Aaron. *Rinaldo*. 1711.

Hooper, George. *A Sermon Preach'd before Both Houses of Parliament, in the Cathedral Church of St. Paul's*. 1713.

Howe, John. *Some consideration of a preface to an enquiry, concerning the occasional conformity of dissenters*. 1701.

Hyde, Edward, First Earl of Clarendon. *The history of the rebellion and civil wars in England, Volume the second*. Oxford, 1703.

Hyde, Henry, Second Earl of Clarendon. *The Correspondence of Henry Hyde, Earl of Clarendon*. 2 vols. Colburn, 1828.

Hymenæus Cantabrigiensis. Cambridge, 1683.

Isaac, Mr. *The Union, A New Dance Compos'd by Mr. Isaac*. 1707.

Isaac, Mr. *The Godolphin. Mr. Isaac's New Dance, made for Her Majesty's Birthday, 1714*. 1714.

Jevon, Thomas. *The Devil of a Wife*. 1686.

Jones, Stephen, ed. *Biographia Dramatica*. 3 vols. Longman, Hurst, etc., 1812.

Jonson, Ben. *The Workes of Benjamin Jonson*. 1616.

Journals of the House of Commons.

Journals of the House of Lords.

Kennett, Basil. *Romae antiquae notitia*. 1696.

Kennett, Basil. *The lives and characters of the ancient Grecian poets dedicated to His Highness the Duke of Glocester*. 1697.

Kennett, White. *Glory to God, and Gratitude to Benefactors. A Sermon Preach'd before the Queen*. 1709.

[Kennett, White]. *A Visit to St. Saviour's*. 1710.

The King of France's Letter to the Cardinal de Noailles, Archbishop of Paris. 1712.

Lake, Edward. *Diary of Dr. Edward Lake*. Ed. George Percy Elliotte. Westminster: Camden Society, 1846.

Lauder, Sir John of Fountainhall. *Historical Observes of Memorable Occurrents*. Edinburgh, 1840.

Lee, Nathaniel. *The Works of Nathaniel Lee*. Ed. Thomas B. Stroup and Arthur L. Cooke. 2 vols. New Brunswick: Scarecrow Press, 1954.

Legg, J. William, ed. *Three Coronation Orders*. Henry Bradshaw Society, 1900.

Leibniz, Gottfried. *Die Werke von Leibniz gemäss seinem handschriftlichen Nachlasse in der Königlichen Bibliothek zu Hannover*. Ed. Onno Klopp. 11 vols. Hanover, 1864–84.

Leti, Gregorio. *Del Teatro Brittanico*. 2 vols. 1683.

Letter-Books of John Hervey, First Earl of Bristol. 3 vols. Wells: Ernest Jackson, 1894.

Leveridge, Richard. *Complete Songs*. Ed. Olive Baldwin and Thelma Wilson. Stainer and Bell, 1997.

Lewis, Jenkin. *Memoirs of Prince William Henry, Duke of Gloucester*. 1789.

Liberty, A Poem. 1705.

Lord, George deForest, ed. *Poems on Affairs of State*. 7 vols. New Haven: Yale University Press, 1963–75.

Lully, Jean-Baptiste. *Cadmus et Hermione... Partition Génerale*. Paris, 1719.

Luttrell, Narcissus. *A Brief Historical Relation of State Affairs, from September 1678 to April 1714*. 6 vols. Oxford: Oxford University Press, 1857.

Macky, John. *A Journey Through England*. 1714.

Macpherson, James. *Original Papers Containing the Secret History of Great Britain*. 2 vols. Dublin, 1775.

The male and female husband: or, A strange and wonderful relation how a midwife living at St. Albans, being brought to bed of an hermophrodite, brought it up in womans apparel, and carryed it with her as her deputy to be assisting at the labours of several women, going under the name of Mary Jewit: and how at last a discovery of it was made by it lying with a maid, and getting her with-child, whom the said hermophrodite was thereupon obliged to marry: with a particular account of the trades and imployments it was put to during its minority. With several pleasant passages that happened. To the tune of, What shall I do, shall I dye for love, & c. n.d. Wing M313.

Mancini, Francesco. *L'Idaspe fidele*. 1710.

Manley, Delarivier. *Secret Memoirs and Manners of Several Persons of Quality of Both Sexes, from the New Atalantis, an Island in the Mediterranean*. 1709.

Manley, Delarivier. *Memoirs of Europe, Towards the Close of the Eighth Century*. 1710.

Manningham, Thomas. *A Sermon Preach'd before the Queen*. 1709.

Mary, Queen of England. *Lettres et Mémoires de Marie Reine D'Angleterre*. Ed. Comtesse de Bentinck. La Haye: Nijhoff, 1880.

Mary, Queen of England. *Memoirs of Mary, Queen of England*. Ed. R. Doebner. Leipzig: Veit & Comp., 1886.

The Mausoleum. 1714.

The Memorial of the Church of England. 1705.

Maynwaring, Arthur. *Prologue for the musick, Spoken on Tuesday, January the 4th, 1703*. 1704.

Maynwaring, Arthur. *Four Letters to a Friend*. 1710.

Middleton, W. Knowles, ed. and trans. *Lorenzo Magalotti at the Court of Charles II*. Waterloo, Ontario: Wilfred Laurier University Press, 1980.

Milton, John. *Milton: Complete Poems and Major Prose*. Ed. Merritt Y. Hughes. Indianapolis: Bobbs-Merrill, 1957.

Misson, Henri. *Memoires et observations faites par un Voyageur en Angleterre*. Paris, 1698. Trans. John Ozell as *M. Misson's memoirs and observations in his travels over England*. 1719.

Morrice, Roger. *The Entring Book of Roger Morrice 1677–1691*. Ed. Mark Goldie. 6 vols. Woodbridge, England: Boydell Press, 2007.

Motteux, Peter. *Europe's Revels for the Peace, and His Majesties Happy Return, a Musical Interlude Performed at the Theatre in Little Lincolns-Inn-Fields*. 1697.

Motteux, Peter. *Words Sung at the Entertainment given by the Right Honorable Sir* Owen Buckingham, *Lord Mayor... Written by Mr* Motteux. *Set to Musick by Mr* Weldon. 1705.

Nicolson, William. *The London Diaries of William Nicolson, Bishop of Carlisle, 1702–1718*. Ed. Clyve Jones and Geoffrey Holmes. Oxford: Clarendon, 1985.

Pepys, Samuel. *The Tangier Papers of Samuel Pepys*. Ed. Edwin Chappell. Navy Records Society, 1935.

Pepys, Samuel. *The Diary of Samuel Pepys*. Ed. Robert Latham and William Matthews. 11 vols. Berkeley: University of California Press, 1970–83.

The Performances of the Antient Music for the Season 1781. 1781.

Philips, Ambrose. *Pastorals, Epistles, Odes*. 1648.

Philips, Ambrose. *Poetical Miscellanies*. London and Cambridge, 1697.

Philips, Ambrose. *The Distrest Mother*. 1712.

Philips, Ambrose. *The Poems of Ambrose Philips*. Ed. M. G. Segar. Oxford: Blackwell, 1937.

Philips, John. *Bleinheim*. 1705.

Philips, John. *The Poems of John Philips*. Ed. M. G. Lloyd Thomas. Oxford, 1927.

Philips, Katherine. *Poems by the most deservedly admired Mrs. Katherine Philips, the matchless Orinda*. 1667.

Pierreville, G[ideon]. *The Present State of Denmark*. 1683.

Pittis, William. *An epistolary poem to John Dryden, Esq. occasion'd by the much lamented death of the Right Honourable James, Earl of Abingdon*. 1699.

[Pittis, William]. *The Generous Muse*. 1701.

[Pittis, William]. *The Loyalist, a funeral poem in memory of William III*. 1702.

Pittis, William. *The Patriots*. 1702.

Pittis, William. *A Hymn to Neptune*. 1705.

Planché, J. R., ed. *Regal records or A chronicle of the coronations of the queens regnant of England*. Chapman and Hall, 1838.

Poems on affairs of state, from 1640 to this present year 1704. 1704.

Poetical Miscellanies. The Sixth Part. 1709.

Pope, Alexander. *The Twickenham Edition of the Works of Alexander Pope*. Ed. John Butt et al. Methuen, 1950–67.

Pope, Alexander. *The Correspondence of Alexander Pope*. Ed. George Sherburn. 5 vols. Oxford: Clarendon, 1956.

Pordage, Samuel. *Azaria and Hushai*. 1681.

Pratt, Samuel. *A Sermon Preach'd At the Savoy-Church on Wednesday the 19th of January, 1703/4*. 1704.

Prince Eugene's Welcome. 1712.

The Prince of Wales: a Poem. 1702.

Principi juventutis Gulielmo celsissimo Duci Glocestriæ præmaturâ morte abrepto Scholæ Westmonasteriensis alumni regii hæc carmina moerentes consecrant. 1700.

Prior, Matthew. *An Ode Humbly Inscrib'd to the Queen*. 1706.

Prior, Matthew. *Poems on Several Occasions*. 1707.

The Proceeding to the Coronation of their Majesties King William and Queen Mary … 11 April 1689. 1689.

Purcell, Henry. *An Opera Perform'd at Mr. Josiah Priest's Boarding-School at Chelsey. By Young Gentlewomen. The Words Made by Mr. Nat. Tate. The Musick Composed by Mr. Henry Purcell*. [1689].

Purcell, Henry. *A choice collection of lessons for the harpsichord or spinnet composed by ye late Mr. Henry Purcell*. 1696.

Purcell, Henry. *Orpheus Britannicus*. 1698.

Purcell, Henry. *The Music in King Arthur*. Ed. Margaret Laurie. Kent: Novello, 1972. In *The Works of Henry Purcell*, XXVI.

Purcell, Henry. *I was glad: anthem for the coronation of James II*. Ed. Bruce Wood. Kent: Novello, 1977.

Purcell, Henry. *Ode on St. Cecilia's Day 1692*. Ed. Peter Dennison. Kent: Novello, 1978. In *The Works of Henry Purcell*, VIII.

Purcell, Henry. *Secular Songs for Solo Voice*. Ed. Margaret Laurie. Kent: Novello, 1985. *The Works of Henry Purcell*, XXV.

Purcell, Henry. *A Song for the Duke of Gloucester's Birthday, 1695*. Ed. Ian Spink. Kent: Novello, 1990. *The Works of Henry Purcell*, IV.

Purcell, Henry. *Birthday Odes for Queen Mary*. Pt. 2. Ed. Bruce Wood. Kent: Novello, 1998. *The Works of Henry Purcell*, XXIV.

Purcell, Henry. *Royal Welcome Songs*. Pt. 1. Ed. Bruce Wood. Kent: Novello, 2000. *The Works of Henry Purcell*, XV.

Purcell, Henry. *Sacred Music, Part II: Nine Anthems with Strings*. Ed. Lionel Pike. Kent: Novello, 2003. *The Works of Henry Purcell*, XIV.

The Queen's and the Duke of Ormond's New Toast. 1712.

The Queen's Famous Progress. 1702.

Queries. 1710.

Raguenet, François. *Parallèle des Italiens et des Français*. Paris, 1705. Translated as *A Comparison between the French and Italian Musick*, with *A Critical Discourse on Opera's and Musick in England*. 1709.

Ravenscroft, Thomas. *The anatomist, or, The sham doctor written by Mr. Ravenscroft; with The loves of Mars and Venus, a play set to music, written by Mr. Motteux*. 1697.

Reports of the Historical Manuscripts Commission: III, VII, VIII, IX, XI, XII, Bath, Buccleuch, Downshire, Egmont, Hastings, Laing, Le Fleming, Ormonde, Portland, Rutland, Various Collections.

Reresby, John. *Memoirs of Sir John Reresby*. Ed. Andrew Browning. Rev. Mary K. Geiter and W. A. Speck. Royal Historical Society, 1991.

The Rights of King and subjects briefly stated: or, Considerations about the royal succession, submitted to the Commons of England in Parliament. 1701.

The Rival Dutchess; or, Court Incendiary in a Dialogue between Madam Maintenon, and Madam M[asham.] 1708.

Rossi, Giacomo. *L. C. Silla. Drama Per Musica.* 1713.

Rowe, Nicholas. *The Ambitious Step-Mother.* 1702.

The Royal Diary. 1705.

Russell, Rachel. *Letters of Rachel, Lady Russell.* Ed. John Lord Russell. 2 vols. Longman, Brown, Green, and Longmans, 1853.

Sacheverell, Henry. *The political union. A discourse shewing the dependance of government on religion in general: and of the English monarchy on the Church of England in particular.* Oxford, 1702.

Sacheverell, Henry. *The Speech of Henry Sacheverell.* 1710.

Sacheverell, Henry. *The Christian Triumph: Or, The Duty of Praying for our Enemies.* 1713.

Sandford, Francis. *The History of the Coronation of . . . James the Second.* 1687.

The Secret History of Queen Zarah. 1705.

Sedley, Charles. *The Poetical and Dramatic Works of Sir Charles Sedley.* Ed. Vivian de Sola Pinto. 2 vols. Constable, 1928.

Settle, Elkanah. *The Female Prelate.* 1680.

Settle, Elkanah. *Memoriæ Fragranti.* 1708.

Sharp, John. *A Sermon Preach'd at the Coronation of Queen Anne.* 1702.

Sheffield, John. *The Works of John Sheffield . . . Duke of Buckingham.* 2 vols. 1723.

Sherlock, Richard. *A Sermon Preach'd before the Queen.* 1704.

Simpson, Claude M., ed. *The British Broadside Ballad and its Music.* New Brunswick: Rutgers University Press, 1966.

Smith, Edmund. *Phædra and Hippolytus.* 1707.

Smith, Edmund. *Poem on the Death of Mr. John Philips.* 1710.

Somers, John. *The true secret history of the lives and reigns of all the kings and queens of England, from King William the first, called the Conqueror, to the end of the reign of the late Queen Anne.* 2nd ed. 2 vols. 1730.

Spanheim, Ezechiel. *Relation de la Cour de France.* Ed. Émile Bourgeois. Paris: Picard et Fils, 1900.

St. John, Henry Viscount Bolingbroke. *A letter to Sir William Windham.* 1753.

St. John, Henry Viscount Bolingbroke. *Letters and Correspondence of Bolingbroke.* Ed. Gilbert Parke. 4 vols. 1798.

Stampiglia, Silvio. *Camilla, Regina de' Volsci.* Venice, 1698.

Stanzani, Tommaso. *Arsinoe drama per musica da recitarsi nel Teatro di S. Angelo l'anno 1678.* Venice, 1678.

Stanhope, George. *A Sermon Preach'd before the Queen.* 1706.

Stanhope, George. *A Sermon Preached Before the Queen.* 1710.

Stanhope, Philip, Second Earl of Chesterfield. *Letters of Philip, Second Earl of Chesterfield.* E. Lloyd and Son, 1829.

Stanhope, Philip, Fourth Earl of Chesterfield. *The Letters of Philip Dormer Stanhope, Fourth Earl of Chesterfield.* Ed. Bonamy Dobrée. 6 vols. Eyre & Spottiswoode, 1932.

Stebbing, Samuel. *A genealogical history of the kings and queens of England, and monarchs of Great Britain, & c. . . . First publish'd to the beginning of King Charles the Second's reign, by Francis Sandford, Esq; Lancaster Herald of Arms: and continued to this time, . . . by Samuel Stebbing, Esq; Somerset Herald.* 1707.

Steele, Richard. *The Crisis.* 1714.

Steele, Richard. *Memoirs of . . . the Marquess of Wharton.* 1715.

Steele, Richard, et al. *The Tatler.* Ed. Donald F. Bond. 3 vols. Oxford: Clarendon, 1987.

Stradling, George. *A Sermon Preached before the King at White-Hall, January 30. 1674/5.* 1675.

[Swift, Jonathan.] *The Conduct of the Allies.* 1711.

[Swift, Jonathan.] *A New Journey to Paris, Together with some Secret Transactions between the Fr—h K—g, and an Eng—Gentleman. Translated from the French.* 1711.

[Swift, Jonathan]. *The Windsor Prophecy.* 1711.

Swift, Jonathan. *The Publick Spirit of the Whigs.* 2nd ed. 1714.

Swift, Jonathan. *An enquiry into the behaviour of the Queen's last ministry.* 1765.

Swift, Jonathan. *A Journal to Stella.* 1768.

Swift, Jonathan. *A Tale of a Tub.* Ed. A. C. Guthkelch and D. Nichol Smith. Oxford: Clarendon, 1920.

Swift, Jonathan. *The Correspondence of Jonathan Swift.* Ed. Harold Williams. 5 vols. Oxford: Clarendon, 1963.

Talbot, William. *A Sermon Preach'd before the Queen.* 1707.

Tate, Nahum. *An Ode upon the Assembling of the New Parliament.* 1702.

Tate, Nahum. *Portrait-Royal. A poem upon Her Majesty's picture set up in Guild-Hall; by order of the Lord Mayor and Court of Aldermen of the City of London.* 1703.

Tate, Nahum. *The song for New-Years-Day, 1703. Perform'd before Her Majesty. Set by Mr. Eccles, Master of her Majesty's Musick. The words by Mr. Tate, Poet Laureat to her Majesty.* 1703.

Tate, Nahum. *The Triumph.* 1705.

Tate, Nahum. *The song for New-Year's-Day, 1706. Perform'd to musick before Her Majesty, at St. James's.* 1706.

Tate, Nahum. *The Song for the New-Year 1708, Set by Mr. Eccles.* 1708.

Tate, Nahum. *The song for Her Majesty's birth-day, February the 6th, 17110/11* [sic]. *Set by Mr. Eccles, master of musick to Her Majesty, the words by Mr. Tate.* 1711.

Tate, Nahum. *A Congratulatory Poem.* 1714.

Thesaurus Musicus. Vol. 5. 1696.

Thibaudeau, A. W., ed. *The Bulstrode Papers.* Privately printed, 1897.

The third part of Miscellany poems. 1716.

Thirtieth Report of the Deputy Keeper of the Public Records. 1869.

Thompson, Edward Maunde, ed. *Correspondence of the Family of Hatton, Being Chiefly Letters Addressed to Christopher, First Viscount Hatton, 1601–1704.* 2 vols. Westminster: Camden Society, 1878.

Threnodia Academiæ Cantabriginesis in Immaturum Obitum Illustrissimi ac Desideratissimi Principi Gulielmi Ducis Glocestrensis. Cambridge, 1700.

Tickell, Thomas. *On the Prospect of Peace.* 1713.

Tilmouth, Michael, ed. *Dramatic Music, with the Music by Humfrey, Banister, Reggio and Hart for "The Tempest." Musica Britannica.* Vol. 51. Stainer and Bell, 1986.

Tindal, Nicholas. *The Continuation of Mr. Rapin de Thoyras's History of England, from the Revolution to the accession of King George II.* 4 vols. 1751.

To the Right Honourable Mr. Harley, Wounded by Guiscard. 1711.

The Traytor's Reward. 1708.

Trimnell, Charles. *A sermon preach'd before the Honourable House of Commons, at the Church of St. Margaret Westminster.* 1708.

The Tryal of William Viscount Stafford for High Treason. 1680/81.

The Tryal of William Viscount Stafford for High Treason. A Sermon Preach'd in the Cathedral Church of Norwich. 1704.

Turner, Francis. *A Sermon Preached before Their Majesties K. James II and Q. Mary at their Coronation.* 1685.

Tutchin, John. *The Foreigners.* 1700.

Vanbrugh, John. *The Provok'd Wife.* 1697.

Vanbrugh, John. *The Works of Sir John Vanbrugh.* Ed. Bonamy Dobrée and Geoffrey Webb. 4 vols. Nonesuch, 1927–28.

Verney, Margaret M., ed. *Memoirs of the Verney Family from the Restoration to the Revolution.* Longmans, Green, and Co., 1899.

Vernon, James. *Letters Illustrative of the Reign of William III.* 2 vols. Colburn, 1841.

Vertue, George. *Vertue Notebooks.* Vol. 6. Oxford: Oxford University Press, 1955.

Wall, Thomas. *An ode for an entertainment of musick on Her Majesty's birth-day, and, the success of Her Majesty's arms by sea and land. The night performance before Her Majesty at St. James's. The words by Mr. Wall. Set to musick by Mr. Abell.* 1703.

Walsh, John. *The SONGS and Symphonys Perform'd before Her MAJESTY…on her Birth Day.* 1703.

Ward, Edward. *Secret History of the Calves-Head Clubb.* 1703.

Warton, Joseph. *An Essay on the Writings and Genius of Pope.* 1756.

Weelkes, Thomas. *Balletts and madrigals to five voyces with one to 6. Voyces.* 1598.

Willis, Richard. *A Sermon Preach'd before the Queen.* 1705.

Wilmot, John, Earl of Rochester. *The Works of John Wilmot, Earl of Rochester.* Ed. Harold Love. Oxford: Oxford University Press, 1999.

Wilson, John Harold, ed. *Court Satires of the Restoration.* Columbus: Ohio State University Press, 1976.

Wright, John Michael. *An Account of his Excellence Roger Earl of Castlemaine's Embassy, From his Sacred Majesty James the IId.…To His Holiness Innocent XI.* 1688.

Zeno, Apostolo. *Hamlet, An Opera.* 1712.

Zimmerman, Franklin B., ed. *The Gostling Manuscript.* Austin: University of Texas Press, 1977.

Secondary Scholarship

Alsop, J. D. "The Quarrel between Sir John Vanbrugh and George Powell." *Restoration and Eighteenth Century Theatre Research,* n.s., 5 (1990): 28–29.

Alsop, J. D. "Victorian Scholarship and the Addison Manuscript." *Harvard Library Bulletin* 8 (1997): 49–62.

Andreadis, Harriette. *Sappho in Early Modern England.* Chicago: University of Chicago Press, 2001.

Andreadis, Harriette. "Re-configuring Early Modern Friendship: Katherine Philips and Homoerotic Desire." *Studies in English Literature* 46 (2006): 523–542.

Arber, Edward, ed. *The Term Catalogues, 1668–1709, With a Number for Easter Term, 1711 A.D. A Contemporary Bibliography of English Literature in the Reigns of Charles II, James II, William and Mary, and Anne.* 3 vols. Edward Arber, 1903/ 1905/ 1906.

Archer, Ian W. "City and Court Connected: The Material Dimensions of Royal Ceremonial, ca. 1480–1625." *Huntington Library Quarterly* 71 (2008): 157–179.

Ashbee, Andrew, and David Lasocki. *Biographical Dictionary of English Court Musicians, 1485–1714.* Aldershot: Ashgate, 1998.

Backscheider, Paula R. *Daniel Defoe: His Life.* Baltimore: Johns Hopkins University Press, 1989.

Backscheider, Paula R. *Spectacular Politics.* Baltimore: Johns Hopkins University Press, 1993.

Backscheider, Paula R. "Powell, George (1668?–1714)." In *Oxford Dictionary of National Biography.* Oxford: Oxford University Press, 2004.

Baird, John D. "Whig and Tory Panegyrics: Addison's *The Campaign* and Philips's Bleinheim Reconsidered." *Lumen* 26 (1997): 163–177.

Baldwin, Olive, and Thelma Wilson. "Who Can from Joy Refraine? Purcell's Birthday Song for the Duke of Gloucester." *Musical Times* 122 (1981): 596–599.

Baldwin, Olive, and Thelma Wilson. "Purcell's Knotting Song." *Musical Times* 128 (1987): 379–381.

Baldwin, Olive, and Thelma Wilson. "Clayton, Thomas." In *The New Grove Dictionary of Music and Musicians*. 2nd ed. Ed. Stanley Sadie. Macmillan, 2001.

Baldwin, Olive, and Thelma Wilson. "Elford, Richard (*bap.* 1677, *d.* 1714)." In *Oxford Dictionary of National Biography*. Oxford: Oxford University Press, 2004.

Baldwin, Olive, and Thelma Wilson. "*England's Glory* and the Celebrations at Court for Queen Anne's Birthday in 1706." *Theatre Notebook* 62 (2008): 7–19.

Baldwin, Olive, and Thelma Wilson. "Music in the Birthday Celebrations at Court in the Reign of Queen Anne: a Documentary Calendar." *A Handbook for Studies in 18th-Century English Music* 19 (2008): 1–24.

Baldwin, Olive, and Thelma Wilson. "Theatre Dancers at the Court of Queen Anne." *Court Historian* 15 (2010): 171–187.

Baldwin, Olive, and Thelma Wilson. "The Harmonious Unfortunate: New Light on Catherine Tofts." *Cambridge Opera Journal* 22 (2011): 217–234.

Baldwin, Olive, and Thelma Wilson. "The Subscription Music of 1703–04." *Musical Times* 153 (2012): 1–17.

Baldwin, Olive, and Thelma Wilson. "Handel, Eccles and the Birthday Celebrations for Queen Anne in 1711." *Musical Times* 154 (2013): 77–84.

Bapasola, Jeri. *Threads of History: The Tapestries at Blenheim Palace*. Oxford: Alden, 2005.

Barash, Carol. *English Women's Poetry, 1649–1714*. Oxford: Clarendon Press, 1996.

Barclay, Andrew. "The Rise of Edward Colman." *Historical Journal* 42 (1999): 109–131.

Barclay, Andrew. "Sedley, Catharine, Suo Jure Countess of Dorchester, and Countess of Portmore (1657–1717)." In *Oxford Dictionary of National Biography*. Oxford: Oxford University Press, 2004.

Barker, G. F. Russell. *The Record of Old Westminsters*. Chiswick Press, 1928.

Barlow, Frank. "Pont l'Évêque, Roger de (*c.*1115–1181)." In *Oxford Dictionary of National Biography*. Oxford: Oxford University Press, 2004.

Barlow, Graham. "Vanbrugh's Queen's Theatre in the Haymarket, 1703–9." *Early Music* 17 (1989): 515–521.

Barnard, John. "Dryden, Tonson, and the Patrons of *The Works of Virgil* (1697)." In *John Dryden: Tercentenary Essays*. Ed. Paul Hammond and David Hopkins. Oxford: Oxford University Press, 2000. 174–239.

Beal, Peter. *In Praise of Scribes*. Oxford: Clarendon Press, 1998.

Bennett, G. V. "Robert Harley, the Godolphin Ministry, and the Bishoprics Crisis of 1707." *English Historical Review*, 82 (1967): 726–746.

Berry, Mary, ed. *Some Account of the Life of Rachael Wriothesley, Lady Russell*. Longman, Hurst, Rees, Orme and Brown, 1820.

Bevan, Bryan. *Nell Gwyn*. Robert Hale, 1969.

Bloxam, John Rouse. *Magdalen College and King James II, 1686–1688*. Oxford: Oxford Historical Society, 1886.

Bolton, A. T., and H. D. Hendry, eds. *The Royal Palaces of Winchester, Whitehall, Kensington, and St. James's*. Oxford: Wren Society, 1930.

Bond, Richmond Pugh. *Queen Anne's American Kings*. Oxford: Clarendon, 1952.

Boswell (Murrie), Eleanor. *The Restoration Court Stage, with a Particular Account of the Production of Calisto*. Cambridge, Mass.: Harvard University Press, 1932.

Brett, Cécile. "Antonio Verrio (c1636–1707): His Career and Surviving Work." *British Art Journal* 10 (2009–10): 4–17.

Brown, Elizabeth C. D. "Announcement Regarding the 'Princess an Lutebook.'" *Lute Society of America Quarterly* 43:3 (September 2008): 38.

Bucholz, R. O. *The Augustan Court: Queen Anne and the Decline of Court Culture*. Stanford: Stanford University Press, 1993.

Bucholz, R. O. "The 'Stomach of a Queen,' or Size Matters: Gender, Body Image, and the Historical Reputation of Queen Anne." In *Queens and Power in Medieval and Early Modern England*. Ed. Carole Levin and Robert Bucholz. Lincoln: University of Nebraska Press, 2009. 242–272.

Burrows, Donald. "Handel and Hanover." In *Bach, Handel, Scarlatti: Tercentenary Essays*. Ed. Peter Williams. Cambridge: Cambridge University Press, 1985. 35–59.

Burrows, Donald. "Orchestras in the New Cathedral." In *St. Paul's: The Cathedral Church of London, 604–2004*. Ed. Derek Keene et al. New Haven: Yale University Press, 2004. 399–402.

Burrows, Donald. *Handel and the English Chapel Royal*. Oxford: Oxford University Press, 2005.

Buttrey, John. "New Light on Robert Cambert in London, and His *Ballet et Musique*." *Early Music* 23 (1995): 199–220.

Cameron, W. J. "Ten New Poems by Ambrose Philips (1674–1749)." *Notes and Queries* 102 (1957): 469–470.

Campbell, John. *The Lives of the Lord Chancellors*. John Murray, 1846.

Cartwright, Julia Mary. *Madame: A Life of Henrietta, Daughter of Charles I*. Seeley, 1900.

Chandler, David G. *Marlborough as Military Commander*. New York: Scribner, 1973.

Childs, John. "Belasyse, Sir Henry (1648–1717)." In *Oxford Dictionary of National Biography*. Oxford: Oxford University Press, 2004.

Chisholm, Duncan. "Handel's 'Lucio Cornelio Silla': Its Problems and Context." *Early Music* 14 (1986): 64–70.

Churchill, Winston. *Marlborough; His Life and Times*. New ed. 2 vols. Chicago: University of Chicago Press, 2002.

Coleridge, H. J. *St. Mary's Convent, Micklegate Bar, York*. Burns and Oates, 1887.

Collins Baker, C. H. "Notes on Pictures in the Royal Collections—XXIV—Anne Killigrew." *Burlington Magazine* 28 (1915): 112–116.

Connell, Neville. *Anne: The Last Stuart Monarch*. Butterworth, 1937.

Cornwall, Robert D. "Birch, Peter (1651/2–1710)." In *Oxford Dictionary of National Biography*. Oxford: Oxford University Press, 2004.

Corp, Edward T. "The Exiled Court of James II and James III: A Centre of Italian Music in France, 1689–1712." *Journal of the Royal Musical Association* 120 (1995): 216–231.

Coxe, William. *Memoirs of John, Duke of Marlborough*. Longman, Hurst, Rees, Orme and Brown, 1918.

Dasent, Arthur Irwin. *The History of St. James's Square*. MacMillan, 1895.

Davies, Kenneth Gordon. *The Royal African Company*. New York: Octagon Books, 1975.

Dean, Winton, and John Merrill Knapp. *Handel's Operas, 1704–1726*. Oxford: Clarendon Press, 1987.

de Jongh, Eddy. "Pearls of Virtue and Pearls of Vice." *Simiolus* 8 (1975–76): 69–97.

Donoghue, Emma. "Imagined More Than Women: Lesbians as Hermaphrodites, 1671–1766." *Women's History Review* 2 (1993): 199–216.

Downes, Kerry. *Sir John Vanbrugh*. Sidgwick and Jackson, 1987.

Downie, J. A. "Arthur Maynwaring and the Authorship of the *Advice to the Electors of Great Britain*: Some Additional Evidence." *British Journal for Eighteenth-Century Studies* 2 (1979): 163–166.

Downie, J. A. *Robert Harley and the Press*. Cambridge: Cambridge University Press, 1979.

Downie, J. A. "Tutchin, John (1660x64–1707)." In *Oxford Dictionary of National Biography*. Oxford: Oxford University Press, 2004.

Downie, J. A. "What If Delarivier Manley Did *Not* Write *The Secret History of Queen Zarah*?" *Library* 5 (2004): 247–264.

Drukker, Tamar. "Thirty-Three Murderous Sisters: A Pre-Trojan Foundation Myth in the Middle English Prose *Brut* Chronicle." *Review of English Studies* 54 (2003): 449–463.

Duffy, Maureen. *The Passionate Shepherdess*. Cape, 1977.

Duffy, Maureen. *Henry Purcell*. Fourth Estate, 1994.

Ellison, Julie. *Cato's Tears*. Chicago: University of Chicago Press, 1999.

English Army Lists and Commission Registers, 1661–1704, vol. IV, 1694–1702. Eyre and Spottiswoode, 1898.

Field, Ophelia. *The Kit-Cat Club: Friends Who Imagined a Nation*. HarperCollins, 2008.

Fisher, Joseph. "The History of Landholding in Ireland." *Transactions of the Royal Historical Society* 5 (1877): 228–326.

Fiske, Roger. *English Theatre Music in the Eighteenth Century*. 2nd ed. Oxford: Oxford University Press, 1986.

Foxon, D. F. "The Stamp Act of 1712." Sandars Lecture for 1978. Typescript. British Library, London, Ac. 2660.m (32).

Foxon, D. F. *English Verse 1701–1750: A Catalogue of Separately Printed Poem*. 2 vols. British Library, 2003.

Freeman, Andrew. "Organs Built for the Royal Palace of Whitehall." *Musical Times* 52 (1911): 521–523; 585–587.

Freeman, Robert. "Apostolo Zeno's Reform of the Libretto." *Journal of the American Musicological Society* 21 (1968): 321–341.

Frey, Linda, and Marsha Frey, eds. *The Treaties of the War of the Spanish Succession: An Historical and Critical Dictionary*. Westport, Conn.; Greenwood, 1995.

Fritz, Paul S. "From 'Public' to 'Private': The Royal Funeral in England, 1500–1830." In *Studies in the Social History of Death*. Ed. Joachim Whaley. Europa, 1981. 61–79.

Gamez, Luis R. "Mocking the Meat It Feeds On: Representing Sarah Churchill's Hystericks in Addison's *Rosamond*." *Comparative Drama* 29 (1995): 270–285.

Garrett, Jane. *The Triumphs of Providence*. Cambridge: Cambridge University Press, 1980.

Gibson, John S. *Playing the Scottish Card: The Franco-Jacobite Invasion of 1708*. Edinburgh: Edinburgh University Press, 1988.

Goff, Moira. *The Incomparable Hester Santlow*. Aldershot: Ashgate, 2007.

Govier, Mark. "The Royal Society, Slavery, and the Island of Jamaica: 1660–1700." *Notes and Records of the Royal Society* 53 (1999): 203–217.

Green, David B. *Gardener to Queen Anne: Henry Wise and the Formal Garden*. Oxford: Oxford University Press, 1956.

Green, David B. *Queen Anne*. Collins, 1970.

Gregg, Edward. "Was Queen Anne a Jacobite?" *History* 62 (1972): 358–375.

Gregg, Edward. *Queen Anne*. Routledge and Kegan Paul, 1980.

Grew, Edwin, and Marion Sharpe Grew. *The Court of William III*. Mills and Boon, 1910.

Griffith, R. H. *Alexander Pope: A Bibliography*. 2 vols. Austin: University of Texas Press, 1922; 1927.

Guerrini, Anita. "Gregory, David (1659–1708)." In *Oxford Dictionary of National Biography*. Oxford: Oxford University Press, 2004.

Haile, Martin. *Queen Mary of Modena: Her Life and Letters*. J. M. Dent, 1905.

Hair, P. E. H., and Robin Law. "The English in Africa to 1700." In *The Origins of Empire*. Ed. Nicholas Canny. Oxford: Oxford University Press, 1998. 241–263.

Haley, K. H. D. *The First Earl of Shaftesbury*. Oxford: Clarendon Press, 1968.

Hall, Kim F. *Things of Darkness: Economies of Race and Gender in Early Modern England*. Ithaca: Cornell University Press, 1995.

Hammond, Brean. "Joseph Addison's Opera *Rosamond:* Britishness in the Early Eighteenth Century." *ELH* 73 (2006): 601–629.

Hammond, Paul. "Dryden's *Albion and Albanius:* The Apotheosis of Charles II." In *The Court Masque.* Ed. David Lindley. Manchester: Manchester University Press, 1984. 169–183.

Handley, Stuart. "Talbot, Charles, Duke of Shrewsbury (1660–1718)." In *Oxford Dictionary of National Biography.* Oxford: Oxford University Press, 2004.

Hanham, A. A. "FitzRoy, Charles, Second Duke of Grafton (1683–1757)." In *Oxford Dictionary of National Biography.* Oxford: Oxford University Press, 2004.

Harris, Frances. "Accounts of the Conduct of Sarah, Duchess of Marlborough, 1704–1742." *British Library Journal* (1982): 7–35.

Harris, Frances. *A Passion for Government: The Life of Sarah, Duchess of Marlborough.* Oxford: Clarendon Press, 1991.

Harris, Frances. *Transformations of Love.* Oxford: Oxford University Press, 2002.

Harris, Frances. "Masham [née Hill], Abigail, Lady Masham (1670?–1734)." In *Oxford Dictionary of National Biography.* Oxford: Oxford University Press, 2004.

Harris, Tim. "Scott [Crofts], James, Duke of Monmouth and First Duke of Buccleuch (1649–1685)." In *Oxford Dictionary of National Biography.* Oxford: Oxford University Press, 2004.

Hattendorf, John B. "Shovell, Sir Cloudesley (*bap.* 1650, *d.* 1707)." In *Oxford Dictionary of National Biography.* Oxford: Oxford University Press, 2004.

Hatton, Ragnhild. *George I, Elector and King.* Cambridge, Mass.: Harvard University Press, 1978.

Hayton, David W., Eveline Cruickshanks, and Stuart Handley, eds. *The History of Parliament: the House of Commons 1690–1715.* 5 vols. Cambridge: Cambridge University Press, 2002.

Herman, Ruth. "Dark Deeds at Night." In *Queer People.* Ed. Chris Mounsey and Caroline Gonda. Lewisburg: Bucknell University Press, 2007. 195–209.

Holman, Peter. "Grabu, Luis." In *The New Grove Dictionary of Music and Musicians.* 2nd ed. Ed. Stanley Sadie. Macmillan, 2001.

Holman, Peter. "Keller, J. Gottfried." In *The New Grove Dictionary of Music and Musicians.* 2nd ed. Ed. Stanley Sadie. Macmillan, 2001.

Holmes, G. E. F., and F. F. Holmes. "William Henry, Duke of Gloucester (1689–1700), Son of Queen Anne (1665–1714), Could Have Ruled Great Britain." *Journal of Medical Biography* 16 (2008): 44–51.

Holmes, G. S., and W. A. Speck. "The Fall of Harley in 1708 Reconsidered." *English Historical Review* 80 (1965): 673–698.

Holmes, Geoffrey. "The Great Ministry." Unpublished thesis. n.d. On deposit at Institute of Historical Research, University of London.

Holmes, Geoffrey. *The Trial of Doctor Sacheverell.* Eyre Methuen, 1973.

Holmes, Geoffrey. *British Politics in the Age of Anne.* Hambledon, 1987.

Hook, Judith. *The Baroque Age in England.* Thames and Hudson, 1976.

Horn, Robert D. *Marlborough: A Survey.* Folkestone: Garland, 1975.

Horwitz, Henry. *Revolution Politicks: The Career of Daniel Finch, Second Earl of Nottingham, 1647–1730.* Cambridge: Cambridge University Press, 1968.

Horwitz, Henry. *Parliament, Policy and Politics in the Reign of William III.* Manchester: Manchester University Press, 1977.

Hudson, Richard, and Meredith Ellis Little. "Sarabande." In *The New Grove Dictionary of Music and Musicians.* 2nd ed. Ed. Stanley Sadie. Macmillan, 2001.

Hume, Robert D. "Jeremy Collier and the Future of the London Theater in 1698." *Studies in Philology* 96 (1999): 480–511.

Hume, Robert D. "The Economics of Culture in London, 1660–1740." *Huntington Library Quarterly* 69 (2006): 487–533.

Hunter, David. "Handel among the Jacobites." *Music and Letters* 82 (2001): 543–556.

Hutton, R. "The Making of the Secret Treaty of Dover." *Historical Journal* 29 (1986): 297–318.

Hutton, Ronald. *Charles the Second*. Oxford: Clarendon Press, 1989.

Johnstone, H. Diack. "Clarke, Jeremiah (1673 x 5–1707)." In *Oxford Dictionary of National Biography*. Oxford: Oxford University Press, 2004.

Jones, Clyve. "Robert Harley and the Myth of the Golden Thread: Family Piety, Journalism and the History of the Assassination Attempt of 8 March 1711." *Electronic British Library Journal* (2010), article 11.

Jones, Peter. "Antoine de Guiscard, 'Abbe de la Bourlie,' 'Marquis de Guiscard.'" *British Library Journal* 8 (1982): 94–113.

Kamen, Henry. "The Destruction of the Spanish Silver Fleet at Vigo in 1702." *Bulletin of the Institute of Historical Research* 39 (1966): 165–173.

Keay, Anna *The Magnificent Monarch*. Continuum, 2008.

Kenyon, J. P. *The Popish Plot*. New York: St. Martin's Press, 1972.

Klopp, Onno. *Der Fall des Hauses Stuart und die Succession des Hauses Hannover in Gross-Britannien und Irland*. 14 vols. Vienna, 1875–88.

Knight, H. R. *Historical Records of the Buffs, East Kent Regiment, 3rd Foot, formerly designated the Holland Regiment and Prince George of Denmark's Regiment*. Vol. 1. 1572–1704. Gale and Polden, 1905.

Lawrence, W. J. "The French Opera in London: A Riddle of 1686." *Times Literary Supplement* (March 28, 1936): 268.

Lee, Maurice, Jr. *The Heiresses of Buccleuch*. East Lothian: Tuckwell Press, 1996.

Lindgren, Lowell. "I Trionfi di Camilla." *Studi Musicali* 6 (1977): 89–160.

Love, Harold. "The Wreck of the *Gloucester*." *Musical Times* 125 (1984): 194–195.

Lowerre, Kathryn. *Music and Musicians on the London Stage, 1695–1705*. Farnham, Surrey: Ashgate, 2009.

Mabbett, Margaret. "Italian Musicians in Restoration England. 1660–90." *Music and Letters* 67 (1986): 237–247.

Macinnes, Allan I. *Union and Empire*. Cambridge: Cambridge University Press, 2007.

Marshall, Ashley. "The Myth of Scriblerus." *Journal for Eighteenth-Century Studies* 31 (2008): 77–99.

Marshall, Ashley. "The Generic Context of Defoe's *The Shortest-Way with the Dissenters* and the Problem of Irony." *Review of English Studies* 61 (2010): 234–258.

McGeary, Thomas. "Thomas Clayton and the Introduction of Italian Opera to England." *Philological Quarterly* 77 (1998): 171–185.

McGuinness, Rosamond. *English Court Odes, 1660–1820*. Oxford: Clarendon Press, 1971.

McLeod, A. L. "The Douai Ms. of Lee's 'Mithridates.'" *Notes and Queries*, n.s., 7 (1960): 69–70.

McTague, John. "'There Is No Such Man as Isaack Bickerstaff': Partridge, Pittis, and Jonathan Swift." *Eighteenth-Century Life* 35 (2011): 83–101.

Menefee, Samuel Pyeatt. "Green, Thomas (1679/80–1705)." In *Oxford Dictionary of National Biography*. Oxford: Oxford University Press, 2004.

Milhous, Judith. "Heidegger, Johann Jakob (1666–1749)." In *Oxford Dictionary of National Biography*. Oxford: Oxford University Press, 2004.

Milhous, Judith, and Robert D. Hume. *Vice-Chamberlain Coke's Theatrical Papers, 1706–1715*. Carbondale: Southern Illinois University Press, 1982.

Milhous, Judith, and Robert D. Hume, eds. *A Register of English Theatrical Documents, 1660–1737*. Carbondale: Southern Illinois University Press, 1991.

Milhous, Judith, and Robert D. Hume, comps. and eds. *The London Stage 1660–1800, Part 2: 1700–1729. Draft of the Calendar for Volume I, 1700–1711*. Available at Professor Hume's website: www.personal.psu.edu/users/h/b/hb1/London%20Stage%202001.

Millar, Oliver. *The Tudor, Stuart, and Early Georgian Pictures in the Collection of Her Majesty the Queen*. Phaidon, 1963.

Miner, Earl. "Dryden's Messianic Eclogue." *Review of English Studies* 11(1960): 299–301.

Murphy, Estelle. "The Fashioning of a Nation: The Court Ode in the Late Stuart Period." Ph.D. diss., National University of Ireland, Cork, 2011.

Neman, Beth S. "Crowne, John. *bap.* 1641, *d.* 1712." In *Oxford Dictionary of National Biography*. Oxford: Oxford University Press, 2004.

The New Grove Dictionary of Music and Musicians. 2nd ed. Ed. Stanley Sadie. Macmillan, 2001.

Novak, Maximillian. *Daniel Defoe, Master of Fictions*. New York: Oxford University Press. 2001.

Ogg, David. *England in the Reign of Charles II*. 2 vols. Oxford: Clarendon Press, 1934; rev. ed. 1955.

Onnekink, David. *The Anglo-Dutch Favourite: The Career of Hans Willem Bentinck, 1st Earl of Portland (1649–1709)*. Farnham, Surrey: Ashgate, 2007.

Orihel, Michele. "'Treacherous Memories' of Regicide: The Calves-Head Club in the Age of Anne." *Historian* 73 (2011): 435–462.

Oxford Dictionary of National Biography. Oxford: Oxford University Press, 2004.

Pellicer, Juan Christian. "John Philips, 1676–1709: Life, Works and Reception." Ph.D. diss, University of Oslo, 2002.

Pellicer, Juan Christian. "Harleian Georgic from Tonson's Press: The Publication of John Philips's *Cyder*, 29 January 1708." *Library* 7 (2006): 185–198.

Pincus, Steve. *1688: The First Modern Revolution*. New Haven: Yale University Press, 2009.

Pinnock, Andrew. "*Deus ex machina*: A Royal Witness to the Court Origin of Purcell's *Dido and Aeneas*." *Early Music* 40 (2012): 265–278.

Piper, David. *A Catalogue of the Seventeenth-Century Portraits in the National Portrait Gallery*. Cambridge: Cambridge University Press, 1963.

Plank, S. E. "Monmouth in Italy: *L'Ambitione Debellata*." *Musical Times* 132 (1991): 280–284.

Price, Curtis. "English Traditions in Handel's *Rinaldo*." In *Handel Tercentenary Collection*. Ed. Stanley Sadie and Anthony Hicks. London: Royal Musical Association, 1987. 120–135.

Price, Curtis. "Political Allegory in Late Seventeenth-Century English Opera." In *Music and Theatre: Essays in Honour of Winton Dean*. Ed. Nigel Fortune. Cambridge: Cambridge University Press, 1987. 1–29.

Price, Curtis A., and Robert D. Hume, eds. *The Island Princess: British Library Add. MS 15318*. Tunbridge Wells: R. Macnutt, 1985.

Range, Matthias. *Music and Ceremonial at British Coronations from James I to Elizabeth II*. Cambridge: Cambridge University Press, 2012.

Roberts, David. *The Ladies*. Oxford: Clarendon Press, 1989.

Roberts, Jane. *Royal Landscape: The Gardens and Parks of Windsor*. New Haven: Yale University Press, 1997.

Rogers, Pat. "Addison, Joseph (1672–1719)." In *Oxford Dictionary of National Biography*. Oxford: Oxford University Press, 2004.

Rogers, Pat. *The Symbolic Design of "Windsor-Forest."* Newark: University of Delaware Press, 2004.

Rogers, Pat. *Pope and the Destiny of the Stuarts*. Oxford: Oxford University Press, 2005.

Rowles, Emilia, Marchesa Campana de Cavelli. *Les Derniers Stuarts*. 2 vols. Paris: Didier, 1871.

Rustici, Craig M. "Gender, Disguise, and Usurpation: 'The Female Prelate' and the Popish Successor." *Modern Philology* 98 (2000): 271–298.

Shaw, Watkins. "Staggins, Nicholas." In *The New Grove Dictionary of Music and Musicians*. 2nd ed. Ed. Stanley Sadie. Macmillan, 2001.

Shaw, Watkins, et al. "Clarke, Jeremiah (i)." In *The New Grove Dictionary of Music and Musicians*. 2nd ed. Ed. Stanley Sadie. Macmillan, 2001.

Sheppard, Edgar. *Memorials of St. James's Palace*. 2 vols. Longmans, Green, and Co., 1894.

Sheppard, F. H. W., ed. *Survey of London: Volumes 29 and 30: St James Westminster. Part 1*. English Heritage, 1960.

Smith, Florence M. *Mary Astell*. New York: Columbia University Press, 1916.

Snyder, Henry L. "Daniel Defoe, the Duchess of Marlborough, and the 'Advice to the Electors of Great Britain.'" *Huntington Library Quarterly* 29 (1965): 53–62.

Snyder, Henry L. "The Duke of Marlborough's Request of his Captain-Generalcy for Life: A Re-examination." *Journal of the Society for Army Historical Research* 45 (1967): 67–83.

Snyder, Henry L. "The Last Days of Queen Anne: The Account of Sir John Evelyn Examined." *Huntington Library Quarterly* 34 (1971): 261–276.

Snyder, Henry L. "Prologues and Epilogues of Arthur Maynwaring." *Philological Quarterly* 50 (1971): 610–619.

Snyder, Henry L., ed. *The Marlborough-Godolphin Correspondence*. 3 vols. Oxford: Clarendon, 1975.

Speck, W. A. *Tory & Whig: The Struggle in the Constituencies, 1701–1715*. London: Macmillan, 1970.

Speck, W. A. "Hyde, Laurence, First Earl of Rochester (*bap.* 1642, *d.* 1711)." In *Oxford Dictionary of National Biography*. Oxford: Oxford University Press, 2004.

Stater, Victor. "Grenville, John, First Earl of Bath (1628–1701)." In *Oxford Dictionary of National Biography*. Oxford: Oxford University Press, 2004.

Stewart, J. Douglas. *Sir Godfrey Kneller*. National Portrait Gallery, 1971.

Stewart, J. Douglas. "Closterman, John (1660–1711)." In *Oxford Dictionary of National Biography*. Oxford: Oxford University Press, 2004.

Strickland, Agnes. *Lives of the Queens of England*. 8 vols. Bell, 1885.

Strizich, Robert, "Corbetta, Francesco." In *The New Grove Dictionary of Music and Musicians*. 2nd ed. Ed. Stanley Sadie. Macmillan, 2001.

Stuart, David, and Greg Skidmore. "Cavalli's *Erismena*." *Early Music* 38 (2010): 482–483.

Sundstrom, Roy A. *Sidney Godolphin, Servant of the State*. Newark: University of Delaware Press, 1992.

Taylor, David A. H. B. "A Rediscovered Portrait of Queen Anne, When a Child, by Sir Peter Lely." *Burlington Magazine* 145 (2003): 501–504.

Taylor, Thomas J. *Thematic Catalog of the Works of Jeremiah Clarke*. Detroit Studies in Music Bibliography, no. 35. Detroit: Information Coordinators, 1977.

Teague, Frances. "Queen Elizabeth in Her Speeches." In *Gloriana's Face*. Ed. S. P. Cerasano and Marion Wynne-Davies. Detroit: Wayne State University Press, 1992. 63–78.

Tempest, Norton Robert. *The Rhythm of English Prose*. Cambridge: Cambridge University Press, 1930.

Thorp, Jennifer, and Ken Pierce. "Three English Chaconnes of the Early Eighteenth Century." *Dance History* 3 (1994): 3–16.

Tilmouth, Michael. "Calendar of References to Music in Newspapers Published in London and the Provinces, 1660–1719." *R.M.A. Research Chronicle* 1 (1961): II–VII, 1–107.

Tomko, Linda J. "Issues of Nation in Isaac's 'The Union.'" *Dance Research* 15 (1997): 99–125.

Toynbee, Margaret. "A Further Note on an Early Correspondence of Queen Mary of Modena." *Notes and Queries* 193 (1948): 292–295.

Traub, Valerie. *The Renaissance of Lesbianism in Early Modern England*. Cambridge: Cambridge University Press, 2002.

Trevelyan, G. M. "The 'Jersey' Period of the Negotiations Leading to the Peace of Utrecht." *English Historical Review* 49 (1934): 100–105.

Trevelyan, George Macaulay. *England under Queen Anne.* 3 vols. Longmans, Green, and Co., 1930–34.

Tuppen, Sandra. "Shrovetide Dancing: Balls and Masques at Whitehall under Charles II." *Court Historian* 15 (2010): 157–169.

van Lennep, William. "The Smock Alley Players of Dublin." *ELH* 13 (1946): 216–222.

van Lennep, William, ed. *The London Stage, 1660–1800.* Pt. 1. *1660–1700.* Carbondale: Southern Illinois University Press, 1965.

Veevers, Erica. *Images of Love and Religion: Queen Henrietta Maria and Court Entertainments.* Cambridge: Cambridge University Press, 1989.

von Maltzahn, Nicholas. "The War in Heaven and the Miltonic Sublime." In *A Nation Transformed: England after the Restoration.* Ed. Alan Houston and Steve Pincus. Cambridge: Cambridge University Press, 2001. 154–179.

Wahl, Elizabeth Susan. *Invisible Relations: Representations of Female Intimacy in the Age of Enlightenment.* Stanford: Stanford University Press, 1999.

Walford, Edward. *Old and New London.* Vol. 6. *The Southern Suburbs.* Cassell, 1893.

Walkling, Andrew. "Masque and Politics at the Restoration Court: John Crowne's 'Calisto.'" *Early Music* 24 (1996): 27–74.

Walkling, Andrew. "Court, Culture, and Politics in Restoration England: Charles II, James II, and the Performance of Baroque Monarchy." Ph.D. diss., Cornell University, 1997.

Webb, Stephen Saunders. *Lord Churchill's Coup.* New York: Knopf, 1995.

Weil, Rachel. *Political Passions.* Manchester: University of Manchester Press, 1999.

Weinbrot, Howard D. "The Thirtieth of January Sermon: Swift, Johnson, Sterne, and the Evolution of Culture." *Eighteenth-Century Life* 34 (2009): 29–55.

Westfall, Richard S. "Newton, Sir Isaac (1642–1727)." In *Oxford Dictionary of National Biography.* Oxford: Oxford University Press, 2004.

White, Bryan. "Music for a 'Brave Livlylike Boy': The Duke of Gloucester, Purcell, and 'The Noise of Foreign Wars.'" *Musical Times* 148 (2007): 75–83.

White, Bryan. "Letter from Aleppo: Dating the Chelsea School Performance of Dido and Aeneas." *Early Music* 37 (2009): 417–428.

White, Eric Walter. *A History of English Opera.* Faber, 1983.

Williams, Abigail. *Poetry and the Creation of a Whig Literary Culture, 1681–1714.* Oxford: Oxford University Press, 2005.

Wilson, John Harold. *A Rake and His Times.* New York: Farrar, Straus, and Young, 1954.

Wilson, John Harold. "Theatre Notes from the Newdigate Newsletters." *Theatre Notebook* 15 (1961): 79–84.

Wilson, John Harold. "More Theatre Notes from the Newdigate Newsletters." *Theatre Notebook* 16 (1962): 59.

Wing, Donald. *A Short-Title Catalogue of Books Printed in England, Scotland, Ireland, Wales, and British America and of the English Books Printed in Other Countries, 1641–1700,* 2nd ed., rev. and enl. 3 vols. New York: Index Committee of the Modern Language Association of America, 1972–88.

Winn, James A. *John Dryden and His World.* New Haven: Yale University Press, 1987.

Winn, James A. *"When Beauty Fires the Blood": Love and the Arts in the Age of Dryden.* Ann Arbor: University of Michigan Press, 1992.

Winn, James A. "Heroic Song: A Proposal for a Revised History of English Theatre and Opera, 1656–1711." *Eighteenth-Century Studies* 30 (1997): 113–137.

Winn, James A. "Dryden and Dorset in 1692: A New Record." *Philological Quarterly* 85 (2006): 391–397.

Winn, James A. "John Dryden, Court Theatricals, and the 'Epilogue to the Faithfull Shepheardess.'" *Restoration* 32 (2008): 45–54.

Winn, James A. *The Poetry of War*. Cambridge: Cambridge University Press, 2008.

Winn, James A. "Style and Politics in the Philips-Handel Ode for Queen Anne's Birthday, 1713." *Music and Letters* 89 (2008): 547–561.

Winn, James A. "'A Versifying Maid of Honour': Anne Finch and the Libretto for *Venus and Adonis*," *Review of English Studies* n.s., 59 (2008): 67–85.

Wood, Bruce. "John Blow's Anthems with Orchestra." 5 vols. Ph.D. diss., University of Cambridge, 1976.

Wood, Bruce. "A Coronation Anthem Lost and Found." *Musical Times* 118 (1977): 466–468.

Wood, Bruce. *Purcell: An Extraordinary Life*. ABRSM, 2009.

Wynne, S. M. "Myddelton, Jane. *bap.* 1646, *d.* 1692." In *Oxford Dictionary of National Biography*. Oxford: Oxford University Press, 2004.

Wynne, S. M. "Palmer, Barbara, Countess of Castlemaine and *Suo Jure* Duchess of Cleveland. *bap.* 1640, *d.* 1709." In *Oxford Dictionary of National Biography*. Oxford: Oxford University Press, 2004.

Zook, Melinda. "The Shocking Death of Mary II: Gender and Political Crisis in Late Stuart England." *British Scholar* 1 (2008): 21–36.

Zwicker, Steven. *Politics and Language in Dryden's Poetry: The Arts of Disguise*. Princeton: Princeton University Press, 1984.

INDEX

Main entries for aristocrats are under their family names, with cross-references to their titles.
QA=Queen Anne; SM=Sarah Churchill, Duchess of Marlborough.

Abell, John, 324

Act for the Encouragement of Learning
(Statute of Anne), 522

Act of Security (Scotland), 349, 352

Act of Settlement (1701), 102, 244, 263–64,
270, 298

Act of Toleration (1689), 297, 318, 335

Addison, Joseph: Harley's attempted coup, 464;
loss of positions, 536; mythology, 106,
387; on opera, 442, 446, 448–89, 552,
589; Steele's defense, 630; Whig beliefs,
384, 560–61

—appointments: Commissioner of Appeals,
383; secretary to Halifax, 430; secretary
to regents, 634; secretary to Wharton,
489; Undersecretary of State, 408

—social relations: with Dryden, 382; with
Kit-Cats, 332; with Ambrose Philips, 247;
with Sacheverell, 382; with Swift, 608

—Works: *The Campaign*, 382–89, 447, 478,
591; *Cato*, 610–14; Latin poem to Halifax,

382; *Letter from Italy*, 416; prologue to
Phædra and Hippolytus, 448; *Rosamond*
(with Clayton), 400, 441–45, 471, 569;
Spectator, 388–89, 536, 552, 557, 559–61,
601, 610; on fame, 576–78; on "Pleasures
of the Imagination," 334, 589–91; *Tatler*,
500; *Whig Examiner*, 536

Advice to the Q＿＿n (anon.), 527

Aire, siege of, 539

Albemarle. *See* Keppel, Arnold Joost van

Almanza, Battle of, 450, 463, 540

Almenara, Battle of, 537–40

Ambleto (pasticcio), 584

Ames, Richard, 196

Anderton, William, 169–70

Anne, Queen of Great Britain and Ireland:
As Princess:
—artistic activities: allusion to Cowley, 176;
attendance at concerts and the theatre,
114, 136, 173, 211, 214, 233, 235; dancing
lessons, 2, 73; dramatic performances, 8,

Anne, Queen of Great Britain (*Continued*)
63–69, 82–83; letter praising Blandford's
dancing, 240; musical studies, 10, 44, 73,
185; organ moved to St. James's Church,
181; subscriber to Dryden's *Virgil*, 219–22
—personal life: alleged robbery victim, 175;
contribution to poor Vaudois, 209; court
as Princess, 84; critical of Maria Beatrice,
126; denied permission to visit Mary, 127;
disdain for Catholicism, 75, 104; dowries
for SM's daughters, 237, 242; exposure to
libertine court, 7; Gloucester's birthday
ball, 211; godmother of second Duke of
Grafton, 92; gracious to Burnett, 228;
"hysterical pregnancies," 130, 191; jealousy
of SM's friendship with Barbara Berkeley,
151, 154, 158, 476; letter to Lady Apsley
from Brussels, 69; letters to Frances
Bathurst, 67, 75, 83; letters to Mary
Cornwallis, 62, 75; letters on Gloucester,
149; opinion of William as a monster, 163,
178, 268, 273; pregnancies, 94–96, 122–24,
128–30, 138, 149, 151, 154, 171–74, 191,
210–11, 221, 226–27, 239–42, 259, 271;
prevented from going to Brussels, 63;
proof of Bathurst's dishonesty, 239;
uncomfortable dissembling, 168; visit to
Brussels, 69; visit to France, 7; visit to
Mary in Holland, 60; visit to Scotland, 58,
82–83; visit to Tunbridge, 172, 177;
wedding, 43–49; 51–57
—politics and the court: additional pension
to SM, 154; alleged letter to James II,
270; hostess for William's birthdays, 211,
225–27, 240–41; interest in courtly
protocol, 6; Irish lands, 223–26; letter to
French court on Gloucester's death, 210;
letter to Godolphin on mourning, 273;
letter to Maria, 168; letters to Mary on
James II, 101, 127; letter to SM on
Sedgemoor, 117; letter to William on
Namur, 193; letter to William promising
support, 169; order forbidding fireworks
after Namur, 193; at Oxford with an
army, 135; popularity, 160; quarrels with
Mary, 155–60, 170–78, 180–84; request

for Garter for Marlborough, 173; return
to St. James's after death of Mary, 194;
skepticism about Maria Beatrice's
pregnancy, 130; support for Revolution,
98, 101
As Queen:
—artistic activities: arrangement of text for
Thanksgiving anthem, 478–79; as Britannia,
308, 317; concerts for, 253; coronation
medal, 290; as Deborah, 312–16, 329,
348, 367; French opera on Ramellies,
374; interest in Thanksgiving liturgy, 313;
monetary support for Haymarket theatre
(?), 391; as Pallas Athena, 290, 309, 374,
393; payments to Elizabeth Dryden, 222;
prayer for Thanksgiving service, 507;
quotation from Cowley, 337; quotation
from Lee's *Sophonisba*, 412, 466; rewards
for actors at court, 284
—personal life: autopsy, 599; complaints
about SM to Godolphin, 379; death, 634;
dispatches physicians to care for
Blandford, 330; efforts to conceive, 244,
350; illnesses, 554, 622; lease to SM, 482;
letter to SM at Margate, 295–97; letters to
SM on Blandford's death, 332; at Abigail
Masham's wedding, 451; private grant to
Marlboroughs, 318; quarrels with SM,
451–52, 473–78, 479–84, 491, 505, 509–10,
522–23; uneasiness in heavy clothes, 481;
will, 599
—politics and the court : addresses to
Parliament, 252, 255, 286, 297, 300, 319,
335, 354, 375, 414, 541, 570, 572, 573,
586, 609, 618, 627; address to Scottish
Parliament, 406; alleged concern for the
Pretender, 468; appointments to House
of Lords, 342; appropriates Whig
rhetoric, 433; arrears to William's
servants, 256; attends House of Lords,
383, 436; choice of bishops, 457; control
of ecclesiastical appointments, 284;
coronation, 250, 286–92, 347–48;
creation of new peers, 579; declaration of
war, 295; desire for freedom from parties,
407, 432; diplomatic correspondence on

George's death, 486; dukedom for Marlborough, 318; forbids duel between Marlborough and Poulett, 586; funeral, 597–99; grant of Woodstock to Marlborough, 397; letter to Dutch on peace terms, 592; letter to George I, 631; letter to Godolphin on sacking Sunderland, 529; letter to Joseph I, 544; letter to Marlborough on Blenheim, 375; letter to SM on politics, 302; letter to Scottish Privy Council, 345; letter to Sunderland, 408; proclamation of indemnity, 348; proclamations against vice, 283; progress to Newmarket and Cambridge, 402; replies to Parliamentary addresses, 468, 490, 510, 633; resentment of Dutch letter, 530; rewards to Daniel Parke, 367; touching for "King's Evil," 251; visit to Oxford, 251–54

Anne-Marie d'Orléans, Duchess of Savoy, QA's cousin, 7, 261, 263, 344

Anne of Denmark, consort of James I, 25, 89

Anne Sophia, daughter of QA, 123, 126

anti-Catholic demonstrations, 71, 74–75, 569, 624

Antioco (pasticcio), 579

Apsley, Frances. *See* Bathurst, Frances

Apsley, Frances Petre, 70

Arbuthnot, John, 433, 451, 627

Archer, Thomas, 555

Architecture, 6, 26, 341, 392, 398, 441, 447, 473, 503, 555; *See also* Archer, Thomas; Hawksmoor, Nicholas; Vanbrugh, Sir John; Wren, Sir Christopher

Argyll. *See* Campbell, Archibald

Arondeaux, Regnier, 117

"Article 37," 504, 518, 568

Arundell, Henry, Third Baron Arundell, 62, 125

Arwaker, Edmund, 397

Asiento. *See* Slave trade

"Associations," 208, 222

Astell, Mary: *Serious Proposal to the Ladies*, 187–88

Athlone. *See* Ginkel, Godart de

Atterbury, Francis, Bishop of Rochester, 599

Augusta, allegorical figure, 12, 20, 23, 109, 110, 388, 628

Aylesbury, 398

Aylesbury, Earls of. *See* Finch, Heneage; Finch, Heneage, Jr.

Ayloffe, William, 54, 403

Bamber, Thomas, 181

Bank of England, 498, 530, 554

Banquet of Musick, The, 158

Barbier, Jane, 513, 588

Barcelona, siege of, 428

Barlow, Joel, 366

Barrier Treaty, 497, 503, 505, 540, 583, 585

Barry, Elizabeth, 63, 78, 212, 360

Bataille de Ramelie, La, 374

Bath: Elizabeth I's visit to, 250; QA's visits to, 130, 149, 156, 181, 249–51, 259, 299, 342, 350–52, 486

Bathurst, Allen, 140, 204, 239, 522

Bathurst, Benjamin, 89, 239, 364

Bathurst, Benjamin, Jr., 194

Bathurst, Frances Apsley, 29–37, 40, 52, 62–63, 87, 239

Bathurst, Peter, 140, 239

Battel of Audenarde, The (anon.), 478

Beachy Head, naval battle, 172

Bedford, Duke of. *See* Russell, William

Bedford, Earl of. *See* Russell, Wriothesley

Behn, Aphra: crypto-Catholic, 104; poem on birth of James Francis Edward, 132–34; *Poem on the Coronation*, 104–07; theatre songs, 234

Belasyse, Henry, 192

Belasyse, John, 125

Bennet, Henry, Earl of Arlington, 14

Bentinck, Jane Temple, Lady Portland, 296

Bentinck, Hans Willem, first Earl of Portland: alleged lover of William III, 158, 163, 209, 267; displaced as ranger of Windsor Great Park, 266, 296; impeached, 265, 342; QA's hostility toward, 266, 296, 342; superintendent of gardens, 297; and Treaty of Ryswick, 208, 228

Berkeley House, 175, 181–83

Berkeley, Barbara Villiers, Viscountess
    Fitzharding ("Loupa"): death, 483, 487;
    escape from Whitehall with QA, 101, 135;
    friend of SM, 151; gossip at court, 153,
    474; governess to QA's children, 123, 153,
    225; lampooned as lesbian, 476;
    messenger from QA to Mary, 175
Berkeley, George, 608, 610, 613, 621
Berkeley, John, Viscount Fitzharding, 89, 101, 153
Bertie, James, first Earl of Abingdon, 274
Berwick. See FitzJames, James
Béthune, siege of, 537
Betterton, Thomas: in All for Love, 360; benefit
    for, 501; in Don Sebastian, 164–67; fined
    for immoral expressions, 284; new theatre
    company, 230; and opera, 107, 425;
    petition to QA, 284; retirement from
    management, 392
Bible, 50, 80, 95, 98–99, 291, 309, 312–13, 316,
    329, 348, 425, 479, 539, 572
Birch, Peter, 181
Birch, Thomas, 468
Blackall, Offspring, Bishop of Exeter, 453–59,
    463, 480
Blackmore, Richard, 518
Blandford. See Churchill, John, Jr.
Blagge. See Godolphin, Margaret
Blenheim, Battle of: 305, 310, 312, 317, 366, 466;
    captured standards on parade, 395; poems
    on, 375, 382–90; prologue by Congreve, 402
Blenheim Palace: 397, 442, 541, 555, 577; in
    Rosamond, 441; tapestries, 518–19
Blount, Charles: Appeal from the Country to the
    City, 78
Blow, John: anthems, 49, 287, 305, 311–12, 449;
    "The Nymphs of the Wells," 214, 220, 242,
    256; ode for QA's birthday, 242; Venus
    and Adonis, 105, 108
Bolingbroke. See St. John, Henry
Bolton. See Paulet, Charles
Bonn, siege of, 352
Bononcini, Giovanni: Camilla, 369, 373, 400,
    426–28, 497; Thomyris, 442
Booth, Barton, 613–14
Boscawen, Hugh, 140, 229
Boschi, Gioseppe, 545

Bothmar, Hans Kaspar, Baron von, 569
Bouchain: siege of, 567
Boufflers, Louis François, duc de Boufflers,
    208, 228
Boyer, Abel, 137, 148–49, 253, 294, 324, 357,
    395, 579, 608, 623
Boyne, Battle of, 142, 172
Bracegirdle, Anne, 333
Brady, Nicholas, 343
Bridges, Ralph, 502–03
Brihuega, Battle of, 541, 544
Briscoe, Samuel, 232
Britannia, allegorical figure, 389, 575, 604, 628
Bromley, William, 414, 520, 530, 619
Brydges, James, Duke of Chandos, 575
Buckhurst. See Sackville, Charles
Buckley, Samuel, 496
Burgess, Daniel, 438
Burnet, Gilbert, Bishop of Salisbury: and
    Astell, 188; attacked in Parliament, 241;
    Harley's attempted coup, 464; opposition
    to occasional conformity bill, 321–22;
    preceptor to Gloucester, 201, 203, 207–08,
    227, 238; relief for poor clergy, 361;
    sermons, 99, 434; and QA, 256, 281, 322,
    619; and Catherine Tofts, 359
Burnet, Gilbert, Jr., 230, 396
Burnet, William, 206, 218
Burridge, Richard: The Consolation of Death, 244
Butler, Charlotte, 26
Butler, James, second Duke of Ormond:
    befriended by Prince Eugene, 579;
    campaign of, 1712, 584; Lord Lieutenant
    of Ireland, 536; marine commander in
    Spain, 300; pictured on fan, 520; praised
    by Tories, 317; "restraining order," 585,
    591, 626; supporter of Haymarket project,
    341; at Thanksgiving for Blenheim, 306;
    wounds Guiscard, 553
Butler, Mary Somerset, Duchess of Ormond,
    598–99
Buys, Willem, 569
Byng, Admiral George, 467–69

cadences (prose), 438–40, 454
Calves-Head Club, 354

Cambert, Robert, 18, 24

Cambridge University: poems on birth of James Francis Edward, 132; poems on death of Gloucester, 203–06; poems on QA's wedding, 52–54, 57; QA's visit to, 402–04

Campbell, Archibald, Ninth Earl of Argyll, 115–16

Campden House, 139, 175, 184, 193

Canada: invasion of, 499, 524, 539, 554, 567

canopies: in Banqueting House, 138; in *Calisto*, 25; at coronation of James II, 91; at coronation of QA, 287, 292; at coronation of William and Mary, 98; at funeral of QA, 598

Capel, Algernon, second Earl of Essex, 256, 509

Carlos II, King of Spain, 236, 265

Carmarthen. *See* Osborne, Thomas

Cartwright, Thomas, Bishop of Chester, 83, 129, 163

Castlecomer. *See* Wandesford, Christopher

Castlemaine. *See* Palmer, Barbara; Palmer, Roger

Catharine of Braganza, Queen of England, 15–16, 29, 135

Catherine Laura, daughter of Maria Beatrice, 60

Catherine, daughter of Anne Hyde, 7

Cavalli, Francesco: *L'Erismena*, 18

Cavendish, Margaret, Duchess of Newcastle, 3

Cavendish, William, first Duke of Devonshire: opposition to occasional conformity bill, 341; patron of art and music, 341, 355, 403, 418; and Revolution, 134–35; supporter of Marlborough, 295

Cavendish, William, Marquess of Hartington and second Duke of Devonshire: and Harley's attempted coup, 457, 461, 466; replaced, 535

Chamberlayne, Edward, 13

Chapel Royal, 118, 155–56, 430–31, 513–14

Charles I, King of England, QA's grandfather, 5, 11, 13, 103, 347

Charles II, King of England, QA's uncle: crypto-Catholic, 14; death, 92, 108; duplicitous policies, 16; illness, 69; libertinism, 2, 22, 27–28, 106; love of arts, 10, 14, 103; opinion of Prince George, 89; promotes African trade, 15; public dining, 13; at QA's wedding, 43; Royal Oak, 215, 255; Rye House plot, 49; Secret Treaty of Dover, 4, 14; speech lessons for QA, 63

Charles III, "King of Spain." *See* Charles VI

Charles VI, Holy Roman Emperor, 406, 428, 433, 497; in Barcelona, 413; division of forces, 450; First Partition Treaty, 237; in Madrid, 538–39; in Portugal, 344; succession, 556; trade agreement favorable to Britain, 462; visit to England, 356–58

Charles, son of Maria Beatrice, 60

Charlotte Maria, daughter of Maria Beatrice, 84–85

Chesterfield. *See* Stanhope, Philip

Christian V, King of Denmark, 47, 148, 240

Christina, Queen of Sweden, 121

Church of England: 284, 620–21; church government, 298; "in danger," 319–21, 414–15; and James II, 95, 97, 101, 127; new churches in London, 555; QA's love for, 15, 39, 62, 181, 287, 298, 302, 335; and Revolution, 102–05

Church of Ireland, 464, 536

Church of Scotland, 298, 345

Churchill, Arabella, mistress of James II, 10, 28, 62, 69, 107, 384, 450

Churchill, Charles, 89, 192

Churchill, George, 294, 404, 456, 488

Churchill, John, Duke of Marlborough: at Blandford's deathbed, 331; courtship of Sarah Jenyns, 10; criticized by Mary, 172; imprisoned, 180; at Lord Mayor's dinner, 395; lover of Castlemaine, 10; marriage, 62; at QA's coronation, 287; at Thanksgiving service, 411; wreck of the *Gloucester*, 84

—and the arts: in Addison's *Campaign*, 383, 387, 390; attacked by Swift, 570; in John Philips's *Bleinheim*, 387; lampooned by Manley, 529; letter to George I re Handel, 589; as Mars in D'Urfey's dialogue, 433; portraits by Kneller, 431, 575; represented in Handel's *Silla*, 615; tapestries, 366, 518, 572; in Tate's *Portrait-Royal*, 328; theatrical politics, 461

Churchill, John, Duke (*Continued*)
—military career: befriends Prince Eugene,
345, 579–80; Blenheim, 305, 316, 366;
campaign of 1702, 250, 299; campaign of
1703, 352; campaign of 1704, 365;
Captain-General, 293; crosses *ne plus
ultra*, 567; dismissed, 574; Grand
Alliance, 268; investigated by House of
Commons, 574; Irish campaign, 172–73;
Line of Brabant, 409; Malplaquet, 504;
opposes Monmouth's rebellion, 116;
Oudenarde, 474; proponent of land war,
254, 294; Ramillies, 428; Schellenberg,
365; siege of Bonn, 336; trip to Hanover,
469; visit to Charles III, 344; visits to
England during War of the Spanish
Succession, 390, 421, 433, 544, 569, 599
—Political career: correspondence with
Godolphin, 268 *et passim*; defection to
William, 101, 135, 166; defense of
MacCartney, 499; departure to
Continent, 594; disloyalty to James II,
166, 169; dismissed by William, 174;
debate on restraining order, 585;
interactions with Harley, 460–64;
plenipotentiary, 518; secret
communications with France, 496;
support for Revolution, 134; suspected
correspondence with exiled court, 174,
180; testimony to House of Lords on
Spain, 461; withdrawal from London, 509
—rewards: annual pension, 318; arrears,
620; lodgings in St. James's, 194; made
Duke, 301, 318; made Earl, 97; Order of
the Garter, 282; Parliamentary grant
extended to heirs, 397
—Relationship with QA: advice about
bishoprics, 456; concern about her public
image, 271, 273, 277; draft treaty shared
with her, 268; enjoined from dueling, 586;
Governor to Gloucester, 201, 203, 208, 227,
238; objections to removal of Sunderland,
528; offer to resign, 466; pension for Prince
George, 318; request for life appointment,
498, 505, 526; trip to Denmark, 89; use of
Albemarle as intermediary, 239

Churchill, John, Jr., Lord Blandford, 204–06,
230, 240, 330–32
Churchill, Sarah Jenyns, Duchess of
Marlborough: Godolphin's affection for,
339; hair, 334; in Holland, 269; imagined
pregnancy, 335–36; impatience with
mourning, 488; jealousy of Abigail
Masham, 451, 456, 475, 482, 543; letters
from Annabella Howard, 476; maid of
honor, 9; marriage, 62; mourning for
Blandford, 332–38, 404; opinions of QA,
97, 406, 485; ranger of Windsor Great
Park, 266, 296; return to England, 599;
support for her indigent cousin Abigail,
229; withdrawals from Privy Purse, 469,
482, 542–44; Woodstock horse race, 413
—and the arts: allusion to Dryden-
Davenant *Tempest*, 524; attends theatre
after Revolution, 136; attacked by Swift,
542; in *Calisto*, 9; cornerstone of London
house, 503; dedicatee of *Rosamond*, 441;
desire to demolish ruins at Woodstock,
447; interest in music and opera, 473,
491; lampooned by Manley, 503, 506; in
Mithridates (?), 83; reading in history and
philosophy, 187; slandered in *Secret
History*, 412; support for Defoe, 379
—political activities and opinions: given
credit for Cowper's appointment, 413;
intervention in Parliamentary election,
413; support for Revolution, 134–37;
Whig partisan, 95, 136, 302, 317, 322, 334,
338, 339, 378, 414, 554
—relations with QA: 69–71, 82, 88–89,
123–25, 151–54, 174–75, 237–39, 306,
336–38, 378–79, 466, 469, 480–82, 485,
522–23
—Works (with Maynwaring): *Advice to the
Electors of Great Britain*, 470; *A New
Ballad, To the Tune of Fair Rosamond*,
471–73, 476, 543
Cifeccio. *See* Grossi
Civil List, monarch's income from, 228–29,
241, 285, 297
Clarke, Jeremiah: anthems, 292, 409, 430, 449;
The Island Princess, 235; "Let Nature

Smile," 258–61; New Year's ode, 411, 418;
ode in praise of Marlborough, 434
Claudian (Claudius Claudianus), 21, 24
Clayton, Thomas: 399, 490; Works: *Arsinoe,
Queen of Cyprus*, 369, 391, 399–400;
Rosamond, 442–45
Closterman, John, portraits by: 185, 325, 333
Clotilda (pasticcio), 497
Coke, Thomas, Vice-Chamberlain, 474
Colbert, Jean-Baptiste, Marquis de Torcy,
502–04, 540–41, 556, 567–68, 580, 583,
592–93
"Cold and Raw" (anon.): 157–60; 180
Collier, Jeremy: *Short View of the Immorality and
Profaneness of the English Stage*, 232–34
Collier, William, 507–08, 545, 551–52
Colman, Edward, 60
Colt, Sir Henry Dutton, 489
Compton, Henry, Bishop of London: death, 619;
forced to alter Chapel Royal service by
Mary, 155; at Gloucester's funeral, 203;
and St. James's Church, 181; sermons,
192, 525; spiritual advisor to QA, 15;
visits to QA after George's death, 488
—Officiant: at christenings, 92, 95, 148; at
coronation of William and Mary, 97; at
QA's wedding, 43
—Political actions: dismissed by James II, 118;
invitation to William, 134; Privy Council,
294; in Revolution 101, 135
Congreve, William: attacked by Collier, 232;
charged by Grand Jury, 232; and Harriet
Godolphin, 332, 401; Kit-Cat, 332; reply
to Collier, 232; resignation from theatre
management, 425; theatrical license from
QA, 392; Works: *The Double Dealer*, 232;
The Judgment of Paris, 263, 427; *Love for
Love*, 212, 501; *The Mourning Bride*, 212,
333; ode on Ramillies, 431; *The Old
Bachelor*, 184, 212; prologue for *Arsinoe*,
400; *The Tears of Amaryllis*, 332–34
Cooper, Anthony Ashley, first Earl of
Shaftesbury, 69–74, 80–83, 89
Cooper, Anthony Ashley, third Earl of
Shaftesbury, 465, 561–63
Corbetta, Francesco, 10

Corelli, Arcangelo, 121
Corneille, Pierre, 34
Cornwallis, Cicely, 61
Cornwallis, Katherine, 61
Cornwallis, Mary, 61, 63, 79, 87
Cotterell, Sir Charles, 34
"Country Whigs," 224, 258, 265
Coventry, Henry, 4
Cowley, Abraham, 176–77, 186, 337
Cowper, Mary Clavering, Countess Cowper, 472
Cowper, Sarah, 616
Cowper, William, 413, 427, 449, 466, 535
Craggs, James, 634
Crew, Nathaniel, Bishop of Durham, 123
Croft, William, 492, 635; on Elford, 259; Italian
influence on, 513; QA's funeral, 598–99;
teacher of Anastasia Robinson, 513;
Works: anthems, 315, 449, 478, 492–96,
507, 539, 617; ode for QA's birthday, 623;
Te Deum and *Jubilate Deo*, 491, 539
Croker, John, 291
Cromwell, Oliver, 11, 354, 386
Crowne, John, attends Harvard, 8; possible
author of birthday ode for Gloucester,
141; Works: *Caligula*, 233; *Calisto*, 1–41,
108–09, 388, 422, 604–06

d'Adda, Count Ferdinando, 119, 129, 131, 135
Dahl, Michael, 185, 563
Dalkeith. *See* Scott, James
Danby. *See* Osborne, Thomas
Dance, 1–3, 11–13, 72–73, 99, 122, 211, 225–26,
238, 240, 250, 369, 436, 546, 623;
See also Gohory, Jeremiah; Isaac, Mr.
Darby, Charles, 449
Dartmouth. *See* Legge, William
d'Aumont de Rochebaron, Louis, duc
d'Aumont, 615–16
Davenant, Charles: *Circe*, 108, 151
Davenant, Sir William: *The Tempest* (with
Dryden), 108, 523
Davis, Mary (Moll), 11, 22, 27
Dawes, William, Bishop of Chester, 455–59,
480, 463
de l'Epine, Margherita, 341–42, 357–59, 423,
448, 497, 553, 584, 588

de Ruvigny, Henri, Earl of Galway, 450, 461
de Villars, Claude Louis Hector, 450, 504, 592
Deborah: in Anne Finch's "Introduction," 317;
        in Symson's poem to QA, 348; in Tate's
        Portrait-Royal, 329; Song of, 312–16, 367
Declarations of Indulgence: Charles II, 17;
        James II, 127–30
Defoe, Daniel, 322, 329, 332, 354, 376, 415,
        433, 626, 632; Works: *The Double
        Welcome*, 379; *The Dyet of Poland*, 376;
        *Enquiry into the occasional conformity of
        Dissenters*, 319; *Hymn to Victory*, 376; *The
        Shortest-Way with the Dissenters*, 320–21;
        *The Succession to the Crown of England
        Considered*, 261–63; *The True-Born
        Englishman*, 267
Delany, Mary Granville, 559
Dennis, John, *Rinaldo and Armida* (with
        Eccles), 235
Derby, Countess of. *See* Stanley, Elizabeth Butler
Dering, Charles, 497
Derry, siege of, 148
Dieupart, Charles, 277, 391
Dillon, Isabella Boynton, Countess of
        Roscommon, 123
Dissenters: establishment of schools, 354, 364,
        632; James II's Indulgence of, 128–29,
        133; mob violence against, 438;
        occasional conformity, 319–22, 377;
        opposition to vice, 283; political
        opposition, 12, 51, 353; support for
        Monmouth, 115, 116, 262
Dives, Annabella. *See* Howard, Annabella
Dorset Garden Theatre, 200
Douai, siege of, 522, 537
Douglas, James, second Duke of Queensberry,
        299, 349, 356
Dover, Secret Treaty of, 14–17
Downes, John, 360, 402, 423, 531
Draghi, Giovanni Baptista, 186, 214, 258, 325
Drama. *See* Congreve, William; Crowne, John;
        Dryden, John; Etherege, George; Lee,
        Nathaniel; Vanbrugh, Sir John
drums and drummers, 91, 96, 145–46, 227,
        289, 344, 598, 600, 624
Drury Lane. *See* King's Theatre

Dryden, Elizabeth, 79, 222
Dryden, John: addressed by Pittis, 274; attacked
        by Collier, 232; conversion, 79; death,
        222; Jacobitism, 221, 276; known to Mary
        II and QA as girls, 32; letter to Etherege,
        126; Rose Alley ambush, 79; Works:
        Absalom and Achitophel, 50, 57; *Albion and
        Albanius* (with Grabu), 107–15, 340, 423,
        606; *All for Love*, 359; *Annus Mirabilis*, 21,
        24, 109, 606; *Aureng-Zebe*, 71; *Britannia
        Rediviva*, 132–34, 270; *Don Sebastian*,
        164–70; epilogue for *The Faithful
        Shepherdess*, 4; *Fables Ancient and Modern*,
        245; *The Indian Emperour*, 33; *King Arthur*
        (with Henry Purcell), 108, 151, 185, 306,
        399, 425, 551; "Parallel of Poetry and
        Painting," 339; *The Secular Masque*, 26;
        The Spanish Fryar, 78–79, 160; *The
        Tempest* (with Davenant), 108, 523;
        Threnodia Augustalis, 104; "To his Sacred
        Majesty," 215; "To Sir Godfrey Kneller,"
        327; "To the Pious Memory of the
        Accomplished Young Lady Mrs. Anne
        Killigrew," 84, 105; *Works of Virgil*
        (trans.), 218–22, 245, 275, 416, 629
Duke, Richard, 52, 350
Dunkirk: demolition of, 497, 616; occupation, 592
Duras, Louis, Earl of Feversham, 116, 123
D'Urfey, Thomas: *Don Quixote* 232; sung
        dialogue, 433; *Wonders in the Sun*, 426–27

Eccles, John: Italian influence on, 513;
        performance of Handel's *Te Deum*, 620;
        "Prize Music," 263; Works: *Acis and
        Galatea*, 325; birthday odes, 308, 324,
        359, 369, 545; *Cato*, 610; *Loves of Mars
        and Venus*, 211; New Year's odes, 278, 323,
        435; *Rinaldo and Armida*, 235
Edgar, Duke of Cambridge, QA's brother, 7
Edwin, Sir Humphrey, 319
Elford, Richard: emphasis on words, 259; Lord
        Mayor's dinners, 395, 433; performances for
        QA, 258, 278, 312, 323–24, 350, 479, 492,
        513, 545, 623; soloist in Handel's *Utrecht
        Te Deum*, 608; song on Blenheim, 375;
        with de l'Epine, 342; with John Shore, 514

Elizabeth I, Queen of England: funeral, 202; imitated by QA, 40, 251, 282, 310, 316; speech at Tilbury, 291; Thanksgiving for defeat of Armada, 311

English Civil War, 5, 8, 26; Clarendon's history of, 6, 339, 352

Erskine, John, Earl of Mar, 619

Etherege, George: *The Man of Mode*, 63, 70

Eugene, Prince of Savoy: military career, 344–45, 365, 433, 450, 461, 474, 567; visit to London, 579–84

Evelyn, John: at *Calisto*, 10; at coronation of William and Mary, 97; fireworks, 133; Italian opera 18; James II's chapel, 125; Marlborough's dismissal by William, 174; sermons by Sharp and Ken, 128; Stop of Exchequer, 16; Thanksgiving for Blenheim, 306

Evelyn, Sir John, 633

Exclusion Bill, 76

Farmer, Anthony, 127

Fiennes, Celia, 287

Filmer, Robert: *Patriarcha*, 168

Finch, Anne Kingsmill, Countess of Winchilsea: maid of honor to Maria Beatrice, 84; Works: "The Introduction," 317; libretto for Blow's *Venus and Adonis*, 105

Finch, Daniel, second Earl of Nottingham: alliance with Whigs, 573; critical of Godolphin, 383; critical of Mary, 161–62; criticized by Mary, 172; and de l'Epine, 341, 355; as "Dismal," 429; mocked in prologue, 429; opposition to land war, 254, 352; opposition to occasional conformity, 319, 363; opposition to Union, 436; pursuit of anonymous author, 183; pursuit of Defoe, 321–22, 377; resignation, 363; Scotch Plot, 356

Finch, Heneage, Jr., later second Earl of Aylesbury: poem for QA, 253–54

Finch, Heneage, MP for Oxford, later first Earl of Aylesbury, 253–54, 342

Finger, Gottfried, "Prize Music," 263; *Loves of Mars and Venus*, 211, 427

Fitzjames, James, Duke of Berwick, 450

Fitzroy, Anne. *See* Palmer, Anne

Fitzroy, Charles, Second Duke of Grafton, 92, 403

Fitzroy, George, Duke of Northumberland, 394

Fitzroy, Henry, First Duke of Grafton: 92, 101, 172

Fitzroy, Isabella Bennet, Duchess of Grafton, 95

Fleetwood, William, 479

Fletcher, Andrew, 433

Fletcher, John: *The Faithful Shepherdess*, 2, 34, 216

Frampton, Robert, Bishop of Gloucester, 94

Fraser, Simon, 356

Frederick IV, Duke of Holstein, 241

Frederick IV, King of Denmark, 486

Freeman, Samuel, 452–53, 459

Frescheville, Anna, 153, 306

Friedrich I, Elector of Brandenburg, 98

Fuller, William, 263

Gallas. *See* Wenzel, Johann

Gallia, Maria, 442, 225

Galliard, John Ernest, *Calypso and Telemachus* (with Hughes), 588

Gallissioner, Marquis de la, 329

Galway. *See* de Ruvigny, Henri

Gape, John, 405, 408

Gardner, William, 146

Garter, Order of the: Bedford, 283; George I, 270; Gloucester, 194, 207–11, 214; Godolphin, 394–95; Marlborough, 282; requested for Marlborough, 173; Oxford, 592; Poulet, 594; QA's insignia, 282

Garth, Samuel: poem on Godolphin, 533–34

Gates, Bernard, 513, 608, 623

Gaultier, François, Abbé, 540–41, 556–67, 593, 620

Gay, John, 622, 627

Gennari, Benedetto, 103

Georg August, Electoral Prince, later King George II of England, 271, 627, 630

Georg Ludwig, Elector of Hanover, later King George I of England: execution of Stafford, 76; opposition to peace proposals, 569–72, 595; Order of the Garter, 270; proclaimed King, 599, 634; proposed match with QA, 65, 76; termination of Handel, 609

Georg Wilhelm, Duke of Zell, 216, 270

George I. *See* Georg Ludwig

George II. *See* Georg August

George, Prince of Denmark, QA's husband: candidate for stadholder, 293; at *Don Sebastian*, 164; Danish estates, 89, 241; death, 484–85; dispatched to meet Charles III, 356; as father of Gloucester, 207; flirtation with Elizabeth Griffith, 153; as Generalissimo, 294–95; illness, 126, 142, 250, 432, 435; at James II's coronation, 91; at Lord Mayor's feast, 129; marriage, 43–44; occasional conformist, 321; Parliamentary pension, 318; at QA's coronation, 293; with QA in Oxford, 135; relations with William, 98, 101, 135, 142, 168, 180, 227, 236, 240, 280–81, 286; subscriber to Dryden's *Virgil*, 219, 222; threatened with investigation, 456; visit to Denmark, 127

Gerard, Charles, second Earl of Macclesfield, 270

Gibbons, Grinling, 181

Gibbs, James, 555, 563

Ginkel, Godart de, Earl of Athlone, 197

Gloucester, Bishop of. *See* Frampton, Robert

Gloucester, Duke of. *See* William, Duke of Gloucester

Gloucester, royal yacht, 64, 86

Godfrey, Sir Edmund Berry, 61

Godolphin, Francis, 230, 237, 364, 403, 408

Godolphin, Harriet, daughter of Francis, 623

Godolphin, Harriet Churchill, wife of Francis: 230, 237, 287; and Congreve, 332–34, 401

Godolphin, Margaret Blagge, 10

Godolphin, Sidney: death, 593; marriage, 10

—and the arts: commissions Addison, 382, 389; lampooned by Manley, 506; lampooned by Swift, 536; as Mammon in D'Urfey's dialogue, 433; praised by John Philips, 381, 387

—political career: betrayed by Harley, 460–64; correspondence with Marlborough, 268 *et passim*; defense of MacCartney, 499; diplomatic nomination, 407; elections, 277, 403; falsely accused, 565; financial support for Victor Amadeus, 344;

funding for Prince Eugene's campaign, 434; impeachment of Halifax, 382; judgeship for Hedges, 432; rapprochement with Whigs, 393, 403; revenge against "Tackers," 378; on Sacheverell, 521; service to James II and William III, 266, 277

—service to QA: advice to her, 257; attempts to protect her from stress, 509; at Bath, 299, 350; criticized by her, 544; dismissed, 532–33, 536; drafts speech for her, 301; Garter, 394–95; house at Windsor used by her, 276; Lord Treasurer, 295; mourning for James II, 271–73; proposed compromise over bishoprics, 456–57; uncertainty about her coming to Parliament, 282

Godolphin, The (dance), 623

Gohory, Jeremiah, 2, 140, 230

Gostling, John, 47, 51, 157, 287, 312

Grabu, Luis: victim of Test Act, 17; Works: *Albion and Albanius*, 107–15; *Ariane*, 18

Grafton. *See* Fitzroy, Charles

Graham, Richard, 43, 107

Grant, John, 316

Granville, George, Lord Lansdowne: dedicatee of *Windsor-Forest*, 601; Works: *The British Enchanters*, 425; *The Jew of Venice*, 546

Granville, John, Earl of Bath, 342

Granville, John, Jr., First Baron Granville, 342

Gray, Ralph: "Coronation Ballad," 162–63, 170

Greber, Jakob: *Gli amori d'Ergasto*, 402

Green, Thomas, 405

Greeting, Edward, 123

Greeting, Thomas, 84, 114

Gregg, William, 463–64, 467, 469–70, 554

Grey, Henry, Earl, then Duke of Kent, 306, 364, 403, 507, 521–23, 627

Griffith, Edward, 153, 187

Griffith, Elizabeth Lawrence ("Duck"), 153

Grimaldi, Nicolo ("Nicolini"): in *Ambleto*, 584; in *Antioco*, 579; benefit for, 497; in *Clotilda*, 497; dedication to Kent, 521; departure, 589; in *Hydaspes*, 521; mocked and praised by Addison, 553, 589; performances at QA's birthdays, 546, 580;

private performances, 488; in *Pyrrhus and Demetrius*, 442, 488–89; in *Tatler*, 440–41
Grossi, Giovanni Francesco ("Siface"), 126, 489
Guiscard, Antoine de, 553
Gwyn, Nell, 80

Halifax, Earl of. *See* Montagu, Charles
Halifax, Marquess of. *See* Savile, George
Hamilton, Anthony, 36
Hamilton, Dr. David: care for QA, 509; conversations with QA, 69, 523, 533, 542–44, 572, 593, 616, 618–19, 622; correspondence with SM, 542–43; praise for Marlborough, 544
Hamilton, Elizabeth Villiers, Countess of Orkney: land in Ireland, 197, 224–25, 241; mistress of William III, 153, 158
Hamilton, James, Fourth Duke of Hamilton: 299, 574, 594
Handel, George Frideric: arrival in London, 545; pension from QA, 620; sacked by George I, 609, 616; Works: *Almira*, 546; "Eternal Source of Light Divine," 513–17; *Il Pastor Fido*, 589; *Rinaldo*, 545–51; *Silla*, 616; *Teseo*, 589; *Utrecht Te Deum* and *Jubilate Deo*, 608, 617, 620
Hanmer, Sir Thomas, 625
Harcourt, Simon: allied with Harley, 457; attacked in ballad, 476; defense attorney for Sacheverell, 438; Lord Chancellor, 630; Lord Keeper, 535; at Oxford, 251; QA's deathbed, 633; resignation, 467
Harcourt, Simon, Jr.: 484; poem for QA, 251–53
Harley, Edward, 565, 620
Harley, Henrietta Holles, 620
Harley, Robert, first Earl of Oxford
—and QA: access through Abigail, 452, 472; advice to her, 257, 285; disapproved by, 620, 632–33; ennobled by, 566; Garter, 592; ghost-written speeches for, 573–74, 587, 609
—political career: Act of Settlement, 263; attempted coup, 460–64; bishopric crisis, 456–57; Chancellor of the Exchequer, 535; communications with Hanover, 631–32; communications with the

Pretender, 620; dismissal of Godolphin, 532; dismissed, 633; Dissenting schools, 364; duplicity, 541, 585; employment of Defoe, 364; expulsion of Steele, 626–27; Gregg's treason, 463; impeachment of Junto Whigs, 265; leader of Country Whigs, 258; Lord Treasurer, 566; opposition to the Tack, 378; peace negotiations, 518, 540–41, 569; slave trade, 568; resignation, 467; restraining order, 585; Secretary of State, 364; Speaker of the House, 258, 277; stabbed by Guiscard, 553; target of Whigs, 456
—and arts: attacked in *Tatler*, 530–31, 536; flattered by Manley, 506; praised in anonymous poem, 364; praised by John Philips, 380, 387; praised by Prior, 436
Harley, Thomas, 585, 631, 632
Harrison, William, 552
Hart, James, 11
Hartington. *See* Cavendish, William
Hasty Widow, The (anon.), 490
Hawksmoor, Nicholas, 297, 555
Hedges, Charles, 407
Hedvig Sophia, Duchess of Holstein, 394
Heinsius, Anthonie, 254, 556
Henrietta Maria, Queen of England, QA's grandmother, 7, 34, 379
Henrietta of England ("Minette"), QA's aunt, 7
Herbert, Philip, seventh Earl of Pembroke, 24
Herbert, Thomas, eighth Earl of Pembroke, 295, 306, 395, 450, 466, 487, 505
Herbert, William, Earl of Powis, 125
Hervey, Elizabeth Felton, countess of Bristol, 468, 558
Hervey, John, Baron Hervey, then first Earl of Bristol, 342, 558
Hesketh, Henry, 530
He's Wellcome Home (anon.), 569
Het Loo, 240, 270
Hill, Aaron: theatre manager, 531–32, 545; Works: *Camillus*, 461; libretto for *Rinaldo*, 550
Hill, Alice, 230
Hill, John, 509, 528, 550, 592. 594
Hoadley, Benjamin, 508
Hobart, Frances, 36

Holles, Denzil: ambassador to the Dutch, 4

Holles, John, first Duke of Newcastle, 395, 457, 461, 466, 566

Holstein, Duchess of. *See* Hedvig Sophia

Holstein, Duke of. *See* Frederick IV

Homer: *Iliad*, 205, 484

homoeroticism, 31, 34–37, 88, 472, 475, 543

Hooper, George, Bishop of Bath and Wells, 617

Horace, 84, 176–77, 337–38, 361, 431

Howard, Annabella Dives: 186, 473, 476, 503

Howard, Dorothy, 37

Howard, Mary Mordaunt, Duchess of Norfolk, 4, 18, 29

Howard, Sir Robert, 186

Howard, William, First Viscount Stafford, 62, 76

Howe, John, 241, 265, 285

Hughes, Francis, 442, 492, 513, 608

Hughes, John: *Calypso and Telemachus*, 588

Hunt, Arabella, 157, 186

hurricane of November, 1703, 355, 390

Hyde, Anne, Duchess of York, QA's mother, 5–7, 15, 34–36, 65, 185

Hyde, Edward, First Earl of Clarendon, QA's grandfather, 5–, 339, 352

Hyde, Flower, 89

Hyde, Henrietta, 73, 89

Hyde, Henry, Second Earl of Clarendon, 89

Hyde, Laurence, first Earl of Rochester, QA's uncle: attack on Godolphin, 383; Church in danger, 414; death, 566; dedication to QA, 352; editor of father's history, 339; godfather to QA's daughter, 95; opposition to Marlborough, 254, 294, 318, 461; opposition to Union, 436; and QA's speech to Parliament, 253; removed from Privy Council, 322; returned to Privy Council, 535

Indian Kings, 524–25, 539, 550, 606

Ingoldsby, Richard, 374

Isaac, Mr., 374, 436, 623

Isabella, daughter of Maria Beatrice, 60, 69, 80

Jacobites: advocacy of Pretender, 243; contacts with QA, 173, 175, 179, 272, 277; hope for restoration of James II, 262; in Parliament, 620; in Scotland, 346–47, 355; opposition to William, 162–63, 169–70; plots against William, 207, 235; *See also* Atterbury, Francis; Dryden, John; Gray, Ralph; Pope, Alexander (suspected); St. John, Henry; Villiers, Edward

James Francis Edward ("James III"), son of James II and Maria Beatrice: authenticity questioned, 131, 217, 625; birth, 130–34; change of religion proposed, 263, 620–21; invasion of Scotland, 467–69, 478; at opera, 593; opposed by Grand Alliance, 293; possible restoration, 541; proposed removal from France, 586, 616; proposed successor, 243; recognized by Louis XIV, 256, 269; refusal to convert, 620–22; reward for, 632

James I, King of England, 11, 93

James II, King of England, QA's father:

—as Duke of York: conversion to Catholicism, 15; denounced as recusant, 73; exile in Brussels, 58, 63, 69; exile in Scotland, 58, 70; illegitimate children, 107, 450; libertinism, 28, 106; naval commander, 16–20; patron of Dryden, 32; reputed lover of Mary Kirk, 9; second marriage, 7; succession opposed, 58; victim of Test Act, 17; wreck of the *Gloucester*, 83

—as King: abandoned by QA, 168; attempts to convert QA, 118, 122, 128; baroque taste, 103; coronation, 91–95; dismissal of Compton, 118; "Dispensing Power," 125; praised for clemency, 121; progress to Bristol, 125; proposed alliance between Dissenters and Catholics, 127, 133; revenge against supporters of Monmouth, 117; Roman Catholic chapel, 104, 125; seditious libel charge against bishops, 131; succession, 92; violation of oaths, 101

—after Revolution: "abdication," 136; assassination plot against William, 207; Battle of the Boyne, 172; death, 269; flight to France, 135; hopes for restoration, 262; invasion of Ireland, 136, 148, 170; planned invasion of England, 179; QA's mourning for, 271

James, Duke of Cambridge, QA's brother, 6, 202

Jeffreys, George, First Baron Jeffreys of Wem, 117

Jersey. *See* Villiers, Edward

Jevon, Thomas: *The Devil of a Wife*, 122

Johnson, Esther ("Stella"), 536, 608

Jones, Inigo, 11, 26

Jonson, Ben: masques, 11, 25, 604

Joseph Ferdinand Leopold of Bavaria, 236–37

Joseph I, Holy Roman Emperor: 406, 450, 544, 556

Junto, 265–66, 382–83, 460–61, 529–30, 573

Keeling, Josiah, 50

Ken, Thomas, Bishop of Bath and Wells, 128, 131, 285

Kennett, Basil, 217

Kennett, White, 507–09

Kensington Palace, 194, 209, 296–97

Kentish Petition, 268

Keppel, Arnold Joost van, Earl of Albemarle, 209, 227, 239–40, 267, 271, 592

Kéroualle, Henriette, Countess of Pembroke, 24

Kéroualle, Louise, Duchess of Portsmouth, 23, 73–74, 80, 114

Killigrew Anne: 84; *Venus attired by the Graces*, 105

Killigrew, Charles, 231, 235

Killigrew, Henry, 405, 408

King of France's Letter to the Cardinal de Noailles, The, (anon.), 575

King, Robert, 158–60

King's Evil, 72, 251

Kingsmill, Anne. *See* Finch, Anne

King's Theatre, 13, 18, 425, 508

Kingston. *See* Pierrepoint, Evelyn

Kirk, Mary, 9

Kirkby, Christopher, 60

Kit-Cat Club, 332, 341

Kneller, Sir Godfrey: Academy of Painting and Drawing, 563; petition refused by QA, 329; Works: allegorical painting for Blenheim, 498; portraits: Gloucester, 150, 204; Kit-Cats, 563; Marlborough,

431, 575; QA with Gloucester, 184; William III, 329

Knight, Mary, 11, 26

knotting, 189–90

Kremberg, James: *England's Glory*, 369, 388, 422–24, 606

La Hogue, Battle of, 180

L'Ambitione Debellata (anon.), 121

Landskrona, Battle of, 47

Lawrence, Thomas, 52

Leake, John, Admiral, 428

Lee, Charlotte, Countess of Litchfield, 54, 82

Lee, Nathaniel: *Mithridates*, 40, 63–69, 82; *Sophonisba*, 30–31, 68, 160, 412, 466

Legge, William, first Earl of Dartmouth: Lord Privy Seal, 619; politics of occasional conformity, 322; Secretary of State, 528, 554, 586, 593–94

Leibniz, Gottfried, 216, 271

Leke, Robert, third Earl of Scarsdale, 137

Lely, Sir Peter, portraits by: Moll Davis, 28; Anne Hyde, 185; Mary II, 3; QA, 6, 54, 58

Lennox, Charles, Duke of Richmond, 598

Leopold I, Holy Roman Emperor: agreement to oppose "James III," 293; death, 406; failure to supply troops to Spain, 344; and Marlborough, 366; QA's mourning for, 406; and Somerset, 363; and Spanish empire, 236

Leveridge, Richard: as composer, 233–35; in *Camilla*, 372; in *Rosamond*, 446; in *Calypso and Telemachus*, 588

Leveson-Gower, John, first Baron Gower, 342

Lewis, Erasmus, 633

Lewis, Jenkin, 139–41, 192, 207, 210–17, 220, 230

Liberty: allegorical figure, 416, 604

Liberty, A Poem (anon.), 416–18

Licensing Acts, 73, 235, 266

Lilliburlero. See Wharton, Thomas

Lincoln's Inn Fields Theatre, 230, 392

Lindelheim, Joanna Maria, 370, 442

Lindsey, Mary, 233, 372, 446

Lisle, siege of, 475

Locke, Matthew, 108

Lord Mayors of London, 129, 319, 395, 433

Louis XIV, King of France: compliments to
QA, 615; guitar playing, 10; invasion of
Holland, 17; joke attributed to, 250; need
for peace, 496; occupation of Spanish
Netherlands, 265; Partition Treaties, 236,
265; recognition of "James III," 256, 269;
recognition of William, 208; revocation of
Edict of Nantes, 119; Secret Treaty of
Dover, 4, 14; subsidies to Charles II, 14;
Treaty of Ryswick, 208, 269

Louis XVI, King of France, 583

Louis, 20th Dauphin of France, 237, 504, 556

Louis, Duke of Burgundy ("le petit Dauphin"),
556, 580

Ludwig, Margrave of Baden, 408, 450

Lully, Jean-Baptiste: *Cadmus et Hermione*, 121

Lund, Battle of, 47

Luttrell, Narcissus: account of Thanksgiving for
Blenheim, 305–06; misinformed about
Gloucester and barges, 202; reports
debate in Privy Council, 405; reports
QA's engagement, 52; reports QA's
miscarriages, 190

MacCartney, George, 499, 525, 558, 594

Malplaquet, Battle of, 504–06, 518, 522, 525

Mancini, Francesco: *Hydaspes*, 521, 545

Manchester. *See* Montagu, Charles

Mancini, Hortense, Duchess of Mazarin, 9

Manley, Delarivier: 553, 564, 576; *The New
Atalantis*, 503, 529; part 2, 506

Manningham, Thomas, 491, 507

Mansell, Thomas, 457, 467

Mar. *See* Erskine, John

Maria Beatrice of Modena, Duchess of York
and Queen of England: alleged meeting
with Bolingbroke, 593; arrival in England,
18; *Calisto*, 2, 14, 29; Catholicism, 18;
complimented in *Ariane*, 19; coronation,
95; flees to France, 135; Godolphin's
affection for, 339; letter to QA on James
II's death, 269; mother of the Pretender,
129–30; music-lover, 107; painted as the
Virgin Mary, 104; proposed payments to,
228; visits Mary in Holland, 60

Marie-Louise, QA's cousin, 7

Markham, Sir Robert, 76

Marlborough, Duke of. *See* Churchill, John

Marlborough, Duchess of. *See* Churchill, Sarah

Marlborough House, 543, 579–80

Mary II, Queen of England, QA's sister:
asceticism, 3, 99, 180; in *Calisto*, 7, 34;
Calvinist tendencies, 98; complaints of
isolation, 171; coronation, 96; criticism of
Privy Council and Cabinet, 171; death,
144, 176, 191; diary entry on her father and
her husband, 169; disapproval of Mary
Cornwallis, 87; at *Don Sebastian*, 164;
embarrassed in theatre, 160; funeral, 191,
486; in *The Faithful Shepherdess*, 2, 34;
gives ball as child, 16; as head of
government, 162, 189; inability to bear
children, 98, 163; knotting, 189–90;
letters as adolescent, 9, 29–30, 32–35, 37,
40; letters on QA and Mulgrave, 87–88;
marriage, 7, 40, 43, 58; new oaths at
coronation, 102; opposition to
independent revenue for QA, 148; poem
by, 33–34; precocious dancer, 2; public
gestures of confidence, 172; quarrel with
QA, 142, 156, 173–75, 545; quotes
Dryden, 32; reads Lee's *Sophonisba*, 30,
68, 160; reform of Chapel Royal, 155, 181;
reprisals against Jacobites, 169; and St.
James's Church, 181; taste in music, 158

Mary, daughter of QA, 95, 126

Masham, Abigail Hill: criticized by
Marlborough, 505; flattered by Manley,
506; glanced at in *Spectator*, 557; intimacy
with QA, 37, 40, 411, 447, 476; Keeper of
Privy Purse, 544; marriage, 451; praised
by Swift, 578; promised a court position,
229; rumored appointment as mall
keeper, 483; share in slave trade, 619, 632

Masham, Samuel, 140, 451, 579

Matignon, Catherine-Thérèse de, Marquise de
Seignelay, 24

Maximilian Emanuel, Elector of Bavaria, 299,
572, 580

Maynwaring, Arthur: interest in music, 473;
letters to SM, 498, 505; proposed address

against Mrs. Masham, 509, 523; urges SM to retain court positions, 469; Works: *Advice to the Electors of Great Britain* (with SM), 470; Epilogue for *Camilla*, 426; "Epilogue to the Ladies," 357; *Medley*, 564; *A New Ballad, To the Tune of Fair Rosamond* (with SM), 471–73, 476

medals, 22, 117, 290, 362

Medlicott, Thomas, 489

Memorial of the Church of England, The (anon.), 380

Mesnager, Nicolas, 567–69

Methuen, John and Paul, 343

Mews, Peter, Bishop of Winchester, 203

Mignard, Pierre, portraits by: Duchess of Portsmouth, 24, 607; Marquise de Seignelay, 24

Milton, John, 385–87, 607

Mindelheim, 366, 542, 570

Misson, Henri, 53

Mohun, Charles, fourth Baron Mohun, 594

Monmouth. *See* Scott, James; Scott, Anne

Montagu House, 543

Montagu, Charles, First Earl of Halifax: awarded LLD, 403; consultations with Godolphin, 382, 407; defense of Godolphin, 383; funds for Gloucester's court, 228; impeached, 265; lobbies SM on behalf of his brother, 473; missions to the Hague, 429, 530; motion against "suspension of arms," 585; poem on QA's wedding, 52; "Prize Music," 266; recoinage, 239; recommends Defoe to SM, 379; removed from Privy Council, 266; school friend of Prior, 361; subscriber to Pope's *Iliad*, 621

Montagu, Charles, fourth Earl and first Duke of Manchester, 210, 269, 277

Montagu, Edward, third Earl of Sandwich, 277

Montagu, Elizabeth Wilmot, Countess of Sandwich, 277

Montagu, James, 438, 464, 473

Montagu, John, second Duke of Montagu, 390

Montagu, Mary Churchill, 391, 543–45, 587

Montagu, Ralph, 9

Montaigne, Michel de, 178, 187, 470

Monthly Mask of Vocal Music, The, 323, 400

Moore, Arthur, 614, 619, 632

Mordaunt, Charles, third Earl of Peterborough, 413, 450, 461, 506, 537, 568

Mordaunt, Henry, Second Earl of Peterborough, 18

Mordaunt, Mary. *See* Howard, Mary

Motteux, Peter (Pierre): *Acis and Galatea*, 325; *Arsinoe*, 399; birthday odes for QA, 308, 324; *The Island Princess*, 235; *The Loves of Mars and Venus*, 211, 426–27; prologue for QA, 212; song for Lord Mayor's dinner, 395; *Temple of Love*, 425; *Thomyris*, 442

mourning, rituals of, 7, 210, 240–41, 271–76, 406–07, 488–91, 597–600

Mulgrave. *See* Sheffield, John

Musgrave, Sir Christopher, 262, 296

Music: at court, 10–14, 44–49, 141–44, 196–200, 214–15, 242, 258–61, 278–80, 323–25, 357–59, 367, 418–21, 434–35, 513–17, 545–46, 620–24; liturgical, 49–51, 95, 126, 156–59, 286–87, 306, 311–14, 409–11, 430, 491–96, 507, 539, 608–09, 620; QA's love of, 158–60, 173, 181, 184–86, 214, 233–34, 253; QA's training in, 1–3, 73, 84, 185–86, 190; *See also* Blow, John; Bononcini, Giovanni; Clarke, Jeremiah; Croft, William; Eccles, John; Handel, George Frideric; opera; Purcell, Henry; Staggins, Nicholas

Namur, siege of, 147, 192, 193

Nantes, Edict of, 119

Needham, Eleanor, 9, 33

New Song to the Tune of Lilly burlaro, A (anon.), 476

Newcastle. *See* Holles, John

Newton, Sir Isaac, 300, 403, 408, 425

Nicolini. *See* Grimaldi, Nicolo

"Night-Bell-Man of Pickadilly to the Princess of Denmark, The" (anon.), 183

Nine Years' War, 143, 147, 192, 208, 224, 226, 250, 428, 430

"No peace without Spain," 462, 556, 569, 583

Nonconformists. *See* Dissenters

non-juring bishops, 165

Northumberland. *See* Fitzroy, George
"nursing mothers," 291–92, 527, 607, 612, 617, 635

Oates, Titus, 60, 69
occasional conformity: bills against, 318–20, 335, 355, 394, 574
October Club, 552
Oldfield, Anne, 426
Onslow, Arthur, 282, 530
Opera. *See* Bononcini, Giovanni; Clayton, Thomas; de L'Epine, Margherita; Galliard, John Ernest; Grabu, Luis; Grimaldi, Nicolo; Handel, George Frideric; de l'Epine, Margherita; Leveridge, Richard; Lindsey, Mary; Purcell, Henry; Tofts, Catherine; Urbani, Valentino
Orinda. *See* Philips, Katherine
Orkney. *See* Hamilton, Elizabeth Villiers
Osborne, Thomas, Earl of Danby and Marquess of Carmarthen, 60, 69, 97, 134, 171
Oudenarde, Battle of, 474
Ovid: *Metamorphoses*, 3, 8, 25, 31, 84, 121, 216, 605
Oxford University: Magdalen College, 127; poems for New Year's Day, 396; poems on death of Gloucester, 203; QA's visits to, 135, 251–54, 298; Sheldonian Theatre, 11, 81, 253, 396

Painting: Academy of, 563–64; aesthetic theories, 339–41, 559, 563, 575; allegories, 26, 32, 54, 138, 393, 498–99; mythological, 105–06; portraits, 3, 6, 24, 58, 103, 184–86, 325–30, 333, 431, 525, 575; religious, 103, 125; *See also* Closterman, John; Dahl, Michael; Lely, Sir Peter; Kneller, Sir Godfrey
Pallas Athena: as model for QA, 290, 309, 316, 374
Palmer, Anne, Countess of Sussex, 2, 9–10, 27, 29
Palmer, Barbara, Countess of Castlemaine and Duchess of Cleveland, 9–10, 34, 92, 394, 503
Palmer, Roger, Earl of Castlemaine, 119–21
Palmes, Guy, 296
Parke, Daniel, 366

Parliament: abolition of Scottish Privy Council, 465; addresses to QA, 467, 490, 496, 508, 566, 573, 616; attack on Barrier Treaty, 583; debate on "restraining order," 585; debate on Spain, 461, 463; declares Church not in danger, 415; elections, 62, 258, 277, 474, 535, 537, 539, 579; impeachment of Clarendon, 6; in Civil War, 11; investigation of Marlborough, 574; motion to dissolve Union, 614; at Oxford, 80–81; prohibition of French wines, 557; refusal to extend Marlborough's grant to heirs, 318; repayment to Prince George, 243; request that QA send Marlborough to Holland, 510; resistance to Charles II, 17; resolutions congratulating Marlborough, 301, 390; revenue designated for QA, 148, 155, 174, 177; revision of coronation oaths, 102; rewards to Marlborough, 397; support for declaration of war, 295
Parliament, Scottish: consideration of Union, 433; first meeting under QA, 298–99; opposition to QA, 349
Partition Treaties, 236–37, 265
Partridge, John, 500
Paulet, Charles, second Duke of Bolton, 403
Peace and Plenty: allegorical figures, 1, 21, 26–27, 32, 133, 603–04
Pepys, Samuel, 2, 22
Perquisite-Monger, The (anon.), 575
Perrin, Pierre: *Ariane*, 18, 20, 112, 606
Peterborough. *See* Mordaunt, Charles; Mordaunt, Henry
Petre, John, Fifth Baron Petre, 62
Philippe of France ("Monsieur"), 7
Philippe, duc d'Anjou ("Felipe V" of Spain), 265, 300, 344, 504, 580, 585–86
Philips, Ambrose: diplomatic post, 247; Works: *The Distrest Mother*, 587, "Eternal Source of Light Divine," 514–17, 607; *Pastorals*, 245–47; theatre song, 233
Philips, John: *Bleinheim*, 380–87
Philips, Katherine, 32–34
Pierrepoint, Evelyn, fifth Earl of Kingston, 403
Pittis, William: pilloried and imprisoned, 380;

Works: *Epistolary Poem to John Dryden*, 274; *The Generous Muse*, 274–76; *Hymn to Neptune*, 379

Poem on the Prospect of a Peace (anon.), 504

Poetry: anonymous, 44–47, 58, 141–47, 182–83, 196–200, 233–34, 242, 255, 258–61, 264, 284, 287, 300, 311, 364, 394, 404–06, 416–17, 422–24, 429, 463, 476–78, 487, 504, 527, 569, 580, 584; University collections, 52–57, 203–06; *See also* Addison, Joseph; Ames, Richard; Arwaker, Edmund; Behn, Aphra; Congreve, William; Cowley, Abraham; Darby, Charles; Defoe, Daniel; Dryden, John; D'Urfey, Thomas; Finch, Heneage, Jr.; Garth, Samuel; Harcourt, Simon, Jr.; Maynwaring, Arthur; Montagu, Charles; Motteux, Peter; Philips, Ambrose; Philips, John; Philips, Katherine; Pittis, William ; Pope, Alexander; Prior, Matthew; Sedley, Sir Charles; Settle, Elkanah; Sheffield, John; Swift, Jonathan; Symson, David; Tate, Nahum; Theobald, Lewis; Tickell, Thomas; Tutchin, John; Turner, Purbeck; Virgil; Wilmot, John

Pope Innocent XI, 121, 135

Pope, Alexander: *The Dunciad*, 635; *Essay on Criticism*, 560–61, 565; letter to Swift, 620–22; *Pastorals*, 399; prologue to *Cato*, 613; *The Rape of the Lock*, 106, 588; translation of Homer, 620; *Windsor-Forest*, 27, 517, 601–12

Popish Plot, 60–63

Portland. *See* Bentinck, Hans Willem

Poulett, John, Earl of Poulett, 585, 594

Powell, Charles, 230

Powell, George, 532

Powell, Martin, 558

Pratt, Samuel, 201, 217–17, 355

Pretender. *See* James Francis Edward

Prior, Matthew, 530, 534, 537, 567–68, 593; Works: ode on Ramillies, 431; poem on Guiscard, 554; prologue for QA's birthday, 360

Privy Council: under Charles II, 60, 69, 71; under James II, 93, 118, 125–26; under

QA: Privy Council of England 266, 281, 286, 293–96, 322, 346–48, 355, 395, 405–06; Privy Council of Great Britain, 450, 455, 463, 466, 468–69, 487, 530, 535, 566, 594, 597, 599, 634; under William and Mary: 171, 222, 255

Privy Council, Scottish: 345, 348, 465

Privy Purse, 286, 297, 318, 336, 341, 357, 451, 469, 482, 542, 544

Protestant succession: 292, 439, 496, 565–66, 625, 627; dependent on Gloucester, 142, 148; dependent on QA and Prince George, 51–53, 107, 129, 138; proposed through Monmouth, 71; in QA's public speeches, 103, 468, 490, 586, 628; in Scotland, 345

Pulteney, Daniel, 247

Purcell, Daniel: *The Island Princess*, 235; music for Gloucester's birthday, 211; "Prize Music," 263; song for QA, 233

Purcell, Frances, 141, 185

Purcell, Henry: death, 200; guitar arrangements of his music, 185; imitated by Handel, 608; performance for Queen Mary, 157; testing of organ, 181; Works: birthday ode for Mary, 179; *The Fairy Queen*, 151, 184; "The Fife and all the Harmony of War" 343; *From Hardy Climes*, 44–47; *I was glad*, 95; *Let the Soldiers Rejoyce*, 395; "Lovely Albina," 196–200, 223; music for Gloucester's birthday, 141–48; music for Mary's funeral, 191; music for *The Old Bachelor*, 184; "The Noise of Foreign Wars," 141; setting of Sedley's song on knotting, 189; solos for John Shore, 146; symphony anthems for Chapel Royal, 156; *Te Deum* and *Jubilate Deo*, 306, 312, 514; welcome songs, 44

Qualification Bill, 590

Queen Anne's Bounty, 317, 361–63, 536–37

Queen's Famous Progress, The (anon.), 249–56

Ramillies, Battle of, 428, 431, 433

Ravenscroft, Edward: *The Anatomist*, 211

Regency Act (1705), 414

Religion, 15–17, 60–62, 76–79, 93, 97, 101, 104, 119, 123–31, 319–22, 345, 348–51, 354–55, 361–64, 377, 414

Restoration, 8, 108

restraining order, 585, 589

Revolution of 1688, 97, 100–06, 134–35, 166, 266, 467, 555, 625

Rich, Christopher, 372, 391, 508

Riley, John: portrait attributed to, 333

Robart, Anthony, 2

Robinson, Anastasia, 513

Robinson, John, Bishop of Bristol, 566, 580, 619

Rochester, first Earl of. *See* Hyde, Laurence

Rochester, second Earl of. *See* Wilmot, John

Romney. *See* Sydney, Henry

Rooke, Admiral Sir George: 300, 317, 375, 380, 396

Roscommon. *See* Dillon, Isabella

Rossi, Giacomo, 551, 553, 616

Rouillé, Pierre, 498

Royal Oak, Boscobel Park, 215–16, 255

Rubens, Peter Paul, 26, 32, 138

Rumbold, Richard, 49, 114–16

Rupert, Prince of the Rhine, 17, 139

Russell, Edward, Earl of Orford, 265–66, 506

Russell, Rachel Wriothesley, 126

Russell, William Baron Russell, 51, 283, 453

Russell, William, first Duke of Bedford, 453

Russell, Wriothesley, second Earl of Bedford, 283

Rye House Plot, 49–51, 114

Ryswick, Treaty of, 208, 221, 228, 269, 313

Sacheverell, Henry: Bank of England elections, 555; depicted on fan, 520; impeached, 438; progress to the West, 527; QA's attitude toward, 510; speaking voice, 439; trial, 437–41, 510, 520–21; Works: *The Duty of Praying for our Enemies*, 608; *The Perils of False Brethren*, 437, 506; *The Political Union*, 319

Sackville, Charles, Sixth Earl of Dorset: censorship, 230; criticized by Mary, 172; at Gloucester's christening, 148; illustration in Dryden's *Virgil*, 220; Lord Chamberlain, 163, 220, 230–31; patron of

Dryden, 163; patron of Prior, 361; role in QA's escape from Whitehall, 101, 135

Sackville, Lionel, seventh Earl and first Duke of Dorset, 204, 220

St. James's Church, Piccadilly, 181

St. James's Palace, 5, 43, 194, 229, 237

St. John, Henry, Viscount Bolingbroke: allied with Harley, 457; attacked in ballad, 476; at *Cato*, 613; commission for John Philips, 380; drafts Latin letter for QA, 544; emissary from QA to Marlborough, 464; ennobled, 592; journey to Paris, 593; memories of Tory victory, 535, 565; peace negotiations, 554, 567–68; at Powell's puppet show, 559; resignation, 467; responsibility for restraining order, 585; Secretary of State, 535; share in slave trade, 619, 632; support for invasion of Canada, 550, 567; testimony about Almanza, 463; wounds Guiscard, 553

St. Venant, siege of, 434

Sancroft, William, Archbishop of Canterbury, 93, 97

Sandford, Francis, 93–95

Sandwich. *See* Montagu, Edward; Montagu, Elizabeth

Sandys, James, 205

Saragossa, Battle of, 537–40

Savile, George, Marquess of Halifax, 138

Saunière, René de, Sieur de L'Hermitage, 257

Scarburgh, Sir Charles, 177

Scarlatti, Alessandro, 442

Schiavonetti, Elisabetta Pilotta, 545, 558

Schooneveld, Battles of, 17

Schütz, Georg, 627, 630

Scotch Plot (1703), 355–56

Scott, Anne, Duchess of Monmouth, QA's godmother, 9, 34, 60, 116–17

Scott, Henrietta Hyde, 163, 558

Scott, James, Duke of Monmouth: alleged legitimacy, 262; dancer, 2, 14; executed, 116; exile, 70; invades England, 115; lover of Eleanor Needham, 33; military career, 16, 20; at Oxford Parliament, 80; proposed as successor by Whigs, 71–72, 80; reputed lover of Mary Kirk, 9

Scott, James, Earl of Dalkeith, 262–63
Scottish Privy Council, 465
Second Dutch Naval War, 4–5, 15–16
Sedgemoor, Battle of, 116
Sedley, Catharine, 107
Sedley, Sir Charles, 179–80, 189
Seignelay. *See* Matignon, Catherine-Thérèse de
Settle, Elkanah: *Pope Joan*, 74–75,
    Memoriæ Fragranti, 483–84, 487
Seven Bishops, case of, 119, 131–33
Seymour, Charles, Duke of Somerset: attacked
    by Nottingham, 363; Chancellor of
    Cambridge, 402; defense of MacCartney,
    499; dismissed, 579; drift toward Tories,
    521; escort for QA in House of Lords,
    383; Harley's attempted coup, 457, 461,
    466; hosts Charles III, 356; hosts QA,
    255; master of the horse, 255; offer of
    Sion House to QA, 175; opposed to
    dissolution of Parliament, 535; patron of
    music, 355, 341, 363, 391, 497; QA's
    funeral, 598; reclaims seat on Privy
    Council, 567; refusal to introduce d'Adda,
    129; speech to QA at Cambridge, 403;
    supporter of Marlborough, 295
Seymour, Edward, fourth Baronet, 241, 364
Seymour, Elizabeth Percy, Duchess of
    Somerset, 363, 474, 521, 523, 543–44,
    572, 578, 580
Shadwell, Thomas: *Psyche*, 108
Shaftesbury. *See* Cooper, Anthony Ashley
Shakespeare, William, 449
Sharp, John, Archbishop of York, 119, 128, 287,
    291, 452, 477
Sheffield, John, Second Earl Mulgrave,
    Marquess of Normanby, Duke of
    Buckingham: dedicatee of Dryden's
    Aeneis, 333; dismissed from office, 395; at
    Gloucester's funeral, 203; Lord Privy Seal,
    294; opposition to Union, 436; poems to
    QA, 85–86; praise of Gloucester's
    manners, 210; Privy Council, 222, 294,
    535, 566
Sherlock, Richard, 305, 309–10
Shore, John, 146, 323, 514, 598
Shovell, Sir Cloudesley, 380, 450, 460

Shrewsbury. *See* Talbot, Charles; Talbot,
    Adelaide
Siface. *See* Grossi, Giovanni Francesco
silk weavers, 497, 508
Sinzendorff. *See* Wenzel, Philipp Ludwig
Sion House, 175
slave trade, 15, 17, 21–22, 25, 565, 568, 586, 619
Smith, Edmund: *Phædra and Hippolytus*, 448
Smith, John, 414, 460
Smock Alley troupe, 82
Sole Bay, Battle of, 17
Somers, John, first Baron Somers: 265–66, 278,
    460, 469, 487, 535
Somerset. *See* Seymour, Charles; Seymour,
    Elizabeth
Sophia Charlotte, Electress of Brandenburg, 98
Sophia Dorothea, Princess of Hanover, 216
Sophia Louise, Queen of Prussia, 394
Sophia, Electress of Hanover, 65, 243, 261, 414,
    630–31
South Sea Company, 565, 614
Spanish Netherlands, 265, 268, 428–30, 580, 609
Spectator. *See* Addison, Joseph
Spencer, Anne Churchill, Countess of
    Sunderland, 242, 287, 411, 544
Spencer, Charles, third Earl of Sunderland:
    blamed for discord between
    Marlboroughs, 447; embassy to Vienna,
    407–08; marriage, 242; partisan fervor,
    407; proposed address against Mrs.
    Masham, 509; prosecution of Manley,
    506; sacked by QA, 528–30; Secretary of
    State, 432; Union negotiations, 427
Spencer, Robert, second Earl of Sunderland,
    224, 231, 234
Stafford. *See* Howard, William
Staggins, Nicholas, 10, 17, 235
Stamp Act, 587, 594, 609
standing army, 208, 228, 258
Stanhope, George, 430, 540
Stanhope, James, 465, 537–41
Stanhope, Philip, second Earl of Chesterfield, 221
Stanley, Elizabeth Butler, Countess of
    Derby, 191
Stanley, Sir John, 508
Stebbing, Samuel, 202–03

Steele, Richard: Academy of Painting and Drawing, 564; attacks on opera, 448; expelled from House of Commons, 626, 630; Gazetteer, 500; Kit-Cat, 332; loss of positions, 536; plan for entertainments, 608; use of Virgil, 629; Works: *The Crisis*, 625, 630; *Englishman*, 625; *Spectator*, 536, 552; *Tatler*, 500–01, 519–21, 530–32, 536, 541, 566, 594; on the Indian Kings, 525–26, 612; on Nicolini, 440

Stradling, George, 11

Strafford. *See* Wentworth, Thomas

Streeter, Robert, 11

Strickland, Sir William, 266

Stuart, Frances, Duchess of Richmond, 22

Sunderland. *See* Spencer, Anne; Spencer, Charles; Spencer, Robert

Swift, Jonathan: and Church of Ireland, 464, 536; corrections to QA's speech, 609; Harley's attempted coup, 464; and William Harrison, 552; and Ambrose Philips, 247; and Alexander Pope, 608, 620; QA's disapproval of, 578, 622; Scriblerian, 627; Works: *The Conduct of the Allies*, 570–71; contributions to *Tatler*, 500; *Examiner*, 535–37, 541, 555, 562–64; *New Journey to Paris*, 568; *The Publick Spirit of the Whigs*, 626–27, 629; *Tale of a Tub*, 564; *The Virtues of Sid Hamet the Magician's Rod*, 536–37; "The Windsor Prophecy," 578

Swiney, Owen, 473, 508, 545, 564, 589, 595

Sydney, Henry, first Earl of Romney, 197

Symson, David: *A poem on Her Sacred Majesty*, 346–48

Tack and Tackers, 378, 403, 405, 408, 414

Talbot, Adelaide Roffeni, Duchess of Shrewsbury 422, 489, 579

Talbot, Charles, Duke of Shrewsbury: ambassador to France, 594; approached by Bolingbroke, 619; architectural knowledge, 503; asked to serve as Gloucester's governor, 227; invitation to William, 134; lampooned by Manley, 503; Lord Chamberlain, 523, 545, 552; Lord Treasurer, 634; QA's funeral, 599; return from abroad, 422; sympathetic to Sacheverell, 521

Talbot, William, 449

Tallard, Camille, Marquis de la Beaume-D'Hostun, 236, 269, 316, 365–66, 540

Tasso, Torquato: *Gerusalemme Liberata*, 551, 553

Tate, Nahum: Works: birthday odes, 369, 545; *Congratulatory Poem*, 628; *Dido and Aeneas* (with Purcell), 279; *The Duke and No Duke*, 532; New Year's odes, 323, 395, 418, 435, 462; *Ode upon the Assembling of the New Parliament*, 278–80; *Portrait-Royal*, 326–40

Tenison, Thomas, Archbishop of Canterbury, 236, 306, 363

Test Act (1673), 17, 117, 490

Texel Bay, Battle of, 17

Thames: allegorical figure, 1, 5, 19–27, 388, 605–07, 628

Thanksgiving services: for Blenheim, 305–17, 349, 367; for breaking Line of Brabant, 409–11; for campaign of 1702, 313; for capture of Lisle, 490–96; for Malplaquet, 507–08; for Oudenarde, 478–81; for Peace of Utrecht, 595, 614–18; for Ramillies, 430–31, 434; for the Union, 443, 449; for victories in Spain, 539–40

Theobald, Lewis, 600, 635

Third Dutch Naval War, 5, 15, 17, 20

Thompson, John, Baron Haversham, 460–61

Thomyris, Queen of Scythia (pasticcio), 442–43, 448

Thornhill, James, 393–94, 399, 563

Tickell, Thomas: *On the Prospect of Peace*, 601–02, 606–08

Tillotson, John, Archbishop of Canterbury, 138, 470

Tofts, Catherine, 355, 357, 359, 369, 391, 442–43, 497, 553

Tonge, Israel, 60

Tonson, Jacob, 219, 232, 245, 332, 502

Torcy. *See* Colbert, Jean-Baptiste

Tory party: in Exclusion Crisis, 83; favored by QA, 253–54; in Parliament, 265, 277–78, 302, 317–19, 376–77, 537, 565, 577, 579; suspected of Jacobitism, 256, 414

Toulon, siege of, 450

Tournai, siege of, 504

Townshend, Charles, second Viscount
    Townshend, 439, 502, 505, 518, 552, 583

Traytor's Reward, The (anon.), 463

Triennial Act (1694), 257, 398

Trimnell, Charles, 452–53, 456, 460, 463

Trumbull, Sir William, 502–03

trumpets and trumpeters, 91, 96, 145–46, 204,
    227, 258, 282, 289, 306, 323, 344, 491,
    514, 598; *See also* Shore, John

Tudor, Lady Mary, 27

Tunbridge Wells, 134, 172–73, 177, 214–17,
    256, 342

Turner, Francis, Bishop of Ely, 94, 99, 131

Turner, Purbeck, 600

Turner, William, 11, 44, 287

Tutchin, John, 266–68, 283–84, 325,
    359–60, 458

two bodies, monarch's, 264, 273, 291

Underhill, Cave, 524

Union of England and Scotland (1707), 345,
    383, 427–36

Union, The, court dance, 369, 374, 435–36

Utrecht, Treaty of, 26, 517, 601, 603, 609, 612,
    614, 625

United Company, 84, 230

Urbani, Valentino ("Valentini"), 369, 442,
    448, 497

Valentini. *See* Urbani, Valentino

Vanbrugh, Sir John, attacked by Collier, 232;
    Blenheim Palace, 397–98, 447, 473;
    Haymarket Theatre, 341, 391–92, 402,
    425–26, 461, 473; Kit-Cat, 332; *The
    Provok'd Wife*, 231

Vanderbank, John, 518

Vanini, Francesca, 545

Vaudois, 209, 344

Venables-Bertie, Anne, countess of Abingdon, 413

Venables-Bertie, Montagu, second Earl of
    Abingdon, 413

Verelst, Jan, 525

Verrio, Antonio, 92, 103, 341

Victor Amadeus, Duke of Savoy, 344, 583–85

Vigo Bay, 300

Villars. *See* de Villars, Claude Louis Hector

Villiers, Edward, Earl of Jersey: death, 566;
    employer of Prior, 361; Lord
    Chamberlain, 272; messages to QA about
    William's death, 281; peace negotiations,
    540–41, 556; proposed as Lord Privy
    Seal, 566; removed from office, 364

Villiers, Elizabeth. *See* Hamilton, Elizabeth

Villiers, Frances, 15, 37, 60, 483

Virgil: *Aeneid*: Ascanius as model for
    Gloucester, 216–19; homoeroticism in,
    32; loved by Gloucester, 206; Nisus and
    Euryalus, 205; on Roman arts, 416, 577,
    611; simile of orator calming crowd, 629;
    source for *Camilla*, 370–73; source for
    Dido and Aeneas, 279; source for *England's
    Glory*, 424; source for Ambrose Philips,
    245; source for Pittis, 275; *Georgics*, 221;
    Pastorals (Eclogues), 221, 255

Wake, William, 181

Wakeman, Sir George, 69

Walpole, Robert, 558, 574, 579

Walsh, John, 325

Walsh, William, 621

Wandesford, Christopher, Viscount
    Castlecomer, 613

War of the Spanish Succession, 249–50,
    253–56, 292–95, 299–302, 344–45,
    365–67, 428–30, 474–75, 504–05,
    537–41; *See also* Churchill, John

Weely, Samuel, 513, 608, 623

Weldon, John, 263, 395, 433

Wentworth, Henrietta, 28, 38, 89, 115, 117

Wentworth, Isabella Apsley, 177, 230, 489

Wentworth, Peter, 230, 490, 565, 599

Wentworth, Thomas, Lord Raby, later Earl of
    Strafford, 552, 567, 580, 592, 595, 626

Wentworth, William, 177

Wenzel, Johann, Count de Gallas, 406, 569

Wenzel, Johann, Count Wratislaw, 282

Wenzel, Philipp Ludwig, Count von
    Sinzendorff, 518

Westminster School: poems on death of
    Gloucester, 203–04

Wharton, Thomas, First Earl of Wharton, 574, 630; attacks on Godolphin, 452, 460; awarded LLD, 403; *Lilliburlero*, 135; Lord Lieutenant of Ireland, 487; removed from Privy Council, 266; return from Ireland, 536

Whig party, 376, 414–18, 516, 521, 552, 588, 613, 625; aesthetic consequences of ideology, 106, 389, 415–18, 560–61; origins in Exclusion Crisis, 71

White, Thomas, Bishop of Peterborough, 131

Whitehall Palace: apartments of Duchess of Portsmouth, 24; Banqueting House, 11, 26, 138, 608; Cockpit, 89, 116–17, 153, 174, 430; fires, 173, 229, 235, 237; lodgings for Gloucester, 155

William III, King of England: addresses to Parliament, 261, 278; alleged homosexuality, 162, 165, 209, 267; assassination plot of 1696, 172, 207, 210, 221, 281; attends QA's chapel, 235; attention to Gloucester, 139, 148, 207, 209–10, 213, 216, 228–30, 238; Battle of the Boyne, 172; contribution to poor Vaudois, 209; coronation, 96; death, 256, 281; disdain for theatre, 212; dismissal of Marlborough, 174; disrespect for Prince George, 142, 172; First Partition Treaty, 236; French invasion of Holland, 17; funeral, 286; grant of land to Countess of Orkney, 197, 223; intolerance of criticism, 232; invasion of England, 101, 134–36; invitation to Georg August, 271; jealousy of QA's popularity, 197; marriage, 33, 40, 58; meeting with QA after Mary's death, 192; mourning for James II, 272; new oaths at coronation, 102; obliquely criticized in song, 197; proclamations against immorality, 232, 284; QA's letter to on Namur, 193; reconciliation with QA, 176, 192; reduction of royal band, 156, 234; refusal to attend coronation of James II, 94; refusal to inform French court of Gloucester's death, 210; refusal to touch for the "King's Evil," 106;

repayment to Prince George for Danish property, 241; sends Marlborough to Holland, 268; sends troops to Windsor, 192; Treaty of Ryswick, 208, 226–27; unpopular, 144; urged to marry, 243; visit to the Electress, 244; visits to QA, 172, 207, 277

William, Duke of Gloucester: as Ascanius, 216, 246; birthdays, 139, 240, 243; books dedicated to, 217; clothing at QA's birthday, 213; contribution to poor Vaudois, 209; court established, 208, 227–29; death, 201, 209, 243; hope for heirs, 216, 242; horseback riding, 206; hydrocephalus, 140, 150, 206; illnesses, 149, 191, 206; illustration in Dryden's *Virgil*, 219; military interests, 191, 208–09; Order of the Garter, 194, 202, 207–11; in pastoral by Ambrose Philips, 245–47; plan to attend Cambridge, 206; pledge of support for William, 208; in poems on Blenheim, 396; as promising branch, 242; provision for family of musician, 238; reading, 206

Willis, Richard, 201, 409

Wilmot, John, second Earl of Rochester, 38, 63, 86

Winchester: project for new castle, 103

Windsor Castle: Charles III's visit to, 356; QA's visits to, 139–47, 207–08, 224–26, 239–40, 257–58, 276–77, 280–81, 566–67, 619–20, 623; St. George's Chapel, 194, 211; St. George's Hall, 140, 211

Wise, Henry, 297

wool trade, 254

Wratislaw. *See* Wenzel, Johann

Wren, Sir Christopher, 11, 305, 437, 503

Wright, John Michael, 119

Wright, Nathan, 306, 408

Wycherley, William, 460

Yard, Robert, 202

York Buildings: concert venue, 173, 214, 355, 434

York House, Twickenham, 5

Younger, John, 127, 177

Zell, Duke of. *See* Georg Wilhelm

Printed and bound by CPI Group (UK) Ltd, Croydon, CR0 4YY